I0131049

UNITED STATES
DEPARTMENT OF AGRICULTURE

NATIONAL AGRICULTURAL STATISTICS SERVICE

AGRICULTURAL

STATISTICS

2015

UNITED STATES
GOVERNMENT PRINTING OFFICE
WASHINGTON: 2015

For sale by the Superintendent of Documents, U.S. Government Printing Office
Internet: bookstore.gpo.gov   Phone: toll free (866) 512-1800;   DC area (202) 512-1800
Fax: (202) 512-2104 Mail: Stop IDCC, Washington, DC 20402-0001
ISBN

Agricultural Statistics 2015

Agricultural Statistics, 2015 was prepared under the direction of Rich Holcomb, Agricultural Statistics Board, National Agricultural Statistics Service. Carolyne Foster, Phoebe Hilliard, Sherrie Pendarvis, and Tanya Ray were responsible for coordination and technical editorial work.

The USDA and NASS invite you to explore their information via their respective web sites: **http://www.usda.gov/** and **http://www.nass.usda.gov/.**

For information on NASS products you may call the **Agricultural Statistics Hotline, 1–800–727–9540 or send e-mail to nass@nass.usda.gov.**

We gratefully acknowledge the cooperation of the contributors to this publication. Source notes below each table credit the various Government agencies which collaborated in providing information.

CONTENTS

Introduction

Agricultural Statistics is published each year to meet the diverse need for a reliable reference book on agricultural production, supplies, consumption, facilities, costs, and returns. Its tables of annual data cover a wide variety of facts in forms suited to most common use.

Inquiries concerning more current or more detailed data, past and prospective revisions, or the statistical methodology used should be addressed directly to the agency credited with preparing the table. Most of the data were prepared or compiled in the U.S. Department of Agriculture.

The historical series in this volume are generally of data from 2005 and later.

Foreign agricultural trade statistics include Government as well as non-Government shipments of merchandise from the United States and Territories to foreign countries. They do not include U.S. shipments to the U.S. Armed Forces abroad for their own use or shipments between the States and U.S. Territories. The world summaries of production and trade of major farm products are prepared by the U.S. Department of Agriculture from reports of the U.S. Department of Commerce, official statistics of foreign governments, other foreign source materials, reports of U.S. Agricultural Attache and Foreign Service Officers, and the result of office research.

Statistics presented in many of the tables represent actual counts of the items covered. Most of the statistics relating to foreign trade and to Government programs, such as numbers and amounts of loans made to farmers, and amounts of loans made by the Commodity Credit Corporation, etc., are data of this type. A large number of other tables, however, contain data that are estimates made by the Department of Agriculture.

The estimates for crops, livestock, and poultry made by the U.S. Department of Agriculture are prepared mainly to give timely current State and national totals and averages. They are based on data obtained by sample surveys of farmers and of people who do business with farmers. The survey data are supplemented by information from the Censuses of Agriculture taken every five years and check data from various sources. Being estimates, they are subject to revision as more data become available from commercial or Government sources. Unless otherwise indicated, the totals for the United States shown in the various tables on area, production, numbers, price, value, supplies, and disposition are based on official Department estimates. They exclude States for which no official estimates are compiled.

DEFINITIONS

"Value of production" as applied to crops in the various tables, is derived by multiplying production by the estimated season average price received by farmers for that portion of the commodity actually sold. In the case of fruits and vegetables, quantities not harvested because of low prices or other economic factors are not included in value of production. The word "Value" is used in the inventory tables on livestock and poultry to mean value of the number of head on the inventory date. It is derived by multiplying the number of head by an estimated value per head as of the date.

The word "Year" (alone) in a column heading means calendar year unless otherwise indicated. "Ton" when used in this book without qualifications means a short ton of 2,000 pounds.

WEIGHTS, MEASURES, AND CONVERSION FACTORS

The following table on weights, measures, and conversion factors covers the most important agricultural products, or the products for which such information is most frequently asked of the U.S. Department of Agriculture. It does not cover all farm products nor all containers for any one product.

The information has been assembled from State schedules of legal weights, various sources within the U.S. Department of Agriculture, and other Government agencies. For most products, particularly fruits and vegetables, there is a considerable variation in weight per unit of volume due to differences in variety or size of commodity, condition and tightness of pack, degree to which the container is heaped, etc. Effort has been made to select the most representative and fairest average for each product. For those commodities which develop considerable shrinkage, the point of origin weight or weight at harvest has been used.

The approximate or average weights as given in this table do not necessarily have official standing as a basis for packing or as grounds for settling disputes. Not all of them are recognized as legal weight. The table was prepared chiefly for use of workers in the U.S. Department of Agriculture who have need of conversion factors in statistical computations.

WEIGHTS, MEASURES, AND CONVERSION FACTORS
(See explanatory text just preceding this table)

WEIGHTS AND MEASURES

Commodity	Unit[1]	Approximate net weight U.S. (Pounds)	Approximate net weight Metric (Kilograms)
Alfalfa seed	Bushel	60	27.2
Apples	....do	48	21.8
Do	Loose pack	38–42	17.2–19.1
Do	Tray pack	40–45	18.1–20.4
Do	Cell pack	37–41	16.8–18.6
Apricots	Lug (brent-wood)[2]	24	10.9
Western	4–basket crate[3]	26	11.8
Artichokes:			
Globe	Ctn, by count and loose pack	20–25	9.1–11.3
Jerusalem	Bushel	50	22.7
Asparagus	Crate (NJ)	30	13.6
Avocados	Lug[4]	12–15	5.4–6.8
Bananas	Fiber folding box[5]	40	18.1
Barley	Bushel	48	21.8
Beans:			
Lima, dry	....do	56	25.4
Other, dry	....do	60	27.2
	Sack	100	45.4
Lima unshelled	Bushel	28–32	12.7–14.5
Snap	....do	28–32	12.7–14.5
Beets:			
Topped	Sack	25	11.3
Bunched	½ crate 2 dz-bchs	36–40	16.3–18.1
Berries frozen pack:			
Without sugar	50–gal. barrel	380	172
3 + 1 pack	....do	425	193
2 + 1 pack	....do	450	204
Blackberries	12, ½-pint basket	6	2.7
Bluegrass seed	Bushel	14–30	6.4–13.6
Broccoli	Wirebound crate	20–25	9.1–11.3
Broomcorn (6 bales per ton)	Bale	333	151
Broomcorn seed	Bushel	44–50	20.0–22.7
Brussels sprouts	Ctn, loose pack	25	11.3
Buckwheat	Bushel	48	21.8
Butter	Block	55,68	25,30.9
Cabbage	Open mesh bag	50	22.7
Do	Flat crate (1¾ bu)	50–60	22.7–27.2
Do	Ctn, place pack	53	24.0
Cantaloups	Crate[6]	40	18.1
Carrots	Film plastic Bags, mesh sacks & cartons holding 48 1 lb. film bags	55	24.9
Without tops	Burlap sack	74–80	33.6–36.3
Castor beans	Bushel	41	18.6
Castor oil	Gallon[7]	8	3.6
Cauliflower	W.G.A. crate	50–60	22.7–27.2
Do	Fiberboard box wrapper leaves removed film-wrapped, 2 layers	23–35	10.4–15.9

Commodity	Unit[1]	Approximate net weight U.S. (Pounds)	Approximate net weight Metric (Kilograms)
Celery	Crate[8]	60	27.2
Cherries	Lug (Camp-bell)[9]	16	7.3
Do	Lug	20	9.1
Clover seed	Bushel	60	27.2
Coffee	Bag	132.3	60
Corn:			
Ear, husked	Bushel[10]	70	31.8
Shelled	....do	56	25.4
Meal	....do	50	22.7
Oil	Gallon[7]	7.7	3.5
Syrup	....do	11.72	5.3
Sweet	Wirebound crate	50	22.7
Do	Ctn, packed 5 oz. ears	50	22.7
Do	WDB crate, 4½–5 oz. (from FL & NJ)	42	19.1
Cotton	Bale[11], gross	500	227
Do	Bale[11], net	480	218
Cottonseed	Bushel[12]	32	14.5
Cottonseed oil	Gallon[7]	7.7	3.5
Cowpeas	Bushel	60	27.2
Cranberries	Barrel	100	45.4
Do	¼–bbl. box[13]	25	11.3
Cream, 40–percent butterfat	Gallon	8.38	3.80
Cucumbers	Bushel	48	21.8
Dewberries	24–qt. crate	36	16.3
Eggplant	Bushel	33	15.0
Eggs, average size	Case, 30 dozen	47.0	21.3
Escarole	Bushel	25	11.3
Figs, fresh	Box single layer[14]	6	2.7
Flaxseed	Bushel	56	25.4
Flour, various	Bag	100	45.4
Do	Ctn or Crate, Bulk	30	13.6
Garlic	Ctn of 12 tubes or 12 film bag pkgs 12 cloves each	10	4.5
Grapefruit: Florida and Texas	½–box mesh bag	40	18.1
Florida	1⅗ bu. box	85	38.6
Texas	1⅗ bu. box	80	36.3
California and Arizona	Box[15,16]	67	30.4
Grapes:			
Eastern	12–qt. basket	20	9.1
Western	Lug	28	12.7
Do	4–basket crate[17]	20	9.1
Hempseed	Bushel	44	20.0
Hickory nuts	....do	50	22.7
Honey	Gallon	11.84	5.4
Honeydew melons	⅔ Ctn	28–32	12.7–14.5
Hops	Bale, gross	200	90.7

See footnotes on page ix.

WEIGHTS AND MEASURES—Continued

Commodity	Unit [1]	Approximate net weight U.S. Pounds	Metric Kilograms	Commodity	Unit [1]	Approximate net weight U.S. Pounds	Metric Kilograms
Horseradish roots	Bushel	35	15.9	Do	Std box, 4/5 bu	45–48	20.4–21.8
Do	Sack	50	22.7	Do	Ctn, Tight-fill pack	36–37	16.3–16.7
Hungarian millet seed	Bushel	48–50	21.8–22.7	Peas: Green,			
Kale	Ctn or crate	25	11.3	unshelled	Bushel	28–30	12.7–13.6
Kapok seed	...do	35–40	15.9–18.1	Dry	...do	60	27.2
Lard	Tierce	375	170	Peppers, green	...do	25–30	11.3–13.6
Lemons:				Do	1½ bu carton	28	12.7
California and Arizona	Box [18]	76	34.5	Perilla seed	Bushel	37–40	16.8–18.1
Do	Carton	38	17.2	Pineapples	Carton	40	18.1
Lentils	Bushel	60	27.2	Plums and prunes:	Ctn & lugs	28	12.7
Lettuce, iceberg	carton packed 24.	43–52	19.5–23.6	Do	½-bu. basket	30	13.6
Lettuce, hot-house	24-qt. basket	10	4.5	Popcorn: On ear	Bushel [10]	70	31.8
Limes (Florida)	Box	88	39.9	Shelled	...do	56	25.4
Linseed oil	Gallon [7]	7.7	3.5	Poppy seed	...do	46	20.9
Malt	Bushel	34	15.4	Potatoes	Bushel	60	27.2
Maple syrup	Gallon	11.02	5.0	Do	Barrel	165	74.8
Meadow fescue seed	Bushel	24	10.9	Do	Box	50	22.7
Milk	Gallon	8.6	3.9	Do	...do	100	45.4
Millet	Bushel	48–60	21.8–27.2	Quinces	Bushel	48	21.8
Molasses: edible	Gallon	11.74	5.3	Rapeseed	...do	50–60	22.7–27.2
inedible	...do	11.74	5.3	Raspberries	½-pint baskets	6	2.7
Mustard seed	Bushel	58–60	26.3–27.2	Redtop seed	Bushel	50–60	22.7–27.2
Oats	...do	32	14.5	Refiners' syrup	Gallon	11.45	5.2
Olives	Lug	25–30	11.3–13.6	Rice: Rough	Bushel	45	20.4
Olive oil	Gallon [7]	7.6	3.4	Do	Bag	100	45.4
Onions, dry	Sack	50	22.7	Do	Barrel	162	73.5
Onions, green bunched	Ctn, 24-dz bchs	10–16	4.5–7.3	Milled	Pocket or bag	100	45.4
Oranges:				Rosin	Drum, net	520	236
Florida	Box	90	40.8	Rutabagas	Bushel	56	25.4
Texas	Box	85	38.5	Rye	...do	56	25.4
California and Arizona	Box [15]	75	34.0	Sesame seed	...do	46	20.9
Do	Carton	38	17.2	Shallots	Crate (4–7 doz. bunches)	20–35	9.1–15.9
Orchardgrass seed	Bushel	14	6.4	Sorgo:			
Palm oil	Gallon [7]	7.7	3.5	Seed	Bushel	50	22.7
Parsnips	Bushel	50	22.7	Syrup	Gallon	11.55	5.2
Peaches	...do	48	21.8	Sorghum grain [19]	Bushel	56	25.4
Do	2 layer ctn or lug	22	10.0	Soybeans	...do	60	27.2
Do	¾-Bu, Ctn/crate	38	17.2	Soybean oil	Gallon [7]	7.7	3.5
Peanut oil	Gallon [7]	7.7	3.5	Spelt	Bushel	40	18.1
Peanuts, unshelled:				Spinach	...do	18–20	8.2–9.1
Virginia type	Bushel	17	7.7	Strawberries	24-qt. crate	36	16.3
Runners, South-eastern	...do	21	9.5	Do	12-pt. crate	9–11	4.1–5.0
Spanish:				Sudangrass seed	Bushel	40	18.1
South-eastern	...do	25	11.3	Sugarcane: Syrup (sulfured or un-sulfured)	Gallon	11.45	5.2
South-western	...do	25	11.3	Sunflower seed	Bushel	24–32	10.9–14.5
Pears:				Sweet potatoes	Bushel [20]	55	24.9
California	Bushel	48	21.8	Do	Crate	50	22.7
Other	...do	50	22.7	Tangerines: Florida	Box	95	43.1
				Arizona	Box	75	34.0
				California	Box	75	34.0

See footnotes on page ix.

WEIGHTS AND MEASURES—Continued

Commodity	Unit [1]	Approximate net weight		Commodity	Unit [1]	Approximate net weight	
		U.S.	Metric			U.S.	Metric
		Pounds	*Kilograms*			*Pounds*	*Kilograms*
Timothy seed	Bushel	45	20.4	Turnips:			
Tobacco:				Without tops ..	Mesh sack	50	22.7
Maryland	Hogshead	775	352	Bunched	Crate [6]	70–80	31.8–36.3
Flue-cured	.....do	950	431	Turpentine	Gallon	7.23	3.3
Burley	.....do	975	442	Velvetbeans			
Dark air-cured	.....do	1,150	522	(hulled)	Bushel	60	27.2
Virginia fire-				Vetch seed	.....do	60	27.2
cured	.....do	1,350	612	Walnuts	Sacks	50	22.7
Kentucky and				Water 60° F	Gallon	8.33	3.8
Tennessee				Watermelons	Melons of aver-		
fire-cured	.....do	1,500	680		age or me-		
Cigar-leaf	Case	250–365	113–166		dium size	25	11.3
Do	Bale	150–175	68.0–79.4	Wheat	Bushel	60	27.2
Tomatoes	Crate	60	27.2	Various com-			
Do	Lug box	32	14.5	modities	Short ton	2,000	907
Do	2-layer flat	21	9.5	Do	Long ton	2,240	1,016
Tomatoes, hot-				Do	Metric ton	2,204.6	1,000
house	12-qt. basket	20	9.1				
Tung oil	Gallon [7]	7.8	3.5				

See footnotes on page ix.

To Convert From Avoirdupois Pounds

To	Multiply by
Kilograms	0.45359237
Metric tons	0.00045359237

Conversion Factors

1 Metric ton=2,204.622 pounds
1 Kilogram=2.2046 pounds
1 Acre=0.4047 hectares
1 Hectare=2.47 acres
1 Square mile=640 acres=259 hectares
1 Gallon=3.7853 liters

CONVERSION FACTORS

Commodity	Unit	Approximate equivalent
Apples	1 pound dried	7 pounds fresh; beginning 1943, 8 pounds fresh
Do	1 pound chops	5 pounds fresh
Do	1 case canned [21]	1.4 bushels fresh
Applesauce	....do [21]	1.2 bushels fresh
Apricots	1 pound dried	6 pounds fresh
Barley flour	100 pounds	4.59 bushels barley
Beans, lima	1 pound shelled	2 pounds unshelled
Beans, snap or wax	1 case canned [22]	0.008 ton fresh
Buckwheat flour	100 pounds	3.47 bushels buckwheat
Calves	1 pound live weight	0.611 pound dressed weight (1999 average)
Cattle	....do	0.607 pound dressed weight (1999 average)
Cane syrup	1 gallon	5 pounds sugar
Cherries, tart	1 case canned [21]	0.023 ton fresh
Chickens	1 pound live weight	0.72 pound ready-to-cook weight
Corn, shelled	1 bushel (56 lbs.)	2 bushels (70 pounds) of husked ear corn
Corn, sweet	1 case canned [22]	0.030 ton fresh
Cornmeal:		
Degermed	100 pounds	3.16 bushels corn, beginning 1946
Nondegermed	....do	2 bushels corn, beginning 1946
Cotton	1 pound ginned	3.26 pounds seed cotton, including trash [23]
Cottonseed meal	1 pound	2.10 pounds cottonseed
Cottonseed oil	....do	5.88 pounds cottonseed
Dairy products:		
Butter	....do	21.1 pounds milk
Cheese	....do	10 pounds milk
Condensed milk, whole	....do	2.3 pounds milk
Dry cream	....do	19 pounds milk
Dry milk, whole	....do	7.6 pounds milk
Evaporated milk, whole	....do	2.14 pounds milk
Malted milk	....do	2.6 pounds milk
Nonfat dry milk	....do	11 pounds liquid skim milk
Ice cream [24]	1 gallon	15 pounds milk
Ice cream [24] (eliminating fat from butter and concentrated milk).	....do	12 pounds milk
Eggs	1 case	47 pounds
Eggs, shell	....do	41.2 pounds frozen or liquid whole eggs
Do	....do	10.3 pounds dried whole eggs
Figs	1 pound dried	3 pounds fresh in California; 4 pounds fresh elsewhere
Flaxseed	1 bushel	About 2½ gallons oil
Grapefruit, Florida	1 case canned juice [22]	0.64 box fresh fruit
Hogs	1 pound live weight	0.737 pound dressed weight, excluding lard (1999 average)
Linseed meal	1 pound	1.51 pounds flaxseed
Linseed oil	....do	2.77 pounds flaxseed
Malt	1 bushel (34 lbs.)	1 bushel barley (48 lbs.)
Maple syrup	1 gallon	8 pounds maple sugar
Nuts:		
Almonds, imported	1 pound shelled	3½ pounds unshelled
Almonds, California	....do	2.22 pounds unshelled through 1949; 2 pounds thereafter
Brazil	....do	2 pounds unshelled
Cashews	....do	4.55 pounds unshelled
Chestnuts	....do	1.19 pounds unshelled
Filberts	....do	2.22 pounds unshelled through 1949; 2.5 pounds thereafter
Pecans:		
Seedling	....do	2.78 pounds unshelled
Improved	....do	2.50 pounds unshelled
Pignolias	....do	1.3 pounds unshelled
Pistachios	....do	2 pounds unshelled
Walnuts:		
Black	....do	5.88 pounds unshelled
Persian (English)	....do	2.67 pounds unshelled
Oatmeal	100 pounds	7.6 bushels oats, beginning 1943
Oranges, Florida	1 case canned juice [22]	0.53 box fresh
Peaches, California, freestone	1 pound dried	5⅓ pounds fresh through 1918; 6 pounds fresh for 1919–28; and 6½ pounds fresh from 1929 to date
Peaches, California, clingstone	....do	7½ pounds fresh
Peaches, clingstone	1 case canned [21]	1 bushel fresh
Do	....do	0.0230 ton fresh
Peanuts	1 pound shelled	1½ pounds unshelled
Pears	1 pound dried	6½ pounds fresh
Pears, Bartlett	1 case canned [22]	1.1 bushels fresh
Do	....do	0.026 ton fresh

See footnotes on page ix.

CONVERSION FACTORS—Continued

Commodity	Unit	Approximate equivalent
Peas, green	1 pound shelled	2½ pounds unshelled
Do	1 case canned [22]	0.009 ton fresh (shelled)
Prunes	1 pound dried	2.7 pounds fresh in California; 3 to 4 pounds fresh elsewhere
Raisins	1 pound	4.3 pounds fresh grapes
Rice, milled (excluding brewers)	100 pounds	152 pounds rough or unhulled rice
Rye flour	......do	2.23 bushels rye, beginning 1947
Sheep and lambs	1 pound live weight	0.504 pound dressed weight (1999 average)
Soybean meal	1 pound	1.27 pounds soybeans
Soybean oil	......do	5.49 pounds soybeans
Sugar	1 ton raw	0.9346 ton refined
Tobacco	1 pound farm-sales weight ..	Various weights of stemmed and unstemmed, according to aging and the type of tobacco (See circular 435, U.S. Dept. of Agr.)
Tomatoes	1 case canned [22]	0.018 ton fresh
Turkeys	1 pound live weight	0.80 pound ready-to-cook weight
Wheat flour	100 pounds	2.30 bushels wheat [25]
Wool, domestic apparel shorn	1 pound greasy	0.48 pounds scoured
Wool, domestic apparel pulled	......do	0.73 pound scoured

[1] Standard bushel used in the United States contains 2,150.42 cubic inches; the gallon, 231 cubic inches; the cranberry barrel, 5,826 cubic inches; and the standard fruit and vegetable barrel, 7,056 cubic inches. Such large-sized products as apples and potatoes sometimes are sold on the basis of a heaped bushel, which would exceed somewhat the 2,150.42 cubic inches of a bushel basket level full. This also applies to such products as sweetpotatoes, peaches, green beans, green peas, spinach, etc.

[2] Approximate inside dimensions, 4⅝ by 12½ by 16⅛ inches.

[3] Approximate inside dimensions, 4½ by 16 by 16⅛ inches.

[4] Approximate dimensions, 4½ by 13½ by 16⅛ inches.

[5] Approximate inside dimensions, 13 by 12 by 32 inches.

[6] Approximate inside dimensions, 13 by 18 by 21⅝ inches.

[7] This is the weight commonly used in trade practices, the actual weight varying according to temperature conditions.

[8] Approximate inside dimensions, 9¾ by 16 by 20 inches.

[9] Approximate inside dimensions, 4⅛ by 11½ by 14 inches.

[10] The standard weight of 70 pounds is usually recognized as being about 2 measured bushels of corn, husked, on the ear, because it required 70 pounds to yield 1 bushel, or 56 pounds, of shelled corn.

[11] For statistical purposes the bale of cotton is 500 pounds or 480 pounds net weight. Prior to Aug. 1, 1946, the net weight was estimated at 478 pounds. Actual bale weights vary considerably, and the customary average weights of bales of foreign cotton differ from that of the American square bale.

[12] This is the average weight of cottonseed, although the legal weight in some States varies from this figure of 32 pounds.

[13] Approximate inside dimensions, 9¼ by 10½ by 15 inches.

[14] Approximate inside dimensions, 1¾ by 11 by 16⅛ inches.

[15] Approximate inside dimensions, 11½ by 11½ by 24 inches.

[16] Beginning with the 1993-94 season, net weights for California Desert Valley and Arizona grapefruit were increased from 64 to 67 pounds, equal to the California other area net weight, making a 67 pound net weight apply to all of California.

[17] Approximate inside dimensions, 4¾ by 16 by 16⅛ inches.

[18] Approximate inside dimensions, 9⅞ by 13 by 25 inches.6 by 16 by 16⅛ inches.

[19] Includes both sorghum grain (kafir, milo, hegari, etc.) and sweet sorghum varieties.

[20] This average of 55 pounds indicates the usual weight of sweetpotatoes when harvested. Much weight is lost in curing or drying and the net weight when sold in terminal markets may be below 55 pounds.

[21] Case of 24 No. 2½ cans.

[22] Case of 24 No. 303 cans.

[23] Varies widely by method of harvesting.

[24] The milk equivalent of ice cream per gallon is 15 pounds. Reports from plants indicate about 81 percent of the butterfat in ice cream is from milk and cream, the remainder being from butter and concentrated milk. Thus the milk equivalent of the milk and cream in a gallon of ice cream is about 12 pounds.

[25] This is equivalent to 4.51 bushels of wheat per barrel (196 pounds) of flour and has been used in conversions, beginning July 1, 1957. Because of changes in milling processes, the following factors per barrel of flour have been used for earlier periods: 1790–1879, 5 bushels; 1880–1908, 4.75 bushels, 1909–17, 4.7 bushels; 1918 and 1919, 4.5 bushels; 1920, 4.6 bushels; 1921–44, 4.7 bushels; July 1944–Feb. 1946, 4.57 bushels; March 1946–Oct. 1946, average was about 4.31 bushels; and Nov. 1946–June 1957, 4.57 bushels.

CHAPTER I

STATISTICS OF GRAIN AND FEED

This chapter contains tables for wheat, rye, rice, corn, oats, barley, sorghum grain, and feedstuffs. Estimates are given of area, production, disposition, supply and disappearance, prices, value of production, stocks, foreign production and trade, price-support operations, animal units fed, and feed consumed by livestock and poultry.

Table 1-1.—Total grain: Supply and disappearance, United States, 2005–2014 [1]

Year [2]	Supply				Disappearance			Ending stocks
	Beginning stocks	Production	Imports	Total	Domestic use	Exports	Total disappearance	
	Million metric tons	Million metric tons	Million metric tons	Million metric tons	Million metric tons	Million metric tons	Million metric tons	Million metric tons
2005	74.7	363.1	4.8	442.6	280.2	90.7	370.9	71.7
2006	71.7	335.5	6.5	413.7	277.8	86.0	363.8	49.9
2007	49.9	412.0	7.3	469.1	307.2	107.6	414.8	54.3
2008	54.3	400.4	7.1	461.9	314.4	81.6	396.0	65.9
2009	66.3	418.0	6.4	490.8	331.1	83.4	414.5	76.3
2010	76.3	399.6	6.0	481.9	333.1	90.8	423.9	58.0
2011	58.0	385.1	6.8	449.9	326.3	74.2	400.0	49.9
2012	49.9	355.7	11.0	416.6	318.7	53.1	371.8	44.7
2013	44.7	433.9	9.0	487.1	345.3	90.2	435.6	51.8
2014 [3]	51.5	442.4	8.4	503.3	348.8	84.8	433.2	....

[1] Aggregate data on corn, sorghum, barley, oats, wheat, rye, and rice.   [2] The marketing year for corn and sorghum begins September 1; for oats, barley, wheat, and rye, June 1; and for rice, August 1.   [3] Estimate.
ERS, Market and Trade Economics Division, (202) 694–5313.

Table 1-2.—Wheat: Area, yield, production, and value, United States, 2005–2014

Year	Area		Yield per harvested acre	Production	Marketing year average price per bushel received by farmers [2]	Value of production [2]
	Planted [1]	Harvested				
	1,000 acres	1,000 acres	Bushels	1,000 bushels	Dollars	1,000 dollars
2005	57,214	50,104	42.0	2,103,325	3.42	7,167,166
2006	57,334	46,800	38.6	1,808,416	4.26	7,694,734
2007	60,460	50,999	40.2	2,051,088	6.48	13,289,326
2008	63,617	56,036	44.8	2,511,896	6.78	16,701,285
2009	59,017	49,841	44.3	2,208,918	4.87	10,607,218
2010	52,620	46,883	46.1	2,163,023	5.70	12,579,125
2011	54,277	45,687	43.6	1,993,111	7.24	14,269,225
2012	55,294	48,758	46.2	2,252,307	7.77	17,383,149
2013	56,236	45,332	47.1	2,134,979	6.87	14,604,442
2014	56,822	46,381	43.7	2,025,651	6.00	11,923,931

[1] Includes area seeded in preceding fall for winter wheat.   [2] Includes allowance for loans outstanding and purchases by the Government valued at the average loan and purchase rate, by States, where applicable.
NASS, Crops Branch, (202) 720–2127.

Table 1-3.—Wheat, by type: Area, yield, production, and value, United States, 2005–2014

Year	Area		Yield per harvested acre	Production	Marketing year average price per bushel received by farmers [2]	Value of production [2]
	Planted [1]	Harvested				
			Winter wheat			
	1,000 acres	*1,000 acres*	*Bushels*	*1,000 bushels*	*Dollars*	*1,000 dollars*
2005	40,418	33,779	44.3	1,497,764	3.32	4,950,001
2006	40,565	31,107	41.6	1,294,461	4.17	5,367,806
2007	45,012	35,938	41.7	1,499,241	6.13	9,077,574
2008	46,781	40,000	47.1	1,885,575	6.57	12,054,269
2009	43,287	34,550	44.0	1,521,077	4.71	7,070,719
2010	36,576	31,219	46.5	1,452,313	5.37	7,835,595
2011	40,596	32,378	46.1	1,493,130	6.81	10,154,257
2012	40,897	34,609	47.1	1,630,387	7.55	12,245,482
2013	43,230	32,650	47.3	1,542,902	6.89	10,590,949
2014	42,399	32,304	42.6	1,377,526	5.95	8,060,580
			Durum wheat			
	1,000 acres	*1,000 acres*	*Bushels*	*1,000 bushels*	*Dollars*	*1,000 dollars*
2005	2,760	2,716	37.2	101,105	3.46	353,223
2006	1,870	1,815	29.5	53,475	4.43	243,992
2007	2,156	2,119	34.1	72,224	9.92	692,512
2008	2,721	2,574	31.3	80,467	9.26	704,365
2009	2,512	2,386	44.0	104,930	5.47	569,360
2010	2,503	2,462	41.2	101,482	5.98	633,469
2011	1,337	1,280	36.8	47,043	9.68	445,186
2012	2,138	2,122	38.4	81,501	8.18	682,317
2013	1,400	1,338	43.3	57,976	7.46	432,733
2014	1,398	1,337	39.7	53,087	8.50	462,316
			Other spring wheat [3]			
	1,000 acres	*1,000 acres*	*Bushels*	*1,000 bushels*	*Dollars*	*1,000 dollars*
2005	14,036	13,609	37.1	504,456	3.66	1,863,942
2006	14,899	13,878	33.2	460,480	4.46	2,082,936
2007	13,292	12,942	37.1	479,623	7.16	3,519,240
2008	14,115	13,462	40.5	545,854	7.31	3,942,651
2009	13,218	12,905	45.2	582,911	5.23	2,967,139
2010	13,541	13,202	46.1	609,228	6.49	4,110,061
2011	12,344	12,029	37.7	452,938	8.24	3,669,782
2012	12,259	12,027	44.9	540,419	8.24	4,455,350
2013	11,606	11,344	47.1	534,101	6.73	3,580,760
2014	13,025	12,740	46.7	595,038	5.80	3,401,035

[1] Seeded in preceding fall for winter wheat.   [2] Obtained by weighting State prices by quantity sold.   [3] Includes small quantities of Durum wheat grown in other States.
NASS, Crops Branch, (202) 720–2127.

Table 1-4.—Wheat: Stocks on and off farms, United States, 2005–2014

Year beginning September	All wheat							
	On farms				Off farms [1]			
	Sept. 1	Dec. 1	Mar. 1	Jun. 1	Sept. 1	Dec. 1	Mar. 1	Jun. 1
	1,000 bushels	*1,000 bushels*	*1,000 bushels*	*1,000 bushels*	*1,000 bushels*	*1,000 bushels*	*1,000 bushels*	*1,000 bushels*
2005	721,360	513,010	256,000	111,010	1,201,931	916,414	716,215	460,180
2006	572,020	403,250	192,450	73,190	1,178,525	911,408	664,278	382,963
2007	495,000	289,540	91,990	25,635	1,221,927	842,398	617,280	280,183
2008	635,700	454,000	280,400	140,745	1,222,183	968,089	759,664	515,760
2009	836,000	558,800	348,250	209,900	1,373,338	1,222,891	1,008,107	765,737
2010	812,100	550,000	288,010	130,915	1,637,517	1,382,946	1,137,292	732,083
2011	633,000	405,200	217,100	112,030	1,513,669	1,257,318	982,245	630,590
2012	572,900	399,500	236,970	120,150	1,542,209	1,271,079	997,860	597,739
2013	555,000	398,400	237,530	96,995	1,314,637	1,076,451	997,860	597,739
2014	713,450	472,550	....	....	1,193,770	1,052,040	....	....

Year beginning September	Durum wheat [2]							
	On farms				Off farms [1]			
	Sept. 1	Dec. 1	Mar. 1	Jun. 1	Sept. 1	Dec. 1	Mar. 1	Jun. 1
	1,000 bushels	*1,000 bushels*	*1,000 bushels*	*1,000 bushels*	*1,000 bushels*	*1,000 bushels*	*1,000 bushels*	*1,000 bushels*
2005	70,200	57,700	39,700	23,100	31,135	24,384	25,795	17,251
2006	31,500	25,900	17,100	8,950	31,524	25,447	21,736	12,430
2007	34,700	17,600	8,100	2,350	35,764	22,170	17,058	5,938
2008	36,200	26,100	18,700	13,300	22,595	18,405	13,571	11,774
2009	74,100	50,600	34,300	23,900	27,686	25,181	21,216	10,749
2010	71,200	46,600	35,700	22,100	28,931	21,742	20,720	13,366
2011	34,900	24,500	17,900	15,200	28,828	23,507	17,899	10,270
2012	43,600	36,700	21,400	13,600	24,842	24,306	21,088	9,450
2013	42,900	32,800	20,700	12,800	23,465	21,175	17,430	8,724
2014	38,700	22,000	....	....	19,121	19,979	....	....

[1] Includes stocks at mills, elevators, warehouses, terminals, and processors. [2] Included in all wheat.
NASS, Crops Branch, (202) 720–2127.

Table 1-5.—Wheat: Supply and disappearance, by class, United States, 2010–2014 [1]

Item	Year beginning June				
	2010	2011	2012	2013	2014
	Million bushels	Million bushels	Million bushels	Million bushels	Million bushels
All wheat:					
Stocks, June 1	976	862	743	718	590
Production	2,207	1,999	2,252	2,135	2,026
Supply [2]	3,279	2,974	3,119	3,026	2,765
Exports [3]	1,291	1,051	1,012	1,176	854
Domestic disappearance	1,126	1,180	1,389	1,260	1,158
Stocks, May 31	862	743	718	590	753
Hard red winter:					
Stocks, June 1	385	386	317	343	237
Production	1,018	780	998	747	738
Supply [2]	1,404	1,166	1,333	1,109	985
Exports [3]	617	397	382	446	269
Domestic disappearance	402	452	608	426	422
Stocks, May 31	386	317	343	237	294
Soft red winter:					
Stocks, June 1	242	171	185	124	113
Production	237	458	413	568	455
Supply [2]	508	661	616	713	582
Exports [3]	109	165	194	282	133
Domestic disappearance	228	310	297	318	296
Stocks, May 31	171	185	124	113	153
Hard red spring:					
Stocks, June 1	234	185	151	165	169
Production	570	398	503	491	556
Supply [2]	832	618	698	733	791
Exports [3]	340	243	233	245	270
Domestic disappearance	307	224	301	319	307
Stocks, May 31	185	151	165	169	213
Durum:					
Stocks, June 1	35	35	25	23	22
Production	106	50	82	58	53
Supply [2]	173	122	145	129	125
Exports [3]	44	27	29	32	37
Domestic disappearance	94	70	93	76	62
Stocks, May 31	35	25	23	22	26
White:					
Stocks, June 1	80	85	64	63	50
Production	275	314	257	271	224
Supply [2]	362	406	328	341	284
Exports [3]	182	219	175	170	146
Domestic disappearance	95	124	90	121	71
Stocks, May 31	85	64	63	50	67

[1] Data except production are approximations.   [2] Total supply includes imports.   [3] Import and exports include flour and products in wheat equivalent.
ERS, Market and Trade Economics Division, (202) 694–5285.

Table 1-6.—Wheat: Supply and disappearance, United States, 2005–2014

Year beginning June	Supply				Disappearance						Ending stocks May 31
	Beginning stocks	Production	Imports [1]	Total	Domestic use				Exports [1]	Total disappearance	
					Food	Seed	Feed [2]	Total			
	Million bushels	Million bushels	Million bushels	Million bushels	Million bushels	Million bushels	Million bushels	Million bushels	Million bushels	Million bushels	Million bushels
2005	540	2,103	81	2,725	917	77	157	1,151	1,003	2,154	571
2006	571	1,808	122	2,501	938	82	117	1,137	908	2,045	456
2007	456	2,051	113	2,620	948	88	16	1,051	1,263	2,314	306
2008	306	2,499	127	2,932	927	78	255	1,260	1,015	2,275	657
2009	657	2,218	119	2,993	919	69	150	1,138	879	2,018	976
2010	976	2,207	97	3,279	926	71	129	1,126	1,291	2,417	862
2011	862	1,999	112	2,974	941	76	162	1,180	1,051	2,231	743
2012	743	2,252	124	3,119	951	73	365	1,389	1,012	2,401	718
2013	718	2,135	173	3,026	955	77	228	1,260	1,176	2,436	590
2014	590	2,026	149	2,765	958	81	120	1,158	854	2,013	753

[1] Imports and exports include flour and other products expressed in wheat equivalent.   [2] Approximates feed and residual use and includes negligible quantities used for distilled spirits.
Totals may not add due to independent rounding.
ERS, Market and Trade Economics Division, (202) 694–5296.

Table 1-7.—All Wheat: Area, yield, and production, by State and United States, 2012–2014

State	Area planted [1]			Area harvested		
	2012	2013	2014	2012	2013	2014
	1,000 acres	1,000 acres	1,000 acres	1,000 acres	1,000 acres	1,000 acres
Alabama	220	310	255	185	285	225
Arizona	114	87	81	110	84	79
Arkansas	550	680	465	445	610	395
California	715	690	495	425	394	205
Colorado	2,363	2,310	2,759	2,212	1,639	2,358
Delaware	80	85	80	76	78	75
Florida	20	25	15	15	19	10
Georgia	290	430	300	230	360	230
Idaho	1,303	1,321	1,271	1,243	1,261	1,196
Illinois	650	880	740	640	840	670
Indiana	330	460	390	285	435	335
Iowa	18	30	26	13	21	15
Kansas	9,400	9,500	9,600	9,100	8,450	8,800
Kentucky	550	700	630	440	610	510
Louisiana	285	265	160	275	255	150
Maryland	310	345	340	210	260	250
Michigan	560	620	570	535	590	485
Minnesota	1,385	1,227	1,262	1,342	1,184	1,212
Mississippi	345	400	230	320	385	215
Missouri	780	1,080	880	680	985	740
Montana	5,800	5,400	5,985	5,615	5,165	5,650
Nebraska	1,370	1,470	1,550	1,300	1,140	1,450
Nevada	26	31	21	15	15	10
New Jersey	27	34	33	23	29	25
New Mexico	440	440	380	105	100	105
New York	100	125	120	85	115	95
North Carolina	810	990	830	740	925	770
North Dakota	7,840	6,105	7,960	7,765	6,025	7,490
Ohio	500	660	620	450	640	545
Oklahoma	5,400	5,600	5,300	4,300	3,400	2,800
Oregon	885	880	830	878	868	818
Pennsylvania	155	185	185	135	155	150
South Carolina	235	280	230	220	265	220
South Dakota	2,395	2,494	2,514	2,225	1,839	2,364
Tennessee	405	640	530	330	575	475
Texas	5,600	6,300	6,000	2,900	2,350	2,250
Utah	140	138	130	122	124	117
Virginia	280	335	290	240	290	260
Washington	2,200	2,210	2,320	2,165	2,175	2,250
West Virginia	8	9	10	4	7	7
Wisconsin	265	315	295	245	265	250
Wyoming	145	150	140	115	120	125
United States	55,294	56,236	56,822	48,758	45,332	46,381

See footnote(s) at end of table.

Table 1-7.—All Wheat: Area, yield, and production, by State and United States, 2012–2014—Continued

State	Yield per harvested acre			Production		
	2012	2013	2014	2012	2013	2014
	Bushels	*Bushels*	*Bushels*	*1,000 bushels*	*1,000 bushels*	*1,000 bushels*
Alabama	59.0	69.0	69.0	10,915	19,665	15,525
Arizona	94.2	99.4	110.0	10,360	8,348	8,692
Arkansas	55.0	62.0	63.0	24,475	37,820	24,885
California	90.9	82.5	83.0	38,645	32,500	17,025
Colorado	31.3	25.3	38.1	69,268	41,488	89,812
Delaware	74.0	64.0	72.0	5,624	4,992	5,400
Florida	42.0	59.0	39.0	630	1,121	390
Georgia	50.0	60.0	49.0	11,500	21,600	11,270
Idaho	78.2	82.2	78.4	97,246	103,592	93,717
Illinois	64.0	67.0	67.0	40,960	56,280	44,890
Indiana	67.0	73.0	76.0	19,095	31,755	25,460
Iowa	50.0	52.0	49.0	650	1,092	735
Kansas	42.0	38.0	28.0	382,200	321,100	246,400
Kentucky	63.0	75.0	71.0	27,720	45,750	36,210
Louisiana	49.0	58.0	62.0	13,475	14,790	9,300
Maryland	68.0	67.0	70.0	14,280	17,420	17,500
Michigan	76.0	75.0	74.0	40,660	44,250	35,890
Minnesota	57.0	56.7	54.8	76,430	67,152	66,468
Mississippi	57.0	58.0	58.0	18,240	22,330	12,470
Missouri	58.0	57.0	58.0	39,440	56,145	42,920
Montana	34.8	39.0	37.1	195,590	201,635	209,470
Nebraska	41.0	35.0	49.0	53,300	39,900	71,050
Nevada	77.8	87.0	105.0	1,167	1,305	1,050
New Jersey	56.0	54.0	53.0	1,288	1,566	1,325
New Mexico	27.0	44.0	28.0	2,835	4,400	2,940
New York	63.0	68.0	63.0	5,355	7,820	5,985
North Carolina	57.0	57.0	58.0	42,180	52,725	44,660
North Dakota	43.8	45.4	46.3	340,100	273,343	347,068
Ohio	68.0	70.0	74.0	30,600	44,800	40,330
Oklahoma	36.0	31.0	17.0	154,800	105,400	47,600
Oregon	65.6	62.1	54.3	57,576	53,904	44,444
Pennsylvania	65.0	68.0	65.0	8,775	10,540	9,750
South Carolina	53.0	54.0	52.0	11,660	14,310	11,440
South Dakota	45.9	42.2	55.5	102,025	77,558	131,260
Tennessee	63.0	71.0	66.0	20,790	40,825	31,350
Texas	33.0	29.0	30.0	95,700	68,150	67,500
Utah	46.3	44.2	50.3	5,643	5,484	5,882
Virginia	64.0	62.0	68.0	15,360	17,980	17,680
Washington	66.6	66.9	48.2	144,125	145,530	108,460
West Virginia	65.0	52.0	64.0	260	364	448
Wisconsin	75.0	58.0	65.0	18,375	15,370	16,250
Wyoming	26.0	24.0	38.0	2,990	2,880	4,750
United States	46.2	47.1	43.7	2,252,307	2,134,979	2,025,651

[1] Includes area planted preceding fall.
NASS, Crops Branch, (202) 720–2127.

Table 1-8.—Wheat, by type: Area, yield, and production, by State and United States, 2012–2014

State	Area planted [1]			Area harvested		
	2012	2013	2014	2012	2013	2014
	Winter wheat					
	1,000 acres	*1,000 acres*	*1,000 acres*	*1,000 acres*	*1,000 acres*	*1,000 acres*
Alabama	220	310	255	185	285	225
Arizona	9	12	8	6	10	7
Arkansas	550	680	465	445	610	395
California	590	620	460	305	345	180
Colorado	2,350	2,300	2,750	2,200	1,630	2,350
Delaware	80	85	80	76	78	75
Florida	20	25	15	15	19	10
Georgia	290	430	300	230	360	230
Idaho	780	780	780	740	740	730
Illinois	650	880	740	640	840	670
Indiana	330	460	390	285	435	335
Iowa	18	30	26	13	21	15
Kansas	9,400	9,500	9,600	9,100	8,450	8,800
Kentucky	550	700	630	440	610	510
Louisiana	285	265	160	275	255	150
Maryland	310	345	340	210	260	250
Michigan	560	620	570	535	590	485
Minnesota	35	27	42	32	24	32
Mississippi	345	400	230	320	385	215
Missouri	780	1,080	880	680	985	740
Montana	2,300	2,000	2,500	2,170	1,900	2,240
Nebraska	1,370	1,470	1,550	1,300	1,140	1,450
Nevada	20	23	15	11	12	9
New Jersey	27	34	33	23	29	25
New Mexico	440	440	380	105	100	105
New York	100	125	120	85	115	95
North Carolina	810	990	830	740	925	770
North Dakota	750	215	870	730	200	555
Ohio	500	660	620	450	640	545
Oklahoma	5,400	5,600	5,300	4,300	3,400	2,800
Oregon	790	790	750	785	780	740
Pennsylvania	155	185	185	135	155	150
South Carolina	235	280	230	220	265	220
South Dakota	1,320	1,300	1,210	1,210	670	1,080
Tennessee	405	640	530	330	575	475
Texas	5,600	6,300	6,000	2,900	2,350	2,250
Utah	125	120	120	109	110	109
Virginia	280	335	290	240	290	260
Washington	1,700	1,700	1,700	1,670	1,670	1,640
West Virginia	8	9	10	4	7	7
Wisconsin	265	315	295	245	265	250
Wyoming	145	150	140	115	120	125
United States	40,897	43,230	42,399	34,609	32,650	32,304
	Other spring wheat					
Colorado	13	10	9	12	9	8
Idaho	510	530	480	490	510	455
Minnesota	1,350	1,200	1,220	1,310	1,160	1,180
Montana	2,950	2,950	3,050	2,900	2,830	2,980
Nevada	6	8	6	4	3	1
North Dakota	5,750	5,100	6,250	5,700	5,060	6,140
Oregon	95	90	80	93	88	78
South Dakota	1,070	1,190	1,300	1,010	1,165	1,280
Utah	15	18	10	13	14	8
Washington	500	510	620	495	505	610
United States	12,259	11,606	13,025	12,027	11,344	12,740
	Durum wheat					
Arizona	105	75	73	104	74	72
California	125	70	35	120	49	25
Idaho	13	11	11	13	11	11
Montana	550	450	435	545	435	430
North Dakota	1,340	790	840	1,335	765	795
South Dakota	5	4	4	5	4	4
United States	2,138	1,400	1,398	2,122	1,338	1,337

See footnote(s) at end of table.

Table 1-8.—Wheat, by type: Area, yield, and production, by State and United States, 2012–2014—Continued

State	Yield per harvested acre			Production		
	2012	2013	2014	2012	2013	2014
		Winter wheat				
	Bushels	Bushels	Bushels	1,000 bushels	1,000 bushels	1,000 bushels
Alabama	59.0	69.0	69.0	10,915	19,665	15,525
Arizona	80.0	80.0	100.0	480	800	700
Arkansas	55.0	62.0	63.0	24,475	37,820	24,885
California	85.0	80.0	80.0	25,925	27,600	14,400
Colorado	31.0	25.0	38.0	68,200	40,750	89,300
Delaware	74.0	64.0	72.0	5,624	4,992	5,400
Florida	42.0	59.0	39.0	630	1,121	390
Georgia	50.0	60.0	49.0	11,500	21,600	11,270
Idaho	80.0	86.0	80.0	59,200	63,640	58,400
Illinois	64.0	67.0	67.0	40,960	56,280	44,890
Indiana	67.0	73.0	76.0	19,095	31,755	25,460
Iowa	50.0	52.0	49.0	650	1,092	735
Kansas	42.0	38.0	28.0	382,200	321,100	246,400
Kentucky	63.0	75.0	71.0	27,720	45,750	36,210
Louisiana	49.0	58.0	62.0	13,475	14,790	9,300
Maryland	68.0	67.0	70.0	14,280	17,420	17,500
Michigan	76.0	75.0	74.0	40,660	44,250	35,890
Minnesota	55.0	43.0	49.0	1,760	1,032	1,568
Mississippi	57.0	58.0	58.0	18,240	22,330	12,470
Missouri	58.0	57.0	58.0	39,440	56,145	42,920
Montana	39.0	43.0	41.0	84,630	81,700	91,840
Nebraska	41.0	35.0	49.0	53,300	39,060	71,050
Nevada	77.0	90.0	110.0	847	1,080	990
New Jersey	56.0	54.0	53.0	1,288	1,566	1,325
New Mexico	27.0	44.0	28.0	2,835	4,400	2,940
New York	63.0	68.0	63.0	5,355	7,820	5,985
North Carolina	57.0	57.0	58.0	42,180	52,725	44,660
North Dakota	56.0	43.0	49.0	40,880	8,600	27,195
Ohio	68.0	70.0	74.0	30,600	44,800	40,330
Oklahoma	36.0	31.0	17.0	154,800	105,400	47,600
Oregon	66.0	62.0	55.0	51,810	48,360	40,700
Pennsylvania	65.0	68.0	65.0	8,775	10,540	9,750
South Carolina	53.0	54.0	52.0	11,660	14,310	11,440
South Dakota	50.0	39.0	55.0	60,500	26,130	59,400
Tennessee	63.0	71.0	66.0	20,790	40,825	31,350
Texas	33.0	29.0	30.0	95,700	68,150	67,500
Utah	47.0	44.0	50.0	5,123	4,840	5,450
Virginia	64.0	62.0	68.0	15,360	17,980	17,680
Washington	70.0	69.0	52.0	116,900	115,230	85,280
West Virginia	65.0	52.0	64.0	260	364	448
Wisconsin	75.0	58.0	65.0	18,375	15,370	16,250
Wyoming	26.0	24.0	38.0	2,990	2,880	4,750
United States	47.1	47.3	42.6	1,630,387	1,542,902	1,377,526
		Other spring wheat				
Colorado	89.0	82.0	64.0	1,068	738	512
Idaho	76.0	77.0	76.0	37,240	39,270	34,580
Minnesota	57.0	57.0	55.0	74,670	66,120	64,900
Montana	33.0	37.0	35.0	95,700	104,710	104,300
Nevada	80.0	75.0	60.0	320	225	60
North Dakota	45.0	46.5	47.5	256,500	235,290	291,650
Oregon	62.0	63.0	48.0	5,766	5,544	3,744
South Dakota	41.0	44.0	56.0	41,410	51,260	71,680
Utah	40.0	46.0	54.0	520	644	432
Washington	55.0	60.0	38.0	27,225	30,300	23,180
United States	44.9	47.1	46.7	540,419	534,101	595,038
		Durum wheat				
Arizona	95.0	102.0	111.0	9,880	7,548	7,992
California	106.0	100.0	105.0	12,720	4,900	2,625
Idaho	62.0	62.0	67.0	806	682	737
Montana	28.0	35.0	31.0	15,260	15,225	13,330
North Dakota	32.0	38.5	35.5	42,720	29,453	28,223
South Dakota	23.0	42.0	45.0	115	168	180
United States	38.4	43.3	39.7	81,501	57,976	53,087

[1] Includes area planted preceding fall.
NASS, Crops Branch, (202) 720–2127.

Table 1-9.—Wheat: Support operations, United States, 2005–2014

Marketing year beginning June 1	Income support payment rates per bushel [1]	Program price levels per bushel		Put under loan		Acquired by CCC under loan program	Owned by CCC at end of marketing year
		Loan [2]	Target [3] [4]	Quantity	Percentage of production [5]		
	Dollars	*Dollars*	*Dollars*	*Million bushels*	*Percent*	*Million bushels*	*Million bushels*
2005/2006 ...	0.52/0.00	2.75	3.92	170	8.1	1	43
2006/2007 ...	0.52/0.00	2.75	3.92	94	5.2	0	41
2007/2008 ...	0.52/0.00	2.75	3.92	36	1.8	0	0
2008/2009 ...	0.52/0.00	2.75	3.92	84	3.4	0	0
2009/2010 ...	0.52/0.00	2.75	3.92	103	4.6	0	0
2010/2011 ...	0.52/0.00	2.94	4.17	67	3.0	0	0
2011/2012 ...	0.52/0.00	2.94	4.17	36	1.8	0	0
2012/2013 ...	0.52/0.00	2.94	4.17	28	1.2	0	0
2013/2014 ...	0.52/0.00	2.94	4.17	25	1.1	0	0
2014/2015 ...	(NA)/0.00	2.94	5.50	43	2.1	0	0

(NA) Not applicable as Direct Payments were eliminated in the 2014 Farm Bill.   [1] Payment rates for 2005/2006 and subsequent crops are calculated according to the Direct and Counter-cyclical program provisions, following enactment of the Farm Security and Rural Investment Act of 2002 (2002 Act). The first entry is the direct payment rate and the second entry is the counter-cyclical payment rate.   [2] Starting in 2009, producers who participate in the Average Crop Revenue Election (ACRE) program get a 30 percent reduction in their loan rate, not calculated in this table.   [3] Target prices were reestablished under the 2002 Act.   [4] Beginning with 2014/2015, Reference price for wheat established under the 2014 Farm Bill for ARC-PLC programs.   [5] Percentage of production is on a grain basis.
FSA, Food Grains, (202) 720–2891.

Table 1-10.—Wheat: Marketing year average price and value, by State and United States, 2012–2014

State	Marketing year average price per bushel			Value of production		
	2012	2013	2014	2012	2013	2014
	Dollars	*Dollars*	*Dollars*	*1,000 dollars*	*1,000 dollars*	*1,000 dollars*
Alabama	6.65	6.85	5.95	72,585	134,705	92,374
Arizona	9.49	8.74	8.36	97,217	71,970	75,600
Arkansas	6.84	7.04	5.62	167,409	266,253	139,854
California	8.00	7.99	7.50	318,506	258,563	138,392
Colorado	7.75	6.97	5.88	536,539	289,581	528,491
Delaware	7.90	6.80	4.90	44,430	33,946	26,460
Florida	6.30	5.75	5.10	3,969	6,446	1,989
Georgia	7.30	6.50	5.35	83,950	140,400	60,295
Idaho	7.92	7.05	6.16	772,673	731,620	582,170
Illinois	7.13	6.52	4.98	292,045	366,946	223,552
Indiana	7.28	6.42	5.22	139,012	203,867	132,901
Iowa	7.00	6.35	5.81	4,550	6,934	4,270
Kansas	7.48	6.99	6.07	2,858,856	2,244,489	1,495,648
Kentucky	7.25	6.57	5.62	200,970	300,578	203,500
Louisiana	6.90	7.10	6.10	92,978	105,009	56,730
Maryland	7.95	6.85	4.90	113,526	119,327	85,750
Michigan	7.91	6.71	5.74	321,621	296,918	199,637
Minnesota	8.13	6.68	5.48	621,278	448,576	363,900
Mississippi	6.85	6.92	5.75	124,944	154,524	71,703
Missouri	6.89	6.55	5.36	271,742	367,750	230,051
Montana	8.15	6.87	6.23	1,600,489	1,386,401	1,298,295
Nebraska	7.87	6.95	5.77	419,471	277,305	409,959
Nevada	7.89	6.92	6.20	9,255	9,022	6,426
New Jersey	7.15	6.60	4.80	9,209	10,336	6,360
New Mexico	7.50	6.80	6.32	21,263	29,920	18,581
New York	8.35	6.60	5.61	44,714	51,612	33,576
North Carolina	6.78	6.28	5.16	285,980	331,113	230,446
North Dakota	8.07	6.62	5.74	2,745,158	1,795,566	1,956,030
Ohio	7.94	6.54	5.60	242,964	292,992	225,848
Oklahoma	7.45	6.99	6.34	1,153,260	736,746	301,784
Oregon	8.10	7.03	6.78	465,217	378,452	300,311
Pennsylvania	7.97	6.83	6.06	69,937	71,988	59,085
South Carolina	6.65	6.00	4.80	77,539	85,860	54,912
South Dakota	8.10	6.84	5.54	821,336	530,269	727,517
Tennessee	6.95	7.00	5.63	144,491	285,775	176,501
Texas	6.72	7.11	6.40	643,104	484,547	432,000
Utah	9.59	7.94	7.07	51,933	42,893	41,040
Virginia	7.39	6.91	5.74	113,510	124,242	101,483
Washington	8.07	6.95	6.55	1,162,209	1,014,032	714,858
West Virginia	7.25	6.75	5.70	1,885	2,457	2,554
Wisconsin	7.55	6.12	4.75	138,731	94,064	77,188
Wyoming	7.59	7.10	5.67	22,694	20,448	26,933
United States	7.77	6.87	5.99	17,383,149	14,604,442	11,914,954

NASS, Crops Branch, (202) 720–2127.

Table 1-11.—International Wheat: Area, yield, and production in specified countries, 2013/2014–2015/2016

Country	Area			Yield per hectare			Production		
	2013/ 2014	2014/ 2015	2015/ 2016	2013/ 2014	2014/ 2015	2015/ 2016	2013/ 2014	2014/ 2015	2015/ 2016
	1,000 hec-tares	*1,000 hec-tares*	*1,000 hec-tares*	*Metric tons*	*Metric tons*	*Metric tons*	*1,000 metric tons*	*1,000 metric tons*	*1,000 metric tons*
Australia	12,613	12,155	12,750	2.01	1.90	1.92	25,303	23,076	24,500
Canada	10,442	9,480	9,600	3.59	3.10	2.88	37,530	29,420	27,600
China	24,117	24,069	24,140	5.06	5.24	5.39	121,930	126,208	130,190
European Union	25,884	26,783	26,846	5.59	5.85	5.90	144,585	156,656	158,457
India	30,003	30,473	30,600	3.12	3.15	2.83	93,506	95,850	86,530
Iran	6,400	6,800	6,800	2.27	1.91	2.06	14,500	13,000	14,000
Pakistan	8,660	9,199	9,180	2.80	2.82	2.78	24,211	25,979	25,478
Russia	23,399	23,636	25,600	2.23	2.50	2.38	52,091	59,080	61,000
Turkey	7,700	7,710	7,860	2.44	1.98	2.48	18,750	15,250	19,500
Ukraine	6,566	6,300	7,100	3.39	3.93	3.84	22,278	24,750	27,250
Others	45,711	45,501	44,744	2.24	2.22	2.28	102,567	101,055	101,971
Total foreign	201,495	202,106	205,220	3.26	3.32	3.30	657,251	670,324	676,476
United States	18,345	18,771	19,058	3.17	2.94	2.93	58,105	55,147	55,840
Total	219,840	220,877	224,278	3.25	3.28	3.27	715,356	725,471	732,316

FAS, Office of Global Analysis, (202) 720-6301. Prepared or estimated on the basis of official USDA production, supply, and distribution statistics from foreign governments.

Table 1-12.—Wheat and flour: United States imports, 2005–2014

Year beginning June	All wheat grain	All wheat flour [1]	All wheat products [2]	Total all wheat [3]
	1,000 bushels	*1,000 bushels [4]*	*1,000 bushels [4]*	*1,000 bushels*
2005	54,073	11,258	16,023	81,354
2006	92,928	11,853	17,089	121,870
2007	85,806	10,710	16,115	112,631
2008	101,964	9,785	15,221	126.970
2009	93,003	9,720	15,868	118,591
2010	69,053	11,283	16,582	96,918
2011	83,336	10,666	18,068	112,069
2012	96,103	10,151	18,063	124,317
2013	141,665	11,535	19,255	172,455
2014	115,239	14,335	19,883	149,457

[1] Includes meal, groats, and durum.   [2] Includes bulgur, couscous, and selected categories of pasta.   [3] Totals may not add due to rounding.   [4] Expressed in grain-equivalent bushels.
ERS, Market and Trade Economics Division, (202) 694–5285.

Table 1-13.—Wheat: International trade, 2013/2014–2015/2016

Country	2013/2014	2014/2015	2015/2016
	1,000 metric tons	*1,000 metric tons*	*1,000 metric tons*
Principle exporting countries:			
Argentina	2,250	5,301	7,000
Australia	18,615	16,605	17,000
Brazil	80	1,691	1,300
Canada	23,270	24,116	22,000
European Union	32,032	35,418	32,500
Kazakhstan	8,100	5,539	6,500
Mexico	1,322	1,104	1,100
Russia	18,568	22,800	23,000
Turkey	4,441	4,062	4,700
Ukraine	9,755	11,269	15,500
Others	15,476	12,986	11,042
Total Foreign	133,909	140,891	141,642
United States	32,001	23,249	21,092
Total	165,910	164,140	162,734
Principle importing countries:			
Algeria	7,484	7,257	7,700
Brazil	7,066	5,374	6,500
Egypt	10,170	11,063	11,000
European Union	3,976	5,975	6,300
Indonesia	7,392	7,478	8,100
Japan	6,123	5,878	5,700
Korea, South	4,288	3,942	4,500
Mexico	4,636	4,446	4,400
Nigeria	4,580	4,244	4,400
Philippines	3,482	5,099	4,300
Others	94,463	93,932	94,176
Total Foreign	153,660	154,688	157,076
United States	4,710	4,068	3,266
Total	158,370	158,756	160,342

FAS, Office of Global Analysis, (202) 720-6301. Prepared or estimated on the basis of official USDA production, supply, and distribution statistics from foreign governments.

Table 1-14.—Wheat and flour: United States exports by country of destination, 2011–2013

Country of destination	Year		
	2011	2012	2013[1]
	Metric tons	*Metric tons*	*Metric tons*
Wheat:			
China	478,926	594,482	4,282,714
Brazil	142,240	46,002	3,929,450
Japan	3,713,747	3,391,142	3,128,611
Nigeria	3,574,153	2,932,294	2,959,160
Mexico	3,200,685	3,623,705	2,901,653
Philippines	2,069,829	1,864,119	1,962,062
Egypt	2,489,363	819,212	1,611,731
Korea, South	1,394,799	2,243,321	1,046,444
Taiwan	963,127	996,657	1,033,844
Colombia	671,868	440,800	732,281
Indonesia	816,042	729,974	722,202
Italy(*)	469,691	358,902	660,633
Chile	430,113	275,535	653,821
Peru	1,006,612	226,314	650,656
Venezuela	671,349	743,283	556,916
Thailand	432,144	546,798	498,499
Guatemala	472,024	444,246	475,965
Dominican Republic	553,506	521,837	468,757
Yemen(*)	578,841	396,182	466,507
Turkey	678,778	21,008	341,297
Honduras	193,113	185,615	235,507
El Salvador	239,106	274,780	229,643
Spain	184,134	496,817	215,129
Israel(*)	451,034	236,505	196,069
Malaysia	432,561	82,838	196,054
Jamaica	175,817	178,614	189,505
Algeria	47,938	316,566	179,315
Ecuador	101,223	187,287	178,712
Sri Lanka	180,222	0	175,935
Costa Rica	179,008	129,982	140,283
Other World Total	5,809,960	2,459,810	1,893,519
World Total	32,801,953	25,764,627	32,912,874
Wheat flour:			
Canada	139,573	162,355	145,086
Mexico	106,166	76,594	111,153
Kenya	23,599	38,094	25,684
Malaysia	716	15,704	16,981
Burkina Faso	0	0	13,699
Dominican Republic	3,405	3,250	3,458
Philippines	287	52	3,449
Panama	193	11	3,374
Netherlands Antilles(*)	3,303	3,261	3,201
Vietnam	232	6,103	2,394
Bahamas, The	3,825	4,355	2,315
Djibouti	2,223	1,082	2,281
Singapore	147	3,874	2,250
Korea, South	1,394	1,955	1,996
Taiwan	2,530	625	1,836
Sweden	521	1,842	1,813
Barbados	1,941	1,804	1,710
Thailand	2,131	4,086	1,591
Indonesia	1,507	12	1,572
Leeward-Windward Islands(*)	1,772	1,553	1,547
Trinidad and Tobago	1,635	1,402	1,524
Australia(*)	332	405	1,516
China	40	16	1,268
Burma	4,914	12,615	1,066
Chad	5,730	1,009	1,010
Liberia	2,603	2,832	705
Hong Kong	624	1,054	692
Kyrgyzstan	0	0	493
Micronesia	539	369	486
Marshall Islands	304	376	482
Other World Total	106,242	55,233	4,378
World Total	418,429	401,921	361,007

[1]2013 data does not reflect 13 month changes.   (*) Denotes a country that is a summarization of its component countries.

FAS, Office of Global Analysis, (202) 720-6301.   Prepared or estimated on the basis of official USDA production, supply, and distribution, supply, and distribution statistics from foreign governments.

Table 1-15.—Rye: Area, yield, production, disposition, and value, United States, 2005–2014

Year	Area		Yield per harvested acre	Production	Marketing year average price per bushel received by farmers	Value of production
	Planted [1]	Harvested				
	1,000 acres	*1,000 acres*	*Bushels*	*1,000 bushels*	*Dollars*	*1,000 dollars*
2005	1,433	279	27.0	7,537	3.30	24,890
2006	1,396	274	26.3	7,193	3.32	23,895
2007	1,334	252	25.0	6,311	5.01	31,604
2008	1,345	286	29.1	8,315	6.35	52,803
2009	1,256	251	27.1	6,791	5.06	34,355
2010	1,256	270	27.7	7,480	5.18	38,767
2011	1,227	239	25.3	6,051	7.81	47,250
2012	1,271	250	26.2	6,542	7.69	50,304
2013	1,451	278	27.4	7,626	7.95	60,598
2014	1,434	258	27.9	7,189	7.76	55,770

[1] Area planted in preceding fall.
NASS, Crops Branch, (202) 720–2127.

Table 1-16.—Rye: Supply and disappearance, United States, 2005–2014

Year begin-ning June	Supply				Disappearance							Ending stocks May 31
	Begin-ning stocks	Produc-tion	Imports	Total	Domestic use					Exports	Total dis-appear-ance [2]	
					Food	Seed	Indus-try [1]	Feed	Total			
	1,000 bushels	*1,000 bushels*	*1,000 bushels*	*1,000 bushels*	*1,000 bushels*	*1,000 bushels*	*1,000 bushels*	*1,000 bushels*	*1,000 bushels*	*1,000 bushels*	*1,000 bushels*	*1,000 bushels*
2005 ..	793	7,537	5,481	13,811	3,300	3,000	3,000	3,791	13 091	14	13,105	706
2006 ..	706	7,193	5,899	13,798	3,300	3,000	3,000	3,947	13,247	70	13,317	481
2007 ..	481	6,311	7,064	13,856	3,300	3,000	3,000	3,909	13,209	251	13,460	396
2008 ..	396	7,979	3,953	12,328	3,300	3,000	3,000	2,203	11,503	316	11,819	509
2009 ..	509	6,993	4,251	11,753	3,300	3,000	3,000	1,448	10,748	73	10,821	932
2010 ..	932	7,480	5,552	13,964	3,300	3,000	3,000	3,714	13,014	149	13,163	801
2011 ..	801	6,051	5,994	12,846	3,310	3,000	3,010	2,917	12,237	157	12,394	452
2012 ..	452	6,542	8,966	15,960	3,400	3,000	3,020	5,829	15,249	310	15,559	401
2013 ..	401	7,669	9,227	17,254	3,430	3,000	3,030	7,241	16,701	268	16,969	285
2014 ..	285	7,189	9,321	16,795	3,460	3,000	3,040	6,466	15,966	240	16,206	589

[1] Includes commercial adhesives, packaging materials, thatching, mattresses, hats, and paper.   [2] Totals may not add due to independent rounding.
ERS, Market and Trade Economics Division, (202) 694–5302.

Table 1-17.—Rye: Area, yield, and production, by State and United States, 2012–2014

State	Area planted [1]			Area harvested		
	2012	2013	2014	2012	2013	2014
	1,000 acres	*1,000 acres*	*1,000 acres*	*1,000 acres*	*1,000 acres*	*1,000 acres*
Georgia	230	190	170	25	40	20
Oklahoma	240	260	240	80	80	55
Other States [2]	801	1,001	1,024	145	158	183
United States	1,271	1,451	1,434	250	278	258

State	Yield per harvested acre			Production		
	2012	2013	2014	2012	2013	2014
	Bushels	*Bushels*	*Bushels*	*1,000 bushels*	*1,000 bushels*	*1,000 bushels*
Georgia	23.0	27.0	27.0	575	1,080	540
Oklahoma	21.0	20.0	9.0	1,680	1,600	495
Other States [2]	29.6	31.3	33.6	4,287	4,946	6,154
United States	26.2	27.4	27.9	6,542	7,626	7,189

[1] Includes area planted preceding fall.　[2] Other States include Illinois, Kansas, Michigan, Minnesota, Nebraska, New York, North Carolina, North Dakota, Pennsylvania, South Carolina, South Dakota, Texas, and Wisconsin.
NASS, Crops Branch, (202) 720–2127.

Table 1-18.—Rye: Marketing year average price and value, by State and United States, 2012–2014

State	Marketing year average price per bushel			Value of production		
	2012	2013	2014	2012	2013	2014
	Dollars	*Dollars*	*Dollars*	*1,000 dollars*	*1,000 dollars*	*1,000 dollars*
Georgia	9.50	8.35	7.75	5,463	9,018	4,185
Oklahoma	7.90	8.40	11.80	13,272	13,440	5,841
Other States [2]	7.36	7.71	7.43	31,569	38,140	45,744
United States	7.69	7.95	7.76	50,304	60,598	55,770

[1] Other States include Illinois, Kansas, Michigan, Minnesota, Nebraska, New York, North Carolina, North Dakota, Pennsylvania, South Carolina, South Dakota, Texas, and Wisconsin.
NASS, Crops Branch, (202) 720-2127.

Table 1-19.—International Rye: Area, yield, and production in specified countries, 2013/2014–2015/2016

Country	Area			Yield per hectare			Production		
	2013/ 2014	2014/ 2015	2015/ 2016	2013/ 2014	2014/ 2015	2015/ 2016	2013/ 2014	2014/ 2015	2015/ 2016
	1,000 hec- tares	*1,000 hec- tares*	*1,000 hec- tares*	*Metric tons*	*Metric tons*	*Metric tons*	*1,000 metric tons*	*1,000 metric tons*	*1,000 metric tons*
Argentina	35	51	32	1.49	1.90	1.91	52	97	61
Australia	35	35	36	0.57	0.57	0.61	20	20	22
Belarus	322	320	325	2.01	2.71	2.46	648	867	800
Canada	87	88	95	2.56	2.48	2.37	223	218	225
European Union ...	2,577	2,114	2,014	3.94	4.19	3.95	10,151	8,858	7,960
Kazakhstan	39	43	38	1.10	1.42	0.97	43	61	37
Norway	3	3	3	3.67	4.00	4.00	11	12	12
Russia	1,777	1,853	1,250	1.89	1.77	1.68	3,360	3,279	2,100
Turkey	140	140	140	2.50	2.50	2.50	350	350	350
Ukraine	279	185	150	2.29	2.57	2.60	638	475	390
Others	38	38	37	1.37	1.34	1.35	52	51	50
Total Foreign	5,332	4,870	4,120	2.92	2.93	2.91	15,548	14,288	12,007
United States	113	104	146	1.72	1.76	2.00	194	183	292
Total	5,445	4,974	4,266	2.89	2.91	2.88	15,742	14,471	12,299

FAS, Office of Global Analysis, (202) 720-6301. Prepared or estimated on the basis of official USDA production, supply, and distribution, supply, and distribution statistics from foreign governments.

Table 1-20.—Rye:[1] International trade, 2013/2014–2015/2016[2]

Country	2013/2014	2014/2015	2015/2016
	1,000 metric tons	*1,000 metric tons*	*1,000 metric tons*
Principle exporting countries:			
Belarus	5	5	5
Canada	118	86	100
European Union	169	184	150
Russia	73	114	80
Ukraine	51	22	20
Others			
Total Foreign	416	411	355
United States	7	6	5
Total	423	417	360
Principle importing countries:			
European Union	77	102	70
Israel	33	25	25
Japan	37	22	25
Korea, South	8	4	10
Norway	17	8	15
Russia	5	5	5
Switzerland	6	6	5
Others	1	5	
Total Foreign	184	177	155
United States	234	237	229
Total	418	414	384

[1] Flour and products reported in terms of grain equivalent.   [2] Year beginning July 1.
FAS, Office of Global Analysis, (202) 720-6301. Prepared or estimated on the basis of official USDA production, supply, and distribution statics from foreign governments.

Table 1-21.—Rice, rough: Area, yield, production, and value, United States, 2005–2014 [1]

Year	Area planted	Area harvested	Yield per acre	Production	Marketing year average price per cwt. received by farmers	Value of production
	1,000 acres	1,000 acres	Pounds	1,000 cwt	Dollars	1,000 dollars
2005	3,384	3,364	6,624	222,833	7.65	1,738,598
2006	2,838	2,821	6,898	194,585	9.96	1,990,783
2007	2,761	2,748	7,219	198,388	12.80	2,600,871
2008	2,995	2,976	6,846	203,733	16.80	3,603,460
2009	3,135	3,103	7,085	219,850	14.40	3,209,236
2010	3,636	3,615	6,725	243,104	12.70	3,183,213
2011	2,689	2,617	7,067	184,941	14.50	2,737,423
2012	2,700	2,679	7,463	199,939	15.10	3,067,365
2013	2,490	2,469	7,694	189,953	16.30	3,181,993
2014	2,954	2,933	7,576	222,215	13.40	3,075,618

[1] Sweet rice yield and production as short grain beginning in 2003.
NASS, Crops Branch, (202) 720–2127.

Table 1-22.—Rice, rough: Stocks on and off farms, United States, 2006–2015

Year beginning previous December	On farms			Off farms [1]		
	Dec. 1	Mar. 1	Aug. 1	Dec. 1	Mar. 1	Aug. 1
	1,000 cwt	1,000 cwt	1,000 cwt	1,000 cwt	1,000 cwt	1,000 cwt
2006	58,630	30,865	1,553	101,518	80,416	35,825
2007	52,420	28,015	1,220	97,706	76,145	33,713
2008	48,250	22,923	395	102,815	81,623	23,981
2009	47,530	21,286	876	91,071	70,042	23,787
2010	51,880	23,465	1,200	104,726	80,516	29,176
2011	63,617	33,895	3,772	109,869	86,720	37,917
2012	41,180	23,825	910	105,689	82,666	35,052
2013	39,385	18,430	640	108,650	85,839	29,880
2014	36,935	14,995	305	96,636	73,959	26,299
2015 [2]	47,865	25,810	1,480	110,061	86,658	41,293

[1] Stocks at mills and in attached warehouses, in warehouses not attached to mills, and in ports or in transit.   [2] Preliminary.
NASS, Crops Branch, (202) 720–2127.

Table 1-23.—Rice, by length of grain: Harvest, yield, and production, United States, 2005–2014

Year	Area harvested			Yield per acre			Production		
	Long grain	Medium grain	Short grain	Long grain	Medium grain	Short grain	Long grain	Medium grain	Short grain
	1,000 acres	1,000 acres	1,000 acres	Pounds	Pounds	Pounds	1,000 cwt	1,000 cwt	1,000 cwt
2005	2,734	575	55	6,479	7,375	6,000	177,125	42,408	3,300
2006	2,186	574	61	6,727	7,631	6,098	147,063	43,802	3,720
2007	2,052	630	66	6,980	8,105	6,197	143,235	51,063	4,090
2008	2,350	575	51	6,522	8,203	6,490	153,257	47,166	3,310
2009	2,265	786	52	6,743	8,052	7,373	152,725	63,291	3,834
2010	2,826	746	43	6,486	7,660	6,195	183,296	57,144	2,664
2011	1,739	834	44	6,691	7,861	6,880	116,352	65,562	3,027
2012	1,979	643	57	7,291	8,059	6,737	144,280	51,819	3,840
2013	1,767	655	47	7,464	8,384	6,685	131,896	54,915	3,142
2014	2,196	700	37	7,407	8,175	6,292	162,665	57,222	2,328

NASS, Crops Branch, (202) 720-2127.

Table 1-24.—Rice, rough, by length of grain: Stocks in all positions, United States, 2006–2015

Year beginning previous December	Dec. 1	Mar. 1	Jun. 1[1]	Aug. 1	Oct. 1[2]
	Long grain				
	1,000 cwt	1,000 cwt	1,000 cwt	1,000 cwt	1,000 cwt
2006	124,485	86,108		28,571	[4]
2007	109,301	76,127		25,738	77
2008	103,620	69,207	35,580	16,101	[4]
2009	96,994	64,226	34,293	17,698	372
2010	103,430	67,910	37,041	19,532	[4]
2011	123,521	86,864	54,636	32,847	[4]
2012	93,027	68,469	37,552	22,034	[4]
2013	99,111	69,313	(NA)	19,439	[4]
2014	85,149	56,125	31,622	14,010	[4]
2015[3]	106,786	71,243	42,295	23,917	[4]
	Medium grain				
	1,000 cwt	1,000 cwt	1,000 cwt	1,000 cwt	1,000 cwt
2006	32,802	23,299		8,012	2,921
2007	37,225	25,857		8,372	2,506
2008	43,520	32,584	16,284	7,196	1,084
2009	37,989	24,755	12,722	6,093	938
2010	49,264	33,395	18,344	9,527	3,053
2011	46,853	31,548	15,327	7,870	1,366
2012	50,935	35,978	20,272	12,983	1,870
2013	45,349	32,558	(NA)	10,057	2,029
2014	45,086	30,481	17,294	11,631	6,691
2015[3]	48,483	39,505	27,988	18,169	7,892
	Short grain				
	1,000 cwt	1,000 cwt	1,000 cwt	1,000 cwt	1,000 cwt
2006	2,861	1,874		795	[4]
2007	3,600	2,176		823	412
2008	3,925	2,755	1,554	1,079	[4]
2009	3,618	2,347	1,301	872	522
2010	3,912	2,676	2,023	1,317	[4]
2011	3,112	2,203	1,410	972	[4]
2012	2,907	2,044	1,282	945	[4]
2013	3,575	2,398	(NA)	1,024	[4]
2014	3,336	2,348	1,435	963	[4]
2015[3]	2,657	1,720	1,057	687	[4]

(NA) Not available. [1] Estimates began in 2008. [2] California only. [3] Preliminary. [4] Not published to avoid disclosing individual reports.
NASS, Crops Branch, (202) 720–2127.

Table 1-25.—Rough and milled rice (rough equivalent): Supply and disappearance, United States, 2004–2013[1]

Year beginning August	Supply				Disappearance					Ending stocks July 31
	Beginning stocks	Production	Imports[2]	Total	Food, industrial, & residual[3]	Seed	Total	Exports[2]	Total disappearance	
	Million cwt	Million cwt	Million cwt	Million cwt	Million cwt	Million cwt	Million cwt	Million cwt	Million cwt	Million cwt
2004 ...	23.7	232.4	13.2	269.2	118.5	4.2	122.7	108.8	231.5	37.7
2005 ...	37.7	222.8	17.1	277.7	116.3	3.5	119.8	114.9	234.7	43.0
2006 ...	43.0	194.6	20.6	258.2	124.7	3.4	128.1	90.8	218.8	39.3
2007 ...	39.3	198.4	23.9	261.6	123.2	3.7	126.8	105.3	232.1	29.5
2008 ...	29.5	203.7	19.2	252.4	123.8	3.9	127.6	94.4	222.0	30.4
2009 ...	30.4	219.9	19.0	269.3	119.9	4.5	124.4	108.3	232.8	36.5
2010 ...	36.5	243.1	18.3	297.9	133.6	3.3	136.9	112.6	249.5	48.5
2011 ...	48.5	184.9	19.4	252.8	107.5	3.3	110.8	100.9	211.7	41.1
2012 ...	41.1	199.5	21.1	261.7	115.6	3.1	118.6	106.6	225.3	36.4
2013 ...	36.4	189.9	23.1	249.4	121.3	3.6	124.9	92.7	217.6	31.8

[1] Consolidated supply and disappearance of rough and milled rice. Milled rice data converted to a rough basis using annually derived extraction rates as factors. [2] Trade data from Bureau of the Census. [3] The residual includes unaccounted losses in transporting, processing, and marketing.
ERS, Market and Trade Economics Division, (202) 694–5292.

Table 1-26.—Rice, by length of grain: Area, yield, and production, by State and United States, 2012–2014

State	Area harvested			Yield per acre			Production		
	2012	2013	2014	2012	2013	2014	2012	2013	2014
	Long grain								
	1,000 acres	1,000 acres	1,000 acres	Pounds	Pounds	Pounds	1,000 cwt	1,000 cwt	1,000 cwt
Arkansas	1,170	950	1,265	7,500	7,560	7,570	87,750	71,820	95,761
California	6	6	4	5,000	5,700	7,300	300	342	292
Louisiana	370	392	389	6,440	7,330	7,150	23,828	28,734	27,814
Mississippi	129	124	189	7,200	7,400	7,420	9,288	9,176	14,024
Missouri	173	154	207	7,000	7,030	6,830	12,110	10,826	14,138
Texas	131	141	138	8,400	7,800	7,500	11,004	10,998	10,350
United States	1,979	1,767	2,192	7,291	7,464	7,408	144,280	131,896	162,379
	Medium grain								
	1,000 acres	1,000 acres	1,000 acres	Pounds	Pounds	Pounds	1,000 cwt	1,000 cwt	1,000 cwt
Arkansas	114	119	214	7,280	7,570	7,540	8,299	9,008	16,136
California	495	510	392	8,350	8,670	8,800	41,333	44,217	34,496
Louisiana	27	21	69	6,340	6,670	7,020	1,712	1,401	4,844
Mississippi	-	-	1	-	-	7,200	-	-	72
Missouri	4	2	6	6,540	7,080	6,700	262	142	402
Texas	3	3	9	7,100	4,900	4,900	213	147	441
United States	643	655	691	8,059	8,384	8,161	51,819	54,915	56,391
	Short grain								
	1,000 acres	1,000 acres	1,000 acres	Pounds	Pounds	Pounds	1,000 cwt	1,000 cwt	1,000 cwt
Arkansas	1	1	1	6,000	6,000	6,000	60	60	60
Calfornia	56	46	35	6,750	6,700	6,300	3,780	3,082	2,205
United States	57	47	36	6,737	6,685	6,292	3,840	3,142	2,265

NASS, Crops Branch, (202) 720–2127.

Table 1-27.—Rice: Area, yield, and production, by State and United States, 2012–2014[1]

State	Area planted			Area harvested		
	2012	2013	2014	2012	2013	2014
	1,000 acres	1,000 acres	1,000 acres	1,000 acres	1,000 acres	1,000 acres
Arkansas	1,291	1,076	1,486	1,285	1,070	1,480
California	562	567	434	557	562	431
Louisiana	402	418	462	397	413	458
Mississippi	130	125	191	129	124	190
Missouri	180	159	216	177	156	213
Texas	135	145	150	134	144	147
United States	2,700	2,490	2,939	2,679	2,469	2,919

State	Yield per harvested acre			Production		
	2012	2013	2014	2012	2013	2014
	Pounds	Pounds	Pounds	1,000 cwt	1,000 cwt	1,000 cwt
Arkansas	7,480	7,560	7,560	96,109	80,888	111,957
California	8,150	8,480	8,580	45,413	47,641	36,993
Louisiana	6,430	7,300	7,130	25,540	30,135	32,658
Mississippi	7,200	7,400	7,420	9,288	9,176	14,096
Missouri	6,990	7,030	6,830	12,372	10,968	14,540
Texas	8,370	7,740	7,340	11,217	11,145	10,791
United States	7,463	7,694	7,572	199,939	189,953	221,035

[1] Sweet rice acreage included with short grain.
NASS, Crops Branch, (202) 720–2127.

Table 1-28.—Rice: Marketing year average price and value, by State and United States, 2012–2014

State	Marketing year average price per cwt.			Value of production		
	2012	2013	2014	2012	2013	2014
	Dollars	Dollars	Dollars	1,000 dollars	1,000 dollars	1,000 dollars
Arkansas	14.30	15.20	12.00	1,374,359	1,229,498	1,343,484
California	18.60	20.90	21.80	844,682	995,697	827,005
Louisiana	14.40	15.50	12.90	367,776	467,093	424,978
Mississippi	14.60	15.40	12.20	135,605	141,310	171,971
Missouri	14.10	15.10	11.00	174,445	165,617	159,940
Texas	15.20	16.40	13.80	170,498	182,778	148,240
United States	15.10	16.30	13.40	3,067,365	3,181,993	3,075,618

NASS, Crops Branch, (202) 720–2127.

Table 1-29.—Rice, milled, by length of grain: Stocks in all positions, United States, 2006–2015

Year beginning previous December	Whole kernels (head rice)				
	Dec. 1	Mar. 1	Jun. 1[1]	Aug. 1	Oct. 1[2]
	Long grain				
	1,000 cwt	1,000 cwt	1,000 cwt	1,000 cwt	1,000 cwt
2006	3,305	2,552	....	2,880	7
2007	2,803	2,454	....	1,989	([4])
2008	2,638	2,546	2,015	2,065	([4])
2009	2,504	2,300	3,251	1,658	([4])
2010	2,022	2,370	2,043	2,511	([4])
2011	2,665	3,038	3,291	1,924	([4])
2012	2,699	1,856	1,906	1,550	1
2013	2,574	3,144	(NA)	1,704	([4])
2014	3,348	2,379	([4])	1,556	([4])
2015[3]	2,308	1,952	2,523	1,792	([4])
	Medium grain				
	1,000 cwt	1,000 cwt	1,000 cwt	1,000 cwt	1,000 cwt
2006	1,247	1,136	....	395	422
2007	653	792	....	536	([4])
2008	958	1,735	850	508	([4])
2009	1,531	978	823	689	([4])
2010	1,496	1,472	1,188	799	454
2011	1,743	1,803	981	845	399
2012	1,406	935	1,041	496	281
2013	1,638	772	(NA)	726	([4])
2014	1,285	1,584	1,601	472	603
2015[3]	1,694	1,139	1,662	878	1,430
	Short grain				
	1,000 cwt	1,000 cwt	1,000 cwt	1,000 cwt	1,000 cwt
2006	75	53	....	53	36
2007	55	98	....	48	([4])
2008	92	69	78	59	([4])
2009	80	69	57	51	36
2010	73	74	47	60	([4])
2011	97	62	53	45	([4])
2012	199	49	60	38	69
2013	99	64	(NA)	61	28
2014	58	48	([4])	47	([4])
2015[3]	51	59	54	37	([4])

See footnote(s) at end of table.

Table 1-29.—Rice, milled, by length of grain: Stocks in all positions, United States, 2006–2015—Continued

Year beginning previous December	Broken kernels [5]				
	Dec. 1	Mar. 1	Jun. 1 [1]	Aug. 1	Oct. 1 [2]
	Second heads				
	1,000 cwt	1,000 cwt	1,000 cwt	1,000 cwt	1,000 cwt
2006	795	370	....	235	128
2007	240	562	....	307	([4])
2008	853	852	906	488	([4])
2009	661	794	828	1,465	([4])
2010	1,374	707	961	670	([4])
2011	888	634	817	992	([4])
2012	1,037	1,021	778	870	([4])
2013	1,231	1,225	(NA)	1,104	([4])
2014	1,243	1,064	1,159	797	([4])
2015 [3]	727	1,663	1,227	1,120	([4])
	Screenings				
	1,000 cwt	1,000 cwt	1,000 cwt	1,000 cwt	1,000 cwt
2006	198	162	....	84	....
2007	90	([4])	....	81	....
2008	195	163	145	206	....
2009	42	64	61	3	....
2010	52	20	34	93	....
2011	110	91	153	75	....
2012	192	82	145	51	....
2013	136	271	(NA)	153	....
2014	96	118	72	92	....
2015 [3]	118	115	153	88	....
	Brewers				
	1,000 cwt	1,000 cwt	1,000 cwt	1,000 cwt	1,000 cwt
2006	320	299	....	297	175
2007	163	([4])	....	150	([4])
2008	533	239	379	249	([4])
2009	437	527	704	211	([4])
2010	662	252	247	247	([4])
2011	799	647	673	786	([4])
2012	710	551	532	573	([4])
2013	1,241	1,189	(NA)	384	([4])
2014	575	651	589	747	([4])
2015 [3]	748	941	1,153	141	([4])

(NA) Not available.   [1] Estimates began in 2008.   [2] California only.   [3] Preliminary.   [4] Not published to avoid disclosing individual operations.   [5] Screenings included in second heads in California.
NASS, Crops Branch, (202) 720–2127.

Table 1-30.—Rice, rough: Support operations, United States, 2005–2014

Marketing year beginning August 1	Income support payment rates per cwt [1]	Program price levels per cwt		Put under loan		Acquired by CCC under loan program	Owned by CCC at end of marketing year
		Loan [2]	Target [3]	Quantity	Percentage of production		
	Dollars	Dollars	Dollars	Million cwt	Percent	Million cwt	Million cwt
2005/2006 ...	2.35/0.50	6.50	10.50	138.3	61.9	0.1	0.0
2006/2007 ...	2.35/0.00	6.50	10.50	92.6	47.8	0.0	0.0
2007/2008 ...	2.35/0.00	6.50	10.50	84.7	42.9	0.0	0.0
2008/2009 ...	2.35/0.00	6.50	10.50	72.4	35.5	0.0	0.0
2009/2010 ...	2.35/0.00	6.50	10.50	67.6	30.7	0.0	0.0
2010/2011 ...	2.35/0.00	6.50	10.50	86.5	35.5	0.0	0.0
2011/2012 ...	2.35/0.00	6.50	10.50	65.8	35.5	0.0	0.0
2012/2013 ...	2.35/0.00	6.50	10.50	65.9	33.0	0.0	0.0
2013/2014 ...	2.35/0.00	6.50	10.50	36.0	18.9	0.0	0.0
2014/2015 ...	(NA)/([4])	6.50	([5])	42.3	19.0	0.0	0.0

(NA) Not applicable as Direct Payments were eliminated in the 2014 Farm Bill. [1] Payment rates for 2005/2006 and subsequent crops are calculated according to the Direct and Counter-cyclical program provisions, following enactment of the Farm Security and Rural Investment Act of 2002 (2002 Act). The first entry is the direct payment rate and the second entry is the counter-cyclical payment rate. [2] Starting in 2009, producers who participate in the Average Crop Revenue Election (ACRE) program get a 30 percent reduction in their loan rate and a 20 percent reduction in their direct payment rate (not calculated in this table). [3] Target prices were reestablished under the 2002 Act for the Counter-cyclical program. [4] Only long grain rice received PLC payment ($2.10) in 2014/2015; medium/short grain and temperate japoinca did not. [5] Reference prices for long grain ($14.00), medium grain ($14.00), and temperate japonica ($16.10) rice established under 2014 Farm Bill for ARC-PLC programs.
FSA, Food Grains, (202) 720-5653.

Table 1-31.—Rice: United States exports (milled basis), by country of destination, 2011–2013 [1]

Country of destination	Year		
	2011	2012	2013 [2]
	Metric tons	Metric tons	Metric tons
Mexico	908,700	848,521	862,461
Haiti	293,457	360,760	324,082
Japan	376,072	342,145	295,860
Venezuela	53,468	226,510	295,644
Canada	232,427	232,844	249,415
Korea, South	163,354	71,911	159,378
Turkey	96,648	152,498	141,248
Saudi Arabia	141,554	114,873	136,734
Iran	0	3,060	125,686
Honduras	155,343	141,259	114,504
Colombia	4,820	97,299	108,538
Ghana	98,255	109,285	103,331
Libya	169,051	33,314	100,980
Jordan	72,716	103,759	87,323
El Salvador	96,252	83,759	73,477
Guatemala	78,151	90,642	67,504
Taiwan	23,634	74,769	66,151
Costa Rica	68,341	95,363	64,688
Iraq	41,109	0	39,957
Pakistan	37,593	52,040	39,544
Panama	61,447	95,586	35,152
United Kingdom	51,505	33,588	26,180
Hong Kong	1,433	6,668	24,347
Israel(*)	23,194	21,711	20,256
Australia(*)	12,303	13,968	13,284
Dominican Republic	17,329	7,843	12,953
Singapore	8,322	9,410	12,017
Liberia	62,421	46,157	11,446
Bahamas, The	8,263	8,599	8,932
Rest of World	351,481	311,437	153,240
World Total [3]	3,708,644	3,789,577	3,774,311

(*) Denotes a country that is a summarization of its component countries. [1] Year beginning Jan 1. [2] 2013 data does not reflect 13 month changes. [3] Includes countries not shown.
FAS, Grain and Feed Division, (202) 720–6219. www.fas.usda.gov/grain/default.html.

Table 1-32.—International Rice, milled: Area, yield, and production in specified countries, 2013/2014–2015/2016

Country	Area			Yield per hectare			Production		
	2013/ 2014	2014/ 2015	2015/ 2016	2013/ 2014	2014/ 2015	2015/ 2016	2013/2014	2014/2015	2015/2016
	1,000 hectares	*1,000 hectares*	*1,000 hectares*	*Metric tons*	*Metric tons*	*Metric tons*	*1,000 metric tons*	*1,000 metric tons*	*1,000 metric tons*
Bangladesh	11,750	11,790	12,000	4.39	4.39	4.33	34,390	34,500	34,600
Brazil	2,400	2,295	2,150	5.09	5.42	5.41	8,300	8,465	7,905
Burma	7,050	7,030	6,800	2.65	2.80	2.80	11,957	12,600	12,200
China	30,312	30,310	30,210	6.72	6.81	6.89	142,530	144,560	145,770
India	44,136	43,740	42,750	3.62	3.62	3.61	106,646	105,480	103,000
Indonesia	12,100	11,830	11,660	4.72	4.73	4.77	36,300	35,560	35,300
Japan	1,621	1,608	1,586	6.72	6.71	6.63	7,931	7,849	7,653
Philippines	4,800	4,705	4,650	3.92	4.02	3.93	11,858	11,915	11,500
Thailand	10,920	10,270	9,460	2.84	2.77	2.55	20,460	18,750	15,900
Vietnam	7,788	7,792	7,660	5.79	5.80	5.89	28,161	28,234	28,200
Others	27,857	28,128	27,742	2.29	2.27	2.27	63,773	63,739	62,956
Total Foreign	160,734	159,498	156,668	2.94	2.96	2.97	472,306	471,652	464,984
United States	999	1,187	1,042	8.62	8.49	8.37	6,117	7,106	6,107
Total	161,733	160,685	157,710	2.96	2.98	2.99	478,423	478,758	471,091

FAS, Office of Global Analysis, (202) 720-6301. Prepared or estimated on the basis of official USDA production, supply, and distribution, supply, and and distribution statistics from foreign governments.

Table 1-33.—Rice, milled equivalent: International trade, 2013/2014–2015/2016

Country	2013/2014	2014/2015	2015/2016
	1,000 metric tons	*1,000 metric tons*	*1,000 metric tons*
Principle exporting countries:			
Argentina	465	325	520
Brazil	819	930	830
Burma	1,688	1,750	1,800
Cambodia	1,000	1,150	900
Guyana	346	502	536
India	10,149	11,871	8,600
Pakistan	3,200	4,000	4,600
Thailand	10,969	9,779	10,000
Uruguay	890	800	950
Vietnam	6,325	6,606	7,000
Others	2,902	2,697	2,746
Total Foreign	38,753	40,410	38,482
United States	3,005	3,207	3,175
Total	41,758	43,617	41,657
Principle importing countries:			
China	4,000	4,700	5,000
European Union	1,530	1,703	1,550
Indonesia	1,225	1,198	2,000
Iran	1,600	1,350	1,450
Iraq	950	1,100	1,200
Malaysia	989	1,000	1,020
Nigeria	2,800	3,500	2,500
Philippines	1,200	1,800	2,000
Saudi Arabia	1,410	1,420	1,450
South Africa	1,144	980	1,080
Others	20,770	21,448	20,062
Total Foreign	37,618	40,199	39,312
United States	734	783	762
Total	38,352	40,982	40,074

FAS, Office of Global Analysis, (202) 720-6301. Prepared or estimated on the basis of official USDA production, supply, and distribution statistics from foreign governments.

Table 1-34.—Food grains: Average price, selected markets and grades, 2005–2013 [1]

Calendar year [2]	Kansas City			Minneapolis (rail)			Portland Wheat No. 1 Soft White	St. Louis Wheat, No. 2 Soft Red Winter (truck)
	Wheat, No. 1 Hard Winter, Ordinary Protein (rail)	Wheat, No. 1 Hard Winter, 13% protein (rail)	Wheat, No. 2 Soft Red Winter (rail)	Wheat, No. 1 Hard Amber Durum (milling) (rail)	Wheat, No. 1 Dark Northern Spring (rail), 14% protein	Rye, No. 2, 20 day delivery (truck)		
	Dollars per bushel	Dollars per bushel	Dollars per bushel	Dollars per bushel	Dollars per bushel	Dollars per bushel	Dollars per bushel	Dollars per bushel
2005	4.10	4.17	3.92	....	4.89	3.63	3.72	3.06
2006	5.11	5.21	4.27	(NA)	5.19	3.25	4.07	3.47
2007	6.85	7.06	6.27	11.33	7.01	6.24	7.29	5.96
2008	8.92	9.82	7.72	23.25	11.16	7.12	7.93	6.32
2009	5.80	6.29	5.06	....	7.21	4.35	5.28	5.55
2010	5.90	6.58	6.03	8.75	7.79	4.58	5.45	5.36
2011	8.44	9.17	7.87	....	11.36	....	7.08	7.49
2012	8.47	8.96	7.25	....	9.69	....	7.74	7.56
2013	7.22	8.60	6.67	(NA)	8.08	(NA)	7.67	6.97

Calendar year [2]	Chicago Wheat, No. 2 Soft Red Winter (rail)	Denver Wheat, No. 1 Hard Winter (truck red)	S.W. Louisiana Milled Rice		Arkansas Milled Rice		Texas Milled Rice
			Medium	Long	Medium	Long	Long
	Dollars per bushel	Dollars per bushel	Dollars per cwt	Dollars per cwt	Dollars per cwt	Dollars per cwt	Dollars per cwt
2005	3.01	3.37	16.55	14.22	15.94	14.32	16.53
2006	3.58	4.47	22.50	71.46	21.56	17.82	19.38
2007	5.85	6.05	23.44	19.28	22.81	19.50	21.58
2008	6.75	7.85	36.49	34.97	38.85	35.93	36.41
2009	4.43	5.04	39.56	24.91	40.57	26.46	27.88
2010	5.36	5.00	30.80	23.12	29.68	23.91	26.46
2011	6.83	7.36	33.47	26.20	34.99	27.10	29.25
2012	7.44	7.44	28.89	25.77	27.91	26.18	27.18
2013	6.84	7.27	30.56	28.48	28.68	28.52	29.61

(NA) Not available. [1] Simple average of daily prices. [2] For wheat and rye, crop year begins in June. For rice, crop year begins in August.
AMS, Livestock and Grain Market News branch, (202) 720–6231.

Table 1-35.—Corn: Area, yield, production, and value, United States, 2005–2014

Year	Corn for grain						Corn for silage		
	Area planted, all purposes	Area harvested	Yield per harvested acre	Production	Marketing year average price per bushel	Value of production	Area harvested	Yield per harvested acre	Production
	1,000 acres	1,000 acres	Bushels	1,000 bushels	Dollars	1,000 dollars	1,000 acres	Tons	1,000 tons
2005 ...	81,779	75,117	147.9	11,112,187	2.00	22,194,287	5,930	18.0	106,486
2006 ...	78,327	70,638	149.1	10,531,123	3.04	32,083,011	6,487	16.2	105,294
2007 ...	93,527	86,520	150.7	13,073,875	4.20	54,666,959	6,060	17.5	106,229
2008 ...	85,982	78,570	153.3	12,043,203	4.06	49,104,148	5,971	18.7	111,792
2009 ...	86,382	79,490	164.4	13,067,156	3.55	46,640,936	5,605	19.3	108,221
2010 ...	88,192	81,446	152.6	12,425,330	5.18	64,529,628	5,567	19.3	107,314
2011 ...	91,936	83,879	146.8	12,313,956	6.22	76,651,242	5,935	18.4	109,091
2012 ...	97,291	87,365	123.1	10,755,111	6.89	74,155,299	7,419	15.7	116,148
2013 ...	95,365	87,451	158.1	13,828,964	4.46	61,927,548	6,281	18.8	118,296
2014 ...	90,597	83,136	171.0	14,215,532	3.65	52,372,215	6,371	20.1	128,048

NASS, Crops Branch, (202) 720–2127.

Table 1-36.—Corn: Area, yield, and production, by State and United States, 2012–2014

State	Area planted for all purposes			Corn for grain		
				Area harvested		
	2012	2013	2014	2012	2013	2014
	1,000 acres	*1,000 acres*	*1,000 acres*	*1,000 acres*	*1,000 acres*	*1,000 acres*
Alabama	310	320	300	295	295	285
Arizona	70	85	75	32	51	28
Arkansas	710	880	540	695	870	530
California	640	600	520	180	180	95
Colorado	1,420	1,220	1,150	1,010	980	1,010
Connecticut	27	27	26	(NA)	(NA)	(NA)
Delaware	185	180	175	178	174	168
Florida	75	115	75	40	78	40
Georgia	345	510	350	310	465	310
Idaho	360	350	320	135	115	80
Illinois	12,800	12,000	11,900	12,250	11,800	11,750
Indiana	6,250	6,000	5,900	6,030	5,830	5,770
Iowa	14,200	13,600	13,700	13,700	13,050	13,300
Kansas	4,700	4,300	4,050	3,950	4,000	3,800
Kentucky	1,650	1,530	1,520	1,530	1,430	1,430
Louisiana	540	680	400	530	670	390
Maine	30	31	31	(NA)	(NA)	(NA)
Maryland	495	480	500	435	420	430
Massachusetts	16	16	16	(NA)	(NA)	(NA)
Michigan	2,700	2,600	2,550	2,380	2,230	2,210
Minnesota	8,750	8,600	8,200	8,330	8,140	7,550
Mississippi	820	860	510	795	830	485
Missouri	3,600	3,350	3,500	3,300	3,200	3,380
Montana	105	120	130	60	75	75
Nebraska	10,000	9,950	9,300	9,100	9,550	8,950
Nevada	8	7	4	(NA)	(NA)	(NA)
New Hampshire	14	14	15	(NA)	(NA)	(NA)
New Jersey	95	90	85	86	80	79
New Mexico	125	120	125	43	38	48
New York	1,170	1,200	1,140	680	690	680
North Carolina	870	930	840	820	860	780
North Dakota	3,640	3,850	2,800	3,460	3,600	2,530
Ohio	3,900	3,900	3,700	3,650	3,730	3,470
Oklahoma	360	370	320	295	310	290
Oregon	85	80	80	52	36	39
Pennsylvania	1,460	1,480	1,460	1,000	1,090	1,030
Rhode Island	2	2	2	(NA)	(NA)	(NA)
South Carolina	330	350	295	310	335	280
South Dakota	6,150	6,200	5,800	5,300	5,860	5,320
Tennessee	1,040	890	920	960	810	840
Texas	1,850	2,350	2,250	1,550	1,950	1,990
Utah	92	83	75	34	31	28
Vermont	91	92	92	(NA)	(NA)	(NA)
Virginia	510	510	500	350	360	350
Washington	195	190	215	115	105	110
West Virginia	51	53	51	35	36	36
Wisconsin	4,350	4,100	4,000	3,300	3,030	3,110
Wyoming	105	100	90	60	67	60
United States	97,291	95,365	90,597	87,365	87,451	83,136

See footnote(s) at end of table.

Table 1-36.—Corn: Area, yield, and production, by State and United States, 2012–2014—Continued

State	Corn for grain					
	Yield per harvested acre			Production		
	2012	2013	2014	2012	2013	2014
	1,000 acres	1,000 acres	1,000 acres	1,000 acres	1,000 acres	1,000 acres
Alabama	98.0	147.0	159.0	28,910	43,365	45,315
Arizona	195.0	177.0	210.0	6,240	9,027	5,880
Arkansas	178.0	186.0	187.0	123,710	161,820	99,110
California	180.0	191.0	165.0	32,400	34,380	15,675
Colorado	133.0	131.0	146.0	134,330	128,380	147,460
Connecticut	(NA)	(NA)	(NA)	(NA)	(NA)	(NA)
Delaware	135.0	166.0	200.0	24,030	28,884	33,600
Florida	115.0	133.0	135.0	4,600	10,374	5,400
Georgia	180.0	175.0	170.0	55,800	81,375	52,700
Idaho	195.0	181.0	200.0	26,325	20,815	16,000
Illinois	105.0	178.0	200.0	1,286,250	2,100,400	2,350,000
Indiana	99.0	177.0	188.0	596,970	1,031,910	1,084,760
Iowa	137.0	164.0	178.0	1,876,900	2,140,200	2,367,400
Kansas	95.0	126.0	149.0	375,250	504,000	566,200
Kentucky	68.0	170.0	158.0	104,040	243,100	225,940
Louisiana	173.0	173.0	183.0	91,690	115,910	71,370
Maine	(NA)	(NA)	(NA)	(NA)	(NA)	(NA)
Maryland	122.0	158.0	175.0	53,070	66,360	75,250
Massachusetts	(NA)	(NA)	(NA)	(NA)	(NA)	(NA)
Michigan	132.0	155.0	161.0	314,160	345,650	355,810
Minnesota	165.0	159.0	156.0	1,374,450	1,294,260	1,177,800
Mississippi	165.0	176.0	185.0	131,175	146,080	89,725
Missouri	75.0	136.0	186.0	247,500	435,200	628,680
Montana	104.0	115.0	100.0	6,240	8,625	7,500
Nebraska	142.0	169.0	179.0	1,292,200	1,613,950	1,602,050
Nevada	(NA)	(NA)	(NA)	(NA)	(NA)	(NA)
New Hampshire	(NA)	(NA)	(NA)	(NA)	(NA)	(NA)
New Jersey	118.0	139.0	157.0	10,148	11,120	12,403
New Mexico	170.0	190.0	195.0	7,310	7,220	9,360
New York	134.0	137.0	148.0	91,120	94,530	100,640
North Carolina	117.0	142.0	132.0	95,940	122,120	102,960
North Dakota	122.0	110.0	124.0	422,120	396,000	313,720
Ohio	120.0	174.0	176.0	438,000	649,020	610,720
Oklahoma	110.0	145.0	147.0	32,450	44,950	42,630
Oregon	205.0	188.0	190.0	10,660	6,768	7,410
Pennsylvania	131.0	146.0	154.0	131,000	159,140	158,620
Rhode Island	(NA)	(NA)	(NA)	(NA)	(NA)	(NA)
South Carolina	122.0	129.0	117.0	37,820	43,215	32,760
South Dakota	101.0	137.0	148.0	535,300	802,820	787,360
Tennessee	85.0	156.0	168.0	81,600	126,360	141,120
Texas	129.0	136.0	148.0	199,950	265,200	294,520
Utah	167.0	170.0	160.0	5,678	5,270	4,480
Vermont	(NA)	(NA)	(NA)	(NA)	(NA)	(NA)
Virginia	103.0	154.0	145.0	36,050	55,440	50,750
Washington	215.0	215.0	215.0	24,725	22,575	23,650
West Virginia	128.0	147.0	149.0	4,480	5,292	5,364
Wisconsin	120.0	145.0	156.0	396,000	439,350	485,160
Wyoming	142.0	127.0	138.0	8,520	8,509	8,280
United States	123.1	158.1	171.0	10,755,111	13,828,964	14,215,532

(NA) Not available.
NASS, Crops Branch, (202) 720–2127.

GRAIN AND FEED

Table 1-37.—Corn: Supply and disappearance, United States, 2005–2014

Year beginning September 1	Supply				Disappearance					Ending stocks Aug. 31
	Beginning stocks	Produc-tion	Imports	Total [1]	Domestic use			Exports	Total dis-appear-ance	
					Feed and residual	Food, seed, and industrial	Total			
	Million bushels	Million bushels	Million bushels	Million bushels	Million bushels	Million bushels	Million bushels	Million bushels	Million bushels	Million bushels
2005	2,114	11,112	9	13,235	6,115	3,019	9,134	2,134	11,268	1,967
2006	1,967	10,531	12	12,510	5,540	3,541	9,081	2,125	11,207	1,304
2007	1,304	13,038	20	14,362	5,858	4,442	10,300	2,437	12,737	1,624
2008	1,624	12,092	14	13,729	5,133	5,025	10,207	1,849	12,056	1,673
2009	1,673	13,067	8	14,749	5,101	5,961	11,062	1,979	13,041	1,708
2010	1,708	12,425	28	14,161	4,777	6,426	11,202	1,831	13,033	1,128
2011	1,128	12,314	29	13,471	4,519	6,424	10,943	1,539	12,482	989
2012	989	10,755	160	11,904	4,315	6,038	10,353	730	11,083	821
2013	821	13,829	36	14,686	5,040	6,493	11,534	1,920	13,454	1,232
2014	1,232	14,216	32	15,479	5,315	6,568	11,883	1,864	13,748	1,731

Latest data may be preliminary or projected. [1] Total may not add due to rounding.
ERS, Market and Trade Economics Division, (202) 694–5313.

Table 1-38.—Corn: Stocks on and off farms, United States, 2006–2015

Year beginning previous December	On farms				Off farms [1]			
	Dec. 1	Mar. 1	Jun. 1	Sep. 1 [2]	Dec. 1	Mar. 1	Jun. 1	Sep. 1 [2]
	1,000 bushels	1,000 bushels	1,000 bushels	1,000 bushels	1,000 bushels	1,000 bushels	1,000 bushels	1,000 bushels
2006	6,325,000	4,055,000	2,350,500	749,500	3,489,957	2,932,328	2,011,199	1,217,661
2007	5,627,000	3,330,000	1,826,600	460,100	3,305,707	2,738,250	1,706,843	843,547
2008	6,530,000	3,780,000	1,970,900	499,950	3,748,085	3,078,722	2,057,117	1,124,200
2009	6,482,000	4,085,000	2,205,400	607,500	3,590,106	2,869,145	2,056,027	1,065,811
2010	7,405,000	4,548,000	2,131,400	485,100	3,497,460	3,145,787	2,178,671	1,222,687
2011	6,302,000	3,384,000	1,681,500	314,950	3,754,769	3,139,228	1,988,832	812,695
2012	6,175,000	3,192,000	1,482,000	313,700	3,471,823	2,831,356	1,666,204	675,327
2013	4,586,000	2,669,200	1,260,100	275,000	3,446,732	2,730,726	1,506,144	546,185
2014	6,380,000	3,860,500	1,863,200	462,000	4,072,532	3,147,623	1,988,516	769,904
2015 [3]	7,087,000	4,380,000	2,275,000	593,000	4,124,380	3,364,906	2,177,988	1,138,164

[1] Includes stocks at mills, elevators, warehouses, terminals, and processors. [2] Old crop only. [3] Preliminary.
NASS, Crops Branch, (202) 720–2127.

Table 1-39.—Corn: Utilization for silage, by State and United States, 2012–2014

State	Silage								
	Area harvested			Yield per acre			Production		
	2012	2013	2014	2012	2013	2014	2012	2013	2014
	1,000 acres	*1,000 acres*	*1,000 acres*	*Tons*	*Tons*	*Tons*	*1,000 tons*	*1,000 tons*	*1,000 tons*
Alabama	7	9	9	12.0	17.0	17.0	84	153	153
Arizona	38	33	46	28.0	30.0	29.0	1,064	990	1,334
Arkansas	3	2	2	7.0	18.0	18.0	21	36	36
California	455	415	420	26.5	26.5	26.0	12,058	10,998	10,920
Colorado	160	100	110	19.0	23.0	25.0	3,040	2,300	2,750
Connecticut	22	23	22	20.0	19.0	20.0	440	437	440
Delaware	5	5	5	17.0	17.0	24.0	85	85	120
Florida	33	35	30	19.0	18.0	13.0	627	630	390
Georgia	30	35	35	21.0	20.0	19.5	630	700	683
Idaho	220	230	235	27.0	26.0	28.0	5,940	5,980	6,580
Illinois	220	100	80	11.0	19.0	22.0	2,420	1,900	1,760
Indiana	170	130	100	13.0	23.0	22.0	2,210	2,990	2,200
Iowa	375	390	310	15.0	19.0	20.0	5,625	7,410	6,200
Kansas	400	150	150	10.0	13.0	14.0	4,000	1,950	2,100
Kentucky	90	80	75	12.5	21.0	21.0	1,125	1,680	1,575
Louisiana	5	3	2	15.0	18.0	18.0	75	54	36
Maine	25	27	27	16.0	17.5	18.5	400	473	500
Maryland	50	55	60	18.0	21.0	22.0	900	1,155	1,320
Massachusetts	13	13	13	19.0	18.0	20.0	247	234	260
Michigan	300	350	320	15.5	17.5	20.5	4,650	6,125	6,560
Minnesota	350	380	500	18.0	16.5	18.0	6,300	6,270	9,000
Mississippi	10	10	10	14.0	16.0	14.0	140	160	140
Missouri	150	80	80	8.0	14.0	18.0	1,200	1,120	1,440
Montana	42	41	51	20.0	23.0	22.0	840	943	1,122
Nebraska	550	260	260	10.0	16.0	21.0	5,500	4,160	5,460
Nevada	6	6	3	24.0	24.0	20.0	144	144	60
New Hampshire	13	13	14	20.0	20.0	21.0	260	260	294
New Jersey	8	9	5	15.0	20.0	20.0	120	180	100
New Mexico	80	79	73	24.0	25.0	26.0	1,920	1,975	1,898
New York	475	500	450	17.0	17.0	18.0	8,075	8,500	8,100
North Carolina	40	45	50	16.0	17.0	19.0	640	765	950
North Dakota	150	140	230	12.0	12.0	14.5	1,800	1,680	3,335
Ohio	200	130	190	15.0	19.5	20.5	3,000	2,535	3,895
Oklahoma	30	37	20	15.0	21.0	17.0	450	777	340
Oregon	32	43	40	27.0	27.0	25.0	864	1,161	1,000
Pennsylvania	430	380	410	18.0	20.5	20.0	7,740	7,790	8,200
Rhode Island	2	2	2	20.0	20.5	20.0	40	41	40
South Carolina	13	10	11	16.0	18.0	14.0	208	180	154
South Dakota	600	280	400	8.5	13.0	15.5	5,100	3,640	6,200
Tennessee	50	60	60	13.0	19.0	21.0	650	1,140	1,260
Texas	190	220	210	19.0	19.0	22.0	3,610	4,180	4,620
Utah	56	49	45	22.0	23.0	22.0	1,232	1,127	990
Vermont	81	85	85	19.0	15.0	18.0	1,539	1,275	1,530
Virginia	130	125	125	15.0	20.0	19.5	1,950	2,500	2,438
Washington	80	85	105	25.0	27.0	28.0	2,000	2,295	2,940
West Virginia	15	16	14	16.0	19.0	18.0	240	304	252
Wisconsin	980	980	850	14.5	16.5	18.5	14,210	16,170	15,725
Wyoming	35	31	27	21.0	24.0	24.0	735	744	648
United States	7,419	6,281	6,371	15.7	18.8	20.1	116,148	118,296	128,048

NASS, Crops Branch, (202) 720–2127.

Table 1-40.—Corn for grain: Marketing year average price and value, by State and United States, 2012–2014

State	Marketing year average price per bushel			Value of production		
	2012	2013	2014	2012	2013	2014
	Dollars	*Dollars*	*Dollars*	*1,000 dollars*	*1,000 dollars*	*1,000 dollars*
Alabama	7.18	4.71	3.80	207,574	204,249	172,197
Arizona	7.84	5.89	5.25	48,922	53,169	30,870
Arkansas	6.81	5.12	4.05	842,465	828,518	401,396
California	6.68	5.33	4.70	216,432	183,245	73,673
Colorado	6.86	4.61	4.10	921,504	591,832	604,586
Delaware	7.55	4.94	3.95	181,427	142,687	132,720
Florida	7.50	4.51	3.60	34,500	46,787	19,440
Georgia	7.90	5.17	4.50	440,820	420,709	237,150
Idaho	7.10	4.91	4.20	186,908	102,202	67,200
Illinois	6.87	4.52	3.65	8,836,538	9,493,808	8,577,500
Indiana	7.23	4.47	3.60	4,316,093	4,612,638	3,905,136
Iowa	6.92	4.49	3.70	12,988,148	9,609,498	8,759,380
Kansas	7.04	4.49	3.75	2,641,760	2,262,960	2,123,250
Kentucky	6.96	4.67	3.75	724,118	1,135,277	847,275
Louisiana	6.90	5.10	4.15	632,661	591,141	296,186
Maryland	7.30	4.84	3.90	387,411	321,182	293,475
Michigan	6.69	4.18	3.65	2,101,730	1,444,817	1,298,707
Minnesota	6.67	4.30	3.65	9,167,582	5,565,318	4,298,970
Mississippi	6.94	5.05	4.30	910,355	737,704	385,818
Missouri	7.34	4.57	3.40	1,816,650	1,988,864	2,137,512
Montana	7.21	4.27	3.75	44,990	36,829	28,125
Nebraska	6.85	4.47	3.75	8,851,570	7,214,357	6,007,688
New Jersey	7.40	4.66	3.80	75,095	51,819	47,131
New Mexico	7.30	5.18	4.35	53,363	37,400	40,716
New York	6.78	4.52	3.90	617,794	427,276	392,496
North Carolina	7.48	4.96	4.05	717,631	605,715	416,988
North Dakota	6.46	3.91	3.30	2,726,895	1,548,360	1,035,276
Ohio	7.09	4.41	3.65	3,105,420	2,862,178	2,229,128
Oklahoma	7.04	5.09	4.10	228,448	228,796	174,783
Oregon	6.96	5.44	4.50	74,194	36,818	33,345
Pennsylvania	7.21	4.47	3.75	944,510	711,356	594,825
South Carolina	7.50	4.67	3.90	283,650	201,814	127,764
South Dakota	6.72	4.05	3.25	3,597,216	3,251,421	2,558,920
Tennessee	7.28	4.87	3.75	594,048	615,373	529,200
Texas	7.12	5.14	4.45	1,423,644	1,363,128	1,310,614
Utah	7.59	5.47	4.60	43,096	28,827	20,608
Virginia	7.30	4.80	3.90	263,165	266,112	197,925
Washington	6.69	5.29	5.10	165,410	119,422	120,615
West Virginia	7.20	4.70	3.80	32,256	24,872	20,383
Wisconsin	6.69	4.38	3.70	2,649,240	1,924,353	1,795,092
Wyoming	7.05	4.08	3.40	60,066	34,717	28,152
United States	6.89	4.46	3.65	74,155,299	61,927,548	52,372,215

NASS, Crops Branch, (202) 720–2127.

Table 1-41.—International Corn: Area, yield, and production in specified countries, 2013/2014–2015/2016

Country	Area			Yield per hectare			Production		
	2013/ 2014	2014/ 2015	2015/ 2016	2013/ 2014	2014/ 2015	2015/ 2016	2013/2014	2014/2015	2015/2016
	1,000 hectares	*1,000 hectares*	*1,000 hectares*	*Metric tons*	*Metric tons*	*Metric tons*	*1,000 metric tons*	*1,000 metric tons*	*1,000 metric tons*
Argentina	3,400	3,300	3,400	7.65	8.18	7.94	26,000	27,000	27,000
Brazil	15,800	15,750	16,200	5.06	5.40	5.19	80,000	85,000	84,000
Canada	1,480	1,227	1,310	9.59	9.36	10.38	14,194	11,487	13,600
China	36,318	37,123	38,120	6.02	5.81	5.89	218,490	215,646	224,580
European Union	9,664	9,530	9,287	6.69	7.95	6.22	64,635	75,793	57,751
India	9,066	9,090	9,000	2.68	2.66	2.33	24,259	24,170	21,000
Indonesia	3,120	3,100	3,180	2.92	2.90	2.96	9,100	9,000	9,400
Mexico	7,052	7,325	7,000	3.24	3.48	3.43	22,880	25,480	24,000
Russia	2,322	2,596	2,650	5.01	4.36	4.91	11,635	11,325	13,000
Ukraine	4,825	4,625	4,080	6.40	6.15	5.71	30,900	28,450	23,300
Others	52,753	51,317	50,234	2.62	2.64	2.53	138,015	135,242	127,018
Total Foreign	145,800	144,983	144,461	4.39	4.47	4.32	640,108	648,593	624,649
United States	35,390	33,644	32,678	9.93	10.73	10.57	351,272	361,091	345,486
Total	181,190	178,627	177,139	5.47	5.65	5.48	991,380	1,009,684	970,135

FAS, Office of Global Analysis, (202) 720-6301. Prepared or estimated on the basis of offical USDA production, supply, and distribution statistics from foreign governments.

Table 1-42.—Corn: International trade, 2013/2014–2015/2016

Country	2013/2014	2014/2015	2015/2016
	1,000 metric tons	*1,000 Metric tons*	*1,000 metric tons*
Principle exporting countries:			
Argentina	17,102	18,500	17,000
Brazil	20,967	34,450	28,000
Burma	700	850	900
Canada	1,949	423	1,000
European Union	2,405	4,026	1,500
Mexico	501	784	1,000
Paraguay	2,372	3,287	2,300
Russia	4,192	3,213	3,800
Serbia	1,736	2,964	1,700
Ukraine	20,004	19,661	15,500
Others	10,393	5,692	5,515
Total Foreign	82,321	93,850	78,215
United States	48,783	47,359	41,912
Total	131,104	141,209	120,127
Principle importing countries:			
Algeria	3,739	4,381	4,200
Colombia	4,436	4,496	4,500
Egypt	8,726	7,826	8,250
European Union	16,015	8,646	16,000
Iran	5,500	6,200	5,000
Japan	15,121	14,656	14,700
Korea, South	10,406	10,168	10,000
Malaysia	3,476	3,221	3,500
Mexico	10,954	11,269	11,500
Taiwan	4,189	3,821	4,100
Others	40,542	47,839	46,125
Total Foreign	123,104	122,523	127,875
United States	909	804	1,270
Total	124,013	123,327	129,145

FAS, Office of Global Analysis, (202) 720-6301. Prepared or estimated on the basis of official USDA production, supply, and distribution statistics from foreign governments.

Table 1-43.—Corn: Support operations, United States, 2005/2006–2014/2015

Marketing year beginning September 1	Income support payment rates per bushel [1]	Program price levels per bushel		Put under loan		Acquired by CCC under loan program [5]	Owned by CCC at end of marketing year
		Loan [2]	Target [3]	Quantity	Percentage of production [4]		
	Dollars	*Dollars*	*Dollars*	*Million bushels*	*Percent*	*Million bushels*	*Million bushels*
2005/2006	0.28/0.35	1.95	2.63	1,064	9.6	2	1.5
2006/2007	0.28/0.00	1.95	2.63	1,108	10.5	0	0
2007/2008	0.28/0.00	1.95	2.63	1,218	9.3	0	0
2008/2009	0.28/0.00	1.95	2.63	1,074	8.9	0	0
2009/2010	0.28/0.00	1.95	2.63	934	7.1	0	0
2010/2011	0.28/0.00	1.95	2.63	801	6.4	0	0
2011/2012	0.28/0.00	1.95	2.63	574	4.6	0	0
2012/2013	0.28/0.00	1.95	2.63	368	3.4	0	0
2013/2014	0.28/0.00	1.95	2.63	460	3.3	0	0
2014/2015	0.00	1.95	3.70	574	4.0	0	0

[1] The first entry is the direct payment rate and the second entry is the counter-cyclical payment rate for 2004/2005-2013/2014. For 2009/2010-2013/2014, producers who participate in the Average Crop Revenue (ACRE) program get a 20 percent reduction in their direct payment, not calculated in this table. For 2014/2015 and after, the entry is the price loss coverage payment rate. Agricultural Risk Coverage (ARC) is also available, but payment rates are established at the county or farm levels. [2] For 2009/2010-2013/2014, producers who participate in the ACRE program get a 30 percent reduction in their loan rate, not calculated in this table. [3] Target applies to 2003/2004-2013/2014 and Reference applies beginning with 2014/2015. [4] Percent of production is on a grain basis. [5] Acquisitions as of December 31, 2015.
FSA, Feed Grains and Oilseeds, (202) 720–2711.

Table 1-44.—Corn: United States exports, specified by country of destination, 2011–2013 [1]

Country of destination	2011	2012	2013 [2]
	Metric tons	*Metric tons*	*Metric tons*
Japan	12,908,304	10,012,409	6,574,428
Mexico	8,596,943	8,475,746	6,537,683
China	2,727,730	4,365,752	3,661,645
Venezuela	832,521	1,389,869	1,123,140
Korea, South	5,946,476	2,002,993	1,001,651
Colombia	541,390	233,835	748,958
Taiwan	2,668,706	1,003,113	667,537
Canada	963,269	596,119	452,450
Guatemala	694,813	446,164	376,004
Saudi Arabia	620,630	313,526	344,709
Peru	39,300	185	253,682
El Salvador	547,842	218,988	242,783
Honduras	462,012	284,226	239,122
Panama	311,203	56,083	238,516
Jamaica	259,969	263,552	237,725
Costa Rica	672,478	394,571	217,883
Cuba	449,952	485,340	185,008
Vietnam	2,440	894	125,659
Egypt	2,326,046	206,857	118,655
Dominican Republic	712,000	146,838	104,803
Trinidad and Tobago	70,563	76,655	91,590
Spain	266,085	776	68,842
Nicaragua	151,854	105,719	48,720
Chile	0	648	35,239
Indonesia	397,483	20,298	31,815
Barbados	28,748	25,067	31,307
Guyana	41,253	32,774	20,318
Hong Kong	22,592	18,572	17,143
Philippines	2,896	17,212	13,730
Haiti	47	4,294	13,000
Other World Total	2,358,945	159,470	41,304
World Total	45,624,490	31,358,545	23,865,049

(*) Denotes a country that is a summarization of its component countries.   [1] Compiled from U.S. Census data. Excludes seed, popcorn.   [2] 2013 data does not reflect 13 month changes.
FAS, Office of Global Analysis, (202) 720-6301.

Table 1-45.—Oats: Area, yield, production, and value, United States, 2005–2014

Year	Area		Yield per harvested acre	Production	Marketing year average price per bushel received by farmers	Value of production
	Planted [1]	Harvested				
	1,000 acres	*1,000 acres*	*Bushels*	*1,000 bushels*	*Dollars*	*1,000 dollars*
2005	4,246	1,823	63.0	114,859	1.63	195,166
2006	4,166	1,564	59.8	93,522	1.87	180,899
2007	3,763	1,504	60.1	90,430	2.63	247,644
2008	3,260	1,414	63.7	90,051	3.15	273,843
2009	3,349	1,340	67.9	91,043	2.02	200,997
2010	3,113	1,267	64.6	81,856	2.52	218,536
2011	2,349	875	57.3	50,126	3.49	175,523
2012	2,700	1,005	61.2	61,486	3.89	243,018
2013	2,980	1,009	64.1	64,642	3.75	239,807
2014	2,753	1,035	67.9	10,232	3.21	241,472

[1] Relates to the total area of oats sown for all purposes, including oats sown in the preceding fall.
NASS, Crops Branch, (202) 720–2127.

Table 1-46.—Oats: Stocks on and off farms, United States, 2005–2014

Year beginning September	On farms				Off farms [1]			
	Sep. 1	Dec. 1	Mar. 1	Jun. 1	Sep. 1	Dec. 1	Mar. 1	Jun. 1
2005	71,700	60,100	42,200	25,190	41,803	35,617	32,673	27,376
2006	60,800	53,000	33,900	18,400	39,284	45,889	37,158	32,198
2007	53,650	43,100	31,000	16,100	34,710	51,331	47,988	50,674
2008	52,800	42,600	30,200	17,480	66,296	72,322	65,250	66,619
2009	54,500	43,000	30,900	17,600	73,875	67,629	67,091	62,716
2010	45,480	34,100	26,950	14,580	70,722	66,911	59,361	53,049
2011	30,300	24,600	19,550	11,070	47,391	54,244	55,044	43,869
2012	34,100	26,100	18,900	11,380	50,872	47,051	33,726	24,957
2013	37,150	25,650	19,800	9,710	26,339	22,394	15,323	15,029
2014	41,400	31,300	20,810	15,120	32,910	35,670	38,609	38,625

[1] Includes stocks at mills, elevators, warehouses, terminals, and processors.
NASS, Crops Branch, (202) 720–2127.

Table 1-47.—Oats: Supply and disappearance, United States, 2005–2014

Year beginning June 1	Supply				Disappearance					Ending stocks May 31
	Beginning stocks	Produc- tion	Imports	Total	Domestic use			Exports	Total dis- appear- ance	
					Feed and residual	Food, seed and industrial	Total			
	Million bushels	*Million bushels*	*Million bushels*	*Million bushels*	*Million bushels*	*Million bushels*	*Million bushels*	*Million bushels*	*Million bushels*	*Million bushels*
2005	58	115	91	264	136	74	209	2	211	53
2006	53	94	106	252	125	74	199	3	202	51
2007	51	90	123	264	120	74	195	3	198	67
2008	67	89	115	270	108	75	183	3	186	84
2009	84	91	95	270	113	74	188	2	190	80
2010	80	82	85	247	103	74	177	3	180	68
2011	68	50	94	212	78	76	154	2	157	55
2012	55	61	93	209	96	76	172	1	173	36
2013	36	65	97	198	98	73	172	2	173	25
2014	25	70	107	202	70	77	147	2	149	54

Latest data may be preliminary or projected. Totals may not add due to rounding.
ERS, Market and Trade Economics Division, (202) 694–5313.

Table 1-48.—Oats: Area, yield, and production, by State and United States, 2012–2014

State	Area planted [1]			Area harvested		
	2012	2013	2014	2012	2013	2014
	1,000 acres	*1,000 acres*	*1,000 acres*	*1,000 acres*	*1,000 acres*	*1,000 acres*
Alabama	60	60	50	15	20	15
Arkansas	12	11	12	7	7	8
California	180	150	110	20	15	10
Colorado	55	55	45	6	12	9
Georgia	60	50	60	20	18	20
Idaho	60	70	70	10	15	15
Illinois	30	40	35	15	25	25
Indiana	15	20	20	5	10	10
Iowa	130	220	145	58	60	55
Kansas	105	100	85	30	20	15
Maine	29	28	32	28	26	31
Michigan	50	50	50	35	30	40
Minnesota	190	240	230	135	105	125
Missouri	20	30	25	8	14	13
Montana	45	50	45	18	22	16
Nebraska	75	150	90	18	25	20
New York	70	75	55	50	46	40
North Carolina	40	35	33	13	13	17
North Dakota	200	225	235	105	135	105
Ohio	70	50	55	46	25	39
Oklahoma	75	60	60	7	7	10
Oregon	35	30	30	19	13	18
Pennsylvania	100	95	90	65	50	60
South Carolina	28	20	21	13	9	10
South Dakota	160	260	250	45	120	100
Texas	500	450	450	65	40	45
Utah	30	40	20	3	5	3
Virginia	11	10	10	4	2	3
Washington	15	20	25	6	5	5
Wisconsin	220	255	255	130	105	140
Wyoming	30	31	30	6	10	7
United States	2,700	2,980	2,723	1,005	1,009	1,029

State	Yield per harvested acre			Production		
	2012	2013	2014	2012	2013	2014
	Bushels	*Bushels*	*Bushels*	*1,000 bushels*	*1,000 bushels*	*1,000 bushels*
Alabama	55.0	60.0	65.0	825	1,200	975
Arkansas	80.0	73.0	90.0	560	511	720
California	90.0	80.0	100.0	1,800	1,200	1,000
Colorado	70.0	65.0	60.0	420	780	540
Georgia	53.0	60.0	54.0	1,060	1,080	1,080
Idaho	65.0	73.0	82.0	650	1,095	1,230
Illinois	76.0	69.0	80.0	1,140	1,725	2,000
Indiana	70.0	71.0	74.0	350	710	740
Iowa	65.0	66.0	64.0	3,770	3,960	3,520
Kansas	33.0	42.0	56.0	990	840	840
Maine	65.0	67.0	70.0	1,820	1,742	2,170
Michigan	60.0	62.0	69.0	2,100	1,860	2,760
Minnesota	62.0	57.0	63.0	8,370	5,985	7,875
Missouri	52.0	53.0	65.0	416	742	845
Montana	45.0	54.0	69.0	810	1,188	1,104
Nebraska	57.0	65.0	80.0	1,026	1,625	1,600
New York	65.0	67.0	63.0	3,250	3,082	2,520
North Carolina	75.0	70.0	67.0	975	910	1,139
North Dakota	62.0	62.0	73.0	6,510	8,370	7,665
Ohio	56.0	63.0	63.0	2,576	1,575	2,457
Oklahoma	45.0	38.0	38.0	315	266	380
Oregon	95.0	100.0	85.0	1,805	1,300	1,530
Pennsylvania	61.0	62.0	58.0	3,965	3,100	3,480
South Carolina	54.0	59.0	62.0	702	531	620
South Dakota	68.0	77.0	93.0	3,060	9,240	9,300
Texas	49.0	46.0	38.0	3,185	1,840	1,710
Utah	76.0	62.0	69.0	228	310	207
Virginia	75.0	70.0	78.0	300	140	234
Washington	82.0	68.0	70.0	492	340	350
Wisconsin	60.0	65.0	62.0	7,800	6,825	8,680
Wyoming	36.0	57.0	59.0	216	570	413
United States	61.2	64.1	67.7	61,486	64,642	69,684

[1] Relates to the total area of oats sown for all purposes, including oats sown in the preceding fall.
NASS, Crops Branch, (202) 720–2127.

Table 1-49.—Oats: Support operations, United States, 2005/2006–2014/2015

Marketing Year beginning June 1	Income support payment rates per bushel [1]	Program price levels per bushel		Put under loan		Acquired by CCC under loan program [5]	Owned by CCC at end of marketing year
		Loan [2]	Target [3]	Quantity	Percentage of production [4]		
	Dollars	Dollars	Dollars	Million bushels	Percent	Million bushels	Million bushels
2005/2006	0.02/0.00	1.33	1.44	3.0	2.6	0.0	0.0
2006/2007	0.02/0.00	1.33	1.44	1.7	1.8	0.0	0.0
2007/2008	0.02/0.00	1.33	1.44	1.2	1.3	0.0	0.0
2008/2009	0.02/0.00	1.33	1.44	1.1	1.3	0.0	0.0
2009/2010	0.02/0.00	1.33	1.44	1.1	1.2	0.0	0.0
2010/2011	0.02/0.00	1.39	1.79	0.7	0.9	0.0	0.0
2011/2012	0.02/0.00	1.39	1.79	0.2	0.4	0.0	0.0
2012/2013	0.02/0.00	1.39	1.79	0.3	0.5	0.0	0.0
2013/2014	0.02/0.00	1.39	1.79	0.3	0.5	0.0	0.0
2014/2015	0.00	1.39	2.40	0.5	0.7	0.0	0.0

[1] The first entry is the direct payment rate and the second entry is the counter-cyclical payment rate for 2004/2005-2013/2014. For 2009/2010-2013/2014, producers who participate in the Average Crop Revenue (ACRE) program get a 20 percent reduction in their direct payment, not calculated in this table. For 2014/2015 and after, the entry is the price loss coverage payment rate. Agricultural Risk Coverage (ARC) is also available, but payment rates are established at the county or farm levels. [2] For 2009/2010-2013/2014, producers who participate in the ACRE program get a 30 percent reduction in their loan rate, not calculated in this table. [3] Target applies to 2003/2004-2013/2014 and Reference applies beginning with 2014/2015. [4] Percent of production is on a grain basis. [5] Acquisitions as of December 31, 2015.
FSA, Feed Grains and Oilseeds, (202) 720–2711.

Table 1-50.—Oats: Marketing year average price and value of production, by State and United States, 2012–2014

State	Marketing year average price per bushel			Value of production		
	2012	2013	2014	2012	2013	2014
	Dollars	Dollars	Dollars	1,000 dollars	1,000 dollars	1,000 dollars
Alabama	3.35	3.90	4.25	2,764	4,680	4,144
Arkansas	3.60	3.40	3.95	2,016	1,737	2,844
California	4.15	3.38	3.40	7,470	4,056	3,400
Colorado	4.22	4.91	3.70	1,772	3,830	1,998
Georgia	3.50	3.80	4.00	3,710	4,104	4,320
Idaho	3.30	3.80	2.45	2,145	4,161	3,014
Illinois	4.39	4.07	4.85	5,005	7,021	9,700
Indiana	4.39	4.25	4.55	1,537	3,018	3,367
Iowa	4.04	3.93	3.60	15,231	15,563	12,672
Kansas	4.40	4.25	3.65	4,356	3,570	3,066
Maine	3.00	2.45	2.35	5,460	4,432	5,100
Michigan	4.02	3.68	3.40	8,442	6,845	9,384
Minnesota	3.67	3.78	3.25	30,718	22,623	25,594
Missouri	4.15	3.85	4.75	1,726	2,857	4,014
Montana	3.74	2.87	3.30	3,029	3,410	3,643
Nebraska	4.21	4.18	3.00	4,319	6,793	4,800
New York	3.71	3.60	3.50	12,058	11,095	8,820
North Carolina	3.75	3.30	3.20	3,656	3,003	3,645
North Dakota	3.36	3.14	2.45	21,874	26,282	18,779
Ohio	4.71	3.75	4.65	12,133	5,906	11,425
Oklahoma	5.10	3.80	4.35	1,607	1,011	1,653
Oregon	3.89	4.61	4.45	7,021	5,993	6,809
Pennsylvania	4.20	3.91	3.65	16,653	12,121	12,702
South Carolina	3.50	3.60	3.60	2,457	1,912	2,232
South Dakota	3.96	3.67	2.95	12,118	33,911	27,435
Texas	5.94	3.63	5.95	18,919	6,679	10,175
Utah	4.40	4.42	3.80	1,003	1,370	787
Virginia	3.50	3.10	3.00	1,050	434	702
Washington	3.50	4.00	2.55	1,722	1,360	893
Wisconsin	3.85	4.07	3.55	30,030	27,778	30,814
Wyoming	4.71	3.95	3.20	1,017	2,252	1,322
United States	3.89	3.75	3.25	243,018	239,807	239,253

NASS, Crops Branch, (202) 720–2127.

Table 1-51.—International Oats: Area, yield, and production in specified countries, 2013/2014–2015/2016

Country	Area			Yield per hectare			Production		
	2013/ 2014	2014/ 2015	2015/ 2016	2013/ 2014	2014/ 2015	2015/ 2016	2013/ 2014	2014/ 2015	2015/ 2016
	1,000 hec- tares	*1,000 hec- tares*	*1,000 hec- tares*	*Metric tons*	*Metric tons*	*Metric tons*	*1,000 metric tons*	*1,000 metric tons*	*1,000 metric tons*
Argentina	215	245	235	2.07	2.14	2.06	445	525	485
Australia	715	683	860	1.76	1.59	1.51	1,255	1,087	1,300
Belarus	133	151	140	2.65	3.46	2.86	352	522	400
Brazil	170	150	190	2.24	2.00	1.84	380	300	350
Canada	1,113	928	1,050	3.51	3.21	3.27	3,906	2,979	3,430
Chile	136	90	85	4.49	4.68	5.53	610	421	470
China	200	200	200	2.90	3.00	3.00	580	600	600
European Union	2,652	2,542	2,627	3.16	3.09	2.91	8,380	7,845	7,640
Russia	3,007	3,077	2,835	1.64	1.71	1.60	4,932	5,267	4,550
Ukraine	241	245	215	1.94	2.49	2.28	467	610	490
Others	687	651	689	1.83	1.82	1.80	1,257	1,187	1,239
Total Foreign	9,269	8,962	9,126	2.43	2.38	2.30	22,564	21,343	20,954
United States	408	419	516	2.30	2.43	2.52	938	1,019	1,300
Total	9,677	9,381	9,642	2.43	2.38	2.31	23,502	22,362	22,254

FAS, Office of Global Analysis, (202) 720-6301. Prepared or estimated on the basis of official USDA production, supply, and distribution, supply, and and distribution statistics from foreign governments.

Table 1-52. Oats: International trade, 2013/2014–2015/2016

Country	2013/2014	2014/2015	2015/2016
	1,000 metric tons	*1,000 metric tons*	*1,000 metric tons*
Principle exporting countries:			
Argentina	2	2	5
Australia	260	250	350
Brazil	6	9	5
Canada	1,662	1,689	1,600
Chile	56	85	75
European Union	316	219	230
Kazakhstan	6	2	5
Russia	6	9	20
Ukraine	6	39	70
Others	1	1	
Total Foreign	2,321	2,305	2,360
United States	23	26	29
Total	2,344	2,331	2,389
Principle importing countries:			
Albania	5	5	5
Algeria	8	16	30
Canada	24	13	10
China	116	162	250
Ecuador	26	21	20
Japan	46	47	50
Mexico	97	84	100
Norway	39	3	40
South Africa	19	50	25
Switzerland	52	52	50
Others	19	28	30
Total Foreign	451	481	610
United States	1,674	1,852	1,637
Total	2,125	2,333	2,247

FAS, Office of Global Analysis, (202) 720-6301. Prepared or estimated on the basis of official USDA production, supply, and distribution statistics from foreign governments.

Table 1-53.—Barley: Area, yield, production, and value, United States, 2005–2014

Year	Area		Yield per harvested acre	Production	Marketing year average price per bushel received by farmers	Value of production
	Planted[1]	Harvested				
	1,000 acres	1,000 acres	Bushels	1,000 bushels	Dollars	1,000 dollars
2005	3,875	3,269	64.8	211,896	2.53	527,633
2006	3,452	2,951	61.1	180,165	2.85	498,691
2007	4,018	3,502	60.0	210,110	4.02	834,954
2008	4,239	3,775	63.3	239,072	5.37	1,253,452
2009	3,568	3,114	72.8	226,603	4.66	968,676
2010	2,872	2,465	73.1	180,241	3.86	691,573
2011	2,564	2,241	69.1	154,788	5.35	808,741
2012	3,660	3,274	66.9	218,990	6.43	1,371,381
2013	3,528	3,040	71.3	216,745	6.06	1,265,798
2014	2,975	2,443	72.4	176,794	5.25	869,742

[1] Barley sown for all purposes, including barley sown in the preceding fall.
NASS, Crops Branch, (202) 720–2127.

Table 1-54.—Barley: Stocks on and off farms, United States, 2005–2014

Year beginning September	On farms				Off farms[1]			
	Sep. 1	Dec. 1	Mar. 1	June 1	Sep. 1	Dec. 1	Mar. 1	June 1
	1,000 bushels	1,000 bushels	1,000 bushels	1,000 bushels	1,000 bushels	1,000 bushels	1,000 bushels	1,000 bushels
2005	137,400	103,650	68,400	30,770	117,511	104,335	98,354	77,161
2006	112,850	83,650	38,310	14,580	99,939	89,171	78,756	54,300
2007	105,600	62,050	28,270	9,950	83,095	73,728	82,154	58,273
2008	127,750	77,050	44,310	27,010	81,669	95,766	84,791	61,723
2009	154,050	114,630	67,370	40,440	85,414	91,759	89,985	75,059
2010	125,070	91,660	57,700	26,040	98,818	88,720	80,424	63,311
2011	93,050	55,320	26,480	9,670	82,007	82,999	67,248	50,317
2012	112,550	72,580	35,180	15,840	85,226	85,473	81,897	64,557
2013	105,620	81,340	43,830	19,110	90,470	88,063	77,734	63,145
2014	97,820	74,510	41,840	....	81,997	81,625	76,059	....

[1] Includes stocks at mills, elevators, warehouses, terminals, and processors.
NASS, Crops Branch, (202) 720–2127.

Table 1-55.—Barley: Supply and disappearance, United States, 2005–2014

Year beginning June 1	Supply				Disappearance					Ending stocks May 31
					Domestic use				Total disappearance	
	Beginning stocks	Production	Imports	Total	Feed and residual	Food, seed, and industrial	Total	Exports		Total
	Million bushels	Million bushels	Million bushels	Million bushels	Million bushels	Million bushels	Million bushels	Million bushels	Million bushels	Million bushels
2005	128	212	5	346	48	162	210	28	238	108
2006	108	180	12	300	49	162	211	20	231	69
2007	69	210	29	308	30	169	199	41	240	68
2008	68	240	29	337	67	169	236	13	249	89
2009	89	227	17	332	47	164	211	6	216	115
2010	115	180	9	305	50	159	208	8	216	89
2011	89	155	16	260	37	155	192	9	200	60
2012	60	219	23	302	66	147	213	9	222	80
2013	80	217	19	316	66	153	219	14	234	82
2014	82	182	24	287	43	151	194	14	209	79

Includes quantity under loan and farmer–owned reserve.   Latest data may be preliminary or projected.   Totals may not add due to independent rounding.
ERS, Market and Trade Economics Division, (202) 694–5313.

Table 1-56.—Barley: Area, yield, and production, by State and United States, 2012–2014

State	Area planted [1]			Area harvested		
	2012	2013	2014	2012	2013	2014
	1,000 acres	1,000 acres	1,000 acres	1,000 acres	1,000 acres	1,000 acres
Arizona	48	75	36	47	69	32
California	120	95	80	80	42	25
Colorado	58	63	57	55	58	54
Delaware	38	43	41	34	33	31
Idaho	620	650	560	600	620	510
Kansas	10	17	16	7	11	10
Maine	17	20	13	16	17	12
Maryland	60	75	70	40	52	45
Michigan	11	10	8	9	9	7
Minnesota	120	90	75	110	75	60
Montana	900	990	920	790	830	770
New York	10	11	12	8	8	8
North Carolina	23	19	20	17	14	15
North Dakota	1,060	760	620	1,010	720	535
Oregon	56	63	40	53	50	30
Pennsylvania	65	75	70	53	60	50
South Dakota	34	37	28	22	19	17
Utah	44	40	32	26	30	20
Virginia	63	72	56	35	44	28
Washington	185	205	115	175	195	105
Wisconsin	33	33	26	18	16	16
Wyoming	85	85	80	69	68	63
United States	3,660	3,528	2,975	3,274	3,040	2,443

State	Yield per harvested acre			Production		
	2012	2013	2014	2012	2013	2014
	Bushels	Bushels	Bushels	1,000 bushels	1,000 bushels	1,000 bushels
Arizona	105.0	118.0	125.0	4,935	8,142	4,000
California	55.0	75.0	73.0	4,400	3,150	1,825
Colorado	122.0	133.0	124.0	6,710	7,714	6,696
Delaware	84.0	78.0	86.0	2,856	2,574	2,666
Idaho	90.0	93.0	94.0	54,000	57,660	47,940
Kansas	58.0	47.0	35.0	406	517	350
Maine	60.0	53.0	68.0	960	901	816
Maryland	82.0	85.0	77.0	3,280	4,420	3,465
Michigan	48.0	52.0	53.0	432	468	371
Minnesota	57.0	69.0	52.0	6,270	5,175	3,120
Montana	51.0	52.0	58.0	40,290	43,160	44,660
New York	46.0	52.0	47.0	368	416	376
North Carolina	61.0	67.0	71.0	1,037	938	1,065
North Dakota	60.0	64.0	67.0	60,600	46,080	35,845
Oregon	72.0	70.0	50.0	3,816	3,500	1,500
Pennsylvania	68.0	68.0	71.0	3,604	4,080	3,550
South Dakota	35.0	54.0	52.0	770	1,026	884
Utah	78.0	78.0	83.0	2,028	2,340	1,660
Virginia	82.0	82.0	79.0	2,870	3,608	2,212
Washington	71.0	72.0	60.0	12,425	14,040	6,300
Wisconsin	44.0	49.0	47.0	792	784	752
Wyoming	89.0	89.0	107.0	6,141	6,052	6,741
United States	66.9	71.3	72.4	218,990	216,745	176,794

[1] Includes area planted in the preceding fall.
NASS, Crops Branch, (202) 720–2127.

Table 1-57.—Barley: Marketing year average price and value, by State and United States, 2012–2014

State	Marketing year average price per bushel			Value of production		
	2012	2013	2014	2012	2013	2014
	Dollars	Dollars	Dollars	1,000 dollars	1,000 dollars	1,000 dollars
Arizona	5.78	5.13	4.45	28,524	41,768	17,800
California	5.97	5.81	5.10	26,268	18,302	9,308
Colorado	6.72	5.73	5.60	45,091	44,201	37,498
Delaware	5.00	4.75	3.05	14,280	12,227	8,131
Idaho	6.53	6.42	4.90	352,620	370,177	234,906
Kansas	6.00	4.52	5.25	2,436	2,337	1,838
Maine	4.25	4.15	3.55	4,080	3,739	2,897
Maryland	4.59	4.13	3.00	15,055	18,255	10,395
Michigan	5.00	4.75	3.50	2,160	2,223	1,299
Minnesota	6.38	6.22	5.10	40,003	32,189	15,912
Montana	6.41	6.32	5.40	258,259	272,771	241,164
New York	5.45	4.61	3.70	2,006	1,918	1,391
North Carolina	4.10	4.00	3.80	4,252	3,752	4,047
North Dakota	6.56	6.09	5.20	397,536	280,627	186,394
Oregon	6.07	4.02	3.20	23,163	14,070	4,800
Pennsylvania	4.28	3.89	3.15	15,425	15,871	11,183
South Dakota	5.54	4.25	3.50	4,266	4,361	3,094
Utah	5.87	4.17	3.15	11,904	9,758	5,229
Virginia	3.88	3.80	3.60	11,136	13,710	7,963
Washington	5.53	4.12	3.25	68,710	57,845	20,475
Wisconsin	5.65	6.49	4.75	4,475	5,088	3,572
Wyoming	6.47	6.71	6.00	39,732	46,609	40,446
United States	6.43	6.06	5.25	1,371,381	1,265,798	869,742

NASS, Crops Branch, (202) 720–2127.

Table 1-58.—International Barley: Area, yield, and production in specified countries, 2013/2014–2015/2016

Country	Area			Yield per hectare			Production		
	2013/ 2014	2014/ 2015	2015/ 2016	2013/ 2014	2014/ 2015	2015/ 2016	2013/ 2014	2014/ 2015	2015/ 2016
	1,000 hectares	1,000 hectares	1,000 hectares	Metric tons	Metric tons	Metric tons	1,000 metric tons	1,000 metric tons	1,000 metric tons
Argentina	1,270	900	1,000	3.74	3.22	3.60	4,750	2,900	3,600
Australia	3,814	3,836	4,100	2.41	2.09	2.12	9,174	8,014	8,700
Canada	2,652	2,136	2,350	3.86	3.33	3.50	10,237	7,119	8,225
European Union	12,408	12,394	12,327	4.81	4.88	4.95	59,674	60,460	60,962
Iran	1,635	1,575	1,600	1.71	2.03	2.06	2,800	3,200	3,300
Kazakhstan	1,837	1,909	2,038	1.38	1.26	1.31	2,539	2,412	2,675
Morocco	1,690	1,440	1,600	1.60	1.18	2.19	2,700	1,700	3,500
Russia	8,024	8,803	8,050	1.92	2.27	2.12	15,389	20,026	17,100
Turkey	3,330	3,400	3,400	2.19	1.18	2.18	7,300	4,000	7,400
Ukraine	3,233	3,200	3,000	2.34	2.95	2.92	7,561	9,450	8,750
Others	9,385	8,932	9,242	1.87	1.98	1.87	17,514	17,712	17,262
Total Foreign	49,278	48,525	48,707	2.83	2.82	2.90	139,638	136,993	141,474
United States	1,230	1,011	1,258	3.84	3.91	3.71	4,719	3,953	4,666
Total	50,508	49,536	49,965	2.86	2.85	2.92	144,357	140,946	146,140

FAS, Office of Global Analysis, (202) 720-6301. Prepared or estimated on the basis of official USDA production, supply, and distribution statistics from foreign governments.

Table 1-59.—Barley: International trade, 2013/2014–2015/2016

Country	2013/2014	2014/2015	2015/2016
	1,000 metric tons	*1,000 metric tons*	*1,000 metric tons*
Principle exporting countries:			
Argentina	2,891	1,552	2,100
Australia	6,216	5,219	6,000
Canada	1,559	1,516	1,350
European Union	5,741	9,547	8,600
India	441	431	200
Kazakhstan	416	483	750
Moldova	10	62	50
Russia	2,681	5,336	3,700
Serbia	28	7	25
Ukraine	2,476	4,456	4,500
Others	54	83	50
Total Foreign	22,513	28,692	27,325
United States	311	312	305
Total	22,824	29,004	27,630
Principle importing countries:			
Algeria	511	876	650
Brazil	318	484	400
China	4,891	9,859	7,500
Iran	900	2,200	1,300
Japan	1,294	1,097	1,300
Jordan	1,009	890	700
Kuwait	436	412	400
Libya	681	1,001	900
Saudi Arabia	9,000	8,200	8,500
Tunisia	646	483	450
Others	2,994	3,942	3,210
Total Foreign	22,680	29,444	25,310
United States	408	513	435
Total	23,088	29,957	25,745

FAS, Office of Global Analysis, (202) 720-6301. Prepared or estimated on the basis of official USDA production, supply, and distribution statistics from foreign governments.

Table 1-60.—Barley: Support operations, United States, 2005/2006–2014/2015

Marketing year beginning June 1	Income support payment rates per bushel [1]	Program price levels per bushel		Put under loan		Acquired by CCC under loan program [5]	Owned by CCC at end of marketing year
		Loan [2]	Target [3]	Quantity	Percentage of production [4]		
	Dollars	*Dollars*	*Dollars*	*Million bushels*	*Percent*	*Million bushels*	*Million bushels*
2005/2006	0.24/0.13	1.85	2.24	12.0	5.7	0.1	0.0
2006/2007	0.24/0.00	1.85	2.24	9.3	5.1	0.0	0.0
2007/2008	0.24/0.00	1.85	2.24	4.4	2.1	0.0	0.0
2008/2009	0.24/0.00	1.85	2.24	6.7	2.8	0.0	0.0
2009/2010	0.24/0.00	1.85	2.24	12.7	5.6	0.0	0.0
2010/2011	0.24/0.00	1.95	2.63	6.4	3.6	0.0	0.0
2011/2012	0.24/0.00	1.95	2.63	2.8	1.8	0.0	0.0
2012/2013	0.24/0.00	1.95	2.63	3.1	1.4	0.0	0.0
2013/2014	0.24/0.00	1.95	2.63	4.2	1.9	0.0	0.0
2014/2015	0.00	1.95	4.95	3.9	2.1	0.0	0.0

[1] The first entry is the direct payment rate and the second entry is the counter-cyclical payment rate for 2004/2005-2013/2014. For 2009/2010-2013/2014, producers who participate in the Average Crop Revenue (ACRE) program get a 20 percent reduction in their direct payment, not calculated in this table. For 2014/2015 and after, the entry is the price loss coverage payment rate. Agricultural Risk Coverage (ARC) is also available, but payment rates are established at the county or farm levels.　[2] For 2009/2010-2013/2014, producers who participate in the ACRE program get a 30 percent reduction in their loan rate, not calculated in this table.　[3] Target applies to 2003/2004-2013/2014 and Reference applies beginning with 2014/2015.　[4] Percent of production is on a grain basis.　[5] Acquisitions as of December 31, 2015.
FSA, Feed Grains and Oilseeds, (202) 720–2711.

Table 1-61.—Grains and grain products: Total and per capita civilian consumption as food, United States, 2003–2013

Calendar year [1]	Wheat			Rye		Rice (milled)	
	Total consumed [2]	Per capita consumption of food products		Total consumed [2]	Per capita consumption of rye flour	Total consumed [4]	Per capita consumption
		Flour [3]	Non-milled product				
	Million bushels	*Pounds*	*Pounds*	*Million bushels*	*Pounds*	*Million cwt.*	*Pounds*
2004	905	135	2.4	3.3	0.5	56.6	19.4
2005	917	134	2.4	3.3	0.5	57.1	19.4
2006	938	136	2.4	3.3	0.5	60.4	20.3
2007	948	138	2.4	3.3	0.5	61.0	20.3
2008	927	137	2.4	3.3	0.5	62.2	20.5
2009	920	135	2.3	3.3	0.5	62.6	20.4
2010	928	135	2.3	3.3	0.5	63.1	20.4
2011	925	133	2.3	3.3	0.5	(NA)	(NA)
2012	952	134	2.3	3.4	0.5	(NA)	(NA)
2013	945	135	2.3	3.4	0.3		

Calendar year [1]	Corn						Oats		Barley	
	Total consumed [5]	Per capita consumption of food products					Total consumed [6]	Per capita consumption of oat food products	Total consumed [7]	Per capita consumption of food products [8]
		Flour and meal	Hominy and grits	Syrup	Dextrose	Starch				
	Million bushels	*Pounds*	*Pounds*	*Pounds*	*Pounds*	*Pounds*	*Million bushels*	*Pounds*	*Million bushels*	*Pounds*
2003	986	18.3	7.4	76.2	3.1	4.6	62.4	4.7	6.5	0.7
2004	973	18.6	7.8	75.6	3.3	4.5	63.0	4.7	6.6	0.7
2005	989	18.8	8.1	74.5	3.2	4.5	62.9	4.6	6.7	0.7
2006	980	19.0	8.5	72.1	3.1	4.4	64.5	4.7	6.6	0.7
2007	958	19.1	8.9	70.0	3.0	4.4	66.0	4.7	6.7	0.7
2008		19.3	9.3	66.6	2.8	4.4	67.6	4.8	6.8	0.7
2009		19.3	9.3		2.7	4.4	74.5	5.3	6.9	0.7
2010		19.3	9.3		2.9	4.5	74.0	5.2	6.8	0.7
2011		19.9	9.6		2.9	4.6	76.0	5.3	6.8	0.7
2012		19.8	9.5		2.7	4.6	76.0	5.2	6.5	0.6

Estimates of corn syrup and sugar are unofficial estimates; industry data were not reported after April 1968. (NA) Not available. [1] Data are in marketing year; for corn, September 1-August 31; for oats and barley, June 1-May 31; and rice, August 1-July 31. Wheat, rye, syrup, and sugar are in calendar year. [2] Excludes quantities used in alcoholic beverages. [3] Includes white, whole wheat, and semolina flour. [4] Does not include shipments to U.S. territories. Excludes rice used in alcoholic beverages. Includes imports and rice used in processed foods and pet foods. [5] Includes an allowance for the quantity used as hominy and grits. This series is not adjusted for trade. [6] Oats used in oatmeal, prepared breakfast foods, infant foods, and food products. [7] Malt for food, breakfast food uses, pearl barley, and flour. [8] Malt equivalent of barley food products.

ERS, Market & Trade Economics Division, (202) 694-5290. All figures are estimates based on data from private industry sources, the U.S. Department of Commerce, the Internal Revenue Service, and other Government agencies.

Table 1-62.—Sorghum: Area, yield, production, and value, United States, 2005–2014

Year	Area planted for all purposes [1]	Sorghum for grain [2]					Sorghum for silage		
		Area harvested	Yield per harvested acre	Production	Marketing year average price per cwt [3]	Value of production [3]	Area harvested	Yield per harvested acre	Production
	1,000 acres	1,000 acres	Bushels	1,000 bushels	Dollars	1,000 dollars	1,000 acres	Tons	1,000 tons
2005 ..	6,454	5,736	68.5	392,739	3.33	736,629	311	13.6	4,224
2006 ..	6,522	4,937	56.1	276,824	5.88	883,204	347	13.3	4,612
2007 ..	7,712	6,792	73.2	497,445	7.28	1,925,312	392	13.4	5,246
2008 ..	8,404	7,312	65.1	475,855	5.72	1,641,963	412	13.9	5,710
2009 ..	6,599	5,502	69.4	381,605	5.75	1,202,331	255	14.5	3,693
2010 ..	5,369	4,806	71.9	345,464	8.96	1,616,773	272	12.5	3,412
2011 ..	5,451	3,945	54.0	212,993	10.70	1,259,635	226	10.4	2,353
2012 ..	6,259	4,995	49.6	247,742	11.30	1,606,237	353	11.9	4,196
2013 ..	8,076	6,585	59.6	392,331	7.64	1,716,927	380	14.3	5,420
2014 ..	7,138	6,401	67.6	432,575	7.20	1,721,330	315	13.1	4,123

[1] Grain and sweet sorghum for all uses, including syrup.   [2] Includes both grain sorghum for grain, and sweet sorghum for grain or seed.   [3] Based on the reported price of grain sorghum.
NASS, Crops Branch, (202) 720–2127.

Table 1-63.—Sorghum grain: Stocks on and off farms, United States, 2006–2015

Year beginning previous Dec.	On farms				Off farms [1]			
	Dec. 1	Mar. 1	Jun. 1	Sep. 1	Dec. 1	Mar. 1	Jun. 1	Sep. 1
	1,000 bushels	1,000 bushels	1,000 bushels	1,000 bushels	1,000 bushels	1,000 bushels	1,000 bushels	1,000 bushels
2006	55,000	26,200	12,650	5,250	235,376	166,936	102,213	60,413
2007	38,100	17,100	5,380	2,150	174,094	125,122	69,490	29,903
2008	51,400	26,100	7,000	3,550	239,850	159,808	94,019	49,200
2009	54,400	32,200	12,000	4,400	243,290	173,650	90,215	50,312
2010	48,000	23,680	10,700	4,500	202,759	151,873	77,162	36,740
2011	30,500	13,020	3,140	2,030	207,168	158,027	76,894	25,420
2012	27,850	12,800	4,120	1,160	123,101	95,266	54,405	21,792
2013	17,600	10,850	2,710	602	122,247	80,685	38,398	14,551
2014	32,950	15,950	4,500	1,945	198,441	159,784	87,924	32,087
2015 [2]	30,500	9,000	2,960	1,895	192,094	110,856	31,329	16,514

[1] Includes stocks at mills, elevators, warehouses, terminals, and processors.   [2] Preliminary.
NASS, Crops Branch, (202) 720–2127.

Table 1-64.—Sorghum: Supply and disappearance, United States, 2005–2014

Year beginning September 1	Supply			Disappearance					Ending stocks Aug. 31
	Beginning stocks	Production	Total	Domestic use			Exports	Total disappearance	
				Feed and residual	Food, seed and industrial	Total			
	Million bushels	Million bushels	Million bushels	Million bushels	Million bushels	Million bushels	Million bushels	Million bushels	Million bushels
2005	57	393	450	140	50	190	194	384	66
2006	66	277	343	113	45	158	153	311	32
2007	32	497	530	165	35	200	277	477	53
2008	53	476	529	233	94	331	143	474	55
2009	55	382	436	141	90	231	164	395	41
2010	41	345	387	123	85	208	152	359	27
2011	27	213	241	69	85	154	63	218	23
2012	23	248	280	93	95	189	76	265	15
2013	15	392	408	93	70	162	211	374	34
2014	34	433	467	80	15	96	353	449	18

Includes quantity under loan and farmer–owned reserve.   Latest data may be preliminary or projected.   Totals may not add due to independent rounding.
ERS, Market and Trade Economics Division, (202) 694–5313.

Table 1-65.—Sorghum: Area, yield, and production, by State and United States, 2012–2014

State	Area planted for all purposes			Sorghum for grain		
				Area harvested		
	2012	2013	2014	2012	2013	2014
	1,000 acres	1,000 acres	1,000 acres	1,000 acres	1,000 acres	1,000 acres
Arizona	31	33	25	10	17	8
Arkansas	140	130	170	135	125	165
Colorado	245	400	345	150	240	280
Georgia	55	55	40	40	40	23
Illinois	30	23	23	27	20	21
Kansas	2,500	3,150	2,850	2,100	2,850	2,700
Louisiana	125	115	100	123	113	96
Mississippi	48	65	110	46	62	105
Missouri	65	70	85	55	60	73
Nebraska	120	250	210	60	145	160
New Mexico	90	125	110	19	68	60
Oklahoma	270	320	370	190	270	310
South Dakota	190	340	200	140	275	150
Texas	2,350	3,000	2,500	1,900	2,300	2,250
United States	6,259	8,076	7,138	4,995	6,585	6,401

State	Yield per harvested acre			Production		
	2012	2013	2014	2012	2013	2014
	Bushels	Bushels	Bushels	1,000 bushels	1,000 bushels	1,000 bushels
Arizona	115.0	75.0	100.0	1,150	1,275	800
Arkansas	84.0	102.0	97.0	11,340	12,750	16,005
Colorado	20.0	24.0	30.0	3,000	5,760	8,400
Georgia	53.0	50.0	41.0	2,120	2,000	943
Illinois	60.0	94.0	106.0	1,620	1,880	2,226
Kansas	39.0	59.0	74.0	81,900	168,150	199,800
Louisiana	100.0	107.0	93.0	12,300	12,091	8,928
Mississippi	84.0	94.0	80.0	3,864	5,828	8,400
Missouri	58.0	82.0	101.0	3,190	4,920	7,373
Nebraska	59.0	67.0	82.0	3,540	9,715	13,120
New Mexico	42.0	34.0	42.0	798	2,312	2,520
Oklahoma	26.0	55.0	56.0	4,940	14,850	17,360
South Dakota	42.0	80.0	63.0	5,880	22,000	9,450
Texas	59.0	56.0	61.0	112,100	128,800	137,250
United States	49.6	59.6	67.6	247,742	392,331	432,575

NASS, Crops Branch, (202) 720–2127.

Table 1-66.—Sorghum: Utilization for silage, by State and United States, 2012–2014

State	Silage								
	Area harvested			Yield per acre			Production		
	2012	2013	2014	2012	2013	2014	2012	2013	2014
	1,000 acres	1,000 acres	1,000 acres	Tons	Tons	Tons	1,000 tons	1,000 tons	1,000 tons
Arizona	20	15	17	25.0	22.0	23.0	500	330	391
Arkansas	2	1	2	9.0	17.0	17.0	18	17	34
Colorado	15	30	10	7.0	13.0	11.0	105	390	110
Georgia	14	10	14	17.0	10.0	11.0	238	100	154
Illinois	2	2	1	15.0	16.0	18.0	30	32	18
Kansas	75	110	70	7.0	14.0	11.0	525	1,540	770
Louisiana	1	1	1	13.0	14.0	13.0	13	14	13
Mississippi	1	2	2	14.0	14.0	12.0	14	28	24
Missouri	6	8	10	8.0	17.0	17.0	48	136	170
Nebraska	11	30	20	10.0	10.0	12.0	110	300	240
New Mexico	19	16	33	15.0	13.0	13.0	285	208	429
Oklahoma	10	10	15	6.0	20.0	10.0	60	200	150
South Dakota	17	25	20	10.0	13.0	11.0	170	325	220
Texas	160	120	100	13.0	15.0	14.0	2,080	1,800	1,400
United States	353	380	315	11.9	14.3	13.1	4,196	5,420	4,123

NASS, Crops Branch, (202) 720–2127.

Table 1-67.—Sorghum grain: Marketing year average price and value of production, by State and United States, 2012–2014

State	Marketing year average price per cwt			Value of production		
	2012	2013	2014	2012	2013	2014
	Dollars	Dollars	Dollars	1,000 dollars	1,000 dollars	1,000 dollars
Arizona	12.80	10.10	9.34	8,243	7,211	4,184
Arkansas	11.10	8.85	7.07	70,489	63,189	63,367
Colorado	12.50	7.66	6.92	21,000	24,708	32,552
Georgia	12.70	9.52	8.52	15,077	10,662	4,499
Illinois	12.00	7.42	5.97	10,886	7,812	7,442
Kansas	12.00	7.46	7.10	550,368	702,463	794,405
Louisiana	11.50	8.70	7.76	79,212	58,907	38,798
Mississippi	10.90	8.62	7.05	23,586	28,133	33,163
Missouri	12.30	8.05	6.35	21,973	22,179	26,218
Nebraska	12.10	7.38	7.17	23,987	40,150	52679
New Mexico	13.30	5.76	6.64	5,944	7,458	9,370
Oklahoma	12.00	7.49	6.94	33,197	62,287	67,468
South Dakota	11.90	6.57	5.95	39,184	80,942	31.487
Texas	11.20	8.33	7.23	703,091	600,826	555,698
United States	11.30	7.64	6.80	1,606,237	1,716,927	1,721,330

NASS, Crops Branch, (202) 720–2127.

Table 1-68.—Sorghum grain: Support operations, United States, 2005/2006–2014/2015

Marketing year beginning September 1	Income support payment rates per cwt[1]	Program price levels per cwt		Put under support		Acquired by CCC under loan program[5]	Owned by CCC at end of marketing year
		Loan[2]	Target[3]	Quantity	Percentage of production[4]		
	Dollars	Dollars	Dollars	Million cwt	Percent	Millions cwt	Million cwt
2005/2006	0.63/0.48	3.48	4.59	5.4	2.4	0.0	0.0
2006/2007	0.63/0.00	3.48	4.59	1.9	1.2	0.0	0.0
2007/2008	0.63/0.00	3.48	4.59	1.8	0.6	0.0	0.0
2008/2009	0.63/0.00	3.48	4.59	4.5	1.7	0.0	0.0
2009/2010	0.63/0.00	3.48	4.59	1.8	0.8	0.0	0.0
2010/2011	0.63/0.00	3.48	4.70	0.5	0.3	0.0	0.0
2011/2012	0.63/0.00	3.48	4.70	0.2	0.2	0.0	0.0
2012/2013	0.63/0.00	3.48	4.70	0.2	0.1	0.0	0.0
2013/2014	0.63/0.00	3.48	4.70	0.3	0.1	0.0	0.0
2014/2015	0.00	3.48	7.05	0.4	0.2	0.0	0.0

[1] The first entry is the direct payment rate and the second entry is the counter-cyclical payment rate for 2004/2005-2013/2014. For 2009/2010-2013/2014, producers who participate in the Average Crop Revenue (ACRE) program get a 20 percent reduction in their direct payment, not calculated in this table. For 2014/2015 and after, the entry is the price loss coverage payment rate. Agricultural Risk Coverage (ARC) is also available, but payment rates are established at the county or farm levels. [2] For 2009/2010-2013/2014, producers who participate in the ACRE program get a 30 percent reduction in their loan rate, not calculated in this table. [3] Target applies to 2003/2004-2013/2014 and Reference applies beginning with 2014/2015. [4] Percent of production is on a grain basis. [5] Acquisitions as of December 31, 2015.
FSA, Feed Grains and Oilseeds, (202) 720–2711.

Table 1-69.—International Sorghum: Area, yield, and production in specified countries, 2013/2014–2015/2016

Country	Area			Yield per hectare			Production		
	2013/ 2014	2014/ 2015	2015/ 2016	2013/ 2014	2014/ 2015	2015/ 2016	2013/ 2014	2014/ 2015	2015/ 2016
	1,000 hec- tares	*1,000 hec- tares*	*1,000 hec- tares*	*Metric tons*	*Metric tons*	*Metric tons*	*1,000 metric tons*	*1,000 metric tons*	*1,000 metric tons*
Argentina	1,000	770	870	4.40	4.55	4.48	4,400	3,500	3,900
Australia	532	651	700	2.41	3.23	3.14	1,282	2,104	2,200
Brazil	730	730	700	2.59	2.74	2.86	1,890	2,000	2,000
Burkina	1,800	1,800	1,800	1.04	1.02	1.06	1,880	1,836	1,900
China	582	619	610	4.97	4.66	4.75	2,892	2,885	2,900
Ethiopia	1,818	1,800	1,800	2.26	2.22	2.11	4,114	4,000	3,800
India	5,793	5,500	6,000	0.96	0.99	0.92	5,542	5,450	5,500
Mexico	2,073	1,715	1,600	4.10	3.66	3.56	8,500	6,270	5,700
Nigeria	5,000	5,500	5,300	1.32	1.22	1.16	6,592	6,700	6,150
Sudan	4,356	8,626	8,000	0.52	0.73	0.69	2,249	6,281	5,500
Others	12,631	12,546	12,459	0.95	0.95	0.96	11,947	11,874	12,000
Total Foreign	36,315	40,257	39,839	1.41	1.31	1.29	51,288	52,900	51,550
United States	2,665	2,590	3,177	3.74	4.24	4.77	9,966	10,988	15,158
Total	38,980	42,847	43,016	1.57	1.49	1.55	61,254	63,888	66,708

FAS, Office of Global Analysis, (202) 720-6301. Prepared or estimated on the basis of official USDA production, supply, and distribution statistics from foreign governments.

Table 1-70.—Sorghum: International trade, 2013/2014–2015/2016

Country	2013/2014	2014/2015	2015/2016
	1,000 metric tons	*1,000 metric tons*	*1,000 metric tons*
Principle exporting countries:			
Argentina	1,279	1,000	1,000
Australia	385	1,650	1,000
Brazil	11	13	30
China	11	9	25
Ethiopia	75	75	25
India	87	121	100
Kenya	56	40	30
Nigeria	50	100	50
South Africa	27	25	25
Ukraine	229	156	100
Others	111	125	90
Total Foreign	2,321	3,314	2,475
United States	5,362	8,965	8,255
Total	7,683	12,279	10,730
Principle importing countries:			
Chile	184	150	100
China	4,161	10,162	7,000
Colombia	104	....	50
Ethiopia	50	75	150
European Union	193	134	80
Japan	1,003	903	950
Kenya	92	98	100
Mexico	162	29	700
Pakistan	15	32	130
Sudan	75	100	75
Others	575	625	385
Total Foreign	6,614	12,308	9,720
United States	2	10	127
Total	6,616	12,318	9,847

FAS, Office of Global Analysis, (202) 720-6301. Prepared or estimated on the basis of official USDA production, supply, and distribution statistics from foreign governments.

Table 1-71.—International Mixed grain: Area, yield, and production in specified countries, 2013/2014–2015/2016

Country	Area			Yield per hectare			Production		
	2013/ 2014	2014/ 2015	2015/ 2016	2013/ 2014	2014/ 2015	2015/ 2016	2013/ 2014	2014/ 2015	2015/ 2016
	1,000 hectares	*1,000 hectares*	*1,000 hectares*	*metric tons*	*metric tons*	*metric tons*	*1,000 metric tons*	*1,000 metric tons*	*1,000 metric tons*
Bangladesh	35	35	35	0.71	0.71	0.71	25	25	25
Canada	66	63	62	2.80	3.00	2.90	185	189	180
European Union ...	3,953	4,035	4,144	3.89	4.17	3.83	15,373	16,808	15,869
Switzerland	9	10	10	5.67	6.00	6.00	51	60	60
Turkey	100	100	100	1.15	1.15	1.15	115	115	115
Total Foreign	4,163	4,243	4,351	3.78	4.05	3.73	15,749	17,197	16,249
Total	4,163	4,243	4,351	3.78	4.05	3.73	15,749	17,197	16,249

FAS, Office of Global Analysis, (202) 720-6301. Prepared or estimated on the basis of official USDA production, supply, and distribution statistics from foreign governments.

Table 1-72.—Commercial feeds: Disappearance for feed, United States, 2005–2014

Year beginning October	Oilseed cake and meal						Animal protein			
	Soybean	Cotton-seed	Linseed	Peanut [1]	Sun-flower	Total	Tankage and meat meal	Fish meal	Dried milk [2]	Total
	1,000 tons	*1,000 tons*	*1,000 tons*	*1,000 tons*	*1,000 tons*	*1,000 tons*	*1,000 tons*	*1,000 tons*	*1,000 tons*	*1,000 tons*
2005	33,195	3,355	269	117	298	37,234	2,254	199	269	2,722
2006	34,355	3,049	275	119	356	38,154	2,375	215	292	2,882
2007	33,232	2,589	210	116	343	36,490	2,398	213	250	2,861
2008	30,752	1,807	129	102	357	33,147	2,271	223	250	2,744
2009	30,639	1,755	210	91	415	33,110	2,343	200	250	2,793
2010	30,301	2,452	209	112	281	33,354	2,350	200	250	2,800
2011	31,541	2,406	194	109	189	34,439	2,444	198	463	3,105
2012	28,999	2,351	199	123	231	31,903	2,445	198	368	3,012
2013	29,547	1,797	152	130	257	31,883	2,445	198	219	2,862
2014	32,300	2,180	212	138	222	35,053	2,535	198	248	2,982

Year beginning October	Mill products [3]					Total commercial feeds
	Wheat millfeeds	Gluten feed and meal [4]	Rice millfeeds	Alfalfa meal	Total	
	1,000 tons	*1,000 tons*	*1,000 tons*	*1,000 tons*	*1,000 tons*	*1,000 tons*
2005	6,753	3,514	641	0	10,908	50,865
2006	6,873	4,624	545	0	12,042	53,078
2007	6,776	4,560	568	0	11,904	51,256
2008	6,464	5,167	570	0	12,201	48,092
2009	6,400	5,075	575	0	12,050	47,953
2010	6,500	5,050	575	0	12,125	48,279
2011	6,168	5,772	580	0	12,521	50,064
2012	6,278	5,707	535	0	12,520	47,435
2013	6,271	5,649	525	0	12,445	47,190
2014	9,101	5,849	525	0	15,475	53,509

[1] Year beginning August 1.　[2] Includes dried skim milk, and whey for feed, but does not include any milk products fed on farms.　[3] Other mill products that are not listed include screenings, hominy, and oats feed etc., for which no statistics are available.　[4] Adjusted for export data.
ERS, Market and Trade Economics Division, (202) 694–5313.

Table 1-73.—High-protein feeds: Quantity for feeding, high-protein animal units, quantity per animal unit, and prices, United States, 2005–2014

Year beginning October	Quantity for feeding [1]						High-protein animal units	Quantity per animal unit	High protein feed prices
	Oilseed meal			Animal protein	Grain protein [3]	Total			
	Soybean meal	Other oilseed meals [2]	Total						
	1,000 tons	1,000 tons	1,000 tons	1,000 tons	1,000 tons	1,000 tons	Million units	Pounds	Index numbers 1992=100
2005	36,515	3,724	40,239	3,047	2,092	45,378	72	1,267	88
2006	37,791	3,497	41,288	3,219	2,753	47,260	72	1,317	105
2007	36,555	3,002	39,557	3,232	2,715	45,505	71	1,273	170
2008	33,827	2,207	36,034	3,092	3,077	42,203	71	1,191	168
2009	33,703	2,263	35,966	3,149	3,022	42,137	70	1,196	150
2010	33,331	2,814	36,145	3,158	3,007	42,310	69	1,220	175
2011	34,695	2,675	37,370	3,334	3,437	44,142	68	1,298	200
2012	31,899	2,680	34,579	3,307	3,398	41,284	68	1,221	235
2013	32,502	2,156	34,658	3,260	3,364	41,282	67	1,237	247
2014	35,530	2,538	38,068	3,379	3,483	44,930	68	1,324	189

Latest data may be preliminary or projected. [1] In terms of 44 percent protein soybean meal equivalent. [2] Includes cottonseed, linseed, peanut meal, and sunflower meal. [3] Beginning 1974, adjusted for exports of corn gluten feed and meal.
ERS, Market and Trade Economics Division, (202) 694–5313.

Table 1-74.—Feed concentrates: Fed to livestock and poultry, 2005–2014

Year beginning October	Feed grains				Wheat [2]	Rye [2]	By-product feeds [3]	Total con-centrates	Grain con-suming animal units	Concen-trates fed per grain-con-suming animal unit
	Corn [1]	Sor-ghum [1]	Oats [2] and barley [2]	Total						
	Million tons	Million tons	Million tons	Million tons	Million tons	Million tons	Million tons	Million tons	Millions	Tons
2005	171.2	3.9	3.9	179.0	3.0	0.1	58.8	240.9	91.5	2.63
2006	155.1	3.2	4.0	162.3	5.1	0.1	60.6	228.1	92.7	2.46
2007	164.0	4.6	3.4	172.0	4.6	0.1	59.0	235.7	95.1	2.48
2008	145.1	6.6	3.4	155.1	3.7	0.1	55.2	214.1	92.7	2.31
2009	133.7	3.9	3.4	141.1	4.5	0.1	54.6	200.3	91.6	2.19
2010	126.5	3.4	3.6	133.6	4.6	0.1	54.6	192.9	92.4	2.09
2011	126.5	1.9	2.6	131.1	11.5	0.1	56.6	199.2	93.1	2.14
2012	120.8	2.6	3.4	126.9	11.4	0.1	53.8	192.1	92.3	2.08
2013	141.1	2.6	2.7	146.4	1.8	0.1	53.9	202.2	91.0	2.22
2014	148.8	2.3	1.4	152.5	4.8	0.1	60.7	218.0	93.2	2.34

Latest data may be preliminary or projected. [1] Marketing year beginning Sept. 1. [2] Marketing year beginning June 1. [3] Oilseed meals, animal protein feeds, mill byproducts, and mineral supplements.
ERS, Market and Trade Economics Division, (202) 694–5313.

Table 1-75.—Feed: Consumed per head and per unit of production, by class of livestock or poultry, with quantity expressed in equivalent feeding value of corn, 2005–2014

Year beginning October	Dairy cattle			Beef cattle				Sheep and lambs	
	Milk cows		Other dairy cattle per head	Cattle on feed per head Jan. 1 [1]	Other beef cattle per head	All beef cattle per head	Cattle and calves per 100 pounds produced [2]	Per head	Per 100 pounds produced [3]
	Per head	Per 100 pounds milk produced							
	Pounds	Pounds	Pounds	Pounds	Pounds	Pounds	Pounds	Pounds	Pounds
2005	13,125	68	6,565	9,978	5,321	6,129	1,301	1,279	1,679
2006	12,775	64	6,506	9,466	5,303	6,037	1,267	1,272	1,691
2007	12,779	64	6,507	9,471	5,303	6,053	1,273	1,272	1,720
2008	12,394	61	6,442	8,909	5,283	5,905	1,215	1,265	1,744
2009	12,226	59	6,409	8,615	5,274	5,844	1,217	1,262	1,683
2010	11,658	55	6,295	7,773	5,244	5,695	1,159	1,252	1,693
2011	11,730	55	6,329	7,836	5,258	5,737	1,136	1,256	1,662
2012	11,721	54	6,341	8,127	5,248	5,765	1,146	1,253	1,650
2013	11,788	54	6,341	8,373	5,255	5,790	1,123	1,256	1,615
2014	12,075	55	6,429	8,410	5,273	5,801	1,136	1,265	1,554

Year beginning October	Poultry								Hogs per 100 pounds produced	Horses and mules two years and over per head
	Hens and pullets		Chickens raised		Broilers produced		Turkeys raised			
	Per head Jan. 1	Per 100 eggs	Per head	Per 100 pounds live weight	Per head	Per 100 pounds produced	Per head	Per 100 pounds produced		
	Pounds	Pounds	Pounds	Pounds	Pounds	Pounds	Pounds	Pounds	Pounds	Pounds
2005	131	50	31	933	12	217	98	357	584	3,875
2006	124	47	30	982	11	202	92	340	552	3,806
2007	124	47	30	1,030	11	200	92	334	564	3,807
2008	116	43	28	984	10	176	87	278	504	3,732
2009	113	42	27	1,068	10	178	84	288	484	9,944
2010	101	37	24	992	9	154	76	264	461	10,018
2011	103	38	25	952	9	155	76	263	464	10,034
2012	100	37	23	935	9	153	79	255	431	9,745
2013	101	37	24	976	9	154	80	259	447	10,271
2014	108	39	26	1,053	10	168	82	274	493	10,489

[1] Feed consumed by all cattle divided by the number on feed Jan. 1. [2] Feed for all cattle, except milk cows, divided by the net live-weight production of cattle and calves. It includes the growth on dairy heifers and calves as well as all beef cattle. [3] Including wool produced.

ERS, Market and Trade Economics Division, (202) 694–5313.

Table 1-76.—Feed: Consumed by livestock and poultry, by type of feed, with quantity expressed in equivalent feeding value of corn, 2005–2014

Year beginning October	Concentrates	Harvested roughage	Pasture	Total
	Million tons	Million tons	Million	Million tons
2005	266	87	157	509
2006	254	82	162	498
2007	261	80	163	504
2008	237	83	158	478
2009	227	83	153	463
2010	203	81	150	435
2011	210	76	153	440
2012	206	76	151	433
2013	206	78	153	437
2014	227	95	140	463

Latest data may be preliminary or projected.
ERS, Market and Trade Economics Division, (202) 694–5313.

Table 1-77.—Animal units fed: Grain-consuming, roughage-consuming, and grain-and-roughage-consuming, United States, 2005–2014 [1]

Year beginning October	Grain-consuming [2]	Roughage-consuming [3]	Grain and roughage-consuming [4]
	1,000 units	1,000 units	1,000 units
2005	91,490	71,647	78,731
2006	92,749	71,753	79,289
2007	95,118	71,479	80,042
2008	92,708	70,887	78,782
2009	91,636	70,386	78,033
2010	92,851	69,233	77,786
2011	93,232	68,023	77,237
2012	92,267	67,593	76,601
2013	90,420	66,756	75,314
2014	92,576	67,409	76,371

Latest data may be preliminary or projected. [1] Index series based on average feeding rates for years 1969–71. In calculations for the feeding years 1969 to date, cattle numbers used are the new categories shown in the Livestock and Poultry Inventory, published by NASS, USDA. [2] Livestock and poultry numbers weighted by all concentrates consumed. [3] Livestock and poultry numbers weighted by all roughage (including pasture) consumed. [4] Livestock and poultry numbers weighted by all feed (including pasture) fed to livestock.
ERS, Market and Trade Economics Division, (202) 694–5313.

Table 1-78.—Feed grains: Average price, selected markets and grades, 2004–2013 [1]

Calendar year	Kansas City			Minneapolis			
	Corn, No. 2 Yellow (truck)	Corn, No. 2 White (rail)	Sorghum, No. 2 Yellow (truck)	Corn, No. 2 Yellow	Barley, No. 3 or Better malting	Duluth Barley, No. 2 Feed	Oats, No. 2 White
	Dollars per bushel	Dollars per bushel	Dollars per cwt.	Dollars per bushel	Dollars per bushel	Dollars per bushel	Dollars per bushel
2004	2.40	2.52	4.23	2.38	2.55	1.79	1.71
2005	1.87	2.19	3.34	1.79	2.53	(NA)	1.84
2006	2.42	2.03	4.27	2.24	3.20	....	2.24
2007	4.61	4.43	6.05	3.38	2.02	3.95	2.98
2008	5.12	5.32	8.41	4.76	6.81	....	3.91
2009	3.60	3.90	5.57	3.46	4.26	....	2.21
2010	4.08	4.27	6.94	3.65	4.70	(NA)	2.74
2011	6.81	7.11	11.73	6.58	6.96	....	3.72
2012	7.17	7.29	11.81	6.87	7.06	....	3.67
2013	6.28	6.35	10.40	5.97	6.35	4.47	3.90

Calendar year	Omaha: Corn, No. 2 Yellow (truck)	Chicago: Corn, No. 2 Yellow	Texas High Plains: Sorghum, No. 2 Yellow	Memphis Corn, No. 2 Yellow	St. Louis: Corn, No. 2 Yellow (truck)
	Dollars per bushel	Dollars per bushel	Dollars per cwt	Dollars per bushel	Dollars per cwt
2004	2.36	2.48	4.70	2.55	2.64
2005	1.77	1.97	3.98	2.11	2.01
2006	2.31	2.43	5.06	2.66	2.34
2007	3.54	3.67	7.10	3.71	3.74
2008	5.04	5.12	9.53	5.07	5.11
2009	3.56	3.76	6.52	3.69	3.78
2010	4.03	4.16	7.81	4.25	4.26
2011	6.72	6.78	12.64	6.85	7.08
2012	7.06	6.86	13.15	6.95	7.08
2013	6.23	5.81	10.51	6.07	6.25

(NA) Not available. [1] Simple average of daily prices.
AMS, Livestock and Grain Market News Branch, (202) 720–6231.

Table 1-79.—Feedstuffs: Average price per ton bulk, in wholesale lots, at leading markets, 2004–2013

Year beginning October	Soybean meal 44% protein Decatur	Soybean meal 48% protein Decatur	Cottonseed meal 41% protein Kansas City	Cottonseed meal 41% protein Memphis	Linseed meal 34% protein Minneapolis	Meat meal 50% protein Kansas City	Fish meal 60% protein Gulf Coast	Wheat bran Kansas City	Wheat middlings Minneapolis
	Dollars per ton	Dollars per ton	Dollars per ton	Dollars per ton	Dollars per ton	Dollars per ton	Dollars per ton	Dollars per ton	Dollars per ton
2004	([1])	237.30	193.58	167.68	148.09	190.63	524.97	67.82	64.19
2005	([1])	188.17	156.59	128.89	115.70	169.19	....	54.34	44.53
2006	([1])	175.60	171.84	141.87	116.12	151.43	707.27	72.68	61.12
2007	([1])	230.39	187.53	166.49	148.36	225.96	850.53	87.31	87.20
2008	([1])	331.09	298.72	265.82	227.05	326.48	866.06	134.33	136.20
2009	([1])	347.73	293.25	265.21	231.77	334.69	861.06	90.17	89.12
2010	([1])	313.47	249.72	212.57	210.80	299.05	1,265.78	94.62	94.44
2011	....	333.73	310.43	275.43	242.60	342.84	1,198.89	176.20	172.74
2012	....	439.77	336.79	303.37	282.67	391.49	1,168.09	175.06	192.91
2013	(NA)	464.61	430.80	333.42	(NA)	467.00	(NA)	129.57	182.40

Year beginning October	Wheat shorts or middlings Kansas City	Wheat millrun Portland	Gluten feed 21% protein Illinois Points	Hominy feed Midwest	Distillers' dried grains Lawrenceburg	Brewers' dried grains Columbus	Alfalfa meal Dehydrated, 17% protein Kansas City	Alfalfa meal Sun-cured Kansas City	Blackstrap molasses New Orleans
	Dollars per ton	Dollars per ton	Dollars per ton	Dollars per ton	Dollars per ton	Dollars per ton	Dollars per ton	Dollars per ton	Dollars per ton
2004	67.82	85.00	68.83	77.02	106.04	([1])	121.35	109.26	57.28
2005	54.23	74.72	68.17	50.50	75.47	([1])	135.83	110.57	(NA)
2006	72.53	84.51	69.51	59.84	89.04	([1])	174.13	161.77	(NA)
2007	....	129.30	81.34	108.64	113.38	([1])	206.53	179.50	(NA)
2008	134.31	185.85	....	153.50	....	([1])	236.28	205.77	(NA)
2009	90.24	120.48	....	100.53	114.23	([1])	224.93	189.19	(NA)
2010	94.62	124.06	....	115.61	122.77	([1])	210.36	178.16	(NA)
2011	176.20	187.71	....	206.85	202.42	....	254.72	243.29	....
2012	174.78	219.71	....	....	200.00	....	347.23	....	....
2013	129.99	228.57	166.35	202.42	236.07	(NA)	339.28	275.70	(NA)

(NA) Not available.   [1] Discontinued.
AMS, Livestock and Grain Market News Branch, (202) 720–6231.

Table 1-80.—International Millet: Area, yield, and production in specified countries, 2013/2014–2015/2016

Country	Area			Yield per hectare			Production		
	2013/ 2014	2014/ 2015	2015/ 2016	2013/ 2014	2014/ 2015	2015/ 2016	2013/ 2014	2014/ 2015	2015/ 2016
	1,000 hectares	*1,000 hectares*	*1,000 hectares*	*metric tons*	*metric tons*	*metric tons*	*1,000 metric tons*	*1,000 metric tons*	*1,000 metric tons*
Burkina	1,327	1,200	1,200	0.81	0.87	0.92	1,079	1,038	1,100
Chad	800	1,000	1,000	0.73	0.68	0.70	582	683	700
China	716	772	750	2.44	2.34	2.40	1,746	1,809	1,800
Ethiopa	455	440	440	1.87	1.70	1.59	850	750	700
India	9,687	8,903	8,950	1.20	1.31	1.19	11,663	11,630	10,680
Mali	1,437	1,600	1,600	0.80	1.00	1.00	1,152	1,600	1,600
Niger	7,100	7,000	7,000	0.42	0.41	0.46	2,995	2,900	3,200
Nigeria	4,000	4,000	4,000	1.25	1.20	1.20	5,000	4,800	4,800
Senegal	714	850	850	0.72	0.48	0.76	515	409	650
Sudan	1,501	2,884	2,500	0.24	0.38	0.28	359	1,085	700
Others	3,898	3,919	3,994	0.79	0.82	0.86	3,090	3,231	3,440
Total Foreign	31,635	32,568	32,284	0.92	0.92	0.91	29,031	29,935	29,370
Total	31,635	32,568	32,284	0.92	0.92	0.91	29,031	29,935	29,370

FAS, Office of Global Analysis, (202) 720-6301. Prepared or estimated on the basis of official USDA production, supply, and distribution statistics from foreign governments.

Table 1-81.—Proso millet: Area, yield, production, and value, United States, 2005–2014

Year	Area		Yield per harvested acre	Production	Marketing year average price per bushel received by farmers	Value of production
	Planted	Harvested				
	1,000 acres	*1,000 acres*	*Bushels*	*1,000 bushels*	*Dollars*	*1,000 dollars*
2005	565	515	26.5	13,670	3.19	43,660
2006	580	475	21.5	10,195	4.09	41,748
2007	570	520	32.5	16,900	4.67	78,975
2008	520	460	32.3	14,880	3.23	48,017
2009	350	265	33.5	8,875	2.87	25,460
2010	390	363	31.8	11,535	4.54	52,419
2011	370	338	27.1	9,149	6.01	54,974
2012	335	205	15.0	3,075	15.10	46,548
2013	720	638	28.9	18,436	4.61	84,915
2014	505	430	31.4	13,483	3.19	43,007

NASS, Crops Branch, (202) 720–2127.

GRAIN AND FEED

Table 1-82.—Proso millet: Area, yield, and production, by State and United States, 2012–2014

State	Area planted			Area harvested		
	2012	2013	2014	2012	2013	20114
	1,000 acres	*1,000 acres*	*1,000 acres*	*1,000 acres*	*1,000 acres*	*1,000 acres*
Colorado	210	370	310	120	330	250
Nebraska	70	160	120	55	143	111
South Dakota	55	190	75	30	165	69
United States	335	720	505	205	638	430

State	Yield per acre			Production		
	2012	2013	2014	2012	2013	2014
	Bushels	*Bushels*	*Bushels*	*1,000 bushels*	*1,000 bushels*	*1,000 bushels*
Colorado	14.0	25.0	32.5	1,680	8,250	8,125
Nebraska	15.0	32.0	29.0	825	4,576	3,219
South Dakota	19.0	34.0	31.0	570	5,610	2,139
United States	15.0	28.9	31.4	3,075	18,436	13,483

NASS, Crops Branch, (202) 720–2127.

Table 1-83.—Proso millet: Marketing year average price and value, by State and United States, 2011–2013

State	Marketing year average price per bushel			Value of production		
	2011	2012	2013	2011	2012	2013
	Dollars	*Dollars*	*Dollars*	*1,000 dollars*	*1,000 dollars*	*1,000 dollars*
Colorado	16.40	4.31	3.15	27,552	35,558	25,594
Nebraska	12.80	4.73	3.15	10,560	21,644	10,140
South Dakota	14.80	4.94	3.40	8,436	27,713	7,273
United States	15.10	4.61	3.19	46,548	84,915	43,007

NASS, Crops Branch, (202) 720–2127.

CHAPTER II

STATISTICS OF COTTON, TOBACCO, SUGAR CROPS, AND HONEY

In addition to tables on cotton, tobacco, sugar, and honey, this chapter includes tables on fibers other than cotton and syrups. Cottonseed data, however, are in the following chapter on oilseeds, fats, and oils.

Table 2-1.—Cotton: Area, yield, production, market year average price, and value, United States, 2005–2014

Year	Area		Yield per harvested acre	Production	Marketing year average price per pound received by farmers	Value of production
	Planted	Harvested				
	1,000 acres	*1,000 acres*	*Pounds*	*1,000 bales*[1]	*Cents*	*1,000 dollars*
2005	14,245.4	13,802.6	831	23,890.2	49.7	5,695,217
2006	15,274.0	12,731.5	814	21,587.8	48.4	5,013,238
2007	10,827.2	10,489.1	879	19,206.9	61.3	5,652,907
2008	9,471.0	7,568.7	813	12,825.4	49.1	3,023,632
2009	9,149.5	7,533.7	776	12,183.0	64.8	3,786,674
2010	10,974.2	10,698.7	812	18,101.8	84.6	7,346,868
2011	14,735.4	9,460.9	790	15,573.2	93.5	6,985,976
2012	12,264.4	9,321.8	892	17,313.8	75.7	6,291,813
2013	10,407.0	7,544.4	821	12,909.2	83.8	5,191,505
2014[2]	11,037.4	9,346.8	838	16,319.4	65.7	5,069,020

[1] 480-pound net weight bales. [2] Preliminary.
NASS, Crops Branch, (202) 720–2127.

Table 2-2.—Cotton: Marketing year average price per pound, and value, by State and United States, 2012–2014

State	Marketing year average price per pound			Value of production		
	2012	2013	2014[1]	2012	2013	2014[1]
Upland:	*Dollars*	*Dollars*	*Dollars*	*1,000 dollars*	*1,000 dollars*	*1,000 dollars*
Alabama	0.726	0.819	0.603	259,618	231,941	192,614
Arizona	0.768	0.780	0.641	223,037	179,712	145,303
Arkansas	0.715	0.794	0.644	445,130	274,406	243,638
California	0.892	0.905	0.853	217,505	144,655	98,700
Florida	0.763	0.820	0.667	73,248	68,880	60,672
Georgia	0.768	0.825	0.654	1,072,742	918,720	770,400
Kansas	0.707	0.774	0.559	23,755	15,232	14,452
Louisiana	0.693	0.784	0.626	159,002	122,680	116,309
Mississippi	0.761	0.815	0.658	362,723	281,273	301,558
Missouri	0.731	0.838	0.650	256,493	199,511	159,782
New Mexico	0.717	0.771	0.655	28,565	22,205	21,154
North Carolina	0.729	0.815	0.668	428,652	299,659	306,806
Oklahoma	0.711	0.781	0.553	52,898	57,732	73,649
South Carolina	0.757	0.819	0.655	215,472	141,523	156,499
Tennessee	0.738	0.799	0.626	263,200	158,777	144,530
Texas	0.698	0.746	0.587	1,675,200	1,493,194	1,753,814
Virginia	0.735	0.802	0.664	69,854	58,129	65,961
United States	0.725	0.779	0.613	5,827,084	4,668,229	4,625,841
American-Pima:						
Arizona	1.200	(D)	(D)	4,205	(D)	(D)
California	1.240	1.720	1.570	448,186	503,616	391,872
New Mexico	1.400	(D)	(D)	3,360	(D)	(D)
Texas	1.290	1.710	1.300	8,978	12,312	25,344
United States	1.240	1.720	1.550	464,729	523,276	443,179
All:						
United States	0.757	0.838	0.657	6,291,813	5,191,505	5,069,020

(D) Withheld to avoid disclosing data for individual operations. [1] Preliminary.
NASS, Crops Branch, (202) 720–2127.

Table 2-3.—Cotton: Area, yield, production, and type by State and United States, 2012–2014

State	Area planted			Area harvested		
	2012	2013	2014[2]	2012	2013	2014[2]
	1,000 acres	1,000 acres	1,000 acres	1,000 acres	1,000 acres	1,000 acres
Upland:						
Alabama	380.0	365.0	350.0	378.0	359.0	348.0
Arizona	200.0	160.0	150.0	197.0	159.0	149.0
Arkansas	595.0	310.0	335.0	585.0	305.0	330.0
California	142.0	93.0	57.0	141.0	92.0	56.0
Florida	108.0	131.0	107.0	107.0	127.0	105.0
Georgia	1,290.0	1,370.0	1,380.0	1,280.0	1,340.0	1,370.0
Kansas	56.0	27.0	31.0	54.0	26.0	29.0
Louisiana	230.0	130.0	170.0	225.0	128.0	168.0
Mississippi	475.0	290.0	425.0	470.0	287.0	420.0
Missouri	350.0	255.0	250.0	330.0	246.0	245.0
New Mexico	45.0	39.0	43.0	38.0	31.0	33.0
North Carolina	585.0	465.0	465.0	580.0	460.0	460.0
Oklahoma	305.0	185.0	240.0	140.0	125.0	210.0
South Carolina	299.0	258.0	280.0	298.0	250.0	278.0
Tennessee	380.0	250.0	275.0	377.0	233.0	270.0
Texas	6,500.0	5,800.0	6,200.0	3,800.0	3,100.0	4,600.0
Virginia	86.0	78.0	87.0	85.0	77.0	86.0
United States	12,026.0	10,206.0	10,845.0	9,085.0	7,345.0	9,157.0
American Pima:						
Arizona	3.0	1.5	15.0	3.0	1.5	14.5
California	225.0	187.0	155.0	224.0	186.0	154.0
New Mexico	2.4	3.5	5.4	2.3	3.4	5.3
Texas	8.0	9.0	17.0	7.5	8.5	16.0
United States	238.4	201.0	192.4	236.8	199.4	189.8
All:						
United States	12,264.4	10,407.0	11,037.4	9,321.8	7,544.4	9,346.8

State	Yield per harvested acre			Production[1]		
	2012	2013	2014[2]	2012	2013	2014[2]
	Pounds	Pounds	Pounds	1,000 bales[3]	1,000 bales[3]	1,000 bales[3]
Upland:						
Alabama	946	789	901	745.0	590.0	653.0
Arizona	1,474	1,449	1,579	605.0	480.0	490.0
Arkansas	1,064	1,133	1,145	1,297.0	720.0	787.0
California	1,729	1,737	1,834	508.0	333.0	214.0
Florida	897	661	878	200.0	175.0	192.0
Georgia	1,091	831	900	2,910.0	2,320.0	2,570.0
Kansas	622	757	794	70.0	41.0	48.0
Louisiana	1,020	1,223	1,154	478.0	326.0	404.0
Mississippi	1,014	1,203	1,232	993.0	719.0	1,078.0
Missouri	1,063	968	1,117	731.0	496.0	570.0
New Mexico	1,048	929	931	83.0	60.0	64.0
North Carolina	1,014	799	1,038	1,225.0	766.0	995.0
Oklahoma	531	591	615	155.0	154.0	269.0
South Carolina	955	691	912	593.0	360.0	528.0
Tennessee	946	853	878	743.0	414.0	494.0
Texas	632	646	644	5,000.0	4,170.0	6,175.0
Virginia	1,118	941	1,239	198.0	151.0	222.0
United States	874	802	826	16,534.0	12,275.0	15,753.0
American Pima:						
Arizona	1,168	1,024	993	7.3	3.2	30.0
California	1,614	1,574	1,558	753.0	610.0	500.0
New Mexico	1,043	847	761	5.0	6.0	8.4
Texas	928	847	840	14.5	15.0	28.0
United States	1,581	1,527	1,432	779.8	634.2	566.4
All:						
United States	892	821	838	17,313.8	12,909.2	16,319.4

[1] Production ginned and to be ginned.   [2] Preliminary.   [3] 480-pound net weight bales.
NASS, Crops Branch, (202) 720–2127.

Table 2-4.—Cotton, American Upland: Support operations, United States, 2007/2008– 2014/2015

Marketing Year beginning August 1	Income support payment rates per pound [1]	Program price levels per pound		Put under Loan		Acquired by CCC under loan program	Owned by CCC at end of marketing year
		Loan [2]	Target [3]	Quantity	Percentage of production		
	Cents	*Cents*	*Cents*	*1,000 bales*	*Percent*	*1,000 bales*	*1,000 bales*
2007/2008	6.67/6.43	52.00	72.40	14,636	81.8	169	0
2008/2009	6.67/12.58	52.00	71.25	10,005	83.0	4	0
2009/2010	6.67/1.68	52.00	71.25	8,278	72.3	0	0
2010/2011	6.67/0	52.00	71.25	11,403	66.5	0	0
2011/2012	6.67/0	52.00	71.25	7,268	50.7	1	0
2012/2013	6.67/0	52.00	71.25	8,330	50.4	0	0
2013/2014	6.67/0	52.00	71.25	3,981	32.4	0	0
2014/2015 [4]	(NA)	52.00	(NA)	7,625	48.4	0	0

(NA) Not available.   [1] The first entry is the direct payment rate and the second entry is the counter-cyclical payment rate for 2004/2005-2013/2014. For 2009/2010-2013/2014, producers who participate in the Average Crop Revenue (ACRE) program get a 20 percent reduction in their direct payment, not calculated in this table. The Agricultural Act of 2014 excludes upland cotton as a covered commodity for the Agricultural Risk Coverage and Price Loss Coverage Programs.   [2] For 2009/ 2010-2013/2014, producers who participate in the ACRE program get a 30 percent reduction in their loan rate, not calculated in this table.   [3] Target applies to 2003/2004-2013/2014 and Reference applies beginning with 2014/ 2015.   [4] Aquisitions as of December 31, 2015.
FSA, Fibers, Peanuts, Tobacco, (202) 401–0062.

Table 2-5.—International Cotton: Area, yield, and production in specified countries, 2013/2014–2015/2016

Country	Area			Yield per hectare			Production		
	2013/ 2014	2014/ 2015	2015/ 2016	2013/ 2014	2014/ 2015	2015/ 2016	2013/ 2014	2014/ 2015	2015/ 2016
	1,000 hectares	*1,000 hectares*	*1,000 hectares*	*Kilograms*	*Kilograms*	*Kilograms*	*1,000 480 lb. bales*	*1,000 480 lb. bales*	*1,000 480 lb. bales*
Argentina	436	205	285	2,047.00	2,443.00	1,910.00	4,100	2,300	2,500
Brazil	1,120	1,020	950	1,555.00	1,494.00	1,536.00	8,000	7,000	6,700
Burkina	647	660	625	421.00	445.00	418.00	1,250	1,350	1,200
China	4,800	4,400	3,400	1,486.00	1,484.00	1,524.00	32,750	30,000	23,800
India	11,700	12,700	11,800	577.00	506.00	494.00	31,000	29,500	26,800
Mali	450	538	580	411.00	433.00	413.00	850	1,070	1,100
Pakistan	2,900	2,950	2,800	713.00	782.00	544.00	9,500	10,600	7,000
Turkey	330	430	370	1,517.00	1,620.00	1,559.00	2,300	3,200	2,650
Turkmenistan	575	545	500	587.00	609.00	566.00	1,550	1,525	1,300
Uzbekistan ...	1,300	1,285	1,285	687.00	661.00	627.00	4,100	3,900	3,700
Others	5,480	5,506	5,062	2.21	2.25	2.08	12,097	12,386	10,528
Total foreign	29,738	30,239	27,657	3.61	3.40	3.16	107,497	102,831	87,278
United States	3,053	3,783	3,261	921.00	939.00	864.00	12,909	16,319	12,943
Total	32,791	34,022	30,918	3.67	3.50	3.24	120,406	119,150	100,221

FAS, Office of Global Analysis, (202) 720–6301.   Prepared or estimated on the basis of official USDA production, supply, and distribution statistics from foreign governments.

Table 2-6.—Cotton: Supply and distribution, United States, 2004–2013

Year beginning August 1	Supply			Distribution				
	Beginning of season total [2]	Ginnings in season [1]	Total supply [2]	Consumption [1]			Exports	Carryover, end of season [2]
				Upland	American Pima	Total		
	1,000 bales	*1,000 bales*	*1,000 bales*	*1,000 bales*	*1,000 bales*	*1,000 bales*	*1,000 bales*	*1,000 bales*
2004	3,381	22,576	25,957	5,968	60	6,028	13,593	5,411
2005	5,368	23,253	28,576	5,604	49	5,653	17,038	5,877
2006	5,878	20,998	26,872	(D)	(D)	4,745	12,631	9,221
2007	9,223	18,713	27,929	(D)	(D)	4,499	13,237	9,699
2008	9,699	12,462	22,154	(D)	(D)	3,439	12,875	6,135
2009	6,136	11,832	17,963	(D)	(D)	3,336	11,687	2,852
2010	2,850	17,643	20,786	(D)	(D)	3,490	13,958	2,940
2011	2,600	15,153	18,190	(D)	(D)	3,300	11,710	3,350
2012	3,350	16,834	20,680	(D)	(D)	3,500	13,030	3,900
2013 [3]	3,900	12,521	16,421	(D)	(D)	3,600	10,400	2,800

(D) Withheld to avoid disclosing data for individual companies. [1] Ginnings during the 12 months, Aug. 1–July 31. Includes an allowance for "city crop" which consists of rebaled samples and pickings from cotton damaged by fire and weather. [2] May include small volume of foreign growths. [3] Preliminary.
AMS, Cotton and Tobacco Program, (901) 384–3016. Compiled from reports of the Bureau of the Census. Bureau of the Census discontinued the report containing this information.

Table 2-7.—Cotton, American Upland: Percentage distribution of fiber strength, United States, 2009–2013

Fiber strength [1]	Year				
	2009	2010	2011	2012	2013
17 and below	-	-	*	-	-
18	*	*	*	*	-
19	*	*	*	*	*
20	*	*	*	*	*
21	*	*	*	*	*
22	*	*	0.1	*	*
23	0.1	*	0.2	0.1	*
24	0.4	0.2	0.3	0.2	0.1
25	1.4	0.6	0.9	0.8	0.4
26	4.9	2.1	2.8	3.1	1.7
27	11.8	5.9	6.9	8.2	5.4
28	19.7	12.5	13.0	13.7	11.8
29	21.9	18.7	17.6	17.2	17.0
30	17.8	20.6	18.6	18.5	19.0
31	11.6	17.1	16.1	16.1	17.7
32	5.9	11.5	10.9	11.1	13.4
33	2.4	6.2	6.5	6.1	7.7
34	1.1	2.9	3.7	3.0	3.7
35	0.6	1.2	1.6	1.3	1.5
36 and above	0.3	0.5	0.7	0.6	0.5
Average	29.1	30.0	30.0	29.9	30.3

[1] Fiber strength expressed in terms of 1/8" gage (grams per tex). *Less than 0.05 percent.
AMS, Cotton and Tobacco Program, (901) 384–3016.

Table 2-8.—Cotton, American Upland: Estimated percentage of the crop forward contracted by growers, by States, 2006–2013

State	Crop of—							
	2006	2007	2008	2009	2010	2011	2012	2013
	Percent	*Percent*	*Percent*	*Percent*	*Percent*	*Percent*	*Percent*	*Percent*
Alabama	15	2	10	3	15	41	32	30
Arizona	-	4	6	-	16	1	5	3
Arkansas	12	3	5	-	17	63	33	18
California	*	*	-	-	14	7	8	4
Florida	-	-	16	10	30	18	8	15
Georgia	2	*	12	16	29	20	18	40
Louisiana	22	39	68	2	64	57	49	15
Mississippi	14	14	6	13	6	54	21	11
Missouri	3	-	19	*	9	78	35	29
New Mexico	-	-	-	-	-	-	-	1
North Carolina	9	1	10	4	29	52	14	33
Oklahoma	-	-	-	-	-	-	-	-
South Carolina	6	6	10	2	22	30	7	34
Tennessee	3	-	1	*	10	69	38	20
Texas	3	3	11	3	22	33	5	5
United States	7	4	12	4	19	38	14	17

*Less than 0.5 percent.
AMS, Cotton and Tobacco Program, (901) 384–3016.

Table 2-9.—Cotton, American Upland: Carryover and crop, running bales, by grade groupings, United States, 2003–2012

Year beginning August 1	White color grades					Light spotted color grades				Other color grades [1]	All grades [2]
	21 and higher	31	41	51	61 and 71	22 and higher	32	42	52 and lower		
	1,000 bales	1,000 bales	1,000 bales	1,000 bales	1,000 bales	1,000 bales	1,000 bales	1,000 bales	1,000 bales	1,000 bales	1,000 bales
Carryover:											
2003	596	988	1,804	502	8	37	193	475	251	115	4,972
2004	435	1,573	1,106	54	1	22	47	51	7	19	3,314
2005	975	1,042	1,609	530	18	42	154	505	186	339	5,402
2006	1,642	2,178	1,466	90	1	68	92	146	62	66	5,810
2007	1,874	3,909	2,611	132	3	59	133	209	127	39	9,096
2008	2,373	4,149	2,466	123	4	77	137	200	126	38	9,692
2009	852	1,999	2,536	236	0	45	64	84	55	3	5,874
2010	336	408	1,547	234	0	42	17	83	98	71	2,838
2011	654	842	666	228	9	21	73	138	222	41	2,899
2012	340	595	1,633	202	0	44	18	97	81	72	3,081
Crop:											
2003	3,971	7,755	4,423	193	2	156	278	319	67	124	17,290
2004	4,063	5,228	7,079	1,955	45	180	605	1,328	567	782	21,832
2005	7,698	8,029	4,297	541	5	303	591	699	312	164	22,638
2006	3,785	8,145	6,842	397	4	146	296	425	198	24	20,262
2007	6,376	3,794	4,788	592	4	188	238	1,184	745	16	17,925
2008	2,160	4,557	4,285	391	2	169	171	161	166	12	12,075
2009	2,696	3,419	3,665	776	21	55	97	241	419	30	11,419
2010	7,099	5,693	2,668	382	7	221	264	402	278	124	17,138
2011	3,475	5,029	4,190	321	4	348	199	416	155	118	14,255
2012	4,075	4,805	5,545	285	1	421	310	374	80	157	16,053

[1] Includes all color grades of Spotted, Tinged, Yellow Stained, and Below Grade. [2] Bales classed as reported by AMS, Cotton and Tobacco Program.
AMS, Cotton and Tobacco Program, (901) 384–3016.

Table 2-10.—Cotton, American Upland: Carryover and crop, running bales, by staple groupings, United States, 2003-2012

Year beginning August 1	Staple										All staples [1]
	26 and shorter	28	29	30	31	32	33	34	35	36 and longer	
	1,000 bales	1,000 bales	1,000 bales	1,000 bales	1,000 bales	1,000 bales	1,000 bales	1,000 bales	1,000 bales	1,000 bales	1,000 bales
Carryover:											
2003	-	(2)	15	35	69	214	708	1,495	1,357	1,079	4,972
2004	-	1	3	14	33	142	389	1,189	869	674	3,314
2005	-	1	4	17	77	213	543	1,128	1,615	1,803	5,402
2006	-	-	(2)	4	32	173	510	1,582	1,849	1,659	5,810
2007	-	(2)	(2)	5	62	382	924	1,873	2,236	3,613	9,096
2008	-	(2)	(2)	6	62	368	892	1,827	2,312	4,225	9,692
2009	-	-	-	3	11	61	337	816	1,423	3,224	5,874
2010	-	-	(2)	-	(2)	63	48	255	825	1,647	2,838
2011	-	(2)	(2)	8	44	176	335	611	765	958	2,899
2012	-	-	(2)	-	(2)	63	47	298	907	1,766	3,081
Crop:											
2003	(2)	1	10	57	202	624	2,205	4,873	4,805	4,512	17,290
2004	(2)	1	9	56	196	723	2,175	4,630	6,543	7,499	21,832
2005	(2)	(2)	1	16	127	650	2,460	5,892	7,261	6,232	22,638
2006	(2)	1	7	29	136	588	1,764	3,735	5,181	8,821	20,262
2007	-	(2)	2	14	113	524	1,574	3,293	4,376	8,030	17,925
2008	-	(2)	1	7	41	195	685	1,675	2,541	6,930	12,075
2009	(2)	(2)	2	11	39	120	488	1,828	3,461	5,468	11,419
2010	-	(2)	1	8	61	317	1,128	2,788	4,371	8,465	17,138
2011	(2)	1	7	32	123	386	947	1,969	3,329	7,461	14,255
2012	(2)	1	4	22	90	285	675	1,574	2,651	9,783	16,052

[1] Carryover as reported by the Bureau of the Census, Crop as reported by AMS, Cotton and Tobacco Program. [2] Less than 500 bales.
AMS, Cotton and Tobacco Program, (901) 384–3016.

Table 2-11.—Cotton, American Pima: Carryover and crop, running bales, by grade and staple, United States, 2007-2012

Year beginning August 1	Grade					Staple				All grades and staples[1]
	01 and 02	03	04	05	06 and 07	42 and shorter	44	46	48 and longer	
	1,000 bales	*1,000 bales*	*1,000 bales*	*1,000 bales*	*1,000 bales*	*1,000 bales*	*1,000 bales*	*1,000 bales*	*1,000 bales*	*1,000 bales*
Carryover:										
2007	76.0	45.1	1.7	1.9	0.1	0.0	51.4	56.1	18.1	125.6
2008	65.5	75.0	0.8	2.9	1.6	0.0	31.7	91.7	22.7	146.2
2009	243.5	15.3	2.1	0.3	0.5	0.1	25.4	128.2	107.8	261.5
2010	14.2	0.5	0.1	0.0	0.0	0.0	1.6	1.9	11.3	14.8
2011	8.5	6.9	20.3	2.5	2.3	0.0	3.8	14.4	23.1	41.3
2012	256.0	8.9	2.4	0.4	0.4	0.0	28.1	35.6	204.3	268.0
Crop:										
2007	784.1	29.0	7.3	1.9	0.3	0.4	51.8	400.7	369.9	822.7
2008	391.1	18.5	1.8	0.3	1.0	0.0	10.5	126.7	275.5	412.7
2009	324.1	51.9	7.7	0.9	0.0	0.0	10.8	118.2	255.5	384.6
2010	411.5	57.9	10.8	3.0	0.4	0.1	8.5	96.8	377.9	483.3
2011	755.3	49.2	11.9	6.4	0.9	0.1	13.6	171.4	638.7	823.8
2012	716.0	31.7	2.3	0.5	0.2	0.3	25.2	212.8	512.5	750.8

[1] Carryover as reported by the Bureau of the Census; crop as reported by AMS, Cotton and Tobacco Program.
AMS, Cotton and Tobacco Program, (901) 384–3016.

Table 2-12.—Cotton, Upland: Average staple length of Upland cotton classed, by State and United States, 2007–2013

State	Average staple length (32ds of an inch)[1]						
	2007	2008	2009	2010	2011	2012	2013
Alabama	33.8	34.3	34.8	34.3	35.6	35.8	35.5
Arizona	35.7	36.3	36.2	36.4	36.0	36.0	36.2
Arkansas	35.0	36.1	35.6	35.5	36.1	36.2	36.8
California	37.2	38.1	38.0	38.2	37.7	37.4	37.5
Florida	34.4	35.0	34.8	35.1	36.1	36.2	35.8
Georgia	34.4	34.5	34.9	34.9	35.9	36.0	36.0
Kansas	35.1	35.7	35.6	35.2	34.9	34.6	34.4
Louisiana	34.8	34.5	35.1	35.0	34.9	35.4	35.6
Mississippi	34.6	35.9	35.5	34.9	35.8	36.1	36.3
Missouri	34.8	36.0	35.7	35.6	36.3	36.1	36.1
New Mexico	37.0	37.2	36.5	36.5	36.5	36.3	36.7
North Carolina	33.9	34.8	35.0	34.8	34.8	35.9	36.1
Oklahoma	35.4	36.0	35.5	35.4	35.2	34.9	35.2
South Carolina	33.6	35.2	35.1	35.5	35.5	36.1	36.2
Tennessee	33.3	35.1	35.0	34.7	35.4	35.1	35.7
Texas	36.0	36.3	35.6	35.7	34.5	35.1	35.4
Virginia	34.0	34.5	35.4	34.3	34.8	36.0	36.3
Other States	(NA)	(NA)	(NA)	(NA)	(NA)	(NA)	(NA)
United States	35.3	35.7	35.5	35.5	35.5	35.7	35.8

(NA) Not available. [1] Average calculated on numerical equivalents of the staple-length designations. For example, 7/8-inch = 28, 29/32-inch = 29, etc.
AMS, Cotton and Tobacco Program, (901) 384–3016.

Table 2-13.—Cotton: United States exports by country of destination, 2011–2013

Country of destination	Year		
	2011	2012	2013 [1]
	Metric tons	Metric tons	Metric tons
Cotton linters:			
China	49,096	19,830	23,882
Japan	1,870	6,716	16,864
Spain	628	1,171	10,165
Germany(*)	3,130	337	870
Brazil	0	20	797
Egypt	0	1,560	503
Belgium-Luxembourg(*)	0	123	197
France(*)	253	177	146
Mexico	3	20	132
United Kingdom	32	45	78
Turkey	0	56	39
Canada	90	63	30
Trinidad and Tobago	0	0	12
Panama	0	0	11
Sweden	29	0	10
Indonesia	701	27	10
Nigeria	33	0	10
Serbia	0	0	9
Kuwait	0	0	9
Argentina	0	0	8
Chile	9	0	7
Guatemala	34	27	7
Vietnam	17	0	4
Leeward-Windward Islands(*)	0	0	2
United Arab Emirates	8	31	0
Australia(*)	246	25	0
Costa Rica	4	25	0
Dominican Republic	6	0	0
El Salvador	26	0	0
Rest of World	1,976	706	0
World Total	58,189	30,957	53,802
Cotton < 1:			
China	68,501	55,332	25,823
Korea, South	16,243	11,620	6,368
Thailand	10,403	12,107	5,618
Vietnam	2,543	2,986	3,878
Japan	1,675	2,166	2,581
Turkey	36,061	9,431	2,516
Indonesia	6,954	2,504	2,351
Mexico	3,376	831	2,229
India	1,820	957	1,286
Taiwan	17,777	11,926	1,236
Peru	504	311	1,150
Bangladesh	8,872	2,230	785
Pakistan	1,736	1,282	785
Philippines	0	116	574
El Salvador	20	0	285
Germany(*)	419	176	100
Ecuador	19	0	98
Portugal)	413	0	20
Malaysia	742	20	19
Dominican Republic	0	0	16
Panama	0	0	12
Spain	455	59	6
Hong Kong	681	0	1
Australia(*)	59	0	0
Austria	20	0	0
Bahrain	96	0	0
Belgium-Luxembourg(*)	100	60	0
Brazil	7,053	1	0
Canada	93	0	0
Rest of World	3,244	355	0
World Total	189,881	114,469	57,736

See footnote(s) at end of table.

Table 2-13.—Cotton: United States exports by country of destination, 2011–2013—Continued

Country of destination	Year		
	2011	2012	2013[1]
	Metric tons	*Metric tons*	*Metric tons*
Cotton > 1 < 1 1/8:			
China	349,736	804,632	402,907
Turkey	192,222	179,374	238,229
Mexico	199,859	160,268	201,825
Vietnam	82,224	80,905	115,999
Indonesia	53,071	23,567	77,499
Pakistan	23,711	22,399	66,928
Taiwan	20,243	44,412	36,563
Thailand	58,727	23,235	30,655
Korea, South	16,795	11,865	25,816
Bangladesh	28,558	19,477	25,677
El Salvador	26,417	25,165	22,732
Guatemala	15,130	15,847	20,865
Colombia	34,525	17,749	17,284
Japan	20,618	8,851	15,005
Peru	21,079	15,423	14,681
Morocco	10,019	10,997	11,799
Malaysia	14,003	9,431	11,659
Ecuador	7,580	4,366	9,372
Brazil	89,194	513	7,234
Philippines	4,293	2,812	5,527
India	2,833	7,405	3,194
Hong Kong	1,226	6,264	2,700
Egypt	2,711	158	1,316
Singapore	2	0	729
Venezuela	920	1,853	709
Germany(*)	1,555	1,371	452
Bahrain	100	0	265
Tunisia	176	119	220
Belgium-Luxembourg(*)	100	577	218
Rest of World	9,044	11,023	726
World Total	1,286,672	1,510,055	1,368,784
Pima >= 1 3/8:			
China	15,981	41,530	67,786
Turkey	3,475	6,499	11,739
India	9,105	8,932	11,110
Pakistan	3,188	8,229	7,161
Korea, South	9,759	7,939	5,750
Peru	2,112	2,896	3,783
Thailand	3,166	3,139	3,681
Germany(*)	4,972	3,802	3,439
Indonesia	3,189	2,308	2,524
Egypt	731	2,078	1,817
Taiwan	1,927	1,897	1,776
Japan	3,936	2,124	1,694
Bangladesh	160	356	1,082
Vietnam	1,861	212	760
Brazil	125	98	582
Italy(*)	295	56	536
Hong Kong	195	0	197
Honduras	0	59	138
Mexico	585	454	113
Colombia	40	123	81
Guatemala	39	122	81
Switzerland(*)	294	24	76
Malaysia	846	334	73
Belgium-Luxembourg(*)	0	142	36
Mauritius	0	40	20
Iraq	0	0	2
Australia(*)	0	0	0
Ecuador	642	120	0
Philippines	0	193	0
Rest of World	2	0	0
World Total	66,627	93,706	126,035

See footnote(s) at and of table.

Table 2-13.—Cotton: United States exports by country of destination, 2011–2013—Continued

Country of destination	Year		
	2011	2012	2013[1]
	Metric tons	*Metric tons*	*Metric tons*
Cotton Other > 1 1/8:			
China	459,387	585,802	579,549
Turkey	171,451	88,222	175,776
Vietnam	46,549	42,474	94,060
Indonesia	93,202	49,985	56,074
Korea, South	69,061	31,409	48,286
Thailand	46,806	31,752	46,618
Peru	41,904	28,613	40,353
Taiwan	21,734	24,857	28,616
Bangladesh	50,183	14,896	22,921
Pakistan	53,406	21,939	21,409
India	9,591	11,453	16,193
Mexico	46,333	31,882	14,711
Hong Kong	3,766	8,447	14,267
Colombia	7,006	7,743	11,246
Morocco	9,921	12,101	11,189
Ecuador	3,931	4,554	11,004
Egypt	7,978	3,813	10,649
Japan	10,889	7,380	6,994
Brazil	26,878	447	5,934
Malaysia	9,130	6,482	3,350
Honduras	313	461	2,996
El Salvador	1,620	1,082	2,857
Bahrain	697	1,198	2,129
Germany(*)	4,948	1,490	1,915
Spain	1,543	1,963	1,657
Philippines	1,693	1,419	1,055
Switzerland(*)	0	15	897
Italy(*)	7,420	2,264	853
Guatemala	48	2,659	821
Rest of World	9,599	6,722	3,099
World Total	1,216,986	1,033,524	1,237,476

(*) Denotes a country that is a summarization of its component countries.   [1]2013 data does not reflect 13 month changes.

Users should use cautious interpretation on quantity reports using mixed units of measure.   Quantity line items will only include statistics on the units of measure that are equal to, or are able to be converted to, the assigned unit of measure of the grouped commodities.

FAS, Office of Global Analysis, (202) 720–6301.

Table 2-14.—Cotton excluding linters: United States exports and imports for consumption, by country of origin, 2010–2012

Country of origin	Year beginning August		
	2010	2011	2012 [1]
	Metric tons	*Metric tons*	*Metric tons*
Exports:			
China	1,057,205	893,605	1,487,296
Turkey	459,486	403,209	283,527
Mexico	315,166	250,154	193,435
Vietnam	132,864	133,17	126,576
Taiwan	100,617	61,681	83,093
Indonesia	151,845	156,416	78,363
Thailand	132,957	119,103	70,233
Korea, South	79,159	111,858	62,832
Pakistan	69,841	82,042	53,850
Peru	76,147	65,600	47,243
Bangladesh	79,754	87,772	36,959
India	28,148	23,349	28,746
El Salvador	30,856	28,057	26,247
Colombia	51,208	41,591	25,617
Morocco	19,990	19,940	23,098
Japan	32,558	37,119	20,522
Guatemala	24,682	15,257	18,709
Malaysia	12,972	24,721	16,266
Hong Kong	19,248	5,868	14,711
Ecuador	13,177	12,172	9,040
Germany(*)	4,278	11,894	6,838
Egypt	4,223	12,425	6,049
Philippines	7,557	5,986	4,540
Lesotho	0	1,808	4,492
Argentina	2,451	692	3,499
Venezuela	4,345	3,665	3,401
Italy(*)	6,153	9,361	3,185
Spain	262	2,006	2,023
Honduras	99	2,156	1,878
Cuba	0	1,480	1,278
Bahrain	0	893	1,198
Brazil	23,608	123,250	1,059
South Africa	0	1,290	1,009
Belgium-Luxembourg(*)	119	512	976
Tunisia	4,728	2,737	516
Canada	1,978	1,680	465
Singapore	1,176	572	454
Switzerland(*)	718	294	433
Portugal	329	990	381
Israel(*)	23	22	301
Gabon	0	0	200
Nicaragua	0	77	178
Russia	60	268	165
United Arab Emirates	1,404	782	145
Tanzania	0	0	118
Netherlands	42	21	103
Dominican Republic	12	70	72
Finland	75	106	62
Georgia	0	39	59
Barbados	34	56	45
Mauritius	0	499	40
Australia(*)	79	207	33
United Kingdom	182	2	24
Greece	0	11	21
Poland	1	0	21
Cyprus	0	0	21
Sweden	0	20	21
Denmark(*)	2	1	20
Chile	3,214	160	20
Bahamas, The	0	4	17
Costa Rica	0	14	12
Saudi Arabia	94	29	7
Panama	79	29	3
Bermuda	0	0	3

See footnote(s) at end of table.

Table 2-14.—Cotton excluding linters: United States exports and imports for consumption, by country of origin, 2010–2012—Continued

Country of origin	Year beginning August		
	2010	2011	2012[1]
	Metric tons	*Metric tons*	*Metric tons*
Leeward-Windward Islands(*)	0	2	2
Cayman Islands	0	0	2
Haiti	2	2	2
Iceland	157	0	1
Trinidad and Tobago	12	4	1
New Zealand(*)	13	0	1
Uganda	0	0	0
Afghanistan	0	98	0
Angola	7	0	0
Austria	0	20	0
Bolivia	495	10	0
Cambodia	79	0	0
Congo (Kinshasa)	79	0	0
Ethiopia(*)	0	3	0
France(*)	120	256	0
Jamaica	8	33	0
Kuwait	1	0	0
Laos	40	0	0
Latvia	0	933	0
Liberia	40	0	0
Norway(*)	4	0	0
Netherlands Antilles(*)	26	0	0
Senegal	20	0	0
Togo	61	0	0
Uruguay	0	6	0
World Total	2,956,365	2,760,166	2,751,754
	1,000 dollars	*1,000 dollars*	*1,000 dollars*
Imports:			
Egypt	1,290	8,710	4,226
Turkey	0	1,580	1,986
India	4	0	268
Pakistan	0	11	149
China	-	1	1
United Kingdom	1	0	1
Canada	0	0	1
Australia(*)	46	0	0
Belgium-Luxembourg(*)	-	0	0
Brazil	61	5,396	0
Costa Rica	-	0	0
Finland	0	0	0
France(*)	0	0	0
Germany(*)	0	0	0
Indonesia	0	0	0
Italy(*)	0	0	0
Japan	0	-	0
Kyrgyzstan	0	0	0
Netherlands	0	0	0
Peru	5	0	0
Rest of World	0	2	0
Grand Total	1,408	15,702	6,632

(*) Denotes a country that is a summarization of its component countries.[1] 2012 data does not reflect 13 month changes. All zeroes for a data item may show that statistics exist in the other import type.

Users should use cautious interpretation on quantity reports using mixed units of measure. Quantity line items will only include statistics on the units of measure that are equal to, or are able to be converted to, the assigned unit of measure of the grouped commodities.

FAS, Office of Global Analysis, (202) 720-6301. Data Source: Department of Commerce, U.S. Census Bureau, Foreign Trade Statistics.

Table 2-15.—Cotton: International trade, 2013/2014–2015/2016 [1]

Country	2013/2014	2014/2015	2015/2016
	1,000 bales	*1,000 bales*	*1,000 bales* [2]
Principle exporting countries:			
Australia	4,852	2,393	2,750
Benin	525	675	675
Brazil	2,230	3,910	4,200
Burkina	1,250	1,125	1,300
Cote d'Ivoire	725	850	800
Greece	1,285	1,168	900
India	9,261	4,199	5,500
Mali	800	750	1,200
Turkmenistan	1,625	1,500	1,000
Uzbekistan	2,700	2,450	2,300
Others	5,030	5,110	4,776
Total foreign	30,283	24,130	25,401
United States	10,530	11,246	9,500
Total	40,813	35,376	34,901
Principle importing countries:			
Bangladesh	5,300	5,400	5,750
China	14,122	8,284	5,000
India	675	1,226	900
Indonesia	2,989	3,345	3,100
Korea, South	1,286	1,321	1,300
Mexico	1,040	830	975
Pakistan	1,200	835	2,300
Thailand	1,546	1,475	1,425
Turkey	4,246	3,675	3,800
Vietnam	3,200	4,300	5,200
Others	5,662	5,009	5,159
Total foreign	41,266	35,700	34,909
United States	13	12	10
Total	41,279	35,712	34,919

[1] Marketing year beginning Aug. 1.   [2] 480-pound net weight.
FAS, Office of Global Analysis, (202) 720–6301.   Prepared or estimated on the basis of official USDA production, supply, and distribution statistics from foreign governments.

Table 2-16.—Cotton, American Upland: High, low, and season average spot prices for the base quality in the designated markets, cents per pound, 2005–2013

Season beginning August 1	Grade 41 Staple 34[1]		
	Average	High	Low
	Cents	Cents	Cents
2005	48.96	53.25	43.46
2006	48.67	60.67	42.84
2007	61.50	79.16	50.34
2008	47.87	62.69	36.28
2009	67.76	78.90	50.98
2010	137.88	209.60	80.18
2011	85.81	110.87	60.71
2012	75.24	87.55	65.11
2013	80.28	89.14	63.53

[1] Prices are for mixed lots, net weight, compressed, FOB car/truck.
AMS, Cotton and Tobacco Program, (901) 384–3016.

Table 2-17.—Cotton, American Upland: Percentage distribution of mike readings, by specified groups, United States, 2004–2013

Year beginning August 1	Mike groups						
	26 and below	27 to 29	30 to 32	33 to 34	35 to 49	50 to 52	53 and above
	Percent						
2004	0.4	1.5	3.4	3.7	83.8	6.4	0.8
2005	*	1.5	4.0	4.4	82.0	6.5	5.8
2006	1.1	1.8	2.7	2.3	79.2	10.8	1.8
2007	0.1	0.6	1.8	2.8	87.4	6.5	0.8
2008	0.5	1.1	2.8	3.9	77.2	9.7	1.4
2009	1.9	2.6	3.9	3.7	81.0	6.0	0.9
2010	0.1	0.4	1.3	1.8	75.6	16.9	3.8
2011	0.1	0.3	0.8	1.1	80.9	14.0	2.9
2012	0.4	0.9	1.8	1.9	75.0	15.7	4.3
2013	0.4	1.3	3.1	3.2	78.2	12.2	1.6

(*) Less than 0.05 percent.
AMS, Cotton and Tobacco Program, (901) 384–3016.

Table 2-18.—Cotton, American Upland: Average spot prices for specified grades of staple 34 in the designated markets for mixed lots, net weight, compressed, FOB car/truck, cents per pound, 2004–2013

Year beginning August 1	White				Light Spotted			Spotted	
	Color 31 Leaf 3	Color 41 Leaf 4	Color 51 Leaf 5	Color 61 Leaf 6	Color 32 Leaf 3	Color 42 Leaf 4	Color 52 Leaf 5	Color 33 Leaf 3	Color 43 Leaf 4
	Cents								
2004	48.40	45.61	41.59	39.11	45.70	43.30	40.38	42.51	40.75
2005	51.33	48.96	44.84	42.34	48.72	46.42	43.41	45.98	44.05
2006	50.83	48.67	44.56	42.12	48.39	46.25	43.24	45.75	43.81
2007	63.46	61.50	57.35	54.95	61.16	59.01	56.09	58.58	56.59
2008	49.83	47.87	43.73	41.33	47.55	45.37	42.48	44.95	42.87
2009	69.97	67.76	63.47	61.21	67.44	65.26	62.37	64.84	62.76
2010	139.98	137.88	133.45	131.28	137.56	135.38	132.49	134.96	132.88
2011	87.64	85.81	81.16	79.29	85.32	81.52	80.16	82.84	79.32
2012	76.87	75.24	70.56	68.76	74.67	70.81	69.46	72.16	68.67
2013	81.68	80.28	75.64	73.83	79.71	77.39	74.49	77.20	75.17

AMS, Cotton and Tobacco Program, (901) 384–3016.

Table 2-19.—Cotton, American Upland: Average spot prices for specified staple lengths of Color 41 Leaf 4 in the designated markets for mixed lots, net weight, compressed, FOB car/truck, cents per pound, 2004–2013

Year beginning August 1	Staple							
	28	29	30	31	32	33	34	35
	Cents							
2004	41.54	41.54	42.13	43.28	43.32	44.07	45.61	47.02
2005	44.26	44.26	44.96	46.13	46.14	46.84	48.96	50.36
2006	43.92	43.92	44.67	45.79	45.89	46.53	48.67	49.97
2007	56.75	56.75	57.50	58.62	58.50	59.27	61.50	62.69
2008	43.12	43.12	43.87	44.99	44.82	45.62	47.87	49.04
2009	62.83	62.83	63.58	64.71	64.71	65.51	67.76	68.98
2010	132.76	132.76	133.51	134.63	134.83	135.63	137.88	139.09
2011	79.54	79.54	79.54	79.54	82.20	82.66	85.81	86.90
2012	69.18	69.18	69.18	69.18	71.52	72.03	75.24	76.52
2013	75.17	75.17	75.17	75.17	75.17	77.05	77.44	80.28	81.58

AMS, Cotton and Tobacco Program, (901) 384–3016.

Table 2-20.—Cotton, American Upland: Season average spot prices for the base quality, by designated markets, cents per pound, 2008–2013 [1]

Market	Color 41, Leaf 4, Staple 34 [2]					
	2008	2009	2010	2011	2012	2013
	Cents					
Southeast	48.97	70.13	139.70	87.75	77.50	82.74
North Delta	47.99	69.30	139.02	86.90	76.56	81.85
South Delta	47.99	69.30	139.02	86.95	76.56	81.85
East TX–OK	47.08	66.57	135.51	83.30	73.78	79.27
West Texas	46.93	66.38	135.10	83.31	73.68	79.13
Desert SW	47.03	65.40	137.91	85.73	73.86	78.23
SJ Valley	49.10	67.20	138.91	86.74	74.74	78.88
Average	47.87	67.76	137.88	85.81	75.21	80.28

[1] Year beginning August 1. [2] Prices are for mixed lots, net weight, compressed, FOB car/truck.
AMS, Cotton and Tobacco Program, (901) 384–3016.

Table 2-21.—Sugarbeets: Area, yield, production, and value, United States, 2005–2014 [1]

Year	Area		Yield per harvested acre	Production	Marketing year average price per ton received by farmers	Value of production
	Planted	Harvested				
	1,000 acres	*1,000 acres*	*Tons*	*1,000 tons*	*Dollars*	*1,000 dollars*
2005	1,299.8	1,242.9	22.1	27,433	43.50	1,109,272
2006	1,366.2	1,303.6	26.1	34,064	44.20	1,193,151
2007	1,268.8	1,246.8	25.5	31,834	42.00	1,337,173
2008	1,090.7	1,004.5	26.8	26,881	48.10	1,294,144
2009	1,185.8	1,148.5	25.9	29,783	51.50	1,532,634
2010	1,171.9	1,156.1	27.7	32,034	66.90	2,142,162
2011	1,232.8	1,213.2	23.8	28,896	69.40	2,004,116
2012	1,230.1	1,204.1	29.3	35,224	66.40	2,338,789
2013	1,198.0	1,154.0	28.4	32,789	46.90	1,536,422
2014	1,161.6	1,147.2	27.4	31,386	43.30	1,356,680

[1] Relates to year of intended harvest for fall planted beets in central California and to year of planting for overwintered beets in central and southern California.
NASS, Crops Branch, (202) 720–2127.

Table 2-22.—Sugarbeets: Area, yield, and production, by State and United States, 2012–2014

State	Area planted			Area harvested			Yield per harvested acre			Production		
	2012	2013	2014	2012	2013	2014	2012	2013	2014	2012	2013	2014
	1,000 acres	*1,000 acres*	*1,000 acres*	*1,000 acres*	*1,000 acres*	*1,000 acres*	*Tons*	*Tons*	*Tons*	*1,000 tons*	*1,000 tons*	*1,000 tons*
California [1] ...	24.5	24.4	24.3	24.4	24.3	22.6	43.7	43.4	42.6	1,066	1,055	1,003
Colorado	31.2	26.8	29.4	29.7	25.7	29.1	31.8	33.5	31.3	944	861	917
Idaho	183.0	175.0	171.0	182.0	174.0	169.0	35.3	36.2	37.3	6,425	6,299	6,338
Michigan	154.0	154.0	151.0	153.0	153.0	150.0	29.0	26.2	29.3	4,437	4,009	4,410
Minnesota	475.0	462.0	440.0	463.0	426.0	434.0	26.5	26.0	22.5	12,270	11,076	9,765
Montana	46.6	43.4	45.0	45.8	42.8	44.5	28.2	29.2	32.3	1,292	1,250	1,437
Nebraska	51.0	46.0	48.0	48.9	44.2	46.5	29.8	29.7	29.1	1,457	1,313	1,339
North Dakota	222.0	227.0	216.0	215.0	225.0	215.0	28.0	25.3	23.8	6,020	5,693	5,117
Oregon	11.0	9.4	6.7	11.0	9.3	6.5	38	38.4	34.5	418	357	226
Wyoming	31.8	30.0	30.2	31.3	29.7	30.0	28.6	29.5	27.8	895	876	834
United States	1,230.1	1,198.0	1,161.6	1,204.1	1,154.0	1,147.2	29.3	28.4	27.3	35,224	32,789	31,386

[1] Relates to year of intended harvest for fall planted beets in central California and to year of planting for overwintered beets in central and southern California.
NASS, Crops Branch, (202) 720–2127.

Table 2-23.—Sugarbeets: Production and value, by State and United States, 2012–2013

State	Production		Marketing year average price per ton received by farmers		Value of production	
	2012	2013	2012	2013	2012	2013
	1,000 tons	*1,000 tons*	*Dollars*	*Dollars*	*1,000 dollars*	*1,000 dollars*
California [1]	1,066	1,055	52.10	52.10	55,539	54,966
Colorado	944	861	55.40	35.60	52,298	30,652
Idaho	6,425	6,299	52.10	40.00	334,743	251,960
Michigan	4,437	4,009	72.40	53.60	321,239	214,882
Minnesota	12,270	11,076	74.20	52.60	910,434	582,598
Montana	1,292	1,250	63.80	39.40	82,430	49,250
Nebraska	1,457	1,313	61.60	37.80	89,751	49,631
North Dakota	6,020	5,693	69.10	44.90	415,982	255,616
Oregon	418	357	52.10	40.00	21,778	14,280
Wyoming	895	876	61.00	37.20	54,595	32,587
United States	35,224	32,789	66.40	46.90	2,338,789	1,536,422

[1] Relates to year of intended harvest for fall planted beets in central California and to year of planting for overwintered beets in central and southern California.
NASS, Crops Branch, (202) 720–2127.

Table 2-24.—Sugarcane for sugar and seed: Area, yield, production, and value, United States, 2005–2014

Year	Area harvested			Yield per acre [1]			Production [1]		
	For sugar	For seed	Total	For sugar	For seed	For sugar and seed	For sugar	For seed	Total
	1,000 acres	*1,000 acres*	*1,000 acres*	*Tons*	*Tons*	*Tons*	*1,000 tons*	*1,000 tons*	*1,000 tons*
2005	858.2	63.7	921.9	28.8	29.5	28.9	24,728	1,878	26,606
2006	846.6	51.1	897.7	33.0	31.4	32.9	27,962	1,602	29,564
2007	827.9	51.7	879.6	34.2	32.8	34.1	28,273	1,696	29,969
2008	821.6	46.4	868.0	31.8	31.7	31.8	26,131	1,472	27,603
2009	817.0	56.9	873.9	34.9	34.1	34.8	28,494	1,938	30,432
2010	825.3	52.2	877.5	31.1	32.5	31.2	25,663	1,697	27,360
2011	827.1	45.5	872.6	33.5	32.7	33.5	27,738	1,486	29,224
2012	854.9	47.5	902.4	35.7	36.4	35.7	30,500	1,727	32,227
2013	859.6	51.2	910.8	33.8	33.9	33.8	29,023	1,738	30,761
2014	829.3	44.8	874.1	35.4	34.4	35.3	29,328	1,541	30,869

Year	Marketing year average price per ton received by farmers	Value of production	
		Of cane used for sugar	Of cane used for sugar and seed [2]
	Dollars	*1,000 dollars*	*1,000 dollars*
2005	28.40	701,920	754,529
2006	30.40	849,157	897,601
2007	29.40	831,218	880,616
2008	29.50	771,134	814,479
2009	34.80	991,424	1,056,613
2010	41.70	1,069,537	1,140,636
2011	47.20	1,308,951	1,379,498
2012	41.90	1,276,631	1,348,361
2013	31.40	910,377	962,807
2014	35.70	1,030,201	1,083,180

[1] Net tons.   [2] Price per ton of cane for sugar used in evaluating value of production for seed.
NASS, Crops Branch, (202) 720–2127.

Table 2-25.—Sugarcane for sugar and seed: Production and value, by State and United States, 2012–2013

State	Sugarcane for sugar						Sugar and seed: Value of production [1]	
	Production [2]		Price per ton		Value of production			
	2012	2013	2012	2013	2012	2013	2012	2013
	1,000 tons	*1,000 tons*	*Dollars*	*Dollars*	*1,000 dollars*	*1,000 dollars*	*1,000 dollars*	*1,000 dollars*
Florida	14,494	13,720	44.50	35.10	644,983	481,572	677,290	505,440
Hawaii	1,262	1,352	58.10	57.50	73,322	77,740	75,937	80,328
Louisiana	13,200	12,505	38.80	25.90	512,160	323,880	548,011	349,158
Texas	1,544	1,446	29.90	18.80	46,166	27,185	47,123	27,881
United States	30,500	29,023	41.90	31.40	1,276,631	910,377	1,348,361	962,807

[1] Price per ton of cane for sugar used in evaluating value of production for seed.   [2] Net tons.
NASS, Crops Branch, (202) 720–2127.

Table 2-26.—Sugarcane for sugar and seed: Area, yield, and production, by State and United States, 2012–2014

State	Area harvested			Yield per acre [1]			Cane production [1]		
	2012	2013	2014	2012	2013	2014	2012	2013	2014
For sugar:	1,000 acres	1,000 acres	1,000 acres	Tons	Tons	Tons	1,000 tons	1,000 tons	1,000 tons
Florida	396.0	400.0	396.0	36.6	34.3	38.4	14,494	13,720	15,206
Hawaii	15.9	15.5	16.8	79.4	87.2	82.0	1,262	1,352	1,378
Louisiana	400.0	410.0	385.0	33.0	30.5	30.0	13,200	12,505	11,550
Texas	43.0	34.1	31.5	35.9	42.4	37.9	1,544	1,446	1,194
United States	854.9	859.6	829.3	35.7	33.8	35.4	30,500	29,023	29,328
For seed:									
Florida	17.0	16.0	16.0	42.7	42.5	42.8	726	680	685
Hawaii	1.5	2.2	2.2	30.0	20.5	20.4	45	45	45
Louisiana	28.0	32.0	25.0	33.0	30.5	30.0	924	976	750
Texas	1.0	1.0	1.6	32.0	37.0	37.9	32	37	61
United States	47.5	51.2	44.8	36.4	33.9	34.4	1,727	1,738	1,541
For sugar and seed:									
Florida	413.0	416.0	412.0	36.9	34.6	38.6	15,220	14,400	15,891
Hawaii	17.4	17.7	19.0	75.1	78.9	74.9	1,307	1,397	1,423
Louisiana	428.0	442.0	410.0	33.0	30.5	30.0	14,124	13,481	12,300
Texas	44.0	35.1	33.1	35.8	42.3	37.9	1,576	1,483	1,255
United States	902.4	910.8	874.1	35.7	33.8	35.3	32,227	30,761	30,869

[1] Net tons.
NASS, Crops Branch, (202) 720–2127.

Table 2-27.—Sugar, cane (raw value [1]): Refiners' raw stocks, receipts, meltings, continental United States, 2005–2014

Year	Jan. 1 stocks	Receipts [2]	Meltings
	1,000 tons	1,000 tons	1,000 tons
2005	244	5,215	5,270
2006	217	5,543	5,405
2007	358	5,388	5,464
2008	304	5,634	5,329
2009	468	5,459	5,577
2010	346	5,753	5,843
2011	257	6,062	5,534
2012	498	6,172	5,805
2013	574	6,025	5,938
2014	592	6,173	6,135

[1] Raw value is the equivalent in terms of 96° sugar. [2] Receipts include refiners' total offshore raw sugar receipts in continental U.S. ports, whether entered through the customs or held pending availability of quota and raw cane sugar produced from sugarcane in the continental United States.
FSA, Dairy and Sweeteners Analysis, (202) 720–3451.

Table 2-28.—Sugar, cane and beet: Domestic marketings, by source of supply, continental United States, 2012–2014

Area of supply	2012	2013	2014
	1,000 tons	1,000 tons	1,000 tons
Domestic areas:			
Mainland (beet)	4,816	6,037	4,998
Mainland and Hawaii (cane)	6,168	6,390	6,591
Total domestic areas	10,984	12,427	11,589

FSA, Dairy and Sweeteners Analysis Division, (202) 720–3451. Source: U.S. Census.

Table 2-29.—Sugar, cane and beet (refined): Stocks, production and receipts, and deliveries, continental United States, 2005–2014

Item and year	Cane sugar refineries	Beet sugar factories	Importers of direct consumption sugar	Mainland cane sugar mills [1]	Total
	1,000 tons	1,000 tons	1,000 tons	1,000 tons	1,000 tons
Jan. 1 Stocks [2]					
2005	368	1,782	0	4	2,154
2006	328	1,429	0	7	1,764
2007	452	1,792	0	3	2,247
2008	400	1,806	0	4	2,210
2009	440	1,464	0	5	1,909
2010	484	1,456	0	8	1,948
2011	466	1,691	0	4	2,161
2012	315	1,597	0	6	1,918
2013	388	2,013	0	3	2,404
2014	572	1,603	0	5	2,180
Production and Receipts					
2005	5,112	4,690	197	19	10,018
2006	5,741	4,758	576	16	11,091
2007	5,525	5,219	733	21	11,498
2008	5,460	4,937	2,961	28	13,386
2009	5,867	4,434	2,848	34	13,183
2010	5,753	4,883	3,396	23	14,055
2011	6,062	4,666	3,891	19	14,638
2012	6,360	5,237	3,431	16	15,044
2013	6,579	5,712	3,319	17	15,627
2014	6,572	5,014	3,326	10	14,922
Deliveries [3]					
2005	5,453	5,012	197	17	10,679
2006	5,587	4,419	576	19	10,601
2007	5,520	5,206	733	20	11,479
2008	5,397	5,258	2,961	27	13,643
2009	5,768	4,441	2,848	32	13,089
2010	6,025	4,631	3,396	20	14,072
2011	6,043	4,755	3,891	17	14,706
2012	6,168	4,816	3,431	18	14,433
2013	6,390	6,037	3,319	15	15,761
2014	6,591	4,998	3,326	11	14,926

[1] Sugar for human consumption only.   [2] Stocks include sugar in bond and in Customs custody and control.   [3] Consists of all refined sugar.
FSA, Dairy and Sweeteners Analysis, (202) 720–3451.

Table 2-30.—Sugar (raw and refined): Average price per pound at specified markets, 2003–2012

Year	Cane sugar		Refined beet: Mid-west	Retail price, granulated: United States
	Raw, 96 centrifugal			
	Intercontinental contract No. 11, average of near-by futures, world price	Intercontinental contract No. 16, average of near-by futures, U.S. price		
	Cents	Cents	Cents	Cents
2003	6.75	21.42	26.21	42.68
2004	7.38	20.46	23.48	42.64
2005	9.99	21.28	29.54	43 54
2006	14.65	22.14	33.10	49.58
2007	9.91	20.99	25.06	51.48
2008	12.11	21.30	32.54	52.91
2009	17.91	24.93	38.10	57.03
2010	22.49	35.97	53.23	62.86
2011	27.22	38.12	56.22	68.30
2012	21.69	28.90	43.38	69.41

ERS, Specialty Crops Branch, (202) 694–5247. Compiled from the following sources: (New York) Coffee, Sugar & Cocoa Exchange; the U.S. Department of Labor, Bureau of Labor Statistics; Milling and Baking News.

Table 2-31.—Sugar, centrifugal: International trade, 2012/2013–2014/2015

Country	2012/2013	2013/2014	2014/2015
	1,000 Metric tons, raw value		
Principle exporting countries:			
Australia	3,100	3,242	3,561
Brazil	27,650	26,200	23,950
Colombia	542	900	845
Cuba	775	992	880
European Union	1,662	1,552	1,610
Guatemala	1,911	2,100	2,200
India	1,261	2,806	2,425
Mexico	2,091	2,661	1,545
South Africa	356	868	772
Thailand	6,693	7,200	8,000
Others	9,236	8,851	8,177
Total Foreign	55,277	57,372	53,965
United States	249	278	168
Total	55,526	57,650	54,133
Principle importing countries:			
Algeria	2,014	1,854	1,844
Bangladesh	1,547	2,085	1,982
China	3,802	4,275	5,058
European Union	3,790	3,262	2,600
India	3,570	3,570	3,050
Indonesia	1,806	1,909	1,881
Iran	1,966	1,897	2,063
Korea, South	1,450	1,470	1,465
Malaysia	1,403	1,320	1,431
United Arab Emirates	2,583	2,108	2,366
Others	25,134	24,120	23,422
Total Foreign	49,065	47,870	47,162
United States	2,925	3,395	3,238
Total	51,990	51,265	50,400

FAS, Office of Global Analysis, (202) 720–6301. Prepared or estimated on the basis of official USDA production, supply, and distribution statistics from foreign governments.

Table 2-32.—Sugar, cane and beet (raw value): Production, stocks, trade, and supply available for consumption in continental United States includes Puerto Rico, 2003–2012

Year	Production	Visible stocks beginning of period	Imports	Exports	Total deliveries
	1,000 short tons	1,000 short tons	1,000 short tons	1,000 short tons	1,000 short tons
2003	8,976	3,429	1,564	354	9,530
2004	8,366	4,086	1,652	459	9,617
2005	7,478	4,029	2,143	404	9,889
2006	7,754	3,357	3,195	436	9,832
2007	8,467	4,039	2,238	574	10,162
2008	7,947	4,009	2,844	325	10,492
2009	7,537	3,984	2,800	329	10,433
2010	8,423	3,559	3,396	491	11,019
2011	7,604	3,869	3,891	548	11,035
2012	8,999	3,780	3,431	369	11,222

ERS, Specialty Crops Branch, (202) 694–5247.

Table 2-33.—Honey: United States exports and imports for consumption, by country of origin, 2011–2013

Country of origin	2011	2012	2013
	Metric tons	Metric tons	Metric tons
Exports:			
Japan	559	761	937
Yemen(*)	567	685	776
Canada	452	377	732
Korea, South	434	431	499
Philippines	266	369	496
Indonesia	254	392	335
Kuwait	238	296	220
United Arab Emirates	307	339	201
China	89	127	183
Hong Kong	112	72	153
Australia(*)	13	2	100
India	298	360	89
Vietnam	365	119	82
Taiwan	35	74	80
Bahamas, The	51	49	59
Singapore	48	59	55
Pakistan	41	42	50
Chile	2	0	44
Thailand	64	248	43
Israel(*)	706	307	41
Bermuda	32	25	31
Netherlands Antilles(*)	42	21	22
Saudi Arabia	148	108	22
Cambodia	3	3	21
Panama	16	21	20
Ukraine	0	0	20
Mexico	15	50	20
Barbados	31	27	20
Qatar	3	0	16
Rest of World	206	211	58
World Total	5,393	5,573	5,422
Imports:			
Argentina	33,502	42,483	44,221
Vietnam	27,826	20,700	33,586
India	26,912	21,454	25,867
Brazil	14,981	11,303	11,677
Canada	7,148	15,971	9,386
Uruguay	7,083	10,877	8,710
Mexico	2,846	6,179	5,648
Ukraine	453	1,302	3,308
Turkey	183	1,073	1,897
Taiwan	903	1,324	1,827
New Zealand(*)	966	966	1,234
Dominican Republic	661	820	1,105
Chile	21	1,706	853
Thailand	1,637	258	846
Latvia	0	0	557
Germany(*)	205	303	450
Pakistan	210	115	325
Spain	122	172	226
Guatemala	132	413	171
Bulgaria	94	112	154
France(*)	157	124	124
Russia	53	67	99
Italy(*)	91	110	95
Greece	53	57	94
Poland	44	105	71
China	1,531	19	60
Egypt	34	10	58
Switzerland(*)	84	96	57
Austria	91	30	44
Rest of World	2,745	2,868	332
World Total	130,765	141,016	153,079

(*) Denotes a country that is a summarization of its component countries.
FAS, Office of Global Analysis, (202) 720-6301.   Data Source: U.S. Census Bureau Trade Data.

Table 2-34.—Honey: Number of colonies, yield, production, stocks, price, and value, United States, 2005–2014 [1]

State	Honey producing colonies [2]	Yield per colony	Production [3]	Stocks Dec 15 [4]	Average price per pound [5]	Value of production
	1,000	Pounds	1,000 pounds	1,000 pounds	Cents	1,000 dollars
2005	2,409	72.5	174,614	62,455	92.2	160,994
2006	2,394	64.7	154,910	60,484	100.5	155,685
2007	2,443	60.7	148,341	52,635	107.7	159,763
2008	2,342	69.9	163,789	51,159	142.1	232,744
2009	2,498	58.6	146,416	37,516	147.3	215,671
2010	2,692	65.6	176,462	45,018	161.9	285,692
2011	2,491	59.6	148,357	36,761	176.5	261,850
2012	2,539	56.0	142,296	31,829	199.2	283,454
2013	2,640	56.6	149,499	38,160	214.1	320,077
2014	2,740	65.1	178,270	41,192	216.1	385,241

[1] For producers with 5 or more colonies. Colonies which produced honey in more than one State were counted in each State. [2] Honey producing colonies are the maximum number of colonies from which honey was taken during the year. It is possible to take honey from colonies which did not survive the entire year. [3] Due to rounding, total colonies multiplied by total yield may not exactly equal production. [4] Stocks held by producers. [5] Average price per pound based on expanded sales.
NASS, Livestock Branch, (202) 720–3570.

Table 2-35.—Honey: Number of colonies, yield, production, stocks, price and value, by State and United States, 2014 [1]

State	Honey producing colonies [2]	Yield per colony	Production	Stocks Dec 15 [3]	Average price per pound [4]	Value of production [5]
	1,000	Pounds	1,000 pounds	1,000 pounds	Cents	1,000 dollars
Alabama	7	53	371	26	340	1,261
Arizona	26	39	1,014	193	202	2,048
Arkansas	21	65	1,365	137	200	2,730
California	320	39	12,480	2,995	203	25,334
Colorado	27	37	999	200	200	1,998
Florida	245	60	14,700	1,029	208	30,576
Georgia	73	62	4,526	362	219	9,912
Hawaii	15	93	1,395	140	228	3,181
Idaho	100	34	3,400	850	203	6,902
Illinois	8	49	392	94	441	1,729
Indiana	5	62	310	115	324	1,004
Iowa	35	43	1,505	933	251	3,778
Kansas	7	75	525	84	233	1,223
Kentucky	5	47	235	56	393	924
Louisiana	48	84	4,032	524	226	9,112
Maine	8	47	376	41	536	2,015
Michigan	91	63	5,733	1,835	250	14,333
Minnesota	132	60	7,920	1,426	206	16,315
Mississippi	20	112	2,240	45	201	4,502
Missouri	12	47	564	96	357	2,013
Montana	162	88	14,256	5,132	205	29,225
Nebraska	50	75	3,750	1,688	210	7,875
New Jersey	12	30	360	119	298	1,073
New York	60	55	3,300	1,518	272	8,976
North Carolina ...	12	43	516	88	347	1,791
North Dakota	490	86	42,140	9,271	200	84,280
Ohio	15	61	915	256	352	3,221
Oregon	71	40	2,840	767	219	6,220
Pennsylvania	17	46	782	203	275	2,151
South Carolina ...	9	54	486	19	383	1,861
South Dakota	280	87	24,360	5,846	209	50,912
Tennessee	7	63	441	88	323	1,424
Texas	116	78	9,048	2,081	223	20,177
Utah	29	28	812	130	213	1,730
Vermont	3	58	174	61	503	875
Virginia	6	41	246	57	507	1,247
Washington	68	44	2,992	1,167	248	7,420
West Virginia	6	31	186	33	404	751
Wisconsin	53	54	2,862	1,030	232	6,640
Wyoming	38	61	2,318	255	206	4,775
Other States [6] [7]	31	45	1,404	202	358	5,026
United States [7] [8]	2,740	65.1	178,270	41,192	216.1	385,241

[1] For producers with 5 or more colonies. Colonies which produced honey in more than one State were counted in each State. [2] Honey producing colonies are the maximum number of colonies from which honey was taken during the year. It is possible to take honey from colonies which did not survive the entire year. [3] Stocks held by producers. [4] Average price per pound based on expanded sales. [5] Value of production is equal to production multiplied by average price per pound. [6] Alaska, Connecticut, Delaware, Maryland, Massachusetts, Nevada, New Hampshire, New Mexico, Oklahoma, and Rhode Island not published separately to avoid disclosing data for individual operations. [7] Due to rounding, total colonies multiplied by total yield may not exactly equal production. [8] United States value of production will not equal summation of States.
NASS, Livestock Branch, (202) 720–3570.

Table 2-36.—U.S. per capita caloric sweeteners estimated deliveries for domestic food and beverage, use by calendar year 2003–2012

| Calendar year | U.S. population (July 1) | Refined sugar | Corn Sweetener | | | | Pure honey | Edible syrups | Total caloric sweeteners |
			HFCS	Glucose syrup	Dextrose	Total			
									Millions
2003	290.3	61.0	61.0	15.2	3.1	79.3	1.0	0.7	141.9
2004	293.0	61.6	59.9	15.6	3.3	78.9	0.9	0.7	142.0
2005	295.8	63.1	58.8	15.3	3.3	77.3	1.1	0.6	142.1
2006	298.8	62.2	57.8	13.7	3.1	74.7	1.2	0.7	138.6
2007	301.7	61.2	55.8	13.7	3.0	72.5	0.9	0.6	135.2
2008	304.5	65.1	52.6	13.4	2.8	68.8	1.0	0.6	135.5
2009	307.2	63.4	49.7	13.0	2.7	65.4	0.9	0.6	130.3
2010	309.8	65.9	48.3	12.6	2.9	63.8	1.0	0.7	131.4
2011	312.0	66.8	46.6	12.2	2.9	61.7	1.1	0.7	130.2
2012	314.3	66.3	46.2	12.5	2.7	61.4	1.1	0.7	129.5

ERS, Market and Trade Economics Division, Specialty Crops Branch, (202) 694–5247.

Table 2-37.—Tobacco: Area, yield, production, price, and value, United States, 2005–2014

Year	Area harvested	Yield per acre	Production[1]	Marketing year average price per pound received by farmers	Value of production
	Acres	*Pounds*	*1,000 pounds*	*Dollars*	*1,000 dollars*
2005	297,080	2,171	645,015	1.642	1,059,324
2006	339,000	2,147	727,897	1.665	1,211,885
2007	356,000	2,213	787,653	1.693	1,329,235
2008	354,490	2,258	800,504	1.859	1,488,069
2009	354,040	2,323	822,581	1.837	1,511,196
2010	337,500	2,128	718,190	1.782	1,279,920
2011	325,040	1,841	598,252	1.857	1,110,737
2012	336,245	2,268	762,709	2.027	1,579,964
2013	355,675	2,034	723,579	2.177	1,574,982
2014	378,360	2,316	876,415	2.094	1,835,308

[1] Production figures are on farm-sales-weight basis.
NASS, Crops Branch, (202) 720–2127.

Table 2-38.—Tobacco: Area, yield, and production, by State and United States, 2012–2014

| State | Area harvested | | | Yield per harvested acre | | | Production | | |
	2012	2013	2014	2012	2013	2014	2012	2013	2014
	Acres	*Acres*	*Acres*	*Pounds*	*Pounds*	*Pounds*	*1,000 pounds*	*1,000 pounds*	*1,000 pounds*
Connecticut	(D)	(D)	(D)	(D)	(D)	(D)	(D)	(D)	(D)
Georgia	10,000	12,800	15,000	2,250	1,750	2,300	22,500	22,400	34,500
Kentucky	87,200	87,200	91,700	2,245	2,147	2,337	195,800	187,240	214,280
Massachusetts	(D)	(D)	(D)	(D)	(D)	(D)	(D)	(D)	(D)
North Carolina	166,100	181,900	193,400	2,295	2,295	2,347	381,190	362,660	453,860
Ohio	1,900	2,100	2,000	2,100	2,200	2,150	3,990	4,620	4,300
Pennsylvania ...	9,600	8,900	9,100	2,394	2,389	2,445	22,985	21,260	22,250
South Carolina	12,000	14,500	15,800	2,100	1,700	2,100	25,200	24,650	33,180
Tennessee	23,900	21,400	24,250	2,218	2,083	2,151	53,000	44,570	52,155
Virginia	23,080	24,250	24,330	2,322	2,170	2,370	53,599	52,613	57,651
United States ...	336,245	355,675	378,360	2,268	2,034	2,316	762,709	723,579	876,415

NASS, Crops Branch, (202) 720–2127.

Table 2-39.—Tobacco: Stocks owned by dealers and manufacturers, by types, United States, 2007–2013 (farm-sales-weight basis)[1]

Type and year	Jan. 1	Apr. 1	July 1	Oct. 1
	1,000 pounds	*1,000 pounds*	*1,000 pounds*	*1,000 pounds*
Flue-cured, types 11–14:				
2007	671,018	570,171	493,248	578,776
2008	581,279	483,696	396,757	452,740
2009	564,889	436,658	360,324	448,901
2010	618,862	449,823	369,054	369,054
2011	561,073	454,548	381,925	363,831
2012	515,681	376,519	319,719	308,391
2013	472,916	372,058	260,393	353,534
Virginia fire-cured, type 21:				
2007	3,167	3,668	3,288	2,717
2008	3,131	3,154	2,833	2,579
2009	3,384	2,894	2,785	2,696
2010	886	1,092	802	802
2011	4,417	4,020	3,729	3,405
2012	3,983	3,848	591	723
2013	829	1,019	975	616
Kentucky and Tennessee fire-cured, types 22–23:				
2007	103,320	117,804	108,637	100,535
2008	111,458	121,405	112,796	103,306
2009	125,167	140,069	136,463	126,011
2010	96,965	102,349	91,278	91,278
2011	161,124	163,421	153,526	144,198
2012	164,412	170,764	104,149	98,740
2013	109,023	113,561	106,232	21,126
Burley, type 31:				
2007	422,568	426,348	361,305	296,177
2008	321,546	337,271	282,561	256,163
2009	283,223	297,075	265,545	239,152
2010	274,244	279,984	237,656	237,656
2011	255,695	275,863	248,528	208,171
2012	239,932	254,687	207,965	170,638
2013	174,645	227,961	194,321	164,151
Maryland, type 32:				
2007	375	1,190	372	1,028
2008	249	971	930	410
2009	116	970	43	30
2010	24	2,048	132	132
2011	20	2,449	87	85
2012	75	2,108	1,851	899
2013	569	700	326	13
One Sucker and Green River, types 35–36:[2]				
2007	39,818	44,456	40,765	35,775
2008	43,183	45,956	43,018	39,047
2009	49,492	53,357	53,517	51,812
2010	38,844	43,502	37,822	37,822
2011	61,528	63,485	59,590	54,906
2012	59,641	62,751	41,870	38,813
2013	39,261	44,603	40,580	7,075
Virginia sun-cured, type 37:				
2007	17	8	0	0
2008	0	5	5	5
2009	5	5	0	13
2010	13	12	12	12
2011	45	45	35	45
2012	45	45	45	45
2013	45	45	66	45
Pennsylvania seedleaf, type 41:				
2007	9,891	10,221	7,899	6,909
2008	6,375	9,953	9,210	7,932
2009	7,666	11,350	10,850	10,620
2010	7,262	13,550	13,547	13,547
2011	13,995	17,941	15,861	15,861
2012	15,467	20,723	14,305	16,499
2013	17,080	20,249	17,608	16,393

See footnote(s) at end of table.

Table 2-39.—Tobacco: Stocks owned by dealers and manufacturers, by types, United States, 2007–2013 (farm-sales-weight basis) [1]—Continued

Type and year	Jan. 1	Apr. 1	July 1	Oct. 1
	1,000 pounds	*1,000 pounds*	*1,000 pounds*	*1,000 pounds*
Connecticut Valley, types 51–52:				
2007	1,713	1,790	1,950	1,762
2008	1,730	1,398	1,837	533
2009	1,554	1,286	1,409	1,671
2010	1,062	953	1,178	943
2011	1,176	593	978	526
2012	149	229	41	155
2013	166	319	320	252
Wisconsin binder, types 54–55:				
2007	6,707	6,564	5,675	4,930
2008	4,826	5,378	4,497	3,777
2009	3,647	4,500	3,805	3,201
2010	2,798	4,492	4,335	4,612
2011	4,778	5,528	5,100	4,866
2012	4,287	5,205	4,008	3,809
2013	3,318	4,055	3,528	3,197
Cigar Wrapper, type 61:				
2007	727	966	511	1,149
2008	768	810	591	779
2009	611	278	239	742
2010	327	222	231	688
2011	1,071	478	356	759
2012	269	316	82	494
2013	354	404	329	290
Perique, type 72:				
2007	27	29	28	43
2008	43	42	22	36
2009	39	36	19	127
2010	105	93	117	165
2011	412	217	200	253
2012	246	216	321	374
2013	356	335	485	458
Other miscellaneous domestic, type 73:				
2007	3,558	1,851	2,661	2,781
2008	1,730	3,101	3,195	3,979
2009	5,351	3,998	2,871	2,024
2010	1,546	2,280	2,359	7,437
2011	8,351	8,611	8,670	8,598
2012	8,846	8,566	8,417	9,116
2013	9,340	9,379	8,956	1,743
Foreign-growth cigar leaf, types 81–89:				
2007	91,323	84,390	82,627	79,698
2008	84,538	85,535	81,340	81,468
2009	99,181	103,158	93,970	91,668
2010	85,370	98,216	77,507	78,171
2011	87,334	76,810	71,096	67,092
2012	71,631	68,683	55,380	83,975
2013	89,706	87,402	79,635	48,256
Foreign-growth cigarette and smoking, types 91–99:				
2007	766,925	753,161	757,311	721,959
2008	711,251	719,283	711,278	670,380
2009	655,356	668,814	621,702	623,288
2010	621,793	609,022	588,708	561,716
2011	587,319	578,762	546,270	530,319
2012	519,810	530,565	500,967	512,542
2013	501,423	492,380	329,528	496,577

[1] Stocks shown have been converted to a farm-sales-weight basis—the equivalent of weight at the time of sale-thereby making these data of leaf-tobacco stocks comparable with the leaf-tobacco production.   [2] One Sucker and Green leaf combined.

AMS Cotton and Tobacco Program, (901) 384–3016.

Table 2-40.—Tobacco products: Cigars, cigarettes, chewing and smoking tobacco, and snuff, manufactured in the United States, 2004–2013

Year	Cigars		Cigarettes		Chewing tobacco			
	Large	Small	Large [1]	Small	Firm	Moist	Twist	Looseleaf
	Millions	*Millions*	*Millions*	*Millions*	*1,000 pounds*	*1,000 pounds*	*1,000 pounds*	*1,000 pounds*
2004	4,341.7	3,359.8	0.0	492,749.4	1,403	271	651	37,012
2005	3,674.2	4,665.1	0.0	498,974.7	1,173	230	601	37,226
2006	4,256.2	5,291.3	0.0	483,678.0	1,098	199	551	36,406
2007	4,797.3	5,870.4	0.0	449,728.5	1,009	176	538	35,066
2008	4,984.4	6,478.0	0.0	396,115.4	909	144	500	30,935
2009	8,231.5	2,729.0	0.0	338,107.6	756	114	470	27,973
2010	10,407.5	1,461.3	0.0	326,653.6	699	86	390	25,974
2011	10,313.9	1,153.5	0.0	318,863.8	674	57	295	23,056
2012	9,910.7	1,258.1	0.0	303,752.3	537	37	320	22,109
2013	7,820.1	1,129.7	0.0	292,720.1	491	29	289	20,524
Taxable removals and domestic invoices [2]								
2004	4,319.2	2,701.6	0.0	374,977.6	1,325	245	656	35,721
2005	4,441.0	3,772.1	0.0	363,260.2	1,166	201	614	35,701
2006	4,499.5	4,233.7	0.0	364,177.7	1,050	174	561	35,486
2007	4,658.7	4,791.3	0.0	347,960.2	978	150	539	32,721
2008	4,771.1	5,440.1	0.0	334,942.7	881	133	512	30,103
2009	7,944.2	2,150.6	0.0	308,117.2	736	72	457	27,002
2010	9,901.8	924.1	0.0	292,714.3	658	68	392	31,429
2011	9,887.0	753.9	0.0	286,315.5	638	42	292	28,606
2012	9,408.6	704.9	0.0	279,830.8	510	23	323	27,148
2013	7,788.4	622.4	0.0	266,205.8	486	19	291	25,639
Tax-free removals and exports								
2004	114.5	658.6	0.0	111,202.4	28	19	0	55
2005	98.2	689.7	0.0	124,117.2	18	19	0	56
2006	100.0	830.7	0.0	116,649.0	21	20	0	59
2007	115.0	1,024.9	0.0	94,935.3	20	18	0	60
2008	152.6	857.0	0.0	61,698.4	19	19	0	96
2009	110.2	674.0	0.0	33,210.5	18	13	0	134
2010	291.6	528.7	0.0	30,369.1	15	13	0	134
2011	257.0	427.2	0.0	28,341.1	13	9	0	150
2012	401.2	492.6	0.0	21,815.9	15	10	0	118
2013	594.3	265.2	0.0	22,544.3	1	6	0	150

Year	Smoking tobacco			Snuff	Total chewing, smoking, and snuff
	Pipe	Granulated	Cigarette cut		
	1,000 pounds	*1,000 pounds*	*1,000 pounds*	*1,000 pounds*	*1,000 pounds*
2004	4,512	0	11,626	79,333	134,808
2005	4,280	0	13,109	81,951	138,570
2006	4,067	0	12,388	86,041	140,750
2007	4,117	0	12,164	90,153	143,223
2008	3,442	0	13,707	94,416	144,053
2009	5,102	0	8,394	95,528	138,337
2010	7,948	0	4,909	99,733	139,739
2011	18,484	0	4,239	106,194	152,999
2012	15,809	0	4,659	108,947	152,418
2013	8,436	0	2,933	113,503	146,205
Taxable removals and domestic invoices [2]					
2004	3,773	0	11,675	74,718	128,113
2005	3,483	0	12,873	79,060	133,098
2006	3,149	0	12,311	83,618	136,349
2007	3,138	0	12,132	88,255	137,913
2008	2,949	0	13,735	93,112	141,425
2009	4,549	0	8,284	93,080	135,491
2010	7,807	0	5,063	97,290	138,164
2011	9,010	0	4,131	102,137	141,713
2012	8,873	0	3,185	106,111	146,173
2013	8,436	0	2,933	111,078	148,882
Tax-free removals and exports					
2004	652	0	0	726	1,480
2005	446	0	0	785	1,324
2006	747	0	0	749	1,596
2007	942	0	0	740	1,780
2008	381	0	0	797	1,312
2009	239	0	0	745	1,156
2010	241	0	4	788	1,176
2011	507	0	11	845	1,520
2012	298	0	8	879	1,328
2013	303	0	5	839	1,304

[1] Weighing more than three pounds per thousand. [2] Includes cigars and cigarettes imported or brought into the United States and Puerto Rico.

AMS Cotton and Tobacco Program, (901) 384–3016.

CHAPTER III

STATISTICS OF OILSEEDS, FATS, AND OILS

This chapter includes information on cottonseed, flaxseed, olive oil, peanuts, soybeans, margarine, and fats and oils. Most butter statistics are included in the chapter on dairy and poultry statistics. Lard data are mostly in the chapter on livestock.

Table 3-1.—Cottonseed: All cotton harvested area and cottonseed production, farm disposition, marketing year average price per ton received by farmers, and value, United States, 2005–2014

Year	Harvested area of all cotton	Cottonseed					
		Production	Farm disposition		Marketing year average price	Value of production
			Sales to oil mills	Other [1]		
	1,000 acres	*1,000 tons*	*1,000 tons*	*1,000 tons*	*Dollars/tons*	*1,000 dollars*
2005	13,802.6	8,172.1	4,588.8	3,583.3	96.00	779,500
2006	12,731.5	7,347.9	3,608.3	3,739.6	111.00	814,151
2007	10,489.1	6,588.7	3,635.1	2,953.6	162.00	1,069,849
2008	7,568.7	4,300.3	2,526.5	1,773.8	223.00	962,708
2009	7,533.7	4,148.8	2,277.9	1,870.9	158.00	670,027
2010	10,698.7	6,096.1	3,252.9	2,843.2	161.00	988,656
2011	9,460.9	5,370.0	2,695.0	2,675.0	260.00	1,413,343
2012	9,321.8	5,666.0	2,985.0	2,681.0	252.00	1,456,245
2013	7,544.4	4,203.0	2,070.0	2,133.0	246.00	1,054,003
2014 [2]	9,707.4	5,314.0	(NA)	(NA)	194.00	1,055,449

(NA) Not available. [1] Includes planting seed, feed, exports, inter-farm sales, shrinkage, losses, and other uses. [2] Preliminary.
NASS, Crops Branch, (202) 720–2127.

Table 3-2.—Cottonseed: Production and farm disposition, by State and United States, 2011–2014

State	Production			Farm disposition				Used for planting [1]		
				Sales to oil mills		Other [4]				
	2012	2013 [2]	2014 [3]	2012	2013	2012	2013	2011	2012	2013
	1,000 tons	*1,000 tons*	*1,000 tons*	*1,000 tons*	*1,000 tons*	*1,000 tons*	*1,000 tons*	*1,000 tons*	*1,000 tons*	*1,000 tons*
Alabama	227.0	165.0	198.0	24.0	15.0	203.0	150.0	1.9	1.8	1.7
Arizona	205.0	163.0	172.0	-	-	205.0	163.0	1.5	1.2	1.1
Arkansas	450.0	252.0	284.0	339.0	220.0	111.0	32.0	3.9	2.1	2.3
California	469.0	355.0	292.0	130.0	78.0	339.0	277.0	3.3	2.5	1.7
Florida	61.0	38.0	60.0	59.0	26.0	2.0	12.0	0.5	0.7	0.6
Georgia	875.0	701.0	751.0	425.0	342.0	450.0	359.0	6.3	6.6	6.5
Kansas	25.0	14.0	18.0	-	-	25.0	14.0	0.3	0.1	0.2
Louisiana	158.0	118.0	139.0	133.0	90.0	25.0	28.0	1.5	0.7	1.0
Mississippi	335.0	220.0	349.0	285.0	155.0	50.0	65.0	3.4	1.9	2.5
Missouri	256.0	205.0	227.0	172.0	145.0	84.0	60.0	2.3	1.7	1.7
New Mexico	31.0	14.0	25.0	-	-	31.0	14.0	0.4	0.3	0.3
North Carolina ...	379.0	255.0	313.0	59.0	29.0	320.0	226.0	3.6	2.7	2.8
Oklahoma	54.0	45.0	91.0	45.0	37.0	9.0	8.0	1.7	1.0	1.2
South Carolina ...	175.0	108.0	159.0	92.0	30.0	83.0	78.0	1.2	1.0	1.0
Tennessee	239.0	139.0	161.0	212.0	122.0	27.0	17.0	2.5	1.6	1.8
Texas	1,669.0	1,368.0	2,009.0	1,010.0	781.0	659.0	587.0	40.0	38.0	42.0
Virginia	58.0	43.0	66.0	-	-	58.0	43.0	0.5	0.5	0.5
United States ...	5,666.0	4,203.0	5,314.0	2,985.0	2,070.0	2,681.0	2,133.0	74.8	64.4	68.9

- Represents zero. [1] Included in 'other' farm disposition. Seed for planting is produced in crop year shown, but used in the following year. [2] Revised. [3] Preliminary. [4] Includes planting seed, feed, exports, inter-farm sales, shrinkage, losses, and other uses.
NASS, Crops Branch, (202) 720–2127.

Table 3-3.—Cottonseed: Marketing year average price per ton and value of production, by State and United States, crop of 2012–2014

State	Marketing year average price per ton			Value of production		
	2012	2013	2014[1]	2012	2013	2014[1]
	Dollars	Dollars	Dollars	1,000 dollars	1,000 dollars	1,000 dollars
Alabama	200.00	218.00	180.00	45,400	35,970	35,640
Arizona	288.00	269.00	263.00	59,040	43,847	45,236
Arkansas	253.00	259.00	221.00	113,850	65,268	62,764
California	366.00	372.00	330.00	171,654	132,060	96,360
Florida	211.00	197.00	171.00	12,871	7,486	10,260
Georgia	212.00	202.00	173.00	185,500	141,602	129,923
Kansas	(D)	(D)	(D)	(D)	(D)	(D)
Louisiana	259.00	245.00	195.00	40,922	28,910	27,105
Mississippi	266.00	243.00	195.00	89,110	53,460	68,055
Missouri	280.00	253.00	210.00	71,680	51,865	47,670
New Mexico	302.00	298.00	241.00	9,362	4,172	6,025
North Carolina	229.00	227.00	198.00	86,791	57,885	61,974
Oklahoma	249.00	226.00	175.00	13,446	10,170	15,925
South Carolina	206.00	203.00	193.00	36,050	21,924	30,687
Tennessee	256.00	255.00	212.00	61,184	35,445	34,132
Texas	265.00	254.00	181.00	442,285	347,472	363,629
Virginia	(D)	(D)	(D)	(D)	(D)	(D)
United States	252.00	246.00	194.00	1,456,245	1,054,003	1,055,449

(D) Withheld to avoid disclosing data for individual operations. [1] Preliminary.
NASS, Crops Branch, (202) 720–2127.

Table 3-4.—Cottonseed: Crushings, output of products and product prices, United States, 2006–2015

Year beginning August	Quantity crushed	Cottonseed products and prices			
		Oil		Cake and meal	
		Quantity	Price[1]	Quantity	Price[2]
	1,000 tons	Million pounds	Cents per pound	1,000 tibs	Dollars per ton
2006	2,680	849	35.7	1,241	150.36
2007	2,706	856	73.6	1,262	253.81
2008	2,240	669	37.1	938	255.23
2009	1,901	617	40.3	883	220.90
2010	2,563	835	54.5	1,163	273.84
2011	2,400	755	53.2	1,090	275.13
2012	2,500	800	48.6	1,125	331.52
2013	2,000	630	60.7	900	377.71
2014	1,900	610	45.7	855	280.00
2015[3]	1,650	530	37.5	745	270.00

[1] Tanks, f.o.b. Valley Points. [2] 41 percent protein, solvent, Memphis. [3] Forecast.
ERS, Field Crops Branch, (202) 694–5300. Compiled from annual reports of the U.S. Department of Commerce.

Table 3-5.—International meal, cottonseed: Production in specified countries, 2013/2014–2015/2016

Country	2013/2014	2014/2015	2015/2016
	1,000 metric tons	1,000 metric tons	1,000 metric tons
Australia	330	294	313
Brazil	1,130	990	950
Burma	168	169	160
China	4,432	4,159	3,306
India	4,269	4,315	4,057
Mexico	160	206	195
Pakistan	1,700	1,860	1,302
Turkey	330	455	380
Turkmenistan	227	222	196
Uzbekistan	660	655	655
Others	1,412	1,341	1,243
Total Foreign	14,818	14,666	12,757
United States	816	776	612
Total	15,634	15,442	13,369

FAS, Office of Global Analysis, (202) 720-6301. Prepared or estimated on the basis of official USDA production, supply, and distribution statistics from foreign governments.

Table 3-6.—Cottonseed, Cottonseed oil, and cottonseed cake and meal: United States exports by country of destination, 2011–2013

Country of destination	2011	2012	2013
	Metric tons	*Metric tons*	*Metric tons*
Cottonseed:			
Mexico	86,512	86,644	100,182
Korea, South	39,840	17,421	35,775
Saudi Arabia	6,262	27,765	30,936
Japan	25,624	1,208	9,019
United Arab Emirates	12,474	3,075	8,493
Canada	8,596	2,515	1,895
Spain	6,986	0	1,440
Lebanon	0	600	251
Qatar	425	350	150
Oman	0	250	75
Taiwan	257	99	48
Costa Rica	0	0	39
Guatemala	0	0	18
China	9,940	0	0
Dominican Republic	119	269	0
Greece	31	0	0
India	0	106	0
Jordan	603	1,204	0
Morocco	0	25	0
Rest of World	94	20	0
World Total	197,762	141,551	188,321
Cottonseed oil:			
Mexico	45,846	73,891	63,533
Canada	39,848	30,698	22,439
Singapore	10	1,376	1,587
Netherlands	0	227	1,170
Malaysia	916	120	974
Trinidad and Tobago	462	567	655
United Arab Emirates	0	0	502
Taiwan	76	0	485
Turkey	3	26	322
Panama	108	75	310
Japan	0	510	223
Honduras	0	0	174
New Zealand(*)	0	7	144
Argentina	131	142	137
Bolivia	21	55	107
Colombia	41	0	92
Brazil	52	166	85
Peru	52	59	69
Portugal	8	13	59
Rest of World	1,157	62	82
World Total	88,731	107,992	93,149
Cottonseed cake & meal:			
Mexico	55,431	98,654	82,791
Korea, South	9,579	256	4,766
Canada	2,471	3,871	4,344
United Kingdom	457	1,108	1,902
Austria	972	1,198	1,156
Italy(*)	62	506	864
Japan	850	555	857
Ecuador	499	0	576
Germany(*)	290	232	337
Brazil	80	265	250
Hungary	20	20	166
Leeward-Windward Islands(*)	0	0	7
France(*)	1	169	3
Colombia	2	0	2
United Arab Emirates	6	0	0
China	14,169	0	0
Dominican Republic	0	1	0
India	0	2	0
Slovakia	0	0	0
Rest of World	1	0	0
World Total	84,889	106,837	98,020

(*) Denotes a country that is a summarization of its component countries.
FAS, Office of Global Analysis, (202) 720-6301. Data Source: U.S. Census Bureau Trade Data

Table 3-7.—International oilseed, cottonseed: Area and production in specified countries, 2013/2014–2015/2016

Country	Area			Production		
	2013/2014	2014/2015	2015/2016	2013/2014	2014/2015	2015/2016
	1,000 hectares	*1,000 hectares*	*1,000 hectares*	*1,000 metric tons*	*1,000 metric tons*	*1,000 metric tons*
Australia	436	205	285	1,881	711	800
Brazil	1,120	1,020	925	2,671	2,360	2,266
Burma	300	300	285	368	370	350
China	4,800	4,400	3,400	12,835	11,757	9,330
European Union	311	355	315	480	523	383
India	11,700	12,700	11,800	12,950	12,500	11,400
Pakistan	2,900	2,950	2,800	4,100	4,600	3,000
Turkey	330	430	370	740	1,030	853
Turkmenistan	575	545	500	607	598	509
Uzbekistan	1,300	1,285	1,285	1,607	1,528	1,450
Others	5,072	5,039	4,785	3,631	3,718	3,230
Total Foreign	28,844	29,229	26,750	41,870	39,695	33,571
United States	3,053	3,783	3,261	3,813	4,649	3,768
Total	31,897	33,012	30,011	45,683	44,344	37,339

FAS, Office of Global Analysis, (202) 720–6301.   Prepared or estimated on the basis of official USDA production, supply, and distribution statistics from foreign governments.

Table 3-8.—International oil, cottonseed: Production in specified countries, 2013/2014–2015/2016 [1]

Country	2013/2014	2014/2015	2015/2016
	1,000 metric tons	*1,000 metric tons*	*1,000 metric tons*
Australia	113	100	109
Brazil	384	336	320
China	60	61	58
European Union	1,487	1,396	1,110
India	1,305	1,320	1,244
Mexico	61	79	74
Pakistan	560	615	430
Turkey	130	185	155
Turkmenistan	85	83	74
Uzbekistan	233	230	230
Others	463	442	409
Total Foreign	4,881	4,847	4,213
United States	286	276	218
Total	5,167	5,123	4,431

[1] Year beginning July 1.
FAS, Office of Global Analysis, (202) 720–6301.   Prepared or estimated on the basis of official USDA production, supply, and distribution statistics from foreign governments.

Table 3-9.—Flaxseed: Area, yield, production, disposition, and value, United States, 2005–2014

Year	Area planted	Area harvested	Yield per harvested acre	Production	Marketing year average price per bushel received by farmers	Value of production
	1,000 acres	*1,000 acres*	*Bushels*	*1,000 bushels*	*Dollars*	*1,000 dollars*
2005	983	955	20.6	19,695	5.94	117,070
2006	813	767	14.4	11,019	5.80	63,961
2007	354	349	16.9	5,896	13.00	76,521
2008	354	340	16.8	5,716	12.70	72,773
2009	317	314	23.6	7,423	8.15	60,373
2010	421	418	21.7	9,056	12.20	110,251
2011	178	173	16.1	2,791	13.90	38,570
2012	349	336	17.3	5,798	13.80	79,919
2013	181	172	19.5	3,356	13.80	46,325
2014	311	302	21.1	6,368	12.00	75,807

NASS, Crops Branch, (202) 720–2127.

Table 3-10.—Flaxseed: Area, yield, and production, by State and United States, 2012–2014

State	Area planted			Area harvested		
	2012	2013	2014	2012	2013	2014
	1,000 acres	*1,000 acres*	*1,000 acres*	*1,000 acres*	*1,000 acres*	*1,000 acres*
Minnesota	3	4	2	3	4	2
Montana	18	20	28	13	16	25
North Dakota	320	150	275	313	146	270
South Dakota	8	7	6	7	6	5
United States	349	181	311	336	172	302

State	Yield per harvested acre			Production		
	2012	2013	2014	2012	2013	2014
	Bushels	*Bushels*	*Bushels*	*1,000 bushels*	*1,000 bushels*	*1,000 bushels*
Minnesota	15.0	19.0	24.0	45	76	48
Montana	12.0	15.0	17.0	156	240	425
North Dakota	17.5	20.0	21.5	5,478	2,920	5,805
South Dakota	17.0	20.0	18.0	119	120	90
United States	17.3	19.5	21.1	5,798	3,356	6,368

NASS, Crops Branch, (202) 720–2127.

Table 3-11.—Flaxseed: Marketing year average price and value of production, by State and United States, 2012–2014

State	Marketing year average price per bushel			Value of production		
	2012	2013	2014	2012	2013	2014
	Dollars	*Dollars*	*Dollars*	*1,000 dollars*	*1,000 dollars*	*1,000 dollars*
Minnesota	14.00	13.80	11.60	630	1,049	557
Montana	13.60	14.00	10.40	2,122	3,360	4,420
North Dakota	13.80	13.80	12.00	75,596	40,296	69,660
South Dakota	13.20	13.50	13.00	1,571	1,620	1,170
United States	13.80	13.80	12.00	79,919	46,325	75,807

NASS, Crops Branch, (202) 720–2127.

Table 3-12.—Flaxseed: Support operations, United States, 2005/2006–2014/2015

Marketin year beginning June 1	Income support payment rates per bushels [1]	Program price levels per bushel		Put under loan		Acquired by CCC under loan program [4]	Owned by CCC at end of marketing year
		Loan [2]	Target [3]	Quantity	Percentage of production		
	Dollars	*Dollars*	*Dollars*	*1,000 bushels*	*Percent*	*1,000 bushels*	*1,000 bushels*
2005/2006	0.45/0.00	5.21	5.66	1,455.4	7.4	0.0	0.0
2006/2007	0.45/0.00	5.21	5.66	598.2	5.4	0.0	0.0
2007/2008	0.45/0.00	5.21	5.66	131.0	2.2	0.0	0.0
2008/2009	0.45/0.00	5.21	5.66	141.1	2.5	0.0	0.0
2009/2010	0.45/0.00	5.21	5.66	80.4	1.1	0.0	0.0
2010/2011	0.45/0.00	5.65	7.10	69.6	0.8	0.0	0.0
2011/2012	0.45/0.00	5.65	7.10	17.9	0.6	0.0	0.0
2012/2013	0.45/0.00	5.65	7.10	26.8	0.5	0.0	0.0
2013/2014	0.45/0.00	5.65	7.10	10.7	0.3	0.0	0.0
2014/2015	0.00	5.65	11.28	37.5	0.6	0.0	0.0

[1] The first entry is the direct payment rate and the second entry is the counter-cyclical payment rate for 2004/2005-2013/2014. For 2009/20010-2013/2014, producers who participate in the Average Crop Revenue (ACRE) program get a 20 percent reduction in their direct payment, not calculated in this table. For 2014/2015 and after, the entry is the price loss coverage payment rate. Agricultural Risk Coverage (ARC) is also available, but payment rates are established at the county or farm levels. [2] For 2009/2010-2013/2014, producers who participate in the ACRE program get a 30 percent reduction in their loan rate, not calculated in this table. [3] Target applies to 2003/2004-2013/2014 and Reference applies beginning with 2014/2015. [4] Acquisitions as of December 31, 2015.
FSA, Feed Grains and Oilseeds, (202) 720–2711.

Table 3-13.—Flaxseed: Supply and disappearance, United States, 2006–2015

Year beginning June	Supply				Disappearance			
	Stocks June 1	Production	Imports	Total	Total used for seed	Exports	Crushings [1]	Total domestic disappearance [2]
	1,000 bushels	*1,000 bushels*	*1,000 bushels*	*1,000 bushels*	*1,000 bushels*	*1,000 bushels*	*1,000 bushels*	*1,000 bushels*
2006	3,535	11,019	5,464	20,018	287	1,788	14,900	15,786
2007	2,444	5,896	8,019	16,359	287	2,221	11,700	12,627
2008	1,512	5,716	4,794	12,022	257	432	8,150	9,038
2009	2,552	7,423	6,283	16,258	341	1,752	12,000	12,949
2010	1,557	9,056	6,040	16,653	144	2,130	11,635	12,352
2011	2,170	2,791	8,286	13,247	279	654	10,500	11,473
2012	1,120	5,709	6,928	13,846	147	1,020	11,000	11,902
2013	924	3,356	6,759	11,309	252	599	8,700	9,677
2014	763	6,368	7,351	14,482	340	528	11,850	13,146
2015	808	8,585	5,425	14,818	328	600	12,200	13,260

[1] From domestic and imported seed. [2] Total supply minus exports and stocks June 1 of following year.
ERS, Field Crops Branch, (202) 694–5300.

Table 3-14.—Flaxseed and linseed oil and meal: Average price Minneapolis, 2006–2015

Year	Average price received by farmers per bushel	Minneapolis	
		Oil, per pound [1]	Meal, per ton [2]
	Dollars	*Cents*	*Dollars*
2006	5.80	53.99	124.61
2007	13.00	44.37	191.54
2008	12.70	70.31	227.66
2009	8.15	86.52	217.24
2010	12.20	67.49	223.23
2011	13.90	(NA)	238.35
2012	13.80	(NA)	320.13
2013	13.80	(NA)	359.42
2014	11.8	(NA)	263.90
2015 [3]	8.65	(NA)	225.00

(NA) Not available.   [1] Raw oil in tank cars.   [2] Bulk carlots, 34 percent protein.   [2] Preliminary.
ERS, Field Crops Branch, (202) 694–5300.

Table 3-15.—Flaxseed and products: Flaxseed crushed; production, imports, and exports of linseed oil, cake, and meal; and June 1 stocks of oil, United States, 2006–2015

Year beginning June	Total flaxseed crushed	Linseed oil			Linseed cake and meal		
		Stocks June 1	Production	Exports	Production	Imports for consumption	Exports
	1,000 bushels	*Million pounds*	*Million pounds*	*Million pounds*	*1,000 tons*	*1,000 tons*	*1,000 tons*
2006	14,900	29	291	76	268	17	10
2007	11,700	51	228	74	211	9	10
2008	8,150	26	159	66	147	10	28
2009	12,000	73	234	103	216	3	10
2010	11,635	37	227	101	209	7	7
2011	10,500	38	205	89	189	8	3
2012	11,000	35	215	94	198	6	5
2013	8,700	35	170	58	157	1	6
2014	11,850	35	231	52	213	3	4
2015	12,200	35	238	54	220	10	6

ERS, Field Crops Branch, (202) 694–5300.

Table 3-16.—Peanuts: Area, yield, production, disposition, marketing year average price per pound received by farmers, and value, United States, 2005–2014

Year	Area planted	Peanuts for nuts				
		Area harvested	Yield per acre	Production [1]	Marketing year average price	Value of production
	1,000 acres	*1,000 acres*	*Pounds*	*1,000 pounds*	*Cents*	*1,000 dollars*
2005	1,657.0	1,629.0	2,989	4,869,860	17.3	843,435
2006	1,243.0	1,210.0	2,863	3,464,250	17.7	612,798
2007	1,230.0	1,195.0	3,073	3,672,250	20.5	758,626
2008	1,534.0	1,507.0	3,426	5,162,400	23.0	1,193,617
2009	1,116.0	1,079.0	3,421	3,691,650	21.7	793,147
2010	1,288.0	1,255.0	3,312	4,156,840	22.5	938,611
2011	1,140.6	1,080.6	3,386	3,658,590	31.8	1,168,587
2012	1,638.0	1,604.0	4,211	6,753,880	30.1	2,026,326
2013	1,067.0	1,043.0	4,001	4,173,170	24.9	1,055,095
2014	1,354.0	1,325.0	3,932	5,210,100	21.3	1,122,276

[1] Estimates comprised of quota and non-quota peanuts.
NASS, Crops Branch, (202) 720–2127.

Table 3-17.—Peanuts, farmer stock: Stocks, production, and quantity milled, United States, 2005–2014

Year beginning August	Stocks Aug. 1 [1]	Production harvested for nuts [1]	Imports	Total supply	Milled [1][2]
	1,000 pounds	*1,000 pounds*	*1,000 pounds*	*1,000 pounds*	*1,000 pounds*
2005	677,436	4,869,860	6	5,547,302	3,896,012
2006	1,402,614	3,464,250	48	4,866,912	3,914,354
2007	730,134	3,672,250	0	4,402,384	3,783,154
2008	346,948	5,162,400	194	5,509,542	3,901,712
2009	1,359,950	3,691,650	1,243	5,052,843	3,930,088
2010	991,394	4,156,840	163	5,148,397	3,976,460
2011	769,016	3,658,590	1,299	4,428,905	3,949,494
2012	272,838	6,753,880	3,117	7,029,835	4,979,182
2013	1,924,996	4,173,170	169	6,098,335	4,955,484
2014	661,774	5,210,100	7	6,248,196	4,775,454

[1] Net weight basis. [2] Includes peanuts milled for seed.
NASS, Crops Branch, (202) 720–2127, ERS, and Foreign trade from the Bureau of the Census.

Table 3-18.—Peanuts: Crushings, and oil and meal stocks, production, and foreign trade, United States, 2005–2014

Year beginning August	Peanuts crushed (shelled basis)	Peanut oil				Peanut cake and meal	
		Stocks Aug. 1 [1]	Production of crude	Imports	Exports [2]	Stocks Aug. 1 [3]	Production
	1,000 pounds	*1,000 pounds*	*1,000 pounds*	*1,000 pounds*	*1,000 pounds*	*1,000 pounds*	*1,000 pounds*
2005	407,817	20,225	181,085	61,926	7,466	1,965	232,868
2006	385,375	11,730	166,450	104,623	11,009	4,908	223,537
2007	372,980	19,824	158,144	75,697	12,979	5,651	211,733
2008	334,296	6,024	142,666	54,155	9,311	4,949	190,748
2009	326,779	4,491	139,903	73,184	10,764	3,792	185,452
2010	441,017	6,888	190,110	60,012	15,923	7,045	250,043
2011	453,835	6,836	188,479	28,290	15,646	9,959	250,037
2012	493,205	2,478	210,702	10,360	12,598	10,446	270,328
2013	497,272	(NA)	209,808	55,265	8,953	(NA)	268,554
2014	506,677	(NA)	214,041	30,041	18,788	(NA)	278,380

(NA) Not available.   [1] Crude plus refined.   [2] Reported as edible peanut oil and crude peanut oil; in this tabulation added without converting.   [3] Holding at producing mills only.
NASS, Crops Branch, (202) 720–2127, ERS, and Foreign trade from the Bureau of the Census.

Table 3-19.—Cleaned peanuts (roasting stock): Supply and disposition, United States, 2005–2014

Year beginning August	Supply				Disposition		
	Stocks Aug. 1	Production	Imports	Total	Exports	Domestic disappearance	
						Total	Per capita
	1,000 pounds	*1,000 pounds*	*1,000 pounds*	*1,000 pounds*	*1,000 pounds*	*1,000 pounds*	*Pounds*
2005	69,655	240,023	6	309,684	36,845	215,846	0.73
2006	56,993	221,618	48	278,659	19,600	216,956	0.72
2007	42,103	257,386	0	299,489	56,323	185,371	0.61
2008	57,795	282,284	194	340,273	67,091	212,695	0.69
2009	60,487	257,414	1,243	319,144	55,430	210,785	0.69
2010	52,929	268,956	163	322,048	78,693	184,385	0.60
2011	58,970	226,481	1,299	286,750	66,819	179,965	0.58
2012	39,966	323,731	3,117	366,814	194,821	100,098	0.32
2013	71,895	323,607	169	395,671	143,875	178,643	0.56
2014	73,153	248,170	7	321,330	168,932	152,398	0.48

NASS, Crops Branch, (202) 720–2127, ERS, and Foreign trade from the Bureau of the Census.

Table 3-20.—Shelled peanuts (all grades): Supply, exports, and quantity crushed, United States, 2005–2014

Year beginning August	Supply						Exports	Crushed
	Stocks Aug. 1		Production		Imports	Total		
	Edible	Oil stock	Edible	Oil stock				
	1,000 pounds	*1,000 pounds*	*1,000 pounds*	*1,000 pounds*	*1,000 pounds*	*1,000 pounds*	*1,000 pounds*	*1,000 pounds*
2005	486,563	15,305	2,411,471	357,600	21,784	3,292,723	341,072	407,817
2006	510,097	21,499	2,415,495	347,243	42,888	3,337,222	437,663	385,375
2007	528,918	33,401	2,291,603	319,186	53,471	3,226,579	520,508	372,980
2008	431,593	39,508	2,442,345	253,778	61,199	3,228,423	494,738	334,296
2009	511,261	22,320	2,547,434	280,888	49,454	3,411,357	402,732	326,779
2010	554,295	35,498	2,450,639	357,130	46,031	3,443,593	395,554	441,017
2011	473,878	43,380	2,399,094	345,565	163,852	3,425,769	352,994	453,835
2012	466,310	52,883	3,125,786	351,284	72,871	4,069,134	741,103	493,205
2013	547,965	33,883	3,098,392	373,008	60,738	4,113,986	708,141	497,272
2014	519,824	25,364	2,997,078	391,728	64,345	3,998,339	676,509	506,677

NASS, Crops Branch, (202) 720–2127, ERS, and Foreign trade from the U.S. Bureau of the Census.

Table 3-21.—Peanuts: Shelled (raw basis) by types, used in primary products and apparent disappearance of peanuts, United States, 2005–2014

Type and year beginning August	Edible grades used in products					Apparent disappear- ance [2]
	Peanut butter [1]	Peanut snack	Peanut candy	Other products	Total	
	1,000 pounds	*1,000 pounds*	*1,000 pounds*	*1,000 pounds*	*1,000 pounds*	*1,000 pounds*
Virginia and Valencia:						
2005	123,402	81,617	25,738	1,136	231,893	....
2006	113,689	75,858	29,542	1,103	220,196	....
2007	125,497	71,059	27,909	979	225,445	....
2008	110,737	52,925	26,342	1,766	191,770	....
2009	(3)	50,812	17,361	(3)	198,770	....
2010	(3)	62,708	16,070	(3)	211,194	....
2011	(3)	78,333	17,856	(3)	203,958	....
2012	82,981	83,722	17,731	8,452	192,888	....
2013	86,759	85,298	17,109	13,373	202,536	....
2014	102,340	91,909	12,079	26,440	232,768	....
Runner:						
2005	849,176	361,176	335,748	10,925	1,557,025	....
2006	869,014	328,167	329,806	8,263	1,535,250	....
2007	878,026	344,551	279,564	9,666	1,511,807	....
2008	981,546	303,730	276,212	8,043	1,569,531	....
2009	1,056,699	290,358	286,277	13,120	1,646,454	....
2010	1,076,521	319,529	365,260	13,036	1,774,346	....
2011	1,091,541	303,631	360,797	14,840	1,770,809	....
2012	1,143,108	309,860	347,428	12,195	1,812,591	....
2013	1,128,206	337,934	(3)	(3)	1,844,490	....
2014	1,196,277	329,930	348,367	26,737	1,901,311	....
Spanish:						
2005	(3)	11,531	15,291	(3)	28,498	....
2006	(3)	11,104	14,335	(3)	36,211	....
2007	(3)	9,556	12,994	(3)	31,321	....
2008	(3)	10,823	13,721	(3)	34,990	....
2009	(3)	11,793	11,957	(3)	31,269	....
2010	(3)	12,940	14,122	(3)	35,207	....
2011	(3)	8,104	16,025	(3)	27,390	....
2012	(3)	6,847	16,755	(3)	25,389	....
2013	(3)	6,564	15,996	(3)	(3)	....
2014	(3)	6,638	15,410	(3)	27,188	....
All types:						
2005	974,223	454,324	376,777	12,092	1,817,416	2,739,343
2006	993,445	415,131	373,684	9,397	1,791,657	2,732,015
2007	1,012,263	425,166	320,467	10,676	1,768,572	2,702,007
2008	1,102,698	367,478	316,275	9,840	1,796,291	2,633,643
2009	1,191,821	352,963	315,595	15,840	1,876,219	2,682,110
2010	1,213,229	395,177	395,452	16,890	2,020,748	2,880,304
2011	1,197,748	390,068	394,678	19,661	2,020,748	2,742,724
2012	1,227,859	400,429	381,914	20,664	2,030,866	3,417,047
2013	1,218,170	429,796	395,726	29,103	2,072,795	3,508,060
2014	1,303,755	428,477	375,856	53,179	2,161,267	3,471,308

[1] Excludes peanut butter made by manufacturers for own use in candy. Includes peanut butter used in spreads, sandwiches, and cookies.   [2] Apparent disappearance represents stocks beginning of year plus production, minus stocks at end of year.   Includes edible grades and oilstocks.   [3] Not published to avoid disclosure of individual operations.
NASS, Crops Branch, (202) 720–2127, and ERS.

**Table 3-22.—Peanuts: Area, yield, and production, by State and
United States, 2012–2014**

State	Area planted			Peanuts for nuts		
	2012	2013	2014	Area harvested		
				2012	2013	2014
	1,000 acres	*1,000 acres*	*1,000 acres*	*1,000 acres*	*1,000 acres*	*1,000 acres*
Alabama	220.0	140.0	175.0	219.0	138.0	173.0
Florida	210.0	140.0	175.0	195.0	131.0	167.0
Georgia	735.0	430.0	600.0	730.0	426.0	591.0
Mississippi	52.0	34.0	32.0	49.0	33.0	31.0
New Mexico	10.0	7.0	5.0	10.0	7.0	5.0
North Carolina	107.0	82.0	94.0	106.0	81.0	93.0
Oklahoma	24.0	17.0	12.0	22.0	16.0	11.0
South Carolina ...	110.0	81.0	112.0	107.0	78.0	108.0
Texas	150.0	120.0	130.0	146.0	117.0	127.0
Virginia	20.0	16.0	19.0	20.0	16.0	19.0
United States	1,638.0	1,067.0	1,354.0	1,604.0	1,043.0	1,325.0

State	Peanuts for nuts					
	Yield per harvested acre			Production		
	2012	2013	2014	2012	2013	2014
	Pounds	*Pounds*	*Pounds*	*1,000 pounds*	*1,000 pounds*	*1,000 pounds*
Alabama	4,000	3,550	3,200	876,000	489,900	553,600
Florida	3,900	3,950	4,000	760,500	517,450	668,000
Georgia	4,580	4,430	4,100	3,343,400	1,887,180	2,423,100
Mississippi	4,400	3,700	4,000	215,600	122,100	124,000
New Mexico	2,600	3,100	3,100	26,000	21,700	15,500
North Carolina	4,030	3,900	4,300	427,180	315,900	399,900
Oklahoma	3,650	3,700	4,000	80,300	59,200	44,000
South Carolina ...	3,900	3,500	3,800	417,300	273,000	410,400
Texas	3,600	3,620	3,850	525,600	423,540	488,950
Virginia	4,100	3,950	4,350	82,000	63,200	82,650
United States	4,211	4,001	3,932	6,753,880	4,173,170	5,210,100

NASS, Crops Branch, (202) 720–2127.

**Table 3-23.—Peanuts: Marketing year average price, and value of production, by State
and United States, 2012–2014**

State	Marketing year average price per pound			Value of production		
	2012	2013	2014 [1]	2012	2013	2014 [1]
	Dollars	*Dollars*	*Dollars*	*1,000 dollars*	*1,000 dollars*	*1,000 dollars*
Alabama	0.275	0.226	0.183	240,900	110,717	101,309
Florida	0.281	0.242	0.217	213,701	125,223	144,956
Georgia	0.287	0.240	0.201	959,556	452,923	487,043
Mississippi	0.314	0.243	0.189	67,698	29,670	23,436
New Mexico	0.489	0.334	(S)	12,714	7,248	(S)
North Carolina	0.347	0.275	0.263	148,231	86,873	105,174
Oklahoma	0.329	0.292	0.265	26,419	17,286	11,660
South Carolina	0.318	0.264	0.222	132,701	72,072	91,109
Texas	0.375	0.321	0.277	197,100	135,956	135,439
Virginia	0.333	0.271	0.268	27,306	17,127	22,150
United States	0.301	0.249	0.212	2,026,326	1,055,095	1,122,276

(S) Insufficient number of reports to establish an estimate.   [1] Based on marketings and monthly prices received from
August 1, 2014 December 31, 2014.
NASS, Crops Branch, (202) 720–2127.

Table 3-24.—Peanuts, farmer's stock: Support operations, United States, 2005/2006–2014/2015

Marketing year beginning August 1	Income support payment rates per short ton [1]	Program price levels per short ton		Put under support		Acquired by CCC under loan program [4]	Owned by CCC at end of marketing year
		Loan [2]	Target Reference [3]	Quantity	Percentage of production		
	Dollars	Dollars	Dollars	1,000 short tons	Percent	1,000 short tons	1,000 short tons
2005/2006	36.00/104.0	355.00	495.00	2,300	96.1	42.0	20.5
2006/2007	36.00/104.0	355.00	495.00	1,694	97.9	0.5	0.0
2007/2008	36.00/49.0	355.00	495.00	1,363	74.2	0.4	0.3
2008/2009	36.00/00.0	355.00	495.00	2,073	80.5	3.6	0.3
2009/2010	36.00/25.0	355.00	495.00	1,674	90.7	3.0	3.0
2010/2011	36.00/9.0	495.00	495.00	1,811	87.1	0.0	0.0
2011/2012	36.00/00.0	495.00	495.00	1,402	76.6	0.0	0.0
2012/2013	36.00/00.0	495.00	495.00	2,640	78.2	55.9	0.0
2013/2014	36.00/00.0	495.00	495.00	1,452	69.6	6.1	2.5
2014/2015	95.00	535.00	535.00	2,123	81.8	172.7	6.8

[1] The first entry is the direct payment rate and the second entry is the counter-cyclical payment rate for 2004/2005-2013/2014. For 2009/2010-2013/2014, producers who participate in the Average Crop Revenue (ACRE) program get a 20 percent reduction in their direct payment, not calculated in this table. For 2014/2015 and after, the entry is the price loss coverage payment rate. Agricultural Risk Coverage (ARC) is also available, but payment rates are established at the county or farm levels.   [2] For 2009/2010-2013/2014, producers who participate in the ACRE program get a 30 percent reduction in their loan rate, not calculated in this table.   [3] Target applies to 2003/2004-2013/2014 and Reference applies beginning with 2014/2015.   [4] Acquisitions as of December 31, 2015.
FSA, Fibers, Peanuts, Tobacco, (202) 401–0062.

Table 3-25.—International oilseed, peanut: Area and production in specified countries, 2013/2014–2015/2016

Country	Area			Production		
	2013/2014	2014/2015	2015/2016	2013/2014	2014/2015	2015/2016
	1,000 hectares	1,000 hectares	1,000 hectares	1,000 metric tons	1,000 metric tons	1,000 metric tons
Argentina	378	341	329	997	1,188	1,070
Burma	885	885	885	1,375	1,375	1,375
Cameroon	463	470	400	636	640	550
China	4,633	4,604	4,600	16,972	16,482	16,700
India	5,400	4,600	4,500	5,650	4,900	4,700
Indonesia	655	630	615	1,160	1,150	1,130
Nigeria	2,500	2,500	2,500	3,000	3,000	3,000
Senegal	917	879	770	677	669	725
Sudan	2,162	1,254	2,184	1,767	963 871	800
Tanzania	944	840	840	900	800	800
Others	6,052	6,116	6,084	6,089	5,898	5,886
Total Foreign	24,989	23,119	23,707	39,223	37,065	37,807
United States	422	535	634	1,893	2,354	2,817
Total	25,411	23,654	24,341	41,116	39,419	40,624

FAS, Office of Global Analysis, (202) 720–6301.   Prepared or estimated on the basis of official USDA production, supply, and distribution statistics from foreign governments.

Table 3-26.—International meal, peanut: Production in specified countries, 2013/2014–2015/2016

Country	2013/2014	2014/2015	2015/2016
	1,000 metric tons	1,000 metric tons	1,000 metric tons
Argentina	90	110	112
Burkina	94	90	90
Burma	325	325	325
Cameroon	57	57	57
China	3,470	3,344	3,462
India	1,410	1,300	1,253
Nigeria	240	240	240
Senegal	120	120	130
Sudan	222	222	260
Tanzania	160	160	160
Others	539	560	545
Total Foreign	6,727	6,528	6,634
United States	122	126	146
Total	6,849	6,654	6,780

FAS, Office of Global Analysis, (202) 720–6301.   Prepared or estimated on the basis of official USDA production, supply, and distribution statistics from foreign governments.

Table 3-27.—Soybeans: Area, yield, production, and value, United States, 2005–2014

Year	Area planted	Soybeans for beans				
		Area har-vested	Yield per acre	Production	Marketing year average price per bushel received by farmers	Value of production
	1,000 acres	*1,000 acres*	*Bushels*	*1,000 bushels*	*Dollars*	*1,000 dollars*
2005	72,032	71,251	43.1	3,068,342	5.66	17,297,137
2006	75,522	74,602	42.9	3,196,726	6.43	20,468,267
2007	64,741	64,146	41.7	2,677,117	10.10	26,974,406
2008	75,718	74,681	39.7	2,967,007	9.97	29,458,225
2009	77,451	76,372	44.0	3,360,931	9.59	32,163,204
2010	77,404	76,610	43.5	3,331,306	11.30	37,571,277
2011	75,046	73,776	42.0	3,097,179	12.50	38,542,177
2012	77,198	76,144	40.0	3,042,044	14.40	43,723,144
2013	76,840	76,253	44.0	3,357,984	13.00	43,582,901
2014	83,701	83,061	47.8	3,968,823	10.20	40,288,536

NASS, Crops Branch, (202) 720–2127.

Table 3-28.—Soybeans: Stocks on and off farms, United States, 2006–2015

Year beginning previous December	On farms				Off farms [1]			
	Dec. 1	Mar. 1	June 1	Sep. 1 [2]	Dec. 1	Mar. 1	June 1	Sep. 1 [2]
	1,000 bushels	*1,000 bushels*	*1,000 bushels*	*1,000 bushels*	*1,000 bushels*	*1,000 bushels*	*1,000 bushels*	*1,000 bushels*
2006	1,345,000	872,000	495,500	176,300	1,156,426	797,206	495,199	273,026
2007	1,461,000	910,000	500,000	143,000	1,240,366	876,887	592,185	430,810
2008	1,128,500	593,000	226,600	47,000	1,231,860	840,982	449,543	158,034
2009	1,189,000	656,500	226,300	35,100	1,086,432	645,289	369,859	103,098
2010	1,229,500	609,200	232,600	35,400	1,109,050	660,868	338,523	115,485
2011	1,091,000	505,000	217,700	48,500	1,187,084	743,800	401,583	166,513
2012	1,139,000	555,000	179,000	38,250	1,230,885	819,488	488,465	131,120
2013	910,000	456,700	171,100	39,550	1,056,161	541,320	263,564	101,007
2014	955,000	381,900	109,100	21,325	1,198,621	611,928	295,945	70,666
2015 [3]	1,218,000	(NA)	(NA)	(NA)	1,305,651	(NA)	(NA)	(NA)

(NA) Not avaliable.   [1] Includes stocks at mills, elevators, warehouses, terminals, and processors.   [2] Old crop only.   [3] Preliminary.
NASS, Crops Branch, (202) 720–2127.

Table 3-29.—Soybeans, soybean meal, and oil: Average price at specified markets, 2006–2015

Year [1]	Soybeans per bushel: No. 1 Yellow Chicago	Soybean oil per pound crude, tanks, f.o.b. Decatur	Soybean meal per short ton: 48 percent protein Decatur
	Dollars	*Cents*	*Dollars*
2006	6.92	31.02	205.44
2007	12.22	52.03	335.94
2008	10.09	32.16	331.17
2009	9.65	35.95	311.27
2010	12.97	53.20	345.52
2011	13.49	51.90	393.53
2012	14.86	47.13	468.11
2013	13.51	38.23	489.94
2014	9.84	31.60	368.49
2015 [2]	(NA)	29.00	330.00

(NA) Not Available.   [1] Year beginning September for soybeans and October for oil and meal.   [2] Preliminary.
ERS, Field Crops Branch, (202) 694–5300.

Table 3-30.—Soybeans: Supply and disappearance, United States, 2006–2015

Year beginning September	Supply				
	Stocks by position			Production	Total [1]
	Farm	Terminal market, interior mill, elevator, and warehouse	Total		
	1,000 bushels	*1,000 bushels*	*1,000 bushels*	*1,000 bushels*	*1,000 bushels*
2006	176,300	273,026	449,326	3,196,726	3,655,086
2007	143,000	430,810	573,810	2,677,117	3,260,798
2008	47,000	158,034	205,034	2,967,007	3,185,3047
2009	35,100	103,098	138,198	3,360,931	3,513,717
2010	35,400	115,485	150,885	3,331,306	3,496,640
2011	48,500	166,513	215,013	3,097,179	3,328,324
2012	38,250	131,120	169,370	3,042,044	3,251,930
2013	39,550	101,007	140,557	3,357,984	3,429,697
2014	21,325	70,666	91,991	3,927,090	3,960,317
2015 [2]	49,700	141,725	191,425	3,888,721	4,109,146

Year beginning September	Disappearance			
	Crushed [3]	Seed, feed and residual	Exports	Total
	1,000 bushels	*1,000 bushels*	*1,000 bushels*	*1,000 bushels*
2006	1,807,706	157,074	1,116,496	3,081,276
2007	1,803,407	93,527	1,158,829	3,055,764
2008	1,661,922	105,890	1,279,294	3,047,106
2009	1,751,686	112,098	1,499,048	3,362,832
2010	1,648,043	128,607	1,504,978	3,281,627
2011	1,703,019	89,601	1,366,335	3,158,954
2012	1,688,903	94,944	1,327,526	3,111,373
2013	1,734,000	106,550	1,637,826	3,478,263
2014	1,845,000	152,378	1,843,376	3,860,883
2015 [2]	1,880,000	129,000	1,675,000	3,864,146

[1] Includes imports.　[2] Preliminary.　[3] Reported by the U.S. Department of Commerce.
ERS, Field Crops Branch, (202) 694–5300.

Table 3-31.—Soybeans: Support operations, United States, 2005/2006–2014/2015

Marketing year beginning September 1	Income support payment rates per bushels [1]	Program price levels per bushel		Put under loan		Acquired by CCC under loan program [4]	Owned by CCC at end of marketing year
		Loan [2]	Target [3]	Quantity	Percentage of production		
	Dollars	*Dollars*	*Dollars*	*Million bushels*	*Percent*	*Million bushels*	*Million bushels*
2005/2006	0.44/0.00	5.00	5.80	464	15.1	8.7	0.1
2006/2007	0.44/0.00	5.00	5.80	397	12.5	0.0	0.0
2007/2008	0.44/0.00	5.00	5.80	181	6.8	0.0	0.0
2008/2009	0.44/0.00	5.00	5.80	189	6.4	0.0	0.0
2009/2010	0.44/0.00	5.00	5.80	123	3.7	0.0	0.0
2010/2011	0.44/0.00	5.00	6.00	108	3.3	0.0	0.0
2011/2012	0.44/0.00	5.00	6.00	98	3.2	0.0	0.0
2012/2013	0.44/0.00	5.00	6.00	58	1.9	0.0	0.0
2013/2014	0.44/0.00	5.00	6.00	49	1.5	0.0	0.0
2014/2015	0.00	5.00	8.40	80	2.0	0.0	0.0

[1] The first entry is the direct payment rate and the second entry is the counter-cyclical payment rate for 2004/2005-2013/2014. For 2009/2010-2013/2014, producers who participate in the Average Crop Revenue (ACRE) program get a 20 percent reduction in their direct payment, not calculated in this table. For 2014/2015 and after, the entry is the price loss coverage payment rate. Agricultural Risk Coverage (ARC) is also available, but payment rates are established at the county or farm levels.　[2] For 2009/2010-2013/2014, producers who participate in the ACRE program get a 30 percent reduction in their loan rate, not calculated in this table.　[3] Target applies to 2003/2004-2013/2014 and Reference applies beginning with 2014/2015.　[4] Acquisitions as of December 31, 2015.
FSA, Feed Grains and Oilseeds, (202) 720–2711.

Table 3-32.—Soybeans for beans: Area, yield, and production, by State and United States, 2012–2014

State	Area planted			Area harvested		
	2012	2013	2014	2012	2013	2014
	1,000 acres	*1,000 acres*	*1,000 acres*	*1,000 acres*	*1,000 acres*	*1,000 acres*
Alabama	340	440	485	335	430	475
Arkansas	3,200	3,270	3,240	3,150	3,240	3,210
Delaware	170	165	185	168	163	183
Florida	21	32	39	20	30	37
Georgia	220	235	300	215	230	290
Illinois	9,050	9,500	9,800	8,930	9,480	9,780
Indiana	5,150	5,200	5,500	5,120	5,190	5,490
Iowa	9,350	9,300	9,900	9,310	9,250	9,820
Kansas	4,000	3,600	4,000	3,820	3,540	3,960
Kentucky	1,480	1,670	1,760	1,470	1,660	1,750
Louisiana	1,130	1,130	1,420	1,115	1,120	1,405
Maryland	480	485	510	475	480	505
Michigan	2,000	1,930	2,150	1,990	1,920	2,140
Minnesota	7,050	6,700	7,350	7,000	6,620	7,270
Mississippi	1,970	2,010	2,220	1,950	1,990	2,200
Missouri	5,400	5,650	5,650	5,270	5,610	5,600
Nebraska	5,050	4,800	5,400	4,990	4,770	5,350
New Jersey	96	90	105	94	88	103
New York	315	280	330	312	278	327
North Carolina	1,590	1,480	1,750	1,580	1,450	1,730
North Dakota	4,750	4,650	5,900	4,730	4,630	5,870
Ohio	4,600	4,500	4,850	4,590	4,490	4,840
Oklahoma	420	345	365	260	335	355
Pennsylvania	530	560	610	520	555	605
South Carolina	380	320	450	370	310	440
South Dakota	4,750	4,600	5,150	4,720	4,580	5,110
Tennessee	1,260	1,580	1,640	1,230	1,550	1,610
Texas	125	105	155	110	92	140
Virginia	590	610	660	580	600	650
West Virginia	21	23	27	20	22	26
Wisconsin	1,710	1,580	1,800	1,700	1,550	1,790
United States	77,198	76,840	83,701	76,144	76,253	83,061

State	Yield per harvested acre			Production		
	2012	2013	2014	2012	2013	2014
	Bushels	*Bushels*	*Bushels*	*1,000 bushels*	*1,000 bushels*	*1,000 bushels*
Alabama	45.0	43.5	40.0	15,075	18,705	19,000
Arkansas	43.5	43.5	50.0	137,025	140,940	160,500
Delaware	42.5	40.5	48.0	7,140	6,602	8,784
Florida	39.0	41.0	43.0	780	1,230	1,591
Georgia	37.5	40.5	40.0	8,063	9,315	11,600
Illinois	43.0	50.0	56.0	383,990	474,000	547,680
Indiana	44.0	51.5	56.0	225,280	267,285	307,440
Iowa	45.0	45.5	51.5	418,950	420,875	505,730
Kansas	23.0	37.0	36.0	87,860	130,980	142,560
Kentucky	40.0	50.0	48.0	58,800	83,000	84,000
Louisiana	46.5	48.5	57.0	51,848	54,320	80,085
Maryland	47.0	39.5	46.0	22,325	18,960	23,230
Michigan	43.0	44.5	43.0	85,570	85,440	92,020
Minnesota	43.5	42.0	42.0	304,500	278,040	305,340
Mississippi	45.0	46.0	52.0	87,750	91,540	114,400
Missouri	30.0	36.0	46.5	158,100	201,960	260,400
Nebraska	41.5	53.5	54.0	207,085	255,195	288,900
New Jersey	39.0	39.5	44.0	3,666	3,476	4,532
New York	46.0	48.0	45.0	14,352	13,344	14,715
North Carolina	39.5	33.5	40.0	62,410	48,575	69,200
North Dakota	34.5	30.5	34.5	163,185	141,215	202,515
Ohio	45.0	49.5	52.5	206,550	222,255	254,100
Oklahoma	15.0	30.5	29.0	3,900	10,218	10,295
Pennsylvania	48.0	49.0	49.0	24,960	27,195	29,645
South Carolina	34.0	28.5	35.0	12,580	8,835	15,400
South Dakota	30.5	40.5	45.0	143,960	185,490	229,950
Tennessee	38.0	46.5	46.0	46,740	72,075	74,060
Texas	26.0	25.5	38.5	2,860	2,346	5,390
Virginia	42.0	38.5	39.5	24,360	23,100	25,675
West Virginia	49.0	46.5	51.0	980	1,023	1,326
Wisconsin	42.0	39.0	44.0	71,400	60,450	78,760
United States	40.0	44.0	47.8	3,042,044	3,357,984	3,968,823

NASS, Crops Branch, (202) 720–2127.

Table 3-33.—Soybeans: Crushings, and oil and meal stocks, production, and foreign trade, United States, 2006–2015

Year beginning October	Soybeans crushed					Soybean oil			Soybean cake and meal		
	Oct.-Dec.	Jan.-Mar.	Apr.-Jun.	Jul.-Sep.	Total	Stocks Oct. 1	Produc-tion	Exports	Stocks Oct. 1	Produc-tion	Ex-ports
	1,000 bushels	*1,000 bushels*	*1,000 bushels*	*1,000 bushels*	*1,000 bushels*	*Million pounds*	*Million pounds*	*Million pounds*	*1,000 tons*	*1,000 tons*	*1,000 tons*
2006	474,220	448,549	445,981	444,926	1,812,676	3,010	20,489	1,877	314	43,032	8,804
2007	484,090	460,817	441,080	393,720	1,779,707	3,085	20,580	2,911	343	42,284	9,242
2008	436,079	424,967	426,566	361,946	1,649,558	2,485	18,745	2,193	294	39,102	8,497
2009	504,875	477,126	398,890	387,833	1,768,724	2,861	19,615	3,358	235	41,707	11,161
2010	464,618	418,849	379,650	370,231	1,633,349	3,406	18,888	3,233	302	39,251	9,081
2011	(NA)	(NA)	(NA)	(NA)	1,712,895	2,425	19,740	1,464	350	41,036	9,750
2012	(NA)	(NA)	(NA)	(NA)	1,677,279	2,540	19,820	2,163	300	39,875	11,146
2013	(NA)	(NA)	(NA)	(NA)	1,724,791	1,705	20,130	1,877	275	40,685	11,546
2014	(NA)	(NA)	(NA)	(NA)	1,905,000	1,165	21,430	2,050	250	45,220	13,200
2015[1]	(NA)	(NA)	(NA)	(NA)	1,880,000	1,620	21,735	2,000	300	44,625	11,650

(NA) Not available.   [1] Preliminary.
ERS, Field Crops Branch, (202) 694–5300. Data from the U.S. Department of Commerce.

Table 3-34.—Soybeans for beans: Marketing year average price and value, by State and United States, 2012–2014

State	Marketing year average price per bushel			Value of production		
	2012	2013	2014	2012	2013	2014
	Dollars	*Dollars*	*Dollars*	*1,000 dollars*	*1,000 dollars*	*1,000 dollars*
Alabama	14.60	12.90	10.20	220,095	241,295	193,800
Arkansas	14.30	13.10	10.70	1,959,458	1,846,314	1,717,350
Delaware	14.40	12.40	9.60	102,816	81,865	84,326
Florida	14.00	11.80	8.90	10,920	14,514	14,160
Georgia	14.60	13.30	10.80	117,720	123,890	125,280
Illinois	14.60	13.20	10.30	5,606,254	6,256,800	5,641,104
Indiana	14.70	13.20	10.30	3,311,616	3,528,162	3,166,632
Iowa	14.40	13.10	10.10	6,032,880	5,513,463	5,107,873
Kansas	14.30	12.80	9.70	1,256,398	1,676,544	1,382,832
Kentucky	14.50	13.10	10.60	852,600	1,087,300	890,400
Louisiana	14.70	13.40	11.00	762,166	727,888	880,935
Maryland	14.20	12.40	9.80	317,015	235,104	227,654
Michigan	14.00	12.90	10.10	1,197,980	1,102,176	929,402
Minnesota	14.30	12.90	10.20	4,354,350	3,586,716	3,114,468
Mississippi	14.50	13.20	11.10	1,272,375	1,208,328	1,269,840
Missouri	14.50	13.10	10.00	2,292,450	2,645,676	2,604,000
Nebraska	14.10	12.70	9.80	2,919,899	3,240,977	2,831,220
New Jersey	13.90	12.40	9.80	50,957	43,102	44,414
New York	13.60	12.80	9.80	195,187	170,803	144,207
North Carolina	14.00	13.10	10.30	873,740	636,333	712,760
North Dakota	14.00	12.40	9.60	2,284,590	1,751,066	1,944,144
Ohio	14.60	13.00	10.40	3,015,630	2,889,315	2,642,640
Oklahoma	14.40	12.90	9.90	56,160	131,812	101,921
Pennsylvania	14.20	13.00	9.80	354,432	353,535	290,521
South Carolina	14.50	13.30	10.40	182,410	117,506	160,160
South Dakota	14.20	12.50	9.40	2,044,232	2,318,625	2,161,530
Tennessee	14.60	13.00	10.60	682,404	936,975	785,036
Texas	14.60	12.60	9.55	41,756	29,560	51,475
Virginia	14.00	13.00	10.10	341,040	300,300	259,318
West Virginia	14.30	12.90	10.30	14,014	13,197	13,658
Wisconsin	14.00	12.80	10.10	999,600	773,760	795,476
United States	14.40	13.00	10.20	43,723,144	43,582,901	40,288,536

NASS, Crops Branch, (202) 720–2127.

Table 3-35.—International oilseed, soybean: Area and production in specified countries, 2013/2014–2015/2016

Country	Area			Production		
	2013/2014	2014/2015	2015/2016	2013/2014	2014/2015	2015/2016
	1,000 hectares	1,000 hectares	1,000 hectares	1,000 metric tons	1,000 metric tons	1,000 metric tons
Argentina	19,400	19,300	20,000	53,500	61,400	58,500
Bolivia	1,000	1,082	1,280	2,400	2,650	3,100
Brazil	30,100	32,100	33,300	86,700	96,200	100,000
Canada	1,860	2,235	2,200	5,359	6,049	6,235
China	6,791	6,800	6,550	11,950	12,150	12,000
India	12,200	10,908	11,650	9,500	8,700	8,000
Paraguay	3,255	3,240	3,400	8,190	8,100	8,800
Russia	1,202	1,907	2,030	1,517	2,362	2,640
Ukraine	1,351	1,800	2,125	2,774	3,900	3,925
Uruguay	1,312	1,333	1,120	3,300	3,109	3,110
Others	3,675	4,011	3,974	6,166	7,067	6,962
Total Foreign	82,146	84,716	87,629	191,356	211,687	213,272
United States	30,858	33,423	33,109	91,389	106,878	106,934
Total	113,004	118,139	120,738	282,745	318,565	320,206

FAS, Office of Global Analysis, (202) 720–6301.   Prepared or estimated on the basis of official USDA production, supply, and distribution statistics from foreign governments.

Table 3-36.—Soybeans: United States exports by country of destination, 2011–2013

Country of destination	2011	2012	2013
	Metric tons	Metric tons	Metric tons
China	20,691,515	26,195,525	24,554,881
Mexico	3,158,106	3,297,985	2,733,295
Japan	1,784,510	1,941,240	1,778,116
Indonesia	1,700,475	1,782,342	1,736,869
Germany(*)	554,509	1,579,104	1,336,474
Taiwan	1,355,388	1,348,951	1,048,205
Spain	361,883	545,734	912,262
Vietnam	227,256	570,450	555,053
Egypt	581,838	1,316,341	500,695
Korea, South	490,164	671,957	474,322
Thailand	335,165	680,778	385,010
Unidentified Countries	279,901	0	359,408
Turkey	246,858	817,490	278,455
Russia	52,520	83,018	272,161
Malaysia	346,916	286,067	264,875
Saudi Arabia	139,942	286,020	208,937
Tunisia	236,369	239,615	186,087
Canada	270,471	231,008	184,184
Netherlands	317,808	87,192	171,344
United Kingdom	25,369	188,410	159,715
Switzerland(*)	0	0	152,294
Israel(*)	135,814	128,534	144,488
Colombia	79,568	158,452	108,646
Costa Rica	231,063	290,162	107,015
Venezuela	49,906	48,841	102,994
France(*)	105,057	106	100,952
Italy(*)	1,342	60,035	79,278
Cuba	108,887	113,460	68,432
Iran	0	0	68,250
Rest of World	507,237	382,620	313,092
World Total	34,375,837	43,331,436	39,345,788

(*) Denotes a country that is a summarization of its component countries.
FAS, Office of Global Analysis, (202) 720–6301.

Table 3-37.—Soybean oil: United States exports by country of destination, 2011–2013

Country of destination	2011	2012	2013
	Metric tons	Metric tons	Metric tons
Mexico	154,843	168,533	182,498
China	102,471	216,369	124,415
Colombia	62,884	29,666	80,170
Dominican Republic	56,661	23,212	42,617
Venezuela	46,293	46,037	40,279
Germany(*)	15	6	40,006
Korea, South	14,657	16,183	36,207
Nicaragua	27,599	50,537	31,014
Egypt	0	18,198	30,002
Canada	31,707	26,497	29,995
India	54	88,099	25,017
Guatemala	42,908	18,275	18,420
Morocco	256,017	135,489	17,999
Malaysia	3	2,003	14,996
Hong Kong	3,415	294	14,753
Mozambique	0	9,400	13,874
Norway(*)	0	0	12,999
Jamaica	20,182	26,989	11,013
Trinidad and Tobago	7,793	8,649	7,695
Panama	6,116	2,385	6,103
Senegal	0	0	4,180
El Salvador	8,747	7,335	3,856
Haiti	7,565	3,161	3,775
Algeria	58,861	13,229	3,497
Japan	5,157	5,737	3,269
Madagascar	0	2,350	2,720
Chile	23	0	2,446
Bahamas, The	2,222	2,568	2,427
Mali	0	0	2,060
Bangladesh	2,929	2,779	1,650
Rest of World	83,803	30,894	8,625
World Total	1,002,926	954,873	818,573

(*) Denotes a country that is a summarization of its component countries.　Users should use cautious interpretation on quantity reports using mixed units of measure.　Quantity line items will only include statistics on the units of measure that are equal to, or are able to be converted to, the assigned unit of measure of the grouped commodities.
FAS, Office of Global Analysis, (202) 720–6301.

Table 3-38.—Soybean cake and meal: United States exports by country of destination, 2011–2013

Country of destination	2011	2012	2013
	Metric tons	Metric tons	Metric tons
Mexico	1,451,234	1,375,594	1,291,920
Philippines	869,526	1,305,854	1,120,642
Canada	1,078,505	1,095,572	914,343
Venezuela	636,066	705,818	755,097
Turkey	115,226	279,540	413,564
Poland	73,426	122,253	397,787
Vietnam	65,646	107,310	377,450
Ecuador	224,283	491,591	366,468
Dominican Republic	358,432	393,912	331,602
Egypt	107,836	392,014	328,499
Colombia	151,770	160,787	326,094
Guatemala	271,895	299,253	317,677
Denmark(*)	25,249	119,136	256,489
Morocco	575,506	443,121	229,861
Italy(*)	33,689	63,243	229,594
Spain	244	50,453	204,354
Japan	338,702	211,644	180,572
Honduras	164,799	172,160	173,125
Panama	93,088	97,711	169,563
Ireland	138,888	161,151	160,062
United Kingdom	98,650	175,771	150,084
El Salvador	142,954	156,466	146,538
Cuba	25,299	79,850	128,875
France(*)	202	270	128,863
Israel(*)	103,979	105,986	101,360
Jamaica	91,921	107,052	93,962
Nicaragua	59,194	79,105	71,158
Indonesia	27,839	137,120	70,833
Australia(*)	544	41,753	68,956
Thailand	17,604	35,543	67,615
Rest of World	647,240	890,783	741,111
World Total	7,989,431	9,857,811	10,314,117

(*) Denotes a country that is a summarization of its component countries.　Users should use cautious interpretation on quantity reports using mixed units of measure.　Quantity line items will only include statistics on the units of measure that are equal to, or are able to be converted to, the assigned unit of measure of the grouped commodities.
FAS, Office of Global Analysis, (202) 720–6301. Data Source: Department of Commerce, U.S. Census Bureau, Foreign Trade Statistics.

Table 3-39.—International oil, soybean: Production in specified countries, 2013/2014–2015/2016

Country	2013/2014	2014/2015	2015/2016
	1,000 metric tons	*1,000 metric tons*	*1,000 metric tons*
Argentina	6,785	7,687	8,710
Bolivia	400	445	475
Brazil	7,070	7,660	7,680
China	12,335	13,347	14,655
European Union	2,553	2,698	2,717
India	1,478	1,245	1,150
Mexico	720	745	745
Paraguay	640	697	783
Russia	609	654	717
Taiwan	355	393	402
Others	2,928	3,668	4,114
Total Foreign	35,873	39,239	42,148
United States	9,131	9,706	9,857
Total	45,004	48,945	52,005

FAS, Office of Global Analysis, (202) 720–6301.　Prepared or estimated on the basis of official USDA production, supply, and distribution statistics from foreign governments.

Table 3-40.—International trade: Meal, soybean in specified countries, 2013/2014–2015/2016

Country	2013/2014	2014/2015	2015/2016
	1,000 metric tons	*1,000 metric tons*	*1,000 metric tons*
Principle exporting countries:			
Argentina	24,972	28,545	32,800
Bolivia	1,608	1,625	1,650
Brazil	13,948	14,390	15,600
Canada	241	212	275
China	2,017	1,595	1,850
European Union	296	362	400
India	2,742	1,072	150
Paraguay	2,504	2,450	2,980
Russia	507	505	450
Ukraine	80	216	250
Others	769	675	699
Total Foreign	49,684	51,647	57,104
United States	10,474	11,929	10,160
Total	60,158	63,576	67,264
Principle importing countries:			
European Union	18,135	19,260	20,700
Indonesia	3,983	3,850	4,500
Iran	2,683	1,948	2,100
Japan	1,976	1,699	1,850
Korea, South	1,825	1,751	1,900
Malaysia	1,397	1,465	1,500
Mexico	1,410	1,795	2,000
Philippines	2,337	2,200	2,400
Thailand	2,665	3,017	3,050
Vietnam	3,342	4,276	4,600
Others	17,825	18,635	19,964
Total Foreign	57,578	59,896	64,564
United States	347	302	340
Total	57,925	60,198	64,904

FAS, Office of Global Analysis, (202) 720–6301.　Prepared or estimated on the basis of official USDA production, supply, and distribution statistics from foreign governments.

Table 3-41.—International trade: Oil, soybean in specified countries, 2013/2014–2015/2016

Country	2013/2014	2014/2015	2015/2016
	1,000 metric tons	*1,000 metric tons*	*1,000 metric tons*
Principle exporting countries:			
Argentina	4,087	5,093	5,925
Bolivia	371	350	370
Brazil	1,378	1,510	1,390
Canada	92	118	170
European Union	766	1,010	1,000
Malaysia	157	170	176
Paraguay	650	660	735
Russia	332	423	445
Ukraine	118	136	160
Vietnam	91	104	100
Others	531	526	524
Total Foreign	8,573	10,100	10,995
United States	851	914	953
Total	9,424	11,014	11,948
Principle importing countries:			
Algeria	629	620	640
Bangladesh	443	508	520
China	1,353	773	850
Colombia	288	315	330
Egypt	230	480	400
India	1,830	2,799	3,700
Iran	551	421	450
Morocco	444	430	460
Peru	355	355	380
Venezuela	403	473	440
Others	2,665	2,772 952	2,772
Total Foreign	9,191	9,946	11,122
United States	75	120	136
Total	9,266	10,066	11,258

FAS, Office of Global Analysis, (202) 720–6301.   Prepared or estimated on the basis of official USDA production, supply, and distribution statistics from foreign governments.

Table 3-42.—International trade: Oil, soybean local in specified countries, 2013/2014–2015/2016

Country	2013/2014	2014/2015	2015/2016
	1,000 metric tons	*1,000 metric tons*	*1,000 metric tons*
Principle exporting countries:			
Argentina	7,190	8,590	8,540
Brazil	7,340	7,740	7,680
Total Foreign	14,530	16,330	16,220
Total	14,530	16,330	16,220

FAS, Office of Global Analysis, (202) 720–6301.   Prepared or estimated on the basis of official USDA production, supply, and distribution statistics from foreign governments.

Table 3-43.—International trade: Oilseed, soybean in specified countries, 2013/2014–2015/2016

Country	2013/2014	2014/2015	2015/2016
	1,000 metric tons	*1,000 metric tons*	*1,000 metric tons*
Principle exporting countries:			
Argentina	7,842	10,573	11,800
Bolivia	141	25	150
Brazil	46,829	50,612	58,000
Canada	3,469	3,853	4,200
China	215	143	200
India	183	234	200
Paraguay	4,800	4,375	4,600
Russia	24	312	350
Ukraine	1,261	2,422	2,200
Uruguay	3,195	2,850	2,850
Others	168	312	351
Total Foreign	68,127	75,711	84,901
United States	44,574	50,169	45,994
Total	112,701	125,880	130,895
Principle importing countries:			
China	70,364	78,350	82,000
Egypt	1,694	1,947	2,050
European Union	13,293	13,388	13,200
Indonesia	2,241	2,000	2,300
Japan	2,894	3,004	2,900
Mexico	3,842	3,819	3,850
Russia	2,048	1,986	2,250
Taiwan	2,335	2,520	2,550
Thailand	1,798	2,411	2,350
Turkey	1,608	2,197	2,400
Others	7,710	9,619	11,497
Total Foreign	109,827	121,241	127,347
United States	1,954	904	816
Total	111,781	122,145	128,163

FAS, Office of Global Analysis, (202) 720–6301. Prepared or estimated on the basis of official USDA production, supply, and distribution statistics from foreign governments.

Table 3-44.—International trade: Oilseed, Soybeans local in specified countries, 2013/2014–2015/2016

Country	2013/2014	2014/2015	2015/2016
	1,000 metric tons	*1,000 metric tons*	*1,000 metric tons*
Principle exporting countries:			
Argentina	7,433	11,800	11,400
Brazil	45,747	54,635	56,650
Total Foreign	53,180	66,435	68,050
Total	53,180	66,435	68,050
Principle importing countries:			
Argentina	2	2	2
Brazil	579	325	300
Total Foreign	581	327	302
Total	581	327	302

FAS, Office of Global Analysis, (202) 720–6301. Prepared or estimated on the basis of official USDA production, supply, and distribution statistics from foreign governments.

OILSEEDS, FATS, AND OILS

Table 3-45.—Sunflower, all: Area, yield, production, and value, United States, 2005–2014

Year	Area planted	Area harvested	Yield per harvested acre	Production	Price per cwt	Value of production
	1,000 acres	*1,000 acres*	*Pounds*	*1,000 pounds*	*Dollars*	*1,000 dollars*
2005	2,709.0	2,610.0	1,539	4,017,155	12.10	487,420
2006	1,950.0	1,770.0	1,211	2,143,613	14.50	308,832
2007	2,070.0	2,012.0	1,426	2,868,870	21.70	614,736
2008	2,516.5	2,396.0	1,429	3,422,840	21.80	704,105
2009	2,030.0	1,953.5	1,554	3,036,460	15.10	458,959
2010	1,951.5	1,873.8	1,460	2,735,570	23.30	633,778
2011	1,543.0	1,457.8	1,398	2,038,275	29.10	589,282
2012	1,920.0	1,840.0	1,487	2,736,060	25.40	699,970
2013	1,575.5	1,464.6	1,380	2,021,765	21.40	443,296
2014	1,560.8	1,507.6	1,469	2,214,835	21.50	504,596

NASS, Crops Branch, (202) 720–2127.

Table 3-46.—Sunflower, oil varieties: Area, yield, production, and value, United States, 2005–2014

Year	Area planted	Area harvested	Yield per harvested acre	Production	Price per cwt.	Value of production
	1,000 acres	*1,000 acres*	*Pounds*	*1,000 pounds*	*Dollars*	*1,000 dollars*
2005	2,104.0	2,032.0	1,564	3,177,635	10.50	340,584
2006	1,658.0	1,514.0	1,181	1,787,966	14.10	249,848
2007	1,765.5	1,719.0	1,445	2,483,585	21.40	527,925
2008	2,163.0	2,062.0	1,452	2,993,510	19.50	572,979
2009	1,698.0	1,653.0	1,563	2,584,010	13.80	359,331
2010	1,463.0	1,422.5	1,458	2,074,500	22.60	457,135
2011	1,289.5	1,233.4	1,397	1,722,675	28.00	480,412
2012	1,658.0	1,589.8	1,484	2,359,775	24.40	580,404
2013	1,279.0	1,200.9	1,363	1,637,205	19.30	322,605
2014	1,172.0	1,138.5	1,461	1,663,170	20.40	323,526

NASS, Crops Branch, (202) 720–2127.

Table 3-47.—Sunflower, non-oil varieties: Area, yield, production, and value, United States, 2004–2013

Year	Area planted	Area harvested	Yield per harvested acre	Production	Price per cwt.	Value of production
	1,000 acres	*1,000 acres*	*Pounds*	*1,000 pounds*	*Dollars*	*1,000 dollars*
2005	605.0	578.0	1,452	839,520	17.30	146,836
2006	292.0	256.0	1,389	355,647	16.80	58,984
2007	304.5	293.0	1,315	385,285	22.90	86,811
2008	353.5	334.0	1,285	429,330	31.30	131,126
2009	332.0	300.5	1,506	452,450	22.10	99,628
2010	488.5	451.3	1,465	661,070	26.60	176,643
2011	253.5	224.4	1,406	315,600	33.80	108,870
2012	262.0	250.2	1,504	376,285	29.60	119,566
2013	296.5	263.7	1,458	384,560	31.30	120,691
2014	388.8	369.1	1,495	551,665	33.70	181,070

NASS, Crops Branch, (202) 720–2127.

Table 3-48.—Sunflower, all: Area, yield, production, and value, by type, State and United States, 2013–2014

Type and State	Area planted		Area harvested		Yield per harvested acre	
	2013	2014	2013	2014	2013	2014
Oil:	*1,000 acres*	*1,000 acres*	*1,000 acres*	*1,000 acres*	*Pounds*	*Pounds*
California	56.0	44.0	55.5	44.0	1,300	1,300
Colorado	50.0	35.0	37.0	33.0	800	1,400
Kansas	55.0	45.0	50.0	42.0	1,160	1,370
Minnesota	33.0	47.0	32.0	45.0	1,600	1,450
Nebraska	28.0	25.0	23.5	23.0	850	1,160
North Dakota	425.0	520.0	400.0	510.0	1,260	1,340
Oklahoma	3.0	3.0	2.9	1.5	1,200	1,400
South Dakota	560.0	410.0	540.0	400.0	1,520	1,670
Texas	69.0	43.0	60.0	40.0	1,300	1,420
United States	1,279.0	1,172.0	1,200.9	1,138.5	1,363	1,461
Non-oil:						
California	2.5	3.0	2.5	3.0	1,200	1,350
Colorado	17.0	9.5	16.0	9.0	1,000	1,900
Kansas	16.0	18.0	15.0	17.0	1,600	2,000
Minnesota	10.0	15.0	9.5	14.5	1,900	1,560
Nebraska	15.0	11.0	13.0	10.5	1,000	1,750
North Dakota	74.0	145.0	71.0	140.0	1,360	1,180
Oklahoma	2.0	1.3	1.7	1.1	1,000	1,000
South Dakota	115.0	125.0	110.0	122.0	1,600	1,710
Texas	45.0	61.0	25.0	52.0	1,450	1,550
United States	296.5	388.8	263.7	369.1	1,458	1,495
Total:						
California	58.5	47.0	58.0	47.0	1,296	1,303
Colorado	67.0	44.5	53.0	42.0	860	1,507
Kansas	71.0	63.0	65.0	59.0	1,262	1,552
Minnesota	43.0	62.0	41.5	59.5	1,669	1,477
Nebraska	43.0	36.0	36.5	33.5	903	1,345
North Dakota	499.0	665.0	471.0	650.0	1,275	1,306
Oklahoma	5.0	4.3	4.6	2.6	1,126	1,231
South Dakota	675.0	535.0	650.0	522.0	1,534	1,679
Texas	114.0	104.0	85.0	92.0	1,344	1,493
United States	1,575.5	1,560.8	1,464.6	1,507.6	1,380	1,469

Type and State	Production		Marketing year average price per cwt		Value of production	
	2013	2014 [1]	2013	2014 [1]	2013	2014 [1]
Oil:	*1,000 lbs*	*1,000 lbs*	*Dollars*	*Dollars*	*1,000 dollars*	*1,000 dollars*
California	72,150	57,200	27.00	25.00	19,481	14,300
Colorado	29,600	46,200	(D)	(D)	(D)	(D)
Kansas	58,000	57,540	18.80	(D)	10,904	(D)
Minnesota	51,200	65,250	22.20	20.20	11,366	13,181
Nebraska	19,975	26,680	17.40	16.90	3,476	4,509
North Dakota	504,000	683,400	20.30	19.90	102,312	135,997
Oklahoma	3,480	2,100	19.10	18.70	665	393
South Dakota	820,800	668,000	18.60	18.60	152,669	124,248
Texas	78,000	56,800	(D)	(D)	(D)	(D)
Other States [1]	....	....	20.20	19.20	21,732	30,898
United States	1,637,205	1,663,170	19.30	20.40	322,605	323,526
Non-oil:						
California	3,000	4,050	29.00	28.00	870	1,134
Colorado	16,000	17,100	(D)	(D)	(D)	(D)
Kansas	24,000	34,000	33.30	(D)	7,992	(D)
Minnesota	18,050	22,620	24.30	36.30	4,386	8,211
Nebraska	13,000	18,375	33.10	33.00	4,303	6,064
North Dakota	96,560	165,200	30.80	33.20	29,740	54,846
Oklahoma	1,700	1,100	33.70	34.00	573	374
South Dakota	176,000	208,620	32.20	32.80	56,672	68,427
Texas	36,250	80,600	(D)	(D)	(D)	(D)
Other States [1]	....	....	30.90	31.90	16,155	42,014
United States	384,560	551,665	31.30	33.70	120,691	181,070
Total:						
California	75,150	61,250	27.10	25.20	20,351	15,434
Colorado	45,600	63,300	25.60	31.00	11,022	14,712
Kansas	82,000	91,540	22.30	26.00	18,896	22,660
Minnesota	69,250	87,870	22.50	20.40	15,752	21,392
Nebraska	32,975	45,055	23.60	23.50	7,779	10,573
North Dakota	600,560	848,600	23.20	22.40	132,052	190,843
Oklahoma	5,180	3,200	23.90	24.00	1,238	767
South Dakota	996,800	876,620	19.60	19.80	209,341	192,675
Texas	114,250	137,400	23.50	25.90	26,865	35,540
Other States [1]	....	....	(X)	(X)	(X)	(X)
United States	2,021,765	2,214,835	21.40	21.50	443,296	504,596

(D) Withheld to avoid disclosing data for individual operations.   (X) Not applicable.   [1] Includes data withheld above.
NASS, Crops Branch, (202) 720–2127.

Table 3-49.—International Oilseed, sunflowerseed: Area and production in specified countries, 2013/2014–2015/2016

Country	Area			Production		
	2013/2014	2014/2015	2015/2016	2013/2014	2014/2015	2015/2016
	1,000 hectares	*1,000 hectares*	*1,000 hectares*	*1,000 metric tons*	*1,000 metric tons*	*1,000 metric tons*
Argentina	1,300	1,440	1,300	2,000	3,160	2,600
Burma	570	540	540	360	450	450
China	930	949	920	2,424	2,492	2,300
European Union	4,615	4,279	4,147	9,052	8,932	7,750
India	750	550	550	670	420	460
Pakistan	822	769	701	573	513	534
Russia	6,795	6,371	6,350	9,842	8,374	9,095
South Africa	600	576	615	832	661	625
Turkey	690	530	490	1,400	1,200	1,000
Ukraine	5,300	5,300	5,235	11,600	10,200	11,300
Others	1,171	1,272	1,273	1,952	2,206	1,978
Total Foreign	23,543	22,576	22,121	40,705	38,608	38,092
United States	593	611	728	917	1,007	1,326
Total	24,136	23,187	22,849	41,622	39,615	39,418

FAS, Office of Global Analysis, (202) 720–6301.　Prepared or estimated on the basis of official USDA production, supply, and distribution statistics from foreign governments.

Table 3-50—Sunflowerseed: United States exports by country of destination, 2011–2013

Country	2011	2012	2013
	Metric tons	*Metric tons*	*Metric tons*
Spain	25,735	18,858	25,092
Canada	28,805	30,634	24,652
Turkey	8,703	8,428	12,232
Mexico	11,584	8,657	11,645
Kuwait	233	440	6,665
Egypt	1,979	3,711	5,654
Jordan	3,953	4,250	5,354
France(*)	471	3,393	4,370
Israel(*)	3,074	2,452	3,567
China	98	35	2,638
Indonesia	120	381	2,559
Romania	5,862	2,112	2,335
Greece	1,789	1,553	1,786
Korea, South	1,065	954	1,710
Morocco	897	1,202	1,220
Germany(*)	6,048	439	1,015
United Arab Emirates	504	1,765	964
Iraq	102	163	874
Ecuador	257	621	856
Japan	789	702	801
United Kingdom	4,713	709	716
Netherlands	504	758	586
Poland	402	387	407
Lebanon	415	325	368
Taiwan	503	618	361
Saudi Arabia	81	0	287
Hungary	1,597	0	285
Tunisia	101	259	246
Russia	0	0	237
Vietnam	0	0	230
Rest of World	5,488	2,651	1,349
World Total	115,868	96,458	121,056

(*) Denotes a country that is a summarization of its component countries.
FAS, Office of Global Analysis, (202) 720–6301.

Table 3-51.—Sunflowerseed oil: United States exports by country of destination, 2011–2013

Country	2011	2012	2013
	Metric tons	Metric tons	Metric tons
Canada	14,060	13,727	15,637
Mexico	3,415	424	9,580
Japan	2,681	794	1,213
Vietnam	95	558	1,161
Korea, South	7	361	993
Costa Rica	1,209	84	478
China	223	386	444
Switzerland(*)	0	0	193
Thailand	2	17	189
Australia(*)	236	480	112
Taiwan	211	99	91
Singapore	49	33	73
Tanzania	89	111	67
Italy(*)	6	2	50
Kyrgyzstan	0	0	50
Norway(*)	0	10	50
Dominican Republic	0	4	40
New Zealand(*)	0	25	34
Chile	18	0	29
Colombia	49	14	28
Indonesia	10	37	23
Netherlands Antilles(*)	4	0	22
Honduras	0	20	19
Brazil	138	0	15
Barbados	2	1	14
Malaysia	0	26	13
United Kingdom	123	443	12
Equatorial Guinea	0	0	10
Poland	0	0	7
India	0	2	7
Rest of World	11,245	654	6
World Total	33,871	18,314	30,659

(*) Denotes a country that is a summarization of its component countries.
FAS, Office of Global Analysis, (202) 720–6301.

Table 3-52.—International oil, sunflowerseed: Production in specified countries, 2013/2014–2015/2016

Country	2013/2014	2014/2015	2015/2016
	1,000 metric tons	1,000 metric tons	1,000 metric tons
Argentina	934	1,135	1,140
Bolivia	113	123	142
Burma	110	150	150
China	481	466	420
European Union	3,170	3,180	2,980
Russia	3,593	3,366	3,530
Serbia	123	161	161
South Africa	347	285	258
Turkey	845	725	595
Ukraine	4,750	4,325	4,663
Others	853	787	783
Total foreign	15,319	14,703	14,822
United States	197	166	258
Total	15,516	14,869	15,080

FAS, Office of Global Analysis, (202) 720–6301.   Prepared or estimated on the basis of official USDA production, supply, and distribution statistics from foreign governments.

Table 3-53.—Sunflowerseed cake and meal: United States exports by country of destination, 2011–2013

Country	2011	2012	2013
	Metric tons	Metric tons	Metric tons
Israel(*)	0	0	14,057
Canada	2,137	3,652	4,823
Dominican Republic	0	0	38
Mexico	825	38	18
Korea, South	0	2	0
World Total	2,962	3,693	18,936

(*) Denotes a country that is a summarization of its component countries.
FAS, Office of Global Analysis, (202) 720–6301.

Table 3-54.—Peppermint oil: Area, yield, production, and value, United States, 2005–2014

Year	Area harvested	Yield per harvested acre	Production	Price per pound	Value of production
	1,000 acres	Pounds	1,000 pounds	Dollars	1,000 dollars
2005	76.0	92	6,980	12.20	85,114
2006	77.7	91	7,105	12.70	89,911
2007	63.6	89	5,636	13.60	76,866
2008	60.0	92	5,499	15.90	87,450
2009	69.8	91	6,379	20.10	128,118
2010	72.8	89	6,495	20.30	131,805
2011	75.5	89	6,700	23.10	154,626
2012	75.7	87	6,549	24.10	158,121
2013	68.5	89	6,115	23.90	146,260
2014	63.1	90	5,692	23.00	130,704

NASS, Crops Branch (202), 720–2127.

Table 3-55.—Spearmint oil: Area, yield, production, and value, United States, 2005–2014

Year	Area harvested	Yield per harvested acre	Production	Price per pound	Value of production
	1,000 acres	Pounds	1,000 pounds	Dollars	1,000 dollars
2005	16.7	108	1,798	10.70	19,230
2006	18.5	110	2,038	11.30	23,044
2007	19.8	126	2,493	12.60	31,495
2008	20.4	118	2,399	14.90	35,765
2009	20.5	132	2,698	16.50	44,597
2010	18.6	125	2,318	16.20	37,553
2011	17.3	132	2,286	18.60	42,438
2012	20.0	119	2,386	19.50	46,521
2013	24.5	119	2,926	18.90	55,283
2014	24.4	114	2,784	19.70	54,977

NASS, Crops Branch, (202) 720–2127.

Table 3-56.—Mint oil: Production and value, by State and United States, 2012–2014

State	Production			Price per pound			Value of production		
	2012	2013	2014	2012	2013	2014	2012	2013	2014
	1,000 pounds	*1,000 pounds*	*1,000 pounds*	*Dollars*	*Dollars*	*Dollars*	*1,000 dollars*	*1,000 dollars*	*1,000 dollars*
Peppermint:									
California	257	153	153	25.70	27.70	26.30	6,605	4,238	4,024
Idaho	1,815	1,550	1,544	23.30	22.30	21.50	42,290	34,565	33,196
Indiana	510	425	510	28.00	27.60	26.00	14,280	11,730	13,260
Michigan	54	42	(D)	27.00	27.60	(D)	1,458	1,159	(D)
Oregon	2,132	1,849	1,800	24.90	24.30	24.80	53,087	44,931	44,640
Washington	1,500	1,925	1,500	22.70	23.60	21.00	34,050	45,430	31,500
Wisconsin	281	171	(D)	22.60	24.60	(D)	6,351	4,207	(D)
Other States	-	-	185	(NA)	(NA)	22.10	(NA)	(NA)	4,084
United States	6,549	6,115	5,692	24.10	23.90	23.00	158,121	146,260	130,704
Spearmint:									
Idaho	96	125	156	18.60	20.00	21.00	1,786	2,500	3,276
Indiana	224	263	226	20.30	20.10	26.00	4,547	5,286	5,876
Michigan	119	119	(D)	19.00	18.00	(D)	2,261	2,142	(D)
Oregon	132	265	325	20.10	20.80	20.90	2,653	5,512	6,793
Washington	1,792	2,133	1,938	19.40	18.50	18.80	34,777	39,402	36,411
Native	1,242	1,365	1,190	19.10	17.50	17.90	23,722	23,888	21,301
Scotch	550	768	748	20.10	20.20	20.20	11,055	15,514	15,110
Wisconsin	23	21	(D)	21.60	21.00	(D)	497	441	(D)
Other States	-	-	139	(NA)	(NA)	18.90	(NA)	(NA)	2,621
United States	2,386	2,926	2,784	19.50	18.90	19.70	46,521	55,283	54,977

- Represents zero.　(D) Withheld to avoid disclosing data for individual operations.　(NA) Not available.
NASS, Crops Branch, (202) 720–2127.

Table 3-57.—International oil, olive: Production in specified countries, 2013/2014–2015/2016

Country	2013/2014	2014/2015	2015/2016
	1,000 metric tons	*1,000 metric tons*	*1,000 metric tons*
Algeria	57	70	73
Australia	14	20	20
European Union	2,475	1,550	2,085
Jordan	25	23	29
Lebanon	18	21	20
Libya	15	15	15
Morocco	120	120	130
Syria	145	105	180
Tunisia	70	340	150
Turkey	140	170	143
Others	16	21	17
Total foreign	3,095	2,455	2,862
United States	5	5	5
Total	3,100	2,460	2,867

FAS, Office of Global Analysis, (202) 720–6301.　Prepared or estimated on the basis of official USDA production, supply, and distribution statistics from foreign governments.

Table 3-58.—Fats and oils: Wholesale price per pound, 2010–2014 [1]

Item and market	2010	2011	2012	2013	2014
	Cents	*Cents*	*Cents*	*Cents*	*Cents*
Castor oil, No. 1, Brazilian, tanks, imported, New York	77.32	(NA)	(NA)	(NA)	(NA)
Coconut oil, crude, tanks, f.o.b. New York	50.69	80.60	54.40	44.26	60.21
Corn oil, crude, tank cars, f.o.b. Decatur	42.50	61.37	55.74	43.13	38.36
Cottonseed oil, crude, tank cars, f.o.b. Valley	42.93	54.60	53.00	46.60	60.33
Linseed oil, raw, tank cars, Minneapolis	64.10	(NA)	(NA)	(NA)	(NA)
Palm oil, U.S. ports, refined	43.93	55.98	48.13	41.13	39.86
Canola oil, Midwest	45.75	59.10	57.56	52.81	42.46
Soybean oil, crude, tank cars, f.o.b. Decatur	39.00	54.05	51.02	44.98	36.83
Sunflower oil, crude, Minneapolis	54.86	93.83	77.98	62.79	59.77
Tallow, edible, number delivered Chicago	35.30	53.40	47.99	42.52	38.91
Tung oil, imported, drums, f.o.b. New York	130.00	(NA)	(NA)	(NA)	(NA)

(NA) Not available.　[1] All prices are calendar year basis.
ERS, Market and Trade Economics Division, Field Crops Branch, (202) 694–5300. Compiled from the Chemical Marketing Reporter, Milling and Baking News, and the Agricultural Marketing Service.

CHAPTER IV
STATISTICS OF VEGETABLES AND MELONS

This chapter contains statistics on potatoes, sweet potatoes, and commercial vegetables and melons.

For potatoes and sweet potatoes, the estimates of area, production, value, and farm disposition pertain to the total crop and include quantities produced both for sale and for use on farms where grown. Potato statistics are shown on a within-year seasonal grouping of winter, spring, summer, and fall crops, by States. Some States have production in more than one seasonal group.

Commercial vegetables for fresh market include 24 principal vegetable and melon crops in the major producing States. These estimates relate to crops which are grown primarily for sale and do not include vegetables and melons produced in farm and non-farm gardens. The bulk of the production of the principal vegetable and melon crops is for consumption in the fresh state. The commercial estimates of these crops include local market production from areas near consuming centers as well as production from well recognized commercial areas which specialize in producing supplies for shipment to distant markets. For fresh market vegetables and melons, value per unit and total value are on a f.o.b. basis.

For processing vegetables, the estimates of area, production, and value for each of 10 crops relate to production used by commercial canners, freezers, and other processors, except dehydrators. These estimates include raw products grown by processors themselves and those grown under contract or purchased on the open market. This production and the actual area harvested are not duplicated in the fresh market estimates for the same commodities. The production of those vegetables used for processing for which regular processing estimates are not made is included in the fresh market estimates. The processed segment of production for asparagus, broccoli, and cauliflower, combined with fresh market production during the year, is published separately at the end of the season. For processed vegetables, value per unit and total value are at processing plant door.

Table 4-1.—Vegetables, commercial: Area, production, and value of principal crops, United States, 2005-2014

Year	Area [1]	
	Fresh market [2]	Processing [3]
	Acres	*Acres*
2005	1,858,420	1,266,460
2006	1,829,840	1,253,350
2007	1,784,290	1,249,230
2008	1,710,884	1,224,410
2009	1,681,774	1,264,849
2010	1,685,155	1,142,000
2011	1,624,535	1,057,480
2012	1,626,510	1,135,605
2013	1,628,010	1,053,160
2014	1,582,960	1,089,920

Year	Production [4]	
	Fresh market [2]	Processing [3]
	1,000 cwt	*Tons*
2005	460,235	15,696,690
2006	460,812	15,910,370
2007	459,421	17,799,410
2008	445,551	17,473,670
2009	437,980	19,518,030
2010	438,324	17,599,990
2011	426,656	17,001,540
2012	429,988	18,225,775
2013	418,011	17,168,580
2014	413,167	19,193,490

Year	Value [5]	
	Fresh market [2]	Processing [3]
	1,000 dollars	*1,000 dollars*
2005	9,567,211	1,252,998
2006	10,150,783	1,343,800
2007	10,047,825	1,609,544
2008	10,297,645	1,896,796
2009	10,757,613	2,102,214
2010	10,777,069	1,659,332
2011	10,532,246	1,771,192
2012	9,797,128	2,002,481
2013	11,488,261	2,092,316
2014	10,889,076	2,171,607

[1] Area for fresh market is area for harvest, including any partially harvested or not harvested because of low prices or other economic factors. Area for processing is area harvested. [2] Area, production, and farm value of the following crops for which regular seasonal estimates are prepared in major producing States: Artichokes, asparagus, snap beans, broccoli, cabbage, cantaloups, carrots, cauliflower, celery, sweet corn, cucumbers, garlic, honeydew melons, head lettuce, leaf lettuce, romaine lettuce, onions, bell peppers, chile peppers, pumpkins, spinach, squash, tomatoes, and watermelons. [3] Area, production, and farm value of the following 8 crops in all States: Lima beans, snap beans, carrots, sweet corn, cucumbers (pickles), green peas, spinach, and tomatoes. Production of other vegetables processed included in fresh market series of estimates. [4] Production for fresh market excludes some quantities not marketed because of low prices or other economic factors. [5] Value for all fresh market vegetables. For processing vegetables, value at processing plant door.
NASS, Crops Branch, (202) 720–2127.

Table 4-2.—Vegetables, commercial: Area of principal crops, by State and United States, 2012–2014[1]

State	Fresh market[2]			Processing[3]		
	2012	2013	2014	2012	2013	2014
	Acres	Acres	Acres	Acres	Acres	Acres
Alabama	5,400	5,100	5,000	....	....	....
Arizona	108,600	105,900	110,000	....	....	....
Arkansas	2,800	2,600	2,500	....	....	....
California	753,300	766,500	741,400	278,460	279,500	308,460
Colorado	17,000	13,400	12,100	....	....	....
Connecticut	3,900	3,600	4,000	....	....	....
Delaware	5,900	6,100	6,000	29,230	26,150	27,800
Florida	157,600	161,600	150,200	....	....	....
Georgia	83,500	87,900	86,300	2,600	3,600	1,900
Idaho	8,500	9,000	6,900	....	....	....
Illinois	25,900	25,000	25,900	32,600	29,200	30,100
Indiana	14,100	15,300	15,520	....	....	....
Maine	1,700	1,500	1,600	....	....	....
Maryland	9,410	9,040	9,180	12,860	10,440	12,990
Massachusetts ..	5,000	4,700	4,300	....	....	....
Michigan	51,900	49,400	48,500	....	....	....
Minnesota	....	....	....	210,510	183,710	178,030
Mississippi	2,300	2,000	2,100	....	....	....
Missouri	2,400	3,000	2,700	1,000	....	(5)
Nevada	3,720	4,050	4,150	....	....	....
New Hampshire .	1,500	1,400	1,400	....	....	....
New Jersey	24,300	23,000	22,900	3,850	4,100	4,200
New Mexico	15,000	14,700	12,800	....	....	....
New York	61,970	63,430	58,470	37,200	30,050	39,320
North Carolina ..	31,400	28,700	30,500	....	....	....
Ohio	23,450	30,640	30,800	12,800	12,100	10,900
Oklahoma	2,900	2,200	2,600	....	....	....
Oregon	27,430	27,550	26,250	54,300	56,650	53,000
Pennsylvania	22,100	22,280	21,860	....	....	....
Rhode Island	850	650	690	....	....	....
South Carolina ..	15,700	15,000	15,500	....	....	....
Tennessee	12,200	8,500	10,130	....	....	....
Texas	58,520	54,850	52,230	8,600	8,800	8,500
Utah	1,500	1,400	1,400	....	....	....
Vermont	1,000	830	910	....	....	....
Virginia	9,560	8,490	8,370	605	(5)	(5)
Washington	45,000	39,600	39,700	132,340	117,090	115,900
Wisconsin	9,200	9,100	8,100	195,600	175,600	177,700
Other States[6] ...	....	....	....	123,050	116,170	121,120
United States	1,626,510	1,628,010	1,582,960	1,135,605	1,053,160	1,089,920

[1] Area for fresh market and for processing is area harvested.   [2] Area of the following crops for which regular seasonal estimates are prepared in major producing States: Artichokes, asparagus, snap beans, broccoli, cabbage, cantaloups, carrots, cauliflower, celery, sweet corn, cucumbers, garlic, honeydew melons, head lettuce, leaf lettuce, romaine lettuce, onions, bell peppers, Chile pepper, spinach, tomatoes, and watermelons.   [3] Includes Lima beans, snap beans, carrots, sweet corn, cucumbers (pickles), green peas, spinach, and tomatoes. Other vegetables processed (dual purpose) included in fresh market series of estimates.   [4] Preliminary.   [5] Withheld to avoid disclosing data for individual operations.   [6] Other States include Alabama, Arkansas, Florida, Iowa, Idaho, Indiana, Massachusetts, Michigan, North Carolina, Pennsylvania, and South Carolina.

NASS, Crops Branch, (202) 720–2127.

Table 4-3.—Vegetables, commercial: Production of principal crops, by State and United States, 2012–2014

State	Fresh market [1]			Processing [2]		
	2012	2013	2014	2012	2013	2014
	1,000 cwt	*1,000 cwt*	*1,000 cwt*	*Tons*	*Tons*	*Tons*
Alabama	835	746	957			
Arizona	31,941	29,829	31,816			
Arkansas	708	486	473			
California	218,418	214,296	214,168	12,782,880	12,258,850	14,150,110
Colorado	5,793	5,234	4,601			
Connecticut	254	234	260			
Delaware	1,382	1,218	1,190	107,600	88,490	104,400
Florida	33,238	31,727	29,317			
Georgia	17,575	18,780	16,222	15,430	16,020	9,790
Idaho	6,205	7,380	5,658			
Illinois	6,059	5,927	8,227	147,525	103,430	148,420
Indiana	3,178	3,377	3,952			
Maine	102	83	112			
Maryland	1,448	1,379	1,484	56,210	49,500	55,620
Massachusetts	325	291	284			
Michigan	8,479	8,015	8,153			
Minnesota				1,038,610	915,250	858,650
Mississippi	403	400	378			
Missouri	960	843	837	1,500		(3)
Nevada	2,706	2,161	1,364			
New Hampshire	90	97	91			
New Jersey	4,536	3,863	3,977	20,400	19,220	19,490
New Mexico	4,418	3,923	4,234			
New York	11,905	11,585	10,097	168,620	129,650	175,150
North Carolina	6,575	5,604	4,284			
Ohio	4,003	4,403	4,599	187,890	205,500	194,950
Oklahoma	348	242	364			
Oregon	14,248	14,922	15,359	384,910	332,070	299,650
Pennsylvania	2,528	2,436	2,612			
Rhode Island	64	36	46			
South Carolina	4,537	4,103	3,547			
Tennessee	1,188	1,397	1,677			
Texas	12,344	13,119	11,337	77,290	75,540	75,270
Utah	810	763	742			
Vermont	50	46	46			
Virginia	1,874	1,440	1,315	2,270	(3)	(3)
Washington	18,810	15,524	17,479	1,088,870	900,650	904,550
Wisconsin	1,651	2,102	1,908	1,126,470	1,117,870	1,068,500
Other States [4]				1,0019,300	956,540	1,128,940
United States	429,988	418,011	413,167	18,225,775	17,168,580	19,193,490

[1] Production of the following crops for which regular seasonal estimates are prepared in major producing States: Artichokes, asparagus, snap beans, broccoli, cabbage, cantaloups, carrots, cauliflower, celery, sweet corn, cucumbers, garlic, honeydew melons, head lettuce, leaf lettuce, romaine lettuce, onions, bell peppers, Chile peppers, spinach, squash, tomatoes, and watermelons.　[2] Includes Lima beans, snap beans, carrots, sweet corn, cucumbers (pickles), green peas, spinach, and tomatoes. Other vegetables processed (dual purpose) included in fresh market series of estimates.　[3] Withheld to avoid disclosing data for individual operations.　[4] Other States include Alabama, Arkansas, Florida, Iowa, Idaho, Indiana, Massachusetts, Michigan, North Carolina, Pennsylvania, and South Carolina.

NASS, Crops Branch, (202) 720–2127.

Table 4-4.—Vegetables, commercial: Value of principal crops, by State and United States, 2012–2014

State	Fresh market [1]			Processing [2]		
	2012	2013	2014	2012	2013	2014
	1,000 dollars	*1,000 dollars*	*1,000 dollars*	*1,000 dollars*	*1,000 dollars*	*1,000 dollars*
Alabama	19,139	15,998	20,111			
Arizona	696,666	1,071,047	685,608			
Arkansas	24,966	11,232	13,646			
California	5,132,243	6,188,036	6,491,170	1,015,298	1,134,826	1,306,796
Colorado	96,206	100,126	67,591			
Connecticut	11,176	9,126	9,620			
Delaware	22,946	19,218	19,754	29,428	21,562	29,255
Florida	959,976	1,253,028	1,044,635			
Georgia	432,828	460,639	403,857	5,714	5,200	3,771
Idaho	52,050	71,478	44,083			
Illinois	50,179	59,810	64,205	33,500	25,441	22,608
Indiana	54,665	68,366	53,230			
Maine	5,202	4,233	5,040			
Maryland	27,839	23,992	26,323	12,772	9,739	12,764
Massachusetts	16,250	15,132	14,200			
Michigan	189,042	187,289	173,562			
Minnesota				194,863	183,765	134,945
Mississippi	4,675	4,200	4,423			
Missouri	9,888	8,683	7,868	360	(3)	(3)
Nevada	86,442	69,213	45,012			
New Hampshire	5,580	5,723	5,005			
New Jersey	137,961	124,187	132,080	5,339	4,526	4,765
New Mexico	121,505	90,397	95,917			
New York	397,744	344,310	289,250	56,682	32,070	53,502
North Carolina	142,014	140,146	112,377			
Ohio	100,819	139,070	127,182	27,709	34,811	29,379
Oklahoma	5,185	3,328	4,295			
Oregon	140,321	160,064	129,180	65,959	54,157	53,692
Pennsylvania	76,408	74,462	80,583			
Rhode Island	3,520	2,160	2,438			
South Carolina	85,925	73,396	78,887			
Tennessee	41,220	53,758	76,184			
Texas	228,459	241,054	213,212	10,360	14,749	16,306
Utah	9,132	8,373	7,835			
Vermont	2,600	2,760	3,128			
Virginia	54,235	53,774	45,118	660	(3)	(3)
Washington	324,600	291,188	259,064	144,066	132,317	115,646
Wisconsin	27,522	39,265	33,403	196,009	255,146	157,920
Other States [4]				203,762	184,007	230,258
United States	9,797,128	11,488,261	10,889,076	2,002,481	2,092,316	2,171,607

[1] Value of the following crops for which regular seasonal estimates are prepared in major producing States: Artichokes, asparagus, snap beans, broccoli, cabbage, cantaloups, carrots, cauliflower, celery, sweet corn, cucumbers, garlic, honeydew melons, head lettuce, leaf lettuce, romaine lettuce, onions, bell peppers, Chile peppers, spinach, tomatoes, and watermelons.   [2] Includes Lima beans, snap beans, carrots, sweet corn, cucumbers (pickles), green peas, spinach, and tomatoes. Other vegetables processed (dual purpose) included in fresh market series of estimates.   [3] Withheld to avoid disclosing data for individual operations.   [4] Other States include Alabama, Arkansas, Florida, Iowa, Idaho, Indiana, Massachusetts, Michigan, North Carolina, Pennsylvania, and South Carolina.
  NASS, Crops Branch, (202) 720–2127.

Table 4-5.— Artichokes for fresh market and processing, commercial crop: Area, yield, production, value, and total value, United States, 2005-2014

Year	Area harvested	Yield per acre	Production	Value Per cwt	Value Total
	Acres	Cwt	1,000 cwt	Dollars	1,000 dollars
2005	7,900	110	869	45.40	39,453
2006	8,700	135	1,175	42.00	49,350
2007	9,600	110	1,056	55.00	58,080
2008	8,800	130	1,144	47.80	54,683
2009	8,600	125	1,075	56.20	60,415
2010	7,200	120	864	50.20	43,373
2011	7,400	135	999	51.10	51,049
2012	7,300	145	1,059	54.30	57,504
2013	7,100	135	959	61.00	58,499
2014	7,300	130	949	58.50	55,517

NASS, Crops Branch, (202) 720–2127.

Table 4-6.—Artichokes for fresh market and processing: Area, production, and value per hundredweight, California, 2012–2014

Crop	Area harvested 2012	Area harvested 2013	Area harvested 2014	Production 2012	Production 2013	Production 2014	Value per unit 2012	Value per unit 2013	Value per unit 2014
	Acres	Acres	Acres	1,000 cwt	1,000 cwt	1,000 cwt	Dollars per cwt	Dollars per cwt	Dollars per cwt
California	7,300	7,100	7,300	1,059	959	949	54.30	61.00	58.50

NASS, Crops Branch, (202) 720–2127.

Table 4-7.—Asparagus for Fresh Market and Processing, commercial crop: Area, production, and value per hundredweight and per ton, by State and United States, 2012–2014

State	Area harvested [1] 2012	Area harvested [1] 2013	Area harvested [1] 2014	Production 2012	Production 2013	Production 2014	Value per unit 2012	Value per unit 2013	Value per unit 2014
	Acres	Acres	Acres	1,000 cwt	1,000 cwt	1,000 cwt	Dollars per cwt	Dollars per cwt	Dollars per cwt
CA [2]	11,500	11,500	11,000	368	368	341	131.00	152.00	115.00
MI	9,100	9,000	9,000	191	206	220	90.40	90.50	93.20
WA	4,700	4,000	3,800	202	188	182	90.00	95.10	75.40
US	25,300	24,500	23,800	761	762	743	110.00	121.00	98.80

State	Fresh market Production 2012	Fresh market Production 2013	Fresh market Production 2014	Fresh market Value per unit 2012	Fresh market Value per unit 2013	Fresh market Value per unit 2014	Processing Production 2012	Processing Production 2013	Processing Production 2014	Processing Value per unit 2012	Processing Value per unit 2013	Processing Value per unit 2014
	1,000 cwt	1,000 cwt	1,000 cwt	Dollars per cwt	Dollars per cwt	Dollars per cwt	Tons	Tons	Tons	Dollars per ton	Dollars per ton	Dollars per ton
CA [2]	368	368	341	131.00	152.00	115.00	....	....	....	....	....	....
Oth Sts [3] ..	252	252	227	96.80	101.00	92.00	7,050	7,100	8,720	1,570.00	1,570.00	1,530.00
US	620	620	568	117.00	131.00	106.00	7,050	7,100	8,750	1,570.00	1,570.00	1,530.00

[1] Asparagus for fresh market and for processing is frequently harvested from the same area; therefore it is not practical to make individual area estimates for these segments. [2] Includes a small amount of processing asparagus. [3] Other States include MI and WA.

NASS, Crops Branch, (202) 720–2127.

Table 4-8.—Asparagus, commercial crop: Area, yield, production, value per hundredweight and per ton, and total value, United States, 2005-2014

Year	Total crop					Fresh market			Processing		
	Area for harvest	Yield per acre	Produc- tion	Value[1]		Produc- tion	Value[1]		Produc- tion	Value[2]	
				Per cwt	Total		Per cwt	Total		Per ton	Total
	Acres	Cwt	1,000 cwt	Dollars	1,000 dollars	1,000 cwt	Dollars	1,000 dollars	Tons	Dollars	1,000 dollars
2005 ...	49,300	31	1,534	78.50	120,436	1,144	87.40	99,988	19,500	1,050.00	20,448
2006 ...	43,200	27	1,153	82.30	94,901	911	88.90	81,027	12,100	1,150.00	13,874
2007 ...	38,600	29	1,125	92.50	104,074	927	98.90	91,642	9,900	1,260.00	12,432
2008 ...	32,200	30	952	94.00	89,451	718	103.00	73,599	11,700	1,360.00	15,852
2009 ...	29,200	31	899	98.80	88,855	703	108.00	75,827	9,800	1,330.00	13,028
2010 ...	28,000	29	799	114.00	90,777	679	122.00	82,597	6,000	1,360.00	8,180
2011 ...	26,800	31	820	112.00	91,896	650	122.00	79,047	8,500	1,510.00	12,849
2012 ...	25,300	30	761	110.00	83,662	620	117.00	72,592	7,050	1,570.00	11,070
2013 ...	24,500	31	762	121.00	92,448	620	131.00	81,332	7,100	1,570.00	11,116
2014 ...	23,800	31	743	98.800	73,441	568	106.00	60,091	8,750	1,530.00	13,350

[1] Price and value at point of first sale. [2] Price and value at processing plant door.
NASS, Crops Branch, (202) 720–2127.

Table 4-9.—Lima beans for processing, commercial crop: Area, yield, production, value per ton, and total value, United States, 2005-2014

Year	Area harvested	Yield per acre	Production	Value[1]	
				Per ton	Total
	Acres	Tons	Tons	Dollars	1,000 dollars
2005	28,820	1.47	42,440	421.00	17,854
2006	43,050	1.31	56,330	398.00	22,444
2007	39,330	1.35	53,100	423.00	22,450
2008	38,270	1.28	49,150	500.00	24,584
2009	34,740	1.38	48,030	519.00	24,945
2010	42,430	1.47	62,230	473.00	29,456
2011	30,960	1.42	45,780	525.00	23,700
2012	32,900	1.85	61,015	524.00	31,950
2013	28,930	1.68	48,620	582.00	28,312
2014	27,760	1.82	50,400	580.00	29,236

[1] Price and value at processing plant door.
NASS, Crops Branch, (202) 720–2127.

Table 4-10.—Lima beans for processing: Area, production, and value per ton, United States, 2012–2014

State	Area harvested			Production			Value per unit		
	2012	2013	2014	2012	2013	2014	2012	2013	2014
	Acres	Acres	Acres	Tons	Tons	Tons	Dollars per ton	Dollars per ton	Dollars per ton
United States ...	32,900	28,930	27,760	61,015	48,620	50,400	524.00	582.00	580.00

NASS, Crops Branch, (202) 720–2127.

Table 4-11.—Snap beans for fresh market, commercial crop: Area, yield, production, value hundredweight, and total value, United States, 2005-2014

Year	Area harvested	Yield per acre	Production	Value[1]	
				Per cwt	Total
	Acres	Cwt	1,000 cwt	Dollars	1,000 dollars
2005	97,300	57	5,511	54.10	298,272
2006	93,900	66	6,213	50.00	310,420
2007	96,400	67	6,502	61.20	397,611
2008	90,600	65	5,849	53.30	312,010
2009	88,300	55	4,823	53.50	257,990
2010	85,800	56	4,770	60.40	287,885
2011	83,500	55	4,591	59.50	273,201
2012	76,700	57	4,340	62.70	271,922
2013	73,100	58	4,252	68.90	293,073
2014	67,700	54	3,684	60.40	222,645

[1] Price and value at point of first sale.
NASS, Crops Branch, (202) 720–2127.

Table 4-12.—Snap beans for fresh market: Area, production, and value per hundredweight, by State and United States, 2012–2014

State	Area harvested			Production			Value per unit		
	2012	2013	2014	2012	2013	2014	2012	2013	2014
	Acres	*Acres*	*Acres*	*1,000 cwt*	*1,000 cwt*	*1,000 cwt*	*Dollars per cwt*	*Dollars per cwt*	*Dollars per cwt*
California	5,700	5,700	4,200	599	570	462	64.60	63.20	78.10
Florida	29,900	28,800	26,600	1,704	1,728	1,330	68.60	80.00	58.20
Georgia	9,600	11,200	8,900	576	616	356	31.90	42.60	39.10
Maryland	1,200	1,100	1,000	66	63	58	46.00	34.00	39.00
Michigan	2,600	2,600	2,600	122	125	182	55.00	57.00	44.90
New Jersey	2,700	2,500	2,600	84	80	86	44.20	50.80	38.20
New York	10,500	10,200	9,800	683	561	617	97.00	89.80	84.50
North Carolina	4,300	4,100	4,300	172	160	172	34.00	67.00	38.00
South Carolina	600	600	600	31	30	35	55.00	78.00	48.70
Tennessee	7,700	4,500	5,400	200	243	308	37.00	50.00	58.00
Virginia	1,900	1,800	1,700	103	76	78	32.00	48.00	42.00
United States	76,700	73,100	67,700	4,340	4,252	3,684	62.70	68.90	60.40

NASS, Crops Branch, (202) 720–2127.

Table 4-13.—Snap beans for processing, commercial crop: Area, yield, production, value per ton, and total value, United States, 2005-2014

Year	Area harvested	Yield per acre	Production	Value [1]	
				Per ton	Total
	Acres	*Tons*	*Tons*	*Dollars*	*1,000 dollars*
2005	204,620	4.00	819,250	140.00	114,648
2006	203,240	3.87	785,950	157.00	123,218
2007	198,770	3.79	753,730	168.00	126,620
2008	196,600	4.08	802,060	219.00	175,697
2009	196,179	4.16	816,440	191.00	156,092
2010	191,660	3.98	762,080	192.00	146,477
2011	158,550	4.20	665,870	235.00	156,563
2012	166,355	4.39	730,680	271.00	197,811
2013	149,770	4.45	666,780	320.00	213,250
2014	159,070	4.28	681,240	250.00	170,066

[1] Price and value at processing plant door.
NASS, Crops Branch, (202) 720–2127.

Table 4-14.—Snap beans for processing, commercial crop: Area, production, and value per ton, by State and United States, 2012–2014

State	Area harvested			Production			Value per unit		
	2012	2013	2014	2012	2013	2014	2012	2013	2014
	Acres	*Acres*	*Acres*	*Tons*	*Tons*	*Tons*	*Dollars per ton*	*Dollars per ton*	*Dollars per ton*
Illinois	7,500	(1)	(1)	34,380	(1)	(1)	232.00	(1)	(1)
Indiana	5,000	5,000	4,700	15,750	14,520	14,100	230.00	247.00	210.00
Michigan	17,800	17,800	(1)	71,200	77,100	(1)	235.00	240.00	(1)
Minnesota	5,700	(1)	(1)	23,910	(1)	(1)	308.00	(1)	(1)
New York	19,000	18,900	20,420	62,540	62,270	81,680	300.00	264.00	338.00
Oregon	13,400	10,550	8,500	91,200	66,850	34,850	223.00	204.00	400.00
Pennsylvania	9,800	7,900	11,400	33,270	21,630	34,310	295.00	284.00	303.00
Wisconsin	70,700	59,800	64,100	317,980	298,570	312,280	242.00	340.00	185.00
Other States [2]	17,455	29,820	49,950	80,450	125,840	204,020	451.00	425.00	282.00
United States	166,355	149,770	159,070	730,680	666,780	681,240	271.00	320.00	250.00

[1] Withheld to avoid disclosing data for individual operations. [2] Includes data withheld above and/or data for States not listed in this table.
NASS, Crops Branch, (202) 720–2127.

Table 4-15.—Broccoli, commercial crop: Area, yield, production, value per hundredweight and per ton, and total value, United States, 2005-2014 [1]

Year	Total crop					Fresh market			Processing		
	Area for harvest	Yield per acre	Produc-tion	Value [2]		Produc-tion	Value [2]		Produc-tion	Value [3]	
				Per cwt	Total		Per cwt	Total		Per ton	Total
	Acres	Cwt	1,000 cwt	Dollars	1,000 dollars	1,000 cwt	Dollars	1,000 dollars	Tons	Dollars	1,000 dollars
2005 ...	127,900	148	18,890	28.50	539,253	[4]	[4]	[4]	[4]	[4]	[4]
2006 ...	130,900	145	19,040	33.30	634,394	18,538	33.70	624,827	25,110	381.00	9,567
2007 ...	129,900	148	19,188	36.20	694,922	18,287	36.70	671,681	45,040	516.00	23,241
2008 ...	126,900	158	20,086	35.90	721,307	19,412	36.20	701,884	33,720	576.00	19,423
2009 ...	126,000	158	19,890	39.90	794,124	19,410	39.80	773,124	24,000	875.00	21,000
2010 ...	130,200	148	19,289	37.70	727,463	18,879	37.60	709,833	20,500	860.00	17,630
2011 ...	123,200	147	18,149	35.20	639,120	17,756	35.40	628,792	19,673	525.00	10,328
2012 ...	126,400	162	20,472	33.60	687,727	20,076	33.80	678,619	19,800	460.00	9,108
2013 ...	131,500	162	21,360	42.80	913,520	20,664	43.20	893,336	34,800	580.00	20,184
2014 ...	128,400	163	20,930	40.00	836,481	20,240	40.60	821,128	34,500	445.00	15,353

[1] Sprouting broccoli only. Does not include broccoli rabe nor heading (cauliflower) broccoli. [2] Price and value at point of first sale. [3] Price and value at processing plant door. [4] Not published to avoid disclosure of individual operations. NASS, Crops Branch, (202) 720–2127.

Table 4-16.—Broccoli, commercial crop: Area, production, and value per hundredweight, and per ton, by State and United States, 2012–2014 [1]

State	Area harvested			Production			Value per unit		
	2012	2013	2014	2012	2013	2014	2012	2013	2014
	Acres	Acres	Acres	1,000 cwt	1,000 cwt	1,000 cwt	Dollars per cwt	Dollars per cwt	Dollars per cwt
Arizona	7,400	7,500	6,400	1,036	900	800	41.20	57.10	37.40
California	119,000	124,000	122,000	19,436	20,460	20,130	33.20	42.10	40.10
United States ...	126,400	131,500	128,400	20,472	21,360	20,930	33.60	42.80	40.00

State	Fresh market						Processing					
	Production			Value per unit			Production			Value per unit		
	2012	2013	2014	2012	2013	2014	2012	2013	2014	2012	2013	2014
	1,000 cwt	1,000 cwt	1,000 cwt	Dollars per cwt	Dollars per cwt	Dollars per cwt	Tons	Tons	Tons	Dollars per ton	Dollars per ton	Dollars per ton
Arizona	1,036	900	800	41.20	57.10	37.40	....	....	....	....	....	....
California	19,040	19,764	19,440	33.40	42.60	40.70	19,800	34,800	34,500	460.00	580.00	445.00
United States ...	20,076	20,664	20,240	33.80	43.20	40.60	19,800	34,800	34,500	460.00	580.00	445.00

[1] Sprouting broccoli only. Does not include broccoli rabe nor heading (cauliflower) broccoli. NASS, Crops Branch, (202) 720–2127.

Table 4-17.—Cabbage for fresh market, commercial crop: Area, yield, production, value and total value, United States, 2005-2014

Year	Area harvested	Yield per acre	Production	Value	
				Per cwt	Total
	Acres	Cwt	1,000 cwt	Dollars	1,000 dollars
2005	71,700	324	23,234	13.70	311,001
2006	69,250	338	23,411	14.10	324,365
2007	69,050	346	23,886	16.40	386,373
2008	65,460	373	24,396	14.70	353,793
2009	63,000	345	21,761	15.60	333,537
2010	66,260	350	23,210	17.40	397,314
2011	58,760	343	20,134	17.60	347,381
2012	56,800	348	19,752	18.50	359,094
2013	59,480	366	21,750	20.10	429,419
2014	62,550	357	22,359	20.40	455,098

NASS, Crops Branch, (202) 720–2127.

Table 4-18.—Cabbage for fresh market: Area, production, and value per hundredweight, by State and United States, 2012–2014

State	Area harvested			Production			Value per unit		
	2012	2013	2014	2012	2013	2014[1]	2012	2013	2014
	Acres	Acres	Acres	1,000 cwt	1,000 cwt	1,000 cwt	Dollars per cwt	Dollars per cwt	Dollars per cwt
Arizona	2,800	2,800	3,700	1,302	1,316	1,906	17.40	29.00	21.70
California	12,500	14,000	16,400	4,750	5,670	6,888	17.10	21.70	25.80
Colorado	1,600	1,200	(2)	720	564	(2)	14.70	16.40	(2)
Florida	9,200	8,300	8,800	3,128	2,739	2,992	16.30	22.70	16.70
Georgia	3,500	5,100	4,700	1,050	1,734	1,598	23.50	15.00	12.00
Michigan	2,800	3,000	3,100	700	690	837	17.00	16.00	16.00
New Jersey	1,500	1,500	1,500	720	570	533	14.60	17.00	17.80
New York	8,800	8,800	8,300	3,696	3,960	3,320	25.30	19.70	21.80
North Carolina	3,400	2,900	2,800	918	783	644	12.30	19.00	15.00
Ohio	900	1,300	1,400	332	436	490	14.90	16.00	13.00
Pennsylvania	1,000	980	960	176	234	212	28.30	16.40	19.80
Texas	6,000	6,100	6,200	1,560	2,074	1,550	19.50	17.90	21.50
Virginia	500	400	(2)	125	112	(2)	12.50	14.00	(2)
Wisconsin	2,300	3,100	2,900	575	868	725	15.00	16.40	14.20
Other States	....	....	1,790	....	....	664	....	....	11.70
United States	56,800	59,480	62,550	19,752	21,750	22,359	18.50	20.10	20.10

[1] Includes some quantities of fall storage in New York harvested but not sold because of shrinkage and loss: 2012, 347,000 cwt; 2013, 334,000 cwt; and 2014.   [2] Not published to avoid disclosure of individual operations.
NASS, Crops Branch, (202) 720–2127.

Table 4-19.—Cantaloups for fresh market, commercial crop: Area, yield, production, value, and total value, United States, 2005-2014

Year	Area harvested	Yield per acre	Production	Value	
				Per cwt	Total
	Acres	Cwt	1,000 cwt	Dollars	1,000 dollars
2005	84,560	242	20,465	15.90	326,201
2006	79,300	246	19,498	17.20	335,526
2007	73,820	277	20,426	14.80	302,485
2008	71,730	269	19,294	18.50	356,781
2009	73,930	258	19,059	18.10	344,122
2010	73,330	256	18,808	16.20	304,896
2011	70,400	266	18,692	18.40	344,832
2012	63,430	263	16,706	19.10	319,348
2013	68,600	265	18,173	17.60	320,029
2014	63,200	236	14,912	22.00	327,934

NASS, Crops Branch, (202) 720–2127.

Table 4-20.—Cantaloups for fresh market: Area, production, and value per hundredweight, by State and United States, 2012–2014

State	Area harvested			Production			Value per unit		
	2012	2013	2014	2012	2013	2014	2012	2013	2014
	Acres	Acres	Acres	1,000 cwt	1,000 cwt	1,000 cwt	Dollars per cwt	Dollars per cwt	Dollars per cwt
Arizona	15,800	15,800	16,000	3,555	3,634	3,840	21.10	20.00	24.30
California	36,000	42,500	36,000	10,800	12,750	9,360	17.20	16.00	21.00
Colorado	600	600	400	150	120	82	32.30	40.00	37.90
Georgia	2,800	2,600	3,300	728	390	396	23.00	20.50	15.00
Indiana	2,100	2,000	1,800	462	460	396	22.70	25.00	15.10
Maryland	630	600	600	54	43	77	29.00	27.00	27.00
Pennsylvania	1,100	1,200	1,200	130	184	144	28.40	25.20	28.10
South Carolina	1,700	1,400	1,600	476	364	352	20.00	17.00	24.70
Texas	2,700	1,900	2,300	351	228	265	33.40	31.00	31.00
United States	63,430	68,600	63,200	16,706	18,173	14,912	19.10	17.60	22.00

NASS, Crops Branch, (202) 720–2127.

Table 4-21.—Carrots for fresh market, commercial crop: Area, production, and value per hundredweight, by State and United States, 2012-2014

State	Area harvested			Production			Value per unit		
	2012	2013	2014	2012	2013	2014	2012	2013	2014
	Acres	Acres	Acres	1,000 cwt	1,000 cwt	1,000 cwt	Dollars per cwt	Dollars per cwt	Dollars per cwt
California	61,500	62,500	65,500	19,065	20,000	20,960	26.90	29.60	27.40
Michigan	1,500	1,500	1,600	420	435	496	16.60	16.60	15.50
Texas	1,300	1,600	1,400	325	336	378	26.00	22.00	20.00
Other States [1]	6,700	5,800	5,700	3,817	3,484	3,545	26.10	24.70	23.20
United States	71,000	71,400	74,200	23,627	24,255	25,379	26.60	28.60	26.50

[1] Other States include Colorado, Georgia, and Washington.
NASS, Crops Branch, (202) 720-2127.

Table 4-22.—Carrots for processing, commercial crop: Area, production, and value per ton, by State and United States, 2012-2014

State	Area harvested			Production			Value per unit		
	2012	2013	2014	2012	2013	2014	2012	2013	2014
	Acres	Acres	Acres	Tons	Tons	Tons	Dollars per tons	Dollars per tons	Dollars per tons
Washington	3,100	4,200	(1)	98,580	127,680	(1)	80.90	104.00	(1)
Wisconsin	4,200	4,100	3,700	118,900	116,850	107,100	87.10	106.00	89.30
Other States [1]	5,810	5,010	7,730	115,870	107,420	214,720	137.00	162.00	129.00
United States	13,110	13,310	11,430	333,350	351,950	321,820	103.00	122.00	116.00

[1] Includes data withheld above and/or data for States not listed in this table.
NASS, Crops Branch, (202) 720–2127.

Table 4-23.—Cauliflower, commercial crop: Area, yield, production, value per hundredweight and per ton, and total value, United States, 2005-2014 [1]

Year	Total crop					Fresh market			Processing		
	Area for harvest	Yield per acre	Produc-tion	Value [2]		Produc-tion	Value [2]		Produc-tion	Value [3]	
				Per cwt.	Total		Per cwt.	Total		Per ton	Total
	Acres	Cwt	1,000 cwt	Dollars	1,000 dollars	1,000 cwt	Dollars	1,000 dollars	Tons	Dollars	1,000 dollars
2005	41,370	174	7,214	30.40	219,411	(4)	(4)	(4)	(4)	(4)	(4)
2006	39,350	176	6,965	31.40	219,008	6,678	32.30	215,607	14,350	237.00	3,401
2007	37,820	181	6,828	34.20	233,413	6,616	34.40	227,689	10,600	540.00	5,724
2008	36,700	181	6,648	40.40	268,531	6,485	40.70	263,912	8,160	566.00	4,619
2009	38,600	186	7,167	44.00	315,551	7,000	44.30	310,290	8,350	630.00	5,261
2010	38,460	184	7,087	41.70	295,186	6,972	41.80	291,647	5,755	615.00	3,539
2011	36,430	183	6,649	46.00	305,539	6,399	46.80	299,164	12,500	510.00	6,375
2012	36,070	185	6,690	35.80	239,203	6,542	35.90	235,059	7,400	560.00	4,144
2013	36,830	181	6,662	44.30	295,450	6,572	44.50	292,615	4,500	630.00	2,835
2014	37,970	186	7,053	49.80	351,191	6,978	50.00	348,903	3,750	610.00	2,288

[1] Includes heading (cauliflower) broccoli.   [2] Price and value at point of first sale.   [3] Price and value at processing plant door.   [4] Not published to avoid disclosure of individual operations.
NASS, Crops Branch, (202) 720–2127.

Table 4-24.—Cauliflower, commercial crop: Area, production, and value per hundredweight and per ton, by State and United States, 2012–2014[1]

State	Area harvested			Production			Value per unit		
	2012	2013	2014	2012	2013	2014	2012	2013	2014
	Acres	*Acres*	*Acres*	*1,000 cwt*	*1,000 cwt*	*1,000 cwt*	*Dollars per cwt*	*Dollars per cwt*	*Dollars per cwt*
Arizona	3,600	3,800	3,600	864	741	720	46.90	56.10	54.90
California	32,000	32,600	33,900	5,760	5,868	6,272	33.70	42.70	49.30
New York	470	430	470	66	53	61	65.00	59.80	43.00
United States	36,070	36,830	37,970	6,690	6,662	7,053	35.80	44.30	49.80

State	Fresh market						Processing					
	Production			Value per unit			Production			Value per unit		
	2012	2013	2014	2012	2013	2014	2012	2013	2014	2012	2013	2014
	1,000 cwt	*1,000 cwt*	*1,000 cwt*	*Dollars per cwt*	*Dollars per cwt*	*Dollars per cwt*	*Tons*	*Tons*	*Tons*	*Dollars per ton*	*Dollars per ton*	*Dollars per ton*
Arizona	864	741	720	46.90	56.10	54.90	....	....	....	....	....	....
California	5,612	5,778	6,197	33.90	42.90	49.50	7,400	4,500	3,750	560.00	630.00	610.00
New York	66	53	61	65.00	59.80	43.00	....	....	....	....	....	....
United States	6,542	6,572	6,978	35.90	44.50	50.00	7,400	4,500	3,750	560.00	630.00	610.00

[1] Includes heading (cauliflower) broccoli.
NASS, Crops Branch, (202) 720–2127.

Table 4-25.—Celery, commercial crop: Area, production, and value per hundredweight, by State and United States, 2012–2014[1]

State	Area harvested			Production			Value per unit		
	2012	2013	2014	2012	2013	2014	2012	2013	2014
	Acres	*Acres*	*Acres*	*1,000 cwt*	*1,000 cwt*	*1,000 cwt*	*Dollars per cwt*	*Doll ars per cwt*	*Dollars per cwt*
California	27,000	27,000	27,200	18,622	16,968	17,408	18.10	25.80	16.60
Michigan	2,000	1,800	1,700	1,130	1,035	985	19.80	19.70	19.10
United States	29,000	28,800	28,900	19,752	18,003	18,393	18.20	25.40	16.70

[1] Mostly for fresh market use, but includes some quantities used for processing.
NASS, Crops Branch, (202) 720–2127.

Table 4-26.—Celery, commercial crop: Area, yield, production, value per hundredweight, and total value, United States, 2005–2014[1]

Year	Area for harvest	Yield per acre	Production	Value[2]	
				Per cwt	Total
	Acres	*Cwt*	*1,000 cwt*	*Dollars*	*1,000 dollars*
2005	26,800	697	18,686	13.90	259,309
2006	27,700	694	19,230	18.20	350,454
2007	28,400	705	20,011	20.40	408,001
2008	28,300	708	20,025	18.50	369,684
2009	28,500	704	20,074	20.10	404,039
2010	28,000	712	19,923	18.60	371,153
2011	28,200	687	19,362	19.70	381,780
2012	29,000	681	19,752	18.20	358,988
2013	28,800	625	18,003	25.40	457,765
2014	28,900	636	18,393	16.70	307,276

[1] Mostly for fresh market use, but includes quantities used for processing.   [2] Price and value at point of first sale.
NASS, Crops Branch, (202) 720–2127.

Table 4-27.—Corn, sweet, commercial crop: Area, production, and value per hundredweight and per ton, by State and United States, 2012–2014

Utilization and State	Area harvested			Production			Value per unit		
	2012	2013	2014	2012	2013	2014	2012	2013	2014
Fresh market:	Acres	Acres	Acres	1,000 cwt	1,000 cwt	1,000 cwt	Dollars per cwt	Dollars per cwt	Dollars per cwt
Alabama	1,400	1,100	1,100	81	72	81	30.30	26.00	21.60
California	33,800	36,000	31,900	5,915	6,120	5,423	20.80	25.70	34.00
Colorado	4,900	4,100	4,000	735	656	680	16.60	18.70	16.20
Connecticut	3,900	3,600	4,000	254	234	260	44.00	39.00	37.00
Delaware	3,100	3,400	3,500	332	332	357	28.00	25.00	25.00
Florida	35,800	39,500	34,000	5,907	5,530	4,590	26.00	27.50	28.30
Georgia	21,700	23,000	22,400	3,689	4,025	2,912	22.80	25.60	25.50
Illinois	5,700	4,900	6,100	496	451	769	35.00	28.00	22.20
Indiana	4,800	5,300	5,300	264	350	440	33.90	42.60	29.90
Maine	1,700	1,500	1,600	102	83	112	51.00	51.00	45.00
Maryland	3,900	3,700	3,900	234	196	230	36.00	38.00	35.00
Massachusetts ..	5,000	4,700	4,300	325	291	284	50.00	52.00	50.00
Minnesota	9,100	9,000	9,200	946	900	828	25.60	26.00	24.70
New Hampshire	1,500	1,400	1,400	90	97	91	62.00	59.00	55.00
New Jersey	6,100	6,000	6,000	580	480	540	33.80	29.30	31.20
New York	18,000	22,600	18,100	1,980	2,486	1,774	30.20	31.40	23.90
North Carolina ..	5,300	4,600	4,600	636	423	308	24.00	22.50	27.00
Ohio	10,500	15,500	15,100	1,103	1,550	1,314	23.60	25.60	29.90
Oregon	4,800	3,900	4,900	653	534	720	21.10	20.00	24.00
Pennsylvania	12,100	12,000	11,300	883	852	791	38.70	31.40	36.30
Rhode Island	850	(D)	690	64	(D)	46	55.00	(D)	53.00
Texas	3,200	2,100	2,950	240	158	280	19.50	21.80	22.00
Vermont	1,000	(D)	910	50	(D)	46	52.00	(D)	68.00
Virginia	2,900	2,800	2,900	128	305	261	30.00	27.00	23.00
Washington	11,400	12,000	11,500	1,767	1,908	1,817	33.00	37.00	27.00
Wisconsin	4,900	4,200	3,500	456	424	392	25.60	29.60	25.60
Other States	(X)	1,480	(X)	(X)	82	(X)	(X)	60.00	(X)
United States	217,350	228,380	215,150	27,910	28,561	25,346	26.30	28.20	28.90
Processing:	Acres	Acres	Acres	Tons	Tons	Tons	Dollars per ton	Dollars per ton	Dollars per ton
Illinois	(D)	(D)	(D)	(D)	(D)	(D)	(D)	(D)	(D)
Minnesota	129,200	118,700	109,400	891,860	799,720	749,440	132.00	150.00	113.00
Oregon	(D)	(D)	23,200	(D)	(D)	220480	(D)	(D)	126.00
Washington	85,600	64,400	69,400	855,880	641,320	692,600	113.00	121.00	108.00
Wiscon	73,200	66,500	65,800	586,340	583,960	542,160	114.00	150.00	96.20
Other States [1] ..	72,480	65,350	44,480	625,270	526,830	363,140	152.00	137.00	138.00
United States	360,480	314,950	312,280	2,959,350	2,551,830	2,567,820	127.00	140.00	113.00

(D) Withheld to avoid disclosing data for individual operations. (X) Not applicable. [1] Includes data withheld above and/or data for States not listed in this table.
NASS, Crops Branch, (202) 720–2127.

Table 4-28.—Corn, sweet, commercial crop: Area, yield, production, value per hundredweight and per ton, and total value, United States, 2005-2014

Year	Fresh market					Processing				
	Area harvested	Yield per acre	Production	Value [1]		Area harvested	Yield per acre	Production	Value [2]	
				Per cwt	Total				Per ton	Total
	Acres	Cwt	1,000 cwt	Dollars	1,000 dollars	Acres	Tons	Tons	Dollars	1,000 dollars
2005 ...	230,600	115	26,416	22.10	582,529	403,910	7.86	3,174,800	68.40	217,111
2006 ...	218,300	118	25,745	23.00	590,859	384,700	8.02	3,085,550	66.80	205,965
2007 ...	234,000	122	28,504	22.70	646,374	367,600	7.88	2,897,430	81.80	236,908
2008 ...	230,280	124	28,501	26.00	739,650	360,600	7.85	2,832,490	120.00	340,486
2009 ...	230,950	122	28,077	29.50	827,941	379,500	8.52	3,234,080	104.00	335,519
2010 ...	235,800	118	27,875	25.90	721,980	335,200	8.04	2,694,210	85.30	229,786
2011 ...	224,050	118	26,336	26.70	702,217	331,650	8.04	2,664,820	116.00	309,622
2012 ...	217,350	128	27,910	26.30	735,104	360,480	8.21	2,959,350	127.00	376,694
2013 ...	228,380	125	28,561	28.20	806,488	314,950	8.10	2,551,830	140.00	357,804
2014 ...	215,150	118	25,346	28.90	806,488	312,280	8.22	2,567,820	113.00	289,573

[1] Price and value at point of first sale. [2] Price and value at processing plant door.
NASS, Crops Branch, (202) 720–2127.

Table 4-29.—Cucumbers for fresh market: Area, production, and value per hundredweight, by State and United States, 2012–2014

State	Area harvested			Production			Value per unit		
	2012	2013	2014	2012	2013	2014	2012	2013	2014
	Acres	*Acres*	*Acres*	*1,000 cwt*	*1,000 cwt*	*1,000 cwt*	*Dollars per cwt*	*Dollars per cwt*	*Dollars per cwt*
California	3,800	3,800	3,800	760	760	684	41.60	25.90	24.20
Florida	10,400	10,700	9,400	2,704	2,408	2,444	24.00	31.70	26.70
Georgia	5,500	6,500	6,500	1,485	1,528	1,008	22.70	28.90	23.20
Maryland	340	300	340	18	17	27	42.00	25.00	28.00
Michigan	4,500	3,500	3,400	765	665	680	23.50	21.00	20.40
New Jersey	3,400	3,200	3,100	731	576	667	21.50	22.00	22.40
New York	1,700	1,700	1,700	357	238	272	42.40	38.50	37.10
North Carolina	4,600	4,600	4,800	874	966	552	15.60	17.00	19.00
South Carolina	1,500	1,600	1,800	195	176	252	20.00	27.40	24.90
Texas	2,100	2,000	2,400	252	230	283	25.00	22.50	18.60
Virginia	460	460	330	41	39	26	20.00	27.50	44.50
United States	38,300	38,360	37,570	8,182	7,603	6,895	25.00	26.80	24.40

NASS, Crops Branch, (202) 720-2127.

Table 4-30.—Cucumbers (for pickles), commercial crop: Area, yield, production, value per ton, total value, and pickle stocks, United States, 2005-2014

Year	Processing					Pickle stocks on hand Dec. 1 [2] [3]
	Area harvested	Yield per acre	Production	Value [1]		
				Per ton	Total	
	Acres	*Tons*	*Tons*	*Dollars*	*1,000 dollars*	*Tons*
2005 ...	110,500	4.89	540,080	256.00	138,391	250,448
2006 ...	103,000	4.90	505,190	305.00	153,968	444,306
2007 ...	101,500	5.33	541,230	325.00	175,822	376,732
2008 ...	96,600	5.87	567,100	316.00	178,998	447,969
2009 ...	97,500	5.63	548,640	328.00	179,836	189,525
2010 ...	87,900	6.27	551,370	337.00	185,928	183,465
2011 ...	82,630	5.83	482,030	360.00	173,425	259,515
2012 ...	84,560	5.68	480,060	342.00	164,151	275,003
2013 ...	82,100	5.76	473,140	313.00	148,101	212,820
2014 ...	76,580	6.29	481,740	365.00	175,634	87,815

[1] Price and value at processing plant door. [2] Stocks in hands of original salters of both salt and dill pickles, sold and unsold, in tanks and barrels, on Dec. 1. [3] Includes stocks of fresh-pack pickles.
NASS, Crops Branch, (202) 720-2127.

Table 4-31.—Cucumbers (for pickles), commercial crop: Area, production, and value per ton, by State and United States, 2012–2014

State	Area harvested			Production			Value per unit		
	2012	2013	2014	2012	2013	2014	2012	2013	2014
	Acres	*Acres*	*Acres*	*Tons*	*Tons*	*Tons*	*Dollars per ton*	*Dollars per ton*	*Dollars per ton*
Florida	16,000	(D)	13,300	108,000	(D)	104,410	442.00	(D)	580.00
Indiana	1,000	1,900	2,300	2,500	5,700	11,500	360.00	350.00	320.00
Michigan	28,700	28,000	27,400	154,980	162,400	167,140	240.00	230.00	210.00
North Carolina	6,300	(D)	(D)	34,710	(D)	(D)	355.00	(D)	(D)
Ohio	7,000	7,000	6,500	31,290	52,500	40,950	320.00	325.00	300.00
South Carolina	2,000	(D)	(D)	6,000	(D)	(D)	220.00	(D)	344.00
Texas	3,300	4,000	4,200	16,500	18,800	19,570	230.00	430.00	540.00
Wisconsin	5,300	5,900	5,400	30,210	38,410	33,800	259.00	288.00	297.00
Other States [1]	14,960	35,300	17,480	95,870	195,330	104,370	449.00	371.00	416.00
United States	84,560	82,100	76,580	480,060	473,140	481,740	342.00	313.00	365.00

(D) Withheld to avoid disclosing data for individual operations. [1] Other States include Alabama, California Delaware, Georgia, and Maryland.
NASS, Crops Branch, (202) 720-2127.

Table 4-32.—Cucumbers for fresh market, commercial crop: Area, yield, production, value, and total value, United States, 2005-2014

Year	Area harvested	Yield per acre	Production	Value	
				Per cwt	Total
	Acres	Cwt	1,000 cwt	Dollars	1,000 dollars
2005	51,970	178	9,265	23.10	214,138
2006	50,740	179	9,079	25.30	229,775
2007	50,960	190	9,700	24.60	238,925
2008	46,600	189	8,830	24.80	218,779
2009	45,420	204	9,269	25.60	237,147
2010	43,410	192	8,351	22.90	190,886
2011	39,000	184	7,194	26.70	191,814
2012	38,300	214	8,182	25.00	204,464
2013	38,360	198	7,603	26.80	203,894
2014	37,570	184	6,895	24.40	168,038

NASS, Crops Branch, (202) 720–2127.

Table 4-33.—Garlic for fresh market and processing, commercial crop: Area, yield, production, value, and total value, United States, 2005-2014

Year	Area harvested	Yield per acre	Production	Value	
				Per cwt	Total
	Acres	Cwt	1,000 cwt	Dollars	1,000 dollars
2005	29,900	160	4,771	43.60	208,018
2006	26,120	165	4,312	29.50	127,067
2007	24,810	165	4,104	41.20	169,218
2008	25,440	168	4,282	43.60	186,807
2009	22,230	174	3,878	49.70	192,872
2010	22,850	164	3,752	71.10	266,884
2011	25,150	167	4,204	68.20	286,820
2012	25,950	166	4,319	52.60	227,090
2013	23,900	162	3,867	60.00	231,977
2014	23,800	163	3,868	67.00	258,981

NASS, Crops Branch, (202) 720–2127.

Table 4-34.—Garlic for fresh market and processing: Area, production, and value per hundredweight, by State and United States, 2012–2014

State	Area harvested			Production			Value per unit		
	2012	2013	2014	2012	2013	2014	2012	2013	2014
	Acres	Acres	Acres	1,000 cwt	1,000 cwt	1,000 cwt	Dollars per cwt	Dollars per cwt	Dollars per cwt
California	25,000	23,000	23,000	4,250	3,795	3,795	52.10	60.30	67.40
Nevada	520	550	550	50	61	61	29.00	33.00	33.00
Oregon	430	350	250	19	11	12	229.00	100.00	90.00
United States	25,950	23,900	23,800	4,319	3,867	3,868	52.60	60.00	67.00

NASS, Crops Branch, (202) 720–2127.

Table 4-35.—Honeydew melons, commercial crop: Area, yield, production, value per hundredweight, and total value, United States, 2005–2014

Year	Area harvested	Yield per acre	Production	Value [1]	
				Per cwt	Total
	Acres	Cwt	1,000 cwt	Dollars	1,000 dollars
2005	19,600	216	4,243	19.00	80,418
2006	18,300	231	4,221	18.20	76,943
2007	17,550	236	4,144	17.70	73,517
2008	17,200	215	3,690	17.80	65,636
2009	15,100	242	3,657	15.60	57,093
2010	16,850	220	3,704	15.50	57,418
2011	15,400	236	3,628	22.10	80,008
2012	13,600	242	3,286	20.70	67,973
2013	14,450	249	3,605	20.90	75,389
2014	14,450	259	3,739	23.70	88,649

[1] Price and value at point of first sale.
NASS, Crops Branch, (202) 720–2127.

Table 4-36.—Honeydew melons, commercial crop: Area, production, and value per hundredweight, by State and United States, 2012–2014

State	Area harvested			Production			Value per unit		
	2012	2013	2014	2012	2013	2014	2012	2013	2014
	Acres	Acres	Acres	1,000 cwt	1,000 cwt	1,000 cwt	Dollars per cwt	Dollars per cwt	Dollars per cwt
Arizona	3,200	3,300	3,500	720	693	805	23.10	21.70	32.60
California	9,400	10,500	10,500	2,256	2,730	2,835	18.80	20.20	21.00
Texas	1,000	650	450	310	182	99	28.80	28.60	29.00
United States	13,600	14,450	14,450	3,286	3,605	3,739	20.70	20.90	23.70

NASS, Crops Branch, (202) 720–2127.

Table 4-37.—Head lettuce, commercial crop: Area, production, and value per hundredweight, by State and United States, 2012–2014

State	Area harvested			Production			Value per unit		
	2012	2013	2014	2012	2013	2014	2012	2013	2014
	Acres	Acres	Acres	1,000 cwt	1,000 cwt	1,000 cwt	Dollars per cwt	Dollars per cwt	Dollars per cwt
Arizona	36,600	33,000	34,500	13,176	11,550	12,248	15.90	31.80	12.80
California	105,000	96,000	87,000	37,800	33,600	32,190	18.30	24.90	29.90
United States	141,600	129,000	121,500	50,976	45,150	44,438	17.70	26.70	25.20

NASS, Crops Branch, (202) 720–2127.

Table 4-38.—Head lettuce, commercial crop: Area, yield, production, value per hundredweight, and total value, United States, 2004–2013

Year	Area harvested	Yield per acre	Production	Value [1]	
				Per cwt	Total
	Acres	Cwt	1,000 cwt	Dollars	1,000 dollars
2005	177,400	368	65,253	15.50	1,011,976
2006	178,800	350	62,494	16.90	1,054,941
2007	161,800	355	57,474	21.70	1,247,941
2008	148,700	356	52,952	20.10	1,063,132
2009	135,000	372	50,180	22.40	1,121,724
2010	132,000	380	50,120	21.10	1,057,504
2011	130,500	381	49,665	23.00	1,142,267
2012	141,600	360	50,976	17.70	901,238
2013	129,100	350	45,150	26.70	1,203,930
2014	121,500	366	44,438	25.20	1,119,255

[1] Price and value at point of first sale.
NASS, Crops Branch, (202) 720–2127.

Table 4-39.—Leaf lettuce for fresh market, commercial crop: Area, yield, production, value per hundredweight, and total value, United States, 2005–2014

Year	Area harvested	Yield per acre	Production	Value [1]	
				Per cwt	Total
	Acres	Cwt	1,000 cwt	Dollars	1,000 dollars
2005	56,900	241	13,701	33.90	463,995
2006	55,900	238	13,317	34.80	463,859
2007	54,600	224	12,240	30.50	373,692
2008	52,300	244	12,781	32.20	411,719
2009	49,100	241	11,845	38.70	458,765
2010	51,200	254	13,004	38.40	499,538
2011	47,400	252	11,939	34.60	413,484
2012	52,500	244	12,825	35.30	452,858
2013	55,000	230	12,650	38.30	484,036
2014	54,100	240	12,984	38.60	501,538

[1] Price and value at point of first sale.
NASS, Crops Branch, (202) 720–2127.

Table 4-40.—Leaf lettuce for fresh market: Area, production, and value per hundredweight, by State and United States, 2012–2014

State	Area harvested			Production			Value per unit		
	2012	2013	2014	2012	2013	2014	2012	2013	2014
	Acres	Acres	Acres	1,000 cwt	1,000 cwt	1,000 cwt	Dollars per cwt	Dollars per cwt	Dollars per cwt
Arizona	7,500	7,500	8,100	1,800	1,725	1,944	41.50	54.50	31.40
California	45,000	47,500	46,000	11,025	10,925	11,040	34.30	35.70	39.90
United States	52,500	55,000	54,100	12,825	12,650	12,984	35.30	38.30	38.60

NASS, Crops Branch, (202) 720–2127.

Table 4-41.—Romaine lettuce for fresh market, commercial crop: Area, yield, production, value per hundredweight, and total value, United States, 2005–2014

Year	Area harvested	Yield per acre	Production	Value [1]	
				Per cwt	Total
	Acres	Cwt	1,000 cwt	Dollars	1,000 dollars
2005	58,400	330	19,272	19.50	375,005
2006	86,400	307	26,500	22.40	593,866
2007	82,400	320	26,409	24.80	655,533
2008	77,400	294	22,774	21.00	479,006
2009	76,100	294	22,355	27.40	612,716
2010	79,300	345	27,389	23.90	655,659
2011	81,900	344	28,142	31.50	886,342
2012	88,900	318	28,256	22.40	633,489
2013	91,100	292	26,620	33.10	880,373
2014	85,400	289	24,679	32.00	788,779

[1] Price and value at point of first sale.
NASS, Crops Branch, (202) 720–2127.

Table 4-42.—Romaine lettuce for fresh market: Area, production, and value per hundredweight, by State and United States, 2012–2014

State	Area harvested			Production			Value per unit		
	2012	2013	2014	2012	2013	2014	2012	2013	2014
	Acres	Acres	Acres	1,000 cwt	1,000 cwt	1,000 cwt	Dollars per cwt	Dollars per cwt	Dollars per cwt
Arizona	19,900	20,100	21,900	6,866	6,030	6,899	20.30	48.00	23.10
California	69,000	71,000	63,500	21,390	20,590	17,780	23.10	28.70	35.40
United States	88,900	91,100	85,400	28,256	26,620	24,679	22.40	33.10	32.00

NASS, Crops Branch, (202) 720–2127.

Table 4-43.—Onions, commercial crop: Area, yield, production, shrinkage and loss, value per hundredweight, and total value, United States, 2005–2014[1]

Year	Area harvested	Yield per acre	Production[2]	Shrinkage and loss	Value[3]	
					Per cwt	Total
	Acres	Cwt	1,000 cwt	1,000 cwt	Dollars	1,000 dollars
2005	163,420	446	72,875	5,098	13.50	839,773
2006	163,780	446	73,066	5,863	16.10	1,084,099
2007	160,080	497	79,638	6,274	11.10	816,061
2008	153,490	489	75,120	5,072	11.90	834,386
2009	151,060	500	75,599	5,170	15.00	1,054,227
2010	149,270	493	73,599	6,112	15.60	1,049,704
2011	147,630	502	74,097	5,882	10.90	742,236
2012	146,870	487	71,495	4,923	14.20	942,340
2013	143,340	486	69,654	4,858	15.00	969,183
2014	139,150	523	72,806	4,147	13.60	933,630

[1] Mostly for fresh market use, but includes some quantities used for processing. [2] Includes storage crop onions harvested but not sold because of shrinkage and loss. [3] Price and value at point of first sale.
NASS, Crops Branch, (202) 720–2127.

Table 4-44.—Onions for fresh market: Area harvested, production, shrinkage and loss, and value per hundredweight, by State and United States, 2012–2014

Season and State	Area harvested			Production			Shrinkage and loss			Value per unit		
	2012	2013	2014	2012	2013	2014	2012	2013	2014	2012	2013	2014
	Acres	Acres	Acres	1,000 cwt	1,000 cwt	1,000 cwt	1,000 cwt	1,000 cwt	1,000 cwt	Dollars per cwt	Dollars per cwt	Dollars per cwt
Spring[1]:												
California	6,200	6,800	6,800	2,480	2,720	2,992	....	....	....	11.60	13.20	12.30
Georgia	10,600	11,100	11,000	2,438	2,997	2,585	....	....	....	41.80	44.10	41.90
Texas	10,300	9,700	9,000	3,090	3,492	2,340	....	....	....	22.50	23.80	24.00
United States	27,100	27,600	26,800	8,008	9,209	7,917	....	....	....	25.00	27.30	25.40
Summer non-storage[1]:												
California	7,100	7,800	7,800	3,870	3,822	3,744	....	....	....	5.00	6.40	7.00
Nevada	(D)	(D)	(D)	(D)	(D)	(D)	....	....	....	(D)	(D)	(D)
New Mexico	5,400	6,100	5,100	2,862	2,623	3,060	....	....	....	19.60	15.60	18.70
Texas	(D)	(D)	(D)	(D)	(D)	(D)	....	....	....	(D)	(D)	(D)
Washington[2]	3,100	2,000	2,000	1,147	900	800	....	....	....	31.80	27.40	34.60
Other States[3]	3,720	4,000	4,250	2,843	2,280	1,622	....	....	....	32.40	32.50	34.10
United States	19,320	19,900	19,150	10,722	9,625	9,226	....	....	....	19.00	17.10	18.00
Summer storage:												
California[4]	28,400	29,300	29,300	12,354	11,700	16,120	250	250	250	10.11	9.10	13.40
Colorado	6,200	4,000	3,600	2,604	1,700	1,800	290	190	190	17.10	18.90	19.00
Idaho	8,500	9,000	6,900	6,205	7,380	5,658	1,000	1,110	1,110	10.00	11.40	8.40
Michigan	2,800	2,700	2,500	644	810	925	48	113	113	13.00	15.90	12.90
New York	8,000	6,500	8,000	2,480	2,015	2,360	407	40	40	16.90	16.00	15.30
Oregon												
Malheur	10,600	10,900	9,300	7,950	7,848	7,440	811	1,020	1,020	10.10	11.30	8.40
Other	8,700	10,000	10,300	5,133	6,100	6,798	739	854	854	9.96	12.60	8.90
Washington	23,500	20,000	20,000	13,865	11,600	13,000	1,248	1,160	1,160	11.70	13.50	8.90
Wisconsin	2,000	1,800	1,700	620	810	791	81	49	49	13.40	16.40	17.50
Other States[3]	1,750	1,640	1,600	910	857	771	49	72	72	11.60	12.00	10.50
United States	100,450	95,840	93,200	54,800	52,765	55,663	4,923	4,858	4,858	11.20	12.10	11.00
Total summer	119,770	115,740	112,350	63,487	60,445	64,889	....	....	....	12.70	12.90	12.10
Total, spring and summer	146,870	143,340	....	71,495	69,654	....	....	....	....	14.20	15.00	....

(D) Withheld to avoid disclosing data for individual operations. (NA) Not available. [1] Primarily fresh market. [2] Includes Walla Walla and other non-storage onions. [3] Other States include Nevada and Texas for Summer Non-storage Onions and Ohio and Utah for Summer Storage Onions. [4] Primarily dehydrated processing.
NASS, Crops Branch, (202) 720–2127.

Table 4-45.—Onions (fresh market): Foreign trade, United States, 2005–2014 [1]

Year beginning July	Imports	Domestic exports
	1,000 cwt	*1,000 cwt*
2005	6,297	6,149
2006	8,656	6,236
2007	7,337	5,368
2008	6,639	6,130
2009	8,177	6,101
2010	8,783	7,478
2011	8,337	6,479
2012	9,306	6,221
2013	10,650	7,223
2014	10,420	6,112

Note: CWT=hundred weight or 100 pounds. [1] Includes bulb onions, onion sets, and pearl onions.
ERS, (202) 694–5253. Compiled from reports of the U.S. Department of Commerce.

Table 4-46.—Peas, green (processing), commercial crop: Area, yield, production, value per ton, and total value, United States, 2005–2014

Year	Area harvested	Yield per acre	Production	Value [1]	
				Per ton	Total
	Acres	*Tons*	*Tons*	*Dollars*	*1,000 dollars*
2005	210,900	1.75	370,050	270.00	99,905
2006	195,900	2.00	392,420	247.00	96,778
2007	202,000	2.07	419,080	259.00	108,702
2008	209,700	1.96	411,780	360.00	148,052
2009	205,400	2.15	441,680	319.00	140,707
2010	172,600	2.00	345,640	287.00	99,216
2011	159,100	1.85	294.920	399.00	117,682
2012	194,500	2.09	407,250	434.00	176,818
2013	178,300	2.00	356,050	427.00	151,928
2014	187,600	1.93	362,860	367.00	133,261

[1] Price and value at processing plant door.
NASS, Crops Branch, (202) 720–2127.

Table 4-47.—Peas, green (processing), commercial crop: Area, production, and value per ton, by State and United States, 2012–2014 [1]

State	Area harvested			Production			Value per unit		
	2012	2013	2014	2012	2013	2014	2012	2013	2014
	Acres	*Acres*	*Acres*	*Tons*	*Tons*	*Tons*	*Dollars per ton*	*Dollars per ton*	*Dollars per ton*
Delaware	5,700	5,000	5,000	12,310	10,800	11,300	350.00	263.00	340.00
Minnesota	74,900	60,800	64,000	111,570	87,630	78,150	617.00	640.00	567.00
Oregon	14,700	21,100	19,600	41,000	40,300	41,430	302.00	265.00	253.00
Washington	40,900	44,500	40,500	128,040	122,380	118,440	275.00	287.00	249.00
Wisconsin	37,300	36,000	36,600	66,300	75,550	70,640	461.00	521.00	378.00
Other States [2]	21,000	10,900	21,900	48,030	19,390	42,900	531.00	403.00	433.00
United States	194,500	178,300	187,600	407,250	356,050	362,860	434.00	427.00	367.00

[1] Shelled basis; 2½ pounds of peas in the shell produce approximately 1 pound of shelled peas. [2] Other States include Illinois, Maryland, New Jersey, and New York.
NASS, Crops Branch, (202) 720–2127.

Table 4-48.—Chile peppers for fresh market and processing: Area, production, and value per hundredweight, by State and United States, 2012–2014 [1] [2]

State	Area harvested			Production			Value per unit		
	2012	2013	2014	2012	2013	2014	2012	2013	2014
	Acres	Acres	Acres	1,000 cwt	1,000 cwt	1,000 cwt	Dollars per cwt	Dollars per cwt	Dollars per cwt
Arizona	1,100	1,300	1,400	60	72	80	53.70	86.50	33.80
California	6,500	6,900	6,900	2,600	2,640	3,186	31.00	38.70	51.80
New Mexico	9,600	8,600	7,700	1,556	1,300	1,174	42.00	38.10	33.00
Texas	3,200	3,200	3,100	99	198	185	69.00	51.50	52.40
United States	20,400	20,000	19,100	4,315	4,210	4,625	36.20	39.90	46.70

[1] Chile peppers are defined as all peppers excluding bell peppers.   [2] Estimates include both fresh and dry product combined.
NASS, Crops Branch, (202) 720–2127.

Table 4-49.—Chile peppers for fresh market and processing, commercial crop: Area, yield, production, value, and total value, United States, 2005–2014 [1]

Year	Area harvested	Yield per acre	Production	Value	
				Per cwt	Total
	Acres	Cwt	1,000 cwt	Dollars	1,000 dollars
2005	32,700	156	5,108	22.90	117,048
2006	28,200	169	4,779	21.90	104,775
2007	24,900	156	3,877	29.90	115,745
2008	25,200	168	4,235	26.60	112,753
2009	28,500	177	5,042	27.80	140,405
2010	23,000	202	4,644	29.80	138,586
2011	22,100	178	3,928	35.00	137,657
2012	20,400	212	4,315	36.20	156,039
2013	20,000	211	4,210	39.90	168,146
2014	19,100	242	4,625	46.70	216,107

[1] Chile peppers are defined as all peppers excluding bell peppers.   Estimates include both fresh and dry product combined.
NASS, Crops Branch, (202) 720–2127.

Table 4-50.—Bell peppers for fresh market and processing: Area, production, and value per hundredweight, by State and United States, 2012–2014

State	Area harvested			Production			Value per unit		
	2012	2013	2014	2012	2013	2014	2012	2013	2014
	Acres	Acres	Acres	1,000 cwt	1,000 cwt	1,000 cwt	Dollars per cwt	Dollars per cwt	Dollars per cwt
California	20,400	20,000	21,900	8,465	8,898	9,242	28.00	41.70	36.00
Florida	12,400	12,300	11,900	3,075	4,400	3,094	46.00	46.00	53.10
Georgia	3,400	3,500	3,800	630	1,445	798	39.90	43.60	51.70
Michigan	1,600	1,500	1,400	375	351	364	38.00	37.00	37.00
New Jersey	3,700	3,100	2,800	977	1,037	952	24.00	28.30	31.00
North Carolina	2,200	1,700	2,100	425	793	441	29.00	37.00	44.00
Ohio	1,800	2,700	2,600	486	1,004	455	40.00	43.00	38.00
United States	45,500	44,800	46,500	14,433	17,928	15,346	32.80	41.60	40.30

NASS, Crops Branch, (202) 720–2127.

Table 4-51.—Bell peppers for fresh market and processing, commercial crop: Area, yield, production, value, hundredweight, and total value, United States, 2005-2014

Year	Area harvested	Yield per acre	Production	Value	
				Per cwt	Total
	Acres	Cwt	1,000 cwt	Dollars	1,000 dollars
2005	56,800	282	16,036	33.30	534,703
2006	53,100	296	15,710	33.70	528,652
2007	54,000	298	16,100	33.10	532,799
2008	50,800	312	15,867	40.10	635,662
2009	49,400	331	16,354	34.10	557,749
2010	49,000	309	15,161	39.10	592,266
2011	46,400	351	16,275	37.80	615,740
2012	45,500	345	15,687	32.80	514,000
2013	44,800	322	14,433	41.60	599,932
2014	46,500	330	15,346	40.30	618,185

NASS, Crops Branch, (202) 720–2127.

Table 4-52.—Potatoes: Area, yield, production, season average price, and value, United States, 2005–2014

Year	Area planted	Area harvested	Yield per harvested acre	Production	Season average price per cwt received by farmers [1]	Value of production
	1,000 acres	1,000 acres	Cwt	1,000 cwt	Dollars	1,000 dollars
2005	1,108.4	1,086.2	390	423,788	7.04	2,981,754
2006	1,139.4	1,120.2	393	440,698	7.31	3,208,632
2007	1,141.9	1,122.2	396	444,875	7.51	3,339,710
2008	1,059.6	1,046.9	396	415,055	9.09	3,770,462
2009	1,071.2	1,044.0	414	432,601	8.25	3,557,574
2010	1,026.7	1,008.9	401	404,549	9.20	3,724,821
2011	1,100.7	1,078.5	399	430,037	9.41	4,044,869
2012	1,154.8	1,138.5	408	464,970	8.63	4,017,245
2013	1,063.9	1,050.9	414	434,652	9.75	4,237,284
2014	1,062.6	1,051.1	421	442,170	8.88	3,928,211

[1] 2002-2007 obtained by weighting State prices by quantity sold. 2008 obtained by weighting State prices by production.
NASS, Crops Branch, (202) 720–2127.

Table 4-53.—Potatoes: Production, seed used, and disposition, United States, 2005–2014

Year	Production	Total used for seed	Used on farms where produced		Sold
			For seed, feed, and household use	Shrinkage and loss	
	1,000 cwt	1,000 cwt	1,000 cwt	1,000 cwt	1,000 cwt
2005	423,788	25,616	4,797	28,572	390,419
2006	440,698	26,374	4,750	29,639	406,309
2007	444,875	24,476	4,105	29,561	411,209
2008	415,055	24,595	4,139	26,438	384,478
2009	432,601	24,027	4,535	29,135	398,931
2010	404,549	25,100	4,227	24,996	375,326
2011	430,037	26,527	4,146	27,789	398,102
2012	464,970	25,656	4,850	28,505	431,615
2013	434,652	25,249	4,323	26,211	404,118
2014	442,170	26,259	4,192	26,762	411,216

NASS, Crops Branch, (202) 720–2127.

Table 4-54.—Potatoes: Area, production, and marketing year price per hundredweight received by farmers, by State and United States, 2012–2014

Season and State	Area harvested			Yield			Production		
	2012	2013	2014	2012	2013	2014	2012	2013	2014
	1,000 acres	*1,000 acres*	*1,000 acres*	*Cwt*	*Cwt*	*Cwt*	*1,000 cwt*	*1,000 cwt*	*1,000 cwt*
Spring:									
Arizona	3.7	3.4	3.5	225	280	310	833	952	1,085
California	29.0	26.5	24.8	400	410	470	11,600	10,865	11,656
Florida	36.6	29.5	29.3	244	240	240	8,917	7,080	7,032
Hastings area [1]	23.3	(NA)	(NA)	222	(NA)	(NA)	5,172	(NA)	(NA)
Other areas [1]	13.3	(NA)	(NA)	282	(NA)	(NA)	3,745	(NA)	(NA)
North Carolina	16.0	13.5	13.5	200	240	210	3,200	3,240	2,835
Texas [2]	9.3	(NA)	(NA)	235	(NA)	(NA)	2,186	(NA)	(NA)
United States	94.6	72.9	71.1	283	304	318	26,736	22,137	22,608
Summer:									
Colorado [3]	5.3	(NA)	(NA)	450	(NA)	(NA)	2,385	(NA)	(NA)
Delaware	1.4	1.4	1.2	255	280	290	357	392	348
Illinois	7.4	6.7	6.4	380	370	415	2,812	2,479	2,656
Kansas	5.2	4.3	4.1	350	350	340	1,820	1,505	1,394
Maryland	2.3	2.1	2.3	380	310	380	874	651	874
Missouri	8.9	9.0	7.9	300	300	270	2,670	2,700	2,133
New Jersey	2.3	2.4	1.9	280	230	225	644	552	428
Texas	10.8	17.7	20.6	490	460	335	5,292	8,142	6,901
Virginia	5.4	3.9	4.5	250	210	250	1,350	819	1,125
United States	49.0	47.5	48.9	372	363	324	18,204	17,240	15,859
Fall:									
California	8.3	7.3	8.3	470	480	470	3,901	3,504	3,901
Colorado	54.0	54.6	59.8	370	372	388	19,980	20,304	23,196
Idaho	344.0	316.0	320.0	412	415	415	141,820	131,131	132,880
10 S.W. counties	20.0	17.0	16.0	530	520	515	10,600	8,840	8,240
Other ID counties	324.0	299.0	304.0	405	409	410	131,220	122,291	124,640
Maine	58.5	54.0	50.5	275	290	290	16,088	15,660	14,645
Massachusetts	3.9	3.9	3.6	330	260	285	1,287	1,014	1,026
Michigan	46.0	44.0	42.5	350	360	370	16,100	15,840	15,725
Minnesota	47.0	45.0	41.0	400	385	400	18,800	17,325	16,400
Montana	11.7	11.1	11.3	320	310	320	3,744	3,441	3,616
Nebraska	23.3	18.3	16.9	445	460	470	10,369	8,418	7,943
Nevada	7.1	(D)	(D)	380	(D)	(D)	2,698	(D)	(D)
New Mexico	6.2	(D)	(D)	460	(D)	(D)	2,852	(D)	(D)
New York	18.0	17.1	15.8	285	290	275	5,130	4,959	4,345
North Dakota	84.0	78.0	77.0	300	290	310	25,200	22,620	23,870
Ohio	2.0	1.8	1.5	220	280	280	440	504	420
Oregon	41.7	39.6	38.9	550	545	580	22,935	21,582	22,562
Pennsylvania	8.6	6.6	5.2	260	290	275	2,236	1,914	1,430
Rhode Island	0.6	0.5	0.5	250	260	245	150	130	123
Washington	164.0	160.0	165.0	585	600	615	95,940	96,000	101,475
Wisconsin	66.0	62.0	64.0	460	420	410	30,360	26,040	26,240
Other States [4]	-	10.7	9.3	-	457	420	-	4,889	3,906
United States	994.9	930.5	931.1	422	425	434	420,030	395,275	403,703
All Potatoes:									
United States	1,138.5	1,050.9	1,051.1	408	414	421	464,970	434,652	442,170

- Represents zero. (D) Withheld to avoid disclosing data for individual operations. (NA) Not available. [1] Estimates discontinued in 2013. [2] Beginning in 2013 Spring estimates included in Summer total for Texas. [3] Beginning in 2013 Summer estimates included in Fall total for Colorado. [4] Includes data withheld above.
NASS, Crops Branch, (202) 720–2127.

Table 4-55.—Fall potatoes: Total stocks held by growers, local dealers, and processors - 13 Fall States: 2013 and 2014[1]

State	Crop of 2013			
	Dec. 1	Feb. 1	Apr. 1	June 1
	1,000 cwt	*1,000 cwt*	*1,000 cwt*	*1,000 cwt*
California	(NA)	(NA)	800	(D)
Colorado	(NA)	(NA)	7,000	2,800
Idaho	(NA)	(NA)	47,000	20,000
Maine	(NA)	(NA)	4,400	(D)
Michigan	(NA)	(NA)	2,100	(D)
Minnesota	(NA)	(NA)	6,000	3,000
Montana	(NA)	(NA)	1,800	(D)
Nebraska	(NA)	(NA)	2,200	(D)
New York	(NA)	(NA)	650	(D)
North Dakota	(NA)	(NA)	6,500	1,800
Oregon	(NA)	(NA)	7,600	3,000
Washington	(NA)	(NA)	26,000	12,500
Wisconsin	(NA)	(NA)	7,000	1,300
Other States[2]	-	-	-	2,485
United States	(NA)	(NA)	119,050	46,885
Klamath Basin[3]	(NA)	(NA)	1,850	(D)

State	Crop of 2014			
	Dec. 1	Feb. 1	Apr. 1	June 1
	1,000 cwt	*1,000 cwt*	*1,000 cwt*	*1,000 cwt*
California	2,500	1,600	700	(D)
Colorado	17,200	13,000	8,500	4,000
Idaho	95,000	74,000	49,000	23,500
Maine	11,600	8,500	5,500	2,200
Michigan	9,400	5,000	2,200	(D)
Minnesota	10,000	7,800	5,000	2,800
Montana	3,500	3,400	2,200	(D)
Nebraska	4,800	3,300	2,100	700
New York	2,100	1,400	500	(D)
North Dakota	16,900	12,200	7,100	2,600
Oregon	17,700	13,200	8,200	2,700
Washington	57,000	44,000	29,000	12,500
Wisconsin	18,000	13,400	8,700	4,500
Other States[2]	-	-	-	835
United States	265,700	200,800	128,700	56,335
Klamath Basin[3]	5,000	3,000	1,500	(D)

- Represents zero. (D) Withheld to avoid disclosing data for individual operations. (NA) Not available. [1] Stocks are defined as the quantity (whether sold or not) remaining in storage for all purposes and uses, including seed potatoes that are not yet moved, and shrinkage, waste, and other losses that occur after the date of each estimate. [2] Includes data withheld above. [3] Includes potato stocks in California and Klamath County, Oregon.
NASS, Crops Branch, (202) 720–2127.

Table 4-56.—Fall potatoes: Production and total stocks held by growers and local dealers, 13 Major States, 2005–2014

Crop year	Production	Total stocks						
		Dec. 1	Following year					
			Jan. 1	Feb. 1	Mar. 1	Apr. 1	May 1	June 1
	1,000 cwt	*1,000 cwt*	*1,000 cwt*	*1,000 cwt*	*1,000 cwt*	*1,000 cwt*	*1,000 cwt*	*1,000 cwt*
2005	378,732	253,800	220,500	189,100	155,500	115,700	75,900	41,560
2006	389,527	258,900	225,800	192,200	159,500	120,900	79,050	44,460
2007	397,753	265,500	232,300	199,300	163,400	125,500	83,960	50,420
2008	369,866	243,700	213,200	183,900	152,700	115,800	78,100	45,300
2009	383,962	265,800	234,300	203,500	169,700	128,700	89,610	55,120
2010	357,467	240,200	209,400	180,300	148,500	111,000	72,000	41,320
2011	382,318	253,000	(NA)	187,500	(NA)	115,650	(NA)	43,340
2012	410,367	271,500	(NA)	204,600	(NA)	(NA)	(NA)	(NA)
2013	386,824	(NA)	(NA)	(NA)	(NA)	119,050	(NA)	46,885
2014	396,798	265,700	(NA)	200,800	(NA)	128,700	(NA)	56,335

(NA) Not available.
NASS, Crops Branch, (202) 720–2127.

Table 4-57.—Potatoes: Utilization and processing, United States, 2013 and 2014

Utilization - 30 Program States	2013	2014
	1,000 cwt	*1,000 cwt*
Sales		
Table stock	106,930	107,344
Processing	273,506	280,330
Other sales		
Livestock feed	1,251	768
Seed	22,431	22,774
Other Sales Total	23,682	23,542
Total sales	404,118	411,216
Non-sales		
Seed used on farms where grown	3,215	3,343
Household use and used for feed on farms where grown	1,108	849
Shrinkage and loss	26,211	26,762
Total non-sales	30,534	30,954
Total production	434,652	442,170
Processing - United States	2013 [1]	2014
	1,000 cwt	*1,000 cwt*
Processing		
Chips and shoestring	60,485	73,364
All Dehydrated (including starch and flour)	47,411	48,708
Frozen french fries	134,966	152,832
Other frozen products	18,451	6,190
Canned potatoes	188	316
Other canned products (hash, stews, soups)	1,089	947
Other (including fresh pack, potato salad, vodka, etc)	10,916	9,450
Total	273,506	291,807

[1] 2013 reflects only 30 program states.
NASS, Crops Branch, (202) 720–2127.

Table 4-58.—Potatoes: Production, seed used, and farm disposition, by seasonal groups, crop of 2013

| Season and State | Production | Total used for seed | Used on farms where produced | | Sold |
			For seed, feed, and household use	Shrinkage and loss	
	1,000 cwt	*1,000 cwt*	*1,000 cwt*	*1,000 cwt*	*1,000 cwt*
Spring					
Arizona	952	(D)	(D)	(D)	(D)
California	10,865	717	2	805	10,058
Florida	7,080	751	-	210	6,870
North Carolina	3,240	(D)	(D)	(D)	(D)
Other States [1]	(NA)	417	3	5	4,184
United States	22,137	1,885	5	1,020	21,112
Summer					
Delaware	392	21	1	1	390
Illinois	2,479	117	10	7	2,462
Kansas	1,505	125	-	60	1,445
Maryland	651	33	1	4	646
Missouri	2,700	102	5	2	2,693
New Jersey	552	37	8	1	543
Texas	8,142	630	-	814	7,328
Virginia	819	74	1	2	816
United States	17,240	1,139	26	891	16,323
Fall					
California	3,504	210	-	70	3,434
Colorado	20,304	1,565	954	1,460	17,890
Idaho	131,131	7,545	1,166	8,525	121,440
Maine	15,660	1,030	230	1,130	14,300
Massachusetts	1,014	89	-	19	995
Michigan	15,840	1,035	310	430	15,100
Minnesota	17,325	900	59	866	16,400
Montana	3,441	286	226	180	3,035
Nebraska	8,418	494	183	429	7,806
Nevada	(D)	(D)	(D)	(D)	(D)
New Mexico	(D)	(D)	(D)	(D)	(D)
New York	4,959	374	29	113	4,817
North Dakota	22,620	1,742	299	2,111	20,210
Ohio	504	34	5	4	495
Oregon	21,582	874	72	1,400	20,110
Pennsylvania	1,914	152	3	13	1,898
Rhode Island	130	10	4	3	123
Washington	96,000	4,175	290	6,000	89,710
Wisconsin	26,040	1,449	421	1,300	24,319
Other States [1]	4,889	261	41	247	4,601
United States	395,275	22,225	4,292	24,300	366,683
All potatoes					
United States	434,652	25,249	4,323	26,211	404,118

- Represents zero.   (D) Withheld to avoid disclosing data for individual operations.   [1] Includes data withheld above.
NASS, Crops Branch, (202) 720–2127.

Table 4-59.—Potatoes, fresh & seed: United States exports by country of destination and imports by country of origin, 2011–2013

Country	2011	2012	2013
	Metric tons	*Metric tons*	*Metric tons*
Imports			
Canada	491,495	352,959	390,719
Belgium-Luxembourg(*)	0	0	23
Ecuador	0	0	3
Peru	25	9	1
Dominican Republic	5	0	0
Germany(*)	45	0	0
India	0	1	0
Mexico	19	0	0
Leeward-Windward Islands(*)	0	1	0
World Total	491,588	352,970	390,746
Exports			
Canada	284,785	240,858	270,969
Mexico	73,570	79,948	82,954
Taiwan	9,300	18,704	18,158
Japan	9,138	14,665	17,312
Korea, South	16,654	18,661	16,291
Malaysia	12,596	17,181	16,105
Philippines	4,431	5,289	10,136
Indonesia	74	3,024	8,323
Singapore	6,136	5,875	6,086
Thailand	8,767	11,533	4,877
Dominican Republic	2,107	5,105	4,676
Hong Kong	3,798	4,030	3,922
Nicaragua	1,139	1,541	2,856
Bahamas, The	1,207	1,883	2,467
Panama	820	984	1,621
Russia	2,284	4,987	1,579
Guatemala	1,809	2,678	1,472
Vietnam	344	2,397	1,284
Brazil	176	0	1,106
Costa Rica	2,695	830	1,069
Leeward-Windward Islands(*)	769	707	999
Trinidad and Tobago	267	731	860
United Arab Emirates	82	164	722
El Salvador	778	565	504
Cayman Islands	125	241	347
Poland	0	0	270
Sri Lanka	197	150	256
Jamaica	105	46	174
Congo (Kinshasa)	0	100	160
Belize	168	153	135
Rest of World	4,726	4,437	1,122
World Total	449,047	447,468	478,809

(*) Denotes a country that is a summarization of its component countries.
FAS, Office of Global Analysis, (202) 720-6301.

Table 4-60.—Potatoes (fresh market): Foreign trade, United States, 2005–2014 [1]

Year beginning July	Imports for consumption	Domestic exports
	1,000 cwt.	*1,000 cwt.*
2005/2006	7,604	5,430
2006/2007	8,152	6,730
2007/2008	10,681	5,798
2008/2009	10,852	6,731
2009/2010	10,550	6,588
2010/2011	9,050	8,183
2011/2012	10,384	9,294
2012/2013	9,041	9,348
2013/2014	7,375	10,467
2014/2015	10,801	10,002

Note: CWT=hundred weight or 100 pounds. [1] Includes seed.
ERS, (202) 694–5253. Based on data from U.S. Department of Commerce, U.S. Census Bureau.

Table 4-61.—Pumpkins for fresh market and processing: Area, production, and value per hundredweight, by State and United States, 2012–2014

State	Area harvested			Production			Value per unit		
	2012	2013	2014	2012	2013	2014	2012	2013	2014
	Acres	*Acres*	*Acres*	*1,000 cwt*	*1,000 cwt*	*1,000 cwt*	*Dollars per cwt*	*Dollars per cwt*	*Dollars per cwt*
California	5,500	5,900	5,400	1,870	1,947	1,922	14.70	15.60	16.10
Illinois	20,200	20,100	15,900	5,563	5,476	7,458	5.90	8.62	6.32
Michigan	6,300	6,300	6,800	945	978	970	14.00	11.50	11.80
New York	6,300	6,000	6,300	1,071	960	690	33.50	31.40	29.70
Ohio	6,000	6,100	6,800	1,440	1,004	1,053	13.40	15.40	17.80
Pennsylvania	6,200	5,900	5,700	1,147	856	1,050	15.10	16.50	15.70
United States	50,500	50,300	50,300	12,036	11,221	13,143	12.10	13.20	11.00

NASS, Crops Branch, (202) 720–2127.

Table 4-62.—Pumpkins for fresh market and processing, commercial crop: Area, yield, production, value, hundredweight, and total value, United States, 2005-2014

Year	Area harvested	Yield per acre	Production	Value	
				Per cwt	Total
	Acres	*Cwt*	*1,000 cwt*	*Dollars*	*1,000 dollars*
2005	43,800	246	10,756	9.64	103,651
2006	43,700	240	10,484	9.98	104,623
2007	45,900	250	11,458	10.80	123,519
2008	43,400	246	10,663	12.90	137,072
2009	44,100	211	9,313	11.00	102,730
2010	48,500	222	10,748	11.00	117,791
2011	46,900	228	10,705	10.60	113,085
2012	50,500	238	12,036	12.10	146,033
2013	50,300	223	11,221	13.20	148,517
2014	49,500	266	13,143	11.00	145,154

NASS, Crops Branch, (202) 720–2127.

Table 4-63.—Spinach for fresh market: Area, production, and value per hundredweight, by State and United States, 2012–2014

State	Area harvested			Production			Value per unit		
	2012	2013	2014	2012	2013	2014	2012	2013	2014
	Acres	Acres	Acres	1,000 cwt	1,000 cwt	1,000 cwt	Dollars per cwt	Dollars per cwt	Dollars per cwt
Arizona	8,000	7,200	8,000	1,360	1,368	1,240	38.80	48.30	39.90
California	22,400	24,300	26,000	3,360	3,645	4,160	44.20	41.60	45.50
New Jersey	1,400	1,300	1,300	259	254	221	48.90	46.60	37.70
Texas	1,500	1,300	1,500	224	260	225	33.40	38.50	44.00
Other States [1]	1,140	840	740	157	92	73	30.60	35.80	37.20
United States	34,440	34,940	37,540	5,360	5,619	5,919	42.20	43.20	43.90

[1] Other States include Colorado and Maryland.
NASS, Crops Branch, (202) 720–2127.

Table 4-64.—Spinach for fresh market, commercial crop: Area, yield, production, value per hundredweight, and total value, United States, 2005-2014

Year	Area harvested	Yield per acre	Production	Value [1]	
				Per cwt	Total
	Acres	Cwt	1,000 cwt	Dollars	1,000 dollars
2005	42,500	167	7,096	22.80	161,732
2006	36,500	166	6,045	29.90	180,774
2007	31,900	159	5,079	32.30	163,952
2008	34,334	161	5,519	34.00	187,497
2009	34,934	192	6,699	39.50	264,564
2010	30,735	184	5,648	42.70	241,050
2011	31,435	191	6,010	40.40	242,823
2012	34,440	156	5,360	42.20	226,232
2013	34,940	161	5,619	43.20	242,846
2014	37,540	158	5,919	43.90	259,700

[1] Price and value at point of first sale.
NASS, Crops Branch, (202) 720–2127.

Table 4-65.—Spinach for processing, commercial crop: Area, yield, production, value per ton, and total value, United States, 2005-2014

Year	Area harvested	Yield per acre	Production	Value [1]	
				Per ton	Total
	Acres	Tons	Tons	Dollars	1,000 dollars
2005	9,600	10.23	98,240	109.00	10,667
2006	9,400	7.40	69,560	127.00	8,809
2007	11,400	8.58	97,800	104.00	10,123
2008	10,200	10.15	103,540	124.00	12,831
2009	10,100	9.47	95,660	127.00	12,144
2010	10,200	8.34	85,050	143.00	12,153
2011	7,500	10.69	80,180	131.00	10,465
2012	7,400	10.18	75,320	137.00	10,320
2013	8,800	10.08	88,710	129.00	11,451
2014	9,100	9.92	90,310	125.00	11,312

[1] Price and value at processing plant door.
NASS, Crops Branch, (202) 720–2127.

Table 4-66.—Spinach for processing: Area, production, and value per ton, by State and United States, 2012-2014

State	Area harvested			Production			Value per unit		
	2012	2013	2014	2012	2013	2014	2011	2012	2013
	Acres	Acres	Acres	Tons	Tons	Tons	Dollars per ton	Dollars per ton	Dollars per ton
California	....	....	....	....	....	....	....	....	....
Other States [1]	....	....	....	....	....	....	....	....	....
United States	7,400	8,800	9,100	75,320	88,710	90,310	137.00	129.00	125.00

[1] Other States include New Jersey and Texas.
NASS, Crops Branch, (202) 720–2127.

Table 4-67.—Sweet Potatoes: Area, yield, production, season average price per hundredweight received by farmers, and value, United States, 2005–2014

Year	Area harvested	Yield per acre	Production	Market year average price [1]	Value of production
	1,000 acres	Cwt	1,000 cwt	Dollars	1,000 dollars
2005	88.4	178	15,730	18.10	284,103
2006	87.3	188	16,401	18.20	298,388
2007	97.4	186	18,070	18.30	330,060
2008	97.3	190	18,443	21.20	390,572
2009	96.9	201	19,469	21.80	423,677
2010	116.9	204	23,845	19.80	472,218
2011	129.7	208	26,964	18.80	505,938
2012	126.6	209	26,482	17.40	461,861
2013	113.2	219	24,785	24.10	597,217
2014	135.2	219	29,584	23.90	706,916

[1] Obtained by weighting State prices by production.
NASS, Crops Branch, (202) 720–2127.

Table 4-68.—Sweet Potatoes: Area, production, and season average price per hundredweight received by farmers, by State and United States, 2012–2014

State	Area harvested			Production			Market year average price per cwt		
	2012	2013	2014	2012	2013	2014	2012	2013	2014
	1,000 acres	1,000 acres	1,000 acres	1,000 cwt	1,000 cwt	1,000 cwt	Dollars	Dollars	Dollars
Alabama	2.6	2.4	2.0	546	415	440	17.30	28.50	24.10
Arkansas	3.9	3.9	3.9	780	702	780	30.60	32.20	(D)
California	18.0	19.0	19.0	6,174	6,840	5,225	22.70	24.60	30.10
Florida	6.3	5.9	5.9	756	838	1,180	(D)	(D)	(D)
Louisiana	9.5	7.5	8.8	1,948	1,650	2,024	18.50	17.90	17.40
Mississippi	22.0	19.5	21.5	3,520	3,510	3,763	17.90	16.40	19.30
New Jersey	1.3	1.2	1.2	208	150	192	24.20	29.50	36.90
North Carolina	62.0	53.0	72.0	12,400	10,600	15,840	13.00	24.90	22.00
Texas	1.0	0.8	0.9	150	80	140	(D)	(D)	27.60
Other States	(X)	(X)	(X)	(X)	(X)	(X)	25.50	42.50	36.60
United States	126.6	113.2	135.2	26,482	24,785	29,584	17.40	24.10	23.90

(D) Withheld to avoid disclosing data for individual operations.
NASS, Crops Branch, (202) 720–2127.

Table 4-69.—Squash for fresh market and processing: Area, production, and value per hundredweight, by State and United States, 2012-2014

State	Area harvested			Production			Value per unit		
	2012	2013	2014	2012	2013	2014	2012	2013	2014
	Acres	Acres	Acres	1,000 cwt	1,000 cwt	1,000 cwt	Dollars per cwt	Dollars per cwt	Dollars per cwt
California	6,200	6,800	6,100	1,240	1,224	1,037	28.70	35.40	35.70
Florida	6,900	7,800	6,800	900	975	800	52.90	72.10	50.80
Georgia	2,700	2,600	3,200	459	390	480	31.80	31.50	31.80
Michigan	7,000	6,100	6,000	1,680	1,220	1,200	14.30	14.50	15.00
New Jersey	2,800	2,600	2,700	392	338	354	40.90	39.30	32.80
New York	5,400	4,500	4,300	1,026	866	691	48.20	43.90	45.40
North Carolina	2,700	1,900	3,000	540	97	162	29.00	47.00	51.90
Ohio	1,500	1,400	1,600	270	238	304	36.00	40.00	34.00
Oregon	2,900	2,400	1,500	493	429	389	12.80	11.70	11.50
South Carolina	1,100	1,300	1,000	160	169	150	30.00	35.00	37.50
Tennessee	700	600	830	38	32	43	40.00	38.00	30.30
Texas	1,900	1,900	1,500	171	171	135	51.00	46.00	55.00
United States	41,800	39,900	38,530	7,369	6,149	5,745	31.80	37.20	33.30

NASS, Crops Branch, (202) 720–2127.

Table 4-70.—Squash for fresh market and processing, commercial crop: Area, yield, production, value and total value, United States, 2005-2014

Year	Area harvested	Yield per acre	Production	Value	
				Per cwt	Total
	Acres	Cwt	1,000 cwt	Dollars	1,000 dollars
2005	48,400	154	7,439	25.40	188,846
2006	48,200	165	7,946	24.20	192,459
2007	41,600	151	6,266	27.80	173,917
2008	42,400	158	6,687	30.50	204,283
2009	42,900	165	7,089	27.90	197,614
2010	42,600	153	6,514	30.40	198,025
2011	42,900	164	7,043	34.30	241,877
2012	41,800	176	7,369	31.80	234,101
2013	39,900	154	6,149	37.20	228,985
2014	38,530	149	5,745	33.30	191,532

NASS, Crops Branch, (202) 720–2127.

Table 4-71.—Taro: Area, total production, price, and value, Hawaii, 2004–2013

Year	Total area	Production	Price per pound	Value of production
	Acres	1,000 pounds	Dollars	1,000 dollars
2004	370	5,200	0.540	2,808
2005	360	4,300	0.540	2,322
2006	380	4,500	0.570	2,565
2007	380	4,000	0.590	2,360
2008	390	4,300	0.620	2,666
2009	445	4,000	0.610	2,440
2010	475	3,900	0.645	2,516
2011	485	4,100	0.670	2,747
2012	400	3,500	0.670	2,345
2013	400	3,100	0.670	1,922

NASS, Crops Branch, (202) 720–2127.

Table 4-72.—Tomatoes: Foreign trade, United States, 2005–2014

Year beginning July	Imports				Domestic exports [2]			
	Fresh	Canned, whole and piece [1]	Catsup and sauces	Paste	Fresh	Canned, whole and piece	Catsup and sauces	Paste
	1,000 cwt	1,000 cwt	1,000 cwt	1,000 cwt	1,000 cwt	1,000 cwt	1,000 cwt	1,000 cwt
2005/2006	22,906	415	3,968	229	3,192	1,056	4,596	2,775
2006/2007	23,056	358	4,544	1,022	3,317	1,069	4,414	2,026
2007/2008	23,905	239	4,097	288	3,641	1,256	4,493	4,721
2008/2009	25,014	336	3,924	179	3,720	1,421	4,971	6,338
2009/2010	32,093	405	3,684	124	3,133	1,128	5,423	5,011
2010/2011	30,904	270	3,839	113	2,794	1,303	5,845	6,426
2011/2012	33,744	265	3,533	111	2,531	1,531	6,064	6,764
2012/2013	33,717	358	3,451	87	2,533	1,312	6,302	9,032
2013/2014	34,834	385	3,526	103	2,345	1,668	7,247	11,035
2014/2015	33,286	306	3,412	129	2,459	1,290	8,727	9,934

Note: CWT=hundred weight or 100 pounds.　[1] Includes all canned tomato and tomato product imports except paste and juice, on a product-weight-basis.　[2] Includes exports for military-civilian feeding abroad.
ERS, (202) 694–5253. Compiled from reports of the U.S. Department of Commerce.

Table 4-73.—Tomatoes, commercial crop: Area, yield, production, value per hundredweight and per ton, and total value, United States, 2005–2014

Year	For fresh market					For processing				
	Area harvested	Yield per acre	Production	Value [1]		Area harvested	Yield per acre	Production	Value [2]	
				Per cwt	Total				Per ton	Total
	Acres	Cwt	1,000 cwt	Dollars	1,000 dollars	Acres	Tons	Tons	Dollars	1,000 dollars
2005 ...	124,000	307	38,033	41.60	1,583,897	281,940	36.15	10,193,120	60.90	620,987
2006 ...	120,200	302	36,274	43.70	1,584,708	299,400	35.44	10,611,820	66.40	704,669
2007 ...	108,100	311	33,627	34.80	1,168,693	313,600	40.37	12,659,890	71.20	901,761
2008 ...	105,250	296	31,137	45.50	1,415,297	296,500	41.50	12,305,820	79.80	982,373
2009 ...	108,700	306	33,235	40.40	1,344,217	327,800	42.62	13,970,560	87.20	1,218,912
2010 ...	103,000	271	27,961	48.40	1,352,315	288,900	44.22	12,776,280	72.50	926,692
2011 ...	94,210	300	28,231	37.00	1,043,491	267,800	46.29	12,396,150	75.60	936,861
2012 ...	101,000	284	28,660	30.50	874,195	276,300	47.70	13,178,750	76.70	1,010,545
2013 ...	99,600	265	26,391	44.60	1,177,592	277,000	45.60	12,631,500	90.10	1,138,462
2014 ...	97,600	280	27,280	41.60	1,134,616	306,100	47.82	14,637,300	90.50	1,325,332

[1] Price and value at point of first sale.　[2] Price and value at processing plant door.
NASS, Crops Branch, (202) 720–2127.

Table 4-74.—Tomatoes, commercial crop: Area, production, and value per hundredweight and per ton, by State and United States, 2012–2014 [1]

Utilization and State	Area harvested			Production			Value per unit		
	2012	2013	2014	2012	2013	2014	2012	2013	2014
Fresh market:	Acres	Acres	Acres	1,000 cwt	1,000 cwt	1,000 cwt	Dollars per cwt	Dollars per cwt	Dollars per cwt
Alabama	1,300	1,100	1,200	416	297	420	30.60	33.60	28.30
Arkansas	1,000	1,000	900	285	150	153	64.00	48.00	62.00
California	36,000	34,000	32,300	11,340	10,200	10,175	22.70	36.20	34.80
Florida	32,000	34,000	33,000	9,600	9,010	9,240	28.00	50.60	47.30
Georgia	(D)	2,200	2,300	(D)	440	575	(D)	35.80	30.40
Indiana	700	900	820	112	153	152	68.00	77.00	48.80
Michigan	2,600	2,400	1,900	520	576	466	40.00	55.00	35.70
New Jersey	2,700	2,800	2,900	567	588	624	54.40	52.60	61.00
New York	2,800	2,700	2,600	546	446	312	86.40	72.60	76.80
North Carolina ..	3,300	3,200	3,400	1,073	1,040	850	34.50	43.50	42.00
Ohio	2,500	3,400	3,600	425	595	954	61.40	75.00	36.60
Pennsylvania	1,700	2,200	2,500	192	310	415	84.60	81.00	65.40
South Carolina	3,300	3,000	3,200	825	630	896	42.00	25.60	32.40
Tennessee	3,800	3,400	3,900	950	1,122	1,326	34.00	36.00	43.00
Texas	(D)	900	780	(D)	90	78	(D)	45.00	57.30
Virginia	3,100	2,400	2,300	1,302	744	644	33.00	50.00	47.00
Other States [2] ...	4,200	(X)	(X)	507	(X)	(X)	42.00	(X)	(X)
United States ...	101,000	99,600	97,600	28,660	26,391	27,280	30.50	44.60	41.60
Processing:	Acres	Acres	Acres	Tons	Tons	Tons	Dollars per ton	Dollars per ton	Dollars per ton
California	258,000	260,000	289,000	12,640,000	12,100,000	14,010,000	75.00	88.80	89.50
Indiana	9,000	8,700	9,300	259,650	269,700	344,100	118.00	121.00	114.00
Michigan	3,500	3,200	3,400	122,500	108,800	129,200	116.00	125.00	117.00
Ohio	5,800	5,100	4,400	156,600	153,000	154,000	113.00	116.00	111.00
United States ...	276,300	277,000	306,100	13,178,750	12,631,500	14,637,300	76.70	90.10	90.50

(D) Withheld to avoid disclosing data for individual operations.　(X) Not applicable.　[1] Cherry, grape, tomatillo, and greenhouse tomatoes are excluded.　[2] Other States includes Georgia and Texas.
NASS, Crops Branch, (202) 720–2127.

Table 4-75.—Watermelon for fresh market: Area, production, and value per hundredweight, by State and United States, 2012–2014

State	Area harvested			Production			Value per unit		
	2012	2013	2014	2012	2013	2014	2012	2013	2014
	Acres	*Acres*	*Acres*	*1,000 cwt*	*1,000 cwt*	*1,000 cwt*	*Dollars per cwt*	*Dollars per cwt*	*Dollars per cwt*
Alabama	2,700	2,900	2,700	338	377	456	11.70	11.00	14.20
Arizona	2,700	3,600	2,900	1,202	1,800	1,334	16.30	16.20	19.40
Arkansas	1,800	1,600	1,600	423	336	320	15.90	12.00	13.00
California	11,100	10,000	8,900	6,771	5,800	5,073	12.80	13.00	14.60
Delaware	2,800	2,700	2,500	1,050	864	833	13.00	12.00	13.00
Florida	21,000	20,200	19,700	6,195	6,262	4,827	18.50	25.00	16.60
Georgia	19,000	18,600	19,000	4,940	5,580	5,130	12.50	10.50	15.60
Indiana	6,500	7,100	7,600	2,340	2,414	2,964	11.80	12.50	9.00
Maryland	3,300	3,300	3,300	1,073	1,056	1,089	13.00	12.00	12.00
Mississippi	2,300	2,000	2,100	403	400	378	11.60	10.50	11.70
Missouri	2,400	3,000	2,700	960	843	837	10.30	10.30	9.40
North Carolina	5,600	5,700	5,500	1,680	1,710	1,155	14.00	13.50	12.00
Oklahoma	2,900	2,200	2,600	348	242	364	14.90	13.75	11.80
South Carolina	7,500	7,100	7,300	2,850	2,734	1,862	11.00	13.90	14.80
Texas	23,500	23,000	20,000	5,405	5,520	5,200	9.60	9.70	9.60
Virginia	700	630	650	175	164	130	10.00	12.50	15.00
United States	115,800	113,630	109,050	36,153	36,102	31,952	13.20	14.20	13.50

NASS, Crops Branch, (202) 720–2127.

Table 4-76.—Watermelon for fresh market, commercial crop: Area, yield, production, value per hundredweight, and total value, United States, 2005-2014

Year	Area harvested	Yield per acre	Production	Value [1]	
				Per cwt	Total
	Acres	*Cwt*	*1,000 cwt*	*Dollars*	*1,000 dollars*
2005	133,800	277	37,023	11.60	429,445
2006	131,000	304	39,865	10.40	414,111
2007	129,000	290	37,349	11.30	422,546
2008	125,550	319	40,003	12.50	499,633
2009	123,900	314	38,911	11.60	450,713
2010	134,300	311	41,736	12.00	499,800
2011	121,400	307	37,215	13.90	518,787
2012	115,800	312	36,153	13.20	476,768
2013	113,630	318	36,102	14.20	513,987
2014	109,050	293	31,952	13.50	431,184

[1] Price and value at point of first sale.
NASS, Crops Branch, (202) 720–2127.

Table 4-77.—Vegetables and melons, fresh: Total reported domestic rail, truck, and air shipments, 2014

Commodity	Jan.	Feb.	Mar.	Apr.	May	June	July	Aug.	Sep.	Oct.	Nov.	Dec.	Total
Vegetables:	1,000 cwt	1,000 cwt	1,000 cwt	1,000 cwt	1,000 cwt	1,000 cwt	1,000 cwt	1,000 cwt	1,000 cwt	1,000 cwt	1,000 cwt.	1,000 cwt	1,000 cwt
Artichokes	63	61	121	97	48	53	71	54	45	52	43	31	739
Asparagus	....	....	54	195	166	59	....	....	....	....	....	....	474
Beans	134	182	313	364	188	150	48	52	37	174	201	256	2,099
Broccoli	697	642	607	586	555	480	515	356	409	471	510	702	6,530
Brussels sprouts	43	18	2	....	2	9	38	55	87	108	101	94	557
Beets	13	10	17	23	17	3	3	2	2	3	2	1	96
Cabbage	1,146	1,153	1,599	959	856	390	441	705	639	676	694	973	10,231
Carrots	694	611	652	672	740	609	608	597	610	661	559	604	7,617
Cauliflower	418	423	461	361	304	285	328	261	270	335	311	391	4,148
Celery	1,498	1,203	1,463	1,475	1,369	1,117	1,073	1,045	1,088	1,314	1,685	1,472	15,802
Chinese cabbage	66	57	55	44	44	58	46	45	57	52	56	59	639
Corn, sweet	433	344	585	1,843	2,613	2,927	1,263	865	398	519	371	167	12,328
Cucumbers	13	1	205	391	393	642	397	597	489	544	296	187	4,155
Cucumbers, greenhouse	19	19	35	34	38	33	38	50	41	29	37	23	396
Eggplant	40	35	45	90	115	144	60	39	84	138	68	59	917
Eggplant-organic	....	....	....	1	5	1	....	....	3	4	....		14
Endive	23	22	25	17	6	4	4	3	4	5	14	14	141
Escarole	29	30	28	21	8	5	5	3	5	6	16	16	172
Greens	241	181	289	279	244	111	89	86	72	126	412	485	2,615
Lettuce, iceberg	2,298	2,312	2,794	2,415	2,339	2,112	2,287	2,120	2,209	2,165	2,187	2,643	27,881
Lettuce, other	387	350	447	289	246	203	216	207	229	268	307	423	3,572
Lettuce, romaine	1,906	1,642	1,965	1,683	1,584	1,338	1,389	1,394	1,466	1,624	1,650	2,010	19,651
Lettuce processed	449	429	566	817	1,248	1,091	983	1,219	1,027	935	927	529	10,220
Onions, dry	4,110	3,373	2,907	2,525	3,710	3,088	3,528	3,427	3,646	3,995	3,505	3,602	41,416
Onions, dry-organic	1	1	1	1	13	11	3	1	1	1	1	1	36
Onions processed	378	387	645	513	622	504	489	331	357	408	591	477	5,702
Onions, green	17	14	15	18	17	29	34	29	18	16	23	16	246
Parsley	46	52	59	49	38	24	26	24	25	31	39	36	449
Peas	....	....	1	1	4	2	2	2	1	1	1	....	15
Peppers, bell	385	384	493	749	968	974	878	731	831	973	671	611	8,648
Peppers, bell-organic	....	....	....	5	8	12	5	....	....	2	6	1	39
Peppers, other	20	28	24	20	20	53	31	8	2	39	18	31	294
Potatoes, table	8,464	7,445	8,154	8,073	8,267	8,072	7,479	8,005	8,123	8,560	9,227	8,396	98,265
Potatoes, table-organic	67	50	55	34	22	5	13	74	51	66	98	84	619
Potatoes, chipper	4,241	4,238	5,142	4,216	4,928	4,264	4,514	5,480	5,248	4,315	5,095	4,186	55,867
Potatoes, seed	391	618	3,634	7,025	3,044	137	3	....	107	44	112	204	15,319
Radishes	46	34	49	44	34	5	9	5	5	8	31	25	295
Spinach	301	297	328	92	58	60	63	54	55	79	145	288	1,820
Squash	56	94	94	168	241	205	128	118	127	171	68	137	1,607
Sweet potatoes	669	656	816	848	636	547	513	476	496	665	1,438	857	8,617
Sweet potatoes-organic	4	8	9	8	7	7	4	....	3	2	10	5	67
Tomatoes	1,336	1,158	1,069	1,407	1,650	1,463	1,593	1,244	1,222	1,161	1,173	1,339	15,815
Tomatoes, greenhouse	122	115	163	161	245	207	194	218	152	155	204	144	2,080
Toms, Grape Type	155	167	190	207	201	144	110	77	98	139	151	120	1,759
Toms, Grape Type-greenhouse	24	22	38	30	40	30	35	55	36	39	39	23	411
Toms, Grape Type-organic	10	10	10	13	10	4	2	....	....	6	11	4	80
Toms, Cherry	52	66	61	71	52	39	30	44	34	33	53	37	572
Toms, Cherry-greenhouse	2	2	1	....	2	2	2	3	2	1	....	....	17
Toms, Plum Type	296	205	175	248	231	129	203	278	257	207	218	199	2,646
Toms, Plum Type-greenhouse	7	8	10	11	10	9	10	13	8	8	11	8	113
Total	31,810	29,157	36,471	39,193	38,206	31,850	29,803	30,452	30,173	31,333	33,390	31,970	393,808
Melons:													
Cantaloupe	....	....	....	31	1,479	2,730	3,081	2,792	2,371	1,010	402	2	13,898
Cantaloupe-organic	....	....	....	....	3	3	25	55	25	17	....	....	128
Honeydews	....	....	....	....	98	402	703	806	927	271	69	....	3,276
Honeydews-organic	....	....	....	....	....	6	14	7	1	....	....	....	28
Mixed & misc. melons	....	....	....	1	25	80	112	119	30	1	1	....	369
Watermelons, seedless	....	....	3	749	4,299	8,909	8,391	7,005	2,214	419	143	....	32,132
Watermelons, seeded	....	....	....	....	169	611	939	678	493	119	38	29	3,076
Watermelons, seeded-organic	....	....	....	....	1	....	14	2	....	....	....	....	17
Total	....	....	3	781	6,074	12,741	13,279	11,464	6,061	1,837	653	31	52,924

AMS, Fruit and Vegetable Programs, Market News Division, (202) 720–9936.

Table 4-78.—Vegetables (fresh), melons, potatoes, sweet potatoes: Per capita civilian utilization (farm-weight basis), United States, 2005–2014[1]

Year	Cabbage	Cucumbers	Tomatoes[2]	Asparagus	Broccoli	Carrots	Head Lettuce	Leaf/romaine
	Pounds	*Pounds*	*Pounds*	*Pounds*	*Pounds*	*Pounds*	*Pounds*	*Pounds*
2005	7.8	6.2	20.2	1.1	5.3	8.7	20.9	9.7
2006	7.8	6.1	19.8	1.1	5.8	8.1	20.1	12.0
2007	8.0	6.4	19.2	1.2	5.6	8.1	18.4	11.5
2008	8.1	6.4	18.5	1.2	6.0	8.1	16.9	10.4
2009	7.3	6.8	19.6	1.3	6.2	7.4	16.1	10.0
2010	7.5	6.7	20.6	1.4	5.6	7.8	15.9	12.0
2011	6.6	6.4	21.0	1.4	5.9	7.5	15.8	11.7
2012	6.3	7.1	20.8	1.4	6.3	7.9	15.9	11.9
2013	6.9	7.3	20.2	1.4	6.9	8.0	14.1	11.4
2014	6.7	7.4	20.5	1.6	6.6	8.5	14.5	10.8

Year	Snap beans	Garlic	Cauliflower	Celery	Sweet Corn	Onions	Spinach	Bell peppers
	Pounds	*Pounds*	*Pounds*	*Pounds*	*Pounds*	*Pounds*	*Pounds*	*Pounds*
2005	1.8	2.4	1.8	5.9	8.7	20.9	2.3	9.2
2006	2.1	2.7	1.7	6.1	8.3	19.9	2.0	9.5
2007	2.2	2.7	1.7	6.3	9.2	21.6	1.6	9.4
2008	2.0	2.8	1.6	6.2	9.1	20.2	1.8	9.6
2009	1.7	2.4	1.7	6.2	9.2	19.6	2.0	9.8
2010	1.9	2.3	1.3	6.1	9.2	19.6	1.7	10.3
2011	1.7	2.3	1.2	6.0	8.2	19.1	1.8	10.6
2012	1.6	2.3	1.2	6.0	8.7	19.5	1.6	10.7
2013	1.6	2.0	1.3	5.5	8.9	18.5	1.6	10.0
2014	1.5	1.9	1.3	5.5	7.6	18.3	1.7	10.7

Year	Others[3]	Total vegetables[4]	Watermelon	Cantaloupe	Honeydew melons	Potatoes	Sweet potatoes
	Pounds	*Pounds*	*Pounds*	*Pounds*	*Pounds*	*Pounds*	*Pounds*
2005	15.29	148.1	13.5	9.6	1.9	41.3	4.5
2006	15.46	148.4	15.1	9.3	1.9	38.6	4.6
2007	15.02	148.1	14.4	9.6	1.8	38.7	5.1
2008	14.31	143.1	15.6	8.9	1.7	37.8	5.1
2009	13.98	141.3	14.9	9.0	1.6	36.7	5.3
2010	14.40	144.3	15.7	8.5	1.7	36.8	6.7
2011	14.78	141.9	13.8	8.6	1.6	34.1	7.5
2012	15.50	144.7	13.9	7.5	1.5	34.4	7.3
2013	15.00	140.6	14.5	8.3	1.6	34.8	6.7
2014	16.65	141.7	....	....	....	....	....

[1] Fresh vegetable consumption computed for total commercial production for fresh market.   Does not include production for home use.   Consumption obtained by dividing the total apparent consumption by total July 1 population as reported by the Bureau of the Census.   All data for calendar year.   [2] After 1996, includes an ERS estimate of domestically produced hothouse tomatoes.   Hothouse imports included in all years.   [3] Includes artichokes, eggplant, radishes, brussels sprouts, squash, green limas, and escarole/endive.   Beginning in 2000, also includes collards, mustard greens, turnip greens, kale, okra, and pumpkins.   [4] Excludes melons, mushrooms, potatoes, and sweet potatoes.

ERS, Market and Trade Economics Division, (202) 694–5253.

Table 4-79.—Vegetables, canning: Per capita utilization (farm weight), United States, 2005–2014

Year	Cabbage for kraut	Asparagus	Snap beans	Carrots	Green peas
	Pounds	*Pounds*	*Pounds*	*Pounds*	*Pounds*
2005	1.2	0.2	4.0	1.1	1.1
2006	1.2	0.2	3.9	1.0	1.2
2007	1.0	0.1	3.5	0.9	1.2
2008	0.9	0.2	3.3	1.0	1.1
2009	0.9	0.2	3.6	0.9	1.3
2010	1.0	0.1	3.7	0.7	1.1
2011	1.0	0.1	3.2	0.8	0.8
2012	1.2	0.1	2.9	0.8	0.8
2013	1.0	0.1	2.9	0.8	0.9
2014	1.0	0.1	2.8	0.7	0.7

Year	Tomatoes	Sweet corn	Pickles	Other [1]	Total [2]
	Pounds	*Pounds*	*Pounds*	*Pounds*	*Pounds*
2005	73.7	8.6	3.8	8.9	102.6
2006	64.5	8.4	3.0	8.9	92.2
2007	68.7	6.9	3.7	8.4	94.5
2008	67.1	6.7	3.5	8.8	92.8
2009	70.3	7.6	5.1	8.9	98.7
2010	71.1	6.9	3.7	9.1	97.4
2011	65.7	5.8	2.8	9.1	89.4
2012	66.5	5.9	3.0	9.8	90.9
2013	65.9	5.8	3.2	9.6	90.1
2014	67.2	5.8	3.9	9.7	91.8

[1] Includes beets, chile peppers (all uses), green lima beans and spinach.   [2] Total excludes mushrooms and potatoes. May not add due to rounding.
ERS, Market and Trade Economics Division, (202) 694–5253.

Table 4-80.—Vegetables, freezing: Per capita utilization (farm weight basis), United States, 2005–2014

Year	Leafy, green, and yellow vegetables					
	Asparagus	Snap beans	Carrots	Peas	Broccoli	Cauliflower
	Pounds	Pounds	Pounds	Pounds	Pounds	Pounds
2005	0.1	1.8	2.0	1.6	2.7	0.4
2006	0.1	1.9	2.1	1.6	2.3	0.4
2007	0.1	2.1	1.5	1.8	2.7	0.4
2008	0.1	2.1	1.5	1.8	2.7	0.4
2009	0.1	1.9	1.5	1.7	2.5	0.4
2010	0.1	2.0	1.5	1.5	2.5	0.4
2011	0.1	1.5	1.6	1.6	2.7	0.4
2012	0.1	1.9	1.2	1.9	2.6	0.3
2013	0.1	2.1	1.7	1.5	2.5	0.3
2014	0.1	1.8	1.2	1.6	2.6	0.4

Year	Sweet Corn	Other [1]	Total vegetables excluding potatoes	Potato products	Grand total [2]
	Pounds	Pounds	Pounds	Pounds	Pounds
2005	9.5	4.1	22.0	54.3	76.3
2006	9.4	4.1	21.8	53.2	75.0
2007	10.0	4.1	22.6	53.2	75.8
2008	9.2	4.0	21.9	51.5	73.4
2009	9.1	4.3	21.4	50.4	71.8
2010	8.5	4.5	20.9	50.2	71.1
2011	9.8	4.3	21.9	48.2	70.1
2012	9.8	4.5	22.3	48.4	70.7
2013	7.0	4.3	19.5	49.3	68.8
2014	7.7	4.6	19.8	....	....

[1] Includes green lima beans, spinach, and miscellaneous freezing vegetables.   [2] Totals may not add due to rounding.
ERS, Market and Trade Economics Division, (202) 694–5253.

Table 4-81.—Commercially produced vegetables: Per capita utilization, United States, 2005–2014

Year	Total fresh and processed	Fresh [2]	Farm weight equivalent				
			Processed [3]				
			Total	Canning	Freezing	Potatoes	Others [1]
	Pounds	Pounds	Pounds	Pounds	Pounds	Pounds	Pounds
2005	407.9	148.1	259.8	102.6	22.0	125.4	9.8
2006	396.4	148.4	248.0	92.2	21.8	123.7	10.3
2007	399.5	148.1	251.5	94.5	22.6	124.3	10.1
2008	386.5	143.1	243.4	92.8	21.9	118.3	10.5
2009	385.5	141.3	244.2	98.7	21.4	113.3	10.8
2010	387.7	144.3	243.3	97.4	20.9	113.8	11.2
2011	375.8	141.9	233.8	89.4	21.9	110.3	12.2
2012	384.8	144.7	240.0	90.9	22.3	114.7	12.2
2013	374.6	140.6	234.0	90.1	19.5	113.3	11.0
2014	378.1	141.7	236.4	91.8	19.8	112.1	12.7

Year	Fresh [2]	Percentage of annual total				
		Processed [3]				
		Total	Canning	Freezing	Potatoes	Others [1]
	Percent	Percent	Percent	Percent	Percent	Percent
2005	36.3	63.7	25.2	5.4	30.7	2.4
2006	37.4	62.6	23.3	5.5	31.2	2.6
2007	37.1	62.9	23.6	5.7	31.1	2.5
2008	37.0	63.0	24.0	5.7	30.6	2.7
2009	36.7	63.3	25.6	5.5	29.4	2.8
2010	37.2	62.8	25.1	5.4	29.4	2.9
2011	37.8	62.2	23.8	5.8	29.4	3.3
2012	37.6	62.4	23.6	5.8	29.8	3.2
2013	37.5	62.5	24.0	5.2	30.2	2.9
2014	37.5	62.5	24.3	5.2	29.6	3.4

[1] Includes potatoes, sweet potatoes, mushrooms, and onions for dehydrating market.   [2] See table 4-78 for items included under Fresh category. Excludes melons.
ERS, Market and Trade Economics Division, (202) 694–5253.

Table 4-82.—Frozen Vegetables and potato products: Cold storage holdings, end of month, United States, 2013 and 2014

Month	Asparagus		Lima beans		Green beans, regular cut		Green beans, french style	
	2013	2014	2013	2014	2013	2014	2013	2014
	1,000 pounds	*1,000 pounds*	*1,000 pounds*	*1,000 pounds*	*1,000 pounds*	*1,000 pounds*	*1,000 pounds*	*1,000 pounds*
January	7,087	9,701	55,077	58,462	230,122	162,305	14,313	13,479
February	6,515	9,497	49,776	54,696	201,608	149,444	14,331	11,607
March	5,517	9,038	43,163	51,382	179,446	139,195	12,910	11,680
April	4,648	7,946	38,938	43,074	164,526	125,882	11,732	10,675
May	6,476	10,252	31,743	39,818	152,338	109,855	8,587	8,790
June	9,900	15,185	29,717	34,333	143,931	96,376	8,749	8,194
July	9,695	15,656	26,868	31,632	166,636	147,470	13,128	15,306
August	9,432	16,324	28,225	35,991	237,400	225,135	20,760	18,840
September	9,378	16,916	52,301	52,979	252,315	253,066	20,563	20,852
October	9,307	14,873	69,060	73,497	224,385	235,830	17,647	18,439
November	9,576	14,572	63,264	69,543	200,790	205,861	15,421	16,975
December	9,758	13,603	60,262	64,530	181,073	182,136	14,248	14,754

Month	Broccoli, spears		Broccoli, chopped & cut		Brussels sprouts		Carrots, diced	
	2013	2014	2013	2014	2013	2014	2013	2014
	1,000 pounds	*1,000 pounds*	*1,000 pounds*	*1,000 pounds*	*1,000 pounds*	*1,000 pounds*	*1,000 pounds*	*1,000 pounds*
January	26,693	19,728	48,011	34,253	13,883	15,327	153,103	153,372
February	23,701	20,956	46,544	33,570	13,534	15,343	143,728	143,648
March	23,110	23,558	41,799	31,421	12,244	14,071	141,134	130,512
April	27,768	30,509	44,958	30,447	11,373	14,283	130,094	114,796
May	27,359	34,882	41,581	32,993	11,119	13,452	120,599	109,991
June	27,359	34,093	41,353	33,394	10,675	12,480	109,846	97,279
July	24,656	34,054	43,215	38,547	9,532	10,911	92,114	81,749
August	20,776	32,216	46,830	41,970	8,058	10,142	79,840	74,944
September	21,245	30,285	43,243	41,131	7,594	9,798	75,125	71,990
October	21,604	30,697	39,861	43,775	7,117	12,149	123,044	130,075
November	22,365	29,339	34,655	37,347	9,258	13,585	153,748	173,870
December	21,705	27,108	34,836	36,143	13,612	15,960	157,220	168,289

Month	Carrots, other		Cauliflower		Corn, cut		Corn, cob	
	2013	2014	2013	2014	2013	2014	2013	2014
	1,000 pounds	*1,000 pounds*	*1,000 pounds*	*1,000 pounds*	*1,000 pounds*	*1,000 pounds*	*1,000 pounds*	*1,000 pounds*
January	154,606	149,956	25,515	21,680	450,464	492,643	219,301	225,426
February	143,605	134,187	24,983	21,139	410,588	460,752	202,672	200,562
March	132,941	121,009	23,370	18,386	369,771	397,092	173,684	174,569
April	123,435	118,973	21,609	17,768	330,335	345,504	150,267	156,311
May	113,051	114,263	21,895	18,035	282,126	296,765	123,501	121,262
June	108,905	102,942	21,738	16,497	249,147	250,726	100,019	101,087
July	97,698	97,360	21,030	15,461	226,862	273,738	83,647	108,477
August	101,655	103,813	16,866	14,427	397,483	462,352	151,447	175,199
September	113,138	130,307	18,745	15,581	585,455	596,616	244,077	258,604
October	155,412	171,014	23,242	22,014	630,849	631,669	271,819	268,087
November	170,679	195,425	26,758	21,897	581,072	576,419	251,382	240,784
December	160,585	180,493	23,139	20,567	550,708	529,586	238,575	223,053

Month	Mixed vegetables		Okra		Onion rings		Onions, other	
	2013	2014	2013	2014	2013	2014	2013	2014
	1,000 pounds	*1,000 pounds*	*1,000 pounds*	*1,000 pounds*	*1,000 pounds*	*1,000 pounds*	*1,000 pounds*	*1,000 pounds*
January	46,003	56,257	19,951	14,964	8,681	9,700	45,201	40,725
February	44,219	54,208	14,701	10,651	10,837	9,135	45,110	37,919
March	40,716	47,594	10,579	7,129	10,957	8,114	41,609	38,309
April	44,956	48,023	9,713	7,353	11,845	8,032	40,990	38,143
May	44,713	47,670	11,107	7,670	11,486	9,154	39,573	40,892
June	46,674	49,422	17,750	14,800	12,287	11,141	38,270	44,632
July	47,610	52,108	23,728	26,511	9,677	9,933	43,371	54,319
August	51,082	58,514	26,156	36,605	8,600	9,755	41,448	51,107
September	51,341	60,248	25,739	46,743	11,049	9,981	39,203	42,755
October	48,420	62,359	28,318	48,448	11,431	10,489	38,075	39,793
November	51,988	59,702	26,182	44,192	10,870	9,127	41,900	36,664
December	50,977	53,082	21,405	39,375	9,889	9,057	39,917	35,944

See footnote(s) at end of table.

Table 4-82.—Frozen Vegetables and potato products: Cold storage holdings, end of month, United States, 2013 and 2014—Continued

Month	Blackeye peas		Green peas		Peas & carrots mixed		Spinach	
	2013	2014	2013	2014	2013	2014	2013	2014
	1,000 pounds	*1,000 pounds*	*1,000 pounds*	*1,000 pounds*	*1,000 pounds*	*1,000 pounds*	*1,000 pounds*	*1,000 pounds*
January	1,650	1,925	195,388	192,134	7,660	6,051	46,726	41,909
February	1,455	1,620	165,683	168,608	7,539	7,608	51,973	43,140
March	1,987	2,072	138,449	136,081	6,546	7,234	49,561	51,886
April	1,415	1,684	112,263	111,179	7,376	7,106	58,951	48,413
May	1,647	2,145	99,542	95,529	6,382	6,494	59,486	54,644
June	1,693	1,655	240,208	284,293	6,951	7,274	55,678	52,579
July	1,787	1,830	392,588	427,634	6,862	7,813	52,155	49,247
August	2,430	1,484	349,572	395,401	6,948	7,840	47,431	46,541
September	3,004	1,784	305,131	354,716	6,476	7,703	43,889	38,924
October	2,249	1,870	285,313	314,577	6,675	7,483	41,713	39,770
November	1,540	1,929	256,457	285,406	6,726	7,525	40,566	39,672
December	1,386	1,565	228,586	243,251	6,250	7,671	39,053	38,024

Month	Squash, summer/zucchini		Southern greens		Other vegetables		Total frozen vegetables	
	2013	2014	2013	2014	2013	2014	2013	2014
	1,000 pounds	*1,000 pounds*	*1,000 pounds*	*1,000 pounds*	*1,000 pounds*	*1,000 pounds*	*1,000 pounds*	*1,000 pounds*
January	57,366	57,592	13,229	11,763	363,899	371,053	2,203,929	2,157,405
February	55,137	56,111	15,199	13,778	352,909	366,772	2,046,347	2,024,951
March	48,824	50,334	15,456	12,126	350,651	359,294	1,874,424	1,842,086
April	48,090	48,985	16,231	13,295	349,274	311,776	1,760,787	1,660,157
May	48,741	47,022	16,469	12,849	301,871	285,450	1,581,392	1,519,877
June	49,657	42,958	17,240	14,873	298,588	281,639	1,646,335	1,607,852
July	46,198	40,448	14,476	13,599	310,171	310,021	1,763,704	1,863,824
August	55,835	53,729	12,445	12,353	369,266	348,093	2,089,985	2,232,775
September	55,229	56,780	9,869	10,597	436,882	402,271	2,430,991	2,530,627
October	57,849	61,649	9,784	9,610	455,362	415,446	2,578,536	2,663,613
November	61,350	63,870	10,006	10,643	433,678	392,454	2,480,231	2,546,801
December	61,133	62,828	11,043	11,253	425,010	381,070	2,360,370	2,359,342

Month	Frozen potatoes					
	French fries		Other frozen potatoes		Total frozen potatoes	
	2013	2014	2013	2014	2013	2014
	1,000 pounds	*1,000 pounds*	*1,000 pounds*	*1,000 pounds*	*1,000 pounds*	*1,000 pounds*
January	958,032	913,426	217,044	191,376	1,175,076	1,104,802
February	1,000,505	924,730	232,226	199,400	1,232,731	1,124,130
March	994,118	840,697	232,719	203,650	1,226,837	1,044,347
April	990,246	806,282	232,128	202,949	1,222,374	1,009,231
May	930,626	780,688	250,653	202,730	1,181,279	983,418
June	1,009,457	807,376	260,865	205,458	1,270,322	1,012,834
July	903,749	725,507	234,641	198,740	1,138,390	924,247
August	874,819	742,033	216,514	194,555	1,091,333	936,588
September	920,034	837,281	217,556	202,414	1,137,590	1,039,695
October	951,207	890,062	224,100	209,443	1,175,307	1,099,505
November	939,267	900,485	211,507	205,070	1,150,774	1,105,555
December	902,139	842,464	193,161	187,967	1,095,300	1,030,431

NASS, Livestock Branch, (202) 720–3570.

CHAPTER V

STATISTICS OF FRUITS, TREE NUTS, AND HORTICULTURAL SPECIALTIES

For most fruits, production is estimated at two levels—total and utilized. Total production is the quantity of fruit harvested plus quantities which would have been acceptable for fresh market or processing but were not harvested or utilized because of economic and other reasons. Utilized production is the amount sold plus the quantities used on farms where grown and quantities held in storage. The difference between total and utilized production is the quantity of marketable fruit not harvested and fruit harvested but not sold or utilized because of economic and other reasons. Production relates to the crop produced on all farms, except for apples and strawberries. In accordance with Congressional enactment, the Department's estimates of apple production since 1938 have related only to commercial production. The estimates for strawberries cover production on area grown primarily for sale. Statistics on utilization of fruit by commercial processors refer to first utilization, not necessarily final utilization. For example, frozen fruit includes fruit which may later be used for preserves.

The price shown for each crop is a marketing year average price for all methods of sales. Prices for most fresh fruit are the average prices producers received at the point of first sale, commonly referred to as the "average price as sold." Since the point of first sale is not the same for all producers, prices for the various methods of sale are weighted by the proportionate quantity sold. For example, if in a given State part of the fruit crop is sold f.o.b. packed by growers, part sold as bulk fruit at the packinghouse door, and some sold retail at roadside stands, the fresh fruit average price as sold is a weighted average of the average price for each method of sale.

The annual estimates are checked and adjusted at the end of each marketing season on the basis of shipment and processing records from transportation agencies, processors, cooperative marketing associations, and other industry organizations. The estimates are reviewed (and revised if necessary) at 5-year intervals, when the Census of Agriculture data become available. The Department's available statistics are limited to the major tree fruits and nuts and to grapes, cranberries, and strawberries, and exclude some States where census data indicate production is of only minor importance.

Table 5-1.—Fruits and planted nuts: Bearing area, United States, 2005–2014

Year	Citrus fruits [1]	Major deciduous fruits [2]	Miscellaneous Noncitrus [3]	Nuts [4]	Total
	1,000 acres	1,000 acres	1,000 acres	1,000 acres	1,000 acres
2005	954.2	1,770.6	303.2	956.3	3,984.3
2006	886.8	1,752.5	309.1	981.2	3,929.6
2007	866.2	1,729.7	292.1	1,016.6	3,904.5
2008	850.9	1,731.5	303.4	1,101.3	3,987.1
2009	844.8	1,739.7	306.3	1,159.7	4,050.5
2010	825.2	1,750.3	310.0	1,206.0	4,091.5
2011	809.2	1,744.2	315.5	1,261.5	4,116.0
2012	801.8	1,734.6	260.7	1,316.0	4,113.1
2013	797.1	1,749.6	331.2	1,379.0	4,256.8
2014	782.3	1,738.4	353.7	1,427.0	4,301.4

[1] Grapefruit, lemons, oranges, tangelos, tangerines, and temples. [2] Commercial apples, apricots, cherries, grapes, nectarines, peaches, pears, plums, and prunes. [3] Avocados, bananas, berries, cranberries, dates, figs, guavas, kiwifruit, olives, papayas, and strawberries. [4] Almonds, hazelnuts, macadamia nuts, pistachios, and walnuts.
NASS, Crops Branch, (202) 720–2127.

Table 5-2.—Fruits: Total production in tons, United States, 2005–2014 [1]

Year	Apples, commercial crop [2]	Peaches	Pears	Grapes (fresh basis)	Sweet cherries	Tart cherries	Apricots
	1,000 tons	*1,000 tons*	*1,000 tons*	*1,000 tons*	*1,000 tons*	*1,000 tons*	*1,000 tons*
2005	4,834	1,185	823	7,814	251	135	82
2006	4,912	1,010	842	6,378	294	131	45
2007	4,545	1,127	873	7,057	311	127	89
2008	4,812	1,135	870	7,279	248	107	82
2009	4,844	1,104	957	7,268	443	180	69
2010	4,641	1,149	814	7,432	313	95	66
2011	4,720	1,071	966	7,409	334	116	67
2012	4,496	968	851	7,531	424	43	61
2013	5,216	904	877	8,632	332	147	61
2014	5,716	853	832	7,772	364	152	65

Year	Figs (fresh basis)	Plums (CA)	Prunes (fresh basis) (CA)	Prunes & Plums (ID,MI,OR,WA)	Olives	Strawberries [3]	Pineapples [3]
	1,000 tons	*1,000 tons*	*1,000 tons*	*1,000 tons*	*1,000 tons*	*1,000 tons*	*1,000 tons*
2005	49	171	296	9	142	1,161	212
2006	43	158	634	22	24	1,202	185
2007	48	152	241	12	133	1,223	(NA)
2008	43	160	368	16	67	1,266	(NA)
2009	44	112	496	19	46	1,401	(NA)
2010	41	142	390	12	206	1,426	(NA)
2011	39	160	444	13	71	1,451	(NA)
2012	35	115	436	13	160	1,526	(NA)
2013	33	95	255	13	166	1,524	(NA)
2014	32	113	312	15	94	1,511	(NA)

Year	Avocados [4]	Nectarines	Oranges [5]	Tangerines and Mandarins [5]	Grapefruit [5]	Lemons [5]	Tangelos [5]	Temples [6]
	1,000 tons	*1,000 tons*	*1,000 tons*	*1,000 tons*	*1,000 tons*	*1,000 tons*	*1,000 tons*	*1,000 tons*
2005	312	251	9,251	335	1,018	870	70	29
2006	147	232	9,020	417	1,232	980	63	32
2007	193	283	7,625	361	1,627	798	56	(NA)
2008	116	303	10,076	527	1,548	619	68	(NA)
2009	299	220	9,128	443	1,304	912	52	(NA)
2010	174	233	8,243	596	1,238	882	41	(NA)
2011	263	225	8,905	657	1,264	920	52	(NA)
2012	(NA)	189	8,268	682	1,204	912	45	(NA)
2013	183	162	6,768	732	1,047	824	40	(NA)
2014	198	205	6,378	843	870	900	31	(NA)

Year	Cranberries	Bananas	Kiwifruit	Dates	Papayas	Berries [7]	Guavas	Total
	1,000 tons	*1,000 tons*	*1,000 tons*	*1,000 tons*	*1,000 tons*	*1,000 tons*	*1,000 tons*	*1,000 tons*
2005	312	11	37	17	17	267	4	29,965
2006	345	11	26	18	14	285	4	28,706
2007	328	13	25	16	17	288	2	27,570
2008	393	9	23	21	17	320	2	30,495
2009	346	9	26	24	16	359	1	30,122
2010	340	9	33	29	15	348	1	28,909
2011	386	9	38	33	14	384	1	30,012
2012	402	(NA)	30	31	(NA)	391	(NA)	28,813
2013	448	7	28	31	12	435	1	28,973
2014	420	7	28	29	12	480	1	28,233

(NA) Not available. [1] For some crops in certain years, production includes some quantities unharvested for economic reasons or excess cullage fruit. [2] Estimates of the commercial crop refer to production in orchards of 100 or more bearing-age trees. [3] Utilized production only. [4] Year of bloom. [5] Year harvest was complete. [6] Temples included in early, midseason, and navel oranges beginning with the 2006-07 season. [7] Excludes strawberries and cranberries.
NASS, Crops Branch, (202) 720–2127.

Table 5-3.—Apples, commercial crop: Production and season average price per pound, by State and United States, 2012–2014

State	Total production			Utilized production			Price per pound [1] for crop of—		
	2012	2013	2014	2012	2013	2014	2012	2013	2014
	Million pounds	*Million pounds*	*Million pounds*	*Million pounds*	*Million pounds*	*Million pounds*	*Dollars*	*Dollars*	*Dollars*
Arizona	8.0	16.5	7.1	8.0	16.3	7.1	0.217	0.274	0.421
California	270.0	270.0	240.0	270.0	270.0	240.0	0.241	0.233	0.238
Colorado	17.0	5.6	8.9	16.0	5.3	8.2	0.304	0.363	0.892
Connecticut	16.5	27.0	19.9	15.5	26.5	19.6	0.654	0.741	0.632
Idaho	75.0	70.6	63.3	75.0	70.0	60.0	0.320	0.331	0.146
Illinois	32.0	16.0	21.0	25.0	15.0	20.2	0.557	0.528	0.764
Indiana	4.5	30.0	17.1	4.5	27.0	16.0	0.396	0.387	0.430
Iowa	0.7	8.1	4.5	0.2	6.8	3.8	0.675	0.699	0.779
Maine	30.0	27.0	38.0	27.5	25.5	36.8	0.560	0.516	0.421
Maryland	35.0	33.0	41.4	34.7	32.6	41.2	0.402	0.187	0.261
Massachusetts	28.0	43.5	43.3	27.5	40.5	40.3	0.623	0.520	0.492
Michigan	115.0	1,260.0	1,025.0	115.0	1,250.0	1,025.0	0.352	0.204	0.215
Minnesota	13.5	26.0	25.0	11.3	22.0	23.0	0.825	0.833	0.842
Missouri	35.0	16.9	20.9	33.0	15.0	19.8	0.471	0.368	0.283
New Hampshire	15.5	25.5	16.9	13.5	24.5	16.5	0.581	0.429	0.616
New Jersey	35.0	29.0	37.0	34.0	28.5	36.0	0.839	0.451	0.847
New York	720.0	1,410.0	1,295.0	710.0	1,390.0	1,285.0	0.352	0.171	0.187
North Carolina	33.5	155.0	125.0	32.0	145.0	125.0	0.313	0.222	0.245
Ohio	33.0	54.0	44.0	26.0	51.0	43.0	0.336	0.418	0.453
Oregon	130.0	141.0	155.0	128.0	137.0	155.0	0.250	0.364	0.279
Pennsylvania	494.0	469.0	493.0	475.0	455.0	482.0	0.281	0.186	0.168
Rhode Island	1.7	2.5	1.8	1.6	2.3	1.7	0.851	0.863	0.740
Tennessee	6.4	6.9	4.7	6.0	6.3	4.2	0.480	0.444	0.440
Utah	14.0	16.5	23.0	13.8	15.8	22.4	0.263	0.481	0.219
Vermont	25.5	34.0	29.4	24.0	31.0	28.2	0.434	0.451	0.407
Virginia	230.0	195.0	195.0	230.0	190.0	195.0	0.297	0.176	0.188
Washington	6,450.0	5,900.0	7,300.0	6,450.0	5,900.0	7,100.0	0.385	0.362	0.267
West Virginia	91.0	95.0	82.0	90.0	95.0	82.0	0.258	0.137	0.152
Wisconsin	32.5	48.0	54.0	29.4	46.0	51.0	0.649	0.508	0.612
United States	8,992.3	10,431.6	11,431.2	8,926.5	10,339.9	11,188.0	0.371	0.303	0.255

[1] Fresh fruit prices are equivalent packinghouse-door returns for California, Michigan, New York, and Washington; prices at point of first sale for other States.   Processing prices are equivalent at processing plant door.
NASS, Crops Branch, (202) 720–2127.

Table 5-4.—Apples: Production and value, United States, 2005–2014

Year	Apples, commercial crop			
	Total production	Utilized production	Marketing year average price [1]	Value
	Million pounds	*Million pounds*	*Cents per pound*	*1,000 dollars*
2005	9,666.9	9,567.2	17.3	1,657,947
2006	9,823.4	9,730.2	22.7	2,213,155
2007	9,089.4	9,045.4	28.8	2,608,220
2008	9,623.3	9,531.7	23.2	2,210,997
2009	9,687.7	9,435.6	23.1	2,182,003
2010	9,282.1	9,205.0	25.1	2,310,982
2011	9,439.6	9,328.8	30.3	2,830,784
2012	8,992.3	8,926.5	37.1	3,314,996
2013	10,431.6	10,339.9	30.3	3,132,936
2014	11,431.2	11,188.0	25.5	2,855,827

[1] Fresh fruit prices are equivalent packinghouse-door returns for California, Michigan, New York, and Washington; prices at point of first sale for other States.   Processing prices are equivalent at processing plant door.
NASS, Crops Branch, (202) 720–2127.

Table 5-5.—International Apples, fresh: Production in specified countries, 2013/2014–2015/2016

Country	Production		
	2013/2014	2014/2015	2015/2016
	metric tons	*metric tons*	*metric tons*
Brazil	1,377,400	1,266,000	1,240,000
Chile	1,310,000	1,350,000	1,350,000
China	39,680,000	40,920,000	43,000,000
European Union	11,864,900	13,618,500	12,220,000
India	2,200,000	2,200,000	2,200,000
Iran	1,693,000	1,693,000	1,693,000
Russia	1,416,500	1,408,600	1,390,000
South Africa	792,500	860,000	865,000
Turkey	2,930,000	2,289,000	2,740,000
Ukraine	1,211,000	1,211,000	1,211,000
Others	4,649,600	4,560,800	4,548,800
Total Foreign	69,124,900	71,376,900	72,457,800
United States	4,690,101	5,074,793	4,561,000
Total	73,815,001	76,451,693	77,018,800

FAS, Office of Global Analysis, (202) 720-6301. Prepared or estimated on the basis of official USDA production, supply, and distribution statistics from foreign governments.

Table 5-6.—Apples, commercial crop: Production and utilization, United States, 2005–2014

Crop of—	Total production	Utilized production	Utilization				
			Fresh	Processed (fresh basis)			
				Canned	Dried	Frozen	Juice, cider & other [1]
	Million pounds	*Million pounds*	*Million pounds*	*Million pounds*	*Million pounds*	*Million pounds*	*Million pounds*
2005	9,666.9	9,567.2	6,096.9	1,163.8	191.1	259.4	1,856.0
2006	9,823.4	9,730.2	6,308.5	1,167.3	252.8	271.8	1,729.8
2007	9,089.4	9,045.4	6,077.3	1,091.2	203.7	257.7	1,415.5
2008	9,623.3	9,531.7	6,265.9	1,253.4	212.7	211.2	1,588.5
2009	9,687.7	9,435.6	6,296.4	1,158.2	161.2	236.2	1,583.6
2010	9,282.1	9,205.0	6,248.8	1,088.3	175.5	206.0	1,486.4
2011	9,439.6	9,328.8	6,312.9	1,123.7	183.5	190.5	1,518.2
2012	8,992.3	8,926.5	6,594.9	748.9	223.0	66.6	1,292.8
2013	10,431.6	10,339.9	6,895.3	1,264.4	161.0	239.3	1,779.9
2014	11,431.2	11,188.0	7,946.6	1,123.0	181.0	222.5	1,714.9

[1] Includes vinegar, wine, and slices for pie making.
NASS, Crops Branch, (202) 720–2127.

Table 5-7.—Apples, commercial crop: Production and utilization, by State and United States, crop of 2013 and 2014

State	Total production	Utilized production	Utilization				
			Fresh	Processed (fresh basis)			
				Canned	Dried	Frozen	Juice, cider & other [1]
	Million pounds	Million pounds	Million pounds	Million pounds	Million pounds	Million pounds	Million pounds
				2013			
Arizona	16.5	16.3	(D)				
California	270.0	270.0	(D)	(D)			(D)
Colorado	5.6	5.3	(D)				
Connecticut	27.0	26.5	25.5				
Idaho	70.6	70.0	50.0				
Illinois	16.0	15.0	(D)				
Indiana	30.0	27.0	17.0				
Iowa	8.1	6.8	(D)				
Maine	27.0	25.5	22.5				
Maryland	33.0	32.6	11.6	13.0			8.0
Massachusetts	43.5	40.5	25.5				
Michigan	1,260.0	1,250.0	500.0	360.0			(D)
Minnesota	26.0	22.0	(D)				
Missouri	16.9	15.0	10.0				
New Hampshire	25.5	24.5	(D)				
New Jersey	29.0	28.5	19.0				
New York	1,410.0	1,390.0	650.0	325.0			340.0
North Carolina	155.0	145.0	75.0	40.0			21.0
Ohio	54.0	51.0	37.0				(D)
Oregon	141.0	137.0	120.0				7.5
Pennsylvania	469.0	455.0	180.0	187.0			81.0
Rhode Island	2.5	2.3	(D)				
Tennessee	6.9	6.3	(D)				
Utah	16.5	15.8	(D)				
Vermont	34.0	31.0	26.0				
Virginia	195.0	190.0	80.0	(D)			(D)
Washington	5,900.0	5,900.0	4,800.0	180.0			660.0
West Virginia	95.0	95.0	20.0	49.0			24.0
Wisconsin	48.0	46.0	41.0				
Other States			185.2	110.4	161.0	239.3	320.2
United States	10,431.6	10,339.9	6,895.3	1,264.4	161.0	239.3	1,761.7
				2014			
Arizona	7.1	7.1	(D)				
California	240.0	240.0	(D)	(D)			
Colorado	8.9	8.2	(D)				
Connecticut	19.9	19.6	19.1				
Idaho	63.3	60.0	34.0				
Illinois	21.0	20.2	(D)				
Indiana	17.1	16.0	9.0				
Iowa	4.5	3.8	(D)				
Maine	38.0	36.8	29.6				
Maryland	41.4	41.2	15.2	(D)			
Massachusetts	43.3	40.3	28.3				
Michigan	1,025.0	1,025.0	425.0	275.0			
Minnesota	25.0	23.0	(D)				
Missouri	20.9	19.8	11.6				
New Hampshire	16.9	16.5	(D)				
New Jersey	37.0	36.0	26.0				
New York	1,295.0	1,285.0	650.0	250.0			
North Carolina	125.0	125.0	65.0	(D)			
Ohio	44.0	43.0	34.0				
Oregon	155.0	155.0	132.0				
Pennsylvania	493.0	482.0	178.0	214.0			
Rhode Island	1.8	1.7	(D)				
Tennessee	4.7	4.2	(D)				
Utah	23.0	22.4	(D)				
Vermont	29.4	28.2	23.8				
Virginia	195.0	195.0	80.0	(D)			
Washington	7,300.0	7,100.0	5,950.0	190.0			
West Virginia	82.0	82.0	18.0	(D)			
Wisconsin	54.0	51.0	42.3				
Other States			175.7	194.0	181.0	222.5	
United States	11,431.2	11,188.0	7,946.6	1,123.0	181.0	222.5	

[1] Includes vinegar, wine, and slices for pie making.
NASS, Crops Branch, (202) 720–2127.

Table 5-8.—Fruits, fresh: United States exports by country of destination and imports by country of origin, 2011–2013

Country	2011	2012	2013
	Metric tons	*Metric tons*	*Metric tons*
Fresh fruits, deciduous:			
Mexico	346,910	410,382	453,255
Canada	354,472	378,790	384,904
Taiwan	111,712	115,852	115,059
Hong Kong	118,203	103,192	111,600
India	79,631	91,160	63,423
United Arab Emirates	34,526	39,640	58,558
Indonesia	82,620	81,230	48,693
Vietnam	19,803	17,553	30,596
Malaysia	23,835	26,776	29,052
Philippines	22,499	24,128	28,863
Thailand	32,865	30,457	28,720
China	21,509	26,182	28,536
Colombia	29,502	28,494	24,830
Russia	18,751	15,254	24,368
Saudi Arabia	22,872	15,437	20,871
Korea, South	13,011	20,762	20,521
Singapore	16,368	14,854	19,361
Australia(*)	10,739	17,018	19,252
Japan	18,842	22,091	18,839
Dominican Republic	15,920	18,022	18,189
United Kingdom	15,540	18,076	17,649
Guatemala	15,576	15,569	15,803
Costa Rica	15,193	14,014	14,816
Honduras	12,969	12,317	11,125
Panama	9,470	8,826	10,117
El Salvador	11,497	10,841	10,028
New Zealand(*)	11,579	11,303	8,608
Israel(*)	8,090	6,959	7,744
Peru	4,280	4,079	7,471
Rest of World	82,499	70,109	59,938
World Total	1,581,281	1,669,367	1,710,789
Fresh fruit, other:			
Canada	199,822	224,529	232,049
Mexico	13,804	18,521	23,469
Japan	12,281	17,492	15,684
Korea, South	10,026	17,524	14,739
United Kingdom	6,138	4,597	6,701
Netherlands	4,386	3,822	5,031
Hong Kong	2,483	3,514	4,119
Chile	140	155	3,275
Bermuda	2,243	2,315	3,052
Taiwan	5,897	2,057	2,661
Russia	1,346	1,456	2,453
Belgium-Luxembourg(*)	1,106	1,404	2,428
Australia(*)	3,498	3,447	2,369
United Arab Emirates	4,224	1,682	1,859
France(*)	1,934	1,874	1,623
New Zealand(*)	710	666	1,349
Singapore	622	1,241	895
China	966	856	704
Saudi Arabia	409	305	618
Germany(*)	965	108	583
Bahamas, The	517	582	554
Cayman Islands	432	839	515
Brazil	604	627	474
Sweden	171	139	446
Costa Rica	137	80	338
Trinidad and Tobago	789	470	336
Colombia	159	214	336
Dominican Republic	598	528	283
Kuwait	686	273	277
Rest of World	5,677	3,576	3,006
World Total	282,768	314,892	332,225

See footnote(s) at end of table.

Table 5-8.—Fruits, fresh: United States exports by country of destination and imports by country of origin, 2011–2013—Continued

Country	2011	2012	2013
	Metric tons	*Metric tons*	*Metric tons*
Fresh melons:			
Canada	239,612	232,092	228,859
Mexico	32,787	17,526	16,141
Japan	13,546	12,905	13,122
Hong Kong	1,747	2,082	3,078
Taiwan	369	849	2,045
Korea, South	2,010	2,054	1,685
United Arab Emirates	326	51	613
Bahamas, The	817	699	554
Panama	79	84	169
Chile	10	53	100
Costa Rica	90	0	33
Ecuador	0	0	33
Netherlands Antilles(*)	16	65	28
Saudi Arabia	0	1	23
Cayman Islands	46	6	22
Turks and Caicos Islands	3	15	17
Singapore	313	65	16
Barbados	21	13	16
Leeward-Windward Islands(*)	7	33	13
Bermuda	176	114	8
China	0	19	7
Bahrain	0	27	6
Trinidad and Tobago	0	0	4
French Pacific Islands(*)	0	0	4
Bulgaria	0	0	4
Haiti	0	0	3
Dominican Republic	4	0	2
Brazil	0	1	0
Guatemala	0	30	0
Rest of World	82	56	0
World Total	292,059	268,837	299,603

(*) Denotes a country that is a summarization of its component countries. All zeroes for a data item may show that statistics exist in the other import type. Consumption or General. Users should use cautious interpretation on Quantity reports using mixed units of measure. Quantity line items will only include statistics on the units of measure that are equal to, or are able to be converted to, the assigned unit of measure of the grouped commodities.

FAS, Office of Global Analysis, (202) 720-6301. Data Source: Department of Commerce, U.S. Census Bureau, Foreign Trade Statistics.

Table 5-9.—Apples: Foreign trade, United States, 2005–2014 [1]

Year beginning October	Imports, fresh and dried, in terms of fresh	Domestic exports	
		Fresh	Dried, in terms of fresh [1]
	Metric tons	Metric tons	Metric tons
2005	198,472	654,138	27,383
2006	255,320	652,827	32,925
2007	238,333	680,618	31,680
2008	206,667	810,984	26,849
2009	225,718	748,054	22,128
2010	184,474	817,906	26,802
2011	219,305	856,819	28,492
2012	243,093	908,752	22,282
2013	243,873	848,664	23,741
2014	209,440	1,057,197	26,091

[1] Dried converted to terms of fresh apples on following basis; 1 pound dried is equivalent to 8 pounds fresh. No re-exports reported.
ERS, Crops Branch, (202) 694–5255.

Table 5-10.—Apricots: Production and value, United States, 2005–2014

Year	Total production	Utilized production	Market year average price per ton	Value
	Tons	Tons	Dollars	1,000 dollars
2005	81,650	76,645	520.00	39,880
2006	44,480	44,455	665.00	29,563
2007	88,460	88,460	477.00	42,227
2008	81,610	77,480	532.00	41,196
2009	68,720	68,690	654.00	44,912
2010	66,380	66,350	722.00	47,876
2011	66,650	66,620	616.00	41,056
2012	60,800	60,770	673.00	40,879
2013	61,035	61,028	737.00	44,987
2014	64,928	64,918	818.00	53,096

NASS, Crops Branch, (202) 720–2127.

Table 5-11.—Apricots: Production and marketing year average price per ton, by State and United States, 2012–2014

State	Total production			Utilized production			Price for crop of—		
	2012	2013	2014	2012	2013	2014	2012	2013	2014
	Tons	Tons	Tons	Tons	Tons	Tons	Dollars	Dollars	Dollars
California	53,800	54,400	55,400	53,800	54,400	55,400	600.00	682.00	777.00
Utah	300	135	228	270	128	218	919.00	1,010.00	1,510.00
Washington	6,700	6,500	9,300	6,700	6,500	9,300	1,250.00	1,190.00	1,050.00
United States ..	60,800	61,035	64,928	60,770	61,028	64,918	673.00	737.00	818.00

NASS, Crops Branch, (202) 720–2127.

Table 5-12.—Apricots: Production and utilization, United States, 2005–2014

Crop of—	Total production	Utilized production	Utilization of quantities sold			
			Fresh	Processed [1]		
				Canned	Dried (fresh basis)	Frozen
	Tons	Tons	Tons	Tons	Tons	Tons
2005	81,650	76,645	23,645	23,500	11,500	[2]
2006	44,480	44,455	13,755	14,900	5,500	[2]
2007	88,460	88,460	29,270	24,000	13,000	[2]
2008	81,610	77,480	25,760	22,000	14,000	[2]
2009	68,720	68,690	25,170	23,100	9,000	[2]
2010	66,380	66,350	23,510	20,100	10,000	[2]
2011	66,650	66,620	23,990	17,150	12,000	[2]
2012	60,800	60,770	23,130	16,500	9,500	[2]
2013	61,035	61,028	25,228	14,550	10,000	[2]
2014	64,928	64,918	25,812	17,550	9,500	[2]

[1] California only. [2] Withheld to avoid disclosure of individual operations.
NASS, Crops Branch, (202) 720–2127.

Table 5-13.—Apricots: Production and utilization, by State and United States, crop of 2014

State	Total production	Utilized production	Utilization			
			Fresh	Processed [1]		
				Canned	Dried (fresh basis)	Frozen
	Tons	Tons	Tons	Tons	Tons	Tons
California	55,400	55,400	18,000	17,550	9,500	[2]
Utah	228	218	[2]	[2]	[2]	[2]
Washington	9,300	9,300	[2]	[2]	[2]	[2]
United States	64,928	64,918	25,812			[2]

[1] California only. [2] Withheld to avoid disclosure of individual operations.
NASS, Crops Branch, (202) 720–2127.

Table 5-14.—Apricots: Foreign trade, United States, 2005–2014

Year beginning October	Domestic exports				
	Fresh	Canned [1]	Dried [1]	Dried, in fruit salad [2]	Total, in terms of fresh [3]
	Metric tons	Metric tons	Metric tons	Metric tons	Metric tons
2005	3,935	1,508	1,142	633	10,887
2006	7,061	1,201	615	364	11,083
2007	7,357	1,217	679	405	11,722
2008	5,047	1,289	602	355	9,064
2009	5,555	1,308	1,011	389	11,691
2010	5,646	1,389	708	470	10,283
2011	7,459	660	634	519	11,191
2012	7,774	646	533	547	10,978
2013	6,843	755	473	504	9,815
2014	5,401	621	367	409	7,732

[1] Net processed weight. [2] Dried apricots are 12⅓ percent of total dried fruit for salad. [3] Dried fruit converted to unprocessed dry weight by dividing by 1.07. Unprocessed dry weight converted to terms of fresh fruit on the basis that 1 pound dried equals 5.5 pounds fresh. Canned apricots converted to terms of fresh on the basis that 1 pound canned equals 0.717 pounds fresh.
ERS, Crops Branch, (202) 694–5255.

Table 5-15.—Avocados: Foreign trade, United States, 2005–2014

Year beginning October	Imports
	Metric tons
2005	197,354
2006	338,559
2007	307,167
2008	413,936
2009	365,146
2010	385,434
2011	475,630
2012	565,127
2013	699,367
2014	832,490

ERS, Crops Branch, (202) 694–5255.

Table 5-16.—Avocados: Production, marketing year average price per ton, and value, United States, 2005/2006 to 2014/2015

Season	California			Florida		
	Production	Price per ton	Value	Production	Price per ton	Value
	Tons	Dollars	1,000 dollars	Tons	Dollars	1,000 dollars
2005/06	300,000	1,140	342,000	12,000	940	11,280
2006/07	132,000	1,890	249,480	14,000	912	12,768
2007/08	165,000	1,990	328,350	27,500	440	12,100
2008/09	88,000	2,280	200,640	27,450	480	13,176
2009/10	274,800	1,510	414,948	23,200	600	13,920
2010/11	151,500	3,040	460,560	22,500	800	18,000
2011/12	231,500	1,650	381,975	31,100	756	23,512
2012/13	(NA)	(NA)	(NA)	(NA)	(NA)	(NA)
2013/14	149,000	2,240	333,760	33,800	796	26,905
2014/15	164,000	2,000	328,000	32,900	656	21,582

Season	Hawaii			United States		
	Production	Price per ton	Value	Production	Price per ton	Value
	Tons	Dollars	1,000 dollars	Tons	Dollars	1,000 dollars
2005/06	400	1,320.00	528	312,400	1,130.00	353,808
2006/07	510	1,360.00	694	146,510	1,800.00	262,942
2007/08	580	1,360.00	789	193,080	1,770.00	341,239
2008/09	500	1,460.00	730	115,950	1,850.00	214,546
2009/10	520	1,380.00	718	298,520	1,440.00	429,586
2010/11	330	1,540.00	508	174,330	2,750.00	479,068
2011/12	350	1,600.00	560	262,950	1,540.00	406,047
2012/13	(NA)	(NA)	(NA)	(NA)	(NA)	(NA)
2013/14	320	2,000.00	640	183,120	1,970.00	361,305
2014/15	550	2,860.00	1,573	197,450	1,780.00	351,155

(NA) Not available.
NASS, Crops Branch, (202) 720–2127.

Table 5-17.—Bananas: Area, yield, utilized production, marketing year average price, and value, Hawaii, 2005–2014

Year	Area harvested	Yield per acre	Production	Price per pound	Value
	Acres	1,000 pounds	1,000 pounds	Cents	1,000 dollars
2005	980	21.3	20,900	43.9	9,175
2006	1,100	20.0	22,000	49.0	10,780
2007	1,300	19.7	25,600	41.0	10,496
2008	1,100	15.8	17,400	46.0	8,004
2009	1,100	16.8	18,500	55.0	10,175
2010	1,100	16.2	17,800	60.0	10,680
2011	1,000	17.4	17,400	65.0	11,310
2012	(NA)	(NA)	(NA)	(NA)	(NA)
2013	900	16.1	14,500	90.0	13,050
2014	900	16.0	14,400	82.0	11,808

NASS, Crops Branch, (202) 720–2127.

Table 5-18.—Kiwifruit: Area, yield, utilized production, marketing year average price, and value, California, 2005–2014

Year	Bearing acreage	Yield [1]	Production	Price per ton	Value
	Acres	Tons	Tons	Dollars	1,000 dollars
2005	4,500	8.27	36,200	620	22,461
2006	4,200	6.21	25,400	911	23,148
2007	4,200	5.83	23,700	950	22,517
2008	4,200	5.48	22,000	888	19,545
2009	4,200	6.10	24,900	847	21,084
2010	4,200	7.79	32,500	768	24,961
2011	4,000	9.43	36,700	775	28,439
2012	3,700	8.00	27,100	1,020	27,508
2013	3,900	7.08	26,900	1,110	29,812
2014	3,900	7.18	27,400	1,190	32,678

[1] Yield based on total production.
NASS, Crops Branch, (202) 720-2127.

Table 5-19.—Cherries: Foreign trade, United States, 2005–2014

Year beginning October	Imports		Domestic exports	
	Fresh	Dried and preserved	Fresh	Canned
	Metric tons	Metric tons	Metric tons	Metric tons
2005	12,062	4,998	47,618	15,831
2006	13,940	5,303	51,182	14,637
2007	22,125	5,403	45,462	14,427
2008	19,410	5,390	64,590	12,678
2009	13,601	5,036	58,737	13,758
2010	23,126	5,076	71,542	13,544
2011	17,250	6,289	101,073	16,127
2012	10,362	6,350	66,953	14,491
2013	12,033	6,613	87,578	17,761
2014	16,092	10,502	74,710	19,039

ERS, Crops Branch, (202) 694–5255.

Table 5-20.—Sweet cherries: Production and value, United States, 2005–2014

Year	Total production	Utilized production	Marketing year average price per ton [1]	Value
	Tons	Tons	Dollars	1,000 dollars
2005	250,830	243,570	1,990.00	484,348
2006	294,160	287,520	1,620.00	465,225
2007	310,680	306,210	1,820.00	557,056
2008	248,060	240,720	2,390.00	574,043
2009	442,870	385,625	1,330.00	513,330
2010	313,220	307,630	2,330.00	715,684
2011	334,415	330,290	2,530.00	834,585
2012	424,000	418,415	2,020.00	843,311
2013	332,090	295,950	2,610.00	771,798
2014	363,850	359,100	2,140.00	767,014

[1] Fresh fruit prices are equivalent packinghouse-door returns for Western States, and the average price as sold for other States. Quantities processed are priced at the equivalent processing plant door level.
NASS, Crops Branch, (202) 720–2127.

Table 5-21.—Tart cherries: Production and value, United States, 2005–2014

Year	Total production	Utilized production	Marketing year average price per pound [1]	Value
	Million pounds	Million pounds	Dollars	1,000 dollars
2005	269.9	267.9	0.238	63,741
2006	262.0	248.6	0.215	53,454
2007	253.2	248.7	0.273	67,923
2008	214.4	213.2	0.377	80,344
2009	359.2	320.8	0.192	61,628
2010	190.4	183.2	0.222	40,741
2011	231.8	230.3	0.300	69,072
2012	85.2	85.0	0.594	50,520
2013	294.2	291.1	0.359	104,395
2014	303.9	300.3	0.355	106,745

[1] Fresh fruit prices are equivalent packinghouse-door returns for Western States, and the average price as sold for other States. Quantities processed are priced at the equivalent processing plant door level.
NASS, Crops Branch, (202) 720–2127.

Table 5-22.—Sweet cherries: Production and season average price, by State and United States, 2012–2014

State	Total production			Utilized production			Price [1]		
	2012	2013	2014	2012	2013	2014	2012	2013	2014
	Tons	Tons	Tons	Tons	Tons	Tons	Dollars per ton	Dollars per ton	Dollars per ton
California	92,300	82,000	33,200	89,300	78,500	29,200	2,890.00	3,390.00	4,840.00
Idaho	3,600	2,300	2,120	3,300	2,200	2,000	2,640.00	2,550.00	2,630.00
Michigan	4,250	22,900	29,860	4,250	21,800	29,460	1,440.00	964.00	941.00
Montana	2,250	2,015	2,090	1,395	1,785	1,930	1,450.00	2,070.00	2,070.00
New York	300	1,045	630	290	845	610	3,700.00	3,750.00	3,290.00
Oregon	56,000	52,000	57,900	54,600	46,000	57,900	1,370.00	1,980.00	1,430.00
Utah	1,300	830	1,050	1,280	820	1,000	1,450.00	2,490.00	1,680.00
Washington	264,000	169,000	237,000	264,000	144,000	237,000	1,860.00	2,630.00	2,120.00
United States	424,000	332,090	363,850	418,415	295,950	359,100	2,020.00	2,610.00	2,140.00

[1] Fresh fruit prices are equivalent packinghouse-door returns for California, Oregon, and Washington, and the average price as sold for other States. Quantities processed are priced at the equivalent processing plant door level.
NASS, Crops Branch, (202) 720–2127.

Table 5-23.—Tart cherries: Production and season average price, by State and United States, 2012–2014

State	Total production			Utilized production			Price [1]		
	2012	2013	2014	2012	2013	2014	2012	2013	2014
	Million pounds	Million pounds	Million pounds	Million pounds	Million pounds	Million pounds	Dollars per Lb.	Dollars per Lb.	Dollars per Lb.
Michigan	11.6	218.7	203.0	11.6	215.8	201.0	1.110	0.345	0.342
New York	2.7	12.0	10.0	2.7	12.0	10.0	1.050	0.358	0.304
Oregon	1.0	4.3	2.4	1.0	4.3	2.3	0.951	0.344	0.372
Pennsylvania	3.3	2.2	0.9	3.2	2.2	0.7	1.110	0.390	0.631
Utah	40.0	26.8	51.0	40.0	26.8	49.8	0.510	0.476	0.432
Washington	24.8	17.9	24.3	24.8	17.9	24.3	0.323	0.344	0.300
Wisconsin	1.8	12.3	12.3	1.7	12.1	12.2	1.110	0.357	0.394
United States	85.2	294.2	303.9	85.0	291.1	300.3	0.594	0.359	0.355

[1] Fresh fruit prices are equivalent packinghouse-door returns for Oregon and Washington, and the average price as sold for other States. Quantities processed are priced at the equivalent processing plant door level.
NASS, Crops Branch, (202) 720–2127.

Table 5-24.—Sweet cherries: Production and utilization, by State and United States, crop of 2014 [1]

State	Total production	Utilized production	Utilization			
			Fresh [1]	Processed		
				Canned	Brined	Other [2]
	Tons	Tons	Tons	Tons	Tons	Tons
California	33,200	29,200	25,000	....	....	....
Idaho	2,120	2,000	(D)	....	....	....
Michigan	29,860	29,460	660	(D)	(D)	12,710
Montana	2,090	1,930	(D)	....	....	....
New York	630	610	(D)	....	....	....
Oregon	57,900	57,900	44,800	(D)	10,000	2,150
Utah	1,050	1,000	(D)	....	(D)	....
Washington	237,000	237,000	193,000	2,000	16,500	25,500
Other States [3]	(X)	(X)	4,740	1,500	20,540	12,710
United States	363,850	359,100	268,200	3,500	47,040	40,360

(D) Withheld to avoid disclosing data for individual operations.   (X) Not applicable.   [1] Includes "Home use."   [2] Includes California canned utilization and other processed utilizations (frozen, juice, etc.) from all States.   [3] Includes data witheld above and/or data for States not listed in this table.
NASS, Crops Branch, (202) 720–2127.

Table 5-25.—Tart cherries: Production and utilization, by State and United States, crop of 2014 [1]

State	Total production	Utilized production	Utilization			
			Fresh [1]	Processed		
				Canned and other-wise processed [2]	Frozen	Other [2]
	Million pounds	Million pounds	Million pounds	Million pounds	Million pounds	Million pounds
Michigan	203.0	201.0	0.1	(D)	141.2	35.3
New York	10.0	10.0	(D)	....	....	....
Oregon	2.4	2.3	(D)	....	....	....
Pennsylvania	0.9	0.7	(D)	....	....	....
Utah	51.0	49.8	....	....	(D)	30.7
Washington	24.3	24.3	(D)	....	....	....
Wisconsin	12.3	12.2	1.1	....	....	....
Other States [3]	....	....	0.7	29.2	57.7	30.7
United States	303.9	300.3	1.9	29.2	198.9	63.3

(D) Withheld to avoid disclosing data for individual operations.   [1] Includes "Home use."   [2] Some quantities used for juice, wine, brined, and dried.   [3] Includes data withheld above and/or data for States not listed in this table.
NASS, Crops Branch, (202) 720–2127.

Table 5-26.—Sweet cherries: Production and utilization, United States, 2005–2014

Crop of—	Total production	Utilized production	Utilization of quantities sold		
			Fresh [1]	Processed	
				Other [2]	Brined
	Tons	*Tons*	*Tons*	*Tons*	*Tons*
2005	250,830	243,570	167,190	30,050	46,330
2006	294,160	287,520	190,770	40,520	56,230
2007	310,680	306,210	222,560	28,930	48,160
2008	248,060	240,720	175,320	20,970	39,750
2009	442,870	385,625	296,750	29,053	51,571
2010	313,220	307,630	244,340	21,905	38,234
2011	334,415	330,290	258,920	25,495	39,625
2012	424,000	418,415	332,555	35,795	47,065
2013	332,090	295,950	217,950	28,535	44,945
2014	363,850	359,100	268,200	40,360	47,040

[1] Includes "Home use."   [2] Includes canned utilization and other processed utilizations from all States.
NASS, Crops Branch, (202) 720–2127.

Table 5-27.—Tart cherries: Production and utilization, United States, 2005–2014

Crop of—	Total production	Utilized production	Utilization of quantities sold		
			Fresh [1]	Processed	
				Other [2]	Frozen
	Million pounds	*Million pounds*	*Million pounds*	*Million pounds*	*Million pounds*
2005	269.9	267.9	1.2	78.7	188.0
2006	262.0	248.6	1.4	90.4	156.8
2007	253.2	248.7	1.6	20.1	179.3
2008	214.4	213.2	1.0	17.4	145.0
2009	359.2	320.8	1.3	35.3	232.0
2010	190.4	183.2	0.8	21.2	125.9
2011	231.8	230.3	0.5	37.3	154.1
2012	85.2	85.0	0.4	18.3	59.8
2013	294.2	291.1	1.2	92.4	158.4
2014	303.9	300.3	1.9	63.3	198.9

[1] Includes "Home use."   [2] Includes canned utilization and other processed utilizations from all states.
NASS, Crops Branch, (202) 720–2127.

Table 5-28.—Citrus fruit: Utilized production and value, United States, for season of 2004/2005 to 2013/2014

Season [1]	Production	Marketing year average returns per box [2]	Value	Quantities processed [3]	Production	Marketing year average returns per box [2]	Value	Quantities processed [3]
		Oranges [4]				Grapefruit		
	1,000 boxes	*Dollars*	*1,000 dollars*	*1,000 boxes*	*1,000 boxes*	*Dollars*	*1,000 dollars*	*1,000 boxes*
2004/2005	216,500	6.68	1,475,381	158,338	25,640	14.93	383,041	9,556
2005/2006	210,750	8.60	1,829,860	157,930	30,600	11.18	345,032	15,086
2006/2007	177,280	12.56	2,216,471	142,030	39,900	7.69	311,914	20,579
2007/2008	234,376	9.36	2,198,828	179,745	37,900	7.15	273,076	18,677
2008/2009	210,709	9.22	1,970,070	163,277	32,025	6.93	224,098	14,661
2009/2010	192,835	10.24	1,997,188	137,628	30,400	9.65	291,424	13,231
2010/2011	204,949	10.90	2,230,412	148,237	30,360	9.29	283,597	14,276
2011/2012	206,119	12.70	2,621,620	149,972	27,650	10.08	279,033	13,121
2012/2013	189,893	10.85	2,073,638	134,799	28,950	8.87	256,524	14,340
2013/2014	155,977	14.29	2,254,303	109,376	25,200	9.60	241,686	12,389
		Lemons				Temples (FL)		
2004/2005	22,900	13.38	306,434	9,772	650	5.10	3,314	437
2005/2006	25,800	15.90	410,338	7,746	700	5.76	4,034	491
2006/2007	21,000	21.40	449,417	8,105	(5)	(5)	(5)	(5)
2007/2008	16,300	32.12	523,528	5,918	(5)	(5)	(5)	(5)
2008/2009	24,000	13.96	335,065	9,986	(5)	(5)	(5)	(5)
2009/2010	23,200	17.04	395,339	10,482	(5)	(5)	(5)	(5)
2010/2011	23,000	16.80	386,514	7,987	(5)	(5)	(5)	(5)
2011/2012	21,250	21.12	448,698	4,869	(5)	(5)	(5)	(5)
2012/2013	22,800	17.56	400,295	7,394	(5)	(5)	(5)	(5)
2013/2014	20,600	31.13	641,259	4,840	(5)	(5)	(5)	(5)
		Tangerines and Mandarins [6]				Tangelos (FL)		
2004/2005	7,750	16.28	127,251	1,633	1,550	5.16	8,004	1,055
2005/2006	9,650	14.11	137,666	2,989	1,400	8.17	11,431	853
2006/2007	8,400	18.30	156,198	2,530	1,250	11.00	13,755	822
2007/2008	12,600	17.91	236,193	3,411	1,500	5.76	8,638	1,068
2008/2009	10,800	18.44	207,202	2,221	1,150	4.81	5,528	646
2009/2010	14,700	18.30	274,519	3,204	900	7.51	6,761	485
2010/2011	15,550	20.87	330,503	3,260	1,150	8.63	9,930	707
2011/2012	15,290	22.34	349,167	3,029	1,150	12.43	14,299	716
2012/2013	16,440	25.60	426,101	2,785	1,000	12.99	12,986	526
2013/2014	17,750	31.05	557,357	2,869	880	11.18	9,839	486

[1] The crop year begins with the bloom of the first year shown and ends with completion of harvest the following year. [2] Equivalent packing-house door returns. [3] Includes quantities used for juice, concentrates, grapefruit segments, and other citrus products. In some seasons, includes appreciable quantities of oranges and lemons in California delivered to processing plants which were not utilized, but for which growers received payment. [4] Includes small quantities of tangerines in Texas and Temples in Florida. [5] Included in early, midseason, and navel orange varieties beginning with the 2006-07 season. [6] Arizona and California tangelos and tangors included.
NASS, Crops Branch, (202) 720–2127.

Table 5-29.—Citrus fruit: Utilized production and marketing year average returns per box, by State, 2012/2013 and 2013/2014[1]

Crop and State	Utilized production		Market year average price[2]	
	2012/2013	2013/2014	2012/2013	2013/2014
	1,000 boxes[3]	*1,000 boxes*[3]	*Dollars*	*Dollars*
Oranges				
Early, midseason, and Navel varieties:[4]				
California	42,500	38,700	12.97	19.13
Florida	67,100	53,300	8.75	11.01
Texas	1,504	1,401	12.50	13.72
Total	111,104	93,401	10.30	14.19
Valencia:				
California	12,000	10,800	13.33	18.68
Florida	66,500	51,400	11.33	13.65
Texas	289	376	11.36	11.31
Total	78,789	62,576	11.61	14.42
All oranges:				
California	54,500	49,500	13.05	19.03
Florida	133,600	104,700	10.03	12.31
Texas	1,793	1,777	12.31	13.21
United States	189,893	155,977	10.85	14.29
Grapefruit				
California	4,500	3,850	8.74	9.82
Florida, all	18,350	15,650	9.19	9.83
Colored[5]	13,100	11,500	9.62	10.18
White	5,250	4,150	8.10	8.85
Texas	6,100	5,700	7.97	8.79
United States	28,950	25,200	8.87	9.60
Lemons				
Arizona	1,800	1,800	(D)	(D)
California	21,000	18,800	(D)	(D)
United States	22,800	20,600	17.56	31.13
Tangelos				
Florida	1,000	880	12.99	11.18
Tangerines and Mandarins				
Arizona[6]	160	150	(D)	(D)
California[6]	13,000	14,700	(D)	(D)
Florida	3,280	2,900	17.05	19.66
United States	16,440	17,750	25.60	31.05

(D) Withheld to avoid disclosing data for individual operations. [1] The crop year begins with the bloom of the first year shown and ends with completion of harvest the following year. [2] Equivalent packinghouse-door returns. [3] Net lbs. per box: oranges—California, 80; Florida, 90; and Texas, 85; grapefruit—California, 80; Florida, 85; Texas, 80; lemons—80; tangelos, tangerines and mandarins—Arizona and California, 80; tangelos—Florida, 90. [4] Includes small quantities of tangerines in Texas and Temples in Florida. [5] Includes seedy grapefruit. [6] Includes tangelos and tangors.
NASS, Crops Branch, (202) 720–2127.

Table 5-30.—International Citrus: Area and production in specified countries, 2013/2014-2015/2016

Country	Area			Production		
	2013/2014	2014/2015	2015/2016	2013/2014	2014/2015	2015/2016
	1,000 hectares	1,000 hectares	1,000 hectares	1,000 metric tons	1,000 metric tons	1,000 metric tons
Oranges, fresh:						
Argentina	40,000	40,000	40,000	800	1,000	1,000
Brazil	612,600	596,100	588,600	17,870	16,320	16,728
China	....	....	....	7,600	6,900	7,000
Egypt	115,000	117,000	122,800	2,570	2,630	2,750
European Union	277,436	272,786	273,373	6,550	5,959	6,107
Mexico	321,683	323,000	320,000	4,533	4,158	3,534
Morocco	45,000	48,067	50,100	1,001	868	920
South Africa	38,100	37,900	37,000	1,715	1,700	1,690
Turkey	50,000	50,000	53,000	1,700	1,650	1,700
Vietnam	....	....	....	520	520	520
Others	25,070	24,770	24,800	1,137	1,153	1,197
Total Foreign	1,524,889	1,509,623	1,509,673	45,996	42,858	43,146
United States	....	....	....	6,140	5,786	4,758
Total	1,524,889	1,509,623	1,509,673	52,136	48,644	47,904
Tangerines/Mandarines:						
Argentina	30,000	30,000	30,000	370	450	450
China	....	....	....	17,850	19,400	20,000
European Union	148,818	153,719	152,440	3,231	3,483	2,917
Israel	6,900	7,300	7,600	139	205	240
Japan	60,600	58,400	57,600	1,124	1,070	1,115
Korea, South	19,342	19,322	19,309	672	697	640
Morocco	42,000	47,140	50,100	1,160	1,005	1,055
South Africa	6,300	6,600	6,600	195	200	205
Thailand	....	....	....	375	375	375
Turkey	27,450	27,450	37,795	880	960	1,040
Others				20	20	20
Total Foreign	341,410	349,931	361,444	26,016	27,865	28,057
United States	....	....	....	700	793	839
Total	341,410	349,931	361,444	26,716	28,658	28,896
Lemons/Limes:						
Argentina	41,000	41,000	41,000	780	1,300	1,450
European Union	66,133	65,906	66,012	1,308	1,599	1,286
Israel	1,870	1,800	1,800	64	65	60
Japan	498	500	500	10	10	10
Mexico	154,803	155,000	156,000	2,187	2,260	2,270
Morocco	3,000	2,800	2,920	43	30	35
South Africa	5,313	5,400	5,600	312	330	330
Turkey	22,900	22,900	24,000	760	725	668
Others	....	....	....	....	....	....
Total Foreign	295,517	295,306	297,832	5,464	6,319	6,109
United States	....	....	....	748	816	784
Total	295,517	295,306	297,832	6,212	7,135	6,893
Grapefruit:						
China	....	....	....	3,717	3,900	4,300
European Union	3,288	2,416	2,494	92	109	95
Israel	3,750	3,050	3,070	236	186	185
Mexico	16,201	16,600	16,700	424	430	432
South Africa	7,943	8,000	8,100	413	400	405
Turkey	5,000	5,000	5,300	235	238	200
Others	....	....	....	....	....	....
Total Foreign	36,182	35,066	35,664	5,117	5,263	5,617
United States	....	....	....	950	789	736
World Total	36,182	35,066	35,664	6,067	6,052	6,353

FAS, Office of Global Analysis, (202) 720-6301. Prepared or estimated on the basis of official USDA production, supply, and distribution statistics from foreign governments.

Table 5-31.—Fresh fruits, citrus: United States exports by country of destination, 2011–2013

Country of destination	2011	2012	2013
	Metric tons	Metric tons	Metric tons
Canada	259,245	245,110	235,313
Japan	255,641	252,301	199,258
Korea, South	166,863	213,767	188,650
Hong Kong	100,252	81,823	106,174
China	64,206	50,305	47,146
Australia(*)	33,641	24,932	36,030
Malaysia	39,699	32,627	34,039
Mexico	21,177	27,007	25,736
Singapore	22,838	18,945	20,839
France(*)	23,848	19,606	17,426
Netherlands	21,868	15,568	16,477
Taiwan	13,407	11,595	15,253
New Zealand(*)	11,070	9,473	11,700
Philippines	9,335	8,180	10,991
United Arab Emirates	14,404	3,054	8,674
Belgium-Luxembourg(*)	6,115	4,741	7,273
Chile	4,973	2,834	5,747
Vietnam	1,742	1,227	3,821
Peru	137	877	3,446
Indonesia	7,000	3,771	3,183
Thailand	1,489	1,876	2,875
Ecuador	1,022	2,404	2,710
United Kingdom	3,823	3,178	2,671
Germany(*)	2,792	2,392	1,873
Bahamas, The	1,517	1,518	1,622
Switzerland(*)	3,861	1,425	1,473
Sri Lanka	4,480	1,981	1,416
Sweden	3,230	912	1,228
Saudi Arabia	2,945	469	1,221
India	14,662	5,902	1,168
Other Partners	21,713	7,653	7,999
World Total	1,138,996	1,057,447	1,023,431

(*) Denotes a country that is a summarization of its component countries. Users should use cautious interpretation on quantity reports using mixed units of measure. Quantity line items will only include statistics on the units of measure that are equal to, or are able to be converted to, the assigned unit of measure of the grouped commodities.

FAS, Office of Global Analysis,(202) 720–6301. Data Source: Department of Commerce, U.S. Census Bureau, Foreign Trade Statistics.

Table 5-32.—Fresh citrus fruits: Foreign trade, United States, 2005–2014

Year [1]	Oranges		Grapefruit		Lemons		Limes		Tangerines	
	Imports	Domestic exports	Imports	Domestic exports	Imports	Domestic exports	Imports	Domestic exports	Imports	Domestic exports
	Metric tons	Metric tons	Metric tons	Metric tons	Metric tons	Metric tons	Metric tons	Metric tons	Metric tons	Metric tons
2005	73,842	589,594	17,580	253,408	35,245	97,445	306,181	2,260	3,434	14,991
2006	112,108	346,936	21,531	331,538	65,656	115,862	337,356	3,413	6,148	12,700
2007	81,033	613,155	15,216	270,363	64,214	155,668	359,020	2,772	7,681	19,321
2008	90,546	495,662	11,697	246,865	37,565	91,459	358,289	2,364	8,027	17,496
2009	101,180	665,157	11,370	245,696	40,848	91,445	362,317	2,317	7,748	18,195
2010	92,159	752,613	7,103	225,836	56,278	97,275	352,956	2,550	6,101	30,419
2011	131,519	694,530	2,869	207,537	50,939	92,081	423,350	3,434	4,202	22,786
2012	130,812	679,663	11,862	182,725	38,152	104,031	438,830	4,389	3,614	23,529
2013	156,257	507,644	13,777	146,666	56,996	122,420	438,273	4,573	2,573	17,628
2014	151,911	534,311	9,291	140,858	85,537	112,081	499,039	3,948	4,570	18,708

[1] Year beginning October for all commodities.
ERS, Crops Branch, (202) 694–5255.

Table 5-33.—Concentrated citrus juices: Annual packs, Florida, 2005–2014

Season beginning December	Frozen concentrated juice [1]		
	Orange [2]	Grapefruit [2]	Tangerine
	1,000 gallons	1,000 gallons	1,000 gallons
2005	84,600	9,717	525
2006	79,054	15,782	446
2007	135,196	13,678	686
2008	120,800	10,731	466
2009	82,260	7,904	740
2010	82,106	9,297	1,374
2011	106,432	9,059	1,083
2012	76,132	7,437	928
2013	35,654	5,745	825
2014	19,224	3,834	763

[1] Net pack. [2] Frozen orange juice reported in 42.0° Brix; Grapefruit 40.0° Brix. Includes concentrated juice for manufacture.
ERS, Crops Branch, (202) 694–5255.

Table 5-34.—Dates: Area, yield, total production, marketing year average price per ton, and value, California, 2005–2014

Year	Bearing acreage	Yield per acre	Production	Price per ton	Value
	Acres	Tons	Tons	Dollars	1,000 dollars
2005	5,700	3.02	17,200	1,430	24,596
2006	5,500	3.22	17,700	2,140	37,878
2007	5,300	3.08	16,300	2,290	37,327
2008	5,700	3.67	20,900	1,260	26,334
2009	6,700	3.54	23,700	1,180	27,966
2010	7,700	3.77	29,000	1,270	36,830
2011	8,400	3.96	33,300	1,320	43,956
2012	8,800	3.53	31,100	1,340	41,674
2013	8,200	3.72	30,500	1,220	37,210
2014	8,200	3.54	29,000	1,190	34,510

NASS, Crops Branch, (202) 720–2127.

Table 5-35.—Dates: Foreign trade, United States, 2005–2014

Year beginning October	Imports
	Metric tons
2005	6,409
2006	9,446
2007	5,123
2008	13,079
2009	12,094
2010	20,113
2011	22,875
2012	23,945
2013	28,974
2014	47,920

ERS, Crops Branch, (202) 694–5255.

Table 5-36.—Cranberries: Area, yield, production, season average price per barrel, value and quantities processed, United States, 2005–2014[1]

Year	Area harvested	Yield per acre[2]	Total production[3]	Utilized production	Price[4]	Value	Quantities processed[5]
	Acres	Barrels[6]	Barrels[6]	Barrels[6]	Dollars	1,000 dollars	Barrels[6]
2005	38,600	161.7	6,243,000	6,243,000	35.20	219,985	5,896,000
2006	38,500	179.0	6,890,000	6,785,000	41.10	278,888	6,429,500
2007	38,100	172.0	6,554,000	6,554,000	50.70	332,092	6,194,000
2008	38,200	205.9	7,865,000	7,865,000	58.10	457,192	7,494,000
2009	38,500	179.6	6,913,000	6,913,000	44.20	305,669	6,580,000
2010	38,500	176.8	6,808,200	6,808,200	43.90	299,123	6,589,000
2011	38,500	200.4	7,713,700	7,713,700	44.80	345,561	7,473,200
2012	40,300	199.6	8,045,000	8,045,000	47.90	385,506	7,791,000
2013	42,000	211.4	8,957,400	8,880,700	32.40	287,322	8,559,300
2014	40,600	202.9	8,400,000	8,236,000	30.90	254,412	7,968,000

[1] Estimates relate to Massachusetts, New Jersey, Oregon, Washington, and Wisconsin. [2] Derived from total production. [3] Differences between utilized and total production are quantities unharvested for economic reasons or excess cullage and/or set-aside production under provisions of the Cranberry Marketing Order. [4] Average price of utilized production. Equivalent returns at first delivery point, screened basis of utilized production. [5] Mainly for canning. [6] Barrels of 100 pounds.
NASS, Crops Branch, (202) 720–2127.

Table 5-37.—Cranberries: Area, yield, production, and season average price per barrel, by State and United States, 2012–2014

State	Area harvested			Yield per acre		
	2012	2013	2014	2012	2013	2014
	Acres	Acres	Acres	Bbl.[2]	Bbl.[2]	Bbl.[2]
Massachusetts	13,000	13,200	12,400	163.3	138.5	164.3
New Jersey	3,000	3,000	3,000	183.3	180.8	204.7
Oregon	2,900	3,000	2,900	139.7	130.0	162.8
Washington	1,700	1,700	1,600	80.6	89.4	97.5
Wisconsin	19,700	21,100	20,700	245.2	282.8	239.5
United States	40,300	42,000	40,600	199.6	211.4	202.9

State	Total production			Price per barrel [1]		
	2012	2013	2014	2012	2013	2014
	Bbl.[2]	Bbl.[2]	Bbl.[2]	Dollars	Dollars	Dollars
Massachusetts	2,123,000	1,852,300	2,070,000	47.00	31.60	37.10
New Jersey	550,000	547,500	652,000	54.40	37.50	36.90
Oregon	405,000	390,000	500,000	40.40	30.60	23.10
Washington	137,000	152,000	156,000	63.50	43.70	44.60
Wisconsin	4,830,000	6,015,600	5,022,000	47.80	32.00	27.90
United States	8,045,000	8,957,400	8,400,000	47.90	32.40	30.90

[1] Average price of utilized production. Equivalent returns at first delivery point, screened basis of utilized production. [2] Barrels of 100 pounds.
NASS, Crops Branch, (202) 720–2127.

Table 5-38.—Figs: Total production, marketing year average price per ton, and value, California, 2005–2014

Year	Dried				Total		
	Production (dry basis)			Price per ton	Production	Price per ton	Value
	Total	Standard	Substandard				
	Tons	1,000 tons	Tons	Dollars	Tons	Dollars	1,000 dollars
2005	15,100	12,500	2,600	847	49,000	404	19,807
2006	13,000	11,100	1,900	829	42,800	426	18,253
2007	14,500	11,100	3,400	873	47,800	401	19,145
2008	13,100	11,800	1,300	1,200	43,300	599	25,954
2009	13,300	12,000	1,300	1,540	43,750	695	30,422
2010	12,320	10,900	1,420	1,220	40,910	542	22,185
2011	11,560	10,140	1,420	1,230	38,660	526	20,336
2012	10,400	9,600	800	1,350	35,200	555	19,520
2013	9,300	8,600	700	1,500	33,000	610	20,143
2014	8,900	8,200	700	1,610	31,700	572	18,141

NASS, Crops Branch, (202) 720–2127.

Table 5-39.—Figs, dried: Foreign trade, United States, 2005–2014

Year beginning October	Imports for consumption	Domestic exports
	Metric tons	Metric tons
2005	5,273	5,355
2006	5,487	3,019
2007	2,978	3,775
2008	6,042	5,019
2009	4,035	5,795
2010	4,042	5,065
2011	4,236	5,449
2012	5,816	4,895
2013	10,294	4,537
2014	7,139	4,665

ERS, Crops Branch, (202) 694–5255.

Table 5-40.—Grapes: Production, price, and value, United States, 2005–2014

Year	Grapes			
	Production (fresh basis)		Market year average price per ton [1]	Value
	Total	Utilized		
	Tons	Tons	Dollars	1,000 dollars
2005	7,813,700	7,810,500	447.00	3,494,095
2006	6,377,470	6,366,170	519.00	3,304,631
2007	7,057,250	7,056,250	489.00	3,453,124
2008	7,279,360	7,265,650	497.00	3,613,420
2009	7,267,890	7,240,310	566.00	4,101,600
2010	7,432,120	7,429,490	542.00	4,023,967
2011	7,408,740	7,401,370	576.00	4,262,945
2012	7,530,883	7,524,443	752.00	5,661,096
2013	8,631,790	8,620,810	712.00	6,135,613
2014	7,771,830	7,759,580	750.00	5,818,678

[1] Fresh fruit prices are equivalent packinghouse-door returns for California and Washington, and the average price as sold for other States. Quantities processed are priced at the equivalent processing plant door level.
NASS, Crops Branch, (202) 720–2127.

Table 5-41.—Grapes: Production and marketing year average price per ton, by State and United States, 2012–2014

State	Total production			Utilized production		
	2012	2013	2014	2012	2013	2014
	Tons	Tons	Tons	Tons	Tons	Tons
Arkansas	1,530	1,790	1,490	1,300	1,640	1,390
California	6,852,000	7,742,000	6,822,000	6,852,000	7,742,000	6,822,000
Wine	4,018,000	4,245,000	3,893,000	4,018,000	4,245,000	3,893,000
Table [1]	1,024,000	1,227,000	1,166,000	1,024,000	1,227,000	1,166,000
Raisin [1]	1,810,000	2,270,000	1,763,000	1,810,000	2,270,000	1,763,000
Georgia	4,700	4,600	4,000	4,000	3,300	3,900
Michigan	38,200	94,000	63,300	38,200	94,000	63,300
Missouri	4,600	5,970	4,030	4,600	5,970	4,030
New York	115,000	206,000	188,000	112,000	202,000	180,000
North Carolina	4,950	5,200	6,000	4,800	4,700	5,400
Ohio	5,293	6,490	3,810	5,293	6,160	3,560
Oregon	46,000	49,000	58,000	46,000	49,000	58,000
Pennsylvania	61,000	110,000	91,000	59,000	106,000	89,000
Texas	9,550	7,240	9,400	9,450	7,040	8,800
Virginia	8,060	7,500	8,800	7,800	7,000	8,200
Washington	380,000	392,000	512,000	380,000	392,000	512,000
Wine	188,000	210,000	227,000	188,000	210,000	227,000
Juice	192,000	182,000	285,000	192,000	182,000	285,000
United States	7,530,883	8,631,790	7,771,830	7,524,443	8,620,810	7,759,580

State	Price per ton [2]		
	2012	2013	2014
	Dollars	Dollars	Dollars
Arkansas	1,170.00	1,010.00	902.00
California	756.00	719.00	768.00
Wine	773.00	753.00	759.00
Table [1]	1,220.00	1,260.00	1,350.00
Raisin [1]	457.00	364.00	402.00
Georgia	1,410.00	1,110.00	1,470.00
Michigan	462.00	378.00	305.00
Missouri	725.00	728.00	790.00
New York	466.00	370.00	385.00
North Carolina	931.00	843.00	807.00
Ohio	630.00	593.00	477.00
Oregon	2,050.00	2,190.00	2,040.00
Pennsylvania	343.00	320.00	318.00
Texas	1,450.00	1,560.00	1,500.00
Virginia	1,630.00	1,800.00	1,850.00
Washington	655.00	708.00	590.00
Wine	1,040.00	1,110.00	1,110.00
Juice	279.00	244.00	175.00
United States	752.00	712.00	750.00

[1] Fresh equivalent of dried and not dried. [2] Fresh fruit prices are equivalent packinghouse-door returns for California and Washington, and the average price as sold for other States. Quantities processed are priced at the equivalent processing plant door level.
NASS, Crops Branch, (202) 720–2127.

Table 5-42.—Grapes: Production and utilization, United States, 2005–2014

Crop of—	Total production [1]	Utilized production	Utilization of quantities sold					
			Fresh	Processed			
				Canned	Dried (fresh basis)	Crushed for wine	Crushed for juice, etc. [2]
	Tons	Tons	Tons	Tons	Tons	Tons	Tons
2005	7,813,700	7,810,500	995,610	([3])	1,645,000	4,550,780	619,110
2006	6,377,470	6,366,170	797,590	21,000	1,424,000	3,725,380	398,200
2007	7,057,250	7,056,250	920,330	21,000	1,621,000	3,920,520	573,400
2008	7,279,360	7,265,650	945,000	25,000	1,873,000	3,943,490	479,130
2009	7,267,890	7,240,310	898,940	20,000	1,510,000	4,373,070	438,300
2010	7,432,120	7,429,490	953,290	25,000	1,777,000	4,270,300	403,900
2011	7,408,740	7,401,370	944,740	25,000	1,807,000	4,154,530	470,100
2012	7,530,883	7,524,443	962,983	20,000	1,488,000	4,706,060	346,950
2013	8,631,790	8,620,810	1,116,940	22,000	1,909,000	5,067,610	504,160
2014	7,771,830	7,759,580	1,116,940	21,000	1,612,000	4,522,320	550,620

[1] Total production includes utilized production plus production not harvested and harvested not sold.   [2] Mostly juice, but includes some quantities used for jam, jelly, etc.   [3] Included with fresh in 2005 to avoid disclosure of individual operations.
NASS, Crops Branch, (202) 720–2127.

Table 5-43.—Grapes: Production and utilization, by State and United States, crop of 2014

State	Total production	Utilized production	Utilization					
			Fresh	Processed			
				Canned	Dried (fresh basis)	Crushed for—	
						Wine	Juice, etc.
	Tons	Tons	Tons	Tons	Tons	Tons	Tons
Arkansas	1,490	1,390	....	....	....	....	....
California	6,822,000	6,822,000	1,046,000	21,000	1,612,000	4,143,000	....
Wine	3,893,000	3,893,000	....	....	....	3,893,000	....
Table	1,166,000	1,166,000	1,003,000	....	68,000	95,000	....
Raisin	1,763,000	1,763,000	43,000	21,000	1,544,000	155,000	....
Georgia	4,000	3,900	....	....	....	....	....
Michigan	63,300	63,300	....	....	....	2,600	60,100
Missouri	4,030	4,030	....	....	....	4,030	....
New York	188,000	180,000	3,000	....	....	44,000	133,000
North Carolina	6,000	5,400	540	....	....	4,860	....
Ohio	3,810	3,560	110	....	....	1,430	2,020
Oregon [1]	58,000	58,000	....	....	....	58,000	....
Pennsylvania	91,000	89,000	1,700	....	....	17,600	69,700
Texas	9,400	8,800	150	....	....	8,650	....
Virginia	8,800	8,200	....	....	....	8,200	....
Washington	512,000	512,000	....	....	....	227,000	285,000
Other States [2]	....	....	1,540	....	....	2,950	800
United States	7,771,830	7,759,580	1,053,040	21,000	1,612,000	4,522,320	550,620

[1] Wine includes small quantities for other uses.   [2] Includes data withheld above and/or data for States not listed in this table.
NASS, Crops Branch, (202) 720–2127.

Table 5-44.—Grapes and raisins: Foreign trade, United States, 2005–2014

Year beginning October	Grapes		Raisins [1]	
	Imports, fresh	Domestic exports, fresh	Imports for consumption	Domestic exports
	Metric tons	Metric tons	Metric tons	Metric tons
2005	580,870	354,731	24,106	118,134
2006	626,189	294,670	29,806	122,349
2007	567,079	299,891	22,647	175,112
2008	600,908	341,205	21,467	160,451
2009	602,273	284,092	24,289	173,049
2010	557,397	304,609	18,813	154,541
2011	557,310	378,536	19,336	142,997
2012	566,038	366,079	17,102	131,987
2013	500,975	421,542	14,904	174,041
2014	554,993	366,198	20,641	131,626

[1] Raisins converted to sweatbox or production basis by multiplying by 1.08.
ERS, Crops Branch, (202) 694–5255.

Table 5-45.—Guavas: Area, yield, utilized production, marketing year average price, and value, Hawaii, 2005–2014

Year	Area harvested	Yield per acre	Production	Price per pound	Value
	Acres	1,000 pounds	1,000 pounds	Cents	1,000 dollars
2005	620	13.1	8,100	13.9	1,126
2006	365	20.3	7,400	14.2	1,051
2007	170	25.3	4,300	15.7	675
2008	160	21.9	3,500	15.8	553
2009	135	15.6	2,100	14.0	294
2010	115	11.3	1,300	16.9	220
2011	110	17.3	1,900	17.0	323
2012	(NA)	(NA)	(NA)	(NA)	(NA)
2013	100	22.0	2,200	17.0	374
2014	100	17.0	1,700	18.0	306

(NA) Not available.
NASS, Crops Branch, (202) 720–2127.

Table 5-46.—Nectarines: Production, utilization, and value, United States, 2005–2014

Crop of—	Production	Utilization		Marketing year average price per ton	Value
		Fresh	Processed (fresh basis)		
	Tons	Tons	Tons	Dollars	1,000 dollars
2005	250,500	250,500	(1)	507.00	126,942
2006	231,900	231,900	(1)	522.00	121,004
2007	283,000	283,000	(1)	340.00	96,305
2008	302,500	302,500	(1)	367.00	110,915
2009	219,800	219,800	(1)	631.00	138,611
2010	233,200	233,200	(1)	553.00	129,075
2011	225,200	225,200	(1)	582.00	130,973
2012	188,900	188,900	(1)	767.00	144,906
2013	162,100	148,300	13,800	772.00	125,113
2014	269,000	196,000	9,300	869.00	178,421

[1] Small quantities of processed nectarines are included in fresh to avoid disclosure of individual operations.
NASS, Crops Branch, (202) 720–2127.

Table 5-47.—Olives: Total production, marketing year average price, value, and processed utilization, California, 2005–2014

Year	Production	Marketing year average price per ton	Value	Processed utilization			
				Crushed for oil	Canned	Limited	Undersized
	Tons	*Dollars*	*1,000 dollars*	*Tons*	*Tons*	*Tons*	*Tons*
2005	142,000	564	80,097	14,000	100,000	21,200	6,300
2006	23,500	771	18,119	4,000	17,000	1,500	500
2007	132,500	654	86,694	12,000	96,000	20,000	4,000
2008	66,800	697	46,587	14,000	45,500	6,000	1,300
2009	46,300	696	32,209	20,000	24,500	1,500	300
2010	206,000	664	136,796	36,000	125,000	37,000	8,000
2011	71,200	733	52,168	42,000	26,500	2,200	500
2012	160,000	813	130,038	74,000	78,500	6,400	1,100
2013	166,000	813	134,881	75,000	78,800	10,500	1,700
2014	94,000	776	72,904	56,700	30,500	5,900	900

NASS, Crops Branch, (202) 720–2127.

Table 5-48.—Olives and olive oil: Foreign trade, United States, 2005–2014

Year beginning October	Imports			
	Olives		Olive oil	
	In brine	Dried	Edible	Inedible
	Metric tons	*Metric tons*	*Metric tons*	*Metric tons*
2005	105,736	423	242,186	295
2006	118,375	1,043	260,398	1,607
2007	118,085	133	262,716	1,575
2008	109,230	289	275,611	594
2009	137,533	184	268,069	114
2010	117,915	206	290,226	258
2011	118,614	145	314,937	788
2012	119,035	131	296,190	379
2013	118,653	202	311,126	351
2014	119,444	130	309,979	163

ERS, Crops Branch, (202) 694–5255.

Table 5-49.—Peaches: Production and value, United States, 2005–2014

Year	Total production	Utilized production	Marketing year average price [1]	Value
	1,000 tons	*1,000 tons*	*Dollars per ton*	*1,000 dollars*
2005	1,184.5	1,145.0	447	511,464
2006	1,010.3	987.2	520	513,093
2007	1,127.2	1,115.9	450	502,087
2008	1,135.0	1,113.2	490	545,499
2009	1,103.5	1,082.4	548	593,387
2010	1,149.4	1,129.8	547	617,459
2011	1,071.2	1,042.3	563	587,228
2012	968.1	955.9	647	618,369
2013	903.9	888.7	617	547,978
2014	852.9	838.0	751	629,134

[1] Fresh fruit prices are equivalent packinghouse-door returns for California and Washington except equivalent returns for bulk fruit at the first delivery point for California Clingstone, and the average price as sold for other States. Quantities processed are priced at the equivalent processing plant door level.
NASS, Crops Branch, (202) 720–2127.

Table 5-50.—Peaches: Production and utilization, United States, 2005–2014

Crop of—	Total production [1]	Utilized production	Utilization of quantities sold				
			Fresh [2]	Processed (fresh basis)			
				Canned	Dried	Frozen	Other [3]
	1,000 tons	*1,000 tons*	*1,000 tons*	*1,000 tons*	*1,000 tons*	*1,000 tons*	*1,000 tons*
2005	1,184.5	1,145.0	502.0	479.7	12.7	101.3	49.4
2006	1,010.3	987.2	481.6	374.1	13.1	96.2	22.2
2007	1,127.2	1,115.9	441.2	484.8	12.7	135.4	41.8
2008	1,135.0	1,113.2	529.8	426.3	9.5	111.4	36.5
2009	1,103.5	1,082.4	502.9	463.7	7.1	92.0	16.9
2010	1,149.4	1,129.8	566.4	428.5	12.7	104.4	17.8
2011	1,071.2	1,042.3	531.1	387.2	4.6	100.6	18.9
2012	968.1	955.9	480.8	364.6	9.8	90.2	10.5
2013	903.9	888.7	397.0	369.8	4.2	103.7	14.0
2014	852.9	838.0	393.3	330.2	4.7	95.3	14.5

[1] Includes harvested not sold and unharvested production for California Clingstone peaches. [2] Includes "Home use." [3] Used for jams, preserves, pickles, wine, brandy, baby food, etc. Includes small quantities frozen for some years.
NASS, Crops Branch, (202) 720–2127.

Table 5-51.—Peaches: Foreign trade, United States, 2005–2014

Year beginning October	Domestic exports				
	Fresh	Canned	Canned, in fruit salad [1]	Dried, in fruit salad [2][3]	Total, in terms of fresh [4]
	Metric tons	*Metric tons*	*Metric tons*	*Metric tons*	*Metric tons*
2005	86,230	27,038	6,162	1,078	125,420
2006	105,559	18,359	5,100	619	132,458
2007	112,352	37,266	10,019	690	163,446
2008	98,911	20,235	9,549	604	132,050
2009	103,038	16,914	11,701	662	135,329
2010	103,523	25,636	15,568	801	149,175
2011	95,798	28,295	17,605	884	146,609
2012	102,140	25,526	21,799	931	154,636
2013	80,251	20,847	19,545	859	125,415
2014	84,924	18,005	20,021	696	126,817

[1] Canned peaches are 40 percent of total canned fruit for salad. [2] Net processed weight. [3] Dried peaches are 21 percent of total dried fruit for salad. [4] Dried fruit converted to unprocessed dry weight by dividing by 1.08. Unprocessed dry weight converted to terms of fresh fruit on the basis that 1 pound dried equals 6.0 pounds fresh. Canned peaches converted to terms of fresh on basis that 1 pound canned equals about 1 pound fresh.
ERS, Crops Branch, (202) 694–5255.

Table 5-52.—Peaches: Production and season average price per pound, by State and United States, 2012–2014

State	Total production			Utilized production			Price per ton[1]		
	2012	2013	2014	2012	2013	2014	2012	2013	2014
	Tons	Tons	Tons	Tons	Tons	Tons	Dollars	Dollars	Dollars
Alabama	4,400	4,140	3,400	3,200	3,840	1,900	1,240.00	1,170.00	1,200.00
Arkansas	1,620	1,300	650	1,510	1,130	570	1,650.00	1,610.00	1,840.00
California	713,000	648,000	620,000	713,000	648,000	620,000	464.00	429.00	574.00
Freestone	344,000	280,000	288,000	344,000	280,000	288,000	588.00	516.00	811.00
Clingstone	369,000	368,000	332,000	369,000	368,000	332,000	348.00	364.00	369.00
Colorado	17,000	7,330	13,260	16,000	7,080	12,650	1,580.00	1,870.00	2,430.00
Connecticut	1,350	1,350	1,770	1,300	1,330	1,750	2,300.00	2,770.00	2,500.00
Georgia	35,300	35,250	35,500	33,100	34,810	33,000	961.00	826.00	1,090.00
Idaho	7,600	6,100	8,200	6,800	5,500	7,800	1,340.00	945.00	1,070.00
Illinois	7,380	3,780	3,700	6,970	3,570	3,550	1,390.00	1,340.00	1,270.00
Maryland	4,340	3,870	3,810	4,260	3,590	3,070	1,190.00	1,060.00	1,040.00
Massachusetts	1,550	1,400	1,249	1,500	1,300	1,187	3,200.00	2,770.00	2,240.00
Michigan	1,980	20,600	8,860	1,980	19,790	8,440	1,330.00	706.00	919.00
Missouri	3,600	4,160	4,090	3,600	4,040	3,940	1,200.00	1,850.00	1,140.00
New Jersey	30,000	18,120	22,450	30,000	18,000	21,050	1,320.00	1,510.00	1,320.00
New York	2,600	7,740	7,270	2,550	7,050	7,070	1,580.00	815.00	1,790.00
North Carolina	5,300	6,000	4,400	5,100	5,200	4,300	1,220.00	1,150.00	1,450.00
Ohio	3,540	5,370	230	3,310	4,960	220	1,710.00	1,480.00	1,680.00
Pennsylvania	20,800	19,500	14,940	20,350	18,300	14,460	1,060.00	1,030.00	1,190.00
South Carolina	66,200	69,650	65,700	61,850	64,150	60,800	1,050.00	1,070.00	1,120.00
Texas	9,090	8,250	3,800	8,400	7,500	3,300	1,850.00	2,570.00	2,000.00
Utah	5,300	5,421	6,500	5,200	5,141	6,200	1,080.00	1,080.00	981.00
Virginia	7,800	7,740	5,300	7,710	6,040	5,020	933.00	926.00	1,170.00
Washington	13,000	13,100	12,500	13,000	12,900	12,500	627.00	770.00	868.00
West Virginia	5,320	5,700	5,360	5,200	5,460	5,250	1,300.00	900.00	1,020.00
United States	968,070	903,871	852,939	955,890	888,681	838,027	647.00	617.00	751.00

[1] Fresh fruit prices are equivalent packing house-door returns for California and Washington except equivalent returns for bulk fruit at the first delivery point for California Clingstone, and the average price as sold for other States. Quantities processed are priced at the equivalent processing plant door level.
NASS, Crops Branch, (202) 720–2127.

Table 5-53.—Peaches: Production and utilization, by State and United States, crop of 2014 [1]

State	Total production	Utilized production [1]	Utilization				
			Fresh [2]	Processed (fresh basis)			
				Canned	Dried	Frozen	Other [3]
	Tons	Tons	Tons	Tons	Tons	Tons	Tons
California, all	620,000	620,000					
Freestone	288,000	288,000	191,200		4,700	82,600	
Clingstone	332,000	332,000		317,000			
Connecticut	1,770	1,750	1,750				
Massachusetts	1,249	1,187	(D)				
Missouri	4,090	(D)	(D)				
South Carolina	65,700	59,300	59,300				
Texas	3,800	3,300	3,300				
Virginia	5,300	(D)	(D)				
West Virginia	5,360	5,250	5,250				
Other States		132,520	132,520	13,220		12,690	
United States	852,939	838,027	393,320	330,220	4,700	95,290	14,497

(D) Withheld to avoid disclosing data for individual operations. [1] Difference between total and utilized production is harvested not sold and unharvested production. [2] Includes "Home use." [3] Used for jams, preserves, brandy, etc.
NASS, Crops Branch, (202) 720–2127.

Table 5-54.—Fruit: Exports, 2011–2013

Country	2011	2012	2013
	Metric tons	*Metric tons*	*Metric tons*
Fruit, processed:			
Canada	76,092	79,711	83,753
Netherlands	34,610	36,597	42,671
Mexico	31,129	29,488	29,103
China	27,077	37,103	14,861
Indonesia	3,543	5,118	5,783
Japan	7,395	6,910	5,550
Korea, South	3,341	4,377	5,284
Australia(*)	4,295	3,924	4,589
Taiwan	5,402	2,941	3,559
Thailand	3,531	3,515	3,493
United Kingdom	2,575	3,290	3,078
Malaysia	1,530	1,966	2,465
Singapore	2,714	3,345	2,379
Philippines	774	2,057	2,344
Poland	2,019	1,253	2,160
Israel(*)	2,337	1,028	2,015
New Zealand(*)	1,485	1,752	1,991
United Arab Emirates	1,337	1,277	1,833
Chile	614	26	1,689
Morocco	25	500	1,392
Germany(*)	2,191	1,202	1,356
Hong Kong	1,124	1,667	1,352
India	704	875	1,351
Russia	144	458	1,020
Panama	1,113	714	860
Guatemala	564	336	827
Belgium-Luxembourg(*)	1,404	896	684
Brazil	112	514	593
Vietnam	1,122	395	528
Rest of World	7,659	8,253	6,998
World Total	227,960	241,486	235,564
Fruit, prepared, misc:			
Canada	47,466	51,888	54,339
Mexico	9,271	8,411	6,893
Vietnam	2,136	3,508	4,930
China	36,199	15,151	4,821
Australia(*)	1,046	1,104	4,509
Saudi Arabia	7,074	7,919	4,065
Japan	3,833	3,710	3,411
Korea, South	9,981	8,003	2,659
Taiwan	1,290	1,166	2,235
United Kingdom	2,691	2,372	1,980
Malaysia	2,184	2,116	1,707
Hong Kong	1,803	1,802	1,683
Panama	3,604	3,157	1,636
Ecuador	126	126	1,084
United Arab Emirates	1,373	1,235	1,053
Costa Rica	896	815	1,039
Philippines	1,588	880	1,009
Thailand	577	1,162	985
Colombia	465	651	885
Bahamas, The	292	808	846
Israel(*)	749	547	719
Singapore	945	1,227	712
Kuwait	330	822	683
Guatemala	751	408	676
Leeward-Windward Islands(*)	263	275	617
Dominican Republic	649	1,099	571
Indonesia	638	517	520
Netherlands Antilles(*)	216	252	465
South Africa	35	141	446
Rest of World	9,333	7,458	6,501
World Total	147,805	128,726	113,677

(*) Denotes a country that is a summarization of its component countries. All zeroes for a data item may show that statistics exist in the other import type. Consumption or General. Users should use cautious interpretation on Quantity reports using mixed units of measure. Quantity line items will only include statistics on the units of measure that are equal to, or are able to be converted to, the assigned unit of measure of the grouped commodities.

FAS, Office of Global Analysis, (202) 720-6301. Data Source: Department of Commerce, U.S. Census Bureau, Foreign Trade Statistics.

Table 5-55.—Pears: Foreign trade, United States, 2005–2014

Year beginning October	Imports for consumption, fresh	Domestic exports				
		Fresh [1]	Canned	Dried, in fruit salad [1][2]	Canned, in fruit salad [3]	Total, in terms of fresh fruit [4]
	Metric tons	Metric tons	Metric tons	Metric tons	Metric tons	Metric tons
2005	85,498	143,024	12,954	856	5,392	166,769
2006	108,587	132,730	6,669	492	4,462	146,964
2007	85,855	165,436	8,028	548	8,767	185,688
2008	82,097	146,252	7,378	479	8,356	165,011
2009	62,808	159,677	7,112	525	10,238	180,342
2010	77,992	154,025	7,958	635	13,622	179,615
2011	64,000	197,633	8,681	702	15,404	226,146
2012	79,034	186,855	7,535	739	19,074	218,126
2013	81,584	200,982	6,283	682	17,102	228,669
2014	89,763	174,680	4,412	552	17,519	200,096

[1] Net processed weight.   [2] Dried pears are 16⅔ percent of total dried fruit for salad.   [3] Canned pears are 35 percent of total canned fruit for salad.   [4] Dried converted to unprocessed dry weight by dividing by 1.03. Unprocessed dry weight converted to terms of fresh on the basis that 1 pound dried equals about 6.5 pounds fresh. Canned converted to terms of fresh on basis that 1 pound of canned equals about 1 pound fresh.
ERS, Crops Branch, (202) 694-5255.

Table 5-56.—Pears: Production and value, United States 2005–2014

Year	Total production	Utilized production	Marketing year average price [1]	Value
	Tons	Tons	Dollars per ton	1,000 dollars
2005	823,320	821,670	358.00	293,863
2006	842,035	831,120	397.00	329,928
2007	872,950	871,850	416.00	363,092
2008	869,850	868,880	456.00	396,081
2009	957,220	955,820	372.00	355,662
2010	813,600	813,400	476.00	386,955
2011	965,720	965,110	380.00	366,552
2012	851,240	851,130	509.00	432,988
2013	877,130	876,520	491.00	430,660
2014	831,610	831,250	550.00	457,146

[1] Fresh fruit prices are equivalent packinghouse-door returns for California, Oregon, and Washington, and the average price as sold for other States. Quantities processed are priced at the equivalent processing plant door level.
NASS, Crops Branch, (202) 720–2127.

Table 5-57.—Pears: Production and season average price per ton, by State and United States, 2012–2014

State and Variety	Total production			Utilized production			Price per ton [1]		
	2012	2013	2014	2012	2013	2014	2012	2013	2014
	Tons	Tons	Tons	Tons	Tons	Tons	Dollars	Dollars	Dollars
California	208,000	220,000	189,000	208,000	220,000	189,000	432.00	391.00	469.00
Bartlett	163,000	177,000	154,000	163,000	177,000	154,000	370.00	348.00	416.00
Other	45,000	43,000	35,000	45,000	43,000	35,000	658.00	571.00	701.00
Michigan	40	5,350	2,720	40	5,180	2,610	625.00	348.00	441.00
New York	3,100	9,200	54,350	3,100	9,100	5,210	758.00	565.00	666.00
Oregon	248,000	207,000	216,000	248,000	207,000	216,000	541.00	537.00	590.00
Bartlett	61,000	55,000	53,000	61,000	55,000	53,000	455.00	511.00	572.00
Other	187,000	152,000	163,000	187,000	152,000	163,000	570.00	546.00	596.00
Pennsylvania	1,100	1,580	2,540	990	1,240	2,430	794.00	923.00	1,100.00
Washington	391,000	434,000	416,000	391,000	434,000	416,000	526.00	519.00	562.00
Bartlett	181,000	185,000	181,000	181,000	185,000	181,000	412.00	435.00	477.00
Other	210,000	249,000	235,000	210,000	249,000	235,000	625.00	582.00	628.00
United States	851,240	877,130	831,610	851,130	876,520	831,250	509.00	491.00	550.00

[1] Fresh fruit prices are equivalent packinghouse-door returns for California, Oregon, and Washington, and the average price as sold for other States. Quantities processed are priced at the equivalent processing plant door level.
NASS, Crops Branch, (202) 720–2127.

Table 5-58.—International Fruits: Production in specified countries, 2013/2014-2015/2016

Country	Production		
	2013/2014	2014/2015	2015/2016
	Metric tons	Metric tons	Metric tons
Apples, fresh:			
Brazil	1,377,400	1,266,000	1,240,000
Chile	1,310,000	1,350,000	1,350,000
China	39,680,000	40,920,000	43,000,000
European Union	11,864,900	13,618,500	12,220,000
India	2,200,000	2,200,000	2,200,000
Iran	1,693,000	1,693,000	1,693,000
Russia	1,416,500	1,408,600	1,390,000
South Africa	792,500	860,000	865,000
Turkey	2,930,000	2,289,000	2,740,000
Ukraine	1,211,000	1,211,000	1,211,000
Others	4,649,600	4,560,800	4,548,800
Total Foreign	69,124,900	71,376,900	72,457,800
United States	4,690,101	5,074,793	4,561,000
Total	73,815,001	76,451,693	77,018,800
Fresh Cherries, sweet and sour:			
Azerbaijan	32,300	30,000	30,000
Chile	85,900	124,184	142,660
China	180,000	220,000	250,000
European Union	723,581	745,417	745,895
Russia	278,000	278,000	278,000
Serbia	126,400	126,000	126,000
Syria	62,400	62,000	62,000
Turkey	510,000	470,000	540,000
Ukraine	282,000	280,000	280,000
Uzbekistan	140,000	140,000	140,000
Others	65,600	65,500	65,500
Total Foreign	2,486,181	2,541,101	2,660,055
United States	400,522	461,984	396,497
Total	2,886,703	3,003,085	3,056,552
Fresh Peaches & nectarines:			
Argentina	291,804	290,000	290,000
Australia	100,000	90,000	90,000
Brazil	217,706	220,000	220,000
Chile	91,000	141,000	151,000
China	11,900,000	13,000,000	13,600,000
European Union	3,730,508	4,182,344	4,026,700
Japan	124,700	136,954	137,000
Mexico	161,268	160,000	160,000
South Africa	174,230	170,000	170,000
Turkey	550,000	500,000	520,000
Others	214,770	198,577	197,900
Total Foreign	17,555,986	19,088,875	19,562,600
United States	953,253	946,491	903,055
Total	18,509,239	20,035,366	20,465,655
Pears, fresh:			
Argentina	690,000	580,000	650,000
Chile	267,000	290,000	300,000
China	17,300,000	18,000,000	19,000,000
European Union	2,523,100	2,594,300	2,450,000
India	340,000	340,000	340,000
Japan	300,000	300,000	300,000
Korea, South	282,200	302,700	259,000
Russia	132,500	160,451	160,000
South Africa	413,600	400,000	410,000
Turkey	415,000	305,000	415,000
Others	339,500	363,800	363,200
Total Foreign	23,002,900	23,636,251	24,647,200
United States	795,166	754,098	665,000
Total	23,798,066	24,390,349	25,312,200

FAS, Office of Global Analysis, (202) 720-6301. Prepared or estimated on the basis of official USDA production, supply, and distribution statistics from foreign governments.

Table 5-59.—Pears: Production and utilization, by State and United States, crop of 2014

State and variety	Total production	Utilized production	Utilization Fresh[1]	Utilization Processed
	Tons	Tons	Tons	Tons
California	189,000	189,000	(D)	(D)
Bartlett	154,000	154,000	48,000	106,000
Other	35,000	35,000	(D)	(D)
Michigan	2,720	2,610	(D)	(D)
New York	5,350	5,210	(D)	(D)
Oregon	216,000	216,000	(D	(D)
Bartlett	53,000	53,000	35,000	18,000
Other	163,000	163,000	(D)	(D)
Pennsylvania	2,540	2,430	(D)	(D)
Washington	416,000	416,000	(D)	(D)
Bartlett	181,000	181,000	76,000	105,000
Other	232,000	235,000	(D)	(D)
United States[2]	831,610	831,250	159,000	229,000

(D) Withheld to avoid disclosing data for individual operations.   [1] Includes "Home use."   [2] Mostly canned, but includes small quantities dried, juiced, and other uses.
NASS, Crops Branch, (202) 720–2127.

Table 5-60.—Pears: Production and utilization, United States, 2005–2014

Crop of—	Total production	Utilized production	Utilization of quantities sold—Fresh[1]
	Tons	Tons	Tons
2005	823,320	821,670	504,400
2006	842,035	831,120	500,720
2007	872,950	871,850	551,960
2008	869,850	868,880	548,930
2009	957,220	955,820	603,800
2010	813,600	813,400	531,430
2011	965,720	965,110	643,710
2012	851,240	851,130	551,820
2013	877,130	876,520	584,730
2014	831,610	831,250	550,080

[1] Includes "Home use."
NASS, Crops Branch, (202) 720–2127.

Table 5-61.—Papayas: Area, utilized production, utilization, marketing year average price, and value, Hawaii, 2005–2014

Year	Area harvested	Utilized production	Utilization Fresh	Utilization Processed	Price per pound	Value
	Acres	1,000 pounds	1,000 pounds	1,000 pounds	Cents	dollars
2005	1,480	32,900	30,700	2,200	34.2	11,241
2006	1,530	28,700	26,600	2,100	38.5	11,049
2007	1,310	33,400	31,200	2,200	39.2	13,094
2008	1,380	33,500	31,500	2,000	43.0	14,393
2009	1,325	31,500	30,300	1,200	45.0	14,186
2010	1,350	30,100	29,200	900	37.0	11,123
2011	1,300	28,600	27,700	900	34.0	9,722
2012	(NA)	(NA)	(NA)	(NA)	(NA)	(NA)
2013	1,300	24,200	23,000	1,200	34.4	8,316
2014	1,500	23,500	23,000	500	48.0	11,285

NASS, Crops Branch, (202) 720–2127.

Table 5-62.—Plums, California: Production, value, and utilization, 2005–2014

Season	Total production	Utilized production	Marketing year average price per ton	Value
	Tons	Tons	Dollars	1,000 dollars
2005	171,000	171,000	541.00	92,463
2006	158,000	158,000	688.00	108,648
2007	152,000	152,000	665.00	101,077
2008	160,000	160,000	356.00	56,960
2009	112,000	112,000	514.00	57,568
2010	141,300	141,300	555.00	78,422
2011	160,000	160,000	402.00	64,320
2012	115,000	115,000	695.00	79,940
2013	95,400	93,400	664.00	62,043
2014	113,000	113,000	913.00	103,167

NASS, Crops Branch, (202) 720–2127.

Table 5-63.—Prunes (dried basis): Production, price and value, California, 2005–2014

Season	Total production	Utilized production	Marketing year average price per ton	Value
	Tons	Tons	Dollars	1,000 dollars
2005	97,000	94,000	1,470.00	138,180
2006	198,000	189,000	1,390.00	262,710
2007	83,000	81,000	1,450.00	117,450
2008	129,000	129,000	1,500.00	193,500
2009	166,000	166,000	1,230.00	204,180
2010	130,000	130,000	1,350.00	175,500
2011	137,000	137,000	1,310.00	179,470
2012	138,000	138,000	1,330.00	183,540
2013	85,000	85,000	2,000.00	170,000
2014	104,000	104,000	2,240.00	232,960

NASS, Crops Branch, (202) 720–2127.

Table 5-64.—Prunes and plums: Production, value, and utilization, 4-States [1], 2005–2014

Year	Total production	Utilized production	Marketing year average price per ton	Value	Utilization of quantities sold			
					Fresh	Processed (fresh basis)		
						Dried and other	Canned	Frozen
	Tons	Tons	Dollars	1,000 dollars	Tons	Tons	Tons	Tons
2005	9,100	9,050	562.00	5,085	5,500	680	2,450	420
2006	21,500	19,200	452.00	8,678	9,550	4,300	3,250	2,100
2007	12,100	10,920	454.00	4,956	6,420	1,300	2,550	650
2008	15,500	15,480	382.00	5,918	8,700	3,540	2,130	1,110
2009	18,600	17,700	327.00	5,787	9,750	5,040	2,130	780
2010	12,100	11,200	439.00	4,915	7,700	1,650	1,395	455
2011	13,300	12,900	370.00	4,767	7,030	3,850	1,460	560
2012	12,935	11,835	531.00	6,288	7,030	3,500	755	550
2013	13,440	12,790	482.00	6,169	6,690	3,980	1,380	740
2014	14,800	14,500	487.00	7,060	7,600	....	690	390

[1] Idaho, Michigan, Oregon, and Washington.
NASS, Crops Branch, (202) 720–2127.

Table 5-65.—Prunes and plums (fresh basis): Production and season average price per ton, by State, 2012–2014

State	Total production			Utilized production			Price per ton		
	2012	2013	2014	2012	2013	2014	2012	2013	2014
	Tons	Tons	Tons	Tons	Tons	Tons	Dollars	Dollars	Dollars
Idaho	2,400	2,400	2,600	2,000	2,350	2,400	673.00	440.00	415.00
Michigan	65	1,890	1,700	65	1,890	1,600	585.00	510.00	535.00
Oregon	7,170	6,800	7,800	6,470	6,250	7,800	538.00	488.00	442.00
Washington	3,300	2,350	2,700	3,300	2,300	2,700	432.00	489.00	652.00
Total, 4 States	12,935	13,440	14,800	11,835	12,790	14,500	531.00	482.00	487.00

NASS, Crops Branch, (202) 720–2127.

Table 5-66.—Prunes and plums: Utilization and marketing year average price per ton, by State, 2008–2014

State and season	Quantity				Price			
	Fresh	Dried and other	Canned	Frozen	Fresh	Dried and other	Canned	Frozen
	Tons	Tons	Tons	Tons	Dollars	Dollars	Dollars	Dollars
Michigan:								
2008	700	(1)	(1)	(1)	775.00	(1)	(1)	(1)
2009	1,000	(1)	(1)	(1)	880.00	(1)	(1)	(1)
2010	1,000	(1)	(1)	(1)	870.00	(1)	(1)	(1)
2011	(1)	(1)	(1)	(1)	(1)	(1)	(1)	(1)
2012	(1)	(1)	(1)	(1)	(1)	(1)	(1)	(1)
2013	(1)	(1)	(1)	(1)	(1)	(1)	(1)	(1)
2014	(1)	(1)	(1)	(1)	(1)	(1)	(1)	(1)
Oregon:								
2008	3,500	(1)	(1)	(1)	407.00	(1)	(1)	(1)
2009	4,200	(1)	(1)	(1)	322.00	(1)	(1)	(1)
2010	2,800	(1)	(1)	(1)	498.00	(1)	(1)	(1)
2011	1,700	(1)	(1)	(1)	441.00	(1)	(1)	(1)
2012	3,220	(1)	(1)	(1)	813.00	(1)	(1)	(1)
2013	2,620	(1)	(1)	(1)	644.00	(1)	(1)	(1)
2014	3,900	(1)	(1)	(1)	554.00	(1)	(1)	(1)
Total States: [2]								
2008	8,700	3,540	2,130	1,110	547.00	153.00	182.00	207.00
2009	9,750	5,040	2,130	780	472.00	129.00	178.00	204.00
2010	7,700	1,650	1,395	455	551.00	163.00	209.00	251.00
2011	7,030	3,850	1,460	560	482.00	240.00	203.00	280.00
2012	7,030	3,500	755	550	739.00	220.00	234.00	265.00
2013	6,690	3,980	1,380	740	608.00	322.00	380.00	400.00
2014	7,600	....	690	390	656.00	....	414.00	367.00

[1] Not published to avoid disclosure of individual operations, but is included in total.   [2] Includes Idaho, Michigan, Oregon, and Washington.
NASS, Crops Branch, (202) 720–2127.

Table 5-67.—Prunes: Foreign trade, United States, 2005–2014

Year beginning October	Imports				Domestic exports			
	Fresh prunes and plums	Otherwise prepared or preserved	Dried prunes [1]	Total, in terms of fresh [2]	Fresh prunes and plums	Dried prunes [1]	Dried, in fruit salad [1][3]	Total, in terms of fresh [2]
	Metric tons	Metric tons	Metric tons	Metric tons	Metric tons	Metric tons	Metric tons	Metric tons
2005	30,606	1,197	6,875	49,531	48,004	48,903	2,208	180,695
2006	36,434	866	840	39,392	46,633	66,253	1,268	221,930
2007	29,104	678	828	31,863	50,551	61,345	1,414	213,483
2008	29,409	829	3,906	40,293	46,215	54,706	1,236	191,451
2009	27,226	805	620	29,559	47,213	65,070	1,355	219,664
2010	29,768	831	497	31,805	59,653	69,110	1,639	243,328
2011	24,105	822	565	26,311	56,788	67,529	1,810	236,801
2012	30,417	680	1,159	34,036	52,333	72,350	1,906	245,164
2013	13,625	821	6,844	32,129	41,752	60,961	1,759	204,581
2014	25,259	792	11,514	55,863	37,204	75,006	1,425	235,630

[1] Net processed weight. [2] Exports and imports of dried prunes converted to unprocessed dry weight by dividing by 1.04. Unprocessed dry weight converted to terms of fresh fruit on the basis that 1 pound dried equals 2.7 pounds fresh. "Otherwise prepared or preserved" converted to terms of fresh fruit on the basis that 1 pound equals 0.899 pound fresh. [3] Dried prunes in salad estimated at 43 percent of total dried fruit for salad.
ERS, Crops Branch, (202) 694–5255.

Table 5-68.—Strawberries, commercial crop: Production and value per hundredweight, by State and United States, 2012–2014

Utilization, season, and State	Production			Value per unit		
	2012	2013	2014	2012	2013	2014
	1,000 cwt	1,000 cwt	1,000 cwt	Dollars per cwt	Dollars per cwt	Dollars per cwt
Fresh market:						
California	21,936	22,398	22,100	88.80	90.40	102.00
Florida	2,226	2,332	2,071	110.00	143.00	148.00
Michigan	32	(D)	(D)	149.00	(D)	(D)
New York	32	38	32	215.00	203.40	235.00
North Carolina	162	110	154	145.00	148.00	152.00
Ohio	25	29	18	168.00	209.00	193.00
Oregon	35	22	25	139.00	167.00	161.00
Pennsylvania	42	51	33	164.00	223.00	160.00
Washington	24	(D)	(D)	177.00	(D)	(D)
Wisconsin	38	39	38	151.00	165.00	165.00
Other States	(X)	66	72	(X)	175.00	180.00
United States	24,552	25,085	24,543	91.80	96.50	107.00
Processing:						
California	5,710	5,175	5,477	32.00	34.00	41.50
Michigan	1	(D)	(D)	58.00	(D)	(D)
Oregon	178	145	130	58.00	48.00	70.00
Washington	79	(D)	(D)	77.00	(D)	(D)
Other States	(X)	65	72	(X)	73.20	75.20
United States	5,968	5,385	5,679	33.40	34.90	42.60

(D) Withheld to avoid disclosing data for individual operations. (X) Not applicable.
NASS, Crops Branch, (202) 720–2127.

Table 5-69.—Strawberries, commercial crop: Area, yield, production, value per hundred weight, and total value, United States, 2005–2014

Year	Fresh market and processing				
	Area for harvest	Yield per acre	Production	Value[2]	
				Per cwt	Total
	Acres	*Cwt*	*1,000 cwt*	*Dollars per cwt*	*1,000 dollars*
2005	52,460	443	23,227	60.10	1,396,385
2006	53,460	450	24,038	63.20	1,519,494
2007	52,180	469	24,453	71.60	1,751,108
2008	54,470	465	25,317	75.80	1,918,288
2009	58,080	482	28,013	76.00	2,129,585
2010	56,890	501	28,520	79.30	2,260,733
2011	57,250	507	29,016	82.40	2,391,406
2012	58,310	523	30,520	80.40	2,453,039
2013	60,410	504	30,470	85.60	2,609,038
2014	59,895	505	30,222	94.80	2,865,432

Year	Fresh market[1]			Processing		
	Production	Value[2]		Production	Value[2]	
		Per cwt	Total		Per cwt	Total
	1,000 cwt	*Dollars per cwt*	*1,000 dollars*	*1,000 cwt*	*Dollars per cwt*	*1,000 dollars*
2005	18,110	68.90	1,248,407	5,117	28.90	147,978
2006	19,109	72.20	1,379,658	4,929	28.40	139,836
2007	19,733	82.10	1,620,241	4,720	27.70	130,867
2008	20,911	84.10	1,759,564	4,406	36.00	158,724
2009	22,880	86.10	1,970,920	5,133	30.90	158,665
2010	23,196	90.80	2,105,492	5,324	29.20	155,241
2011	23,324	94.00	2,193,379	5,692	34.80	198,027
2012	24,552	91.80	2,253,854	5,968	33.40	199,185
2013	25,085	96.50	2,421,370	5,385	34.90	187,668
2014	24,543	107.00	2,623,625	5,679	42.60	241,807

[1] Fresh market price and value at point of first sale. Processing price and value at processing plant door.   [2] Mostly for fresh market, but includes some quantities used for processing in States for which processing estimates are not prepared. NASS, Crops Branch, (202) 720–2127.

Table 5-70.—Strawberries, commercial crop: Area harvested, production, value per hundred weight, by State and United States, 2012–2014[1]

Season and State	Area harvested			Production			Value per unit		
	2012	2013	2014	2012	2013	2014	2012	2013	2014
	Acres	*Acres*	*Acres*	*1,000 cwt*	*1,000 cwt*	*1,000 cwt*	*Dollars per cwt*	*Dollars per cwt*	*Dollars per cwt*
California	39,000	41,500	41,500	27,646	27,573	27,577	77.10	79.80	90.00
Florida	10,600	10,600	10,900	2,226	2,332	2,071	110.00	143.00	148.00
Michigan	650	750	750	33	44	45	146.00	161.00	161.00
New York	1,400	1,400	1,000	32	38	32	215.00	203.00	235.00
North Carolina	1,200	1,100	1,100	162	110	154	145.00	148.00	152.00
Ohio	660	590	480	25	29	18	168.00	209.00	193.00
Oregon	2,000	1,700	1,700	213	167	155	71.30	63.70	84.70
Pennsylvania	820	950	735	42	51	33	164.00	223.00	160.00
Washington ...	1,300	1,100	1,100	103	87	99	100.00	106.00	112.00
Wisconsin	740	720	630	38	39	38	151.00	165.00	165.00
United States	58,310	60,410	59,895	30,520	30,470	30,222	80.40	85.60	94.80

[1] Includes quantities used for fresh market and processing. NASS, Crops Branch, (202) 720–2127.

Table 5-71.—Fruits, noncitrus: Production, utilization, and value, United States, 2005–2014 [1]

Year	Utilized production	Fresh [2]	Processed						Value of utilized production
			Canned	Dried	Juice	Frozen	Wine	Other	
	1,000 tons	1,000 tons	1,000 tons	1,000 tons	1,000 tons	1,000 tons	1,000 tons	1,000 tons	1,000 dollars
2005	18,272	7,188	1,575	2,101	1,555	712	4,551	277	9,805,757
2006	16,816	6,930	1,400	2,219	1,256	710	3,726	235	10,510,417
2007	17,023	7,008	1,453	2,030	1,257	748	3,921	278	11,397,171
2008	17,603	7,248	1,406	2,413	1,228	682	3,944	290	11,270,860
2009	18,069	7,562	1,394	2,148	1,235	742	4,373	269	11,811,298
2010	17,879	7,458	1,386	2,318	1,103	706	4,270	298	12,367,607
2011	18,147	7,702	1,301	2,399	1,153	737	4,154	316	13,910,375
2012	17,635	7,443	1,100	2,091	1,213	707	4,707	374	15,611,441
2013	19,433	7,718	1,373	2,321	1,631	875	5,068	448	16,220,752
2014	19,035	8,324	1,202	2,076	1,609	876	4,522	460	16,329,920

[1] Includes the following crops: Apples, apricots, avocados, bananas, berries, cherries, cranberries, dates, figs, grapes, guavas, kiwifruit, nectarines, olives, papayas, peaches, pears, pineapples, plums, prunes, and strawberries. [2] Includes "Home Use," local and roadside sales.
NASS, Crops Branch, (202) 720–2127.

Table 5-72.—Fruits, fresh: Total reported domestic rail, truck, and air shipments, 2014

Commodity	Jan.	Feb.	Mar.	Apr.	May	Jun.	Jul.	Aug.	Sep.	Oct.	Nov.	Dec.	Total
	1,000 cwt	1,000 cwt	1,000 cwt	1,000 cwt	1,000 cwt	1,000 cwt	1,000 cwt	1,000 cwt	1,000 cwt	1,000 cwt	1,000 cwt	1,000 cwt	1,000 cwt
Citrus:													
Grapefruit	1,207	1,108	975	585	253	22	18	13	36	771	964	1,126	7,078
Grapefruit-organic	8	7	7	6	1								29
Lemons	26	22	32	46	50	46	41	32	16	15	12	28	366
Oranges	991	838	867	859	745	444	202	104	137	475	819	1,040	7,521
Oranges-organic	4	1											5
Tangelos	102	13		1							30	92	238
Tangerines	234	171	152	78					29	222	226	250	1,362
Temples	29	36	12	2									79
Total	2,601	2,196	2,045	1,577	1,049	512	261	149	218	1,483	2,051	2,536	16,678
Noncitrus:													
Apples	5,261	5,252	6,486	4,833	5,154	3,150	2,508	4,040	4,887	5,864	7,035	5,469	59,939
Apples-organic	376	326	387	248	93	10	7	106	362	431	503	394	3,243
Apricots				1	64	50	98	13					226
Apricots-organic						5	19						24
Avocados	65	70	261	407	737	593	542	498	241	105	48	40	3,607
Blueberries	1	3	11	136	629	808	536	241	119	16			2,500
Blueberries-organic ..	1	1	5	17	46	57	68	28	4	1			228
Cherries				17	338	2,039	2,808	205	2				5,409
Cherries-organic					2	58	57	2					119
Cranberries									9	40	149	25	223
Grapes										1	3		4
Grapes-organic	275	26		5	382	676	2,366	3,177	3,385	3,185	2,295	1,227	16,999
Kiwifruit				1	43	84	11						139
Kiwifruit-organic	11	1								14	25	22	73
Nectarines				3	339	574	605	495	75				2,091
Peaches				6	393	949	1,362	1,205	516	50			4,481
Peaches-organic						4	50	26					80
Pears	1,201	1,107	1,052	873	543	305	367	590	1,101	1,329	1,580	1,153	11,201
Pears-organic	60	45	13	3			7	45	76	86	95	61	491
Persimmons	1								9	47	20	4	81
Plums					68	362	435	326	147	13			1,351
Pomegranates									39	59	31	20	149
Prunes									29	12	1		42
Raspberries	55	52	48	86	186	220	227	280	182	159	116	76	1,687
Raspberries-organic ..	7	8	9	11	21	27	26	37	21	18	12	9	206
Strawberries	669	1,226	1,979	2,199	2,580	1,950	1,910	1,311	984	896	329	503	16,536
Strawberries-organic	13	19	33	70	145	162	169	113	82	54	21	12	893
Total	7,996	8,136	10,284	8,916	11,763	12,083	14,178	12,767	12,253	12,369	12,262	9,015	132,022
Grand total	10,597	10,332	12,329	10,493	12,812	12,595	14,439	12,916	12,471	13,852	14,313	11,551	148,700

AMS, Fruit and Vegetable Programs, Market News Division, (202) 720–9936.

Table 5-73.—Fruits, dried: Production (dry basis), California, 2005–2014

Year	Apricots	Figs [1]	Peaches [2]	Pears [3]	Prunes	Grapes [4]	Total
	Tons	Tons	Tons	Tons	Tons	Tons	Tons
2005	1,360	15,100	1,160	400	94,000	357,500	469,520
2006	640	13,000	1,290	(D)	189,000	309,500	513,430
2007	1,970	14,500	1,365	(D)	81,000	360,000	458,835
2008	1,830	13,100	1,050	(D)	129,000	390,300	535,280
2009	1,090	13,300	850	(D)	166,000	335,500	516,740
2010	1,400	12,320	2,010	(D)	130,000	394,800	540,530
2011	1,810	11,560	470	(D)	137,000	384,300	535,140
2012	1,210	10,400	1,230	(D)	138,000	345,900	496,740
2013	1,080	9,300	420	(D)	85,000	406,100	501,900
2014	1,500	8,900	610	(D)	104,000	343,100	458,110

(D) Withheld to avoid disclosing data for individual operations. [1] Standard and substandard. [2] Freestone only. [3] Bartlett only. [4] Raisin and table type.
NASS, Crops Branch, (202) 720–2127.

Table 5-74.—International Raisins: Production in specified countries, 2013/2014–2015/2016

Country	2013/2014	2014/2015	2014/2016
	Metric tons	Metric tons	Metric tons
Afghanistan	34,300	40,000	42,000
Argentina	20,500	33,000	32,000
Australia	10,000	10,000	10,000
Chile	69,200	64,000	65,000
China	165,000	180,000	190,000
European Union	10,000	10,000	10,000
Iran	160,000	130,000	150,000
South Africa	46,000	58,000	55,000
Turkey	242,635	320,000	200,000
Uzbekistan	18,000	51,000	35,000
Others	10,000	10,000	10,000
Total Foreign	785,635	906,000	799,000
United States	368,408	311,255	340,000
Total	1,154,043	1,217,255	1,139,000

FAS, Office of Global Analysis, (202) 720-6301. Prepared or estimated on the basis of official USDA production, supply, and distribution statistics from foreign governments.

Table 5-75.—Fruits: Per capita consumption, United States, 2005–2014 [1]

Year	Fruits used fresh		Canned fruits [4]	Juice [5]	Frozen fruit [6]	Dried fruits [7]
	Citrus fruit [2]	Noncitrus fruits [3]				
	Pounds	Pounds	Pounds	Gallons	Pounds	Pounds
2005	21.6	78.3	14.4	7.7	5.4	2.3
2006	21.6	79.5	13.2	7.8	5.2	2.3
2007	17.9	79.4	14.1	7.6	5.5	2.2
2008	20.6	79.2	13.4	7.6	5.1	2.2
2009	20.7	77.2	13.5	7.1	5.1	2.1
2010	21.6	80.7	13.1	7.2	5.7	2.3
2011	22.6	82.0	12.1	6.1	5.3	2.4
2012	23.6	84.8	11.5	6.4	5.0	2.4
2013	24.0	87.3	12.9	6.2	5.2	2.5
2014	23.4	89.7	11.7	6.0	6.5	2.4

[1] Fresh citrus fruits, canned fruit, and fruit juices are on a crop-year basis. Dried fruits are on a pack-year basis. The per capita consumption was obtained by dividing the total consumption by total population.　[2] Oranges and temples, tangerines and tangelos, lemons, limes, and grapefruit.　[3] Apples, apricots, avocados, bananas, cherries, cranberries, grapes, kiwifruit, mangoes, peaches and nectarines, pears, pineapples, papayas, plums and prunes, and strawberries.　[4] Apples, apricots, cherries, olives, peaches, pears, pineapples, and plums and prunes.　[5] Orange, grapefruit, lemon, lime, apple, grape, pineapple, prune, and cranberry.　[6] Blackberries, blueberries, raspberries, strawberries, other berries, apples, apricots, cherries, and peaches.　[7] Apples, apricots, dates, figs, peaches, pears, prunes, and raisins. Dried data in terms of processed weight.
ERS, Crops Branch, (202) 694–5255.

Table 5-76.—All tree nuts: Supply and utilization, United States, 2005/2006–2014/2015

Market year[1]	Beginning stocks	Marketable production[2]	Imports	Total supply	Exports	Ending stocks	Domestic consumption	
							Total	Per capita Pounds
	—Million pounds (shelled)—							
2005/2006	262.9	1,502.4	431.9	2,197.2	1,125.6	267.7	803.9	2.70
2006/2007	267.7	1,655.8	438.3	2,361.8	1,129.8	243.1	988.9	3.29
2007/2008	243.1	2,062.5	489.8	2,795.4	1,311.8	405.9	1,077.8	3.55
2008/2009	405.9	2,259.5	439.2	3,104.6	1,466.3	543.7	1,094.6	3.57
2009/2010	543.7	2,113.3	467.6	3,124.6	1,546.4	422.2	1,155.9	3.74
2010/2011	422.2	2,482.2	488.0	3,392.4	1,786.1	407.3	1,199.1	3.86
2011/2012	407.3	2,787.2	444.9	3,639.4	1,976.9	480.1	1,182.4	3.78
2012/2013	480.1	2,762.6	515.6	3,758.0	1,971.6	462.1	1,324.4	4.20
2013/2014	462.1	2,806.7	579.5	3,848.3	2,068.5	505.4	1,274.4	4.01
2014/2015[3] ..	505.4	2,745.6	732.2	3,983.3	2,054.5	587.5	1,341.3	4.19

[1] Marketing season begins July 1 for almonds, hazelnuts, macadamias, pecans, and other nuts; August 1 for walnuts; and September 1 for pistachios.　[2] Utilized production (NASS data) minus inedibles and noncommercial useage.　[3] Preliminary.
ERS, Crops Branch, (202) 694–5255.

Table 5-77.—International Nuts: Production in specified countries, 2013/2014–2015/2016

Country	Production		
	2013/2014	2014/2015	2015/2016
	Metric tons	Metric tons	Metric tons
Almonds:			
Australia	65,100	75,000	82,000
Chile	3,900	11,000	12,000
China	7,000	9,500	10,000
European Union	58,800	79,700	85,000
India	1,100	1,200	1,100
Turkey	18,000	13,000	14,000
Total Foreign	153,900	189,400	204,100
United States	911,720	848,220	816,470
Total	1,065,620	1,037,620	1,020,570
Walnuts, Inshell basis:			
Australia	2,500	2,500	2,500
Brazil	5,200	6,000	6,000
Chile	60,000	54,000	60,000
China	780,000	900,000	1,000,000
European Union	110,000	111,000	117,000
India	43,000	35,000	38,000
Moldova	23,100	32,000	35,000
Turkey	75,000	40,000	60,000
Ukraine	115,790	102,740	102,000
Total Foreign	1,214,590	1,283,240	1,420,500
United States	446,335	517,095	521,631
Total	1,660,925	1,800,335	1,942,131

FAS, Office of Global Analysis, (202) 720-6301. Prepared or estimated on the basis of official USDA production, supply, and distribution statistics from foreign governments.

Table 5-78.—Almonds (shelled basis): Bearing acreage, yield, production, price, and value, California, 2005–2014[1]

Year	Bearing Acreage	Yield per acre[2]	Utilized production	Price per pound	Value
	Acres	Pounds	1,000 pounds	Dollars	1,000 dollars
2005	590,000	1,550	915,000	2.81	2,525,909
2006	610,000	1,840	1,120,000	2.06	2,258,790
2007	640,000	2,170	1,390,000	1.75	2,401,875
2008	710,000	2,300	1,630,000	1.45	2,343,200
2009	750,000	1,880	1,410,000	1.65	2,293,500
2010	770,000	2,130	1,640,000	1.79	2,903,380
2011	800,000	2,540	2,030,000	1.99	4,007,860
2012	820,000	2,310	1,890,000	2.58	4,816,860
2013	840,000	2,390	2,010,000	3.21	6,384,690
2014	860,000	2,170	1,870,000	3.50	6,464,500

[1] Price and value are based on edible portion of the crop only. Production includes inedible quantities of no value as follows (million pounds): 2004-14.5; 2005-16.1; 2006-23.5; 2007-17.5; 2008-14.0; 2009-20.0; 2010-18.0; 2011-16.0; 2012-23; 2013-21.0. [2] Yield is based on utilized production.
NASS, Crops Branch, (202) 720–2127.

Table 5-79.—Almonds (shelled basis): Foreign trade, United States, 2005–2014[1]

Year beginning October	Imports	Domestic exports
	Metric tons	Metric tons
2005	2,076	324,798
2006	1,515	342,046
2007	1,722	397,105
2008	796	439,759
2009	776	462,276
2010	2,391	527,228
2011	5,729	615,258
2012	15,653	579,564
2013	14,724	581,283
2014	10,133	545,839

[1] Imports of unshelled nuts converted to shelled basis at ratio of 1.67 to 1. Exports of unshelled nuts converted to shelled basis at ratio of 1.67 to 1.0.
ERS, Crops Branch, (202) 694–5255.

Table 5-80.—Macadamia nuts (in-shell basis): Bearing acreage, yield, production, price, and value, Hawaii, 2005–2014

Year	Bearing Acreage	Yield per acre	Utilized production	Price per pound	Value
	Acres	Pounds	1,000 pounds	Cents	1,000 dollars
2005	18,000	3,000	54,000	81.0	43,740
2006	15,000	3,870	58,000	67.0	38,860
2007	15,000	2,730	41,000	60.0	24,600
2008	15,000	3,330	50,000	67.0	33,500
2009	15,000	2,800	42,000	70.0	29,400
2010	15,000	2,670	40,000	75.0	30,000
2011	15,000	3,270	49,000	78.0	38,220
2012	15,000	2,930	44,000	80.0	35,200
2013	16,000	2,560	41,000	87.0	35,670
2014	16,000	2,500	40,000	87.0	34,800

NASS, Crops Branch, (202) 720–2127.

Table 5-81.—Hazelnuts (in-shell basis): Bearing acreage, yield, production, price, and value, Oregon, 2005–2014

Year	Bearing Acreage	Yield per acre	Utilized production	Price per ton	Value
	Acres	Tons	Tons	Dollars	1,000 dollars
2005	28,300	0.98	27,600	2,240	61,824
2006	28,200	1.52	43,000	1,080	46,440
2007	28,600	1.29	37,000	2,040	75,480
2008	28,300	1.13	32,000	1,620	51,840
2009	28,700	1.64	47,000	1,690	79,430
2010	29,000	0.97	28,000	2,410	67,480
2011	28,500	1.35	38,500	2,330	89,705
2012	29,000	1.22	35,500	1,830	64,965
2013	30,000	1.50	45,000	2,680	120,600
2014	30,000	1.20	36,000	3,600	129,600

NASS, Crops Branch, (202) 720–2127.

Table 5-82.—Hazelnuts (shelled basis): Foreign trade, United States, 2005–2014 [1]

Year beginning October	Imports	Domestic exports
	Metric tons	Metric tons
2005	5,383	11,183
2006	4,344	11,187
2007	4,979	10,031
2008	2,969	9,715
2009	2,533	13,917
2010	4,417	7,691
2011	3,118	10,031
2012	5,392	11,243
2013	4,747	14,862
2014	1,761	20,309

[1] Imports of unshelled nuts converted to shelled basis at ratio of 2.22 to 1. Exports of unshelled nuts converted to shelled basis at ratio of 2.50 to 1.
ERS, Crops Branch, (202) 694–5255.

Table 5-83.—Pecans (in-shell basis): Production, price per pound, and value, United States, 2005–2014

Year	Improved varieties [1]			Native and seedling			All pecans		
	Utilized production	Price per pound	Value	Utilized production	Price per pound	Value	Utilized production	Price per pound	Value
	1,000 pounds	Dollars	1,000 dollars	1,000 pounds	Dollars	1,000 dollars	1,000 pounds	Dollars	1,000 dollars
2005 [2]	228,700	1.540	351,353	51,550	1.080	55,567	280,250	1.450	406,920
2006	152,130	1.730	262,544	55,170	1.090	59,949	207,300	1.560	322,493
2007	303,462	1.230	373,131	83,843	0.722	60,513	387,305	1.120	433,644
2008	173,660	1.420	246,590	28,420	0.883	25,097	202,080	1.340	271,687
2009	249,720	1.530	381,550	52,300	0.934	48,838	302,020	1.430	430,388
2010	232,560	2.490	578,149	61,180	1.580	96,679	293,740	2.300	674,828
2011	227,030	2.590	587,064	42,670	1.610	68,825	269,700	2.430	655,889
2012	247,100	1.730	427,473	55,200	0.879	48,518	302,300	1.570	475,991
2013	220,000	1.900	417,758	46,330	0.920	42,632	266,330	1.730	460,390
2014	227,410	2.120	482,323	36,740	0.933	34,268	264,150	1.960	516,591

[1] Budded, grafted or topworked varieties.   [2] Missouri added.
NASS, Crops Branch, (202) 720–2127.

Table 5-84.—Pecans (in-shell basis): Production and marketing year average price per pound, by State and United States, 2012–2014

Item and State	Utilized production			Price per pound		
	2012	2013	2014	2012	2013	2014
	1,000 pounds	*1,000 pounds*	*1,000 pounds*	*Dollars*	*Dollars*	*Dollars*
Improved Varieties [1]						
Alabama	3,400	2,500	1,500	1.400	1.940	2.060
Arizona	20,000	22,500	21,000	1.600	1.900	2.000
Arkansas	1,600	2,000	2,200	1.540	1.600	1.910
California	4,300	5,000	5,000	1.580	2.060	2.140
Florida	1,100	700	100	1.100	1.720	1.750
Georgia	96,000	83,000	74,000	1.940	1.960	2.340
Louisiana	5,000	1,500	2,500	1.300	1.400	1.520
Mississippi	2,000	3,800	700	1.250	1.230	1.570
Missouri	200	500	210	1.450	1.340	1.930
New Mexico	65,000	72,000	67,000	1.700	1.900	2.100
Oklahoma	5,000	3,000	4,000	1.550	2.050	1.630
South Carolina	1,500	1,500	200	1.750	2.000	2.160
Texas	42,000	22,000	49,000	1.520	1.790	1.960
United States	247,100	220,000	227,410	1.730	1.900	2.120
Native and Seedling						
Alabama	600	770	200	0.830	1.020	1.140
Arkansas	600	700	1,300	0.850	0.830	0.860
Florida	900	(D)	(D)	0.750	(D)	(D)
Georgia	4,000	6,000	2,000	1.220	1.240	1.380
Kansas	3,000	(D)	(D)	1.350	(D)	(D)
Louisiana	10,000	9,500	11,500	0.700	0.860	0.790
Mississippi	500	1,700	300	0.850	0.950	0.900
Missouri	2,300	2,240	460	0.950	1.010	1.040
Oklahoma	20,000	17,000	8,000	0.850	0.801	0.923
South Carolina	300	60	50	1.250	1.500	1.270
Texas	13,000	6,000	12,000	0.840	0.900	0.980
Other States	-	2,360	930	-	1.130	1.210
United States	55,200	46,330	36,740	0.879	0.920	0.933
All Pecans						
Alabama	4,000	3,270	1,700	1.310	1.720	1.950
Arizona	20,000	22,500	21,000	1.600	1.900	2.000
Arkansas	2,200	2,700	3,500	1.350	1.400	1.520
California	4,300	5,000	5,000	1.580	2.060	2.140
Florida	2,000	(D)	(D)	0.943	(D)	(D)
Georgia	100,000	89,000	76,000	1.910	1.910	2.310
Kansas	3,000	(D)	(D)	1.350	(D)	(D)
Louisiana	15,000	11,000	14,000	0.900	0.934	0.920
Mississippi	2,500	5,500	1,000	1.170	1.140	1.370
Missouri	2,500	2,740	670	0.990	1.070	1.320
New Mexico	65,000	72,000	67,000	1.700	1.900	2.100
Oklahoma	25,000	20,000	12,000	0.990	0.988	1.160
South Carolina	1,800	1,560	250	1.670	1.980	1.980
Texas	55,000	28,000	61,000	1.360	1.600	1.770
Other States	-	3,060	1,030	-	1.270	1.260
United States	302,300	266,330	264,150	1.570	1.730	1.960

- Represents zero. (D) Withheld to avoid disclosing data for individual operations. [1] Budded, grafted or topworked varieties.
NASS, Crops Branch, (202) 720–2127.

Table 5-85.—Pecans (shelled basis): Foreign trade, United States, 2005–2014 [1]

Year beginning October	Imports	Domestic exports
	Metric tons	*Metric tons*
2005	30,983	16,419
2006	23,923	19,145
2007	33,689	29,409
2008	26,831	22,037
2009	33,735	30,607
2010	35,906	25,531
2011	30,449	31,141
2012	33,525	37,873
2013	39,000	33,107
2014	43,736	40,990

[1] Imports of unshelled nuts converted to shelled basis at ratio of 2.50 to 1. Exports of unshelled nuts converted to shelled basis at ratio of 2.50 to 1.
ERS, Crops Branch, (202) 694–5255.

Table 5-86.—Pistachios (in-shell basis): Bearing acreage, yield, production, price, and value, California, 2005–2014

Year	Bearing Acreage	Yield per acre	Utilized production	Price per pound	Value
	Acres	Pounds	1,000 pounds	Dollars	1,000 dollars
2005	105,000	2,700	283,000	2.05	580,150
2006	112,000	2,130	238,000	1.89	449,820
2007	115,000	3,620	416,000	1.41	586,560
2008	118,000	2,360	278,000	2.05	569,900
2009	126,000	2,820	355,000	1.67	592,850
2010	137,000	3,810	522,000	2.22	1,158,840
2011	153,000	2,900	444,000	1.98	879,120
2012	182,000	3,030	551,000	2.61	1,438,110
2013	203,000	2,320	470,000	3.48	1,635,600
2014	215,000	2,390	514,000	2.51	1,290,140

NASS, Crops Branch, (202) 720–2127.

Table 5-87.—Walnuts, English (in-shell basis): Bearing acreage, yield, production, price, and value, California, 2005–2014

Year	Bearing Acreage	Yield per acre [1]	Utilized production	Price per ton	Value
	Acres	Tons	Tons	Dollars	1,000 dollars
2005	215,000	1.65	355,000	1,570	557,350
2006	216,000	1.60	346,000	1,630	563,980
2007	218,000	1.50	328,000	2,290	751,120
2008	230,000	1.90	436,000	1,280	558,080
2009	240,000	1.82	437,000	1,710	747,270
2010	255,000	1.98	504,000	2,040	1,028,160
2011	265,000	1.74	461,000	2,900	1,336,900
2012	270,000	1.84	497,000	3,030	1,505,910
2013	280,000	1.76	492,000	3,710	1,825,320
2014	290,000	1.97	570,000	3,230	1,841,100

[1]Yield is based on utilized production.
NASS, Crops Branch, (202) 720–2127.

Table 5-88.—Walnuts (shelled basis): Foreign trade, United States, 2005–2014 [1]

Year beginning October	Imports	Domestic exports
	Metric tons	Metric tons
2005	561	89,668
2006	974	69,062
2007	4,059	64,467
2008	837	96,313
2009	1,529	101,865
2010	186	133,868
2011	2,442	117,031
2012	3,957	133,049
2013	5,266	134,380
2014	9,787	157,704

[1]Imports of unshelled nuts converted to shelled basis at ratio of 2.50 to 1. Exports of unshelled nuts converted to shelled basis at ratio of 2.50 to 1.
ERS, Crops Branch, (202) 694–5255.

Table 5-89.—Coffee, green: International trade, exports from principal producing countries, 2012/2013-2014/2015

Country of origin	2012/2013	2013/2014	2014/2015
	1,000 bags	*1,000 bags*	*1,000 bags*
Principle exporting countries:			
Brazil	30,660	34,146	36,570
Colombia	8,855	11,040	12,125
Ethiopia	3,500	3,285	3,500
Guatemala	3,770	3,175	3,070
Honduras	4,480	3,940	4,700
India	4,858	4,983	4,700
Indonesia	8,900	7,800	7,040
Malaysia	2,150	2,110	2,780
Uganda	3,575	3,600	3,400
Vietnam	24,643	28,289	22,072
Others	23,318	20,605	18,949
Total Foreign	118,709	122,973	118,906
United States	365	580	390
Total	119,074	123,553	119,296
Principle importing countries:			
Algeria	1,945	2,300	2,155
Australia	1,660	1,615	1,775
Canada	4,230	4,605	4,505
China	1,560	1,705	1,940
European Union	45,070	44,650	45,110
Japan	8,345	7,870	8,075
Korea,South	1,825	2,160	2,305
Philippines	3,880	3,185	3,790
Russia	4,130	4,230	4,050
Switzerland	2,310	2,300	2,420
Others	17,369	16,789	16,762
Total Foreign	92,324	91,409	92,887
United States	23,700	24,915	24,010
Total	116,024	116,324	116,897

FAS, Office of Global Analysis, (202) 720-6301. Prepared or estimated on the basis of official USDA production, supply, and distribution statistics from foreign governments. Data Source: Department of Commerce, U.S. Census Bureau, Foreign Trade Statistics.

Table 5-90.—Coffee: Area, yield, production, marketing year average price, and value, Hawaii, 2005/2006–2014/2015

Year	Area Harvested	Yield per acre	Production [1]	Price per pound	Value
	Acres	*Pounds*	*1,000 pounds*	*Dollars*	*1,000 dollars*
Hawaii					
2005/2006	6,100	1,340	8,200	4.55	37,310
2006/2007	6,300	1,170	7,400	4.30	31,820
2007/2008	6,400	1,170	7,500	4.25	31,875
2008/2009	6,900	1,260	8,700	3.40	29,580
2009/2010	7,200	1,210	8,700	3.60	31,320
2010/2011	7,500	1,170	8,800	3.80	33,440
2011/2012	7,700	990	7,600	4.15	31,540
2012/2013	7,900	890	7,000	5.90	41,300
2013/2014	8,200	1,020	8,400	6.20	52,080
2014/2015	7,800	1,030	8,100	....	62,622

[1] Parchment basis.
NASS, Crops Branch, (202) 720–2127.

Table 5-91.—Coffee and tea: U.S. imports, 2011–2013

Country	2011	2012	2013
	Metric tons	*Metric tons*	*Metric tons*
Coffee and coffee products:			
Brazil	418,257	334,905	365,420
Colombia	213,147	180,563	254,441
Vietnam	202,971	261,543	225,594
Mexico	98,323	119,203	115,375
Guatemala	94,545	107,208	101,789
Indonesia	59,413	79,706	80,627
Peru	63,046	51,755	52,170
Costa Rica	42,401	44,948	45,734
Honduras	39,920	62,369	44,838
Nicaragua	39,306	44,644	42,893
Germany(*)	35,591	33,286	42,758
Canada	37,765	37,468	39,686
El Salvador	39,420	23,842	25,645
Ethiopia(*)	16,972	12,401	16,090
Papua New Guinea	13,045	16,992	15,313
Uganda	8,530	7,910	13,870
Kenya	5,191	8,492	7,013
Italy(*)	5,925	6,797	6,807
Tanzania	4,599	4,320	6,346
India	7,157	6,324	4,639
China	5,361	5,460	4,510
Rwanda	4,596	4,291	3,893
Ecuador	4,399	2,681	3,264
Switzerland(*)	2,110	2,225	2,414
Malaysia	3,131	3,605	2,366
Dominican Republic	1,547	4,403	2,067
Panama	1,528	1,451	1,366
Korea, South	1,326	1,302	1,294
Sweden	3,892	2,070	1,281
Rest of World	21,142	17,809	11,357
World Total	1,494,552	1,489,973	1,540,860
Tea, except herbal tea:			
Canada	58,870	55,723	59,842
Argentina	50,819	50,205	51,158
China	29,147	29,527	28,080
India	14,719	13,906	15,790
Vietnam	4,638	8,164	9,549
Mexico	4,783	9,225	7,610
Germany(*)	8,891	7,160	7,286
Sri Lanka	3,984	4,141	4,542
Malawi	4,437	3,729	4,474
Indonesia	5,690	4,435	4,452
Kenya	3,725	3,502	3,501
Thailand	829	805	2,851
Japan	1,521	1,326	1,776
Chile	1,653	1,610	1,395
United Kingdom	1,794	1,090	1,332
Taiwan	1,098	1,035	1,167
Brazil	1,627	1,199	1,003
Netherlands	432	273	979
Zimbabwe	599	1,676	910
Poland	606	537	689
Egypt	677	736	687
Ecuador	544	629	669
Nigeria	495	429	637
Hong Kong	466	515	576
Korea, South	683	670	549
South Africa	325	183	473
Papua New Guinea	869	434	462
Pakistan	321	333	411
Mozambique	121	468	395
Rest of World	7,166	7,288	3,920
World Total	211,529	210,956	217,164

Data Source: Department of Commerce, U.S. Census Bureau, Foreign Trade Statistics. (*) Denotes a country that is a summarization of its component countries. All zeroes for a data item may show that statistics exist in the other import type. Consumption or General. Users should use cautious interpretation on Quantity reports using mixed units of measure. Quantity line items will only include statistics on the units of measure that are equal to, or are able to be converted to, the assigned unit of measure of the grouped commodities.
FAS, Office of Global Analysis, (202) 720-6301.

Table 5-92.—Specialty mushrooms: Number of growers, total production, volume of sales, price per pound, and value of sales, United States: 2011/2012-2013/2014

Year and variety	Growers[1]	Total Production[2]	All sales		
			Volume of sales[3]	Price per pound[4]	Value of sales
	Number	1,000 pounds	1,000 pounds	Dollars	1,000 dollars
2011/2012					
Shiitake	162	8,413	7,999	3.42	27,377
Oyster	80	7,505	7,031	2.56	18,008
Other	22	3,414	3,083	4.82	14,856
United States[5]	194	19,332	18,113	3.33	60,241
2012/2013					
Shiitake	179	8,875	8,277	3.32	27,468
Oyster	97	7,414	6,975	3.02	21,050
Other	28	3,659	3,375	4.99	16,827
United States[5]	209	19,948	18,627	3.51	65,345
2013/2014					
Shiitake	206	9,327	8,952	3.21	28,759
Oyster	119	7,499	7,165	3.74	26,783
Other	37	1,846	1,641	6.16	10,114
United States[5]	260	18,672	17,758	3.70	65,656

[1] Growers counted only once for United States total if growing more than one specialty type mushroom. Growers growing Agaricus and specialty mushrooms are included.   [2] Total production includes all fresh market and processing sales plus amount harvested but not sold (shrinkage, cullage, dumped, etc.).   [3] Virtually all specialty mushroom sales are for fresh market.   [4] Prices for mushrooms are the average prices producers receive at the point of first sale, commonly referred to as the average price as sold. For example, if in a given State, part of the fresh mushrooms are sold F.O.B. packed by growers, part are sold bulk to brokers or repackers, and some are sold retail at roadside stands, the mushroom average price as sold is a weighted average of the average price for each method of sale.   [5] 2011-2012: Arkansas, California, Colorado, Connecticut, Florida, Georgia, Hawaii, Illinois, Indiana, Kansas, Kentucky, Maine, Maryland, Massachusetts, Michigan, Minnesota, Missouri, Montana, New York, North Carolina, Ohio, Oregon, Pennsylvania, South Carolina, Tennessee, Texas, Vermont, Virginia, Washington, West Virginia, and Wisconsin. 2012-2013: Arkansas, California, Colorado, Connecticut, Florida, Georgia, Hawaii, Illinois, Indiana, Kansas, Kentucky, Maine, Maryland, Massachusetts, Michigan, Minnesota, Missouri, Montana, New York, North Carolina, Ohio, Oregon, Pennsylvania, South Carolina, Tennessee, Texas, Vermont, Virginia, Washington, West Virginia, and Wisconsin. 2013-2014: Arkansas, California, Colorado, Connecticut, Delaware, Florida, Georgia, Hawaii, Illinois, Indiana, Kansas, Kentucky, Maine, Maryland, Massachusetts, Michigan, Minnesota, Missouri, Nebraska, New Hampshire, New York, North Carolina, Ohio, Oregon, Pennsylvania, South Carolina, Tennessee, Texas, Vermont, Virginia, Washington, West Virginia, and Wisconsin.
NASS, Crops Branch, (202) 720–2127.

Table 5-93.—Agaricus mushrooms: Area, volume of sales, marketing year average price, and value of sales, United States: 2005-2014[1]

Year	Area in production	Volume of sales	Price per pound	Value of sales		
				Total	Fresh market	Processing
	1,000 sq. ft.	1,000 pounds	Dollars	1,000 dollars	1,000 dollars	1,000 dollars
2005/2006	142,550	833,677	1.020	848,836	793,538	55,298
2006/2007	145,743	813,849	1.120	915,561	840,560	75,001
2007/2008	136,011	797,348	1.150	917,607	841,753	75,854
2008/2009	134,533	803,896	1.130	910,658	841,021	69,637
2009/2010	129,268	777,064	1.140	884,390	821,472	62,918
2010/2011	134,266	845,951	1.140	964,192	887,839	76,353
2011/2012	139,331	881,857	1.180	1,039,159	969,847	69,312
2012/2013	139,846	869,625	1.190	1,038,541	969,278	69,263
2014/2015	134,685	882,075	1.190	1,049,972	971,521	78,451

[1] Marketing year begins July 1 and ends June 30 the following year.
NASS, Crops Branch, (202) 720–2127.

Table 5-94.—Cut flowers: Sales and wholesale value for operations with $100,000+ sales, Surveyed States, 2005–2014

Year	Quantity sold	Wholesale price	Value of sales at wholesale [1]	Quantity sold	Wholesale price	Value of sales at wholesale [1]	Quantity sold	Wholesale price	Value of sales at wholesale [1]
	Alstromeria			Carnations, standard			Chrysanthemums pompon		
	1,000 stems	Cents per stem	1,000 dollars	1,000 stems	Cents per stem	1,000 dollars	1,000 bunches	Cents per bunch	1,000 dollars
2005 ...	7,313	35.4	2,588	8,955	20.3	1,816	12,320	1.40	17,246
2006 [2]	8,595	21.9	1,885	5,428	17.6	955	10,338	1.26	12,985
2007 ...	9,879	20.8	2,057	3,328	18.8	626	18,059	0.76	13,810
2008 ...	10,774	17.9	1,927	3,343	17.0	567	10,058	1.34	13,428
2009 ...	8,800	18.5	1,629	2,837	16.9	480	7,920	1.43	11,298
2010 ...	9,868	16.7	1,650	1,893	16.7	317	8,347	1.40	11,705
2011 ...	8,764	19.1	1,676	1,441	16.2	233	7,823	1.41	11,048
2012 ...	10,964	21.0	2,307	715	23.4	167	9,167	1.43	13,115
2013 ...	10,164	20.7	2,104	624	24.5	153	9,009	1.53	13,816
2014 ...	8,898	19.9	1,770	797	30.6	244	6,821	1.69	11,497
	Delphinium & Larkspur			Gerbera Daisy			Gladioli		
	1,000 stems	Cents per stem	1,000 dollars	1,000 stems	Cents per stem	1,000 dollars	1,000 spikes	Cents per spike	1,000 dollars
2005 ...	34,150	23.7	8,087	104,682	30.9	32,314	105,432	22.8	24,074
2006 [2]	26,142	23.5	6,133	112,587	30.2	33,997	95,350	23.8	22,694
2007 ...	32,158	24.4	7,842	117,403	30.6	35,939	85,471	27.0	23,081
2008 ...	31,221	24.0	7,505	120,836	29.8	35,976	76,850	25.9	19,935
2009 ...	22,373	27.1	6,071	106,805	30.9	33,027	94,951	24.1	22,880
2010 ...	27,173	26.5	7,193	107,678	30.4	32,737	89,672	25.4	22,801
2011 ...	19,639	30.5	5,981	113,655	28.5	32,385	60,167	27.1	16,299
2012 ...	19,448	37.4	7,265	107,899	30.6	33,067	60,747	25.3	15,349
2013 ...	16,929	38.6	6,542	98,535	31.0	30,552	59,435	34.1	20,244
2014 ...	17,012	35.3	6,005	97,015	32.0	31,065	61,675	32.8	20,221
	Iris			Lilies, all			Lisianthus		
	1,000 stems	Cents per stem	1,000 dollars	1,000 stems	Cents per stem	1,000 dollars	1,000 stems	Cents per stem	1,000 dollars
2005 ...	88,803	22.5	20,021	114,188	67.4	77,009	12,333	39.8	4,906
2006 [2]	81,194	22.6	18,315	107,044	70.5	75,459	8,518	43.1	3,670
2007 ...	90,890	22.4	20,349	111,185	67.4	74,954	13,956	38.2	5,338
2008 ...	92,404	22.1	20,462	116,797	67.3	78,609	15,180	35.6	5,406
2009 ...	64,114	24.3	15,550	101,339	63.5	64,392	8,689	38.3	3,327
2010 ...	57,576	25.2	14,518	93,373	65.5	61,165	7,650	38.8	2,966
2011 ...	62,414	26.1	16,303	141,337	56.5	79,798	7,502	42.1	3,160
2012 ...	55,025	24.5	13,477	99,743	66.7	66,553	9,846	43.1	4,240
2013 ...	54,635	24.4	13,356	87,094	68.4	59,558	9,216	45.2	4,167
2014 ...	45,520	26.5	12,072	77,146	76.6	59,109	8,568	44.9	3,844
	Orchids, all			Roses, all			Snapdragons		
	1,000 blooms	Cents per bloom	1,000 dollars	1,000 stems	Cents per stem	1,000 dollars	1,000 spikes	Cents per spike	1,000 dollars
2005 ...	10,228	66.9	6,847	99,771	39.1	38,969	47,016	27.9	13,132
2006 [2]	10,332	120.3	12,428	82,138	37.7	30,974	36,559	28.0	10,244
2007 ...	11,209	99.5	11,150	67,701	41.5	28,110	41,887	29.1	12,202
2008 ...	7,882	98.2	7,737	57,999	38.8	22,481	42,696	27.6	11,790
2009 ...	7,637	185.1	14,133	42,031	42.0	17,662	37,473	27.0	10,118
2010 ...	7,852	99.8	7,834	39,497	42.9	16,950	31,475	27.1	8,524
2011 ...	7,166	83.0	5,949	37,004	48.4	17,912	34,777	25.1	8,744
2012 ...	6,498	90.9	5,909	32,736	49.4	16,184	35,061	29.7	10,396
2013 ...	5,846	163.6	9,564	28,626	56.3	16,105	42,013	25.4	10,652
2014 ...	6,292	237.9	14,971	29,104	58.1	16,896	45,414	23.2	10,552

Year	Tulips			Other cut flowers		
	1,000 stems	Cents per stem	1,000 dollars	1,000 stems	Cents per stem	1,000 dollars
2005 ...	128,978	32.7	42,121	....	....	124,832
2006 [2]	141,893	34.1	48,391	....	....	134,198
2007 ...	157,992	35.9	56,719	....	....	133,017
2008 ...	170,854	37.6	64,285	....	....	126,990
2009 ...	150,228	38.1	57,185	....	....	103,687
2010 ...	155,667	36.6	56,900	(NA)	(NA)	129,466
2011 ...	169,219	35.3	59,788	(NA)	(NA)	99,824
2012 ...	161,802	37.2	60,172	(NA)	(NA)	171,159
2013 ...	161,926	36.8	59,535	(NA)	(NA)	116,509
2014 ...	160,966	36.5	58,699	(NA)	(NA)	107,460

(NA) Not available. [1] Equivalent wholesale value of all sales. [2] Beginning in 2006, program was reduced to 15 States from 36.

NASS, Crops Branch, (202) 720–2127.

Table 5-95.—Cut Cultivated Greens: Sales and wholesale value for operations with $100,000+ sales, Surveyed States, 2005–2014

Year	Leatherleaf Ferns			Other cut cultivated greens
	Quantity sold	Wholesale price	Value of sales at wholesale [1]	Value of sales at wholesale [1]
	1,000 bunches	Dollars per bunch	1,000 dollars	1,000 dollars
2005	49,213	1.03	50,668	56,776
2006 [2]	44,183	1.04	45,902	51,706
2007	39,437	1.00	39,543	58,527
2008	34,761	0.98	33,924	57,824
2009	31,800	0.94	29,942	43,993
2010	28,474	1.03	29,312	47,713
2011	26,277	0.97	25,499	46,537
2012	32,063	0.99	31,706	43,811
2013	32,209	1.02	32,779	42,706
2014	31,410	1.01	31,580	40,386

[1] Equivalent wholesale value of all sales. [2] Beginning in 2006, program was reduced to 15 States from 36.
NASS, Crops Branch, (202) 720–2127.

Table 5-96.—Foliage Plants for Indoor or Patio Use: Sales and Wholesale value for operations with $100,000+ sales, Surveyed States, 2005–2014

Year	Foliage, Hanging Baskets			Foliage, Pots
	Quantity Sold	Wholesale price	Value of sales at wholesale	Value of sales at wholesale
	1,000 baskets	Dollars per basket	1,000 dollars	1,000 dollars
2005	19,713	4.55	89,719	619,793
2006 [1] ...	13,341	4.60	61,303	466,609
2007	14,118	4.66	65,857	589,545
2008	11,003	4.90	53,949	456,362
2009	12,072	5.29	63,881	493,148
2010	14,530	5.39	78,247	507,882
2011	14,483	5.42	78,438	534,943
2012	10,323	6.12	63,158	576,778
2013	11,493	5.92	67,996	544,562
2014	10,134	6.10	61,784	537,020

[1] Beginning in 2006, program was reduced to 15 States from 36.
NASS, Crops Branch, (202) 720–2127.

Table 5-97.— Potted Flowering Plants for Indoor or Patio Use: Sales and wholesale value for operations with $100,000+ sales, Surveyed States, 2005–2014

Year	Quantity sold		Wholesale price		Value of sales at wholesale [1]
	Less than 5 inches	5 inches or more	Less than 5 inches	5 inches or more	
	African violets				
	1,000 pots	1,000 pots	Dollars per pot	Dollars	1,000 dollars
2005	11,931	522	1.16	2.33	15,010
2006 [2]	5,997	434	1.20	1.92	8,046
2007	4,357	430	1.37	1.95	6,809
2008	2,946	9	1.35	3.34	3,993
2009	2,313	38	1.49	3.48	3,580
2010	2,727	23	1.31	1.88	3,614
2011	2,582	51	1.25	3.84	3,414
2012	2,632	27	1.55	2.38	4,150
2013	2,572	33	1.47	2.53	3,870
2014	2,531	9	1.53	4.13	3,906
	Florist azaleas				
	1,000 pots	1,000 pots	Dollars per pot	Dollars per pot	1,000 dollars
2005	2,410	6,443	2.27	4.86	36,750
2006 [2]	2,237	6,844	2.10	4.41	34,909
2007	1,514	5,081	2.34	4.90	28,435
2008	1,095	7,188	2.24	4.65	35,897
2009	2,345	5,214	2.30	4.92	31,044
2010	1,348	3,289	2.59	5.67	22,138
2011	1,266	3,012	2.32	6.01	21,022
2012	1,129	3,544	2.68	5.28	21,734
2013	1,109	3,313	2.48	5.05	19,471
2014	1,040	3,043	2.46	5.38	18,938
	Florist chrysanthemums				
	1,000 pots	1,000 pots	Dollars per pot	Dollars	1,000 dollars
2005	4,421	18,891	1.75	3.23	68,797
2006 [2]	1,299	12,693	1.82	3.03	40,815
2007	1,810	11,363	1.65	3.15	38,777
2008	1,927	9,902	1.57	3.21	34,762
2009	1,314	6,181	1.90	3.61	24,842
2010	2,225	4,526	1.82	3.97	22,029
2011	1,351	5,210	2.43	3.54	21,720
2012	1,654	4,400	2.00	4.14	21,535
2013	613	5,343	2.82	3.99	23,045
2014	880	4,865	2,75	3.98	21,767
	Easter lilies				
	1,000 pots	1,000 pots	Dollars per pot	Dollars per pot	1,000 dollars
2005	34	8,251	3.21	4.25	35,204
2006 [2]	2	6,334	6.53	4.12	26,106
2007	....	6,546	....	4.05	26,512
2008	31	5,824	4.05	4.33	25,335
2009	93	6,196	3.16	4.38	27,405
2010	147	5,891	3.29	4.29	25,764
2011	99	5,094	2.73	4.35	22,436
2012	37	5,011	3.48	4.36	21,958
2013	295	5,901	2.80	4.23	25,758
2014	713	5,027	3.86	4.56	25,677
	Potted Orchids				
	1,000 pots	1,000 pots	Dollars per pot	Dollars per pot	1,000 dollars
2005	11,535	5,975	6.46	10.87	139,482
2006 [2]	10,140	4,615	6.90	10.96	120,521
2007	10,661	6,655	6.95	9.89	139,960
2008	10,689	5,415	7.16	9.23	126,509
2009	12,503	7,135	7.36	9.70	161,208
2010	13,395	7,933	7.10	9.71	172,196
2011	15,415	8,520	6.78	10.19	191,306
2012	15,915	12,389	7.01	9.62	230,695
2013	18,934	12,750	7.34	8.83	251,559
2014	18,540	14,128	7.68	8.78	266,396

See footnote(s) at end of table.

Table 5-97.—Potted flowering for indoor or patio use: Sales and wholesale value for operations with $100,000+ sales, Surveyed States, 2005–2014—Continued

Year	Quantity sold		Wholesale price		Value of sales at wholesale [1]
	Less than 5 inches	5 inches or more	Less than 5 inches	5 inches or more	
	1,000 pots	*1,000 pots*	*Dollars per pot*	*Dollars per pot*	*1,000 dollars*

Poinsettias

Year	1,000 pots	1,000 pots	Dollars per pot	Dollars per pot	1,000 dollars
2005	11,251	47,494	2.04	4.60	241,705
2006 [2]	7,762	33,743	1.98	4.61	171,012
2007	7,130	31,901	2.07	4.60	161,409
2008	6,373	28,922	2.07	4.82	152,611
2009	6,679	28,649	2.13	4.69	148,579
2010	7,710	26,942	2.02	4.65	140,841
2011	7,470	27,259	1.84	4.60	139,274
2012	6,620	27,301	2.12	4.77	144,309
2013	6,610	26,797	2.06	4.82	142,805
2014	6,270	26,909	2.15	4.73	140,713

Potted florist roses

Year	1,000 pots	1,000 pots	Dollars per pot	Dollars	1,000 dollars
2005	8,396	1,897	2.01	4.64	25,706
2006 [2]	6,389	1,901	1.90	4.90	21,446
2007	6,834	2,364	1.94	5.16	25,425
2008	7,252	1,064	2.74	5.34	25,569
2009	6,924	1,031	2.57	5.14	23,115
2010	5,599	2,167	2.50	5.83	26,669
2011	5,183	2,550	2.16	4.87	23,619
2012	5,729	2,828	2.18	5.74	28,741
2013	5,976	2,750	2.40	6.14	31,214
2014	6,003	2,680	2.32	6.51	31,349

Potted spring flowering bulbs

Year	1,000 pots	1,000 pots	Dollars per pot	Dollars	1,000 dollars
2005	14,051	9,581	1.50	3.55	55,132
2006 [2]	13,061	8,469	1.41	3.43	47,447
2007	10,073	8,624	1.91	3.66	50,861
2008	13,317	10,958	1.69	3.56	61,532
2009	4,689	11,234	1.74	3.43	46,662
2010	9,766	12,382	1.46	3.52	57,903
2011	8,162	11,637	1.52	3.54	53,638
2012	5,095	11,434	1.74	3.63	50,376
2013	4,623	11,013	1.96	3.77	50,614
2014	4,962	10,559	1.78	3.83	49,264

Other flowering

Year	1,000 pots	1,000 pots	Dollars per pot	Dollars per pot	1,000 dollars
2005	33,669	31,032	1.91	4.20	194,572
2006 [2]	23,220	27,703	2.01	3.77	151,158
2007	27,176	36,862	2.09	4.51	223,111
2008	22,529	31,482	2.10	4.91	201,962
2009	19,531	29,173	2.13	4.62	176,570
2010	17,162	25,695	2.71	5.00	175,006
2011	24,663	21,896	1.88	5.36	163,903
2012	22,670	25,625	2.57	5.99	211,766
2013	24,868	26,835	2.67	5.87	223,931
2014	25,413	31,082	2.71	5.18	229,982

[1] Equivalent wholesale value of all sales except for potted foliage which is value of sales less cost of plant material purchased from other growers for growing on.　[2] Beginning in 2006, program was reduced to 15 States from 36.
NASS, Crops Branch, (202) 720–2127.

Table 5-98.—Annual Bedding and Garden Hanging Baskets: Sales and wholesale value for operations with $100,000+ sales, Surveyed States, 2005–2014

Year	Quantity sold	Wholesale price	Value of sales at wholesale [1]	Quantity sold	Wholesale price	Value of sales at wholesale [1]
		Begonias			Geraniums from vegetative cuttings	
	1,000 baskets	*Dollars*	*1,000 dollars*	*1,000 baskets*	*Dollars*	*1,000 dollars*
2005	2,834	5.82	16,505	4,802	7.02	33,732
2006 [2]	3,199	5.97	19,091	3,285	6.75	22,186
2007	1,701	5.76	9,796	3,296	6.87	22,640
2008	1,707	5.80	9,899	3,056	7.32	22,366
2009	1,531	5.84	8,944	3,564	7.44	26,523
2010	1,650	5.96	9,839	3,753	7.10	26,659
2011	1,622	5.99	9,723	3,561	7.13	25,390
2012	1,823	5.94	10,830	3,280	7.49	24,562
2013	2,016	6.33	12,770	3,126	7.39	23,113
2014	1,805	5.97	10,770	3,251	7.54	24,522
		Geraniums from seeds			Impatiens, Other	
	1,000 baskets	*Dollars*	*1,000 dollars*	*1,000 baskets*	*Dollars*	*1,000 dollars*
2005	724	5.88	4,260	3,824	5.51	21,087
2006 [2]	246	6.03	1,483	2,846	5.19	14,761
2007	316	5.63	1,778	2,597	5.22	13,548
2008	267	6.05	1,616	2,375	5.29	12,561
2009	455	5.95	2,708	2,098	5.79	12,146
2010	286	7.01	2,005	2,534	5.63	14,260
2011	337	6.61	2,227	2,385	5.72	13,639
2012	475	6.56	3,115	2,479	5.44	13,494
2013	415	7.28	3,020	2,065	5.33	11,015
2004	448	7.49	3,355	3,732	5.43	20,257
		New Guinea Impatiens			Marigolds	
	1,000 baskets	*Dollars*	*1,000 dollars*	*1,000 baskets*	*Dollars*	*1,000 dollars*
2005	4,558	6.62	30,169	21	5.14	108
2006 [2]	3,174	6.81	21,624	162	6.41	1,039
2007	2,987	6.96	20,797	184	6.08	1,118
2008	2,668	7.23	19,280	202	6.30	1,272
2009	2,556	7.09	18,122	55	6.33	348
2010	2,615	7.11	18,581	83	6.01	499
2011	2,456	7.14	17,526	77	5.77	444
2012	2,380	7.32	17,420	87	4.92	428
2013	2,254	7.37	16,613	117	4.38	513
2014	2,242	7.25	16,256	128	5.76	737
		Pansies/Violas			Petunias	
	1,000 baskets	*Dollars*	*1,000 dollars*	*1,000 baskets*	*Dollars*	*1,000 dollars*
2005	1,131	6.51	7,368	4,891	6.18	30,218
2006 [2]	510	5.15	2,625	3,673	5.74	21,081
2007	694	5.02	3,485	4,011	5.99	24,017
2008	695	5.20	3,612	3,969	5.98	23,752
2009	1,077	5.43	5,848	4,186	6.38	26,711
2010	911	5.59	5,091	5,066	6.16	31,225
2011	941	5.83	5,483	5,047	6.29	31,767
2012	1,096	5.75	6,299	5,028	6.21	31,240
2013	1,085	5.62	6,096	4,986	6.11	30,459
2014	1,153	5.88	6,782	5,390	6.24	33,660
		Other flowering hanging baskets and foliar				
	1,000 baskets		*Dollars*		*1,000 dollars*	
2005	21,284		6.55		139,480	
2006 [2]	14,910		6.22		92,736	
2007	15,153		6.95		105,330	
2008	14,718		6.92		101,856	
2009	14,451		7.36		106,323	
2010	13,483		7.67		103,399	
2011	12,759		7.56		96,500	
2012	14,865		7.33		109,030	
2013	14,797		7.73		114,409	
2014	12,912		8.38		108,252	

[1] Equivalent wholesale value of all sales.   [2] Beginning in 2006, program was reduced to 15 States from 36.
NASS, Crops Branch, (202) 720–2127.

Table 5-99.—Annual bedding garden plants flats: Sales and wholesale value for operations with $100,000+ sales, Surveyed States, 2005–2014

Year	Quantity sold	Wholesale price	Value of sales at wholesale [1]	Quantity sold	Wholesale price	Value of sales at wholesale [1]
	Begonias			Geraniums from vegetative cuttings		
	1,000 flats	Dollars	1,000 dollars	1,000 flats	Dollars	1,000 dollars
2005	7,043	8.06	56,757	654	11.87	7,763
2006 [2]	4,947	8.17	40,429	520	11.54	5,999
2007	4,094	8.17	33,444	417	12.32	5,138
2008	4,360	8.49	36,999	396	12.57	4,979
2009	4,055	8.75	35,490	353	15.09	5,326
2010	4,218	8.13	34,313	306	13.12	4,015
2011	3,983	7.97	31,738	264	14.08	3,716
2012	3,865	8.56	33,005	237	13.57	3,215
2013	3,758	8.15	30,640	325	11.65	3,785
2014	3,869	8.61	33,317	249	14.01	3,488
	Geraniums from seeds			Impatiens, other		
	1,000 flats	Dollars	1,000 dollars	1,000 flats	Dollars	1,000 dollars
2005	606	10.86	6,584	12,409	8.09	100,334
2006 [2]	398	10.99	4,373	9,884	7.77	76,771
2007	380	11.54	4,387	8,915	8.11	72,320
2008	384	11.00	4,223	8,547	8.52	72,815
2009	424	9.23	3,915	7,973	8.67	69,093
2010	465	10.29	4,784	8,641	8.24	71,160
2011	332	10.62	3,526	8,353	7.96	66,519
2012	394	9.81	3,866	6,852	9.08	62,230
2013	475	7.51	3,565	5,055	8.17	41,300
2014	356	9.24	3,291	4,623	8.36	38,670
	New Guinea Impatiens			Marigolds		
	1,000 flats	Dollars	1,000 dollars	1,000 flats	Dollars	1,000 dollars
2005	468	10.97	5,134	6,158	8.54	52,569
2006 [2]	305	10.14	3,093	4,032	8.13	32,788
2007	243	11.09	2,696	3,694	8.39	31,001
2008	218	11.55	2,518	3,933	8.69	34,190
2009	290	10.77	3,124	3,976	8.98	35,713
2010	276	9.69	2,675	4,100	8.89	36,444
2011	190	10.56	2,006	3,884	8.45	32,807
2012	226	9.86	2,229	3,436	8.49	29,188
2013	335	10.01	3,355	3,488	8.24	28,733
2014	603	9.89	5,964	3,603	8.37	30,170
	Pansies/Violas			Petunias		
	1,000 flats	Dollars	1,000 dollars	1,000 flats	Dollars	1,000 dollars
2005	13,340	8.41	112,165	10,821	8.72	94,351
2006 [2]	8,238	8.03	66,168	7,349	8.12	59,682
2007	8,047	8.33	67,050	7,023	8.52	59,808
2008	8,169	8.82	72,036	7,402	8.80	65,129
2009	7,430	9.15	67,957	7,006	9.32	65,317
2010	7,538	8.88	66,916	7,448	8.92	66,404
2011	7,266	8.66	62,936	7,227	8.56	61,891
2012	7,343	9.02	66,245	6,667	8.64	57,618
2013	6,369	8.94	56,926	6,581	8.36	55,034
2014	7,048	8.48	59,734	6,724	9.13	61,400
	Other flowering and foliar plants			Vegetable type plants		
	1,000 flats	Dollars	1,000 dollars	1,000 flats	Dollars	1,000 dollars
2005	34,837	8.83	307,711	7,845	9.66	75,747
2006 [2]	25,652	8.02	205,649	4,776	9.55	45,604
2007	21,350	8.70	185,788	4,135	9.39	38,822
2008	19,441	9.00	175,027	4,545	10.25	46,573
2009	16,331	9.45	154,342	5,025	10.53	52,911
2010	17,898	9.40	168,261	4,862	10.20	49,603
2011	17,836	9.50	169,484	5,102	10.53	53,740
2012	16,934	9.10	154,089	6,297	9.64	60,714
2013	16,275	8.71	141,740	4,998	10.18	50,858
2014	14,578	9.30	135,570	4,682	10.54	49,350

[1] Equivalent wholesale value of all sales.   [2] Beginning in 2006, program was reduced to 15 States from 36.
NASS, Crops Branch, (202) 720–2127.

Table 5-100.—Potted annual bedding and garden plants: Sales and wholesale value for operations with $100,000+ sales, Surveyed States, 2005–2014

Year	Quantity sold		Wholesale price		Value of sales at wholesale [1]
	Less than 5 inches	5 inches or more	Less than 5 inches	5 inches or more	
	Begonias				
	1,000 pots	*1,000 pots*	*Dollars*	*Dollars*	*1,000 dollars*
2005	23,381	5,185	0.88	2.07	31,275
2006 [2]	19,939	4,387	0.85	2.28	27,004
2007	16,748	3,683	0.84	2.06	21,645
2008	16,481	4,296	0.91	2.17	24,293
2009	17,821	3,272	0.86	2.34	22,907
2010	14,709	3,163	0.92	2.22	20,617
2011	14,763	3,374	0.91	2.24	20,973
2012	15,837	3,323	0.91	2.40	22,340
2013	18,296	4,118	0.94	2.58	27,922
2014	16,349	3,541	1.02	2.42	25,290
	Geraniums from cuttings				
	1,000 pots	*1,000 pots*	*Dollars*	*Dollars*	*1,000 dollars*
2005	40,105	21,679	1.59	2.97	127,998
2006 [2]	23,991	12,246	1.58	3.29	78,244
2007	22,785	13,253	1.66	3.35	82,364
2008	23,094	13,050	1.76	3.35	84,300
2009	22,985	14,209	1.79	3.18	86,303
2010	23,339	13,431	1.81	3.54	89,770
2011	21,156	12,844	1.85	3.57	85,031
2012	21,563	13,560	1.85	3.38	85,842
2013	20,429	11,554	1.88	3.62	80,293
2014	20,525	11,029	1.92	3.67	79,899
	Geraniums from seed				
	1,000 pots	*1,000 pots*	*Dollars*	*Dollars*	*1,000 dollars*
2005	34,039	844	0.88	2.62	32,251
2006 [2]	31,377	456	0.81	2.20	26,545
2007	28,897	343	0.83	2.86	25,071
2008	25,114	367	0.87	3.31	23,186
2009	24,622	495	0.92	2.78	23,923
2010	18,748	1,248	1.03	4.67	25,097
2011	23,673	1,648	0.93	5.20	30,680
2012	16,449	728	0.88	3.42	16,988
2013	17,825	393	1.12	3.49	21,604
2014	16,621	489	1.11	3.67	20,262
	Other impatiens				
	1,000 pots	*1,000 pots*	*Dollars*	*Dollars*	*1,000 dollars*
2005	30,819	4,457	0.73	2.08	31,867
2006 [2]	23,555	5,804	0.73	1.87	28,130
2007	19,575	5,575	0.81	1.69	25,267
2008	20,606	4,973	0.78	1.91	25,663
2009	21,923	5,075	0.76	1.87	26,065
2010	21,955	4,033	0.77	2.43	26,702
2011	20,480	4,220	0.77	2.25	25,334
2012	13,941	4,834	0.82	2.11	21,678
2013	8,825	3,629	0.94	1.90	15,245
2014	7,214	3,537	0.96	1.92	13,727
	New guinea impatiens				
	1,000 pots	*1,000 pots*	*Dollars*	*Dollars*	*1,000 dollars*
2005	19,105	7,074	1.44	2.65	46,320
2006 [2]	12,411	5,404	1.49	2.97	34,498
2007	11,885	4,735	1.58	2.83	32,180
2008	12,630	4,283	1.57	3.18	33,459
2009	12,439	3,834	1.59	3.25	32,177
2010	10,919	3,961	1.50	3.28	29,376
2011	9,794	3,658	1.59	3.44	28,130
2012	11,640	4,236	1.47	3.27	30,956
2013	13,325	4,045	1.51	3.46	34,105
2014	12,465	4,130	1.57	3.37	33,515

See footnote(s) at end of table.

Table 5-100.—Potted annual bedding and garden plants: Sales and wholesale value for operations with $100,000+ sales, Surveyed States, 2005–2014—Continued

Year	Quantity sold		Wholesale price		Value of sales at wholesale [1]
	Less than 5 inches	5 inches or more	Less than 5 inches	5 inches or more	
	1,000 pots	*1,000 pots*	*Dollars*	*Dollars*	*1,000 dollars*

Marigolds

Year	*1,000 pots*	*1,000 pots*	*Dollars*	*Dollars*	*1,000 dollars*
2005	9,954	2,672	0.69	1.58	11,045
2006 [2]	7,928	2,207	0.69	1.79	9,392
2007	8,372	2,150	0.68	1.59	9,125
2008	7,600	1,704	0.72	1.61	8,185
2009	8,837	1,826	0.78	1.76	10,124
2010	7,901	2,463	0.76	1.88	10,621
2011	7,180	2,272	0.81	1.82	9,947
2012	8,871	1,792	0.79	2.10	10,762
2013	8,637	1,819	0.80	2.09	10,688
2014	9,181	1,218	0.97	2.29	11,698

Pansies/violas

Year	*1,000 pots*	*1,000 pots*	*Dollars*	*Dollars*	*1,000 dollars*
2005	38,362	10,729	0.73	1.88	48,188
2006 [2]	27,824	7,144	0.80	1.75	34,615
2007	28,021	6,145	0.74	2.13	33,788
2008	25,980	5,989	0.75	2.09	31,966
2009	27,054	5,529	0.74	2.06	31,363
2010	23,394	6,159	0.80	2.02	31,035
2011	24,573	6,130	0.80	2.12	32,692
2012	23,416	6,918	0.81	2.19	34,078
2013	21,953	6,155	0.86	2.19	32,308
2014	22,112	6,170	0.86	2.15	32,208

Petunias

Year	*1,000 pots*	*1,000 pots*	*Dollars*	*Dollars*	*1,000 dollars*
2005	22,714	9,664	0.92	2.28	43,000
2006 [2]	13,630	8,106	0.91	2.04	28,894
2007	18,551	6,935	0.98	2.37	34,558
2008	16,310	6,796	1.01	2.27	31,852
2009	18,088	7,527	0.98	2.20	34,301
2010	19,152	9,142	1.07	2.11	39,732
2011	18,212	8,843	1.12	2.07	38,629
2012	20,830	8,651	1.14	2.30	43,546
2013	18,713	8,251	1.23	2.64	44,844
2014	17,258	7,723	1.27	2.69	42,670

Other flowering and foliar plants

Year	*1,000 pots*	*1,000 pots*	*Dollars*	*Dollars*	*1,000 dollars*
2005	169,646	69,500	1.12	2.46	360,109
2006 [2]	110,614	57,880	1.09	2.73	278,296
2007	117,723	50,605	1.13	3.08	288,890
2008	108,251	55,789	1.20	2.65	278,250
2009	93,289	48,271	1.18	3.06	257,709
2010	104,633	57,937	1.26	3.04	301,479
2011	108,661	54,133	1.25	2.96	296,030
2012	127,328	64,961	1.20	3.02	348,961
2013	111,363	50,025	1.32	3.30	309,160
2014	101,469	45,874	1.33	3.34	288,042

Vegetable type plants [3]

Year	*1,000 pots*	*1,000 pots*	*Dollars*	*Dollars*	*1,000 dollars*
2005	48,033	10,491	0.84	2.17	63,270
2006 [2]	18,507	4,410	0.96	2.19	27,374
2007	27,676	3,874	1.01	2.22	36,668
2008	35,998	7,497	1.06	2.49	56,697
2009	38,534	12,794	1.07	2.51	73,307
2010	38,453	14,155	1.12	2.64	80,411
2011	40,176	7,478	1.29	3.19	75,761
2012	31,100	12,211	1.22	2.98	74,478
2013	31,816	10,057	1.24	3.16	71,249
2014	38,509	6,583	1.38	3.89	76,683

[1] Equivalent wholesale value of all sales.　[2] Beginning in 2006, program was reduced to 15 States from 36.　[3] Does not include vegetable transplants grown for use in commercial vegetable production.
NASS, Crops Branch, (202) 720–2127.

Table 5-101.—Potted herbaceous perennial plants: Sales and wholesale value for operations with $100,000+ sales, Surveyed States, 2005–2014

Year	Quantity sold		Wholesale price		Value of sales at wholesale [1]
	Less than 5 inches	5 inches or more	Less than 5 inches	5 inches or more	
	Hardy/Garden Chrysanthemums				
	1,000 pots	*1,000 pots*	*Dollars*	*Dollars*	*1,000 dollars*
2005	12,661	59,137	1.03	2.20	143,318
2006 [2]	10,545	40,303	0.99	2.31	103,656
2007	9,763	35,148	1.06	2.66	103,831
2008	9,217	34,689	1.10	2.61	100,868
2009	8,049	35,833	1.25	2.81	110,747
2010	11,352	34,531	1.10	2.93	113,620
2011	11,962	36,634	1.03	2.77	113,747
2012	13,327	35,792	1.03	3.08	124,097
2013	15,558	33,176	1.08	2.89	112,552
2014	14,648	33,091	1.06	3.08	117,540

Year	Quantity sold			Wholesale price			Value of sales at wholesale [1]
	Less than 1 gallon	1-2 gallons	2 gallons or more	Less than 1 gallon	1-2 gallons	2 gallons or more	
	Hosta						
	1,000 pots	*1,000 pots*	*1,000 pots*	*Dollars*	*Dollars*	*Dollars*	*1,000 dollars*
2005	4,098	7,943	483	2.36	3.42	7.52	40,481
2006 [2]	1,724	6,661	399	2.10	3.25	6.66	27,924
2007	4,374	6,589	271	1.74	3.50	7.69	32,723
2008	4,451	6,793	173	1.91	3.43	9.10	33,391
2009	4,279	6,340	582	2.15	3.36	6.47	34,283
2010	1,448	6,783	337	2.11	3.26	7.54	27,704
2011	2,112	6,270	281	2.27	3.19	8.53	27,195
2012	2,365	5,535	363	2.34	3.40	8.04	27,240
2013	2,511	5,898	382	2.64	3.39	7.98	29,671
2014	5,242	3,309	473	2.71	3.86	7.75	30,620
	Other Herbaceous Perennials						
	1,000 pots	*1,000 pots*	*1,000 pots*	*Dollars*	*Dollars*	*Dollars*	*1,000 dollars*
2005	97,471	95,692	7,123	1.70	3.15	6.51	513,099
2006 [2]	49,602	85,660	5,075	1.55	3.14	6.97	381,511
2007	68,640	69,843	6,442	1.71	3.33	6.84	394,407
2008	65,928	74,574	7,533	1.59	3.43	6.65	410,867
2009	50,229	80,234	4,975	1.68	3.42	6.92	392,847
2010	53,613	86,180	6,257	1.63	3.38	7.11	423,266
2011	56,970	83,944	5,459	1.75	3.35	7.43	421,276
2012	56,936	65,596	10,001	1.77	3.78	7.33	422,282
2013	62,721	72,430	6,983	1.90	3.90	8.41	460,375
2014	59,733	58,785	6,206	2.24	3.88	8.28	413,426

[1] Equivalent wholesale value of all sales.   [2] Beginning in 2006, program was reduced to 15 States from 36.
NASS, Crops Branch, (202) 720–2127.

Table 5-102.—Floriculture: Number of Producers and Area Used for Production by Type of Cover, operations with $10,000+ sales, 15 Program States: 2013–2014

State	Total number of producers		Glass greenhouses		Fiberglass and other rigid greenhouses		Film plastic (single/ multi) greenhouses	
	2013	2014	2013	2014	2013	2014	2013	2014
	Number	Number	1,000 square feet	1,000 square feet	1,000 square feet	1,000 square feet	1,000 square feet	1,000 square feet
California	732	582	12,246	12,341	35,454	36,911	66,113	68,863
Florida	695	597	4,712	4,007	8,661	9,000	37,977	36,874
Hawaii	303	298	(D)	(D)	(D)	(D)	2,932	3,152
Illinois	261	226	2,890	3,119	2,032	1,831	9,101	9,712
Maryland	157	128	1,230	1,333	700	906	5,126	5,330
Michigan	604	454	3,890	3,605	3,856	3,580	39,355	38,947
New Jersey	317	258	4,609	5,453	1,095	1,023	19,369	19,859
New York	622	477	4,445	3,723	1,367	1,453	19,764	14,484
North Carolina	279	211	(D)	(D)	(D)	(D)	12,881	13,707
Ohio	525	349	7,780	7,497	1,784	1,600	17,464	15,903
Oregon	295	230	2,930	2,544	2,747	2,420	13,724	12,400
Pennsylvania	725	549	2,298	2,442	3,800	3,746	14,424	12,721
South Carolina	76	56	(D)	(D)	(D)	(D)	2,894	2,696
Texas	278	226	1,345	1,158	3,110	3,570	28,616	28,378
Washington	246	208	2,258	2,221	1,002	828	8,180	7,728
Other States ..	-	-	6,791	7,051	2,094	2,146	-	-
15 State total	6,115	4,849	57,424	56,494	67,702	69,014	297,920	290,754

State	Total greenhouse cover		Shade and temporary cover		Total covered area		Open ground[2]	
	2013	2014	2013	2014	2013	2014	2013	2014
	1,000 square feet	1,000 square feet	1,000 square feet	1,000 square feet	1,000 square feet	1,000 square feet	Acres	Acres
California	113,813	118,115	31,521	29,455	145,334	147,570	11,943	10,844
Florida	51,350	49,881	247,650	249,399	299,000	299,280	4,484	5,206
Hawaii	(D)	(D)	(D)	(D)	18,559	19,004	873	918
Illinois	14,023	14,662	316	675	14,339	15,337	631	1,666
Maryland	7,056	7,569	375	470	7,431	8,039	2,536	2,646
Michigan	47,101	46,132	484	599	47,585	46,731	3,270	3,999
New Jersey	25,073	26,335	604	353	25,677	26,688	4,196	4,720
New York	25,576	19,660	440	319	26,016	19,979	798	835
North Carolina	19,745	20,862	1,034	1,128	20,779	21,990	648	1,668
Ohio	27,028	25,000	506	485	27,534	25,485	1,253	1,530
Oregon	19,401	17,364	2,319	5,079	21,720	22,443	4,290	4,589
Pennsylvania	20,522	18,909	474	492	20,996	19,401	1,306	1,445
South Carolina	(D)	(D)	(D)	(D)	6,026	5,555	226	426
Texas	33,071	33,106	9,232	11,482	42,303	44,588	1,457	1,960
Washington	11,440	10,777	255	227	11,695	11,004	2,578	2,622
Other States [1]	7,847	7,890	16,738	16,669	-	-	-	-
15 State total	423,046	416,262	311,948	316,832	734,994	733,094	40,490	45,073

- Represents zero. (D) Withheld to avoid disclosure of individual operations. [1] Includes data withheld above. [2] Totals may not add due to rounding.
NASS, Crops Branch, (202) 720-2127.

Table 5-103.—Floriculture Crops: Wholesale value of sales by category - 15 Program States, operations with $100,000+ sales: 2013–2014

State	Annual bedding/ garden plants		Herbaceous perennial plants		Total bedding/ garden plants [1]	
	2013	2014	2013	2014	2013	2014
	1,000 dollars	*1,000 dollars*	*1,000 dollars*	*1,000 dollars*	*1,000 dollars*	*1,000 dollars*
California	197,485	196,307	81,599	76,684	279,084	272,991
Florida	90,391	101,766	41,343	41,042	131,734	142,808
Hawaii	2,868	2,499	1,588	1,607	4,456	4,106
Illinois	36,717	46,063	38,894	28,913	75,611	74,976
Maryland	62,102	58,724	23,934	23,385	86,036	82,109
Michigan	220,542	203,840	61,195	62,337	281,737	266,177
New Jersey	65,475	70,451	44,146	52,830	109,621	123,281
New York	80,779	71,926	29,384	26,402	110,163	98,328
North Carolina	137,355	131,667	44,113	34,882	181,468	166,549
Ohio	82,510	71,375	47,977	45,483	130,487	116,858
Oregon	50,441	49,045	28,464	29,397	78,905	78,442
Pennsylvania	61,690	59,760	16,552	17,616	78,242	77,376
South Carolina	5,715	6,183	53,737	45,833	59,452	52,016
Texas	125,124	124,721	44,722	37,202	169,846	161,923
Washington	64,074	67,476	44,960	37,973	109,034	105,449
15 State total	1,281,362	1,259,752	602,598	561,586	1,883,960	1,821,338

State	Potted flowering plants		Foliage plants for indoor or patio use		Cut flowers	
	2013	2014	2013	2014	2013	2014
	1,000 dollars	*1,000 dollars*	*1,000 dollars*	*1,000 dollars*	*1,000 dollars*	*1,000 dollars*
California	280,032	288,028	106,549	116,313	275,356	274,632
Florida	175,970	189,162	431,922	420,421	4,249	3,352
Hawaii	14,816	14,936	8,606	8,702	8,467	6,164
Illinois	23,723	12,600	1,190	1,352	(D)	1,237
Maryland	3,702	4,298	369	327	(D)	(D)
Michigan	34,394	37,127	7,085	7,289	4,786	5,368
New Jersey	33,156	33,964	1,806	997	12,435	14,594
New York	30,691	25,886	2,944	2,095	669	958
North Carolina	29,822	31,255	16,512	15,176	5,328	3,500
Ohio	50,513	58,212	4,255	7,436	(D)	(D)
Oregon	16,594	16,082	6,964	3,591	15,373	13,726
Pennsylvania	29,886	28,965	4,384	2,024	(D)	(D)
South Carolina	9,863	8,559	302	108	(D)	(D)
Texas	30,795	28,906	18,709	12,091	(D)	(D)
Washington	8,310	10,012	961	882	21,210	20,857
Other States [2]	-	-	-	-	14,984	10,017
15 State total	772,267	787,992	612,558	598,804	362,857	354,405

State	Cut cultivated greens		Propagative floriculture material		Total wholesale value of all plant categories [3]	
	2013	2014	2013	2014	2013	2014
	1,000 dollars	*1,000 dollars*	*1,000 dollars*	*1,000 dollars*	*1,000 dollars*	*1,000 dollars*
California	12,409	9,488	90,190	79,733	1,043,620	1,041,185
Florida	59,224	58,693	71,753	66,649	874,852	881,085
Hawaii	458	450	(D)	1,416	38,352	35,774
Illinois	(D)	(D)	3,719	(D)	108,864	90,165
Maryland	(D)	(D)	9,315	9,340	99,983	96,295
Michigan	(D)	(D)	78,612	82,794	406,631	398,755
New Jersey	(D)	(D)	23,429	18,425	180,447	191,261
New York	(D)	(D)	25,202	16,922	169,687	143,748
North Carolina	(D)	-	2,821	(D)	235,951	219,301
Ohio	(D)	-	27,499	4,472	212,754	186,978
Oregon	2,232	2,908	9,189	8,692	129,257	123,441
Pennsylvania	(D)	(D)	18,443	18,772	139,452	135,559
South Carolina	-	-	(D)	-	69,617	60,683
Texas	(D)	(D)	9,767	8,387	229,117	211,307
Washington	13	31	25,816	19,493	165,344	156,724
Other States [2]	1,149	396	1,679	5,578	15,700	15,991
15 State total	75,485	71,966	397,425	340,673	4,119,628	3,976,788

- Represents zero.   (D) Withheld to avoid disclosure of individual operations.   [1] Includes Annual Bedding Plants and Herbaceous Perennials.   [2] Includes data withheld above.   [3] State total wholesale value excludes plant category values denoted by (D).
NASS, Crops Branch, (202) 720-2127.

Table 5-104.—Fruit and orange juice: Cold storage holdings, end of month, United States, 2013–2014

Month	Apples		Apricots		Blackberries, IQF		Blackberries, pails & tubs	
	2013	2014	2013	2014	2013	2014	2013	2014
	1,000 pounds	1,000 pounds	1,000 pounds	1,000 pounds	1,000 pounds	1,000 pounds	1,000 pounds	1,000 pounds
January	51,297	56,312	3,395	3,532	21,807	15,649	2,206	1,549
February	48,411	60,384	2,340	3,406	16,721	15,146	1,935	1,399
March	46,119	61,220	1,907	3,380	16,236	13,441	1,733	1,247
April	42,047	60,693	1,452	2,384	13,991	12,446	1,569	936
May	39,547	58,866	1,668	1,974	10,987	13,067	1,519	1,013
June	34,354	56,046	11,874	12,488	13,253	14,845	1,661	1,220
July	34,202	55,517	7,871	9,847	24,668	28,169	2,086	1,992
August	31,733	52,050	7,204	7,852	23,467	26,634	1,667	2,107
September	32,414	49,676	6,276	7,533	22,669	24,528	1,313	1,972
October	37,339	53,072	4,639	6,471	18,739	22,839	1,218	1,718
November	50,486	52,828	4,501	6,191	17,305	20,939	1,649	1,632
December	49,831	55,400	3,895	5,941	15,890	20,281	1,774	1,550

Month	Blackberries, barrels		Blackberries, concentrate		Blackberries, total		Blueberries	
	2013	2014	2013	2014	2013	2014	2013	2014
	1,000 pounds	1,000 pounds	1,000 pounds	1,000 pounds	1,000 pounds	1,000 pounds	1,000 pounds	1,000 pounds
January	8,043	11,114	965	511	33,021	28,823	165,932	172,718
February	6,903	10,134	416	504	25,975	27,183	152,187	150,626
March	5,976	7,828	302	478	24,247	22,994	137,358	130,825
April	5,983	7,245	249	483	21,792	21,110	119,814	117,065
May	5,228	6,494	153	533	17,887	21,107	100,876	98,716
June	3,678	5,429	135	559	18,727	22,053	103,559	102,012
July	13,696	11,636	156	784	40,606	42,581	166,382	171,661
August	13,610	10,503	493	1,095	39,237	40,339	260,094	269,537
September	13,668	10,103	230	891	37,880	37,494	251,279	265,303
October	13,246	9,331	265	868	33,468	34,756	235,007	240,830
November	12,483	9,033	611	764	32,048	32,368	217,393	229,225
December	11,874	8,396	528	698	30,066	30,925	201,834	208,324

Month	Boysenberries		Cherries, Tart (RTP)		Cherries, Sweet		Grapes	
	2013	2014	2013	2014	2013	2014	2013	2014
	1,000 pounds	1,000 pounds	1,000 pounds	1,000 pounds	1,000 pounds	1,000 pounds	1,000 pounds	1,000 pounds
January	1,345	1,648	44,651	99,639	18,822	14,477	3,014	4,108
February	1,635	1,906	38,315	91,631	19,224	14,136	2,393	4,226
March	1,059	1,213	33,746	82,926	19,586	13,065	1,825	3,856
April	1,113	960	26,644	71,746	18,445	12,245	1,672	3,322
May	930	865	19,127	58,869	16,486	10,659	1,676	2,831
June	1,078	1,016	14,227	50,181	14,985	9,448	3,376	3,403
July	2,400	2,049	114,938	103,362	23,530	13,469	3,833	3,306
August	2,809	1,918	150,224	178,542	22,674	27,390	3,968	3,540
September	2,764	1,984	139,064	164,429	20,371	23,525	4,498	3,699
October	2,413	1,931	128,171	153,521	18,416	23,173	4,301	3,972
November	2,103	1,577	114,676	144,280	17,893	22,722	4,783	3,465
December	1,918	1,441	112,101	134,908	18,051	22,226	4,850	3,404

Month	Peaches		Raspberries, Black		Red Raspberries, IQF		Red Raspberries, pails & tubs	
	2013	2014	2013	2014	2013	2014	2013	2014
	1,000 pounds	1,000 pounds	1,000 pounds	1,000 pounds	1,000 pounds	1,000 pounds	1,000 pounds	1,000 pounds
January	45,535	53,367	619	710	17,514	25,341	7,336	5,801
February	40,062	47,862	543	677	14,692	22,537	6,833	4,497
March	33,489	39,621	421	620	13,733	20,300	5,657	4,202
April	28,880	32,936	320	592	13,276	18,519	5,352	3,868
May	22,290	25,714	354	462	11,862	18,294	4,726	3,712
June	19,137	19,497	763	1,442	13,112	18,159	4,340	3,608
July	36,193	34,001	1,518	2,027	31,017	36,855	9,161	10,779
August	59,642	54,810	1,395	1,401	41,792	36,201	9,276	9,475
September	72,610	63,033	1,121	1,381	39,125	34,803	8,466	8,057
October	73,147	57,543	1,050	1,353	35,257	33,491	7,797	6,709
November	65,548	52,384	985	1,245	32,041	30,861	7,394	6,024
December	61,092	47,465	852	1,145	30,527	29,517	6,651	6,027

See footnotes(s) at end of table.

Table 5-104.—Fruit and orange juice: Cold storage holdings, end of month, United States, 2013 and 2014—Continued

Month	Red Raspberries, barrels		Red Raspberries, concentrate		Red Raspberries, total		Strawberries, IQF & Poly	
	2013	2014	2013	2014	2013	2014	2013	2014
	1,000 pounds	1,000 pounds	1,000 pounds	1,000 pounds	1,000 pounds	1,000 pounds	1,000 pounds	1,000 pounds
January	18,619	20,019	1,057	1,569	44,526	52,730	103,448	91,367
February	17,448	16,643	842	1,394	39,815	45,071	99,481	81,716
March	12,030	12,497	1,496	1,419	32,916	38,418	96,904	86,100
April	11,894	10,074	1,144	1,212	31,666	33,673	132,720	108,405
May	9,213	8,133	1,119	1,214	26,920	31,353	170,446	123,274
June	7,061	7,119	856	1,340	25,369	30,226	175,747	154,588
July	31,219	37,278	1,050	2,580	72,447	87,492	203,299	165,509
August	30,831	33,746	1,085	2,119	82,984	81,541	196,672	148,359
September	30,074	29,997	1,814	2,001	79,479	74,858	172,438	131,035
October	27,706	24,924	2,028	1,971	72,788	67,095	143,980	119,620
November	24,222	23,541	1,438	1,911	65,095	62,337	130,997	101,207
December	23,332	19,996	1,592	1,758	62,102	57,298	108,740	92,172

Month	Strawberries, pails & tubs		Strawberries, barrels & drums		Strawberries, juice stock		Strawberries, total	
	2013	2014	2013	2014	2013	2014	2013	2014
	1,000 pounds	1,000 pounds	1,000 pounds	1,000 pounds	1,000 pounds	1,000 pounds	1,000 pounds	1,000 pounds
January	71,645	67,354	79,003	67,007	11,154	14,654	265,250	240,382
February	60,732	60,666	71,026	59,391	8,844	13,395	240,083	215,168
March	53,628	55,797	60,740	55,287	6,877	13,880	218,149	211,064
April	88,998	57,051	100,253	53,629	12,388	14,062	334,359	233,147
May	106,241	61,592	111,685	60,147	8,980	12,770	397,352	257,783
June	116,029	92,845	121,108	95,041	8,244	15,052	421,128	357,526
July	124,062	89,369	123,168	95,398	13,169	11,851	463,698	362,127
August	111,891	82,167	104,646	87,713	14,951	12,427	428,160	330,666
September	107,550	72,340	94,512	80,575	17,532	11,019	392,032	294,969
October	96,708	66,004	86,270	72,941	18,194	11,988	345,152	270,553
November	90,985	59,902	83,211	64,535	14,843	11,184	320,036	236,828
December	79,511	49,966	75,978	55,264	15,748	9,439	279,977	206,841

Month	Other fruit		Total frozen fruit		Orange juice	
	2013	2014	2013	2014	2013	2014
	1,000 pounds	1,000 pounds	1,000 pounds	1,000 pounds	1,000 pounds	1,000 pounds
January	444,506	528,790	1,123,466	1,261,124	781,594	750,467
February	417,678	475,527	1,030,107	1,140,370	875,350	799,317
March	382,611	440,532	934,920	1,051,950	946,751	813,007
April	355,428	389,071	984,995	981,069	1,021,312	877,826
May	316,247	341,283	962,602	912,114	1,042,263	872,936
June	284,810	305,249	954,134	972,152	996,154	853,656
July	277,685	286,727	1,251,339	1,176,038	915,029	815,884
August	238,619	264,490	1,335,033	1,317,864	864,592	773,000
September	224,171	293,231	1,269,963	1,286,143	795,828	712,015
October	470,098	542,534	1,431,119	1,461,405	785,905	721,880
November	589,226	576,843	1,488,953	1,426,813	732,567	676,846
December	575,025	535,775	1,405,632	1,315,421	739,466	734,784

NASS, Livestock Branch, (202) 720–3570.

Table 5-105.—Nuts: Cold storage holdings, end of month, United States, 2013-2014

Month	Pecans			
	Shelled		In-shell	
	2013	2014	2013	2014
	1,000 pounds	1,000 pounds	1,000 pounds	1,000 pounds
January	42,480	46,212	162,239	164,037
February	47,292	47,989	209,428	204,365
March	49,564	48,497	216,594	196,843
April	54,467	51,514	194,670	183,169
May	54,355	53,431	175,623	158,555
June	55,342	55,610	154,153	137,685
July	57,210	52,184	117,631	103,286
August	51,233	53,125	94,804	73,275
September	43,800	52,871	75,446	51,450
October	36,884	43,061	54,970	27,102
November	37,341	40,344	63,439	33,063
December	36,672	45,067	93,565	84,740

NASS, Livestock Branch, (202) 720-3570.

STATISTICS OF HAY, SEEDS, AND MINOR FIELD CROPS

Chapter VI deals with hay, pasture, seeds, and various minor field crops.

Table 6-1.—Hay, all: Area, yield, and production, by State and United States, 2012–2014

State	Area harvested			Yield per harvested acre			Production		
	2012	2013	2014	2012	2013	2014	2012	2013	2014
	1,000 acres	1,000 acres	1,000 acres	Tons	Tons	Tons	1,000 tons	1,000 tons	1,000 tons
Alabama	860	790	750	2.60	2.70	2.80	2,236	2,133	2,100
Arizona	295	285	300	7.82	7.65	8.03	2,307	2,179	2,410
Arkansas	1,450	1,335	1,225	1.21	2.10	2.01	1,750	2,810	2,458
California	1,500	1,370	1,375	5.42	5.58	5.37	8,130	7,646	7,388
Colorado	1,390	1,310	1,340	2.28	2.25	2.66	3,167	2,941	3,566
Connecticut	56	47	53	1.98	2.26	1.92	111	106	102
Delaware	16	18	13	2.63	3.28	2.62	42	59	34
Florida	320	300	320	2.50	2.20	2.60	800	660	832
Georgia	580	580	580	2.50	2.70	2.60	1,450	1,566	1,508
Idaho	1,340	1,480	1,390	3.53	3.36	3.51	4,730	4,976	4,881
Illinois	540	660	520	2.54	3.07	3.38	1,370	2,024	1,755
Indiana	560	640	600	2.36	2.80	3.25	1,324	1,792	1,950
Iowa	1,120	1,170	1,155	2.48	2.89	3.18	2,780	3,377	3,675
Kansas	2,600	2,750	2,300	1.65	2.38	2.17	4,280	6,545	5,000
Kentucky	2,130	2,400	2,265	2.08	2.29	2.10	4,422	5,500	4,761
Louisiana	460	400	470	2.60	2.20	2.70	1,196	880	1,269
Maine	130	135	150	1.78	1.46	1.55	231	197	233
Maryland	175	225	195	2.42	2.33	2.65	424	524	517
Massachusetts	69	84	75	1.96	2.12	1.72	135	178	129
Michigan	970	940	980	1.88	2.68	2.62	1,820	2,518	2,570
Minnesota	1,750	1,900	1,910	2.28	2.05	2.35	3,995	3,895	4,486
Mississippi	750	720	600	2.50	2.50	2.60	1,875	1,800	1,560
Missouri	3,640	4,030	3,480	1.53	1.97	2.04	5,580	7,921	7,100
Montana	2,200	2,800	2,730	1.87	1.95	1.97	4,120	5,460	5,381
Nebraska	2,570	2,500	2,580	1.73	1.97	2.34	4,457	4,935	6,028
Nevada	415	345	430	3.22	3.37	3.29	1,336	1,161	1,416
New Hampshire	52	50	54	1.90	2.50	1.74	99	125	94
New Jersey	103	97	106	2.20	2.42	2.46	227	235	261
New Mexico	285	230	305	4.47	4.18	3.93	1,273	962	1,198
New York	1,340	1,430	1,370	1.87	2.05	1.97	2,506	2,930	2,698
North Carolina	655	858	830	2.42	2.41	2.40	1,583	2,064	1,996
North Dakota	2,190	2,620	2,700	1.44	1.94	2.02	3,156	5,090	5,460
Ohio	1,030	1,000	960	2.15	2.50	2.82	2,214	2,495	2,710
Oklahoma	2,800	3,130	3,590	1.39	1.59	1.71	3,880	4,971	6,121
Oregon	1,000	1,020	1,030	2.91	3.14	3.08	2,912	3,204	3,172
Pennsylvania	1,420	1,260	1,400	2.24	2.32	2.28	3,182	2,918	3,185
Rhode Island	8	8	7	1.88	1.88	1.64	15	15	12
South Carolina	300	290	270	2.20	2.20	2.30	660	638	621
South Dakota	2,850	3,050	3,250	1.31	1.94	2.05	3,740	5,905	6,665
Tennessee	1,764	1,915	1,766	2.01	2.31	2.20	3,545	4,427	3,893
Texas	5,100	5,640	5,440	1.85	1.57	2.16	9,460	8,880	11,746
Utah	660	725	680	3.62	3.77	3.52	2,386	2,730	2,396
Vermont	180	180	185	2.02	1.72	1.68	363	310	311
Virginia	1,290	1,240	1,175	2.17	2.49	2.28	2,800	3,084	2,675
Washington	710	760	870	3.88	4.24	3.72	2,753	3,223	3,234
West Virginia	595	590	618	1.63	1.97	1.83	972	1,165	1,132
Wisconsin	1,500	1,600	1,640	2.23	2.35	2.97	3,350	3,760	4,866
Wyoming	935	990	1,060	2.06	2.11	2.12	1,928	2,088	2,243
United States	54,653	57,897	57,092	2.14	2.33	2.45	117,072	135,002	139,798

NASS, Crops Branch, (202) 720–2127.

Table 6-2.—Hay, all: Area, yield, production, and value, United States, 2005–2014

Year	Area harvested	Yield per acre	Production	Marketing year average price per ton received by farmers	Value of production
	1,000 acres	Tons	1,000 tons	Dollars	1,000 dollars
2005	61,637	2.44	150,461	98.20	12,533,762
2006	60,632	2.32	140,783	110.00	13,633,837
2007	61,006	2.41	146,901	127.00	16,842,233
2008	60,152	2.43	146,270	152.00	18,638,748
2009	59,775	2.47	147,700	108.00	14,715,559
2010	59,574	2.43	145,000	114.00	14,606,696
2011	55,204	2.35	129,880	178.00	18,085,074
2012	54,653	2.14	117,072	191.00	18,613,183
2013	57,897	2.33	135,002	176.00	19,814,822
2014	57,092	2.45	139,798	180.00	19,185,254

NASS, Crops Branch, (202) 720–2127.

Table 6-3.—Alfalfa and alfalfa mixtures for hay: Area, yield, and production, by State and United States, 2012–2014

State	Area harvested			Yield per harvested acre			Production		
	2012	2013	2014	2012	2013	2014	2012	2013	2014
	1,000 acres	1,000 acres	1,000 acres	Tons	Tons	Tons	1,000 tons	1,000 tons	1,000 tons
Arizona	250	250	260	8.40	8.10	8.50	2,100	2,025	2,210
Arkansas	10	5	5	2.20	3.30	3.60	22	17	18
California	900	830	875	6.70	7.00	6.50	6,030	5,810	5,688
Colorado	680	650	740	3.30	2.90	3.40	2,244	1,885	2,516
Connecticut	5	7	8	2.80	2.00	2.00	14	14	16
Delaware	6	6	4	2.70	3.50	2.70	16	21	11
Idaho	1,040	1,120	1,090	4.00	3.80	3.90	4,160	4,256	4,251
Illinois	290	340	270	3.00	3.60	4.00	870	1,224	1,080
Indiana	260	280	240	2.90	3.70	4.00	754	1,036	960
Iowa	730	730	810	2.90	3.30	3.60	2,117	2,409	2,916
Kansas	600	550	600	2.80	3.50	3.80	1,680	1,925	2,280
Kentucky	180	200	165	2.90	3.30	3.40	522	660	561
Maine	10	10	10	1.50	2.20	2.30	15	22	23
Maryland	30	30	35	3.50	3.80	3.80	105	114	133
Massachusetts	9	9	10	2.30	3.10	1.80	21	28	18
Michigan	660	610	640	2.10	3.10	2.90	1,386	1,891	1,856
Minnesota	850	950	1,100	2.90	2.60	2.90	2,465	2,470	3,190
Missouri	240	330	280	2.00	2.70	2.50	480	891	700
Montana	1,500	1,800	1,850	2.00	2.20	2.10	3,000	3,960	3,885
Nebraska	770	700	830	3.10	3.45	4.10	2,387	2,415	3,403
Nevada	240	210	280	4.40	4.50	4.20	1,056	945	1,176
New Hampshire	5	5	4	2.00	1.60	2.30	10	8	9
New Jersey	15	17	14	3.40	3.00	3.50	51	51	49
New Mexico	200	145	210	5.30	5.40	4.80	1,060	783	1,008
New York	380	350	290	2.30	2.20	2.60	874	770	754
North Carolina	10	8	10	3.50	3.00	2.80	35	24	28
North Dakota	1,290	1,620	1,650	1.40	2.00	2.10	1,806	3,240	3,465
Ohio	360	330	310	2.80	3.50	3.50	1,008	1,155	1,085
Oklahoma	200	230	290	2.50	2.70	2.90	500	621	841
Oregon	380	400	350	4.40	4.60	4.40	1,672	1,840	1,540
Pennsylvania	400	340	350	2.60	2.90	2.80	1,040	986	980
Rhode Island	1	1	1	1.50	2.00	2.50	2	2	3
South Dakota	1,600	1,800	1,900	1.40	2.10	2.30	2,240	3,780	4,370
Tennessee	14	15	16	3.20	3.80	2.70	45	57	43
Texas	100	140	140	4.60	4.50	4.40	460	630	616
Utah	500	550	520	4.10	4.20	3.90	2,050	2,310	2,028
Vermont	30	35	35	2.10	1.80	1.60	63	63	56
Virginia	70	90	75	3.40	3.60	3.40	238	324	255
Washington	380	410	420	4.90	5.30	4.70	1,862	2,173	1,974
West Virginia	25	20	18	2.40	4.10	2.90	60	82	52
Wisconsin	1,100	1,100	1,250	2.50	2.60	3.30	2,750	2,860	4,125
Wyoming	475	450	490	2.80	3.20	2.60	1,330	1,440	1,274
United States	16,795	17,673	18,445	3.01	3.24	3.33	50,600	57,217	61,446

NASS, Crops Branch, (202) 720–2127.

Table 6-4.—Hay, all other: Area, yield, and production, by State and United States, 2012–2014

State	Area harvested			Yield per harvested acre			Production		
	2012	2013	2014	2012	2013	2014	2012	2013	2014
	1,000 acres	*1,000 acres*	*1,000 acres*	*Tons*	*Tons*	*Tons*	*1,000 tons*	*1,000 tons*	*1,000 tons*
Alabama[1]	860	790	750	2.60	2.70	2.80	2,236	2,133	2,100
Arizona	45	35	40	4.60	4.40	5.00	207	154	200
Arkansas	1,440	1,330	1,220	1.20	2.10	2.00	1,728	2,793	2,440
California	600	540	500	3.50	3.40	3.40	2,100	1,836	1,700
Colorado	710	660	600	1.30	1.60	1.75	923	1,056	1,050
Connecticut	51	40	45	1.90	2.30	1.90	97	92	86
Delaware	10	12	9	2.60	3.20	2.50	26	38	23
Florida[1]	320	300	320	2.50	2.20	2.60	800	660	832
Georgia[1]	580	580	580	2.50	2.70	2.60	1,450	1,566	1,508
Idaho	300	360	300	1.90	2.00	2.10	570	720	630
Illinois	250	320	250	2.00	2.50	2.70	500	800	675
Indiana	300	360	360	1.90	2.10	2.75	570	756	990
Iowa	390	440	345	1.70	2.20	2.20	663	968	759
Kansas	2,000	2,200	1,700	1.30	2.10	1.60	2,600	4,620	2,720
Kentucky	1,950	2,200	2,100	2.00	2.20	2.00	3,900	4,840	4,200
Louisiana[1]	460	400	470	2.60	2.20	2.70	1,196	880	1,269
Maine	120	125	140	1.80	1.40	1.50	216	175	210
Maryland	145	195	160	2.20	2.10	2.40	319	410	384
Massachusetts	60	75	65	1.90	2.00	1.70	114	150	111
Michigan	310	330	340	1.40	1.90	2.10	434	627	714
Minnesota	900	950	810	1.70	1.50	1.60	1,530	1,425	1,296
Mississippi[1]	750	720	600	2.50	2.50	2.60	1,875	1,800	1,560
Missouri	3,400	3,700	3,200	1.50	1.90	2.00	5,100	7,030	6,400
Montana	700	1,000	880	1.60	1.50	1.70	1,120	1,500	1,496
Nebraska	1,800	1,800	1,750	1.15	1.40	1.50	2,070	2,520	2,625
Nevada	175	135	150	1.60	1.60	1.60	280	216	240
New Hampshire	47	45	50	1.90	2.60	1.70	89	117	85
New Jersey	88	80	92	2.00	2.30	2.30	176	184	212
New Mexico	85	85	95	2.50	2.10	2.00	213	179	190
New York	960	1,080	1,080	1.70	2.00	1.80	1,632	2,160	1,944
North Carolina	645	850	820	2.40	2.40	2.40	1,548	2,040	1,968
North Dakota	900	1,000	1,050	1.50	1.85	1.90	1,350	1,850	1,995
Ohio	670	670	650	1.80	2.00	2.50	1,206	1,340	1,625
Oklahoma	2,600	2,900	3,300	1.30	1.50	1.60	3,380	4,350	5,280
Oregon	620	620	680	2.00	2.20	2.40	1,240	1,364	1,632
Pennsylvania	1,020	920	1,050	2.10	2.10	2.10	2,142	1,932	2,205
Rhode Island	7	7	6	1.90	1.90	1.50	13	13	9
South Carolina[1]	300	290	270	2.20	2.20	2.30	660	638	621
South Dakota	1,250	1,250	1,350	1.20	1.70	1.70	1,500	2,125	2,295
Tennessee	1,750	1,900	1,750	2.00	2.30	2.20	3,500	4,370	3,850
Texas	5,000	5,500	5,300	1.80	1.50	2.10	9,000	8,250	11,130
Utah	160	175	160	2.10	2.40	2.30	336	420	368
Vermont	150	145	150	2.00	1.70	1.70	300	247	255
Virginia	1,220	1,150	1,100	2.10	2.40	2.20	2,562	2,760	2,420
Washington	330	350	450	2.70	3.00	2.80	891	1,050	1,260
West Virginia	570	570	600	1.60	1.90	1.80	912	1,083	1,080
Wisconsin	400	500	390	1.50	1.80	1.90	600	900	741
Wyoming	460	540	570	1.30	1.20	1.70	598	648	969
United States	37,858	40,224	38,647	1.76	1.93	2.03	66,472	77,785	78,352

[1] Alfalfa and alfalfa mixtures included in all other hay.
NASS, Crops Branch, (202) 720–2127.

Table 6-5.—Hay, all: Stocks on farms, United States, 2005–2014

Crop year	Dec. 1	May 1[1]
	1,000 tons	*1,000 tons*
2005	105,181	21,345
2006	96,400	14,990
2007	104,089	21,585
2008	103,658	22,065
2009	107,222	20,931
2010	101,667	22,217
2011	89,723	21,381
2012	75,175	14,156
2013	89,304	19,176
2014	92,052	24,517

[1] Following year.
NASS, Crops Branch, (202) 720–2127.

Table 6-6.—Hay, all: Marketing year average price and value of production, by State and United States, 2012–2014

State	Marketing year average price per ton, baled			Value of production		
	2012	2013	2014	2012	2013	2014
	Dollars	Dollars	Dollars	1,000 dollars	1,000 dollars	1,000 dollars
Alabama	82.00	88.00	100.00	183,352	187,704	210,000
Arizona	222.00	201.00	216.00	511,800	437,979	521,160
Arkansas	137.00	128.00	115.00	233,090	360,904	284,200
California	204.00	199.00	235.00	1,650,600	1,521,832	1,737,024
Colorado	237.00	236.00	209.00	736,607	687,513	738,994
Connecticut	237.00	235.00	170.00	26,048	24,940	17,324
Delaware	227.00	179.00	165.00	10,032	10,533	5,607
Florida	167.00	167.00	160.00	133,600	110,220	133,120
Georgia	75.00	75.00	90.00	108,750	117,450	135,720
Idaho	189.00	191.00	203.00	881,540	943,808	984,855
Illinois	160.00	166.00	155.00	212,010	328,368	268,380
Indiana	219.00	178.00	146.00	281,886	305,508	280,920
Iowa	203.00	176.00	139.00	564,783	599,445	533,832
Kansas	196.00	164.00	155.00	694,440	893,200	665,120
Kentucky	113.00	121.00	116.00	449,412	609,840	491,451
Louisiana	120.00	93.00	100.00	143,520	81,840	126,900
Maine	183.00	172.00	169.00	42,285	33,938	39,440
Maryland	227.00	181.00	161.00	99,071	94,686	82,621
Massachusetts	219.00	200.00	189.00	29,502	35,674	24,414
Michigan	173.00	165.00	149.00	316,148	433,823	398,488
Minnesota	175.00	171.00	122.00	713,490	668,705	578,592
Mississippi	70.00	66.00	71.00	131,250	118,800	110,760
Missouri	118.00	118.00	88.50	610,980	862,088	585,800
Montana	143.00	138.00	126.00	579,120	741,360	672,312
Nebraska	203.00	148.00	97.00	846,624	698,775	570,231
Nevada	204.00	207.00	241.00	266,040	240,543	339,744
New Hampshire	212.00	172.00	169.00	20,963	21,559	15,905
New Jersey	166.00	133.00	175.00	37,434	31,225	45,567
New Mexico	249.00	242.00	252.00	316,283	231,930	298,486
New York	141.00	157.00	160.00	375,714	494,810	458,034
North Carolina	108.00	110.00	107.00	172,811	227,184	214,320
North Dakota	121.00	103.00	81.50	344,130	481,270	410,235
Ohio	193.00	171.00	139.00	428,220	426,410	370,790
Oklahoma	126.00	106.00	141.00	506,580	536,208	629,125
Oregon	210.00	200.00	223.00	607,216	636,360	703,080
Pennsylvania	164.00	184.00	201.00	537,930	541,096	640,675
Rhode Island	226.00	214.00	178.00	3,384	3,215	2,133
South Carolina	100.00	110.00	110.00	66,000	70,180	68,310
South Dakota	204.00	143.00	114.00	729,040	819,405	732,318
Tennessee	96.50	95.50	92.00	341,500	422,807	359,552
Texas	121.00	120.00	107.00	1,000,480	884,820	978,257
Utah	189.00	182.00	190.00	440,572	484,260	441,992
Vermont	166.00	140.00	127.00	60,504	43,450	38,522
Virginia	161.00	128.00	128.00	447,986	393,732	345,095
Washington	228.00	209.00	221.00	625,982	675,050	720,678
West Virginia	109.00	120.00	112.00	107,160	139,551	126,208
Wisconsin	175.00	192.00	145.00	592,600	722,680	732,198
Wyoming	208.00	184.00	144.00	394,714	378,144	316,765
United States	191.00	176.00	180.00	18,613,183	19,814,822	19,185,254

NASS, Crops Branch, (202) 720–2127.

Table 6-7.—Hay: Area and production, by type, United States, 2005–2014

Year	Area harvested			Production		
	Alfalfa	All other hay	All hay	Alfalfa	All other hay	All hay
	1,000 acres	1,000 acres	1,000 acres	1,000 tons	1,000 tons	1,000 tons
2005	22,359	39,278	61,637	75,610	74,851	150,461
2006	21,138	39,494	60,632	70,548	70,235	140,783
2007	21,126	39,880	61,006	69,880	77,021	146,901
2008	21,060	39,092	60,152	70,180	76,090	146,270
2009	21,247	38,528	59,775	71,072	76,628	147,700
2010	19,968	39,606	59,574	67,977	77,023	145,000
2011	19,044	36,160	55,204	64,815	65,065	129,880
2012	16,795	37,858	54,653	50,600	66,472	117,072
2013	17,673	40,224	57,897	57,217	77,785	135,002
2014	18,445	38,647	57,092	61,446	78,352	139,798

NASS, Crops Branch, (202) 720–2127.

Forage production is the sum of all dry hay production and haylage/greenchop production after converting the haylage/greenchop production to a dry equivalent basis (13 percent moisture) by multiplying the green weight (weight at harvest) by 0.4943. The conversion factor (0.4943) is based on the assumption that one ton of dry hay is 0.87 ton of dry matter, one ton of haylage is 0.45 ton dry matter and one ton of greenchop is 0.25 ton dry matter. The total haylage/greenchop production is assumed to be comprised of 90 percent haylage and 10 percent greenchop. Therefore, the conversion factor used to adjust haylage/greenchop production to a dry equivalent basis = ((0.45*0.9)+(0.25*0.1))/0.87 = 0.4943. The factors assumed here may vary by State and can be adjusted. Adjustments would result in a slightly different conversion factor.

Table 6-8.—All forage: Area harvested, yield, and production, by State and 18 State total, 2012–2014 [1]

State	Area harvested			Yield		
	2012	2013	2014	2012	2013	2014
	1,000 acres	1,000 acres	1,000 acres	Tons	Tons	Tons
California	1,740	1,565	1,560	5.58	5.98	5.69
Idaho	1,405	1,520	1,460	3.77	3.62	3.78
Illinois	570	680	540	2.67	3.12	3.54
Iowa	1,145	1,220	1,220	2.68	3.07	3.39
Kansas	2,740	2,780	2,420	1.63	2.41	2.24
Michigan	1,150	1,180	1,210	2.26	3.02	3.07
Minnesota	1,980	2,165	2,210	2.48	2.25	2.56
Missouri	3,680	4,085	3,570	1.57	2.00	2.05
Nebraska	2,590	2,530	2,610	1.77	2.00	2.37
New Mexico	311	244	330	4.44	4.16	4.00
New York	1,860	2,020	1,830	2.36	2.47	2.58
Ohio	1,100	1,050	1,030	2.35	2.70	2.96
Pennsylvania	1,690	1,540	1,720	2.58	2.79	2.65
South Dakota	2,900	3,085	3,280	1.35	1.98	2.09
Texas	5,240	5,744	5,545	1.93	1.63	2.20
Vermont	280	310	290	3.40	2.73	2.59
Washington	770	805	930	4.06	4.44	3.88
Wisconsin	2,490	2,650	2,700	2.81	2.65	3.54
18 State Total	33,641	35,173	34,455	2.37	2.53	2.77

State	Production		
	2012	2013	2014
	1,000 tons	1,000 tons	1,000 tons
California	9,704	9,362	8,883
Idaho	5,291	5,496	5,524
Illinois	1,524	2,120	1,909
Iowa	3,073	3,747	4,135
Kansas	4,468	6,710	5,413
Michigan	2,594	3,568	3,719
Minnesota	4,918	4,882	5,657
Missouri	5,771	8,158	7,319
Nebraska	4,584	5,062	6,192
New Mexico	1,381	1,014	1,320
New York	4,392	4,998	4,728
Ohio	2,588	2,838	3,044
Pennsylvania	4,355	4,294	4,562
South Dakota	3,914	6,093	6,859
Texas	10,128	9,345	12,178
Vermont	951	847	751
Washington	3,126	3,573	3,609
Wisconsin	7,009	7,022	9,570
18 State Total	79,771	89,129	95,372

[1] All forage production is the sum of the following dry equivalents: alfalfa hay harvested as dry hay, all other hay harvested as dry hay, alfalfa haylage and greenchop, all other hay haylage and greenchop; after converting alfalfa and all other haylage and greenchop to a dry equivalent basis.
NASS, Crops Branch, (202) 720–2127.

Table 6-9.—All alfalfa forage: Area harvested, yield, and production, by State and 18 State total, 2012–2014 [1]

State	Area harvested			Yield		
	2012	2013	2014	2012	2013	2014
	1,000 acres	*1,000 acres*	*1,000 acres*	*Tons*	*Tons*	*Tons*
California	940	865	900	6.70	7.09	6.62
Idaho	1,085	1,135	1,120	4.26	4.10	4.20
Illinois	310	360	290	3.18	3.59	4.17
Iowa	760	770	860	3.11	3.56	3.85
Kansas	640	560	650	2.89	3.50	3.72
Michigan	830	840	850	2.53	3.43	3.48
Minnesota	1,040	1,185	1,360	3.17	2.86	3.12
Missouri	250	345	320	2.15	2.80	2.34
Nebraska	780	710	850	3.15	3.48	4.12
New Mexico	205	145	215	5.28	5.50	4.87
New York	680	650	500	3.16	3.16	3.83
Ohio	410	360	350	3.18	3.91	3.71
Pennsylvania	580	490	560	3.22	4.11	3.52
South Dakota	1,630	1,820	1,910	1.44	2.15	2.32
Texas	110	144	145	4.59	4.47	4.41
Vermont	70	90	70	4.03	3.28	3.27
Washington	390	425	430	4.91	5.25	4.80
Wisconsin	2,000	2,000	2,200	3.06	2.88	3.84
18 State Total	12,710	12,894	13,580	3.31	3.54	3.76

State	Production		
	2012	2013	2014
	1,000 tons	*1,000 tons*	*1,000 tons*
California	6,299	6,136	5,955
Idaho	4,622	4,658	4,706
Illinois	986	1,294	1,210
Iowa	2,366	2,738	3,314
Kansas	1,852	1,959	2,421
Michigan	2,104	2,879	2,961
Minnesota	3,295	3,386	4,249
Missouri	538	965	749
Nebraska	2,460	2,474	3,498
New Mexico	1,082	797	1,048
New York	2,146	2,055	1,914
Ohio	1,305	1,408	1,300
Pennsylvania	1,867	2,015	1,969
South Dakota	2,343	3,909	4,431
Texas	505	644	640
Vermont	282	295	229
Washington	1,915	2,232	2,064
Wisconsin	6,121	5,766	8,455
18 State Total	42,088	45,610	51,113

[1] All alfalfa forage production is the sum of alfalfa harvested as dry hay; and alfalfa haylage and greenchop production after converting it to a dry equivalent basis.
NASS, Crops Branch, (202) 720–2127.

Table 6-10.—All haylage and greenchop: Area harvested, yield, and production, by State and 18 State total, 2012–2014[1]

State	Area harvested			Yield		
	2012	2013	2014	2012	2013	2014
	1,000 acres	*1,000 acres*	*1,000 acres*	*Tons*	*Tons*	*Tons*
California	280	265	240	11.37	13.10	12.60
Idaho	105	90	120	10.81	11.68	10.83
Illinois	55	49	49	5.64	3.95	6.38
Iowa	90	105	155	6.60	7.13	6.01
Kansas	160	66	165	4.21	5.06	5.07
Michigan	250	295	290	6.26	7.20	8.02
Minnesota	280	331	370	6.67	6.03	6.40
Missouri	120	80	90	3.23	6.00	4.92
Nebraska	65	50	55	3.94	5.16	6.05
New Mexico	26	17	32	8.38	6.21	7.66
New York	660	760	660	5.78	5.51	6.22
Ohio	142	112	133	5.32	6.20	5.06
Pennsylvania	410	465	450	5.79	5.98	6.19
South Dakota	100	55	60	3.53	6.91	6.55
Texas	293	110	157	4.61	8.54	5.57
Vermont	175	165	140	6.81	6.59	6.36
Washington	100	83	103	7.56	8.53	7.36
Wisconsin	1,220	1,230	1,335	5.93	5.37	7.13
18 State Total	4,531	4,328	4,604	6.19	6.50	6.98

State	Production		
	2012	2013	2014
	1,000 tons	*1,000 tons*	*1,000 tons*
California	3,184	3,472	3,025
Idaho	1,135	1,051	1,300
Illinois	310	194	313
Iowa	594	749	931
Kansas	673	334	836
Michigan	1,566	2,123	2,326
Minnesota	1,868	1,996	2,368
Missouri	387	480	443
Nebraska	256	258	333
New Mexico	218	106	245
New York	3,816	4,184	4,106
Ohio	755	694	674
Pennsylvania	2,374	2,783	2,785
South Dakota	353	380	393
Texas	1,351	940	874
Vermont	1,192	1,087	890
Washington	756	708	758
Wisconsin	7,240	6,600	9,516
18 State Total	28,028	28,139	32,116

[1] Includes all types of forage harvested as haylage or greenchop (green weight). Forage harvested as dry hay and corn and sorghum silage/greenchop are not included.
NASS, Crops Branch, (202) 720–2127.

Table 6-11.—Alfalfa haylage and greenchop: Area harvested, yield, and production, by State and 18 State total, 2012–2014 [1]

State	Area harvested			Yield		
	2012	2013	2014	2012	2013	2014
	1,000 acres	1,000 acres	1,000 acres	Tons	Tons	Tons
California	80	75	65	6.80	8.80	8.30
Idaho	85	65	80	11.00	12.50	11.50
Illinois	36	38	40	6.50	3.70	6.60
Iowa	70	90	130	7.20	7.40	6.20
Kansas	35	16	65	6.70	4.30	4.40
Michigan	220	270	260	6.60	7.40	8.60
Minnesota	240	285	315	7.00	6.50	6.80
Missouri	30	25	20	3.90	6.00	5.00
Nebraska	30	25	35	4.90	4.80	5.50
New Mexico	5	3	10	8.80	9.50	8.00
New York	390	400	340	6.60	6.50	6.90
Ohio	100	80	85	6.00	6.40	5.10
Pennsylvania	270	285	290	6.20	7.30	6.90
South Dakota	55	40	30	3.80	6.50	4.10
Texas	13	4	7	7.00	7.00	7.00
Vermont	60	70	50	7.40	6.70	7.00
Washington	20	23	23	5.40	5.20	7.90
Wisconsin	1,100	1,050	1,200	6.20	5.60	7.30
18 State Total	2,839	2,844	3,045	6.49	6.49	7.16

State	Production		
	2012	2013	2014
	1,000 tons	1,000 tons	1,000 tons
California	544	660	540
Idaho	935	813	920
Illinois	234	141	264
Iowa	504	666	806
Kansas	235	69	286
Michigan	1,452	1,998	2,236
Minnesota	1,680	1,853	2,142
Missouri	117	150	100
Nebraska	147	120	193
New Mexico	44	29	80
New York	2,574	2,600	2,346
Ohio	600	512	434
Pennsylvania	1,674	2,081	2,001
South Dakota	209	260	123
Texas	91	28	49
Vermont	444	469	350
Washington	108	120	182
Wisconsin	6,820	5,880	8,760
18 State Total	18,412	18,449	21,812

[1] Includes only alfalfa and alfalfa mixtures that were harvested as haylage or greenchop (green weight). Alfalfa harvested as dry hay is not included.
NASS, Crops Branch, (202) 720–2127.

Table 6-12.—Hay: Supply and disappearance, prices, and number of animal units fed annually, United States, 2005–2014 [1]

Year beginning May	Farm carryover May 1	Production	Total supply	Disappearance	Roughage-consuming animal units	Supply per animal unit	Disappearance per animal unit	Price received per ton
	Million tons	Million tons	Million tons	Million tons	Million tons	Tons	Tons	Dollars
2005	27.8	150.5	178.2	156.9	71.6	2.49	2.19	98.20
2006	21.3	140.8	162.1	147.1	71.8	2.26	2.05	110.00
2007	15.0	146.9	161.9	140.3	71.5	2.26	1.96	127.00
2008	21.6	146.3	167.9	145.8	71.0	2.36	2.05	152.00
2009	22.1	147.7	169.8	148.8	70.5	2.41	2.11	108.00
2010	20.9	145.0	144.3	144.3	69.4	2.40	2.08	114.00
2011	22.2	129.9	132.1	132.1	68.0	2.26	1.94	178.00
2012	21.4	117.1	127.1	127.1	67.6	1.88	1.88	191.00
2013	14.2	135.0	149.2	130.0	66.8	2.23	1.95	176.00
2014	19.2	139.9	159.1	134.6	67.9	2.34	1.98	173.00

[1] Excludes trade.
ERS, Market and Trade Economics Division, (202) 694-5313.

Table 6-13.—Field seeds: Average retail price paid by farmers for seed, Mar. 15, United States, 2005–2014 [1]

Kind of seed	2005	2006	2007	2008	2009	2010	2011	2012	2013	2014
	Price per 100 pounds									
	Dollars	Dollars	Dollars	Dollars	Dollars	Dollars	Dollars	Dollars	Dollars	Dollars
Alfalfa:										
Public and common ...	177.00	181.00	201.00	246.00	262.00	273.00	284.00	308.00	316.00	326.00
Proprietary	281.00	286.00	292.00	342.00	379.00	379.00	411.00	442.00	456.00	469.00
Clover, ladino	280.00	306.00	316.00	344.00	394.00	349.00	321.00	337.00	348.00	356.00
Clover, red	174.00	177.00	202.00	241.00	289.00	213.00	200.00	218.00	226.00	231.00
Lespedeza:										
Korean	79.30	87.00	126.00	184.00	127.00	105.00	123.00	248.00	263.00	277.00
Striate, Kobe	83.10	89.50	113.00	263.00	198.00	141.00	128.00	280.00	298.00	317.00
Sericea	220.00	181.00	(4)	(4)	(4)	(4)	(4)	(4)	(4)	(4)
Timothy	105.00	106.00	112.00	133.00	149.00	135.00	146.00	191.00	193.00	198.00
Orchardgrass	137.00	158.00	189.00	321.00	329.00	185.00	170.00	187.00	197.00	199.00
Bluegrass, Kentucky:										
Public and common ...	180.00	161.00	175.00	227.00	269.00	224.00	189.00	223.00	230.00	236.00
Proprietary, including Merion	235.00	224.00	232.00	251.00	326.00	284.00	259.00	260.00	266.00	270.00
Rye grass, annual	59.30	69.60	71.80	78.80	78.90	70.30	73.40	95.20	99.90	101.00
Tall fescue	100.00	124.00	146.00	158.00	143.00	99.00	102.00	146.00	147.00	150.00
Sudangrass	57.40	50.20	56.70	62.10	72.50	73.60	75.70	100.00	103.00	105.00
Potatoes	9.30	11.80	12.00	13.10	15.60	12.90	14.40	15.90	14.80	15.53
Peanuts	56.40	57.70	60.70	83.10	76.50	75.40	91.00	95.40	74.50	77.60
Sunflower	476.00	520.00	616.00	718.00	749.00	729.00	897.00	931.00	940.00	948.00
Cottonseed, all	309.00	356.00	408.00	455.00	521.00	570.00	684.00	702.00	735.00	734.00
Biotech [2]	390.00	443.00	500.00	525.00	609.00	648.00	702.00	754.00	739.00	789.00
Non-biotech	110.00	118.00	97.10	88.50	113.00	130.00	242.00	249.00	323.00	331.00
Grain sorghum, hybrid ..	114.00	116.00	120.00	142.00	161.00	165.00	162.00	203.00	207.00	212.00
Rice	20.80	27.30	30.20	33.50	48.60	48.90	49.80	50.60	60.30	68.10
	Price per bushel									
	Dollars	Dollars	Dollars	Dollars	Dollars	Dollars	Dollars	Dollars	Dollars	Dollars
Corn, hybrid, all [3]	111.00	118.00	133.00	165.00	217.00	229.00	237.00	258.00	274.00	283.00
Biotech [2][3]	131.00	137.00	154.00	184.00	235.00	247.00	249.00	268.00	285.00	293.00
Non-biotech [3]	93.40	95.10	100.00	115.00	139.00	152.00	163.00	182.00	197.00	197.00
Wheat, spring	7.30	7.60	8.40	20.50	11.80	10.00	14.20	15.20	15.60	16.20
Wheat, winter	9.06	9.32	10.60	14.80	16.00	13.70	15.40	17.50	18.00	18.40
Oats, spring	5.54	5.83	6.81	8.19	8.19	7.78	8.34	10.30	10.50	10.70
Barley, spring	6.72	6.58	7.18	10.10	9.78	8.52	10.30	13.10	13.90	13.90
Soybeans for seed, all ..	27.60	28.90	34.80	38.80	48.30	51.90	49.70	54.90	57.80	58.40
Biotech [2]	34.60	34.10	36.70	40.00	49.60	53.50	51.00	55.90	59.10	59.80
Non-biotech	19.10	21.10	20.50	26.30	33.70	33.90	33.50	38.80	40.50	40.70
Flaxseed	14.40	8.80	9.73	19.80	13.80	13.80	19.10	17.50	19.00	19.50

[1] Beginning in 2009 program changed from April 15 to March 15. [2] Biotech varieties are made to be resistant to herbicides, insects, or both. A technology fee is included within the price. [3] Price per 80,000 kernels. [4] Estimate discontinued in 2007.
NASS, Environmental, Economics, and Demographics Branch, (202) 720–6146.

Table 6-14.—Beans, dry edible (clean basis): Production, by classes, United States, 2012–2014 [1]

Class	2012	2013	2014
	1,000 cwt	*1,000 cwt*	*1,000 cwt*
Navy (pea beans)	4,906	3,402	4,421
Great northern	1,222	1,515	2,351
Small white	33	([2])	42
Pinto	13,534	8,486	9,834
Red kidney, light	802	845	1,206
Red kidney, dark	905	838	1,160
Pink	612	476	366
Small red	838	548	708
Cranberry	69	53	76
Black	3,739	2,545	3,997
Large lima (CA)	227	189	190
Baby lima (CA)	302	178	300
Blackeye	546	639	433
Small chickpeas (Garbanzo)	1,147	813	904
Large chickpeas (Garbanzo)	2,185	2,746	1,904
Chickpeas, all (Garbanzo)	3,332	3,559	2,808
Other	858	1,303	1,314
Total	31,925	24,576	29,206

[1] Excludes beans grown for garden seed.   [2] Data are included in "Other" class to avoid disclosing data for individual operations.
NASS, Crops Branch, (202) 720–2127.

Table 6-15.—Beans, dry edible: Area, yield, and production, by State and United States, 2012–2014 [1]

State	Area planted			Area harvested		
	2012	2013	2014	2012	2013	2014
	1,000 acres	*1,000 acres*	*1,000 acres*	*1,000 acres*	*1,000 acres*	*1,000 acres*
Arizona	13.5	10.0	11.0	13.4	10.0	10.9
California	58.5	50.0	48.0	57.5	49.5	47.5
Colorado	50.0	39.0	46.0	45.0	36.0	44.0
Idaho	145.0	125.0	125.0	144.0	124.0	124.0
Kansas	8.0	5.0	7.5	7.5	4.8	6.9
Michigan	200.0	175.0	250.0	197.0	172.0	245.3
Minnesota	160.0	125.0	155.0	155.0	120.0	148.0
Montana	32.0	24.0	37.5	31.1	23.6	37.0
Nebraska	145.0	130.0	165.0	133.0	117.0	152.0
New Mexico	9.8	10.0	10.5	9.8	9.5	10.5
New York	10.0	9.0	8.0	9.5	8.8	7.7
North Dakota	700.0	440.0	630.0	685.0	430.0	615.0
Oregon	10.5	8.3	8.5	10.5	8.2	8.5
South Dakota	13.0	12.0	14.0	12.9	11.5	12.9
Texas	22.0	33.0	23.0	17.0	30.0	21.0
Washington	115.0	120.0	130.0	115.0	119.0	129.0
Wisconsin	5.2	5.4	7.9	5.2	5.4	7.9
Wyoming	45.0	39.0	42.0	42.0	37.0	37.6
United States	1,742.5	1,359.7	1,718.9	1,690.4	1,316.3	1,665.7

State	Yield per acre (clean basis)			Production (clean basis)		
	2012	2013	2014	2012	2013	2014
	Pounds	Pounds	Pounds	*1,000 cwt*	*1,000 cwt*	*1,000 cwt*
Arizona	2,070	1,680	1,940	277	168	211
California	2,270	2,320	2,190	1,304	1,150	1,040
Colorado	1,840	1,500	1,900	828	540	835
Idaho	2,100	1,900	1,800	3,024	2,356	2,232
Kansas	2,110	1,790	1,710	158	86	118
Michigan	1,790	1,900	1,940	3,526	3,270	4,749
Minnesota	2,000	1,950	1,950	3,103	2,340	2,887
Montana	1,500	1,920	1,630	466	453	603
Nebraska	2,400	2,350	2,500	3,193	2,750	3,800
New Mexico	2,200	2,040	1,900	216	194	200
New York	1,920	1,820	1,490	182	160	115
North Dakota	1,700	1,650	1,430	11,660	7,095	8,795
Oregon	2,460	2,260	2,260	258	185	192
South Dakota	2,060	2,000	1,880	266	230	243
Texas	800	1,220	1,220	136	366	256
Washington	1,930	1,820	1,500	2,220	2,165	1,935
Wisconsin	1,940	1,810	2,480	101	98	196
Wyoming	2,400	2,620	2,130	1,007	970	799
United States	1,889	1,867	1,753	31,925	24,576	29,206

[1] Excludes beans grown for garden seed.
NASS, Crops Branch, (202) 720–2127.

Table 6-16.—Beans, dry edible: Area, yield, production, price, and value, United States, 2005–2014 [1]

Year	Area planted	Area harvested	Yield per acre [2]	Production [2]	Marketing year average price per 100 pounds received by farmers	Value of production
	1,000 acres	*1,000 acres*	*Pounds*	*1,000 cwt.*	*Dollars*	*1,000 dollars*
2005	1,623.0	1,526.6	1,741	26,576	18.50	512,833
2006	1,622.8	1,531.6	1,577	24,155	22.10	554,154
2007	1,527.4	1,479.2	1,730	25,586	28.80	748,680
2008	1,495.0	1,445.2	1,768	25,558	34.60	910,200
2009	1,540.0	1,464.0	1,737	25,427	30.00	790,250
2010	1,911.4	1,842.7	1,726	31,801	28.00	899,258
2011	1,217.9	1,167.9	1,703	19,890	42.10	851,131
2012	1,742.5	1,690.4	1,889	31,925	38.00	1,235,255
2013	1,359.7	1,316.3	1,867	24,576	39.10	982,385
2014	1,718.9	1,665.7	1,753	29,206	34.50	1,015,485

[1] Excludes beans grown for garden seed.　[2] Clean basis.
NASS, Crops Branch, (202) 720–2127.

Table 6-17.—Beans, dry edible (clean basis): Marketing year average price and value of production, by State and United States, 2012–2014 [1]

State	Marketing year average price per cwt.			Value of production		
	2012	2013	2014	2012	2013	2014
	Dollars	*Dollars*	*Dollars*	*1,000 dollars*	*1,000 dollars*	*1,000 dollars*
Arizona	51.30	42.20	54.30	14,210	7,090	11,457
California	52.10	56.80	66.80	67,938	65,320	69,472
Colorado	39.00	39.70	26.20	32,292	21,438	21,877
Idaho	36.20	34.30	31.90	109,469	80,811	71,201
Kansas	36.00	36.90	(D)	5,688	3,173	(D)
Michigan	39.90	43.10	34.70	140,687	140,937	164,790
Minnesota	42.60	50.30	48.70	132,188	117,702	140,597
Montana	37.60	30.10	28.00	17,522	13,635	16,884
Nebraska	38.70	43.80	31.60	123,569	120,450	120,080
New Mexico	60.00	60.00	60.00	12,960	11,640	12,000
New York	51.20	48.70	(D)	9,318	7,792	(D)
North Dakota	35.10	35.30	28.60	409,266	250,454	251,537
Oregon	36.90	38.30	40.10	9,520	7,086	7,699
South Dakota	36.90	36.00	33.20	9,815	8,280	8,068
Texas	45.00	46.00	46.00	6,120	16,836	11,776
Washington	41.50	33.10	32.10	92,130	71,662	62,114
Wisconsin	54.50	55.00	54.00	5,505	5,390	10,584
Wyoming	36.80	33.70	34.10	37,058	32,689	27,246
Other States	(NA)	(NA)	34.80	(NA)	(NA)	8,103
United States	38.00	39.10	34.50	1,235,255	982,385	1,015,485

(NA) Not Available. [1] Excludes beans grown for garden seed.
NASS, Crops Branch, (202) 720–2127.

Table 6-18.—Beans, dry edible: Season average wholesale (dealer) price per 100 pounds, selected markets, 2005/2006–2014/2015

Year beginning September	F.o.b. California points			F.o.b. Northern Colorado points: Pinto	F.o.b. Western Nebraska points: Great northern	F.o.b. Southern Idaho points: Small red	F.o.b. Michigan points:		
	Baby lima	Large lima	Blackeye				Pea bean (Navy)	Black	Light red kidney
	Dollars	*Dollars*	*Dollars*	*Dollars*	*Dollars*	*Dollars*	*Dollars*	*Dollars*	*Dollars*
2005/2006	38.28	47.62	44.26	23.47	24.32	27.33	24.44	29.54	27.74
2006/2007	47.25	66.26	47.38	29.52	31.61	30.95	29.07	30.94	35.33
2007/2008	42.39	65.64	41.51	38.66	47.65	44.52	44.48	43.47	53.71
2008/2009	58.87	73.39	51.97	40.85	54.00	52.71	36.63	46.70	57.67
2009/2010	43.98	71.59	45.12	39.45	41.57	43.32	40.37	46.04	43.56
2010/2011	40.13	59.53	42.47	36.08	41.81	47.74	41.94	43.05	48.25
2011/2012	57.88	60.50	(NA)	62.72	54.75	61.25	58.61	52.09	69.30
2012/2013	(NA)	60.00	54.75	45.54	53.96	53.36	45.57	46.36	63.32
2013/2014	(NA)	(NA)	(NA)	45.65	(NA)	52.13	55.25	52.50	68.88
2014/2015	56.50	(NA)	70.00	32.59	48.60	55.20	38.71	45.45	64.85

(NA) Not available.
ERS, Specialty Crops Branch, (202) 694–5253. Compiled from the Bean Market Summary, Agricultural Marketing Service, U.S. Department of Agriculture, Greeley, Colorado.

Table 6-19.—Beans, dry edible: United States exports to specified countries, 2010–2012[1]

Country	2010	2011	2012
	Metric tons	*Metric tons*	*Metric tons*
Mexico	134,205.1	110,246.7	214,730.2
Canada	40,737.0	48,625.7	49,751.0
United Kingdom	44,718.0	35,440.9	48,622.7
Taiwan	35,089.6	39,271.9	31,076.8
Dominican Republic	28,585.9	34,208.4	29,179.8
Italy(*)	9,464.5	19,094.4	14,031.6
Japan	16,035.5	14,083.7	12,322.0
France(*)	6,836.9	5,652.8	10,042.1
New Zealand(*)	328.2	8,104.8	9,034.0
Yemen(*)	2,130.0	205.3	6,100.3
Guatemala	8,364.1	6,902.4	5,765.7
Angola	7,975.9	7,969.5	5,382.2
Australia(*)	3,216.2	3,712.3	4,506.8
Haiti	16,919.4	4,366.4	3,846.6
Belgium-Luxembourg(*)	4,865.8	2,258.5	3,560.6
Mozambique	0.0	0.0	2,912.0
Jamaica	1,667.7	2,971.5	2,774.4
Algeria	2,322.6	1,642.6	2,739.1
Turkey	4,554.0	125.7	2,550.1
Malaysia	1,447.6	2,368.4	2,526.3
Russia	124.5	478.5	2,170.3
Netherlands	2,328.5	827.2	2,035.7
Malawi	1,248.1	948.2	1,865.9
French West Indies(*)	1,799.5	1,988.2	1,605.5
Cote d'Ivoire	0.0	0.0	1,520.0
Africa, not elsewhere specified(*)	1,867.6	1,482.3	1,414.2
Korea, South	2,315.2	1,443.3	1,399.6
Hong Kong	758.4	904.4	1,137.9
South Africa	162.2	97.5	1,067.4
Spain	1,855.6	556.2	992.7
Rest of World	30,389.1	31,549.6	12,360.8
World Total	412,312.4	387,527.2	489,024.3

(*) Denotes a country that is a summarization of its component countries. [1] Excluding seed bean exports.
FAS, Office of Global Analysis, (202) 720-6301. Compiled from U.S. Census data.

Table 6-20.—Chickpeas & lentils, dried: United States exports by class and quantity, 2010–2012[1]

Country	2010	2011	2012
	Metric tons	*Metric tons*	*Metric tons*
Dried chickpeas:			
Spain	14,846.60	15,304.00	19,137.00
India	6,596.40	6,350.60	8,457.60
Turkey	968.00	1,282.50	7,391.70
Canada	3,695.10	7,502.20	4,484.30
Pakistan	2,213.80	3,180.70	3,664.00
Portugal	0.00	362.00	3,447.70
Italy(*)	3,237.50	6,896.10	2,895.60
Peru	1,035.40	2,085.10	2,882.60
Algeria	1,857.60	1,703.10	2,617.70
Lebanon	1,545.90	1,842.00	2,144.50
Israel(*)	433.00	792.40	2,022.10
Japan	242.90	1,126.80	1,697.10
New Zealand(*)	351.10	697.90	1,635.00
Philippines	252.20	438.50	1,610.70
United Arab Emirates	105.30	180.30	1,034.50
United Kingdom	513.30	172.90	843.50
Malaysia	217.40	221.30	808.90
France(*)	0.00	0.00	717.90
Colombia	1,178.90	3,410.90	635.80
Belgium-Luxembourg(*)	0.00	408.50	468.30
Sri Lanka	0.00	0.00	408.00
Taiwan	222.80	348.40	318.30
Trinidad and Tobago	108.70	315.30	301.90
Indonesia	0.00	88.70	261.40
Tunisia	0.00	372.80	231.90
Thailand	0.00	62.00	229.60
Russia	0.00	172.00	222.60
Vietnam	0.00	139.20	191.70
Greece	0.00	21.80	185.50
Venezuela	0.00	2.80	185.50
Rest of World	1,916.40	2,294.80	1,302.60
World Total	41,538.40	57,776.00	72,435.20
Dried lentils:			
India	40,164.00	12,011.80	31,212.80
Spain	26,173.30	20,647.90	25,411.30
Peru	10,403.50	14,725.90	10,084.60
Sudan(*)	10,051.80	22,444.20	9,539.10
Germany(*)	2,441.40	3,990.70	9,247.50
Ethiopia(*)	4,857.60	368.90	8,131.00
Canada	14,676.50	13,573.00	7,542.70
Italy(*)	3,698.80	10,038.70	7,321.00
Mexico	5,093.10	3,207.10	7,244.10
Belgium-Luxembourg(*)	1,328.80	3,904.10	3,737.30
Turkey	10,467.50	2,252.80	3,411.00
Djibouti	0	0	3,334.00
Somalia	0	0	3,255.40
Syria	0	0	2,800.00
Cameroon	0	0	2,440.00
Bangladesh	127.80	543.10	2,071.20
Israel(*)	2	51.90	1,875.30
Greece	3,117.90	1,887.30	1,874.90
Jordan	0	136.60	1,872.30
French Pacific Islands(*)	1,329.60	1,158.20	1,698.90
Netherlands	1,000.50	1,995.80	1,417.00
Sierra Leone	144.60	180.00	1,185.70
Chad	0	0	1,107.30
Pakistan	6,117.50	2,211.30	1,048.00
Burkina Faso	224.40	188.40	935.90
Egypt	3,244.90	2,193.80	752.40
Sri Lanka	8,867.60	1,391.70	731.90
Mali	0	0	609.10
Haiti	4,662.40	1,859.10	578.00
Algeria	4,198.50	1,019.00	574.80
Rest of World	27,430.70	16,616.10	5,186.60
World Total	189,824.60	138,597.20	158,231.00

(*) Denotes a country that is a summarization of its component countries.　　[1] Excluding seed pea exports.
FAS, Office of Global Analysis, (202) 720-6301.

Table 6-21.—Peas, dry: United States exports to specified countries, 2010–2012 [1]

Country	2010	2011	2012
	Metric tons	Metric tons	Metric tons
India	166,003	65,038	127,120
China	56,869	12,433	26,301
Kenya	22,008	32,575	26,169
Philippines	24,488	16,324	17,079
Pakistan	43,658	10,197	14,874
Peru	9,637	10,524	12,945
Ethiopia(*)	27,131	28,774	11,741
Canada	27,962	13,432	11,431
Djibouti	8,133	13,004	8,055
South Africa	12,645	3,431	7,712
Korea, South	3,935	4,881	5,829
Mexico	6,125	3,759	4,584
Mozambique	87	749	4,289
Indonesia	8,708	7,572	3,867
Colombia	6,176	2,970	3,684
Taiwan	6,152	6,696	3,602
Belgium-Luxembourg(*)	186	70	3,508
Somalia	0	3,109	2,948
Chad	0	5,209	2,833
Mali	488	550	2,655
Sri Lanka	3,282	6,545	2,393
Spain	1,001	438	2,365
Zimbabwe	1,338	2,306	2,063
Cameroon	4,625	3,860	1,970
Congo (Kinshasa)	0	2,088	1,956
Uganda	220	3,506	1,631
Togo	0	1,248	1,610
Russia	1,943	1,363	1,487
Tanzania	4,076	1,731	1,360
Bangladesh	4,424	2,152	1,359
Rest of World	45,693	38,376	12,977
World Total	496,994	304,908	332,398

(*) Denotes a country that is a summarization of its component countries. [1] Excluding seed pea exports.
FAS, Office of Global Analysis, (202) 720-6301.

Table 6-22.—Hops: Area, yield, production, price, value, and Sept. 1 stocks, United States, 2005–2014

Year	Area harvested	Yield per acre	Production	Marketing year average price per pound received by farmers	Value of production	Stocks Sept. 1	Stocks Mar. 1
	1,000 acres	Pounds	1,000 pounds	Dollars per pound	1,000 dollars	1,000 pounds	1,000 pounds
2005	29.5	1,796	52,915	1.94	102,818	60,000	76,000
2006	29.4	1,964	57,672	2.05	118,008	49,000	69,000
2007	30.9	1,949	60,253	2.99	179,978	47,000	70,000
2008	40.9	1,971	80,630	4.03	325,092	47,000	66,000
2009	39.7	2,383	94,678	3.57	337,874	65,000	82,000
2010	31.3	2,093	65,493	3.28	214,589	83,000	102,000
2011	29.8	2,175	64,782	3.14	203,378	87,000	121,000
2012	29.7	1,985	58,911	3.17	186,876	96,000	120,000
2013	35.3	1,962	69,246	3.35	232,308	(NA)	115,000
2014	38.0	1,868	70,996	3.83	271,992	90,000	121,000

(NA) Not available.
NASS, Crops Branch, (202) 720–2127.

Table 6-23.—Hops: Area, yield, and production, by State and United States, 2012–2014

State	Area harvested			Yield per acre			Production		
	2012	2013	2014	2012	2013	2014	2012	2013	2014
	1,000 acres	1,000 acres	1,000 acres	Pounds	Pounds	Pounds	1,000 pounds	1,000 pounds	1,000 pounds
Idaho	2,596	3,356	3,743	1,841	1,740	1,847	4,778.2	5,837.9	6,913.8
Oregon	4,391	4,835	5,410	1,746	1,764	1,520	7,667.6	8,530.5	8,221.0
Washington	22,696	27,097	28,858	2,047	2,025	1,936	46,465.6	54,877.7	55,861.1
United States ...	29,683	35,288	38,011	1,985	1,962	1,868	58,911.4	69,246.1	70,995.9

NASS, Crops Branch, (202) 720–2127.

Table 6-24.—Hops: Marketing year average price and value of production, by State and United States, 2012–2014

State	Marketing year average price per pound			Value of production		
	2012	2013	2014	2012	2013	2014
	Dollars	Dollars	Dollars	1,000 dollars	1,000 dollars	1,000 dollars
Idaho	2.69	2.62	2.75	12,853	15,295	19,013
Oregon	3.91	3.76	4.34	29,980	32,075	35,679
Washington	3.10	3.37	3.89	144,043	184,938	217,300
United States ...	3.17	3.35	3.83	186,876	232,308	271,992

NASS, Crops Branch, (202) 720–2127.

Table 6-25.—Hops: United States exports by country of destination and imports by country of origin, 2010–2012

Country	2010	2011	2012
	Metric tons	Metric tons	Metric tons
United Kingdom	1,344	1,206	1,561
Mexico	1,192	1,156	1,258
Germany(*)	1,328	1,001	1,200
Brazil	1,147	1,031	1,047
Belgium-Luxembourg(*)	1,331	1,086	939
Colombia	803	781	804
Canada	1,613	760	742
Japan	755	663	525
China	522	426	334
Argentina	249	239	330
Venezuela	135	135	297
Hong Kong	214	272	271
Australia(*)	222	214	203
Korea, South	154	195	176
South Africa	97	86	162
Peru	222	269	143
Philippines	277	179	116
Chile	69	119	111
Ecuador	307	134	97
Netherlands	41	44	97
Dominican Republic	71	106	85
Bolivia	118	23	79
India	208	178	58
Guatemala	57	38	50
Russia	169	70	49
Nigeria	64	55	44
Vietnam	184	112	44
Tanzania	48	33	38
Ireland	2	60	38
Thailand	66	93	34
Indonesia	8	21	33
Panama	60	32	31
Costa Rica	26	12	26
Kenya	52	9	26
Uruguay	0	21	23
New Zealand(*)	8	9	22
Malaysia	74	36	18
El Salvador	26	17	16
Cambodia	8	7	15
Singapore	5	18	14
Rest of World	388	314	119
World Total	13,661	11,257	11,274

(*) Denotes a country that is a summarization of its component countries.
FAS, Office of Global Analysis, (202) 720-6301.

CHAPTER VII

STATISTICS OF CATTLE, HOGS, AND SHEEP

This chapter contains information about most kinds of farm livestock and livestock products, with the exception of dairy and poultry. The information relates to inventories, production, disposition, prices, and income for farm animals, and to livestock slaughter, meat production, and market statistics for meat animals.

Table 7-1.—All cattle and calves: Operations, inventory, and value, United States, Jan. 1, 2006–2015

Year	Operations [1]	Inventory	Value	
			Per head	Total
	Number	*Thousands*	*Dollars*	*1,000 dollars*
2006	971,400	96,342	1,009	97,230,415
2007	965,510	96,573	922	89,063,310
2008	955,500	96,035	990	95,112,820
2009	946,000	94,721	872	82,435,620
2010	935,000	94,081	832	78,150,010
2011	922,000	92,887	947	87,786,137
2012	915,000	91,160	1,111	100,817,090
2013		90,095	1,139	101,731,742
2014		88,526	1,223	108,255,950
2015 [2]		89,800	1,587	142,548,460

[1] Operation estimates discontinued after 2012. [2] Preliminary.
NASS, Livestock Branch, (202) 720–3570.

Table 7-2.—All cattle and calves: Number by class, United States, Jan. 1, 2006–2015

Year	All cattle and calves [1]	Cows and heifers that have calved		500 pounds and over					Calves under 500 pounds
		Beef cows	Milk cows	Heifers			Steers	Bulls	
				Beef cow replacements	Milk cow replacements	Other			
	Thousands	*Thousands*	*Thousands*	*Thousands*	*Thousands*	*Thousands*	*Thousands*	*Thousands*	*Thousands*
2006	96,342	32,703	9,104	5,864	4,298	9,788	16,988	2,258	15,339
2007	96,573	32,644	9,145	5,835	4,325	9,914	17,185	2,214	15,311
2008	96,035	32,435	9,257	5,647	4,415	9,793	17,163	2,207	15,118
2009	94,721	31,794	9,333	5,550	4,410	9,644	16,809	2,188	14,994
2010	94,081	31,440	9,087	5,443	4,551	9,784	16,568	2,190	15,019
2011	92,887	30,913	9,156	5,135	4,577	9,938	16,394	2,165	14,610
2012	91,160	30,282	9,236	5,281	4,618	9,546	15,957	2,100	14,141
2013	90,095	29,631	9,221	5,429	4,546	9,281	15,931	2,074	13,983
2014	88,526	29,085	9,208	5,551	4,549	8,869	15,668	2,038	13,558
2015 [2]	89,800	29,693	9,307	5,777	4,615	8,847	15,779	2,104	13,677

[1] Totals may not add due to rounding. [2] Preliminary.
NASS, Livestock Branch, (202) 720–3570.

　　STATISTICS OF CATTLE, HOGS, AND SHEEP

Table 7-3.—All cattle and calves: Inventory and value, by State and
United States, Jan. 1, 2014–2015

| State | Inventory | | Value | | | |
| | 2014 | 2015[1] | Value per head | | Total value | |
			2014	2015[1]	2014	2015[1]
	Thousands	Thousands	Dollars	Dollars	1,000 dollars	1,000 dollars
Alabama	1,270.0	1,220.0	1,000	1,380	1,270,000	1,683,600
Alaska	10.0	10.0	1,120	1,220	11,200	12,200
Arizona	920.0	880.0	1,150	1,470	1,058,000	1,293,600
Arkansas	1,650.0	1,640.0	1,110	1,500	1,831,500	2,460,000
California	5,250.0	5,150.0	1,140	1,510	5,985,000	7,776,500
Colorado	2,550.0	2,600.0	1,310	1,670	3,340,500	4,342,000
Connecticut	47.0	47.0	1,110	1,430	52,170	67,210
Delaware	16.0	17.0	1,200	1,330	19,200	22,610
Florida	1,670.0	1,700.0	1,090	1,530	1,820,300	2,601,000
Georgia	1,040.0	1,040.0	1,050	1,380	1,092,000	1,435,200
Hawaii	133.0	135.0	980	1,060	130,340	143,100
Idaho	2,240.0	2,300.0	1,240	1,670	2,777,600	3,841,000
Illinois	1,130.0	1,140.0	1,210	1,590	1,367,300	1,812,600
Indiana	860.0	870.0	1,110	1,430	954,600	1,244,100
Iowa	3,800.0	3,900.0	1,250	1,530	4,750,000	5,967,000
Kansas	5,800.0	6,000.0	1,250	1,490	7,250,000	8,940,000
Kentucky	2,110.0	2,060.0	1,060	1,400	2,236,600	2,884,000
Louisiana	790.0	790.0	1,170	1,530	924,300	1,208,700
Maine	85.0	85.0	1,110	1,300	94,350	110,500
Maryland	182.0	185.0	1,160	1,460	211,120	270,100
Massachusetts	39.0	38.0	1,050	1,300	40,950	49,400
Michigan	1,130.0	1,140.0	1,220	1,600	1,378,600	1,824,000
Minnesota	2,300.0	2,330.0	1,170	1,470	2,691,000	3,425,100
Mississippi	930.0	910.0	1,000	1,350	930,000	1,228,500
Missouri	3,850.0	4,000.0	1,190	1,570	4,581,500	6,280,000
Montana	2,550.0	2,500.0	1,530	2,120	3,901,500	5,300,000
Nebraska	6,250.0	6,300.0	1,350	1,600	8,437,500	10,080,000
Nevada	460.0	435.0	1,250	1,740	575,000	756,900
New Hampshire	32.0	30.0	1,150	1,390	36,800	41,700
New Jersey	27.0	28.0	1,260	1,380	34,020	38,640
New Mexico	1,310.0	1,340.0	1,260	1,680	1,650,600	2,251,200
New York	1,450.0	1,450.0	1,160	1,490	1,682,000	2,160,500
North Carolina	810.0	800.0	950	1,240	769,500	992,000
North Dakota	1,750.0	1,650.0	1,640	2,140	2,870,000	3,531,000
Ohio	1,250.0	1,250.0	1,180	1,410	1,475,000	1,762,500
Oklahoma	4,300.0	4,600.0	1,180	1,590	5,074,000	7,314,000
Oregon	1,280.0	1,300.0	1,210	1,650	1,548,800	2,145,000
Pennsylvania	1,610.0	1,530.0	1,180	1,500	1,899,800	2,295,000
Rhode Island	5.0	5.0	1,040	1,380	5,200	6,900
South Carolina	335.0	335.0	1,030	1,340	345,050	448,900
South Dakota	3,700.0	3,700.0	1,510	2,040	5,587,000	7,548,000
Tennessee	1,760.0	1,730.0	1,060	1,420	1,865,600	2,456,600
Texas	11,100.0	11,800.0	1,150	1,520	12,765,000	17,936,000
Utah	810.0	780.0	1,350	1,750	1,093,500	1,365,000
Vermont	260.0	260.0	1,210	1,510	314,600	392,600
Virginia	1,510.0	1,470.0	1,070	1,390	1,615,700	2,043,300
Washington	1,110.0	1,150.0	1,180	1,530	1,309,800	1,759,500
West Virginia	385.0	370.0	1,150	1,460	442,750	540,200
Wisconsin	3,400.0	3,500.0	1,240	1,630	4,216,000	5,705,000
Wyoming	1,270.0	1,300.0	1,530	2,120	1,943,100	2,756,000
United States	88,526.0	89,800.0	1,223	1,587	108,255,950	142,548,460

[1] Preliminary.
NASS, Livestock Branch, (202) 720–3570.

Table 7-4.—Cattle and calves, Jan. 1: Number by class, State and United States, 2014–2015

State	Cows and heifers that have calved				Heifers, 500 pounds and over					
	Beef cows		Milk cows		Beef cow replacements		Milk cow replacements		Other	
	2014	2015[1]	2014	2015[1]	2014	2015[1]	2014	2015[1]	2014	2015[1]
	1,000 head	*1,000 head*	*1,000 head*	*1,000 head*	*1,000 head*	*1,000 head*	*1,000 head*	*1,000 head*	*1,000 head*	*1,000 head*
Alabama	681.0	672.0	9.0	8.0	110.0	110.0	4.0	3.0	31.0	32.0
Alaska	4.3	4.3	0.3	0.3	0.8	0.9	0.1	0.1	0.1	0.1
Arizona	178.0	175.0	192.0	195.0	30.0	34.0	74.0	65.0	21.0	21.0
Arkansas	862.0	863.0	8.0	7.0	137.0	141.0	5.0	4.0	78.0	60.0
California	600.0	600.0	1,780.0	1,780.0	110.0	120.0	750.0	750.0	230.0	180.0
Colorado	710.0	745.0	140.0	145.0	150.0	160.0	100.0	100.0	490.0	490.0
Connecticut	4.0	5.0	19.0	19.0	1.5	2.0	9.0	8.0	0.5	1.0
Delaware	2.8	2.5	4.7	5.0	0.5	0.7	2.6	2.5	0.6	0.7
Florida	907.0	916.0	123.0	124.0	115.0	125.0	35.0	35.0	30.0	35.0
Georgia	500.0	489.0	80.0	81.0	82.0	83.0	25.0	25.0	29.0	34.0
Hawaii	71.8	69.8	2.2	2.2	9.0	11.0	1.0	1.0	4.0	5.0
Idaho	465.0	481.0	565.0	579.0	110.0	110.0	270.0	300.0	190.0	190.0
Illinois	355.0	376.0	95.0	94.0	63.0	64.0	45.0	50.0	102.0	101.0
Indiana	187.0	199.0	178.0	181.0	39.0	45.0	68.0	78.0	53.0	47.0
Iowa	895.0	920.0	205.0	210.0	160.0	170.0	120.0	130.0	640.0	640.0
Kansas	1,414.0	1,477.0	136.0	143.0	240.0	260.0	100.0	80.0	1,400.0	1,380.0
Kentucky	992.0	1,007.0	68.0	63.0	150.0	135.0	45.0	45.0	125.0	110.0
Louisiana	450.0	466.0	15.0	14.0	84.0	73.0	5.0	5.0	21.0	23.0
Maine	11.0	11.0	30.0	30.0	3.0	4.0	17.0	16.0	2.0	3.0
Maryland	38.0	41.0	50.0	50.0	9.5	8.0	25.0	24.0	7.5	10.0
Massachusetts	6.0	5.5	12.0	12.5	2.0	2.0	7.5	7.0	0.5	1.0
Michigan	119.0	112.0	381.0	403.0	29.0	23.0	164.0	167.0	47.0	40.0
Minnesota	340.0	350.0	460.0	460.0	80.0	85.0	280.0	280.0	170.0	165.0
Mississippi	477.0	468.0	13.0	12.0	91.0	95.0	6.0	6.0	43.0	35.0
Missouri	1,820.0	1,881.0	90.0	89.0	305.0	310.0	50.0	60.0	215.0	230.0
Montana	1,476.0	1,506.0	14.0	14.0	430.0	425.0	9.0	7.0	211.0	198.0
Nebraska	1,807.0	1,786.0	53.0	54.0	400.0	390.0	20.0	20.0	1,280.0	1,300.0
Nevada	231.0	217.0	29.0	28.0	36.0	37.0	9.0	9.0	31.0	29.0
New Hampshire	3.0	3.0	13.5	14.0	1.0	1.0	7.0	5.5	0.5	0.5
New Jersey	7.0	7.5	7.0	7.0	1.0	1.3	3.0	3.8	1.0	0.9
New Mexico	407.0	407.0	323.0	323.0	70.0	80.0	120.0	105.0	70.0	80.0
New York	105.0	115.0	615.0	615.0	45.0	40.0	355.0	350.0	40.0	45.0
North Carolina	355.0	363.0	45.0	47.0	72.0	69.0	20.0	18.0	24.0	28.0
North Dakota	923.0	904.0	17.0	16.0	170.0	164.0	10.0	6.0	210.0	185.0
Ohio	293.0	282.0	267.0	268.0	55.0	50.0	130.0	125.0	60.0	55.0
Oklahoma	1,795.0	1,900.0	45.0	40.0	325.0	405.0	20.0	25.0	340.0	390.0
Oregon	516.0	525.0	124.0	125.0	105.0	110.0	60.0	60.0	120.0	105.0
Pennsylvania	160.0	150.0	530.0	530.0	50.0	50.0	315.0	305.0	70.0	60.0
Rhode Island	1.5	1.5	0.9	0.9	0.5	0.5	0.5	0.5	0.2	0.2
South Carolina	169.0	170.0	16.0	15.0	30.0	30.0	6.0	5.0	12.0	12.0
South Dakota	1,635.0	1,632.0	95.0	98.0	340.0	380.0	50.0	65.0	490.0	495.0
Tennessee	864.0	883.0	46.0	47.0	130.0	135.0	30.0	25.0	85.0	70.0
Texas	3,910.0	4,180.0	440.0	470.0	660.0	710.0	220.0	240.0	1,420.0	1,480.0
Utah	340.0	324.0	95.0	96.0	70.0	78.0	46.0	48.0	69.0	64.0
Vermont	12.0	12.0	132.0	132.0	4.5	4.0	56.0	56.0	5.5	5.0
Virginia	637.0	637.0	93.0	93.0	115.0	105.0	40.0	43.0	70.0	47.0
Washington	214.0	198.0	266.0	277.0	50.0	51.0	125.0	133.0	130.0	136.0
West Virginia	191.0	185.0	9.0	9.0	35.0	32.0	5.0	4.0	24.0	21.0
Wisconsin	250.0	275.0	1,270.0	1,275.0	70.0	75.0	680.0	710.0	70.0	55.0
Wyoming	694.0	694.0	6.0	6.0	175.0	183.0	4.0	5.0	106.0	152.0
United States	29,085.4	29,693.1	9,207.6	9,306.9	5,551.3	5,777.4	4,548.7	4,615.4	8,869.4	8,847.4

See footnote(s) at end of table.

STATISTICS OF CATTLE, HOGS, AND SHEEP

Table 7-4.—Cattle and calves, Jan. 1: Number by class, State and United States, 2014–2015—Continued

State	Steers, 500 pounds and over		Bulls, 500 pounds and over		Calves under 500 pounds	
	2014	2015[1]	2014	2015[1]	2014	2015[1]
	Thousands	*Thousands*	*Thousands*	*Thousands*	*Thousands*	*Thousands*
Alabama	60.0	50.0	50.0	45.0	325.0	300.0
Alaska	0.4	0.3	1.9	2.4	2.1	1.6
Arizona	305.0	275.0	20.0	20.0	100.0	95.0
Arkansas	145.0	130.0	55.0	55.0	360.0	380.0
California	640.0	570.0	70.0	70.0	1,070.0	1,080.0
Colorado	780.0	790.0	45.0	55.0	135.0	115.0
Connecticut	2.0	2.0	0.5	0.5	10.5	9.5
Delaware	2.0	2.2	0.3	0.4	2.5	3.0
Florida	25.0	30.0	60.0	60.0	375.0	375.0
Georgia	36.0	45.0	28.0	28.0	260.0	255.0
Hawaii	7.0	9.0	4.0	4.0	34.0	33.0
Idaho	260.0	290.0	40.0	40.0	340.0	310.0
Illinois	250.0	220.0	25.0	25.0	195.0	210.0
Indiana	108.0	118.0	17.0	17.0	210.0	185.0
Iowa	1,270.0	1,310.0	60.0	60.0	450.0	460.0
Kansas	1,770.0	1,930.0	90.0	90.0	650.0	640.0
Kentucky	200.0	200.0	70.0	65.0	460.0	435.0
Louisiana	24.0	25.0	30.0	30.0	161.0	154.0
Maine	5.0	4.5	1.5	1.5	15.5	15.0
Maryland	15.0	16.0	4.0	4.0	33.0	32.0
Massachusetts	2.0	2.0	1.0	1.0	8.0	7.0
Michigan	175.0	175.0	15.0	15.0	200.0	205.0
Minnesota	490.0	500.0	35.0	35.0	445.0	455.0
Mississippi	62.0	61.0	38.0	38.0	200.0	195.0
Missouri	380.0	400.0	100.0	110.0	890.0	920.0
Montana	220.0	175.0	100.0	100.0	90.0	75.0
Nebraska	2,300.0	2,360.0	95.0	95.0	295.0	295.0
Nevada	44.0	44.0	13.0	12.0	67.0	59.0
New Hampshire	1.0	1.0	0.5	0.5	5.5	4.5
New Jersey	2.0	2.0	1.0	1.0	5.0	4.5
New Mexico	90.0	95.0	35.0	35.0	195.0	215.0
New York	32.0	35.0	18.0	15.0	240.0	235.0
North Carolina	44.0	36.0	30.0	29.0	220.0	210.0
North Dakota	270.0	215.0	55.0	50.0	95.0	110.0
Ohio	195.0	200.0	25.0	25.0	225.0	245.0
Oklahoma	910.0	870.0	125.0	140.0	740.0	830.0
Oregon	160.0	165.0	36.0	40.0	159.0	170.0
Pennsylvania	185.0	145.0	25.0	25.0	275.0	265.0
Rhode Island	0.5	0.5	0.1	0.1	0.8	0.8
South Carolina	12.0	9.0	14.0	14.0	76.0	80.0
South Dakota	690.0	680.0	95.0	100.0	305.0	250.0
Tennessee	135.0	120.0	60.0	60.0	410.0	390.0
Texas	2,370.0	2,500.0	280.0	320.0	1,800.0	1,900.0
Utah	85.0	78.0	23.0	22.0	82.0	70.0
Vermont	4.0	4.0	3.0	3.0	43.0	44.0
Virginia	170.0	155.0	40.0	40.0	345.0	350.0
Washington	160.0	180.0	19.0	18.0	146.0	157.0
West Virginia	45.0	44.0	14.0	13.0	62.0	62.0
Wisconsin	380.0	375.0	30.0	35.0	650.0	700.0
Wyoming	150.0	135.0	40.0	40.0	95.0	85.0
United States	15,667.9	15,778.5	2,037.8	2,104.4	13,557.9	13,676.9

[1] Preliminary.
NASS, Livestock Branch, (202) 720–3570.

Table 7-5.—Cows and calf crop: Cows and heifers that have calved, Jan. 1, 2014–2015, and calves born, by State and United States, 2013–2014

State	Cows and heifers that have calved		Calves born	
	Jan. 1		2013	2014
	2014	2015[1]		
	Thousands	Thousands	Thousands	Thousands
Alabama	690.0	680.0	600.0	570.0
Alaska	4.6	4.6	3.3	3.3
Arizona	370.0	370.0	280.0	290.0
Arkansas	870.0	870.0	750.0	730.0
California	2,380.0	2,380.0	2,010.0	1,950.0
Colorado	850.0	890.0	740.0	760.0
Connecticut	23.0	24.0	18.5	19.0
Delaware	7.5	7.5	5.0	6.0
Florida	1,030.0	1,040.0	830.0	830.0
Georgia	580.0	570.0	480.0	480.0
Hawaii	74.0	72.0	60.0	56.0
Idaho	1,030.0	1,060.0	940.0	950.0
Illinois	450.0	470.0	385.0	410.0
Indiana	365.0	380.0	325.0	330.0
Iowa	1,100.0	1,130.0	1,020.0	1,050.0
Kansas	1,550.0	1,620.0	1,280.0	1,320.0
Kentucky	1,060.0	1,070.0	950.0	950.0
Louisiana	465.0	480.0	370.0	360.0
Maine	41.0	41.0	32.0	32.0
Maryland	88.0	91.0	67.0	70.0
Massachusetts	18.0	18.0	18.0	17.0
Michigan	500.0	515.0	395.0	395.0
Minnesota	800.0	810.0	780.0	780.0
Mississippi	490.0	480.0	400.0	375.0
Missouri	1,910.0	1,970.0	1,730.0	1,760.0
Montana	1,490.0	1,520.0	1,470.0	1,480.0
Nebraska	1,860.0	1,840.0	1,680.0	1,610.0
Nevada	260.0	245.0	210.0	195.0
New Hampshire	16.5	17.0	13.5	13.5
New Jersey	14.0	14.5	9.5	9.0
New Mexico	730.0	730.0	560.0	560.0
New York	720.0	730.0	540.0	510.0
North Carolina	400.0	410.0	355.0	365.0
North Dakota	940.0	920.0	890.0	860.0
Ohio	560.0	550.0	480.0	460.0
Oklahoma	1,840.0	1,940.0	1,670.0	1,780.0
Oregon	640.0	650.0	620.0	630.0
Pennsylvania	690.0	680.0	570.0	520.0
Rhode Island	2.4	2.4	2.2	2.2
South Carolina	185.0	185.0	150.0	160.0
South Dakota	1,730.0	1,730.0	1,680.0	1,620.0
Tennessee	910.0	930.0	830.0	840.0
Texas	4,350.0	4,650.0	3,800.0	4,000.0
Utah	435.0	420.0	380.0	385.0
Vermont	144.0	144.0	116.0	107.0
Virginia	730.0	730.0	640.0	650.0
Washington	480.0	475.0	425.0	410.0
West Virginia	200.0	194.0	180.0	180.0
Wisconsin	1,520.0	1,550.0	1,350.0	1,400.0
Wyoming	700.0	700.0	640.0	660.0
United States	38,293.0	39,000.0	33,730.0	33,900.0

[1] Preliminary.
NASS, Livestock Branch, (202) 720–3570.

Table 7-6.—Cattle and calves: All cattle on feed, United States, Jan. 1, 2006–2015 [1]

Year	Inventory
	Thousands
2006	14,392
2007	14,647
2008	14,827
2009	13,900
2010	13,728
2011	14,132
2012	14,355
2013	13,703
2014	12,949
2015[2]	13,025

[1] Cattle and calves on feed are animals for slaughter market being fed a ration of grain or other concentrates and are expected to produce a carcass that will grade select or better. [2] Preliminary.
NASS, Livestock Branch, (202) 720–3570.

Table 7-7.—Cattle and calves: Total number on feed by State and United States, Jan. 1, 2014–2015

State	2014	2015 [1]
	1,000 head	*1,000 head*
Arizona	274.0	252.0
California	510.0	425.0
Colorado	960.0	930.0
Idaho	235.0	245.0
Illinois	260.0	230.0
Indiana	110.0	100.0
Iowa	1,230.0	1,220.0
Kansas	2,130.0	2,180.0
Kentucky	18.0	15.0
Maryland	10.0	10.0
Michigan	150.0	160.0
Minnesota	375.0	385.0
Missouri	75.0	70.0
Montana	54.0	40.0
Nebraska	2,420.0	2,530.0
Nevada	4.0	4.0
New York	23.0	26.0
North Dakota	38.0	44.0
Ohio	160.0	170.0
Oklahoma	265.0	265.0
Oregon	75.0	85.0
Pennsylvania	110.0	90.0
South Dakota	375.0	385.0
Tennessee	3.0	5.0
Texas	2,450.0	2,510.0
Utah	26.0	24.0
Virginia	20.0	20.0
Washington	195.0	210.0
West Virginia	5.0	4.0
Wisconsin	260.0	260.0
Wyoming	75.0	75.0
Other States [2]	54.3	56.0
United States	12,949.3	13,025.0

[1] Preliminary.   [2] Individual state estimates not available for states not shown, but are included in Other States.
NASS, Livestock Branch, (202) 720–3570.

Table 7-8.—Cattle: Average price per 100 pounds, by grades, at Nebraska Direct, Worthing, SD and Louisville, KY, 2005–2015

Year	Nebraska		Worthing, SD [1]		Louisville, KY	
	Choice		Cows [2]		Cows	
	Steers [3]	Heifers [4]	Commercial	Breaking utility	Breaking utility	85-95% Lean
	Dollars	*Dollars*	*Dollars*	*Dollars*	*Dollars*	*Dollars*
2005 65-80%	86.54	87.35	61.89	57.82		
2006 65-80%	85.55	86.58	58.72	54.19		
2007 65-80%	91.87	91.86	60.91	56.85	47.02	45.22
2008	93.07	93.04	63.15	61.32	52.80	42.99
2009	82.70	82.71	53.94	54.32	46.61	37.95
2010	95.81	95.41	NA	61.49	53.98	41.70
2011	111.52	111.55	74.25	71.34	67.20	53.92
2012	123.11	124.18	83.95	78.90	76.55	62.71
2013	127.13	127.37	84.83	78.52	79.22	71.00
2014	154.03	154.67	108.79	(NA)	(NA)	83.56
2015	148.71	148.09	100.39	(NA)	(NA)	78.27

(NA) Not available.   [1] 2004-2007 Sioux Falls, SD; 2008 to present Worthing, SD.   [2] All weights; simple average of price range.   [3] 1,100 to 1,500 pound weight range; weighted average of price range.   [4] 1,000 to 1,300 pound weight range; simple average of price range.
AMS, Livestock and Grain Market News, (202) 720–7316.

Table 7-9.—Cattle and calves: Production, disposition, cash receipts, and gross income, United States, 2005–2014

| Year | Calf crop [1] | Death loss | | Marketings [2] | | Inshipments [3] | Farm slaughter |
		Cattle	Calves	Cattle	Calves		Cattle and calves
	1,000 head	1,000 head	1,000 head	1,000 head	1,000 head	1,000 head	1,000 head
2005	37,106	1,718	2,335	43,665	8,888	21,010	188
2006	37,016	1,818	2,348	44,789	8,856	21,213	187
2007	36,759	1,856	2,394	45,008	8,956	21,104	188
2008	36,158	1,760	2,314	44,238	8,752	19,769	176
2009	35,939	1,741	2,323	43,369	8,530	19,550	167
2010	35,740	1,736	2,265	44,658	8,874	20,757	157
2011	35,357	1,787	2,230	44,875	8,401	20,357	148
2012	34,469	1,752	2,171	43,578	8,337	20,443	139
2013	33,730	1,730	2,140	43,259	8,007	19,965	128
2014	33,900	1,720	2,130	41,024	7,833	20,204	124

| Year | Production (live weight) [4] | Value of production | Cash receipts [5] | Value of home consumption | Gross income [6] | Average price per 100 pounds received by farmers | |
						Cattle	Calves
	1,000 pounds	1,000 dollars	1,000 dollars	1,000 dollars	1,000 dollars	Dollars	Dollars
2005	41,246,788	36,348,156	49,283,098	459,077	49,742,175	89.70	135.00
2006	41,824,568	35,490,732	49,110,330	447,857	49,558,187	87.20	133.00
2007	41,437,021	35,973,068	49,843,322	441,051	50,284,373	89.90	119.00
2008	41,586,134	35,597,898	48,394,131	404,745	48,798,876	89.10	110.00
2009	41,033,359	31,897,074	43,720,324	368,285	44,088,609	80.30	105.00
2010	41,379,839	36,850,474	51,246,136	405,789	51,651,925	92.20	117.00
2011	41,483,945	45,059,200	62,321,217	478,871	62,800,088	113.00	142.00
2012	40,920,479	48,059,904	66,090,126	525,630	66,615,756	121.00	172.00
2013	40,695,232	48,478,687	67,457,442	509,175	67,966,617	125.00	181.00
2014	40,279,611	60,770,098	81,251,415	620,827	81,872,242	153.00	264.00

[1] Calves born during the year.　[2] Includes custom slaughter for use on farms where produced and State outshipments, but excludes interfarm sales within the State.　[3] Includes cattle shipped in from other States, but excludes cattle for immediate slaughter.　[4] Adjustments made for changes in inventory and for inshipments.　[5] Receipts from marketings and sale of farm slaughter.　[6] Cash receipts from sales of cattle, calves, beef, and veal plus value of cattle and calves slaughtered for home consumption.

NASS, Livestock Branch, (202) 720–3570.

Table 7-10.—Cattle: Weighted average weight and price per 100 pounds, Texas-Oklahoma, Kansas, Colorado, Nebraska, Iowa-So. Minnesota Feedlots, 2005–2015 [1]

| Year | Steers SE/CH 65-80% | | | Steers SE/CH 35-65% | | |
	Price	Average Weight	Number of Head	Price	Average Weight	Number of Head
	Dollars	Pounds		Dollars	Pounds	
2005 ...	86.28	1,336	326,751	87.66	1,265	2,492,108
2006 ...	85.51	1,358	317,732	85.75	1,282	2,319,896
2007 ...	92.21	1,366	359,511	92.10	1,289	2,081,144
2008 ...	93.37	1,360	344,633	93.16	1,294	1,757,049
2009 ...	82.81	1,376	476,823	83.59	1,314	1,474,925
2010 ...	95.00	1,359	561,173	95.95	1,301	1,329,021
2011 ...	114.45	1,364	518,689	114.92	1,304	1,101,808
2012 ...	122.84	1,402	458,382	123.06	1,312	743,859
2013 ...	126.27	1,408	384,642	126.35	1,338	517,782
2014 ...	154.25	1,410	548,667	152.15	1,339	386,051
2015 ...	147.64	1,432	314,078	149.00	1,366	228,126

| Year | Heifers SE/CH 65-80% | | | Heifers SE/CH 35-65% | | |
	Price	Average Weight	Number of Head	Price	Average Weight	Number of Head
	Dollars	Pounds		Dollars	Pounds	
2005 ...	87.23	1,219	313,240	87.90	1,145	1,901,730
2006 ...	86.57	1,245	247,902	86.06	1,165	1,781,077
2007 ...	92.01	1,241	357,880	93.09	1,165	1,582,183
2008 ...	92.95	1,229	342,547	93.22	1,170	1,317,211
2009 ...	82.88	1,252	498,481	83.63	1,180	1,136,234
2010 ...	95.41	1,227	562,788	96.22	1,166	1,159,191
2011 ...	114.05	1,222	508,487	114.64	1,167	928,633
2012 ...	123.38	1,255	412,483	123.31	1,173	577,535
2013 ...	126.09	1,266	320,285	126.36	1,198	335,205
2014 ...	154.37	1,279	322,272	152.18	1,204	218,658
2015 ...	148.20	1,289	220,073	147.73	1,235	97,078

[1] Sales FOB the feedyard.　Estimated net weights after 3-4% shrink.
AMS, Livestock and Grain Market News, (202) 720–7316.

Table 7-11.—Cattle: Receipts at selected markets, 2005–2015

Year	Oklahoma City	Fort Collins [1]	Amarillo	South St. Joseph	Sioux Falls
	Thousands	Thousands	Thousands	Thousands	Thousands
2005	491	77	87	97	198
2006	471	85	69	114	179
2007	422	82	65	52	115
2008	465	80	43	84	90
2009	501	67	56	96	43
2010	492	63	74	105	153
2011	468	30	60	94	104
2012	399	72	43	121	153
2013	409	46	35	90	156
2014	382	(NA)	37	86	140
2015	368	(NA)	21	88	139

[1] Switch to Fort Collins market 2005.
AMS, Livestock & Grain Market News, (202) 720–7316.

Table 7-12.—Cattle and calves: Number slaughtered, United States, 2005–2014

Year	Cattle slaughter					Calf slaughter				
	Commercial			Farm	Total	Commercial			Farm	Total
	Federally inspected	Other	Total [1]			Federally inspected	Other	Total [1]		
	Thousands	Thou-sands	Thousands	Thou-sands	Thousands	Thousands	Thou-sands	Thou-sands	Thou-sands	Thou-sands
2005 ...	31,832	556	32,388	152	32,539	718	17	734	38	772
2006 ...	33,145	553	33,698	150	33,849	699	13	711	37	748
2007 ...	33,721	543	34,264	150	34,414	745	13	758	37	795
2008 ...	33,805	560	34,365	140	34,505	942	15	957	36	993
2009 ...	32,765	573	33,338	132	33,470	930	14	944	35	979
2010 ...	33,702	547	34,249	124	34,373	864	14	879	33	912
2011 ...	33,555	532	34,087	119	34,205	839	14	853	30	882
2012 ...	32,426	525	32,951	112	33,062	760	12	772	27	800
2013 ...	31,947	515	32,462	103	32,565	751	11	762	26	788
2014 ...	29,684	486	30,170	99	30,268	558	8	566	26	591

[1] Totals are based on unrounded numbers.
NASS, Livestock Branch, (202) 720-3570.

Table 7-13.—Cattle and calves: Number slaughtered under Federal inspection, and average live weight, 2005–2014

Year	Cattle		Calves	
	Number slaughtered	Average live weight [1]	Number slaughtered	Average live weight [1]
	Thousands	Pounds	Thousands	Pounds
2005	31,832	1,259	718	352
2006	33,145	1,277	699	344
2007	33,721	1,275	745	304
2008	33,805	1,284	942	255
2009	32,765	1,296	930	248
2010	33,702	1,282	864	260
2011	33,555	1,280	839	260
2012	32,426	1,305	760	257
2013	31,947	1,317	751	248
2014	29,684	1,333	558	281

[1] Excludes postmortem condemnations.
NASS, Livestock Branch, (202) 720-3570.

Table 7-14.—Cattle and calves: Number slaughtered commercially, total and average live weight, by State and United States, 2014[1]

State	Cattle			Calves		
	Number slaughtered	Total live weight[2]	Average live weight[2]	Number slaughtered	Total live weight[2]	Average live weight[2]
	Thousands	1,000 pounds	Pounds	Thousands	1,000 pounds	Pounds
Alabama	5.9	5,957	1,013	0.1	24	422
Alaska	0.6	645	1,025	(Y)	(Y)	(Y)
Arizona	523.2	701,960	1,345	(Y)	(Y)	(Y)
Arkansas	5.6	5,408	959	(D)	(D)	(D)
California	1,360.1	1,770,700	1,312	122.8	11,733	97
Colorado	2,464.9	3,343,473	1,357	(Y)	(Y)	(Y)
Delaware-Maryland	33.5	42,837	1,281	(D)	(D)	(D)
Florida	(D)	(D)	(D)	(D)	(D)	(D)
Georgia	(D)	(D)	(D)	1.1	598	541
Hawaii	10.4	11,627	1,115	(D)	(D)	(D)
Idaho	30.3	33,826	1,182	0.2	79	444
Illinois	(D)	(D)	(D)	11.3	4,860	430
Indiana	37.4	39,771	1,064	5.5	1,520	279
Iowa	(D)	(D)	(D)	(D)	(D)	(D)
Kansas	5,907.5	7,856,257	1,330	0.1	44	393
Kentucky	14.7	14,713	1,002	0.3	135	443
Louisiana	6.0	4,867	809	0.8	396	496
Michigan	522.8	711,825	1,370	1.5	448	299
Minnesota	664.2	954,718	1,444	(D)	(D)	(D)
Mississippi	1.3	1,045	814	(D)	(D)	(D)
Missouri	57.1	63,165	1,107	0.2	75	368
Montana	21.3	24,008	1,129	(Y)	(Y)	(Y)
Nebraska	6,683.7	9,299,912	1,393	(D)	(D)	(D)
Nevada	1.4	1,460	1,024	(D)	(D)	(D)
New England[3]	21.1	22,510	1,071	5.8	877	151
New Jersey	34.2	37,028	1,086	58.0	24,672	426
New Mexico	3.7	3,945	1,056	(D)	(D)	(D)
New York	33.8	38,554	1,155	65.9	8,020	123
North Carolina	70.5	85,062	1,214	0.8	365	430
North Dakota	9.8	11,993	1,229	(D)	(D)	(D)
Ohio	103.9	121,122	1,176	(D)	(D)	(D)
Oklahoma	22.8	22,978	1,010	0.3	118	455
Oregon	66.0	79,834	1,226	(D)	(D)	(D)
Pennsylvania	962.2	1,159,584	1,209	106.7	44,414	416
South Carolina	169.4	196,414	1,170	(D)	(D)	(D)
South Dakota	(D)	(D)	(D)	(D)	(D)	(D)
Tennessee	53.4	47,243	903	0.1	59	433
Texas	5,322.0	6,770,855	1,275	6.0	3,400	570
Utah	563.7	758,430	1,347	(D)	(D)	(D)
Virginia	12.2	12,649	1,040	0.3	111	436
Washington	1,059.0	1,414,031	1,339	(D)	(D)	(D)
West Virginia	8.7	8,646	992	(D)	(D)	(D)
Wisconsin	1,327.3	1,824,374	1,382	73.9	34,012	462
Wyoming	6.3	6,939	1,096	(D)	(D)	(D)
United States	30,169.7	40,045,321	1,330	565.8	159,090	283

(Y) Less than level of precision shown. (D) Withheld to avoid disclosing data for individual operations. [1] Includes slaughter in federally inspected and other slaughter plants; excludes animals slaughtered on farms. Average live weight is based on unrounded numbers. Totals may not add due to rounding. [2] Excludes postmortem condemnations. [3] New England includes Connecticut, Maine, Massachusetts, New Hampshire, Rhode Island, and Vermont.
NASS, Livestock Branch, (202) 720-3570.

Table 7-15.—Cattle and calves: Production, disposition, cash receipts, and gross income, by State and United States, 2014

State	Marketings [1]		Inship-ments [2]	Farm slaugh-ter [3]	Production (live weight) [4]	Value of production	Cash receipts [5]	Value of home con-sump-tion	Gross income [6]
	Cattle	Calves							
	1,000 head	1,000 head	1,000 head	1,000 head	1,000 pounds	1,000 dollars	1,000 dollars	1,000 dollars	1,000 dollars
Alabama	486.0	88.0	7.0	2.0	478,169	616,002	669,559	4,346	673,905
Alaska	1.3	0.1	-	0.3	1,991	2,849	2,073	411	2,484
Arizona	546.0	112.0	370.0	1.0	538,327	841,131	1,165,143	2,979	1,168,122
Arkansas	604.0	227.0	161.0	1.0	469,397	624,530	775,583	7,344	782,927
California	2,002.0	491.0	670.0	7.0	1,894,827	2,630,197	3,719,100	13,329	3,732,429
Colorado	1,877.0	87.0	1,370.0	1.0	1,582,555	2,409,626	3,831,976	15,788	3,847,764
Connecticut	10.4	8.1	2.0	0.4	13,434	21,330	21,938	1,257	23,195
Delaware	3.3	1.5	1.0	0.2	4,175	6,499	6,274	438	6,712
Florida	241.0	561.0	64.0	1.0	461,886	818,405	867,792	4,073	871,865
Georgia	242.0	221.0	27.0	2.0	342,763	528,610	547,284	6,179	553,463
Hawaii	16.0	33.0	-	0.5	35,983	64,887	61,021	803	61,824
Idaho	1,085.0	152.0	435.0	4.0	1,134,200	1,731,000	2,041,176	15,215	2,056,391
Illinois	361.0	81.0	96.0	6.0	457,027	751,184	810,029	22,534	832,563
Indiana	258.0	112.0	98.0	4.0	261,556	381,266	437,502	18,821	456,323
Iowa	2,207.0	101.5	1,535.0	1.5	1,909,156	2,854,242	4,665,691	17,393	4,683,084
Kansas	4,389.0	3.0	3,485.0	3.0	3,707,120	4,687,210	8,972,196	22,104	8,994,300
Kentucky	505.0	434.0	45.0	3.0	571,419	962,296	1,040,853	14,713	1,055,566
Louisiana	131.0	195.0	2.0	1.0	202,945	357,142	354,783	2,053	356,836
Maine	15.3	15.0	3.5	1.0	17,018	27,042	27,783	3,655	31,438
Maryland	47.6	18.1	7.0	0.6	63,768	96,631	101,003	3,986	104,989
Massachusetts	8.6	9.1	2.0	0.3	7,862	12,577	14,756	1,507	16,263
Michigan	329.0	45.0	60.0	3.0	434,337	630,490	664,566	20,798	685,364
Minnesota	894.0	106.0	390.0	5.0	1,106,642	1,604,194	1,932,975	38,414	1,971,389
Mississippi	229.0	131.0	12.0	2.0	183,757	273,628	294,831	7,726	302,557
Missouri	742.0	781.0	104.0	6.0	1,170,413	2,119,651	2,047,430	30,372	2,077,802
Montana	1,376.0	220.0	159.0	3.0	1,115,644	1,776,184	1,999,274	14,743	2,014,017
Nebraska	5,986.0	83.0	4,710.0	1.0	5,123,860	7,414,063	12,854,372	15,221	12,869,593
Nevada	183.5	89.0	69.0	0.5	172,530	289,470	392,550	3,234	395,784
New Hampshire	7.1	7.0	0.5	0.3	8,379	13,931	15,381	1,431	16,812
New Jersey	3.8	4.3	1.4	0.3	6,270	10,460	9,519	1,051	10,570
New Mexico	692.0	104.5	315.0	1.5	532,694	876,860	1,092,753	5,417	1,098,170
New York	188.5	270.5	22.0	3.0	262,818	424,407	414,612	12,958	427,570
North Carolina	212.5	139.5	6.0	1.0	292,733	419,441	431,161	5,218	436,379
North Dakota	882.2	101.0	84.0	0.8	674,214	1,085,847	1,334,430	6,762	1,341,192
Ohio	344.0	120.0	60.0	4.0	407,418	611,561	654,667	29,854	684,521
Oklahoma	2,080.0	330.0	1,150.0	5.0	2,029,020	3,295,225	4,001,477	29,111	4,030,588
Oregon	454.0	189.0	100.0	7.0	568,075	922,031	976,374	17,871	994,245
Pennsylvania	454.0	190.5	110.0	6.5	461,170	708,834	904,395	35,375	939,770
Rhode Island	1.2	1.0	0.4	0.1	1,262	1,948	1,974	492	2,466
South Carolina	135.0	16.0	8.0	2.0	157,961	201,035	203,709	5,101	208,810
South Dakota	1,746.0	415.0	680.0	1.0	1,523,888	2,538,536	3,183,825	13,688	3,197,513
Tennessee	497.0	323.0	30.0	3.0	525,846	773,774	825,052	14,990	840,042
Texas	5,430.0	252.0	2,950.0	8.0	6,005,807	9,197,494	11,011,347	34,772	11,046,119
Utah	526.0	44.0	191.0	2.0	328,739	488,740	800,004	13,058	813,062
Vermont	36.4	62.1	5.0	1.5	56,412	92,769	83,540	4,017	87,557
Virginia	370.0	256.0	9.5	3.5	451,053	679,914	714,077	11,468	725,545
Washington	485.0	10.0	170.0	6.0	568,600	820,392	947,712	19,709	967,421
West Virginia	125.0	75.0	20.0	2.0	134,658	219,366	254,043	6,363	260,406
Wisconsin	836.0	370.2	107.0	3.8	1,263,321	1,918,114	1,868,820	38,272	1,907,092
Wyoming	742.0	146.5	300.0	0.5	556,512	937,083	1,203,030	4,413	1,207,443
United States	41,023.7	7,832.5	20,204.3	124.1	40,279,611	60,770,098	81,251,415	620,827	81,872,242

- Represents zero.   [1] Includes custom slaughter for use on farms where produced and State outshipments, but excludes interfarm sales within the State.   [2] Includes cattle shipped in from other states, but excludes cattle for immediate slaughter.   [3] Excludes custom slaughter for farmers at commercial establishments.   [4] Adjustments made for changes in inventory and for inshipments.   [5] Includes receipts from marketings and sales of farm-slaughter.   [6] Includes cash receipts from sales of cattle, calves, beef, and veal plus value of cattle and calves slaughtered for home consumption.

NASS, Livestock Branch, (202) 720–3570.

Table 7-16.—Cattle and calves: Inventory Jan 1, 2014–2015, and number of operations, 2012, by State and United States [1]

State	January 1 Cattle inventory		Operations with cattle [2]
	2014	2015 [3]	2012
	1,000 head	*1,000 head*	*Number*
Alabama	1,270	1,220	21,149
Alaska	10	10	134
Arizona	920	880	6,029
Arkansas	1,650	1,640	25,866
California	5,250	5,150	16,764
Colorado	2,550	2,600	13,970
Connecticut	47	47	1,452
Delaware	16	17	431
Florida	1,670	1,700	21,255
Georgia	1,040	1,040	17,188
Hawaii	133	135	1,314
Idaho	2,240	2,300	10,957
Illinois	1,130	1,140	16,550
Indiana	860	870	17,370
Iowa	3,800	3,900	26,827
Kansas	5,800	6,000	27,568
Kentucky	2,110	2,060	40,141
Louisana	790	790	13,687
Maine	85	85	2,423
Maryland	182	185	3,499
Massachusetts	39	38	1,423
Michigan	1,130	1,140	13,626
Minnesota	2,300	2,330	23,702
Mississippi	930	910	15,940
Missouri	3,850	4,000	53,401
Montana	2,550	2,500	11,845
Nebraska	6,250	6,300	23,280
Nevada	460	435	1,822
New Hampshire	32	30	1,091
New Jersey	27	28	1,224
New Mexico	1,310	1,340	12,796
New York	1,450	1,450	13,559
North Carolina	810	800	19,548
North Dakota	1,750	1,650	9,868
Ohio	1,250	1,250	25,501
Oklahoma	4,300	4,600	51,043
Oregon	1,280	1,300	14,351
Pennsylvania	1,610	1,530	25,189
Rhode Island	5	5	300
South Carolina	335	335	8,121
South Dakota	3,700	3,700	15,583
Tennessee	1,760	1,730	38,826
Texas	11,100	11,800	151,362
Utah	810	780	8,625
Vermont	260	260	2,784
Virginia	1,510	1,470	23,911
Washington	1,110	1,150	11,861
West Virginia	385	370	12,067
Wisconsin	3,400	3,500	29,908
Wyoming	1,270	1,300	6,115
United States	88,526	89,800	913,246

[1] An operation is any place having one or more head of cattle on hand on December 31. [2] State level estimates only available in conjunction with the Census of Agriculture every 5 years. [3] Preliminary.
NASS, Livestock Branch, (202) 720–3570.

Table 7-17.—Cattle: Number slaughtered under Federal inspection and percentage distribution, by classes, 2005–2014[1]

Year	Number						Percentage of total					
	Steers	Heif-ers	Cows			Bulls	Steers	Heif-ers	Cows			Bulls
			Dairy cows	Other cows	Total cows				Dairy cows	Other cows	Total cows	
	Thou-sands	Thou-sands	Thou-sands	Thou-sands	Thou-sands	Thou-sands	Per-cent	Per-cent	Per-cent	Per-cent	Per-cent	Per-cent
2005 ...	16,797	9,761	2,252	2,523	4,775	498	52.8	30.7	7.1	7.9	15.0	1.6
2006 ...	17,478	9,820	2,354	2,983	5,336	511	52.7	29.6	7.1	9.0	16.1	1.5
2007 ...	17,285	10,207	2,497	3,178	5,675	554	51.3	30.3	7.4	9.4	16.8	1.6
2008 ...	16,949	10,091	2,591	3,569	6,161	605	50.1	29.9	7.7	10.6	18.2	1.8
2009 ...	16,312	9,743	2,815	3,325	6,140	570	49.8	29.7	8.6	10.1	18.7	1.7
2010 ...	16,596	10,047	2,807	3,630	6,437	622	49.2	29.8	8.3	10.8	19.1	1.8
2011 ...	16,539	9,726	2,914	3,798	6,712	579	49.3	29.0	8.7	11.3	20.0	1.7
2012 ...	16,160	9,269	3,102	3,344	6,446	551	49.8	28.6	9.6	10.3	19.9	1.7
2013 ...	16,003	9,132	3,125	3,130	6,255	557	50.1	28.6	9.8	9.8	19.6	1.7
2014 ...	15,378	8,378	2,816	2,565	5,380	548	51.8	28.2	9.5	8.6	18.1	1.8

[1] Totals and percentages based on unrounded data and may not equal sum of classes due to rounding.
NASS, Livestock Branch, (202) 720-3570.

Table 7-18.—Cattle and calves: Average dressed weight under Federal inspection, 2005–2014[1]

Year	Cattle					Calves
	All cattle	Steers	Heifers	Cows	Bulls	
	Pounds	Pounds	Pounds	Pounds	Pounds	Pounds
2005	769	817	750	621	905	216
2006	781	833	767	622	914	207
2007	776	830	764	617	893	182
2008	778	838	772	609	888	150
2009	784	847	782	610	878	147
2010	773	835	768	607	875	154
2011	773	841	773	596	868	154
2012	790	859	792	608	877	152
2013	796	863	794	620	880	146
2014	808	872	800	627	898	166

[1] Excludes postmortem condemnations.
NASS, Livestock Branch, (202) 720-3570.

Table 7-19.—Beef cows: Inventory Jan 1, 2014–2015, and number of operations, 2012, by State and United States [1]

State	January 1 beef cow inventory		Operations with beef cows [2]
	2014	2015 [3]	2012
	1,000 head	*1,000 head*	*Number*
Alabama	681	672	19,685
Alaska	4	4	98
Arizona	178	175	4,851
Arkansas	862	863	23,385
California	600	600	10,925
Colorado	710	745	11,267
Connecticut	4	5	1,003
Delaware	3	3	296
Florida	907	916	18,433
Georgia	500	489	15,175
Hawaii	72	70	1,173
Idaho	465	481	8,336
Illinois	355	376	12,646
Indiana	187	199	11,218
Iowa	895	920	19,677
Kansas	1,414	1,477	23,272
Kentucky	992	1,007	33,823
Louisana	450	466	12,115
Maine	11	11	1,354
Maryland	38	41	2,403
Massachusetts	6	6	849
Michigan	119	112	8,016
Minnesota	340	350	13,547
Mississippi	477	468	14,644
Missouri	1,820	1,881	46,161
Montana	1,476	1,506	10,598
Nebraska	1,807	1,786	19,313
Nevada	231	217	1,508
New Hampshire	3	3	683
New Jersey	7	8	871
New Mexico	407	407	11,004
New York	105	115	6,579
North Carolina	355	363	16,059
North Dakota	923	904	8,964
Ohio	293	282	16,922
Oklahoma	1,795	1,900	44,106
Oregon	516	525	11,557
Pennsylvania	160	150	11,880
Rhode Island	2	2	212
South Carolina	169	170	7,232
South Dakota	1,635	1,632	13,327
Tennessee	864	883	33,556
Texas	3,910	4,180	133,924
Utah	340	324	6,827
Vermont	12	12	1,295
Virginia	637	637	19,596
Washington	214	198	9,285
West Virginia	191	185	10,156
Wisconsin	250	275	13,020
Wyoming	694	694	5,080
United States	29,085	29,693	727,906

[1] An operation is any place having one or more beef cows on hand on December 31.　[2] State level estimates only available in conjunction with the Census of Agriculture every 5 years.　[3] Preliminary.
NASS, Livestock Branch, (202) 720–3570.

Table 7-20.—Hogs and pigs: Inventory and value, Dec. 1, 2013–2014, and number of operations, 2013, by State and United States

State	Inventory		Value				Operations [1]
	2013	2014	Value per head		Total value		2012
			2013	2014	2013	2014	
	Thousands	Thousands	Dollars	Dollars	1,000 dollars	1,000 dollars	Number
Alabama	85.0	110.0	145	150	12,325	16,500	689
Alaska	1.0	1.2	200	205	200	246	37
Arizona	170.0	139.0	145	150	24,650	20,850	509
Arkansas	115.0	115.0	155	165	17,825	18,975	752
California	95.0	110.0	180	185	17,100	20,350	1,437
Colorado	690.0	700.0	130	140	89,700	98,000	1,001
Connecticut	3.5	2.6	180	185	630	481	318
Delaware	6.0	4.0	145	150	870	600	59
Florida	15.0	17.0	145	150	2,175	2,550	1,642
Georgia	141.0	155.0	110	120	15,510	18,600	866
Hawaii	11.5	9.0	160	170	1,840	1,530	231
Idaho	(D)	(D)	(D)	(D)	(D)	(D)	680
Illinois	4,550.0	4,700.0	130	140	591,500	658,000	2,045
Indiana	3,650.0	3,700.0	140	145	511,000	536,500	2,757
Iowa	20,200.0	21,300.0	145	150	2,929,000	3,195,000	6,266
Kansas	1,750.0	1,840.0	120	125	210,000	230,000	1,010
Kentucky	315.0	340.0	105	105	33,075	35,700	1,284
Louisiana	8.0	8.0	145	150	1,160	1,200	658
Maine	4.5	4.5	145	150	653	675	752
Maryland	22.0	21.0	145	150	3,190	3,150	333
Massachusetts	8.5	9.0	145	150	1,233	1,350	478
Michigan	1,060.0	1,170.0	150	155	159,000	181,350	2,198
Minnesota	7,800.0	8,100.0	160	170	1,248,000	1,377,000	3,355
Mississippi	500.0	575.0	145	150	72,500	86,250	540
Missouri	2,750.0	2,850.0	115	125	316,250	356,250	2,128
Montana	166.0	176.0	145	150	24,070	26,400	406
Nebraska	3,050.0	3,200.0	145	145	442,250	464,000	1,476
Nevada	2.0	2.0	180	185	360	370	81
New Hampshire	3.8	3.6	155	160	589	576	359
New Jersey	9.0	10.0	155	160	1,395	1,600	298
New Mexico	1.2	1.3	145	150	174	195	211
New York	66.0	70.0	125	130	8,250	9,100	1,912
North Carolina	8,500.0	8,800.0	115	120	977,500	1,056,000	2,217
North Dakota	135.0	140.0	145	150	19,575	21,000	218
Ohio	2,200.0	2,230.0	145	155	319,000	345,650	3,494
Oklahoma	1,980.0	2,120.0	125	130	247,500	275,600	1,947
Oregon	8.5	9.0	145	150	1,233	1,350	1,124
Pennsylvania	1,080.0	1,140.0	125	130	135,000	148,200	3,097
Rhode Island	1.9	1.6	145	150	276	240	77
South Carolina	245.0	255.0	115	125	28,175	31,875	838
South Dakota	1,200.0	1,270.0	145	155	174,000	196,850	681
Tennessee	170.0	210.0	125	130	21,250	27,300	1,297
Texas	590.0	810.0	120	125	70,800	101,250	4,905
Utah	700.0	610.0	145	150	101,500	91,500	669
Vermont	3.2	3.5	180	185	576	648	450
Virginia	260.0	280.0	115	115	29,900	32,200	1,265
Washington	(D)	(D)	(D)	(D)	(D)	(D)	934
West Virginia	5.0	4.0	145	150	725	600	725
Wisconsin	295.0	310.0	120	125	35,400	38,750	2,270
Wyoming	90.0	83.0	155	160	13,950	13,280	270
Idaho and Washington	62.0	57.0	145	150	8,990	8,550	....
United States	64,774.6	67,776.3	138	144	8,921,822	9,754,191	63,246

(D) Withheld to avoid disclosing data for individual operations.   [1] State level estimates only available in conjunction with the Census of Agriculture every 5 years.   An operation is any place having one or more hogs and pigs on hand December 31.   Totals may not add due to rounding.
NASS, Livestock Branch, (202) 720–3570.

Table 7-21.—Hogs and pigs: Operations, inventory and value, United States, Dec. 1, 2005–2014

Year	Operations [1][2]	Inventory	Value Per head	Value Total
	Number	Thousands	Dollars	1,000 dollars
2005	67,280	61,463	95.00	5,833,763
2006	65,940	62,516	90.00	5,598,613
2007	75,450	68,177	73.00	4,986,206
2008	73,150	67,048	89.00	5,948,761
2009	71,450	64,687	83.00	5,399,951
2010	69,100	64,725	106.00	6,876,276
2011	69,100	66,259	123.00	8,145,260
2012	68,300	66,224	116.00	7,683,152
2013		64,775	138.00	8,921,842
2014		67,777	144.00	9,754,191

[1] An operation is any place having one or more hogs and pigs on hand December 31. [2] Operation estimates discontinued after 2012.
NASS, Livestock Branch, (202) 720–3570.

Table 7-22.—Sows farrowing and pig crop: Number, United States 2005-2014

Year	Sows farrowing Dec.-May	Sows farrowing June-Nov.	Pig crop Dec.-May	Pig crop June-Nov.	Total
	Thousands	Thousands	Thousands	Thousands	Thousands
2005	5,715	5,817	51,340	52,636	103,975
2006	5,769	5,861	52,259	53,374	105,633
2007	5,935	6,312	54,266	58,608	112,874
2008	6,077	6,103	56,583	58,010	114,593
2009	5,982	5,874	57,111	56,977	114,088
2010	5,749	5,824	55,770	57,358	113,128
2011	5,694	5,846	56,469	58,616	115,085
2012	5,759	5,810	57,749	58,906	116,655
2013	5,595	5,670	57,020	58,115	115,135
2014	5,573	5,985	53,821	61,035	114,856

NASS, Livestock Branch, (202) 720–3570.

Table 7-23.—Hogs and pigs: Number for breeding and market, United States, 2005–2014

Year	All hogs and pigs	Kept for breeding	Market hogs by weight groups Under 50 pounds	Market hogs by weight groups 50 to 119 pounds	Market hogs by weight groups 120 to 179 pounds	Market hogs by weight groups 180 pounds and over	Total
			June 1				
	Thousands	Thousands	Thousands	Thousands	Thousands	Thousands	Thousands
2005	60,744	5,988			11,143	9,813	54,756
2006	61,701	6,080			11,483	9,642	55,621
2007	63,947	6,169			11,789	9,920	57,777
2008	67,100	6,131	19,782	17,637	12,790	10,761	60,969
2009	66,709	5,968	19,514	17,778	12,604	10,847	60,742
2010	64,650	5,788	19,224	16,832	12,154	10,653	58,862
2011	65,320	5,803	19,423	17,241	12,254	10,599	59,517
2012	66,469	5,862	19,746	17,924	12,243	10,694	60,607
2013	65,188	5,884	19,145	17,068	12,414	10,678	59,304
2014	61,568	5,855	18,254	15,801	11,491	10,166	55,713
			Dec. 1				
	Thousands	Thousands	Thousands	Thousands	Thousands	Thousands	Thousands
2005	61,463	6,031			11,291	10,566	55,432
2006	62,516	6,116			11,274	10,738	56,399
2007	68,177	6,233			12,658	11,569	61,944
2008	67,048	6,062	19,428	17,396	12,656	11,508	60,987
2009	64,687	5,850	18,705	16,782	12,199	11,152	58,837
2010	64,725	5,778	18,864	16,519	12,183	11,381	58,947
2011	66,259	5,803	19,447	16,618	12,473	11,918	60,456
2012	66,224	5,819	19,299	16,752	12,614	11,741	60,405
2013	64,775	5,757	18,389	16,080	12,576	11,972	59,018
2014	67,776	5,939	19,801	17,366	13,000	11,671	61,838

NASS, Livestock Branch, (202) 720–3570.

Table 7-24.—Cattle and swine: Production, 2013–2015

Country	2013	2014	2015
	1,000 head	*1,000 head*	*1,000 head*
Cattle:			
Argentina	14,000	13,300	13,700
Australia	10,783	11,063	9,664
Brazil	50,185	49,600	48,220
Canada	4,516	4,606	4,400
China	48,800	47,900	49,000
European Union	29,050	29,280	29,550
India	65,000	66,000	67,000
Mexico	6,700	6,750	6,850
New Zealand	4,923	5,440	5,040
Russia	6,820	6,670	6,635
Others	14,914	14,429	10,334
Total Foreign	255,691	255,038	250,393
United States	33,730	33,900	34,300
Total	289,421	288,938	284,693
Swine:			
Belarus	5,325	4,850	5,150
Brazil	37,900	38,470	39,050
Canada	27,376	27,078	28,630
China	720,971	729,927	696,600
European Union	257,000	261,750	266,500
Japan	17,350	17,050	17,150
Korea, South	16,953	16,812	17,600
Mexico	17,800	17,600	18,000
Russia	36,000	37,000	39,760
Ukraine	9,465	9,527	9,200
Others	4,737	4,985	4,850
Total Foreign	1,150,877	1,165,049	1,142,490
United States	115,135	114,856	120,079
Total	1,266,012	1,279,905	1,262,569

FAS, Office of Global Analysis, (202) 720-6301. Prepared or estimated on the basis of official USDA production, supply, and distribution statistics from foreign governments.

Table 7-25.—Hogs: Number slaughtered, United States, 2005–2014

Year	Commercial			Farm	Total
	Federally inspected	Other	Total [1]		
	Thousands	*Thousands*	*Thousands*	*Thousands*	*Thousands*
2005	102,519	1,063	103,582	107	103,690
2006	103,689	1,048	104,737	105	104,842
2007	108,138	1,033	109,172	106	109,278
2008	115,421	1,031	116,452	106	116,558
2009	112,613	1,006	113,619	114	113,732
2010	109,315	945	110,260	107	110,367
2011	109,956	904	110,860	96	110,956
2012	112,265	898	113,163	83	113,247
2013	111,248	829	112,077	84	112,161
2014	106,123	753	106,876	82	106,958

[1] Totals are based on unrounded number.
NASS, Livestock Branch, (202) 720-3570.

Table 7-26.—Sows farrowing and pig crop: Number by State and United States, 2013–2014

State	Sows farrowing							
	December [1]–February		March–May		June–August		September–November	
	2013	2014	2013	2014	2013	2014	2013	2014
	Thousands	Thousands	Thousands	Thousands	Thousands	Thousands	Thousands	Thousands
Colorado	70	71	69	73	70	72	72	70
Illinois	245	245	250	250	250	255	235	250
Indiana	135	120	125	125	125	140	130	145
Iowa	465	480	465	470	485	510	455	485
Kansas	79	80	79	82	81	84	80	85
Michigan	53	49	50	52	50	50	49	51
Minnesota	275	275	290	290	290	280	290	280
Missouri	180	180	180	185	195	195	180	195
Nebraska	165	165	160	170	165	170	165	175
North Carolina	440	435	460	440	470	460	445	445
Ohio	86	90	80	80	90	85	85	87
Oklahoma	185	180	185	185	190	195	185	190
Pennsylvania	44	44	44	48	48	48	47	48
South Dakota	86	82	88	90	86	88	82	84
Texas	37	41	38	43	42	42	38	47
Utah	43	40	41	41	43	41	40	37
Other States [2]	200	186	202	186	210	191	202	197
United States [3][4]	2,788	2,763	2,806	2,810	2,890	2,906	2,780	2,871

State	Pig crop							
	December [1]–February		March–May		June–August		September–November	
	2013	2014	2013	2014	2013	2014	2013	2014
	Thousands	Thousands	Thousands	Thousands	Thousands	Thousands	Thousands	Thousands
Colorado	672	625	656	679	665	680	677	679
Illinois	2,475	2,450	2,575	2,475	2,550	2,601	2,397	2,563
Indiana	1,289	1,104	1,231	1,156	1,263	1,372	1,307	1,479
Iowa	4,813	4,752	4,883	4,982	5,141	5,457	4,823	5,190
Kansas	774	732	786	759	814	832	740	876
Michigan	543	451	510	463	505	505	497	520
Minnesota	2,901	2,888	3,103	3,074	3,132	3,038	3,132	3,066
Missouri	1,863	1,638	1,890	1,647	2,028	1,911	1,854	1,853
Nebraska	1,733	1,741	1,720	1,785	1,790	1,853	1,774	1,925
North Carolina	4,180	3,654	4,623	3,828	4,747	4,370	4,228	4,450
Ohio	869	720	824	760	936	850	884	901
Oklahoma	1,887	1,647	1,906	1,776	1,957	1,892	1,841	1,938
Pennsylvania	453	458	449	494	490	485	484	494
South Dakota	912	873	959	963	937	937	882	911
Texas	318	353	338	404	349	416	325	395
Utah	426	400	422	431	430	426	404	248
Other States [2]	1,991	1,840	2,046	1,819	2,128	1,909	2,004	1,885
United States [3][4]	28,099	26,326	28,921	27,495	29,862	29,534	28,253	29,373

[1] December preceding year.　[2] Individual State estimates not available for the 34 other States.　[3] Totals may not add due to rounding.

NASS, Livestock Branch, (202) 720–3570.

Table 7-27.—Hogs: Production, disposition, cash receipts, and gross income, United States, 2005–2014

Year	Mar-ketings [1]	Inshipments [2]	Farm slaugh-ter [3]	Production (live weight) [4]	Value of produc-tion [5]	Cash receipts [6]	Value of home consump-tion	Gross income	Average price per 100 pounds received by farmers
	1,000 head	1,000 head	1,000 head	1,000 pounds	1,000 dollars	1,000 dollars	1,000 dollars	1,000 dollars	Dollars
2005 ...	129,027	33,396	107	27,368,993	13,591,029	14,970,027	34,713	15,004,740	50.20
2006 ...	132,384	36,323	105	28,182,382	12,714,218	14,105,864	31,344	14,137,208	46.00
2007 ...	137,519	39,433	106	29,606,420	13,468,332	14,750,490	32,148	14,782,638	46.60
2008 ...	148,813	42,221	106	31,335,313	14,419,170	16,027,805	33,526	16,061,331	47.00
2009 ...	150,034	42,598	114	31,235,019	12,536,325	14,640,502	31,121	14,671,623	41.60
2010 ...	144,362	40,004	107	30,284,630	16,012,200	17,898,063	38,306	17,936,369	54.10
2011 ...	145,420	40,522	96	30,836,171	20,014,277	21,631,894	44,004	21,675,898	65.30
2012 ...	151,835	44,027	83	32,060,619	20,285,027	22,092,108	40,007	22,132,115	64.20
2013 ...	154,923	47,864	84	32,620,264	21,666,015	23,761,227	37,428	23,798,655	67.20
2014 ..	148,342	45,937	82	32,011,688	24,152,893	26,419,703	43,556	26,463,259	76.50

[1] Includes custom slaughter for use on farms where produced and State outshipments, but excludes interfarm sales within the State.   [2] Includes hogs and pigs shipped in from other states but excludes animals for immediate slaughter.   [3] Excludes custom slaughter for farmers at commercial establishments.   [4] Adjustments made for changes in inventory and for inshipments.   [5] Includes allowance for higher average price of State inshipments and outshipments of feeder pigs.   [6] Receipts from marketings and sale of farm slaughter.
NASS Livestock Branch, (202) 720–3570.

Table 7-28.—Hogs: Direct receipts at interior markets, 2005–2015

Year	All receipts (live and carcass basis)			
	National	Iowa/ Southern Minnesota [1]	Western Region	Eastern Region
	Thousands	Thousands	Thousands	Thousands
2005	77,905	42,609	49,757	25,174
2006	76,527	41,773	48,089	25,405
2007	78,475	41,446	49,929	25,740
2008	80,890	42,546	51,846	24,830
2009	81,443	44,628	53,331	23,065
2010	75,104	40,143	48,413	22,896
2011	75,514	41,479	49,649	22,643
2012	75,459	42,343	50,607	22,192
2013	71,599	40,744	48,202	20,929
2014	73,182	41,687	49,180	21,341
2015	78,445	44,997	53,076	22,298

[1] Iowa / Southern Minnesota is a subset of the Western Region.
AMS, Livestock & Grain Market News, (202) 720–7316.

Table 7-29.—Hogs and corn: Hog-corn price ratio and average price received by farmers for corn, United States, 2005–2014

Year	Hog-corn price ratio [1]	Price of corn per bushel [2]
		Dollars
2005	25.3	1.96
2006	20.3	2.28
2007	13.8	3.39
2008	10.0	4.78
2009	11.2	3.75
2010	14.4	3.83
2011	11.0	6.02
2012	9.6	6.67
2013	10.9	6.15
2014	18.8	4.11

[1] Number of bushels of corn equal in value to buy 100 pounds of live hogs at local markets, based on average prices received by farmers for hogs and corn. Annual average is a simple average of monthly ratios for the calendar year.   [2] Annual average is a simple average of monthly prices for the calendar year.
NASS, Environmental, Economics, and Demographics Branch, (202) 720–6146.

Table 7-30.—Hogs: Production, disposition, cash receipts, and gross income, by State and United States, 2014

State	Mar-ketings [1]	Inship-ments [2]	Farm slaugh-ter [3]	Production (live weight) [4]	Value of production [5]	Cash receipts [5][6]	Value of home consump-tion	Gross income
	1,000 head	*1,000 head*	*1,000 head*	*1,000 pounds*	*1,000 dollars*	*1,000 dollars*	*1,000 dollars*	*1,000 dollars*
Alabama	298.0	131.0	1.0	45,565	35,079	38,433	407	38,840
Alaska	1.5	0.7	0.5	504	401	309	99	408
Arizona	286.0	10.0	1.0	66,385	54,303	58,884	323	59,207
Arkansas	1,126.0	20.0	1.0	71,066	83,396	88,918	590	89,508
California	194.0	170.0	3.0	39,304	22,747	37,809	1,028	38,837
Colorado	2,811.0	260.0	1.0	246,115	235,645	256,137	409	256,546
Connecticut	4.3	0.3	0.1	984	736	702	91	793
Delaware	10.1	2.0	0.1	1,129	1,137	1,557	70	1,627
Florida	29.4	6.0	0.7	4,119	3,114	3,115	133	3,248
Georgia	545.0	170.0	2.0	70,760	54,824	61,438	876	62,314
Hawaii	15.8	-	3.5	4,201	3,465	3,194	707	3,901
Idaho	(D)	(D)	(D)	(D)	(D)	(D)	(D)	(D)
Illinois	11,935.0	2,488.0	3.0	1,949,324	1,610,615	1,737,987	1,030	1,739,017
Indiana	7,674.0	2,846.0	2.0	1,639,654	1,199,250	1,347,350	1,194	1,348,544
Iowa	43,718.0	26,800.0	7.0	11,548,962	8,017,968	9,214,817	4,308	9,219,125
Kansas	3,074.0	295.0	2.0	773,202	607,795	623,137	1,079	624,216
Kentucky	686.0	45.0	3.0	170,721	128,686	133,145	1,941	135,086
Louisiana	7.9	2.0	1.0	1,621	1,239	1,135	144	1,279
Maine	8.0	1.8	0.1	2,075	1,490	1,430	186	1,616
Maryland	60.4	15.0	0.1	11,519	8,644	10,219	205	10,424
Massachusetts	12.9	1.8	0.1	3,016	2,199	2,129	86	2,215
Michigan	2,070.0	250.0	2.0	524,658	393,428	402,618	807	403,425
Minnesota	17,296.0	6,400.0	4.0	3,785,444	2,784,251	3,161,396	2,651	3,164,047
Mississippi	938.0	4.0	4.0	144,323	116,817	109,225	1,043	110,268
Missouri	7,645.5	920.0	1.5	1,481,513	1,200,854	1,234,688	1,336	1,236,024
Montana	491.3	38.5	2.0	83,619	71,353	78,079	533	78,612
Nebraska	7,247.0	340.0	2.0	1,188,096	1,004,858	1,031,039	2,244	1,033,283
Nevada	7.5	5.1	0.3	1,667	1,073	1,485	81	1,566
New Hampshire	6.0	2.3	0.1	1,420	945	1,103	78	1,181
New Jersey	19.2	12.2	0.3	1,414	262	1,357	132	1,489
New Mexico	3.3	0.7	0.2	744	579	592	81	673
New York	123.5	11.3	1.2	28,016	20,977	20,598	901	21,499
North Carolina	15,308.0	578.0	2.0	3,558,499	2,854,413	2,929,464	729	2,930,193
North Dakota	796.9	40.0	0.5	52,281	66,738	71,823	206	72,029
Ohio	4,024.0	900.0	8.0	1,046,439	767,231	817,316	4,023	821,339
Oklahoma	7,425.0	700.0	1.0	1,262,803	1,002,181	1,023,970	439	1,024,409
Oregon	9.1	0.6	0.9	2,420	2,017	1,666	392	2,058
Pennsylvania	2,083.0	351.0	1.0	516,772	383,495	404,870	1,167	406,037
Rhode Island	3.5	-	0.1	704	537	477	33	510
South Carolina	264.5	89.0	1.5	50,136	37,706	39,070	1,773	40,843
South Dakota	4,024.0	499.0	2.0	606,351	537,480	584,562	1,838	586,400
Tennessee	383.0	111.0	2.0	94,251	70,078	71,313	1,097	72,410
Texas	2,169.0	920.0	6.0	309,408	241,847	252,224	3,481	255,705
Utah	1,479.5	1.0	0.5	267,002	230,964	240,313	198	240,511
Vermont	4.0	0.3	0.2	1,316	989	759	136	895
Virginia	323.5	315.0	1.5	64,875	46,300	57,578	869	58,447
Washington	(D)	(D)	(D)	(D)	(D)	(D)	(D)	(D)
West Virginia	4.7	0.6	1.0	1,266	961	644	492	1,136
Wisconsin	762.0	155.0	1.0	143,196	122,235	136,313	630	136,943
Wyoming	767.0	4.0	1.0	101,832	87,032	89,067	425	89,492
Idaho & Wash-ington	167.0	23.8	2.0	40,997	32,559	34,249	835	35,084
United States	148,342.3	45,937.0	82.0	32,011,688	24,152,893	26,419,703	43,556	26,463,259

- Represents zero. (D) Withheld to avoid disclosing data for individual operations. [1] Includes custom slaughter for use on farms where produced and State outshipments,but excludes interfarm sales within the State. [2] Includes hogs and pigs shipped in from other states but excludes animals for immediate slaughter. [3] Excludes custom slaughter for farmers at commercial establishments. [4] Adjustments made for changes in inventory and for inshipments. [5] Includes allowance for higher average price of State inshipments and outshipments of feeder pigs. [6] Receipts from marketings and sale of farm-slaughter.
NASS, Livestock Branch, (202) 720–3570.

Table 7-31.—Hogs: Number slaughtered commercially, total and average live weight, by State and United States, 2014[1]

State	Number slaughtered	Total live weight[2]	Average live weight[2]
	Thousands	*1,000 pounds*	*Pounds*
Alabama	22.6	8,618	381
Alaska	1.0	264	259
Arizona	1.8	458	258
Arkansas	9.3	2,382	256
California	2,344.7	586,816	250
Colorado	16.6	3,902	236
Delaware & Maryland	18.6	4,612	249
Florida	40.7	6,617	163
Georgia	70.9	17,196	243
Hawaii	13.7	3,327	243
Idaho	129.3	33,902	263
Illinois	10,437.7	3,008,036	288
Indiana	8,206.2	2,301,137	280
Iowa	28,644.7	8,197,146	286
Kansas	(D)	(D)	(D)
Kentucky	(D)	(D)	(D)
Louisiana	11.9	2,436	205
Michigan	184.0	72,603	395
Minnesota	9,708.4	2,670,789	275
Mississippi	42.4	7,974	188
Missouri	8,429.7	2,450,372	291
Montana	14.2	3,117	220
Nebraska	7,139.0	2,014,836	282
Nevada	0.8	201	250
New England[3]	29.4	7,275	248
New Jersey	104.4	9,858	94
New Mexico	2.1	569	269
New York	36.4	8,376	230
North Carolina	(D)	(D)	(D)
North Dakota	3.8	1,104	290
Ohio	909.7	257,744	284
Oklahoma	4,845.3	1,362,893	281
Oregon	164.5	43,253	263
Pennsylvania	2,829.5	760,167	269
South Carolina	(D)	(D)	(D)
South Dakota	(D)	(D)	(D)
Tennessee	713.8	321,773	451
Texas	261.8	65,780	251
Utah	43.6	7,873	180
Virginia	(D)	(D)	(D)
Washington	(D)	(D)	(D)
West Virginia	7.1	1,864	263
Wisconsin	613.1	274,959	449
Wyoming	4.0	1,033	258
United States[4]	106,875.7	30,431,080	285

(D) Withheld to avoid disclosing data for individual operations.   [1] Includes slaughter in federally inspected and other slaughter plants; excludes animals slaughtered on farms. Average live weight is based on unrounded numbers. Totals may not add due to rounding.   [2] Excludes postmortem condemnations.   [3] Connecticut, Maine, Massachusetts, New Hampshire, Rhode Island, and Vermont.   [4] States with no data printed are still included in US total. Data are not printed to avoid disclosing individual operations.

NASS, Livestock Branch, (202) 720-3570.

Table 7-32.—Hogs: Number slaughtered, average dressed and live weights, Federally inspected, 2005–2014 [1]

Year	Federally inspected											
	Barrows and gilts			Sows			Boars			Total		
	Head	Percent of total	Avg. dressed weight [2]	Head	Percent of total	Avg. dressed weight [2]	Head	Percent of total	Avg. dressed weight [2]	Head	Avg. dressed weight [2]	Avg. live weight [2]
	1,000		Pounds	1,000		Pounds	1,000		Pounds	1,000	Pounds	Pounds
2005 ..	99,123	96.7	197	3,116	3.0	310	280	0.3	213	102,519	201	269
2006 ..	100,113	96.6	198	3,227	3.1	309	348	0.3	227	103,689	202	269
2007 ..	104,352	96.5	198	3,309	3.1	308	477	0.4	213	108,138	202	269
2008 ..	111,461	96.6	198	3,502	3.0	308	458	0.4	208	115,421	201	268
2009 ..	108,951	96.7	200	3,243	2.9	306	419	0.4	199	112,613	203	271
2010 ..	105,983	97.0	201	2,966	2.7	305	366	0.3	200	109,315	204	273
2011 ..	106,600	96.9	203	3,027	2.8	305	329	0.3	210	109,956	206	275
2012 ..	108,912	97.0	203	3,009	2.7	306	344	0.3	208	112,265	206	275
2013 ..	107,965	97.0	205	2,932	2.6	304	351	0.3	204	111,248	207	277
2014 ..	102,998	97.1	212	2,788	2.6	305	337	0.3	204	106,123	214	285

[1] All weights calculated using unrounded totals.　Totals and percentages based on unrounded data and may not equal sum of classes due to rounding.　[2] Excludes postmortem condemnations.
NASS, Livestock Branch, (202) 720-3570.

Table 7-33.—Lard: Supply and disappearance, United States, 2005–2014

Calendar year	Supply				Disappearance		
	Beginning stocks [1]	Production [2]	Imports	Total	Domestic	Exports	Total
	Million lbs	Million lbs	Million lbs	Million lbs	Million lbs	Million lbs	Million lbs
2005	14	779	5	798	695	94	789
2006	9	788	7	805	719	72	790
2007	14	821	9	844	757	73	830
2008	14	874	7	894	801	81	882
2009	12	860	17	889	788	83	871
2010	18	840	15	873	776	72	847
2011	26	852	13	891	794	77	871
2012	20	871	14	905	830	55	885
2013	20	867	14	901	816	65	881
2014 [3]	20	852	16	888	821	47	868

[1] Domestic disappearance data are computed by ERS.　[2] Includes edible tallow direct use beginning in 1979.　[3] Preliminary.　[4] Including paint, varnish, resin, plastic, and lubricants.
ERS, Market and Trade Economics Division, Field Crops Branch, (202) 694–5300.

Table 7-34.—Lard: United States exports by country of destination, 2011–2013

Country	2011	2012	2013[1]
	Metric tons	Metric tons	Metric tons
Mexico	32,878	23,487	28,347
Canada	1,016	598	596
Trinidad and Tobago	236	488	234
Micronesia	0	3	131
Marshall Islands	3	2	40
Barbados	4	0	34
Korea, South	0	0	19
Cayman Islands	4	0	13
Bermuda	65	49	11
Palau	0	0	9
Argentina	0	3	5
Panama	0	0	4
Mayotte	0	0	2
Colombia	0	0	1
Bahamas, The	107	0	0
Belize	2	0	0
China	0	29	0
Ireland	0	18	0
France(*)	5	20	0
Guyana	0	13	0
Haiti	70	64	0
Hong Kong	2	2	0
Honduras	3	0	0
Japan	16	0	0
Jamaica	4	4	0
Lebanon	79	0	0
Netherlands Antilles(*)	167	6	0
Nicaragua	2	0	0
Saudi Arabia	25	0	0
United Kingdom	0	10	0
Rest of World	90	30	0
World Total	34,776	24,826	29,445

(*) Denotes a country that is a summarization of its component countries.   [1] 2013 data does not reflect 13 month changes.   Users should use cautious interpretation on quantity reports using mixed units of measure.   Quantity line items will only include statistics on the units of measure that are equal to, or are able to be converted to, the assigned unit of measure of the grouped commodities.
FAS, Office of Global Analysis, (202) 720-6301.   Data Source: Department of Commerce, U.S. Census Bureau, Foreign Trade Statistics.

Table 7-35.—Sheep and lambs: Operations, inventory, and value, United States, Jan. 1, 2006–2015

Year	Operations[1]	Inventory	Value	
			Per head	Total
	Number	1,000 head	Dollars	1,000 dollars
2006	69,180	6,200	141.00	872,351
2007	83,130	6,120	134.00	818,491
2008	82,500	5,950	138.00	823,424
2009	82,000	5,747	133.00	765,194
2010	81,000	5,620	135.00	761,115
2011	80,000	5,470	170.00	931,008
2012	79,500	5,375	221.00	1,185,075
2013		5,360	177.00	946,194
2014		5,245	188.00	984,236
2015[2]		5,280	214.00	1,129,447

[1] Operations discontinued.   [2] Preliminary.
NASS, Livestock Branch, (202) 720–3570.

Table 7-36.—Sheep and lambs: Number by class, United States, Jan. 1, 2006–2015

Year	All sheep and lambs	Breeding sheep			
		Total[1]	Replacement lambs	1 year and over	
				Ewes	Rams
	1,000 head	1,000 head	1,000 head	1,000 head	1,000 head
2006	6,200	4,616	786	3,630	200
2007	6,120	4,553	735	3,620	199
2008	5,950	4,432	697	3,540	195
2009	5,747	4,247	647	3,405	196
2010	5,620	4,185	655	3,335	195
2011	5,470	4,070	665	3,215	190
2012	5,375	3,995	660	3,165	170
2013	5,360	3,985	670	3,135	180
2014	5,245	3,900	635	3,090	175
2015[2]	5,280	3,935	650	3,110	175

[1] Categories may not add to total due to rounding.   [2] Preliminary.
NASS, Livestock Branch, (202) 720–3570.

Table 7-37.—Lamb mutton, goat, etc. meat: U.S. imports, 2011–2013

Country	2011	2012	2013
	1,000 metric tons	*1,000 metric tons*	*1,000 metric tons*
Australia(*)	57,389	59,011	63,312
New Zealand(*)	23,569	19,227	21,192
Canada	672	805	952
Chile	0	63	354
Iceland	138	185	181
Mexico	129	99	82
Ireland	22	0	0
Finland	13	0	0

(*) Denotes a country that is a summarization of its component countries.   Users should use cautious interpretation on quantity reports using mixed units of measure.   Quantity line items will only include statistics on the units of measure that are equal to, or are able to be converted to, the assigned unit of measure of the grouped commodities.
FAS, Office of Global Analysis, (202) 720-6301.   Data Source: Department of Commerce, U.S. Census Bureau, Foreign Trade Statistics.

Table 7-38.—Breeding sheep: Number by class, State and United States, Jan. 1, 2014–2015

State	Under one year old		One year and over			
	Replacement lambs		Ewes		Rams	
	2014	2015[1]	2014	2015[1]	2014	2015[1]
	1,000 head	*1,000 head*	*1,000 head*	*1,000 head*	*1,000 head*	*1,000 head*
Arizona	22.0	24.0	80.0	76.0	7.0	7.0
California	45.0	45.0	270.0	275.0	10.0	10.0
Colorado	23.0	30.0	142.0	184.0	5.0	6.0
Idaho	30.0	31.0	155.0	150.0	5.0	6.0
Illinois	8.0	7.0	36.0	38.0	3.0	3.0
Indiana	6.0	6.0	34.0	34.0	3.0	3.0
Iowa	15.0	20.0	90.0	100.0	5.0	5.0
Kansas	7.0	6.0	39.0	36.0	2.0	2.0
Kentucky	7.0	6.0	31.0	30.0	2.0	2.0
Michigan	13.0	12.0	43.0	40.0	3.0	3.0
Minnesota	15.0	15.0	79.0	73.0	4.0	4.0
Missouri	12.0	11.0	57.0	58.0	3.0	4.0
Montana	37.0	34.0	155.0	153.0	6.0	6.0
Nebraska	8.0	9.0	54.0	55.0	3.0	3.0
Nevada	12.0	10.0	55.0	48.0	2.0	2.0
New England[2]	7.0	6.0	27.0	26.0	2.0	2.0
New Mexico	12.0	14.0	53.0	58.0	3.0	4.0
New York	14.0	16.0	47.0	51.0	3.0	3.0
North Carolina	4.0	4.0	15.0	18.0	2.0	2.0
North Dakota	7.0	6.0	41.0	42.0	2.0	2.0
Ohio	15.0	17.0	72.0	73.0	6.0	6.0
Oklahoma	9.0	8.0	36.0	31.0	3.0	3.0
Oregon	22.0	24.0	97.0	110.0	6.0	6.0
Pennsylvania	11.0	10.0	63.0	56.0	5.0	5.0
South Dakota	31.0	32.0	172.0	162.0	7.0	6.0
Tennessee	6.0	6.0	25.0	28.0	3.0	3.0
Texas	105.0	105.0	440.0	435.0	35.0	30.0
Utah	37.0	40.0	215.0	220.0	8.0	10.0
Virginia	10.0	9.0	53.0	50.0	3.0	3.0
Washington	8.0	8.0	34.0	31.0	3.0	3.0
West Virginia	4.0	4.0	22.0	22.0	1.0	1.0
Wisconsin	14.0	12.0	52.0	50.0	3.0	3.0
Wyoming	38.0	43.0	220.0	210.0	7.0	7.0
Other States[3]	21.0	20.0	86.0	87.0	10.0	10.0
United States	635.0	650.0	3,090.0	110.0	175.0	175.0

[1]Preliminary.   [2]New England includes Connecticut, Maine, Massachusetts, New Hampshire, Rhode Island, and Vermont.   [3]Individual state estimates not available for states not shown, but are included in Other States.
NASS, Livestock Branch, (202) 720–3570.

Table 7-39.—Sheep and lambs: Average price per 100 pounds at San Angelo, 2005–2015[1]

Year	Sheep			Slaughter lambs choice & prime			
	Good	Utility	Cull	Wooled		Shorn	
				90-110 lbs	110-130 1bs	90-110 lbs	110-130 1bs
2005	54.21	56.59	41.39	98.26	97.69	98.24	97.50
2006	42.16	42.33	26.41	80.41	78.99	78.17	78.16
2007	41.06	41.31	25.16	85.36	85.36	85.13	85.18
2008	36.91	37.62	18.01	86.02	85.62	86.06	85.66
2009	40.27	40.53	21.20	90.49	90.24	90.55	90.32
2010	59.51	59.50	41.12	114.66	115.12	115.18	115.68
2011	66.22	66.62	41.43	161.09	161.08	161.53	161.24
2012	64.30	65.80	42.84	113.64	114.01	114.56	114.68
2013	47.68	49.68	28.21	107.34	107.50	107.44	107.69
2014	65.66	67.88	43.76	157.08	157.14	157.19	157.30
2015	79.11	80.63	54.70	143.97	143.97	144.02	144.12

[1] Simple average of monthly bulk-of-sales prices from data of the livestock reporting service. AMS, Livestock & Grain Market News, (202) 720–7316.

Table 7-40.—Sheep and lambs: Number of breeding and market sheep, by State and United States, Jan. 1, 2014–2015

State	Breeding sheep and lambs		Market sheep and lambs	
	2014	2015[1]	2014	2015[1]
	1,000 head	1,000 head	1,000 head	1,000 head
Arizona	109.0	107.0	41.0	43.0
California	325.0	330.0	265.0	270.0
Colorado	170.0	220.0	195.0	200.0
Idaho	190.0	187.0	60.0	73.0
Illinois	47.0	48.0	9.0	9.0
Indiana	43.0	43.0	7.0	7.0
Iowa	110.0	125.0	45.0	50.0
Kansas	48.0	44.0	27.0	22.0
Kentucky	40.0	38.0	9.0	10.0
Michigan	59.0	55.0	22.0	21.0
Minnesota	98.0	92.0	37.0	38.0
Missouri	72.0	73.0	11.0	12.0
Montana	198.0	193.0	22.0	22.0
Nebraska	65.0	67.0	11.0	14.0
Nevada	69.0	60.0	11.0	9.0
New England[2]	36.0	34.0	8.0	9.0
New Mexico	68.0	76.0	13.0	14.0
New York	64.0	70.0	11.0	10.0
North Carolina	21.0	24.0	6.0	6.0
North Dakota	50.0	50.0	16.0	14.0
Ohio	93.0	96.0	24.0	25.0
Oklahoma	48.0	42.0	11.0	11.0
Oregon	125.0	140.0	70.0	55.0
Pennsylvania	79.0	71.0	15.0	15.0
South Dakota	210.0	200.0	60.0	55.0
Tennessee	34.0	37.0	5.0	7.0
Texas	580.0	570.0	150.0	150.0
Utah	260.0	270.0	20.0	20.0
Virginia	66.0	62.0	17.0	13.0
Washington	45.0	42.0	10.0	10.0
West Virginia	27.0	27.0	5.0	6.0
Wisconsin	69.0	65.0	14.0	12.0
Wyoming	265.0	260.0	90.0	85.0
Other States[3]	117.0	117.0	28.0	28.0
United States	3,900.0	3,935.0	1,345.0	1,345.0

[1] Preliminary. [2] New England includes Connecticut, Maine, Massachusetts, New Hampshire, Rhode Island, and Vermont. [3] Individual state estimates not available for states not shown, but are included in Other States. NASS, Livestock Branch, (202) 720–3570.

Table 7-41.—Lamb crop: Per 100 ewes 1+, number and percent of previous year, by State and United States, 2013–2014

State	Breeding ewes 1 year & older, Jan. 1		Lambs per 100 ewes 1+, Jan. 1		Lamb crop [1]		
	2013	2014	2013	2014	2013	2014	2014 as % of 2013
	1,000 head	*1,000 head*	*Number*	*Number*	*1,000 head*	*1,000 head*	*Percent*
Arizona	75.0	80.0	60	61	45.0	49.0	109
California	275.0	270.0	84	89	230.0	240.0	104
Colorado	160.0	142.0	109	141	175.0	200.0	114
Idaho	152.0	155.0	125	119	190.0	185.0	97
Illinois	35.0	36.0	137	139	48.0	50.0	104
Indiana	37.0	34.0	119	126	44.0	43.0	98
Iowa	100.0	90.0	135	167	135.0	150.0	111
Kansas	33.0	39.0	136	108	45.0	42.0	93
Kentucky	31.0	31.0	132	129	41.0	40.0	98
Michigan	43.0	43.0	147	140	63.0	60.0	95
Minnesota	79.0	79.0	171	158	135.0	125.0	93
Missouri	57.0	57.0	123	125	70.0	71.0	101
Montana	155.0	155.0	129	129	200.0	200.0	100
Nebraska	53.0	54.0	134	135	71.0	73.0	103
Nevada	50.0	55.0	104	85	52.0	47.0	90
New England [2]	33.0	27.0	97	107	32.0	29.0	91
New Mexico	52.0	53.0	73	85	38.0	45.0	118
New York	42.0	47.0	114	117	48.0	55.0	115
North Carolina	15.0	15.0	113	127	17.0	19.0	112
North Dakota	44.0	41.0	125	134	55.0	55.0	100
Ohio	77.0	72.0	119	136	92.0	98.0	107
Oklahoma	37.0	36.0	111	100	41.0	36.0	88
Oregon	110.0	97.0	114	132	125.0	128.0	102
Pennsylvania	58.0	63.0	119	97	69.0	61.0	88
South Dakota	180.0	172.0	128	125	230.0	215.0	93
Tennessee	24.0	25.0	125	136	30.0	34.0	113
Texas	420.0	440.0	75	77	315.0	340.0	108
Utah	225.0	215.0	100	109	225.0	235.0	104
Virginia	56.0	53.0	104	104	58.0	55.0	95
Washington	32.0	34.0	141	121	45.0	41.0	91
West Virginia	22.0	22.0	141	132	31.0	29.0	94
Wisconsin	53.0	52.0	136	131	72.0	68.0	94
Wyoming	225.0	220.0	100	109	225.0	240.0	107
Other States [3]	95.0	86.0	82	95	78.0	82.0	105
United States	3,135.0	3,090.0	107	111	3,370.0	3,440.0	102

[1] Lamb crop is defined as lambs born in the Eastern States and lambs docked or branded in the Western States. [2] New England includes Connecticut, Maine, Massachusetts, New Hampshire, Rhode Island, and Vermont. [3] Unpublished states. NASS, Livestock Branch, (202) 720–3570.

Table 7-42—Sheep and lambs: Production, disposition, cash receipts, and gross income, United States, 2006–2015[1]

| Year | Lamb crop[2] | Marketings[3] | | Inshipments | Farm slaughter | Production (live weight)[4] |
		Sheep	Lambs			
	1,000 head	*1,000 head*	*1,000 head*	*1,000 head*	*1,000 head*	*1,000 pounds*
2006	3,950	743	4,035	1,465	80	460,580
2007	3,895	780	3,927	1,398	85	440,286
2008	3,710	737	3,652	1,232	92	417,019
2009	3,690	625	3,532	1,070	95	421,615
2010	3,600	645	3,429	1,089	97	405,289
2011	3,510	....	....	....	93	....
2012	3,450	....	....	....	93	....
2013	3,370	....	....	....	94	....
2014	3,440	....	....	....	95	....
2015[5]	3,440	....	....	....	95	....

[1] Monthly sheep and lamb prices were discontinued after September 2011 prices were published. Production, Disposition, and Income estimates for sheep and lambs were discontinued after the 2011 publication. [2] Lamb crop defined as lambs born in the native States and lambs docked or branded in the Western States. [3] Includes custom slaughter for use on farms where produced and State outshipments, but excludes interfarm sales within the State. [4] Adjustments made for changes in inventory and for inshipments. [5] Preliminary.
NASS, Livestock Branch, (202) 720–3570.

Table 7-43.—Sheep and lambs: Receipts at selected markets, 2005–2015

Year	Sioux Falls, SD	Billings, MT	San Angelo, TX	New Holland, PA
	Thousands	*Thousands*	*Thousands*	*Thousands*
2005	41	56	199	71
2006	48	58	217	98
2007	40	58	186	108
2008	42	50	192	107
2009	28	54	144	102
2010	41	48	143	92
2011	38	42	156	94
2012	35	53	89	101
2013	48	52	110	109
2014	52	49	107	80
2015	82	63	1,098	84

AMS, Livestock & Grain Market News, (202) 720–7316.

Table 7-44.—Sheep and lambs: Number slaughtered, United States, 2005–2014

| Year | Commercial | | | Farm | Total |
	Federally inspected	Other	Total[1]		
	Thousands	*Thousands*	*Thousands*	*Thousands*	*Thousands*
2005	2,554	143	2,698	75	2,763
2006	2,547	151	2,699	80	2,766
2007	2,529	165	2,694	85	2,779
2008	2,394	162	2,556	92	2,647
2009	2,323	193	2,516	95	2,611
2010	2,261	196	2,458	95	2,553
2011	2,000	164	2,164	93	2,258
2012	2,012	171	2,183	93	2,275
2013	2,120	199	2,319	94	2,412
2014	2,104	205	2,309	95	2,404

[1] Totals are based on unrounded numbers.
NASS, Livestock Branch, (202) 720–3570.

Table 7-45.—Sheep and lambs: Number slaughtered commercially, total and average live weight, by State and United States, 2014[1]

State	Number slaughtered	Total live weight	Average live weight[2]
	Thousands	*1,000 pounds*	*Pounds*
Alabama	0.4	35	84
Alaska	0.1	15	126
Arizona	3.2	416	129
Arkansas	0.7	66	90
California	290.2	40,124	138
Colorado	945.1	148,110	157
Delaware-Maryland	47.4	4,532	96
Florida	7.8	474	61
Georgia	12.3	807	65
Hawaii	0.8	108	132
Idaho	2.2	300	135
Illinois	146.8	21,494	146
Indiana	51.6	5,816	113
Iowa	2.8	452	161
Kansas	5.4	524	97
Kentucky	14.7	1,785	122
Louisiana	4.4	316	71
Michigan	198.6	26,944	136
Minnesota	4.9	529	109
Mississippi	4.0	296	73
Missouri	9.4	979	104
Montana	4.9	642	131
Nebraska	0.5	62	126
Nevada	0.9	120	129
New England[3]	37.2	3,522	95
New Jersey	120.7	9,703	80
New Mexico	9.2	1,334	146
New York	51.7	5,025	97
North Carolina	15.6	1,073	69
North Dakota	0.5	67	128
Ohio	16.2	1,677	104
Oklahoma	2.5	251	101
Oregon	33.6	4,692	140
Pennsylvania	71.8	7,245	101
South Carolina	(D)	(D)	(D)
South Dakota	3.1	473	154
Tennessee	13.5	919	68
Texas	109.4	11,480	105
Utah	(D)	(D)	(D)
Virginia	4.6	433	94
Washington	11.6	1,529	132
West Virginia	(D)	(D)	(D)
Wisconsin	11.1	1,396	126
Wyoming	1.3	192	146
United States	2,309.5	310,893	135

(D) Withheld to avoid disclosing data for individual operations. [1] Includes slaughter in federally inspected and in other slaughter plants; exludes animals slaughtered on farms. Excludes postmortem condemnations. [2] Averages are based on unrounded data. [3] New England includes Connecticut, Maine, Massachusetts, New Hampshire, Rhode Island, and Vermont.

NASS, Livestock Branch, (202) 720–3570.

Table 7-46.—Sheep and lambs: Number slaughtered, average dressed and live weights, percentage distribution, by class, Federally inspected, 2005–2014[1]

Year	Federally inspected								
	Lambs and yearlings			Mature sheep			Total		
	Head	Pct. of total	Avg. dressed weight[2]	Head	Pct. of total	Avg. dressed weight[2]	Head	Avg. dressed weight[2]	Avg. live weight[2]
	1,000		Pounds	1,000		Pounds	1,000	Pounds	
2005	2,425	94.9	71	129	5.1	69	2,554	70	140
2006	2,429	95.4	70	118	4.6	67	2,547	70	138
2007	2,413	95.4	69	116	4.6	67	2,529	69	138
2008	2,271	94.9	69	122	5.1	67	2,394	69	138
2009	2,165	93.2	70	158	6.8	64	2,323	70	139
2010	2,105	93.1	69	156	6.9	65	2,261	68	137
2011	1,860	93.0	71	141	7.0	66	2,000	70	141
2012	1,869	92.9	74	143	7.1	64	2,012	74	147
2013	1,988	93.7	69	133	6.3	64	2,120	69	137
2014	1,968	94.3	69	135	5.7	64	2,104	66	137

[1] All percents and weights calculated using unrounded totals.   [2] Excludes postmortem condemnations.
NASS, Livestock Branch, (202) 720–3570.

Table 7-47.—Sheep and lambs: Inventory Jan 1, 2014–2015, and number of operations, 2012, by State and United States[1]

State	January 1 Sheep inventory		Operations with sheep[2]
	2014	2015[3]	2012
	1,000 head	1,000 head	Number
Alabama			712
Alaska			50
Arizona	150.0	150.0	7,447
Arkansas			778
California	590.0	600.0	4,224
Colorado	365.0	420.0	1,509
Delaware			69
Florida			1,161
Georgia			688
Hawaii			353
Idaho	250.0	260.0	1,241
Illinois	56.0	57.0	1,751
Indiana	50.0	50.0	2,109
Iowa	155.0	175.0	2,904
Kansas	75.0	66.0	1,160
Kentucky	49.0	48.0	1,743
Louisiana			643
Maryland			663
Michigan	81.0	76.0	2,312
Minnesota	135.0	130.0	2,171
Mississippi			499
Missouri	83.0	85.0	2,454
Montana	220.0	215.0	1,338
Nebraska	76.0	81.0	1,464
Nevada	80.0	69.0	508
New England[4]	44.0	43.0	3566
New Jersey			819
New Mexico	81.0	90.0	3,385
New York	75.0	80.0	2,017
North Carolina	27.0	30.0	1,311
North Dakota	66.0	64.0	661
Ohio	117.0	121.0	3,568
Oklahoma	59.0	53.0	1,779
Oregon	195.0	195.0	2,753
Pennsylvania	94.0	86.0	3,590
South Carolina			549
South Dakota	270.0	255.0	1,798
Tennessee	39.0	44.0	1,476
Texas	730.0	720.0	10,674
Utah	280.0	290.0	1,755
Virginia	83.0	75.0	2,315
Washington	55.0	52.0	1,967
West Virginia	32.0	33.0	1,043
Wisconsin	83.0	77.0	2,590
Wyoming	355.0	345.0	771
Other States[5]	145.0	145.0	
United States	5,245.0	5,280.0	88,338

[1] An operation is any place having one or more head of sheep on hand December 31.   [2] State level estimates only available in conjunction with the Census of Agriculture every 5 years.   [3] Preliminary.   [4] New England includes Connecticut, Maine, Massachusetts, New Hampshire, Rhode Island, and Vermont.   [5] Individual state estimates not available for states not shown, but are included in Other States.
NASS, Livestock Branch, (202) 720–3570.

Table 7-48.—Wool: Number of sheep shorn, weight per fleece, production, average price per pound received by farmers, value of production, exports, imports, total new supply of apparel wool, and imports of carpet wool, United States, 2005–2014

Year	Sheep and lambs shorn [1]	Weight per fleece	Shorn wool production	Price per pound [2]	Value of production [3]
	Thousands	Pounds	1,000 pounds	Cents	1,000 dollars
2005	5,061	7.4	37,182	0.71	26,249
2006	4,847	7.4	35,899	0.68	24,300
2007	4,657	7.5	34,723	0.87	30,242
2008	4,434	7.4	32,963	0.99	32,486
2009	4,195	7.4	30,860	0.79	24,337
2010	4,180	7.3	30,360	1.15	35,013
2011	4,030	7.3	29,280	1.67	48,920
2012	3,790	7.3	27,630	1.52	41,972
2013	3,700	7.3	26,990	1.45	39,209
2014	3,680	7.3	26,700	1.46	38,949

Year	Shorn wool production	Raw wool supply (clean)				Total new supply [8]
		Domestic production [4]	Exports [5]	Imports for consumption		
				48's and Finer [6]	Not Finer than 46's [7]	
	1,000 pounds	1,000 pounds	1,000 pounds	1,000 pounds	1,000 pounds	
2005	37,182	19,632	12,573	6,220	12,155	25,434
2006	35,899	18,955	17,998	7,324	9,929	18,210
2007	34,723	18,334	17,077	5,245	9,025	15,527
2008	32,963	17,404	10,307	4,551	8,631	20,279
2009	30,860	16,294	10,207	3,306	6,046	15,439
2010	30,370	16,035	9,973	3,108	4,928	14,098
2011	29,290	15,465	9,586	3,791	4,694	14,364
2012	27,400	14,467	7,741	4,564	4,551	15,841
2013	26,990	14,251	9,998	3,858	3,746	11,857
2014	26,680	14,087	7,916	3,917	3,159	13,247

[1] Includes sheep shorn at commercial feeding yards.　[2] Price computed by weighting State average prices for all wool sold during the year by sales of shorn wool.　[3] Production by States multiplied by annual average price.　[4] Conversion factor from grease basis to clean basis are as follows: Shorn wool production—52.8 percent (Stat. Bull. 616) from 1987-1997.　[5] Includes carpet wool exports.　[6] Prior to 1989, known as dutiable imports.　[7] Prior to 1989, known as duty-free imports. In 1994 includes 24,645,306 pounds of imported raw wool not finer than 46's and 2,182,576 pounds of miscellaneous imported raw wool.　[8] Production minus exports plus imports; stocks not taken into consideration.
NASS, Livestock Branch, (202) 720–3570 and ERS, Field Crops Branch, (202) 694–5300.　Imports and exports from reports of the U.S. Department of Commerce.

Table 7-49.—Wool: Price-support operations, United States, 2005–2014 [1]

Year	Income support payment rates per pound	Program price levels per pound		Put under loan		Acquired by CCC under loan program [2]	Owned by CCC at end of marketing year
		Graded wool loan	Nongraded loan	Quantity	Percentage of production		
	Dollars	Dollars	Dollars	1,000 pounds	Percent	1,000 pounds	1,000 pounds
2005	(NA)	1.00	0.40	76.2	0.20	5.0	0.0
2006	(NA)	1.00	0.40	3.2	0.01	0.0	0.0
2007	(NA)	1.00	0.40	3.0	0.01	0.0	0.0
2008	(NA)	1.00	0.40	8.6	0.03	0.0	0.0
2009	(NA)	1.00	0.40	28.9	0.09	0.0	0.0
2010	(NA)	1.15	0.40	27.8	0.09	0.0	0.0
2011	(NA)	1.15	0.40	0.0	0.00	0.0	0.0
2012	(NA)	1.15	0.40	0.0	0.00	0.0	0.0
2013	(NA)	1.15	0.40	14.0	0.05	0.0	0.0
2014	(NA)	1.15	0.40	11.0	0.04	0.0	0.0

(NA) Not available.　[1] Nonrecourse Marketing Loan Program authorized by the Farm Security and Rural Investment Act of 2002, as amended, for marketing years 2002-2007, the Food, Conservation, and Energy Act of 2008, as amended, for marketing years 2008-2013, and the Agricultural Act of 2014, as amended, for marketing years 2014-2018.　[2] Acquisitions as of December 31, 2015.
FSA, Fibers, Peanuts, Tobacco, (202) 401–0062.

Table 7-50.—Wool: United States imports (for consumption), clean content, by grades, 2005–2014 [1] [2]

Grade	2005	2006	2007	2008	2009	2010	2011	2012	2013	2014
	Million pounds	Million pounds	Million pounds	Million pounds	Million pounds	Million pounds	Million pounds	Million pounds	Million pounds	Million pounds
48's and finer:										
Finer than 58's [3]	5.6	6.5	4.7	4.0	3.0	2.7	3.2	3.7	2.9	3.0
48's–58's [4]	0.6	0.8	0.5	0.5	0.3	0.4	0.6	0.9	1.0	0.9
Total	6.2	7.3	5.2	4.6	3.3	3.1	3.8	4.6	3.9	3.9
Not Finer than 46's:										
Wool for special use [5]	3.1	1.1	0.7	0.6	0.2	0.2	0.3	0.4	0.2	0.4
Not finer than 40's [6]	2.4	2.6	2.6	1.8	1.5	1.1	1.2	1.2	0.9	0.9
Finer than 40's– 44's [7]	4.5	5.4	4.4	5.0	3.6	3.2	2.3	2.5	1.4	1.4
46's [8]	2.1	0.8	1.4	1.3	0.7	0.5	0.9	0.5	1.2	0.5
Total	12.2	9.9	9.0	8.6	6.0	4.9	4.7	4.6	3.7	3.2
Miscellaneous [9]	0	0	0	0	0	0	0	0	0	0
Grand total	18.4	17.3	14.3	13.2	9.4	8.0	8.5	9.1	7.6	7.1

[1] Natural fiber grown by sheep or lambs.   [2] Beginning 1989 the following Harmonized Tariff Schedule numbers are in the above 7 wool import groups: 5101.19.606060, 5101.19.6060, 5101.21.4000, 5101.21.4000, 5101.29.4060, 0.5(5101.30.4000).   [4] 5101.11.6030, 5101.19.6030, 5101.21.4030, 5101.29.4030, 0.5(5101.30.4000).   [5] 5101.11.1000, 5101.19.1000, 5101.21.1000, 5101.29.1000.   [6] 5101.11.2000, 5101.19.2000, 5101.21.1500, 5101.29.1500, 5101.30.1000.   [7] 5101.11.4000, 5101.19.4000, 5101.21.3000, 5101.29.3000, 5101.30.1500.   [8] 5101.11.5000, 5101.19.5000, 5101.21.3500, 5101.29.3500, 5101.30.3000.   [9] 5101.21.6000, 5101.29.6000, 5101.30.6000. They include wool not carded or combed but processed beyond the scoured or carbonized condition, e.g. dyed. This wool is not identified by use or grade.
ERS, Field Crops Branch, (202) 694–5300. Compiled from reports of the U.S. Department of Commerce.

Table 7-51.—Wool: United States imports (for consumption), clean content, by country of origin, 2005–2014 [1]

Country of origin	2005	2006	2007	2008	2009	2010	2011	2012	2013	2014
	Million pounds	Million pounds	Million pounds	Million pounds	Million pounds	Million pounds	Million pounds	Million pounds	Million pounds	Million pounds
48's and finer:										
Argentina	0.1	0.0	0.1	0.0	0.0	0.0	0.3	0.0	0.0	0.0
Australia	4.5	5.5	3.7	2.9	2.0	2.2	2.0	2.5	2.3	1.6
Canada	0.6	0.6	0.5	0.5	0.9	0.3	0.4	0.9	0.6	0.9
Chile	0.0	0.0	0.0	0.0	0.0	0.0	0.0	0.0	0.0	0.0
New Zealand	0.4	0.4	0.2	0.2	0.0	0.2	0.1	0.3	0.2	0.4
South Africa	0.3	0.2	0.3	0.4	0.1	0.0	0.3	0.2	0.0	0.0
United Kingdom	0.1	0.0	0.0	0.1	0.0	0.1	0.0	0.1	0.0	0.0
Uruguay	0.1	0.3	0.3	0.2	0.1	0.1	0.3	0.4	0.3	0.4
Other	0.1	0.3	0.1	0.3	0.2	0.2	0.4	0.2	0.5	0.6
Total	6.2	7.3	5.2	4.6	3.3	3.1	3.8	4.6	3.9	3.9
Not finer than 46's:										
Argentina	0.7	0.3	0.2	0.1	0.4	0.4	0.2	0.1	0.0	0.0
Australia	0.4	0.2	0.0	0.2	0.1	0.4	1.1	0.3	0.2	0.1
Canada	0.1	0.0	0.0	0.0	0.0	0.0	0.0	0.0	0.0	0.0
New Zealand	9.7	7.9	7.2	6.5	4.6	3.3	2.3	3.0	2.8	2.4
Uruguay	0.0	0.0	0.0	0.0	0.0	0.0	0.0	0.0	0.0	0.0
South Africa	0.2	0.2	0.1	0.2	0.2	0.3	0.2	0.2	0.1	0.1
United Kingdom	1.0	1.2	1.4	1.4	0.5	0.3	0.7	1.0	0.5	0.4
Other	0.1	0.1	0.1	0.2	0.2	0.2	0.2	0.0	0.1	0.2
Total	12.2	9.9	9.0	8.6	6.0	4.9	4.7	4.6	3.7	3.2
Grand total	18.4	17.3	14.3	13.2	9.4	8.0	8.5	9.1	7.6	7.1

[1] Wool not advanced in any manner or by any process of manufacture beyond washed, scoured, or carbonized condition.
ERS, Field Crops Branch, (202) 694–5300. Compiled from reports of the U.S. Department of Commerce.

Table 7-52.—Wool: Average price per pound, clean basis, delivered to United States mills, 2005–2014[1]

| Year | Territory[2] | | Australian 64's good topmaking (in bond, American yield) |
	64's (20.60–22.04 microns)	Avg. 58's–56's (24.95–27.84 microns)	
	Cents	*Cents*	*Cents*
2005	186	126	257
2006	179	115	265
2007	265	157	373
2008	309	204	347
2009	227	155	302
2010	327	203	410
2011	425	374	630
2012	281	346	590
2013	423	259	534
2014	417	274	489

[1] Beginning January 1976 the unit designation terminology for wool prices changed to microns. For example 64's (20.60–22.04 microns) formerly was fine good French combing and staple. Two designations 56's (26.40–27.84 microns) and 58's (24.95–26.39 microns) have been averaged in the price data shown here and together were formerly the category fleece ⅜ blood good French combing and staple.   [2] Wool grown in the range areas of California, Oregon, Washington, Texas, the intermountain States (including Arizona and New Mexico), and parts of the Dakotas, Kansas, Nebraska, and Oklahoma. These wools vary considerably in shrinkage and color.
ERS, Field Crops Branch, (202) 694–5300 and AMS.

Table 7-53.—Wool: Number of sheep shorn, weight per fleece, and production, by State and United States, 2013–2014

| State | Sheep | | Weight per fleece | | Shorn wool production | |
	2013	2014	2013	2014	2013	2014
	1,000 head	*1,000 head*	*Pounds*	*Pounds*	*1,000 pounds*	*1,000 pounds*
Arizona	110.0	115.0	6.0	5.9	660	680
California	400.0	460.0	6.5	6.3	2,600	2,900
Colorado	310.0	340.0	6.8	7.1	2,100	2,400
Idaho	200.0	200.0	9.0	8.5	1,800	1,700
Illinois	42.0	43.0	7.1	7.1	300	305
Indiana	36.0	35.0	6.1	6.0	220	210
Iowa	155.0	165.0	5.5	5.5	850	900
Kansas	45.0	39.0	6.3	6.2	285	240
Kentucky	11.0	11.0	6.4	6.5	70	71
Michigan	65.0	63.0	6.2	6.0	400	380
Minnesota	135.0	125.0	6.3	6.4	850	800
Missouri	43.0	44.0	6.0	6.0	260	265
Montana	200.0	185.0	8.9	9.0	1,770	1,660
Nebraska	59.0	62.0	7.1	7.2	420	445
Nevada	60.0	54.0	9.8	10.4	585	560
New England[1]	33.0	30.0	6.7	6.8	220	205
New Mexico	74.0	81.0	8.0	7.8	590	630
New York	38.0	40.0	6.3	6.5	240	260
North Carolina	8.0	7.0	5.0	5.0	40	35
North Dakota	60.0	58.0	8.2	7.9	490	460
Ohio	80.0	83.0	6.1	5.9	490	490
Oklahoma	24.0	21.0	5.6	5.5	135	115
Oregon	160.0	158.0	6.9	6.3	1,100	1,000
Pennsylvania	56.0	48.0	6.6	6.7	370	320
South Dakota	250.0	230.0	7.3	7.6	1,830	1,750
Tennessee	18.0	18.0	5.6	5.6	100	100
Texas	310.0	290.0	7.4	7.2	2,300	2,100
Utah	240.0	245.0	9.2	9.2	2,200	2,250
Virginia	32.0	27.0	5.9	5.6	190	150
Washington	38.0	36.0	7.8	7.5	295	270
West Virginia	19.0	20.0	5.5	5.7	105	114
Wisconsin	59.0	50.0	6.8	7.0	400	350
Wyoming	285.0	250.0	8.6	9.2	2,450	2,300
Other States[2]	45.0	47.0	6.1	6.1	275	285
United States	3,700.0	3,680.0	7.3	7.3	26,990	26,700

[1] New England includes Connecticut, Maine, Massachusetts, New Hampshire, Rhode Island, and Vermont.   [2] Unpublished states.
NASS, Livestock Branch, (202) 720–3570.

Table 7-54.—Wool: Price and value, by State and United States, 2013–2014

State	Price per pound		Value [1]	
	2013	2014	2013	2014
	Dollars	*Dollars*	*1,000 Dollars*	*1,000 dollars*
Arizona	0.80	1.10	528	748
California	1.45	1.35	3,770	3,915
Colorado	1.90	1.85	3,990	4,440
Idaho	1.35	1.54	2,430	2,618
Illinois	0.52	0.57	156	174
Indiana	0.82	0.46	180	97
Iowa	0.65	0.58	553	522
Kansas	0.85	0.95	242	228
Kentucky	0.50	0.75	35	53
Michigan	0.85	0.86	340	327
Minnesota	0.84	0.82	714	656
Missouri	0.57	0.56	148	148
Montana	2.20	2.05	3,894	3,403
Nebraska	1.05	1.06	441	472
Nevada	2.10	1.95	1,229	1,034
New England [2]	0.80	0.85	176	174
New Mexico	1.35	1.65	797	1,040
New York	0.60	0.70	144	182
North Carolina	1.00	1.30	40	46
North Dakota	1.25	1.45	613	667
Ohio	0.69	0.59	338	289
Oklahoma	0.60	0.70	81	81
Oregon	1.11	1.36	1,221	1,360
Pennsylvania	0.46	0.50	170	160
South Dakota	1.57	1.52	2,873	2,660
Tennessee	0.77	0.96	77	96
Texas	1.76	1.57	4,048	3,297
Utah	1.60	1.80	3,520	4,068
Virginia	0.85	0.80	162	120
Washington	1.10	1.80	325	486
West Virginia	0.86	0.86	90	98
Wisconsin	0.70	0.75	280	263
Wyoming	2.13	1.97	5,219	4,531
Other States [3]	1.40	1.60	385	456
United States	1.45	1.46	39,209	38,909

[1] Production multiplied by marketing year average price.   [2] New England includes Connecticut, Maine, Massachusetts, New Hampshire, Rhode Island, and Vermont.   [3] Unpublished states.
NASS, Livestock Branch, (202) 720–3570.

Table 7-55.—Mohair: Price-support operations, United States, 2005–2014[1]

Year	Income support payment rates per pound	Program price levels per pound		Put under loan		Acquired by CCC under loan program[2]	Owned by CCC at end of marketing year
		Loan	Target	Quantity	Percentage of production		
	Dollars	*Dollars*	*Dollars*	*1,000 pounds*	*Percent*	*1,000 pounds*	*1,000 pounds*
2005	NA	4.20	NA	36.4	2.35	0.0	0.0
2006	NA	4.20	NA	25.0	1.85	0.0	0.0
2007	NA	4.20	NA	20.4	1.79	0.0	0.0
2008	NA	4.20	NA	8.7	0.73	0.0	0.0
2009	NA	4.20	NA	14.5	1.37	0.0	0.0
2010	NA	4.20	NA	4.2	0.38	0.0	0.0
2011	NA	4.20	NA	0.0	0.0	0.0	0.0
2012	NA	4.20	NA	0.0	0.0	0.0	0.0
2013	NA	4.20	NA	0.0	0.0	0.0	0.0
2014	NA	4.20	NA	0.0	0.0	0.0	0.0

(NA) Not available.   [1] Nonrecourse Marketing Loan Program authorized by the Farm Security and Rural Investment Act of 2002, as amended, for marketing years 2002-2007, the Food , Conservation, and Energy Act of 2008, as amended, for marketing years 2008-2013, and the Agricultural Act of 2014, as amended, for marketing years 2014-2018.   [2] Acquisitions as of December 31, 2015.
FSA, Fibers, Peanuts, Tobacco, (202) 401–0062.

Table 7-56.—Mohair: Goats clipped, production, price, and value, by State and United States, 2013–2014

State	Goats clipped		Average clip per goat		Production		Price per pound		Value[1]	
	2013	2014	2013	2014	2013	2014	2013	2014	2013	2014
	Head	*Head*	*Pounds*	*Pounds*	*1,000 pounds*	*1,000 pounds*	*Dollars*	*Dollars*	*1,000 dollars*	*1,000 dollars*
Arizona	30,000	33,000	3.5	3.6	105	120	1.35	1.15	142	138
California	2,200	2,000	4.5	5.0	10	10	6.00	6.00	60	60
New Mexico	7,500	9,000	4.0	3.9	30	35	1.60	1.20	48	42
Texas	80,000	92,000	6.1	6.3	490	580	5.50	6.30	2,695	3,654
Other States[2]	23,800	23,000	6.1	5.9	145	135	2.45	2.80	355	378
United States	143,500	159.000	5.4	5.5	780	880	4.23	4.85	3,300	4,272

[1] Production multiplied by marketing year average price.   U.S. value is summation of State values.   [2] Unpublished states.
NASS, Livestock Branch, (202) 720–3570.

Table 7-57—Angora goats: Inventory Jan 1, 2014–2015, and number of operations, 2012, by State and United States [1]

State	January 1 angora goats inventory		Operations with angora goats [2]
	2014	2015 [3]	2012
	Head	Head	Number
Alabama			152
Alaska			5
Arizona	33,000	36,000	3,218
Arkansas			25
California	3,600	3,400	314
Colorado			182
Delaware			3
Florida			165
Georgia			140
Hawaii			23
Idaho			70
Illinois			84
Indiana			85
Iowa			67
Kansas			45
Kentucky			143
Louisiana			49
Maryland			59
Michigan			177
Minnesota	1,000	(NA)	125
Mississippi			77
Missouri	1,500	(NA)	152
Montana			59
Nebraska			47
Nevada			27
New England [4]			664
New Jersey			75
New Mexico	10,000	11,000	904
New York			176
North Carolina			195
North Dakota			24
Ohio			189
Oklahoma			61
Oregon	2,500	(NA)	166
Pennsylvania			268
South Carolina			121
South Dakota			22
Tennessee			28
Texas	76,000	85,000	629
Utah			275
Virginia			169
Washington			151
Wisconsin	900	(NA)	75
West Virginia			158
Wyoming			16
Other States [5]	19,500	24,600	
United States	148,000	160,000	9,859

(NA) Not Available. [1] An operation is any place having one or more head of angora goats on hand December 31. [2] State level estimates only available in conjunction with the Census of Agriculture every 5 years. [3] Preliminary. [4] New England includes Connecticut, Maine, Massachusetts, New Hampshire, Rhode Island, and Vermont. [5] Unpublished states.
NASS, Livestock Branch, (202) 720–3570.

Table 7-58.—Milk goats: Inventory Jan 1, 2014–2015, and number of operations, 2012, by State and United States [1]

State	January 1 milk goats inventory		Operations with milk goats [2]
	2014	2015 [3]	2012
	Head	Head	Number
Alabama	3,500	3,800	359
Alaska	(NA)	(NA)	34
Arizona	3,000	(NA)	642
Arkansas	4,200	4,400	567
California	38,000	40,000	1,416
Colorado	9,000	10,000	756
Delaware	(NA)	(NA)	24
Florida	6,200	6,400	852
Georgia	4,500	4,000	396
Hawaii	(NA)	(NA)	79
Idaho	4,000	3,900	435
Illinois	3,400	5,700	593
Indiana	11,800	11,500	1,123
Iowa	30,000	31,000	639
Kansas	4,800	4,200	518
Kentucky	4,500	5,700	822
Louisiana	1,200	(NA)	234
Maryland	2,200	(NA)	234
Michigan	11,400	11,300	1,194
Minnesota	13,000	13,500	575
Mississippi	2,000	(NA)	234
Missouri	9,600	9,900	1,083
Montana	3,000	(NA)	311
Nebraska	3,800	3,700	361
Nevada	(NA)	(NA)	143
New England [4]	14,600	14,500	3,901
New Jersey	2,100	(NA)	182
New Mexico	2,500	(NA)	377
New York	13,100	(NA)	1,091
North Carolina	7,100	13,400	803
North Dakota	(NA)	8,000	154
Ohio	9,500	10,000	1,341
Oklahoma	5,900	6,900	929
Oregon	11,200	9,500	842
Pennsylvania	12,000	13,000	1,288
South Carolina	3,100	3,400	453
South Dakota	3,300	(NA)	276
Tennessee	7,200	6,300	587
Texas	20,000	23,000	2,591
Utah	2,500	(NA)	298
Virginia	3,300	4,500	708
Washington	8,400	7,200	934
West Virginia	2,000	(NA)	380
Wisconsin	46,000	44,000	994
Wyoming	2,000	(NA)	258
Other States [5]	9,100	32,300	
United States	358,000	365,000	32,011

(NA) Not Available.　[1] An operation is any place having one or more head of milk goats on hand December 31.　[2] State level estimates only available in conjunction with the Census of Agriculture every 5 years.　[3] Preliminary.　[4] New England includes Connecticut, Maine, Massachusetts, New Hampshire, Rhode Island, and Vermont.　[5] Unpublished states.
NASS, Livestock Branch, (202) 720–3570.

Table 7-59.—Meat and other goats: Inventory Jan 1, 2014–2015, and number of operations, 2012, by State and United States [1]

State	January 1 meat and other goats inventory		Operations with Meat goats [2]
	2014	2015 [3]	2012
	Head	Head	Number
Alabama	50,000	47,000	2,469
Alaska	(NA)	(NA)	35
Arizona	25,000	28,000	2,387
Arkansas	38,000	38,000	2,083
California	85,000	85,000	3,330
Colorado	22,000	25,000	1,591
Delware	(NA)	(NA)	136
Florida	37,000	41,000	3,022
Georgia	58,000	67,000	2,951
Hawaii	10,500	(NA)	336
Idaho	14,000	(NA)	859
Illinois	18,000	16,700	1,698
Indiana	31,400	31,000	2,026
Iowa	25,000	25,500	1,383
Kansas	37,000	40,000	1,653
Kentucky	58,000	60,000	3,092
Louisiana	19,000	20,000	1,225
Maryland	11,600	(NA)	687
Michigan	16,500	(NA)	1,669
Minnesota	23,000	20,500	1,121
Mississippi	19,000	19,000	1,329
Missouri	85,200	78,600	3,161
Montana	8,000	(NA)	435
Nebraska	19,500	(NA)	1,247
Nevada	7,300	(NA)	406
New England [4]	11,000	(NA)	9,368
New Jersey	6,000	(NA)	581
New Mexico	20,000	(NA)	1,629
New York	22,000	18,700	1,535
North Carolina	45,000	43,000	3,659
North Dakota	2,800	(NA)	227
Ohio	47,000	46,000	3,401
Oklahoma	75,000	95,000	4,020
Oregon	23,000	24,000	1,672
Pennsylvania	39,000	37,000	2,989
South Carolina	36,000	34,000	2,447
South Dakota	11,500	(NA)	514
Tennessee	110,000	118,000	4,514
Texas	810,000	800,000	23,107
Utah	11,000	(NA)	812
Virginia	45,000	46,000	2,742
Washington	24,000	21,000	1,792
West Virginia	19,000	21,000	1,276
Wisconsin	22,000	(NA)	1,518
Wyoming	4,700	(NA)	410
Other States [5]	3,000	179,000	
United States	2,105,000	2,125,000	108,544

(NA) Not Available.   [1] An operation is any place having one or more head of meat goats on hand December 31.   [2] State level estimates only available in conjunction with the Census of Agriculture every 5 years.   [3] Preliminary.   [4] New England includes Connecticut, Maine, Massachusetts, New Hampshire, Rhode Island, and Vermont.   [5] Unpublished states.
NASS, Livestock Branch, (202) 720–3570.

Table 7-60.—All goats: Number of operations, 2012, by State and United States [1]

State	2012 [2]
	Number
Alabama	2,832
Alaska	56
Arizona	5,525
Arkansas	2,450
California	4,474
Colorado	2,168
Delware	154
Florida	3,746
Georgia	3,329
Hawaii	420
Idaho	1,208
Illinios	2,193
Indiana	2,883
Iowa	1,921
Kansas	1,995
Kentucky	3,797
Louisiana	1,412
Maryland	903
Michigan	2,623
Minnesota	1,580
Mississippi	1,533
Missouri	3,955
Montana	698
Nebraska	1,509
Nevada	523
New England [3]	3,096
New Jersey	766
New Mexico	2,638
New York	2,449
North Carolina	4,387
North Dakota	350
Ohio	4,485
Oklahoma	4,629
Oregon	2,350
Pennsylvania	4,088
South Carolina	2,861
South Dakota	748
Tennessee	4,929
Texas	25,063
Utah	1,249
Virginia	3,376
Washington	2,506
West Virginia	1,586
Wisconsin	2,419
Wyoming	594
United States	128,456

[1] An operation is any place having one or more head of goats on hand December 31. [2] State level estimates only available in conjunction with the Census of Agriculture every 5 years. [3] New England includes Connecticut, Maine, Massachusetts, New Hampshire, Rhode Island, and Vermont.
NASS, Livestock Branch, (202) 720–3570.

Table 7-61.—Red meat: Production, by class of slaughter, United States, 2005–2014

Year	Commercial			Farm	Total
	Federally inspected	Other [1]	Total [2]		

Beef

	Million pounds	Million pounds	Million pounds	Million pounds	Million pounds
2005	24,328	355	24,683	104	24,786
2006	25,792	360	26,152	104	26,256
2007	26,070	351	26,421	103	26,524
2008	26,200	361	26,561	96	26,657
2009	25,598		25,966	90	26,056
2010	25,954		26,305	84	26,389
2011	25,854		26,195	75	26,270
2012	25,573		25,913	76	25,989
2013	25,385		25,720	70	25,790
2014	23,934		24,251	68	24,318

Pork, excluding lard

	Million pounds	Million pounds	Million pounds	Million pounds	Million pounds
2005	20,506	179	20,685	20	20,705
2006	20,877	177	21,054	20	21,073
2007	21,768	175	21,943	20	21,962
2008	23,170	177	23,347	20	23,367
2009	22,827		22,999	21	23,020
2010	22,275		22,437	19	22,456
2011	22,599		22,758	17	22,775
2012	23,090		23,253	15	23,268
2013	23,040		23,187	16	23,203
2014	22,710		22,843	15	22,858

Veal

	Million pounds	Million pounds	Million pounds	Million pounds	Million pounds
2005	152	4	156	9	165
2006	144	3	147	9	155
2007	134	3	137	9	146
2008	140	3	143	9	152
2009	135		138	8	147
2010	131		134	8	143
2011	126		130	7	136
2012	115		118	7	125
2013	109		111	6	117
2014	92		94	6	100

Lamb and Mutton

	Million pounds	Million pounds	Million pounds	Million pounds	Million pounds
2005	180	7	187	4	192
2006	177	8	185	5	190
2007	175	8	183	6	189
2008	166	8	174	6	180
2009	162		171	5	175
2010	154		164	5	168
2011	141		149	5	153
2012	148		156	5	161
2013	146		156	5	161
2014	145		156	5	161

All meat, excluding lard

	Million pounds	Million pounds	Million pounds	Million pounds	Million pounds
2005	45,166	545	45,711	138	45,848
2006	46,990	547	47,537	137	47,675
2007	48,147	537	48,684	137	48,820
2008	49,675	550	50,225	131	50,355
2009	48,721		49,274	124	49,398
2010	48,514		49,039	116	49,155
2011	48,721		49,232	103	49,335
2012	48,925		49,440	103	49,543
2013	48,679		49,174	97	49,271
2014	46,881		47,343	93	47,437

[1] Other class no longer reported.　　[2] Totals are based on unrounded data.
NASS, Livestock Branch, (202) 720–3570.

Table 7-62.—Meat: United States exports and imports into the United States, carcass weight equivalent, 2004–2013 [1]

Year	Exports				Imports			
	Beef and veal	Lamb and mutton	Pork [2]	All meat	Beef & veal	Lamb and mutton	Pork [2]	All meat
	Million pounds	Million pounds	Million pounds	Million pounds	Million pounds	Million pounds	Million pounds	Million pounds
2004	460	8	2,181	2,649	3,679	181	1,099	4,960
2005	697	9	2,666	3,373	3,599	180	1,024	4,803
2006	1,145	18	2,995	4,158	3,085	190	990	4,265
2007	1,434	9	3,141	4,585	3,052	203	968	4,223
2008	1,887	12	4,667	6,566	2,538	183	832	3,553
2009	1,935	16	4,095	6,046	2,626	171	834	3,631
2010	2,300	16	4,223	6,539	2,298	166	859	3,323
2011	2,785	19	5,196	7,994	2,057	162	803	3,022
2012	2,452	11	5,380	7,843	2,220	154	802	3,176
2013	2,590	7	4,992	7,589	2,250	173	880	3,302

[1] Carcass weight equivalent of all meat, including the meat content of minor meats and of mixed products.   Shipments to U.S. Territories are included in domestic consumption.   [2] The pork series has been revised to a dressed weight equivalent rather than "Pork, excluding lard."

ERS, Market and Trade Economics Division, Animal Products and Cost of Production Branch, (202) 694–5409. Data on imports and commercial exports are computed from records of the U.S. Department of Commerce, those on exports by the U.S. Department of Agriculture are separately estimated from deliveries and stocks.

Table 7-63.—International Meat: Production, 2013–2015

Country	2013	2014	2015
	1,000 metric tons	1,000 metric tons	1,000 metric tons
Beef and veal:			
Argentina	2,850	2,700	2,740
Australia	2,359	2,595	2,547
Brazil	9,675	9,723	9,425
Canada	1,049	1,099	1,050
China	6,730	6,890	6,700
European Union	7,388	7,443	7,670
India	3,800	4,100	4,100
Mexico	1,807	1,827	1,850
Pakistan	1,630	1,675	1,725
Russia	1,380	1,370	1,355
Others	9,063	9,232	8,402
Total Foreign	47,731	48,654	47,564
United States	11,751	11,076	10,861
Total	59,482	59,730	58,425
Swine:			
Brazil	3,335	3,400	3,519
Canada	1,822	1,805	1,890
China	54,930	56,710	54,870
European Union	22,359	22,540	23,350
Japan	1,309	1,264	1,254
Korea, South	1,252	1,200	1,217
Mexico	1,284	1,290	1,323
Philippines	1,340	1,353	1,370
Russia	2,400	2,510	2,615
Vietnam	2,349	2,425	2,450
Others	5,918	5,692	5,337
Total Foreign	98,298	100,189	99,195
United States	10,525	10,370	11,121
Total	108,823	110,559	110,316

FAS, Office of Global Analysis, (202) 720-6301.   Prepared or estimated on the basis of official USDA production, supply, and distribution statistics from foreign governments.

Table 7-64.—Meat: U.S. exports, 2011–2013

Country	2011	2012	2013
	Metric tons	Metric tons	Metric tons
Beef & veal, fr/ch/fz:			
Japan	138,945	137,769	207,586
Canada	145,535	132,954	130,652
Mexico	156,083	111,614	128,437
Hong Kong	44,020	63,765	120,869
Korea, South	135,553	111,991	94,404
Taiwan	35,354	19,365	32,046
Egypt	33,814	32,169	17,341
Netherlands	14,589	11,131	11,710
Chile	3,988	8,906	10,235
Philippines	6,780	5,962	7,049
Italy(*)	6,397	5,308	5,719
United Arab Emirates	7,999	5,113	4,930
Vietnam	43,306	39,644	3,891
Dominican Republic	4,142	3,579	3,772
Germany(*)	3,812	2,975	3,230
Bahamas, The	3,470	3,197	2,887
Kuwait	3,905	2,084	2,560
Indonesia	5,241	1,030	2,045
Guatemala	2,519	2,022	1,870
Netherlands Antilles(*)	1,932	1,841	1,851
Jamaica	2,135	1,835	1,533
Singapore	2,894	1,216	1,371
Peru	896	1,744	1,353
Cayman Islands	1,377	1,332	1,332
Qatar	2,539	868	1,198
Colombia	1,087	331	1,148
Angola	2,471	317	1,117
Trinidad and Tobago	1,095	1,067	1,103
Honduras	627	646	961
Rest of World	68,943	61,525	11,456
World Total	881,448	773,297	815,656
Beef & veal, prep/pres:			
Canada	30,715	32,898	34,306
Hong Kong	2,811	458	4,010
Mexico	521	866	893
Germany(*)	533	285	840
Australia(*)	923	793	710
Panama	330	396	561
Philippines	30	548	252
Brazil	352	0	184
Guatemala	122	135	136
New Zealand(*)	54	78	115
United Arab Emirates	130	128	111
Suriname	123	162	88
Turks and Caicos Islands	188	180	71
Netherlands Antilles(*)	76	76	70
United Kingdom	103	25	67
Angola	0	8	65
Bahamas, The	242	200	63
Colombia	7	5	61
Costa Rica	6	31	60
Italy(*)	21	0	55
Lebanon	37	38	51
Leeward-Windward Islands(*)	10	47	46
Trinidad and Tobago	25	27	42
Palau	28	32	35
Kuwait	63	18	33
Jamaica	25	40	33
Peru	73	0	31
Dominican Republic	31	38	29
Netherlands	95	32	28
Rest of World	2,385	522	345
World Total	40,058	38,065	43,390

See footnote(s) at end of table.

Table 7-64.—Meat: U.S. exports, 2011–2013—Continued

Country	2011	2012	2013
	Metric tons	Metric tons	Metric tons
Pork, fr/ch/fz:			
Mexico	286,080	409,868	427,968
Japan	465,636	421,235	401,950
China	219,502	198,995	153,405
Canada	120,932	130,672	111,999
Korea, South	148,885	132,603	87,239
Australia(*)	56,080	59,788	48,706
Hong Kong	36,672	38,295	45,753
Colombia	9,444	16,198	29,969
Philippines	29,561	26,000	28,169
Honduras	17,827	17,850	20,824
Dominican Republic	12,054	13,892	17,028
Chile	8,192	12,223	16,815
Ukraine	3,791	2,236	14,456
Taiwan	14,583	9,690	11,927
Guatemala	5,885	7,776	8,465
New Zealand(*)	4,587	7,643	7,411
Panama	2,756	3,014	7,006
Singapore	8,375	7,549	6,800
Russia	63,679	89,324	5,315
Albania	1,137	5,128	3,498
Bahamas, The	2,899	2,831	3,374
Costa Rica	850	1,342	3,276
El Salvador	1,541	2,469	2,943
Trinidad and Tobago	2,353	2,518	2,442
Ecuador	1,733	1,737	2,265
Cuba	3,007	2,692	2,212
Leeward-Windward Islands(*)	1,306	1,236	1,346
Uruguay	617	747	1,242
Vietnam	2,855	1,766	1,226
Rest of World	15,528	17,639	13,375
World Total	1,548,345	1,644,953	1,488,403
Pork, hams/shldrs,cured:			
Canada	25,984	35,135	36,134
China	5,045	5,545	6,796
Mexico	70,518	2,041	2,456
Panama	534	1,432	2,102
Japan	1,543	1,294	2,025
Trinidad and Tobago	750	858	798
Belize	338	473	589
Colombia	277	642	576
Bahamas, The	1,131	411	384
Netherlands Antilles(*)	314	413	330
Philippines	278	74	198
Australia(*)	74	0	148
Honduras	71	72	123
Leeward-Windward Islands(*)	90	162	119
Haiti	147	149	109
Barbados	138	198	88
Korea, South	78	94	52
Bolivia	33	0	48
Italy(*)	8	0	35
United Kingdom	54	15	33
Bermuda	0	13	33
Netherlands	160	35	24
Chile	0	34	18
Singapore	87	30	17
Guyana	0	3	15
Costa Rica	63	7	9
Suriname	4	2	6
Dominican Republic	3	1	4
El Salvador	0	0	3
Rest of World	2,662	3,437	11
World Total	110,382	52,571	53,284

See footnote(s) at end of table.

Table 7-64.—Meat: U.S. exports, 2011–2013—Continued

Country	2011	2012	2013
	Metric tons	*Metric tons*	*Metric tons*
Pork, bacon, cured:			
Mexico	15,973	13,291	12,596
Canada	3,343	5,794	3,513
Japan	4,610	3,415	1,951
Korea, South	426	977	1,552
Dominican Republic	518	494	547
Bahamas, The	367	404	370
Colombia	120	226	363
Guatemala	397	373	339
Costa Rica	275	360	304
Australia(*)	130	225	273
Ecuador	114	110	272
Netherlands	109	80	258
Panama	125	159	216
Chile	99	79	214
Singapore	392	358	209
Hong Kong	164	316	184
Netherlands Antilles(*)	149	85	149
Honduras	175	151	140
Philippines	60	64	119
Italy(*)	110	12	118
China	6	20	114
Leeward-Windward Islands(*)	113	104	112
New Zealand(*)	238	141	108
El Salvador	37	74	101
United Arab Emirates	66	35	80
Bermuda	74	79	73
Trinidad and Tobago	98	190	67
Peru	25	1	60
Nicaragua	84	92	59
Rest of World	596	689	370
World Total	28,992	28,395	24,827
Pork, prep/pres, nt/cn:			
Canada	32,653	42,651	56,414
Mexico	6,109	11,604	17,998
Chile	25	850	880
Colombia	210	550	858
Dominican Republic	301	215	349
Panama	112	137	326
Netherlands Antilles(*)	131	151	301
Philippines	726	492	279
Ecuador	198	211	276
Bahamas, The	106	258	271
Singapore	261	72	211
Korea, South	265	321	208
Honduras	410	228	201
Japan	565	723	187
Micronesia	146	140	174
Hong Kong	234	195	173
Trinidad and Tobago	46	94	138
Costa Rica	224	196	120
Guatemala	318	402	111
Peru	14	93	91
Ukraine	0	168	82
Palau	64	61	80
Marshall Islands	82	97	78
Belize	0	1	66
Leeward-Windward Islands(*)	35	39	61
El Salvador	34	35	50
Netherlands	4	4	32
Italy(*)	0	0	29
Nicaragua	12	15	27
Rest of World	1,004	219	171
World Total	44,287	60,223	80,241

See footnote(s) at end of table.

Table 7-64.—Meat: U.S. exports, 2011–2013—Continued

Country	2011	2012	2013
	Metric tons	*Metric tons*	*Metric tons*
Pork, prep/pres, canned:			
Philippines	4,310	4,463	6,572
Japan	6,467	5,927	4,134
Australia(*)	2,524	2,983	3,011
Canada	2,198	2,561	2,168
Hong Kong	1,116	1,823	1,987
Mexico	521	1,174	1,181
Korea, South	1,065	1,059	1,052
China	205	258	1,035
Panama	709	705	808
New Zealand(*)	459	411	560
Guatemala	166	368	470
Singapore	260	310	416
Colombia	241	132	351
Costa Rica	81	73	279
Honduras	70	217	264
United Arab Emirates	93	98	249
Netherlands Antilles(*)	65	169	213
Thailand	59	134	179
Dominican Republic	72	147	175
Bahamas, The	202	187	143
Trinidad and Tobago	49	17	106
French Pacific Islands(*)	67	72	89
El Salvador	38	18	81
Taiwan	58	30	66
Vietnam	35	63	61
Jamaica	14	19	46
Haiti	69	16	44
Palau	31	37	41
Bermuda	31	15	39
Rest of World	1,352	886	235
World Total	22,626	24,372	26,055
Lamb & mutton; fr/ch/fz:			
Mexico	3,027	3,140	1,909
Canada	560	369	383
Leeward-Windward Islands(*)	419	172	130
Bahamas, The	564	248	97
Dominican Republic	128	148	81
Bermuda	149	18	63
Honduras	12	7	59
Trinidad and Tobago	166	108	48
Panama	99	42	30
Netherlands Antilles(*)	520	124	29
Germany(*)	28	6	28
Costa Rica	124	36	23
Spain	29	33	20
Singapore	89	8	17
Philippines	0	17	16
Hong Kong	130	14	14
Australia(*)	7	6	13
Barbados	92	8	12
Turks and Caicos Islands	22	15	10
Guatemala	115	18	10
United Arab Emirates	84	27	9
Malaysia	0	0	7
Netherlands	943	12	5
Mayotte	0	0	5
Equatorial Guinea	27	5	4
Jamaica	99	15	4
Saudi Arabia	43	0	4
Italy(*)	296	9	4
Uruguay	5	0	4
Rest of World	333	79	23
World Total	8,108	4,680	3,060

See footnote(s) at end of table.

Table 7-64.—Meat: U.S. exports, 2011–2013—Continued

Country	2011	2012	2013
	Metric tons	*Metric tons*	*Metric tons*
Sausages & bologna:			
Canada	29,908	33,435	37,369
Japan	29,103	24,631	26,751
China	5,150	15,341	18,543
Mexico	6,914	8,266	8,787
Hong Kong	23,018	11,456	3,128
Korea, South	3,011	2,329	2,332
Philippines	1,579	1,553	2,186
Belize	631	770	854
Bahamas, The	941	1,001	768
Panama	332	495	683
Guatemala	432	403	538
United Kingdom	151	322	420
Uruguay	311	447	403
Taiwan	811	247	337
Singapore	223	216	311
El Salvador	265	283	302
Peru	102	262	291
Netherlands Antilles(*)	314	356	278
Dominican Republic	317	253	254
Marshall Islands	170	202	252
Australia(*)	111	97	193
Trinidad and Tobago	100	94	163
Chile	104	104	148
Colombia	55	67	130
Bermuda	159	157	126
Netherlands	100	12	79
Thailand	58	67	76
Costa Rica	60	44	72
Ecuador	87	91	68
Rest of World	887	790	604
World Total	105,402	103,790	106,443
Other meat products, fr/ch/fz:			
Mexico	61	0	244
Hong Kong	37	143	35
Leeward-Windward Islands(*)	34	40	32
Dominican Republic	0	5	20
Singapore	21	21	16
Brazil	0	0	6
Cayman Islands	21	2	6
Netherlands Antilles(*)	27	14	4
Barbados	1	0	2
Costa Rica	9	1	1
Bahamas, The	0	19	1
Bermuda	0	0	1
Trinidad and Tobago	1	0	1
Netherlands	0	0	1
Turks and Caicos Islands	0	2	1
Panama	2	10	0
Bahrain	3	1	0
China	0	25	0
Ireland	0	2	0
Germany(*)	0	1	0
Guatemala	0	5	0
Israel(*)	0	1	0
Jamaica	0	1	0
Jordan	0	3	0
Malaysia	52	30	0
Saudi Arabia	50	0	0
Timor-Leste	1	0	0
Taiwan	24	0	0
United Kingdom	0	1	0
Rest of World	143	252	0
World Total	488	578	369

See footnote(s) at end of table.

Table 7-64.—Meat: U.S. exports, 2011–2013—Continued

Country	2011	2012	2013
	Metric tons	*Metric tons*	*Metric tons*
Variety meats, beef:			
Egypt	113,381	105,299	122,973
Mexico	100,144	80,324	87,542
Japan	19,738	14,921	27,071
Peru	9,931	11,155	16,005
Korea, South	18,469	13,622	10,966
Canada	14,766	13,711	9,656
Angola	8,903	10,220	7,188
Hong Kong	4,931	3,516	5,018
Philippines	5,938	5,127	4,077
Gabon	2,688	3,155	3,634
Jamaica	5,347	3,703	3,129
Indonesia	12,555	617	2,986
Cote d'Ivoire	4,522	5,935	2,690
Chile	260	2,481	2,624
Moldova	1,834	2,954	2,527
Ukraine	998	779	2,025
Colombia	331	581	1,526
Ecuador	1,210	1,248	1,239
Trinidad and Tobago	528	523	608
Guatemala	864	1,621	571
Vietnam	272	497	567
Costa Rica	353	540	493
Bahrain	543	654	420
Mozambique	515	516	418
Panama	72	58	311
Zambia	1,039	1,333	308
Honduras	389	385	278
Libya	0	0	268
Nicaragua	194	179	225
Rest of World	32,589	34,258	2,308
World Total	363,303	319,909	319,653
Variety meats, pork:			
China	136,784	134,633	156,841
Mexico	144,853	148,940	148,751
Hong Kong	69,353	34,846	35,481
Canada	18,421	17,794	16,268
Philippines	3,970	6,478	14,327
Japan	15,594	22,713	14,108
Singapore	963	259	9,375
Korea, South	37,869	14,212	6,603
Taiwan	11,764	7,744	5,782
Chile	4,338	3,333	5,741
Panama	1,499	2,968	2,860
Haiti	1,270	1,141	2,494
Colombia	1,124	1,868	1,926
Cuba	468	497	1,789
Guatemala	1,337	726	1,120
Peru	158	186	1,043
Albania	231	1,039	988
Honduras	908	1,626	957
Trinidad and Tobago	1,015	643	668
Benin	0	0	544
Dominican Republic	871	942	544
Australia(*)	4,676	3,975	477
El Salvador	301	350	367
Germany(*)	7	0	328
Vietnam	733	821	306
Netherlands Antilles(*)	401	286	289
Jamaica	53	25	288
Gabon	0	104	226
Uruguay	0	144	167
Rest of World	7,936	4,784	959
World Total	466,895	413,076	431,617

See footnote(s) at end of table.

Table 7-64.—Meat: U.S. exports, 2011–2013—Continued

Country	2011	2012	2013
	Metric tons	*Metric tons*	*Metric tons*
Variety meats, other:			
Mexico	11,405	11,836	12,129
Netherlands	568	2,780	3,340
Canada	2,974	2,302	3,169
Hong Kong	3,159	2,526	2,045
Korea, South	572	1,149	1,092
Venezuela	0	38	699
Taiwan	9	0	330
Vietnam	0	59	282
Peru	13	0	264
China	219	360	221
Saudi Arabia	1	8	209
Japan	4	34	171
Trinidad and Tobago	12	0	163
Dominican Republic	283	31	140
Colombia	67	25	89
Philippines	13	40	74
Netherlands Antilles(*)	280	111	68
Germany(*)	180	248	68
Nigeria	24	51	49
Brazil	1	0	41
Barbados	15	21	26
Leeward-Windward Islands(*)	66	26	25
Singapore	14	17	22
Bahamas, The	43	21	21
Denmark(*)	127	15	21
Uruguay	28	12	20
Bermuda	39	37	19
United Arab Emirates	75	48	19
Australia(*)	20	3	16
Rest of World	834	158	93
World Total	21,042	21,954	24,922

(*) Denotes a country that is a summarization of its component countries.   Users should use cautious interpretation on quantity reports using mixed units of measure.   Quantity line items will only include statistics on the units of measure that are equal to, or are able to be converted to, the assigned unit of measure of the grouped commodities.
    FAS, Office of Global Analysis, (202) 720-6301.   Data Source: Department of Commerce, U.S. Census Bureau, Foreign Trade Statistics.

Table 7-65.—Meat, beef, veal, and swine: International trade, imports and exports, 2013–2015

Country	2013	2014	2015
	1,000 metric tons	*1,000 metric tons*	*1,000 metric tons*
Principle exporters, beef and veal:			
Australia	1,593	1,851	1,854
Belarus	220	184	213
Brazil	1,849	1,909	1,705
Canada	332	378	391
European Union	244	301	303
India	1,765	2,082	1,806
Mexico	166	194	228
New Zealand	529	579	639
Paraguay	326	389	380
Uruguay	340	350	372
Others	588	605	627
Total Foreign	7,952	8,822	8,518
United States	1,174	1,167	1,035
Total	9,126	9,989	9,553
Principle importers, beef and veal:			
Canada	296	284	280
Chile	245	241	245
China	412	417	663
Egypt	195	270	360
European Union	376	372	365
Hong Kong	473	646	339
Japan	760	739	708
Korea, South	375	392	414
Malaysia	194	205	235
Russia	1,023	929	625
Others	2,096	2,066	1,814
Total Foreign	6,445	6,561	6,048
United States	1,020	1,337	1,559
Total	7,465	7,898	7,607
Principle exporters, swine:			
Australia	36	37	36
Belarus	585	556	627
Brazil	1,246	1,218	1,234
Canada	164	163	180
Chile	244	276	231
China	2,227	2,164	2,400
European Union	111	117	128
Mexico	4	25	19
Norway	7	13	36
Vietnam	40	40	40
Others	100	62	46
Total Foreign	4,764	4,671	4,977
United States	2,262	2,203	2,242
Total	7,026	6,874	7,219
Principle importers, swine:			
Australia	183	191	220
Canada	220	214	216
China	770	761	1,029
Hong Kong	399	347	397
Japan	1,223	1,332	1,269
Korea, South	388	480	599
Mexico	783	818	981
Philippines	172	199	175
Russia	868	515	407
Ukraine	98	117	116
Others	1,085	891	756
Total Foreign	6,189	5,865	6,165
United States	399	457	504
Total	6,588	6,322	6,669

FAS, Office of Global Analysis, (202) 720-6301. Prepared or estimated on the basis of official USDA production, supply, and distribution statistics from foreign governments.

Table 7-66.—Meats and lard: Production and consumption, United States, 2004–2013 [1]

Year	Beef			Veal			Lamb and mutton		
	Production	Consumption		Produc-tion	Consumption		Produc-tion	Consumption	
		Total	Per capita		Total	Per capita		Total	Per capita
	Million pounds	Million pounds	Pounds	Million pounds	Million pounds	Pounds	Million pounds	Million pounds	Pounds
2004	24,650	27,750	94.6	176	177	0.6	200	373	1.3
2005	24,787	27,754	93.8	165	164	0.6	191	356	1.2
2006	26,256	28,137	94.2	156	155	0.5	190	356	1.2
2007	26,523	28,141	93.3	146	145	0.5	189	385	1.3
2008	26,664	27,303	89.6	152	150	0.5	180	343	1.1
2009	26,068	26,836	87.3	147	147	0.5	177	338	1.1
2010	26,412	26,390	85.2	145	150	0.5	168	318	1.0
2011	26,281	25,538	81.8	136	137	0.4	153	295	0.9
2012	25,995	25,755	82.0	125	123	0.4	161	299	1.0
2013	25,791	25,475	80.5	118	119	0.4	161	324	1.0

Year	Pork			All meats		
	Production	Consumption		Production	Consumption	
		Total	Per capita		Total	Per capita
	Million pounds	Million pounds	Pounds	Million pounds	Million pounds	Pounds
2004	20,531	19,446	66.3	45,557	47,746	163
2005	20,705	19,093	64.5	45,848	47,366	160
2006	21,074	19,055	63.8	47,675	47,703	160
2007	21,962	19,763	65.5	48,817	48,434	160
2008	23,367	19,415	63.8	50,362	47,211	155
2009	23,020	19,870	64.7	49,412	47,191	154
2010	22,456	19,076	61.6	49,181	45,934	148
2011	22,775	18,388	58.9	49,345	44,358	142
2012	23,268	18,607	59.2	49,549	44,783	143
2013	23,200	19,095	60.3	49,270	45,013	142

[1] Carcass weight equivalent or dressed weight. Beginning 1977, pork production was no longer reported as "pork, excluding lard." This series has been revised to reflect pork production in prior years on a dressed weight basis that is comparable with the method used to report beef, veal, and lamb and mutton. Edible offals are excluded. Shipments to the U.S. territories are included in domestic consumption.
ERS, Animal Products, Grains and Oilseeds Branch, (202) 694–5409.

Table 7-67.—Hides, packer: Average price per piece, Central U.S., 2004–2013

Year	Steers				Heifers	
	Heavy native	Heavy Texas	Butt branded	Colorado branded	Heavy native	Branded
	Dollars	Dollars	Dollars	Dollars	Dollars	Dollars
2004	67.09	64.91	64.39	61.48	57.07	54.02
2005	65.64	63.50	63.53	60.90	57.89	54.20
2006	68.87	67.76	67.79	65.99	60.30	57.52
2007	72.01	70.51	70.72	67.79	65.70	61.85
2008	63.94	63.22	62.62	59.35	58.35	57.18
2009	45.29	44.10	42.70	31.84	29.00	31.86
2010	71.93	72.30	70.77	67.31	63.44	67.57
2011	82.17	81.70	80.77	76.42	74.39	71.17
2012	84.53	84.23	84.28	79.83	71.77	70.19
2013	98.73	95.74	98.56	94.38	84.68	82.90

AMS, Livestock & Grain Market News, (202) 720–7316.

Table 7-68.—Hides and skins: United States imports by country of origin, 2011–2013

Country of origin	2011	2012	2013
	Pieces	Pieces	Pieces
Hides and skins, mixed:			
Canada	931,947	1,209,375	1,007,569
Mexico	196,290	240,792	432,885
China	16,484	36,891	80,638
Turkey	48,515	17,273	22,030
Brazil	4,676	36,896	15,216
Italy(*)	18,929	3,939	12,227
Belgium-Luxembourg(*)	10,002	9,951	11,367
India	4	5,658	7,134
Thailand	6,868	6,833	5,324
Argentina	333	1,432	5,115
New Zealand(*)	16,621	7,538	4,377
Germany(*)	782	17	3,088
Australia(*)	321	7,165	2,647
Pakistan	24,660	2,555	2,514
Singapore	1,659	410	2,391
Taiwan	0	0	1,800
Lebanon	900	800	1,000
Colombia	6,204	10,336	889
France(*)	931	241	786
United Kingdom	145	1,916	625
Malaysia	40	1,661	575
Uruguay	524	31	547
Guinea	1,205	200	540
Korea, South	1,539	26	421
Dominican Republic	0	0	360
Spain	3,365	1,071	343
South Africa	4,980	258	203
Cote d'Ivoire	0	1,760	200
Denmark(*)	0	6	48
Rest of World	7,734	4,634	133
World Total	1,305,658	1,609,665	1,622,992
	Number	Number	Number
Furskins:			
Canada	1,874,531	2,543,217	2,288,602
Netherlands	387,273	483,686	390,630
Belgium-Luxembourg(*)	263,860	75,336	190,823
Poland	16,335	35,765	190,022
Sweden	133,255	129,624	124,520
Ukraine	0	97,000	50,148
Spain	28,418	35,162	44,123
Germany(*)	34,632	167	43,623
Finland	35,487	28,613	24,441
Denmark(*)	9,308	5,373	17,145
Greece	81,799	4,539	13,955
Russia	5,969	7,666	12,375
Mexico	27,696	3,477	11,025
Italy(*)	172	2	3,358
Ireland	0	0	3,019
Bosnia and Herzegovina	1,728	1,739	1,937
Switzerland(*)	4,350	8	574
China	1,026	8,540	497
Latvia	0	4	233
United Kingdom	0	0	59
Lithuania	0	138	35
South Africa	21	38	30
Uruguay	0	0	22
United Arab Emirates	0	0	13
Namibia	6	0	8
France(*)	1,446	864	6
Hong Kong	0	746	5
Austria	0	0	4
New Zealand(*)	7	0	4
Rest of World	93,759	96,776	0
World Total	3,001,078	3,558,480	3,411,236

(*) Denotes a country that is a summarization of its component countries.
FAS, Office of Global Analysis, (202) 720–6301.

Table 7-69.—Hides: U.S. trade exports, 2011–2013

Country	2011	2012	2013
	Pieces	*Pieces*	*Pieces*
Cattle hides, whole:			
China	10,539,676	12,009,559	17,052,725
Korea, South	4,383,022	4,137,583	4,356,831
Taiwan	1,496,401	1,098,726	1,870,784
Mexico	1,299,132	1,506,203	1,740,158
Italy(*)	2,347,259	1,154,127	1,129,983
Hong Kong	1,522,844	495,545	844,279
Japan	605,802	711,187	625,791
Vietnam	1,138,348	650,162	478,776
Thailand	692,901	500,532	309,296
Belgium-Luxembourg(*)	42,240	78,298	220,809
Turkey	292,970	270,603	213,326
Israel(*)	95,806	123,957	91,471
Netherlands	88,688	35,248	89,113
Indonesia	5,700	4,183	80,795
Germany(*)	72,251	40,842	77,561
Canada	184,116	99,987	72,476
India	14,128	11,506	41,713
Pakistan	18,790	0	30,321
Croatia	19,179	8,560	25,890
Spain	54,403	7,318	22,101
Portugal	4,800	1,680	18,605
Haiti	4,000	3,800	12,358
France(*)	42,528	5,480	7,932
Macau	5,879	0	6,469
Slovenia	0	0	4,059
Poland	2,217	0	3,525
Philippines	0	0	3,318
Austria	0	0	2,559
Chile	2,550	0	2,420
Rest of World	122,044	67,615	6,806
World Total	25,097,674	23,022,701	29,442,250
Sheep & lambskins:			
China	1,173,215	1,010,317	980,503
Mexico	43,255	222,824	151,017
Turkey	63,307	129,514	144,851
Russia	4,860	66,075	85,690
Vietnam	0	0	34,125
Pakistan	0	8,036	31,321
India	0	7,400	10,200
France(*)	0	349	9,450
Morocco	0	0	9,000
Canada	13,498	6,451	8,790
Germany(*)	1,400	3,000	7,900
Guatemala	0	0	7,474
Ethiopia(*)	0	0	5,098
United Kingdom	207	3,466	3,600
Argentina	0	0	700
Netherlands Antilles(*)	15	508	150
United Arab Emirates	100	0	0
Barbados	0	10	0
Belgium-Luxembourg(*)	111	0	0
Guyana	30	0	0
Italy(*)	0	10,311	0
Japan	782	0	0
Lebanon	0	53	0
Poland	0	7,425	0
Spain	0	3,296	0
Switzerland(*)	1,192	391	0
Leeward-Windward Islands(*)	0	630	0
World Total	1,301,972	1,480,056	1,489,869
Pig and hog skins, pieces:			
Mexico	2,204,647	2,359,767	2,523,738
Taiwan	1,367,474	1,079,508	1,470,387
Vietnam	550,345	442,702	643,800
Thailand	114,426	560,787	425,200
United Kingdom	56,317	43,745	85,905
Japan	20,939	12,665	72,125
Slovenia	14,631	15,245	61,997
Hong Kong	390,447	143,878	24,276
Italy(*)	9,270	1,360	6,989
Greece	6,931	0	6,344
China	117,555	2,600	3,721
Ecuador	0	0	2,688
El Salvador	0	0	1,995
Canada	5,393	0	0
Dominican Republic	1,067	0	0
France(*)	0	2,400	0
Germany(*)	1,650	0	0
Korea, South	107,561	66,730	0
World Total	4,968,653	4,731,387	5,329,165

See footnote(s) at end of table.

Table 7-69.—Hides: U.S. trade exports, 2011–2013—Continued

Country	2011	2012	2013
	Number	Number	Number
Mink furskins, undressed:			
China	3,678,292	3,626,923	4,942,895
Hong Kong	1,107,203	2,743,323	3,664,569
Canada	1,833,404	2,316,857	3,285,175
Korea, South	1,290,403	2,504,559	1,816,284
Greece	394,578	625,060	610,844
Germany(*)	196,763	45,971	269,869
Italy(*)	51,089	61,612	76,373
Denmark(*)	0	7,580	65,201
United Kingdom	20,781	12,070	54,696
France(*)	5,327	25,901	53,542
United Arab Emirates	10,258	48,988	42,316
Poland	9,224	50,441	17,732
Malaysia	22,840	18,236	16,363
Russia	7,172	6,016	4,804
Japan	3,767	4,084	4,147
Haiti	0	0	4,006
Finland	459	0	3,450
Switzerland(*)	1,272	0	1,538
Ukraine	6,828	9,805	1,458
Turkey	1,491	0	1,409
Mexico	316	2,423	1,400
Brazil	0	0	1,292
Australia(*)	0	374	0
Belize	7,878	0	0
Cyprus	23,526	0	0
Czech Republic	25,177	0	0
Lithuania	2,282	0	0
Macau	4,912	0	0
New Zealand(*)	0	2,832	0
World Total	8,705,242	12,113,055	14,939,363
Other furskins, whole:			
Canada	1,639,155	1,945,633	2,035,197
China	837,207	1,052,347	1,103,397
Germany(*)	100,935	162,938	125,626
Italy(*)	38,613	56,435	119,973
Greece	16,594	3,801	83,534
Hong Kong	43,831	182,017	79,071
Poland	78,049	102,855	70,587
Czech Republic	59,226	73,521	31,010
Estonia	12,473	19,007	23,512
Portugal	5,986	2,471	11,954
Korea, South	690	942	6,897
Turkey	12,740	7,264	5,117
Venezuela	0	128	3,766
Belgium-Luxembourg(*)	1,915	10,442	3,468
Taiwan	0	0	2,723
Pakistan	1,277	1,571	1,509
Austria	500	0	1,116
France(*)	0	0	973
United Kingdom	2,000	5,898	785
Brazil	0	0	698
Guatemala	3,400	5,100	611
Suriname	0	0	576
Panama	0	0	547
Lithuania	2,000	0	500
Malaysia	0	0	334
Netherlands	0	2,092	256
Singapore	65	0	51
United Arab Emirates	1,866	2,718	0
Australia(*)	2,204	746	0
Rest of World	16,689	27,057	0
World Total	2,877,415	3,664,983	3,713,788

See footnote(s) at end of table.

Table 7-69.—Hides: U.S. trade exports, 2011–2013—Continued

Country	2011	2012	2013
	Pieces	Pieces	Pieces
Other hides & skins, mixed:			
China	5,378,381	5,606,765	6,606,123
Korea, South	2,298,612	1,941,925	2,473,377
Taiwan	904,180	549,675	469,238
Thailand	351,699	236,534	266,663
Vietnam	376,378	232,105	242,790
France(*)	133,990	136,165	214,068
Italy(*)	266,746	142,152	190,938
Germany(*)	156,706	82,726	152,641
Hong Kong	350,766	159,310	141,698
Singapore	41,706	24,363	114,521
Haiti	76,179	85,870	66,126
Turkey	186,624	90,016	47,671
Pakistan	31,061	30,934	43,524
Mexico	116,508	25,528	39,364
Canada	39,600	16,903	28,556
Japan	11,320	18,365	24,600
Malaysia	0	0	12,062
India	3,216	0	6,101
Israel(*)	0	0	6,056
Portugal	1,600	855	2,632
Indonesia	0	0	1,680
Belgium-Luxembourg(*)	4,080	5,425	1,360
Kuwait	19	0	1,080
Spain	9	8,568	477
Estonia	0	0	333
United Kingdom	17	40	298
Brazil	0	2,115	249
Colombia	398	100	157
Sri Lanka	0	0	150
Rest of World	24,725	24,018	138
World Total	10,754,520	9,420,457	11,154,671

(*) Denotes a country that is a summarization of its component countries.
FAS, Office of Global Analysis, (202) 720-6301.

Table 7-70.—Mink: Farms, pelts produced, average price, and value, United States, 2005–2014

Year	Mink farms	Pelts produced	Average marketing price	Value of mink pelts
	Number	*Number*	*Dollars*	*Dollars*
2005	275	2,637,800	60.90	160,642,020
2006	279	2,858,800	48.40	138,365,920
2007	283	2,828,200	65.70	185,812,740
2008	274	2,820,700	41.60	117,341,120
2009	278	2,866,700	65.10	186,622,170
2010	265	2,840,200	81.90	232,612,380
2011	268	3,091,470	94.30	291,525,621
2012[1]	(NA)	(NA)	(NA)	(NA)
2013	(NA)	3,544,610	56.30	199,561,543
2014	(NA)	3,763,250	57.70	217,139,525

(NA) Not available.　　[1] Due to sequestration the Mink report was suspended.
NASS, Livestock Branch, (202) 720–3570.

Table 7-71.—Mink pelts: Pelts produced by color class, selected States, and United States, 2014

State	Black	Demi/Wild	Pastel	Sapphire	Blue Iris	Mahogany
	Number	*Number*	*Number*	*Number*	*Number*	*Number*
Idaho	139,000	7,500	4,300	17,500	(D)	164,000
Illinois	68,000	-	-	(D)	-	(D)
Iowa	45,000	-	(D)	(D)	(D)	34,000
Michigan	36,000	-	(D)	(D)	(D)	2,300
Minnesota	84,000	27,000	(D)	(D)	40,000	82,000
Montana	9,000	(D)	(D)	-	(D)	9,500
Ohio	68,000	(D)	-	(D)	(D)	18,500
Oregon	215,000	-	-	(D)	80,000	(D)
Pennsylvania	36,000	(D)	8,000	9,000	19,000	(D)
South Dakota	(D)	(D)	(D)	-	(D)	(D)
Utah	320,000	37,000	(D)	40,000	1,500	425,000
Washington	73,000	-	(D)	-	(D)	(D)
Wisconsin	800,000	1,100	31,000	39,000	138,000	117,000
Other States [1]	4,600	7,860	70,450	15,830	26,740	57,350
United States	1,897,600	80,460	113,750	121,330	305,240	909,650

State	Pearl	Lavender	Violet	White	Other	Total [2]
	Number	*Number*	*Number*	*Number*	*Number*	*Number*
Idaho	-	(D)	(D)	-	(D)	357,970
Illinois	(D)	-	(D)	(D)	-	97,740
Iowa	-	-	-	(D)	-	85,700
Michigan	-	-	-	8,000	-	53,200
Minnesota	(D)	-	(D)	(D)	-	255,930
Montana	-	-	-	(D)	(D)	25,730
Ohio	-	-	-	(D)	-	95,800
Oregon	-	-	(D)	-	-	333,050
Pennsylvania	(D)	-	(D)	(D)	(D)	87,430
South Dakota	(D)	-	-	-	-	(D)
Utah	(D)	(D)	(D)	(D)	(D)	958,760
Washington	-	-	-	-	-	104,100
Wisconsin	(D)	7,500	(D)	115,000	3,900	1,268,760
Other States [1]	103,970	6,090	43,100	32,180	15,480	39,080
United States	103,970	13,590	43,100	155,180	19,380	3,763,250

- Represents zero.　　(D) Withheld to avoid disclosing data for individual operations.　　[1] Other States include Indiana, New Hampshire, New Jersey, New York, North Carolina, Virginia, and some pelts from the above listed States that were not published to avoid disclosing individual operations.　　[2] Published color classes may not add to the State total to avoid disclosing individual operations.
NASS, Livestock Branch, (202) 720–3570.

Table 7-72.—Livestock: Number of animals slaughtered under Federal inspection and number of whole carcasses condemned, 2005–2014[1]

Year	Cattle		Calves		Sheep and lambs	
	Total head	Condemned	Total head	Condemned	Total head	Condemned
	1,000	*1,000*	*1,000*	*1,000*	*1,000*	*1,000*
2005	31,847	145.8	757	12.1	2,582	5.4
2006	32,861	143.1	682	11.1	2,534	4.7
2007	33,473	141.5	769	13.6	2,497	4.1
2008	34,220	146.8	866	24.0	2,447	5.2
2009	32,714	143.1	951	23.0	2,297	3.3
2010	33,295	149.4	908	22.7	2,285	3.5
2011	29,530	143.2	740	33.0	1.684	3.1
2012	32,062	142.3	742	26.7	1,978	4.2
2013	31,631	154.0	761	36.7	2,129	5.0
2014	30,721	157.9	645	36.7	2,171	4.1

Year	Goats		Hogs		Horses[2]	
	Total head	Condemned	Total head	Condemned	Total head	Condemned
	1,000	*1,000*	*1,000*	*1,000*	*1,000*	*1,000*
2005	553	1.1	103,849	414.8	88	0.7
2006	561	0.9	103,600	417.0	102	0.9
2007	613	0.7	105,611	404.8	58	0.4
2008	654	0.9	115,600	393.0	0	0
2009	660	0.8	113,395	333.6	0	0
2010	617	0.7	109,346	316.6	0	0
2011	509	0.5	91,541	266.2	0	0
2012	576	0.5	111,440	256.7	0	0
2013	540	0.5	111,935	296.3	0	0
2014	499	0.7	108,650	320.5	0	0

[1] Data are reported by the Food Safety and Inspection Service, USDA for the fiscal year ending September 30. Condemnations include ante-mortem and post-mortem inspection.   [2] Equine slaughter was discontinued during the week of September 22, 2007.
NASS, Livestock Branch, (202) 720–3570.

Table 7-73.—Livestock: Inventory and value, United States, Jan. 1, 2013–2015

Class of livestock and poultry	Inventory			Value					
				Per head[1]			Total		
	2013	2014	2015[2]	2013	2014	2015[2]	2013	2014	2015[2]
	1,000	*1,000*	*1,000*	*Dollars*	*Dollars*	*Dollars*	*1,000 Dollars*	*1,000 Dollars*	*1,000 Dollars*
Angora goats[3]	136	148	160	87.70	105	124	12,694	12,807	16,850
Cattle	90,095	88,526	89,143	1,139.00	1,223.00	1,584.00	101,731,742	108,255,950	141,211,070
Chickens[4]	474,902	483,530	470,915	4.15	4.11	4.36	1,971,590	1,989,495	2,055,503
Hogs[4]	64,775	67,776	68,299	138	144	96	8,921,822	9,754,191	6,566,642
Sheep and lambs	5,360	5,245	5,280	221.00	188	214	946,194	984,236	1,129,447

[1] Based on reporters' estimates of average price per head in their localities.   [2] Preliminary.   [3] Four state total for angora goats (Arizona, California, New Mexico, Texas).   [4] Dec. 1 of preceding year.
NASS, Livestock Branch, (202) 720–3570.

Table 7-74.—Livestock: Market year for specified commodities

Cattle market year average price received: United States marketing years 2005–2014[1]

Year	Cows[2]	Steers and heifers	Calves	Beef cattle[3]	Milks cows[4]
	Dollars	Dollars	Dollars	Dollars	Dollars
2005	51.70	94.30	135.00	89.70	1,770.00
2006	46.60	92.30	133.00	87.20	1,730.00
2007	47.90	95.40	119.00	89.90	1,830.00
2008	50.60	94.50	110.00	89.10	1,950.00
2009	44.80	85.40	105.00	80.30	1,390.00
2010	54.80	97.70	117.00	92.20	1,330.00
2011	71.20	117.00	142.00	113.00	1,420.00
2012	81.70	123.00	172.00	121.00	1,430.00
2013	82.30	126.00	181.00	125.00	1,380.00
2014	107.00	153.00	261.00	152.00	1,830.00

Hog market year average price received: United States marketing years 2005–2014[5]

Year	Barrows and gilts	Sows	All Hogs
	Dollars	Dollars	Dollars
2005	50.70	41.30	50.20
2006	46.60	33.20	46.00
2007	47.40	32.00	46.60
2008	47.90	29.20	47.00
2009	42.00	36.10	41.60
2010	54.40	48.70	54.10
2011	65.70	57.50	65.30
2012	64.60	51.30	64.20
2013	67.30	62.90	67.20
2014	76.50	77.70	76.50

[1] Market year for cattle January 1-December 31 for United States and all States. [2] Cows includes beef cows and cull dairy cows sold for slaughter. [3] All beef includes steer and heifers combined and cows. [4] Milk cow prices are calendar year average. [5] Market year for hogs December 1-November 30 for United States and all States.
NASS, Livestock Branch, (202) 720–3570.

Table 7-75.—Frozen meat: Cold storage holdings, end of month, United States, 2013–2014

Month	Boneless beef		Beef cuts		Total beef	
	2013	2014	2013	2014	2013	2014
	1,000 pounds	*1,000 pounds*	*1,000 pounds*	*1,000 pounds*	*1,000 pounds*	*1,000 pounds*
January	420,786	389,031	63,824	40,266	484,610	429,297
February	433,261	365,804	56,717	43,703	489,978	409,507
March	459,354	364,771	51,879	41,016	511,233	405,787
April	460,043	360,079	50,086	42,202	510,129	402,281
May	437,035	336,099	45,533	41,544	482,568	377,643
June	434,090	320,350	47,158	37,819	481,248	358,169
July	418,721	328,572	43,876	39,370	462,597	367,942
August	384,710	308,350	45,526	38,206	430,236	346,556
September ...	401,443	337,357	43,716	40,813	445,159	378,170
October	394,820	342,898	45,286	38,030	440,106	380,928
November	407,596	365,351	43,162	35,474	450,768	400,825
December	400,816	406,484	38,552	37,892	439,368	444,376

Month	Picnics		Bellies		Butts	
	2013	2014	2013	2014	2013	2014
	1,000 pounds	*1,000 pounds*	*1,000 pounds*	*1,000 pounds*	*1,000 pounds*	*1,000 pounds*
January	12,267	9,920	36,425	87,171	31,091	21,179
February	16,814	11,716	42,976	87,675	28,710	26,094
March	16,544	9,080	51,473	79,721	24,458	20,163
April	21,152	13,204	56,352	83,579	23,854	19,771
May	16,265	9,413	54,829	85,888	21,804	21,732
June	13,669	7,638	42,033	83,936	16,165	19,999
July	12,719	6,909	28,177	64,644	15,639	21,116
August	13,808	8,505	19,335	45,562	16,737	23,778
September ...	13,115	10,513	23,491	34,311	17,756	22,035
October	11,192	10,893	26,674	29,006	19,058	23,458
November	8,810	10,860	48,298	35,894	19,887	22,549
December	7,889	8,827	80,367	47,455	17,979	19,567

Month	Hams					
	Bone-in		Boneless		Total	
	2013	2014	2013	2014	2013	2014
	1,000 pounds	*1,000 pounds*	*1,000 pounds*	*1,000 pounds*	*1,000 pounds*	*1,000 pounds*
January	50,539	42,570	57,911	63,613	108,450	106,183
February	53,474	48,511	57,289	68,953	110,763	117,464
March	35,976	37,661	58,511	51,791	94,487	89,452
April	54,137	34,580	72,794	47,205	126,931	81,785
May	64,148	44,989	89,831	65,010	153,979	109,999
June	62,530	56,394	99,118	70,099	161,648	126,493
July	85,080	69,161	95,597	79,744	180,677	148,905
August	103,615	86,106	103,391	93,377	207,006	179,483
September ...	121,270	96,916	100,363	97,161	221,633	194,077
October	102,054	83,095	90,893	78,940	192,947	162,035
November	54,582	49,067	61,494	47,330	116,076	96,397
December	26,737	26,898	50,036	39,451	76,773	66,349

Month	Loins					
	Bone-in		Boneless		Total	
	2013	2014	2013	2014	2013	2014
	1,000 pounds	*1,000 pounds*	*1,000 pounds*	*1,000 pounds*	*1,000 pounds*	*1,000 pounds*
January	13,755	16,424	30,234	26,372	43,989	42,796
February	15,224	16,290	27,123	29,083	42,347	45,373
March	14,424	15,218	28,525	26,252	42,949	41,470
April	15,481	16,239	30,659	29,711	46,140	45,950
May	13,562	12,788	25,068	26,674	38,630	39,462
June	10,915	9,327	17,930	18,264	28,845	27,591
July	10,125	7,908	15,563	16,367	25,688	24,275
August	8,934	6,859	16,004	14,054	24,938	20,913
September ...	7,510	7,508	16,152	12,759	23,662	20,267
October	10,278	10,006	18,170	13,519	28,448	23,525
November	15,524	15,310	24,774	18,059	40,298	33,369
December	17,588	16,543	27,112	21,256	44,700	37,799

See end of table.

Table 7-75.—Frozen meat: Cold storage holdings, end of month, United States, 2013–2014—Continued

Month	Ribs		Trimmings		Other frozen pork	
	2013	2014	2013	2014	2013	2014
	1,000 pounds	*1,000 pounds*	*1,000 pounds*	*1,000 pounds*	*1,000 pounds*	*1,000 pounds*
January	114,370	112,246	57,826	41,577	109,891	110,199
February	119,439	122,859	64,372	37,448	111,855	110,102
March	122,396	120,606	66,070	36,871	122,958	94,722
April	120,593	115,957	66,050	42,023	129,912	97,321
May	91,153	89,596	59,226	47,940	118,339	91,231
June	56,652	59,943	48,516	43,581	105,002	86,547
July	57,631	55,140	36,927	42,413	96,881	87,745
August	48,298	49,621	36,642	40,440	97,662	90,271
September ...	56,107	53,957	38,273	35,143	92,479	90,627
October	75,746	69,374	34,775	37,337	94,496	97,433
November	98,853	76,897	38,606	41,110	91,839	98,139
December	106,589	87,020	39,134	50,943	104,042	100,625

Month	Variety meats		Unclassified pork		Total pork	
	2013	2014	2013	2014	2013	2014
	1,000 pounds	*1,000 pounds*	*1,000 pounds*	*1,000 pounds*	*1,000 pounds*	*1,000 pounds*
January	28,109	32,442	64,007	55,033	606,425	618,746
February	32,562	36,807	63,561	59,174	633,399	654,712
March	34,712	35,427	71,737	48,027	647,784	575,539
April	32,926	38,733	77,067	45,568	700,977	583,891
May	32,808	35,819	71,914	44,738	658,947	575,818
June	27,672	32,170	64,861	49,549	565,063	537,447
July	31,041	31,906	58,288	50,206	543,668	533,259
August	28,882	33,587	55,667	51,506	548,975	543,666
September ...	27,971	35,068	53,340	54,624	567,827	550,622
October	26,717	28,769	54,967	51,246	565,020	533,076
November	28,696	32,769	54,875	44,768	546,238	492,752
December	31,539	39,177	45,316	46,030	554,328	503,792

Month	Veal		Lamb & mutton		Total red meat	
	2013	2014	2013	2014	2013	2014
	1,000 pounds	*1,000 pounds*	*1,000 pounds*	*1,000 pounds*	*1,000 pounds*	*1,000 pounds*
January	5,012	3,285	18,768	25,658	1,114,815	1,076,986
February	4,858	3,190	19,833	26,191	1,148,068	1,093,600
March	5,774	2,921	17,624	28,076	1,182,415	1,012,323
April	5,404	3,212	21,463	26,536	1,237,073	1,015,920
May	4,996	2,752	19,793	25,208	1,166,304	981,421
June	5,633	3,324	19,307	31,119	1,071,251	930,059
July	5,897	3,952	23,324	33,968	1,035,486	939,121
August	3,839	3,581	21,988	40,157	1,005,038	933,960
September ...	4,571	2,326	23,444	39,693	1,041,001	970,811
October	3,885	3,797	23,967	38,686	1,032,978	956,487
November	3,208	5,315	21,697	31,366	1,021,901	930,258
December	3,957	6,435	24,508	33,942	1,022,161	988,545

NASS, Livestock Branch, (202) 720–3570.

CHAPTER VIII

DAIRY AND POULTRY STATISTICS

Dairy statistics in this chapter include series relating to many phases of production, movement, prices, stocks, and consumption of milk and its products. Two series of number of milk cows on farms are included in this publication. One series is an inventory number of a specific classification estimated as one of the major groups making up the total cattle population on January 1. The other series identified as "milk cows" is an annual average number of milk cows during the year (excluding any not yet fresh) and is used in estimating milk production.

In comparing the several series of milk prices, it is important to note that prices received by farmers for all whole milk sold are for milk or milkfat content as actually sold, while certain prices paid by dealers for milk for fluid purposes or for specified manufacturing purposes may be quoted on a 3.5 percent butterfat basis, or for some types of manufacturing milk on the test of the milk used for that particular purpose.

Poultry and poultry products statistics include inventory numbers of chickens by classes; the production, disposition, cash receipts, and gross income from chickens and eggs; poultry and egg receipts at principal markets; commercial broiler production; turkey production, disposition, and gross income; poultry and eggs under Federal inspection; and the National Poultry Improvement Plan. Estimates relating to inventories, production, and income exclude poultry and eggs produced on places not classified as farms.

Table 8-1.—Milk cows and heifers: Number that have calved and heifers 500 pounds and over kept for milk cow replacements, United States, Jan. 1, 2006–2015

Year	Milk cows and heifers that have calved	Heifers 500 pounds and over kept for milk cow replacements
	Thousands	*Thousands*
2006	9,104	4,298
2007	9,145	4,325
2008	9,257	4,415
2009	9,333	4,410
2010	9,087	4,551
2011	9,156	4,577
2012	9,236	4,618
2013	9,221	4,546
2014	9,208	4,549
2015[1]	9,307	4,710

[1] Preliminary.
NASS, Livestock Branch, (202) 720–3570.

Table 8-2.—Milk cows and heifers: Number that have calved and heifers 500 pounds and over kept for milk cow replacements, by State and United States, Jan. 1, 2014 and 2015

State	Milk cows and heifers that have calved		Heifers 500 pounds and over kept for milk cow replacements	
	2014	2015[1]	2014	2015[1]
	Thousands	Thousands	Thousands	Thousands
Alabama	9.0	8.0	4.0	3.0
Alaska	0.3	0.3	0.1	0.1
Arizona	192.0	195.0	74.0	65.0
Arkansas	8.0	7.0	5.0	4.0
California	1,780.0	1,780.0	750.0	770.0
Colorado	140.0	145.0	100.0	100.0
Connecticut	19.0	19.0	9.0	8.0
Delaware	4.7	5.0	2.6	2.5
Florida	123.0	124.0	35.0	35.0
Georgia	80.0	81.0	25.0	27.0
Hawaii	2.2	2.2	1.0	1.0
Idaho	565.0	579.0	270.0	320.0
Illinois	95.0	94.0	45.0	52.0
Indiana	178.0	181.0	68.0	80.0
Iowa	205.0	210.0	120.0	130.0
Kansas	136.0	143.0	100.0	90.0
Kentucky	68.0	63.0	45.0	45.0
Louisiana	15.0	14.0	5.0	5.0
Maine	30.0	30.0	17.0	16.0
Maryland	50.0	49.0	25.0	25.0
Massachusetts	12.0	12.5	7.5	7.0
Michigan	381.0	403.0	164.0	167.0
Minnesota	460.0	460.0	280.0	280.0
Mississippi	13.0	12.0	6.0	6.0
Missouri	90.0	89.0	50.0	60.0
Montana	14.0	14.0	9.0	7.0
Nebraska	53.0	54.0	20.0	20.0
Nevada	29.0	28.0	9.0	9.0
New Hampshire	13.5	14.0	7.0	5.5
New Jersey	7.0	7.0	3.0	3.8
New Mexico	323.0	323.0	120.0	110.0
New York	615.0	615.0	355.0	350.0
North Carolina	45.0	47.0	20.0	18.0
North Dakota	17.0	16.0	10.0	6.0
Ohio	267.0	268.0	130.0	125.0
Oklahoma	45.0	40.0	20.0	25.0
Oregon	124.0	125.0	60.0	60.0
Pennsylvania	530.0	530.0	315.0	305.0
Rhode Island	0.9	0.9	0.5	0.5
South Carolina	16.0	15.0	6.0	5.0
South Dakota	95.0	99.0	50.0	65.0
Tennessee	46.0	47.0	30.0	25.0
Texas	440.0	470.0	220.0	250.0
Utah	95.0	96.0	46.0	48.0
Vermont	132.0	132.0	56.0	56.0
Virginia	93.0	93.0	40.0	43.0
Washington	266.0	277.0	125.0	136.0
West Virginia	9.0	9.0	5.0	4.0
Wisconsin	1,270.0	1,275.0	680.0	730.0
Wyoming	6.0	6.0	4.0	5.0
United States	9,207.6	9,306.9	4,548.7	4,710.4

[1] Preliminary.
NASS, Livestock Branch, (202) 720–3570.

Table 8-3.—Milk and milkfat production: Number of milk cows, production per cow, and total quantity produced, by State and United States, 2013 [1]

State	Number of milk cows [2]	Production of milk and milkfat [3]				
		Per milk cow		All milk percent of fat	Total	
		Milk	Milkfat		Milk	Milkfat
	Thousands	*Pounds*	*Pounds*	*Percent*	*Million pounds*	*Million pounds*
Alabama	9.0	13,000	491	3.78	117.0	4.4
Alaska	0.3	10,667	427	4.00	3.2	0.1
Arizona	190.0	23,626	832	3.52	4,489.0	158.0
Arkansas	9.0	11,667	426	3.65	105.0	3.8
California	1,780.0	23,178	869	3.75	41,256.0	1,547.1
Colorado	137.0	24,292	865	3.56	3,328.0	118.5
Connecticut	18.0	20,556	785	3.82	370.0	14.1
Delaware	4.8	19,521	736	3.77	93.7	3.5
Florida	123.0	19,374	705	3.64	2,383.0	86.7
Georgia	80.0	19,600	729	3.72	1,568.0	58.3
Hawaii	2.2	13,409	464	3.46	29.5	1.0
Idaho	573.0	23,440	884	3.77	13,431.0	506.3
Illinois	96.0	19,063	724	3.80	1,830.0	69.5
Indiana	176.0	21,761	816	3.75	3,830.0	143.6
Iowa	208.0	22,149	842	3.80	4,607.0	175.1
Kansas	134.0	21,881	803	3.67	2,932.0	107.6
Kentucky	71.0	15,070	561	3.72	1,070.0	39.8
Louisiana	16.0	12,875	470	3.65	206.0	7.5
Maine	31.0	19,548	733	3.75	606.0	22.7
Maryland	50.0	19,440	733	3.77	972.0	36.6
Massachusetts	13.0	17,692	679	3.84	230.0	8.8
Michigan	380.0	24,116	892	3.70	9,164.0	339.1
Minnesota	464.0	19,694	764	3.88	9,138.0	354.6
Mississippi	14.0	13,286	490	3.69	186.0	6.9
Missouri	92.0	14,663	548	3.74	1,349.0	50.5
Montana	14.0	21,286	794	3.73	298.0	11.1
Nebraska	54.0	21,574	828	3.84	1,165.0	44.7
Nevada	29.0	22,034	787	3.57	639.0	22.8
New Hampshire	13.0	20,923	789	3.77	272.0	10.3
New Jersey	7.0	18,143	686	3.78	127.0	4.8
New Mexico	323.0	24,944	891	3.57	8,057.0	287.6
New York	610.0	22,070	825	3.74	13,463.0	503.5
North Carolina	46.0	20,326	754	3.71	935.0	34.7
North Dakota	18.0	18,944	720	3.80	341.0	13.0
Ohio	270.0	20,178	775	3.84	5,448.0	209.2
Oklahoma	45.0	17,311	630	3.64	779.0	28.4
Oregon	123.0	20,439	793	3.88	2,514.0	97.5
Pennsylvania	533.0	19,797	738	3.73	10,552.0	393.6
Rhode Island	0.9	19,000	760	4.00	17.1	0.7
South Carolina	16.0	16,500	639	3.87	264.0	10.2
South Dakota	94.0	21,521	850	3.95	2,023.0	79.9
Tennessee	48.0	15,938	591	3.71	765.0	28.4
Texas	437.0	21,991	842	3.83	9,610.0	368.1
Utah	95.0	22,432	843	3.76	2,131.0	80.1
Vermont	134.0	19,448	739	3.80	2,606.0	99.0
Virginia	95.0	18,337	678	3.70	1,742.0	64.5
Washington	266.0	23,820	924	3.88	6,336.0	245.8
West Virginia	10.0	15,200	567	3.73	152.0	5.7
Wisconsin	1,271.0	21,693	822	3.79	27,572.0	1,045.0
Wyoming	6.0	21,367	750	3.51	128.2	4.5
United States	9,224.0	21,816	820	3.76	201,231.0	7,557.2

[1] May not add due to rounding.   [2] Average number during year, excluding heifers not yet fresh.   [3] Excludes milk sucked by calves.

NASS, Livestock Branch, (202) 720–3570.

Table 8-4.—Milk and milkfat production: Number of milk cows, production per cow, and total quantity produced, by State and United States, 2014[1]

State	Number of milk cows[2]	Production of milk and milkfat[3]				
		Per milk cow		All milk percent of fat	Total	
		Milk	Milkfat		Milk	Milkfat
	Thousands	*Pounds*	*Pounds*	*Percent*	*Million pounds*	*Million pounds*
Alabama	8.0	13,625	511	3.75	109.0	4.1
Alaska	0.3	11,667	462	3.96	3.5	0.1
Arizona	193.0	24,368	845	3.47	4,703.0	163.1
Arkansas	7.0	13,714	495	3.61	96.0	3.5
California	1,780.0	23,786	880	3.70	42,339.0	1,566.5
Colorado	144.0	24,951	886	3.55	3,593.0	127.6
Connecticut	19.0	20,158	782	3.88	383.0	14.9
Delaware	4.8	20,104	743	3.69	96.5	3.6
Florida	123.0	20,390	734	3.60	2,508.0	90.3
Georgia	81.0	20,877	759	3.65	1,691.0	61.5
Hawaii	2.2	13,591	472	3.47	29.9	1.0
Idaho	575.0	24,127	905	3.75	13,873.0	520.2
Illinois	94.0	19,681	744	3.78	1,850.0	69.9
Indiana	178.0	21,865	809	3.70	3,892.0	144.0
Iowa	207.0	22,449	842	3.75	4,647.0	174.2
Kansas	141.0	22,085	812	3.68	3,114.0	114.5
Kentucky	63.0	15,905	574	3.61	1,002.0	36.2
Louisiana	15.0	13,600	496	3.65	204.0	7.4
Maine	30.0	19,967	754	3.77	599.0	22.6
Maryland	50.0	19,740	740	3.75	987.0	37.0
Massachusetts	13.0	17,923	686	3.83	233.0	8.9
Michigan	390.0	24,638	912	3.70	9,609.0	355.5
Minnesota	460.0	19,841	772	3.89	9,127.0	355.0
Mississippi	13.0	14,462	538	3.72	188.0	7.0
Missouri	89.0	15,539	580	3.73	1,383.0	51.6
Montana	14.0	21,500	808	3.76	301.0	11.3
Nebraska	54.0	22,130	841	3.80	1,195.0	45.4
Nevada	29.0	23,793	849	3.57	690.0	24.6
New Hampshire	14.0	20,143	776	3.85	282.0	10.9
New Jersey	7.0	18,143	679	3.74	127.0	4.7
New Mexico	323.0	25,093	891	3.55	8,105.0	287.7
New York	615.0	22,325	842	3.77	13,730.0	517.7
North Carolina	46.0	20,891	754	3.61	961.0	34.7
North Dakota	16.0	20,250	765	3.78	324.0	12.2
Ohio	267.0	20,318	770	3.79	5,425.0	205.6
Oklahoma	40.0	18,150	629	3.61	726.0	25.2
Oregon	124.0	20,565	799	3.88	2,550.0	99.1
Pennsylvania	530.0	20,121	754	3.74	10,664.0	399.5
Rhode Island	0.9	19,000	766	4.03	17.1	0.7
South Carolina	16.0	16,438	626	3.82	263.0	10.0
South Dakota	97.0	21,753	857	3.94	2,110.0	83.1
Tennessee	46.0	16,196	589	3.61	745.0	27.1
Texas	463.0	22,268	853	3.83	10,310.0	394.9
Utah	95.0	22,968	854	3.72	2,184.0	81.2
Vermont	132.0	20,197	767	3.80	2,666.0	101.3
Virginia	93.0	19,129	701	3.66	1,779.0	65.1
Washington	273.0	24,088	936	3.88	6,576.0	255.5
West Virginia	9.0	15,556	576	3.70	140.0	5.2
Wisconsin	1,271.0	21,869	827	3.78	27,795.0	1,050.7
Wyoming	6.0	21,583	822	3.81	129.5	4.9
United States	9,257.0	22,259	832	3.74	206,054.0	7,698.5

[1] May not add due to rounding.   [2] Average number during year, excluding heifers not yet fresh.   [3] Excludes milk sucked by calves.

NASS, Livestock Branch, (202) 720–3570.

Table 8-5.—Milk: Quantities used and marketed by producers, by State and United States, 2013[1]

State	Milk used where produced			Milk marketed by producers	
	Fed to calves[2]	Used for milk cream & butter	Total	Total quantity[3]	Fluid grade[4]
	Million pounds	*Million pounds*	*Million pounds*	*Million pounds*	*Percent*
Alabama	0.7	0.3	1.0	116.0	100
Alaska	0.1	0.1	0.2	3.0	100
Arizona	12.0	1.0	13.0	4,476.0	100
Arkansas	1.7	0.3	2.0	103.0	100
California	30.0	5.0	35.0	41,221.0	98
Colorado	21.0	1.0	22.0	3,306.0	100
Connecticut	2.5	0.5	3.0	367.0	100
Delaware	0.9	0.1	1.0	92.7	100
Florida	5.0	1.0	6.0	2,377.0	100
Georgia	7.0	1.0	8.0	1,560.0	100
Hawaii	0.1	0.1	0.2	29.3	100
Idaho	30.0	1.0	31.0	13,400.0	100
Illinois	10.0	2.0	12.0	1,818.0	98
Indiana	23.0	4.0	27.0	3,803.0	100
Iowa	12.0	1.0	13.0	4,594.0	99
Kansas	10.0	1.0	11.0	2,921.0	100
Kentucky	9.0	1.0	10.0	1,060.0	100
Louisiana	3.0	1.0	4.0	202.0	100
Maine	3.0	1.0	4.0	602.0	100
Maryland	6.0	1.0	7.0	965.0	100
Massachusetts	1.5	0.5	2.0	228.0	100
Michigan	26.0	2.0	28.0	9,136.0	100
Minnesota	100.0	5.0	105.0	9,033.0	99
Mississippi	1.0	1.0	2.0	184.0	100
Missouri	17.0	4.0	21.0	1,328.0	97
Montana	3.0	2.0	5.0	293.0	100
Nebraska	7.0	1.0	8.0	1,157.0	99
Nevada	5.0	1.0	6.0	633.0	100
New Hampshire	1.5	0.5	2.0	270.0	100
New Jersey	1.5	0.5	2.0	125.0	100
New Mexico	42.0	4.0	46.0	8,011.0	100
New York	35.0	2.0	37.0	13,426.0	100
North Carolina	5.0	1.0	6.0	929.0	100
North Dakota	6.5	0.5	7.0	334.0	96
Ohio	20.0	4.0	24.0	5,424.0	97
Oklahoma	7.0	1.0	8.0	771.0	100
Oregon	21.0	1.0	22.0	2,492.0	100
Pennsylvania	50.0	15.0	65.0	10,487.0	100
Rhode Island	0.2	-	0.2	16.9	100
South Carolina	2.0	1.0	3.0	261.0	100
South Dakota	6.0	1.0	7.0	2,016.0	99
Tennessee	4.0	1.0	5.0	760.0	100
Texas	23.0	1.0	24.0	9,586.0	100
Utah	12.0	1.0	13.0	2,118.0	100
Vermont	13.0	2.0	15.0	2,591.0	100
Virginia	7.0	2.0	9.0	1,733.0	100
Washington	15.0	1.0	16.0	6,320.0	100
West Virginia	1.0	1.0	2.0	150.0	100
Wisconsin	255.0	19.0	274.0	27,298.0	98
Wyoming	1.3	0.2	1.5	126.7	93
United States	877.0	100.0	977.0	200,254.0	99

- Represents zero. [1] May not add due to rounding. [2] Excludes milk sucked by calves. [3] Milk sold to plants and dealers as whole milk and equivalent amounts of milk for cream. Includes milk produced by dealers' own herds and milk sold directly to consumers. Also includes milk produced by institutional herds. [4] Percentage of milk sold that is eligible for fluid use (Grade A in most States). Includes fluid grade milk used in manufacturing dairy products.
NASS, Livestock Branch, (202) 720–3570.

Table 8-6.—Milk: Quantities used and marketed by producers, by State and United States, 2014[1]

State	Milk used where produced			Milk marketed by producers	
	Fed to calves[2]	Used for milk cream & butter	Total	Total quantity[3]	Fluid grade[4]
	Million pounds	*Million pounds*	*Million pounds*	*Million pounds*	*Percent*
Alabama	0.7	0.3	1.0	108.0	100
Alaska	0.1	0.1	0.2	3.3	100
Arizona	12.0	1.0	13.0	4,686.0	100
Arkansas	1.7	0.3	2.0	94.0	100
California	26.0	5.0	31.0	42,306.0	99
Colorado	21.0	1.0	22.0	3,571.0	100
Connecticut	2.5	0.5	3.0	380.0	100
Delaware	0.9	0.1	1.0	95.7	100
Florida	5.0	1.0	6.0	2,501.0	100
Georgia	7.0	1.0	8.0	1,676.0	100
Hawaii	0.1	0.1	0.2	29.7	100
Idaho	30.0	1.0	31.0	13,842.0	100
Illinois	10.0	2.0	12.0	1,838.0	98
Indiana	23.0	4.0	27.0	3,865.0	100
Iowa	13.0	1.0	14.0	4,632.0	99
Kansas	11.0	1.0	12.0	3,099.0	100
Kentucky	8.0	1.0	9.0	993.0	100
Louisiana	3.0	1.0	4.0	200.0	100
Maine	3.0	1.0	4.0	596.0	100
Maryland	6.0	1.0	7.0	980.0	100
Massachusetts	1.5	0.5	2.0	231.0	100
Michigan	24.0	2.0	26.0	9,583.0	100
Minnesota	100.0	5.0	105.0	9,022.0	99
Mississippi	1.0	1.0	2.0	186.0	100
Missouri	17.0	4.0	21.0	1,362.0	97
Montana	3.0	2.0	5.0	296.0	100
Nebraska	6.0	1.0	7.0	1,188.0	100
Nevada	5.0	1.0	6.0	684.0	100
New Hampshire	1.5	0.5	2.0	280.0	100
New Jersey	1.5	0.5	2.0	125.0	100
New Mexico	39.0	3.0	42.0	8,063.0	100
New York	40.0	2.0	42.0	13,691.0	100
North Carolina	5.0	1.0	6.0	955.0	100
North Dakota	5.5	0.5	6.0	318.0	97
Ohio	18.0	4.0	22.0	5,403.0	97
Oklahoma	6.0	1.0	7.0	690.0	100
Oregon	21.0	1.0	22.0	2,533.0	100
Pennsylvania	54.0	12.0	66.0	10,617.0	100
Rhode Island	0.2	-	0.2	16.9	100
South Carolina	2.0	1.0	3.0	259.0	100
South Dakota	5.0	1.0	6.0	2,103.0	99
Tennessee	4.0	1.0	5.0	745.0	100
Texas	27.0	1.0	28.0	10,282.0	100
Utah	12.0	1.0	13.0	2,169.0	100
Vermont	13.0	2.0	15.0	2,651.0	100
Virginia	6.0	2.0	8.0	1,772.0	100
Washington	16.0	1.0	17.0	6,567.0	100
West Virginia	1.0	1.0	2.0	138.0	100
Wisconsin	248.0	16.0	264.0	27,531.0	99
Wyoming	1.3	0.2	1.5	128.0	100
United States	869.0	93.0	962.0	205,085.0	99

- Represents zero.   [1] May not add due to rounding.   [2] Excludes milk sucked by calves.   [3] Milk sold to plants and dealers as whole milk and equivalent amounts of milk for cream.   Includes milk produced by dealers' own herds and milk sold directly to consumers.   Also includes milk produced by institutional herds.   [4] Percentage of milk sold that is eligible for fluid use (Grade A in most States).   Includes fluid grade milk used in manufacturing dairy products.
NASS, Livestock Branch, (202) 720–3570.

Table 8-7.—Milk and cream: Marketings and income, by State and United States, 2013[1]

State	Milk utilized	All milk Average returns per cwt[2]	Returns per lb milkfat	Cash receipts from marketings
	Million pounds	Dollars	Dollars	1,000 dollars
Alabama	116.0	23.70	6.27	27,492
Alaska	3.0	22.00	5.50	660
Arizona	4,476.0	19.50	5.54	872,820
Arkansas	103.0	20.80	5.70	21,424
California	41,221.0	18.48	4.93	7,617,641
Colorado	3,306.0	20.20	5.67	667,812
Connecticut	367.0	21.60	5.65	79,272
Delaware	92.7	20.50	5.44	19,004
Florida	2,377.0	23.90	6.57	568,103
Georgia	1,560.0	21.60	5.81	336,960
Hawaii	29.3	34.40	9.94	10,079
Idaho	13,400.0	19.20	5.09	2,572,800
Illinois	1,818.0	20.70	5.45	376,326
Indiana	3,803.0	20.80	5.55	791,024
Iowa	4,594.0	20.50	5.39	941,770
Kansas	2,921.0	20.20	5.50	590,042
Kentucky	1,060.0	21.50	5.78	227,900
Louisiana	202.0	21.90	6.00	44,238
Maine	602.0	22.30	5.95	134,246
Maryland	965.0	20.90	5.54	201,685
Massachusetts	228.0	21.80	5.68	49,704
Michigan	9,136.0	20.50	5.54	1,872,880
Minnesota	9,033.0	20.40	5.26	1,842,732
Mississippi	184.0	21.90	5.93	40,296
Missouri	1,328.0	20.50	5.48	272,240
Montana	293.0	18.70	5.01	54,791
Nebraska	1,157.0	21.00	5.47	242,970
Nevada	633.0	20.30	5.69	128,499
New Hampshire	270.0	21.50	5.70	58,050
New Jersey	125.0	20.60	5.45	25,750
New Mexico	8,011.0	18.80	5.27	1,506,068
New York	13,426.0	21.20	5.67	2,846,312
North Carolina	929.0	21.40	5.77	198,806
North Dakota	334.0	19.90	5.24	66,466
Ohio	5,424.0	21.20	5.52	1,149,888
Oklahoma	771.0	21.50	5.91	165,765
Oregon	2,492.0	21.20	5.46	528,304
Pennsylvania	10,487.0	21.60	5.79	2,265,192
Rhode Island	16.9	21.80	5.45	3,684
South Carolina	261.0	23.00	5.94	60,030
South Dakota	2,016.0	21.00	5.32	423,360
Tennessee	760.0	21.50	5.80	163,400
Texas	9,586.0	20.40	5.33	1,955,544
Utah	2,118.0	19.50	5.19	413,010
Vermont	2,591.0	21.30	5.61	551,883
Virginia	1,733.0	22.90	6.19	396,857
Washington	6,320.0	20.50	5.28	1,295,600
West Virginia	150.0	20.30	5.44	30,450
Wisconsin	27,298.0	20.30	5.36	5,541,494
Wyoming	126.7	20.10	5.73	25,467
United States	200,254.0	20.11	5.35	40,276,790

[1] May not add due to rounding.　[2] Cash receipts divided by milk or milkfat in combined marketings.
NASS, Livestock Branch, (202) 720–3570.

Table 8-8.—Milk and cream: Marketings and income, by State and United States, 2014[1]

State	Milk utilized	All milk Average returns per cwt[2]	Returns per lb milkfat	Cash receipts from marketings
	Million pounds	Dollars	Dollars	1,000 dollars
Alabama	108.0	27.80	7.41	30,024
Alaska	3.3	21.90	5.53	723
Arizona	4,686.0	23.20	6.69	1,087,152
Arkansas	94.0	25.50	7.06	23,970
California	42,306.0	22.12	5.98	9,358,087
Colorado	3,571.0	24.00	6.76	857,040
Connecticut	380.0	26.10	6.73	99,180
Delaware	95.7	24.10	6.53	23,064
Florida	2,501.0	28.20	7.83	705,282
Georgia	1,676.0	26.40	7.23	442,464
Hawaii	29.7	35.40	10.20	10,514
Idaho	13,842.0	23.10	6.16	3,197,502
Illinois	1,838.0	24.70	6.53	453,986
Indiana	3,865.0	24.30	6.57	939,195
Iowa	4,632.0	24.60	6.56	1,139,472
Kansas	3,099.0	24.00	6.52	743,760
Kentucky	993.0	25.80	7.15	256,194
Louisiana	200.0	26.20	7.18	52,400
Maine	596.0	26.80	7.11	159,728
Maryland	980.0	24.80	6.61	243,040
Massachusetts	231.0	26.10	6.81	60,291
Michigan	9,583.0	24.10	6.51	2,309,503
Minnesota	9,022.0	24.80	6.38	2,237,456
Mississippi	186.0	26.80	7.20	49,848
Missouri	1,362.0	24.60	6.60	335,052
Montana	296.0	22.00	5.85	65,120
Nebraska	1,188.0	25.00	6.58	297,000
Nevada	684.0	24.80	6.95	169,632
New Hampshire	280.0	25.90	6.73	72,520
New Jersey	125.0	24.90	6.66	31,125
New Mexico	8,063.0	22.30	6.28	1,798,049
New York	13,691.0	25.40	6.74	3,477,514
North Carolina	955.0	25.70	7.12	245,435
North Dakota	318.0	23.60	6.24	75,048
Ohio	5,403.0	24.60	6.49	1,329,138
Oklahoma	690.0	25.90	7.17	178,710
Oregon	2,533.0	25.70	6.62	650,981
Pennsylvania	10,617.0	25.70	6.87	2,728,569
Rhode Island	16.9	26.40	6.55	4,462
South Carolina	259.0	27.30	7.15	70,707
South Dakota	2,103.0	24.70	6.27	519,441
Tennessee	745.0	25.80	7.15	192,210
Texas	10,282.0	24.60	6.42	2,529,372
Utah	2,169.0	23.70	6.37	514,053
Vermont	2,651.0	25.50	6.71	676,005
Virginia	1,772.0	27.00	7.38	478,440
Washington	6,567.0	24.70	6.37	1,622,049
West Virginia	138.0	24.40	6.59	33,672
Wisconsin	27,531.0	24.50	6.48	6,745,095
Wyoming	128.0	23.40	6.14	29,952
United States	205,085.0	24.07	6.44	49,349,226

[1] May not add due to rounding.   [2] Cash receipts divided by milk or milkfat in combined marketings.
NASS, Livestock Branch, (202) 720–3570.

Table 8-9.—Milk production: Value, by State and United States, 2013[1]

State	Used for milk, cream, & butter where produced		Gross producer income[3]	Value of milk produced[2][4]
	Milk utilized	Value[2]		
	Million pounds	1,000 Dollars	1,000 Dollars	1,000 Dollars
Alabama	0.3	71	27,563	27,729
Alaska	0.1	22	682	704
Arizona	1.0	195	873,015	875,355
Arkansas	0.3	62	21,486	21,840
California	5.0	924	7,618,565	7,624,109
Colorado	1.0	202	668,014	672,256
Connecticut	0.5	108	79,380	79,920
Delaware	0.1	21	19,025	19,209
Florida	1.0	239	568,342	569,537
Georgia	1.0	216	337,176	338,688
Hawaii	0.1	34	10,113	10,148
Idaho	1.0	192	2,572,992	2,578,752
Illinois	2.0	414	376,740	378,810
Indiana	4.0	832	791,856	796,640
Iowa	1.0	205	941,975	944,435
Kansas	1.0	202	590,244	592,264
Kentucky	1.0	215	228,115	230,050
Louisiana	1.0	219	44,457	45,114
Maine	1.0	223	134,469	135,138
Maryland	1.0	209	201,894	203,148
Massachusetts	0.5	109	49,813	50,140
Michigan	2.0	410	1,873,290	1,878,620
Minnesota	5.0	1,020	1,843,752	1,864,152
Mississippi	1.0	219	40,515	40,734
Missouri	4.0	820	273,060	276,545
Montana	2.0	374	55,165	55,726
Nebraska	1.0	210	243,180	244,650
Nevada	1.0	203	128,702	129,717
New Hampshire	0.5	108	58,158	58,480
New Jersey	0.5	103	25,853	26,162
New Mexico	4.0	752	1,506,820	1,514,716
New York	2.0	424	2,846,736	2,854,156
North Carolina	1.0	214	199,020	200,090
North Dakota	0.5	100	66,566	67,859
Ohio	4.0	848	1,150,736	1,154,976
Oklahoma	1.0	215	165,980	167,485
Oregon	1.0	212	528,516	532,968
Pennsylvania	15.0	3,240	2,268,432	2,279,232
Rhode Island	-	-	3,684	3,728
South Carolina	1.0	230	60,260	60,720
South Dakota	1.0	210	423,570	424,830
Tennessee	1.0	215	163,615	164,475
Texas	1.0	204	1,955,748	1,960,440
Utah	1.0	195	413,205	415,545
Vermont	2.0	426	552,309	555,078
Virginia	2.0	458	397,315	398,918
Washington	1.0	205	1,295,805	1,298,880
West Virginia	1.0	203	30,653	30,856
Wisconsin	19.0	3,857	5,545,351	5,597,116
Wyoming	0.2	40	25,507	25,768
United States	100.0	20,629	40,297,419	40,476,608

- Represents zero.   [1] May not add due to rounding.   [2] Value at average returns per 100 pounds of milk in combined marketings of milk and cream.   [3] Cash receipts from marketings of milk and cream plus value of milk used for home consumption.   [4] Includes value of milk fed to calves.
NASS, Livestock Branch, (202) 720–3570.

Table 8-10.—Milk production: Value, by State and United States, 2014 [1]

State	Used for milk, cream, & butter where produced		Gross producer income [3]	Value of milk produced [2] [4]
	Milk utilized	Value [2]		
	Million pounds	*1,000 Dollars*	*1,000 Dollars*	*1,000 Dollars*
Alabama	0.3	83	30,107	30,302
Alaska	0.1	22	745	767
Arizona	1.0	232	1,087,384	1,090,168
Arkansas	0.3	77	24,047	24,480
California	5.0	1,106	9,359,193	9,364,944
Colorado	1.0	240	857,280	862,320
Connecticut	0.5	131	99,311	99,963
Delaware	0.1	24	23,088	23,305
Florida	1.0	282	705,564	706,974
Georgia	1.0	264	442,728	444,576
Hawaii	0.1	35	10,549	10,585
Idaho	1.0	231	3,197,733	3,204,663
Illinois	2.0	494	454,480	456,950
Indiana	4.0	972	940,167	945,756
Iowa	1.0	246	1,139,718	1,142,916
Kansas	1.0	240	744,000	746,640
Kentucky	1.0	258	256,452	258,516
Louisiana	1.0	262	52,662	53,448
Maine	1.0	268	159,996	160,800
Maryland	1.0	248	243,288	244,776
Massachusetts	0.5	131	60,422	60,813
Michigan	2.0	482	2,309,985	2,315,769
Minnesota	5.0	1,240	2,238,696	2,263,496
Mississippi	1.0	268	50,116	50,384
Missouri	4.0	984	336,036	340,218
Montana	2.0	440	65,560	66,220
Nebraska	1.0	250	297,250	298,750
Nevada	1.0	248	169,880	171,120
New Hampshire	0.5	130	72,650	73,038
New Jersey	0.5	125	31,250	31,623
New Mexico	3.0	669	1,798,718	1,807,415
New York	2.0	508	3,478,022	3,488,182
North Carolina	1.0	257	245,692	246,977
North Dakota	0.5	118	75,166	76,464
Ohio	4.0	984	1,330,122	1,334,550
Oklahoma	1.0	259	178,969	180,523
Oregon	1.0	257	651,238	656,635
Pennsylvania	12.0	3,084	2,731,653	2,745,531
Rhode Island	-	-	4,462	4,514
South Carolina	1.0	273	70,980	71,526
South Dakota	1.0	247	519,688	520,923
Tennessee	1.0	258	192,468	193,500
Texas	1.0	246	2,529,618	2,536,260
Utah	1.0	237	514,290	517,134
Vermont	2.0	510	676,515	679,830
Virginia	2.0	540	478,980	480,600
Washington	1.0	247	1,622,296	1,626,248
West Virginia	1.0	244	33,916	34,160
Wisconsin	16.0	3,920	6,749,015	6,809,775
Wyoming	0.2	47	29,999	30,303
United States	93.0	22,918	49,372,144	49,585,330

- Represents zero.   [1] May not add due to rounding.   [2] Value at average returns per 100 pounds of milk in combined marketings of milk and cream.   [3] Cash receipts from marketings of milk and cream plus value of milk used for home consumption.   [4] Includes value of milk fed to calves.
NASS, Livestock Branch, (202) 720–3570.

Table 8-11.—Milk cows, milk, and fat in cream: Average prices received by farmers, United States, 2005–2014

Year	Milk cows, per head [1]	Milk per 100 pounds [2]						
		Eligible for fluid market [3]		Of manufacturing grade		All milk wholesale	
		Price per 100 lb.	Fat test	Price per 100 lb.	Fat test	Price per 100 lb.	Fat test
	Dollars	*Dollars*	*Percent*	*Dollars*	*Percent*	*Dollars*	*Percent*
2005	1,770.00	15.19	3.66	14.42	3.84	15.19	3.66
2006	1,730.00	12.96	3.68	12.19	3.93	12.96	3.69
2007	1,830.00	19.22	3.68	18.31	3.99	19.21	3.68
2008	1,950.00	18.45	3.68	17.91	4.01	18.45	3.68
2009	1,390.00	12.94	3.67	12.03	4.00	12.93	3.67
2010	1,330.00	16.37	3.65	14.56	4.00	16.35	3.66
2011	1,420.00	(NA)	(NA)	(NA)	(NA)	20.24	3.71
2012	1,430.00	(NA)	(NA)	(NA)	(NA)	18.56	3.72
2013	1,380.00	(NA)	(NA)	(NA)	(NA)	20.11	3.76
2014	1,830.00	(NA)	(NA)	(NA)	(NA)	24.07	3.74

(NA) Not available.   [1] Simple average of quarterly prices, by States, weighted by the number of milk cows on farms Jan. 1 of the current year.   [2] Average price at average fat test for all milk sold at wholesale to plants and dealers, based on reports from milk-market administrators, cooperative milk-market associations, whole-milk distributors, and milk-products manufacturing plants, f.o.b. plant or receiving station (whichever is the customary place for determining prices) before hauling costs are deducted and including all premiums.   [3] Includes fluid milk surplus diverted to manufacturing.
NASS, Livestock Branch, (202) 720–3570.

Table 8-12—Milk-feed price ratios: All milk price; Dairy feed price, 16% protein; Milk-feed price ratios, United States, annual 2005–2014

Year	All milk price	Dairy feed price 16% protein [1]	Milk-feed price ratio [2]
	Dollars/cwt	*Dollars/ton*	*Pounds*
2005	15.19	197	3.24
2006	12.96	210	2.57
2007	19.21	249	2.80
2008	18.45	313	2.01
2009	12.93	293	1.78
2010	16.35	274	2.26
2011	20.24	369	1.90
2012	18.56	442	1.52
2013	20.11	481	1.75
2014	24.07	502	2.54

[1] Commercially prepared 16%protein dairy ration price collected from March annual Prices Paid Survey.   [2] Annual ratios based on average of monthly ratios.   Pounds of 16% protein mixed dairy feed equal in value to one pound of whole milk.   Feed price component (16% protein) calculated using U.S. price received for corn (51 lbs), soybeans (8 1b), and alfalfa hay (41 lbs).
NASS, Environmental, Economics, and Demographics Branch, (202) 720–6146.

Table 8-13.—Fluid beverage milk: Total and per capita consumption, United States, 2004–2014

Year	Consumption	
	Total	Per capita
	Billion pounds	*Pounds*
2004	54.5	186
2005	54.6	185
2006	54.8	184
2007	54.6	181
2008	54.5	179
2009	54.7	178
2010	54.9	177
2011	54.2	174
2012	53.4	170
2013	52.2	165
2014	50.7	159

ERS, Animal Products and Cost of Production Branch, (202) 694–5171.

Table 8-14.—Federal milk order markets: Measures of growth, 2005–2014 [1]

Year	Number of markets [2]	Population of Federal milk marketing areas	Number of handlers [2]	Number of producers [3]	Receipts of producer milk	Producer milk used in Class I	Percentage of producer milk used in Class I
	Number	*Thousands*	*Number*	*Number*	*Million pounds*	*Million pounds*	*Percent*
2005	10	238,428	302	53,036	114,682	44,570	38.9
2006	10	239,142	314	52,725	120,618	45,304	37.6
2007	10	241,000	312	49,782	114,407	45,226	39.5
2008	10	242,988	333	47,859	115,867	44,989	38.8
2009	10	245,445	251	46,677	123,430	45,262	36.7
2010	10	247,031	251	45,918	126,909	44,970	35.4
2011	10	247,675	241	43,654	126,879	44,383	35.0
2012	10	250,724	237	40,750	122,388	43,492	35.5
2013	10	251,201	225	40,048	132,100	42,742	32.4
2014	10	255,184	223	38,391	129,420	41,420	32.0

Year	Prices at 3.5 percent butterfat content per hundredweight [4]		Receipts as percentage of milk sold to plants and dealers		Daily deliveries of milk per producer	Gross value of receipts of producer milk [5]	
	Class I	Blend	Fluid grade	All milk		Per producer	All producer
	Dollars	*Dollars*	*Percent*	*Percent*	*Pounds*	*Dollars*	*1,000 dollars*
2005	17.13	15.07	66	65	5,904	334,626	17,747,577
2006	14.59	12.86	68	67	6,264	303,429	15,998,288
2007	20.81	19.19	63	62	6,297	452,097	22,507,219
2008	20.78	18.24	61	62	6,613	453,886	21,772,538
2009	14.40	12.44	66	66	7,242	339,698	15,856,077
2010	18.25	16.07	67	66	7,572	444,038	20,389,201
2011	21.97	19.87	66	65	7,963	577,538	25,211,996
2012	20.39	18.05	62	61	8,229	542,121	22,091,337
2013	21.80	19.44	67	66	9,047	641,295	25,682,588
2014	26.14	23.54	63	63	9,236	793,728	30,472,016

[1] Over this period, handler selected periodically not to pool substantial volumes of milk that normally would have been pooled under Federal orders. This decision resulted from disadvantageous blend/class price relationships and qualification circumstances. This fact should be kept in mind if year-to-year comparisons are made using the various "producer deliveries" measures of growth. [2] End of year. [3] Average for year. [4] Prices are weighted averages. [5] Based on blend (uniform) price adjusted for butterfat content, and in later years, other milk components of producer milk.
AMS, Dairy Programs, (202) 720–7461.

Table 8-15.—Milk production: Marketings, income and value, United States, 2005–2014

Year	Combined marketings of milk and cream				Used for milk, cream, and butter on farms where produced		Gross farm income from dairy products [3]	Farm value of all milk produced [2][4]
	Milk utilized	Average returns [1]		Cash receipts from marketings	Milk utilized	Value [2]		
		Per 100 pounds milk	Per pound milkfat					
	Million pounds	*Dollars*	*Dollars*	*1,000 dollars*	*Million pounds*	*1,000 dollars*	*1,000 dollars*	*1,000 dollars*
2005	175,836	15.19	4.15	26,704,863	146	22,787	26,727,650	26,874,301
2006	180,700	12.96	3.51	23,412,552	138	18,591	23,431,143	23,556,102
2007	184,565	19.21	5.22	35,453,399	137	27,073	35,480,472	35,665,894
2008	188,911	18.45	5.01	34,846,236	124	23,743	34,869,979	35,048,242
2009	188,189	12.93	3.52	24,321,032	112	15,224	24,336,256	24,455,900
2010	191,897	16.35	4.47	31,372,346	107	18,269	31,390,615	31,535,575
2011	195,290	20.24	5.46	39,531,306	98	20,561	39,551,867	39,730,346
2012	199,687	18.56	4.99	37,064,731	98	18,779	37,083,510	37,247,542
2013	200,254	20.11	5.35	40,276,790	100	20,629	40,297,419	40,476,608
2014	205,085	24.07	6.44	49,349,226	93	22,918	49,372,144	49,585,330

[1] Cash receipts divided by milk or milkfat represented in combined marketings [2] Valued at average returns per 100 pounds of milk in combined marketings of milk and cream. [3] Cash receipts from marketings of milk and cream plus value of milk used for home consumption. [4] Includes value of milk fed to calves.
NASS, Livestock Branch, (202) 720–3570.

Table 8-16.—Official Dairy Herd Information test plans: Numbers of herds and cows and milk, fat, and protein production, United States, 2005–2014

Year	Herds	Cows	Cows per herd	Average production			Cows with protein information	Average protein production	Average protein production
				Milk	Fat	Fat			
	Number	Number	Number	Pounds	Percent	Pounds	Percent	Percent	Pounds
2005 ...	18,349	3,537,857	192.8	22,077	3.67	812	95	3.08	680
2006 ...	17,606	3,602,719	204.6	22,282	3.69	825	95	3.09	688
2007 ...	17,174	3,749,257	218.3	22,371	3.68	826	95	3.09	693
2008 ...	16,602	3,804,216	229.1	22,437	3.69	830	96	3.10	696
2009 ...	15,331	3,665,911	239.1	22,501	3.68	831	98	3.09	698
2010 ...	15,067	3,746,177	248.6	22,765	3.66	836	98	3.09	706
2011 ...	14,490	3,800,410	262.3	22,961	3.71	855	98	3.11	714
2012 ...	13,894	3,762,925	270.8	23,328	3.72	871	98	3.12	728
2013 ...	13,329	3,712,080	278.5	23,695	3.77	894	98	3.13	742
2014 ...	13,043	3,829,273	293.6	24,101	3.76	907	98	3.14	757

Council on Dairy Cattle Breeding, (301) 525–2006, https://www.cdcb.us.

Table 8-17.—Milk and milkfat production: Number of producing cows, production per cow, and total quantity produced, United States, 2005–2014

Year	Number of milk cows [1]	Production of milk and milkfat [2]				
		Per milk cow		Percentage of fat in all milk produced	Total	
		Milk	Milkfat		Milk	Milkfat
	Thousands	Pounds	Pounds	Percent	Million pounds	Million pounds
2005	9,050	19,550	716	3.66	176,931	6,480
2006	9,137	19,895	734	3.69	181,782	6,700
2007	9,189	20,204	744	3.68	185,654	6,832
2008	9,314	20,397	751	3.68	189,978	6,998
2009	9,202	20,561	755	3.67	189,202	6,944
2010	9,123	21,142	774	3.66	192,877	7,054
2011	9,199	21,334	791	3.71	196,255	7,284
2012	9,237	21,722	808	3.72	200,642	7,463
2013	9,224	21,816	820	3.76	201,231	7,557
2014	9,257	22,259	832	3.74	206,054	7,699

[1] Average number during year, excluding heifers not yet fresh. [2] Excludes milk sucked by calves.
NASS, Livestock Branch, (202) 720–3570.

Table 8-18.—Milk: Quantities used and marketed by farmers, United States, 2005–2014

Year	Milk used on farms where produced			Milk marketed by producers	
	Fed to calves [1]	Consumed as fluid milk or cream	Total	Total [2]	Fluid grade [3]
	Million pounds	Million pounds	Million pounds	Million pounds	Percent
2005	949	146	1,095	175,836	98
2006	943	138	1,081	180,700	99
2007	952	137	1,089	184,565	99
2008	944	124	1,068	188,911	99
2009	901	112	1,013	188,189	98
2010	873	107	980	191,897	98
2011	867	98	965	195,290	99
2012	858	98	956	199,687	99
2013	877	100	977	200,254	99
2014	869	93	962	205,085	99

[1] Excludes milk sucked by calves. [2] Milk sold to plants and dealers as whole milk and equivalent amounts of milk for cream. Includes milk produced by dealers' own herds and small amounts sold directly to consumers. Also includes milk produced by institutional herds. [3] Percentage of milk sold that is eligible for fluid use (Grade A in most States). Includes fluid-grade milk used in manufacturing dairy products.
NASS, Livestock Branch, (202) 720–3570.

Table 8-19.—Milk markets under Federal order program: Whole milk and fat-reduced milk products sold for fluid consumption within defined marketing areas, 2011–2013[1]

Federal milk order marketing area	Whole milk products[2]		Fat-reduced milk products[3]		Total fluid milk products	
	Quantity	Butterfat content	Quantity	Butterfat content	Quantity	Butterfat content
	Million pounds	*Percent*	*Million pounds*	*Percent*	*Million pounds*	*Percent*
2011						
Northeast	2,999	3.29	6,110	1.08	9,109	1.81
Appalachian	1,041	3.30	2,538	1.29	3,580	1.87
Southeast	1,607	3.34	3,291	1.33	4,898	1.99
Florida	1,021	3.33	1,879	1.18	2,900	1.94
Mideast	1,263	3.32	4,725	1.31	5,988	1.24
Upper Midwest	578	3.31	3,643	1.10	4,221	1.40
Central	1,005	3.32	3,543	1.24	4,548	1.70
Southwest	1,522	3.32	2,953	1.36	4,476	2.03
Arizona	308	3.26	872	1.20	1,179	1.74
Pacific Northwest	457	3.40	1,757	1.30	2,214	1.73
Combined areas	11,802	3.32	31,311	1.23	43,113	1.80
2012						
Northeast	2,976	3.30	6,055	1.08	9,030	1.81
Appalachian	1,022	3.27	2,477	1.29	3,498	1.87
Southeast	1,538	3.34	3,232	1.31	4,770	1.96
Florida	1,016	3.35	1,839	1.18	2,855	1.95
Mideast	1,254	3.32	4,620	1.29	5,874	1.73
Upper Midwest	568	3.33	3,551	1.10	4,120	1.41
Central	1,002	3.33	3,525	1.23	4,527	1.70
Southwest	1,482	3.34	2,960	1.35	4,442	2.01
Arizona	306	3.23	848	1.16	1,154	1.71
Pacific Northwest	462	3.41	1,708	1.31	2,170	1.76
Combined areas	11,625	3.32	30,814	1.22	42,440	1.79
2013						
Northeast	2,979	3.29	5,892	1.10	8,871	1.83
Appalachian	1,019	3.25	2,357	1.31	3,376	1.89
Southeast	1,512	3.34	3,133	1.32	4,646	1.97
Florida	1,013	3.34	1,785	1.20	2,797	1.97
Mideast	1,244	3.32	4,415	1.30	5,659	1.74
Upper Midwest	577	3.32	3,411	1.12	3,988	1.44
Central	1,000	3.34	3,418	1.25	4,417	1.72
Southwest	1,495	3.34	2,982	1.36	4,477	2.02
Arizona	311	3.24	816	1.17	1,128	1.74
Pacific Northwest	470	3.42	1,618	1.32	2,089	1.79
Combined areas	11,620	3.32	29,828	1.23	41,448	1.82

[1] In-area sales include total sales in each of the areas by handlers regulated under the respective order, by handlers regulated under other orders, by partially regulated handlers, by exempt handlers, and by producer-handlers. Sales routes of handlers may extend outside defined marketing areas; therefore, some handlers' in-area sales are partially estimated. [2] Plain, organic, flavored, and miscellaneous whole milk products, and eggnog. [3] Plain, fortified, organic, and flavored reduced fat milk (2%), low fat milk (1%), and fat-free milk (skim), and miscellaneous fat-reduced milk products, and buttermilk.

AMS, Dairy Programs, (202) 720–7461.

Table 8-20.—Milk markets under Federal order program: Uniform and Class I milk prices at 3.5 percent fat test, number of producers, producer milk receipts, producer milk used in Class I, Class I percentage, daily milk deliveries per producer, average fat test of producer milk receipts, by markets, 2013–2014

Federal milk order marketing area	Class I $ / cwt[1]	Uniform $ / cwt[1][2]	Average number of producers	Receipts of producer milk	Producer milk used in Class I	Class I utilization	Daily milk deliveries per producer	Average fat test of producer milk
	Dollars	Dollars	Number	Million pounds	Million pounds	Percent	Pounds	Percent
				2013				
Northeast[3]	22.09	20.23	12,353	25,420	9,508	37.40	5,638	3.76
Appalachian[4]	22.24	21.34	2,307	5,729	3,845	67.12	6,816	3.71
Florida[5]	24.24	23.53	262	2,833	2,424	85.54	30,731	3.64
Southeast[6]	22.64	21.74	2,320	6,129	4,163	67.92	7,336	3.72
Upper Midwest[7][8]	20.64	18.29	12,467	34,315	3,686	10.74	7,545	3.81
Central[8][9]	20.85	18.82	3,040	15,199	4,867	32.02	13,707	3.75
Mideast[8][10]	20.85	19.17	6,155	16,719	6,448	38.57	7,447	3.76
Pacific Northwest[8][11]	20.74	18.83	566	8,239	2,120	25.74	40,104	3.88
Southwest[8][12]	21.85	19.59	487	12,901	4,324	33.51	72,981	3.69
Arizona[13]	21.18	19.41	92	4,615	1,357	29.40	137,341	3.52
All markets combined	21.80	19.44	40,048	132,100	42,742	32.36	9,047	3.76
				2014				
Northeast[3]	26.53	24.28	12,178	25,793	9,123	35.37	5,803	3.78
Appalachian[4]	26.68	25.62	2,244	5,593	3,783	67.63	6,834	3.65
Florida[5]	28.67	27.82	214	2,771	2,343	84.56	37,006	3.60
Southeast[6]	27.07	26.20	2,109	5,289	3,905	73.83	6,870	3.66
Upper Midwest[7][8]	25.08	22.54	12,219	32,785	3,587	10.94	7,552	3.80
Central[8][9]	25.28	22.90	3,093	15,063	4,816	31.97	13,364	3.73
Mideast[8][10]	25.28	23.13	5,958	17,279	6,245	36.10	7,954	3.75
Pacific Northwest[8][11]	25.18	22.71	537	7,892	2,021	25.61	39,849	3.88
Southwest[8][12]	26.29	23.66	504	12,137	4,310	35.51	65,929	3.67
Arizona[13]	25.62	23.25	93	4,800	1,287	26.81	142,220	3.47
All markets combined	26.14	23.54	38,391	129,420	41,420	32.00	9,239	3.74

[1] Prices are for milk of 3.5 percent butterfat content and for the principal pricing point of the market. See footnotes 3-13.   [2] For those orders that use the component pricing system for paying producers (orders 1, 30, 32, 33, 124,and 126), the figures are the statistical uniform price (the sum of the producer price differential and the Class III price). For those orders that use the skim milk/butterfat pricing system for paying producers (orders 5, 6, 7, and 131), the figures are the uniform price (the sum of the uniform butterfat price times 3.5 and the uniform skim milk price times 0.965).   [3] Suffolk Co. (Boston), MA.   [4] Mecklenburg Co. (Charlotte), NC.   [5] Hillsborough Co. (Tampa), FL.   [5] Fulton Co. (Atlanta), GA.   [7] Cook Co. (Chicago), IL.   [8] Due to the disadvantageous intraorder class and uniform price relationships in some months in these markets, handlers elected not to pool milk that normally would have been pooled under these orders.   [9] Jackson Co. (Kansas City), MO.   [10] Cuyahoga Co. (Cleveland), OH.   [11] King Co. (Seattle), WA.   [12] Dallas Co. (Dallas), TX.   [13] Maricopa Co. (Phoenix), AZ.

AMS, Dairy Programs, (202) 720–7461.

Table 8-21.—Dairy products: Quantities manufactured, United States, 2010–2014

Product	2010	2011	2012	2013	2014[1]
	1,000 pounds	*1,000 pounds*	*1,000 pounds*	*1,000 pounds*	*1,000 pounds*
Butter	1,563,972	1,809,751	1,859,537	1,862,516	1,856,330
Cheese:					
American types	4,289,341	4,226,670	4,355,252	4,419,848	4,534,237
Cheddar	3,234,991	3,096,350	3,143,443	3,189,859	3,263,258
Other American	1,054,350	1,130,320	1,211,809	1,230,009	1,270,979
Blue and Gorgonzola	84,133	85,867	87,932	92,401	92,817
Brick	6,706	11,420	12,482	9,312	2,942
Cream and Neufchatel	744,864	714,594	807,681	842,264	851,711
Feta	77,560	107,323	109,310	103,609	105,622
Gouda	19,000	16,158	37,227	47,799	47,264
Hispanic	215,313	224,396	223,893	241,420	250,263
Italian types	4,415,714	4,585,327	4,632,825	4,735,476	4,949,601
Mozzarella	3,479,441	3,574,428	3,614,848	3,699,989	3,923,480
Parmesan	233,792	287,705	296,963	319,741	301,848
Provolone	354,857	351,460	356,079	360,069	361,575
Ricotta	261,305	260,229	247,853	241,117	245,284
Romano	33,639	44,705	48,481	45,052	45,021
Other Italian types	52,680	66,800	68,601	69,608	72,393
Muenster cheese	117,647	146,585	152,516	163,220	163,650
Swiss cheese	336,458	329,145	320,599	294,495	297,797
All other types	136,662	147,521	146,524	151,894	154,213
Total cheese[2]	10,443,397	10,595,006	10,886,241	11,101,669	11,450,117
Cottage cheese:					
Curd[3]	432,881	423,683	423,900	389,396	382,587
Creamed[4]	331,348	322,099	323,220	307,391	303,972
Lowfat[5]	387,689	381,499	386,105	370,323	366,600
Sour cream	1,227,947	1,255,008	1,281,432	1,281,366	1,304,529
Yogurt plain & flavored	4,180,688	4,271,395	4,416,986	4,717,076	4,756,545
Bulk condensed milk:					
Skim, sweetened	38,405	42,503	39,635	38,190	43,593
Skim, unsweetened	1,557,612	1,575,211	1,619,260	1,623,159	1,661,446
Whole, sweetened	79,840	82,650	87,322	89,681	88,607
Whole, unsweetened	89,125	64,440	95,642	75,645	65,596
Condensed or evaporated buttermilk	75,983	76,502	81,278	94,499	109,044
Canned milk:					
Evaporated and condensed whole[6] ...	502,665	494,853	470,615	495,844	315,290
Evaporated skim	18,853	18,946	20,903	20,387	27,856
Dry milk products:					
Dry buttermilk, total	82,042	100,138	109,132	119,273	111,097
Dry skim milk animal	8,350	8,535	9,792	10,350	11,303
Dry whole milk	71,056	65,787	58,132	72,053	103,122
Milk protein concentrate, total	88,617	94,489	102,318	101,747	126,017
Nonfat dry milk, human	1,562,518	1,499,477	1,764,449	1,477,864	1,764,510
Skim milk powder, total[7]	253,804	446,017	380,672	630,689	543,504
Dry whey, total	1,012,983	1,010,117	998,898	961,020	869,660
	1,000 gallons	*1,000 gallons*	*1,000 gallons*	*1,000 gallons*	*1,000 gallons*
Ice cream, regular, total	929,128	888,378	894,033	897,363	872,091
Ice cream, lowfat, total[8]	415,496	415,464	457,273	400,925	411,617
Ice cream, nonfat, total	15,961	17,159	17,166	14,225	18,468
Sherbet, total	49,270	45,387	43,563	46,096	45,650
Frozen yogurt, total	50,058	62,715	57,555	74,483	66,760

[1] Preliminary. [2] Excluding cottage cheese. [3] Mostly used for processing into creamed or lowfat cottage cheese. [4] Fat content 4 percent or more. [5] Fat content less than 4 percent. [6] Combined to avoid disclosing individual plant operations. [7] Includes protein standardized and blends. [8] Includes freezer-made milkshake.
NASS, Livestock Branch, (202) 720–3570.

Table 8-22.—Dairy Products: Factory production of specified items, by State and United States, 2013–2014

State	Butter 2013	Butter 2014[1]	Total American cheese[2] 2013	Total American cheese[2] 2014[1]	Total cheese[3] 2013	Total cheese[3] 2014[1]
	1,000 pounds	1,000 pounds	1,000 pounds	1,000 pounds	1,000 pounds	1,000 pounds
California	634,397	612,658	616,996	647,081	2,312,895	2,444,260
Idaho			597,814	587,502	871,640	895,189
Illinois					65,134	75,135
Iowa			183,814	180,525	267,249	263,627
Minnesota					661,293	666,537
New Mexico					751,280	758,729
New York					777,355	784,666
Ohio					196,415	202,350
Oregon			194,182	200,838		
Pennsylvania	89,233	93,844			426,985	415,790
South Dakota					264,899	263,618
Vermont					127,346	123,534
Wisconsin			837,517	848,876	2,855,881	2,910,299
Other States[4]	1,138,886	1,149,828	1,989,555	2,069,415	1,523,297	1,646,383
United States	1,862,516	1,856,330	4,419,848	4,534,237	11,101,669	11,450,117

State	Ice cream, regular (hard) 2013	Ice cream, regular (hard) 2014[1]	Nonfat dry milk for human food 2013	Nonfat dry milk for human food 2014[1]
	Gallons	Gallons	Pounds	Pounds
California	127,508	129,002	583,106	719,044
Missouri	21,970	26,251		
Ohio	21,844	21,151		
Oregon	11,873	12,393		
Pennsylvania	36,521	37,020		
Wisconsin	23,067	18,779		
Other States[4]	548,579	523,251	894,758	1,045.466
United States	791,362	767,847	1,477,864	1,764,510

[1] Preliminary. [2] Includes Cheddar, Colby, washed curd, stirred curd, Monterey, and Jack. [3] Excluding cottage cheese. [4] States not shown when fewer than 3 plants reported or individual plant operations could be disclosed. NASS, Livestock Branch, (202) 720–3570.

Table 8-23.—Dairy products: Average price per pound for specified products, 2010–2014

Item and market	2010	2011	2012	2013	2014
	Dollars	Dollars	Dollars	Dollars	Dollars
Butter, Chicago Mercantile Exchange: Grade AA:					
High[1]	2.2350	2.1800	1.9525	1.7875	3.0600
Low[1]	1.3100	1.5950	1.3000	1.3600	1.5325
Butter, Agricultural Marketing Service, Grade AA:[2]	1.7020	1.9498	1.5943	1.5451	2.1341
Cheese, Cheddar, Chicago Mercantile Exchange, Barrels:					
High[1]	1.7350	2.1350	2.0800	1.9700	2.4900
Low	1.2500	1.3400	1.4075	1.5300	1.4200
Cheese, Cheddar, Chicago Mercantile Exchange, 40-lb blocks:					
High[1]	1.7700	2.1550	2.1200	2.0000	2.4500
Low[1]	1.2675	1.3425	1.4600	1.5500	1.5200
Cheese, Cheddar, Agricultural Marketing Service, Barrels:[2]	1.5033	1.8146	1.6888	1.7456	2.1283
Cheese, Cheddar, Agricultural Marketing Service, 40-lb blocks:[2]	1.5138	1.8084	1.6972	1.7620	2.1341
Nonfat dry milk, Agricultural Marketing Service:					
Low/medium heat[2]	1.1687	1.5058	1.3279	1.7066	1.7592
Dry whey, Agricultural Marketing Service:					
Edible nonhygroscopic[2]	0.3716	0.5325	0.5935	0.5902	0.6526

[1] Figures are the high and low prices for any trading day during the year. [2] Prices used in Federal milk order price formulas. Prior to April 2012, the product prices were published by the National Agricultural Statistics Service. AMS, Dairy Programs, (202) 720–9351.

Table 8-24.—Dairy products: Manufacturers' stocks, end of month, United States, 2013–2014 [1]

Month	Evaporated and condensed whole milk [2]		Dry whole milk		Nonfat dry milk, human	
	2013	2014	2013	2014	2013	2014
	1,000 pounds	*1,000 pounds*	*1,000 pounds*	*1,000 pounds*	*1,000 pounds*	*1,000 pounds*
January	58,165	52,954	6,692	6,925	194,791	149,021
February	60,831	60,456	6,887	9,196	224,637	182,101
March	66,101	62,094	3,683	7,381	217,779	215,974
April	78,395	78,889	4,479	5,757	208,557	239,792
May	90,392	86,239	4,895	10,497	231,931	221,121
June	97,155	85,172	6,120	14,405	231,259	227,248
July	105,161	96,381	9,220	14,817	210,568	248,469
August	106,797	99,668	10,148	19,860	196,070	236,424
September	97,526	90,157	7,081	24,968	147,617	169,819
October	69,867	67,282	8,777	21,657	114,818	186,309
November	45,959	50,320	8,662	21,957	115,252	218,942
December	37,256	32,402	7,591	23,244	135,128	239,029

[1] Stocks held by manufacturers at all points and in transit.   [2] Combined to avoid disclosing individual plant operations.
NASS, Livestock Branch, (202) 720–3570.

Table 8-25.—Dairy products: Total disappearance, and total and per capita consumption, United States, 2005–2014 [1]

Year	Butter			Cheese [2]			Condensed and evaporated milk [3]		
	Total disappearance	Consumption		Total disappearance	Consumption		Total disappearance	Consumption	
		Total	Per capita		Total	Per capita		Total	Per capita
	Million pounds	*Million pounds*	*Pounds*	*Million pounds*	*Million pounds*	*Pounds*	*Million pounds*	*Million pounds*	*Pounds*
2005	1,355	1,337	4.5	9,481	9,278	31.3	767	695	2.4
2006	1,418	1,395	4.7	9,841	9,617	32.2	732	678	2.3
2007	1,503	1,414	4.7	10,150	9,868	32.7	716	628	2.1
2008	1,693	1,516	5.0	10,162	9,799	32.1	787	712	2.3
2009	1,574	1,522	5.0	10,248	9,917	32.3	771	703	2.3
2010	1,623	1,521	4.9	10,605	10,136	32.7	718	607	2.0
2011	1,795	1,676	5.4	10,893	10,301	33.0	711	598	1.9
2012	1,828	1,730	5.5	11,123	10,461	33.3	715	627	2.0
2013	1,914	1,731	5.5	11,365	10,578	33.4	723	594	1.9
2014	1,888	1,753	5.5	11,722	10,824	33.9	537	446	1.4

Year	Reg hard ice cream (product weight)			Dry whole milk			Nonfat dry milk (human food)		
	Total disappearance	Consumption		Total disappearance	Consumption		Total disappearance	Consumption	
		Total	Per capita		Total	Per capita		Total	Per capita
	Million pounds	*Million pounds*	*Pounds*	*Million pounds*	*Million pounds*	*Pounds*	*Million pounds*	*Million pounds*	*Pounds*
2005	4,047	3,989	13.5	64	45	0.15	1,807	1,186	4.0
2006	4,122	4,063	13.6	60	33	0.11	1,487	846	2.8
2007	4,016	3,959	13.1	73	50	0.16	1,424	843	2.8
2008	3,949	3,893	12.8	86	29	0.09	1,786	903	3.0
2009	3,860	3,804	12.4	97	78	0.25	1,789	1,227	4.0
2010	3,689	3,618	11.7	86	64	0.21	1,864	998	3.2
2011	3,603	3,522	11.3	84	67	0.21	1,926	943	3.0
2012	3,608	3,504	11.1	79	53	0.17	2,132	1,136	3.6
2013	3,565	3,430	10.8	88	54	0.17	2,160	921	2.9
2014	3,455	3,313	10.4	101	63	0.20	2,207	988	3.1

[1] Total disappearance is based on production, imports, and change in stocks during the year. Production statistics for these commodities appear in other tables in this chapter. The total apparent consumption was obtained by subtracting ending stocks, shipments, and exports, from the total supply. The per capita consumption for each year was obtained by dividing the total apparent consumption by the number of persons. [2] Includes all kinds of cheese except cottage cheese. [3] The evaporated milk is unskimmed, unsweetened, case goods. The condensed milk is unsweetened, unskimmed, bulk goods; and sweetened condensed milk, unskimmed, case and bulk goods.
ERS, Animal Products and Cost of Production Branch, (202) 694–5171.

Table 8-26.—Dairy products: Dec. 31 stocks, United States, 2005–2014

Year	Butter [1][2]	Cheese [1][3]	Canned milk [1]	Dry whole milk	Nonfat dry milk for human consumption [1]
	Million pounds	Million pounds	Million pounds	Million pounds	Million pounds
2005	59	758	44	2	185
2006	109	817	31	2	107
2007	155	798	37	4	166
2008	119	852	42	5	253
2009	133	967	45	7	289
2010	82	1,048	52	8	145
2011	107	992	37	7	165
2012	153	1,023	38	7	183
2013	112	1,009	37	8	135
2014	105	1,018	32	23	240

[1] Includes Government holdings.   [2] Includes anhydrous milkfat and butter oil.   [3] Excludes processed cheese and cottage cheese.
ERS, Animal Products and Cost of Production Branch, (202) 694–5171.

Table 8-27.—International dairy: Butter production, 2013–2015

Country	2013	2014	2015
	1,000 metric tons	1,000 metric tons	1,000 metric tons
Australia	117	125	122
Belarus	99	105	120
Brazil	83	85	87
Canada	95	88	91
European Union	2,100	2,250	2,310
India	4,745	4,887	5,035
Mexico	190	192	195
New Zealand	535	580	570
Russia	219	252	265
Ukraine	93	115	105
Others	128	116	118
Total Foreign	8,404	8,795	9,018
United States	845	842	830
Total	9,249	9,637	9,848

FAS, Office of Global Analysis, (202) 720-6301. Prepared or estimated on the basis of official USDA production, supply, and distribution statistics from foreign governments.

Table 8-28.—International dairy: Cheese production, 2013–2015

Country	2013	2014	2015
	1,000 metric tons	1,000 metric tons	1,000 metric tons
Argentina	556	564	570
Australia	320	320	330
Belarus	140	170	190
Brazil	722	736	751
Canada	388	396	400
European Union	9,368	9,560	9,610
Mexico	270	275	282
New Zealand	311	325	347
Russia	713	760	850
Ukraine	140	104	100
Others	73	72	68
Total Foreign	13,001	13,282	13,498
United States	5,036	5,194	5,299
Total	18,037	18,476	18,797

FAS, Office of Global Analysis, (202) 720-6301. Prepared or estimated on the basis of official USDA production, supply, and distribution statistics from foreign governments.

Table 8-29.—Dairy products: United States imports by country of origin, 2011–2013

Commodity and country of origin	2011	2012	2013
	Metric tons	Metric tons	Metric tons
Licensed cheese items 1:			
Netherlands	4,740	5,221	5,502
United Kingdom	2,472	2,566	3,124
Denmark(*)	1,844	1,962	2,182
Ireland	879	1,442	1,484
Canada	1,869	958	1,023
Germany(*)	664	670	707
New Zealand(*)	711	5,249	683
Italy(*)	340	436	457
Australia(*)	331	560	386
France(*)	245	233	260
Israel(*)	0	3	146
Austria	34	72	137
Dominican Republic	109	211	118
Jamaica	116	12	108
Bahrain	29	141	80
Spain	34	81	61
India	37	58	42
Lithuania	30	46	40
Finland	70	65	38
Mexico	0	0	38
Poland	24	56	27
Argentina	26	21	18
Philippines	5	12	15
Portugal	3	3	3
Egypt	8	0	2
Rest of World	75	4	1
World Total	14,694	20,080	16,682
Licensed cheese items 2:			
France(*)	18,712	18,088	19,344
Italy(*)	15,634	16,157	16,209
Switzerland(*)	5,374	6,090	8,069
Norway(*)	6,286	6,375	6,421
Ireland	5,111	6,101	5,537
Denmark(*)	5,125	5,166	5,536
Netherlands	6,668	6,025	5,238
Canada	3,021	3,309	4,304
Finland	7,164	6,134	3,699
Spain	1,081	1,922	3,562
Nicaragua	3,207	3,647	3,554
Germany(*)	1,901	1,695	2,973
Mexico	4,301	3,565	2,935
United Kingdom	1,880	1,901	2,146
Australia(*)	209	1,146	1,872
Poland	1,769	1,651	1,456
Uruguay	1,309	666	927
Austria	872	941	894
Argentina	2,989	2,510	853
Belgium-Luxembourg(*)	968	689	821
Egypt	496	573	642
Sweden	592	687	620
Lithuania	200	365	387
Portugal	445	334	351
Israel(*)	600	388	263
Rest of World	3,738	9,437	2,121
World Total	99,650	105,560	100,732
Licensed dairy, misc :			
Mexico	19,026	21,510	25,679
Canada	7,130	10,084	14,249
Chile	2,146	1,874	2,035
New Zealand(*)	3,409	3,333	1,675
Germany(*)	267	2,411	1,520
Netherlands	835	599	1,212
France(*)	211	346	889
Belgium-Luxembourg(*)	989	994	883
Australia(*)	882	2,204	658
Korea, South	452	449	589
Honduras	0	200	403
Ireland	515	1	394
Spain	60	26	325
Peru	120	205	264
Colombia	117	279	250
Argentina	158	361	234
United Kingdom	177	140	178
Denmark(*)	170	167	163
Italy(*)	160	54	150
Pakistan	0	0	136
Brazil	132	187	118
Ecuador	13	28	95
Japan	22	23	52
Israel(*)	200	1,753	49
Costa Rica	0	12	45
Rest of World	471	1,003	164
World Total	37,660	48,241	52,406

See footnote(s) at end of table.

Table 8-29.—Dairy products: United States imports by country of origin, 2011–2013—Continued

Commodity and country of origin	2011	2012	2013
	Metric tons	*Metric tons*	*Metric tons*
Non-licensed dairy, misc:			
Germany(*)	1,356	8,877	15,050
Mexico	15,409	18,513	15,016
Canada	4,526	5,722	6,471
Peru	3,123	3,935	5,936
Chile	4,842	4,468	5,221
New Zealand(*)	2,240	5,967	3,527
Denmark(*)	1,699	1,679	1,309
Greece	328	228	674
Netherlands	1,031	1,451	587
Israel(*)	44	425	343
Belgium-Luxembourg(*)	340	340	308
Ukraine	50	78	170
Brazil	287	134	131
United Kingdom	130	586	111
Norway(*)	46	181	100
Australia(*)	295	107	90
Russia	207	96	78
Nicaragua	76	40	70
Ireland	47	13	66
Poland	55	63	62
Argentina	273	20	39
Colombia	0	2	32
Spain	381	401	19
Italy(*)	0	8	19
Yemen(*)	0	0	18
Rest of World	63	275	76
World Total	36,849	53,609	55,520
Non-licensed cheese:			
Italy(*)	12,978	14,015	12,984
Spain	3,966	3,587	4,244
France(*)	3,165	2,757	3,399
Greece	2,519	2,827	2,986
Bulgaria	2,672	2,756	2,685
Turkey	315	585	995
Lithuania	0	40	769
Israel(*)	474	565	571
United Kingdom	486	431	483
Romania	169	157	319
Cyprus	298	244	277
Norway(*)	156	140	172
Netherlands	142	115	171
Macedonia	26	17	66
Egypt	18	29	44
Portugal	31	15	19
El Salvador	0	30	13
Jordan	31	12	9
Switzerland(*)	0	0	4
Croatia	5	4	4
Germany(*)	25	2	3
Poland	3	5	2
Bosnia and Herzegovina	0	0	1
Austria	1	4	1
Guatemala	0	0	1
Rest of World	1,194	34	0
World Total	28,672	28,368	30,222
Casein:			
New Zealand(*)	30,262	31,136	30,222
Netherlands	8,001	10,191	13,797
Poland	6,856	5,689	8,007
India	4,730	5,534	7,480
Ireland	13,641	10,664	7,143
Argentina	10,552	4,142	4,237
Germany(*)	5,868	4,472	4,135
France(*)	3,294	5,468	2,688
Uruguay	146	2,959	1,914
Denmark(*)	2,353	2,156	1,664
Australia(*)	1,439	565	996
China	74	631	237
Ukraine	183	253	155
Malaysia	0	0	71
Russia	0	0	20
Portugal	0	0	1
Belgium-Luxembourg(*)	0	19	0
Belarus	2,150	195	0
Canada	0	0	0
Japan	0	-	0
Mexico	5	0	0
United Kingdom	85	249	0
World Total	89,640	84,322	82,767

See footnote(s) at end of table.

Table 8-29.—Dairy products: United States imports by country of origin, 2011–2013—Continued

Commodity and country of origin	2011	2012	2013
	Metric tons	Metric tons	Metric tons
Lactose:			
Canada	3,193	2,435	2,798
Germany(*)	2,878	2,618	1,737
Netherlands	1,377	252	873
New Zealand(*)	127	102	137
France(*)	1	7	45
China	208	124	22
Belarus	66	44	22
Russia	9	0	7
Bosnia and Herzegovina	0	5	4
Thailand	0	0	3
Ireland	0	0	3
South Africa	0	2	3
Hong Kong	0	0	2
United Kingdom	7	1	2
Argentina	0	0	2
Japan	17	0	2
India	1	1	0
Belgium-Luxembourg(*)	2	0	0
Guatemala	15	0	0
Honduras	0	51	0
Israel(*)	-	0	0
Italy(*)	0	0	0
Singapore	0	0	0
Spain	-	-	0
Ukraine	0	6	0
World Total	7,900	5,646	5,661
Butter:			
New Zealand(*)	8,823	10,328	5,725
Ireland	1,856	2,391	3,391
Mexico	6	1,125	1,544
Australia(*)	627	1,860	1,123
France(*)	313	1,121	901
Germany(*)	239	182	352
Canada	228	279	285
Denmark(*)	242	230	219
India	277	171	141
Malaysia	0	14	135
Poland	122	114	133
United Kingdom	112	102	116
Italy(*)	61	55	61
Belgium-Luxembourg(*)	14	159	38
Argentina	10	139	37
Israel(*)	0	0	26
Turkey	10	13	17
Lithuania	13	15	17
Netherlands	5	5	13
Iceland	48	56	12
Portugal	12	11	10
Other Pacific Islands, NEC(*)	10	2	6
Bangladesh	0	0	6
Pakistan	0	0	5
Kenya	0	1	4
Rest of World	99	227	5
World Total	13,125	18,600	14,322

- Represents zero.　(*) Denotes a country that is a summarization of its component countries.　Note: All zeroes for a data item may show that statistics exist in the other importtype.　Consumption or General.　Users should use cautious in-terpretation on quantity reports using mixed units of measure.　Quantity line items will only include statistics on the units of measure that are equal to, or are able to be converted to the assigned unit of measure of the grouped commodities.
　FAS, Office of Global Analysis, (202) 720-6301.　Data Source: Department of Commerce, U.S. Census Bureau, Foreign Trade Statistics

Table 8-30.—Dairy products: United States exports by country of destination, 2011–2013

Commodity and country of destination	2011	2012	2013
	Metric tons	*Metric tons*	*Metric tons*
Condensed & evap milk:			
Mexico	15,002	12,585	13,643
Vietnam	413	554	11,056
China	347	1,016	3,572
Philippines	55	882	3,497
Indonesia	0	194	2,035
Algeria	0	0	1,573
Canada	1,054	1,690	1,269
Bahamas, The	1,978	692	761
Hong Kong	553	458	759
Panama	117	266	583
Malaysia	48	633	571
Korea, South	270	435	562
Venezuela	38	32	518
Dominican Republic	367	341	424
Taiwan	540	388	382
Trinidad and Tobago	127	189	270
Bermuda	114	189	211
Australia(*)	452	539	199
El Salvador	18	6	185
Singapore	50	154	152
Honduras	1,057	166	135
Sweden	0	14	122
Belize	10	124	106
Thailand	0	141	100
Japan	8	39	94
Barbados	101	44	91
Leeward-Windward Islands(*)	74	60	86
Colombia	30	146	81
Netherlands Antilles(*)	110	115	73
Peru	9	3	69
Rest of World	1,249	2,151	432
World Total	24,188	24,243	43,610
Non-fat dry milk:			
Mexico	173,107	195,718	182,779
China	14,843	15,425	60,686
Philippines	51,363	45,689	57,708
Indonesia	44,790	31,543	56,145
Vietnam	41,868	24,335	37,403
Malaysia	23,303	16,494	30,712
Egypt	8,793	12,420	19,358
Algeria	0	8,335	17,554
Thailand	11,081	6,935	10,593
Peru	6,213	11,128	9,374
Pakistan	9,332	11,409	7,752
Dominican Republic	4,795	8,396	6,125
Korea, South	374	1,480	5,524
Japan	7,974	6,784	5,330
Chile	4,901	9,568	4,683
Singapore	5,629	3,418	4,263
Sri Lanka	416	2,621	3,997
Morocco	1,158	4,941	3,844
Canada	2,416	2,271	2,733
Libya	0	552	2,329
Colombia	422	2,330	2,197
Venezuela	1,527	2,530	2,141
Panama	1,293	1,821	1,827
Saudi Arabia	760	573	1,538
Russia	256	411	1,401
Taiwan	878	898	1,353
Hong Kong	130	561	1,197
Jamaica	115	740	1,116
Nigeria	1,349	824	1,033
Ukraine	471	19	993
Rest of World	15,543	14,181	11,433
World Total	435,098	444,349	555,122

See footnote(s) at end of table.

Table 8-30.—Dairy products: United States exports by country of destination, 2011–2013—Continued

Commodity and country of destination	2011	2012	2013
	Metric tons	Metric tons	Metric tons
Dry whole milk & cream:			
Algeria	0	0	12,828
China	63	1,591	6,179
Mexico	6,858	5,326	4,177
Vietnam	694	1,836	3,487
Philippines	65	1,005	1,803
Canada	1,036	650	1,271
Israel(*)	2,005	909	1,035
Japan	1,019	743	911
Thailand	256	1	759
Korea, South	114	44	572
Panama	232	290	507
Egypt	1,854	313	500
Djibouti	0	0	480
Malaysia	7	329	387
Colombia	325	552	364
Australia(*)	0	26	323
Hong Kong	491	837	323
Singapore	119	51	320
Indonesia	764	394	318
Guatemala	216	404	226
Tanzania	0	0	200
Pakistan	916	1,219	172
Trinidad and Tobago	3	123	145
Nicaragua	200	877	138
United Arab Emirates	22	32	130
Peru	370	283	128
South Africa	57	591	121
Italy(*)	0	4	115
Belize	41	102	114
Saudi Arabia	170	318	112
Rest of World	3,658	2,081	998
World Total	21,555	20,932	39,141
Butter and milkfat:			
Saudi Arabia	13,065	16,643	19,182
Iran	2,871	6,561	11,791
Morocco	3,747	3,878	8,081
Ukraine	0	0	7,817
Egypt	3,661	3,063	7,066
Turkey	478	19	5,905
Korea, South	3,631	507	3,693
Canada	5,625	1,539	3,307
Mexico	6,785	3,226	3,201
United Arab Emirates	445	1,566	2,178
Bahrain	557	927	1,514
Lithuania	0	4	1,512
France(*)	894	459	1,448
Vietnam	5	1	1,373
Denmark(*)	2,966	334	1,267
Belgium-Luxembourg(*)	3,295	148	991
China	503	240	946
Dominican Republic	1,074	1,106	795
Israel(*)	630	537	709
Lebanon	213	44	636
Algeria	0	94	631
Nigeria	132	5	505
Uruguay	257	105	482
Indonesia	499	0	458
Bahamas, The	169	1,603	440
Taiwan	489	195	412
Moldova	0	0	396
Netherlands	546	67	385
Panama	773	285	358
Georgia	19	0	323
Rest of World	10,341	5,575	3,850
World Total	63,669	48,730	91,649

See footnote(s) at end of table.

Table 8-30.—Dairy products: United States exports by country of destination, 2011–2013—Continued

Commodity and country of destination	2011	2012	2013
	Metric tons	*Metric tons*	*Metric tons*
Ice cream:			
Mexico	18,857	21,265	22,798
Saudi Arabia	62	1,446	6,471
United Arab Emirates	451	2,750	4,948
Canada	3,643	3,599	3,876
Australia(*)	965	1,955	3,370
China	283	782	1,641
Malaysia	164	673	1,442
Trinidad and Tobago	1,007	1,035	1,262
Korea, South	833	903	1,220
Bahamas, The	1,218	1,160	1,213
Kuwait	85	384	937
Chile	540	1,150	837
Indonesia	14	230	781
Jamaica	828	1,185	769
Netherlands Antilles(*)	687	691	741
Singapore	789	849	719
Qatar	66	256	601
Philippines	423	519	576
Dominican Republic	451	409	527
Netherlands	685	299	456
Russia	15	13	424
Leeward-Windward Islands(*)	482	445	415
Bahrain	45	134	381
Bermuda	583	394	372
Nigeria	148	170	356
Taiwan	290	327	332
Japan	159	310	321
United Kingdom	81	168	238
Panama	93	114	230
Cayman Islands	252	289	227
Rest of World	2,706	2,927	2,637
World Total	36,904	46,829	61,116
Cheese and curd:			
Mexico	48,407	65,483	82,234
Korea, South	35,431	39,411	49,215
Japan	22,882	25,913	31,189
Canada	11,177	13,946	14,314
Australia(*)	9,973	11,059	12,105
Saudi Arabia	10,989	11,333	11,881
China	6,678	8,798	11,343
Egypt	7,443	4,003	8,509
Panama	5,182	6,542	7,651
Taiwan	5,071	6,355	7,028
Philippines	5,545	4,913	6,469
Chile	2,764	4,594	6,122
Dominican Republic	4,264	3,542	4,993
Morocco	3,751	3,483	4,961
Bahrain	1,424	3,588	4,546
Indonesia	4,598	5,377	4,338
Guatemala	3,084	3,383	3,133
Honduras	2,420	2,331	2,635
Hong Kong	1,906	2,462	2,298
Peru	2,099	2,246	2,176
Colombia	581	1,213	2,128
Kuwait	1,323	1,440	2,093
United Arab Emirates	1,628	1,653	2,055
United Kingdom	336	491	1,953
Netherlands	1,486	372	1,952
Algeria	0	180	1,879
Libya	486	1,284	1,874
Bahamas, The	1,946	1,783	1,634
Singapore	1,769	1,396	1,599
Costa Rica	1,127	1,625	1,566
Rest of World	19,295	19,765	20,315
World Total	225,064	259,962	316,185

See footnote(s) at end of table.

Table 8-30.—Dairy products: United States exports by country of destination, 2011–2013—Continued

Commodity and country of destination	2011	2012	2013
	Liters	*Liters*	*Liters*
Fluid milk and cream:			
Canada	30,188,599	27,065,590	32,347,609
Mexico	26,687,323	24,992,377	32,177,942
Peru	32,164	2,269,686	5,059,489
Taiwan	255,755	165,260	3,209,351
Hong Kong	853,282	1,823,650	2,856,649
China	430,502	1,408,906	2,393,649
Singapore	340,419	602,266	2,311,769
Dominican Republic	67,330	2,917	1,387,323
Bahamas, The	1,447,509	1,448,556	1,040,446
Philippines	26,718	358,912	780,511
Vietnam	1,683,492	747,290	485,296
Malaysia	618,444	339,584	413,033
Turks and Caicos Islands	226,227	191,817	276,883
Netherlands Antilles(*)	419,894	152,575	272,314
Leeward-Windward Islands(*)	170,578	196,311	271,720
Cayman Islands	630,190	458,872	269,753
Korea, South	10,735,241	197,858	226,629
Pakistan	232,200	303,180	200,047
Saudi Arabia	156,000	321,753	156,000
Palau	200,433	133,431	150,200
Panama	18,368	5,604	103,948
Colombia	4,526	6,839	81,929
Guatemala	20,859	76,935	73,073
Equatorial Guinea	42,942	17,208	69,974
United Arab Emirates	6,259	0	57,342
Australia(*)	0	2,781	52,946
Uruguay	0	16,227	47,257
Thailand	14,934	36,337	43,604
French Pacific Islands(*)	66,522	435	41,026
Bangladesh	8,724	42,885	36,883
Rest of World	535,507	274,665	171,326
World Total	76,120,941	63,660,707	87,065,921
	Metric tons	*Metric tons*	*Metric tons*
Whey:			
China	152,214	154,558	183,079
Mexico	63,340	65,823	59,126
Canada	41,726	38,666	39,691
Japan	29,155	26,181	26,154
Indonesia	22,218	21,504	25,585
New Zealand(*)	3,227	11,517	22,627
Philippines	14,509	22,396	21,866
Korea, South	16,341	21,173	20,654
Vietnam	19,816	27,043	18,976
Malaysia	20,945	14,612	15,087
Morocco	6,578	8,590	14,287
Thailand	14,141	8,944	10,808
Taiwan	5,753	6,725	8,732
Australia(*)	7,027	3,878	8,573
Brazil	6,424	8,576	4,490
Singapore	5,083	4,902	4,110
Egypt	2,930	2,050	4,083
Peru	1,024	3,408	3,540
Dominican Republic	2,591	3,113	2,481
Guatemala	2,101	2,638	2,375
Venezuela	2,059	1,672	2,102
Chile	2,358	3,076	1,714
El Salvador	2,355	2,108	1,621
Switzerland(*)	272	1,079	1,535
Uruguay	526	358	1,380
Belgium-Luxembourg(*)	1,599	2,803	1,242
United Kingdom	379	1,463	1,158
Ghana	0	60	1,120
Panama	759	749	1,112
Colombia	422	1,073	1,008
Rest of World	14,905	17,247	11,080
World Total	462,772	487,984	521,396
Grand Total	1,269,249	1,333,029	1,628,219

(*) Denotes a country that is a summarization of its component countries. Note: Users should use cautious interpretation on quantity reports using mixed units of measure. Quantity line items will only include statistics on the units of measure that are equal to, or are able to be converted to, the assigned unit of measure of the grouped commodities.
FAS, Office of Global Analysis, (202) 720-6301. Data Source: Department of Commerce, U.S. Census Bureau, Foreign Trade Statistics.

Table 8-31.—Chickens: Layers, pullets, and other chickens, by State and United States, December 1, 2013 and 2014

State	Total layers		Total pullets		Other Chickens	
	2013	2014	2013	2014	2013	2014
	Thousands	Thousands	Thousands	Thousands	Thousands	Thousands
Alabama	9,175	9,279	5,596	5,820	943	961
Arkansas	11,794	12,529	6,783	7,284	1,100	1,097
California	17,003	14,890	3,752	2,704	21	19
Colorado	5,052	4,791	905	1,052	52	50
Connecticut	2,419	2,418	559	558	7	9
Florida	8,556	8,998	1,795	2,053	24	26
Georgia	18,158	18,797	8,078	8,442	1,061	909
Illinois	4,763	5,026	405	212	28	24
Indiana	27,339	26,913	8,210	7,522	91	115
Iowa	58,867	59,889	12,893	14,038	78	69
Kentucky	4,656	4,583	2,047	2,306	200	161
Louisiana	1,994	2,086	680	651	115	100
Maine	3,535	3,535	61	24	-	-
Maryland	2,888	2,844	687	676	10	7
Massachusetts	139	144	8	8	-	-
Michigan	13,195	13,192	3,080	2,819	3	-
Minnesota	10,714	11,277	3,941	3,379	40	37
Mississippi	5,650	5,571	3,294	3,446	500	492
Missouri	8,578	9,138	3,696	3,139	209	167
Montana	455	458	184	162	-	-
Nebraska	9,339	9,571	2,138	1,983	-	-
New York	5,116	5,155	1,009	1,346	13	8
North Carolina	13,311	14,441	7,053	6,523	870	850
Ohio	29,977	31,542	7,975	7,584	42	40
Oklahoma	3,065	3,072	1,041	1,186	198	179
Oregon	2,291	2,253	410	554	-	-
Pennsylvania	26,320	25,900	4,637	4,666	132	143
South Carolina	4,414	4,218	1,199	1,443	133	110
South Dakota	2,872	2,715	384	716	-	-
Tennessee	1,491	1,495	1,050	1,076	165	132
Texas	19,069	19,116	5,610	5,564	424	380
Utah	3,940	4,473	761	773	-	-
Vermont	143	141	12	11	3	1
Virginia	2,875	2,939	1,079	979	185	135
Washington	6,867	7,094	1,186	1,320	2	-
West Virginia	1,187	1,207	744	715	135	102
Wisconsin	5,619	5,626	1,285	1,408	35	36
Other States [2]	8,577	8,729	2,419	2,460	34	44
United States	361,403	366,045	106,646	106,602	6,853	6,403

- Represents zero. [1] Alaska, Arizona, Delaware, Hawaii, Idaho, Kansas, New Hampshire, New Jersey, New Mexico, Nevada, North Dakota, and Rhode Island combined to avoid disclosing individual operations.
NASS, Livestock Branch, (202) 720–3570.

Table 8-32.—Chickens: Inventory number and value, United States, Dec. 1, 2005–2014 [1]

Year	Total layers	Total pullets	Other chickens	All chickens	Value per head	Total value
	Thousands	Thousands	Thousands	Thousands	Dollars	1,000 dollars
2005	349,764	97,544	8,264	455,572	2.52	1,149,736
2006	352,316	97,459	8,038	457,813	2.60	1,189,978
2007	346,613	103,816	8,164	458,593	2.95	1,351,549
2008	340,811	101,016	7,589	449,416	3.38	1,518,547
2009	342,058	104,069	8,487	454,614	3.32	1,510,038
2010	342,782	107,025	7,390	457,197	3.58	1,637,016
2011	343,283	104,159	6,922	454,364	3.79	1,721,671
2012	354,977	105,140	6,827	466,944	4.04	1,885,904
2013	361,403	106,646	6,853	474,902	4.15	1,971,590
2014	366,045	106,602	6,403	479,050	4.10	1,962,126

[1] Does not include commercial broilers.
NASS Livestock Branch, (202) 720-3570.

Table 8-33.—Chicken inventory: Number, value per head, and total value, by State and United States, December 1, 2013 and 2014[1]

State	Number		Value per bird		Total value	
	2013	2014	2013	2014	2013	2014
	1,000 Head	*1,000 Head*	*Dollars*	*Dollars*	*1,000 Dollars*	*1,000 Dollars*
Alabama	15,714	16,060	7.70	7.60	120,998	122,056
Arkansas	19,677	20,910	7.10	7.70	139,707	161,007
California	20,776	17,613	3.40	2.80	70,638	49,316
Colorado	6,009	5,893	2.30	2.30	13,821	13,554
Connecticut	2,985	2,985	2.90	2.90	8,657	8,657
Florida	10,375	11,077	2.40	2.30	24,900	25,477
Georgia	27,297	28,148	6.40	5.50	174,701	154,814
Illinois	5,196	5,262	3.00	3.90	15,588	20,522
Indiana	35,640	34,550	2.10	2.90	74,844	100,195
Iowa	71,838	73,996	3.40	2.60	244,249	192,390
Kentucky	6,903	7,050	4.70	5.00	32,444	35,250
Louisiana	2,789	2,837	4.60	5.10	12,829	14,469
Maine	3,596	3,559	2.70	2.70	9,709	9,609
Maryland	3,585	3,527	3.30	3.30	11,831	11,639
Massachusetts	147	152	6.30	6.80	926	1,034
Michigan	16,278	16,011	2.10	2.20	34,184	35,224
Minnesota	14,695	14,693	4.30	3.90	63,189	57,303
Mississippi	9,444	9,509	7.00	7.20	66,108	68,465
Missouri	12,483	12,444	4.30	5.30	53,677	65,953
Montana	639	620	4.70	5.00	3,003	3,100
Nebraska	11,477	11,554	3.60	3.10	41,317	35,817
New York	6,138	6,509	2.10	2.90	12,890	18,876
North Carolina	21,234	21,814	9.00	8.10	191,106	176,693
Ohio	37,994	39,166	2.80	3.80	106,383	148,831
Oklahoma	4,304	4,437	6.90	7.00	29,698	31,059
Oregon	2,701	2,807	2.80	2.90	7,563	8,140
Pennsylvania	31,089	30,709	3.60	3.40	111,920	104,411
South Carolina	5,746	5,771	3.70	4.40	21,260	25,392
South Dakota	3,256	3,431	3.30	2.30	10,745	7,891
Tennessee	2,706	2,703	7.50	7.70	20,295	20,813
Texas	25,103	25,060	4.00	3.80	100,412	95,228
Utah	4,701	5,246	2.60	2.50	12,223	13,115
Vermont	158	153	5.90	5.40	932	826
Virginia	4,139	4,053	6.00	6.30	24,834	25,534
Washington	8,055	8,414	3.20	3.30	25,776	27,766
West Virginia	2,066	2,024	7.60	8.00	15,702	16,192
Wisconsin	6,939	7,070	3.30	2.60	22,899	18,382
Other States[2]	11,030	11,233	3.59	3.31	39,632	37,126
United States	474,902	479,050	4.15	4.10	1,971,590	1,962,126

[1] Excludes commercial broilers.   Totals may not add due to rounding.   [2] Alaska, Arizona, Delaware, Hawaii, Idaho, Kansas, New Hampshire, New Jersey, New Mexico, Nevada, North Dakota, Rhode Island and Wyoming combined to avoid disclosing data for individual operations.

NASS, Livestock Branch, (202) 720-3570.

Table 8-34.—Chickens: Lost, sold for slaughter, and value of sales, by State and United States, 2013 and 2014[1]

State	Number lost[2]		Number sold		Pounds sold		Value of sales	
	2013	2014	2013	2014	2013	2014	2013	2014
	1,000 head	*1,000 head*	*1,000 head*	*1,000 head*	*1,000 pounds*	*1,000 pounds*	*1,000 dollars*	*1,000 dollars*
Alabama	2,628	2,762	10,893	10,855	82,787	83,584	12,749	13,624
Arkansas	3,866	3,834	12,058	13,270	89,229	100,852	13,563	16,136
California	7,289	6,405	5,848	3,569	19,298	12,135	174	206
Colorado	462	484	2,968	3,536	12,169	14,144	694	834
Connecticut ...	1,805	1,818	34	25	194	123	23	12
Florida	3,603	3,378	2,556	1,964	9,713	7,463	447	343
Georgia	4,229	4,636	16,025	15,226	107,368	106,582	15,032	16,094
Illinois	751	625	2,607	2,410	9,125	8,194	219	197
Indiana	4,322	7,781	13,263	11,768	43,768	38,834	481	505
Iowa	26,396	25,811	9,717	15,502	32,066	49,606	160	149
Kentucky	2,450	1,591	2,385	4,278	18,842	25,668	2,996	3,363
Louisiana	272	340	1,674	2,014	10,211	12,688	1,307	1,738
Maine	507	507	1,225	1,225	3,920	3,920	4	4
Maryland	250	234	1,752	892	5,957	3,300	107	129
Massachusetts	9	7	83	97	266	310	(Z)	(Z)
Michigan	1,129	2,232	5,737	6,206	18,358	19,859	18	20
Minnesota	2,217	1,952	5,072	7,457	17,245	25,354	310	482
Mississippi	1,346	1,410	5,849	6,062	42,113	44,253	6,233	6,859
Missouri	1,086	1,173	6,155	6,916	32,006	35,963	3,329	3,812
Montana	281	324	52	55	166	176	(Z)	(Z)
Nebraska	807	1,054	5,862	5,624	18,758	17,997	19	18
New York	384	708	4,111	3,801	13,155	12,163	26	36
North Carolina	3,319	2,900	11,021	12,524	76,045	83,911	10,874	12,251
Ohio	9,035	11,206	11,393	8,236	37,597	28,002	376	476
Oklahoma	729	709	2,558	2,176	18,418	16,538	2,744	2,663
Oregon	1,116	1,045	495	207	1,634	642	15	1
Pennsylvania .	3,033	2,786	12,062	10,404	42,217	36,414	929	947
South Carolina	1,526	1,337	2,839	2,626	18,454	16,281	2,528	2,214
South Dakota .	907	780	707	1,150	2,262	3,680	2	4
Tennessee	287	424	1,846	1,987	14,583	15,300	2,319	2,479
Texas	5,758	4,138	12,964	12,091	62,227	59,246	5,600	5,747
Utah	788	1,201	2,281	1,857	7,299	5,942	7	6
Vermont	12	18	159	92	588	405	19	31
Virginia	887	890	2,521	2,268	17,143	16,103	2,417	2,448
Washington ...	4,781	5,267	32	146	109	496	2	9
West Virginia .	217	284	1,443	1,599	11,255	12,632	1,767	2,072
Wisconsin	546	378	2,799	3,496	10,076	12,935	312	504
Other States[3]	2,136	2,090	4,791	4,801	15,925	15,804	137	144
United States	101,166	104,519	185,837	188,412	922,546	947,499	87,939	96,557

(Z) Less than half of the unit shown. [1] Annual estimates cover the period December 1 previous year through November 30. Exclude broilers. Totals may not add due to rounding. [2] Includes rendered, died, destroyed, composted, or disappeared for any reason except sold during the 12-month period. [3] Alaska, Arizona, Delaware, Hawaii, Idaho, Kansas, Nevada, New Hampshire, New Jersey, New Mexico, North Dakota, Rhode Island, and Wyoming combined to avoid disclosing data for individual operations.

NASS, Livestock Branch, (202) 720–3570.

Table 8-35.—Mature chickens: Lost, sold for slaughter, price, and value, United States, 2005–2014[1]

Year	Number		Pounds (live weight) sold[3]	Price per pound live weight[3][4]	Value of sales[3]
	Lost[2]	Sold[3]			
	1,000 head	*1,000 head*	*1,000 pounds*	*Dollars*	*1,000 dollars*
2005	93,445	193,938	1,005,838	0.065	65,072
2006	101,611	173,883	924,993	0.059	54,141
2007	101,152	168,283	912,875	0.056	51,498
2008	102,071	176,023	940,221	....	62,456
2009	99,596	176,266	910,333	....	65,381
2010	108,356	173,404	903,750	....	73,099
2011	106,361	182,153	943,142	....	81,110
2012	103,758	179,162	901,411	....	79,208
2013	101,166	185,837	922,546	....	87,939
2014	104,519	188,412	947,499	....	96,557

[1] Annual estimates cover the period December 1 previous year through November 30. Excludes broilers. Totals may not add due to rounding. [2] Includes rendered, died, destroyed, composted, or disappeared for any reason (excluding sold for slaughter) during the 12-month period. [3] Sold for slaughter.

NASS, Livestock Branch, (202) 720–3570.

Table 8-36.—Poultry, meat, and broiler: International trade, 2013–2015

Country	2013	2014	2015
	1,000 metric tons	1,000 metric tons	1,000 metric tons
Principle exporting:			
Argentina	334	278	187
Belarus	105	113	135
Brazil	3,482	3,558	3,841
Canada	150	137	133
Chile	88	87	99
China	420	430	401
European Union	1,083	1,133	1,177
Thailand	504	546	622
Turkey	337	379	321
Ukraine	141	167	159
Others	298	340	331
Total Foreign	6,942	7,168	7,406
United States	3,332	3,312	2,866
Total	10,274	10,480	10,272
Principle importing:			
China	244	260	268
European Union	671	712	728
Hong Kong	272	299	312
Iraq	673	730	630
Japan	854	888	936
Mexico	682	722	790
Russia	535	465	249
Saudi Arabia	838	775	930
South Africa	355	369	436
United Arab Emirates	217	192	262
Others	3,288	3,474	3,059
Total Foreign	8,629	8,886	8,600
United States	55	53	59
Total	8,684	8,939	8,659

FAS, Office of Global Analysis, (202) 720-6301.   Prepared or estimated on the basis of official USDA production, supply, and distribution statistics from foreign governments.

Table 8-37.—Broilers: Production and value, United States, 2005–2014 [1] [2] [3]

Year	Number produced	Pounds produced	Price per pound [4] [5]	Value of production
	1,000 head	1,000 pounds	Cents	1,000 dollars
2005	8,872,000	47,855,600	43.6	20,877,916
2006	8,867,800	48,829,900	36.3	17,739,234
2007	8,906,700	49,330,700	43.6	21,513,536
2008	9,009,300	50,441,600		23,203,136
2009	8,550,200	47,752,300		21,822,804
2010	8,623,600	49,152,600		23,691,553
2011	8,607,600	50,082,400		22,987,822
2012	8,463,000	49,655,600		24,827,800
2013	8,533,800	50,678,200		30,761,669
2014	8,544,100	51,373,100		32,724,667

[1] December 1, previous year through November 30, current year. [2] Broiler production including other domestic meat-type strains. [3] Excludes States producing less than 500,000 broilers. [4] Live weight equivalent prices, derived from ready-to-cook (RTC) prices, minus processing costs, then multiplied by a dressing percentage. [5] Price per pound discontinued in 2008.
NASS, Livestock Branch, (202) 720–3570.

Table 8-38.—Chickens: Supply, distribution, and per capita consumption, ready-to-cook basis, United States, 2004–2013

Year	Production			Commercial storage at beginning of year	Exports	Commercial storage at end of year	Consumption	
	Commercial broilers	Other chickens	Total [1]				Total [1] [2]	Per capita
	Million pounds	Million pounds	Million pounds	Million pounds	Million pounds	Million pounds	Million pounds	Pounds
2004	33,699	504	34,203	600	4,997	705	29,129	99
2005	34,986	516	35,502	705	5,332	913	29,997	101
2006	35,120	504	35,624	913	5,365	738	30,484	102
2007	35,772	498	36,270	737	6,072	721	30,280	100
2008	36,511	559	37,070	721	7,110	748	30,036	99
2009	35,131	500	35,631	748	7,226	618	28,948	94
2010	36,515	503	37,018	618	6,841	777	30,130	97
2011	36,804	521	37,325	777	7,061	592	30,558	98
2012	36,643	517	37,160	592	7,364	652	29,850	95
2013	37,425	523	37,948	652	7,453	675	30,596	97

[1] Totals may not add due to rounding. [2] Shipments to territories now included in total consumption.
ERS Markets and Trade Economics Division, Animal Products and Cost of Production Branch, (202) 694–5308.

Table 8-39.—Poultry: Feed-price ratios, United States, 2005–2014

Year	Ratios [1]		
	Egg-feed	Broiler-feed	Turkey-feed
	Pounds	Pounds	Pounds
2005	7.0	7.0	7.8
2006	7.5	5.7	7.8
2007	10.2	5.0	6.0
2008	8.6	3.7	4.6
2009	7.2	4.1	5.0
2010	7.5	4.5	6.2
2011	6.0	3.1	4.9
2012	5.4	3.1	4.7
2013	6.5	3.7	4.6
2014	10.2	5.0	6.3

[1] Number of pounds of poultry feed equivalent in value at local market prices to 1 dozen market eggs, or 1 pound of broiler or 1 pound of turkey live weight. Simple average of monthly feed-price ratios. Egg feed= corn (75 lbs) and soybeans (25 lbs); broiler feed= corn (58 lbs); soybeans (42 lbs); turkey feed= corn (51 lbs), soybeans (28 lbs), and wheat (21 lbs). Monthly equivalent prices of commercial prepared feeds are based on current U.S. prices received for corn, soybeans, and wheat.
NASS, Environmental, Economics, and Demographics Branch, (202) 720–6146.

Table 8-40.—Broilers: Production and value, by State and Total, 2013–2014 [1]

State	2013			2014		
	Number produced	Pounds produced	Value of production	Number produced	Pounds produced	Value of production
	1,000 head	*1,000 pounds*	*1,000 dollars*	*1,000 head*	*1,000 pounds*	*1,000 dollars*
Alabama	1,048,600	5,872,200	3,564,425	1,061,500	6,050,600	3,854,232
Arkansas	996,400	5,978,400	3,628,889	969,800	6,012,800	3,830,154
Delaware	215,600	1,530,800	929,196	244,100	1,733,100	1,103,985
Florida	64,400	392,800	238,430	66,700	386,900	246,455
Georgia	1,334,600	7,607,200	4,617,570	1,324,200	7,547,900	4,808,012
Kentucky	309,500	1,671,300	1,014,479	308,000	1,724,800	1,098,698
Maryland	305,200	1,617,600	981,883	287,800	1,554,100	989,962
Minnesota	48,200	284,400	172,631	46,800	280,800	178,870
Mississippi	734,100	4,478,000	2,718,146	727,200	4,508,600	2,871,978
Missouri	277,400	1,331,500	808,221	288,500	1,384,800	882,118
North Carolina ..	786,600	5,899,500	3,580,997	795,200	6,043,500	3,849,710
Ohio	69,800	404,800	245,714	75,600	430,900	274,483
Oklahoma	206,100	1,360,300	825,702	205,300	1,334,500	850,077
Pennsylvania	170,700	955,900	580,231	181,300	997,200	635,216
South Carolina ..	226,700	1,586,900	963,248	232,500	1,650,800	1,051,560
Tennessee	182,500	949,000	576,043	180,600	939,100	598,207
Texas	610,100	3,599,600	2,184,957	591,800	3,550,800	2,261,860
Virginia	250,100	1,350,500	819,754	262,000	1,441,000	917,917
West Virginia	96,300	385,200	233,816	95,300	371,700	236,773
Wisconsin	51,300	215,500	130,809	53,400	224,300	142,879
Other States [2] ...	549,600	3,206,800	1,946,528	546,500	3,204,900	2,041,521
19 State Total [3]	8,235,800	49,080,800	29,792,046	8,241,500	49,759,000	31,696,483
United States	8,533,800	50,678,200	30,761,669	8,544,100	51,373,100	32,724,667

[1] Annual estimates cover the period December 1 previous year through November 30. Broiler production including other domestic meat-type strains. Excludes States producing less than 500,000 broilers. [2] California, Illinois, Indiana, Iowa, Louisiana, Michigan, Nebraska, New York, Oregon, and Washington combined to avoid disclosing individual operations. [3] 19 states in the weekly estimating program: Alabama, Arkansas, California, Delaware, Florida, Georgia, Kentucky, Louisiana, Maryland, Mississippi, Missouri, North Carolina, Oklahoma, Pennsylvania, South Carolina, Tennessee, Texas, Virginia, and West Virginia.
NASS, Livestock Branch, (202) 720–3570.

Table 8-41.—Chicks hatched by commercial hatcheries: Number, average price, and value, United States, 2005–2014

Year	Chicks hatched			Average price of baby chicks per 100		Value of chick production
	Broiler-type	Egg-type	All	Broiler-type	Egg-type	
	Thousands	*Thousands*	*Thousands*	*Dollars*	*Dollars*	*1,000 dollars*
2005	9,483,918	437,066	9,920,984	20.60	53.50	2,070,602
2006	9,414,070	427,373	9,841,443	22.90	66.50	2,297,924
2007	9,590,018	446,562	10,036,580	25.60	69.40	2,610,002
2008	9,468,133	467,763	9,935,896	26.30	75.60	2,666,933
2009	9,116,802	467,981	9,584,783	26.60	81.20	2,615,070
2010	9,276,240	484,393	9,760,633	27.00	83.00	2,705,608
2011	9,057,461	478,606	9,536,067	28.20	86.70	2,761,680
2012	8,965,425	483,443	9,448,868	29.50	89.70	2,861,625
2013	9,078,764	514,479	9,593,243	29.90	93.40	2,954,812
2014	9,160,978	518,346	9,679,324	31.00	74.80	3,033,765

NASS, Environmental, Economics, and Demographics Branch, (202) 720–6146 and Livestock Branch, (202) 720–3570.

Table 8-42.—Poultry: Slaughtered under Federal inspection, by class, United States, 2012–2014

Class	Number inspected			Pounds inspected (live weight)		
	2012	2013	2014	2012	2013	2014
	Thousands	Thousands	Thousands	Thousands	Thousands	Thousands
Young chickens	8,428,999	8,503,750	8,525,393	49,350,169	50,357,463	51,225,964
Mature chickens	147,196	145,006	144,235	814,905	812,167	822,537
Total chickens	8,576,195	8,648,756	8,669,628	50,165,074	51,169,630	52,048,501
Young turkeys	248,590	237,964	235,189	7,420,590	7,220,540	7,150,782
Old turkeys	1,602	1,440	1,428	42,566	39,347	39,442
Total turkeys	250,192	239,404	236,617	7,463,156	7,259,887	7,190,224
Ducks	24,183	24,575	26,368	164,388	168,223	181,068
Other poultry [1]	(NA)	(NA)	(NA)	4,555	3,518	3,143
Total poultry	(NA)	(NA)	(NA)	57,797,173	58,601,258	59,422,936

Class	Pounds condemned					
	Ante-mortem (live weight)			Post-mortem (Carcass and parts)		
	2012	2013	2014	2012	2013	2014
	Thousands	Thousands	Thousands	Thousands	Thousands	Thousands
Young chickens	96,144	99,945	108,109	294,920	316,386	341,079
Mature chickens	8,661	7,844	8,853	24,820	24,825	27,984
Total chickens	104,805	107,789	116,962	319,740	341,211	369,063
Young turkeys	17,076	15,728	16,491	78,248	79,430	77,912
Old turkeys	430	434	536	1,316	1,640	1,417
Total turkeys	17,506	16,162	17,027	79,564	81,070	79,329
Ducks	492	531	469	3,216	3,391	3,342
Other poultry	6	7	4	30	22	23
Total poultry	122,809	124,489	134,462	402,550	425,694	451,757

Class	Pounds certified (ready-to-cook)		
	2012	2013	2014
	Thousands	Thousands	Thousands
Young chickens	37,039,355	37,830,041	38,565,192
Mature chickens	516,573	523,332	521,176
Total chickens	37,555,928	38,535,373	39,086,368
Young turkeys	5,934,977	5,775,814	5,725,668
Old turkeys	32,285	29,725	29,963
Total turkeys	5,967,262	5,805,539	5,755,631
Ducks	118,781	121,398	130,950
Other poultry [2]	3,027	2,346	2,098
Total poultry	43,644,998	44,282,656	44,975,047

(NA) Not available. [1] Includes geese, guineas, ostriches, emus, rheas, and squab. [2] Includes geese, guineas, and squab.
NASS, Livestock Branch, (202) 720–3570.

Table 8-43.—Turkeys: Supply, distribution, and per capita consumption, ready-to-cook basis, United States, 2004–2013

Year	Production	Commercial storage at beginning of year	Exports	Commercial storage at end of year	Consumption	
					Total [1] [2]	Per capita
	Million pounds	Million pounds	Million pounds	Million pounds	Million pounds	Pounds
2004	5,383	354	442	288	5,010	17.1
2005	5,432	288	570	206	4,954	16.7
2006	5,607	206	547	218	5,064	16.9
2007	5,873	218	547	261	5,300	17.5
2008	6,165	261	676	396	5,367	17.6
2009	5,589	396	534	262	5,210	17.0
2010	5,570	262	581	192	5,084	16.4
2011	5,715	192	702	211	5,014	16.1
2012	5,889	211	797	296	5,030	16.0
2013	5,729	296	759	237	5,051	16.0

[1] Totals may not add due to rounding.   [2] Shipments to territories now included in consumption.
ERS Markets and Trade Economics Division, Animal Products and Cost of Production Branch, (202) 694–5308.

Table 8-44.—Poultry, meat, and turkey: International trade, 2013–2014

Country	2013	2014
	1,000 metric tons	1,000 metric tons
Principle exporting:		
Others	329	281
Total Foreign	329	281
United States	344	366
Total	673	647
Principle importing:		
Others	339	276
Total Foreign	339	276
United States	10	13
Total	349	289

FAS, Office of Global Analysis, (202) 720-6301. Prepared or estimated on the basis of official USDA production, supply, and distribution statistics from foreign governments.

Table 8-45.—Turkeys: Production and value, United States, 2005–2014

Year	Number raised	Pounds (live weight) produced	Price per pound live weight [1]	Value of production
	1,000 head	*1,000 pounds*	*Cents*	*1,000 dollars*
2005	249,666	6,991,599	44.5	3,107,875
2006	256,334	7,223,675	48.0	3,467,534
2007	266,828	7,566,315	52.3	3,954,472
2008	273,088	7,911,797		4,471,046
2009	247,359	7,149,314		3,573,324
2010	244,188	7,108,222		4,372,438
2011	248,500	7,313,205		4,987,608
2012	253,500	7,561,905		5,452,135
2013	240,000	7,277,536		4,839,562
2014	237,500	7,217,056		5,304,537

[1] Price per pound discontinued in 2008.
NASS, Livestock Branch, (202) 720–3570.

Table 8-46.—Turkeys: Production and value, by State and United States, 2013–2014 [1]

State	2013			2014		
	Number raised	Pounds produced	Value of production	Number raised	Pounds produced	Value of production
	1,000 head	*1,000 pounds*	*1,000 dollars*	*1,000 head*	*1,000 pounds*	*1,000 dollars*
Arkansas	28,000	560,000	372,400	30,000	612,000	449,820
California	13,000	365,300	242,925	11,000	310,200	227,997
Indiana	17,500	663,250	441,061	19,000	754,300	554,411
Michigan	5,200	210,600	140,049	10,500	435,750	320,276
Minnesota	44,000	1,126,400	749,056	5,100	205,530	151,065
Missouri	17,000	544,000	361,760	45,500	1,178,450	866,161
North Carolina	33,500	1,139,000	757,435	17,000	544,000	399,840
Ohio	5,700	233,130	155,031	28,500	997,500	733,163
Pennsylvania	7,000	170,800	113,582	5,100	209,100	153,689
South Carolina	12,000	478,800	318,402	7,000	175,700	129,140
South Dakota	4,300	176,300	117,240	4,500	188,550	138,584
Utah	4,000	108,800	72,352	4,000	96,800	71,148
Virginia	15,500	403,000	267,995	16,800	443,520	325,987
West Virginia	3,100	80,600	53,599	3,100	81,840	60,152
Other States [2]	30,200	1,017,556	676,675	30,400	983,816	723,104
United States	240,000	7,277,536	4,839,562	237,500	7,217,056	5,304,537

(D) Withheld to avoid disclosure of individual operations. [1] Based on turkeys placed September 1 through August 31. Excludes young turkeys lost. [2] Includes State estimates not shown and States withheld to avoid disclosing data for individual operations.
NASS, Livestock Branch, (202) 720–3570.

Table 8-47.—Turkeys: Net poults placements, United States, Monthly, 2013–2014 [1]

Month	Total all breeds		Percent of Previous Year
	2013	2014	
	Thousands	*Thousands*	*Percent*
January	23,545	22,096	94
February	21,608	20,889	97
March	21,391	21,557	101
April	22,410	22,621	101
May	21,931	23,310	106
June	21,251	23,452	110
July	24,025	24,234	101
August	22,724	23,224	102
September	19,624	21,169	108
October	20,908	21,695	104
November	20,042	20,379	102
December	21,138	22,516	107
Total	260,597	267,142	103

[1] Includes imports and excludes exports.
NASS, Livestock Branch, (202) 720–3570.

Table 8-48.—Turkeys: Poults hatched by commercial hatcheries, United States by Month, 2013–2014

Month	2013	2014	Percent of Previous Year
	Thousands	*Thousands*	*Percent*
January	24,102	23,430	97
February	22,232	21,486	97
March	21,908	22,380	102
April	23,263	22,800	98
May	22,342	24,189	108
June	21,422	23,647	110
July	23,893	24,405	102
August	23,011	23,500	102
September	20,974	22,844	109
October	22,928	23,744	104
November	21,308	21,936	103
December	22,074	24,660	112
Total	269,457	279,021	104

NASS, Livestock Branch, (202) 720–3570.

Table 8-49.—Eggs: Supply, distribution, and per capita consumption, United States, 2004–2013 [1]

Year	Total egg production	Storage at beginning of the year [1]	Imports [2]	Exports [2]	Eggs used for hatching	Consumption		
						Storage at end of the year [2]	Total [3]	Per capita
	Million dozen	*Million dozen*	*Million dozen*	*Million dozen*	*Million dozen*	*Million dozen*	*Million dozen*	*Number*
2004	7,450	14	13	168	988	15	6,319	258
2005	7,538	15	9	203	997	16	6,349	257
2006	7,650	16	9	202	992	13	6,472	260
2007	7,588	13	14	250	1,016	11	6,351	252
2008	7,519	11	14	206	996	17	6,338	250
2009	7,569	17	11	242	955	18	6,390	250
2010	7,656	18	12	259	982	19	6,436	249
2011	7,715	19	21	276	950	28	6,501	250
2012	7,883	28	18	302	941	21	6,666	255
2013	8,145	21	18	372	960	23	6,828	259

[1] Calendar years.   [2] Shell eggs and the approximate shell-egg equivalent of egg product.   [3] Shipments to territories now included in total consumption.
ERS Markets and Trade Economics Division, Animal Products and Cost of Production Branch, (202) 694–5308.

Table 8-50.—Eggs, shell: Average price per dozen on consumer Grade A cartoned white eggs to volume buyers, store-door delivery, New York, 2005–2015

Year	Large
	Cents
2005	65.51
2006	71.76
2007	114.36
2008	128.32
2009	102.97
2010	106.29
2011	115.31
2012	117.46
2013	124.69
2014	142.33
2015	181.74

AMS, Livestock, Poultry and Seed Programs, Livestock, Poultry and Grain Market News Division, (515) 284-4460.

Table 8-51.—All layers and egg production: Annual average number of layers, eggs per layer, and total production, by State and United States, 2013–2014[1]

State	Average number of layers		Eggs per layer[2]		Total egg production	
	2013	2014	2013	2014	2013	2014
	Thousands	*Thousands*	*Number*	*Number*	*Millions*	*Millions*
Alabama	9,286	9,280	238	232	2,207	2,148
Arkansas	12,069	12,131	245	244	2,952	2,962
California	18,010	16,173	280	281	5,048	4,551
Colorado	4,460	4,845	289	299	1,289	1,450
Connecticut	2,369	2,367	282	283	668	669
Florida	8,177	8,610	269	278	2,198	2,390
Georgia	17,748	18,270	255	259	4,525	4,723
Illinois	4,399	4,832	276	292	1,216	1,409
Indiana	26,664	27,400	277	283	7,382	7,747
Iowa	58,007	59,154	279	278	16,156	16,449
Kentucky	4,443	4,717	257	258	1,143	1,219
Louisiana	1,938	2,006	275	270	532	541
Maine	3,524	3,524	281	281	989	989
Maryland	2,458	2,782	279	282	686	785
Massachusetts	152	140	317	315	48	44
Michigan	12,959	13,044	295	297	3,818	3,867
Minnesota	10,348	10,926	280	281	2,899	3,071
Mississippi	5,753	5,626	243	240	1,395	1,351
Missouri	8,519	8,666	281	278	2,396	2,407
Montana	436	455	328	314	143	143
Nebraska	9,292	9,466	299	302	2,776	2,860
New York	4,795	5,048	295	296	1,416	1,493
North Carolina	12,990	13,458	245	251	3,184	3,381
Ohio	29,180	30,624	280	285	8,171	8,731
Oklahoma	3,139	3,054	238	233	746	712
Oregon	2,336	2,323	308	313	719	727
Pennsylvania	25,347	25,529	295	297	7,467	7,570
South Carolina	4,311	4,260	264	262	1,139	1,117
South Dakota	2,730	2,632	298	286	814	752
Tennessee	1,443	1,530	228	223	329	341
Texas	18,801	18,932	271	270	5,098	5,109
Utah	3,793	4,144	286	285	1,084	1,180
Vermont	162	143	260	252	42	36
Virginia	2,878	2,977	250	257	719	765
Washington	6,842	6,928	287	282	1,962	1,950
West Virginia	1,085	1,188	219	227	238	270
Wisconsin	5,377	5,105	285	284	1,532	1,449
Other States[3]	8,626	8,585	282	281	2,429	2,410
United States	354,844	360,873	275	277	97,555	99,768

[1] Annual estimates cover the period December 1 previous year through November 30. Totals may not add due to rounding. [2] Total egg production divided by average number of layers on hand. [3] Alaska, Arizona, Delaware, Hawaii, Idaho, Kansas, New Hampshire, New Jersey, New Mexico, Nevada, North Dakota, Rhode Island, and Wyoming combined to avoid disclosing data for individual operations.
NASS, Livestock Branch, (202) 720–3570.

Table 8-52.—Eggs: Broken under Federal inspection, United States, 2013–2014

Item	Quantity	
	2013	2014
	1,000 dozen	*1,000 dozen*
Shell eggs broken	2,134,068	2,262,138
	1,000 pounds	*1,000 pounds*
Edible product from shell eggs broken		
Whole	1,663,149	1,696,633
White	730,059	821,741
Yolk	366,399	405,616
Total	2,759,607	2,923,990
Inedible product from shell eggs broken	220,874	233,471

NASS, Livestock Branch, (202) 720–3570.

Table 8-53.—Eggs: Number, rate of lay, production, and value, United States, 2005–2014 [1]

Year	Layers average number	Rate of lay per layer [2]	Eggs, total produced	Price per dozen [3][4]	Value of production
	Thousands	Number	Millions	Dollars	1,000 dollars
2005	345,027	262	90,343	0.540	4,066,669
2006	349,700	263	91,788	0.583	4,460,211
2007	346,498	263	91,101	0.885	6,718,853
2008	339,933	266	90,239	....	8,239,313
2009	338,846	268	90,737	....	6,191,040
2010	341,505	269	91,811	....	6,553,087
2011	340,598	271	92,450	....	7,355,873
2012	394,844	274	94,364	....	7,929,104
2013	354,844	275	97,555	....	8,678,859
2014	360,873	277	99,768	....	10,166,321

[1] Annual estimates cover the period December 1 previous year through November 30.   [2] Total egg production divided by average number of layers on hand.   [3] Average mid-month price of all eggs sold by producers including hatching eggs.   [4] Price per dozen discontinued in 2008.
NASS, Livestock Branch, (202) 720–3570.

Table 8-54.—All Eggs: Production and value by State and United States, 2013–2014 [1]

State	Eggs produced		Value of production	
	2013	2014	2013	2014
	Millions	Millions	1,000 dollars	1,000 dollars
Alabama	2,207	2,148	388,780	400,702
Arkansas	2,952	2,962	454,913	482,351
California	5,048	4,551	382,690	419,135
Colorado	1,289	1,450	103,782	130,584
Connecticut	668	669	52,024	61,646
Florida	2,198	2,390	167,335	218,994
Georgia	4,525	4,723	585,797	665,866
Illinois	1,216	1,409	92,194	124,258
Indiana	7,382	7,747	545,130	674,076
Iowa	16,156	16,449	1,166,457	1,403,504
Kentucky	1,143	1,219	131,969	154,849
Louisiana	532	541	62,904	72,828
Maine	989	989	72,208	86,266
Maryland	686	785	52,925	70,753
Massachusetts	48	44	3,496	3,844
Michigan	3,818	3,867	271,400	325,322
Minnesota	2,899	3,071	214,011	265,908
Mississippi	1,395	1,351	222,415	234,653
Missouri	2,396	2,407	225,228	252,305
Montana	143	143	10,705	12,966
Nebraska	2,776	2,860	197,279	240,418
New York	1,416	1,493	107,145	133,257
North Carolina	3,184	3,381	431,359	500,989
Ohio	8,171	8,731	587,562	744,317
Oklahoma	746	712	97,227	102,226
Oregon	719	727	56,228	65,781
Pennsylvania	7,467	7,570	599,377	715,299
South Carolina	1,139	1,117	116,175	130,060
South Dakota	814	752	57,804	63,293
Tennessee	329	341	61,387	67,997
Texas	5,098	5,109	471,264	526,459
Utah	1,084	1,180	81,139	106,640
Vermont	42	36	3,701	4,275
Virginia	719	765	99,390	114,346
Washington	1,962	1,950	147,396	176,805
West Virginia	238	270	46,209	55,886
Wisconsin	1,532	1,449	115,879	129,890
Other States [2]	2,429	2,410	195,975	227,573
United States	97,555	99,768	8,678,859	10,166,321

[1] Annual estimates cover the period December 1 previous year through November 30.   Includes hatching and market (table) eggs.   Totals may not add due to rounding.   [2] Alaska, Arizona, Delaware, Hawaii, Idaho, Kansas, Nevada, New Hampshire, New Jersey, New Mexico, North Dakota, Rhode Island, and Wyoming combined to avoid disclosing individual operations.
NASS, Livestock Branch, (202) 720–3570.

Table 8-55.—Poultry and poultry products: Cold storage holdings, end of month, United States, 2013– 2014

Month	Frozen eggs							
	Whites		Yolks		Whole & mixed		Unclassified	
	2013	2014	2013	2014	2013	2014	2013	2014
	1,000 pounds	1,000 pounds	1,000 pounds	1,000 pounds	1,000 pounds	1,000 pounds	1,000 pounds	1,000 pounds
January	3,225	4,099	2,473	2,176	8,271	12,367	15,690	16,045
February	2,934	4,478	2,229	1,727	7,988	12,162	15,469	16,264
March	3,384	4,117	2,412	1,906	6,274	10,437	15,068	12,584
April	3,065	3,427	2,318	1,627	8,609	9,279	15,347	13,097
May	3,053	3,462	2,370	1,302	8,057	10,172	15,376	13,364
June	4,138	3,590	2,794	1,478	7,803	10,649	15,856	14,425
July	3,507	3,912	1,702	1,760	8,278	10,576	12,631	15,205
August	3,690	3,615	1,635	1,756	11,503	10,585	13,316	13,864
September ...	5,140	4,146	1,721	1,791	11,841	10,385	14,875	14,804
October	4,896	4,447	1,604	1,540	12.509	10,171	14,823	15,772
November	4,108	4,036	1,823	1,458	11,620	10,685	12,203	14,170
December	3,474	3,574	1,965	1,471	11,718	10,148	13,193	15,525

Month	Frozen eggs, total		Frozen chicken					
	2013	2014	Broilers (Whole)		Hens		Breast and breast meat	
			2013	2014	2013	2014	2013	2014
	1,000 pounds	1,000 pounds	1,000 pounds	1,000 pounds	1,000 pounds	1,000 pounds	1,000 pounds	1,000 pounds
January	26,659	34,687	18,741	16,750	3,474	7,084	129,741	113,677
February	28,620	34,631	16,409	13,053	1,505	7,492	128,153	122,830
March	27,138	29,044	14,888	11,117	1,526	5,099	122,331	113,032
April	29,339	27,430	16,305	8,448	4,162	5,472	121,075	108,812
May	28,856	28,300	13,978	7,138	5,044	4,850	108,360	117,089
June	30,591	30,142	15,469	7,932	5,229	4,541	101,812	113,318
July	26,118	31,453	21,631	13,578	4,337	5,536	98,536	108,948
August	30,144	29,820	22,482	12,603	4,592	6,946	96,011	110,520
September ...	33,577	31,126	23,244	11,092	3,155	6,934	89,739	114,033
October	33,832	31,960	27,583	11,723	5,414	4,972	104,816	126,303
November	29,754	30,349	21,607	10,771	4,873	2,257	114,376	146,185
December	30,350	30,718	13,791	11,425	5,955	3,030	110,357	159,121

Month	Frozen chicken							
	Drumsticks		Leg quarters		Legs		Thigh and thigh quarters	
	2013	2014	2013	2014	2013	2014	2013	2014
	1,000 pounds	1,000 pounds	1,000 pounds	1,000 pounds	1,000 pounds	1,000 pounds	1,000 pounds	1,000 pounds
January	17,032	27,248	128,213	158,922	13,055	8,846	8,836	9,590
February	13,403	23,320	123,087	152,883	10,020	8,193	7,682	11,281
March	15,316	23,383	110,481	106,551	6,632	9,514	8,597	8,647
April	19,263	25,127	136,978	100,723	8,884	13,320	7,792	8,403
May	16,902	28,396	165,098	118,697	10,569	13,957	7,476	8,128
June	17,337	22,836	157,088	99,556	10,538	13,613	7,644	9,104
July	17,400	17,934	161,962	124,248	9,218	13,816	8,445	8,810
August	17,536	18,030	162,467	127,116	8,177	11,327	7,166	8,115
September ...	17,919	17,445	153,233	118,616	7,214	11,859	6,200	8,434
October	24,129	21,308	150,543	129,762	8,707	12,270	9,445	8,877
November	26,464	26,001	154,318	128,192	8,747	10,597	8,667	11,211
December	28,690	26,331	154,400	128,638	9,393	15,748	8,625	13,088

Month	Frozen chicken							
	Thigh meat		Wings		Paws and feet		Other	
	2013	2014	2013	2014	2013	2014	2013	2014
	1,000 pounds	1,000 pounds	1,000 pounds	1,000 pounds	1,000 pounds	1,000 pounds	1,000 pounds	1,000 pounds
January	17,914	22,169	59,737	62,433	22,546	23,416	250,105	239,006
February	17,836	22,265	63,305	58,935	19,995	23,491	251,195	237,200
March	13,554	17,618	75,351	55,699	19,556	22,102	239,901	218,807
April	16,870	17,759	83,811	61,373	28,116	21,380	243,877	213,276
May	14,680	16,130	89,108	66,719	22,876	22,727	240,762	208,234
June	15,218	17,659	83,636	64,938	21,723	22,930	244,748	214,923
July	15,934	19,593	94,176	64,462	25,767	26,232	246,259	255,592
August	17,007	17,690	102,772	63,781	20,570	25,228	250,322	224,565
September ...	15,796	16,970	90,926	62,014	23,130	25,356	246,364	232,493
October	19,617	21,880	97,745	64,322	23,289	27,671	250,074	229,532
November	20,985	23,657	101,564	70,126	23,969	30,252	252,286	237,866
December	20,290	24,547	88,145	58,720	23,701	29,346	234,982	242,512

See end of table.

Table 8-55.—Poultry and poultry products: Cold storage holdings, end of month, United States, 2013–2014—Continued

Month	Total chicken		Frozen turkey					
			Toms		Hens		Total whole	
	2013	2014	2013	2014	2013	2014	2013	2014
	1,000 pounds	1,000 pounds	1,000 pounds	1,000 pounds	1,000 pounds	1,000 pounds	1,000 pounds	1,000 pounds
January	669,394	689,141	68,418	53,681	78,549	53,873	146,967	107,554
February	652,590	680,943	82,841	72,426	88,093	67,950	170,934	140,376
March	628,133	591,569	96,247	77,979	92,724	85,038	188,971	163,017
April	687,133	584,093	122,022	88,096	110,136	104,883	232,158	192,979
May	694,853	612,065	153,563	107,122	131,669	129,404	285,232	236,526
June	680,442	591,350	168,792	118,638	142,362	150,261	311,154	268,899
July	703,665	628,749	183,368	131,617	144,984	157,002	328,352	288,619
August	709,102	625,921	192,205	136,686	143,348	164,098	335,553	300,784
September	676,920	625,246	188,007	141,964	137,334	155,259	325,341	297,223
October	721,362	658,440	141,835	112,734	97,895	112,045	239,730	224,779
November	737,856	697,115	45,677	39,855	16,579	28,047	62,256	67,902
December	698,329	712,506	44,409	30,715	23,477	28,841	67,886	59,556

Month	Frozen turkey							
	Breasts		Legs		Mechanically deboned meat		Other	
	2013	2014	2013	2014	2013	2014	2013	2014
	1,000 pounds	1,000 pounds	1,000 pounds	1,000 pounds	1,000 pounds	1,000 pounds	1,000 pounds	1,000 pounds
January	63,914	56,457	20,930	10,001	9,660	7,809	33,232	28,399
February	66,655	56,448	19,515	8,018	12,924	5,779	30,789	24,782
March	70,105	53,024	18,742	8,127	11,004	5,919	30,497	22,880
April	73,892	51,436	16,324	7,471	13,470	5,079	31,950	25,924
May	78,750	53,904	13,216	7,979	10,088	6,180	37,014	26,994
June	83,591	54,594	13,008	8,326	12,534	9,022	37,330	29,771
July	83,392	54,820	14,022	9,852	9,977	9,566	35,639	31,157
August	76,562	50,394	15,624	9,350	7,324	6,261	34,203	27,545
September	64,925	48,599	13,330	7,309	6,011	6,107	32,853	25,134
October	51,526	36,441	10,510	7,827	7,306	7,750	31,083	27,474
November	45,777	27,884	11,691	9,835	8,694	8,122	30,035	26,355
December	48,352	29,860	11,811	9,964	7,465	6,582	30,865	28,465

Month	Frozen turkey				Ducks		Total frozen poultry	
	Unclassified		Total turkey		2013	2014	2013	2014
	2013	2014	2013	2014				
	1,000 pounds	1,000 pounds	1,000 pounds	1,000 pounds	1,000 pounds	1,000 pounds	1,000 pounds	1,000 pounds
January	85,315	65,567	360,018	275,787	1,444	2,019	1,030,856	966,947
February	93,938	75,353	394,755	310,756	1,482	2,021	1,048,827	993,720
March	81,927	83,416	401,246	336,383	1,553	1,782	1,030,932	929,734
April	89,781	92,124	457,575	375,013	2,311	1,793	1,147,019	960,899
May	97,256	90,919	521,556	422,502	1,249	1,426	1,217,658	1,035,993
June	108,858	91,974	566,475	462,586	1,711	1,824	1,248,628	1,055,760
July	109,975	95,744	581,357	489,758	2,574	1,853	1,287,596	1,120,360
August	110,803	100,452	580,069	494,786	2,480	2,588	1,291,651	1,123,295
September	98,723	100,175	541,183	484,547	2,027	2,887	1,220,130	1,112,680
October	94,338	86,383	434,493	390,654	1,720	2,317	1,157,575	1,051,411
November	62,768	47,465	221,221	187,563	1,985	2,296	961,062	886,974
December	71,028	59,002	237,407	193,429	1,940	2,231	937,676	908,166

NASS, Livestock Branch, (202) 720–3570.

Table 8-56.—Dairy products: Cold storage holdings, end of month, United States, 2013–2014

Month	Butter		American cheese	
	2013	2014	2013	2014
	1,000 pounds	*1,000 pounds*	*1,000 pounds*	*1,000 pounds*
January	207,075	143,890	643,184	630,820
February	238,342	171,773	661,019	628,679
March	254,991	191,755	684,653	639,067
April	309,719	186,914	698,655	648,900
May	321,954	209,430	714,637	656,446
June	318,893	199,248	710,604	655,239
July	295,751	180,834	701,964	660,438
August	263,928	172,789	668,361	648,784
September	233,031	152,361	661,046	631,279
October	181,799	147,956	626,161	623,336
November	121,627	107,566	613,965	635,776
December	112,467	104,728	618,265	627,769

Month	Swiss cheese		Other	
	2013	2014	2013	2014
	1,000 pounds	*1,000 pounds*	*1,000 pounds*	*1,000 pounds*
January	30,401	25,421	358,611	358,812
February	30,130	26,942	377,607	354,511
March	30,589	27,425	390,483	351,798
April	28,503	28,316	394,135	360,370
May	29,051	30,538	406,351	378,556
June	31,347	27,972	407,426	372,231
July	32,715	24,593	411,452	369,861
August	32,006	27,085	399,984	365,539
September	29,975	25,684	379,676	356,819
October	27,923	25,600	365,632	346,730
November	26,102	24,419	356,542	356,997
December	24,688	21,282	366,428	368,885

Month	Total natural cheese	
	2013	2014
	1,000 pounds	*1,000 pounds*
January	1,032,196	1,015,053
February	1,068,756	1,010,132
March	1,105,725	1,018,290
April	1,121,293	1,037,586
May	1,150,039	1,065,540
June	1,149,377	1,055,442
July	1,146,131	1,054,892
August	1,100,351	1,041,408
September	1,070,697	1,013,782
October	1,019,716	995,666
November	996,609	1,017,192
December	1,009,381	1,017,936

NASS, Livestock Branch, (202) 720–3570.

CHAPTER IX

FARM RESOURCES, INCOME, AND EXPENSES

The statistics in this chapter deal with farms, farm resources, farm income, and expenses. Many of the series are estimates developed in connection with economic research activities of the Department.

Table 9-1.—Economic trends: Data relating to agriculture, United States, 2004–2013

| Year | Prices paid by farmers [1] | | | Farm income [2] | | |
	Total including interest, taxes, and wage rates (PPITW)	Production items	Prices received by farmers [1]	Gross farm income [3]	Production expenses	Net farm income
	Index numbers 2011=100	Index numbers 2011=100	Index numbers 2011=100	Billion dollars	Billion dollars	Billion dollars
2004	66	62	73	294.9	207.5	87.4
2005	70	65	71	298.5	219.7	78.8
2006	74	69	71	290.2	232.7	57.4
2007	79	75	84	339.6	269.5	70.0
2008	90	88	92	377.7	292.6	85.1
2009	87	85	81	343.3	280.3	63.0
2010	90	88	82	365.6	285.2	80.4
2011	100	100	100	428.5	310.6	117.9
2012	104	105	105	....	....	....
2013	106	107	107	....	....	....

Year	National income [5]	Personal income [5]	Industrial production [6]	Consumer prices all items [7]	Producer prices consumer foods [7]
	Billion dollars	Billion dollars	Index numbers 2007=100	Index numbers 1982–84=100	Index numbers 1982=100
2004	10,541.9	10,049.2	92.5	188.9	152.7
2005	11,240.8	10,610.3	95.5	195.3	155.7
2006	12,005.6	11,389.8	97.6	201.6	156.7
2007	12,322.3	11,995.7	100.0	207.3	167.0
2008	12,430.8	12,430.6	96.6	215.3	178.3
2009	12,124.5	12,082.1	85.7	214.5	175.5
2010	12,739.5	12,435.2	90.6	218.1	182.4
2011	13,395.7	13,191.3	93.6	224.9	....
2012	13,971.6	13,743.8	97.1	229.6	....
2013	14,542.4	14,134.7	99.9	233.0	....

[1] U.S. Department of Agriculture - NASS. [2] U.S. Department of Agriculture - ERS. [3] Includes cash receipts from farm marketings, government payments, nonmoney income (gross rental value of dwelling and value of home consumption), other income (machine hire custom work and recreational income), and value of change in farm inventories. [4] Forecast. [5] Department of Commerce, Bureau of Economic Analysis. [6] Federal Reserve Board. [7] U.S. Department of Labor, Bureau of Labor Statistics.

ERS, Farm and Rural Business Branch, (202) 694–5446. E-mail contact is Timothy Park at tapark@ers.usda.gov. For National Income, Personal Income, Industrial Production and Consumer Price Indexes, Contact David Torgerson at (202) 694-5334. E-mail contact is dtorg@ers.usda.gov.

Table 9-2.—Farms: Number, land in farms, and average size of farm, United States, 2005–2014

Year	Farms [1]	Land in farms	Average size farm
	Number	1,000 acres	Acres
2005	2,098,690	927,940	442
2006	2,088,790	925,790	443
2007	2,204,600	921,460	418
2008	2,184,500	918,600	421
2009	2,169,660	917,590	423
2010	2,149,520	915,660	426
2011	2,131,240	914,420	429
2012	2,109,810	914,600	433
2013	2,102,010	914,030	435
2014	2,084,000	913,000	438

[1] A farm is any establishment from which $1,000 or more of agricultural products were sold or would normally be sold during the year.
NASS, Environmental, Economics, and Demographics Branch, (202) 720–6146.

Table 9-3.—Farms: Percent of farms, land in farms, and average size, by economic sales class, United States, 2013–2014

Economic sales class	Percent of total				Average size farm	
	Farms		Land		2013	2014[1]
	2013	2014[1]	2013	2014[1]		
	Percent	Percent	Percent	Percent	Acres	Acres
$ 1,000 - $ 9,999	51.5	50.6	10.4	9.9	88	86
$ 10,000 - $ 99,999	29.5	29.9	21.2	21.2	313	312
$100,000 - $249,999	6.8	7.0	14.4	14.1	918	889
$250,000 - $499,999	4.6	4.7	13.7	13.7	1,300	1,290
$500,000 - $999,999	3.8	4.0	16.7	17.1	1,913	1,887
$1,000,000 or more	3.9	3.9	23.7	23.9	2,637	2,655
Total	100.0	100.0	100.0	100.0	435	438

[1]Preliminary.
NASS, Environmental, Economics, and Demographics Branch, (202) 720–6146.

Table 9-4.—Land in farms: Classification by tenure of operator, United States, 1935–2012

Year	Land in farms	Tenure of operator			
		Full owners	Part owners	Managers	All tenants
	Acres	Percent	Percent	Percent	Percent
1935[1]	1,054,515,111	37.1	25.2	5.8	31.9
1940	1,065,113,774	35.9	28.2	6.5	29.4
1945[1]	1,141,615,364	36.1	32.5	9.3	22.0
1950	1,161,419,720	36.1	36.4	9.2	18.3
1954[1]	1,158,191,511	34.2	40.7	8.6	16.5
1959	1,123,507,574	31.0	44.0	9.8	14.8
1964	1,110,187,000	28.7	48.0	10.2	13.1
1969	1,062,892,501	35.3	51.8	....	13.0
1974	1,017,030,357	35.3	52.6	....	12.0
1978	1,014,777,234	32.7	55.3	....	12.0
1982	986,796,579	34.7	53.8	....	11.5
1987	964,470,625	32.9	53.9	....	13.2
1992	945,531,506	31.3	55.7	....	13.0
1997	931,795,255	33.9	54.5	....	11.6
2002[2]	938,279,056	38.0	52.8	....	9.2
2007[2]	922,095,843	37.3	53.8	....	8.9
2012[2]	914,527,657	36.8	53.7	....	9.5

[1] Excludes Alaska and Hawaii.   [2] The 2002 Census of Agriculture introduced new methodology to account for all farms in the United States.   All 2002 published census items were reweighted for undercoverage.   Strictly speaking, data for 2002 and subsequent years are not fully comparable with data from earlier years.
ERS, Resource and Rural Economics Division, (202) 694–5572.   Data from the Census of Agriculture, National Agricultural Statistics Service.

Table 9-5.—Number of farms and land in farms by economic sales class by State and United States, 2013–2014

State	Economic Sales Class: $1,000-$9,999			
	Number of Farms		Land in Farms	
	2013	2014	2013	2014
	Number	Number	1,000 Acres	1,000 Acres
Alabama	26,000	25,600	2,850	2,750
Alaska	380	380	270	270
Arizona	14,800	14,900	800	800
Arkansas	22,600	22,000	1,900	1,650
California	30,400	29,800	1,500	1,400
Colorado	19,500	19,100	2,500	2,400
Connecticut	4,000	4,000	150	150
Delaware	830	870	20	20
Florida	28,800	27,400	1,410	1,260
Georgia	24,000	23,000	2,250	2,150
Hawaii	3,850	3,850	100	100
Idaho	12,300	12,200	800	800
Illinois	30,500	30,000	1,500	1,400
Indiana	28,200	27,900	1,070	1,000
Iowa	27,500	27,100	1,200	1,200
Kansas	23,700	23,000	2,600	2,500
Kentucky	43,700	42,700	3,100	3,000
Louisiana	16,600	16,600	1,300	1,300
Maine	5,000	5,000	480	480
Maryland	6,800	6,600	310	300
Massachusetts	5,000	5,000	210	210
Michigan	26,300	25,800	1,370	1,100
Minnesota	27,000	26,600	2,100	2,100
Mississippi	21,800	21,700	2,800	2,800
Missouri	47,300	45,500	4,200	3,900
Montana	12,200	11,900	3,100	2,900
Nebraska	13,400	13,000	1,000	900
Nevada	2,300	2,300	150	150
New Hampshire	3,100	3,100	240	240
New Jersey	5,600	5,600	160	160
New Mexico	16,300	16,200	4,400	4,200
New York	16,700	16,700	1,400	1,400
North Carolina	28,400	28,000	1,600	1,500
North Dakota	9,800	9,300	1,700	1,600
Ohio	37,300	33,200	1,920	1,650
Oklahoma	43,200	42,500	5,250	5,150
Oregon	21,300	21,000	1,500	1,500
Pennsylvania	29,000	26,700	1,790	1,800
Rhode Island	720	710	30	20
South Carolina	17,100	16,700	1,800	1,700
South Dakota	8,900	8,300	1,300	1,200
Tennessee	44,100	43,400	3,200	3,050
Texas	160,500	156,000	19,000	18,200
Utah	10,700	10,600	650	650
Vermont	4,100	4,050	340	340
Virginia	26,500	26,300	2,000	1,850
Washington	22,400	22,200	1,000	1,000
West Virginia	15,200	15,100	1,600	1,600
Wisconsin	31,000	30,500	2,100	2,000
Wyoming	5,200	4,900	1,100	1,000
United States	1,081,880	1,054,860	95,120	90,800

See footnote(s) at end of table.

Table 9-5.—Number of farms and land in farms by economic sales class by State and United States, 2013–2014—Continued

State	Economic Sales Class: $10,000-$99,999			
	Number of Farms		Land in Farms	
	2013	2014	2013	2014
	Number	*Number*	*1,000 Acres*	*1,000 Acres*
Alabama	12,600	12,700	3,300	3,300
Alaska	(D)	290	(D)	450
Arizona	(D)	3,200	(D)	8,200
Arkansas	14,200	14,000	3,300	3,600
California	26,900	26,000	4,400	4,300
Colorado	10,000	10,200	6,800	7,200
Connecticut	(D)	1,550	(D)	110
Delaware	(D)	(D)	(D)	(D)
Florida	13,600	14,700	1,800	1,900
Georgia	10,400	10,500	2,200	2,200
Hawaii	(D)	2,600	(D)	260
Idaho	7,000	7,000	2,100	2,050
Illinois	19,300	18,700	2,700	2,700
Indiana	15,700	15,300	1,720	1,800
Iowa	23,600	23,600	3,100	3,100
Kansas	21,700	21,500	8,000	8,000
Kentucky	26,000	26,900	4,600	4,700
Louisiana	7,400	7,300	1,800	1,800
Maine	(D)	2,400	(D)	400
Maryland	(D)	3,500	(D)	400
Massachusetts	(D)	2,000	(D)	140
Michigan	15,300	14,800	1,680	1,700
Minnesota	22,000	21,900	3,650	3,700
Mississippi	10,700	10,600	2,950	2,950
Missouri	38,800	38,200	9,300	9,000
Montana	8,300	8,000	9,100	9,100
Nebraska	14,300	13,900	5,200	5,000
Nevada	(D)	900	(D)	330
New Hampshire	(D)	1,050	(D)	150
New Jersey	(D)	2,350	(D)	160
New Mexico	6,400	6,200	11,900	11,500
New York	11,600	11,600	1,780	1,780
North Carolina	13,000	12,800	1,500	1,500
North Dakota	7,200	6,600	3,300	3,000
Ohio	22,100	25,300	2,470	2,650
Oklahoma	28,200	28,300	11,600	11,500
Oregon	9,100	9,100	2,900	2,860
Pennsylvania	18,200	19,900	2,280	2,300
Rhode Island	(D)	(D)	(D)	(D)
South Carolina	5,600	5,600	1,300	1,350
South Dakota	9,500	9,700	5,200	5,100
Tennessee	19,700	19,500	3,700	3,700
Texas	69,500	70,000	41,600	41,700
Utah	5,400	5,500	1,850	1,900
Vermont	(D)	2,100	(D)	320
Virginia	14,700	14,700	2,900	2,900
Washington	8,400	8,400	2,000	1,900
West Virginia	(D)	5,300	(D)	1,400
Wisconsin	21,200	21,000	2,900	2,900
Wyoming	(D)	3,900	(D)	4,800
Other States[1]	31,790	1,010	17,000	60
United States	619,390	622,150	193,880	193,820

See footnote(s) at end of table.

Table 9-5.—Number of farms and land in farms by economic sales class by State and United States, 2013–2014—Continued

State	Economic Sales Class: $100,000-$249,999			
	Number of Farms		Land in Farms	
	2013	2014	2013	2014
	Number	Number	1,000 Acres	1,000 Acres
Alabama	1,000	1,050	650	700
Alaska	(D)	50	(D)	70
Arizona	(D)	610	(D)	11,200
Arkansas	1,350	1,700	1,000	1,050
California	6,800	6,300	3,700	3,800
Colorado	2,550	2,500	5,400	5,100
Connecticut	(D)	(D)	(D)	(D)
Delaware	(D)	(D)	(D)	(D)
Florida	2,100	2,200	930	940
Georgia	1,300	1,400	630	630
Hawaii	(D)	280	(D)	160
Idaho	1,900	1,900	1,600	1,650
Illinois	8,700	8,700	3,000	3,000
Indiana	5,300	5,400	1,560	1,560
Iowa	10,300	10,400	3,000	3,000
Kansas	6,500	6,600	7,300	7,300
Kentucky	3,200	3,100	1,300	1,200
Louisiana	710	710	450	450
Maine	(D)	340	(D)	100
Maryland	(D)	600	(D)	230
Massachusetts	(D)	380	(D)	50
Michigan	3,900	4,200	1,000	1,050
Minnesota	8,400	8,600	2,550	2,500
Mississippi	900	900	550	550
Missouri	5,900	6,700	4,000	4,100
Montana	2,950	3,100	10,000	9,800
Nebraska	7,300	7,400	6,100	5,900
Nevada	(D)	270	(D)	610
New Hampshire	(D)	(D)	(D)	(D)
New Jersey	(D)	450	(D)	80
New Mexico	980	1,100	7,100	7,400
New York	3,300	3,500	900	900
North Carolina	1,900	2,000	550	600
North Dakota	3,700	3,500	4,300	3,900
Ohio	7,100	7,200	1,900	1,900
Oklahoma	4,300	4,400	5,700	5,700
Oregon	1,750	1,700	2,900	2,900
Pennsylvania	5,600	5,500	1,070	1,050
Rhode Island	(D)	(D)	(D)	(D)
South Carolina	600	600	270	270
South Dakota	4,500	4,400	6,200	5,500
Tennessee	1,600	1,750	700	750
Texas	8,000	8,400	20,600	20,200
Utah	1,000	900	1,200	1,400
Vermont	(D)	490	(D)	140
Virginia	1,750	1,850	900	950
Washington	2,150	2,200	1,560	1,600
West Virginia	(D)	400	(D)	240
Wisconsin	7,500	7,400	2,000	1,950
Wyoming	(D)	1,300	(D)	4,700
Other States[1]	5,730	530	18,290	100
United States	142,520	144,960	130,860	128,930

See footnote(s) at end of table.

Table 9-5.—Number of farms and land in farms by economic sales class by State and United States, 2013–2014—Continued

State	Economic Sales Class: $250,000-$499,999			
	Number of Farms		Land in Farms	
	2013	2014	2013	2014
	Number	*Number*	*1,000 Acres*	*1,000 Acres*
Alabama	900	950	450	500
Alaska	(D)	(D)	(D)	(D)
Arizona	(D)	240	(D)	2,500
Arkansas	1,450	1,100	700	600
California	4,100	4,500	2,300	2,500
Colorado	1,650	1,400	6,000	5,500
Connecticut	(D)	(D)	(D)	(D)
Delaware	(D)	(D)	(D)	(D)
Florida	1,150	1,250	910	950
Georgia	1,000	900	470	470
Hawaii	(D)	120	(D)	60
Idaho	1,300	1,300	1,400	1,400
Illinois	6,800	7,100	4,300	4,400
Indiana	3,900	4,000	2,000	2,100
Iowa	9,700	9,600	5,000	5,000
Kansas	4,300	4,300	7,600	7,600
Kentucky	1,500	1,500	1,000	1,000
Louisiana	540	540	450	450
Maine	(D)	220	(D)	110
Maryland	(D)	650	(D)	250
Massachusetts	(D)	(D)	(D)	(D)
Michigan	2,600	2,700	1,100	1,200
Minnesota	6,400	6,400	3,300	3,300
Mississippi	800	800	500	500
Missouri	3,050	3,200	3,400	3,500
Montana	2,300	2,400	12,300	12,200
Nebraska	5,300	5,100	7,600	7,300
Nevada	(D)	420	(D)	960
New Hampshire	(D)	(D)	(D)	(D)
New Jersey	(D)	270	(D)	90
New Mexico	480	550	6,200	6,300
New York	1,900	1,700	800	800
North Carolina	1,500	1,500	650	700
North Dakota	2,900	2,900	5,100	5,000
Ohio	3,700	3,850	1,870	1,900
Oklahoma	2,050	2,050	4,550	4,550
Oregon	1,050	1,000	2,300	2,290
Pennsylvania	3,350	3,550	910	950
Rhode Island	(D)	(D)	(D)	(D)
South Carolina	300	300	230	230
South Dakota	3,800	3,500	8,000	7,200
Tennessee	950	950	700	700
Texas	4,200	4,500	16,300	16,700
Utah	550	600	1,400	1,550
Vermont	(D)	350	(D)	150
Virginia	1,200	1,200	700	700
Washington	1,250	1,250	2,250	2,250
West Virginia	(D)	150	(D)	110
Wisconsin	5,000	4,900	2,100	2,050
Wyoming	(D)	850	(D)	6,600
Other States[1]	3,620	560	10,630	150
United States	96,540	97,170	125,470	125,320

See footnote(s) at end of table.

Table 9-5.—Number of farms and land in farms by economic sales class by State and United States, 2013–2014—Continued

State	Economic Sales Class: $500,000-$999,999			
	Number of Farms		Land in Farms	
	2013	2014	2013	2014
	Number	Number	1,000 Acres	1,000 Acres
Alabama	1,500	1,650	650	500
Alaska	(D)	(D)	(D)	(D)
Arizona	250	300	500	400
Arkansas	1,300	1,500	1,200	1,200
California	3,300	3,300	2,500	2,600
Colorado	950	850	5,000	5,600
Connecticut	(D)	(D)	(D)	(D)
Delaware	370	370	100	100
Florida	820	820	700	650
Georgia	2,900	2,900	1,630	1,630
Hawaii	70	70	240	240
Idaho	800	800	1,800	1,900
Illinois	5,300	5,500	6,300	6,300
Indiana	2,800	3,000	2,950	2,840
Iowa	10,000	10,000	8,800	8,700
Kansas	3,000	2,900	9,600	9,600
Kentucky	1,000	1,100	1,140	1,240
Louisiana	850	950	1,000	1,000
Maine	120	110	90	90
Maryland	370	400	270	270
Massachusetts	(D)	(D)	(D)	(D)
Michigan	2,100	2,250	1,700	1,800
Minnesota	5,300	5,300	4,770	4,800
Mississippi	1,200	1,200	1,000	1,000
Missouri	1,950	2,200	3,500	3,700
Montana	1,450	1,450	13,000	13,500
Nebraska	4,700	4,900	9,700	9,800
Nevada	150	170	1,300	1,000
New Hampshire	(D)	(D)	(D)	(D)
New Jersey	210	210	80	80
New Mexico	310	320	7,900	8,100
New York	1,000	1,000	650	650
North Carolina	1,600	1,600	950	950
North Dakota	3,800	4,600	9,800	10,600
Ohio	2,700	2,850	2,300	2,400
Oklahoma	1,350	1,350	3,920	4,000
Oregon	850	850	2,710	2,650
Pennsylvania	1,900	1,900	750	770
Rhode Island	(D)	(D)	(D)	(D)
South Carolina	400	400	390	450
South Dakota	2,900	3,300	10,000	11,200
Tennessee	800	800	780	850
Texas	2,950	3,250	15,100	15,500
Utah	270	220	4,900	4,500
Vermont	160	150	100	90
Virginia	1,000	1,050	830	830
Washington	1,200	1,050	2,990	2,950
West Virginia	170	170	100	110
Wisconsin	2,800	2,900	2,000	2,050
Wyoming	460	500	6,600	6,800
Other States[1]	260	260	75	80
United States	79,640	82,720	152,365	156,070

See footnote(s) at end of table.

Table 9-5.—Number of farms and land in farms by economic sales class by State and United States, 2013–2014—Continued

State	Economic Sales Class: $1,000,000 or more			
	Number of Farms		Land in Farms	
	2013	2014	2013	2014
	Number	*Number*	*1,000 Acres*	*1,000 Acres*
Alabama	1,500	1,450	1,000	1,150
Alaska	(D)	(D)	(D)	(D)
Arizona	430	350	2,900	2,900
Arkansas	3,700	3,700	5,700	5,700
California	6,400	6,500	11,100	10,900
Colorado	950	950	6,000	6,000
Connecticut	90	90	100	100
Delaware	380	380	270	270
Florida	1,230	1,230	3,800	3,800
Georgia	2,400	2,400	2,320	2,320
Hawaii	80	80	300	300
Idaho	1,200	1,200	4,100	4,000
Illinois	4,500	4,500	9,100	9,100
Indiana	2,600	2,600	5,400	5,400
Iowa	7,400	7,300	9,500	9,500
Kansas	2,600	2,700	11,000	11,000
Kentucky	1,100	1,100	1,860	1,860
Louisiana	1,200	1,100	2,800	2,800
Maine	120	130	270	270
Maryland	530	550	580	580
Massachusetts	80	80	50	50
Michigan	1,800	1,850	3,100	3,100
Minnesota	5,300	5,200	9,530	9,500
Mississippi	1,900	1,900	3,100	3,100
Missouri	2,000	1,900	4,000	4,100
Montana	900	950	12,200	12,200
Nebraska	4,600	4,800	15,700	16,300
Nevada	140	140	2,600	2,900
New Hampshire	(D)	(D)	(D)	(D)
New Jersey	220	220	150	150
New Mexico	330	330	5,700	5,700
New York	1,000	1,000	1,650	1,650
North Carolina	3,600	3,600	3,150	3,150
North Dakota	3,400	3,400	15,100	15,200
Ohio	2,100	2,100	3,540	3,500
Oklahoma	1,000	1,000	3,380	3,400
Oregon	950	950	4,190	4,200
Pennsylvania	1,250	1,250	900	850
Rhode Island	(D)	(D)	(D)	(D)
South Carolina	800	800	1,010	1,000
South Dakota	2,400	2,500	12,600	13,100
Tennessee	850	900	1,820	1,850
Texas	3,350	3,350	17,500	17,700
Utah	280	280	1,000	1,000
Vermont	160	160	210	210
Virginia	850	800	970	970
Washington	1,600	1,600	5,000	5,000
West Virginia	180	180	150	140
Wisconsin	2,300	2,300	3,500	3,550
Wyoming	250	250	6,400	6,500
Other States[1]	40	40	35	40
United States	82,040	82,140	216,335	218,060

(D) Withheld to avoid disclosing data for individual operations.   (NA) Not available.   [1] Includes data withheld above.
NASS, Environmental, Economics, and Demographics Branch, (202) 720–6146.

Table 9-6.—Number of farms and land in farms by State and United States, 2013–2014

State	Number of Farms [1]		Land in farms		Average farm size	
	2013	2014	2013	2014	2013	2014
	Number	*Number*	*1,000 acres*	*1,000 acres*	*Acres*	*Acres*
Alabama	43,500	43,400	8,900	8,900	205	205
Alaska	760	760	830	830	1,092	1,092
Arizona	19,600	19,600	26,200	26,000	1,337	1,327
Arkansas	44,600	44,000	13,800	13,800	309	314
California	77,900	76,400	25,500	25,500	327	334
Colorado	35,600	35,000	31,700	31,800	890	909
Connecticut	6,000	6,000	440	440	73	73
Delaware	2,450	2,500	500	500	204	200
Florida	47,700	47,600	9,550	9,500	200	200
Georgia	42,000	41,100	9,500	9,400	226	229
Hawaii	7,000	7,000	1,120	1,120	160	160
Idaho	24,500	24,400	11,800	11,800	482	484
Illinois	75,100	74,500	26,900	26,900	358	361
Indiana	58,500	58,200	14,700	14,700	251	253
Iowa	88,500	88,000	30,600	30,500	346	347
Kansas	61,800	61,000	46,100	46,000	746	754
Kentucky	76,500	76,400	13,000	13,000	170	170
Louisiana	27,300	27,200	7,800	7,800	286	287
Maine	8,200	8,200	1,450	1,450	177	177
Maryland	12,400	12,300	2,030	2,030	164	165
Massachusetts	7,800	7,800	520	520	67	67
Michigan	52,000	51,600	9,950	9,950	191	193
Minnesota	74,400	74,000	25,900	25,900	348	350
Mississippi	37,300	37,100	10,900	10,900	292	294
Missouri	99,000	97,700	28,400	28,300	287	290
Montana	28,100	27,800	59,700	59,700	2,125	2,147
Nebraska	49,600	49,100	45,300	45,200	913	921
Nevada	4,150	4,200	5,950	5,950	1,434	1,417
New Hampshire ...	4,400	4,400	470	470	107	107
New Jersey	9,100	9,100	720	720	79	79
New Mexico	24,800	24,700	43,200	43,200	1,742	1,749
New York	35,500	35,500	7,180	7,180	202	202
North Carolina	50,000	49,500	8,400	8,400	168	170
North Dakota	30,800	30,300	39,300	39,300	1,276	1,297
Ohio	75,000	74,500	14,000	14,000	187	188
Oklahoma	80,100	79,600	34,400	34,300	429	431
Oregon	35,000	34,600	16,500	16,400	471	474
Pennsylvania	59,300	58,800	7,700	7,720	130	131
Rhode Island	1,250	1,240	70	70	56	56
South Carolina	24,800	24,400	5,000	5,000	202	205
South Dakota	32,000	31,700	43,300	43,300	1,353	1,366
Tennessee	68,000	67,300	10,900	10,900	160	162
Texas	248,500	245,500	130,100	130,000	524	530
Utah	18,200	18,100	11,000	11,000	604	608
Vermont	7,300	7,300	1,250	1,250	171	171
Virginia	46,000	45,900	8,300	8,200	180	179
Washington	37,000	36,700	14,800	14,700	400	401
West Virginia	21,400	21,300	3,600	3,600	168	169
Wisconsin	69,800	69,000	14,600	14,500	209	210
Wyoming	11,500	11,700	30,200	30,400	2,626	2,598
United States	2,102,010	2,084,000	914,030	913,000	435	438
Puerto Rico	10,400	10,400	450	450	43	43

[1] A farm is any establishment from which $1,000 or more of agricultural products were sold or would normally be sold during the year.
NASS, Environmental, Economics, and Demographics Branch, (202) 720–6146.

Table 9-7.—Farms: Classification by tenure of operator, United States, 1935–2012

Year	Farms	Tenure of operator			
		Full owners	Part owners	Managers	All tenants
	Number	Percent	Percent	Percent	Percent
1935 [1]	6,812,350	47.1	10.1	0.7	42.1
1940	6,102,417	50.6	10.1	0.6	38.8
1945 [1]	5,859,169	56.4	11.3	0.7	31.7
1950	5,388,437	57.4	15.3	0.4	26.9
1954 [1]	4,783,021	57.4	18.2	0.4	24.0
1959	3,710,503	57.1	21.9	0.6	20.5
1964	3,157,857	57.6	24.8	0.6	17.1
1969	2,730,250	62.5	24.6		12.9
1974	2,314,013	61.5	27.2		11.3
1978	2,257,775	57.5	30.2		12.3
1982	2,240,976	59.2	29.3		11.6
1987	2,087,759	59.3	29.2		11.5
1992	1,925,300	57.7	31.0		11.3
1997	1,911,859	60.0	30.0		10.0
2002 [2]	2,128,982	67.1	25.9		7.0
2007 [2]	2,204,792	69.0	24.6		6.4
2012 [2]	2,109,303	67.7	25.3		7.0

[1] Excludes Alaska and Hawaii.　[2] The 2002 Census of Agriculture introduced new methodology to account for all farms in the United States.　All 2002 published census items were reweighted for undercoverage.　Strictly speaking, data for 2002 and subsequent years are not fully comparable with data from earlier years.

ERS, Resource and Rural Economics Division, (202) 694–5572.　Data from the Census of Agriculture, National Agricultural Statistics Service.

Table 9-8.—Farmland Rented: Classification by tenants and part owners, United States, 1910–2012

Year	Land in farms	Land rented by tenure of operator [1]			Percentage of land rented
		Tenants	Part owners	Total	
	Million acres	Million acres	Million acres	Million acres	Percent
1910	878.8	225.5	[2] 51.3	277.8	31.6
1920	958.7	[3] 265.0	[4] 54.7	319.7	33.3
1925	924.3	264.9	96.3	361.2	39.1
1930	990.1	307.3	125.2	432.5	43.7
1935	1,054.5	336.8	134.3	471.1	44.7
1940	1,065.1	313.2	155.9	469.1	44.0
1945	1,141.6	251.6	178.9	430.5	37.7
1950	1,161.4	212.2	196.2	408.4	35.2
1954	1,158.2	192.6	212.3	404.9	35.0
1959	1,123.0	166.8	234.1	400.9	35.7
1964	1,110.2	144.9	248.1	[5] 393.0	35.4
1969	1,063.3	137.6	241.8	379.4	35.7
1974	1,017.0	122.3	258.4	380.7	37.4
1978	1,029.7	124.1	282.2	406.2	39.4
1982	986.2	113.6	269.9	383.5	38.9
1987	964.5	126.9	275.4	402.3	41.7
1992	945.5	122.7	282.2	404.9	42.8
1997	931.8	108.1	270.0	378.1	40.6
2002 [6]	938.3	86.5	266.8	353.3	37.7
2007 [6]	922.1	81.8	269.0	350.8	38.0
2012 [6]	914.5	82.9	268.1	351.0	38.4

[1] Columns 3, 4, and 5 refer only to land rented from others and operated, so subleased land is not included.　Acres of land rented are comparable in the same year, but definitions change over time.　Basic sources are 1969 Census of Agriculture, table 5, p.14; 1974 Census of Agriculture, table 3, pp.1-6; 1978 Census of Agriculture, vol. 1, part 51, table 5, pp. 124-127; 1982 Census of Agriculture, vol. 1, part 51, table 48, p. 49; 1987 Census of Agriculture vol. 1 part 51, table 48, p. 49; 1992 Census of Agriculture vol. 1, part 51, table 46, p. 53; 1997 Census of Agriculture, vol. 1, part 51, chapter 1, table 46, p. 57; 2002 Census of Agriculture, vol. 1, part 51, chapter 1, table 61, p. 214; 2007 Census of Agriculture, vol. 1, part 51, chapter 1, table 65, p. 262; 2012 Census of Agriculture, vol. 1, part 51, table 70, p. 231; and earlier census volumes as noted.　[2] Assumes land leased by part-owners is the difference between the average size of full-owner and part-owner farms.　Acreage leased by part-owners is this difference times the number of part-owners.　1910 Census of Agriculture, chapter 11, table 1 and 3, pp.97-99.　[3] 1920 Census of Agriculture, vol. VI, part 1, table 5, p. 19.　[4] Assumes same proportion of owner and part-owner as in 1910.　[5] 1964 Census of Agriculture, vol. II, chapter 8, p.757.　[6] The 2002 Census of Agriculture introduced new methodology to account for all farms in the United States.　All 2002 published census items were reweighted for undercoverage.　Strictly speaking, data for 2002 and subsequent years are not fully comparable with data from earlier years.

ERS, Resource and Rural Economics Division, (202) 694–5572.　Data from the Census of Agriculture, National Agricultural Statistics Service.

Table 9-9.—Land: Utilization, by State and United States, 2007

| State | Cropland | | | Grassland pasture | Forest land |
	Used for crops	Idle	Used only for pasture		
	1,000 acres	*1,000 acres*	*1,000 acres*	*1,000 acres*	*1,000 acres*
AL	2,070	406	627	2,642	22,587
AK	31	48	7	738	93,801
AZ	818	96	0	40,648	16,780
AR	7,409	94	736	3,293	18,596
CA	8,084	657	809	27,524	26,983
CO	8,110	2,076	1,242	28,871	18,236
CT	111	13	13	33	1,413
DE	404	10	9	23	383
DC	0	0	0	0	0
FL	2,098	90	571	5,558	15,649
GA	3,665	364	590	1,292	24,267
HI	72	49	23	738	1,552
ID	4,680	789	511	18,082	17,455
IL	22,778	970	309	1,940	4,363
IN	12,201	262	284	1,642	4,533
IA	24,277	1,608	845	2,460	2,864
KS	24,649	2,608	1,292	16,438	2,104
KY	5,395	676	1,550	3,516	11,686
LA	3,340	460	635	1,860	14,142
ME	341	85	37	105	17,355
MD	1,208	71	0	464	2,386
MA	139	14	16	54	2,240
MI	7,145	553	316	1,697	19,019
MN	19,857	1,745	740	3,020	15,572
MS	4,411	376	769	2,055	19,579
MO	13,301	1,372	1,887	8,423	14,838
MT	12,631	3,558	1,678	46,051	19,875
NE	19,495	1,221	896	23,191	1,234
NV	516	30	185	46,850	10,436
NH	76	10	17	90	4,422
NJ	415	24	40	51	1,472
NM	1,174	545	648	52,122	14,977
NY	3,594	266	280	2,414	16,168
NC	4,258	247	339	1,231	18,037
ND	23,290	3,569	817	11,935	699
OH	10,141	431	352	1,924	7,666
OK	9,169	890	2,781	18,707	7,620
OR	3,560	696	677	22,726	27,813
PA	4,325	513	427	1,123	16,119
RI	18	2	2	8	313
SC	1,536	201	264	795	12,646
SD	17,026	1,516	1,311	23,263	1,640
TN	4,406	410	1,203	2,093	13,913
TX	21,515	4,663	7,938	101,735	17,159
UT	1,137	198	403	26,120	16,058
VT	413	27	47	261	4,504
VA	2,570	194	487	2,463	15,350
WA	5,733	1,521	372	6,789	19,225
WV	678	51	192	1,249	11,833
WI	9,069	738	395	2,768	16,168
WY	1,657	141	420	44,653	7,661
US [1]	334,996	37,154	35,989	613,733	671,390

[1] Distributions may not add to totals due to rounding.
ERS, Resource and Rural Economics Division, (202) 694–5626. See notes to Table 9-13 for definitions and data sources. Estimates developed for years coinciding with a Census of Agriculture.

FARM RESOURCES, INCOME, AND EXPENSES

Table 9-10.—Land in farms: Irrigated land, by State and United States, 1969–2007 [1]

State	1969	1974	1978[2]	1982	1987	1992	1997	2002	2007
	1,000 acres	1,000 acres	1,000 acres	1,000 acres	1,000 acres	1,000 acres	1,000 acres	1,000 acres	1,000 acres
AL	11	14	59	66	84	82	80	109	113
AK	1	1	1	1	2	2	3	3	4
AZ	1,178	1,153	1,196	1,098	914	956	1,075	932	876
AR	1,010	949	1,683	2,022	2,406	2,702	3,785	4,150	4,461
CA	7,240	7,749	8,506	8,461	7,596	7,571	8,887	8,709	8,016
CO	2,895	2,874	3,431	3,201	3,014	3,170	3,374	2,591	2,868
CT	9	7	7	7	7	6	8	10	10
DE	20	20	34	44	61	62	75	97	105
FL	1,365	1,559	1,980	1,585	1,623	1,783	1,874	1,815	1,552
GA	79	112	463	575	640	725	773	871	1,018
HI	146	142	159	146	149	134	77	69	59
ID	2,761	2,859	3,475	3,450	3,219	3,260	3,544	3,289	3,300
IL	51	54	130	166	208	328	352	391	474
IN	34	33	75	132	170	241	256	313	397
IA	21	39	101	91	92	116	133	142	190
KS	1,522	2,010	2,686	2,675	2,463	2,680	2,696	2,678	2,763
KY	20	11	14	23	38	28	60	37	59
LA	702	702	681	694	647	898	961	939	954
ME	6	6	7	6	6	10	22	20	21
MD	22	23	28	39	51	57	69	81	93
MA	19	19	17	17	20	20	27	24	23
MI	77	97	226	286	315	366	407	456	500
MN	36	78	272	315	354	370	403	455	506
MS	150	162	309	431	637	883	1,110	1,176	1,369
MO	156	150	320	403	535	709	921	1,033	1,200
MT	1,841	1,759	2,070	2,023	1,997	1,978	2,102	1,976	2,013
NE	2,857	3,967	5,683	6,039	5,682	6,312	7,066	7,625	8,559
NV	753	778	881	830	779	556	764	747	691
NH	2	2	2	1	3	2	3	2	2
NJ	72	89	77	83	91	80	94	97	95
NM	823	867	891	807	718	738	852	845	830
NY	55	55	56	52	51	47	74	75	68
NC	59	51	90	81	138	113	156	264	232
ND	63	71	141	163	168	187	183	203	236
OH	22	22	25	28	32	29	35	41	38
OK	524	515	602	492	478	512	509	518	535
OR	1,519	1,561	1,881	1,808	1,648	1,622	1,963	1,908	1,845
PA	19	18	15	18	30	23	40	43	38
RI	2	2	3	2	4	3	3	4	4
SC	15	10	32	81	81	76	89	96	132
SD	148	152	335	376	362	371	367	401	374
TN	12	10	13	18	38	37	47	61	81
TX	6,888	6,594	6,947	5,576	4,271	4,912	5,764	5,075	5,010
UT	1,025	970	1,169	1,082	1,161	1,143	1,218	1,091	1,134
VT	(3)	1	1	1	2	2	3	2	2
VA	37	28	42	43	79	62	86	99	82
WA	1,224	1,309	1,639	1,638	1,519	1,641	1,787	1,823	1,736
WV	3	2	1	1	3	3	4	2	2
WI	106	128	235	259	285	331	358	386	377
WY	1,523	1,460	1,662	1,565	1,518	1,465	1,750	1,542	1,551
US	39,122	41,243	50,350	49,003	46,386	49,404	56,289	55,316	56,599
PR	91	70	54	42	36	46	35	43	40
VI	(3)	(3)	(4)	(4)	(4)	(4)	(4)	(3)	(3)
Total	39,213	41,313	50,350	49,002	46,386	49,404	55,058	55,360	56,639

[1] Data may not add because of rounding.   [2] Data for 1978 not directly comparable with earlier censuses as it includes estimates from the direct enumeration sample for farms not represented on the mail list.   [3] Less than 500 acres.   [4] Not available.   Note: Data from the Census of Agriculture, U.S. Department of Commerce.   Beginning in 1997 Census of Agriculture, U.S. Department of Agriculture.   Estimates developed for years coinciding with a Census of Agriculture.
ERS, Resource and Rural Economics Division, (202) 694–5626.

Table 9-11.—Land utilization, United States, selected years, 1959–2007

Major land uses	1959	1969	1978	1987	1992	1997	2002	2007
	Million acres	Million acres	Million acres	Million acres	Million acres	Million acres	Million acres	Million acres
Cropland used for crops [1]	359	333	369	331	338	349	340	335
Idle cropland	34	51	26	68	56	39	40	37
Cropland used for pasture [2]	66	88	76	65	67	68	62	36
Grassland pasture [3]	633	604	587	591	591	580	587	614
Forest land [4]	745	723	703	648	648	641	651	671
Special uses [5]	115	143	158	279	281	286	297	313
Urban areas [6]	27	31	45	57	59	66	60	61
Other land [7]	293	291	301	227	224	236	228	197
Total land area [8]	2,271	2,264	2,264	2,265	2,263	2,263	2,264	2,264

[1] Cropland harvested, crop failure, and cultivated summer fallow. [2] The 2007 estimate declined due to a change in the methodology for determining cropland used for pasture for non-respondents. [3] Grassland and other nonforest pasture and range. [4] Excludes reserved and other forest land duplicated in parks and special uses of land. Includes forested grazing land. [5] Includes rural transportation areas, Federal and State areas used primarily for recreation and wildlife purposes, military areas, farmsteads, and farm roads and lanes. [6] The 2002 urban acreage estimate is not directly comparable to estimates in prior years due to a change in the definition of urban areas in the 2000 Census of Population and Housing. The apparent change in "urban" acreage between 1997 and 2002 reflects a definitional change, rather than a decline in acreage. [7] Miscellaneous areas such as marshes, open swamps, bare rock areas, deserts, and other uses not inventoried. [8] Remeasurement and increases in reservoirs account for changes in total land areas except for the major increase in 1949 when data for Alaska and Hawaii were added.

ERS, Rural and Resource Economics Division, (202) 694–5626. Estimates based on reports and records of the U.S. Agriculture and Commerce Departments, and public land administering and conservation agencies. Estimates developed for years coinciding with a Census of Agriculture. See http://www.ers.usda.gov/data/majorlanduses for data and more information.

FARM RESOURCES, INCOME, AND EXPENSES

Table 9-12.—Farm real estate: Value of farmland and buildings, Region, State, and United States, 2009–2013 [1]

Region and State	Total value of land and buildings				
	2009	2010	2011	2012	2013
	Million dollars	*Million dollars*	*Million dollars*	*Million dollars*	*Million dollars*
Northeast:					
Connecticut	5,040	4,715	4,872	4,928	4,884
Delaware	4,366	4,065	4,151	4,157	4,085
Maine	2,982	2,870	2,912	3,002	3,150
Maryland	15,203	14,309	14,015	13,723	14,207
Massachusetts	6,240	5,936	5,777	5,408	5,408
New Hampshire	2,242	2,204	2,098	2,087	2,026
New Jersey	9,936	9,301	9,216	8,856	9,216
New York	17,040	17,040	17,395	19,027	18,720
Pennsylvania	39,424	38,633	38,380	40,810	41,811
Rhode Island	1,106	1,022	1,008	966	966
Vermont	3,542	3,596	3,695	3,825	4,000
Lake:					
Michigan	36,590	34,830	36,000	38,706	42,785
Minnesota	74,465	75,481	82,476	97,240	111,370
Wisconsin	55,130	53,655	56,648	60,006	59,860
Corn Belt:					
Illinois	119,705	126,968	145,530	167,049	190,990
Indiana	58,568	61,674	74,529	85,848	94,080
Iowa	116,046	133,110	165,546	199,818	235,620
Missouri	62,208	65,149	68,970	76,693	80,940
Ohio	52,807	53,284	57,408	64,960	71,400
Northern Plains:					
Kansas	46,662	48,972	57,164	69,611	80,675
Nebraska	60,060	66,738	83,536	109,626	126,840
North Dakota	30,373	32,430	36,735	45,588	60,915
South Dakota	38,237	41,013	47,197	57,589	73,177
Appalachian:					
Kentucky	37,800	37,252	36,300	36,920	39,260
North Carolina	35,785	34,608	36,022	36,415	36,456
Tennessee	35,534	37,368	37,908	38,368	38,913
Virginia	38,475	36,900	35,670	35,358	35,773
West Virginia	8,732	8,388	9,288	9,169	9,180
Southeast:					
Alabama	20,025	20,470	20,826	21,271	22,500
Florida	49,555	47,846	48,479	49,278	49,660
Georgia	39,494	36,569	35,017	31,296	31,350
South Carolina	14,357	14,750	14,900	14,960	14,811
Delta States:					
Arkansas	32,058	32,880	33,428	36,156	37,260
Louisiana	15,662	16,298	17,270	18,960	20,018
Mississippi	21,816	22,672	23,980	24,525	24,743
Southern Plains:					
Oklahoma	40,135	41,640	43,344	47,128	49,880
Texas	201,807	210,560	219,605	220,038	218,568
Mountain:					
Arizona [2]	15,846	13,298	13,796	17,960	18,506
Colorado	34,430	34,020	34,760	37,323	40,576
Idaho	25,300	24,265	23,896	25,252	26,196
Montana	42,350	42,420	43,097	45,448	47,163
Nevada [2]	4,882	4,877	4,838	5,071	5,113
New Mexico [2]	18,861	18,597	18,814	20,641	19,929
Utah [2]	12,773	12,840	12,773	12,773	13,439
Wyoming	15,900	16,200	16,800	17,936	18,120
Pacific:					
California	167,790	169,830	170,752	176,128	175,950
Oregon	28,851	29,646	30,780	31,948	32,505
Washington	29,054	29,638	30,076	33,222	34,040
United States [3]	1,845,244	1,890,827	2,027,677	2,223,067	2,397,034

[1] Total value of land and buildings is derived by multiplying average value per acre of farm real estate by the land in farms.   [2] Value of all land and buildings adjusted to include American Indian reservation land value.   [3] Excludes Alaska and Hawaii.

NASS, Environmental, Economics, and Demographics Branch, (202) 720–6146.

Table 9-13.—Farm real estate: Average value per acre - Region, State, and United States, 2010–2014

Region and State	2010	2011	2012	2013	2014
	Dollars	*Dollars*	*Dollars*	*Dollars*	*Dollars*
Northeast:	4,690	4,690	4,790	4,850	4,930
Connecticut	11,500	11,600	11,200	11,100	11,200
Delaware	8,130	8,140	8,150	8,170	8,180
Maine	2,050	2,080	2,070	2,100	2,080
Maryland	6,980	6,870	6,760	6,930	6,900
Massachusetts	11,200	10,900	10,400	10,400	10,400
New Hampshire	4,690	4,560	4,440	4,310	4,280
New Jersey	13,100	12,800	12,300	12,800	12,800
New York	2,400	2,450	2,650	2,600	2,700
Pennsylvania	5,050	5,070	5,300	5,430	5,600
Rhode Island	14,600	14,400	13,800	13,800	13,700
Vermont	2,900	2,980	3,060	3,200	3,260
Lake:	3,220	3,450	3,880	4,240	4,640
Michigan	3,490	3,600	3,890	4,300	4,700
Minnesota	2,870	3,160	3,740	4,300	4,750
Wisconsin	3,650	3,880	4,110	4,100	4,400
Corn Belt:	3,830	4,460	5,190	5,880	6,370
Illinois	4,720	5,390	6,210	7,100	7,520
Indiana	4,170	5,070	5,840	6,400	6,950
Iowa	4,350	5,410	6,530	7,700	8,500
Missouri	2,270	2,420	2,710	2,850	3,100
Ohio	3,850	4,160	4,640	5,100	5,550
Northern Plains:	1,080	1,290	1,620	1,960	2,280
Kansas	1,060	1,240	1,510	1,750	2,050
Nebraska	1,470	1,840	2,420	2,800	3,120
North Dakota	821	930	1,160	1,550	1,820
South Dakota	945	1,090	1,330	1,690	2,070
Appalachian:	3,480	3,520	3,530	3,610	3,690
Kentucky	2,780	2,750	2,840	3,020	3,150
North Carolina	4,120	4,340	4,330	4,340	4,510
Tennessee	3,460	3,510	3,520	3,570	3,600
Virginia	4,500	4,350	4,260	4,310	4,320
West Virginia	2,330	2,580	2,540	2,550	2,560
Southeast:	3,630	3,610	3,530	3,590	3,630
Alabama	2,300	2,340	2,390	2,500	2,600
Florida	5,090	5,130	5,160	5,200	5,250
Georgia	3,770	3,610	3,260	3,300	3,300
South Carolina	2,950	2,980	3,010	2,980	3,010
Delta:	2,210	2,300	2,440	2,520	2,640
Arkansas	2,400	2,440	2,620	2,700	2,850
Louisiana	2,050	2,200	2,400	2,550	2,670
Mississippi	2,080	2,200	2,250	2,270	2,340
Southern Plains:	1,520	1,580	1,620	1,630	1,790
Oklahoma	1,200	1,260	1,370	1,450	1,580
Texas	1,600	1,670	1,690	1,680	1,850
Mountain:	902	899	953	1,010	1,070
Arizona[1]	3,390	3,330	3,370	3,500	3,740
Colorado	1,080	1,100	1,170	1,280	1,350
Idaho	2,110	2,060	2,140	2,220	2,360
Montana	700	710	760	790	860
Nevada[1]	997	995	1,040	1,040	1,080
New Mexico[1]	460	470	520	500	540
Utah[1]	1,810	1,800	1,800	1,900	2,030
Wyoming	540	560	590	600	630
Pacific:	4,070	4,100	4,270	4,290	4,520
California	6,660	6,670	6,880	6,900	7,300
Oregon	1,830	1,900	1,960	1,970	2,050
Washington	2,030	2,060	2,260	2,300	2,500
United States[2]	2,150	2,300	2,520	2,730	2,950

[1] Excludes American Indian Reservation Land.   [2] Excludes Alaska and Hawaii.
NASS, Environmental, Economics, and Demographics Branch, (202) 720–6146.

Table 9-14.—Land values, cropland and pasture: Region, State, and United States, 2010–2014

Region and State	Cropland				
	2010	2011	2012	2013	2014
	Dollars	Dollars	Dollars	Dollars	Dollars
Northeast:	5,270	5,200	5,280	5,260	5,260
Delaware	7,930	7,840	7,850	7,870	7,880
Maryland	6,790	6,680	6,570	6,470	6,470
New Jersey	13,300	12,900	12,400	12,900	13,000
New York	2,400	2,400	2,600	2,550	2,530
Pennsylvania	5,710	5,630	5,760	5,840	5,840
Other States [1] ..	7,220	7,170	7,120	7,060	7,020
Lake:	3,010	3,310	3,790	4,240	4,670
Michigan	3,160	3,370	3,660	4,120	4,500
Minnesota	2,710	3,070	3,740	4,390	4,870
Wisconsin	3,550	3,780	4,000	4,010	4,350
Corn Belt:	4,090	4,810	5,600	6,470	7,000
Illinois	4,720	5,480	6,300	7,190	7,700
Indiana	4,270	5,070	5,840	6,590	7,050
Iowa	4,450	5,600	6,810	8,000	8,750
Missouri	2,600	2,790	3,120	3,500	3,810
Ohio	3,900	4,160	4,640	5,190	5,650
Northern Plains:	1,410	1,730	2,210	2,720	3,090
Kansas	1,110	1,340	1,650	1,930	2,260
Nebraska	2,430	3,130	4,190	4,860	5,180
North Dakota	840	987	1,260	1,750	2,050
South Dakota ...	1,520	1,790	2,200	2,840	3,430
Appalachian:	3,490	3,440	3,550	3,690	3,780
Kentucky	3,070	3,080	3,210	3,430	3,550
North Carolina ..	3,650	3,610	3,850	4,050	4,200
Tennessee	3,310	3,270	3,260	3,340	3,400
Virginia	4,600	4,350	4,500	4,450	4,460
West Virginia	3,300	3,340	3,250	3,200	3,210
Southeast:	3,800	3,810	3,710	3,690	3,730
Alabama	2,630	2,680	2,750	2,750	2,850
Florida	6,550	6,580	6,420	6,450	6,500
Georgia	3,390	3,360	3,130	3,080	3,080
South Carolina	2,560	2,590	2,620	2,440	2,460
Delta:	1,890	2,020	2,160	2,380	2,510
Arkansas	1,910	1,990	2,180	2,380	2,540
Louisiana	1,800	1,970	2,120	2,260	2,380
Mississippi	1,950	2,100	2,180	2,470	2,570
Southern Plains:	1,400	1,450	1,500	1,480	1,630
Oklahoma	1,130	1,130	1,280	1,390	1,500
Texas	1,510	1,580	1,590	1,520	1,680
Mountain:	1,520	1,540	1,600	1,780	1,690
Arizona [2]	7,750	7,610	7,960	8,290	8,320
Colorado	1,290	1,340	1,450	1,770	1,840
Idaho	2,480	2,470	2,580	2,850	3,040
Montana	779	806	852	890	987
Nevada [2]	(D)	(D)	(D)	(D)	2,670
New Mexico [2] ...	1,750	1,740	1,550	1,450	1,450
Utah [2]	2,720	2,690	2,690	3,230	3,260
Wyoming	1,230	1,320	1,360	1,360	1,370
Pacific:	4,980	5,070	5,310	5,690	5,860
California	8,960	9,130	9,400	9,860	10,140
Oregon	2,210	2,180	2,340	2,400	2,500
Washington	1,870	1,930	2,190	2,420	2,560
United States [4]	2,700	2,980	3,350	3,810	4,100

See footnote(s) at end of table.

Table 9-14.—Land values, cropland and pasture: Region, State, and United States, 2010–2014—Continued

Region, State, and land type	Irrigated and Non-Irrigated Cropland				
	2010	2011	2012	2013	2014
	Dollars	Dollars	Dollars	Dollars	Dollars
Corn Belt:					
Missouri all cropland	2,600	2,790	3,120	3,500	3,810
Irrigated	3,140	3,320	3,640	4,140	4,750
Non-irrigated	2,560	2,750	3,080	3,450	3,730
Northern Plains:					
Kansas all cropland	1,110	1,340	1,650	1,930	2,260
Irrigated	1,540	1,810	2,250	2,760	3,280
Non-irrigated	1,060	1,290	1,590	1,840	2,150
Nebraska all cropland	2,430	3,130	4,190	4,860	5,180
Irrigated	3,050	4,080	5,610	6,700	7,100
Non-irrigated	2,030	2,510	3,270	3,730	4,000
South Dakota all cropland	1,520	1,790	2,200	2,840	3,430
Irrigated	(D)	(D)	(D)	(D)	(D)
Non-irrigated	1,510	1,780	2,190	2,820	3,400
Southeast:					
Florida all cropland	6,550	6,580	6,420	6,450	6,500
Irrigated	7,100	7,090	7,180	7,280	7,430
Non-irrigated	6,040	6,110	5,720	5,660	5,630
Georgia all cropland	3,390	3,360	3,130	3,080	3,080
Irrigated	3,090	3,140	2,980	3,120	3,430
Non-irrigated	3,480	3,420	3,170	3,070	2,950
Delta:					
Arkansas all cropland	1,910	1,990	2,180	2,380	2,540
Irrigated	2,160	2,300	2,530	2,790	3,000
Non-irrigated	1,630	1,640	1,790	1,760	1,840
Louisiana all cropland	1,800	1,970	2,120	2,260	2,380
Irrigated	1,700	1,850	2,000	2,150	2,270
Non-irrigated	1,830	2,000	2,150	2,300	2,420
Mississippi all cropland	1,950	2,100	2,180	2,470	2,570
Irrigated	2,020	2,330	2,440	2,760	2,930
Non-irrigated	1,930	2,020	2,090	2,330	2,390
Southern Plains:					
Oklahoma all cropland	1,130	1,130	1,280	1,390	1,500
Irrigated	(D)	(D)	(D)	(D)	(D)
Non-irrigated	1,120	1,120	1,270	1,370	1,480
Texas all cropland	1,510	1,580	1,590	1,520	1,680
Irrigated	1,680	1,670	1,660	1,700	1,880
Non-irrigated	1,480	1,560	1,580	1,490	1,650

See footnote(s) at end of table.

Table 9-14.—Land values, cropland and pasture: Region, State, and United States, 2010–2014—Continued

Region, State, and land type	Irrigated and Non-Irrigated Cropland				
	2010	2011	2012	2013	2014
	Dollars	*Dollars*	*Dollars*	*Dollars*	*Dollars*
Mountain:					
Arizona all cropland[2]	7,750	7,610	7,960	8,290	8,320
Irrigated	7,750	7,610	7,960	8,290	8,320
Colorado all cropland	1,290	1,340	1,450	1,770	1,840
Irrigated	3,100	3,160	3,400	4,100	4,450
Non-irrigated	840	880	960	1,200	1,200
Idaho all cropland	2,480	2,470	2,580	2,850	3,040
Irrigated	3,820	3,820	4,040	4,240	4,600
Non-irrigated	1,230	1,210	1,210	1,310	1,320
Montana all cropland	779	806	852	890	987
Irrigated	2,690	2,690	2,690	2,780	2,950
Non-irrigated	600	630	680	710	800
Nevada all cropland[2]	(D)	(D)	(D)	(D)	2,670
Irrigated	(D)	(D)	(D)	(D)	2,670
New Mexico all cropland[2]	1,750	1,740	1,550	1,450	1,450
Irrigated	5,290	5,190	4,450	3,910	3,930
Non-irrigated	390	410	430	400	390
Utah all cropland[2]	2,720	2,690	2,690	3,230	3,260
Irrigated	5,050	5,000	5,000	5,200	5,250
Non-irrigated	1,040	1,030	1,030	1,100	1,120
Wyoming all cropland	1,230	1,320	1,360	1,360	1,370
Irrigated	2,010	2,140	2,170	2,140	2,190
Non-irrigated	720	(D)	(D)	(D)	780
Pacific:					
California all cropland	8,960	9,130	9,400	9,860	10,140
Irrigated	10,900	11,100	11,500	11,800	12,100
Non-irrigated	3,420	3,480	3,390	3,400	3,650
Oregon all cropland	2,210	2,180	2,340	2,400	2,500
Irrigated	3,520	3,470	3,920	3,940	4,140
Non-irrigated	1,730	1,710	1,770	1,830	1,900
Washington all cropland	1,870	1,930	2,190	2,420	2,560
Irrigated	4,650	5,130	6,190	7,240	7,670
Non-irrigated	1,140	1,080	1,130	1,170	1,230

See footnote(s) at end of table.

Table 9-14.—Land values, cropland and pasture: Region, State, and United States, 2010–2014-Continued

Region and State	Pasture				
	2010	2011	2012	2013	2014
	Dollars	Dollars	Dollars	Dollars	Dollars
Northeast:	3,170	3,220	3,240	3,370	3,460
Maryland	(D)	(D)	(D)	(D)	6,000
New Jersey	14,200	14,000	13,600	13,500	13,500
New York	1,100	1,200	1,250	1,240	1,330
Pennsylvania	2,530	2,640	2,650	2,770	2,900
Other States [5]	5,800	5,730	5,760	5,840	5,790
Lake:	1,710	1,710	1,740	1,870	1,950
Michigan	2,290	2,340	2,290	2,420	2,500
Minnesota	1,340	1,320	1,390	1,580	1,600
Wisconsin	2,000	2,000	2,010	2,000	2,150
Corn Belt:	1,900	2,000	2,130	2,290	2,360
Illinois	2,500	2,650	2,870	3,370	3,400
Indiana	2,340	2,390	2,450	2,500	2,550
Iowa	2,030	2,520	2,800	3,220	3,400
Missouri	1,600	1,610	1,700	1,790	1,850
Ohio	2,890	2,840	2,970	3,010	3,100
Northern Plains:	502	531	648	754	954
Kansas	761	773	938	1,150	1,300
Nebraska	459	503	617	643	900
North Dakota	357	389	458	578	750
South Dakota	429	453	561	667	860
Appalachian:	3,240	3,170	3,110	3,210	3,280
Kentucky	2,360	2,290	2,330	2,560	2,700
North Carolina	4,410	4,590	4,330	4,530	4,760
Tennessee	3,510	3,460	3,410	3,380	3,400
Virginia	4,400	4,060	3,920	3,930	3,930
West Virginia	1,840	2,010	1,980	1,990	2,000
Southeast:	4,190	3,900	3,700	3,770	3,790
Alabama	1,810	1,830	1,850	2,000	2,100
Florida	5,360	4,910	4,820	4,850	4,910
Georgia	5,220	4,750	3,910	3,850	3,650
South Carolina	2,950	2,980	2,960	2,820	2,900
Delta:	2,110	2,120	2,130	2,190	2,270
Arkansas	2,210	2,160	2,110	2,160	2,240
Louisiana	2,100	2,200	2,300	2,400	2,500
Mississippi	1,980	2,000	2,030	2,070	2,110
Southern Plains:	1,300	1,350	1,390	1,410	1,540
Oklahoma	987	985	1,060	1,210	1,360
Texas	1,370	1,430	1,460	1,450	1,580
Mountain:	518	523	550	594	611
Arizona [2]	920	(D)	(D)	(D)	940
Colorado	650	640	640	680	760
Idaho	1,260	1,230	1,220	1,220	1,220
Montana	530	530	570	580	640
Nevada [2]	(D)	(D)	(D)	(D)	(D)
New Mexico [2]	280	290	330	320	360
Utah [2]	920	920	920	950	1,050
Wyoming	420	450	480	470	490
Pacific:	1,660	1,620	1,590	1,590	1,610
California	2,790	2,710	2,680	2,650	2,700
Oregon	650	640	600	620	630
Washington	810	810	800	800	810
United States [4]	1,060	1,070	1,110	1,170	1,300

(D) Withheld to avoid disclosing data for individual operations.
[1] Includes: Connecticut, Maine, Massachusetts, New Hampshire, Rhode Island, and Vermont.   [2] Excludes American Indian Reservation land.   [3] Not published due to insufficient reports.   [4] Excludes Alaska and Hawaii.   [5] Other pasture States include Connecticut, Maine, Massachusetts, New Hampshire, Rhode Island, and Vermont.
NASS, Environmental, Economics, and Demographics Branch, (202) 720–6146.

Table 9-15.—Cash rents, cropland and pasture: By State, 2013–2014

State	2013				2014			
	Cropland	Irrigated cropland	Non-irrigated cropland	Pasture	Cropland	Irrigated cropland	Non-irrigated cropland	Pasture
	Dollars	Dollars	Dollars	Dollars	Dollars	Dollars	Dollars	Dollars
Alabama	54.50	119.00	51.00	20.00	54.50	93.00	53.00	21.00
Arizona	225.00	225.00	(S)	2.00	220.00	220.00	....	1.80
Arkansas	95.50	122.00	50.00	18.00	102.00	125.00	50.00	18.00
California	280.00	365.00	30.00	12.00	313.00	405.00	32.00	13.50
Colorado	72.00	125.00	27.00	4.60	74.50	140.00	28.00	4.80
Connecticut	(S)	(S)	64.00	(S)	(S)	(S)	62.00	(S)
Delaware	88.50	130.00	76.50	(S)	98.50	133.00	82.50	(S)
Florida	87.00	202.00	41.00	16.00	103.00	192.00	54.00	13.00
Georgia	98.50	174.00	62.00	24.00	111.00	195.00	62.00	27.00
Hawaii	264.00	330.00	175.00	13.50	254.00	375.00	140.00	15.00
Idaho	139.00	177.00	56.00	13.00	151.00	197.00	61.00	12.00
Illinois	223.00	228.00	223.00	53.00	234.00	262.00	233.00	38.00
Indiana	192.00	240.00	190.00	37.00	195.00	260.00	193.00	40.00
Iowa	255.00	245.00	255.00	49.00	260.00	255.00	260.00	50.00
Kansas	62.50	137.00	53.00	17.50	62.00	126.00	54.00	17.50
Kentucky	149.00	225.00	148.00	27.00	148.00	215.00	147.00	27.00
Louisiana	80.00	101.00	68.00	15.00	84.50	104.00	70.00	16.00
Maine	(S)	(S)	43.00	(S)	(S)	(S)	48.00	(S)
Maryland	91.00	132.00	89.00	39.50	94.50	143.00	92.00	43.50
Massachusetts	65.00	185.00	51.00	(S)	73.00	190.00	62.00	(S)
Michigan	118.00	220.00	110.00	26.00	123.00	225.00	115.00	30.00
Minnesota	178.00	205.00	177.00	28.00	186.00	210.00	185.00	26.00
Mississippi	104.00	130.00	79.00	17.00	113.00	135.00	83.00	17.00
Missouri	121.00	176.00	113.00	29.00	132.00	173.00	127.00	29.00
Montana	31.50	86.00	23.50	6.00	32.50	81.00	25.50	5.60
Nebraska	203.00	260.00	147.00	20.00	205.00	262.00	149.00	20.50
Nevada	155.00	155.00	(S)	14.00	150.00	150.00	....	13.00
New Hampshire	(S)	(S)	37.00	(S)	(S)	(S)	34.00	(S)
New Jersey	67.50	95.00	60.00	28.00	66.00	100.00	57.00	(S)
New Mexico	105.00	145.00	19.00	2.80	93.00	150.00	17.00	3.00
New York	53.50	155.00	52.00	17.50	55.50	160.00	54.00	20.00
North Carolina	77.50	90.00	77.00	26.00	84.50	100.00	84.00	26.00
North Dakota	65.00	165.00	64.00	15.00	68.00	166.00	67.00	16.00
Ohio	139.00	150.00	139.00	25.00	144.00	165.00	144.00	25.00
Oklahoma	33.50	70.00	32.00	12.00	33.50	64.00	32.00	12.00
Oregon	122.00	180.00	65.00	18.00	149.00	200.00	90.00	15.00
Pennsylvania	73.50	128.00	73.00	35.00	78.50	130.00	78.00	27.00
Rhode Island	(S)	(S)	(S)	(S)	(S)	(S)	(S)	(S)
South Carolina	41.50	79.00	39.00	18.00	43.00	85.00	40.00	18.00
South Dakota	105.00	190.00	104.00	20.00	116.00	193.00	114.00	22.00
Tennessee	92.00	160.00	89.00	20.00	101.00	165.00	98.00	20.00
Texas	35.50	82.00	24.00	6.50	38.50	87.00	27.00	6.50
Utah	57.50	82.00	21.00	6.00	68.00	91.00	25.00	5.00
Vermont	(S)	(S)	43.00	23.00	(S)	(S)	48.00	21.00
Virginia	52.00	85.00	50.00	21.00	56.00	100.00	54.00	21.00
Washington	212.00	360.00	67.00	11.00	205.00	340.00	74.00	9.00
West Virginia	(S)	(S)	40.00	12.00	40.00	....	40.00	13.00
Wisconsin	124.00	220.00	120.00	35.00	135.00	240.00	130.00	34.00
Wyoming	64.50	89.00	14.00	4.50	61.00	91.00	14.00	5.00

(S) Not published due to insufficient reports.
NASS, Environmental, Economics, and Demographics Branch, (202) 720–6146.

Table 9-16.—Farm assets and claims: Comparative balance sheet of the farming sector, excluding operator households, United States, Dec. 31, 2005–2014

Item	2005	2006	2007	2008	2009
Assets	Billion dollars	Billion dollars	Billion dollars	Billion dollars	Billion dollars
Physical assets:					
Real estate	1,372.6	1,536.6	1,549.0	1,566.6	1,554.1
Non-real estate:					
Livestock and poultry [1]	87.8	86.7	89.4	86.2	80.3
Machinery and motor vehicles [2]	144.3	155.3	194.8	188.7	191.2
Crops [3]	33.4	41.1	54.2	58.8	53.4
Purchased inputs	10.7	11.7	16.0	19.5	18.7
Financial	56.5	70.1	55.6	78.8	67.0
Total	1,709.4	1,906.7	1,961.9	2,003.6	1,970.1
Claims					
Liabilities:					
Real estate	113.9	113.4	131.7	147.9	146.0
Non-real estate	95.2	102.3	109.0	113.2	122.4
Total liabilities [4]	209.1	215.7	240.7	261.1	268.3
Equity	1,500.3	1,691.0	1,721.2	1,742.5	1,701.7
Ratio:	Percent	Percent	Percent	Percent	Percent
Debt/equity	13.9	12.8	14.0	15.0	15.8
Debt/assets	12.2	11.3	12.3	13.0	13.6

Item	2010	2011	2012	2013	2014
Assets	Billion dollars	Billion dollars	Billion dollars	Billion dollars	Billion dollars
Physical assets:					
Real estate	1,651.4	1,795.1	2,073.1	2,252.9	2,378.7
Non-real estate:					
Livestock and poultry [1]	90.7	101.4	95.7	110.8	127.8
Machinery and motor vehicles [2]	206.9	223.3	244.0	247.0	245.1
Crops [3]	57.2	62.5	64.8	60.5	61.7
Purchased inputs	19.8	21.0	21.5	20.6	20.1
Financial	129.6	101.5	131.9	78.4	103.1
Total	2,161.4	2,310.6	2,637.7	2,777.8	2,944.3
Claims					
Liabilities:					
Real estate	154.1	167.2	173.2	184.8	196.3
Non-real estate debt to	124.9	127.3	123.8	130.2	149.4
Total liabilities [4]	278.9	294.5	297.0	315.0	345.7
Equity	1,882.4	2,016.2	2,340.7	2,462.8	2,598.6
Ratio:	Percent	Percent	Percent	Percent	Percent
Debt/equity	14.8	14.6	12.7	12.8	13.3
Debt/assets	12.9	12.7	11.3	11.3	11.7

Note: Data as of February 9, 2016. [1] The U.S. total exceeds the sum of the states because NASS does not release state data for some minor producing states due to disclosure issues. Horses and mules are excluded. [2] Includes only farm share value for trucks and autos. [3] All non-CCC crops held on farms plus the value above loan rate for crops held under CCC. [4] Excludes debt for nonfarm purposes.
ERS, Farm Income Team. http://www.ers.usda.gov/data-products/farm-income-and-wealth-statistics.aspx.

Table 9-17.—Farm labor: Number of workers on farms and average wage rates, United States, 2006–2014

Year	Ag service workers [1]	Hired workers [2]	Wage rate [3]
	Thousands	*Thousands*	*Dollars Per Hour*
2006			
Jan	180	614	10.10
Apr	241	720	9.78
July	320	876	9.72
Oct	286	800	9.96
Annual average	([4])	751.8	9.87
2007			
Jan	([5])	([5])	([5])
Apr	253	736	10.20
July	363	843	9.99
Oct	329	817	10.38
Annual average	([4])	746.5	10.23
2008			
Jan	179	594	10.81
Apr	219	700	10.57
July	345	847	10.37
Oct	316	813	10.72
Annual average	([4])	738.5	10.60
2009			
Jan	190	603	10.93
Apr	223	694	10.86
July	363	892	10.66
Oct	285	829	10.93
Annual average	([4])	754.5	10.83
2010			
Jan	190	612	11.08
Apr	261	746	10.82
July	360	885	10.79
Oct	330	827	11.13
Annual average	([4])	767.5	10.95
2011			
Jan	205	603	11.30
Apr	([5])	([5])	([5])
July	350	834	10.93
Oct	313	828	11.15
Annual average	([4])	748.8	11.07
2012			
Jan		575	11.52
Apr		748	11.41
July		906	11.36
Oct		876	11.75
Annual average		776.3	11.51
2013			
Jan		596	12.02
Apr		736	11.89
July		906	11.68
Oct		871	11.96
Annual average		777.3	11.87
2014			
Jan		540	12.23
Apr		690	12.01
July		838	11.96
Oct		782	12.12
Annual average		712.5	12.07

[1] Includes all workers who performed any farm-related service on a farm or ranch on a contract or fee basis, paid during the survey week. This data series was discontinued after year 2011. [2] Includes all workers, other than agricultural service workers, who were paid for at least one hour of agricultural work on a farm or ranch during the survey week. [3] Applies to hired workers only (excludes pay for agricultural service workers). [4] Annual average not computed. [5] The Farm Labor Survey was not conducted for this quarter.

NASS, Economic, Environmental and Demographics Branch, (202) 720–6146.

Table 9-18.—Farm labor: Number of hired workers on farms and average wage rates, by regions and United States, 2014 [1]

Region [2]	Workers on farms	Farm wage rates			
	Hired	Type of worker			
		Field	Livestock	Field and livestock	All hired workers [3]
	Thousands	*Dollars per hour*	*Dollars per hour*	*Dollars per hour*	*Dollars per hour*
January 12–18, 2014					
Northeast I	23	11.46	10.62	10.95	12.38
Northeast II	25	12.09	11.64	11.90	12.80
Appalachian I	21	10.64	10.33	10.50	11.52
Appalachian II	14	9.18	10.38	9.75	10.68
Southeast	19	10.30	9.99	10.20	11.23
Florida	47	10.15	10.50	10.20	11.33
Lake	42	12.43	11.34	11.65	12.52
Cornbelt I	22	12.52	11.16	11.70	12.82
Cornbelt II	13	14.78	13.37	13.90	15.25
Delta	22	10.40	10.13	10.30	10.56
Northern Plains	28	14.15	12.60	13.35	14.07
Southern Plains	39	10.29	10.70	10.50	11.15
Mountain I	18	11.17	11.14	11.15	12.29
Mountain II	12	11.42	12.41	12.20	12.62
Mountain III	15	10.67	11.54	10.95	11.60
Pacific	42	11.66	12.06	11.75	12.83
California	131	10.75	11.80	10.92	12.13
Hawaii	7	13.45	14.55	13.55	15.96
United States	540	11.10	11.36	11.20	12.23
April 6–12, 2014					
Northeast I	36	11.28	10.96	11.15	12.20
Northeast II	35	11.59	12.10	11.75	12.55
Appalachian I	27	10.59	10.13	10.45	11.30
Appalachian II	20	9.86	10.30	10.10	11.02
Southeast	28	9.82	9.64	9.78	10.50
Florida	50	10.10	10.65	10.16	11.28
Lake	53	11.42	11.57	11.50	12.23
Cornbelt I	32	12.34	11.08	11.80	12.59
Cornbelt II	21	13.22	13.41	13.30	14.25
Delta	28	10.12	9.85	10.05	10.30
Northern Plains	34	13.43	12.82	13.15	13.84
Southern Plains	49	9.75	10.58	10.10	10.66
Mountain I	24	11.11	10.82	10.95	11.68
Mountain II	16	10.86	12.12	11.58	11.91
Mountain III	13	10.30	11.95	10.90	11.66
Pacific	54	11.45	12.05	11.55	12.29
California	163	11.00	11.70	11.09	12.28
Hawaii	7	13.30	14.65	13.42	15.85
United States	690	11.02	11.35	11.12	12.01

See footnote(s) at end of table.

Table 9-18.—Farm labor: Number of hired workers on farms and average wage rates, by regions and United States, 2014[1]—Continued

Region[2]	Workers on farms	Type of worker			
	Hired	Field	Livestock	Field and livestock	All hired workers[3]
	Thousands	*Dollars per hour*	*Dollars per hour*	*Dollars per hour*	*Dollars per hour*
July 6–12, 2014					
Northeast I	47	11.60	10.73	11.30	12.04
Northeast II	44	10.52	11.17	10.70	11.25
Appalachian I	46	10.09	10.33	10.15	10.69
Appalachian II	31	9.99	11.07	10.35	10.99
Southeast	27	9.80	10.86	10.00	10.68
Florida	36	10.05	10.65	10.13	11.03
Lake	61	11.30	11.40	11.35	11.87
Cornbelt I	35	11.39	11.27	11.35	11.92
Cornbelt II	19	11.77	11.84	11.80	13.01
Delta	27	10.20	9.99	10.15	10.47
Northern Plains	36	14.09	12.99	13.65	14.09
Southern Plains	59	10.15	10.35	10.25	10.74
Mountain I	28	11.53	11.03	11.30	11.74
Mountain II	20	11.00	10.99	11.00	11.49
Mountain III	20	9.91	11.25	10.35	11.25
Pacific	118	12.70	12.78	12.70	13.03
California	177	11.50	11.90	11.57	12.42
Hawaii	7	12.35	13.75	12.48	14.96
United States	838	11.36	11.26	11.33	11.96
October 12–18, 2014					
Northeast I	45	11.77	10.74	11.45	12.09
Northeast II	34	11.27	11.20	11.25	11.88
Appalachian I	43	10.32	10.45	10.35	10.87
Appalachian II	28	10.42	10.83	10.55	11.11
Southeast	24	9.93	10.76	10.10	10.82
Florida	40	10.25	10.45	10.28	11.00
Lake	63	12.09	11.35	11.75	12.24
Cornbelt I	38	11.82	11.19	11.65	12.08
Cornbelt II	25	12.24	12.12	12.20	13.07
Delta	28	10.34	9.94	10.25	10.50
Northern Plains	36	14.55	13.17	14.05	14.52
Southern Plains	55	10.61	10.48	10.55	10.91
Mountain I	28	11.43	10.85	11.15	11.66
Mountain II	18	11.01	11.10	11.05	11.68
Mountain III	20	9.67	11.21	10.15	10.98
Pacific	81	13.04	12.55	13.00	13.42
California	169	11.45	12.05	11.56	12.54
Hawaii	7	12.30	13.95	12.46	15.04
United States	782	11.52	11.29	11.46	12.12

[1] Includes all workers, other than agricultural service workers, who were paid for at least one hour of agricultural work on a farm or ranch during the survey week.   [2] Multi-state regions consist of the following: Northeast I: Connecticut, Maine, Massachusetts, New Hampshire, New York, Rhode Island, Vermont; Northeast II: Delaware, Maryland, New Jersey, Pennsylvania; Appalachian I: North Carolina, Virginia; Appalachian II: Kentucky, Tennessee, West Virginia; Southeast: Alabama, Georgia, South Carolina; Lake: Michigan, Minnesota, Wisconsin; Cornbelt I: Illinois, Indiana, Ohio; Cornbelt II: Iowa, Missouri; Delta: Arkansas, Louisiana, Mississippi; Northern Plains: Kansas, Nebraska, North Dakota, South Dakota; Southern Plains: Oklahoma, Texas; Mountain I: Idaho, Montana, Wyoming; Mountain II: Colorado, Nevada, Utah; Mountain III: Arizona, New Mexico; Pacific: Oregon, Washington.   [3] Includes field workers, livestock workers, supervisors, and others, excluding agricultural service workers.

NASS, Economic, Environmental and Demographics Branch, (202) 720–6146.

Table 9-19.—Farm production and output: Index numbers of total output, and production of livestock, crops, and secondary output, by groups, United States, 2000–2009

[2005=100]

Year	Total farm output	Livestock and products			
		All livestock and products [1]	Meat animals [2]	Dairy products [3]	Poultry and eggs [4]
2000	0.9662	0.9764	1.0143	0.9446	0.9040
2001	0.9681	0.9743	1.0169	0.9334	0.9187
2002	0.9509	0.9862	1.0022	0.9608	0.9555
2003	0.9730	1.0014	1.0022	0.9624	1.0088
2004	1.0128	0.9803	0.9957	0.9652	0.9680
2005	1.0000	1.0000	1.0000	1.0000	1.0000
2006	0.9882	1.0244	1.0147	1.0277	1.0299
2007	1.0200	1.0252	1.0186	1.0496	1.0388
2008	1.0326	1.0323	1.0108	1.0744	1.0552
2009	1.0590	1.0227	1.0128	1.0709	1.0068

Year	Crops				
	All crops	Food Grains	Feed crops	Oil crops [5]	Vegetables and melons
2000	0.9525	1.0127	0.9485	0.8783	1.0110
2001	0.9503	0.9330	0.9303	0.9345	0.9761
2002	0.9114	0.8004	0.8779	0.8768	1.0053
2003	0.9486	1.0662	0.9633	0.7998	0.9828
2004	1.0399	1.0291	1.0616	0.9957	1.0299
2005	1.0000	1.0000	1.0000	1.0000	1.0000
2006	0.9482	0.8626	0.9388	1.0066	0.9806
2007	1.0231	0.9613	1.0997	0.8578	0.9834
2008	1.0450	1.1408	1.0492	0.9440	0.9735
2009	1.1012	1.0504	1.1018	1.0469	0.9584

Year	Crops		Farm-related output [5]
	Fruits and nuts	Other crops	
2000	1.0808	0.9098	1.0285
2001	1.0544	0.9190	1.0999
2002	1.0603	0.9425	1.0616
2003	1.0696	0.9627	0.9921
2004	1.1021	1.0150	1.0394
2005	1.0000	1.0000	1.0000
2006	1.0910	0.8320	1.0606
2007	1.1719	1.0426	0.9241
2008	1.2539	1.1742	0.8838
2009	1.2241	1.4187	0.8416

[1] Includes wool, mohair, horses, mules, honey, beeswax, bees, goats, rabbits, aquaculture, and fur animals.　These items are not included in the separate groups of livestock and products shown.　[2] Cattle and calves, sheep and lambs, and hogs.　[3] Butter, butterfat, wholesale milk, retail milk, and milk consumed on farms.　[4] Chicken eggs, commercial broilers, chickens, and turkeys.　[5] These activities are defined as activities closely linked to agriculture for which information on production and input use cannot be separately observed.

ERS, Agricultural Structure and Productivity Branch, (202) 694–5460, (202) 694–5601.

Table 9-20.—Hired farmworkers: Number of Workers and Median Weekly Earnings, 2012–2014 [1]

Characteristics	Workers			Median Weekly Earnings [2]		
	2012	2013	2014	2012	2013	2014
	Thousands	Thousands	Thousands	Dollars	Dollars	Dollars
All workers	787	759	828	400	400	400
15–19 years old	80	78	72	184	200	184
20–24 years old	119	112	101	360	362	400
25–34 years old	189	195	203	450	468	450
35–44 years old	154	145	161	400	450	438
45–54 years old	128	122	142	433	461	462
55 years old and older	118	107	149	423	478	470
Male	646	615	670	420	440	447
Female	141	144	158	320	330	360
White [3]	397	359	404	425	460	461
Black and other races [3]	35	45	44	*	*	*
Hispanic	355	354	380	400	400	400
Schooling completed						
Less than 5th grade	71	71	69	360	380	360
5th-8th grade	145	127	155	365	368	400
9th-12th grade (no diploma)	150	140	156	400	350	380
High school diploma	227	242	238	441	450	440
Beyond high school	194	179	211	440	500	550
Full-time (35 or more hours per week) [4]	635	619	681	448	462	455
Part-time (less than 35 hours per week) [4]	147	138	146	174	162	201

* Insufficient number of reports to publish data.   [1] Represents annual average number of persons 15 years old and over in the civilian noninstitutional population who were employed as hired farm managers, supervisors, or laborers.   Employment estimates based on 12 monthly Current Population Survey microdata files.   Earnings estimates based on 12 monthly Current Population Survey Outgoing Rotation Group microdata files.   [2] "Median weekly earnings" is the earnings value that divides farmworkers into two equal-sized groups, one group having earnings above the median and the other group having earnings below the median.   "Earnings" refers to the weekly earnings the farmworker usually earns at a farmwork job, before deductions, and includes any overtime pay or commissions.   [3] Excludes persons of Hispanic origin.   [4] The sum of full-time and part-time workers will not equal the total because usual hours worked varies for some individuals.
ERS, Rural Economy Branch, (202) 694–5416.

Table 9-21.—Crops: Area, United States, 2005–2014

Year	Principal crops			Area planted total [3]	Commercial vegetables, harvested area	Fruits and nuts, bearing area [4]
	Area harvested					
	Feed grains [1]	Food grains [2]	Total [3]			
	1,000 acres	1,000 acres	1,000 acres	1,000 acres	1,000 acres	1,000 acres
2005	85,945	53,747	303,566	317,640	3,124.9	3,984.3
2006	80,090	49,895	294,453	315,645	3,083.2	3,929.6
2007	98,318	53,999	304,376	320,369	3,033.5	3,904.5
2008	91,071	59,298	309,225	325,632	2,935.3	3,987.1
2009	89,446	53,195	301.172	319,022	2,946.6	4,050.5
2010	89,984	50,768	303,619	315,414	2,827.2	4,091.5
2011	90,940	48,543	292,652	314,343	2,682.0	4,132.6
2012	96,639	51,687	306,855	324,304	2,762.1	4,113.1
2013	98,085	48,079	303,717	324,869	2,681.2	4,256.8
2014	93,009	49,558	309,047	326,786	2,672.9	4,301.4

[1] Corn for grain, oats, barley, and sorghum for grain.   [2] Wheat, rye, and rice.   [3] Crops included in area planted and area harvested are corn, sorghum, oats, barley, winter wheat, rye, durum wheat, other spring wheat, rice, soybeans, peanuts, sunflower, cotton, dry edible beans, potatoes, canola, proso millet, and sugarbeets. Harvested acreage for all hay, tobacco, and sugarcane are used in computing total area planted.   [4] Includes the following fruits and nuts: Citrus fruits—oranges, tangerines, Temples, grapefruit, lemons and tangelos; area is for the year of harvest; deciduous fruits—commercial apples, peaches, pears, grapes, cherries, plums, prunes, apricots, bananas, nectarines, figs, kiwifruit, olives, avocados, papayas, dates, berries, guavas, cranberries, pineapples (discontinued as of 2007 crop) and strawberries; nuts—almonds, hazelnuts, macadamias, pistachios, and walnuts.
NASS, Crops Branch, (202) 720–2127.

Table 9-22.—Crops: Area harvested and yield, United States, 2013–2014

Crop	Area harvested			Yield per acre	
	2013	2014	Unit	2013	2014
	1,000 acres	1,000 acres			
Grains and hay:					
Barley	3,040	2,443	Bushels	71.3	72.4
Corn for grain	87,451	83,136	Bushels	158.1	171.0
Corn for silage	6,281	6,371	Tons	18.8	20.1
Hay, all	57,897	57,092	Tons	2.33	2.45
Alfalfa	17,673	18,445	Tons	3.24	3.33
All other	40,224	38,647	Tons	1.93	2.03
Oats	1,009	1,029	Bushels	64.1	67.7
Proso millet	638	430	Bushels	28.9	31.4
Rice	2,469	2,919	Pounds	7,694	7,572
Rye	278	258	Bushels	27.4	27.9
Sorghum for grain	6,585	6,401	Bushels	59.6	67.6
Sorghum for silage	380	315	Tons	14.3	13.1
Wheat, all	45,332	46,381	Bushels	47.1	43.7
Winter	32,650	32,304	Bushels	47.3	42.6
Durum	1,338	1,337	Bushels	43.3	39.7
Other spring	11,344	12,740	Bushels	47.1	46.7
Oilseeds:					
Canola	1,264.5	1,555.7	Pounds	1,748	1,614
Cottonseed	(X)	(X)	Tons	(X)	(X)
Flaxseed	172	302	Bushels	19.5	21.1
Mustard Seed	43.4	31.2	Pounds	846	930
Peanuts	1,043.0	1,325.0	Pounds	4,001	3,932
Rapeseed	1.7	2.1	Pounds	1,141	1,233
Safflower	170.7	170.2	Pounds	1,232	1,226
Soybeans for beans	76,253	83,061	Bushels	44.0	47.8
Sunflower	1,464.6	1,507.6	Pounds	1,380	1,469
Cotton, tobacco and sugar crops:					
Cotton,	7,544.4	9,707.4	Pounds	821	795
Upland	7,345.0	9,518.0	Pounds	802	781
American Pima	199.4	189.4	Pounds	1,527	1,490
Sugarbeets	1,154.0	1,147.2	Tons	28.4	27.4
Sugarcane	910.8	874.1	Tons	33.8	35.3
Tobacco	355.7	378.4	Pounds	2,034	2,316
Dry beans, peas and lentils:					
Austrian winter peas [1]	14.1	16.8	Cwt	1,617	1,339
Dry edible beans [1]	1,316.3	1,665.7	Cwt	1,867	1,753
Dry edible peas [1]	797.0	899.5	Cwt	1,960	1,907
Lentils	347.0	259.0	Cwt	1,446	1,300
Wrinkled seed peas	(NA)	(NA)	Cwt	(NA)	(NA)
Potatoes and miscellaneous:					
Coffee (Hawaii)	8.2	7.9	Pounds	1,020	1,030
Hops	35.3	38.0	Pounds	1,962	1,868
Peppermint oil	68.5	63.1	Pounds	89	90
Potatoes, all	1,050.9	1,049.5	Cwt	414	426
Spring	72.9	71.1	Cwt	304	318
Summer	47.5	48.9	Cwt	363	322
Fall	930.5	929.5	Cwt	425	439
Spearmint oil	24.5	24.4	Pounds	119	114
Sweet potatoes	113.2	135.2	Cwt	219	219
Taro (Hawaii)	0.4	0.4	Pounds	(NA)	(NA)

(X) Not applicable.   (NA) Not available.
NASS, Crops Branch, (202) 720–2127.

Table 9-23.—Crops: Production and value, United States, 2013–2014

Crop	Unit	Production 2013	Production 2014	Value of production 2013	Value of production 2014
		Thousands	*Thousands*	*1,000 dollars*	*1,000 dollars*
Grains and hay:					
Barley	Bushels	216,745	176,794	1,265,798	869,742
Corn for grain	Bushels	13,828,964	14,215,532	61,927,548	52,372,215
Corn for silage	Bushels	118,296	128,048	(X)	(X)
Hay, all	Tons	135,002	139,798	19,814,822	19,185,254
Alfalfa	Tons	57,217	61,446	10,676,113	10,770,299
All other	Tons	77,785	78,352	9,138,709	8,414,955
Oats	Bushels	64,642	69,684	239,807	239,253
Proso millet	Bushels	18,436	13,483	84,915	43,007
Rice	Cwt	189,953	221,035	3,181,993	3,104,623
Rye	Bushels	7,626	7,189	60,598	55,770
Sorghum for grain	Bushels	392,331	432,575	1,716,927	1,670,431
Sorghum for silage	Bushels	5,420	4,123	(X)	(X)
Wheat, all	Bushels	2,134,979	2,025,651	14,604,442	11,923,931
Winter	Bushels	1,542,902	1,377,526	10,590,949	8,060,580
Durum	Bushels	57,976	53,087	432,733	462,316
Other Spring	Bushels	534,101	595,038	3,580,760	3,401,035
Oilseeds:					
Canola	Pounds	2,210,505	2,510,995	456,448	425,796
Cottonseed	Tons	4,203.0	5,314.0	1,054,003	1,055,449
Flaxseed	Bushels	3,356	6,368.0	46,325	75,807
Mustard Seed	Pounds	36,727	29,004	13,648	10,089
Peanuts	Pounds	4,173,170	5,210,100	1,055,095	1,122,276
Rapeseed	Pounds	1,940	2,590	486	903
Safflower	Pounds	210,238	208,643	58,615	52,146
Soybeans for beans	Bushels	3,357.984	3,968,823	43,582,901	40,288,536
Sunflower	Pounds	2,021,765	2,214,835	443,296	504,596
Cotton, tobacco and sugar crops:					
Cotton, all	Bales	12,909.2	16,084.0	5,191,505	5,069,020
Upland	Bales	12,275.0	15,496.0	4,668,229	4,625,841
American Pima	Bales	634.2	588.0	523,276	443,179
Sugarbeets	Tons	32,789	31,386	1,536,422	....
Sugarcane	Tons	30,761	30,869	962,807	....
Tobacco[1]	Pounds	723,579	876,415	1,574,982	1,837,981
Dry Beans, peas and lentils:					
Austrian winter peas	Cwt	228	225	5,088	5,577
Dry edible beans	Cwt	24,576	29,206	982,385	1,015,485
Chickpeas, all[2]	Cwt	3,559	2,808	101,776	65,738
Large[3]	Cwt	2,746	1,904	83,213	46,265
Small[4]	Cwt	813	904	18,563	19,473
Dry edible peas	Cwt	15,620	17,155	227,601	192,899
Lentils	Cwt	5,019	3,367	100,032	77,939
Wrinkled seed peas	Cwt	275	618	7,453	17,208
Potatoes and miscellaneous:					
Coffee (Hawaii)	Pounds	8,400	8,100	52,080	54,270
Hops	Pounds	69,246.1	70,995.9	232,308	271,992
Maple syrup	Gallon	3,523	3,167	131,766	....
Mushrooms	Pounds	888,252	899,833	1,103,886	1,115,381
Peppermint oil	Pounds	6,115	5,692	146,260	130,704
Potatoes, all	Cwt	434,652	446,693	4,222,628	3,847,616
Spring	Cwt	22,137	22,608	389,961	....
Summer	Cwt	17,240	15,756	252,837	....
Fall	Cwt	395,275	408,329	3,579,830	....
Spearmint oil	Pounds	2,926	2,784	55,283	54,977
Sweet potatoes	Cwt	24,785	29,584	597,217	698,928
Taro (Hawaii)	Pounds ...	3,100	3,240	1,922	1,944

(X) Not applicable.   [1] Excludes estimated 2012 value of production for Connecticut Massachusetts.   [2] Chickpeas included with dry edible beans.   [3] Chickpeas (or Garbanzo beans) larger than 20/64 inches.   [4] Chickpeas (or Garbanzo beans) smaller than 20/64 inches.
NASS, Crops Branch, (202) 720–2127.

Table 9-24.—Fruits and nuts: Bearing acreage and yield, United States, 2013–2014

Crop	Bearing acreage		Yield per acre		
	2013	2014	Unit	2012	2014
	Acres	*Acres*			
Noncitrus fruits:					
Apples	328,620	327,380	Tons	15.80	17.20
Apricots	10,850	10,840	Tons	5.63	5.92
Avocados	59,600	....	Tons	3.02	....
Bananas (Hawaii)[1]	900	....	Tons	8.06	....
Blackberries (Oregon)[1][2]	6,000	6,100	Tons	4.25	3.65
Blueberries					
Cultivated[1]	80,460	82,630	Tons	3.24	3.35
Wild (Maine)[3]	(NA)	21,400	Tons	(NA)	2.44
Boysenberries (Oregon)[1]	500	500	Tons	2.30	2.55
Raspberries[1]					
Black (Oregon)	1,000	1,650	Tons	1.33	2.50
Red	11,200	16,400	Tons	3.28	5.26
All (California)	5,600	18,050	Tons	8.40	5.01
Cherries, Sweet	90,100	90,000	Tons	3.69	4.24
Cherries, Tart	38,150	37,950	Tons	3.86	3.81
Cranberries	42,000	40,500	Tons	10.70	10.80
Dates (California)	8,200	8,200	Tons	3.41	3.66
Figs (California)	7,300	7,200	Tons	4.64	4.40
Grapes	1,046,920	1,049,600	Tons	8.24	7.40
Guava (Hawaii)[1]	100	....	Tons	10.50	....
Kiwifruit (California)	3,800	3,900	Tons	7.92	7.44
Nectarines	19,600	22,600	Tons	8.27	9.24
Olives (California)	40,000	40,000	Tons	4.15	2.06
Papayas (Hawaii)[1]	1,300	....	Tons	9.31	....
Peaches	105,890	102,750	Tons	8.54	8.24
Pears	49,600	49,300	Tons	17.70	16.40
Plums (California)	18,000	18,000	Tons	5.30	7.00
Prunes, dried (California)	50,000	48,000	Tons	5.10	5.94
Prunes and plums[4]	2,600	2,500	Tons	5.17	5.92
Strawberries[1]	60,410	59,895	Tons	25.20	25.30
Tree nuts:					
Almonds (California)[5]	840,000	860,000	Tons	2.06	1.79
Hazelnuts (Oregon)[5]	30,000	30,000	Tons	1.50	1.20
Macadamia (Hawaii)[5]	16,000	16,000	Tons	1.28	1.25
Pecans[2]	(NA)	(NA)	Tons	(NA)	(NA)
Pistachios (California)[5]	203,000	215,000	Tons	1.16	1.20
Walnuts (California)[5]	280,000	290,000	Tons	1.76	1.95
Citrus fruits:					
Oranges[6]	612,200	595,700	Boxes	310	263
Grapefruit[6]	71,900	70,100	Boxes	403	362
Lemons[6]	54,000	54,500	Boxes	422	382
Tangelos (Florida)[6]	3,900	3,600	Boxes	256	244
Tangerines and Mandarins[6]	55,100	58,400	Boxes	299	301

(NA) Not available. [1]Harvested acreage. Yield based on utilized production. [2]Cultivated. [3]Bearing acreage and yield not estimated. [4]Idaho, Michigan, Oregon, and Washington. [5]Yield based on in-shell basis. Almond shelling ratios are: 2012, 0.571; 2013, 0.580. [6]Crop year begins with bloom in one year and ends with completion of harvest the following year. Citrus production is for the the year of harvest.

NASS, Crops Branch, (202) 720–2127.

Table 9-25.—Fruits and nuts: Production and value, United States, 2013–2014

Crop	Total production		Value of utilized production	
	2013	2014	2013	2014
	1,000 tons [1]	*1,000 tons [1]*	*1,000 dollars*	*1,000 dollars*
Noncitrus fruits:				
Apples	5,199.6	5,625.6	3,113,126	2,963,981
Apricots	61.0	64.1	44,987	52,513
Avocados	180.0		358,837	
Bananas (Hawaii) [2]	(NA)		13,050	
Blackberries (Oregon)	25.8	22.4	42,268	43,197
Blueberries				
Cultivated	270.4	283.4	729,532	811,625
Wild (Maine)	43.9	52.2	65,984	63,480
Boysenberries (Oregon)	1.2	1.3	2,503	3,034
Raspberries				
Black (Oregon)	1.3	4.1	6,866	16,868
Red	36.7	86.9	63,656	371,677
All (California)	47.1	91.1	239,020	388,545
Cherries, Sweet	332.1	381.9	771,798	806,095
Cherries, Tart	147.1	144.4	104,395	105,438
Cranberries	447.9	435.9	287,050	266,173
Dates (California)	28.0	30.0	33,880	38,700
Figs (California)	33.9	31.7	23,092	21,941
Grapes	8,630.9	7,769.6	6,133,369	5,758,390
Guava (Hawaii) [2]	(NA)		357	
Kiwifruit (California)	30.1	29.0	32,595	
Nectarines	162.1	208.8	122,155	181,580
Olives (California)	166.0	82.3	134,881	66,299
Papayas (Hawaii) [2]	(NA)		8,316	
Peaches	903.9	846.6	547,978	616,473
Pears	877.1	808.2	430,660	457,833
Plums (California)	95.4	126.0	62,043	115,760
Prunes, dried (California)	255.0	285.0	170,000	209,000
Prunes and plums [3]	13.4	14.8	6,169	7,401
Strawberries [2]	(NA)	(NA)	2,609,038	2,865,432
Tree nuts:				
Almonds (California) [2][4]	(NA)	(NA)	6,384,690	6,464,500
Hazelnuts (Oregon) [2]	(NA)	(NA)	120,600	129,600
Macadamia (Hawaii) [2]	(NA)	(NA)	35,670	34,800
Pecans [2]	(NA)	(NA)	460,390	507,990
Pistachios (California) [2]	(NA)	(NA)	1,635,600	1,290,140
Walnuts (California) [2]	(NA)	(NA)	1,825,320	
Citrus fruits:				
Oranges [2][5]	8,269	6,783	2,073,374	1,960,080
Grapefruit [2][5]	1,204	1,053	257,280	231,897
Lemons [2][5]	912	832	400,295	647,737
Tangelos (Florida) [2][5]	45	40	12,986	9,839
Tangerines and mandarins [2][5]	684	726	426,573	543,435

(NA) Not available.   [1] Tons refers to the 2,000 lb. short Tons.   [2] Only utilized production estimated.   [3] Idaho, Michigan, Oregon, and Washington.   [4] Production is shelled basis, almond shelling ratios are: 2012, 0.571; 2013, 0.580.   [5] Value of production is packinghouse-door equivalent.
NASS, Crops Branch, (202) 720–2127.

Table 9-26.—Vegetables: Area harvested and yield, United States, 2013–2014

Crop	Area harvested		Yield per harvested acre		
	2013	2014	Unit	2013	2014
	Acres	*Acres*			
Commercial Vegetables					
Fresh market:					
Artichokes [1]	7,100	7,300	Cwt	135	130
Asparagus [1]	24,500	23,800	Cwt	31	31
Beans, snap	73,100	67,700	Cwt	58	54
Broccoli [1]	131,500	128,400	Cwt	162	163
Cabbage	59,480	62,550	Cwt	366	357
Cantaloups	68,600	63,200	Cwt	265	236
Carrots	71,400	74,200	Cwt	340	342
Cauliflower [1]	36,830	37,970	Cwt	181	186
Celery [1]	28,800	28,900	Cwt	625	636
Corn, sweet	228,380	215,150	Cwt	125	118
Cucumbers	38,360	37,570	Cwt	198	184
Garlic [1]	23,900	23,800	Cwt	162	163
Honeydew melons	14,450	14,450	Cwt	249	259
Lettuce					
Head	129,000	121,500	Cwt	350	366
Leaf	55,000	54,100	Cwt	230	240
Romaine	91,100	85,400	Cwt	292	289
Onions [1]	143,340	139,150	Cwt	486	523
Peppers, bell [1]	44,800	46,500	Cwt	322	330
Peppers, chile [1]	20,000	19,100	Cwt	211	242
Pumpkins [1]	50,300	49,500	Cwt	223	266
Spinach	34,940	37,540	Cwt	161	158
Squash [1]	39,900	38,530	Cwt	154	149
Tomatoes	99,600	97,600	Cwt	265	280
Watermelons	113,630	109,050	Cwt	318	293
Processing:					
Beans, lima	28,930	27,760	Tons	1.68	1.82
Beans, snap	149,770	159,070	Tons	4.45	4.28
Carrots	13,310	11,430	Tons	26.44	28.16
Corn, sweet	314,950	312,280	Tons	8.10	8.22
Cucumbers for pickles	82,100	76,580	Tons	5.76	6.29
Peas, green	178,300	187,600	Tons	2.00	1.93
Spinach	8,800	9,100	Tons	10.08	9.92
Tomatoes	277,000	306,100	Tons	45.60	47.82

[1] Includes processing total for dual usage crops.
NASS, Crops Branch, (202) 720–2127.

Table 9-27.—Vegetables: Production and value, United States, 2013–2014

Crop	Unit	Production		Value of production	
		2013	2014	2013	2014
Commercial Vegetables		*Thousands*	*Thousands*	*1,000 dollars*	*1,000 dollars*
Fresh market:					
Artichokes [1]	Cwt	959	949	58,499	55,517
Asparagus [1]	Cwt	762	743	92,448	73,441
Beans, snap	Cwt	4,252	3,684	293,073	222,645
Broccoli [1]	Cwt	21,360	20,930	913,520	836,481
Cabbage	Cwt	21,750	22,359	429,419	455,098
Cantaloups	Cwt	18,173	14,912	320,029	327,934
Carrots	Cwt	24,255	25,379	692,783	671,656
Cauliflower [1]	Cwt	6,662	7,053	295,450	351,191
Celery [1]	Cwt	18,003	18,393	457,765	307,276
Corn, sweet	Cwt	28,561	25,346	806,488	732,489
Cucumbers	Cwt	7,603	6,895	203,894	168,038
Garlic [1]	Cwt	3,867	3,868	231,977	258,981
Honeydew melons	Cwt	3,605	3,739	75,389	88,649
Lettuce					
Head	Cwt	45,150	44,438	1,203,930	1,119,255
Leaf	Cwt	12,650	12,984	484,036	501,538
Romaine	Cwt	26,620	24,679	880,373	788,779
Onions [1]	Cwt	69,652	72,806	969,170	933,630
Peppers, bell [1]	Cwt	14,433	15,346	599,932	618,185
Peppers, chile [1]	Cwt	4,210	4,625	168,146	216,107
Pumpkins [1]	Cwt	11,221	13,143	148,517	145,154
Spinach	Cwt	5,619	5,919	242,846	259,700
Squash [1]	Cwt	6,149	5,745	228,985	191,532
Tomatoes	Cwt	26,391	27,280	1,177,592	1,134,616
Watermelons	Cwt	36,102	31,952	513,987	431,184
Processing:					
Beans, lima	Tons ...	48,620	50,400	28,312	29,236
Beans, snap	Tons ...	666,780	681,240	213,250	170,066
Carrots	Tons ...	351,950	321,820	43,008	37,193
Corn, sweet	Tons ...	2,551,830	2,567,820	357,804	289,573
Cucumbers for pickles	Tons ...	473,140	481,740	148,101	175,634
Peas, green	Tons ...	356,050	362,860	151,928	133,261
Spinach	Tons ...	88,710	90,310	11,451	11,312
Tomatoes	Tons ...	12,631,500	14,637,300	1,138,462	1,325,332

[1] Includes processing total for dual usage crops.
NASS, Crops Branch, (202) 720–2127.

Table 9-28.—Total farm input: Index numbers of farm input, by major subgroups, United States, 2000–2009

[2005=100]

Year	Total farm input	Capital					Labor		
		All	Durable equipment	Service buildings	Inven- tories	Land	All	Hired labor	Self- employed
2000 ...	1.0231	1.0051	0.9159	1.0838	1.0355	0.9599	1.0720	1.0874	1.0629
2001 ...	1.0168	1.0001	0.9142	1.0708	1.0280	0.9683	1.0708	1.1009	1.0527
2002 ...	1.0073	1.0000	0.9250	1.0501	1.0202	0.9798	1.0813	1.1123	1.0627
2003 ...	1.0048	0.9934	0.9358	1.0331	1.0131	0.9482	1.0446	1.0915	1.0163
2004 ...	0.9890	0.9934	0.9596	1.0153	1.0065	0.9242	1.0066	1.0037	1.0083
2005 ...	1.0000	1.0000	1.0000	1.0000	1.0000	1.0000	1.0000	1.0000	1.0000
2006 ...	0.9823	1.0009	1.0232	0.9826	0.9934	0.9977	0.9399	0.9566	0.9298
2007 ...	1.0332	0.9941	1.0224	0.9636	0.9865	0.9732	0.9612	1.0397	0.9140
2008 ...	0.9937	1.0085	1.0362	1.1512	0.9794	0.9809	0.9351	0.9906	0.9018
2009 ...	0.9966	1.0118	1.0745	1.1378	0.9724	1.0133	0.8927	0.9772	0.8417

Year	Materials				
	All	Farm origin	Energy	Chemicals	Purchased services
2000 ...	1.0121	1.0110	1.1329	0.9276	1.0304
2001 ...	1.0033	0.9791	1.1048	0.9288	1.0539
2002 ...	0.9832	0.9736	1.2022	0.8539	0.9930
2003 ...	0.9941	1.0064	1.0045	0.9856	0.9593
2004 ...	0.9796	0.9901	1.0826	0.9713	0.9523
2005 ...	1.0000	1.0000	1.0000	1.0000	1.0000
2006 ...	0.9924	1.0114	0.9530	0.8769	1.0203
2007 ...	1.0760	1.0452	1.0757	1.0338	1.1189
2008 ...	1.0074	0.9736	0.9804	1.0362	1.0476
2009 ...	1.0254	0.9791	1.1946	1.0616	1.0084

ERS, Agricultural Structure and Productivity Branch, (202) 694–5460, (202) 694–5601.

Table 9-29.—Livestock and livestock products: Production and value, United States, 2012–2014

Product	Production [1]			Value of production		
	2012	2013	2014	2012	2013	2014
	Millions	*Millions*	*Millions*	*1,000 dollars*	*1,000 dollars*	*1,000 dollars*
Eggs	94,364	97,555	100,879	7,929,104	8,678,859	10,166,321
	1,000 pounds	*1,000 pounds*	*1,000 pounds*	*1,000 dollars*	*1,000 dollars*	*1,000 dollars*
Cattle and calves	40,920,479	40,695,232	40,279,611	48,059,904	48,478,687	60,770,098
Hogs	32,060,619	32,620,264	32,011,688	20,285,027	21,666,015	24,152,893
Broilers [2]	49,655,600	50,678,200	51,373,100	24,827,800	30,761,669	32,724,667
Mature chickens	901,411	922,546	947,499	79,208	87,939	96,557
Turkeys [3]	7,561,905	7,277,536	7,217,050	5,452,135	4,839,562	5,304,537
Milk	200,642,000	201,231,000	205,085,00	37,247,542	40,476,608	49,585.330
Catfish [3][4]	355,990	351,314	320,741	340,564	356,734	351,940
Trout [3][4]	57,776	58,212	62,720	93,104	97,414	103,216
Honey	142,936	149,499	178,270	283,454	320,077	387,381
Wool (shorn)	27,630	26,990	26,680	41,972	39,209	38,909
Mohair	750	780	880	2,903	3,300	4,272

[1] For cattle, sheep, and hogs, the quantity of net production is the live weight actually produced during the year, adjustments having been made for animals shipped in and changes in inventory. Estimates for broilers and eggs cover the 12-month period Dec. 1, previous year through Nov. 30. [2] Young chickens of meat–type strains raised for meat production. [3] Live weight. [4] Value of fish sold, excludes eggs.
NASS, Livestock Branch, (202) 720–3570.

Table 9-30.—Agricultural productivity: Index numbers (2005=100) of farm output per unit of input, United States, 2000–2009

Year	Productivity [1]
2000	0.9444
2001	0.9521
2002	0.9440
2003	0.9683
2004	1.0240
2005	1.0000
2006	1.0060
2007	0.9872
2008	1.0392
2009	1.0626

[1] Productivity is the output-input ratio.
ERS, Agricultural Structure and Productivity Branch (202) 694–5601, (202) 694–5460.

Table 9-31.—Farm product prices: Marketing year average prices received by farmers; Parity prices for January, United States, 2012–2013

Commodity	Unit	Marketing year average price [1]		Parity price [2]	
		2012	2013	2012	2013
		Dollars	*Dollars*	*Dollars*	*Dollars*
Basic commodities:					
Cotton:					
Upland	pound	.725	.779	1.99	2.12
Extra long staple(American Pima)	pound	1.24	1.72	3.89	3.91
Wheat	bushel	7.77	6.87	17.50	18.70
Rice	cwt	15.10	16.30	40.30	48.50
Corn	bushel	6.89	4.46	11.40	12.80
Peanuts	pound	0.301	0.249	0.718	0.794
Tobacco:					
Flue-cured, types (class 1)	pound	1.983	2.115	5.41	5.44
Types 21	pound	2.578	2.661	7.01	7.47
Burley, type 31	pound	1.968	2.061	5.58	5.53
Maryland, type 32 [3]	pound	1.750	1.900	4.80	4.91
Dark air-cured, types 35–36	pound	(NA)	(NA)	7.78	8.29
Sun-cured, type 37	pound	(NA)	(NA)	6.49	6.91
Pa., seedleaf, type 41	pound	1.95	2.100	5.02	5.17
Cigar binder type 51	pound	6.538	(NA)	17.70	17.90
Puerto Rican filler, type 46	pound	(NA)	(NA)	4.28	4.56
Cigar wrapper, type 61	pound	(NA)	(NA)	79.50	71.10
Designated nonbasic commodities:					
All milk, sold to plants	cwt	18.56	20.11	49.70	49.60
Honey, all	pound	199.2	214.1	3.84	4.15
Wool and mohair:					
Wool [4]	pound	1.520	1.450	2.87	3.15
Mohair [5]	pound	3.87	4.23	9.19	9.88
Other nonbasic commodities:					
Field crops and miscellaneous:					
Austrian winter peas	cwt	20.70	23.50	(NA)	(NA)
Barley	bushel	6.43	6.06	12.00	13.10
Beans, dry edible	cwt	38.00	39.10	83.10	85.30
Cottonseed	ton	252.00	246.00	480.00	504.00
Crude pine gum	barrel	(NA)	(NA)	384.00	407.00
Flaxseed	bushel	13.80	13.80	30.40	31.50
Hay, all, baled	ton	191.00	176.00	362.00	388.00
Hops	pound	3.17	3.35	8.45	8.91
Lentils	cwt	20.70	19.80	(NA)	(NA)
Oats	bushel	3.89	3.75	7.26	7.79
Peas, dry edible	cwt	15.70	14.60	(NA)	(NA)
Peppermint oil	pounds	24.10	23.90	49.40	52.60
Popcorn, shelled basis	cwt	(NA)	(NA)	50.00	53.20
Potatoes	cwt	8.63	9.75	23.60	24.20
Rye	bushel	7.69	7.95	14.50	15.70
Sorghum grain	cwt	11.30	7.64	20.10	22.30
Soybeans	bushel	14.40	13.00	27.60	30.30
Spearmint oil	pound	19.50	18.90	41.40	44.10
Sweet potatoes	cwt	17.40	24.10	60.70	61.20
Fruits:					
Citrus (equiv. on-tree): [6]					
Grapefruit	box	7.65	6.51	19.00	20.50
Lemons	box	15.13	12.05	37.80	38.80
Oranges	box	10.14	8.27	19.30	20.90
Tangelos	box	9.65	10.21	(NA)	(NA)
Tangerines	box	19.16	22.45	41.10	43.80
Temples, Florida	box	(NA)	(NA)	10.30	10.90
Deciduous and other:					
Apples:					
For fresh consumption [7]	pound	0.453	0.303	0.911	0.941
For processing [8]	ton	281.00	197.00	455.00	488.00
Apricots:					
For fresh consumption [9]	ton	1,140.00	1,190.00	3,390.00	3,260.00
Dried, California (dried basis) [8]	ton	2,470.00	2,980.00	7,150.00	7,410.00
For processing (excl dried) [8]	ton	387.00	415.00	1,020.00	1,050.00
Avocados [9]	ton	(NA)	1,970.00	5,630.00	5,360.00

See footnote(s) at end of table.

Table 9-31.—Farm product prices: Marketing year average prices received by farmers; Parity prices for January, United States, 2012–2013—Continued

Commodity	Unit	Marketing year average price [1]		Parity price [2]	
		2012	2013	2012	2013
		Dollars	Dollars	Dollars	Dollars
Deciduous and other—Continued					
Berries for processing:					
Blackberries (Oregon)	pound	0.720	0.740	17.10	18.20
Boysenberries (California & Oregon)	pound	1.03	1.07	2.43	2.59
Gooseberries	pound	(NA)	(NA)	1.02	1.09
Loganberries (Oregon)	pound	(NA)	(NA)	1.66	1.76
Raspberries, black (Oregon)	pound	2.65	(NA)	2.93	3.12
Raspberries, red (Oregon & Washington)	pound	0.745	0.945	2.32	2.47
Cherries:					
Sweet	ton	2,020.00	(NA)	5,930.00	6,030.00
Tart	pound	0.594	(NA)	0.938	0.970
Cranberries [10]	barrel	47.90	(NA)	140.00	138.00
Dates, California [9]	ton	1,340.00	(NA)	4,890.00	4,730.00
Figs, California	ton	555.00	(NA)	(NA)	(NA)
Grapes:					
For all sales	ton	752.00	712.00	(NA)	(NA)
Raisin varieties dried, California (dried basis) [8]	ton	1,880.00	1,630.00	3,450.00	3,910.00
Other dried grapes	ton	435.00	347.00	1,550.00	1,620.00
Kiwi	ton	1,020.00	1,110.00	2,600.00	2,600.00
Nectarines (California):					
For fresh consumption [17]	ton	777.00	(NA)	1,490.00	1,610.00
For processing [18]	ton	(NA)	(NA)	116.00	58.50
Olives (California): [11]					
For all sales	ton	813.00	813.00	(NA)	(NA)
Crushed for oil	ton	550.00	582.00	1,550.00	1,640.00
For all sales (excl crushed)	ton	(NA)	(NA)	2,180.00	2,320.00
For canning	ton	1,110.00	1,110.00	2,470.00	2,580.00
Papayas	pound	(NA)	(NA)	1.21	1.12
Peaches:					
For all sales	ton	647.00	(NA)	(NA)	(NA)
For fresh consumption [7]	ton	967.00	(NA)	2,260.00	2,360.00
Dried, California (dried basis) [8]	ton	327.00	(NA)	1,480.00	1,430.00
For processing California (excl dried):					
Clingstone [11]	ton	348.00	364.00	919.00	929.00
Freestone [8]	ton	242.00	272.00	729.00	738.00
Pears:					
For all sales	ton	509.00	491.00	(NA)	(NA)
For fresh consumption [7]	ton	656.00	599.00	1,530.00	1,660.00
Dried, California (dried basis) [8]	ton	(NA)	(NA)	4,720.00	4,410.00
For processing (excl dried) [8]	ton	238.00	276.00	1,080.00	1,350.00
Plums (California):					
For all sales [9]	ton	695.00	664.00	(NA)	(NA)
For fresh consumption [17]	ton	(NA)	(NA)	1,620.00	1,710.00
For processing [18]	ton	(NA)	(NA)	192.00	253.00
Prunes, dried (California) [8]	ton	421.00	(NA)	4,080.00	4,250.00
Prunes and plums (excl California):					
For fresh consumption [12]	ton	739.00	608.00	1,720.00	1,820.00
For processing (excl dried) [8]	ton	228.00	345.00	696.00	700.00
Strawberries:					
For fresh consumption [13]	cwt	91.80	96.50	254.00	258.00
For processing [8]	cwt	33.40	34.90	97.20	96.70
Sugar crops:					
Sugarbeets	ton	66.40	46.90	145.00	154.00
Sugarcane for sugar	ton	41.90	31.40	95.20	98.50
Tree nuts: [14]					
Almonds	pound	2.58	3.21	5.88	6.20
Hazelnuts	ton	1,830.00	2,180.00	5,410.00	5,620.00
Macadamia	pound	0.800	0.870	(NA)	(NA)
Pecans, all	pound	1.57	1.73	4.91	5.06
Pistachios	pound	2.61	3.48	5.41	5.70
Walnuts	ton	3,030.00	3,710.00	4,940.00	5,440.00

See footnote(s) at end of table.

Table 9-31.—Farm product prices: Marketing year average prices received by farmers; Parity prices for January, United States, 2012–2013—Continued

Commodity	Unit	Marketing year average price [1]		Parity price [2]	
		2012	2013	2012	2013
		Dollars	Dollars	Dollars	Dollars
Vegetables for fresh market: [13]					
Artichokes, California	cwt	54.30	61.00	126.00	134.00
Asparagus	cwt	110.00	121.00	326.00	326.00
Broccoli	cwt	33.80	43.20	111.00	111.00
Cabbage	cwt	18.50	20.10	38.10	40.60
Cantaloups	cwt	19.10	17.60	58.80	62.60
Carrots [15]	cwt	26.60	28.60	74.20	75.60
Cauliflower [15]	cwt	35.90	44.50	119.00	119.00
Celery [15]	cwt	18.20	25.40	55.50	57.00
Cucumbers	cwt	25.00	26.80	62.90	67.00
Eggplant	cwt	(NA)	(NA)	66.50	70.90
Escarole/Endive	cwt	(NA)	(NA)	85.60	91.10
Garlic	cwt	52.60	60.00	80.90	86.10
Green peppers [15]	cwt	32.80	41.60	99.40	106.00
Honeydew melons	cwt	20.70	20.90	57.70	57.90
Lettuce	cwt	17.70	26.70	63.20	61.40
Onions [15]	cwt	14.20	15.00	41.10	41.50
Snap beans	cwt	62.70	68.90	124.00	133.00
Spinach	cwt	42.20	43.20	109.00	116.00
Sweet corn	cwt	26.30	28.20	74.80	76.10
Tomatoes	cwt	30.50	44.60	129.00	126.00
Watermelons	cwt	13.20	14.20	23.30	24.90
Vegetables for processing: [8]					
Asparagus	ton	1,570.00	1,570.00	4,000.00	4,090.00
Beets	ton	66.40	46.90	215.00	229.00
Cabbage	ton	(NA)	(NA)	166.00	177.00
Cucumbers	ton	342.00	313.00	(NA)	67.00
Green peas	ton	434.00	427.00	930.00	976.00
Lima beans	ton	524.00	582.00	1,850.00	1,970.00
Snap beans	ton	271.00	320.00	569.00	597.00
Spinach	ton	137.00	129.00	400.00	426.00
Sweet corn	ton	127.00	140.00	273.00	290.00
Tomatoes	ton	76.70	90.10	221.00	225.00
Livestock and livestock products:					
All beef cattle	cwt	121.00	125.00	292.00	294.00
Cows	cwt	81.70	82.30	(NA)	(NA)
Steers and heifers	cwt	123.00	126.00	(NA)	(NA)
Calves	cwt	172.00	81.00	384.00	403.00
Beeswax	pound	(NA)	(NA)	8.03	8.56
Chickens:					
Broilers, live [18]	pound	0.511	0.604	1.35	(NA)
All Eggs	dozen	0.999	1.09	2.63	2.62
Hogs	cwt	64.20	67.20	160.00	161.00
Lambs	cwt	([19])	([19])	323.00	344.00
Milk cows [16]	head	1,430	1,380.00	(NA)	(NA)
Sheep	cwt	([19])	([19])	119.00	129.00
Turkeys, live	pound	0.719	0.665	1.650	1.68

(NA) Not available. [1] Unless otherwise noted, these prices are for marketing year average or calendar year average computed by weighing State prices by quantities sold, or by production for those commodities for which the production is sold. [2] Parity prices are for January of the year shown as published in the January issue of Agricultural Prices. [3] Previous year. [4] Average local market price for wool sold excluding incentive payment. [5] Average local market price for mohair sold excluding incentive payment. [6] Crop year begins with bloom in one year and ends with completion of harvest the following year. Prices refer to the year harvest begins. [7] Equivalent packinghouse-door returns for California, Oregon (pears only), Washington, and New York (apples only), and prices as sold for other States. [8] Equivalent returns at processing plant-door. [9] Equivalent returns at packinghouse-door. [10] Weighted average of co-op and independent sales. Co-op prices represent pool proceeds excluding returns from non-cranberry products and before deductions for capital stock and other retains. [11] Equivalent per unit returns for bulk fruit at first delivery point. [12] Average price as sold. [13] FOB shipping point when available. Weighted average of prices at points of first sale. [14] Prices are in-shell basis except almonds which are shelled basis. [15] Includes some processing. [16] Simple average of States weighted by estimated Jan. 1 head for U.S. average. [17] Prices for fresh and processing breakdown no longer published to avoid disclosure of individual operations. [18] Live weight equivalent price. [19] Estimates discontinued in 2011.

NASS, Environmental, Economics, and Demographics Branch (202) 720–6146.

Table 9-32.—Producer prices: Index numbers, by groups of commodities, United States, 2005–2014

[1982=100]

Year	Total finished goods	Consumer foods	Total consumer goods	Total intermediate materials	Total crude materials
2005	155.7	155.7	160.4	154.0	182.2
2006	160.4	156.7	166.0	164.0	184.8
2007	166.6	167.0	173.5	170.7	207.1
2008	177.1	178.3	186.3	188.3	251.8
2009	172.5	175.5	179.1	172.5	175.2
2010	179.8	182.4	189.1	183.4	212.2
2011	190.5	193.9	203.3	199.8	249.4
2012	194.3	199.1	207.5	200.7	241.4
2013	196.7	203.5	210.3	200.8	246.7
2014	200.4	212.5	214.7	201.9	249.3

ERS, Food Marketing Branch, (202) 694–5349. Compiled from reports of the U.S. Department of Labor.

Table 9-33.—Prices received by farmers: Index numbers by groups of commodities and parity ratio, United States, 2005–2014 [1]

[1910–14=100]

Year	Food grain	Feed grain	Cotton	Tobacco	Oilseed	Fruit & tree nut[2]	Vegetable & melon	Other crop
2005	351	338	361	1,417	579	894	932	558
2006	425	388	402	1,377	550	1,074	974	572
2007	590	541	423	1,392	748	1,103	1,128	582
2008	820	734	515	1,409	1,107	1,038	1,076	604
2009	590	579	416	1,569	971	977	1,153	609
2010	560	587	601	1,557	944	1,031	1,161	622
2011	758	902	745	1,497	1,225	1,162	1,224	645
2012	779	1,010	673	1,576	1,356	1,339	1,040	649
2013	759	943	651	1,760	1,343	1,311	1,330	645
2014	(NA)	(NA)	(NA)	(NA)	(NA)	(NA)	(NA)	(NA)

Year	Potato & dry edible bean	Crop Production	Meat animal	Dairy	Poultry & egg	Livestock Production	Agricultural Production	Parity ratio[3]
2005	554	546	1,201	931	347	910	726	38
2006	634	593	1,180	793	312	850	730	37
2007	637	706	1,204	1,177	393	994	862	40
2008	797	836	1,195	1,128	424	1,000	947	39
2009	761	747	1,075	790	390	857	832	35
2010	708	690	1,256	1,000	427	1,002	850	37
2011	867	872	1,540	1,239	422	1,161	1,032	38
2012	846	933	1,633	1,140	459	1,190	1,083	38
2013	901	922	1,669	1,230	515	1,260	1,104	38
2014	(NA)	802	(NA)	(NA)	(NA)	1,495	1,112	37

(NA) Not available. [1] These indexes are computed using the price estimates of averages for all classes and grades for individual commodities being sold in local farm markets. In computing the group indexes, prices of individual commodities have been compared with 2011 weighted average prices. The resulting ratios are seasonally weighted by average quantities sold for the most recent 5–year period. For example, 2013 indexes use quantities sold for the period 2007–11. Then, the 2011 indexes are used to adjust the 1910–14 base period. [2] Fresh market for noncitrus, and fresh market and processing for citrus. [3] Ratio of Index of Prices Received to the Index of Prices Paid by Farmers for Commodities and Services, Interest, Taxes, and Farm Wage Rates.

NASS, Environmental, Economics, and Demographics Branch, (202) 720–6146.

Table 9-34.—Prices received by farmers: Index numbers by groups of commodities and ratio, United States, 2005–2014 [1]

(2011=100)

Year	Food grain	Feed grain	Cotton [2]	Tobacco [2]	Oilseed	Fruit & tree nut [3]	Vegetable & melon	Other crop
2005	46.7	38.0	48.5	90.1	49.8	76.8	83.1	86.1
2006	56.4	43.6	54.0	87.6	47.3	92.2	86.8	88.3
2007	78.4	60.8	56.8	88.5	64.4	94.7	100.5	89.9
2008	109.1	82.6	69.1	89.6	95.2	89.1	95.9	93.3
2009	78.5	65.1	55.9	99.7	83.5	83.9	102.8	94.1
2010	74.4	66.0	80.6	98.9	81.2	88.5	103.5	95.9
2011	100.0	100.0	(NA)	(NA)	100.0	100.0	100.0	100.0
2012	103.8	110.8	(NA)	(NA)	111.9	112.4	91.9	102.7
2013	101.5	102.4	(NA)	(NA)	111.6	119.1	103.8	100.5
2014	90.4	69.1	(NA)	(NA)	98.8	133.5	103.3	94.7

Year	Potato [4] & dry edible bean [5]	Crop Production	Meat animal	Dairy product	Poultry & egg	Livestock Production	Agricultural Production	Parity ratio [6]
2005	64.3	62.63	78.1	75.2	82.6	78.4	71.0	91.2
2006	73.5	68.0	76.7	64.0	74.3	73.2	71.0	86.6
2007	73.9	81.0	78.3	95.0	93.6	85.7	84.0	96.8
2008	92.5	95.9	77.6	91.0	101.0	86.1	92.0	93.3
2009	88.3	85.7	69.9	63.7	93.0	73.8	81.0	84.4
2010	82.1	87.0	81.6	80.7	101.6	85.7	82.0	88.2
2011	(NA)	100.0	100.0	100.0	100.0	100.0	100.0	100.0
2012	(NA)	107.0	103.9	92.1	109.0	102.5	105.0	101.7
2013	(NA)	105.7	106.8	99.8	123.3	108.5	107.0	100.0
2014	(NA)	92.0	131.1	119.2	133.2	128.8	107.7	96.8

[1] These indexes are computed using the price estimates of averages for all classes and grades for individual commodities being sold in local farm markets. In computing the group indexes, prices of individual commodities have been compared with 2011 weighted average prices. The resulting ratios are seasonally weighted by average quantities sold for the most recent previous 5–year period. For example, 2013 indexes use quantities sold for the period 2007–11. [2] Included in Other crop index group beginning in 2010. [3] Fresh market for noncitrus, and fresh market and processing for citrus. [4] Included in Vegetable and melon index group beginning 2010. [5] Included in Food grain index group beginning 2010. [6] Ratio of Index of Prices Received (2011=100) to Index of Prices Paid by Farmers for Commodities & Services, Interest, Taxes, and Wage Rates (2007–11=100).

NASS, Environmental, Economics, and Demographics Branch, (202) 720–6146.

Table 9-35.—Prices paid by farmers: Index numbers, by groups of commodities, United States, 2005–2014

(2011=100)

	Production indexes [1]								
Year	Production all commodities	Feed	Livestock & Poultry	Seeds	Fertilizer	Agricultural chemicals	Fuels	Supplies & Repairs	Autos & trucks
2005	65.4	51.8	89.1	50.5	49.9	84.9	59.7	84.4	98.6
2006	68.9	55.1	86.4	54.8	53.5	88.2	66.0	87.2	97.3
2007	74.6	65.8	84.7	61.6	65.6	89.2	72.9	89.9	96.0
2008	88.3	85.8	80.4	78.0	119.2	95.7	94.9	92.5	93.8
2009	84.8	82.5	74.6	90.1	83.8	102.5	63.1	94.3	94.9
2010	87.7	79.7	86.0	93.4	76.8	99.5	78.3	96.1	97.3
2011	100.0	100.0	100.0	100.0	100.0	100.0	100.00	100.0	100.0
2012	105.4	115.3	106.6	105.5	101.3	105.3	99.3	102.9	101.9
2013	107.4	117.5	108.3	110.3	96.6	108.6	98.3	103.8	103.4
2014	114.1	114.8	153.6	113.5	94.7	109.7	97.8	105.7	104.4

	Production indexes [1] - continued							Production, interest, taxes, & wage rates	Family living	Commodities, interest, taxes, & wage rates [2]
Year	Farm machinery	Building materials	Farm services	Rent	Interest	Taxes	Wage rates			
2005	70.9	83.0	81.3	62.7	76.0	69.9	86.0	67.4	86.8	69.9
2006	74.6	88.5	84.8	68.4	91.3	79.7	89.2	71.6	89.6	73.9
2007	78.5	90.5	89.1	71.8	97.6	90.2	92.4	77.2	92.2	79.0
2008	85.6	96.5	89.0	80.2	101.9	94.3	96.6	89.5	95.7	90.0
2009	91.2	95.4	95.3	89.6	94.2	91.9	97.9	86.4	95.4	87.3
2010	94.3	96.6	98.1	92.6	91.6	95.9	98.9	89.0	96.9	90.0
2011	100.0	100.0	100.0	100.0	100.0	100.0	100.0	100.0	100.0	100.0
2012	105.3	102.7	101.8	101.7	99.3	101.0	102.9	104.8	102.1	104.4
2013	108.1	104.8	105.5	105.5	93.3	103.4	106.3	106.7	103.6	106.3
2014	112.0	106.8	109.1	114.2	92.8	116.3	108.0	113.1	105.3	112.0

[1] Annual price index computed using annual weights. Base period (2011=100) are now being published to one decimal digit. [2] Family Living component included.

NASS, Environmental, Economics, and Demographics Branch, (202) 720–6146.

Table 9-36.—Prices paid by farmers: Index numbers, by groups of commodities, United States, 2005–2014 [1]

[1910–14=100]

Year	Family living	Production indexes							
		Production all commodities	Feed	Livestock & poultry	Seed	Fertilizer	Agricultural chemicals	Fuels	Supplies & repairs
2005	1,855	1,361	571	1,759	1,661	601	762	1,668	995
2006	1,915	1,434	607	1,706	1,802	644	792	1,845	1,029
2007	1,969	1,552	725	1,671	2,024	790	801	2,038	1,060
2008	2,045	1,839	945	1,587	2,563	1,436	859	2,653	1,091
2009	2,038	1,766	909	1,472	2,960	1,009	921	1,765	1,113
2010	2,071	1,825	879	1,698	3,070	925	893	2,191	1,134
2011	2,136	2,082	1,102	1,974	3,286	1,204	898	2,797	1,180
2012	2,181	2,193	1,270	2,104	3,468	1,221	946	2,779	1,214
2013	2,213	2,236	1,295	2,137	3,622	1,164	974	2,752	1,225
2014	2,249	2,376	1,266	3,032	3,729	1,138	983	2,739	1,247

Year	Production indexes—Continued				Interest	Taxes	Wage rates	Production, interest, taxes, & wage rates	Commodities, interest, taxes, & wage rates [2]
	Autos & trucks	Farm machinery	Building materials	Farm services & rent					
2005	3,031	4,329	1,930	1,569	2,772	4,150	6,158	1,900	1,891
2006	2,991	4,556	2,059	1,664	3,328	4,729	6,390	2,019	1,999
2007	2,949	4,794	2,104	1,746	3,560	5,356	6,618	2,178	2,138
2008	2,882	5,231	2,245	1,818	3,727	5,598	6,917	2,522	2,434
2009	2,917	5,575	2,218	1,976	3,436	5,453	7,007	2,435	2,364
2010	2,992	5,762	2,248	2,036	3,339	5,694	7,079	2,509	2,434
2011	3,074	6,111	2,326	2,123	3,646	5,935	7,161	2,820	2,706
2012	3,131	6,432	2,387	2,162	3,620	5,993	7,366	2,954	2,824
2013	3,179	6,609	2,434	2,240	3,402	6,137	7,607	3,010	2,876
2014	3,209	6,845	2,486	2,360	3,383	6,904	7,730	3,189	3,031

[1] Based on Consumer Price Index-Urban of Bureau of Labor Statistics. [2] The index known as the Parity Index is the Index of Prices Paid by Farmers for Commodities and Services, Interest, Taxes, and Wage Rates expressed on the 1910–14=100 base.
NASS, Environmental, Economics, and Demographics Branch, (202) 720–6146.

Table 9-37.—Prices paid by farmers: April prices, by commodities, United States, 2012–2014 [1]

Commodity	Unit	2012	2013	2014
		Dollars	Dollars	Dollars
Fuels and energy:				
Diesel fuel [2][3]	Gal	3.740	3.570	3.537
Gasoline, service station, unleaded [4]	Gal	3.837	3.684	3.595
Gasoline, service station, bulk delivery [4]	Gal	3.862	3.696	3.569
L. P. gas, bulk delivery [2]	Gal	2.233	2.009	2.151
Feeds:				
Alfalfa Meal	Cwt	26.60	31.20	32.10
Alfalfa Pellets	Cwt	27.10	30.90	31.90
Bran	Cwt	26.40	29.70	30.70
Beef Cattle Concentrate.				
32-36% Protein	Ton	525.00	602.00	617.00
Corn Meal	Cwt	20.40	22.30	23.00
Cottonseed Meal, 41%	Cwt	27.80	31.40	32.90
Dairy Feed				
14% Protein	Ton	437.00	474.00	487.00
16% Protein	Ton	442.00	481.00	502.00
18% Protein	Ton	431.00	447.00	470.00
20% Protein	Ton	407.00	414.00	434.00
32% Protein Conc.	Ton	550.00	630.00	654.00
Hog Feed				
14-18% Protein	Ton	475.00	490.00	507.00
38-42% Protein Conc.	Ton	592.00	646.00	666.00
Molasses, Liquid	Cwt	23.20	24.70	25.70
Poultry Feed				
Broiler Grower	Ton	591.00	639.00	654.00
Chick Starter	Ton	597.00	628.00	644.00
Laying Feed	Ton	527.00	552.00	581.00
Turkey Grower	Ton	589.00	604.00	619.00
Soybean meal				
44%	Cwt	26.50	32.50	34.00
over 44%	Cwt	24.10	29.40	31.00
Stock Salt	50 Lb	6.33	6.43	6.60
Trace mineral blocks	50 Lb	7.59	7.80	8.07

See footnote(s) at end of table.

Table 9-37.—Prices paid by farmers: April prices, by commodities, United States, 2012–2014 [1]—Continued

Commodity	Unit	2012	2013	2014
		Dollars	*Dollars*	*Dollars*
Fertilizer: [5]				
0-15-40	Ton	(NA)	(NA)	(NA)
0-18-36	Ton	621.00	595.00	595.00
0-20-20	Ton	(NA)	(NA)	(NA)
3-10-30	Ton	527.00	504.00	480.00
5-10-10	Ton	(NA)	(NA)	(NA)
5-10-15	Ton	(NA)	(NA)	(NA)
5-10-30	Ton	547.00	596.00	600.00
5-20-20	Ton	601.00	590.00	580.00
6- 6- 6	Ton	(NA)	(NA)	(NA)
6- 6-18	Ton	555.00	571.00	575.00
6-12-12	Ton	(NA)	(NA)	(NA)
6-24-24	Ton	687.00	703.00	690.00
8- 8- 8	Ton	(NA)	(NA)	(NA)
8-20- 5	Ton	(NA)	(NA)	(NA)
8-32-16	Ton	(NA)	(NA)	(NA)
9-23-30	Ton	654.00	626.00	623.00
10- 3- 3	Ton	(NA)	(NA)	(NA)
10- 6- 4	Ton	(NA)	(NA)	(NA)
10-10-10	Ton	514.00	535.00	518.00
10-20-10	Ton	(NA)	(NA)	(NA)
10-20-20	Ton	638.00	613.00	572.00
10-34- 0	Ton	755.00	629.00	611.00
11-52- 0	Ton	719.00	691.00	620.00
13-13-13	Ton	601.00	606.00	620.00
15-15-15	Ton	(NA)	(NA)	(NA)
16- 0-13	Ton	(NA)	(NA)	(NA)
16- 4- 8	Ton	585.00	593.00	616.00
16- 6-12	Ton	537.00	529.00	522.00
16-16-16	Ton	(NA)	(NA)	(NA)
16-20- 0	Ton	626.00	646.00	619.00
17-17-17	Ton	641.00	640.00	598.00
18-46- 0 (DAP)	Ton	675.00	640.00	611.00
19-19-19	Ton	662.00	637.00	590.00
24- 8- 0	Ton	443.00	427.00	436.00
Ammonium Nitrate	Ton	574.00	544.00	560.00
Anhydrous Ammonia	Ton	785.00	847.00	851.00
Aqua Ammonia	Ton	266.00	262.00	253.00
Limestone, Spread on field	Ton	57.50	54.90	56.60
Muriate of Potash, 60–62% K2O	Ton	665.00	595.00	601.00
Nitrate of Soda	Ton	(NA)	(NA)	(NA)
Nitrogen Solutions.				
28% N	Ton	388.00	397.00	372.00
30% N	Ton	403.00	410.00	359.00
32% N	Ton	425.00	441.00	416.00
Sulfate of Ammonia	Ton	503.00	522.00	533.00
Superphosphate, 44-46% P2O5	Ton	729.00	701.00	621.00
Urea, 44-46% Nitrogen	Ton	644.00	592.00	571.00
Farm Machinery:				
Baler, Pick-Up, Automatic Tie, P.T.O.				
Square Conventional, Under 200 Lb Bales	Each	23,000	24,100	24,900
Round, 1200-1500 Lb Bale	Each	28,000	28,500	29,700
Round, 1900-2200 Lb Bale	Each	38,900	40,400	42,400
Chisel Plow, Maxiumum 1 Foot Depth				
Tillage, Chisel or Sweep Type, Drawn.				
Mounted, 16-20 Foot	Each	27,800	29,100	29,600
Mounted, 21-25 Foot	Each	39,300	41,600	42,100
Combine, Self Propelled with Grain head				
Extra-large capacity	Each	363,000	371,000	388,000
Large capacity	Each	295,000	305,000	315,000
Corn Head for combine				
6 Row	Each	42,700	45,300	47,400
8 Row	Each	57,800	60,200	62,100
Cotton Picker, Self Propelled, with spindle,				
6-Row	Each	585,000	602,000	610,000
Cultivator, Row Crop				
6-Row	Each	(NA)	(NA)	(NA)
8-Row	Each	18,000	18,200	18,600
12-Row, Flexible	Each	32,700	33,000	33,800
Disk Harrow, Tandem, Drawn [6]				
15-17 Foot	Each	21,800	22,100	22,300
18-20 foot	Each	31,400	31,800	32,800
21-25 foot	Each	38,800	39,600	41,700

See footnote(s) at end of table.

**Table 9-37.—Prices paid by farmers: April prices, by commodities,
United States, 2012–2014 [1]—Continued**

Commodity	Unit	2012	2013	2014
		Dollars	*Dollars*	*Dollars*
Farm Machinery (continued):				
Elevator, Portable, Without Power Unit,				
Auger Type, 8 Inch Diameter, 60 Foot	Each	9,030	9,350	9,740
Feed Grinder-Mixer, Trailer Mtd., P.T.O.	Each	34,700	37,200	37,800
Field Cultivator, Mounted or Drawn				
17-19 Foot	Each	21,800	23,100	23,800
20-25 Foot, Flexible	Each	30,600	31,700	32,500
Forage Harvester, P.T.O., Shear Bar,				
With Pick-Up Attachment	Each	47,600	49,500	51,600
With Row Crop Unit, 2-Row	Each	51,200	53,600	57,300
Forage Harvester, Self-propelled, Shear Bar				
With 4–6 row	Each	414,000	422,000	454,000
Front-End Loader, Hydraulic, Tractor Mounted				
1800-2500 Lb. Capacity, 60 Inch Bucket	Each	7,140	7,160	7,360
Grain Drill, Most Common Spacing				
Plain, 15-17 Openers	Each	21,000	22,100	23,600
Press, 23-25 Openers	Each	40,500	41,400	44,300
With Fertilizer Attachment, 20-24 Openers	Each	32,700	34,000	34,700
Min/No-Till W/Fert. Attach., 15 Foot	Each	42,300	44,300	45,100
Hayrake, Side-Delivery, or Wheel Rake,				
Traction Drive, 8-12 Foot Working Width	Each	7,430	7,880	7,960
Hay Tedder, 15-18 Foot	Each	7,090	7,570	7,610
Manure Spreader, Conveyor Type, P.T.O.,				
2-Wheel, with Tires.				
141-190 Bushel Capacity	Each	10,300	11,300	12,200
225-300 Bushel Capacity	Each	15,700	16,200	17,100
Mower-Conditioner, P.T.O., Pull Type, with				
8-10 Foot, Sickle (Cutter) Bar or Disc	Each	21,700	22,400	23,400
14-16 Foot, Sickle (Cutter) Bar or Disc	Each	33,500	34,200	36,200
Mower, Mounted or Drawn,				
7-8 ft Sickle (Cutter) Bar	Each	7,930	8,020	8,440
13-14 Foot, Sickle (Cutter) Bar or Disc	Each	17,600	17,900	19,000
Planter, Row Crop				
With Fertilizer Attachment, 4-Row	Each	24,300	25,700	26,500
With Fertilizer Attachment, 8-Row	Each	47,800	49,600	50,400
With Fertilizer Attachment, 24-Row	Each	164,000	173,000	190,000
12-Row Conservation (No-Till Cond), w/Fert ..	Each	86,100	87,400	88,900
Rotary Hoe, 20-25 Foot	Each	13,900	14,300	15,900
Rotary Cutter, 7-8 Foot	Each	4,200	4,330	4,450
Sprayer, Field Crop, Power, Boom Type				
(Excl. Self-Propelled and Orchard).				
Tractor Mounted, w/ 300 Gal. Spray Tank	Each	7,530	7,960	8,310
Trailer Type, w/ 500-700 Gal. Spray Tank	Each	17,000	17,000	17,300
Tractor, 2-Wheel Drive				
30-39 P.T.O. horsepower	Each	19,000	19,900	20,600
50-59 P.T.O. horsepower	Each	25,800	26,700	27,500
70-89 P.T.O. horsepower	Each	43,000	44,000	45,100
110 - 129 P.T.O. horsepower	Each	81,400	84,000	85,800
140 - 159 P.T.O. horsepower	Each	128,000	133,000	135,000
190 - 220 P.T.O. horsepower	Each	185,000	190,000	197,000
Tractor, 4-Wheel Drive				
200 - 280 P.T.O. horsepower	Each	217,000	226,000	233,000
281 - 350 Engine horsepower	Each	272,000	277,000	294,000
51-500 Engine horsepower	Each	301,000	309,000	321,000
Wagon, Gravity Unload, W/Box and Running				
Gear, and Tires,				
200-400 Bushel Capacity				
Without Side Extensions	Each	7,850	8,350	8,820
Wagon, Running Gear, W/O Box				
8-10 Ton Capacity	Each	2,450	2,480	2,600
Windrower, Self-Propelled,				
14-16 Foot	Each	115,000	119,000	129,000

See footnote(s) at end of table.

Table 9-37.—Prices paid by farmers: April prices, by commodities, United States, 2012–2014 [1]—Continued

Commodity	Unit	2012	2013	2014
		Dollars	*Dollars*	*Dollars*
Agricultural Chemicals: [7]				
Fungicides:				
Calcium Polysulfide (Lime Sulfur) Liq.Conc	Gal	(NA)	(NA)	(NA)
Captan 50% WP	Lb	7.84	7.92	8.14
Captan 80% WP	Lb	8.47	8.61	8.75
Chlorothalonil (Bravo), 6 pounds/gallon EC	Gal	43.80	45.30	47.20
Copper Hydroxide (Kocide 200), 35% WP	Lb	6.40	6.64	6.88
Copper Hydroxide (Kocide 101), 77% WP	Lb	5.29	5.40	5.51
Dodine (Cyprex), 65% WP	Lb	(NA)	(NA)	(NA)
Fenarimol (Rubigan), 1 pounds/gallon EC	Gal	375.00	386.00	392.00
Ferbam (Carbamate), 76% WP	Lb	4.81	5.03	5.17
Fosethyl-AL (Aliette), 80% WP	Lb	15.10	15.30	15.80
Mancozeb (Dithane 80% WP,Manzate 75% DF)	Lb	5.11	5.23	5.40
Maneb (Manex), 4 pounds/gallon	Lb	40.10	41.80	42.40
Maneb, 80% WP, 75% DF	Lb	(NA)	(NA)	(NA)
Myclobutanil (Systhane, Nova, Rally), 40% WP	Lb	68.90	71.50	73.20
Oxytetraycline (Mycoshield), 17% WP	Lb	22.50	22.90	23.80
Sulfur, 80% - Microthiol Disperssm Kumulus DF	Lb	0.89	0.93	0.99
Triadimefon (Bayleton), 50% WP	Lb	107.00	109.00	113.00
Ziram, 76% WP	Lb	4.44	4.52	4.67
Herbicides:				
2,4–D, 4 pounds/gallon EC	Gal	20.10	20.40	20.90
Acetochlor (Surpass), 6.4–7 pounds/gallon EC	Gal	70.80	74.50	78.40
Alachlor (Lasso), 4 pounds/gallon EC	Gal	29.60	30.40	31.40
Atrazine(AAtrex), 4 pounds/gallon L	Gal	17.60	17.80	18.40
Bentazon (Basagran), 4 pounds/gallon EC	Gal	110.00	111.00	114.00
Butylate (Sutan), 6.7 pounds/gallon EC	Gal	34.40	35.40	37.30
Chlorimuron–ethyl (Classic), 25% DF	oz	16.00	16.60	17.10
Chlorsulfuron (Glean), 75%	oz	21.30	22.30	23.10
DCPA (Dacthal), 75% WP	Lb	21.50	22.00	23.10
Dicamba (Banvel), 4 pounds/gallon EC	Gal	(NA)	(NA)	(NA)
Diuron (Karmex, Diurex), 80% WP	Lb	6.38	6.52	6.67
EPTC (Eptan), 7E–(Eradicane),6.7 pounds/gallon EC	Gal	46.00	47.60	48.40
Glyphosate (Roundup), 4.5 pounds/gallon EC	Gal	17.90	18.20	18.70
Glyphosate (Roundup), 5 pounds/gallon EC	Gal	26.00	26.10	26.80
Linuron (Lorox, Linex), 50% DF	Lb	21.60	22.60	23.00
MCPA, 4 pounds/gallon EC	Gal	21.90	22.10	22.90
Metribuzin (Lexone or Sencor), 75% DF	Lb	17.40	17.80	18.00
Napropamide (Devrinol), 50% WP	Lb	12.10	12.40	12.60
Pendimethalin (Prowl), 3.3–3.8 pounds/gallon EC	Gal	40.40	41.60	42.60
Sethoxydim (Poast), 1.5 pounds/gallon EC	Gal	87.00	89.10	91.50
Simazine (Princep), 4 pounds/gallon EC	Gal	25.40	26.40	26.80
Terbacil (Sinbar), 80% WP	Lb	43.60	45.20	46.20
Trifluralin (Treflan), 4 pounds/gallon EC	Gal	26.20	26.80	27.60

See footnote(s) at end of table.

Table 9-37.—Prices paid by farmers: April prices, by commodities, United States, 2012–2014 [1]—Continued

Commodity	Unit	2012	2013	2014
		Dollars	Dollars	Dollars
Insecticides:				
Acephate (Orthene), 75% SP	Lb	11.50	12.20	12.60
Acephate (Orthene), 90% SP	Lb	9.13	9.41	9.62
Aldicarb (Temik), 15% G	Lb	4.03	4.27	4.32
Azinphos–methyl (Guthion), 50% WP	Lb	14.50	15.10	15.70
Bt (Dipel 2X), WP	Lb	12.50	13.50	14.00
Carbaryl, (Sevin), 80% S, SP or WP	Lb	7.29	7.45	7.61
Carbaryl, (Sevin), 4 pounds/gallon 4F or XLR Plus WP	Lb	46.90	48.80	50.40
Carbofuran (Furadan), 4F	Gal	83.50	87.30	91.70
Chlorpyrifos (Lorsban), 4 pounds/gallon EC	Gal	37.60	38.80	40.10
Cyfluthrin (Baythroid) 2 pounds/gallon EC	Gal	302.00	303.00	308.00
Dicofol, 4 pounds/gallon 4E WP	Lb	44.90	47.90	49.00
Dicrotophos (Bidrin), 8 pounds/gallon EC	Gal	134.00	138.00	143.00
Dimethoate (Cygon), 2.67 pounds/gallon EC	Gal	49.00	49.60	51.00
Disulfoton (Di-Syston), 8 pounds/gallon EC	Gal	(NA)	(NA)	(NA)
Endosulfon (Thiodan, Phaser), 3 pounds/gallon EC	Gal	32.40	33.40	34.10
Esfenvalerate (Asana XL),0.66 pounds/gallon EC	Gal	101.00	102.00	105.00
Malathion, 5 pounds/gallon EC	Gal	44.00	46.80	48.30
Malathion,(Fyfanon ULV AG), 9.9 pounds/gallon EC	Gal	58.10	61.50	63.70
Methidathion (Supracide), 25% WP	Lb	10.50	10.60	10.80
Methomyl (Lannate LV), 2.4 pounds/gallon EC	Gal	70.50	71.10	73.10
Methyl Parathion (Penncap–M), 2 pounds/gallon EC	Gal	40.20	44.80	46.40
Oil(Oil, Superior Oil, Supreme, Volck)	Gal	10.40	10.70	11.20
Oxamyl (Vydate–L), 2 pounds/gallon L	Gal	101.00	104.00	107.00
Oxydemeton–methyl (MSR Spray),.				
2 pounds/gallon EC	Gal	138.00	146.00	150.00
Phorate (Thimet), 20% G	Lb	2.95	3.06	3.14
Phosmet (Imidan), 50% WSP	Lb	10.40	10.10	9.86
Phosmet (Imidan), 70% WSP	Lb	10.60	11.40	12.30
Propargite (Comite, Omite), 32% WP	Lb	7.70	7.91	8.01
Synthetic Pyrethroids,.				
(Pounce, Ambush) 2–3.2 pounds/gallon	Gal	86.30	93.30	95.45
Terbufos (Counter), 15% G	Lb	3.07	3.38	3.48
Zeta–Cyermethrin (Zeta –cype), 0.8 pounds/gallon EC	Gal	136.00	134.00	133.00
Zeta–Cyermethrin (Fury), 1.5 pounds/gallon EC	Gal	178.00	187.00	191.00
Other:				
Gibberellic Acid (Pro–Gibb)4.0% L	Gal	118.00	114.00	113.00
NAD Napthaleneacetamide (Amid–Thin W), 8.4% WP	Lb	69.00	84.40	63.80

(NA) Not available.   [1] Prices paid by famers are collected, for the most part, from retail establishments located in smaller cities and towns in rural areas.   Prior to 1995, recorded prices reflected a modified annual average based on frequency item was surveyed during the year.   Recorded item values, 1995-99, are the U.S. April average price.   [2] Includes Federal, State, and local per gallon taxes where applicable.   [3] Excludes Federal excise tax.   [4] Includes Federal, State, and local per gallon taxes.   [5] Excludes cost of application, except for limestone.   [6] With hydraulic lift, transport wheels, and tires.   [7] Active Ingredient, (Common Names),and Formulation abbreviations: EC-Emulsifiable Concentrate, DF-Dry Flowable, DG-Dry Granular, G-Granular, L-Liquid, S-Solution, P-Soluble Powder, and WP-Wettable Powder.   [8] Insufficient data.
NASS, Environmental, Economics, and Demographics Branch, (202) 720–6146.

Table 9-38.—Agricultural commodities: Support prices per unit, United States, 2005–2014[1]

Commodity	Unit	2005	2006	2007	2008	2009
		Dollars	Dollars	Dollars	Dollars	Dollars
Basic commodities:						
Corn:						
Target/reference price	Bushel	2.63	2.63	2.63	2.63	2.63
Loan rate	do	1.95	1.95	1.95	1.95	1.95
Cotton:						
American upland:						
Target price	Cwt	72.40	72.40	72.40	71.25	71.25
Loan rate	do	52.00	52.00	52.00	52.00	52.00
Extra-long staple:						
Target price	do	(NA)	(NA)	(NA)	(NA)	(NA)
Loan rate	do	79.77	79.77	79.77	79.77	79.77
Peanuts:						
Target/reference price	Short tons	495.00	495.00	495.00	495.00	495.00
Loan rate	do	355.00	355.00	355.00	355.00	355.00
Rice:						
Target/reference price [3]	Cwt	10.50	10.50	10.50	10.50	10.50
Loan rate	do	6.50	6.50	6.50	6.50	6.50
Wheat:						
Target/reference price	Bushel	3.92	3.92	3.92	3.92	3.92
Loan rate	do	2.75	2.75	2.75	2.75	2.75
Barley:						
Target/reference price	Bushel	2.24	2.24	2.24	2.24	2.24
Loan rate	do	1.85	1.85	1.85	1.85	1.85
Sorghum grain:						
Target/reference price	Cwt	4.59	4.59	4.59	4.59	4.59
Loan rate	do	3.48	3.48	3.48	3.48	3.48
Oats:						
Target/reference price	Bushel	1.44	1.44	1.44	1.44	1.44
Loan rate	do	1.33	1.33	1.33	1.33	1.33
Other oilseeds: [4]						
Target/reference price	Cwt	10.10	10.10	10.10	10.10	10.10
Loan rate	do	9.30	9.30	9.30	9.30	9.30
Soybeans:						
Target/reference price	Bushel	5.80	5.80	5.80	5.80	5.80
Loan rate	do	5.00	5.00	5.00	5.00	5.00
Dry Peas:						
Target/reference price	Cwt	(NA)	(NA)	(NA)	(NA)	8.32
Loan rate	do	6.22	6.22	6.22	6.22	5.40
Small chick peas:						
Target/reference price	Cwt	(NA)	(NA)	(NA)	(NA)	10.36
Loan rate	do	7.43	7.43	7.43	7.43	7.43
Large chick peas:						
Target/reference price	Cwt	(NA)	(NA)	(NA)	(NA)	12.81
Loan rate	do	(NA)	(NA)	(NA)	(NA)	11.28
Lentils:						
Target/reference price	do	(NA)	(NA)	(NA)	(NA)	12.81
Loan rate	do	11.72	11.72	11.72	11.72	11.28
Sugar, raw cane:						
Loan rate	Pound	0.180	0.180	0.180	0.180	0.183
Sugar, refined beet:						
Loan rate	do	0.229	0.229	0.229	0.229	0.235
Honey, extracted:						
Loan rate	Pound	0.60	0.60	0.60	0.60	0.60
Mohair:						
Loan rate	do	4.20	4.20	4.20	4.20	4.20
Wool, graded:						
Loan rate	Pound	1.00	1.00	1.00	1.00	1.00
Wool, nongraded:						
Loan rate	Pound	0.40	0.40	0.40	0.40	0.40
Milk for manufacturing: [5]						
Support price	Cwt	9.90	9.90	9.35[3]	9.35	9.35

See footnote(s) at end of table.

Table 9-38.—Agricultural commodities: Support prices per unit, United States, 2005–2014 [1]—Continued

Commodity	Unit	2010	2011	2012	2013	2014[2]
		Dollars	Dollars	Dollars	Dollars	Dollars
Basic commodities:						
Corn:						
Target/reference price	Bushel	2.63	2.63	2.63	2.63	3.70
Loan rate	do	1.95	1.95	1.95	1.95	1.95
Cotton:						
American upland:						
Target price	Cwt	71.25	71.25	71.25	71.25	(NA)
Loan rate	do	52.00	52.00	52.00	52.00	52.00
Extra-long staple:						
Target price	do	(NA)	(NA)	(NA)	(NA)	(NA)
Loan rate	do	79.77	79.77	79.77	79.77	79.77
Peanuts:						
Target/reference price	Short tons	495.00	495.00	495.00	495.00	535.00
Loan rate	do	355.00	355.00	355.00	355.00	355.00
Rice:						
Target/reference price [3]	Cwt	10.50	10.50	10.50	10.50	14.00
Loan rate	do	6.50	6.50	6.50	6.50	6.50
Wheat:						
Target/reference price	Bushel	4.17	4.17	4.17	4.17	5.50
Loan rate	do	2.94	2.94	2.94	2.94	2.94
Barley:						
Target/reference price	Bushel	2.63	2.63	2.63	2.63	4.95
Loan rate	do	1.95	1.95	1.95	1.95	1.95
Sorghum grain:						
Target/reference price	Cwt	4.70	4.70	4.70	4.70	7.05
Loan rate	do	3.48	3.48	1.95	1.95	3.48
Oats:						
Target/reference price	Bushel	1.79	1.79	1.79	1.79	2.40
Loan rate	do	1.39	1.39	1.39	1.39	1.39
Other oilseeds: [4]						
Target/reference price	Cwt	12.68	12.68	12.68	12.68	20.15
Loan rate	do	10.09	10.09	10.09	10.09	10.09
Soybeans:						
Target/reference price	Bushel	6.00	6.00	6.00	6.00	8.40
Loan rate	do	5.00	5.00	5.00	5.00	5.00
Dry Peas:						
Target/reference price	Cwt	8.32	8.32	8.32	8.32	11.00
Loan rate	do	5.40	5.40	5.40	5.40	5.40
Small chick peas:						
Target/reference price	Cwt	10.36	10.36	10.36	10.36	19.04
Loan rate	do	7.43	7.43	7.43	7.43	7.43
Large chick peas:						
Target/reference price	Cwt	12.81	12.81	12.81	12.81	21.54
Loan rate	do	11.28	11.28	11.28	11.28	11.28
Lentils:						
Target/reference price	do	12.81	12.81	12.81	12.81	19.97
Loan rate	do	11.28	11.28	11.28	11.28	11.28
Sugar, raw cane:						
Loan rate	Pound	0.185	0.187	0.187	0.187	0.188
Sugar, refined beet:						
Loan rate	do	0.238	0.241	0.241	0.241	0.241
Honey, extracted:						
Loan rate	Pound	0.69	0.69	0.69	0.69	0.69
Mohair:						
Loan rate	do	4.20	4.20	4.20	4.20	4.20
Wool, graded:						
Loan rate	Pound	1.15	1.15	1.15	1.15	1.15
Wool, nongraded:						
Loan rate	Pound	0.40	0.40	0.40	0.40	0.40
Milk for manufacturing: [5]						
Support price	Cwt	9.35	9.35	9.35	9.35	(NA)

(NA) Not available.   [1] National averages during the marketing years for the individual crops.   [2] Target price is applicable for crop years 2003-2013 and reference price is applicable beginning with crop year 2014.   [3] Target and reference price shown is for long grain and medium (including short) grain rice.   The reference price for temperate japonica rice equals 115 percent of the medium (including short) grain rice (16.10 per Cwt) beginning with crop year 2014.   [4] Other oilseeds are flaxseed, sunflower seed (oil and other types), safflower, rapeseed, canola, mustard seed, crambe, and sesame seed.   [5] Effective support price calculated from product prices specified in 2008 Farm Bill, effective January 1, 2008. the Dairy Product Price Support Program expired December 31, 2013.

FSA, Feed Grains and Oilseeds, (202) 720–2711.

Table 9-39.—Farm income: Cash receipts by commodity groups and selected commodities, United States, 2005–2014 [1]

Commodity	2005	2006	2007	2008	2009
	1,000 dollars	*1,000 dollars*	*1,000 dollars*	*1,000 dollars*	*1,000 dollars*
All commodities	240,897,821	240,623,888	288,545,936	314,424,441	291,605,777
Livestock and products	124,931,103	118,498,682	138,478,570	140,500,928	119,998,586
Cattle and calves	49,283,094	49,110,334	49,843,326	48,394,131	43,720,324
Hogs	14,970,027	14,105,864	14,750,486	16,027,805	14,640,502
Sheep and lambs	560,047	471,896	466,670	451,081	447,237
Dairy products	26,704,863	23,412,552	35,453,399	34,846,236	24,321,032
Broilers	20,877,923	17,852,894	21,513,538	23,203,136	21,822,804
Farm chickens	65,072	54,141	51,498	62,456	65,381
Chicken eggs	4,066,669	4,460,211	6,718,853	8,239,313	6,191,040
Turkeys	3,025,891	3,451,528	3,929,008	4,471,046	3,573,324
Miscellaneous livestock	4,579,063	4,754,102	4,851,248	5,256,805	5,664,179
	2010	**2011**	**2012**	**2013**	**2014**
All commodities	321,195,035	365,849,626	401,437,418	403,034,491	421,505,060
Livestock and products	140,824,967	164,799,514	169,818,778	182,606,111	212,210,798
Cattle and calves	51,246,136	62,321,217	66,090,126	67,457,442	81,251,415
Hogs	17,898,063	21,631,894	22,092,108	23,761,227	26,419,703
Sheep and lambs	544,379	(X)	(X)	(X)	(X)
Dairy products	31,372,346	39,531,306	37,064,731	40,276,790	49,349,226
Broilers	23,691,553	22,987,822	24,827,800	30,761,669	32,724,667
Farm chickens	73,099	81,110	79,208	87,939	96,557
Chicken eggs	6,553,087	7,355,873	7,929,104	8,678,859	10,166,321
Turkeys	4,372,438	4,987,608	5,452,135	4,839,562	5,304,537
Miscellaneous livestock	5,618,245	5,902,684	6,283,566	6,742,623	6,898,372

Commodity	2005	2006	2007	2008	2009
Crops	115,966,718	122,125,206	150,067,366	173,923,513	171,607,190
Food grains	8,611,410	9,089,720	13,559,548	17,750,842	15,269,993
Feed crops	24,589,872	29,386,073	42,321,639	58,432,876	51,059,719
Cotton	6,402,504	5,545,956	6,457,260	5,252,889	4,280,531
Tobacco	1,097,081	1,156,674	1,284,098	1,371,512	1,465,580
Oil crops	18,387,789	18,545,958	24,603,108	28,279,442	36,315,294
Vegetables	17,291,250	18,074,300	19,320,989	17,048,920	17,797,884
Fruits/nuts	17,137,528	17,254,259	18,651,692	18,645,523	19,178,580
All other crops	22,449,284	23,072,266	23,869,032	27,141,508	26,239,610
	2010	**2011**	**2012**	**2013**	**2014**
Crops	180,370,068	201,050,111	231,618,640	220,428,381	209,294,263
Food grains	14,317,317	16,531,761	19,300,697	17,236,104	16,172,133
Feed crops	55,143,504	71,734,962	82,137,199	70,836,182	66,041,777
Cotton	7,464,640	7,303,972	8,230,448	6,515,834	7,301,851
Tobacco	1,335,561	1,139,738	1,347,847	1,546,501	1,696,384
Oil crops	36,543,865	35,324,476	46,925,389	47,274,513	42,682,668
Vegetables	17,406,924	17,617,985	17,409,430	19,425,462	18,852,397
Fruits/nuts	21,612,927	24,166,286	28,107,818	29,904,646	30,101,275
All other crops	26,545,330	27,230,931	28,159,812	27,689,138	26,445,777

Data as of February 9, 2016. (X) Data are not available/applicable. [1] USDA estimates and publishes individual cash receipt values only for major commodities and major producing States. The U.S. receipts for individual commodities, computed as the sum of the reported States, may understate the value of sales for some commodities, with the balance included in the appropriate category labeled "other" or "miscellaneous". The degree of underestimation in some of the minor commodities can be substantial.

ERS, Farm Income Team, (202) 694–5344. FarmIncomeTeam@ers.usda.gov. http://www.ers.usda.gov/data-products/farm-income-and-wealth-statistics.aspx.

Table 9-40.—Farm income: United States, 2005–2014

Item [3]	2005	2006	2007	2008	2009
	Billion dollars	Billion dollars	Billion dollars	Billion dollars	Billion dollars
Total gross farm income	298.5	290.2	339.6	364.6	336.5
Value of Production	274.1	274.4	327.7	352.3	324.3
Crops	114.4	118.7	151.1	173.8	164.6
Livestock and products	126.5	119.3	138.4	139.4	119.5
Services and forestry	33.2	36.4	38.1	39.1	40.2
Direct government payments	24.4	15.8	11.9	12.2	12.2
Total production expenses [1]	219.7	232.7	269.5	286.3	274.3
Net farm income	78.8	57.4	70.0	78.2	62.3
Gross cash income	279.7	273.2	318.0	349.5	327.3
Cash expenses	193.1	204.8	240.6	264.5	253.0
Net cash income	86.7	68.4	77.4	85.0	74.3
Item	2010	2011	2012	2013	2014
Total gross farm income	356.5	420.4	449.8	483.3	480.9
Value of production	344.1	409.9	439.1	472.3	471.1
Crops	168.1	199.3	212.9	233.2	204.7
Livestock and product	140.2	163.7	169.1	180.9	214.7
Services and forestry	35.8	46.9	57.1	58.2	51.7
Direct government payments	12.4	10.4	10.6	11.0	9.8
Total production expenses [1]	279.4	306.5	353.3	360.0	390.3
Net farm income	77.1	113.9	96.5	123.3	90.5
Gross cash income	353.6	407.0	451.3	455.0	466.7
Cash expenses	257.3	283.6	316.0	320.0	338.5
Net cash income	96.3	123.4	135.3	135.1	128.1

Data as of February 9, 2016. [1] Includes expenses associated with operator dwellings.
ERS, Farm Income Team. FarmIncomeTeam@ers.usda.gov. http://www.ers.usda.gov/data-products/farm-income-and-wealth-statistics.aspx.

Table 9-41.—Expenses: Farm production expenses, United States, 2007–2014

Item	2007	2008	2009	2010
	Billion dollars	Billion dollars	Billion dollars	Billion dollars
Total production expenses	269.5	286.3	274.3	279.4
Feed purchased	41.9	46.9	45.0	45.4
Livestock and poultry purchased	18.8	18.9	17.9	20.4
Seed purchased	12.6	15.1	15.5	16.3
Fertilizer and lime	17.7	22.5	20.1	21.0
Pesticides	10.5	11.7	11.5	10.7
Fuel and oil	13.8	16.9	13.2	13.8
Electricity	4.3	4.6	4.6	4.6
Other [1]	60.2	61.8	59.1	56.8
Interest [2]	15.1	16.8	17.6	16.9
Contract and hired labor expenses	29.0	29.9	29.0	27.5
Net rent to landlords [3]	9.0	13.1	13.6	16.9
Capital consumption [2]	27.0	16.8	16.0	17.6
Property taxes and fees [2]	11.0	11.3	11.1	11.5
Item	2011	2012	2013	2014
Total production expenses	306.5	353.3	360.0	390.3
Feed purchased	54.6	60.5	62.4	63.7
Livestock and poultry purchased	23.7	24.8	25.5	30.8
Seed purchased	17.8	20.9	21.9	22.1
Fertilizer and lime	25.1	28.9	28.3	28.1
Pesticides	11.8	14.0	14.6	15.8
Fuel and oil	16.2	16.5	17.3	17.7
Electricity	4.9	5.4	5.5	5.9
Other [1]	61.4	66.3	64.2	71.0
Interest [2]	16.0	16.9	14.9	15.6
Contract and hired labor expenses	27.0	32.1	32.3	34.5
Net rent to landlords [3]	17.4	20.5	22.9	21.1
Capital consumption [2]	18.4	34.2	37.7	49.7
Property taxes and fees [2]	12.0	12.2	12.4	14.3

Data as of February 9, 2016. [1] Includes repair and maintenance, machine hire and custom work, marketing, storage and transportation, insurance premiums, and miscellaneous other expenses. [2] Includes expenses associated with operator dwellings. [3] Data includes landlord capital consumption. Prior to 2008, net rent to landlords only included the portion paid to nonoperator.
ERS, Farm Income Team. FarmIncomeTeam@ers.usda.gov. http://www.ers.usda.gov/data-products/farm-income-and-wealth-statistics.aspx.

Table 9-42.—Principal Farm Operator Households: Farm and Off-farm Income, United States, 2009–2012

Item	2009	2010	2011	2012[1]
	Dollars per farm operator household			
Median household income from farming	(2,740)	(2,020)	(2,250)	(1,453)
Median off-farm income	47,500	49,490	53,424	58,750
Earned income	30,161	31,779	32,500	38,750
Unearned income	9,250	8,750	12,500	17,500
Median household income of farm operators	52,235	54,162	57,050	68,298
Average household income of farm operators	77,169	84,459	87,290	108,844
	Dollars per farm operator household			
U.S. Median household income	49,777	49,445	50,054	51,017
U.S. Average household income	67,976	67,530	69,677	71,274
	Percent			
Median farm household incomeas a percent of median U.S. household income	104.9	109.5	114.0	133.9
Average farm household incomeas a percent of average U.S. household income	113.5	125.1	125.3	152.7

[1] Differences between 2012 estimates and estimates from prior years reflect changes in survey methodology and implementation associated with the 2012 Agricultural Resource Management Survey in addition to changes in the economic situation of farm households..

ERS, Farm and Rural Household Well-Being Branch, (202) 694-5583. Source: 2009-2012 USDA Agricultural Resource Management Survey.

Table 9-43.—Grazing fees: Rates for cattle by selected States and regions, 2013–2014

State	Monthly lease rates for private non-irrigated grazing land [1]					
	Animal unit [2]		Cow-calf		Per head	
	2013	2014	2013	2014	2013	2014
	Dollars per month	Dollars per month	Dollars per month	Dollars per month	Dollars per month	Dollars per month
Arizona	9.00	9.00	(S)	(S)	12.00	(S)
California	19.50	20.00	23.50	25.10	21.00	22.50
Colorado	17.50	17.00	20.00	20.00	19.00	19.00
Idaho	15.50	16.50	19.00	19.00	15.50	18.50
Kansas	17.00	18.00	21.00	22.00	18.50	21.50
Montana	21.00	23.00	23.60	26.00	20.80	23.00
Nebraska	33.50	38.00	40.50	44.50	34.00	35.00
Nevada	(S)	11.50	(S)	(S)	(S)	(S)
New Mexico	13.00	13.50	(S)	(S)	14.00	15.50
North Dakota	18.00	19.20	21.50	22.00	18.00	18.00
Oklahoma	(S)	(S)	(S)	(S)	(S)	14.00
Oregon	15.00	17.00	17.80	19.50	19.00	19.00
South Dakota	27.90	30.00	33.30	35.00	28.50	32.50
Texas	(S)	(S)	(S)	(S)	12.00	14.00
Utah	14.50	15.00	18.50	19.00	16.00	16.50
Washington	13.50	13.50	15.00	16.50	14.50	15.00
Wyoming	18.70	20.00	21.00	22.00	19.40	21.00
17-State [3]	18.30	19.90	21.40	23.20	18.90	20.70
16-State [4]	20.10	21.60	23.80	25.40	21.00	22.60
11-State [5]	17.50	18.20	20.30	21.60	18.50	19.70
9-State [6]	18.50	20.30	21.50	23.50	18.90	20.90

(S) Insufficient number of reports to establish an estimate.
[1] The average rates are estimates (rates over $10.00 are rounded to the nearest dime) based on survey indications of monthly lease rates for private, non-irrigated grazing land from the January Cattle Survey.   [2] Includes animal unit plus cow-calf rates. Cow-calf rate converted to animal unit (AUM) using (1 aum=cow-calf *0.833).   [3] Seventeen Western States: All States listed.   [4] Sixteen Western States: All States, except Texas.   [5] Eleven Western States: Arizona, California, Colorado, Idaho, Montana, Nevada , New Mexico, Oregon, Utah, Washington and Wyoming.   [6] Nine Great Plains States: Colorado, Kansas, Nebraska, New Mexico, North Dakota, Oklahoma, South Dakota, Texas and Wyoming.

NASS, Environmental, Economics, and Demographics Branch, (202) 720–6146.

CHAPTER X
INSURANCE, CREDIT, AND COOPERATIVES

The statistics in this chapter deal with insurance, agricultural credit and farm cooperatives. Some of the series were developed in connection with research activities of the Department, while others, such as data from agricultural credit agencies, are primarily records of operations.

Table 10-1.—Crop losses: Average percentage of indemnities attributed to specific hazards, by crops, 1948–2015

Crop	Year	Drought heat (excess)	Hail	Precip. (excess poor drainage)	Frost freeze (other cold damage)	Flood	Cyclone, tornado, wind, hot wind	Insects	Disease	All others
					Percent					
Adj. gross revenue	2001-2013	13	10	15	33	0	2	0	0	28
Adj. gross revenue-lite	1981-2013	5	6	12	42	0	1	0	0	34
Alfalfa seed	2002-2014	5	41	8	23	0	19	1	0	3
All other citrus trees	2000-2014	0	0	2	12	0	2	0	0	84
Almonds	1981-2014	2	4	51	37	0	6	0	0	0
Annual Forage	2014-2014	0	0	0	0	0	0	0	0	100
Apiculture	2009-2014	0	0	0	0	0	0	0	0	100
Apples	1963-2014	11	25	10	46	0	3	0	1	4
Avocado trees	1996-2013	0	0	4	9	0	87	0	0	0
Avocados	1998-2015	26	0	0	51	0	14	0	0	8
Banana	2012-2013	54	0	0	0	0	0	0	0	46
Barley	1956-2014	37	19	23	8	1	3	1	3	4
Blueberries	1995-2014	5	8	31	53	0	0	0	1	1
Buckwheat	2010-2014	44	22	30	2	0	1	0	0	0
Burley tobacco	1997-2014	35	7	27	4	6	6	0	14	1
Cabbage	1999-2014	15	2	44	13	0	6	17	1	1
Camelina	2012-2012	100	0	0	0	0	0	0	0	0
Canola	1995-2014	25	15	30	19	0	6	1	1	2
Cherries	1963-2014	4	7	19	55	0	5	0	0	9
Cigar binder tobacco	1997-2014	2	20	23	2	0	2	0	50	1
Cigar filler tobacco	1998-2010	86	0	6	0	0	0	1	7	0
Cigar wrapper tobacco	1997-2012	0	0	51	3	0	0	0	46	0
Citrus	1989-1997	18	5	1	74	0	2	0	0	0
Citrus I	1998-2012	0	0	0	3	0	97	0	0	0
Citrus II	2000-2013	0	0	0	27	0	73	0	0	0
Citrus III	2001-2013	0	0	0	13	0	87	0	0	0
Citrus IV	1998-2011	0	6	0	13	0	81	0	0	0
Citrus V	1999-2013	0	1	0	13	0	85	0	0	0
Citrus VI	2005-2006	0	0	0	0	0	100	0	0	0
Citrus VII	1998-2013	0	4	0	15	0	81	0	0	0
Citrus VIII	2009-2012	0	13	0	87	0	0	0	0	0
Citrus trees	1990-1997	0	0	0	100	0	0	0	0	0
Citrus trees I	2008-2010	0	0	70	0	0	30	0	0	0
Citrus trees II	2008-2010	0	0	100	0	0	0	0	0	0
Citrus trees III	2010-2010	0	0	99	0	0	0	0	0	1
Citrus trees IV	2004-2010	0	0	100	0	0	0	0	0	0
Citrus trees V	2010-2010	0	0	100	0	0	0	0	0	0
Clams	2001-2014	0	0	0	6	0	5	0	0	89
Coffee	2009-2013	82	0	0	0	0	0	12	0	5
Corn	1948-2014	59	29	27	45	22	43	6	19	65
Cotton	1948-2014	181	113	109	111	45	171	23	9	139
Cotton ex long staple	1984-2014	7	6	19	17	0	5	5	0	42
Cranberries	1984-2014	13	13	24	42	1	0	3	1	3
Cucumbers	2014-2014	0	0	100	0	0	0	0	0	0
Cultivated wild rice	1999-2014	8	16	4	11	1	26	1	1	33
Dark air tobacco	1997-2014	42	5	34	1	0	5	0	11	0
Dry beans	1948-2014	18	29	23	23	1	3	0	2	1
Dry peas	1963-2014	44	28	19	7	0	1	1	1	0
Early, midseason oranges	1998-2014	0	7	9	48	0	35	0	0	0
Figs	1988-2014	14	0	47	31	0	2	0	0	6
Fire cured tobacco	1997-2014	35	9	33	6	0	5	0	5	8
Flax	1948-2014	33	6	56	3	0	1	0	0	0
Flue cured tobacco	1997-2014	24	12	15	5	1	19	0	23	1
Forage production	1979-2014	43	4	11	31	1	0	2	0	8
Forage seeding	1978-2014	43	0	24	32	0	1	0	0	0
Fresh apricots	1997-2014	2	24	12	58	0	3	0	0	0
Fresh freestone peaches	1997-2014	4	21	15	59	0	1	0	0	0
Fresh market beans	2000-2013	0	0	72	15	0	9	0	4	0
Fresh market sweet corn	1985-2014	10	1	42	29	0	15	0	1	2
Fresh market tomatoes	1984-2014	11	8	45	21	0	7	1	7	0
Fresh nectarines	1997-2014	7	50	19	24	0	1	0	0	0
Grain sorghum	1959-2014	32	8	22	14	1	13	2	0	8

See note(s) at end of table.

Table 10-1.—Crop losses: Average percentage of indemnities attributed to specific hazards, by crops, 1948–2015—Continued

Crop	Year	Drought heat (ex-cess)	Hail	Precip. (excess poor drainage)	Frost freeze, (other cold damage)	Flood	Cyclone, tornado, wind, hot wind	In-sects	Dis-ease	All others
Grapefruit	1997-2015	27	0	0	47	0	25	0	0	0
Grapefruit trees	2000-2014	0	0	1	5	0	0	0	0	93
Grapes	1967-2014	19	3	16	61	0	1	0	0	0
Grass Seed	2012-2012	53	0	0	0	0	47	0	0	0
Green peas	1962-2014	44	3	48	2	0	1	0	1	0
Hybrid corn seed	1983-2014	44	4	31	3	0	16	0	2	0
Hybrid sorghum seed	1988-2014	38	6	1	16	0	38	0	0	1
Late oranges	1998-2015	0	1	18	9	0	72	0	0	0
Lemon trees	2005-2005	0	0	0	0	0	100	0	0	0
Lemons	1997-2014	3	0	0	96	0	0	0	0	0
Lime trees	1998-2005	0	0	0	1	0	0	0	0	99
Macadamia nuts	1996-2014	76	0	3	0	0	0	13	0	7
Macadamia trees	2000-2012	0	0	56	0	0	36	0	0	8
Mandarins	1997-2014	16	3	1	79	0	2	0	0	0
Mango trees	1997-2010	0	0	0	59	0	41	0	0	0
Maryland tobacco	1997-2014	59	9	7	4	0	6	0	14	1
Millet	1996-2014	71	15	11	1	0	1	0	0	0
Minneola tangelos	1998-2014	11	1	1	86	0	1	0	0	0
Mint	2000-2014	49	1	13	33	1	2	0	1	0
Mustard	1999-2014	65	28	3	3	0	1	0	0	0
Navel oranges	1998-2014	42	2	7	45	0	1	0	0	2
Nursery	1990-1999	24	0	7	11	7	42	3	5	0
Nursery (fg&c)	2001-2014	2	13	26	19	4	29	4	1	1
Oats	1956-2014	45	13	34	4	0	1	1	1	1
Olives	2012-2014	57	1	10	26	0	6	0	0	0
Onions	1988-2014	14	14	47	5	0	4	0	13	3
Orange trees	1996-2014	0	0	3	7	0	1	0	0	89
Oranges	1997-2015	28	0	0	32	0	18	0	0	22
Orlando tangelos	1998-2012	0	0	0	100	0	0	0	0	0
Papaya	2007-2009	0	0	56	0	0	31	12	0	0
Pastures/Rangeland Forage	2007-2014	0	0	0	0	0	0	0	0	100
Peaches	1957-2014	5	33	5	52	0	0	0	0	5
Peanuts	1962-2014	44	0	21	5	0	7	0	18	3
Pears	1989-2014	1	28	2	68	0	0	0	0	0
Pecans	1998-2014	27	1	19	35	0	16	0	1	2
Peppers	1984-2014	0	5	62	26	0	5	0	1	0
Pistachios	2012-2014	58	0	12	16	0	13	0	0	0
Plums	1998-2014	9	33	16	38	0	4	0	0	0
Popcorn	1984-2014	59	12	19	3	1	2	1	1	2
Potatoes	1962-2014	25	8	24	22	1	1	0	17	2
Prevented planting endorse	1990-1994	31	0	11	0	53	0	0	0	5
Processing apricots	1997-2014	1	7	48	26	0	18	0	0	0
Processing beans	1988-2014	42	3	46	5	0	2	0	1	0
Processing cling peaches	1997-2014	27	10	31	31	0	2	0	0	0
Processing cucumbers	2000-2005	45	1	47	2	0	1	1	4	0
Processing freestone	1998-2014	12	27	4	55	0	1	0	0	0
Prunes	1986-2014	28	1	11	49	0	10	0	0	1
Pumpkins	2009-2014	22	0	59	18	0	0	0	0	1
Raisins	1961-2013	0	0	100	0	0	0	0	0	0
Rangeland	1999-2008	0	0	0	0	0	0	0	0	100
Raspberry and blackberry	2002-2006	40	0	22	27	0	12	0	0	0
Revenue coverage corn	1996-1996	20	44	3	5	26	0	0	1	0
Revenue coverage soybeans	1996-1996	1	24	55	5	13	0	0	3	0
Rice	1960-2014	16	0	45	6	6	9	0	3	13
Rio red & star ruby	1998-2015	0	3	40	30	0	27	0	0	1
Ruby red grapefruit	1998-2015	0	5	25	26	0	44	0	0	0
Rye	1980-2014	44	8	36	11	0	0	0	0	0
Safflower	1964-2014	40	7	20	15	0	15	1	1	0
Sesame	2011-2014	91	1	3	0	0	5	0	0	0
Silage sorghum	1965-2014	83	5	0	0	0	11	0	0	1
Soybeans	1955-2014	209	101	140	125	76	61	11	26	117
Special citrus	1992-1994	6	12	0	82	0	0	0	0	0
Stonefruit	1989-1996	1	28	44	19	0	2	0	0	6
Strawberries	2000-2012	9	0	66	7	0	0	0	17	0
Sugar beets	1965-2014	11	7	29	27	2	11	1	11	1
Sugarcane	1967-2014	21	0	25	17	0	5	1	12	20
Sunflowers	1976-2014	24	15	24	13	0	8	3	6	7
Sweet corn	1978-2014	52	1	29	13	0	4	0	0	1
Sweet oranges	1998-2014	11	0	10	75	0	4	0	0	1
Sweet potatoes	1998-2011	39	0	43	0	0	13	4	0	1
Table grapes	1984-2014	28	7	27	37	0	1	0	0	0
Tangelos	1997-2015	3	0	0	93	0	0	0	0	4
Tobacco	1989-1996	17	20	20	1	0	18	0	20	2
Tomatoes	1963-2014	33	0	54	3	1	1	0	7	1
Valencia oranges	1998-2014	34	2	3	57	0	3	0	0	0
Walnuts	1984-2014	33	3	45	17	0	2	0	0	0
Watermelons	1999-1999	8	7	38	1	0	14	0	29	2
Wheat	1948-2014	46	22	25	74	10	30	7	21	29
Winter squash	1999-2005	10	13	75	0	2	0	0	0	1

GRP crops do not have any specific cause of loss.
RMA, Requirements, Analysis and Validation Branch, (816) 926–7910.

Table 10-2.—Crop insurance programs: Coverage, amount of premiums and indemnities, by crops, United States, 2012–2014

Commodity and year	Coverage				Amount of premium	Indemnities		
	County programs	Insured units [1]	Area insured [2]	Maximum insured production		Number	Area in-demnified [2]	Amount
	Number	*Number*	*1,000 acres*	*1,000 dollars*	*1,000 dollars*		*1,000 acres*	*1,000 dollars*
Adjusted gross revenue:								
2012	230	372	0	353,530	12,565	30	....	7,798
2013	230	365	0	363,911	12,969	35	....	4,865
2014	230	354	0	396,832	14,503	0	....	0
Adjusted gross revenue-lite:								
2012	1,706	428	0	106,263	4,544	53	....	2,717
2013	1,708	389	0	104,888	4,394	65	....	4,459
2014	1,706	414	0	116,315	4,922	0	....	0
Alfalfa seed:								
2012	12	322	24	17,366	1,516	68	4	844
2013	12	376	28	27,942	2,081	100	5	1,856
2014	13	432	30	36,039	2,766	7	0	243
All other citrus trees:								
2012	28	825	0	42,677	775	10	0	105
2013	28	848	0	51,551	932	3	0	105
2014	28	779	0	47,933	850	2	0	13
All other grapefruit:								
2012	3	1	0	1	0	0	....	0
2013	3	1	0	1	0	0	....	0
2014	3	1	0	0	0	0	....	0
Almonds:								
2012	16	5,612	664	1,229,339	48,502	274	19	6,787
2013	16	5,907	695	1,516,336	55,320	203	12	4,596
2014	16	6,181	721	2,188,496	82,871	104	6	4,315
Annual Forage:								
2014	648	1,942	497	21,613	4,971	1,140	0	6,316
Apiculture:								
2012	2,061	614	0	13,554	2,852	340	76	3,183
2013	2,059	2,091	0	33,792	7,153	1,362	204	9,983
2014	2,059	5,208	0	77,470	17,036	1,738	0	10,912
Apples:								
2012	360	6,767	239	830,352	74,529	2,835	69	153,488
2013	360	7,037	239	932,005	85,261	1,171	26	58,562
2014	334	7,252	248	1,089,083	101,859	125	2	4,632
Avocado trees:								
2012	1	186	0	21,573	802	1	0	55
2013	1	183	0	22,590	782	10	0	199
2014	1	174	0	21,403	765	0	....	0
Avocados:								
2012	7	1,254	38	80,295	9,877	134	3	2,531
2013	7	1,247	38	76,283	8,841	90	1	861
2014	7	1,207	38	84,390	9,371	148	2	1,969
Banana tree:								
2012	4	2	0	625	38	0	....	0
2013	4	2	0	674	41	0	....	0
2014	4	2	0	462	26	0	....	0
Bananas:								
2012	4	7	0	1,155	35	1	0	1
2013	4	7	0	1,393	35	1	0	1
2014	4	5	0	1,487	36	0	....	0
Barley:								
2012	3,036	29,616	2,689	640,520	86,290	5,157	549	45,618
2013	3,030	28,212	2,580	607,635	81,089	7,427	765	68,965
2014	3,021	23,997	2,167	437,022	52,708	4,575	432	32,750
Blueberries:								
2012	67	1,212	57	136,677	11,009	196	5	6,136
2013	74	1,322	63	155,631	12,443	231	5	7,126
2014	76	1,376	66	177,024	13,523	102	2	2,520
Buckwheat:								
2012	23	223	20	2,213	514	86	9	460
2013	22	140	10	1,830	358	50	3	252
2014	22	140	11	1,899	395	17	1	63
Burley tobacco:								
2012	253	8,213	82	196,346	26,537	2,370	31	35,818
2013	253	6,510	63	166,364	20,545	2,157	24	33,389
2014	253	7,959	87	261,690	35,677	78	1	2,509

See footnote(s) at end of table.

Table 10-2.—Crop insurance programs: Coverage, amount of premiums and indemnities, by crops, United States, 2012–2014—Continued

Commodity and year	Coverage					Indemnities		
	County programs	Insured units [1]	Area insured [2]	Maximum insured production	Amount of premium	Number	Area indemnified [2]	Amount
	Number	Number	1,000 acres	1,000 dollars	1,000 dollars		1,000 acres	1,000 dollars
Cabbage:								
2012	30	348	14	21,951	1,558	61	1	1,270
2013	29	309	13	21,432	1,974	25	1	516
2014	29	366	14	25,733	2,197	35	1	1,554
Camelina:								
2012	52	3	1	34	6	1	0	7
2013	52	4	0	22	4	0		0
Canola:								
2012	489	16,629	1,713	440,607	68,624	3,700	419	39,929
2013	489	16,347	1,682	418,973	73,684	7,699	804	117,815
2014	504	17,190	1,698	349,407	59,338	6,466	634	62,785
Carambola trees:								
2012	1	7	0	682	23	0		0
2013	1	6	0	511	16	0		0
2014	2	11	0	1,716	59	0		0
Cherries:								
2012	35	2,971	65	379,430	33,422	761	17	40,824
2013	51	3,106	69	417,476	37,829	974	20	40,839
2014	63	3,550	89	463,948	42,218	654	17	44,650
Chile Peppers:								
2012	3	32	4	1,282	70	0		0
2013	3	33	3	1,351	80	0		0
2014	3	24	2	939	54	0		0
Cigar binder tobacco:								
2012	16	385	3	17,381	4,620	109	1	3,409
2013	16	376	3	17,891	4,951	145	1	5,331
2014	16	341	3	16,018	4,347	35	0	2,412
Cigar filler tobacco:								
2012	3	9	0	214	4	0		0
2013	3	13	0	273	5	0		0
2014	3	8	0	231	4	0		0
Cigar wrapper tobacco:								
2012	5	24	1	8,075	631	17	0	2,266
2013	5	20	1	8,799	616	0		0
2014	5	14	0	5,600	448	0		0
Clams:								
2012	13	147	0	19,635	517	14		558
2013	13	119	0	22,689	726	19		530
2014	13	121	0	20,158	668	7		486
Coffee:								
2012	4	70	4	4,468	213	10	0	69
2013	4	72	4	4,968	186	31	0	265
2014	4	80	4	8,540	269	0		0
Corn:								
2012	12,387	1,157,945	81,449	53,639,149	4,329,988	555,348	49,965	11,842,466
2013	12,369	1,199,368	84,878	56,545,320	4,692,102	481,273	47,550	5,840,271
2014	12,771	1,153,312	78,831	43,884,551	3,637,484	82,577	5,314	742,756
Cotton:								
2012	2,352	163,180	11,431	4,831,942	836,730	66,825	15,658	1,096,015
2013	2,352	148,936	9,910	3,780,834	682,478	59,043	13,941	1,002,238
2014	2,352	154,353	10,348	4,041,847	721,846	13,248	3,200	308,249
Cotton exlong staple:								
2012	31	961	236	197,519	14,136	285	43	20,069
2013	31	879	213	147,815	12,447	334	61	26,845
2014	29	1,320	287	260,220	35,201	305	97	58,310
Cranberries:								
2012	30	700	32	92,792	3,051	64	2	2,083
2013	30	709	32	127,433	4,122	55	1	1,547
2014	30	692	32	99,927	3,042	23	1	581
Cucumbers:								
2014	40	351	24	17,051	1,301	3	0	140
Cultivated wild rice:								
2012	11	96	24	11,900	649	18	3	529
2013	11	96	25	14,853	826	12	2	393
2014	11	80	23	15,683	987	4	1	875
Dark air tobacco:								
2012	30	687	3	12,883	457	48	0	367
2013	30	690	4	13,909	486	108	1	930
2013	30	809	4	18,085	656	2	0	60
Dry beans:								
2012	276	18,273	1,337	693,280	98,316	2,712	211	38,479
2013	437	15,537	1,118	463,963	70,172	4,079	332	63,727
2014	499	18,126	1,353	574,642	84,697	2,265	186	31,562
Dry Peas:								
2012	140	10,742	1,157	223,951	31,968	1,829	235	15,693
2013	418	12,398	1,367	264,372	38,838	2,633	353	29,306
2014	429	11,766	1,344	206,516	30,240	1,789	240	13,939

See footnote(s) at end of table.

Table 10-2.—Crop insurance programs: Coverage, amount of premiums and indemnities, by crops, United States, 2012–2014—Continued

Commodity and year	Coverage				Amount of premium	Indemnities		
	County programs	Insured units [1]	Area insured [2]	Maximum insured production		Number	Area indemnified [2]	Amount
	Number	*Number*	*1,000 acres*	*1,000 dollars*	*1,000 dollars*		*1,000 acres*	*1,000 dollars*
Early and Midseason oranges:								
2012	3	250	3	2,122	128	71	1	166
2013	3	251	3	2,178	135	19	0	63
2014	3	275	4	2,776	160	25	0	86
Figs:								
2012	4	57	5	4,110	183	1	0	10
2013	4	51	4	4,134	178	0		0
2014	4	66	4	5,821	295	2	0	53
Fired cured tobacco:								
2012	41	1,176	11	46,152	1,991	99	1	1,894
2013	41	1,172	11	50,873	2,145	195	2	3,578
2014	41	1,396	14	70,750	3,047	10	0	205
Flax:								
2012	152	4,000	323	59,595	8,268	1,070	98	5,734
2013	150	2,658	219	35,760	5,698	1,155	96	9,481
2014	142	3,415	296	47,575	7,021	589	45	3,501
Flue cured tobacco:								
2012	146	11,479	201	545,963	38,822	1,794	34	40,805
2013	146	12,274	221	651,853	47,534	3,916	72	78,815
2014	146	13,117	241	868,445	63,956	865	16	24,541
Forage production:								
2012	783	38,521	3,304	502,440	47,288	17,057	1,628	64,743
2013	774	38,018	3,302	606,393	62,676	3,646	302	26,188
2014	772	33,800	3,068	648,149	73,906	1,476	159	13,988
Forage seeding:								
2012	592	4,723	185	31,279	3,966	2,085	83	9,437
2013	589	4,536	190	32,267	4,211	1,021	38	3,838
2014	589	4,000	158	26,383	3,485	91	4	463
Fresh apricots:								
2012	29	148	3	9,609	1,290	31	1	1,466
2013	29	151	3	10,051	1,364	18	0	745
2014	29	149	3	9,726	1,290	5	0	451
Fresh freestone peaches:								
2012	25	777	20	25,396	844	64	2	801
2013	25	846	18	26,292	899	32	0	186
2014	25	838	19	33,070	1,216	13	0	74
Fresh market beans:								
2012	15	37	5	2,633	326	5	1	168
2013	15	52	4	1,812	222	1	0	4
2014	15	41	3	1,604	203	0		0
Fresh market sweet corn:								
2012	230	898	52	44,517	4,146	101	3	1,975
2013	230	838	53	49,586	4,654	105	4	1,918
2014	230	774	51	48,557	4,537	54	4	2,266
Fresh market tomatoes:								
2012	59	716	47	197,106	24,182	354	18	60,432
2013	59	853	45	208,654	26,958	209	7	16,905
2014	59	785	44	176,947	20,733	133	4	9,675
Fresh nectarines:								
2012	24	743	16	24,867	1,712	114	3	2,223
2013	24	829	16	27,736	2,033	34	1	311
2014	24	809	17	34,536	2,467	22	0	227
Grain sorghum:								
2012	3,879	82,836	4,682	1,064,658	214,164	43,869	4,224	402,312
2013	3,879	98,623	5,805	1,307,900	277,810	42,346	4,839	363,711
2014	3,852	91,574	5,296	947,557	209,943	9,085	997	48,608
Grapefruit:								
2012	11	239	7	10,548	396	28	1	831
2013	11	265	8	11,845	432	25	1	656
2014	41	925	47	79,438	4,062	22	0	377
Grapefruit trees:								
2012	31	1,488	0	152,270	4,000	22	0	161
2013	31	1,536	0	188,090	4,865	8	0	55
2014	31	1,478	0	178,676	4,773	1	0	5

See footnote(s) at end of table.

Table 10-2.—Crop insurance programs: Coverage, amount of premiums and indemnities, by crops, United States, 2012–2014—Continued

Commodity and year	Coverage					Indemnities		
	County programs	Insured units [1]	Area insured [2]	Maximum insured production	Amount of premium	Number	Area indemnified [2]	Amount
	Number	Number	1,000 acres	1,000 dollars	1,000 dollars		1,000 acres	1,000 dollars
Mint:								
2012	31	318	29	27,755	1,291	85	4	1,037
2013	31	266	23	21,219	1,060	46	3	1,001
2014	31	332	25	23,955	1,102	48	3	652
Mustard:								
2012	45	316	37	6,002	1,368	72	11	744
2013	45	220	31	5,337	1,296	45	8	808
2014	45	113	16	2,390	509	28	6	416
Nursery (FG & C):								
2012	2,802	4,521	0	2,017,258	43,379	69		6,495
2013	2,802	3,980	0	1,803,698	38,427	16		1,359
2014	2,799	3,192	0	1,551,010	33,774	13		2,009
Oats:								
2012	1,512	10,626	434	49,481	8,291	1,922	88	4,956
2013	1,509	10,636	462	54,894	9,885	2,115	94	5,575
2014	1,505	10,979	494	50,103	9,069	1,640	67	3,453
Olives:								
2012	20	599	24	31,349	3,110	144	5	3,453
2013	22	620	26	26,873	2,594	86	2	1,284
2014	22	586	26	28,808	2,901	167	5	3,963
Onions:								
2012	93	1,632	79	149,772	24,999	447	14	23,552
2013	93	1,850	92	164,046	33,047	700	20	25,591
2014	101	2,068	110	210,458	39,647	608	19	26,319
Orange trees:								
2012	31	5,791	12	1,115,667	18,711	38	0	434
2013	31	5,986	12	1,325,361	22,493	25	0	329
2014	31	5,807	0	1,310,800	20,663	3	0	33
Oranges:								
2014	29	5,785	369	451,350	13,735	0		0
Papaya:								
2012	4	6	0	253	5	0		0
2013	4	6	0	355	6	0		0
2014	4	6	0	242	4	0		0
Papaya tree:								
2012	4	4	0	81	1	0		0
2013	4	3	0	105	1	0		0
2014	4	3	0	133	4	0		0
Pasture/Range-land/Forage:								
2012	2,061	133,074	48,265	790,074	164,038	74,010	28,925	182,323
2013	2,059	154,135	54,280	978,761	196,249	66,420	26,858	177,223
2014	2,059	141,529	52,715	964,957	199,056	49,394	0	147,558
Peaches:								
2012	232	1,525	34	72,928	16,591	565	10	11,204
2013	232	1,556	35	78,973	17,558	488	9	14,065
2014	222	1,531	34	80,450	18,411	525	12	22,136
Peanuts:								
2012	345	30,049	1,325	908,150	87,868	2,626	125	26,799
2013	360	21,100	954	496,004	46,304	2,641	112	25,512
2014	355	25,564	1,228	689,329	64,458	865	37	8,588
Pears:								
2012	29	2,240	33	83,621	1,759	67	1	614
2013	29	2,222	34	87,690	1,905	81	1	913
2014	29	2,299	34	98,007	2,184	16	0	82
Pecans:								
2012	143	1,750	166	166,793	12,670	244	18	5,493
2013	143	1,760	167	189,994	13,413	641	44	15,400
2014	147	1,809	152	230,180	14,303	3	0	19
Peppers:								
2012	13	157	7	24,074	3,508	26	1	1,904
2013	13	128	7	26,334	4,382	33	1	2,433
2014	13	121	6	23,868	3,808	12	0	1,136

See footnote(s) at end of table.

Table 10-2.—Crop insurance programs: Coverage, amount of premiums and
indemnities, by crops, United States, 2012–2014—Continued

Commodity and year	Coverage				Amount of premium	Indemnities		
	County programs	Insured units [1]	Area insured [2]	Maximum insured production		Number	Area indemnified [2]	Amount
	Number	Number	1,000 acres	1,000 dollars	1,000 dollars		1,000 acres	1,000 dollars
Grapes:								
2012	105	16,697	583	997,038	39,803	2,098	43	19,224
2013	105	17,317	593	1,263,367	46,647	680	13	7,797
2014	110	18,841	601	1,455,452	57,099	456	8	7,017
Grass seed:								
2012	6	97	16	2,077	300	3	0	8
2013	6	111	18	2,408	352	0		0
2014	6	175	29	4,064	637	0		0
Green peas:								
2012	166	2,340	150	62,375	7,212	759	48	8,832
2013	170	2,211	149	71,379	8,139	811	58	11,267
2014	170	2,027	136	60,191	6,618	794	58	9,842
Hybrid corn seed:								
2012	230	8,828	557	567,301	37,139	2,491	202	62,740
2013	229	9,678	617	702,336	47,643	645	49	14,103
2014	229	5,407	355	302,853	19,305	116	9	3,438
Hybrid sorghum seed:								
2012	23	775	58	37,068	4,345	173	17	3,695
2013	23	946	71	51,330	5,721	37	3	1,110
2014	23	660	43	23,495	2,611	2	0	110
Late oranges:								
2012	3	85	1	572	92	8	0	13
2013	3	94	1	691	121	7	0	26
2014	3	104	1	889	145	4	0	13
Lemons:								
2012	15	781	43	90,507	4,902	52	7	2,738
2013	15	802	43	98,710	5,036	26	2	1,237
2014	19	830	43	118,439	6,443	40	2	1,473
Macadamia nuts:								
2012	3	105	13	21,679	653	18	2	683
2013	3	63	12	19,042	555	14	1	467
2014	3	62	12	18,957	552	30	3	1,325
Macadamia trees:								
2012	3	108	13	59,135	603	5	1	43
2013	3	106	12	57,554	587	0		0
2014	3	107	13	57,698	588	0		0
Mandarins/Tangerines:								
2014	29	334	5	7,022	297	0		0
Mango trees:								
2012	1	16	0	326	8	0		0
2013	1	13	0	393	15	0		0
2014	1	13	0	401	16	0		0
Maryland tobacco:								
2012	6	1	0	11	1	0		0
2013	6	24	0	132	7	3	0	7
2014	6	25	0	211	10	2	0	4
Millet:								
2012	68	3,716	293	20,333	4,737	2,791	322	10,512
2013	68	6,245	544	69,804	16,752	2,015	268	14,725
2014	68	5,245	412	43,117	10,249	487	60	2,403

See footnote(s) at end of table.

Table 10-2.—Crop insurance programs: Coverage, amount of premiums and indemnities, by crops, United States, 2012–2014—Continued

Commodity and year	Coverage					Indemnities		
	County programs	Insured units [1]	Area insured [2]	Maximum insured production	Amount of premium	Number	Area indemnified [2]	Amount
	Number	*Number*	*1,000 acres*	*1,000 dollars*	*1,000 dollars*		*1,000 acres*	*1,000 dollars*
Pistachios:								
2012	24	505	85	193,330	7,337	22	1	650
2013	24	538	89	201,333	7,473	117	9	4,581
2014	24	576	92	296,256	11,483	18	3	8,667
Plums:								
2012	27	1,005	17	30,594	3,514	169	3	2,758
2013	27	973	15	27,427	3,155	116	1	967
2014	27	912	14	22,936	2,739	40	0	380
Popcorn:								
2012	663	2,237	185	127,040	9,047	933	88	20,394
2013	660	2,366	209	131,642	10,680	255	29	4,385
2014	624	2,929	254	153,196	12,382	170	13	1,577
Potatoes:								
2012	317	7,663	916	1,153,958	94,365	862	54	39,405
2013	316	7,117	858	1,123,833	94,291	1,082	75	45,578
2014	315	7,153	853	1,156,124	96,336	366	21	14,137
Processing apricots:								
2012	13	69	3	3,719	545	6	1	557
2013	13	64	3	3,599	528	5	0	183
2014	13	68	3	4,685	721	1	0	10
Processing beans:								
2012	151	1,691	102	49,552	4,921	250	13	2,941
2013	148	1,444	86	42,814	4,009	238	13	3,221
2014	148	1,650	97	46,647	4,521	161	11	2,505
Processing cling peaches:								
2012	10	1,125	17	38,832	1,581	133	2	1,476
2013	10	1,076	16	42,845	1,764	48	1	417
2014	10	1,009	16	46,991	2,036	27	0	213
Processing freestone:								
2012	8	94	3	5,497	196	5	0	63
2013	8	98	3	5,988	216	2	0	95
2014	8	101	3	6,116	263	1	0	3
Prunes:								
2012	14	923	51	57,608	11,354	91	4	1,435
2013	14	862	48	55,193	10,868	449	23	12,687
2014	14	828	46	78,889	15,543	36	2	2,033
Pumpkins:								
2012	11	179	8	6,623	385	33	2	434
2013	11	146	6	5,386	319	58	4	530
2014	11	152	6	4,136	246	6	0	14
Rice:								
2012	402	17,028	2,101	1,097,214	55,086	957	142	41,260
2013	405	18,726	2,656	1,278,975	62,501	4,773	616	123,080
2014	402	23,453	3,352	1,781,165	93,631	3,109	371	111,224
Rio Red & Star Ruby:								
2012	3	382	10	10,810	2,259	104	4	740
2013	3	387	10	11,534	2,475	42	1	479
2014	3	418	12	14,388	3,062	49	1	395
Ruby red grapefruit:								
2012	3	64	1	477	80	16	0	22
2013	3	66	1	476	81	5	0	30
2014	3	71	1	481	79	7	0	15
Rye:								
2012	48	343	27	2,155	389	68	5	149
2013	48	374	32	3,160	616	101	7	484
2014	48	418	32	3,330	602	217	21	935

See footnote(s) at end of table.

Table 10-2.—Crop insurance programs: Coverage, amount of premiums and
indemnities, by crops, United States, 2012–2014—Continued

Commodity and year	Coverage				Amount of premium	Indemnities		
	County programs	Insured units[1]	Area insured[2]	Maximum insured production		Number	Area indemnified[2]	Amount
	Number	*Number*	*1,000 acres*	*1,000 dollars*	*1,000 dollars*		*1,000 acres*	*1,000 dollars*
Safflower:								
2012	83	753	108	12,587	2,459	156	25	971
2013	83	772	121	13,505	2,777	128	21	744
2014	83	792	124	13,598	3,009	81	11	794
Sesame:								
2012	29	143	11	1,104	228	97	10	465
2013	35	386	27	4,632	784	226	22	2,455
2014	35	730	43	7,786	1,315	53	5	275
Silage Sorghum:								
2012	39	302	21	4,852	804	170	14	1,469
2013	97	997	82	23,361	3,589	197	21	2,245
2014	97	1,043	82	19,916	2,880	46	4	405
Soybeans:								
2012	8,016	1,038,175	65,195	25,655,505	2,351,157	297,887	22,875	2,129,146
2013	8,010	1,092,507	67,497	27,808,389	2,494,306	219,945	15,061	1,205,267
2014	8,010	1,159,067	73,682	27,424,681	2,253,976	89,453	5,464	355,502
Strawberries:								
2012	6	6	0	7,278	202	2	0	954
2013	6	3	0	2,520	75	0	....	0
2014	6	1	0	325	22	0	....	0
Sugar beets:								
2012	132	15,283	1,118	1,097,991	62,227	1,532	116	23,762
2013	120	14,987	1,103	1,106,332	62,002	2,164	213	63,733
2014	120	14,246	1,054	730,642	40,076	731	54	6,915
Sugarcane:								
2012	52	5,481	753	220,964	5,970	201	10	1,279
2013	52	5,282	758	292,302	7,515	138	6	1,509
2014	31	4,935	580	256,653	7,159	13	2	602
Sunflowers:								
2012	906	16,438	1,724	462,571	77,266	4,068	443	39,789
2013	915	15,378	1,691	417,709	76,038	7,773	1,022	128,722
2014	915	14,569	1,589	333,553	56,269	3,350	316	33,529
Sweet corn:								
2012	167	2,979	227	105,739	5,641	309	22	3,627
2013	167	2,857	225	110,466	5,950	358	29	8,414
2014	166	2,790	225	101,329	5,182	332	23	3,970
Sweet potatoes:								
2012	9	37	8	6,866	1,241	0	....	0
2013	9	47	7	5,441	819	0	....	0
2014	9	43	6	5,515	710	0	....	0
Table grapes:								
2012	9	1,185	80	217,274	9,806	70	2	2,294
2013	9	1,244	85	251,429	9,695	58	1	2,449
2014	10	1,294	81	286,861	10,829	5	0	218
Tangelos:								
2014	29	247	2	1,535	68	0	....	0
Tangerine Trees:								
2012	3	13	0	245	9	0	....	0
2013	3	16	0	390	14	0	....	0
2014	3	16	0	394	15	0	....	0
Tangors:								
2014	29	305	6	9,998	541	0	....	0
Tomatoes:								
2012	78	2,746	258	430,138	9,210	151	10	3,832
2013	78	2,799	268	468,200	8,873	175	18	8,618
2014	93	3,268	297	557,109	11,606	50	4	1,154
Walnuts:								
2012	26	1,678	136	217,173	6,861	26	1	370
2013	26	1,713	140	257,593	7,720	82	3	1,111
2014	26	1,822	149	349,202	10,400	4	0	233
Wheat:								
2012	8,556	578,829	46,557	10,607,723	1,789,631	113,516	13,274	760,513
2013	8,394	613,379	48,640	11,748,624	1,983,872	243,058	28,375	2,274,990
2014	8,376	589,951	47,804	9,238,607	1,443,307	228,066	26,724	1,492,581

[1] Number of farms on which the insured crop was planted including duplication where both the landlord and tenant are insured. Insured farms on which no insured crop was planted are not included. [2] The insured's share of the planted area on the farm.

RMA, Requirements, Analysis and Validation Branch, (816) 926–7910.

Table 10-3.—Farm real estate debt: Amount outstanding by lender, United States, Dec. 31, 2005–2014 [1]

Year	Farm Credit System	Farm Service Agency	Farmer Mac	Commercial banks [1]
	Billion dollars	Billion dollars	Billion dollars	Billion dollars
2005	47.9	2.5	0.8	37.2
2006	49.7	2.4	1.5	37.5
2007	57.8	2.6	2.8	41.1
2008	62.8	2.5	2.4	46.4
2009	69.1	2.6	2.1	44.2
2010	72.5	3.5	3.6	51.2
2011	75.3	3.3	3.8	52.9
2012	80.3	3.7	3.8	64.5
2013	85.3	3.7	4.1	68.9
2014	88.8	4.3	4.5	73.2

Year	Individuals and others [1]	Life insurance companies	Storage facility loans	Total farm mortgage debt
	Billion dollars	Billion dollars	Billion dollars	Billion dollars
2005	14.1	11.3	0.2	113.9
2006	10.1	12.0	0.3	113.4
2007	16.3	10.8	0.3	131.7
2008	19.6	13.7	0.4	147.9
2009	14.2	13.3	0.5	146.0
2010	10.2	12.4	0.6	154.1
2011	18.1	13.0	0.7	167.2
2012	8.7	11.5	0.7	173.2
2013	10.1	12.0	0.7	184.8
2014	12.8	11.9	0.8	196.3

Data as of February 9, 2016.
[1] Beginning with 2012 estimates, farm sector debt held by savings associations is reported with the commercial bank lender group instead of the individuals and others grouping.
ERS, Farm Farm Income Team, (202) 694–5586. FarmIncomeTeam@ers.usda.gov. http://www.ers.usda.gov/data-products/farm-income-and-wealth-statistics.aspx.

Table 10-4.—Nonreal estate farm debt: Amount outstanding, by lender, United States, Dec. 31, 2005–2014

Year	Commericial banks [1]	Farm Credit System	Farm Service Agency	Individuals and others [1]	Total nonreal estate debt
	Billion dollars	Billion dollars	Billion dollars	Billion dollars	Billion dollars
2005	48.7	24.1	3.0	19.5	95.2
2006	48.4	27.0	2.7	24.2	102.3
2007	54.0	31.4	3.1	20.5	109.0
2008	56.3	36.0	3.0	17.9	113.2
2009	57.2	39.0	3.3	22.9	122.4
2010	56.2	39.2	3.6	25.8	124.9
2011	59.2	41.1	3.5	23.5	127.3
2012	59.9	42.7	3.4	17.9	123.8
2013	63.7	44.0	2.8	19.6	130.2
2014	71.0	48.1	3.6	26.7	149.4

Data as of February 9, 2016.
[1] Beginning with 2012 estimates, farm sector debt held by savings associations is reported with the commercial bank lender group instead of the individuals and others grouping.
ERS, Farm Farm Income Team, (202) 694–5586. FarmIncomeTeam@ers.usda.gov. http://www.ers.usda.gov/data-products/farm-income-and-wealth-statistics.aspx.

Table 10-5.—Farm Service Agency: Loans made to individuals and associations for farming purposes, and amount outstanding, United States and Territories, 2005–2014 [1]

Year	Loans to individuals						
	Farm ownership			Soil and water			Recreation
	New borrowers	Loans made	Outstanding Jan. 1	New borrowers	Loans made	Outstanding Jan. 1	Outstanding Jan. 1
	Number	1,000 dollars	1,000 dollars	Number	1,000 dollars	1,000 dollars	1,000 dollars
2005	4,199	1,298,943	8,190,313	0	0	27,341	875
2006	3,878	1,223,725	8,343,554	0	0	21,451	714
2007	3,865	1,268,809	8,518,399	0	0	18,477	674
2008	4,335	1,552,303	8,876,232	0	0	13,954	514
2009	5,048	1,832,709	9,800,441	0	0	12,469	267
2010	6,281	2,308,813	10,875,039	0	0	10,364	4,632
2011	5,945	2,486,929	11,872,786	0	0	8,053	208
2012	4,976	2,029,778	12,498,221	0	0	6,585	191
2013	4,224	1,946,912	12,842,052	0	0	5,483	133
2014	7,418	3,012,450	13,768,000	0	0	4,617	102

Year	Loans to individuals					
	Operating			Emergency		
	New borrowers	Loans made	Outstanding Jan. 1	New borrowers	Loans made	Outstanding Jan. 1
	Number	1,000 dollars	1,000 dollars	Number	1,000 dollars	1,000 dollars
2005	8,891	1,723,953	6,404,277	235	23,569	1,150,557
2006	9,623	1,849,894	6,131,132	494	51,525	975,594
2007	8,673	1,789,590	5,732,012	691	74,898	920,453
2008	8,207	1,710,441	5,731,149	385	44,994	792,120
2009	11,778	2,611,248	6,500,532	177	30,401	726,370
2010	12,056	2,934,097	7,047,105	187	35,598	661,950
2011	10,064	2,285,131	6,953,778	176	32,610	578,846
2012	10,325	2,103,112	6,594,239	155	31,436	537,640
2013	10,685	1,960,150	6,254,820	224	23,340	479,869
2014	12,039	2,201,420	6,214,490	118	18,106	428,304

Year	Loans to associations					Economic opportunity individual loans	Economic emergency loans
	Indian tribe land acquisition			Grazing association	Irrigation, drainage, and soil conservation		
	New borrowers	Loans made	Outstanding Jan. 1	Outstanding Jan. 1	Outstanding Jan. 1	Outstanding Jan. 1	Outstanding Jan. 1
	Number	1,000 dollars	1,000 dollars	1,000 dollars	1,000 dollars	1,000 dollars	1,000 dollars
2005	0	0	55,205	4,883	1,471	8	249,039
2006	0	360	52,134	3,613	1,263	8	198,266
2007	0	0	47,914	3,317	1,184	7	173,095
2008	0	0	43,764	2,945	1,045	6	135,303
2009	0	0	38,510	2,590	860	6	117,942
2010	0	0	34,306	2,232	707	6	100,515
2011	0	0	29,539	1,848	605	6	85,915
2012	0	0	25,112	1,618	511	6	76,843
2013	0	0	24,246	1,014	468	6	65,040
2014	0	0	19,825	798	284	6	57,053

[1] Includes loans made directly by FmHA and those guaranteed by the Agency. Amounts of loans made represent obligations and include loans to new borrowers and subsequent loans to borrowers who received an initial loan in a prior year. Amounts outstanding are loan advances less principal repayments for loans made directly by the Agency.

FSA, Loan Making Division, (202) 690–4006.

Table 10-6.—Farmers' marketing, farm supply, and related service cooperatives: Number, memberships, and business volume, United States, 2005–2014

Year[1]	Cooperatives[2]				Estimated memberships[4]			
	Marketing	Farm supply	Related service[3]	Total	Marketing	Farm supply	Related service[3]	Total
	Number	*Number*	*Number*	*Number*	*1,000 members*	*1,000 members*	*1,000 members*	*1,000 members*
2005	1,553	1,161	181	2,895	1,005	1,561	39	2,605
2006	1,454	1,146	135	2,735	939	1,609	48	2,596
2007	1,385	1,094	116	2,595	814	1,605	40	2,459
2008	1,354	1,011	110	2,475	809	1,509	36	2,354
2009	1,277	992	121	2,390	754	1,448	35	2,237
2010	1,215	974	125	2,314	737	1,463	35	2,234
2011	1,222	935	128	2,285	846	1,398	36	2,279
2012	1,200	916	120	2,236	652	1,426	37	2,115
2013	1,195	871	120	2,186	655	1,284	37	1,977
2014	1,114	876	116	2,106	627	1,333	35	1,996

Year[1]	Marketing volume		Farm supply volume		Service	Total marketing and farm supply volume and service receipts	
	Gross[5]	Net[6]	Gross[5]	Net[6]	Receipts[8]	Gross[5]	Net[6]
	Billion dollars	*Billion dollars*	*Billion dollars*	*Billion dollars*	*Billion dollars*	*Billion dollars*	*Billion dollars*
2005	76.902	71.189	37.246	26.376	4.328	118.475	101.893
2006	77.613	71.484	44.916	34.871	4.225	126.754	110.580
2007	94.103	86.129	49.784	38.569	4.132	148.019	128.830
2008	118.197	111.699	70.525	51.172	4.744	193.465	167.615
2009	101.386	94.558	62.999	47.362	4.940	169.325	146.860
2010	103.031	95.756	63.842	47.118	4.930	171.803	147.805
2011	128.041	121.784	80.898	57.322	4.453	213.391	187.100
2012	140.900	133.200	92.200	64.700	4.700	237.800	202.600
2013	144.615	135.810	95.933	67.175	5.572	246.120	208.557
2014	147.731	138.340	92.624	65.638	6.315	246.670	210.293

[1] Reports of cooperatives are included for the calendar year.   [2] Includes independent local cooperatives, centralized cooperatives, federations of cooperatives, and cooperatives with mixed organizational structures.   Cooperatives are classified according to their major activity.   If, for example, more than 50 percent of a cooperative's business is derived from marketing activities, it is included as a marketing cooperative.   [3] Includes cooperatives whose major activity is providing services related to marketing and farm supply activities.   [4] Includes members (those entitled to vote for directors) but does not include nonvoting patrons. (Some duplication exists because some farmers belong to more than one cooperative.)   [5] Estimated gross business includes all business reported between cooperatives, such as the wholesale business of farm supply cooperatives with other cooperatives or terminal market sales for local cooperatives.   [6] Estimated net business represents the value at the first level at which cooperatives transact business for farmers, adjusted for duplication resulting from intercooperative business.   [7] Receipts for services related to marketing or purchasing activities but not included in the volumes reported for those activities, plus other operting and non-operating income and losses and extraordinary items..
Rural Development, Cooperative Programs, (202) 720-7395.

Table 10-7.—Farmers' cooperatives: Business volume of marketing, farm supply, and related service cooperatives, United States, 2013–2014

Item	Gross business		Net business [1]	
	2013	2014	2013	2014
	Billion dollars	*Billion dollars*	*Billion dollars*	*Billion dollars*
Products marketed:				
Beans and peas (dry edible)	0.247	0.238	0.243	0.234
Cotton and cotton products	3.079	2.730	2.987	2.627
Dairy products	42.729	52.394	40.184	49.636
Fish	0.185	0.215	0.185	0.215
Fruits and vegetables	8.157	8.362	5.890	5.848
Grain and oilseeds [2]	67.007	58.837	66.252	57.898
Livestock and livestock products	3.345	4.948	3.345	4.947
Nuts	1.337	1.569	1.334	1.566
Poultry products	0.727	1.353	0.727	1.353
Rice	1.732	0.935	1.732	0.936
Sugar products	8.706	7.758	6.030	5.146
Tobacco	0.137	0.339	0.137	0.339
Wool and mohair	0.005	0.005	0.005	0.005
Other products [3]	7.211	8.048	6.759	7.590
Total farm products	144.615	147.731	135.810	138.340
Supplies purchased:				
Crop protectants	11.530	11.530	7.332	7.504
Feed	16.180	13.674	12.717	10.800
Fertilizer	17.660	16.251	14.016	13.116
Petroleum	38.520	39.211	24.397	25.558
Seed	5.540	5.791	3.357	3.444
Other supplies [4]	6.440	6.167	5.356	5.216
Total farm supplies	95.930	92.624	67.175	65.638
Receipts for services: [5]				
Trucking, cotton ginning, storage, grinding, locker plants, miscellaneous	5.572	6.315	5.572	6.315
Total business	246.117	246.670	208.557	210.293

[1] Represents value at the first level at which cooperatives transact business for farmers; adjusted for inter-cooperative business.　[2] Excludes oilseed meal and oil.　Oilseed meal is included in feed sales while oil sales are included in other products sales.　[3] Includes coffee, forest products, hay, hops, seed marketed for growers, nursery stock, other farm products not separately classified, and sales of farm products not received directly from member-patrons.　Also includes manufactured food products and resale items marketed by cooperatives.　[4] Includes automotive supplies, building material, chicks, containers, farm machinery and equipment, hardware, meats and groceries, and other supplies not separately classified.　[5] Trucking, cotton ginning, storage, grinding, locker plants, and/or miscellaneous services related to marketing or purchasing but not included in the volume reported for those activities, plus other operating and non-operating income and losses and extraordinary items.

Rural Development, Cooperative Programs, (202) 690–1414.

Table 10-8.—Farmers' cooperatives: Number of cooperatives, memberships, and business volume of marketing, farm supply, and related service cooperatives, by State, United States and Foreign, 2013–2014

State	Cooperatives headquartered in State		Memberships in State [1]		Net business [1]	
	2013	2014	2013	2014	2013	2014
	Number	*Number*	*Thousand*	*Thousand*	*Billion dollars*	*Billion dollars*
Alabama	48	47	27.90	28.12	0.83	0.79
Arizona	32	32	37.20	35.05	2.82	2.58
California	112	109	34.40	34.44	11.43	13.12
Colorado	27	26	20.50	19.55	1.75	1.61
Florida	30	29	19.60	18.99	1.46	1.24
Georgia	14	12	13.40	14.45	1.00	1.23
Hawaii	13	13	0.60	0.60	0.02	0.02
Idaho	23	23	12.10	12.22	1.83	1.91
Illinois	109	104	113.90	116.29	14.63	15.64
Indiana	33	33	42.10	44.82	4.86	4.75
Iowa	93	91	105.10	104.75	24.36	22.74
Kansas	89	89	95.60	100.75	8.81	8.85
Kentucky	26	26	169.40	169.37	1.26	1.54
Louisiana	34	32	10.60	10.44	2.11	2.05
Maryland	14	14	36.10	36.09	0.68	0.73
Massachusetts	8	8	3.90	4.26	0.29	0.25
Michigan	43	40	39.40	39.06	4.11	4.63
Minnesota	194	186	133.10	130.37	27.68	26.95
Mississippi	51	47	49.00	80.64	1.59	1.37
Missouri	60	57	96.80	91.09	8.87	10.63
Montana	44	42	20.10	23.43	2.78	2.68
Nebraska	51	48	69.70	66.41	12.06	11.42
New York	55	51	5.70	5.51	3.19	3.43
North Carolina	12	11	22.10	23.13	0.90	0.84
North Dakota	146	142	80.30	77.40	11.06	10.44
Ohio	41	40	39.80	39.27	5.76	5.51
Oklahoma	53	50	38.80	37.66	2.07	2.11
Oregon	32	32	31.70	32.98	5.27	5.33
Pennsylvania	36	32	8.10	8.04	2.19	2.36
South Dakota	71	70	67.30	68.88	8.56	7.63
Tennessee	61	60	71.80	70.24	1.99	1.93
Texas	181	177	72.90	74.38	5.94	6.20
Utah	12	12	11.20	10.05	0.79	1.01
Virginia	53	52	124.30	127.64	1.84	1.85
Washington	60	60	26.50	29.04	6.55	6.69
West Virginia	14	13	61.60	60.94	0.36	0.34
Wisconsin	125	113	133.30	118.69	11.23	12.17
Wyoming	10	10	4.30	4.31	0.67	0.63
Other States [2]	76	73	26.30	25.98	4.13	4.43
United States	2,186	2,106	1,976.50	1,995.33	207.74	209.63
Foreign [3]	....	....	0.40	0.42	0.82	0.66
Total	2,186	2,106	1,976.90	1,995.75	208.56	210.29

[1] Represents value at the first level at which cooperatives transact business for farmers. Totals may not add due to rounding.   [2] Dollar volume or membership is not shown to avoid disclosing operations of individual cooperatives.   [3] Sales outside the United States and sales of certain products not received directly from member-patrons.
Rural Development, Cooperative Programs, (202) 690–1414.

Table 10-9.—Rural Utilities Service: Long-term electric financing approved by purpose, by States and United States as of December 31, 2011

State	Borrowers	Total financing approved						Loan estimates	
		Non-RUS financing			Financing approved by purpose			Miles of line	Con-sumers
		RUS loans [1]	With RUS guar-antee [2]	Without RUS guar-antee [3]	Distribu-tion	Genera-tion and trans-mission [3]	Consumer facilities		
	Number	1,000 dollars	1,000 dollars	1,000 dollars	1,000 dollars	1,000 dollars	1,000 dollars	Number	Number
AL	27	902,681	1,808,680	280,177	1,296,291	1,693,889	1,359	69,762	658,661
AK	18	864,376	670,188	198,024	678,309	1,053,190	1,089	11,157	197,575
AZ	15	423,646	957,481	220,448	705,799	895,285	490	23,372	243,293
AR	20	1,086,615	2,708,733	813,414	1,892,049	2,712,241	4,471	78,753	614,860
CA	10	95,586	56,513	7,216	117,757	41,501	56	6,828	80,037
CO	25	1,377,508	4,034,083	794,956	1,804,302	4,402,171	74	78,247	514,191
CT	-	-	-	-	-	-	-	-	-
DE	1	85,430	57,300	31,266	173,132	861	3	7,646	99,435
FL	18	1,467,692	2,565,326	1,153,744	2,448,286	2,735,958	2,519	77,937	1,048,309
GA	52	2,540,840	10,562,822	1,852,266	5,342,708	9,610,261	2,959	186,166	2,126,681
HI	1	215,000	142,928	8,240	282,314	83,854	-	872	31,099
ID	10	196,308	92,542	36,612	285,187	39,078	1,197	13,079	72,575
IL	29	628,023	1,352,350	638,935	709,872	1,909,224	212	55,715	256,959
IN	46	526,088	2,894,224	707,487	831,699	3,295,383	717	60,054	498,583
IA	45	857,085	1,000,326	173,640	911,243	1,119,411	397	67,365	219,974
KS	31	782,940	1,053,657	206,156	1,061,806	980,531	415	78,735	293,224
KY	26	1,766,221	5,430,379	1,581,746	2,726,967	6,050,220	1,159	94,386	969,693
LA	20	772,408	3,134,623	425,178	1,267,910	3,064,122	177	56,828	565,227
ME	5	41,737	22,350	20,396	51,425	33,014	44	2,183	20,708
MD	2	368,228	144,253	140,356	536,899	115,937	-	15,312	1 189,187
MA	-	-	-	-	-	-	-	-	-
MI	10	665,087	1,090,491	92,692	893,022	954,775	473	40,471	334,575
MN	46	1,687,889	2,749,021	556,717	2,492,135	2,497,134	4,357	124,632	717,487
MS	29	969,263	1,764,166	361,096	1,365,474	1,728,357	694	90,200	753,265
MO	48	1,863,673	3,437,021	600,270	2,346,124	3,554,019	821	127,495	790,878
MT	25	442,360	160,143	66,866	568,825	100,315	229	47,711	146,603
NE	35	483,130	38,616	42,711	449,732	114,163	562	76,004	177,923
NV	8	75,008	1,241	10,441	65,315	21,127	248	6,265	24,889
NH	1	81,213	143,839	8,696	87,335	146,380	32	4,616	64,601
NJ	2	18,173	-	5,377	22,250	1,295	4	1,000	13,334
NM	18	655,808	345,257	78,251	941,363	134,944	3,010	47,420	250,430
NY	6	46,782	30,205	20,114	87,731	9,286	85	5,298	29,533
NC	33	2,040,634	2,845,230	560,907	2,946,394	2,495,742	4,635	106,205	1,142,335
ND	23	1,179,286	4,845,541	953,122	1,060,313	5,915,651	1,986	71,164	588,129
OH	27	652,958	1,582,082	472,666	1,005,120	1,702,367	218	49,071	380,290
OK	29	1,197,869	1,621,525	328,543	1,577,044	1,568,217	2,676	101,801	538,851
OR	18	309,173	142,611	93,022	393,129	151,440	237	25,001	146,978
PA	13	462,705	689,683	132,794	658,902	626,041	239	28,276	234,175
RI	1	-	3,940	-	334	3,606	-	4	160
SC	28	1,884,073	1,684,010	379,965	3,110,289	835,527	2,231	79,910	860,908
SD	30	814,091	471,391	155,806	1,123,535	316,872	881	68,396	191,151
TN	33	782,429	491,626	190,919	1,429,703	35,048	223	94,631	1,170,176
TX	99	2,424,164	5,081,218	1,681,403	3,360,478	5,823,783	2,524	274,809	1,535,995
UT	6	72,455	1,031,811	216,171	62,920	1,257,393	124	5,860	25,033
VT	3	75,437	52,370	7,310	72,238	61,975	903	3,011	25,878
VA	19	939,353	5,107,913	251,378	5,889,353	408,803	488	57,555	585,053
WA	23	250,753	47,692	40,181	311,427	26,947	252	21,122	112,830
WV	1	26,236	3,000	1,059	29,443	847	5	970	8,663
WI	26	569,792	1,255,217	464,963	588,244	1,699,931	1,798	47,007	249,640
WY	13	384,512	235,722	27,216	524,882	122,467	101	33,270	105,968
AS	1	-	3,000	-	-	3,000	-	-	-
MH	1	-	11,857	-	-	11,857	-	161	3,426
PW	-	-	-	-	-	-	-	-	-
PR	1	300,981	-	31,424	292,851	39,554	-	16,633	624,343
VI	1	430	-	-	234	197	-	85	912
US [4]	1,058	36,354130	75,656,195	17,122,336	56,880,093	72,205,194	47,374	2,640,451	20,534,683

[1] Includes $628,992,093 discounted principal from 226 prepaid borrowers. [2] Includes RUS Section 313A loan guarantees. [3] Includes loans obtained by RUS borrowers' affiliates specifically organized to facillitate non-RUS finanacing. [4] Includes figures not shown elsewhere in this table for two borrowers whose loans have been foreclosed. The amount of these loans was $37,237. Note: Territories are American Samoa, Marshall Island, Palau, Puerto Rico and Virgin Islands.

Rural Development, Rural Utilities Service, Electric Program, (202) 692-0163.

Table 10-10.—Rural Utilities Service: Composite revenues and patronage capital, average number of consumers and megawatt-hour sales reported by RUS electric borrowers operating distribution systems—calendar years 2009–2011

Item	2009 Amount	2009 Percent of total	2010 Amount	2010 Percent of total	2011 Amount	2011 Percent of total
Number of borrowers reporting	580	....	571	....	566	....
Average number of consumers served:						
Residential service (farm & non-farm) ...	10,952,374	88.4	10,826,192	88.3	10,885,204	88.3
Commercial & industrial, small	1,248,412	10.1	1,241,357	10.1	1,248,623	10.1
Commercial & industrial, large	9,660	0.1	8,879	0.1	9,296	0.1
Irrigation	106,753	0.9	110,902	0.9	112,587	0.9
Other electric service	79,019	0.6	73,367	0.6	73,330	0.6
To others for resale	188	*	184	*	261	*
Total	12,396,406	100.0	12,260,881	100.0	12,329,301	100.0
Megawatt-hour sales:						
Residential service (farm & non-farm) ...	152,105,577	57.3	161,245,731	57.5	156,164,256	56.1
Commercial & industrial, small	49,551,825	18.7	52,539,103	18.7	52,524,707	18.9
Commercial & industrial, large	55,247,184	20.8	58,063,409	20.7	59,679,110	21.5
Irrigation	4,350,266	1.6	4,200,967	1.5	5,297,215	1.9
Other electric service	2,707,597	1.0	2,681,929	1.0	2,527,060	0.9
To others for resale	1,330,927	0.5	1,651,962	0.6	1,962,944	0.7
Total	265,293,361	100.0	280,383,115	100.0	278,155,291	100.0
	1,000 dollars		*1,000 dollars*		*1,000 dollars*	
Revenue and patronage capital:						
Residential service (farm & non-farm) ...	16,141,422	62.7	17,085,401	62.6	17,083,438	61.3
Commercial & industrial, small	4,854,339	18.8	5,161,990	18.9	5,340,980	19.2
Commercial & industrial, large	3,495,396	13.6	3,710,526	13.6	3,948,978	14.2
Irrigation	405,528	1.6	429,483	1.6	515,794	1.9
Other electric service	289,136	1.1	297,010	1.1	288,713	1.0
To others for resale	80,712	0.3	96,606	0.4	113,155	0.4
Total from sales of electric energy	25,266,534	98.1	26,781,016	98.2	27,291,058	98.0
Other operating revenue	494,890	1.9	495,333	1.8	558,911	2.0
Total operating revenue	25,761,424	100.0	27,276,349	100.0	27,849,969	100.0

* Less than 0.05 percent.
Rural Development, Rural Utilities Service, Electric Program, (202) 692-0163.

Table 10-11.—Rural Utilities Service: Annual revenues and expenses reported by
electric borrowers, United States, 2002–2011

Year	Operating revenue	Operating expense	Interest expense	Depreciation and amortiza- tion expense	Net margins	Total utility plant
	1,000 dollars	*1,000 dollars*	*1,000 dollars*	*1,000 dollars*	*1,000 dollars*	*1,000 dollars*
2002	27,458,144	22,568,763	1,867,431	1,992,415	1,382,964	72,481,696
2003	31,821,409	26,393,809	2,153,155	2,314,811	1,303,510	84,991,605
2004	30,649,839	25,646,721	1,919,835	2,181,541	1,340,317	79,508,979
2005	34,330,831	29,164,368	2,075,557	2,271,565	1,441,751	83,405,976
2006	36,765,064	31,213,044	2,247,071	2,375,325	1,747,997	88,112,547
2007	38,423,386	32,659,447	2,311,524	2,369,896	1,989,271	90,936,276
2008	42,087,440	36,048,847	2,372,255	2,462,420	2,068,523	97,191,799
2009	42,189,052	35,680,844	2,456,980	2,656,212	2,751,860	104,286,469
2010	45,261,487	38,315,046	2,474,526	2,821,453	2,486,432	109,572,949
2011	46,146,088	39,129,741	2,515,389	2,969,391	2,461,388	115,047,960

Rural Development, Rural Utilities Service, Electric Program, (202) 692-0163.

Table 10-12.—Loans to farmers' cooperative organizations: Outstanding amounts held
by the agricultural credit bank classified by type of loan, United States,
Jan. 1, 2005-2014

Year	Operating capital loans	Facility loans
	1,000 dollars	*1,000 dollars*
2005	11,549,929	12,406,423
2006	12,293,156	14,004,128
2007	10,956,633	22,119,209
2008	13,263,702	27,226,859
2009	11,769,457	32,780,415
2010	10,743,647	33,430,718
2011	10,871,732	35,413,410
2012	32,789,008	39,191,450
2013	32,449,687	41,153,688
2014	32,171,519	48,210,977

FCA, Office of Management Services, (703) 883–4073.

STABILIZATION AND PRICE-SUPPORT PROGRAMS

The statistics in this chapter relate to activities of the Commodity Credit Corporation (CCC), loan and inventory acquisition and disposition programs, the CCC and Farm Service Agency payment programs, and marketing agreements and order programs for fruits and vegetables. Statistics for Federal Milk Marketing Order programs are contained in chapter VIII.

Table 11-1.—Commodity Credit Corporation: Price-supported commodities owned as of September 2014[1] (Inventory quantity)

Year	Barley	Butter and butter oil	Cheese and products	Corn	Cotton extra long staple	Cotton upland	Sorghum and products
	Million bushels	Million pounds	Million pounds	Million bushels	1,000 bales	1,000 bales	Million bushels
2005	0	0	1	1	0	2	0
2006	(2)	(2)	0	1	0	5	(2)
2007	0	0	0	1	0	0	(3)
2008	0	0	0	0	0	0	(2)
2009	0	0	0	0	0	0	0
2010	0	(3)	0	0	0	0	(3)
2011	0	0	0	0	0	0	(3)
2012	0	0	0	0	0	0	0
2013	0	0	0	0	0	0	(3)
2014	0	0	0	0	0	0	0

Year	Milk and products	Oils and oilseeds	Oats and products	Rice and products[4]	Peanut and products	Soybeans	Beans, dry edible
	Million pounds	Million cwt	Million bushels	Million cwt	Million pounds	Million bushels	Million bushels
2005	116	0	0	(3)	65	(2)	(2)
2006	49	(2)	(2)	(3)	51	1	(2)
2007	14	(2)	(2)	(3)	0	1	(3)
2008	0	0	0	(2)	0	0	(2)
2009	224	0	0	(2)	(2)	0	0
2010	7	0	0	(3)	0	0	(5)
2011	0	0	0	(2)	0	0	(2)
2012	0	0	0	0	0	0	0
2013	0	0	0	(3)	0	0	0
2014	0	0	0	(3)	4	0	0

Year	Wheat	Blended Foods	Poultry	Meat	Fish	Vegetable Oil Products	Value of all commodities owned
	Million bushels	Million pounds	Million pounds	Million pounds	Million pounds	Million pounds	Million dollars
2005	46	10	0	0	0	22	304
2006	43	3	0	0	0	4	226
2007	39	0	0	0	0	6	185
2008	0	8	0	0	0	2	11
2009	0	13	0	0	0	6	205
2010	(2)	16	0	0	0	5	48
2011	0	16	0	0	0	33	53
2012	0	2	0	0	0	12	14
2013	0	25	0	0	0	23	71
2014	0	18	0	0	0	32	40

[1] Commodities which were owned by CCC in some years but not shown in this table are as follows: tobacco, honey, sugar and products, dry whole peas, potatoes, and wool and mohair. [2] Less than 50,000 units. [3] Less than 500,000 units. [4] Total value of all commodities owned by CCC, including price-supported commodities not shown and commodities acquired under programs other than price-support programs, less, reserve for losses on inventory. [5] Less than 500 units. [6] Prior years data were not available.

FSA, Office and Budget and Finance, Budget Division, (202) 720–0174.

Table 11-2.—Commodity Credit Corporation: Loans pledge made, by quantity and face amount United States and Territories, by crop year 2011–2014 [1]

Commodity	Unit	2011		2012	
		Quantity pledged	Face amount	Quantity pledged	Face amount
		1,000	*1,000 dollars*	*1,000*	*1,000 dollars*
Barley	1,000 bushels	2,812	4,856	3,088	5,452
Corn	1,000 bushels	574,224	1,050,954	367,998	675,046
Cotton, ELS & Upland [2]	1,000 bales	7,645	2,063,757	8,756	2,340,767
Seed cotton, ELS & Upland	1,000 pounds ..	171,598	2,333	203,741	2,368
Sugar Cane and Beet	1,000 pounds ..	4,554,339	959,537	5,523,966	1,203,630
Flaxseed	1,000 cwt	10	101	15	151
Honey	1,000 pounds ..	5,655	3,898	5,363	3,698
Oats	1,000 bushels	220	288	335	441
Peanuts	1,000 pounds ..	2,804,063	489,961	5,279,721	949,952
Rice	1,000 cwt	65,825	421,813	65,922	419,095
Wool	1,000 pounds ..	0	0	0	0
Grain sorghum	1,000 bushels	437	806	329	628
Soybeans	1,000 bushels	98,468	476,107	58,437	284,078
Wheat	1,000 bushels	35,961	98,497	27,541	73,798
Sunflower Seed	1,000 cwt	104	921	415	3,646
Canola Seed	1,000 cwt	229	2,102	378	3,723
Safflower Seed	1,000 cwt	0	0	0	0
Mustard Seed	1,000 cwt	0	0	0	0
Sunflower Seed (non-oil)	1,000 cwt	83	627	23	214
Crambe Oilseed	1,000 cwt	0	0	0	0
Mohair	1,000 pounds ..	0	0	0	0
Chickpeas	1,000 cwt	19	117	18	132
Dry Whole Peas	1,000 cwt	90	426	171	866
Lentil Dry	1,000 cwt	280	2,989	219	2,372

Commodity	Unit	2013		2014 [3]	
		Quantity pledged	Face amount	Quantity pledged	Face amount
		1,000	*1,000 dollars*	*1,000*	*1,000 dollars*
Barley	1,000 bushels	4,163	7,719	995	1,900
Corn	1,000 bushels	460,885	823,153	7,822	16,432
Cotton, ELS & Upland [2]	1,000 bales	4,283	1,083,352	270	71,822
Seed cotton, ELS & Upland	1,000 pounds ..	2,032	983	0	0
Sugar Cane and Beet	1,000 pounds ..	3,755,863	758,801	0	0
Flaxseed	1,000 cwt	6	50	0	0
Honey	1,000 pounds ..	4,228	2,825	2,082	1,437
Oats	1,000 bushels	347	435	273	362
Peanuts	1,000 pounds ..	2,904,469	500,765	89,190	15,805
Rice	1,000 cwt	36,116	226,567	1,602	10,474
Wool	1,000 pounds ..	14	5	0	0
Grain sorghum	1,000 bushels	578	921	98	194
Soybeans	1,000 bushels	49,453	232,113	83	422
Wheat	1,000 bushels	24,649	70,520	15,696	45,513
Sunflower Seed	1,000 cwt	322	2,995	0	0
Canola Seed	1,000 cwt	355	3,307	80	802
Safflower Seed	1,000 cwt	0	0	0	0
Mustard Seed	1,000 cwt	7	68	0	0
Sunflower Seed (non-oil)	1,000 cwt	16	124	0	0
Crambe Oilseed	1,000 cwt	0	0	0	0
Mohair	1,000 pounds ..	0	0	0	0
Chickpeas	1,000 cwt	20	136	0	0
Dry Whole Peas	1,000 cwt	301	1,539	106	568
Lentil Dry	1,000 cwt	172	1,807	37	413

[1] Includes loans pledge directly by Commodity Credit Corporation.   [2] Includes extra long staple cotton and upland cotton.   [3] Loan pledges are made through fiscal year 2014.
FSA, Office and Budget and Finance, Budget Division, (202) 720–0174.

Table 11-3.—Commodity Credit Corporation: Loan transactions for fiscal year 2014, by commodities[1]

Commodity	Unit	Loans outstanding Oct. 1, 2012[2]	New loans made	Loans repayments	Collateral acquired in settlement	Loans written off and transferred to accounts receivable[3]	Loans outstanding Sept. 30, 2014	
							Value	Quantity collateral remaining pledged
		1,000 dollars	*1,000 dollars*	*1,000 dollars*	*1,000 dollars*	*1,000 dollars*	*1,000 dollars*	*1,000 units*
Basic commodities:								
Corn	Bushel	32,866	824,588	(783,241)	0	(879)	73,334	40,166
Cotton	Bale	13,114	1,130,161	(1,102,852)	0	(2,762)	37,661	140
Seed cotton	Pound	0	983	(983)	0	0	0	0
Peanuts	Pound	60,407	502,668	(507,033)	(13,434)	(21,339)	21,269	121,519
Rice	Cwt	45,175	196,446	(225,379)	0	0	16,242	2,622
Tobacco	Pound	0	0	0	0	0	0	0
Wheat	Bushel	35,582	82,040	(69,899)	0	(86)	47,637	16,368
Total[4]		187,144	2,736,886	(2,689,387)	(13,434)	(25,066)	196,143	180,815
Designated nonbasic commodities								
Barley	Bushel	4,143	5,504	(7,431)	0	(2)	2,214	1,177
Sorghum	Bushel	41	1,074	(898)	0	0	217	111
Honey	Pound	1,134	3,081	(2,755)	0	(4)	1,456	2,114
Oats	Bushel	194	573	(362)	0	0	405	313
Raw sugar, cane	Pound	17,514	253,081	(253,081)	(17,514)	0	0	0
Refined sugar, cane	Pound	0	0	0	0	0	0	0
Raw sugar beet	Pound	7,456	159,968	(159,968)	(7,456)	0	0	0
Refined sugar beet	Pound	111,966	360,431	(360,431)	(111,966)	0	0	0
FlaxSeed	Cwt	0	50	(50)	0	0	0	0
Sunflower seed (oil)	Cwt	100	2,995	(2,950)	0	0	145	15
Canola seed	Cwt	702	3,216	(3,117)	0	(1)	802	80
Safflower seed	Cwt	0	0	0	0	0	0	0
Rapeseed	Cwt	0	0	0	0	0	0	0
Mustard seed	Cwt	0	68	(68)	0	0	0	0
Crambe oilseed	Cwt	0	0	0	0	0	0	0
Sunflower seed, non oil	Cwt	0	124	(124)	0	0	0	0
Total[4]		143,250	790,165	(791,235)	(136,936)	(5)	5,239	3,810
Other nonbasic commodities:								
Soybeans	Bushel	5,253	232,376	(230,925)	0	(93)	6,611	1,397
Mohair	Pound	0	0	0	0	0	0	0
Chickpeas	Pound	14	136	(107)	0	0	43	4
Lentils	Pound	412	1,903	(1,902)	0	0	413	37
Peas, dry whole	Pound	614	1,586	(1,498)	0	1	702	133
Wool	Pound	0	5	(5)	0	0	0	0
Total[4]		6,293	236,006	(234,437)	0	(93)	7,769	1,571
Grand total[5]		336,687	3,763,057	(3,715,059)	(150,370)	(25,164)	209,151	186,196

[1] Loans made directly by Commodity Credit Corporation. [2] Book value of outstanding loans; includes face amounts and any charges paid. [3] Includes transfers to accounts receivable. [4] Totals do not include allowance for losses. [5] Table may not add due to rounding.

FSA, Office and Budget and Finance, Budget Division, (202) 720–0174.

Table 11-4.—Commodity Credit Corporation: Selected inventory transactions, programs and commodity, as of September 30, 2014

Program and commodity	Unit	Quantity					
		Inventory Oct. 1, 2013	Purchases	Collateral acquired from loans	Other addition deduction	Sales and other dis-positions [1]	Inventory Sept. 30, 2014
		Thousands	Thousands	Thousands	Thousands	Thousands	Thousands
Feed grains:							
Barley	Bushel	0	0	0	0	0	0
Corn	Bushel	0	24	0	0	24	0
Corn products	Pound	0	73,199	0	0	73,199	0
Grain sorghum	Bushel	138	16,308	0	0	16,446	0
Sorghum grits	Pound	0	0	0	0	0	0
Oats	Bushel	0	0	0	0	0	0
Food grains, cotton and to-bacco:							
Wheat	Bushel	0	14,725	0	0	14,725	0
Wheat flour	Pound	0	55,675	0	0	55,675	0
Bulgur	Pound	6,380	2,869	0	0	9,249	0
Rice, milled	Cwt	88	1,582	0	0	1,543	127
Rice, rough	Cwt	0	0	0	0	0	0
Cotton, extra long staple	Bale	0	0	0	0	0	0
Upland cotton	Bale	0	0	1	(1)	0	0
Tobacco Products	Pound	0	0	0	0	0	0
Dairy products:							
Butter	Pound	0	0	0	0	0	0
Cheese	Pound	0	0	0	0	0	0
Milk, dried	Pound	0	0	0	0	0	0
Milk, UHT	Pound	0	0	0	0	0	0
Dry whole milk	Pound	0	0	0	0	0	0
Non fat dry milk	Pound	0	0	0	0	0	0
Oils and oilseeds:							
Crambe oilseed	Cwt	0	0	0	0	0	0
Canola seed	Cwt	0	0	0	0	0	0
Sunflower seed	Cwt	0	0	0	0	0	0
Sunflower seed, non-oil	Cwt	0	0	0	0	0	0
Peanuts	Pound	0	0	74,676	(70,194)	0	4,482
Peanut butter	Pound	0	0	0	0	0	0
Soybeans	Bushel	0	0	0	0	0	0
Soybean products	Pound	0	130,821	0	0	130,821	0
Dry edible beans	Cwt	0	168	0	0	168	0
Flaxseed	Cwt	0	0	0	0	0	0
Blended foods	Pound	24,542	94,869	0	0	100,947	18,464
Dry whole peas and lentils	Cwt	331	2,133	0	0	2,251	213
Sugar cane and beet	Pound	170,750	0	593,000	(593,000)	170,750	0
Vegetable oil products	Pound	23,327	175,866	0	0	166,946	32,347
Wool	Pound	0	0	0	0	0	0
Mohair	Pound	0	0	0	0	0	0
Other [2]	....	714	11,285	0	0	10,341	1,658

See footnote(s) at end of table.

Table 11-4.—Commodity Credit Corporation: Selected inventory transactions, programs and commodity, as of September 30, 2014—Continued

Program and commodity	Unit	Inventory Oct. 1, 2013	Purchases	Collateral acquired from loans	Other addition deduction	Sales and other disposi- tions[1]	Inventory Sept. 30, 2014
		1,000 dollars	1,000 dollars	1,000 dollars	1,000 dollars	1,000 dollars	1,000 dollars
Feed grains:							
Barley	Bushel	0	0	0	0	0	0
Corn	Bushel	0	186	0	0	186	0
Corn products	Pound	0	13,767	0	0	13,767	0
Grain sorghum	Bushel	849	97,765	0	0	98,614	0
Sorghum grits	Pound	0	0	0	0	0	0
Oats	Bushel	0	0	0	0	0	0
Food grains, cotton and tobacco:							
Wheat	Bushel	0	123,557	0	0	123,557	0
Wheat flour	Pound	0	12,254	0	0	12,254	0
Bulgur	Pound	1,039	579	0	0	1,618	0
Rice, milled	Cwt	2,180	40,727	0	0	39,851	3,056
Rice, rough	Cwt	0	0	0	0	0	0
Cotton, extra long staple	Bale ...	0	0	0	0	0	0
Upland cotton	Bale ...	11	0	0	(11)	0	0
Tobacco Products	Pound	0	0	0	0	0	0
Dairy products:							
Butter	Pound	0	0	0	0	0	0
Cheese	Pound	0	0	0	0	0	0
Milk, dried	Pound	0	0	0	0	0	0
Milk, UHT	Pound	0	0	0	0	0	0
Dry whole milk	Pound	0	0	0	0	0	0
Non fat dry milk	Pound	0	0	0	0	0	0
Oils and oilseeds:							
Crambe oilseed	Cwt	0	0	0	0	0	0
Canola seed	Cwt	0	0	0	0	0	0
Sunflower seed	Cwt	0	0	0	0	0	0
Sunflower seed, non-oil	Cwt	0	0	0	0	0	0
Peanuts	Pound	0	0	13,434	(12,712)	0	722
Peanut butter	Pound	0	0	0	0	0	0
Soybeans	Bushel	0	0	0	0	0	0
Soybean products	Pound	0	34,407	0	0	34,407	0
Dry edible beans	Cwt	0	7,634	0	0	7,634	0
Flaxseed	Cwt	0	0	0	0	0	0
Blended foods	Pound	7,974	29,921	0	0	31,130	6,765
Dry whole peas and lentils	Cwt	7,662	51,950	0	0	55,602	4,010
Sugar, cane and beet	Pound	34,569	0	136,936	0	171,505	0
Vegetable oil products	Pound	15,368	104,632	0	(1)	99,925	20,074
Wool	Pound	0	0	0	0	0	0
Mohair	Pound	0	0	0	0	0	0
Other[2]	....	1,470	22,436	0	2,892	21,305	5,493
Total inventory operations	....	71,122	539,815	150,370	(9,832)	711,355	40,120

[1] Includes sales, commodity donations, transfers to other government agencies and inventory adjustment.   [2] Includes tomato, vegetable, and cartons of soup.

FSA, Office and Budget and Finance, Budget Division, (202) 720–0174.

Table 11-5.—Commodity Credit Corporation: Cost value of export and domestic commodity dispositions, by type of disposition, fiscal year 2014 [1]

(In Thousands)

Commodity	Domestic				
	Dollar sales (Costs)	Transfers to other Government agencies	Donations [1]	Inventory adjustments and other recoveries (domestic)	Total domestic
Feed grains:					
Barley	0	0	0	0	0
Corn	0	0	0	0	0
Corn products	0	0	0	0	0
Grain sorghum	0	0	0	0	0
Sorghum grits	0	0	0	0	0
Oats	0	0	0	0	0
Food grains, cotton and tobacco:					
Tobacco products	0	0	0	0	0
Bulgur	0	0	0	0	0
Wheat	0	0	0	1	1
Wheat flour	0	0	0	0	0
Wheat product, Other	0	0	0	0	0
Rice, milled	0	0	0	0	0
Rice, rough	0	0	0	0	0
Rice, brown and Textured soy	0	0	0	0	0
Cotton, extra long staple & upland	0	0	0	0	0
Dairy products:					
Butter oil	0	0	0	0	0
Butter	0	0	0	0	0
Cheese Products	0	0	0	0	0
Nonfat dry milk	0	0	0	(1)	(1)
Milk, dried. UT high temp	0	0	0	0	0
Oils and oilseeds:					
Peanuts	0	0	0	0	0
Peanut butter	0	0	0	0	0
Peanuts farmer's stock & products	0	0	0	0	0
Soya flour	0	0	0	0	0
Flaxseed	0	0	0	0	0
Sunflower Seed (oil & non-oil)	0	0	0	0	0
Soybeans & Soybean products	0	0	0	0	0
Fruit fresh apples	0	0	0	0	0
Blended foods	0	0	0	0	0
Potatoes	0	0	0	0	0
Grains and seeds:					
Feed for Government facilities	0	0	0	0	0
Foundation seeds	0	0	0	0	0
Lentils dry	0	0	0	0	0
Vegetable Seeds	0	0	0	0	0
Canola seed	0	0	0	0	0
Crambe oil seed	0	0	0	0	0
Peas, dried whole	0	0	0	0	0
Dry edible beans	0	0	0	0	0
Honey	0	0	0	0	0
Sugar	0	0	0	0	0
Vegetable oil products	0	0	0	0	0
Mohair	0	0	0	0	0
Meat (and products)	0	0	0	0	0
Veg. canned tomato sauce	0	0	0	0	0
Wool	0	0	0	0	0
Other (rice products, fish, canned salmon)	0	0	0	0	0
Total	0	0	0	0	0

See footnote(s) at end of table.

Table 11-5.—Commodity Credit Corporation: Cost value of export and domestic commodity dispositions, by type of disposition, fiscal year 2014 [1]—Continued

(In Thousands)

Commodity	Export				Total export and domestic
	Dollar sales (Costs)	Public law 480 (Costs)	Donations [1]	Total export	
Feed grains:					
Barley	0	0	0	0	0
Corn	0	186	0	186	186
Corn products	0	13,767	0	13,767	13,767
Grain sorghum	0	98,614	0	98,614	98,614
Sorghum grits	0	0	0	0	0
Oats	0	0	0	0	0
Food grains, cotton and tobacco:					
Tobacco Products	0	0	0	0	0
Bulgur	0	1,618	0	1,618	1,618
Wheat	0	83,529	40,028	123,557	123,558
Wheat flour	0	12,254	0	12,254	12,254
Wheat product, Other	0	0	0	0	0
Rice, milled	0	36,545	3,307	39,852	39,852
Rice, rough	0	0	0	0	0
Rice, brown and textured soy	0	0	0	0	0
Cotton, extra long staple & upland	0	0	0	0	0
Dairy products:					
Butter oil	0	0	0	0	0
Butter	0	0	0	0	0
Cheese Products	0	0	0	0	0
Nonfat dry milk	0	0	0	(1)	(1)
Milk, dried UT high temp	0	0	0	0	0
Oils and oilseeds:					
Peanuts	0	0	0	0	0
Peanut butter	0	0	0	0	0
Peanuts farmer's stock & products	0	0	0	0	0
Soya flour	0	0	0	0	0
Flaxseed	0	0	0	0	0
Sunflower Seed (oil & non-oil)	0	0	0	0	0
Soybeans & Soybean products	0	0	34,407	34,407	34,407
Fruit fresh apples	0	0	0	0	0
Blended foods	0	31,130	0	31,130	31,130
Potatoes	0	6,108	0	6,108	6,108
Grains and seeds:					
Feed for Government facilities	0	0	0	0	0
Foundation seeds	0	0	0	0	0
Lentils dry	0	10,276	0	10,276	10,276
Vegetable Seeds	0	0	0	0	0
Canola seed	0	0	0	0	0
Crambe oil seed	0	0	0	0	0
Peas, dried whole	0	45,325	0	45,325	45,325
Dry edible beans	0	7,634	0	7,634	7,634
Honey	0	0	0	0	0
Sugar	0	0	0	0	0
Vegetable oil products	0	75,548	24,377	99,925	99,925
Mohair	0	0	0	0	0
Meat (and products)	0	0	0	0	0
Veg. canned tomato sauce	0	0	0	0	0
Wool	0	0	0	0	0
Other (rice products, fish, canned salmon)	0	15,058	104	15,198	15,198
Total	0	437,592	102,259	539,851	539,851

[1] Includes donations under section 202,407,416, Section 210, P.L. 85-540, miscellaneous donations under various other authorizations.
FSA, Office and Budget and Finance, Budget Division, (202) 720–0174.

Table 11-6.—Commodity Credit Corporation: Investment in price-support operations, March 30 and June 30, 2005–2014 [1]

Year Month	Inventory investment	Loan investment	Total investment
	Million dollars	*Million dollars*	*Million dollars*
2005:			
March	592	4,705	5,297
June	95	2,956	3,051
2006:			
March	84	5,503	5,587
June	93	3,016	3,109
2007:			
March	72	7,031	7,103
June	48	2,902	2,950
2008:			
March	168	5,926	6,094
June	11	3,335	3,346
2009:			
March	174	4,647	4,821
June	209	2,215	2,424
2010:			
March	119	4,054	4,173
June	70	1,996	2,066
2011:			
March	41	3,259	3,300
June	66	1,588	1,654
2012:			
March	63	2,740	2,803
June	27	1,260	1,287
2013:			
March	28	2,981	3,009
June	43	1,664	1,707
2014:			
March	188	2,094	2,282
June	94	890	984

[1] Reflects total CCC loans and inventories investment.
FSA, Office and Budget and Finance, Budget Division, (202) 720–0174.

Table 11-7.—Commodity Credit Corporation: Loans made in fiscal year 2014 as of September 30, by State and Territories [1]

State or Territory	Barley	Corn	Cotton	Flaxseed	Honey	Oats
	1,000 dollars	*1,000 dollars*	*1,000 dollars*	*1,000 dollars*	*1,000 dollars*	*1,000 dollars*
Alabama	0	842	15,082	0	0	0
Alaska	0	0	0	0	0	0
Arizona	0	1,164	0	0	8	0
Arkansas	0	5,134	35,033	0	0	0
California	11	222	266,946	0	382	0
Colorado	0	6,134	0	0	76	0
Connecticut	0	0	0	0	0	0
Delaware	0	171	0	0	0	0
Florida	0	353	4	0	81	0
Georgia	47	4,923	1,733	0	68	6
Hawaii	0	0	0	0	0	0
Idaho	647	376	0	0	188	0
Illinois	13	58,595	0	0	0	0
Indiana	0	99,130	0	0	0	0
Iowa	0	137,635	0	0	584	2
Kansas City Commod	0	0	0	0	0	0
Kansas	3	5,715	0	0	0	0
Kentucky	85	13,601	0	0	0	0
Louisiana	0	2,786	1,806	0	3	0
Maine	121	0	0	0	0	239
Maryland	70	4,367	0	0	0	0
Massachusetts	0	30	0	0	0	0
Michigan	0	49,104	0	0	0	0
Minnesota	128	172,861	0	0	145	14
Mississippi	0	3,672	221,588	0	0	0
Missouri	0	17,736	2,571	0	0	0
Montana	2,889	55	0	27	248	5
Nebraska	0	42,944	0	0	0	0
Nevada	0	0	0	0	0	0
New Hampshire	0	0	0	0	0	0
New Jersey	0	639	0	0	0	0
New Mexico	0	0	0	0	0	0
New York	0	24,106	0	0	20	5
North Carolina	7	3,992	58,425	0	0	0
North Dakota	1,227	13,761	0	23	57	20
Ohio	0	49,844	0	0	0	0
Oklahoma	0	314	0	0	0	0
Oregon	13	0	0	0	178	0
Pennsylvania	22	9,379	0	0	0	29
Rhode Island	0	0	0	0	0	0
South Carolina	0	815	229	0	0	49
South Dakota	12	46,949	0	0	730	193
Tennessee	0	3,350	117,392	0	0	0
Texas	0	6,477	409,352	0	124	0
Utah	0	367	0	0	86	0
Vermont	0	0	0	0	0	0
Virginia	128	4,531	0	0	0	0
Washington	62	0	0	0	75	0
West Virginia	0	867	0	0	0	0
Wisconsin	3	31,034	0	0	28	11
Wyoming	16	613	0	0	0	0
Adjustments	....	....	....	....	....	....
Peanut Associations	....	....	....	....	....	....
Total [2]	5,504	824,588	1,130,161	50	3,081	573

See footnote(s) at end of table.

Table 11-7.—Commodity Credit Corporation: Loans made in fiscal year 2014 as of September 30, by State and Territories [1]—Continued

State or Territory	Oilseeds	Peanuts	Rice	Seed cottton	Sorghum	Soybeans
	1,000 dollars	*1,000 dollars*	*1,000 dollars*	*1,000 dollars*	*1,000 dollars*	*1,000 dollars*
Alabama	0	2,979	0	0	0	226
Alaska	0	0	0	0	0	0
Arizona	0	0	0	0	0	0
Arkansas	0	0	73,730	0	18	1,954
California	0	0	99,784	0	0	0
Colorado	0	0	0	0	0	81
Connecticut	0	0	0	0	0	0
Delaware	0	0	0	0	0	151
Florida	0	10,112	0	0	0	0
Georgia	0	375,037	0	0	4	15
Hawaii	0	0	0	0	0	0
Idaho	152	0	0	0	0	0
Illinois	0	0	0	0	7	17,656
Indiana	0	0	0	0	13	38,171
Iowa	0	0	0	0	0	41,699
Kansas City Commod	0	0	0	0	0	0
Kansas	0	0	0	0	190	2,218
Kentucky	0	0	0	0	0	5,193
Louisiana	0	0	5,794	0	0	48
Maine	0	0	0	0	0	0
Maryland	0	0	0	0	0	1,426
Massachusetts	0	0	0	0	0	0
Michigan	0	0	0	0	0	10,435
Minnesota	148	0	0	0	0	28,460
Mississippi	0	5,191	4,206	0	0	1,897
Missouri	0	0	4,132	0	242	11,586
Montana	731	0	0	0	0	0
Nebraska	79	0	0	0	23	6,264
Nevada	0	0	0	0	0	0
New Hampshire	0	0	0	0	0	0
New Jersey	0	0	0	0	9	93
New Mexico	0	1,159	0	0	0	0
New York	1	0	0	0	0	4,416
North Carolina	0	28,218	0	42	0	1,451
North Dakota	3,426	0	0	0	0	2,865
Ohio	0	0	0	0	0	32,899
Oklahoma	0	1,838	0	0	60	0
Oregon	0	0	0	0	0	0
Pennsylvania	0	0	0	0	0	3,286
Rhode Island	0	0	0	0	0	0
South Carolina	0	8,280	0	0	0	1,232
South Dakota	1,867	0	0	0	353	8,771
Tennessee	0	0	0	0	0	2,365
Texas	0	45,637	8,800	941	155	0
Utah	0	0	0	0	0	0
Vermont	0	0	0	0	0	0
Virginia	0	24,217	0	0	4	1,947
Washington	0	0	0	0	0	0
West Virginia	0	0	0	0	0	459
Wisconsin	0	0	0	0	0	5,112
Wyoming	0	0	0	0	0	0
Adjustments	....	....	....	....	....	....
Peanut Associations	....	....	....	....	....	....
Total [2]	6,403	502,668	196,446	983	1,074	232,376

See footnote(s) at end of table.

Table 11-7.—Commodity Credit Corporation: Loans made in fiscal year 2014 as of September 30, by State and Territories [1]—Continued

State or Territory	Sugar	Wheat	Mohair	Dry whole peas	Wool
	1,000 dollars	*1,000 dollars*	*1,000 dollars*	*1,000 dollars*	*1,000 dollars*
Alabama	0	0	0	0	0
Alaska	0	0	0	0	0
Arizona	0	0	0	0	0
Arkansas	0	401	0	0	0
California	0	0	0	0	0
Colorado	79,121	2,429	0	0	0
Connecticut	0	0	0	0	0
Delaware	0	53	0	0	0
Florida	70,821	0	0	0	0
Georgia	0	40	0	0	0
Hawaii	0	0	0	0	0
Idaho	205,520	2,458	0	172	0
Illinois	0	262	0	0	0
Indiana	0	139	0	0	0
Iowa	0	0	0	0	0
Kansas City Commod	0	0	0	0	0
Kansas	0	1,080	0	0	0
Kentucky	0	1,687	0	0	0
Louisiana	182,260	0	0	0	0
Maine	0	162	0	0	0
Maryland	0	130	0	0	0
Massachusetts	0	0	0	0	0
Michigan	106,594	929	0	0	0
Minnesota	78,806	8,850	0	0	0
Mississippi	0	524	0	0	0
Missouri	0	935	0	0	0
Montana	0	22,128	0	2,558	5
Nebraska	0	313	0	0	0
Nevada	0	0	0	0	0
New Hampshire	0	0	0	0	0
New Jersey	0	26	0	0	0
New Mexico	0	0	0	0	0
New York	0	1,118	0	0	0
North Carolina	0	1,533	0	0	0
North Dakota	46,344	13,137	0	766	0
Ohio	0	274	0	0	0
Oklahoma	0	182	0	0	0
Oregon	0	1,698	0	35	0
Pennsylvania	0	128	0	0	0
Rhode Island	0	0	0	0	0
South Carolina	0	149	0	0	0
South Dakota	0	13,828	0	0	0
Tennessee	0	246	0	0	0
Texas	0	963	0	0	0
Utah	0	373	0	0	0
Vermont	0	0	0	0	0
Virginia	0	1,398	0	0	0
Washington	0	3,237	0	129	0
West Virginia	0	0	0	0	0
Wisconsin	0	1,161	0	0	0
Wyoming	4,014	69	0	0	0
Adjustments	....	....	....	....	....
Peanut Associations	....	....	....	....	....
Total [2]	773,480	82,040	0	3,625	5

[1] Loans made directly by Commodity Credit Corporation. As much as possible, loans have been distributed according to the location of producers receiving the loans. Direct loans to cooperative associations for the benefit of members have been distributed according to the location of the association. [2] Totals may not add due to rounding.
FSA, Office and Budget and Finance, Budget Division, (202) 720–0174.

Table 11-8.—Farm Service Agency programs: Payments to producers, by program and commodity, United States, calendar year 2013–2014

Program and commodity	2013	2014
	1,000 dollars	*1,000 dollars*
Acreage grazing payments	0	0
Additional interest	0	0
Agricultural management assistance	0	0
American indian - livestock feed	0	0
Aquaculture block grant	0	0
Auto conservation reserve program (crp)-cost shares	74,593	80,871
Avg crop revenue election program	469,183	266,139
Bioenergy program	0	0
Biomass crop assistance	7,242	5,795
Cotton transition program	0	460,320
Cottonseed payment program	0	0
Crop assistance program	18	7
Crop disaster - North Carolina	0	0
Crop disaster - Virginia	0	0
Crop disaster program	0	0
Crop disaster program - 2005	0	0
Crop hurricane damage program	0	0
Crp annual rental	1,595,673	1,580,605
Crp incentives	31,273	35,785
Crp transition incentive	8,112	2,857
Dairy economic loss assistance	45	15
Dairy indemnity	1,596	379
Dairy market loss assistance	0	0
Direct and counter cyclical program	4,106,196	75,340
Durum wheat quality program	0	0
Extra long staple special provision program	0	0
Emergency Assistance program	377	26,831
Emergency conservation program	30,181	24,986
Emergency forest restoration	3,975	1,964
Environment quality incentives	0	0
Feed indemnity program	0	0
Finalty rule	0	0
Fl hurricane citrus disaster	0	0
Forestry conservation reserve	3,655	5,178
Fl nursery disaster	0	0
Fl vegetable disaster	0	0
Florida sugarcane program	0	0
Grasslands reserve program	10,641	10,671
Geographic disadvantaged program	1,945	1,837
Hard white winter wheat	0	0
Hawaii sugar disaster	0	0
Hurricane indemnity program	0	0
Interest payments	0	0
Lamb meat adjustment assistance	0	0
Livestock assistance grant	0	0
Livestock assistance program	0	0
Livestock compensation program	0	0
Livestock emergency assistance	0	0
Livestock forage program	1,145	4,396,383
Livestock indemnity program	595	77,188
Loan deficiency	17	62,378
Louisiana sugarcane program	0	0
Market gains	0	34,308
Marketing loss assistance-asparagus	0	0
Marketing loss assistance	0	0
Milk income loss contract transitional	0	0
Milk income loss contract	0	0
Milk income loss II	235,518	1,079
Noninsured assistance program	259,116	184,410
Peanut quota buyout program	0	0
Pima cotton trust fund program	0	16,000
Soil/water conservation assistance	0	0
Speciality crop - nursery	0	0
Speciality crop - tropical fruit	0	0
Specialty crop - citrus	0	0
Specialty crop - fruit/vegetable	0	0
Storage forgiven	0	1,992
Sugar beet disaster program	0	0
Supplemental assistance program	1,642,331	31,528
Texas sugarcane storage & transportation	0	0
Tobacco quota holder-interest	1	23
Trade adjustment assistance	7,600	6,354
Tree assistance program	1,403	3,413
Tree indemnity program	0	0
Ttpp tobacco producer	285,331	286,835
Upland cotton assistance	48,192	47,553
Wetlands reserve	0	0
01 - 02 crop disaster assistance	0	0
05 - 07 crop disaster assistance	5	2
05 - 07 dairy disaster prog	0	0
05 - 07 livestock compensation	0	0
05 - 07 livestock indemnity prog	0	0
Grand Total	8,825,955	7,729,025

FSA, Office and Budget and Finance, Budget Division, (202) 720–0174.

Table 11-9.—Farm Service Agency programs: Payments received, by States, calendar year 2013–2014

State	Payments	
	2013	2014
	1,000 dollars	*1,000 dollars*
Alabama	66,937	97,286
Alaska	1,189	1,146
Arizona	28,894	51,349
Arkansas	247,637	221,862
California	159,429	171,285
Colorado	189,200	235,429
Connecticut	2,481	1,620
Delaware	6,183	1,033
District of Columbia	0	0
Florida	24,484	60,284
Georgia	156,565	188,340
Hawaii	6,974	19,610
Idaho	91,561	47,797
Illinois	575,611	161,442
Indiana	291,411	71,066
Iowa	713,154	375,624
Kansas	632,170	596,887
Kentucky	158,098	109,312
Louisiana	132,328	78,673
Maine	5,205	3,909
Maryland	31,028	11,992
Massachusetts	3,194	2,234
Michigan	112,785	35,184
Minnesota	442,657	174,420
Mississippi	158,741	121,105
Missouri	359,631	443,227
Montana	199,224	107,273
Nebraska	521,238	623,533
Nevada	3,716	35,371
New Hampshire	1,127	380
New Jersey	4,418	1,697
New Mexico	78,027	192,026
New York	51,212	7,647
North Carolina	192,759	127,764
North Dakota	528,206	137,663
Ohio	221,045	51,670
Oklahoma	295,619	957,512
Oregon	62,361	70,596
Pennsylvania	60,787	21,471
Rhode Island	237	219
South Carolina	48,027	49,104
South Dakota	244,027	397,736
Tennessee	82,584	60,018
Texas	1,038,891	1,074,627
Utah	20,041	58,420
Vermont	8,798	2,383
Virginia	49,977	25,082
Washington	161,332	91,624
West Virginia	4,190	2,290
Wisconsin	176,462	50,189
Wyoming	23,967	135,753
KCCO	145,295	162,228
Puerto Rico	4,807	2,550
Virgin Islands	8	19
Guam	15	47
MI	6	12
AS	5	2
Total [1]	8,825,955	7,729,025

[1] Total may not add due to rounding.
FSA, Office and Budget and Finance, Budget Division, (202) 720–0174.

Table 11-10.—Fruit, vegetable, and tree nut and specialty crop marketing orders and peanut program, 2013-14 season

Program	Estimated number of producers	Farm value
	Number	*1,000 dollars*
Citrus fruits		
Florida oranges, grapefruit, tangerines, and tangelos ...	8,000	241,922
Texas oranges and grapefruit	170	73,554
Deciduous fruits		
California olives	1,000	134,881
California desert grapes	41	63,497
California kiwifruit	175	29,812
Florida avocados	300	26,905
Washington apricots	94	7,767
Washington sweet cherries	1,500	350,900
Washington and Oregon pears [1]	1,500	301,256
Tart cherries (7 States) [2]	600	104,395
Cranberries (10 States) [3]	1,200	287,322
Dried fruits		
California dates	70	37,210
California plums	800	170,000
California raisins	3,000	826,921
Vegetables		
Florida tomatoes	100	348,013
Idaho and Eastern Oregon onions	250	148,634
South Texas onions	85	83,110
Georgia onions (Vidalia)	80	97,610
Onions (Walla Walla, Washington, and Oregon)	21	6,043
Potatoes [4]		
Colorado	180	128,168
Idaho and Eastern Oregon	450	293,136
Washington	267	84,824
Tree Nuts		
California almonds	6,400	6,384,690
California, Arizona, and New Mexico pistashios [5]	1,040	1,635,600
California walnuts	4,100	1,825,320
Oregon and Washington hazelnuts	650	120,600
Spearmint oil [5]	130	44,914
Peanuts [7]	6,182	1,055,095
Total 28 programs [8]		14,912,100

[1] Includes fresh and processed pears.   [2] The tart cherry order covers the States of Michigan, New York, Pennsylvania, Oregon, Utah, Washington, and Wisconsin.   [3] The cranberry order covers Massachusetts, Rhode Island, Connecticut, New Jersey, Wisconsin, Michigan, Minnesota, Oregon, Washington, and Long Island in New York.   [4] The farm values of fresh potatoes regulated under the three potato marketing orders are based on the season average grower prices for all potatoes (fresh and processed utilization combined) in Colorado, Idaho, and Washington, respectively. NASS grower prices for fresh potato utilization were not available for all of the states regulated under the marketing order.   [5] Pistachio farm value is for California only.   [6] The marketing order regulates the handling of spearmint oil produced in the States of Washington, Idaho, Oregon and designated parts of Nevada and Utah. The farm value is the sum of crop values for Washington, Idaho and Oregon, and excludes the minor level of production in Nevada and Utah, which is not published by NASS.   [7] The Farm Security and Rural Investment Act of 2002 terminated the Peanut Administrative Committee (which locally administered Marketing Agreement No. 146). As a result, the marketing agreement was terminated and and new quality standards were established for domestic and imported peanuts, administered by the Peanut Standards Board.   [8] The total number of producers cannot be determined from totals for individual commodities; some producers may produce more than one commodity.
AMS, Fruit and Vegetable Programs, (202) 720–9915.

CHAPTER XII

AGRICULTURAL CONSERVATION AND FORESTRY STATISTICS

Statistics in this chapter concern conservation of various natural resources, particularly soil, water, timber, wetlands, wildlife, and improvement of water quality. Forestry statistics include area of private and public-owned forest land, timber production, imports and exports, pulpwood consumption and paper and board production, area burned over by forest fires, livestock grazing, and recreational use of national forest lands.

Conservation Practices on Active CRP Contracts

Practice code	Practice	Acres
CP1	Introduced grasses and legumes	3,300,553
CP2	Native grasses	6,280,904
CP3	Tree planting	959,416
CP4	Wildlife habitat with woody vegetation	1,916,100
CP5	Field windbreaks	92,326
CP6	Diversions	18
CP7	Erosion control structures	19
CP8	Grass waterways	126,346
CP9	Shallow water areas for wildlife	29,490
CP10	Existing grasses and legumes[1]	4,018,927
CP11	Existing trees	376,490
CP12	Wildlife food plots	48,158
CP15	Contour grass strips	63,628
CP16	Shelterbelts	34,445
CP17	Living snow fences	6,566
CP18	Salinity reducing vegetation	220,412
CP21	Filter strips (grass)	838,057
CP22	Riparian buffers (trees)	811,407
CP23	Wetland restoration	1,053,132
CP24	Cross wind trap strips	98
CP25	Rare and declining habitat	1,556,229
CP26	Sediment retention	63
CP27	Farmable wetland pilot (wetland)	92,062
CP28	Farmable wetland pilot (upland)	206,844
CP29	Wildlife habitat buffer (marginal pasture)	120,375
CP30	Wetland buffer (marginal pasture)	43,521
CP31	Bottomland hardwood	130,456
CP32	Hardwood trees	9,075
CP33	Upland bird habitat buffers	257,160
CP34	Flood control structure	69
CP36	Longleaf pine	139,254
CP37	Duck nesting habitat	300,415
CP38	State acres for wildlife enhancement	1,016,323
CP39	FWP–Constucted wetlands	381
CP40	FWP–Aquaculture wetlands	17,166
CP41	FWP–Flooded prairie wetlands	43,750
CP42	Pollinator Habitat[2]	92,953
	Total	24,202,586

[1] Includes both introduced grasses and legumes and native grasses. [2] Does not include about 40,000 acres from Signup 39 before CP42 was implemented.
FSA, Conservation and Environmental Programs Division, (530) 792-5594.

CRP enrollment: By sign up and initial contract year[1], as of August 2015

Sign up	Before 2007	2007	2007	2009	2010	2011
1-27	2,196,642					
28	187,008					
29	963,239	56,905				
30	375,111					
31	188,812	140,70				
32	155		2,194,765	821,337	523,332	238,008
33	0	802,781	78			
35	0	150,239	347,781			
36	22		202,282	171,831		
37	22			223,946	225,072	
38		2			216,903	382,440
39						3,703,621
40						171,335
41						
42						
43						
44						
45						
46						
47						
All	3,911,011	1,150,626	2,744,907	1,217,113	965,307	4,495,403

Sign up	2012	2013	2014	2015	Total
1-27					2,196,642
28					187,008
29					1,020,144
30					375,111
31					329,512
32					3,777,597
33					802,859
35					498,020
36					374,134
37		90			449,130
38					599,344
39					3,703,621
40	309,290				480,625
41	2,509,411				2,509,411
42	117,411	493,447			610,859
43		3,491,432			3,491,432
44	34	23,096	509,916		533,046
45			1,560,573		1,560,573
46			3,211	527,575	530,786
47				167,778	167,778
All	2,936,146	4,008,066	2,070,489	695,353	24,197,633

[1] For CRP, contract year is the same as fiscal year, which begins October 1.
General Signup Numbers: 1-13, 15, 16, 18, 20, 26, 29, 33, 39, 41, 43, 45. Continuous Sign-up Numbers: 14, 17, 19, 21-25, 27, 28, 30, 31, 35-38, 40, 42, 44, 46, 47.
FSA, Conservation and Environmental Programs Division, (530) 792–5594.

Table 12-1.—Conservation Reserve Program (CRP): Enrollment by practice, under contract, August 2015

(CP1 and CP2)

State	CP1 Establishment of permanent introduced grasses and legumes			CP2 Establishment of permanent native grasses		
	Total acres treated	Total cost share	Avg cost share per acre treated [1]	Total acres treated	Total cost share	Avg cost share per acre treated [1]
Alabama	13,722	794,388	71.09	3,674	180,872	77.89
Alaska	2,033	0				
Arkansas	4,076	260,290	84.90	4,441	710,116	191.15
California	21,025	821,890	136.16	253	32,374	314.95
Colorado	67,235	3,386,169	65.68	853,863	49,405,544	70.58
Delaware	31	11,105	358.23	23	16,310	700.00
Florida	85	0		108	3,718	143.00
Georgia	754	53,778	97.64	177	17,165	204.83
Hawaii		0			0	
Idaho	208,868	13,795,782	77.86	44,745	3,127,392	78.61
Illinois	176,613	7,775,348	66.14	53,214	8,106,413	220.06
Indiana	23,435	1,243,506	83.58	17,010	1,960,103	182.02
Iowa	191,602	5,789,865	46.05	130,723	18,802,814	219.59
Kansas	12,348	491,080	51.96	738,126	31,123,377	48.26
Kentucky	38,060	3,075,361	126.88	26,167	2,361,810	138.53
Louisiana	862	31,838	67.02	1,474	194,232	204.20
Maine	2,921	458,339	194.71		0	
Maryland	8,919	672,850	161.18	2,462	282,935	208.61
Massachusetts		0			0	
Michigan	26,279	2,748,049	132.95	20,597	3,042,920	198.78
Minnesota	72,772	2,087,505	44.10	59,313	2,610,754	89.55
Mississippi	20,586	252,257	113.74	2,788	71,630	133.41
Missouri	468,562	21,928,510	86.49	166,654	14,314,954	161.63
Montana	439,290	5,232,955	21.95	352,380	5,289,743	33.33
Nebraska	29,846	2,819,701	104.52	304,118	20,241,253	80.35
Nevada	*	*	*	*	*	*
New Hampshire		0			0	
New Jersey	303	5,620	200.00	124	0	
New Mexico	43,654	3,051,940	88.72	288,317	21,417,745	114.47
New York	6,792	1,569,291	273.98	757	321,899	561.98
North Carolina	1,069	58,728	86.58	465	109,285	418.56
North Dakota	174,137	6,237,189	48.65	29,771	1,830,804	79.34
Ohio	15,160	936,978	127.12	52,794	4,679,930	116.83
Oklahoma	112,877	5,473,133	61.08	349,891	18,302,339	71.23
Oregon	211,531	12,628,865	70.91	104,529	8,437,711	91.85
Pennsylvania	84,977	10,240,570	151.43	29,371	3,766,962	178.88
Puerto Rico	108	17,550	162.50		0	
South Carolina	899	46,742	215.30	182	0	
South Dakota	53,925	1,532,526	34.39	87,279	5,198,675	86.60
Tennessee	31,373	1,417,184	117.23	25,449	3,090,587	195.00
Texas	264,549	15,534,927	82.98	1,840,234	126,423,395	86.01
Utah	74,154	2,513,606	42.77	14,652	1,060,598	77.39
Vermont	9	1,080	800.00		0	
Virginia	2,932	520,590	340.50	1,387	312,804	505.09
Washington	253,870	13,309,041	61.85	641,963	44,068,435	92.18
West Virginia	208	17,792	134.89		0	
Wisconsin	38,014	2,616,877	94.88	29,666	2,836,859	159.33
Wyoming	99,938	1,870,235	31.40	1,739	49,436	86.38
United States	3,300,553	153,343,838	67.96	6,280,904	403,803,889	84.74

[1] Not including acres which receive no cost share.
Total acres treated may not add due to rounding.
FSA, Conservation and Environmental Programs Division, (530) 792-5594.

Table 12-2.—Conservation Reserve Program (CRP): Enrollment by practice, under contract, August 2015

(CP3 and CP4)

State	CP3 Tree planting			CP4 Permanent wildlife habitat		
	Total acres treated	Total cost share	Avg cost share per acre treated [1]	Total acres treated	Total cost share	Avg cost share per acre treated [1]
Alabama	136,850	12,485,255	118.07	7,648	903,451	289.53
Alaska	0	0	....	0	0	....
Arkansas	47,985	4,309,802	111.43	2,400	136,917	76.55
California	55	0	....	9,851	1,275	250.00
Colorado	37	11,793	589.65	430,685	25,377,387	82.78
Delaware	3,392	1,154,143	361.06	991	279,826	368.04
Florida	20,192	1,232,448	139.76	1,180	0	....
Georgia	110,966	13,596,763	143.04	2,782	270,915	225.73
Hawaii	13	55,854	4,168.21	0	0	....
Idaho	6,525	540,363	102.53	83,870	2,577,173	50.99
Illinois	48,027	9,635,654	267.55	109,977	25,098,302	347.11
Indiana	18,001	3,333,550	281.96	8,182	1,042,839	244.70
Iowa	16,030	4,440,793	369.37	131,481	3,484,473	138.44
Kansas	450	45,385	191.34	318,572	16,607,861	57.32
Kentucky	4,590	878,145	222.47	331	67,372	335.52
Louisiana	81,841	7,482,194	113.54	32,713	3,170,826	125.75
Maine	129	84,326	938.00	38	0	....
Maryland	989	244,539	487.04	1,583	167,008	239.16
Massachusetts	0	0	....	0	0	....
Michigan	6,513	869,681	217.86	12,659	484,436	121.89
Minnesota	27,392	2,741,526	143.16	167,524	2,030,096	93.32
Mississippi	260,741	7,187,684	111.73	4,507	312,287	360.03
Missouri	14,702	1,104,478	220.32	3,295	228,099	147.11
Montana	45	0	....	12,543	588,147	217.70
Nebraska	664	70,385	250.83	45,482	2,973,116	75.49
Nevada	*	*	*	*	*	*
New Hampshire	0	0	....	0	0	....
New Jersey	99	12,750	250.00	0	0	....
New Mexico	0	0	....	140	16,800	120.00
New York	895	391,141	564.43	529	276,127	646.52
North Carolina	31,212	6,700,097	283.54	986	493,292	888.49
North Dakota	456	36,482	183.51	299,946	14,455,178	75.07
Ohio	8,554	2,470,915	494.86	13,257	620,992	111.14
Oklahoma	286	21,405	111.89	623	31,681	98.22
Oregon	2,196	161,252	303.28	10,678	1,050,042	151.50
Pennsylvania	1,144	948,973	1,047.43	4,342	1,446,558	405.71
Puerto Rico	16	1,510	151.00	20	0	....
South Carolina	34,675	1,690,934	87.02	1,547	62,780	182.02
South Dakota	48	946	220.00	55,905	3,234,065	73.97
Tennessee	25,378	1,785,814	161.30	3,635	128,080	122.61
Texas	1,465	49,738	95.48	20,730	799,532	76.11
Utah	0	0	....	13	0	....
Vermont	0	0	....	0	0	....
Virginia	8,947	1,120,034	176.87	488	104,512	435.46
Washington	2,185	178,703	90.83	110,211	7,972,909	126.18
West Virginia	22	4,602	464.85	0	0	....
Wisconsin	35,706	6,635,429	287.06	4,163	430,317	280.40
Wyoming	1	0	....	591	0	....
United States	959,416	93,715,489	163.34	1,916,100	116,924,670	98.88

[1] Not including acres which receive no cost share.
Total acres treated may not add due to rounding.
FSA, Conservation and Environmental Programs Division, (530) 792-5594.

Table 12-3.—Conservation Reserve Program (CRP): Enrollment by practice, under contract, August 2015

(CP5, CP6, and CP7)

State	CP5 Establishment of field windbreaks			CP6 Diversions			CP7 Erosion control structures		
	Total acres treated	Total cost share	Avg cost share per acre treated[1]	Total acres treated	Total cost share	Avg cost share per acre treated[1]	Total acres treated	Total cost share	Avg cost share per acre treated[1]
Alabama	0.0	0	....	....	0	....	....	0	....
Alaska	0.0	0	....	....	0	....	....	0	....
Arkansas	0.0	0	....	....	0	....	....	0	....
California	0.0	0	....	....	0	....	....	0	....
Colorado	1,547	1,189,875	1,011.77	....	0	....	....	0	....
Delaware	0	0	....	....	0	....	....	0	....
Florida	0	0	....	....	0	....	....	0	....
Georgia	0	0	....	....	0	....	....	0	....
Hawaii	0	0	....	....	0	....	....	0	....
Idaho	263	621,952	2,733.85	....	0	....	....	0	....
Illinois	2,401	460,333	253.04	15	0	....	4	0	....
Indiana	1,970	374,331	215.29	....	0	....	0	0	....
Iowa	6,460	1,607,833	305.76	....	0	....	10	2,484	709.57
Kansas	1,805	740,333	523.61	....	0	....	....	0	....
Kentucky	0	0	....	....	0	....	....	0	....
Louisiana	0	0	....	....	0	....	....	0	....
Maine	0	0	....	....	0	....	....	0	....
Maryland	0	0	....	....	0	....	....	0	....
Massachusetts	0	0	....	....	0	....	....	0	....
Michigan	2,467	682,310	310.37	1	0	....	....	0	....
Minnesota	8,930	2,675,459	350.58	....	0	....	0	0	....
Mississippi	0	0	....	....	0	....	....	0	....
Missouri	82	23,330	481.03	3	0	....	3	0	....
Montana	186	74,634	477.72	....	0	....	....	0	....
Nebraska	32,942	17,855,924	707.83	....	0	....	....	0	....
Nevada	*	*	*	*	*	*	*	*	*
New Hampshire	0	0	....	....	0	....	....	0	....
New Jersey	7	37,144	5,306.29	....	0	....	....	0	....
New Mexico	0	0	....	....	0	....	....	0	....
New York	7	2,836	436.31	....	0	....	....	0	....
North Carolina	23	2,558	127.90	....	0	....	....	0	....
North Dakota	4,539	2,620,728	658.44	....	0	....	....	0	....
Ohio	3,493	1,175,264	384.18	....	0	....	....	0	....
Oklahoma	30	6,348	869.59	....	0	....	....	0	....
Oregon	4	525	145.83	....	0	....	....	0	....
Pennsylvania	0	0	....	....	0	....	....	0	....
Puerto Rico	0	0	....	....	0	....	....	0	....
South Carolina	36	2,709	90.60	....	0	....	....	0	....
South Dakota	24,652	17,267,723	833.80	....	0	....	....	0	....
Tennessee	0	0	....	....	0	....	....	0	....
Texas	41	29,371	861.32	....	0	....	....	0	....
Utah	1	2,437	1,740.71	....	0	....	....	0	....
Vermont	0	0	....	....	0	....	....	0	....
Virginia	3	500	1,250.00	....	0	....	....	0	....
Washington	12	3,000	476.19	....	0	....	....	0	....
West Virginia	0	0	....	....	0	....	....	0	....
Wisconsin	149	49,907	426.27	....	0	....	1	0	....
Wyoming	277	265,656	1,276.58	....	0	....	....	0	....
United States	92,326	47,773,019	636.25	18	....	....	19	2,484	709.57

[1] Not including acres which receive no cost share.
Total acres treated may not add due to rounding.
FSA, Conservation and Environmental Programs Division, (530) 792-5594.

Table 12-4.—Conservation Reserve Program (CRP): Enrollment by practice, under contract, August 2015

(CP8 and CP9)

State	CP8 Grass waterways			CP9 Shallow water areas for wildlife		
	Total acres treated	Total cost share	Avg cost share per acre treated [1]	Total acres treated	Total cost share	Avg cost share per acre treated [1]
Alabama	1	0		102	39,771	872.94
Alaska	0	0			0	
Arkansas	5	66	12.74	557	58,925	267.72
California	0	0		40	17,389	434.40
Colorado	519	6,739	157.01	18	0	
Delaware	6	0		221	251,097	1,671.75
Florida	0	0			0	
Georgia	35	17,047	906.76	23	14,424	1,109.54
Hawaii	0	0			0	
Idaho	3	0		23	224	70.00
Illinois	32,217	29,313,301	1,724.97	4,727	1,291,099	646.00
Indiana	18,892	57,069,750	5,509.75	979	303,084	1,063.04
Iowa	36,632	30,532,911	1,368.87	10,285	957,365	210.44
Kansas	8,401	2,846,628	515.68	1,051	145,804	434.13
Kentucky	4,401	9,212,974	2,957.55	1,897	455,754	806.22
Louisiana	5	0		442	70,256	380.79
Maine	59	329,918	6,858.99		0	
Maryland	252	847,999	6,307.64	1,153	1,679,852	2,437.04
Massachusetts	0	0			0	
Michigan	598	1,261,122	4,855.14	1,856	1,031,131	744.54
Minnesota	3,547	1,765,336	1,116.83	243	14,498	233.09
Mississippi	58	300	93.75	539	31,731	480.04
Missouri	2,005	1,310,080	1,304.73	1,854	95,421	324.02
Montana	83	1,990	50.90	11	0	
Nebraska	1,294	315,729	415.21	187	50,060	533.91
Nevada	*	*	*	*	*	*
New Hampshire	0	0			0	
New Jersey	151	1,799,022	12,676.31		0	
New Mexico	0	0			0	
New York	42	88,343	3,424.14	3	3,462	1,018.24
North Carolina	268	620,112	2,779.40	350	241,127	887.15
North Dakota	95	22,004	449.07	1	0	
Ohio	11,111	35,412,109	5,564.57	560	248,033	1,262.25
Oklahoma	166	8,784	358.53	79	16,109	449.97
Oregon	27	10,680	726.53		0	
Pennsylvania	341	741,243	3,188.69	33	17,602	1,248.37
Puerto Rico	0	0			0	
South Carolina	36	34,448	1,299.93	44	42,836	1,457.01
South Dakota	1,328	472,032	555.84	41	0	
Tennessee	162	199,206	2,388.85	73	8,000	800.00
Texas	1,603	1,123,264	1,018.09	92	42,514	920.22
Utah	14	347	43.38		0	
Vermont	16	12,615	1,025.61		0	
Virginia	88	181,450	2,382.48	69	142,381	2,256.43
Washington	376	4,390	55.36	51	3,151	201.47
West Virginia	0	0			0	
Wisconsin	1,513	2,021,724	2,611.68	1,884	873,267	919.49
Wyoming	0	0			0	
United States	126,346	177,583,663	2,457.01	29,490	8,146,366	645.65

[1] Not including acres which receive no cost share.
Total acres treated may not add due to rounding.
FSA, Conservation and Environmental Programs Division, (530) 792-5594.

Table 12-5.—Conservation Reserve Program (CRP): Enrollment by practice, under contract, August 2015

(CP10, CP11, and CP12)

State	CP10 Vegetative-cover-grass-already established			CP11 Vegetative-cover-trees-already established			CP12 Wildlife food plots		
	Total acres treated	Total cost share	Avg cost share per acre treated [1]	Total acres treated	Total cost share	Avg cost share per acre treated [1]	Total acres treated	Total cost share	Avg cost share per acre treated [1]
Alabama	22,589	667,627	73.26	40,259	2,501,994	128.51	1,077	0	
Alaska	14,919	0		0	0		0	0	
Arkansas	4,726	64,373	158.36	12,392	88,861	227.50	397	0	
California	45,989	0		303	0		6	0	
Colorado	487,854	4,464,034	28.67	22	0		257	0	
Delaware	25	0		0	0		8	0	
Florida	308	0		12,456	12,500	690.61	58	0	
Georgia	1,172	24,000	568.72	24,331	480,714	133.80	777	0	
Hawaii		0		0	0		0	0	
Idaho	119,986	17,652	9.57	1,117	0		227	0	
Illinois	77,033	56,675	58.34	10,947	12,219	62.92	5,508	0	
Indiana	18,962	6,298	17.77	5,535	8,834	42.17	656	30	50.00
Iowa	188,516	2,872,708	109.00	6,485	585,354	714.89	4,750	0	
Kansas	206,903	217,136	10.06	223	12,000	2,926.83	3,369	12	12.00
Kentucky	9,263	20,149	22.58	983	1,012	34.66	783	0	
Louisiana	1,455	638	11.71	13,725	4,135	7.88	1,044	0	
Maine	2,633	0		274	0		0	0	
Maryland	1,736	8,518	116.53	310	634	36.86	37	0	
Massachusetts		0		0	0		0	0	
Michigan	15,891	19,331	53.14	2,558	8,243	32.16	1,154	0	
Minnesota	62,961	33,137	52.21	9,063	162,192	263.56	3,964	1,013	63.28
Mississippi	32,015	1,764	32.30	161,788	1,096,965	196.29	2,705	0	
Missouri	139,965	125,242	64.27	6,341	15,871	160.48	3,580	0	
Montana	444,412	242,713	4.54	442	0		1,726	24	24.00
Nebraska	98,973	1,001,308	44.98	858	38,165	481.28	811	50	50.00
Nevada	*	*	*	*	*	*	*	*	*
New Hampshire		0		0	0		0	0	
New Jersey	22	0		0	0		2	0	
New Mexico	91,508	1,955	6.50	0	0		1	0	
New York	14,974	454,994	112.22	738	45,310	216.48	77	0	
North Carolina	1,187	0		10,520	1,493,353	358.14	28	0	
North Dakota	320,912	2,134,639	23.24	342	103	42.96	2,482	0	
Ohio	25,457	398,426	684.00	2,615	2,200	35.15	468	0	
Oklahoma	233,579	614,035	11.63	173	0		1,008	0	
Oregon	123,558	703,713	25.71	518	152,111	987.73	120	300	600.00
Pennsylvania	14,053	372,030	114.89	296	2,079	44.05	1,155	0	
Puerto Rico	224	0		117	0		0	0	
South Carolina	1,755	1,185	28.07	21,393	129,911	34.92	263	0	
South Dakota	88,251	34,384	13.85	210	138	43.23	4,019	0	
Tennessee	19,457	6,004	44.24	8,024	52	43.23	384	0	
Texas	756,897	11,866,765	112.80	3,028	0		3,215	1,880	100.00
Utah	82,055	5,454	3.00	0	0		19	0	
Vermont	45	0		0	0		0	0	
Virginia	3,419	67,468	258.99	5,233	100,579	139.37	28	0	
Washington	117,821	137,346	23.01	781	4,168	54.14	597	80	80.00
West Virginia	164	0		0	0		0	0	
Wisconsin	50,872	462,733	76.97	12,079	96,941	195.29	1,379	0	
Wyoming	74,425	0		12	0		20	0	
United States	4,018,927	27,104,432	45.31	376,490	7,056,640	169.75	48,158	3,389	84.92

[1] Not including acres which receive no cost share.
Total acres treated may not add due to rounding.
FSA, Conservation and Environmental Programs Division, (530) 792-5594.

Table 12-6.—Conservation Reserve Program (CRP): Enrollment by practice, under contract, August 2015

(CP15, CP16, and CP17)

State	CP15 Contour grass strips			CP16 Shelter belts			CP17 Living snow fences		
	Total acres treated	Total cost share	Avg cost share per acre treated [1]	Total acres treated	Total cost share	Avg cost share per acre treated [1]	Total acres treated	Total cost share	Avg cost share per acre treated [1]
Alabama	11	0	....	0.0	0	....	0.0	0	....
Alaska	0	0	....	0.0	0	....	0.0	0	....
Arkansas	0	0	....	0.0	0	....	0.0	0	....
California	0	0	....	0.0	0	....	0.0	0	....
Colorado	12	0	....	4,419	4,010,964	1,037.40	35	18,880	1,026.09
Delaware	4	1,290	300.00	0	0	....	0	0	....
Florida	0	0	....	0	0	....	0	0	....
Georgia	0	0	....	0	0	....	0	0	....
Hawaii	0	0	....	0	0	....	0	0	....
Idaho	261	6,964	37.14	101	175,876	1,843.56	62	41,357	668.13
Illinois	935	22,615	62.03	144	33,204	302.16	56	11,532	241.76
Indiana	26	674	89.87	18	3,393	273.85	1	0	....
Iowa	12,527	361,753	101.66	2,250	1,946,475	1,082.23	656	151,289	268.70
Kansas	3,435	78,569	46.73	808	336,693	541.99	67	32,182	569.59
Kentucky	42	1,901	162.48	0	0	....	0	0	....
Louisiana	0	0	....	0	0	....	0	0	....
Maine	0	0	....	0	0	....	0	0	....
Maryland	0	0	....	0	0	....	0	0	....
Massachusetts	0	0	....	0	0	....	0	0	....
Michigan	3	1,069	509.05	54	12,013	322.06	14	4,232	313.48
Minnesota	748	20,279	57.52	3,951	1,281,989	389.21	4,209	809,161	229.40
Mississippi	27	0	....	0	0	....	0	0	....
Missouri	886	14,760	84.93	70	26,696	523.35	0	0	....
Montana	0	0	....	232	136,326	650.47	41	26,264	634.40
Nebraska	326	10,505	63.62	2,121	1,126,126	601.93	114	34,255	420.30
Nevada	*	*	*	*	*	*	*	*	*
New Hampshire	0	0	....	0	0	....	0	0	....
New Jersey	0	0	....	0	0	....	0	0	....
New Mexico	0	0	....	0	0	....	0	0	....
New York	3	0	....	0	0	....	0	0	....
North Carolina	0	0	....	5	0	....	0	0	....
North Dakota	0	0	....	5,109	3,304,152	717.55	667	360,547	644.22
Ohio	14	0	....	99	25,050	288.59	0	0	....
Oklahoma	9	0	....	21	4,783	226.68	0	0	....
Oregon	0	0	....	0	0	....	0	0	....
Pennsylvania	60	3,202	119.92	0	0	....	0	0	....
Puerto Rico	60	0	....	0	0	....	0	0	....
South Carolina	0	0	....	0	0	....	0	0	....
South Dakota	33	154	33.06	14,948	11,729,874	899.97	601	361,683	767.77
Tennessee	17	161	107.33	0	0	....	0	0	....
Texas	104	1,412	129.54	5	4,833	1,074.00	0	0	....
Utah	40	0	....	0	0	....	0	0	....
Vermont	0	0	....	0	0	....	0	0	....
Virginia	4	286	130.00	0	0	....	0	0	....
Washington	43,451	531,573	70.69	8	24,588	7,025.14	0	0	....
West Virginia	0	0	....	0	0	....	0	0	....
Wisconsin	593	9,917	109.23	27	8,125	303.17	39	8,824	239.12
Wyoming	0	0	....	55	74,819	1,370.31	3	729	214.41
United States	63,628	1,067,085	75.33	34,445	24,265,979	814.24	6,566	1,860,934	339.44

[1] Not including acres which receive no cost share.
Total acres treated may not add due to rounding.
FSA, Conservation and Environmental Programs Division, (530) 792-5594.

Table 12-7.—Conservation Reserve Program (CRP): Enrollment by practice, under contract, August 2015

(CP18 and CP21)

State	CP18 Salt tolerant grasses			CP21 Alternative perennials		
	Total acres treated	Total cost share	Avg cost share per acre treated [1]	Total acres treated	Total cost share	Avg cost share per acre treated [1]
Alabama	0	0		589	41,376	135.00
Alaska	0	0			0	
Arkansas	0	0		5,594	375,358	95.10
California	0	0			0	
Colorado	7	0		115	10,287	229.01
Delaware	0	0		1,031	337,194	352.03
Florida	0	0			0	
Georgia	0	0		314	4,025	838.54
Hawaii	0	0			0	
Idaho	0	0		797	60,559	117.84
Illinois	4	261	104.40	114,699	5,945,276	86.27
Indiana	0	0		50,471	4,436,133	151.86
Iowa	0	0		195,758	11,542,548	99.58
Kansas	875	0		26,143	1,149,329	63.34
Kentucky	0	0		23,025	1,823,014	144.34
Louisiana	0	0		484	14,321	47.03
Maine	0	0		61	850	404.76
Maryland	0	0		29,431	3,505,166	159.84
Massachusetts	0	0		10	7,074	714.55
Michigan	0	0		42,203	5,677,880	156.87
Minnesota	4,528	181,678	57.22	123,856	6,914,299	84.54
Mississippi	0	0		6,917	441,745	99.12
Missouri	0	0		32,611	1,379,873	87.84
Montana	95,493	166,287	8.91	225	4,877	25.13
Nebraska	503	9,685	37.47	16,258	850,072	66.20
Nevada	*	*	*	*	*	*
New Hampshire	0	0			0	
New Jersey	0	0		364	75,890	234.00
New Mexico	0	0			0	
New York	0	0		431	164,210	455.35
North Carolina	0	0		1,928	498,950	315.54
North Dakota	101,809	1,366,060	37.53	8,291	292,818	50.96
Ohio	0	0		70,903	4,216,488	88.29
Oklahoma	1,862	11,560	72.39	601	15,690	71.31
Oregon	0	0		1,852	141,546	149.59
Pennsylvania	0	0		1,334	183,314	205.24
Puerto Rico	0	0			0	
South Carolina	0	0		2,030	40,944	78.91
South Dakota	14,869	549,343	46.90	9,058	380,582	54.63
Tennessee	0	0		7,378	703,975	145.16
Texas	436	20	0.13	1,233	192,893	259.33
Utah	0	0		38	1,413	94.83
Vermont	0	0		215	50,584	243.08
Virginia	0	0		4,281	477,231	125.08
Washington	24	0		35,662	1,646,773	90.63
West Virginia	0	0		562	152,062	696.25
Wisconsin	0	0		21,304	2,303,668	139.66
Wyoming	0	0			0	
United States	220,412	2,284,894	32.40	838,057	56,060,288	105.01

[1] Not including acres which receive no cost share.
Total acres treated may not add due to rounding.
FSA, Conservation and Environmental Programs Division, (530) 792-5594.

Table 12-8.—Conservation Reserve Program (CRP): Enrollment by practice, under contract, August 2015

(CP22 and CP23)

State	CP22 Riparian buffer			CP23 Wetland restoration		
	Total acres treated	Total cost share	Avg cost share per acre treated [1]	Total acres treated	Total cost share	Avg cost share per acre treated [1]
Alabama	32,784	4,316,343	153.58	5	0	
Alaska	145	21,880	230.80	0	0	
Arkansas	61,577	5,128,995	115.64	46,832	15,262,043	505.12
California	1,534	615,932	463.77	569	0	
Colorado	676	728,736	1,196.04	779	24,355	95.75
Delaware	102	38,188	381.88	327	269,836	911.30
Florida	64	0		0	0	
Georgia	1,040	576,492	791.94	403	0	
Hawaii	987	3,616,588	3,664.59	0	0	
Idaho	5,609	2,478,207	525.68	507	12,915	39.87
Illinois	107,513	18,961,456	231.01	42,431	6,539,224	195.86
Indiana	5,568	1,046,767	278.13	8,303	1,369,490	282.63
Iowa	54,436	16,037,871	378.04	112,185	17,116,171	198.04
Kansas	2,974	202,195	156.85	8,681	327,996	56.23
Kentucky	23,163	7,949,768	363.21	134	21,706	214.49
Louisiana	5,408	566,553	128.48	102,183	8,654,895	176.78
Maine	49	126,632	5,147.64	0	0	
Maryland	15,705	5,821,553	515.58	2,669	2,197,012	1,050.90
Massachusetts		0		0	0	
Michigan	3,155	1,104,633	403.89	22,589	5,554,994	268.69
Minnesota	40,821	6,786,915	212.63	267,786	20,913,203	104.47
Mississippi	170,943	8,930,374	73.85	12,751	673,263	155.88
Missouri	29,080	4,999,444	268.94	14,082	1,057,890	150.89
Montana	3,082	357,050	184.87	2,140	33,183	37.41
Nebraska	2,544	773,451	366.28	5,933	374,423	108.40
Nevada	*	*	*	*	*	*
New Hampshire	13	11,593	1,332.53	0	0	
New Jersey	249	199,730	802.19	0	0	
New Mexico	5,280	2,217,812	485.76	0	0	
New York	12,580	10,953,125	1,003.61	95	9,634	296.43
North Carolina	22,554	2,043,615	107.11	2,535	354,815	164.67
North Dakota	399	207,202	660.98	202,878	1,969,518	44.09
Ohio	7,069	1,664,602	336.17	11,225	5,655,333	739.16
Oklahoma	1,856	549,615	427.71	2,050	95,490	59.71
Oregon	36,356	20,004,706	724.56	243	52,256	307.03
Pennsylvania	24,658	30,198,640	1,362.19	947	1,132,916	1,278.69
Puerto Rico	297	12,180	60.00	0	0	
South Carolina	14,796	806,587	83.77	172	0	
South Dakota	5,730	3,095,324	696.46	167,774	3,597,749	34.86
Tennessee	6,051	1,155,638	241.00	628	28,818	101.79
Texas	29,844	5,425,161	239.70	7,153	54,125	101.02
Utah	102	36,843	443.36	0	0	
Vermont	2,588	3,261,312	1,336.99	0	0	
Virginia	24,394	30,420,291	1,418.25	178	61,655	375.26
Washington	23,723	23,205,233	1,203.21	266	29,616	120.63
West Virginia	5,577	5,006,566	979.22	0	0	
Wisconsin	13,663	4,616,745	397.29	5,699	781,749	268.81
Wyoming	4,639	1,398,796	308.49	0	0	
United States	811,407	237,677,338	381.03	1,053,132	94,226,273	153.52

[1] Not including acres which receive no cost share.
Total acres treated may not add due to rounding.
FSA, Conservation and Environmental Programs Division, (530) 792-5594.

Table 12-9.—Conservation Reserve Program (CRP): Enrollment by practice, under contract, August 2015

(CP25, CP26, and CP27)

State	CP25 Rare and declining habitat			CP26 Sediment retention			CP27 Farmable wetland pilot (wetland)		
	Total acres treated	Total cost share	Avg cost share per acre treated[1]	Total acres treated	Total cost share	Avg cost share per acre treated[1]	Total acres treated	Total cost share	Avg cost share per acre treated[1]
Alabama	422	19,234	125.71	....	0	....	....	0	....
Alaska	....	0	....	....	0	....	....	0	....
Arkansas	....	0	....	....	0	....	....	0	....
California	....	0	....	....	0	....	....	0	....
Colorado	1,802	60,639	95.77	....	0	....	2	0	....
Delaware	....	0	....	....	0	....	....	0	....
Florida	....	0	....	....	0	....	....	0	....
Georgia	....	0	....	....	0	....	....	0	....
Hawaii	....	0	....	....	0	....	....	0	....
Idaho	79	4,120	100.00	....	0	....	4	606	173.14
Illinois	2,461	368,086	158.02	....	0	....	317	62,200	253.10
Indiana	2,318	428,688	185.47	....	0	....	333	517,305	1,966.19
Iowa	163,061	38,415,230	259.80	....	0	....	23,133	4,852,676	252.41
Kansas	730,864	45,772,661	70.15	....	0	....	724	16,216	124.26
Kentucky	38,695	8,669,377	231.10	....	0	....	....	0	....
Louisiana	....	0	....	....	0	....	....	0	....
Maine	....	0	....	....	0	....	....	0	....
Maryland	416	117,676	282.60	....	0	....	1	1,062	885.00
Massachusetts	....	0	....	....	0	....	....	0	....
Michigan	199	22,643	143.55	49	149,562	3,844.79	25	3,047	507.83
Minnesota	162,468	16,741,771	113.46	....	0	....	16,182	1,758,331	139.84
Mississippi	....	0	....	....	0	....	40	5,109	129.34
Missouri	56,323	7,341,520	153.79	....	0	....	6	2,258	525.12
Montana	109,770	5,946,584	64.98	....	0	....	203	344	23.24
Nebraska	176,590	17,462,619	106.67	....	0	....	1,570	69,056	144.07
Nevada	*	*	*	*	*	*	*	*	*
New Hampshire	....	0	....	....	0	....	....	0	....
New Jersey	....	0	....	....	0	....	....	0	....
New Mexico	....	0	....	....	0	....	....	0	....
New York	....	0	....	....	0	....	....	0	....
North Carolina	....	0	....	....	0	....	....	0	....
North Dakota	11,547	992,767	89.78	....	0	....	21,772	937,226	66.89
Ohio	6,595	2,185,601	421.88	....	0	....	82	395,261	5,028.77
Oklahoma	24,294	2,063,392	91.21	....	0	....	9	7,316	2,090.29
Oregon	34,216	1,081,639	98.09	....	0	....	....	0	....
Pennsylvania	....	0	....	....	0	....	....	0	....
Puerto Rico	....	0	....	....	0	....	....	0	....
South Carolina	....	0	....	....	0	....	....	0	....
South Dakota	18,553	1,384,824	99.26	14	0	....	27,628	823,715	62.76
Tennessee	....	0	....	....	0	....	....	0	....
Texas	....	0	....	....	0	....	....	0	....
Utah	....	0	....	....	0	....	....	0	....
Vermont	....	0	....	....	0	....	....	0	....
Virginia	....	0	....	....	0	....	....	0	....
Washington	1,166	88,535	156.98	....	0	....	2	0	....
West Virginia	....	0	....	....	0	....	....	0	....
Wisconsin	14,391	4,043,886	314.09	....	0	....	29	1,072	126.12
Wyoming	....	0	....	....	0	....	....	0	....
United States	1,556,229	153,211,492	111.69	63	149,562	3,844.79	92,062	9,452,801	156.99

[1] Not including acres which receive no cost share.
Total acres treated may not add due to rounding.
FSA, Conservation and Environmental Programs Division, (530) 792-5594.

Table 12-10.—Conservation Reserve Program (CRP): Enrollment by practice, under contract, August 2015

(CP28, CP29, and CP30)

State	CP28 Farmable wetland pilot (buffer)			CP29 Wildlife habitat buffer (marginal pastureland)			CP30 Wetland buffer (marginal pastureland)		
	Total acres treated	Total cost share	Avg cost share per acre treated [1]	Total acres treated	Total cost share	Avg cost share per acre treated [1]	Total acres treated	Total cost share	Avg cost share per acre treated [1]
Alabama	0	0		214	3,001	130.48		0	
Alaska		0			0		422	128,957	305.51
Arkansas	0	0		509	236,058	497.59	3,389	6,502	6,502.00
California		0		115	34,205	297.95		0	
Colorado	4	0		94	630	420.00	38	8,221	437.29
Delaware		0			0			0	
Florida		0			0			0	
Georgia		0		28	9,463	4,301.36		0	
Hawaii		0			0			0	
Idaho	2	62	31.00	229	62,987	593.10	162	14,845	99.76
Illinois	545	59,787	137.32	266	44,038	199.90	24	2,368	101.63
Indiana	614	74,736	136.23	67	81,387	1,285.73	51	9,398	185.00
Iowa	55,162	4,394,773	94.39	9,714	2,789,879	378.11	2,188	285,774	192.76
Kansas	1,390	51,675	49.33	19	4,056	209.07		0	
Kentucky		0		71,764	11,160,245	162.42	5	1,508	295.69
Louisiana	0	0			0		151	0	
Maine		0		5	18,088	36,176.00	12	37,630	3,084.43
Maryland	4	0		1,009	233,380	489.90	149	7,992	583.36
Massachusetts		0			0			0	
Michigan	52	3,444	186.16	5	0		296	285,145	1,092.30
Minnesota	35,622	2,794,778	96.20	837	35,841	84.43	7,469	378,670	117.66
Mississippi	157	20,462	130.17	24	3,564	2,741.54	24	2,466	104.49
Missouri	12	2,416	525.22	1,327	459,543	451.10	2,009	1,203,996	780.65
Montana	184	1,819	33.14	98	5,876	62.38		0	
Nebraska	2,493	146,892	69.28	1,399	348,643	281.52	238	34,166	193.14
Nevada	*	*	*	*	*	*	*	*	*
New Hampshire		0			0			0	
New Jersey		0			0			0	
New Mexico		0			0			0	
New York		0		2,572	1,910,552	838.63	1,124	777,606	772.81
North Carolina	0	0		55	72,972	1,600.26		0	
North Dakota	52,125	2,286,669	71.40	35	0			0	
Ohio	179	17,383	99.27	2,864	352,848	155.76	131	206,106	2,605.97
Oklahoma	21	465	62.84	6	4,324	697.42	9	850	100.00
Oregon		0		13,565	2,892,996	358.58	659	905,601	1,373.18
Pennsylvania		0		1,229	513,191	573.53	467	123,820	395.21
Puerto Rico		0		545	12,180	60.00		0	
South Carolina		0		47	128,607	2,730.51	77	156,170	2,030.82
South Dakota	58,228	2,990,413	63.04	5,104	348,429	103.01	24,184	539,660	48.61
Tennessee		0		36	16,884	1,110.77		0	
Texas		0		2,303	400,071	183.81	2	2,973	1,351.36
Utah		0		35	6,563	321.72		0	
Vermont		0			0		3	9,394	2,846.67
Virginia		0		691	961,333	1,507.19	20	0	
Washington	8	0		956	285,230	729.12	190	227,527	1,224.12
West Virginia		0			0			0	
Wisconsin	41	2,077	112.27	1,175	274,428	271.66	28	16,619	595.66
Wyoming		0		1,435	308,037	400.72		0	
United States	206,844	12,847,851	80.47	120,375	24,019,529	234.15	43,521	5,373,965	257.54

[1] Not including acres which receive no cost share.
Total acres treated may not add due to rounding.
FSA, Conservation and Environmental Programs Division, (530) 792-5594.

Table 12-11.—Conservation Reserve Program (CRP): Enrollment by practice, under contract, August 2015

(CP31, CP32, and CP33)

State	CP31 Bottomland hardwood			CP32 Hardwood trees			CP33 Upland bird habitat buffers		
	Total acres treated	Total cost share	Avg cost share per acre treated [1]	Total acres treated	Total cost share	Avg cost share per acre treated [1]	Total acres treated	Total cost share	Avg cost share per acre treated [1]
Alabama	1,208	89,829	117.25		0		1,179	73,231	101.78
Alaska		0			0			0	
Arkansas	15,442	1,131,161	120.75	980	6,000	594.06	5,511	500,367	132.72
California		0		160	0			0	
Colorado		0			0		344	16,357	94.57
Delaware		0			0			0	
Florida		0			0			0	
Georgia	25	2,000	103.63		0		2,221	92,280	81.25
Hawaii		0			0			0	
Idaho		0			0			0	
Illinois	4,481	870,881	212.35	636	0		66,065	7,192,256	122.51
Indiana	5,764	1,179,388	253.53	518	7,527	46.26	14,145	1,908,283	148.62
Iowa	3,208	925,669	342.39	1,546	53,465	283.48	26,546	4,056,452	178.56
Kansas	215	37,640	235.84		0		40,407	1,437,284	44.20
Kentucky	276	98,849	372.31	234	9	0.50	7,727	1,068,489	150.17
Louisiana	48,604	3,240,857	106.28	913	0		382	23,012	100.49
Maine		0			0			0	
Maryland		0			0		741	108,107	153.76
Massachusetts		0			0			0	
Michigan	11	7,300	675.93	6	610	100.00	859	117,470	191.22
Minnesota	596	16,340	246.83	1,684	12,859	82.32	503	44,279	93.59
Mississippi	45,162	1,224,550	94.56	775	0		2,113	154,959	99.12
Missouri	1,471	118,421	167.64	541	0		34,687	2,723,105	99.12
Montana		0			0			0	
Nebraska	9	4,778	542.95		0		6,199	428,298	79.21
Nevada	*	*	*	*	*	*	*	*	*
New Hampshire		0			0			0	
New Jersey		0			0			0	
New Mexico		0			0			0	
New York	2	2,000	869.57		0			0	
North Carolina	42	1,978	139.30		0		8,612	528,206	87.47
North Dakota		0			0			0	
Ohio	106	23,856	343.25	39	473	105.11	15,755	1,534,741	109.84
Oklahoma	443	63,174	152.04	80	0		1,063	45,067	58.26
Oregon		0			0			0	
Pennsylvania		0			0		26	3,900	150.00
Puerto Rico		0			0			0	
South Carolina	8	379	48.01		0		5,441	307,952	66.18
South Dakota		0		17	0		1,473	91,050	67.98
Tennessee	3,002	248,409	118.30	1	0		5,277	402,888	86.05
Texas	381	53,558	140.54		0		7,557	652,982	130.86
Utah		0			0			0	
Vermont		0			0			0	
Virginia		0			0		1,638	127,362	97.39
Washington		0			0		399	25,782	109.34
West Virginia		0			0			0	
Wisconsin		0		945	71	16.14	290	53,386	184.28
Wyoming		0			0			0	
United States	130,456	9,341,018	134.87	9,075	81,014	147.14	257,160	23,717,545	110.59

[1] Not including acres which receive no cost share.
Total acres treated may not add due to rounding.
FSA, Conservation and Environmental Programs Division, (530) 792-5594.

Table 12-12.—Conservation Reserve Program (CRP): Enrollment by practice, under contract, August 2015

(CP34, CP36, and CP37)

State	CP34 Flood control structure			CP36 Longleaf pine			CP37 Duck nesting habitat		
	Total acres treated	Total cost share	Avg cost share per acre treated[1]	Total acres treated	Total cost share	Avg cost share per acre treated[1]	Total acres treated	Total cost share	Avg cost share per acre treated[1]
Alabama		0		13,550	2,460,974	206.72		0	
Alaska		0			0			0	
Arkansas		0			0			0	
California		0			0			0	
Colorado		0			0			0	
Delaware		0			0			0	
Florida		0		1,847	453,663	250.60		0	
Georgia		0		104,928	19,468,997	294.01		0	
Hawaii		0			0			0	
Idaho		0			0			0	
Illinois		0		2	247	117.76		0	
Indiana		0			0			0	
Iowa		0			0		2,476	219,005	129.31
Kansas		0			0			0	
Kentucky		0			0			0	
Louisiana		0		59	7,030	119.97		0	
Maine		0			0			0	
Maryland		0			0			0	
Massachusetts		0			0			0	
Michigan		0			0			0	
Minnesota	69	5,623	112.91		0		12,740	1,073,534	93.95
Mississippi		0		418	32,207	97.27		0	
Missouri		0			0			0	
Montana		0			0		1,978	23,211	18.39
Nebraska		0			0			0	
Nevada	*	*	*	*	*	*	*	*	*
New Hampshire		0			0			0	
New Jersey		0			0			0	
New Mexico		0			0			0	
New York		0			0			0	
North Carolina		0		6,715	1,072,047	220.96		0	
North Dakota		0			0		137,523	3,927,184	47.82
Ohio		0			0			0	
Oklahoma		0			0			0	
Oregon		0			0			0	
Pennsylvania		0			0			0	
Puerto Rico		0			0			0	
South Carolina		0		11,208	1,295,700	140.73		0	
South Dakota		0			0		145,698	4,847,260	41.201
Tennessee		0			0			0	
Texas		0			0			0	
Utah		0			0			0	
Vermont		0			0			0	
Virginia		0		527	62,573	127.31		0	
Washington		0			0			0	
West Virginia		0			0			0	
Wisconsin		0			0			0	
Wyoming		0			0			0	
United States	69	5,623	112.91	139,254	24,853,439	261.95	300,415	10,090,194	47.12

[1] Not including acres which receive no cost share.
Total acres treated may not add due to rounding.
FSA, Conservation and Environmental Programs Division, (530) 792-5594.

Table 12-13.—Conservation Reserve Program (CRP): Enrollment by practice, under contract, August 2015

(CP38 and CP39)

State	CP38 State acres for wildlife enhancement			CP39 Constructed wetlands		
	Total acres treated	Total cost share	Avg cost share per acre treated[1]	Total acres treated	Total cost share	Avg cost share per acre treated[1]
Alabama	2,114	126,966	116.01	0	0	
Alaska	0	0		0	0	
Arkansas	15,404	791,285	171.06	0	0	
California	0	0		0	0	
Colorado	29,267	1,631,956	72.29	0	0	
Delaware	0	0		0	0	
Florida	0	0		0	0	
Georgia	10,449	748,469	108.59	0	0	
Hawaii	0	0		0	0	
Idaho	108,395	7,840,264	76.90	0	0	
Illinois	20,540	3,432,062	228.00	17	0	
Indiana	27,988	3,470,261	144.68	0	0	
Iowa	80,626	10,885,131	154.82	251	60,210	284.55
Kansas	82,585	2,344,175	42.82	4	1,150	261.36
Kentucky	10,765	956,730	208.41	0	0	
Louisiana	215	21,000	150.00	0	0	
Maine	2,135	384,722	419.21	0	0	
Maryland	0	0		0	0	
Massachusetts	0	0		0	0	
Michigan	6,314	1,465,682	357.40	0	0	
Minnesota	50,484	4,477,436	107.15	71	18,278	258.53
Mississippi	8,418	1,696,133	384.88	0	0	
Missouri	30,423	4,193,165	225.43	0	0	
Montana	34,667	3,188,025	191.32	0	0	
Nebraska	57,532	4,114,563	86.25	0	0	
Nevada	*	*	*	*	*	*
New Hampshire	0	0		0	0	
New Jersey	705	138,645	235.24	0	0	
New Mexico	2,749	0		0	0	
New York	1,252	129,204	220.45	0	0	
North Carolina	880	109,686	219.50	0	0	
North Dakota	116,448	2,569,478	44.94	0	0	
Ohio	17,664	1,448,431	132.52	38	54,829	2,383.89
Oklahoma	7,038	2,749,021	498.80	0	0	
Oregon	1,046	49,637	55.35	0	0	
Pennsylvania	0	0		0	0	
Puerto Rico	0	0		0	0	
South Carolina	1,105	189,901	214.32	0	0	
South Dakota	101,763	2,665,017	41.89	0	0	
Tennessee	6,047	766,608	138.63	0	0	
Texas	88,057	7,358,065	93.49	0	0	
Utah	0	0		0	0	
Vermont	0	0		0	0	
Virginia	308	37,305	121.05	0	0	
Washington	73,032	9,549,456	137.32	0	0	
West Virginia	0	0		0	0	
Wisconsin	10,219	1,465,836	178.16	0	0	
Wyoming	9,688	852,240	87.97.	0	0	
United States	1,016,323	81,846,552	108.72	381	134,467	434.19

[1] Not including acres which receive no cost share.
Total acres treated may not add due to rounding.
FSA, Conservation and Environmental Programs Division, (530) 792-5594.

Table 12-14.—Conservation Reserve Program (CRP): Enrollment by practice, under contract, August 2015

(CP40, CP41, and CP42)

State	CP40 Aquaculture wetlands			CP41 Flooded prairie wetlands			CP42 Pollinator Habitat [2]		
	Total acres treated	Total cost share	Avg cost share per acre treated [1]	Total acres treated	Total cost share	Avg cost share per acre treated [1]	Total acres treated	Total cost share	Avg cost share per acre treated [1]
Alabama	37	504	36.52	0	0	....	21	3,800	200.00
Alaska	0	0	....	0	0	....	0	0	....
Arkansas	2,191	573,522	314.28	0	0	....	32	6,553	412.15
California	0	0	....	0	0	....	1,821	0	....
Colorado	446	29,853	67.01	0	0	....	13,289	1,073,401	104.59
Delaware	0	0	....	0	0	....	4	2,800	700.00
Florida	0	0	....	0	0	....	0	0	....
Georgia	0	0	....	0	0	....	0	0	....
Hawaii	0	0	....	0	0	....	0	0	....
Idaho	0	0	....	0	0	....	7,828	767,212	103.54
Illinois	0	0	....	0	0	....	12,887	5,688,018	453.60
Indiana	0	0	....	0	0	....	1,910	244,482	137.52
Iowa	0	0	....	125	23,200	185.30	15,304	7,804,973	517.15
Kansas	0	0	....	0	0	....	1,763	90,400	78.57
Kentucky	0	0	....	0	0	....	302	57,898	201.30
Louisiana	3,324	609,562	183.36	0	0	....	17	1,413	83.60
Maine	0	0	....	0	0	....	0	0	....
Maryland	0	0	....	0	0	....	19	0	....
Massachusetts	0	0	....	0	0	....	0	0	....
Michigan	0	0	....	0	0	....	280	45,858	175.95
Minnesota	0	0	....	700	37,490	63.95	879	149,019	200.76
Mississippi	10,816	1,645,072	180.91	0	0	....	0	0	....
Missouri	206	0	....	0	0	....	3,829	448,401	152.03
Montana	0	0	....	0	0	....	4,900	188,718	48.91
Nebraska	88	0	....	0	0	....	5,734	392,920	85.11
Nevada	*	*	*	*	*	*	*	*	*
New Hampshire	0	0	....	0	0	....	0	0	....
New Jersey	0	0	....	0	0	....	1	244	407.00
New Mexico	0	0	....	0	0	....	742	84,804	120.00
New York	0	0	....	0	0	....	23	9,825	514.37
North Carolina	58	692	197.71	0	0	....	4	3,510	900.00
North Dakota	0	0	....	32,803	929,661	40.40	1,791	286,724	174.27
Ohio	0	0	....	0	0	....	1,323	72,080	106.71
Oklahoma	0	0	....	0	0	....	142	7,088	105.33
Oregon	0	0	....	0	0	....	352	13,728	85.85
Pennsylvania	0	0	....	0	0	....	0	0	....
Puerto Rico	0	0	....	0	0	....	0	0	....
South Carolina	0	0	....	0	0	....	0	0	....
South Dakota	0	0	....	10,121	413,700	44.22	1,131	164,800	160.91
Tennessee	0	0	....	0	0	....	417	35,062	178.77
Texas	0	0	....	0	0	....	12,131	975,905	126.98
Utah	0	0	....	0	0	....	766	64,790	84.58
Vermont	0	0	....	0	0	....	0	0	....
Virginia	0	0	....	0	0	....	61	3,576	236.82
Washington	0	0	....	0	0	....	3,005	325,008	123.73
West Virginia	0	0	....	0	0	....	0	0	....
Wisconsin	0	0	....	0	0	....	215	49,375	304.92
Wyoming	0	0	....	0	0	....	15	2,310	150.00
United States	17,166	2,859,205	194.43	43,750	1,404,051	42.45	92,953	19,067,488	248.31

* Data withheld to avoid disclosure of individual operations.   [1] Not including acres which receive no cost share.   [2] Does not include about 40,000 acres from Signup 39 before CP42 was implemented.
Total acres treated may not add due to rounding.
FSA, Conservation and Environmental Programs Division, (530) 792-5594.

Table 12-15.—Emergency Conservation Program: Assistance, fiscal years 2005–2014 [1]

Year	Emergency Conservation Program
2005	56,376
2006	58,973
2007	30,754
2008	27,845
2009	73,028
2010	76,735
2011	32,262
2012	56,114
2013	41,206
2014	22,548

[1] Totals are from unrounded data.
FSA, Conservation and Environmental Protection Division, (202) 720-0048.

Table 12-16.—Conservation Reserve Program (CRP): Enrollment by State, August 2015

State [1]	Number of contracts	Number of farms	Acres	Annual rent ($1,000)	Avg Payments [2] ($/acre)
Alabama	6,723	4,855	278,058	12,762	45.90
Alaska	37	28	17,518	619	35.32
Arkansas	5,744	3,212	234,443	16,310	69.57
California	298	226	81,722	3,661	44.80
Colorado	10,807	5,579	1,894,647	66,041	34.86
Connecticut	6	5	52	4	69.51
Delaware	570	305	6,166	729	118.17
Florida	899	736	36,299	1,686	46.46
Georgia	7,950	5,412	260,424	14,540	55.83
Hawaii	19	15	1,000	50	49.64
Idaho	4,299	2,451	589,817	30,624	51.92
Illinois	77,953	43,036	894,671	135,752	151.73
Indiana	35,327	19,775	231,719	32,593	140.66
Iowa	100,779	51,030	1,484,096	243,576	164.12
Kansas	40,428	23,304	2,192,408	92,340	42.12
Kentucky	14,349	7,622	262,607	35,902	136.72
Louisiana	4,787	3,086	295,392	23,390	79.18
Maine	342	243	8,315	385	46.31
Maryland	5,931	3,286	67,588	10,948	161.98
Massachusetts	3	3	10	2	207.20
Michigan	12,727	7,145	166,681	17,888	107.32
Minnesota	55,576	29,669	1,151,977	102,505	88.98
Mississippi	17,821	11,191	744,311	44,861	60.27
Missouri	31,207	18,201	1,014,671	102,486	101.00
Montana	8,696	3,823	1,504,134	44,810	29.79
Nebraska	22,694	13,167	794,829	56,375	70.93
Nevada	*	*	*	*	*
New Hampshire	3	3	13	1	69.04
New Jersey	314	208	2,026	173	85.20
New Mexico	2,000	1,282	432,391	16,141	37.33
New York	2,526	1,824	42,896	3,332	77.68
North Carolina	6,578	4,309	89,498	6,524	72.89
North Dakota	24,246	12,526	1,525,887	67,790	44.43
Ohio	36,172	20,163	267,555	37,994	142.01
Oklahoma	6,424	4,324	738,215	25,374	34.37
Oregon	4,365	2,327	541,450	32,489	60.00
Pennsylvania	9,926	6,566	164,432	18,760	114.09
Puerto Rico	18	18	1,387	104	74.91
Rhode Island	*	*	*	*	*
South Carolina	4,856	2,699	95,714	3,844	40.16
South Dakota	29,679	13,769	922,585	72,001	78.04
Tennessee	5,837	3,861	142,790	12,142	85.04
Texas	19,768	14,449	3,041,690	111,817	36.76
Utah	869	535	171,887	5,851	34.04
Vermont	413	300	2,876	297	103.25
Virginia	5,437	4,149	54,694	3,442	62.94
Washington	11,640	5,174	1,309,759	76,152	58.14
West Virginia	514	421	6,534	513	78.59
Wisconsin	17,015	10,692	244,083	25,281	103.58
Wyoming	810	537	192,839	5,129	26.60
United States	655,384	367,543	24,204,930	1,615,993	66.77

*Data withheld to avoid disclosure of individual operations.   [1] State in which land is located.   [2] Payments scheduled to be made October 2015.
FSA, Conservation and Environmental Programs Division, (530) 792-5594.

Table 12-17.—Forest land: Total forest land and area and ownership of timberland, by regions, Jan. 1, 2007 [1]

Region	Total forest land [2]	Timberland [3]							
		All own-erships	Federal			State, county, and mu-nicipal	Private		
			Total	National forest	Other		Total	Forest industry	Farmer and other private [4]
	1,000 acres	1,000 acres	1,000 acres	1,000 acres	1,000 acres	1,000 acres	1,000 acres	1,000 acres	1,000 acres
Northeast	84,796	79,803	2,971	2,401	570	9,308	67,523	20,860	46,663
North Central	87,243	84,215	8,926	7,725	1,201	15,944	59,345	7,297	52,048
North	172,039	164,018	11,897	10,126	1,771	25,252	126,868	28,157	98,711
Southeast	87,889	85,665	7,559	4,969	2,589	4,689	73,417	24,711	48,706
South Central	126,756	118,365	9,605	7,255	2,350	3,191	105,569	32,291	73,278
South	214,645	204,030	17,164	12,225	4,939	7,880	178,986	57,002	121,984
Great Plains	5,757	5,287	1,294	1,056	238	198	3,795	79	3,716
Intermountain	144,905	65,681	47,318	44,330	2,988	2,987	15,375	3,870	11,505
Rocky Mountains	150,662	70,968	48,612	45,386	3,226	3,185	19,170	3,949	15,221
Alaska	126,869	11,865	4,750	3,772	978	4,344	2,771	2,022	749
Pacific Northwest	52,449	43,489	20,403	17,937	2,466	3,704	19,383	10,681	8,702
Pacific Southwest [5] ..	34,565	19,843	9,907	9,275	632	629	9,308	4,320	4,988
Pacific Coast	213,883	75,197	35,060	30,984	4,076	8,677	31,462	17,023	14,439
All regions	751,229	514,213	112,733	98,721	14,012	44,994	356,486	106,131	250,355

[1] Forest Resources of the United States, 2007. Data may not add to totals because of rounding.   [2] Forest land is land at least 10 percent stocked by forest trees of any size, including land that formerly had such tree cover and that will be naturally or artificially regenerated. Forest land includes transition zones, such as areas between heavily forested and nonforested lands that are at least 10 percent stocked with forest trees, and forest areas. The minimum area for classification of forest land is 1 acre. Roadside, streamside, and shelterbelt strips of timber must have a crown width at least 120 feet wide to qualify as forest land. Unimproved roads and trails, streams, and clearings in forest areas are classified as forest if less than 120 feet in width.   [3] Timberland is forest land that is producing or is capable of producing crops of industrial wood and that is not withdrawn from timber utilization by statute or administrative regulation. Areas qualifying as timberland have the capability of producing more than 20 cubic feet per acre per year of industrial wood in natural stands. Currently inaccessible and inoperable areas are included.   [4] Includes Indian lands.   [5] Includes Hawaii.
FS, Economics & Statistics Research, RWU-4851, (608) 231–9376.

Table 12-18.—Timber volume: Net volume of growing stock and sawtimber on timberland, by softwoods and hardwoods, and regions, 2007 [1]

Region	Growing stock [2]			Sawtimber [3]		
	All species	Softwoods	Hardwoods	All species	Softwoods	Hardwoods
	Million cubic feet	*Million cubic feet*	*Million cubic feet*	*Million board feet*	*Million board feet*	*Million board feet*
Northeast	137,585	34,252	103,333	145,976	36,805	109,171
North Central	110,422	21,614	88,808	122,328	22,896	99,432
North	248,007	55,866	192,141	268,304	59,701	208,603
Southeast	126,747	56,722	70,025	142,582	58,462	84,120
South Central	161,775	61,749	100,026	182,486	64,226	118,260
South	288,522	118,471	170,051	325,068	122,688	202,380
Great Plains	4,539	1,641	2,898	6,591	1,812	4,779
Intermountain	137,724	123,168	9,556	152,549	141,869	10,680
Rocky Mountains	137,263	124,809	12,454	159,140	143,681	15,459
Alaska	31,998	29,125	2,873	34,267	31,191	3,076
Pacific Northwest	158,896	146,006	12,890	159,047	146,048	12,999
Pacific Southwest [4]	67,410	54,926	12,484	67,580	54,983	12,597
Pacific Coast	258,304	230,057	28,247	260,894	232,222	28,672
All regions	932,096	529,203	402,893	1,013,406	558,292	455,114

[1] Forest Resources of the United States, 2007. Data may not add to totals because of rounding.   [2] Live trees of commercial species meeting specified standards of quality or vigor. Cull trees are excluded. Includes only trees 5.0-inches diameter or larger at 4½ feet above ground.   [3] Live trees of commercial species containing at least one 12-foot sawlog or two non-contiguous 8-foot logs, and meeting regional specifications for freedom from defect. Softwood trees must be at least 9.0-inches diameter and hardwood trees must be at least 11.0-inches diameter at 4½ feet above ground.   [4] Includes Hawaii.
FS, Economics & Statistics Research, RWU-4851, (608) 231–9376.

Table 12-19.—Timber removals: Roundwood product output, logging residues and other removals from growing stock and other sources, by softwoods and hardwoods, 2006 [1]

Roundwood products, logging residues, and other removals	All sources			Growing stock[2]			Other sources[3]		
	All species	Soft-woods	Hard-woods	All species	Soft-woods	Hard-woods	All species	Soft-woods	Hard-woods
	Million cubic feet	Million cubic feet	Million cubic feet	Million cubic feet	Million cubic feet	Million cubic feet	Million cubic feet	Million cubic feet	Million cubic feet
Roundwood products:									
Sawlogs	7,179	5,289	1,890	6,781	5,030	1,752	398	260	138
Pulpwood	4,394	2,634	1,760	3,872	2,345	1,527	522	289	233
Veneer logs	1,211	1,068	143	1,156	1,020	136	55	48	7
Other products[4]	255	215	40	217	183	35	37	32	5
Fuelwood[5]	1,408	477	931	490	86	404	918	391	526
Total	14,447	9,684	4,763	12,517	8,663	3,854	1,930	1,021	909
Logging residues[6]	4,543	2,253	2,290	1,253	552	701	3,290	1,700	1,589
Other removals[7]	1,658	489	1,170	1,278	409	869	380	80	301
Total	6,201	2,741	3,460	2,531	962	1,569	3,670	1,780	1,890

[1] Forest Resources of the United States, 2007. Data may not add to totals because of rounding.   [2] Includes live trees of commercial species meeting specified standards of quality or vigor. Cull trees are excluded. Includes only trees 5.0-inches diameter or larger at 4½ feet above ground.   [3] Includes salvable dead trees, rough and rotten trees, trees of noncommercial species, trees less than 5.0-inches diameter at 4½ feet above ground, tops, and roundwood harvested from nonforest land (for example, fence rows).   [4] Includes such items as cooperage, pilings, poles, posts, shakes, shingles, board mills, charcoal and export logs.   [5] Downed and dead wood volume left on the ground after trees have been cut on timberland.   [6] Net of wet rot or limbs.   [7] Unutilized wood volume from cut or otherwise killed growing stock, from non-growing stock sources on timberland (for example, precommercial thinnings), or from timberland clearing. Does not include volume removed from inventory through reclassification of timberland to reserved timberland.
FS, Economics & Statistics Research, RWU-4851, (608) 231–9376.

Table 12-20.—Timber growth, removals and mortality: Net annual growth, removals, and mortality of growing stock on timberland by softwoods and hardwoods and regions, 2006 [1]

Region	Growth[2]			Removals[3]			Mortality[4]		
	All species	Soft-woods	Hard-woods	All species	Soft-woods	Hard-woods	All species	Soft-woods	Hard-woods
	Million cubic feet	Million cubic feet	Million cubic feet	Million cubic feet	Million cubic feet	Million cubic feet	Million cubic feet	Million cubic feet	Million cubic feet
Northeast	3,249	836	2,412	1,169	353	815	935	300	636
North Central	3,327	652	2,675	1,651	324	1,328	1,098	247	851
North	6,576	1,489	5,087	2,820	677	2,034	1,683	547	1,487
Southeast	6,115	3,876	2,239	4,306	2,961	1,345	1,192	611	581
South Central	7,157	3,756	3,401	5,391	3,357	2,034	1,668	754	913
South	13,272	7,632	5,640	9,696	6,317	3,379	2,860	1,366	1,494
Great Plains	72	27	45	41	25	16	54	11	43
Intermountain	1,689	1,550	139	502	496	6	1,310	1,227	83
Rocky Mountains	1,761	1,577	184	543	521	22	1,364	1,238	126
Alaska	248	130	118	66	59	7	256	236	20
Pacific Northwest	3,340	3,039	301	1,939	1,818	121	950	836	114
Pacific Southwest[5]	1,548	1,374	174	469	466	3	363	288	75
Pacific Coast	5,135	4,543	593	2,474	2,344	131	1,569	1,360	209
All regions	26,744	15,241	11,503	15,533	9,859	5,675	7,826	4,511	3,316

[1] Forest Resources of the United States, 2007. Data may not add to totals because of rounding.   [2] The net increase in the volume of trees during a specified year. Components include the increment in net volume of trees at the beginning of the specific year surviving to its end, plus the net volume of trees reaching the minimum size class during the year, minus the volume of trees that died during the year, and minus the net volume of trees that became cull trees during the year.   [3] The net volume of trees removed from the inventory during a specified year by harvesting, cultural operations such as timber stand improvement, or land clearing.   [4] The volume of sound wood in trees that died from natural causes during a specified year.   [5] Includes Hawaii.
FS, Economics & Statistics Research, RWU-4851, (608) 231–9376.

Table 12-21.—Timber volume: Net volume of sawtimber on timberland in the West, by regions and species, Jan. 1, 2007 [1]

Species	Total West	Inter-mountain	Alaska	Pacific Northwest	Pacific South-west [2]	Great Plains
	Million board feet	Million board feet	Million board feet	Million board feet	Million board feet	Million board feet
Softwoods:						
Douglas-fir	124,628	30,504	....	75,516	18,608	....
Ponderosa and Jeffrey pines	41,589	17,383	....	12,420	10,379	1,407
True fir	53,046	23,024	6	17,213	12,803	....
Western hemlock	33,940	941	11,224	21,697	78	....
Sugar pine	3,394	....	....	677	2,717	....
Western white pine	1,162	443	....	436	283	....
Redwood	4,711	....	....	1	4,710	....
Sitka spruce	10,233	....	8,641	1,486	106	....
Engelmann and other spruces	25,128	18,934	4,287	1,889	18	....
Western larch	6,099	3,961	3	2,135	....	....
Incense cedar	4,031	....	....	695	3,336	....
Lodgepole pine	26,537	21,855	81	3,678	923	....
Western redcedar	....	....	....	....	....	....
Other	20,369	6,123	4,884	8,164	964	234
Total	354,867	123,168	29,126	146,007	54,925	1,641
Hardwoods:						
Cottonwood and aspen	12,163	9,198	843	969	124	1,029
Red alder	6,791	68	73	6,317	333	....
Oak	7,427	18	....	777	6,068	564
Other	14,317	272	1,957	4,826	5,957	1,305
Total	40,698	9,556	2,873	12,889	12,482	2,898
All species	395,565	132,724	31,999	158,896	67,407	4,539

[1] Forest Resources of the United States, 2007. International ¼-inch rule. Data may not add to totals because of rounding.   [2] Includes Hawaii.
FS, Economics & Statistics Research, RWU-4851, (608) 231–9376.

Table 12-22.—Timber volume: Net volume of sawtimber on timberland in the East, by regions and species, Jan. 1, 2007 [1]

Species	Total East	North			South		
		Total	Northeast	North Central	Total	Southeast	South Central
	Million board feet	Million board feet	Million board feet	Million board feet	Million board feet	Million board feet	Million board feet
Softwoods:							
Longleaf and slash pines	16,830	....	....	....	16,830	12,212	4,618
Loblolly and shortleaf pines	84,313	1,584	658	926	82,729	32,873	49,856
Other yellow pines	8,979	1,984	1,605	379	6,995	4,907	2,088
White and red pines	21,456	18,759	11,093	7,666	2,697	2,180	517
Jack pine	1,172	1,172	3	1,169	....	....	....
Spruce and balsam fir	13,599	13,554	9,413	4,141	45	45	....
Eastern hemlock	10,509	9,558	8,281	1,277	951	502	449
Cypress	6,543	13	6	7	6,530	3,529	3,001
Other	10,928	9,240	3,193	6,047	1,688	474	1,214
Total	174,329	55,864	34,252	21,612	118,465	56,722	61,743
Hardwoods:							
Select white oaks	34,050	15,375	5,395	9,980	18,675	7,056	11,619
Select red oaks	25,241	16,236	9,775	6,461	9,005	3,190	5,815
Other white oaks	21,759	7,075	4,785	2,290	14,684	5,300	9,384
Other red oaks	44,029	13,149	5,141	8,008	30,880	11,338	19,542
Hickory	21,023	8,334	3,499	4,835	12,689	3,591	9,098
Yellow birch	4,231	4,162	3,355	807	69	58	11
Hard maple	24,409	22,100	12,696	9,404	2,309	470	1,839
Soft maple	38,480	30,239	20,418	9,821	8,241	5,149	3,092
Beech	8,350	6,075	4,922	1,153	2,275	770	1,505
Sweetgum	19,361	877	658	219	18,484	7,637	10,847
Tupelo and black gum	11,583	985	697	288	10,598	6,005	4,593
Ash	17,258	12,086	5,881	6,205	5,172	1,545	3,627
Basswood	5,741	5,031	1,846	3,185	710	316	394
Yellow-poplar	27,826	8,218	5,780	2,438	19,608	12,009	7,599
Cottonwood and aspen	15,451	14,744	3,740	11,004	707	99	608
Black walnut	2,563	1,912	358	1,554	651	196	455
Black cherry	8,964	7,881	5,688	2,193	1,083	427	656
Other	31,871	17,660	8,696	8,964	14,211	4,866	9,345
Total	362,190	192,139	103,330	88,809	170,051	70,022	100,029
All species	536,519	248,003	137,582	110,421	288,516	126,744	161,772

[1] Forest Resources of the United States, 2007. International ¼-inch rule. Data may not add to totals because of rounding.
FS, Economics & Statistics Research, RWU-4851, (608) 231–9376.

Table 12-23.—National Forest System: National Forest System lands and other lands in States and Territories, 2012

State or other area	Gross acreage	National Forest System acreage [1]	Other acreage [2]
	1,000 acres	*1,000 acres*	*1,000 acres*
Alabama	1,289	671	617
Alaska	3,553	2,599	954
Arizona	11,891	11,265	627
Arkansas	3,553	2,599	954
California	24,444	20,828	3,616
Colorado	16,035	14,537	1,498
Connecticut	24	24	-
Florida	1,435	1,178	257
Georgia	1,858	868	990
Hawaii	1	1	-
Idaho	21,658	20,465	1,193
Illinois	923	298	625
Indiana	644	203	441
Kansas	116	108	8
Kentucky	2,208	814	1,394
Louisiana	1,025	604	420
Maine	93	54	40
Michigan	4,894	2,876	2,018
Minnesota	5,466	2,841	2,625
Mississippi	3,492	1,174	2,318
Missouri	3,060	1,494	1,567
Montana	19,145	17,116	2,029
Nebraska	560	352	208
Nevada	6,276	5,766	510
New Hampshire	828	736	92
New Mexico	10,457	9,412	1,045
New York	16	16	-
North Carolina	3,165	1,256	1,909
North Dakota	1,111	1,107	4
Ohio	834	241	593
Oklahoma	755	401	354
Oregon	17,580	15,692	1,888
Pennsylvania	743	513	230
South Carolina	1,379	631	748
South Dakota	2,452	2,018	435
Tennessee	1,276	721	555
Texas	1,994	755	1,239
Utah	9,213	8,209	1,004
Vermont	823	401	421
Virginia	3,223	1,664	1,559
Washington	10,115	9,292	823
West Virginia	1,896	1,045	851
Wisconsin	2,023	1,534	489
Wyoming	9,706	9,241	465
Puerto Rico	56	28	28
Virgin Islands	0	0	-
Total	213,292	173,649	39,642

- Represents zero.

[1] *National Forest System acreage.*—A nationally significant system of Federally owned units of forest, range, and related land consisting of national forests, purchase units, national grasslands, land utilization project areas, experimental forest areas, experimental range areas, designated experimental areas, other land areas; water areas, and interests in lands that are administered by USDA Forest Service or designated for administration through the Forest Service.

National forests.—Units formally established and permanently set aside and reserved for national forest purposes.

Purchase units.—Units designated by the Secretary of Agriculture or previously approved by the National Forest Reservation Commission for purposes of Weeks Law Acquisition.

National grasslands.—Units designated by the Secretary of Agriculture and permanently held by the Department of Agriculture under Title III of the Bankhead-Jones Farm Tenant Act.

Land utilization projects.—Units designated by the Secretary of Agriculture for conservation and utilization under Title III of the Bankhead-Jones Farm Tenant Act.

Research and experimental areas.—Units reserved and dedicated by the Secretary of Agriculture for forest or range research and experimentation.

Other areas.—Units administered by the Forest Service that are not included in the above groups.

[2] *Other acreage.*—Lands within the unit boundaries in private, State, county, and municipal ownership and Federal lands over which the Forest Service has no jurisdiction. Areas of such lands which have been offered to the United States and have been approved for acquisition and subsequent Forest Service administration, but to which title had not yet been accepted by the United States.

FS, Economics & Statistics Research, RWU-4851, (608) 231–9376.

Table 12-24.—Forest products cut on National Forest System lands: Volume and value of timber cut and value of all products, United States, fiscal years 2003–2012

Year[1]	Timber cut[2]		Value of miscellaneous forest products[4]	Total value including free-use timber[5]
	Volume	Value[3]		
	Million bd. ft.	1,000 dollars	1,000 dollars	1,000 dollars
2003	1,818	157,323	3,262	160,585
2004	2,032	217,534	3,262	220,796
2005	2,098	224,143	3,262	227,405
2006	2,296	218,520	3,262	221,512
2007	1,960	173,774	3,262	169,992
2008	2,049	131,261	3,262	141,231
2009	1,954	98,088	3,262	78,050
2010	2,137	104,809	3,262	80,265
2011	2,240	131,904	3,262	108,374
2012	2,500	140,428	3,262	117,712

[1] U.S. Timber Production, Trade, Consumption, and Price Statistics. Fiscal years Oct. 1–Sept. 30.   [2] Commercial and cost sales and land exchanges.   [3] Includes collections for forest restoration or improvement under the Knutson-Vandenberg Act, 1930.   [4] Includes materials not measurable in board feet, such as Christmas trees, tanbark, turpentine, seedlings, Spanish moss, etc.   [5] Total value including free-use timber from 1996-2002 has been estimated.
FS, Economics & Statistics Research, RWU-4851, (608) 231–9376.

Table 12-25.—Lumber: Production, United States, 2004–2013

Year	Total	Softwoods	Hardwoods
	Billion bd. ft.	Billion bd. ft.	Billion bd. ft.
2004	50.134	39.075	11.059
2005	50.928	39.770	11.158
2006	49.740	38.726	11.014
2007	45.766	35.158	10.608
2008	35.964	29.177	6.787
2009	30.229	23.240	6.989
2010	30.461	24.802	5.659
2011	33.304	26.754	6.550
2012	34.791	28.256	6.535
2013	37.300	30.000	7.300

FS, Economics & Statistics Research, RWU-4851, (608) 231–9376. From data published by the American Forest and Paper Association.

Table 12-26.—Timber products: Production, imports, exports, and consumption, United States, 2004–2013[1]

Year	Industrial roundwood used for—										Other in-dustrial products, produc-tion and consump-tion[4]
	Lumber				Plywood and veneer				Pulp-wood chip imports	Pulp-wood chip exports	
	Pro-duction	Imports	Exports	Con-sump-tion	Produc-tion	Imports	Exports	Con-sump-tion			
	Million cu. ft.[3]	Million cu. ft.[3]	Million cu. ft.[3]	Million cu. ft.[3]	Million cu. ft.[3]	Million cu. ft.[3]	Million cu. ft.[3]	Million cu. ft.[3]	Million cu. ft.[3]	Million cu. ft.[3]	Million cu. ft.[3]
2004	7,563	3,704	348	10,919	1,082	354	43	1,393	5	168	318
2005	7,680	3,744	362	11,063	1,068	373	37	1,403	9	166	318
2006	7,505	3,415	390	10,530	989	339	35	1,293	4	151	320
2007	6,921	2,743	359	9,305	898	264	40	1,122	3	205	325
2008	5,395	1,894	345	6,945	754	184	45	884	5	257	290
2009	4,576	1,347	288	5,636	616	146	34	728	9	196	250
2010	4,569	1,422	341	5,650	655	161	55	760	9	235	245
2011	5,005	1,403	387	6,022	653	163	52	764	9	235	239
2012	5,219	1,480	374	6,324	679	160	57	782	9	235	222
2013	5,607	1,699	406	6,901	702	171	57	815	9	234	230

Year	Industrial roundwood used for—									
	Pulpwood-based products				Logs		Total			
	Produc-tion	Imports[2]	Exports[2]	Consump-tion	Imports	Exports	Produc-tion	Imports	Exports	Consump-tion
	Million cu. ft.[3]	Million cu. ft.[3]	Million cu. ft.[3]	Million cu. ft.[3]	Million cu. ft.[3]	Million cu. ft.[3]	Million cu. ft.[3]	Million cu. ft.[3]	Million cu. ft.[3]	Million cu. ft.[3]
2004	4,388	1,268	521	5,135	73	366	13,884	5,404	1,445	17,844
2005	4,498	1,272	560	5,211	113	345	14,075	5,511	1,470	18,116
2006	4,528	1,229	564	5,193	94	339	13,832	5,081	1,479	17,434
2007	4,727	1,144	692	5,180	67	350	13,427	4,221	1,647	16,001
2008	4,720	1,029	791	4,959	35	313	11,721	3,148	1,751	13,117
2009	4,423	857	731	4,550	28	322	10,384	2,388	1,571	11,201
2010	4,617	873	802	4,688	32	407	10,727	2,496	1,840	11,384
2011	4,682	861	881	4,661	30	485	11,299	2,466	2,040	11,725
2012	4,824	879	875	4,842	49	432	11,611	2,577	1,960	12,227
2013	4,766	672	1,033	4,406	47	432	11,971	2,597	2,161	12,407

Year	Fuelwood production and consumption	Production, all products	Consumption, all products
	Million cu. ft.[3]	Million cu. ft.[3]	Million cu. ft.[3]
2004	1,540	15,424	19,384
2005	1,550	15,625	19,666
2006	1,555	15,387	18,989
2007	1,605	15,032	17,606
2008	1,510	13,231	14,627
2009	1,400	11,784	12,601
2010	1,380	12,107	12,764
2011	1,366	12,665	13,091
2012	1,440	13,051	13,667
2013	1,520	13,491	13,927

[1] U.S. Timber Production, Trade, Consumption, and Price Statistics. Data may not add to totals because of round-ing.   [2] Includes both pulpwood and the pulpwood equivalent of wood pulp, paper, and board.   [3] Roundwood equiva-lent.   [4] Includes cooperage logs, poles and piling, fence posts, hewn ties, round mine timbers, excelsior bolts, chemical wood, shingle bolts, and miscellaneous items.

FS, Economics and Statistics Research, RWU-4851, (608) 231–9376.

Table 12-27.—Timber products: Producer price indexes, selected products, United States, 2004–2013

[2009=100]

Year	Lumber	Softwood plywood	Woodpulp	Paper	Paperboard
2004	203.6	146.0	88.0	83.2	82.1
2005	198.6	130.0	91.9	88.9	84.7
2006	188.6	110.8	95.9	93.2	92.7
2007	174.7	115.1	107.5	94.3	97.3
2008	163.5	112.3	114.1	102.6	105.2
2009	149.4	100.0	100.0	100.0	100.0
2010	167.3	114.7	123.8	101.4	108.5
2011	166.6	108.1	129.7	106.5	111.2
2012	172.5	127.2	123.8	106.7	110.0
2013	198.7	137.8	120.3	106.2	117.6

FS, Economics & Statistics Research, RWU-4851, (608) 231–9376. Compiled from reports of the U.S. Department of Labor, Bureau of Labor Statistics.

Table 12-28.—Timber prices: Average stumpage prices for sawtimber sold from national forests, by selected species, 2003–2012

Year	Douglas-fir [1]	Southern pine [2]	Ponderosa pine [3]	Western hemlock [4]	All eastern hardwoods [5]	Oak, white, red, and black [5]	Maple, sugar [6]
	Dollars per 1,000 bd. ft.	Dollars per 1,000 bd. ft.	Dollars per 1,000 bd. ft.	Dollars per 1,000 bd. ft.	Dollars per 1,000 bd. ft.	Dollars per 1,000 bd. ft.	Dollars per 1,000 bd. ft.
2003	279.00	163.62	111.18	86.00	284.84	303.71	560.20
2004	114.00	182.99	65.39	63.20	427.22	291.21	618.00
2005	320.50	192.82	103.34	70.10	415.09	329.21	648.00
2006	(NA)	112.46	39.17	101.10	275.31	180.26	533.30
2007	(NA)	176.38	60.90	26.30	276.62	220.35	361.60
2008	(NA)	152.65	33.52	19.70	198.25	156.27	479.60
2009	(NA)	(NA)	(NA)	24.00	171.43	119.53	275.00
2010	(NA)	(NA)	(NA)	65.90	118.80	214.32	432.50
2011	(NA)	(NA)	(NA)	83.30	105.30	370.80	504.30
2012	(NA)	(NA)	(NA)	88.70	94.10	389.20	491.70

(NA) Not available. [1] Western Washington and western Oregon. [2] Southern region. [3] Pacific Southwest region. Includes Jeffrey pine. [4] Pacific Northwest region. [5] Eastern and Southern regions. [6] Eastern region.

Forest Service National Forest prices in this table are for timber sold on a Scribner Decimal C log rule basis, except in the Northeastern States where International ¼-inch log rule is used. Prices include KV payments; exclude timber sold by land exchanges and from land utilization project lands. Data for 1983 are statistical high bid prices; beginning in 1984, data are high bid prices which include specified road costs.

FS, Economics & Statistics Research, RWU-4851, (608) 231–9376. U.S. Timber Production, Trade, Consumption, and Price Statistics.

Table 12-29.—Timber products: Pulpwood consumption, woodpulp production, and paper and board production and consumption, United States, 2004–2013 [1]

Year	Pulpwood consumption [2]	Woodpulp production [3]	Paper and board [4]		
			Production	Consumption or new supply [5]	Per capita consumption
	1,000 cords [6]	*1,000 tons*	*1,000 tons*	*1,000 tons*	*Pounds*
2004	86,903	59,065	91,899	104,193	709
2005	86,284	60,267	91,031	101,864	687
2006	85,883	60,568	91,800	102,439	707
2007	82,696	55,636	91,570	99,825	662
2008	80,341	52,899	87,619	93,640	615
2009	79,992	48,939	78,299	81,767	532
2010	80,307	47,715	82,968	85,331	551
2011	80,040	48,135	82,003	83,342	534
2012	81,422	48,135	81,051	82,456	525
2013	81,422	48,135	80,670	78,795	498

[1] Revised to match data from American Forest and Paper Association and American Pulpwood Association.   [2] Includes changes in stocks.   [3] Excludes defibrated and exploded woodpulp used for hard pressed board.   [4] Excludes hardboard. Includes wet machine board and construction grades.   [5] Production plus imports and minus exports (excludes products); changes in inventories not taken into account.   [6] One cord equals 128 cubic feet.
U.S. Timber Production, Trade, Consumption, and Price Statistics.FS, Economic & Statistics Research, RWU-4851, (608) 231–9376. Compiled from U.S. Department of Commerce and American Forest and Paper Association.

Table 12-30.—Lumber and competing engineered wood products: Production by type of product, 2004–2013

Year	Laminated veneer lumber [1]	Wood glulam [1]	Structural Panels [1]		Lumber [2]	
			Oriented strandboard	Softwood Plywood	Hardwood	Softwood
	Million cubic feet	*Million board feet*	*Million square feet (3/8-in. basis)*	*Million square feet (3/8-in. basis)*	*Billion board feet*	*Billion board feet*
2004	86	402	14,271	14,665	11.1	39.1
2005	91	491	14,985	14,330	11.2	39.8
2006	80	461	14,960	13,428	11.0	38.7
2007	68	358	14,763	12,243	10.6	35.2
2008	47	256	13,003	10,237	6.8	29.2
2009	30	167	9,598	8,608	7.0	23.2
2010	37	176	10,299	9,131	5.7	24.8
2011	38	184	10,039	8,980	6.6	26.8
2012	46	204	11,038	9,181	6.5	28.3
2013	54	230	12,492	9,346	7.3	30.0

[1] APA-The Engineered Wood Association.   [2] US Department of Commerce, Bureau of the Census; American Forest and Paper Association; Luppold and Dempsey. Hardwood Market Report: 2008-present.
FS, Economics & Statistics Research, RWU-4851, (608) 231–9376.

CHAPTER XIII

CONSUMPTION AND FAMILY LIVING

The statistics in this chapter deal with the consumption of food by both rural and urban people, retail price levels, and other aspects of family living of farm people. Data presented here on quantities of food available for consumption are based on material presented in the earlier commodity chapters, but they are shown here at the retail level, a form that is more useful for an analysis of the demand situation faced by the producer. Data on quantities of farm-produced food consumed directly by farm households are presented in the commodity chapters. Its value and the rental value of the farm home are given in the section on farm income.

Table 13-1.—Population: Number of people eating from civilian food supplies, United States, Jan. 1 and July 1, 2005-2014

Year	Jan. 1	July 1
	Millions	Millions
2005	293.2	294.6
2006	296.0	297.4
2007	299.0	300.4
2008	301.9	303.2
2009	304.6	305.8
2010	307.2	308.1
2011	309.4	310.5
2012	311.8	312.9
2013	314.2	315.3
2014	316.5	317.5

Monthly Population Estimates for the United States: April 1, 2010 to December 1, 2015. Source: U.S. Census Bureau, Population Division. Release Dates: Monthly, April 2010 to December 2015.
ERS, Rural Economy Branch (202) 694–5435.

Table 13-2.—Macronutrients: Quantities available for consumption per capita per day, United States, 2001–2010 [1]

Year	Food energy	Carbo-hydrate	Dietary fiber	Protein	Total fat	Saturated fatty acids	Monounsaturated fatty acids	Polyunsat-urated fatty acids	Choles-terol
	Kilo-calories	Grams	Grams	Grams	Grams	Grams	Grams	Grams	Milli-grams
2001	4,100	500	24	122	192	61	84	38	470
2002	4,200	495	24	123	199	63	87	40	480
2003	4,200	492	24	124	202	64	88	40	480
2004	4,200	491	25	125	202	64	88	40	490
2005	4,100	488	25	123	194	61	84	40	470
2006	4,100	485	25	124	196	62	83	41	480
2007	4,100	480	24	123	196	61	82	43	470
2008	4,100	478	24	121	194	60	80	45	470
2009	4,000	471	24	120	185	57	75	42	460
2010	4,000	474	25	120	190	59	77	44	460

[1] Data are based on Economic Research Service estimates of per capita quantities of food available for consumption. Center for Nutrition Policy and Promotion (CNPP), (703) 305–7600.

Table 13-3.—Vitamins: Quantities available for consumption per capita per day, United States, 2001–2010 [1]

Year	Vitamin A	Caro-tenes	Vitamin E	Vitamin C	Thiamin	Ribo-flavin	Niacin	Vitamin B_6	Folate	Folate, Dfe	Vitamin B_{12}
	Micro-grams RAE	Micro-grams RE	Milli-grams ATE	Milli-grams	Milli-grams	Milli-grams	Milli-grams	Milli-grams	Micro-grams	Micro-grams	Micro-grams
2001	960	670	20.6	113	3	3.1	35	2.6	690	900	10
2002	940	630	21.7	112	3	3.1	35	2.6	682	888	10
2003	950	660	21.7	114	3	3.1	35	2.6	690	899	10
2004	960	670	21.7	113	3	3.1	35	2.7	685	893	10.1
2005	910	650	21.4	111	3	3.1	35	2.6	682	889	9.9
2006	930	650	21.4	109	3	3.1	35	2.6	684	892	9.9
2007	940	630	22.1	107	3	3.1	35	2.6	678	886	9.8
2008	930	630	22.4	106	2.9	3	34	2.5	673	881	9.6
2009	920	610	21.3	105	2.9	3	34	2.5	673	881	9.6
2010	920	630	21.9	105	2.9	3	34	2.5	681	889	9.3

[1] Data are based on USDA Economic Research Service estimates of per capita quantities of food available for consumption. Seafood estimates from the National Oceanic and Atmospheric Administration. Game harvest estimates from the individual States or from the Wildlife Management Institute. Imputed data for foods no longer reported or available. Values in the USDA Agricultural Research, National Nutrient Database for Standard Reference, Release 26. Components may not add to 100 because of rounding.
Calculated by USDA/Center for Nutrition Policy and Promotion, (703) 305–7600. Data last updated May 15, 2014.

Table 13-4.—Minerals: Quantities available for consumption per capita per day, United States, 2001–2010 [1]

Year	Calcium	Phosphorus	Magnesium	Iron	Zinc	Copper	Potassium	Sodium	Selenium
	Milligrams	Milligrams	Milligrams	Milli-grams	Milli-grams	Milli-grams	Milligrams	Milli-grams	Micro-grams
2001	1020	1850	410	24.8	18.1	2.1	3,960	1,270	191.8
2002	1020	1840	410	24.7	18.1	2.1	3,930	1,280	192.2
2003	1020	1870	410	24.9	18.2	2.1	3,970	1,340	195.8
2004	1030	1880	420	25	18.3	2.2	3,990	1,340	195.7
2005	1010	1840	410	24.9	18.1	2.2	3,890	1,250	191.2
2006	1020	1850	420	25.1	18.1	2.2	3,890	1,230	192.9
2007	1030	1850	410	24.9	18.2	2.2	3,870	1,240	193.7
2008	1030	1830	410	24.6	17.8	2.1	3,800	1,210	189.4
2009	1040	1820	400	24.4	17.7	2.1	3,770	1,220	188.8
2010	1030	1810	410	24.6	17.6	2.1	3,760	1,210	187.2

[1] Data are based on USDA Economic Research Service estimates of per capita quantities of food available for consumption. Seafood estimates from the National Oceanic and Atmospheric Administration. Game harvest estimates from the individual States or from the Wildlife Management Institute. Imputed data for foods no longer reported or available. Values in the USDA Agricultural Research, National Nutrient Database for Standard Reference, Release 26. Components may not add to 100 because of rounding.
Calculated by USDA/Center for Nutrition Policy and Promotion, (703) 305–7600. Data last updated May 15, 2014.

Table 13-5.—Food nutrients: Percentage of total contributed by major food groups, 2006 [1]

Nutrient	Meat, poultry, fish	Dairy products	Eggs	Legumes, nuts, soy	Grain products	Fruits		
						Citrus	Non-citrus	Total
	Percent	Percent	Percent	Percent	Percent	Percent	Percent	Percent
Kilocalories	16.9	907	1.3	3.0	22.7	0.7	2.1	2.8
Carbohydrate	0.1	6.1	0.1	2.1	40.2	1.5	4.3	5.9
Fiber	0.0	1.2	0.0	14.1	34.5	2.1	9.3	11.4
Protein	45.0	17.9	3.7	5.7	20.0	0.4	0.7	1.1
Total fat	25.8	11.2	1.8	3.6	2.2	0.0	0.4	0.4
Saturated fatty acids	29.6	21.9	1.8	2.1	1.5	0.0	0.2	0.2
Monounsaturated fatty acids	28.0	7.3	1.7	3.8	1.2	0.0	0.5	0.5
Polyunsaturated fatty acids	12.9	1.9	1.2	5.1	3.9	0.0	0.3	0.4
Cholesterol	48.5	15.0	31.8	0.0	0.0	0.0	0.0	0.0
Vitamin A (RAE)	21.2	21.2	5.5	0.0	6.5	0.5	2.0	2.5
Carotene	0.0	2.2	0.0	0.1	0.8	1.1	6.8	7.9
Vitamin E	4.1	2.1	1.8	5.6	4.2	0.6	2.1	2.7
Vitamin C	1.9	1.2	0.0	0.1	5.7	25.8	16.5	42.3
Thiamin	18.9	5.5	0.7	4.6	59.0	1.6	1.4	2.9
Riboflavin	18.6	27.6	5.6	1.7	37.3	0.4	1.5	1.9
Niacin	40.0	1.3	0.1	3.8	42.0	0.4	1.5	1.9
Vitamin B$_6$	41.7	6.4	2.0	3.5	18.8	1.2	5.1	6.3
Folate (DFE)	3.4	2.7	1.9	7.5	70.2	2.8	1.6	4.4
Vitamin B$_{12}$	73.4	21.6	4.7	0.0	0.1	0.0	0.0	0.0
Calcium	3.8	71.4	1.9	4.2	4.8	1.1	1.3	2.4
Phosphorus	28.0	30.8	3.7	5.9	18.4	0.6	1.2	1.8
Magnesium	14.5	13.8	1.1	13.1	23.3	1.6	4.0	5.7
Iron	18.2	1.7	2.7	7.0	50.0	0.4	1.6	2.0
Zinc	43.3	15.5	2.2	4.9	23.9	0.2	0.8	1.1
Copper	21.7	2.9	1.7	18.8	21.1	1.3	3.7	5.0
Potassium	20.6	17.7	1.3	9.0	9.5	3.2	6.7	9.9
Sodium	19.8	37.4	4.2	0.3	1.1	0.1	1.4	1.5
Selenium	31.0	12.4	6.0	7.0	39.2	0.1	0.2	0.3

Nutrient	Vegetables					Fats, oils	Sugars, sweeteners	Miscellaneous
	White potatoes	Dark green, deep yellow	Tomatoes	Other	Total			
	Percent	Percent	Percent	Percent	Percent	Percent	Percent	Percent
Kilocalories	2.0	0.3	0.5	1.1	4.0	22.6	16.1	1.0
Carbohydrate	3.9	0.6	0.9	2.1	7.6	0.0	36.4	1.7
Fiber	7.2	3.8	3.5	9.2	23.7	0.0	0.0	15.2
Protein	1.8	0.5	0.6	1.6	4.5	0.1	0.0	2.0
Total fat	0.1	0.0	0.1	0.2	0.3	53.6	0.0	1.0
Saturated fatty acids	0.1	0.0	0.0	0.1	0.2	41.5	0.0	1.2
Monounsaturated fatty acids	0.0	0.0	0.0	0.1	0.1	56.6	0.0	0.8
Polyunsaturated fatty acids	0.1	0.1	0.1	0.3	0.6	73.2	0.0	0.7
Cholesterol	0.0	0.0	0.0	0.0	0.0	4.6	0.0	0.0
Vitamin A (RAE)	0.0	23.7	1.8	6.0	31.5	9.1	0.0	2.5
Carotene	0.0	67.7	3.9	8.3	79.9	2.0	0.0	7.2
Vitamin E	0.3	1.4	2.7	1.3	5.7	73.2	0.0	0.6
Vitamin C	15.2	14.1	6.1	11.9	47.3	0.0	0.0	1.5
Thiamin	3.7	0.8	0.6	2.4	7.5	0.0	0.1	0.7
Riboflavin	0.8	1.0	0.8	2.2	4.8	0.1	0.7	1.7
Niacin	3.9	0.7	1.4	1.9	8.0	0.0	0.0	3.0
Vitamin B$_6$	9.3	2.7	2.1	4.8	19.0	0.0	0.2	2.1
Folate (DFE)	1.6	1.9	0.9	4.1	8.5	0.0	0.0	1.3
Vitamin B$_{12}$	0.0	0.0	0.0	0.0	0.0	0.2	0.0	0.0
Calcium	0.9	1.4	0.9	3.4	6.6	0.3	0.6	4.1
Phosphorus	2.4	0.8	0.8	2.6	6.7	0.1	0.1	4.3
Magnesium	4.4	1.8	1.8	4.4	12.4	0.1	0.6	15.5
Iron	2.9	0.9	1.5	2.9	8.3	0.1	0.6	9.3
Zinc	1.6	0.6	0.6	1.9	4.7	0.1	0.2	4.1
Copper	3.9	1.3	2.3	3.1	10.7	0.0	1.5	16.8
Potassium	9.7	2.9	4.1	5.8	22.6	0.1	0.4	8.9
Sodium	3.3	1.4	10.8	9.2	24.7	7.4	3.0	0.7
Selenium	0.7	0.1	0.1	0.6	1.6	0.0	1.0	1.6

[1] Data are based on USDA Economic Research Service estimates of per capita quantities of food available for consumption. Seafood estimates from the National Oceanic and Atmospheric Administration. Game harvest estimates from the individual States or from the Wildlife Management Institute. Imputed data for foods no longer reported or available. Values in the USDA Agricultural Research, National Nutrient Database for Standard Reference, Release 26. Components may not add to 100 because of rounding.

Calculated by USDA/Center for Nutrition Policy and Promotion, (703) 305–7600. Data last updated May 15, 2014.

Table 13-6.—Food nutrients: Percentage of total contributed by major food groups, 2010 [1]

Nutrient	Meat, poultry, fish	Dairy products	Eggs	Legumes, nuts, soy	Grain products	Fruits		
						Citrus	Non-citrus	Total
	Percent	*Percent*	*Percent*	*Percent*	*Percent*	*Percent*	*Percent*	*Percent*
Kilocalories	16.1	10.0	1.2	3.4	23.4	0.7	2.1	2.8
Carbohydrate	0.1	6.0	0.1	2.4	41.5	1.4	4.4	5.8
Fiber	0.0	1.1	0.0	16.2	35.1	2.1	9.3	11.3
Protein	43.1	18.9	3.6	6.4	20.7	0.4	0.7	1.1
Total fat	24.8	11.5	1.8	4.1	2.3	0.0	0.5	0.5
Saturated fatty acids	28.9	23.1	1.8	2.4	1.6	0.0	0.3	0.3
Monounsaturated fatty acids	28.0	7.8	1.7	4.6	1.3	0.0	0.7	0.7
Polyunsaturated fatty acids	11.5	1.8	1.1	5.2	3.7	0.0	0.4	0.4
Cholesterol	47.7	15.7	31.9	0.0	0.0	0.0	0.0	0.0
Vitamin A (RAE)	21.0	21.5	5.2	0.0	6.5	0.5	2.0	2.5
Carotene	0.0	2.3	0.0	0.1	0.8	1.1	6.8	7.9
Vitamin E	4.1	2.1	1.8	5.6	4.2	0.6	2.1	2.7
Vitamin C	1.9	1.4	0.0	0.1	6.0	24.2	17.8	42.0
Thiamin	18.1	5.3	0.7	5.1	60.0	1.4	1.4	2.8
Riboflavin	17.7	27.5	5.4	2.1	38.2	0.4	1.6	1.9
Niacin	38.6	1.3	0.1	4.3	43.4	0.4	1.5	1.9
Vitamin B$_6$	40.6	6.4	2.0	4.1	19.8	1.1	5.3	6.4
Folate (DFE)	3.2	2.8	1.8	8.2	70.7	2.5	1.6	4.1
Vitamin B$_{12}$	72.2	22.8	4.8	0.0	0.1	0.0	0.0	0.0
Calcium	3.6	71.8	1.8	4.6	4.8	1.0	1.3	2.3
Phosphorus	26.7	31.6	3.7	6.7	18.9	0.5	1.2	1.8
Magnesium	13.9	13.9	1.0	14.7	24.1	1.5	4.1	5.6
Iron	17.1	1.8	2.6	7.8	51.2	0.3	1.7	2.1
Zinc	41.7	16.2	2.2	5.5	24.7	0.2	0.9	1.1
Copper	21.5	3.0	1.6	20.4	21.5	1.2	3.8	5.0
Potassium	19.8	17.8	1.2	10.1	9.9	2.9	6.9	9.8
Sodium	19.0	37.5	4.0	0.3	1.1	0.1	2.7	2.8
Selenium	30.0	12.5	5.9	7.1	40.4	0.1	0.3	0.3

Nutrient	Vegetables				Fats, oils	Sugars, sweeteners	Miscellaneous
	White potatoes	Dark green, deep yellow	Tomatoes	Other	Total			
	Percent	*Percent*	*Percent*	*Percent*	*Percent*	*Percent*	*Percent*	*Percent*
Kilocalories	1.9	0.4	0.5	1.1	3.8	22.5	15.8	0.9
Carbohydrate	3.6	0.8	1.0	2.0	7.4	0.0	35.3	1.5
Fiber	6.5	4.0	3.8	8.4	22.7	0.0	0.0	13.5
Protein	1.7	0.6	0.6	1.5	4.4	0.1	0.0	1.8
Total fat	0.1	0.1	0.1	0.1	0.3	53.8	0.0	0.9
Saturated fatty acids	0.1	0.0	0.0	0.1	0.2	40.6	0.0	1.1
Monounsaturated fatty acids	0.0	0.0	0.0	0.1	0.1	54.9	0.0	0.8
Polyunsaturated fatty acids	0.1	0.1	0.1	0.3	0.5	75.2	0.0	0.6
Cholesterol	0.0	0.0	0.0	0.0	0.0	4.6	0.0	0.0
Vitamin A (RAE)	0.0	25.9	1.9	5.5	33.3	8.2	0.0	1.7
Carotene	0.0	70.4	4.3	7.8	82.5	1.7	0.0	4.7
Vitamin E	0.3	1.4	2.7	1.3	5.7	72.8	0.0	0.4
Vitamin C	14.4	15.2	6.8	11.1	47.4	0.0	0.0	1.3
Thiamin	3.5	0.9	0.7	2.2	7.2	0.0	0.1	0.6
Riboflavin	0.8	1.2	0.9	2.0	4.9	0.1	0.6	1.5
Niacin	3.6	0.8	1.6	1.8	7.8	0.0	0.0	2.7
Vitamin B$_6$	8.9	3.0	2.4	4.5	18.8	0.0	0.2	1.8
Folate (DFE)	1.4	1.9	1.0	3.7	8.0	0.0	0.0	1.2
Vitamin B$_{12}$	0.0	0.0	0.0	0.0	0.0	0.2	0.0	0.0
Calcium	0.8	1.5	0.9	3.1	6.4	0.3	0.5	3.9
Phosphorus	2.2	1.0	0.9	2.4	6.5	0.1	0.1	3.9
Magnesium	4.1	2.1	1.9	4.1	12.1	0.1	0.6	14.1
Iron	2.7	1.1	1.6	2.7	8.2	0.1	0.6	8.7
Zinc	1.5	0.7	0.6	1.8	4.6	0.1	0.2	3.7
Copper	3.6	1.7	2.6	2.9	10.7	0.0	1.3	14.9
Potassium	9.1	3.5	4.6	5.4	22.5	0.1	0.5	8.3
Sodium	2.9	1.4	12.1	9.0	25.3	6.5	2.8	0.6
Selenium	0.6	0.2	0.2	0.6	1.5	0.0	0.9	1.4

[1] Data are based on USDA Economic Research Service estimates of per capita quantities of food available for consumption. Seafood estimates from the National Oceanic and Atmospheric Administration. Game harvest estimates from the individual States or from the Wildlife Management Institute. Imputed data for foods no longer reported or available. Values in the USDA Agricultural Research, National Nutrient Database for Standard Reference, Release 26. Components may not add to 100 because of rounding.
Calculated by USDA/Center for Nutrition Policy and Promotion, (703) 305–7600. Data last updated May 15, 2014.

Table 13-7.—Consumption: Per capita consumption of major food commodities, United States, 2006–2013 [1]

Commodity	2006	2007	2008	2009	2010	2011	2012	2013
	Pounds	Pounds	Pounds	Pounds	Pounds	Pounds	Pounds	Pounds
Red meats [2][3]	109.9	110.5	106.4	105.7	102.1	97.7	97.9	97.9
Beef	62.8	62.1	59.4	58.1	56.7	54.4	54.5	53.5
Veal	0.4	0.3	0.3	0.3	0.3	0.3	0.3	0.3
Lamb and mutton	0.8	0.8	0.7	0.7	0.7	0.6	0.6	0.7
Pork	46.0	47.2	45.9	46.6	44.4	42.3	42.5	43.4
Fish [2]	16.5	16.3	15.9	15.8	15.8	14.9	14.2	14.3
Canned	3.9	3.9	3.9	3.7	3.9	3.7	3.4	3.6
Fresh and frozen	12.3	12.0	11.7	11.7	11.5	10.9	10.5	10.4
Cured	0.3	0.3	0.3	0.3	0.3	0.3	0.3	0.3
Poultry [2][3]	74.2	73.7	72.6	69.4	70.6	71.0	69.2	70.2
Chicken	60.9	59.9	58.7	56.1	58.0	58.4	56.6	57.6
Turkey	13.3	13.8	13.9	13.3	12.6	12.6	12.6	12.5
Eggs	33.8	33.0	32.5	32.6	32.5	32.0	32.8	33.3
Dairy products [4]								
Total dairy products	611.8	612.1	606.8	607.3	603.1	603.6	613.5	605.3
Fluid milk and cream	204.3	202.3	203.0	202.9	201.8	196.7	194.6	190.4
Plain and flavored whole milk	58.7	56.0	53.2	52.1	49.2	47.5	46.5	46.2
Plain reduced fat and light milk (2%, 1%, and 0.5%)	82.6	83.2	83.9	84.9	86.3	85.7	84.7	82.5
Plain fat free milk (skim)	27.3	27.4	27.3	26.9	27.3	26.5	24.8	22.6
Flavored lower fat free milk	12.7	12.4	12.5	12.8	13.0	12.7	12.5	12.3
Buttermilk	1.7	1.7	1.8	1.5	1.5	1.5	1.5	1.6
Eggnog	0.5	0.5	0.5	0.5	0.5	0.5	0.4	0.4
Yogurt (excl. frozen)	11.1	11.6	11.7	12.5	13.4	13.6	14.0	14.9
Heavy cream, light cream and half and half	8.2	NA	NA	NA	NA	NA	NA	NA
Sour cream and dip	3.8	3.8	3.8	3.9	4.0	4.0	4.1	4.0
Cheese (excluding cottage) [5]	32.2	32.7	32.1	32.3	32.7	33.0	33.3	33.4
American	13.1	12.8	13.1	13.4	13.3	13.0	13.3	13.3
Cheddar	0.0	0.0	0.0	0.0	0.0	0.0	0.0	0.0
Italian	0.0	0.0	0.0	0.0	0.0	0.0	0.0	0.0
Mozzarella	0.0	0.0	0.0	0.0	0.0	0.0	0.0	0.0
Cottage cheese	2.6	2.6	2.3	2.4	2.3	2.3	2.3	2.0
Condensed and evaporated milk	6.5	7.7	7.4	7.3	7.2	7.1	7.3	7.2
Ice cream	14.8	14.2	13.7	13.4	13.5	12.8	12.8	12.7
Fats and oils [6]	84.5	84.7	85.0	77.7	82.2	NA	NA	NA
Butter	4.7	4.7	5.0	5.0	4.9	5.4	5.5	5.5
Margarine	4.6	4.5	4.2	3.7	3.5	NA	NA	NA
Shortening	24.8	20.9	18.0	15.9	15.3	NA	NA	NA
Lard (direct use)	1.7	1.6	1.0	1.5	1.5	NA	NA	NA
Edible tallow (direct use)	3.9	2.9	2.9	0.7	3.3	NA	NA	NA
Salad and cooking oils	44.6	50.2	54.0	51.0	53.6	NA	NA	NA
Fruits and vegetables [3][7]	672.9	668.2	649.5	645.5	648.6	627.3	641.9	645.5
Fruits	269.3	262.1	257.0	253.7	252.2	244.8	249.8	261.1
Fresh	127.9	123.6	126.4	124.0	128.6	129.3	131.6	136.2
Citrus	21.6	17.9	20.6	20.7	21.6	22.8	23.5	23.9
Noncitrus	106.3	105.7	105.8	103.3	107.0	106.6	108.2	112.2
Processing	141.4	138.5	130.6	129.8	123.6	115.5	118.2	124.8
Citrus	71.4	67.2	62.0	63.7	57.0	54.2	61.0	65.2
Noncitrus	70.0	71.4	68.6	66.0	66.6	61.3	57.6	60.1
Vegetables	403.6	406.1	392.6	391.8	396.4	382.6	392.1	384.4
Fresh	194.1	194.3	188.3	185.5	190.4	186.2	189.6	184.9
Processing	209.5	211.8	204.2	206.3	206.0	196.3	202.5	199.6
Flour and cereal products [4]	193.9	196.9	195.9	193.9	194.2	172.5	174.1	174.7
Wheat flour [8]	135.8	138.3	136.6	134.7	134.8	132.5	134.3	135.0
Rice (milled basis) [9]	20.3	20.3	20.5	20.4	20.4	NA	NA	NA
Corn products	31.9	32.4	33.0	33.0	33.1	34.1	33.9	33.9
Oat products	4.7	4.7	4.7	4.7	4.7	4.8	4.7	4.5
Barley and rye products	1.2	1.2	1.2	1.2	1.1	1.1	1.1	1.2
Caloric sweeteners (dry weight basis) [3]	140.8	137.0	137.2	132.3	133.7	131.2	131.1	130.1
Sugar (refined)	62.1	61.1	65.0	63.4	65.9	65.8	66.6	67.9
Corn sweeteners [10]	76.9	74.3	70.5	67.5	66.0	63.6	62.8	60.4
Honey and edible syrups	1.8	1.6	1.6	1.5	1.7	1.7	1.7	1.8
Others								
Coffee (green bean equivalent)	9.5	9.6	9.5	9.1	9.2	9.6	9.7	9.9
Cocoa (chocolate liquor equivalent) [11]	5.1	4.8	4.5	4.4	4.4	4.4	4.2	4.2
Tea (dry leaf equivalent)	0.9	0.9	1.0	1.0	1.0	1.0	0.9	0.9
Peanuts (shelled)	6.6	6.3	6.4	6.6	7.0	7.0	6.7	6.9
Tree nuts (shelled)	3.4	3.6	3.6	3.8	3.9	3.8	4.2	4.0

[1] Quantity in pounds, retail weight unless otherwise shown. [2] Boneless, trimmed weight equivalent. [3] Total may not add due to rounding. [4] Total dairy products reported on a milk-equivalent, milkfat basis. All other dairy categories reported on a product weight basis. [5] Natural equivalent of cheese and cheese products. [6] Total fats and oils reported on a fat content basis. All other fats and oils categories reported on a product weight basis. Due to the termination of select Current Industrial Reports (CIR) by the Census Bureau, data on some added fats and oils could not be updated beyond 2010 in the Food Availability Data System. This means that certain summary estimates-such as per capita daily amounts of calories and food pattern equivalents (or servings)-cannot be calculated beyond 2010 for the added fats & oils group. Additionally, the summary estimates or totals across all food groups cannot be calculated beyond 2010. [7] Farm weight. [8] White, whole wheat, semolina, and durum flour. [9] Annual data and per capita estimates for rice are unavailable beyond 2010 due to a large and unexplained decline in the implied total domestic and residual use estimate. Residual use accounts for all reported losses in the milling, transporting, and marketing of rice, and also offsets any statistical error in another supply and use account. [10] High fructose, glucose, and dextrose. [11] Chocolate liquor is what remains after cocoa beans have been roasted and hulled; it is sometimes called ground or bitter chocolate.

ERS, Food Economics Division, (202) 694-5400. Historical consumption and supply-disappearance data for food may be found at http://www.ers.usda.gov/data-products/food-availability-(per-capita)-data-system.aspx, ERS, USDA, 2016.

Table 13-8.—Food plans: Food cost at home, at four cost levels, for families and individuals in the United States, for week and month, December 2014[1]

Age-gender groups	Weekly cost[2]				Monthy cost[2]			
	Thrifty plan	Low-cost plan	Moderate-cost plan	Liberal plan	Thrifty plan	Low-cost plan	Moderate-cost plan	Liberal plan
	Dollars	*Dollars*	*Dollars*	*Dollars*	*Dollars*	*Dollars*	*Dollars*	*Dollars*
Individuals: [3]								
Child:								
1 year	22.00	29.80	33.60	41.10	95.10	129.10	145.80	177.90
2-3 year	24.00	30.80	37.10	45.40	104.10	133.70	161.00	196.60
4-5 years	25.40	31.90	39.60	48.20	109.90	138.20	171.70	209.00
6-8 years	32.50	45.50	54.10	63.90	140.70	197.20	234.40	276.90
9-11 years	36.60	48.20	62.70	72.90	158.70	209.00	271.90	316.10
Male:								
12-13 years	39.10	55.50	69.70	81.70	169.60	240.30	302.00	354.20
14-18 years	40.10	56.10	71.80	82.80	173.80	243.20	311.10	358.70
19-50 years	43.50	56.30	70.50	86.90	188.30	243.70	305.40	376.70
51-70 years	39.60	53.00	66.10	79.80	171.50	229.50	286.40	345.60
71+ years	39.90	52.70	65.20	80.70	172.80	228.20	282.50	349.60
Female:								
12-13 years	39.10	47.80	57.80	70.80	169.30	206.90	250.30	306.90
14-18 years	38.40	48.00	58.30	71.70	166.50	208.10	252.50	310.60
19-50 years	38.60	48.80	60.40	77.00	167.10	211.60	261.60	333.50
51-70 years	38.10	47.40	59.00	71.40	164.90	205.60	255.80	309.20
71+ years	37.30	47.20	58.60	70.60	161.80	204.50	254.10	306.10
Families:								
Family of 2: [4]								
19-50 years	90.20	115.60	144.00	180.30	391.00	500.90	623.80	781.20
51-70 years	85.40	110.40	137.70	166.20	370.10	478.50	596.50	720.30
Family of 4:								
Couple, 19-50 years and children.								
2-3 and 4-5 years	131.40	167.90	207.60	257.50	569.40	727.30	899.70	1,115.80
6-8 and 9-11 years	151.10	198.90	247.70	300.80	654.90	861.60	1,073.40	1,303.20

[1] The Food Plans represent a nutritious diet at four different cost levels. The nutritional bases of the Food Plans are the 1997-2005 Dietary References Intakes, 2005 Dietary Guidelines for Americans, and 2005 MyPyramid food intake recommendations. In addition to cost, differences among plans are in specific foods and quantities of foods. Another basis of the Food Plans is that all meals and snacks are prepared at home. For specific foods and quantities of foods in the Food Plans, see *Thrifty Food Plan, 2006* and *The Low-Cost, Moderate-Cost, and Liberal Food Plans, 2007.* All four Food Plans are based on 2001-02 data and updated to current dollars by using the Consumer Price Index for specific food items.   [2] All costs are rounded to nearest 10 cents.   [3] The costs given are for individuals in 4–person families. For individuals in other size families, the following adjustments are suggested: 1 person-add 20 percent; 2 person-add 10 percent; 3 person-add 5 percent; 4 person-no adjustment; 5- or 6-person–subtract 5 percent; 7- (or more) person-subtract 10 percent. To calculate overall household food costs, (1) adjust food costs for each person in household and then (2) sum these adjusted food costs.   [4] Ten percent added for family size adjustment.

Center for Nutrition Policy and Promotion, (703) 305–7600. This file and the referenced Food Plans may be accessed on CNPP's home page at http://www.cnpp.usda.gov.

Table 13-9.—SNAP: Participation and federal costs, fiscal years 2005–2014

Fiscal year [1]	Average monthly participation [2]		Recipient benefits	Total cost [3]	Average monthly benefit [4]	
	Persons	Housholds			Per person	Per household
	1,000	1,000	1,000 dollars	1,000 dollars	Dollars	Dollars
2005	25,628	11,196	28,567,876	31,072,112	92.89	212.64
2006	26,549	11,733	30,187,347	32,903,063	94.75	214.41
2007	26,316	11,788	30,373,271	33,174,484	96.18	214.72
2008	28,223	12,727	34,608,397	37,642,040	102.19	226.60
2009	33,490	15,232	50,359,919	53,620,011	125.31	275.51
2010	40,302	18,618	64,702,165	68,283,942	133.79	289.60
2011	44,709	21,072	71,810,924	75,687,179	133.85	283.99
2012	46,609	22,330	74,619,345	78,411,049	133.41	278.48
2013	47,636	23,052	76,066,319	79,929,150	133.07	274.98
2014	46,536	22,700	69,999,805	74,138,720	125.35	256.98

SNAP is the Special Nutrition Assistance Program, formerly known as the Food Stamp Program.   [1] October 1 to September 30.   [2] Participation data are 12-month averages.   [3] Total cost includes matching funds for state administrative expenses (e.g., certification of households, quality control, anti-fraud activities; employment and training); and for other Federal costs (e.g., benefit redemption processing; computer support; electronic benefit transfer systems; retailer redemption and monitoring; certification of SSI recipients; nutrition education and program information).   [4] The sharprise in FY 2009 reflects April 2009 implementation of higher benefits mandated by the American Recovery Reinvestment Act.

FNS, Budget Division/Program Reports, Analysis and Monitoring Branch, (703) 305–2165.

Table 13-10.—Food and Nutrition Service Programs: Federal costs of the National School Lunch, School Breakfast, Child Care Food, Summer Food Service, WIC, Special Milk, and Food Distribution Programs, fiscal years 2005–2014 [1]

Fiscal year [2]	Child Nutrition				Cost of food distribution programs [5]	WIC [6]	Special Milk	Food Distribution Programs [7]
	Cash payments							
	School Lunch	School Breakfast	Child & Adult Care [3]	Summer Food [4]				
	1,000 dollars	1,000 dollars	1,000 dollars	1,000 dollars	1,000 dollars	1,000 dollars	1,000 dollars	1,000 dollars
2005	7,055,303	1,927,154	2,040,478	264,957	1,047,234	4,992,568	16,437	626,462
2006	7,387,935	2,041,914	2,079,250	274,309	876,545	5,072,736	14,581	528,994
2007	7,706,080	2,163,483	2,160,391	288,631	1,112,559	5,409,580	13,619	487,968
2008	8,264,807	2,365,485	2,315,216	324,914	1,141,080	6,188,804	14,859	543,025
2009	8,874,491	2,582,654	2,438,500	345,119	1,216,491	6,471,624	14,112	873,582
2010	9,751,636	2,859,268	2,544,633	357,252	1,223,305	6,690,915	11,926	895,761
2011	10,105,035	3,034,245	2,621,413	371,662	1,298,930	7,178,702	12,296	829,817
2012	10,414,185	3,277,119	2,740,793	397,313	1,278,946	6,799,675	12,295	756,034
2013	11,057,440	3,514,032	2,869,745	426,072	1,288,905	6,476,802	10,719	998,061
2014 [8]	11,353,307	3,685,531	2,994,385	463,364	1,437,475	6,293,079	10,502	939,260

[1] See table 13-9 for Food Stamp Program costs.   [2] October 1–September 30.   [3] Includes sponsor administrative, audit, and startup costs.   [4] Includes sponsor administrative, State administrative and health clinic costs.   [5] Includes entitlement commodities, bonus commodities, and cash-in-lieu for the National School Lunch, School Breakfast, Child and Adult Care Food, and Summer Food Service Programs.   [6] Includes food costs, administrative costs, program evaluation funds, special grants, and Farmer's Market projects for the Special Supplemental Food Program for Women, Infants and Children.   [7] Includes entitlement and bonus commodities, cash-in-lieu of commodities, and administrative costs of the following programs: Food Distribution to Indian Reservations, Nutrition Services Incentive Program (formerly Nutrition Program for the Elderly), Commodity Supplemental Food, Charitable Institutions, Summer Camps, Emergency Food Assistance Program (TEFAP), Disaster Feeding, Bureau of Federal Prisons, Veteran Affairs Administration, and the Food Stamp Program Elderly Pilot Project.   [8] Preliminary.

FNS, Budget Division/Program Reports, Analysis and Monitoring Branch, (703) 305–2165.

Table 13-11.—Food and Nutrition Service program benefits: Cash payments made under the National School Lunch, School Breakfast, Child and Adult Care, Summer Food and Special Milk Programs and the value of food benefits provided under the SNAP, WIC, Commodity Distribution and The Emergency Feeding Food Assistance Programs, fiscal year 2014 [1]

State/Territory	Child Nutrition Program (cash payments only) [2]					Special Supplemental Food (WIC)	SNAP (formerly Food Stamp Program) [4]	Emergency food assistance (TEFAP)	Commodity distribution [3]	Total [4]
	Child and Adult Care Food	Summer Food	Special Milk	National School Lunch	School Breakfast					
	1,000 dollars	1,000 dollars	1,000 dollars	1,000 dollars	1,000 dollars	1,000 dollars	1,000 dollars	1,000 dollars	1,000 dollars	1,000 dollars
Alabama	38,468	5,550	29	205,936	66,975	71,140	1,318,134	9,015	28,182	1,743,429
Alaska	8,888	1,471	2	31,999	9,353	12,964	174,242	937	3,297	243,154
Amer. Samoa [4]	0	0	0	0	0	5,452	0	0	0	5,452
Arizona	43,668	5,018	52	263,817	83,331	91,657	1,476,762	12,249	41,673	2,018,227
Arkansas	62,709	9,906	0	127,866	47,003	44,001	663,719	6,005	22,701	983,910
California	345,714	21,418	364	1,431,994	465,296	765,860	7,411,484	72,589	187,978	10,702,697
Colorado	22,556	4,053	138	130,365	43,394	45,248	765,737	8,238	17,762	1,037,490
Connecticut	14,168	2,395	209	91,552	26,733	29,400	697,436	5,479	11,532	878,903
Delaware	13,442	1,810	31	30,513	10,094	9,555	220,353	2,036	5,620	293,454
District of Columbia	7,630	2,722	7	24,992	10,292	7,569	222,604	1,627	3,965	281,408
Florida	207,789	30,343	25	717,073	215,564	245,503	5,472,834	35,519	78,176	7,002,825
Georgia	103,398	11,836	9	483,503	169,111	133,563	2,827,854	20,619	53,169	3,803,062
Guam	380	0	0	7,485	2,749	6,976	108,434	487	32	126,544
Hawaii	6,297	471	1	45,672	11,416	21,616	525,398	2,015	3,648	616,533
Idaho	6,737	3,800	163	52,148	17,668	17,989	295,663	2,729	7,075	403,972
Illinois	129,639	11,385	2,139	436,514	124,252	152,742	3,202,510	22,154	55,679	4,137,014
Indiana	47,700	8,029	167	247,278	68,287	71,136	1,311,468	10,423	36,446	1,800,935
Iowa	25,164	2,719	79	101,621	23,314	28,261	532,085	3,885	18,570	735,697
Kansas	29,167	3,149	62	103,306	28,713	31,210	395,210	4,168	15,479	610,464
Kentucky	30,739	5,134	36	191,915	73,505	59,774	1,170,990	8,927	29,978	1,570,998
Louisiana	77,373	11,624	33	207,370	71,029	76,546	1,288,316	8,454	37,804	1,778,550
Maine	8,681	1,642	20	33,435	11,596	12,277	321,551	2,333	5,384	396,919
Maryland	48,932	7,121	324	150,611	56,116	70,049	1,133,136	7,364	18,453	1,492,106
Massachusetts	58,269	7,072	300	169,122	46,053	54,454	1,272,977	8,263	26,926	1,643,435
Michigan	57,513	10,254	293	293,528	100,653	124,816	2,576,165	18,476	59,887	3,241,585
Minnesota	55,241	6,892	790	152,223	42,151	64,219	670,203	6,562	29,136	1,027,416
Mississippi	37,377	6,110	3	166,278	60,590	55,969	912,986	6,352	20,849	1,266,513
Missouri	45,563	10,412	469	199,870	68,813	63,553	1,236,445	9,991	35,847	1,670,963
Montana	9,079	1,513	21	26,171	7,322	9,029	176,170	1,598	8,507	239,411
Nebraska	30,448	2,503	56	67,052	15,670	21,660	238,904	2,302	14,482	393,076
Nevada	7,811	1,524	112	91,979	27,142	33,208	536,711	6,784	12,465	717,736
New Hampshire	4,257	777	195	23,319	5,317	5,740	140,719	1,633	5,366	187,322
New Jersey	65,721	7,590	449	241,237	76,492	104,708	1,290,688	17,594	34,484	1,838,964
New Mexico	28,432	5,662	0	90,649	39,309	26,399	630,130	4,641	15,803	841,024
New York	213,653	51,130	846	659,203	190,244	325,035	5,200,758	38,063	92,897	6,771,829
North Carolina	83,758	9,958	162	357,384	119,549	143,156	2,383,572	23,132	48,511	3,169,182
North Dakota	8,840	554	23	18,330	4,559	7,273	75,765	881	8,437	124,662
Northern Marianas [4]	0	0	0	0	0	3,247	0	0	0	3,247
Ohio	82,792	10,092	395	342,712	106,621	108,242	2,582,758	20,193	51,625	3,305,430
Oklahoma	52,066	4,321	25	155,137	55,741	54,949	865,050	6,154	47,322	1,240,765
Oregon	30,480	5,788	119	105,059	34,622	48,445	1,161,871	7,420	14,376	1,408,179
Pennsylvania	96,296	13,148	389	331,348	89,391	126,421	2,573,657	19,472	64,034	3,314,156
Puerto Rico [4]	26,691	10,902	0	121,521	33,164	173,944	0	9,231	13,903	389,355
Rhode Island	7,903	1,023	74	29,447	9,303	11,852	279,843	1,972	3,271	344,689
South Carolina	29,865	7,896	12	189,483	73,738	63,546	1,235,696	9,048	21,214	1,630,498
South Dakota	7,912	1,161	33	28,450	7,225	11,440	148,938	1,062	11,693	217,914
Tennessee	59,591	10,300	25	245,651	93,733	81,342	1,951,919	11,700	31,691	2,485,952
Texas	303,751	43,777	22	1,352,142	518,914	322,530	5,330,651	40,931	180,673	8,093,390
Utah	25,791	1,627	78	95,311	18,967	26,757	316,672	3,893	12,448	501,542
Vermont	5,100	1,073	91	15,150	5,409	9,097	130,324	748	3,139	170,132
Virginia	40,250	9,424	195	221,878	68,396	67,303	1,303,282	9,422	26,992	1,747,142
Virgin Islands	1,250	388	0	5,300	1,137	4,266	55,099	261	657	68,357
Washington	41,865	5,039	260	190,980	51,478	92,813	1,547,546	11,327	28,537	1,969,845
West Va	14,002	1,480	21	64,956	30,654	20,669	476,134	3,850	9,336	621,102
Wisconsin	35,787	6,868	1,124	162,474	43,920	58,625	1,112,981	9,365	27,266	1,458,411
Wyoming	4,746	627	30	14,323	3,460	4,609	49,273	662	2,485	80,214
DoD [5]	0	0	0	8,676	6	0	0	0	1,997	10,679
Total [4]	2,851,340	408,482	10,502	11,353,307	3,685,531	4,339,802	69,999,805	560,233	1,648,861	94,857,864

[1] Excludes all administrative and program evaluation costs. [2] Excludes $3.1 million for Food Safety Education and $14.8 million for Team Nutrition. [3] Includes distribution of bonus and entitlement commodities to the National School Lunch, Child and Adult Care, Summer Food Service, Charitable Institutions, Summer Camps, Food Distribution on Indian Reservations, Nutrition Services Incentive Program (NSIP, formerly Nutrition Program for the Elderly), Commodity Supplemental Food, and Disaster Feeding Programs. Also includes cash-in-lieu of commodities for the National School Lunch and the Child and Adult Care Food programs (NSIP cash grants were transferred to the Agency on Aging, DHHS, in FY 2003). [4] Excludes Nutrition Assistance grants of $2,001 million for Puerto Rico, $22.6 million for the Northern Marianas, and $27.3 million for American Samoa. [5] Dept. of Defense represents food service to children of armed forces personnel in overseas schools.
FNS, Budget Division/Program Reports, Analysis and Monitoring Branch (703) 305–2165. May 8, 2014.

Table 13-12.—Food and Nutrition Service Programs: Persons participating, fiscal years 2005–2014

Fiscal year	National School Lunch Program [1]	School Breakfast Program [1]	Child and Adult Care Program [2]	Summer Food Service [3]	WIC Program [4]
	Thousands	Thousands	Thousands	Thousands	Thousands
2005	29,646	9,357	3,108	1,946	8,023
2006	30,128	9,760	3,112	1,912	8,088
2007	30,630	10,119	3,207	1,977	8,285
2008	31,016	10,608	3,254	2,130	8,705
2009	31,310	11,076	3,320	2,260	9,122
2010	31,753	11,669	3,411	2,304	9,175
2011	31,841	12,175	3,426	2,278	8,961
2012	31,653	12,868	3,547	2,348	8,908
2013	30,674	13,200	3,680	2,427	8,663
2014	30,407	13,603	3,892	2,648	8,259

[1] Average monthly participation (excluding summer months). [2] Average daily attendance (data reported quarterly). [3] Average daily attendance for peak month (July). [4] Average monthly participation. WIC is an abbreviation for the Special Supplemental Food Program for Women, Infants and Children.
FNS, Budget Division/Program Reports, Analysis and Monitoring Branch, (703) 305–2165.

Table 13-13.—Consumers' prices: Index number of prices paid for goods and services, United States, 2005–2014 [1]

[1982–84=100]

Year	Food	Nonfood items					All items
		Apparel and upkeep	Housing		Transportation	Medical care	
			Total	Rent			
2005	190.7	119.5	195.7	233.7	173.9	323.2	195.3
2006	195.2	119.5	203.2	241.9	180.9	336.2	201.6
2007	202.9	118.9	209.6	250.8	184.7	351.1	207.3
2008	214.1	118.9	216.3	257.2	195.5	364.1	215.3
2009	218.0	120.1	217.1	259.9	179.3	375.6	214.5
2010	219.6	119.5	216.3	258.8	193.4	388.4	218.1
2011	227.8	122.1	219.1	262.2	212.4	400.3	224.9
2012	233.8	126.3	222.7	267.8	217.3	414.9	229.6
2013	237.0	127.4	227.4	274.0	217.4	425.1	233.0
2014	242.7	127.5	233.2	281.8	215.9	435.3	236.7

[1] Reflects retail prices of goods and services usually bought by average families in urban areas of the United States. This index is the official index released monthly by the U.S. Department of Labor. Data are for all urban consumers.
ERS, Food Markets Branch, (202) 694–5349. Compiled from data of the U.S. Department of Labor.

CHAPTER XIV

STATISTICS OF FERTILIZERS AND PESTICIDES

This chapter contains statistics on percentages of crop acres treated by various types of fertilizers and pesticides. Nitrogen, phosphate, potash, and sulfur are the most common fertilizers; herbicides, insecticides, fungicides, and other chemicals are the main categories of pesticides. Other chemicals include soil fumigants, vine killers, and desiccants. The tables show data for field crops for 2003–2013, fruits for 2011, and vegetables for 2010. NASS collects data for field crops on an annual basis; data collection for fruits and vegetables was suspended for fiscal year 2013. The surveyed States are generally the major producing States for each crop shown in the tables and represent 65–95 percent of the U.S. planted acres, depending on the selected crop. Application data for specific pesticide active ingredients and additional fertilizer data are available in the series of NASS "Agricultural Chemical Usage" reports and data sets.

Table 14-1.—Field crops: Fertilizer, and percent of area receiving applications, all States surveyed, 2006–2013 [1]

Crop	Nitrogen	Phosphate	Potash	Sulfur
	Percent	*Percent*	*Percent*	*Percent*
2006:				
Rice	97	67	54	18
Soybeans	18	23	25	3
Wheat, Durum	92	74	7	4
Wheat, Other Spring	95	85	27	13
Wheat, Winter	80	57	17	14
2007:				
All Cotton	92	67	52	42
2009:				
Wheat, Durum	99	85	11	9
Wheat, Other Spring	94	84	21	14
Wheat, Winter	83	54	16	16
2010:				
Corn	97	78	61	15
Cotton, Upland	90	62	52	42
Potatoes, Fall	99	96	90	73
2011:				
Barley	86	68	28	30
Sorghum	81	54	9	16
2012:				
Soybeans	27	37	37	7
Wheat, Durum	98	89	12	12
Wheat, Other Spring	97	87	27	20
Wheat, Winter	85	55	13	19
2013:				
Rice	97	75	54	23
Peanuts	40	42	42	17

[1] Refers to percent of planted acres receiving one or more applications of a specific fertilizer ingredient.   See tables 14-2 through 14-21 for surveyed States.   Note: See planted acreage estimates in tables 1-56 for barley, 1-36 for corn, 2-2 for upland and all cotton, 1-49 for oats, 3-16 for peanuts, 1-27 for rice, 1-65 for sorghum, 3-32 for soybeans and 1-8 for wheat.
NASS, Environmental, Economics, and Demographics Branch, (202) 720–6146.

Table 14-2.—Barley: Pesticide usage, 2003 and 2011 [1]

State and Year	Percent treated and amount applied							
	Herbicide		Insecticide		Fungicide		Other Chemicals	
	Area applied	Pounds applied	Area applied	Pounds applied	Area applied	Pounds applied	Area applied	Pounds applied
	Percent	*Thousands*	*Percent*	*Thousands*	*Percent*	*Thousands*	*Percent*	*Thousands*
AZ:								
2011	37	16	*	*	....	....	....	....
CA:								
2003	67	32	*	*	*	*	*	*
2011	39	48	*	*	....	....	....	....
CO:								
2011	96	36	22	1	25	2	....	....
ID:								
2003	94	573	3	16	*	*	5	9
2011	91	302	11	1	18	11	14	27
MN:								
2003	89	88	8	3	39	9	....	....
2011	58	19	10	2	32	3	....	....
MT:								
2003	93	1,005	2	5	*	*	*	*
2011	92	1,065	*	*	26	16	*	*
ND:								
2003	98	1,067	4	12	11	20	....	....
2011	95	236	6	4	48	26	....	....
OR:								
2011	74	21	*	*	31	1	*	*
PA:								
2003	32	8	....	....	....	....	....	....
2011	39	7	*	*	3	**	....	....
SD:								
2003	86	34	....	....	*	*	....	....
UT:								
2003	75	17	*	*	....	....	....	....
VA:								
2011	59	29	20	**	15	1	*	*
WA:								
2003	94	358	....	....	....	....	*	*
2011	93	111	....	....	19	2	....	....
WI:								
2003	21	5	....	....	....	....	....	....
2011	25	4	....	....	....	....	....	....
WY:								
2003	83	57	10	**	....	....	....	....
2011	76	32	*	*	13	1	....	....

* Insufficient number of reports to publish data.   ** Amount applied is less than 500 lbs.   [1] Data not available for all States for all years.   Note: Planted acres are in table 1-56.
NASS, Environmental, Economics, and Demographics Branch, (202) 720–6146.

Table 14-3.—Barley: Fertilizer usage, 2003 and 2011 [1]

State	Percent treated and amount applied							
	Nitrogen		Phosphate		Potash		Sulfur [2]	
	Area applied	Pounds applied	Area applied	Pounds applied	Area applied	Pounds applied	Area applied	Pounds applied
	Percent	Millions	Percent	Millions	Percent	Millions	Percent	Millions
AZ:								
2011	97	8.2	39	1.5	*	*	21	0.3
CA:								
2003	72	5.2	32	0.6	2	***	....	....
2011	41	2.6	*	*	....	....	14	0.2
CO:								
2011	82	7.2	40	1.5	28	0.6	36	0.4
ID:								
2003	91	56.2	58	15.4	25	5.7	....	....
2011	93	44.2	66	10.0	37	4.9	65	9.6
MN:								
2003	91	11.4	87	5.6	66	4.0	....	....
2011	60	3.3	56	1.3	44	1.0	11	0.1
MT:								
2003	92	44.2	88	30.2	52	9.7	....	....
2011	90	29.1	83	16.6	37	3.6	16	1.2
ND:								
2003	98	116.5	91	50.7	20	4.2	....	....
2011	96	28.3	92	11.1	16	1.0	4	0.1
OR:								
2011	77	1.6	26	0.1	*	*	36	0.1
PA:								
2003	69	2.2	39	1.1	40	1.2	....	....
2011	64	1.9	32	0.8	32	0.8	10	0.1
SD:								
2003	82	2.6	78	1.9	13	0.2	....	....
UT:								
2003	58	2.1	14	0.3	**	***	....	....
VA:								
2011	77	4.9	39	1.7	35	1.7	24	0.3
WA:								
2003	99	22.5	58	2.5	8	0.5	....	....
2011	91	9.0	59	1.1	9	0.2	90	1.6
WI:								
2003	37	0.5	36	0.7	44	1.8	....	....
2011	34	0.2	*	*	34	1.0	14	0.1
WY:								
2003	78	7.3	60	2.4	22	0.7	....	....
2011	73	5.2	55	1.8	30	0.8	18	0.4

* Insufficient number of reports to publish data.   ** Area applied is less than 0.5 percent.   *** Amount applied is less than 50,000 lbs.   [1] Data not available for all States for all years.   [2] Estimates began in 2005.   Note: Planted acres are in table 1-56.

NASS, Environmental, Economics, and Demographics Branch, (202) 720–6146.

STATISTICS OF FERTILIZERS AND PESTICIDES

Table 14-4.—Corn: Pesticide usage, 2005–2014[1][2]

State	Percent treated and amount applied							
	Herbicide		Insecticide[2]		Fungicide[2]		Other Chemicals	
	Area applied	Pounds applied	Area applied	Pounds applied	Area applied	Pounds applied	Area applied	Pounds applied
	Percent	Thousands	Percent	Thousands	Percent	Thousands	Percent	Thousands
CO:								
2005	90	1,494	24	252				
2010	95	3,176	12	81				
GA:								
2005	91	495	14	25				
2010	97	559	30	58	*	*		
IL:								
2005	99	30,967	52	1,426				
2010	99	29,354	28	399	23	339	*	*
2014	98	26,870	23	237	21	321	*	*
IN:								
2005	97	14,136	41	722				
2010	97	15,060	14	114	5	31		
2014	100	14,609	9	45	12	80	*	*
IA:								
2005	96	24,726	11	187				
2010	100	26,195	8	148	11	149		
2014	95	30,240	13	122	19	296	*	*
KS:								
2005	87	7,436	11	89				
2010	96	14,727	7	93	*	*	*	*
2014	97	11,432	10	244	3	13		
KY:								
2005	100	3,187	18	26				
2010	98	4,661	39	12	*	*	*	*
2014	94	4,102	29	15	11	19	*	*
MI:								
2005	99	5,145	14	153				
2010	98	4,520	*	*	*	*	*	*
2014	98	5,710	4	5	12	36		
MN:								
2005	100	10,361	12	214				
2010	95	11,619	7	108	*	*		
2014	98	13,596	2	26	*	*	*	*
MO:								
2005	96	7,707	11	41				
2010	94	8,304	17	7	*	*		
2014	98	8,517	24	43	14	61		
NE:								
2005	98	18,416	20	456				
2010	97	20,418	4	231	8	100	*	*
2014	95	21,320	16	213	10	118	*	*
NY:								
2005	96	2,325	21	146				
2010	98	2,721	13	23				
NC:								
2005	98	1,669	17	130				
2010	98	2,349	40	30	*	*		
ND:								
2005	99	1,094						
2010	100	3,761	*	*				
2014	97	4,489	*	*	4	16		
OH:								
2005	99	9,322	9	215				
2010	99	9,149	8	93				
2014	99	9,231	13	64	9	81	*	*
PA:								
2005	97	3,346	21	154				
2010	99	4,668	30	31				
2014	97	4,080	20	46	4	6	4	2
SD:								
2005	100	6,036	12	239				
2010	100	8,480	1	4				
2014	98	10,803	*	*	9	47		
TX:								
2005	94	3,344	24	236				
2010	97	3,755	13	133	*	*		
2014	89	4,338	14	528	23	27	*	*
WI:								
2005	97	6,369	22	134				
2010	97	8,676	11	64	*	*		
2014	90	6,952	8	22	*	*	*	*

* Insufficient number of reports to publish data.   [1] Data not available for all States for all years.   [2] Amount applied excludes Bt (bacillus thuringiensis) and other biologicals.   Note: Planted acres are in table 1-36.
NASS, Environmental, Economics, and Demographics Branch, (202) 720–6146.

Table 14-5.—Corn: Fertilizer usage, 2005–2014 [1]

State and Year	Nitrogen		Phosphate		Potash		Sulfur [2]	
	Area applied	Pounds applied	Area applied	Pounds applied	Area applied	Pounds applied	Area applied	Pounds applied
	Percent	Millions	Percent	Millions	Percent	Millions	Percent	Millions
CO:								
2005	89	126.2	63	24.4	21	4.2	33	3.3
2010	98	165.1	52	19.3	8	1.6	19	3.4
GA:								
2005	98	38.7	86	16.1	87	24.5	53	2.5
2010	90	46.7	74	14.8	78	22.6	51	2.4
IL:								
2005	98	1,728.3	84	780.4	84	1,160.5	4	14.9
2010	98	2,061.5	85	988.1	81	1,080.0	9	20.5
2014	99	1,918.3	85	938.4	81	1,066.9	8	17.5
IN:								
2005	100	869.3	93	420.2	88	648.2	14	8.1
2010	99	1,041.0	90	366.5	87	613.5	10	10.4
2014	96	877.7	81	351.1	79	530.5	22	16.0
IA:								
2005	92	1,653.2	70	579.0	71	762.3	5	4.5
2010	95	1,806.6	72	620.3	68	734.7	8	11.5
2014	96	1,842.2	64	600.5	63	705.3	18	40.2
KS:								
2005	97	482.1	81	112.7	26	34.9	17	5.3
2010	99	629.7	81	146.7	37	72.1	29	20.3
2014	98	549.6	87	148.5	35	60.5	29	10.1
KY:								
2005	98	210.5	78	75.5	77	86.9	....	....
2010	96	210.6	88	116.8	88	124.6	*	*
2014	98	214.1	88	109.0	87	119.0	14	4.5
MI:								
2005	97	277.8	88	89.6	81	148.4	21	3.7
2010	99	288.8	93	72.1	83	186.9	35	4.5
2014	98	338.7	84	89.2	82	192.6	25	7.4
MN:								
2005	94	953.9	86	378.1	77	400.3	9	8.2
2010	87	835.4	72	277.3	68	327.7	9	8.5
2014	94	1,091.8	86	491.4	80	570.2	51	72.5
MO:								
2005	99	489.5	79	149.5	78	180.1	19	10.0
2010	99	392.5	89	177.3	61	109.9	15	4.0
2014	98	603.3	81	191.1	83	228.0	32	16.2
NE:								
2005	99	1,162.5	75	237.3	22	38.8	30	35.0
2010	99	1,270.1	69	256.4	20	46.1	23	28.4
2014	99	1,359.9	77	329.9	29	100.8	42	71.6
NY:								
2005	94	62.2	88	33.2	79	34.9	....	....
2010	86	52.2	75	28.3	59	23.2	*	*
NC:								
2005	97	90.5	74	25.5	86	53.1	18	1.1
2010	94	109.3	83	30.6	81	57.6	29	5.2
ND:								
2005	99	169.3	94	58.8	38	13.3	8	0.9
2010	100	326.7	94	85.5	53	35.1	8	2.2
2014	99	349.7	88	132.1	44	34.7	43	12.3
OH:								
2005	99	551.7	87	224.9	76	264.5	12	3.2
2010	100	481.8	90	198.8	83	257.8	18	11.2
2014	98	558.8	85	228.9	80	282.2	15	5.1
PA:								
2005	88	108.4	64	40.7	58	37.4	6	3.0
2010	94	109.2	39	25.0	46	32.2	28	5.9
2014	96	137.7	67	39.7	66	40.5	35	5.6
SD:								
2005	95	477.7	79	154.2	37	41.9	13	5.5
2010	99	580.8	85	196.0	35	46.6	19	11.7
2014	97	684.8	83	216.4	50	113.2	35	24.0
TX:								
2005	94	282.0	81	73.9	28	10.6	29	6.9
2010	99	292.0	72	59.5	32	12.2	32	8.8
2014	95	310.5	77	77.9	37	19.2	43	10.7
WI:								
2005	93	380.9	84	118.8	84	191.7	22	9.1
2010	93	330.9	72	121.1	77	159.1	20	7.3
2014	98	407.6	85	127.9	88	222.2	49	31.7

*Insufficient number of reports to publish data.　[1] Data not available for all States for all years.　[2] Estimates began in 2005.　Note: Planted acres are in table 1-36.
NASS, Environmental, Economics, and Demographics Branch, (202) 720–6146.

Table 14-6.—Cotton, Upland: Pesticide usage, 2003–2010 [1] [2]

State and Year	Percent treated and amount applied							
	Herbicide		Insecticide [3]		Fungicide		Other Chemicals	
	Area applied	Pounds applied	Area applied	Pounds applied	Area applied	Pounds applied	Area applied	Pounds applied
	Percent	Thousands	Percent	Thousands	Percent	Thousands	Percent	Thousands
AL:								
2003	99	1,336	84	260	15	44	93	930
2005	98	1,186	74	192	2	3	89	697
2007	98	941	55	88	*	*	75	423
AZ:								
2003	94	382	74	374	*	*	80	323
AR:								
2003	96	2,703	89	3,575	17	64	92	1,947
2005	95	2,997	84	2,669	6	18	87	1,910
2007	97	2,399	92	1,092	2	16	96	1,780
2010	92	1,587	97	655	*	*	98	1,473
CA:								
2003	97	1,005	95	899	7	13	96	2,091
2005	92	551	96	574	4	2	96	1,570
2007	90	565	90	506	2	1	93	1,414
GA:								
2003	96	2,994	73	746	4	43	91	2,709
2005	99	2,958	88	1,145	**	1	95	2,539
2007	100	3,163	85	956	*	*	96	3,955
2010	100	4,098	75	1,121	*	*	95	4,300
LA:								
2003	100	1,448	97	2,007	17	11	99	690
2005	98	1,897	94	1,358	3	7	99	888
2007	98	992	99	562	*	*	100	567
MS:								
2003	100	3,475	94	1,534	17	63	99	1,590
2005	100	3,947	92	1,917	6	28	98	1,880
2007	100	2,132	97	1,231	2	3	99	1,146
2010	100	1,457	92	634	....	....	100	853
MO:								
2003	96	636	74	146	*	*	95	822
2007	100	995	83	270	*	*	100	867
2010	100	1,191	92	279	*	*	99	556
NC:								
2003	97	2,118	88	420	7	41	90	2,041
2005	99	2,181	82	597	7	41	92	1,642
2007	100	1,479	79	300	3	15	99	896
2010	100	1,581	83	315	*	*	95	1,103
SC:								
2003	92	470	97	141	3	4	79	307
2007	100	535	92	85	13	13	86	291
TN:								
2003	98	1,270	88	422	20	33	90	863
2005	99	1,339	87	253	11	23	94	1,030
2007	100	1,482	94	228	*	*	99	985
2010	98	1,291	94	146	*	*	97	790
TX:								
2003	99	7,701	36	3,102	2	22	31	1,400
2005	93	8,677	53	5,946	*	*	47	3,075
2007	96	11,532	43	2,624	*	*	74	5,702
2010	99	13,111	35	2,891	*	*	80	5,425

* Insufficient number of reports to publish data.   ** Area applied is less than 0.5 percent.   [1] Data not available for all States for all years.   [2] 2007 data are for all cotton (pima and upland).   [3] Amount applied excludes Bt (bacillus thuringiensis) and other biologicals.   Note: Planted acres are in table 2-2.
NASS, Environmental, Economics, and Demographics Branch, (202) 720–6146.

Table 14-7.—Cotton, Upland: Fertilizer usage, 2003–2010 [1] [2]

State and Year	Percent treated and amount applied							
	Nitrogen		Phosphate		Potash		Sulfur [3]	
	Area applied	Pounds applied	Area applied	Pounds applied	Area applied	Pounds applied	Area applied	Pounds applied
	Percent	*Millions*	*Percent*	*Millions*	*Percent*	*Millions*	*Percent*	*Millions*
AL:								
2003	97	51.9	84	31.2	83	33.4	....	....
2005	98	51.4	87	27.0	90	37.0	39	3.4
2007	97	34.2	87	17.0	90	23.3	46	2.1
AZ:								
2003	93	35.3	35	4.6	11	0.8	....	....
AR:								
2003	97	89.7	84	33.5	90	79.9	....	....
2005	96	112.8	73	33.3	82	71.2	33	8.5
2007	98	94.1	83	29.4	85	63.9	46	5.5
2010	98	57.6	83	19.3	86	34.7	27	1.6
CA:								
2003	94	72.9	47	14.3	25	11.6	....	....
2005	96	79.8	32	10.2	22	8.3	4	0.2
2007	96	53.6	39	13.2	20	4.3	*	*
GA:								
2003	100	124.5	90	65.8	91	105.8	....	....
2005	97	112.6	88	63.8	90	103.7	56	11.7
2007	98	90.9	91	56.3	91	81.3	67	10.5
2010	97	122.7	86	66.9	91	127.0	53	8.1
LA:								
2003	99	45.1	45	8.8	59	16.1	....	....
2005	99	47.5	47	12.3	49	23.3	35	1.3
2007	100	29.3	70	8.1	63	16.1	*	*
MS:								
2003	99	119.8	45	23.0	70	82.2	....	....
2005	99	144.5	35	22.6	58	82.7	17	2.8
2007	100	77.3	33	12.4	54	37.7	28	2.0
2010	95	40.0	32	6.4	53	20.2	29	1.4
MO:								
2003	100	35.5	73	11.6	81	26.2	....	....
2007	98	36.1	88	10.3	95	24.5	64	2.6
2010	100	40.2	81	12.2	93	25.2	61	3.7
NC:								
2003	97	59.9	74	24.4	93	79.7	....	....
2005	95	57.9	74	25.7	95	79.0	40	7.1
2007	92	31.3	71	11.0	89	44.2	25	2.9
2010	98	35.7	68	17.2	87	45.6	38	2.6
SC:								
2003	95	16.0	78	7.9	90	21.6	....	....
2007	99	16.2	79	6.5	94	16.0	33	0.8
TN:								
2003	97	50.0	92	27.3	96	46.4	....	....
2005	100	60.6	90	31.1	99	58.3	42	2.1
2007	100	52.3	95	25.2	100	45.1	60	2.8
2010	100	36.9	96	19.1	99	33.4	75	3.2
TX:								
2003	61	258.0	50	141.7	20	28.6	....	....
2005	77	310.9	64	144.9	32	35.4	40	32.3
2007	86	347.7	60	109.8	24	19.8	42	26.2
2010	85	296.6	52	92.0	30	25.0	38	26.8

*Insufficient number of reports to publish data.　[1] Data not available for all States for all years.　[2] 2007 data are for all cotton (pima and upland).　[3] Estimates began in 2005.　Note: Planted acres are in table 2-2.
NASS, Environmental, Economics, and Demographics Branch, (202) 720–6146.

STATISTICS OF FERTILIZERS AND PESTICIDES

Table 14-8.—Peanuts: Pesticide usage, 2004 and 2013 [1]

	Percent treated and amount applied							
State and Year	Herbicide		Insecticide		Fungicide		Other Chemicals	
	Area applied	Pounds applied	Area applied	Pounds applied	Area applied	Pounds applied	Area applied	Pounds applied
	Percent	Thousands	Percent	Thousands	Percent	Thousands	Percent	Thousands
Alabama:								
2004	100	277	81	200	100	896	....	....
2013	99	219	32	33	95	632	*	*
Florida:								
2004	100	298	88	199	100	835	*	*
2013	93	237	59	28	100	670	*	*
Georgia:								
2004	99	878	77	569	99	2,275	*	*
2013	100	853	48	177	97	1,692	*	*
North Carolina:								
2004	100	221	92	161	96	164	43	1,404
2013	99	190	71	54	87	144	*	*
South Carolina:								
2013	96	150	60	33	81	261	....	....
Texas:								
2004	94	258	3	2	67	154	....	....
2013	65	93	11	2.0	33	42	....	....

*Insufficient number of reports to publish data.   [1] Data not available for all States for all years.   Note: Planted acres are in table 3-16.
NASS, Environmental, Economics, and Demographics Branch, (202) 720–6146.

Table 14-9.—Peanuts: Fertilizer usage, 2004 and 2013 [1]

	Percent treated and amount applied							
State and Year	Nitrogen		Phosphate		Potash		Sulfur [2]	
	Area applied	Pounds applied	Area applied	Pounds applied	Area applied	Pounds applied	Area applied	Pounds applied
	Percent	Millions	Percent	Millions	Percent	Millions	Percent	Millions
Alabama:								
2004	70	4.3	79	8.6	75	12.4	....	....
2013	48	1.5	54	3.0	57	5.2	19	0.6
Florida:								
2004	71	3.3	80	5.4	94	12.7	....	....
2013	81	2.2	86	4.9	93	11.7	36	1.3
Georgia:								
2004	48	5.3	59	17.5	51	23.7	....	....
2013	27	2.1	31	6.5	26	6.5	*	*
North Carolina:								
2004	37	1.0	35	1.2	64	6.7	....	....
2013	21	0.5	22	0.7	51	4.1	23	0.5
South Carolina:								
2013	13	0.5	14	0.4	22	1.5	*	*
Texas:								
2004	86	14.4	77	10.6	62	9.3	....	....
2013	57	5.3	47	2.4	34	1.4	37	0.7

*Insufficient number of reports to publish data.   [1] Data not available for all States for all years.   [2] Estimates began in 2005.   Note: Planted acres are in table 3-16.
NASS, Environmental, Economics, and Demographics Branch, (202) 720–6146.

Table 14-10.—Oats: Pesticide usage, 2005 [1][2]

State and Year	Herbicide		Insecticide		Fungicide	
	Area applied	Pounds applied	Area applied	Pounds applied	Area applied	Pounds applied
	Percent	Thousands	Percent	Thousands		
California: 2005	36	59				
Idaho: 2005	26	17	*	*		
Illinois: 2005	7	1	*	*		
Iowa: 2005	3	2	*	*		
Kansas: 2005	27	13				
Michigan: 2005	61	26				
Minnesota: 2005	21	26				
Montana: 2005	34	18				
Nebraska: 2005	7	4				
New York: 2005	51	23	*	*		
North Dakota: 2005	54	167			*	*
Pennsylvania: 2005	58	46	*	*		
South Dakota: 2005	37	52				
Texas: 2005	26	80	18	35	*	*
Wisconsin: 2005	18	25	*	*		

[1] Data not available for all States for all years. [2] Insufficient number of reports to publish data for fungicides and other chemicals. Note: Planted acres are in table 1-49.
NASS, Environmental, Economics, and Demographics Branch, (202) 720–6146.

Table 14-11.—Oats: Fertilizer usage, 2005 [1]

State and Year	Nitrogen		Phosphate		Potash		Sulfur [2]	
	Area applied	Pounds applied	Area applied	Pounds applied	Area applied	Pounds applied	Area applied	Pounds applied
	Percent	Millions	Percent	Millions	Percent	Millions	Percent	Millions
California: 2005	26	4.4	*	*	*	*	*	*
Idaho: 2005	42	1.6	22	1.4	5	0.1	12	0.2
Illinois: 2005	15	0.4	12	0.4	26	1.7	*	*
Iowa: 2005	31	1.8	30	2.5	40	6.9	*	*
Kansas: 2005	84	4.4	39	1.4	17	0.8	*	*
Michigan: 2005	82	2.6	72	2.8	77	3.4	*	*
Minnesota: 2005	28	4.2	22	2.4	28	5.9	5	0.2
Montana: 2005	53	2.0	35	1.0	14	0.4	9	0.1
Nebraska: 2005	68	4.5	24	1.3	7	0.1	5	**
New York: 2005	75	1.9	72	2.7	72	2.8	*	*
North Dakota: 2005	71	15.8	49	5.7	9	0.7	5	0.1
Pennsylvania: 2005	90	4.5	81	4.9	82	5.1	2	0.1
South Dakota: 2005	64	11.8	46	5.6	17	1.7	*	*
Texas: 2005	79	45.4	56	12.7	39	4.9	25	1.7
Wisconsin: 2005	23	2.1	24	3.9	35	15.1	8	0.4

[1] Data not available for all States for all years. [2] Estimates began in 2005. ** Amount applied is less than 50,000 lbs. Note: Planted acres are in table 1-49.
NASS, Environmental, Economics, and Demographics Branch, (202) 720–6146.

Table 14-12.—Potatoes, Fall: Pesticide usage, 2005–2014 [1]

State and Year	Percent treated and amount applied							
	Herbicide		Insecticide [2]		Fungicide		Other Chemicals	
	Area applied	Pounds applied	Area applied	Pounds applied	Area applied	Pounds applied	Area applied	Pounds applied
	Percent	*Thousands*	*Percent*	*Thousands*	*Percent*	*Thousands*	*Percent*	*Thousands*
CO:								
2005	78	101	57	10	78	87	34	9,678
2010	92	173	93	108	98	191	74	5,156
2014	78	83	50	37	96	120	74	5,696
ID:								
2005	90	694	65	331	81	813	49	37,732
2010	98	829	67	190	93	983	63	36,080
2014	89	717	89	287	95	1,618	57	36,437
ME:								
2005	100	35	91	18	100	607	12	46
2010	93	36	91	8	100	373	73	30
2014	97	30	84	9	90	329	78	37
MI:								
2005	98	68	97	20	98	391	2	55
2010	90	70	90	18	96	298	67	46
2014	99	86	96	32	99	442	73	35
MN:								
2005	97	33	97	10	98	578	8	7
2010	90	44	99	9	100	586	48	3,099
2014	91	34	93	13	91	612	52	4,067
ND:								
2005	89	57	76	11	96	854	7	15
2010	89	71	85	13	96	874	60	6,872
2014	90	71	89	10	99	801	30	1,653
WA:								
2005	96	328	97	517	99	1,394	70	17,171
2010	98	376	97	392	99	1,197	80	16,901
2014	92	566	98	489	99	1,109	87	16,635
WI:								
2005	99	78	97	62	99	810	49	3,327
2010	82	73	91	12	96	866	92	2,742
2014	95	96	99	16	100	987	96	4,913

[1] Data not available for all States for all years. [2] Amount applied excludes Bt (bacillus thuringiensis) and other biologicals.

NASS, Environmental, Economics, and Demographics Branch, (202) 720–6146.

Table 14-13.—Potatoes, Fall: Fertilizer usage, 2005–2014 [1]

State and Year	Percent treated and amount applied							
	Nitrogen		Phosphate		Potash		Sulfur [2]	
	Area applied	Pounds applied	Area applied	Pounds applied	Area applied	Pounds applied	Area applied	Pounds applied
	Percent	*Millions*	*Percent*	*Millions*	*Percent*	*Millions*	*Percent*	*Millions*
Colorado:								
2005	92	9.4	86	7.9	64	3.2	89	2.6
2010	97	10.0	92	10.4	66	3.9	93	5.2
2014	94	9.2	93	7.2	70	1.6	94	2.6
Idaho:								
2005	100	72.9	99	56.9	92	40.0	82	21.7
2010	100	75.0	96	53.2	91	35.9	81	30.0
2014	99	78.1	98	47.5	85	36.3	90	23.6
Maine:								
2005	100	10.2	100	10.1	100	11.9	....	....
2010	99	8.8	99	8.2	95	10.2	*	*
2014	98	8.3	98	7.1	98	8.7	12	0.1
Michigan:								
2005	99	9.2	94	4.9	100	10.2	58	1.4
2010	100	8.6	98	3.5	100	8.6	*	*
2014	100	7.9	99	3.8	100	9.6	52	1.7
Minnesota:								
2005	100	8.2	100	5.0	81	7.7	55	0.7
2010	98	9.2	100	4.6	100	14.6	80	1.3
2014	100	6.2	88	2.8	80	5.9	66	0.9
North Dakota:								
2005	100	14.7	100	8.4	96	13.7	54	1.3
2010	100	15.1	89	7.9	84	14.3	44	1.3
2014	100	12.3	97	8.9	100	8.7	79	1.7
Washington:								
2005	100	37.8	98	30.2	92	38.2	89	9.5
2010	100	32.6	99	24.9	94	36.0	90	9.7
2014	100	29.2	100	20.1	97	18.2	82	7.2
Wisconsin:								
2005	100	17.9	99	9.1	99	20.5	72	4.1
2010	100	16.5	100	5.3	93	17.7	91	3.9
2014	100	15.0	96	5.4	99	20.8	89	4.2

*Insufficient number of reports to publish data.　[1] Data not available for all States for all years.　[2] Estimates began in 2005.

NASS, Environmental, Economics, and Demographics Branch, (202) 720–6146.

Table 14-14.—Rice: Pesticide usage, 2006 and 2013[1]

State and Year	Percent treated and amount applied							
	Herbicide		Insecticide		Fungicide		Other Chemicals	
	Area applied	Pounds applied	Area applied	Pounds applied	Area applied	Pounds applied	Area applied	Pounds applied
	Percent	Thousands	Percent	Thousands	Percent	Thousands	Percent	Thousands
Arkansas:								
2006	95	3,054	10	14	37	109	5	269
2013	97	2,646	30	10	45	103	5	251
California:								
2006	93	2,500	14	2	50	738	....	....
2013	96	2,986	28	6	45	553	*	*
Louisiana:								
2006	96	475	42	49	46	30	*	*
2013	99	680	17	13	73	82	*	*
Mississippi:								
2006	100	502	55	14	46	16	3	36
2013	100	364	51	2	35	9	6	37
Missouri:								
2006	100	454	....	....	25	12	*	*
2013	100	512	18	1	55	22	20	159
Texas:								
2006	97	496	77	83	55	21	....	....
2013	88	263	35	3	35	11	*	*

* Insufficient number of reports to publish data.   [1] Data not available for all States for all years.   Note: Planted acres are in table 1-27.
NASS, Environmental, Economics, and Demographics Branch, (202) 720–6146.

Table 14-15.—Rice: Fertilizer usage, 2006 and 2013[1]

State and Year	Percent treated and amount applied							
	Nitrogen		Phosphate		Potash		Sulfur	
	Area applied	Pounds applied	Area applied	Pounds applied	Area applied	Pounds applied	Area applied	Pounds applied
	Percent	Millions	Percent	Millions	Percent	Millions	Percent	Millions
Arkansas:								
2006	97	281.2	68	54.7	60	64.9	9	6.0
2013	96	195.8	76	53.2	56	51.3	14	2.1
California:								
2006	94	61.4	75	18.2	40	7.2	31	4.0
2013	98	83.9	81	21.2	38	7.2	41	4.4
Louisiana:								
2006	99	52.8	78	14.6	75	16.2	4	0.3
2013	100	63.9	87	16.0	79	23.0	14	1.3
Mississippi:								
2006	99	35.8	29	2.5	4	0.5	42	1.5
2013	100	23.3	13	0.8	*	*	50	1.2
Missouri:								
2006	100	45.2	47	5.5	42	5.7	29	0.7
2013	100	32.7	56	4.7	*	*	29	0.6
Texas:								
2006	97	29.2	92	5.8	89	6.0	30	0.6
2013	90	22.3	82	5.5	79	5.4	11	0.1

* Insufficient number of reports to publish data.   [1] Data not available for all States for all years.   Note: Planted acres are in table 1-27.
NASS, Environmental, Economics, and Demographics Branch, (202) 720–6146.

Table 14-16.—Sorghum: Pesticide usage, 2003 and 2011 [1] [2]

State and Year	Percent treated and amount applied							
	Herbicide		Insecticide		Fungicide		Other chemicals	
	Area applied	Pounds applied	Area applied	Pounds applied	Area applied	Pounds applied	Area applied	Pounds applied
	Percent	Thousands	Percent	Thousands				
Colorado:								
2003	52	132	*	*	....	....	....	....
2011	75	285	....	....	....	....	....	....
Kansas:								
2003	90	9,014	....	....	....	....	....	....
2011	96	9,411	4	3	....	....	....	....
Missouri:								
2003	98	571	6	4	....	....	*	*
Nebraska:								
2003	98	2,030	4	29	....	....	....	....
2011	84	362	*	*	....	....	....	....
Oklahoma:								
2003	84	329	*	*	....	....	....	....
2011	74	505	*	*	....	....	....	....
South Dakota:								
2003	87	430	*	*	....	....	....	....
2011	89	289	*	*	....	....	....	....
Texas:								
2003	78	2,881	20	208	....	....	....	....
2011	72	1,901	10	9	*	*	....	....

* Insufficient number of reports to publish data. [1] Data not available for all States for all years. [2] Insufficient number of reports to publish data for fungicides and other chemicals. Note: Planted acres are in table 1-65.
NASS, Environmental, Economics, and Demographics Branch, (202) 720–6146.

Table 14-17.—Sorghum: Fertilizer usage, 2003 and 2011 [1]

State	Percent treated and amount applied							
	Nitrogen		Phosphate		Potash		Sulfur [2]	
	Area applied	Pounds applied	Area applied	Pounds applied	Area applied	Pounds applied	Area applied	Pounds applied
	Percent	Millions	Percent	Millions	Percent	Millions	Percent	Millions
Colorado:								
2003	61	7.8	39	5.5	**	***	....	....
2011	75	7.4	41	1.5	*	*	*	*
Kansas:								
2003	97	261.8	55	57.5	4	4.7	....	....
2011	83	135.7	51	32.8	8	2.9	9	1.5
Missouri:								
2003	100	25.0	75	9.1	72	10.8	....	....
Nebraska:								
2003	99	56.7	40	6.1	1	0.1	....	....
2011	88	11.0	41	1.9	15	0.2	22	0.4
Oklahoma:								
2003	69	15.5	36	3.6	11	0.8	....	....
2011	81	11.9	58	3.8	13	0.2	13	0.3
South Dakota:								
2003	84	13.0	54	4.4	3	0.1	....	....
2011	88	8.9	45	1.9	*	*	*	*
Texas:								
2003	63	182.8	43	45.5	14	5.5	....	....
2011	77	94.1	63	27.2	11	3.7	29	5.1

* Insufficient number of reports to publish data. ** Area applied is less than 0.5 percent. *** Amount applied is less than 50,000 lbs. [1] Data not available for all States for all years. [2] Estimates began in 2005. Note: Planted acres are in table 1-65.
NASS, Environmental, Economics, and Demographics Branch, (202) 720–6146.

Table 14-18.—Soybeans: Pesticide usage, 2005–2012 [1]

State and Year	Percent treated and amount applied							
	Herbicide		Insecticide [2]		Fungicide		Other Chemicals [2]	
	Area applied	Pounds applied	Area applied	Pounds applied	Area applied	Pounds applied	Area applied	Pounds applied
	Percent	Thousands	Percent	Thousands	Percent	Thousands	Percent	Thousands
Arizona:								
2005	95	4,152	14	344	8	21		
2006	88	4,317	12	96	9	26	*	*
2012	97	7,531	36	238	27	132		
Illinois:								
2005	99	11,767	9	384				
2006	99	13,794	5	141	2	12		
2012	98	15,478	16	384	11	105	*	*
Indiana:								
2005	99	6,511	18	209				
2006	100	8,910	*	*	6	44		
2012	99	8,730	16	362	13	95	*	*
Iowa:								
2005	96	11,281	16	509	*	*		
2006	99	13,946	9	127	*	*		
2012	99	16,093	21	486	16	173	*	*
Kansas:								
2005	100	3,549						
2006	100	4,386	6	7				
2012	96	7,337	*	*	*	*		
Kentucky:								
2005	89	1,385	2	9	*	*		
2006	97	1,978	7	1	8	40		
2012	98	2,553	13	6	7	9		
Louisiana:								
2005	97	1,285	44	277	13	15		
2006	97	1,664	75	499	37	66		
2012	99	3,224	84	604	71	130	*	*
Michigan:								
2005	92	2,061	42	172	*	*		
2006	98	2,390	*	*	*	*		
2012	97	3,650	25	194	*	*		
Minnesota:								
2005	99	7,310	30	125	*	*		
2006	99	9,715	56	896	*	*	*	*
2012	100	11,017	26	493	8	54	*	*
Mississippi:								
2005	100	2,860	10	9				
2006	100	3,770	26	65	12	30	*	*
2012	100	5,448	38	364	33	60	*	*
Missouri:								
2005	99	5,382	*	*	*	*		
2006	95	6,577	8	28	6	70		
2012	91	9,287	15	120	4	18		
Nebraska:								
2005	100	5,856						
2006	97	7,837	5	129	*	*		
2012	98	8,947	*	*	5	23		
North Carolina:								
2005	86	1,427	11	94				
2006	92	1,968	22	30	6	12		
2012	90	2,852	31	40	14	29		
North Dakota:								
2006	100	4,982	57	480	*	*		
2012	99	8,719	10	125	3	17		
Ohio:								
2005	99	5,358	18	152	3	13		
2006	99	6,871	4	23	4	19		
2012	98	7,941	6	45	8	40	*	*
South Dakota:								
2005	98	5,046	13	12	*	*		
2006	99	5,620	21	111				
2012	97	7,771	17	363	5	77		
Tennessee:								
2005	96	1,436	15	5	25	39		
2006	98	1,866	25	8	35	43		
2012	95	2,861	12	6	23	33		
Virginia:								
2005	97	521	*	*	*	*		
2006	99	842	23	4	*	*		
2012	99	1,138	37	29	26	17		
Wisconsin:								
2006	98	2,058	4	13	*	*		
2012	100	2,404	29	177	5	8		

* Insufficient number of reports to publish data. [1] Data not available for all States for all years. [2] Amount applied excludes Bt (bacillus thuringiensis) and other biologicals. Note: Planted acres are in table 3-32.
NASS, Environmental, Economics, and Demographics Branch, (202) 720–6146.

Table 14-19.—Soybeans: Fertilizer usage, 2006 and 2012[1]

State and Year	Percent treated and amount applied							
	Nitrogen		Phosphate		Potash		Sulfur[2]	
	Area applied	Pounds applied	Area applied	Pounds applied	Area applied	Pounds applied	Area applied	Pounds applied
	Percent	Millions	Percent	Millions	Percent	Millions	Percent	Millions
Arizona:								
2006	3	0.9	34	60.4	36	94.4	*	*
2012	7	8.5	49	84.2	53	149.2	*	*
Illinois:								
2006	11	18.1	16	96	31	290.2	*	*
2012	19	44.7	23	148.8	39	387.5	4	8.6
Indiana:								
2006	16	15.2	20	54.6	32	177.4	*	*
2012	18	13.8	30	83.9	47	224.5	....	....
Iowa:								
2006	7	10.8	12	64.4	20	172.6	1	0.9
2012	13	19.2	26	134.5	36	270.0	7	8.8
Kansas:								
2006	21	10.5	25	32.0	8	8.8	*	*
2012	29	14.7	31	44.0	14	24.3	3	1.1
Kentucky:								
2006	28	14.6	40	35.3	41	44.5	*	*
2012	24	5.1	44	34.6	54	64.9	*	*
Louisiana:								
2006	4	0.4	13	4.9	16	9.3	*	*
2012	6	0.9	22	10.3	24	17.8	*	*
Michigan:								
2006	28	5.9	28	19.5	56	96.7	3	0.2
2012	44	11.2	43	30.4	69	107.2	*	*
Minnesota:								
2006	16	15.3	18	53.2	16	57.4	*	*
2012	27	24.0	30	80.2	27	101.0	6	4.4
Mississippi:								
2006	6	1.0	14	9.0	19	25.6	*	*
2012	14	6.2	13	12.0	26	43.7	*	*
Missouri:								
2006	12	10.9	19	45.7	22	76.2	*	*
2012	24	23.3	45	130.4	46	190.9	8	3.3
Nebraska:								
2006	32	20.2	32	70.4	12	15.8	12	8.0
2012	42	27.4	52	129.6	14	24.6	21	10.1
North Carolina:								
2006	39	11.0	42	25.6	44	50.8	*	*
2012	50	15.8	44	31.6	61	80.3	16	2.3
North Dakota:								
2006	43	22.6	42	58.3	3	1.9	*	*
2012	51	27.3	61	106.0	14	12.2	3	0.9
Ohio:								
2006	19	11.9	20	40.5	40	171.4	2	1.7
2012	25	17.2	31	74.1	58	267.4	4	1.8
South Dakota:								
2006	29	19.7	31	49.4	8	8.6	*	*
2012	43	25.4	49	110.5	22	33.4	2	1.2
Tennessee:								
2006	42	12.0	48	28.1	63	63.8	8	0.7
2012	48	15.7	68	45.4	72	73.6	13	3.2
Virginia:								
2006	32	3.9	34	7.4	39	15.1	4	0.3
2012	53	7.3	50	13.3	56	27.3	9	1.5
Wisconsin:								
2006	31	7.4	33	18.0	55	74.2	10	2.3
2012	45	13.4	42	25.5	75	114.9	28	11.6

* Insufficient number of reports to publish data.　[1] Data not available for all States for all years.　[2] Estimates began in 2005.　Note: Planted acres are in table 3-32.

NASS, Environmental, Economics, and Demographics Branch, (202) 720–6146.

Table 14-20.—Wheat: Pesticide usage, 2006–2012[1]

State and Year	Percent treated and amount applied							
	Herbicide		Insecticide		Fungicide[2]		Other Chemicals[2]	
	Area applied	Pounds applied	Area applied	Pounds applied	Area applied	Pounds applied	Area applied	Pounds applied
	Percent	Thousands	Percent	Thousands	Percent	Thousands	Percent	Thousands
Winter								
Colorado:								
2006	54	1,018	*	*	....	....	....	....
2009	75	2,535	17	160	*	*	....	....
2012	81	3,875	*	*	*	*	....	
Idaho:								
2006	84	349	*	*	5	3	....	
2009	100	478	*	*	16	12	*	*
2012	95	444	*	*	46	45	*	*
Illinois:								
2006	46	62	*	*	6	7	....	
2009	40	31	*	*	11	10	....	
2012	50	59	15	4	36	32	....	
Kansas:								
2006	53	2,600	*	*	....	....	....	
2009	51	4,789	*	*	*	*	....	
2012	67	4,567	*	*	21	227	....	
Michigan:								
2006	71	148	3	**	23	17	....	
2009	52	113	*	*	17	25	....	
Minnesota:								
2009	83	51	*	*	30	3	....	
Missouri:								
2006	28	49	12	12	6	10	....	
2009	42	57	16	3	18	16	....	
2012	36	54	21	5	30	33	....	
Montana:								
2006	92	2,315	*	*	*	*	....	
2009	100	3,746	*	*	5	8	....	
2012	95	2,365	....	....	7	16	....	
Nebraska:								
2006	56	399	....	....	4	8	....	
2009	61	787	....	....	12	25	....	
2012	61	588	*	*	17	30	....	
North Dakota:								
2009	99	652	*	*	66	41	....	
Ohio:								
2006	44	93	*	*	*	*	....	
2009	31	78	*	*	*	*	....	
2012	39	37	9	1	23	18	....	
Oklahoma:								
2006	20	495	7	138	....	....	....	
2009	53	2,359	12	159	*	*	....	
2012	41	1,089	*	*	*	*	....	
Oregon:								
2006	87	366	*	*	3	3	....	
2009	94	690	*	*	4	5	....	
2012	98	886	*	*	39	44	*	*
South Dakota:								
2006	74	749	*	*	21	27	....	
2009	91	1,183	*	*	37	54	....	
2012	75	799	6	1	56	61	....	
Texas:								
2006	22	1,299	4	92	....	....	....	
2009	36	2,323	9	228	*	*	....	
2012	27	997	4	81	8	68	....	
Washington:								
2006	94	1,077	*	*	2	5	....	
2009	99	1,723	....	....	4	8	*	*
2012	99	1,181	*	*	62	166	....	

See footnote(s) at end of table.

Table 14-20.—Wheat: Pesticide usage, 2006–2012[1]—Continued

State and Year	Herbicide		Insecticide		Fungicide[2]		Other Chemicals[2]	
	Area applied	Pounds applied	Area applied	Pounds applied	Area applied	Pounds applied	Area applied	Pounds applied
	Percent	Thousands	Percent	Thousands	Percent	Thousands	Percent	Thousands
Durum								
Idaho:								
2009	*	*			*	*	*	*
Montana:								
2006	89	250			*	*		
2009	100	522	*	*	*	*		
2012	96	604			9	3		
North Dakota:								
2006	97	862	*	*	*	*		
2009	100	1,618	*	*	30	47		
2012	100	1,146	5	8	51	88		
South Dakota:								
2009	*	*			*	*		
Other Spring								
Colorado:								
2009	50	5	*	*				
Idaho:								
2006	95	272	8	9	12	6	*	*
2009	96	298	4	4	15	7	*	*
Minnesota:								
2006	96	952	5	12	40	45		
2009	97	786	23	118	59	136		
2012	97	664	41	37	76	144		
Montana:								
2006	91	2,172			*	*		
2009	96	2,306	*	*	*	*		
2012	93	2,642	*	*	10	25		
North Dakota:								
2006	95	4,723			14	88		
2009	98	4,824	*	*	47	309		
2012	99	3,855	10	81	64	460		
Oregon:								
2009	88	114	10	1	6	1	*	*
South Dakota:								
2006	84	943	*	*	24	31		
2009	96	864	13	29	43	62		
2012	93	519	*	*	39	43		
Washington:								
2006	96	261	11	19	12	5		
2009	99	505	*	*	*	*		

*Insufficient number of reports to publish data. [1] Data not available for all States for all years. [2] Amount applied excludes biologicals. Note: Planted acres are in table 1-8.
NASS, Environmental, Economics, and Demographics Branch, (202) 720–6146.

STATISTICS OF FERTILIZERS AND PESTICIDES

Table 14-21.—Wheat: Fertilizer usage, 2006–2012 [1]

State and Year	Percent treated and amount applied							
	Nitrogen		Phosphate		Potash		Sulfur [2]	
	Area applied	Pounds applied	Area applied	Pounds applied	Area applied	Pounds applied	Area applied	Pounds applied
	Percent	Millions	Percent	Millions	Percent	Millions	Percent	Millions
Winter Wheat								
Colorado:								
2006	54	36.8	36	13.5	*	*	4	0.7
2009	54	49.6	33	15.1	*	*	6	1.1
2012	72	59.2	40	21.3	3	1.4	11	1.2
Idaho:								
2006	93	80.9	66	13.7	16	2.2	63	9.6
2009	99	85.4	54	11.2	24	5.5	64	8.5
2012	94	91.9	61	14.0	34	6.2	58	10.4
Illinois:								
2006	93	82.1	76	49.8	76	68.4	3	0.5
2009	99	84.2	80	47.3	73	56.8	4	1.0
2012	88	63.3	78	41.2	81	54.2	10	1.3
Kansas:								
2006	88	493.0	66	197.5	8	29.0	5	5.3
2009	94	466.8	62	170.6	7	18.0	10	6.3
2012	94	456.2	65	183.1	8	24.4	9	4.4
Michigan:								
2006	98	57.6	74	22.2	85	33.9	37	3.0
2009	96	48.4	58	17.2	67	31.1	26	1.9
Minnesota:								
2009	92	3.3	67	1.3	46	0.6	15	0.1
Missouri:								
2006	97	90.7	73	35.5	74	44.8	12	1.8
2009	91	67.7	75	30.2	80	39.8	15	1.6
2012	99	72.3	85	37.6	82	47.0	33	3.3
Montana:								
2006	87	96.8	84	46.2	31	9.9	12	2.0
2009	96	130.4	87	54.8	22	4.9	16	2.7
2012	91	135.3	88	57.4	21	5.2	23	3.9
Nebraska:								
2006	75	73.3	57	34.0	4	1.4	13	1.9
2009	84	80.9	65	33.4	6	1.8	19	3.3
2012	83	63.0	64	30.7	7	1.3	23	3.1
North Dakota:								
2009	100	53.9	97	19.2	26	2.0	24	0.7
Ohio:								
2006	98	86.2	84	53.0	82	57.5	23	7.2
2009	98	93.5	72	39.2	73	46.9	32	6.7
2012	89	39.6	83	22.5	80	25.1	25	1.6
Oklahoma:								
2006	89	283.4	65	130.9	8	9.8	*	*
2009	95	295.7	55	95.5	13	7.7	*	*
2012	85	288.8	43	72.1	8	5.7	5	2.6
Oregon:								
2006	95	46.2	12	2.8	10	1.4	48	4.9
2009	97	39.5	23	3.6	*	*	41	3.6
2012	100	64.2	22	3.7	11	3.4	50	7.5
South Dakota:								
2006	82	78.7	57	28.1	15	4.7	12	1.1
2009	83	99.9	55	25.9	15	2.9	*	*
2012	84	81.5	75	29.7	9	1.3	34	3.3
Texas:								
2006	44	152.1	29	47.3	8	20.8	11	5.3
2009	47	141.4	29	46.2	11	6.3	19	10.2
2012	65	203.5	32	55.6	7	6.6	21	14.5
Washington:								
2006	99	140.8	36	12.0	10	3.5	71	18.0
2009	100	130.0	27	8.8	7	3.3	60	13.9
2012	97	133.3	40	13.4	8	2.6	74	15.7

See footnote(s) at end of table.

Table 14-21.—Wheat: Fertilizer usage, 2006–2012 [1]—Continued

State and Year	Nitrogen		Phosphate		Potash		Sulfur [2]	
	Area applied	Pounds applied	Area applied	Pounds applied	Area applied	Pounds applied	Area applied	Pounds applied
	Percent	*Millions*	*Percent*	*Millions*	*Percent*	*Millions*	*Percent*	*Millions*
Spring Durum Wheat								
Idaho:								
2009	*	*	*	*	*	*	*	*
Montana:								
2006	93	20.6	82	7.3	8	0.3	4	0.1
2009	97	29.8	82	11.2	9	1.1	8	0.2
2012	98	32.2	90	12.7	12	0.6	15	0.5
North Dakota:								
2006	92	77.4	71	21.3	7	0.8	4	0.1
2009	99	101.1	87	35.3	11	1.4	9	0.8
2012	99	95.0	89	31.4	12	1.7	11	0.6
South Dakota:								
2009	*	*	*	*	*	*	*	*
Other Spring Wheat								
Colorado:								
2009	*	*	*	*	....	....	....	....
Idaho:								
2006	96	60.7	56	9.5	25	3.5	59	8.5
2009	98	59.1	78	12.5	18	3.0	74	7.7
Minnesota:								
2006	99	148.5	97	64.0	72	31.6	2	0.4
2009	94	148.2	88	56.5	56	31.9	9	0.9
2012	98	151.8	88	48.8	58	23.1	13	2.2
Montana:								
2006	86	129.5	81	57.7	21	9.0	10	2.5
2009	85	115.6	80	45.8	15	3.6	10	2.0
2012	93	146.4	84	70.4	17	7.3	28	8.7
North Dakota:								
2006	99	504.6	88	202.2	21	13.0	11	4.3
2009	96	461.2	89	172.0	18	18.8	6	3.7
2012	98	515.0	90	195.3	29	45.3	18	8.9
Oregon:								
2009	97	8.4	*	*	11	0.4	68	1.1
South Dakota:								
2006	90	119.4	80	55.6	22	11.9	10	3.5
2009	*	*	86	48.7	19	5.9	9	0.8
2012	97	84.8	78	32.9	10	3.8	24	3.0
Washington:								
2006	100	43.6	60	4.7	9	1.6	89	6.4
2009	99	45.8	62	6.0	6	0.7	87	7.8

* Insufficient number of reports to publish data.   [1] Data not available for all States for all years.   Note: Planted acres are in table 1-8.
NASS, Environmental, Economics, and Demographics Branch, (202) 720–6146.

Table 14-22.—Fruits, Pesticides: Percent of bearing acres receiving applications, for surveyed States, 2011 [1]

Crop	Herbicide	Insecticide	Fungicide	Other
		Percent		
Apples	40	84	84	76
Apricots	32	72	79	55
Avocados	23	18	*	22
Blackberries	84	89	88	8
Blueberries	64	84	87	23
Cherries, Sweet	37	85	80	72
Cherries, Tart	40	87	91	79
Dates	19	*		
Figs	21	*		
Grapefruit	60	71	74	67
Grapes, All	50	39	68	36
Grapes, Raisin	35	33	51	28
Grapes, Table	54	67	85	80
Grapes, Wine	53	36	73	32
Kiwifruit	26	*	*	12
Lemons	44	27	25	42
Nectarines	41	59	69	49
Olives	45	24	30	10
Oranges	66	77	61	60
Peaches	33	61	81	35
Pears	36	84	88	88
Plums	35	35	39	40
Prunes	12	14	20	10
Raspberries	87	91	93	19
Tangelos	45	60	55	63
Tangerines	73	62	57	62

* Insufficient number of reports to publish data. [1] Refers to acres receiving one or more applications of a specific agricultural chemical.
NASS, Environmental, Economics, and Demographics Branch, (202) 720–6146.

Table 14-23.—Fruit, Fertilizers: Percent of acres receiving applications, for surveyed States, 2009 [1]

Crop	Nitrogen	Phosphate	Potash	Sulfur
		Percent		
Apples	67	33	34	*
Apricots	67	14	34	*
Avocados	83	47	45	*
Blackberries	78	67	67	*
Blueberries	89	69	77	*
Cherries, Sweet	77	44	49	*
Cherries, Tart	82	40	62	*
Dates	26	13	*	*
Figs	48	19	20	*
Grapefruit	88	65	67	*
Grapes, All	57	26	36	*
Grapes, Raisin	52	15	20	*
Grapes, Table	77	51	53	*
Grapes, Wine	54	27	40	*
Kiwifruit	85	54	65	*
Lemons	85	22	27	*
Nectarines	67	17	22	*
Olives	61	8	24	*
Oranges	68	54	67	*
Peaches	80	23	43	*
Pears	75	27	29	*
Plums	66	27	37	*
Prunes	84	12	49	*
Raspberries	50	47	47	*
Tangelos	97	83	96	*
Tangerines	58	47	55	*

* Insufficient number of reports to publish data. [1] Refers to acres receiving one or more applications of a specific agricultural chemical.
NASS, Environmental, Economics, and Demographics Branch, (202) 720–6146.

Table 14-24.—Vegetables, Pesticides: Percent of acres receiving applications, for surveyed States, 2010[1]

Crop	Herbicide	Insecticide	Fungicide	Other
	Percent			
Asparagus	77	70	34	*
Beans, Snap, Fresh	64	86	84	5
Beans, Snap, Proc	91	75	57	*
Broccoli	71	76	64	*
Cabbage, Fresh	61	95	64	15
Cantatoupes	57	81	45	*
Carrots, Fresh	71	26	74	14
Carrots, Proc	93	86	93	*
Cauliflower	60	59	*	
Celery	58	82	71	*
Sweet Corn, Fresh	71	92	24	4
Sweet Corn, Proc	96	69	24	*
Cucumbers, Fresh	57	68	85	22
Cucumbers, Pickles	80	29	90	6
Eggplant	21	81	71	*
Garlic	69	*	66	
Honeydews	54	*	46	*
Head Lettuce	47	86	86	*
Other Lettuce	33	66	62	*
Onions	88	75	82	29
Green Peas, Proc	93	23	3	
Bell Peppers	32	85	87	34
Pumpkins	63	55	66	11
Spinach	56	68	51	*
Squash	43	60	63	3
Strawberries	16	87	95	32
Tomatoes, Fresh	33	76	76	26
Tomatoes, Proc	72	82	82	19
Watermelons	54	64	86	14

* Insufficient number of reports to publish data.　[1] Refers to acres receiving one or more applications of a specific agricultural chemical.
NASS, Environmental, Economics, and Demographics Branch, (202) 720–6146.

Table 14-25.—Vegetables, Fertilizers: Percent of acres receiving applications, for surveyed States, 2010[1]

Crop	Nitrogen	Phosphate	Potash	Sulfur
	Percent			
Asparagus	95	33	59	13
Beans, Snap, Fresh	86	84	79	13
Beans, Snap, Proc	95	81	86	39
Broccoli	90	37	31	16
Cabbage, Fresh	92	87	81	14
Cantatoupes	98	95	44	32
Carrots, Fresh	80	77	19	3
Carrots, Proc	91	86	87	75
Cauliflower	100	9	96	*
Celery	100	69	93	25
Sweet Corn, Fresh	98	93	77	26
Sweet Corn, Proc	92	70	64	31
Cucumbers, Fresh	94	66	82	8
Cucumbers, Pickles	99	80	61	32
Eggplant	81	67	81	17
Garlic	86	55	16	*
Honeydews	*	*	42	*
Head Lettuce	98	65	*	38
Other Lettuce	98	66	*	41
Onions	97	71	67	28
Green Peas, Proc	71	41	44	19
Bell Peppers	99	88	92	6
Pumpkins	93	67	87	14
Spinach	96	35	21	57
Squash	92	80	87	13
Strawberries	95	90	93	17
Tomatoes, Fresh	98	89	93	30
Tomatoes, Proc	98	74	29	7
Watermelons	99	91	88	25

* Insufficient number of reports to publish data.　[1] Refers to acres receiving one or more applications of a specific agricultural chemical.
NASS, Environmental, Economics, and Demographics Branch, (202) 720–6146.

CHAPTER XV

MISCELLANEOUS AGRICULTURAL STATISTICS

This chapter contains miscellaneous data which do not fit into the preceding chapters. Included here are summary tables on foreign trade in agricultural products; statistics on fishery products; tables on refrigerated warehouses; and statistics on crops in Alaska.

Foreign Agricultural Trade Statistics

Agricultural products, sometimes referred to as food and fiber products, cover a broad range of goods from unprocessed bulk commodities like soybeans, feed corn and wheat to highly-processed, high-value foods and beverages like sausages, bakery goods, ice cream, or beer sold in retail stores and restaurants. All of the products found in Chapters 1-24 (except for fishery products in Chapter 3) of the U.S. Harmonized Tariff Schedule are considered agricultural products. These products generally fall into the following categories: grains, animal feeds, and grain products (like bread and pasta); oilseeds and oilseed products (like canola oil); livestock, poultry and dairy products including live animals, meats, eggs, and feathers; horticultural products including all fresh and processed fruits, vegetables, tree nuts, as well as nursery products and beer and wine; unmanufactured tobacco; and tropical products like sugar, cocoa, and coffee. Certain other products are considered "agricultural," the most significant of which are essential oils (Chapter 33), protein isolates and modified starches (Chapter 35), raw rubber (Chapter 40), raw animal hides and skins (Chapter 41), and wool and cotton (Chapters 51-52). Manufactured products derived from plants or animals, but which are not considered "agricultural" by USDA's definition are cotton yarn, textiles and clothing; leather and leather articles of apparel; and cigarettes and spirits. The World Trade Organization's definition of agricultural products varies in that it includes some products like spirits and tobacco products.

U.S. foreign agricultural trade statistics are based on documents filed by exporters and importers and compiled by the Bureau of the Census. Puerto Rico is a Customs district within the U.S. Customs territory, and its trade with foreign countries is included in U.S. export and import statistics. U.S. export and import statistics include merchandise trade between the U.S. Virgin Islands and foreign countries even though the Virgin Islands of the United States are not officially a part of the U.S. Customs territory.

The export value, the value at the port of exportation, is based on the selling price and includes inland freight, insurance, and other charges to the port. The country of destination is the country of ultimate destination or where the commodities are consumed or further processed.

Agricultural products, like manufactured goods, are often transhipped from the one country to another. Shippers are asked to identify the ultimate destination of a shipment. However, transhipment points are often recorded as the ultimate destination even though the actual point of consumption may be in a neighboring state. Thus, exports to countries which act as transhipment points are generally overstated, while exports to neighboring countries are often understated. Major world transhipment points include the Netherlands, Hong Kong, and Singapore. In such cases, exports are over reported for the Netherlands, but under reported for Germany, Belgium and the United Kingdom. They are overstated to Hong Kong, but under reported to China, and they are overstated to Singapore, but understated to Malaysia and Indonesia.

Imports for consumption are a combination of entries for immediate consumption and withdrawals from bonded warehouses for consumption. The import value, defined generally as the market value in the foreign country, excludes import duties, ocean freight, and marine insurance. The country of origin is defined as the country where the commodities were grown or processed. Where the country of origin is not known, the imports are credited to the country of shipment.

Table 15-1.—Foreign trade: Value of total agricultural exports and imports, United States, fiscal years 2005–2014

Fiscal year ending Sep. 30 [1]	U.S. total domestic exports			U.S. total imports for consumption, customs value			Surplus agricultural exports over agricultural imports
	Total merchandise exports	Agricultural exports [2]	Agricultural exports share of total exports	Total merchandise imports	Agricultural imports	Agricultural imports share of total imports	
	Million dollars	Million dollars	Percent	Million dollars	Million dollars	Percent	Million dollars
2005	877,710	62,517	7	1,618,937	57,711	4	4,806
2006	993,203	68,593	7	1,834,339	64,026	3	4,567
2007	1,110,804	82,220	7	1,906,928	70,063	4	12,157
2008	1,297,574	114,911	9	2,152,782	79,320	4	35,591
2009 [1] ...	1,058,869	96,296	9	1,594,328	73,404	5	22,892
2010	1,224,652	108,529	9	1,844,486	78,963	4	29,566
2011	1,446,591	137,465	10	2,147,138	94,511	4	42,955
2012	1,534,887	135,907	9	2,272,484	103,371	5	32,536
2013	1,562,962	141,144	9	2,262,446	103,872	5	37,272
2014	1,616,778	152,312	9	2,328,525	109,221	5	43,091

[1] Fiscal years Oct. 1–Sept. 30 revised.   [2] Includes food exported for relief or charity by individuals and private agencies.
ERS, Market and Trade Economics Division, (202) 694–5257.

Table 15-2.—Foreign trade: Value and quantity of bulk commodity exports, United States, fiscal years 2006–2014 [1]

Fiscal year	Wheat, unmilled	Rice, milled	Feed grains [2]	Oilseeds [3]	Tobacco unmanufactured	Cotton and linters	Bulk commodities
	Value						
	Million dollars	Million dollars	Million dollars	Million dollars	Million dollars	Million dollars	Million dollars
2006	4,289	1,291	6,808	7,161	1,058	4,678	25,286
2007	6,579	1,273	9,783	9,339	1,143	4,305	32,423
2008	12,332	2,010	15,750	15,580	1,280	4,762	51,714
2009	5,997	2,241	9,982	14,790	1,199	3,561	37,771
2010	5,840	2,296	9,806	17,951	1,223	4,836	41,951
2011	11,504	2,117	13,969	21,571	1,116	8,982	59,260
2012	8,376	1,963	11,719	21,101	1,051	6,551	50,761
2013	10,126	2,212	6,198	22,456	1,193	5,649	47,834
2014	8,257	2,002	12,486	25,753	1,114	4,614	54,226
	Quantity						
	1,000 metric tons	1,000 metric tons	1,000 metric tons	1,000 metric tons	1,000 metric tons	1,000 metric tons	1,000 metric tons
2006	25,005	4,014	61,363	27,593	169	3,707	121,851
2007	29,636	3,306	59,051	31,592	180	3,128	126,893
2008	32,847	3,899	68,205	32,148	184	2,970	140,253
2009	22,545	3,388	51,442	35,713	168	2,805	116,062
2010	25,698	4,260	53,849	42,499	185	2,746	129,236
2011	34,583	3,920	49,170	41,365	174	3,113	132,325
2012	26,969	3,578	40,024	39,247	167	2,731	112,716
2013	31,110	3,848	20,460	35,862	165	2,921	94,366
2014	27,081	3,355	56,605	46,031	152	2,202	135,426

[1] Fiscal years, Oct. 1–Sept. 30.   [2] Corn, barley, sorghum, rye, and oats.   [3] Soybeans, peanuts, rapeseed, cottonseed, sunflowerseed, safflowerseed, and others.
ERS, Market and Trade Economics Division, (202) 694–5257.

Table 15-3.—Agricultural exports: Value to top 50 countries of destination, United States, fiscal years 2012–2014[1]

Country	2012	2013	2014
	Million dollars	Million dollars	Million dollars
China	23,381.4	23,360.9	25,699.4
Canada	20,048.3	21,458.3	21,786.9
Mexico	18,874.2	17,938.5	19,498.2
Japan	13,775.9	12,419.4	13,360.0
European Union-28	8,916.8	11,548.6	12,709.9
Korea, South	6,196.6	5,203.4	6,867.5
Hong Kong	3,386.4	3,630.1	4,052.4
Taiwan	3,088.3	3,178.9	3,491.3
Indonesia	2,474.1	2,619.5	2,964.7
Philippines	2,306.4	2,428.7	2,774.3
Turkey	1,886.5	2,176.9	2,066.3
Egypt	1,788.2	1,661.1	1,851.4
Venezuela	1,528.7	1,600.4	1,322.9
Russia	1,504.1	1,316.1	1,165.2
Vietnam	1,499.3	2,066.1	2,231.9
Thailand	1,305.0	1,445.9	1,613.5
Australia(*)	1,227.3	1,345.0	1,536.4
Saudi Arabia	1,134.8	1,128.4	1,405.0
Nigeria	1,077.4	1,110.7	901.2
Dominican Republic	1,043.4	1,132.3	1,281.2
United Arab Emirates	1,023.4	1,173.8	1,259.1
Guatemala	958.2	939.9	1,101.4
Malaysia	879.1	1,024.5	1,010.1
Colombia	845.3	1,418.0	2,310.8
India	764.3	971.6	987.8
Morocco	686.0	455.5	444.6
Singapore	664.1	734.4	801.2
Costa Rica	644.5	482.9	600.8
Chile	631.2	902.2	856.7
Honduras	619.5	588.7	619.0
Israel(*)	583.4	625.6	715.9
Peru	577.0	682.4	958.3
Panama	529.6	571.4	668.2
Brazil	528.9	1,556.7	1,642.3
El Salvador	527.0	466.4	525.3
Cuba	417.5	415.3	300.6
Jamaica	412.8	447.0	418.1
Ecuador	391.0	466.0	437.9
New Zealand(*)	359.1	394.8	424.0
Trinidad and Tobago	334.1	380.4	398.1
Haiti	329.2	408.1	363.9
Pakistan	327.4	360.7	271.2
Switzerland(*)	283.4	459.3	389.6
South Africa	270.6	279.8	281.3
Jordan	249.5	238.9	237.7
Bahamas, The	247.5	243.9	240.2
Angola	241.1	282.8	276.3
Nicaragua	234.2	216.1	212.9
Tunisia	226.2	178.5	158.6
Bangladesh	198.1	248.6	289.7
Other countries	4,480.6	4,760.4	4,530.4
World Total[2]	135,906.7	141,143.7	152,311.6

[1] Fiscal years Oct. 1–Sept. 30.   [2] Totals may not add due to rounding.
ERS, Market and Trade Economics Divison, (202) 694–5257.

Table 15-4.—Foreign trade in agricultural products: Value of exports by principal commodity groups, United States, fiscal years 2011–2014 [1]

Commodity	2011	2012	2013	2014
	1,000 dollars	*1,000 dollars*	*1,000 dollars*	*1,000 dollars*
Total Merchandise Exports	1,446,591,062	1,534,887,100	1,562,961,800	1,616,777,930
Nonagricultural U.S. Exports (Na)	1,309,125,623	1,398,980,407	1,421,818,086	1,464,466,319
Total Agricultural exports	137,465,439	135,906,693	141,143,714	152,311,611
Animals and animal products	26,696,837	28,951,218	30,563,844	32,967,495
Animals, live	693,576	792,824	826,574	660,926
Cattle	299,741	375,719	365,913	194,661
Horses,mules,burros-live	369,794	379,217	423,082	442,306
Swine, live	17,919	32,920	30,833	17,899
Sheep, live	5,374	3,605	5,621	4,930
Other live Animals	747	1,364	1,125	1,129
Red meat and products	11,418,923	12,426,938	12,629,569	14,054,351
Beef and Veal	4,555,357	4,770,766	5,217,247	6,036,279
Beef and Veal, fresh/frozen	4,387,110	4,596,817	5,019,369	5,757,388
Beef prep/pres	168,247	173,949	197,879	278,891
Horsemeat, fresh/frozen	11	27	58	60
Lamb and Goat, fr/frozen	17,678	16,326	16,734	17,318
Pork	4,910,184	5,549,347	5,167,839	5,672,702
Pork, fresh/frozen	4,271,994	4,957,912	4,470,063	4,919,156
Pork, prep/pres	638,191	591,435	697,776	753,546
Variety meats	1,273,117	1,456,200	1,557,060	1,674,100
Beef variety meats	654,371	712,544	720,139	783,918
Pork variety meats	579,537	691,389	778,117	825,558
Other variety meats	39,209	52,268	58,805	64,624
Other meats, fresh/frozen	662,576	634,271	670,630	653,892
Poultry and products	5,485,626	6,153,107	6,489,572	6,406,657
Poultry, live	193,359	198,750	206,944	211,355
Baby chicks	180,067	187,288	193,219	196,389
Other live poultry	13,292	11,462	13,724	14,966
Poultry meats	4,265,286	4,918,546	5,190,337	5,045,749
Chickens, fresh/frozen	3,348,639	3,897,792	4,070,972	3,857,742
Turkeys, fresh/frozen	494,097	577,831	590,751	634,181
Other poultry, fresh/frozen	19,135	9,674	5,752	5,103
Poultry meats, prep	403,415	433,249	522,862	548,722
Poultry, misc	589,550	573,574	469,847	524,690
Eggs	437,431	462,236	622,445	624,864
Dairy products	4,616,234	5,274,236	6,212,803	7,499,843
Evaporated/condensed milk	38,412	47,817	92,844	67,067
Nonfat dry milk	1,450,988	1,418,128	1,875,632	2,435,597
Butter and milkfat	232,694	165,302	247,159	309,429
Cheese	896,931	1,104,752	1,242,158	1,703,060
Whey,fluid/dried	657,204	812,526	896,067	1,046,924
Other dairy products	1,340,005	1,725,711	1,858,944	1,937,767
Fats, oils, and greases	1,313,878	977,229	716,282	672,082
Lard	61,014	64,264	51,211	60,315
Tallow, inedible	737,011	534,282	371,983	373,629
Other animal fats	515,852	378,682	293,088	238,138
Hides and skins	2,626,741	2,770,110	3,058,069	2,989,633
Bovine hides, whole	1,089,967	1,123,174	1,289,832	1,435,506
Other cattle hides	72,072	68,544	90,244	53,050
Calf skins, whole	332,322	227,170	116,369	98,323
Horse hides, whole	408,344	431,316	445,581	404,630
Sheep and lamb skins	31,763	30,534	23,133	21,011
Other hides and Skin	326,708	361,408	487,213	478,489
Furskins	365,564	527,964	605,697	498,624
Mink pelts	333,088	480,372	541,561	418,697
Other furskins	32,476	47,592	64,136	79,926
Wool and mohair	25,577	19,309	22,948	21,811
Sausage casings	211,852	197,714	225,866	241,421
Bull semen	118,601	131,784	136,458	157,350
Misc animal products	185,830	207,967	245,703	263,420
Grains and feeds	38,110,186	33,678,863	31,694,568	36,681,392
Wheat,unmilled	11,504,420	8,375,731	10,126,210	8,257,060
Wheat flour	166,283	150,795	142,726	132,983
Other wheat products	163,218	170,846	180,993	186,792
Rice-paddy, milled	2,117,116	1,962,970	2,212,059	2,001,730
Feed grains and products	14,474,075	12,289,277	6,739,813	13,001,684
Feed grain	13,969,132	11,719,232	6,198,202	12,486,009
Barley	45,083	59,416	46,522	87,072
Corn	12,882,255	11,216,737	5,570,678	11,088,625
Grain sorghum	1,033,386	431,331	570,124	1,297,689
Oats	5,445	5,054	4,147	6,595
Rye	2,963	6,694	6,731	6,028

See footnote(s) at end of table.

Table 15-4.—Foreign trade in agricultural products: Value of exports by principal commodity groups, United States, fiscal years 2011–2014 [1]—Continued

Commodity	2011	2012	2013	2014
	1,000 dollars	*1,000 dollars*	*1,000 dollars*	*1,000 dollars*
Feed grains and products--Continued				
Feed grain products	504,942	570,046	541,611	515,675
Popcorn	77,571	90,015	103,944	119,579
Blended food products	75,998	118,372	69,710	60,014
Other grain products	3,141,147	3,519,141	3,754,795	3,893,572
Feeds and fodders	6,390,358	7,001,716	8,364,318	9,027,980
Corn by-products	730,789	718,565	914,538	923,183
Alfalfa meal and cubes	41,623	58,516	59,124	63,557
Beef pulp	81,183	99,055	110,911	114,386
Citrus pulp pellets	45,409	30,740	36,643	19,938
Other feeds and fodders	5,491,354	6,094,841	7,243,102	7,906,917
Fruit and prep	5,897,072	6,430,836	6,603,903	6,752,461
Fruits, fresh	4,396,191	4,829,857	4,987,769	4,998,833
Citrus fruits, fresh	1,036,101	1,008,711	1,004,071	973,927
Grapefruit, fresh	177,467	158,852	144,746	125,390
Lemons and limes, fresh	128,595	126,292	140,851	219,313
Oranges and tanger, fresh	711,930	709,795	704,456	621,251
Other citrus, fresh	18,108	13,773	14,017	7,972
Noncitrus Fruits, fresh	3,360,090	3,821,146	3,983,698	4,024,906
Apples, fresh	904,672	1,025,215	1,161,541	1,052,325
Berries, fresh	635,967	696,356	746,736	752,005
Cherries, fresh	415,059	502,294	412,312	469,986
Grapes, fresh	671,566	799,994	827,400	949,466
Melons, fresh	164,244	161,513	159,238	163,124
Peaches, fresh	149,160	168,287	173,358	167,217
Pears, fresh	163,120	203,678	223,261	224,493
Plums-fresh	75,873	79,410	72,233	67,105
Other noncitrus, fresh	180,430	184,399	207,620	179,185
Fruits, dried	679,694	690,630	659,410	711,964
Raisin, dried	366,966	386,351	364,571	432,677
Prunes, dried	176,798	170,865	187,258	172,651
Other dried fruits	135,931	133,414	107,582	106,636
Fruits, canned	493,076	532,129	547,351	581,479
Fruits, frozen	114,018	129,127	147,750	158,842
Other fruits, prep	214,091	249,093	261,624	301,344
Fruits juices	1,327,596	1,295,231	1,284,983	1,252,045
Apple juice	34,961	36,856	39,186	39,527
Grape juice	83,515	97,209	97,668	84,969
Grapefruit juice	61,650	56,574	56,303	46,886
Orange juice	561,108	457,338	461,506	465,846
Other fruit juices	586,362	647,254	630,319	614,817
Wine	1,232,920	1,285,765	1,474,169	1,447,068
Nuts and prep	5,419,551	6,435,595	7,767,580	8,646,761
Almonds	2,669,458	3,301,381	3,876,728	4,552,878
Filberts	64,413	86,576	93,185	113,445
Peanuts	273,452	324,399	603,484	513,114
Pistachios	804,005	916,303	1,131,652	1,236,453
Walnuts	989,671	1,051,572	1,258,140	1,421,835
Pecans	325,683	435,558	430,842	372,702
Other nuts	292,870	319,806	373,550	436,334
Vegetables and prep	5,739,095	6,107,950	6,587,469	7,028,460
Vegetables fresh	2,251,302	2,153,699	2,329,931	2,404,896
Aspargus, fresh	31,345	36,000	32,540	30,417
Broccoli, fresh	121,474	128,279	129,714	135,231
Carrots, fresh	132,765	121,957	122,427	116,165
Cabbage, fresh	22,852	28,483	42,182	35,589
Celery, fresh	78,913	74,251	96,514	81,309
Cauliflower, fresh	121,999	124,706	132,155	142,525
Corn sweet, fresh	58,756	52,561	52,422	46,327
Cucumbers, fresh	22,837	17,740	16,589	16,421
Garlic, fresh	20,553	11,452	13,055	15,957
Lettuce, fresh	467,245	455,254	493,796	473,155
Mushrooms, fresh	37,433	36,668	33,478	33,728
Onions and shallots, fresh	184,372	170,847	186,731	205,965
Peppers, fresh	87,794	82,141	86,815	91,828
Potatoes, fresh	218,418	208,230	213,332	201,937
Tomatoes, fresh	197,951	150,308	152,265	165,666
Other vegetables, fresh	446,595	454,821	525,916	612,676
Vegetables, frozen	1,105,705	1,303,749	1,352,405	1,435,236
Corn, sweet, frozen	80,787	87,627	89,164	93,305
Potatoes, frozen	839,025	1,023,842	1,064,105	1,131,200
Other vegetables, frozen	185,893	192,281	199,136	210,731
Vegetables, canned	504,215	545,417	651,418	764,985
Pulses	587,465	682,027	747,062	797,204
Dried Beans	275,069	361,126	361,821	358,772
Dried Peas	158,138	166,627	178,971	252,473
Dried Lentils	115,875	103,007	138,152	141,155
Dried chickpeas	38,384	51,267	68,117	44,804
Other vegetables, prep/pres	1,290,407	1,423,058	1,506,653	1,626,139

See footnote(s) at end of table.

Table 15-4.—Foreign trade in agricultural products: Value of exports by principal commodity groups, United States, fiscal years 2011–2014 [1]—Continued

Commodity	2011	2012	2013	2014
	1,000 dollars	*1,000 dollars*	*1,000 dollars*	*1,000 dollars*
Oilseeds and products	29,388,327	28,813,150	31,992,749	34,881,752
Oilcake and meal	3,445,156	3,955,009	5,587,337	5,810,383
Bran and residues	25,536	32,117	29,152	19,163
Corn oilcake and meal	40,177	22,358	8,543	47,558
Soybean meal	3,332,698	3,844,954	5,472,503	5,687,203
Other oilcake and meal	46,745	55,579	77,139	56,459
Oilseeds	21,570,968	21,100,708	22,455,538	25,753,288
Rapeseed	142,144	150,566	105,708	110,359
Safflower seeds	0	143	1,433	1,438
Soybeans	20,379,550	19,856,690	20,886,753	24,099,072
Sunflowerseeds	139,901	110,978	156,398	138,988
Peanuts, oilstock	85,028	68,698	215,846	174,413
Other oilseeds	136,486	90,572	121,978	113,385
Protein substances	687,859	823,060	967,424	1,115,633
Vegetable oils	4,372,203	3,757,434	3,949,874	3,318,081
Soybean oil	1,733,588	829,936	1,147,763	809,767
Cottonseed oil	45,963	72,287	60,005	41,029
Sunflower oil	55,814	36,799	44,545	57,629
Corn oil	510,645	619,427	567,261	464,861
Peanut oil	5,936	8,237	13,840	10,438
Rapeseed oil	259,045	346,219	246,541	123,320
Safflower oil	24,016	28,650	32,303	19,799
Other vegetable oils/waxes	1,737,197	1,815,878	1,837,614	1,791,239
Tobacco, unmfg	1,116,154	1,051,037	1,192,610	1,113,706
Tobacco, light air	257,743	236,807	262,622	210,593
Tobacco, flue	612,283	553,811	705,626	685,739
Other tobacco, unmfg	246,128	260,419	224,362	217,374
Cotton, ex linters	8,819,611	6,533,609	5,604,211	4,598,448
Cotton linters	162,599	17,692	44,764	15,464
Essential oils	1,479,421	1,582,468	1,688,297	1,711,321
Seeds, field and garden	1,355,532	1,444,510	1,573,728	1,692,488
Sugar and tropical products	4,586,182	5,181,578	5,258,495	5,267,221
Sugar and related products	1,767,532	1,977,000	2,017,478	1,857,763
Sugar, cane or beet	161,998	169,688	162,624	151,250
Related sugar products	1,605,534	1,807,312	1,854,854	1,706,513
Coffee	886,873	1,079,304	983,628	959,746
Cocoa	200,043	220,200	218,457	218,178
Chocolate and prep	1,153,780	1,284,533	1,424,038	1,557,370
Tea, including herbal	350,033	377,424	391,511	423,930
Spices	133,027	148,332	153,931	175,170
Rubber, crude	91,526	91,957	66,312	71,635
Fibers, ex cotton	3,368	2,827	3,140	3,428
Other hort products	4,533,467	5,208,711	5,710,532	5,998,229
Hops, including extract	251,866	205,155	206,611	204,794
Starches, not wheat/corn	115,965	113,843	126,163	141,556
Yeasts	84,154	95,745	93,135	99,988
Misc hort products	4,081,481	4,793,968	5,284,622	5,551,892
Nursery & greenhouse	368,923	376,962	390,306	399,269
Beverages ex juice	1,231,966	1,511,519	1,711,507	1,858,031

[1] Fiscal years, Oct. 1–Sept. 30. Totals may not add due to rounding.
ERS, Market and Trade Economics Division, (202) 694–5257. Compiled from reports of the U.S. Department of Commerce.

Table 15-5.—Foreign trade in agricultural products: Value of imports by principal groups, United States, fiscal years 2011–2014 [1]

Product	2011	2012	2013	2014
	1,000 dollars	*1,000 dollars*	*1,000 dollars*	*1,000 dollars*
Total merchandise imports	2,147,137,809	2,272,483,900	2,262,445,800	2,328,524,585
Non-agricultural U.S. imports	2,052,627,151	2,169,113,214	2,158,574,083	2,219,303,985
Total agricultural imports	94,510,658	103,370,686	103,871,717	109,220,600
Animals & prods.	11,948,291	13,354,489	13,859,277	16,155,248
Animals - live ex. poultry	2,092,092	2,356,798	2,466,606	2,909,811
Cattle and calves	1,451,045	1,676,472	1,784,224	2,128,025
Horses, mules, burros	251,158	302,206	327,427	333,505
Swine	355,076	347,527	329,321	410,090
Sheep, Live	1027	396	273	482
Other live animals	33,786	30,198	25,361	37,709
Red meat & products	5,303,879	5,863,576	6,009,357	7,483,945
Beef & veal	3,010,592	3,620,358	3,672,658	4,727,055
Beef & veal - fr. or froz.	2,747,964	3,278,264	3,363,683	4,407,107
Beef & veal - prep. or pres.	262,628	342,094	308,975	319,948
Pork	1,253,830	1,294,023	1,381,328	1,654,193
Pork - fr. or froz.	949,501	1,003,072	1,092,292	1,343,235
Pork - prep. or pres.	304,329	290,951	289,036	310,958
Mutton, goat & lamb	745,330	617,676	623,144	726,861
Horsemeat - fr. or froz.	1194	1769	1,482	1,799
Variety meats - fr. or froz.	156,337	207,992	210,473	262,604
Other meats - fr. or froz.	49,805	32,117	41,185	45,469
Other meats & prods.	86,791	89,640	79,087	65,964
Poultry and prods.	519,818	612,979	650,271	699,909
Poultry - live	35,624	41,267	45,456	42,887
Poultry meat	282,757	306,244	360,170	376,987
Eggs	43,439	42,653	40,955	57,218
Poultry, misc.	157,997	222,814	203,690	222,817
Dairy products.	2,857,556	3,136,708	3,173,471	3,442,205
Milk & cream, fr. or dried	79,885	105,237	110,713	110,054
Butter & butterfat mixtures	32,173	75,826	64,415	67,670
Cheese	1,061,286	1,059,462	1,148,953	1,230,481
Casein & mixtures	623,877	690,476	621,859	702,819
Other dairy prods.	1,060,333	1,205,707	1,227,531	1,331,181
Fats, oils, & greases	166,428	192,847	190,787	181,339
Hides & skins	196,727	218,841	282,069	293,240
Sheep & lamb skins	542	868	760	867
Other hides & skins	53,588	48,678	51,344	58,266
Furskins	142,598	169,296	229,966	234,107
Wool - unmfg.	29,516	34,067	24,209	21,718
Apparel grade wool	14,969	19,692	14,650	11,844
Carpet grade wool	14,548	14,375	9,559	9,874
Sausage casings	123,757	140,509	166,277	192,720
Bull semen	34,197	28,500	31,827	41,741
Misc. animal prods	623,777	769,335	864,117	888,227
Silk, raw	545	328	286	392
Grains & feeds	8,494,118	9,669,851	11,453,460	11,007,832
Wheat, ex. seed	508,185	832,264	1,003,536	1,086,258
Corn, unmilled	155,471	186,685	1,176,437	150,532
Oats, unmilled	348,508	410,820	361,101	516,729
Barley, unmilled	35,789	139,386	135,746	151,536
Rice	601,220	659,227	712,847	772,381
Biscuits & wafers	2,629,793	2,819,593	2,996,181	3,102,120
Pasta & noodles	488,464	549,131	566,383	613,896
Other grains & preps.	2,362,273	2,492,291	2,790,631	2,894,382
Feeds & fodders, ex. oilcake	1,364,413	1,580,455	1,710,549	1,719,998
Fruits & preps.	9,733,344	10,425,400	11,410,624	12,584,861
Fruits - fr. or froz.	7,629,891	8,215,160	8,977,530	10,129,635
Apples, fresh	132,950	160,670	219,653	237,193
Avocados	864,921	846,883	1,003,422	1,480,924
Berries, excl. strawberries	964,505	1,154,711	1,231,621	1,415,920
Bananas & plantains - fr. or froz.	1,970,399	2,056,919	2,141,374	2,185,461
Citrus, fresh	525,188	515,688	588,558	782,151
Grapes, fresh	988,344	1,089,336	1,190,056	1,195,201
Kiwifruit, fresh	56,594	68,615	85,324	100,522
Mangoes	346,583	361,332	450,658	467,746
Melons	480,782	450,002	539,482	560,572
Peaches	50,183	53,654	48,490	40,388
Pears	95,213	78,480	106,961	119,466
Pineapples - fr. or froz.	483,970	526,363	555,252	655,172
Plums	44,064	34,077	42,912	30,259
Strawberries - fr. or froz.	334,424	494,337	446,977	503,926
Other fruits - fr. or froz.	291,771	324,091	326,787	354,734
Fruits - prep. or pres.	2,103,453	2,210,240	2,433,094	2,455,226
Bananas & plantains - prep. or pres.	90,630	111,499	116,561	125,050
Pineapples - canned or prep.	344,089	311,425	328,325	303,818
Other fruits - prep. or pres.	1,668,734	1,787,316	1,988,208	2,026,357
Fruit juices	1,839,712	1,763,695	1,894,440	1,839,942
Apple juice	734,259	677,973	680,949	597,027
Grape juice	118,295	133,202	169,039	129,266
Grapefruit juice	639	888	1391	652
Lemon juice	117,553	70,287	59,067	90,055
Lime juice	24,702	24,963	22,090	28,870
Orange juice	406,300	392,304	567,613	587,723
Pineapple juice	117,874	109,984	114,120	113,823
Other fruit juice	320,090	354,094	280,172	292,526

See footnote(s) at end of table.

Table 15-5.—Foreign trade in agricultural products: Value of imports by principal groups, United States, fiscal years 2011–2014 [1]—Continued

Product	2011	2012	2013	2014
	1,000 dollars	*1,000 dollars*	*1,000 dollars*	*1,000 dollars*
Nuts & preps	1,777,245	1,981,078	1,922,555	2,187,791
Brazil nuts	57,688	53,091	52,616	60,683
Cashew nuts	913,506	900,198	933,191	986,209
Chestnuts	11,915	13,824	13,014	13,733
Coconut meat	153,372	175,891	151,125	196,116
Filberts	36,775	31,793	46,702	53,090
Macadamia nuts	89,563	85,058	111,438	116,480
Pecans	266,784	318,029	243,447	298,087
Pistachio nuts	4,906	7,650	8,304	6,068
Other nuts	242,737	395,544	362,719	457,325
Vegetables & preps.	9,999,068	10,423,843	11,192,105	11,453,086
Vegetables, fresh	5,724,475	5,837,365	6,551,970	6,660,226
Tomatoes, fresh	2,067,045	1,885,713	1,935,648	1,936,263
Asparagus fresh	419,141	443,125	578,374	497,581
Beans, fresh	76,531	80,115	96,128	96,076
Cabbage, fresh	30,405	20,344	32,179	33,716
Carrots, fresh	78,247	66,435	73,577	74,816
Cauliflower & broccoli, fresh	130,819	128,651	157,531	176,819
Celery, fresh	17,546	15,954	25,845	22,509
Cucumbers, fresh	375,220	482,080	556,948	627,885
Eggplant, fresh	63,586	64,262	64,267	58,927
Endive, fresh	4,238	4,715	4,650	4,648
Garlic, fresh	114,636	126,612	191,795	131,122
Lettuce, fresh	162,371	164,738	190,079	202,298
Okra, fresh	21,442	17,114	19,730	27,099
Onions, fresh	288,426	282,383	338,304	354,206
Peas, fresh	61,509	66,490	78,598	72,164
Peppers, fresh	933,115	1,030,965	1,183,174	1,273,512
Potatoes, fresh	167,819	149,048	126,043	172,820
Radishes, fresh	15,398	20,068	19,713	19,263
Squash, fresh	210,545	278,197	305,618	303,461
Other vegetables, fresh	486,435	510,356	573,771	575,041
Vegetables - prep. or pres.	2,567,088	2,712,460	2,719,501	2,813,471
Bamboo shoots, preserved	32,918	38,212	34,353	28,104
Cucumbers, preserved	48,995	58,572	52,123	43,131
Garlic, dried	62,001	49,949	63,663	63,219
Olives - prep. or pres.	412,213	385,610	384,794	428,568
Mushrooms, canned	118,247	127,220	102,113	110,666
Mushrooms, dried	32,012	27,724	26,891	32,679
Onions, preserved	30,324	33,975	38,383	38,924
Artichokes - prep.	175,098	174,682	137,132	137,813
Asparagus- prep.	29,125	32,271	41,569	24,450
Tomatoes, incl. paste & sauce	156,476	168,441	173,760	180,805
Waterchestnuts	21,583	25,854	30,652	30,854
Peppers & pimentos, prep.	92,174	85,033	99,393	95,195
Veg Starches, excl. wheat & corn	122,993	142,134	137,829	147,075
Soups & sauces	295,906	326,297	361,011	396,709
Other vegetables - prep. or pres.	937,023	1,036,487	1,035,835	1,055,281
Vegetables, frozen	1,507,711	1,632,290	1,701,398	1,714,823
Tomatoes, frozen	6,162	5,861	5,127	6,395
Asparagus, frozen	15,126	18,699	13,970	15,667
Beans, frozen	61,740	74,039	84,402	78,246
Carrots, frozen	4,033	4,555	4,601	4,839
Cauliflower & broccoli, frozen	313,090	320,723	299,442	321,294
Okra, frozen	11,437	8,765	7,487	10,184
Peas, frozen	32,106	36,417	39,036	42,499
Potatoes, frozen	655,572	709,333	795,787	753,509
Other vegetables, frozen	408,444	453,900	451,547	482,192
Pulses	199,795	241,728	219,236	264,565
Dried peas	31,093	35,915	53,662	67,733
Dried beans	128,862	162,879	124,154	140,940
Dried lentils	20,521	23,695	19,552	30,915
Dried chickpeas	19,318	19,239	21,867	24,977
Sugar & related prods.	4,816,301	4,986,478	4,340,821	4,473,561
Sugar - cane & beet	2,534,637	2,556,359	1,714,158	1,645,665
Molasses	146,411	168,505	184,901	144,233
Confectionery prods.	1,387,248	1,454,170	1,534,290	1,655,518
Other sugar & related prods.	748,004	807,445	907,472	1,028,146
Cocoa & products	4,685,534	4,168,761	4,083,919	4,739,945
Coffee & products	7,337,215	7,782,441	6,056,712	6,011,339
Tea	622,310	660,930	704,044	695,123
Spices & herbs	1,210,909	1,291,457	1,420,601	1,581,211
Pepper	607,978	707,710	764,392	816,148
Other spices & herbs	602,931	583,747	656,209	765,063

See footnote(s) at end of table.

Table 15-5.—Foreign trade in agricultural products: Value of imports by principal groups, United States, fiscal years 2011–2014 [1]—Continued

Product	2011	2012	2013	2014
	1,000 dollars	*1,000 dollars*	*1,000 dollars*	*1,000 dollars*
Drugs, crude & natural	1,392,995	1,473,700	1,564,449	1,638,011
Essential oils	2,090,317	2,163,315	2,374,077	2,585,283
Fibers, excl. cotton	84,266	90,759	78,292	89,314
Rubber & gums	4,430,322	3,790,943	2,672,674	2,138,416
Tobacco - unmfg.	756,763	865,069	866,192	889,594
Tobacco - filler	732,559	838,622	834,275	855,269
Tobacco - scrap	14,622	20,707	23,714	22,892
Other tobacco	9,582	5,740	8,203	11,434
Beverages, ex. fruit juice	10,395,887	11,171,323	11,569,825	12,358,058
Wine	4,738,880	5,037,869	5,306,943	5,430,147
Malt beverages	3,526,256	3,736,505	3,595,254	4,101,669
Other beverages	2,130,752	2,396,949	2,667,628	2,826,242
Oilseeds & prods.	7,491,336	8,293,413	8,539,795	9,647,789
Oilseeds & oilnuts	681,868	892,520	1,266,536	1,983,568
Flaxseed	105,558	130,408	118,234	126,670
Rapeseed	265,475	299,758	259,468	468,415
Soybeans	197,966	266,620	684,079	1,098,150
Sunflower seeds	31,380	35,617	42,735	46,586
Other oilseeds & oilnuts	81,489	160,117	162,021	243,748
Oils & waxes - vegetable	6,165,783	6,426,713	5,959,013	6,101,733
Castor oil	104,287	86,171	79,187	80,634
Coconut oil	824,863	765,640	561,591	734,355
Cottonseed oil	60	4532	9337	13,498
Olive oil	945,850	953,317	1,070,099	1,145,266
Palm oil	1,060,917	1,125,463	1,142,199	1,029,905
Palm kernel oil	481,858	439,969	282,433	312,751
Peanut oil	26,594	23,732	21,577	27,752
Rapeseed oil	1,760,654	1,906,072	1,619,207	1,598,346
Soybean oil	88,317	83,628	114,527	79,161
Sesame oil	58,766	60,294	65,420	70,003
Other vegetable oils	813,618	977,896	993,436	1,010,061
Oilcake & meal	643,684	974,180	1,314,246	1,562,488
Cotton, excl. linters	9521	13080	6,679	9,143
Cotton, linters	2,594	2,177	0	488
Seeds - field & garden	924,913	1,283,962	1,644,131	1,379,586
Cut flowers	867,850	962,416	1,000,903	1,013,218
Nursery stock, bulbs, etc.	656,947	663,073	669,436	704,908
Other hort products	2,942,900	6,089,030	4,546,706	4,036,853
Hops, including extract	32,006	33,356	41,373	43,828
Starches, ex wheat/corn	108,904	100,487	105,419	117,403
Yeasts	239,278	254,195	278,700	292,709
Misc hort products	2,562,712	5,700,993	4,121,215	3,582,914

[1] Fiscal years, Oct. 1–Sept. 30.

ERS, Market and Trade Economics Division, (202) 694–5257. Compiled from reports of the U.S. Department of Commerce.

Table 15-6.—Agricultural exports: Value of U.S. exports to the top market, China, by commodity, fiscal years 2012–2014 [1]

Commodity	Value		
	2012	2013	2014
	1,000 dollars	*1,000 dollars*	*1,000 dollars*
Total agricultural exports	23,381,366	23,360,863	25,699,412
Animals and animal products	3,066,484	3,703,483	3,381,282
Animals Live-Ex Poultry	20,034	17,240	9,878
Cattle, live	12	0	0
Horses, live	2,582	490	3,652
Swine, Live	17,440	16,750	6,226
Other live animals	0	0	0
Red meat and Products	813,683	789,101	569,331
Beef and Veal	161	0	121
Beef and Veal-fresh or frozen	0	0	121
Beef-prep or pres	161	0	0
Lamb, goat-fr-ch-froz	0	0	0
Pork	559,230	345,563	287,046
Pork-fresh or frozen	547,073	320,058	279,180
Pork-prep or pres	12,158	25,505	7,866
Variety meats, Ed Offals	202,280	340,673	205,351
Beef variety meats	963	159	150
Pork variety meats	200,133	340,114	204,284
Other variety meats	1184	400	917
Other meats-fr or froz	52,012	102,865	76,813
Poultry and poultry products	375,853	529,405	379,918
Poultry-Live	36,715	49,552	31,212
Baby chicks	36,378	47,069	28,436
Other live poultry	337	2482	2775
Poultry meats	171,515	247,506	210,425
Chickens-fresh or frozen	103,988	164,945	144,451
Turkeys-fresh or frozen	64,398	72,344	52,591
Other poultry-fresh or frozen	401	371	191
Poultry meats-prep or pres.	2,727	9,847	13,191
Poultry misc.	165,228	229,925	136,667
Eggs	2,396	2,422	1,614
Dairy prods	431,740	607,814	767,078
Evap and condensed milk	1323	4774	4,924
Nonfat dry milk	50,401	165,929	245,078
Butter and Milkfat	601	846	1633
Cheese	36,967	39,537	58,954
Whey, fluid or dried	194,408	220,542	267,593
Other dairy products	148,039	176,185	188,896
Fats, oils and greases	3,064	3,305	2,937
Lard	51	2182	2088
Other animal fats	3,013	1,123	849
Hides and skins include furs	1,302,601	1,617,190	1,507,167
Bovine hides, whole	617,811	797,668	919,772
Other cattle hides-pieces	21,857	51,166	34,686
Calf skins, whole	97,634	53,480	31,587
Horse hides whole	251,268	294,130	245,501
Sheep and lamb skins	25,759	16,349	15,230
Other hides and skins, ex.furs	154,434	222,718	186,826
Furskins	133,839	181,680	73,564
Mink pelts	124,119	162,576	66,121
Other furskins	9,720	19,103	7,443
Wool and Mohair	9,544	10,247	6,929
Sausage casings	84,823	94,107	96,855
Bull semen	7,743	8,288	15,500
Misc animal products-other	17,399	26,787	25,690
Grains and feeds	2,946,691	3,296,030	4,587,554
Wheat, unmilled	257,968	1,038,466	439,795
Wheat flour	25	407	145
Other wheat products	1,846	1,831	2,349
Rice-paddy,milled parb	136	353	253
Feed grains and products	1,598,160	709,365	1,670,566
Feed grains	1,595,145	705,663	1,665,355
Corn	1,595,145	678,214	571,144
Grain sorghums	0	27433	1094194
Oats	0	16	18
Rye	0	0	0
Feed grain products	3,015	3,702	5,211
Popcorn	9,539	10,878	17,422
Blended food products	54137	1,765	1,290
Other grain prods	56,843	71,821	84,395
Feeds and fodders, ex.oilcakes	968,037	1,461,145	2,371,339
Corn by-products	1436	1,520	1,779
Alfalfa meal and cubes	1,385	1,614	14,836
Citrus pulp pellet	1178	32	0
Other feeds and fodder	964,038	1,457,980	2,354,723

See footnote(s) at end of table.

Table 15-6.—Agricultural exports: Value of U.S. exports to the top market, China, by commodity, fiscalyears 2012–2014 [1]—Continued

Commodity	Value		
	2012	2013	2014
	1,000 dollars	*1,000 dollars*	*1,000 dollars*
Fruits and prep. ex.juice	203,611	164,950	171,942
Fruits-fresh	117,615	104,424	103,842
Fruits-fresh-citrus	35,901	33,382	13,374
Grapefruit-fresh	312	523	411
Lemons and limes-fresh	3,825	5,105	7,446
Oranges and tangerines fresh	29,388	26,927	5,518
Other citrus-fresh	2,376	826	0
Fruits-fresh-noncitrus	81,713	71,042	90,467
Apple-fresh	5,537	1,011	933
Berries-fresh	725	692	157
Cherries-fresh	40,468	33,399	49,894
Grapes, fresh	26,807	28,829	32,752
Melons-fresh	0	22	0
Peaches-fresh	4,357	289	116
Pears-fresh	81	897	2851
Plums-fresh	1,818	4,881	2,518
Other noncitrus-fresh	1,921	1,022	1,246
Fruits, dried	33,014	35,099	32,499
Raisins, dried	21,922	20,823	22,953
Prunes,dried	6,710	5,921	2,099
Other dried-fruits	4,382	8,354	7,447
Fruits-canned excl. juice	50,902	22,986	31,257
Fruits-frozen excl. juice	787	634	881
Other fruits-prep. or pres	1,294	1,806	3,464
Fruit juices, including frozen	26,504	44,392	51,221
Apple juice	197	185	314
Grape juice	3,349	2,362	3,108
Grapefruit juice	590	3,033	2344
Orange juice	4,965	4,648	4,741
Other fruit juices	17,403	34,163	40,714
Wine	70,068	71,052	74,999
Nuts and prep	278,701	386,380	308,702
Almonds	100,032	142,158	104,828
Filberts	2,540	4,880	2,870
Peanuts, shelled or prep	639	2,130	3031
Pistachios	88,469	62,385	84,681
Walnuts	73,779	164,252	102,508
Pecans	9,996	7,420	2,364
Other nuts	3,245	3,156	8,420
Vegetables and prep	147,600	174,983	191,949
Vegetables-fresh	2,867	3,283	2,536
Asparagus-fresh	0	0	0
Broccoli-fresh	0	193	0
Carrots-fresh	0	20	0
Celery-fresh	691	211	442
Cauliflower-fresh	0	0	0
Corn, sweet-fresh	172	236	180
Cucumbers-fresh	0	0	0
Garlic-fresh	0	0	139
Lettuce-fresh	0	0	0
Mushrooms-fresh	0	0	0
Onion and Shallots-fresh	70	48	3
Peppers-fresh	52	66	79
Potatoes-fresh	0	48	11
Tomatoes-fresh	1,684	314	713
Other fresh vegetables	198	2,148	970
Vegetables-frozen	113,033	107,010	112,034
Corn, sweet-frozen	11,384	7,219	10,237
Potatoes-frozen	98,552	98,032	100,714
Other frozen vegetables	3,098	1,759	1,084
Vegetables-canned	6,665	19,292	25,560
Pulses	6,334	25,155	27,277
Dried beans	130	222	524
Dried peas	6,205	24,798	25,917
Dried lentils	0	16	836
Dried chick peas	0	118	0
Other veg-prep or pres	18,701	20,243	24,542

See footnote(s) at end of table.

Table 15-6.—Agricultural exports: Value of U.S. exports to the top market, China, by commodity, fiscal years 2012–2014 [1]—Continued

Commodity	Value		
	2012	2013	2014
	1,000 dollars	*1,000 dollars*	*1,000 dollars*
Oilseeds and products	12,471,342	12,505,524	14,846,034
Oilcake and meal	17,879	1,652	37,986
Bran and residues	0	15	0
Corn oilcake and meal	16,316	0	31,449
Soybean meal	1,559	1,607	6,501
Other oilcake and meal	4	30	36
Oilseeds	12,214,431	12,211,483	14,592,965
Rapeseed	0	0	0
Soybeans	12,202,126	12,191,031	14,556,765
Sunflowerseeds	53	1,104	2,134
Peanuts, including oilstock	7	2,718	9,851
Other oilseeds	1,111	1,793	4,916
Protein substances	11,133	14,836	19,299
Vegetable oils	239,032	292,390	215,083
Soybean oil	133,991	232,329	164,943
Cottonseed oil	0	0	0
Sunflower oil	327	359	570
Corn oil	332	173	225
Peanut oil	93	430	1,360
Rapeseed oil	46,730	6,835	312
Safflower oil	106	1,128	139
Other Vegetable oils and Waxes	57,453	51,136	47,534
Tobacco-unmanufactured	119,295	172,492	213,475
Tobacco-light air cured	18,030	0	460
Tobacco-flue cured	100,119	171,340	205,465
Other tobacco-unmanufactured	1,146	1,153	7,549
Cotton, excluding linters	3,546,514	2,236,056	1,249,616
Cotton linters	9,269	25,617	4,001
Essential oils	111,449	137,766	129,013
Seeds-field and garden	102,053	94,846	118,070
Sugar and tropical products	99,240	115,942	103,128
Sugar and related products	14,174	15,137	18,464
Sugar, cane or beet	204	367	1,157
Related sugar product	13,971	14,770	17,307
Coffee	21,375	21,327	15,007
Cocoa	26,656	43,777	17,058
Chocolate and prep	16,814	13,532	23,552
Tea, including herbal	17,673	19,620	25,790
Spices	1,627	1,655	1,855
Rubber, crude	742	771	1,390
Fibers, excluding cotton	179	122	11
Other hort products	162,988	202,575	238,224
Hops, including extract	11,258	11,645	15,332
Starches, not wheat/corn	935	671	549
Yeasts	4,002	8,878	5,780
Misc hort products	146,793	181,381	216,563
Nursery and greenhouse	3,862	3,547	4,914
Beverages, excluding juice	15,695	25,229	25,288

[1] Fiscal years Oct. 1–Sept. 30.
ERS, Market and Trade Economics Division, (202) 694–5257.

Table 15-7.—Agricultural imports for consumption: Value of Top 50 countries of origin, United States, fiscal years 2012–2014 [1]

Country	2012	2013	2014
	1,000 dollars	*1,000 dollars*	*1,000 dollars*
Canada	19,986,433	21,555,694	22,819,837
Mexico	16,276,724	17,218,508	18,863,749
European Union-28	16,636,005	17,329,270	18,744,268
China	4,349,766	4,459,021	4,343,127
Brazil	3,791,141	3,759,965	3,674,507
Australia	2,557,550	2,720,569	3,343,874
Indonesia	3,665,521	3,127,109	3,093,719
India	5,392,444	3,696,291	2,971,621
Chile	2,498,884	2,842,554	2,742,661
New Zealand	2,174,219	2,177,524	2,460,561
Colombia	2,336,081	2,142,268	2,358,266
Thailand	2,458,800	2,217,847	2,241,561
Guatemala	1,985,417	1,867,379	1,825,719
Vietnam	1,371,648	1,450,047	1,658,565
Argentina	1,731,992	1,821,288	1,566,335
Peru	1,358,347	1,239,315	1,556,807
Costa Rica	1,524,298	1,469,319	1,552,097
Malaysia	2,032,453	1,689,724	1,501,893
Cote d'Ivoire	837,101	889,883	1,136,841
Philippines	1,292,991	1,002,441	1,098,989
Switzerland	790,023	1,045,945	1,095,311
Ecuador	1,001,524	939,721	1,074,279
Turkey	551,209	708,800	784,324
Honduras	673,199	574,532	600,516
Japan	583,193	577,819	555,840
Nicaragua	508,848	431,199	503,699
South Korea	371,155	413,919	441,767
Dominican Republic	485,858	355,690	367,590
Israel	311,135	323,314	344,422
Taiwan	300,511	321,416	331,940
Uruguay	238,183	273,569	264,720
South Africa	238,964	266,624	260,667
Ghana	231,195	212,410	210,975
Bolivia	87,270	142,169	206,940
El Salvador	375,754	276,130	206,209
Paraguay	83,594	185,551	170,688
Morocco	115,759	117,212	164,830
Ethiopia	96,870	113,591	114,115
Pakistan	125,856	121,753	112,621
Sri Lanka	94,608	95,492	110,538
Singapore	88,460	106,371	101,801
Kenya	98,331	100,433	99,251
Egypt	88,603	92,859	96,294
Liberia	137,717	103,935	86,063
Norway	73,515	79,074	84,817
Hong Kong	86,498	91,036	84,589
Jamaica	91,841	69,683	81,562
Papua New Guinea	126,503	65,519	80,817
Madagascar	45,837	60,002	79,618
Tunisia	102,298	132,657	78,115
Other countries	908,557	797,280	870,690
Total U.S. Agricultural Imports [2]	103,370,288	103,878,801	109,183,999

[1] Fiscal years Oct. 1–Sept. 30. [2] Totals may not add due to rounding.
ERS, Market and Trade Economics Division, (202) 694–5257. Compiled from reports of the U.S. Department of Commerce.

Table 15-8.—European Union: Value of agricultural imports by origin, 2005–2014

Year[1]	United States	EU countries[2]	Other countries	Total
	Million dollars	Million dollars	Million dollars	Million dollars
2005	8,740	218,164	78,448	305,352
2006	8,907	238,982	85,191	333,080
2007	10,272	285,452	106,474	402,198
2008	12,232	335,191	129,786	477,209
2009	8,679	295,746	107,970	412,395
2010	10,026	304,902	114,668	429,596
2011	11,894	361,397	143,195	516,486
2012	11,078	347,447	133,459	491,984
2013	13,660	380,670	134,518	528,848
2014	14,382	381,143	136,738	532,263

[1] Data on calendar year basis. Users should use cautious interpretation on reports that include summarized reporter groupings. These groupings will only include the members that have reported data for any particular year. [2] EU-28. Based on import data from the United Nations.

ERS, Market and Trade Economics Division, (202) 694–5257. Data Source: United National Commodity Trade Statistics, United Nations Statistics Division.

Table 15-9.—Fisheries: Landings and value of principal species: 2006–2013 [1]

Species	Landings							
	2006	2007	2008	2009	2010	2011	2012	2013
	Million pounds	Million pounds	Million pounds	Million pounds	Million pounds	Million pounds	Million pounds	Million pounds
Fish:								
Cod, Atlantic	13	17	19	20	18	18	11	5
Flounder	446	483	663	575	625	707	703	717
Haddock	7	8	14	13	22	13	4	4
Halibut	71	70	67	60	56	43	34	30
Herring, sea	290	232	259	313	254	276	270	298
Jack mackerel	3	1	1	0	0	0	*	2
Menhaden	1,307	1,482	1,341	1,567	1,472	1,875	1,771	1,466
Ocean perch, Atlantic	1	2	3	3	4	4	8	7
Pollock	3,414	3,085	2,298	1,883	1,959	2,827	2,872	3,003
Salmon, Pacific	664	885	658	705	788	780	636	1,069
Tuna	50	51	48	49	48	50	60	56
Whiting (silver hake)	12	14	14	17	18	17	16	14
Shellfish:								
Clams (meats)	111	116	108	101	89	86	91	91
Crabs	340	294	325	326	350	369	367	332
Lobsters, American	93	81	82	96	115	126	150	149
Oysters (meats)	34	38	30	36	28	29	33	45
Scallops (meats)	59	59	54	58	57	59	57	41
Shrimp	320	281	257	301	259	313	303	283
	Value							
	Million dollars	Million dollars	Million dollars	Million dollars	Million dollars	Million dollars	Million dollars	Million dollars
Fish:								
Cod, Atlantic	20	27	31	25	28	33	22	10
Flounder	151	154	184	153	146	160	177	198
Haddock	11	12	16	14	22	16	8	6
Halibut	202	227	218	139	139	213	152	117
Herring, sea	30	35	45	56	44	38	49	49
Jack mackerel	(2)	(2)	(2)	(2)	(2)	(2)	(2)	(2)
Menhaden	66	93	91	98	107	144	128	129
Ocean perch, Atlantic	1	1	1	2	2	3	6	4
Pollock	337	306	334	281	282	363	343	406
Salmon, Pacific	311	381	395	370	555	618	489	757
Tuna	87	94	107	96	108	136	164	146
Whiting (silver hake)	7	8	8	9	11	11	10	9
Shellfish:								
Clams (meats)	189	194	187	191	201	187	193	209
Crabs	414	472	562	485	573	650	681	714
Lobsters, American	395	376	306	300	397	424	429	460
Oysters (meats)	121	140	132	137	118	132	155	217
Scallops (meats)	386	387	372	382	457	587	561	470
Shrimp	441	433	442	370	414	518	490	565

*Total is less than the weight threshhold.   [1] Landings are reported in round (live) weight for all items except univalve and bivalve mullusks such as clams, oysters, and scallops, which are reported in weight of meats (excluding the shell). Landings for Mississippi River drainage are not available.   [2] Less than $500,000.

Note: Data are preliminary. Totals may not add due to rounding. Data do not include landings by U.S.-flag vessels at Puerto Rico or other ports outside the 50 States. Data do not include aquaculture products, except oysters and clams.

U.S. Department of Commerce, NOAA, NMFS, Fisheries Statistics Division, (301) 427–8103.

Table 15-10.—Fresh and frozen fishery products: Production and value, 2006–2013

Product	Production							
	2006	2007	2008	2009	2010	2011 [2]	2012	2013
	Million pounds	Million pounds	Million pounds	Million pounds	Million pounds	Million pounds	Million pounds	Million pounds
Fish fillets and steaks [1]	631	632	656	511	585	775	692	753
Cod	42	32	39	36	49	66	64	69
Flounder	18	21	21	18	32	18	16	14
Haddock	16	11	9	14	23	26	11	11
Ocean perch, Atlantic	1	1	1	1	1	1	1	1
Rockfish	2	2	2	3	2	2	2	2
Pollock, Atlantic	2	2	3	3	2	2	2	2
Pollock, Alaska	398	401	364	277	290	461	415	473
Other	152	162	217	159	186	199	181	181
	Value							
	Million dollars	Million dollars	Million dollars	Million dollars	Million dollars	Million dollars	Million dollars	Million dollars
Fish fillets and steaks [1]	1,300	1,304	1,392	1,223	1,486	1,773	1,844	2,074
Cod	123	102	112	102	131	173	216	232
Flounder	73	69	69	57	53	55	51	61
Haddock	70	59	44	60	89	101	54	56
Ocean perch, Atlantic	3	3	3	3	3	5	4	5
Rockfish	5	6	4	6	6	6	8	6
Pollock, Atlantic	4	5	8	8	7	7	8	8
Pollock, Alaska	488	494	450	341	368	568	643	714
Other	564	566	702	646	829	858	861	992

[1] Fresh and frozen. [2] Data for 2012 has been revised.
U.S. Department of Commerce, NOAA, NMFS, Fisheries Statistics Division, (301) 427–8103.

Table 15-11.—Canned fishery products: Production and value, 2006–2013

Product	Production							
	2006	2007	2008	2009	2010	2011	2012	2013
	Million pounds	Million pounds	Million pounds	Million pounds	Million pounds	Million pounds	Million pounds	Million pounds
Tuna [1]	445	436	474	369	395	385	387	384
Salmon	152	142	124	142	146	148	120	203
Clam products [2]	112	110	105	100	110	106	72	73
Sardines, Maine	(4)	(4)	(4)	(4)	(4)	(4)	(4)	(4)
Shrimp [3]	(5)	(5)	(5)	(4)	(4)	(4)	(4)	(4)
Crabs	(5)	(5)	(5)	(5)	1	1	(5)	(5)
Oysters	(5)	(5)	(5)	(5)	(4)	(4)	(4)	(4)
Total [6]	1,081	1,070	1,316	934	956	947	881	961
	Value							
	Million dollars	Million dollars	Million dollars	Million dollars	Million dollars	Million dollars	Million dollars	Million dollars
Tuna [1]	705	702	845	756	724	769	886	852
Salmon	250	274	225	322	356	377	410	572
Clam products [2]	123	89	95	89	98	100	66	90
Sardines, Maine	(4)	(4)	(4)	(4)	(4)	(4)	(4)	(4)
Shrimp [4]	1	1	(4)	(4)	(4)	(4)	(4)	(4)
Crabs	(5)	(5)	(5)	(5)	9	(5)	2	(5)
Oysters	(5)	(5)	(5)	(5)	(4)	(4)	(4)	(4)
Total [6]	1,330	1,324	1,422	1,408	1,414	1,476	1,615	1,775

[1] Flakes included with chunk. [2] "Cut out" or "drained" weight of can contents are given for whole or minced clams, and net contents for other clam products. [3] Drained weight. [4] Confidential data. [5] Less than 500,000 pounds or $500,000. [6] Includes other products not shown separately.
U.S. Dept. of Commerce, NOAA, NMFS, Fisheries Statistics Division, (301) 427–8103.

Table 15-12.—Fisheries: Fishermen and craft, 1977, and catch, 2008–2013 by area

Area	1977 [1]			2008		2009	
	Fishermen	Fishing vessels	Fishing boats [2]	Total catch	Value	Total catch	Value
	1,000	*Number*	*1,000*	*Million pounds*	*Million dollars*	*Million pounds*	*Million dollars*
New England States	31.7	929	15.4	590	792	646	784
Middle Atlantic States	17.3	573	11.3	201	233	200	202
Chesapeake Bay States	27.9	2,086	19.0	477	219	473	222
South Atlantic States	11.6	1,463	6.7	116	167	113	149
Gulf States	29.3	5,328	11.0	1,273	698	1,583	623
Pacific Coast States	54.0	7,643	15.4	5,619	2,174	4,972	1,824
Great Lakes States	1.2	217	0.5	18	17	17	17
Hawaii	2.7	101	1.3	31	85	27	71
United States	182.1	17,545	89.2	8,326	4,384	8,031	3,891

Area	2010		2011		2012		2013	
	Total catch	Value	Total catch	Value	Total catch	Value	Total catch	Value
	Million pounds	*Million dollars*	*Million pounds*	*Million dollars*	*Million pounds*	*Million dollars*	*Million pounds*	*Million dollars*
New England States	576	954	622	1,109	664	1,191	636	1,162
Middle Atlantic States	194	218	208	257	751	487	583	435
Chesapeake Bay States	593	295	572	269	....	....	92	....
South Atlantic States	119	165	125	176	108	172	92	160
Gulf States	1,283	635	1,754	790	1,643	754	1,457	905
Pacific Coast States	5,418	2,150	6,531	2,580	6,418	2,366	7,061	2,697
Great Lakes States	19	18	18	17	18	20	19	23
Hawaii	28	84	29	92	31	112	32	108
United States	8,231	4,520	9,858	5,289	9,634	5,103	9,880	5,490

[1] Exclusive of duplication among regions. Computation of area amounts will not equal U.S. total. Mississippi River data included with total.   [2] Refers to craft having capacity of less than 5 net tons.   Note: Table may not add due to rounding.
U.S. Department of Commerce, NOAA, NMFS, Fisheries Statistics Division, (301) 427–8103.

Table 15-13.—Fisheries: Quantity and value of domestic catch, 2004–2013

Year	Quantity [1]			Ex-vessel value	Average price per lb.
	Total	For human food	For industrial products [2]		
	Million pounds	*Million pounds*	*Million pounds*	*Million dollars*	*Cents*
2004	9,683	7,794	1,889	3,756	38.8
2005	9,707	7,997	1,710	3,942	40.6
2006	9,483	7,842	1,641	4,024	42.4
2007	9,309	7,490	1,819	4,192	45.0
2008	8,325	6,633	1,692	4,383	52.6
2009	8,031	6,198	1,833	3,891	48.4
2010	8,231	6,526	1,705	4,520	54.9
2011	9,858	7,909	1,949	5,289	53.7
2012	9,634	7,477	2,157	5,103	53.0
2013	9,880	8,053	1,827	5,490	55.6

[1] Live weight.   [2] Meals, oil, fish solubles, homogenized condensed fish, shell products, bait, and animal food.
U.S. Department of Commerce, NOAA, NMFS Fisheries Statistics Division, (301) 427–8103.

Table 15-14.—Fishery products: Supply,[1] 2004–2013[2]

Item	2004	2005	2006	2007	2008
	Million pounds	Million pounds	Milion pounds	Million pounds	Million pounds
For human food	17,648	18,155	18,594	18,253	17,037
Finfish	12,959	13,567	13,484	13,339	12,295
Shellfish[3]	4,689	4,588	5,110	4,914	4,742
For industrial use	2,765	2,457	2,366	2,308	2,163
Domestic catch	9,683	9,707	9,483	9,309	8,326
Percent of total	47.4	47.1	45.2	45.3	43.4
For human food	7,794	7,997	7,842	7,490	6,633
Finfish	6,641	6,914	6,671	6,415	5,590
Shellfish[3]	1,153	1,084	1,171	1,075	1,043
For industrial use	1,889	1,710	1,641	1,819	1,692
Imports[4]	10,730	10,905	11,477	11,252	10,927
Percent of total	52.6	52.9	54.8	54.7	56.6
For human food	9,854	10,158	10,752	10,763	10,404
Finfish	6,318	6,653	6,813	6,925	6,705
Shellfish[3]	3,536	3,505	3,939	3,838	3,699
For industrial use[5]	876	747	725	489	471
Total	20,413	20,612	20,960	20,561	19,200

Item	2009	2010	2011	2012	2013
	Million pounds	Million pounds	Million pounds	Million pounds	Million pounds
For human food	16,637	17,560	18,732	18,066	18,582
Finfish	11,701	12,504	13,644	13,159	13,786
Shellfish[3]	4,936	5,056	5,088	4,906	4,795
For industrial use	2,263	2,188	2,374	2,692	2,416
Domestic catch	8,031	8,231	9,858	9,634	9,880
Percent of total	42.5	41.7	46.7	46.4	47
For human food	6,198	6,526	7,909	7,478	8,053
Finfish	4,930	5,216	6,540	6,163	6,777
Shellfish[3]	1,268	1,310	1,369	1,314	1,275
For industrial use	1,833	1,705	1,949	2,157	1,827
Imports[4]	10,869	11,517	11,248	11,123	11,118
Percent of total	57.5	58.3	53.3	53.6	53
For human food	10,439	11,034	10,823	10,588	10,529
Finfish	6,771	7,288	7,104	6,996	7,009
Shellfish[3]	3,668	3,746	3,719	3,592	3,520
For industrial use[5]	430	483	425	535	589
Total	18,900	19,748	21,106	20,757	20,998

[1] Supply totals are the domestic catch and imports without accounting for exports taken out.   [2] Live weight, except percent. May not add due to rounding.   [3] For univalve and bivalves mollusks (conchs, clams, oysters, scallops, etc.), the weight of meats, excluding the shell is reported.   [4] Excluding imports of edible fishery products consumed in Puerto Rico; includes landings of tuna caught by foreign vessels in American Samoa.   [5] Fish meal and sea herring.
U.S. Department of Commerce, NOAA, NMFS, Fisheries Statistics Division, (301) 427–8103.

Table 15-15.—Fisheries: Disposition of domestic catch, 2005–2013[1]

Disposition	2005	2006	2007	2008	2009	2010	2011	2012	2013
	Million pounds	Million pounds	Million pounds	Million pounds	Million pounds	Million pounds	Million pounds	Million pounds	Million pounds
Fresh and frozen	7,776	7,627	7,450	6,538	6,204	6,515	7,817	7,541	8,019
Canned	563	573	514	336	392	373	371	299	365
Cured	160	117	121	138	103	102	52	82	45
Reduced to meal, oil, etc	1,208	1,166	1,224	1,313	1,332	1,241	1,618	1,712	1,451
Total	9,707	9,483	9,309	8,326	8,031	8,231	9,858	9,634	9,880

[1] Live weight catch. In addition to whole fish, a large portion of waste (400–500 mil. lb.) derived from canning, filleting, and dressing fish and shellfish is utilized in production of fish meal and oil in each year shown.
U.S. Department of Commerce, NOAA, NMFS, Fisheries Statistics Division, (301) 427–8103.

Table 15-16.—Processed fishery products: Production and value, 2006–2013 [1]

Item	Production							
	2006	2007	2008	2009	2010	2011	2012	2013
	Million pounds	*Million pounds*	*Million pounds*	*Million pounds*	*Million pounds*	*Million pounds*	*Million pounds*	*Million pounds*
Fresh and frozen:.								
Fillets	617	617	643	498	574	767	687	746
Steaks	14	15	13	13	10	8	5	8
Fish sticks	59	74	82	80	74	80	58	58
Fish portions	179	194	204	141	142	172	152	127
Breaded shrimp	140	86	74	97	117	92	80	105
Canned products [2]	1,081	1,070	1,316	934	956	947	880	961
Fish and shellfish	721	699	714	621	656	641	582	662
Animal feed	360	371	602	313	299	306	299	299
Industrial products	(X)	(X)	(X)	(X)	(X)	(X)	(X)	(X)
Meal and scrap	583	563	493	473	488	621	586	508
Oil (body and liver)	143	152	190	168	136	143	115	176
Other	(X)	(X)	(X)	(X)	(X)	(X)	(X)	(X)

Item	Value							
	2006	2007	2008	2009	2010	2011	2012	2013
	Million dollars	*Million dollars*	*Million dollars*	*Million dollars*	*Million dollars*	*Million dollars*	*Million dollars*	*Million dollars*
Fresh and frozen:.								
Fillets	1,246	1,249	1,340	1,159	1,443	1,738	1,818	2,029
Steaks	54	55	52	64	43	35	26	44
Fish sticks	62	105	121	125	113	105	87	86
Fish portions	303	300	310	292	277	346	260	223
Breaded shrimp	347	200	159	252	563	241	194	297
Canned products [2]	1,330	1,324	1,422	1,408	1,414	1,476	1,615	1,775
Fish and shellfish	1,101	1,090	1,191	1,190	1,196	1,251	1,373	1,534
Animal feed	229	234	231	218	218	225	242	242
Industrial products	242	340	310	289	283	435	498	479
Meal and scrap	152	218	182	187	189	239	280	242
Oil (body and liver)	34	60	63	40	30	63	55	57
Other	57	62	65	62	64	134	162	180

(X) Not applicable.   [1] Includes cured fish.   [2] Includes salmon eggs for baits.
U.S. Department of Commerce, NOAA, NMFS, Fisheries Statistics Division, (301) 427–8103.

Table 15-17.—Selected fishery products: Imports and exports, 2006–2013 [1]

Product	Quantity							
	2006	2007	2008	2009	2010	2011	2012	2013
	Million pounds	Million pounds	Million pounds	Million pounds	Million pounds	Million pounds	Million pounds	Million pounds
Imports								
Edible	5,400	5,346	5,226	5,161	5,447	5,349	5,383	5,422
Fresh and frozen	4,529	4,497	4,363	4,297	4,526	4,451	4,525	4,561
Salmon [2]	200	204	201	218	228	291	242	225
Tuna	429	417	372	320	426	303	316	314
Groundfish fillets, blocks [3]	350	341	298	315	312	331	318	328
Other fillets and steaks	944	1,040	1,027	1,046	1,112	1,135	1,236	1,292
Scallops (meats)	59	55	56	54	50	55	34	60
Lobster, American and spiny	94	65	96	88	100	102	106	110
Shrimp and prawn	1,297	1,224	1,241	1,206	1,228	1,265	1,173	1,115
Canned	724	702	707	716	770	752	685	682
Sardines, in oil	17	19	21	20	21	20	25	26
Sardines and herring, not in oil	39	38	40	47	46	51	46	38
Tuna	420	378	378	398	442	413	354	347
Oysters	13	14	12	12	12	15	9	10
Pickled or salted	52	49	54	49	51	51	51	58
Cod, haddock, hake, pollock, cusk	9	7	7	4	6	4	7	8
Nonedible scrap and meal	129	87	84	77	86	76	96	105
Exports								
Canned salmon	116	114	117	97	91	112	91	100
Fish oil, nonedible	148	123	126	108	175	149	93	152

Product	Value							
	2006	2007	2008	2009	2010	2011	2012	2013
	Million dollars	Million dollars	Million dollars	Million dollars	Million dollars	Million dollars	Million dollars	Million dollars
Imports								
Edible	13,355	13,696	14,171	13,124	14,811	16,618	16,691	18,043
Fresh and frozen	11,738	11,954	12,138	11,314	12,820	14,411	14,225	15,665
Salmon [2]	494	523	516	562	652	633	627	712
Tuna	611	584	601	502	680	578	749	745
Groundfish fillets, blocks [3]	602	614	570	551	560	648	581	656
Other fillets and steaks	2,333	2,642	2,793	2,616	3,107	3,466	3,637	3,931
Scallops (meats)	238	231	239	225	233	294	220	366
Lobster, American and spiny	928	935	914	685	871	900	895	928
Shrimp and prawn	4,104	3,896	4,084	3,746	4,272	5,148	4,442	5,278
Canned	1,259	1,367	1,625	1,416	1,581	1,781	1,923	1,838
Sardines, in oil	32	35	41	34	37	39	61	68
Sardines and herring, not in oil	36	37	45	58	62	70	63	56
Tuna	526	524	661	613	660	720	762	762
Oysters	28	31	28	28	30	44	28	30
Pickled or salted	85	85	95	90	86	87	95	106
Cod, haddock, hake, pollock, cusk	20	16	15	11	14	11	19	21
Nonedible scrap and metal	41	33	33	30	56	48	56	73
Exports								
Canned salmon	182	203	218	194	179	224	222	229
Fish oil, nonedible	57	64	101	52	96	103	100	147

[1] Includes Puerto Rico. [2] Excludes fillets. [3] Includes cod, cusk, haddock, hake, pollock, ocean perch, and whiting.
U.S. Dept. of Commerce, NOAA, NMFS, Fisheries Statistics Division (301) 427–8103.

Table 15-18.—Fishery products: Imports and exports, 2004–2013 [1]

Year	Imports [2]				Exports			
	Total value	Edible products		Non-edible, value	Total value	Edible products		Non-edible, value
		Quantity	Value			Quantity	Value	
	Million dollars	*Million pounds*	*Million dollars*	*Million dollars*	*Million dollars*	*Million pounds*	*Million dollars*	*Million dollars*
2004	22,949	4,951	11,331	11,618	13,592	2,888	3,708	9,884
2005	25,120	5,115	12,099	13,021	15,431	2,929	4,074	11,357
2006	27,712	5,401	13,355	14,357	17,760	2,967	4,238	13,522
2007	28,777	5,346	13,696	15,081	20,054	2,869	4,269	15,785
2008	28,457	5,226	14,171	14,286	23,367	2,650	4,257	19,110
2009	23,554	5,161	13,124	10,430	19,636	2,546	3,980	15,656
2010	27,352	5,447	14,811	12,542	22,386	2,733	4,389	17,997
2011	30,943	5,349	16,618	14,326	26,183	3,265	5,442	20,742
2012	31,108	5,384	16,691	14,417	27,388	3,254	5,470	21,917
2013	33,196	5,422	18,043	15,154	29,104	3,324	5,583	23,521

[1] Includes Puerto Rico.   [2] Includes landings of tuna by foreign vessels in American Samoa.
U.S. Department of Commerce, NOAA, NMFS, Fisheries Statistics Division, (301) 427–8103.

Table 15-19.—Fish trips: Estimated number of fishing trips taken by marine recreational fishermen by subregion and year, Atlantic, Gulf, and Pacific Coasts, 2010–2013

Subregion	2010	2011	2012	2013
	Thousands	*Thousands*	*Thousands*	*Thousands*
Atlantic and Gulf:				
North Atlantic	7,213	6,059	6,164	6,286
Mid-Atlantic	16,587	15,974	14,434	14,217
South Atlantic [1]	19,064	17,676	17,793	16,618
Gulf	22,039	23,701	24,331	26,384
Total	64,903	63,410	62,722	63,505

Subregion	2010	2011	2012	2013
	Thousands	*Thousands*	*Thousands*	*Thousands*
Pacific: [2]				
Southern California	2,646	2,011	3,857	3,784
Northern California	1,086	1,691	1,579	1,592
Oregon	156	148	173	196
Washington	107	104	113	109
Hawaii	2,391	1,382	1,520	1,513
Alaska	523	491	473	595
Total	6,909	5,827	7,715	7,789

[1] Does not include trips from headboats (party boats) in the South Atlantic or Gulf of Mexico.   [2] Pacific state estimates do not include salmon data collected by recreational surveys.
U.S. Department of Commerce, NOAA, NMFS, Fisheries Statistics Division, (301) 427–8103.

Table 15-20.—Fish harvested: Estimated number of fish harvested by marine recreational anglers by subregion and year, Atlantic, Gulf Coasts, and Pacific Coasts, 2010–2013

Subregion	2010	2011	2012	2013
	Thousands	Thousands	Thousands	Thousands
Atlantic and Gulf:				
North Atlantic	10,532	11,262	11,099	13,048
Mid-Atlantic	24,988	21,451	22,015	26,280
South Atlantic [1]	27,689	32,888	29,632	36,211
Gulf	64,401	62,012	65,015	82,018
Total	127,610	127,613	127,761	157,557
Subregion	2010	2011	2012	2013
	Thousands	Thousands	Thousands	Thousands
Pacific: [2]				
Southern California	4,693	4,540	5,678	5,120
Northern California	1,788	3,795	2,468	2,961
Oregon	453	367	455	490
Washington	433	294	302	310
Hawaii	4,897	2,503	2,763	3,651
Alaska	1,315	1,314	1,203	1,572
Total	13,579	12,813	12,869	14,104

[1] Does not include trips from headboats (party boats) in the South Atlantic or Gulf of Mexico.　[2] Data do not include recreational trips in Hawaii or Alaska.　Pacific state estimates do not include salmon data collected by recreational surveys.　Note: "Harvested" includes dead discards and fish used for bait but does not include fish released alive; totals may not match due to rounding.

U.S. Department of Commerce, NOAA, NMFS, Fisheries Statistics Division, (301) 427–8103.

Table 15-21.—Fish harvested: Estimated number of fish harvested by marine recreational anglers by mode and year, Atlantic, Gulf Coasts, and Pacific Coasts, 2010–2013

Mode	2010	2011	2012	2013
	Thousands	Thousands	Thousands	Thousands
Atlantic and Gulf: [1]				
Shore	30,979	37,916	40,258	49,377
Party/charter [2]	8,901	9,789	10,921	12,626
Private/rental	87,730	79,908	76,582	95,554
Total	127,610	127,613	127,761	157,557
Mode	2010	2011	2012	2013
	Thousands	Thousands	Thousands	Thousands
Pacific: [2]				
Shore	6,915	6,373	5,426	5,794
Party/charter	1,906	2,924	3,267	3,487
Private/rental	3,443	2,202	2,973	3,251
Total	12,264	11,499	11,666	12,532

[1] Does not include trips from headboats (party boats) in the South Atlantic or Gulf of Mexico.　[2] Data do not include recreational trips in Alaska.　Pacific state estimates do not include salmon data collected by recreational surveys.　Note: "Harvested" includes dead discards and fish used for bait but does not include fish released alive; totals may not match due to rounding.

U.S. Department of Commerce, NOAA, NMFS, Fisheries Statistics Division, (301) 427–8103.

Table 15-22.—Fish harvested: Estimated number of fish harvested by marine recreational anglers by species group and year, Atlantic and Gulf coasts, 2010–2013[1]

Species group	2010	2011	2012	2013
	Thousands	*Thousands*	*Thousands*	*Thousands*
Atlantic Cod	550	580	338	392
Atlantic Croaker	8,347	7,315	7,193	9,449
Atlantic Mackerel	3,473	5,336	3,282	3,713
Black Drum	1,091	1,238	1,126	1,431
Black Sea Bass	2,884	1,513	2,408	1,715
Blue Runner	613	1,268	998	2,955
Conger Eels	6	4	1	22
Crevalle Jack	311	175	319	756
Cunner	22	45	23	99
Epinephelus Groupers	147	123	322	480
Florida Pompano	471	308	385	858
Freshwater Catfishes	554	504	708	461
Gray Snapper	737	731	1,297	2,230
Greater Amberjack	108	62	90	93
Gulf Flounder	219	229	335	364
King Mackerel	440	342	443	400
Kingfishes	5,359	5,543	5,978	7,122
Lane Snapper	77	64	206	368
Little Tunny/Atlantic Bonito	178	261	374	319
Moray Eels	-	-	-	-
Mycteroperca Groupers	274	140	188	278
Pigfish	662	840	876	697
Pinfishes	5,815	4,546	5,320	5,064
Pollock	382	410	208	570
Red Drum	4,130	4,385	3,518	4,896
Red Hake	133	224	76	103
Red Porgy	171	308	274	537
Red Snapper	367	557	633	1,308
Saltwater Catfishes	426	557	1,034	843
Sand Seatrout	4,659	6,224	5,191	3,344
Scup	5,147	3,058	3,670	5,030
Sheepshead	1,907	2,937	2,126	1,971
Silver Perch	98	195	504	147
Skates/Rays	60	69	44	72
Southern Flounder	1,351	1,331	1,249	1,503
Spanish Mackerel	2,670	2,454	2,672	4,472
Spot	5,008	6,004	4,759	8,179
Spotted Seatrout	11,824	15,827	15,413	13,883
Striped Bass	1,964	2,278	1,492	2,139
Striped Mullet	2,409	4,203	4,882	3,545
Summer Flounder	1,509	1,844	2,277	2,544
Tautog	1,121	430	495	530
Vermilion Snapper	337	664	365	835
Weakfish	80	36	236	137
White Grunt	1,052	1,509	1,825	2,184
White Perch	2,987	2,124	1,907	2,582
Winter Flounder	161	192	98	51
Yellowtail Snapper	423	282	439	818
Other Barracudas	52	93	93	84
Other Bluefish	6,242	5,219	5,640	6,023
Other Cods/Hakes	262	234	233	311
Other Dolphins	1,036	1,271	1,132	1,217
Other Drum	244	162	60	394
Other Eels	134	7	38	11
Other Flounders	115	180	108	123
Other Grunts	348	250	360	960
Other Herrings	26,693	20,698	22,165	31,202
Other Jacks	505	781	1,404	2,021
Other Mullets	4,335	4,185	4,175	6,419
Other Porgies	166	214	313	344
Other Puffers	252	1,197	708	494
Other Sculpins	-	-	-	3
Other Sea Basses	75	146	132	141
Other Searobins	87	110	120	354
Other Sharks	190	193	158	269
Other Snappers	141	75	124	142
Other Temperate Basses	-	-	-	-
Other Toadfishes	34	8	17	42
Other Triggerfishes/Filefishes	274	267	266	356
Other Tunas/Mackerels	259	383	545	580
Other Wrasses	168	69	203	174
Other fishes	3,284	2,636	2,170	4,404
Total[2]	127,610	127,613	127,761	157,557

- Represents zero.   [1] Data do not include headboats (party boats) in the South Atlantic and the Gulf of Mexico.   [2] Totals may not add due to rounding.   Note: "Harvested" includes dead discards and fish used for bait but does not include fish released alive.

U.S. Department of Commerce, NOAA, NMFS, Fisheries Statistics Division (301) 427–8103.

Table 15-23.—Fish harvested: Estimated number of fish harvested by marine recreational anglers by species group and year, Pacific coast, 2010–2013[1]

Species group	2010	2011	2012	2013
	Thousands	*Thousands*	*Thousands*	*Thousands*
Albacore	-	-	-	-
Barred Sand Bass	140	238	152	64
Barred Surfperch	48	340	544	368
Bigeye Scad	676	656	347	810
Bigeye Trevally	2	1	2	3
Bigscale Soldierfish	41	2	8	11
Black Perch	38	66	42	33
Black Rockfish	686	621	718	1,022
Blackspot Sergeant	14	8	29	12
Blacktail Snapper	34	29	31	23
Blue Rockfish	157	177	161	272
Bluefin Trevally	75	76	60	88
Bluestripe Snapper	67	17	22	21
Bocaccio	64	164	209	188
Brown Rockfish	117	146	132	138
Cabezon	24	30	32	29
California Corbina	5	-	9	6
California Halibut	49	25	38	24
California Sheephead	31	31	31	48
Canary Rockfish	27	41	42	37
Chilipepper Rockfish	10	23	38	30
Chub Mackerel	1,179	1,115	848	576
Conger Eels	1	-	6	3
Convict Tang	253	138	141	109
Copper Rockfish	58	89	118	158
Giant Trevally	37	20	36	34
Goldring Surgeonfish	112	54	136	95
Gopher Rockfish	210	180	133	95
Greater Amberjack	18	-	3	2
Green Jobfish	23	18	30	8
Greenspotted Rockfish	31	49	52	32
Halfmoon	15	25	26	37
Hawaiian Flagtail	224	67	105	143
Hawaiian Hogfish	3	2	6	4
Highfin Rudderfish	23	6	21	7
Island Jack	5	1	8	10
Jacksmelt	303	366	239	248
Kawakawa	8	2	6	5
Kelp Bass	88	131	132	55
Kelp Greenling	38	55	35	35
Lingcod	120	192	229	279
Mackerel Scad	165	6	260	79
Manybar Goatfish	45	15	41	23
Moray Eels	4	-	6	8
Northern Anchovy	197	207	54	356
Olive Rockfish	17	39	67	49
Opaleye	21	11	41	31
Pacific Barracuda	64	46	50	18
Pacific Bonito	77	2	-	9
Pacific Cod	37	48	42	38
Pacific Hake	-	-	-	-
Pacific Herring	17	49	184	128
Pacific Tomcod	-	-	-	-
Pile Perch	4	5	10	8
Pink Snapper	115	26	47	46
Queenfish	71	40	66	34
Quillback Rockfish	8	11	15	7
Razorfishes	46	14	94	63
Redtail Surfperch	5	43	50	39
Rock Sole	-	-	1	-
Sanddabs	296	537	441	603
Shiner Perch	164	92	72	59
Silver Surfperch	7	28	16	21
Skates/Rays	9	2	6	8
Skipjack Tuna	288	125	197	380
Smallmouth Bonefish	55	14	27	23
Spiny Dogfish	-	2	-	1
Spotted Sand Bass	11	10	23	5
Squirrel Fishes	-	1	3	1
Starry Flounder	-	-	-	-
Striped Bass	9	30	14	7
Striped Mullet	67	13	16	34

See footnote(s) at end of table.

Table 15-23.—Fish harvested: Estimated number of fish harvested by marine recreational anglers by species group and year, Pacific coast, 2010–2013 [1]—Continued

Species group	2010	2011	2012	2013
	Thousands	*Thousands*	*Thousands*	*Thousands*
Striped Seaperch	19	36	25	34
Surf Smelt	1	1,278	4	-
Unicornfishes	19	183	10	5
Wahoo	40	16	31	36
Walleye Surfperch	111	90	149	144
White Croaker	86	48	86	73
White Seaperch	22	10	17	7
Whitemouth Trevally	1	-	-	-
Whitesaddle Goatfish	11	7	11	4
Whitetip Soldierfish	5	6	3	3
Widow Rockfish	-	2	10	40
Yellowfin Tuna	302	141	182	150
Yellowstripe Goatfish	165	112	96	791
Yellowtail	4	-	13	16
Yellowtail Rockfish	104	173	168	171
Other Anchovies	235	135	61	19
Other Barracudas	3	5	9	2
Other Cods/Hakes	-	-	-	-
Other Damselfishes	59	5	27	20
Other Dolphins	164	63	163	94
Other Drum	86	43	140	92
Other Flounders	417	409	409	477
Other Goatfishes	50	38	11	54
Other Greenlings	2	1	14	1
Other Groupers	2	4	10	10
Other Herrings	910	470	855	634
Other Jacks	291	76	40	38
Other Mullets	32	13	9	39
Other Rockfishes	755	1,119	1,409	1,559
Other Sablefishes	9	10	18	18
Other Scorpionfishes	132	197	261	245
Other Sculpins	2	39	13	14
Other Sea Basses	3	-	-	-
Other Sea Chubs	36	5	16	33
Other Sharks	10	6	8	16
Other Silversides	192	74	195	207
Other Smelts	79	43	94	50
Other Snappers	101	24	67	55
Other Soldierfishes	2	3	2	45
Other Sturgeons	1	1	-	-
Other Surfperches	41	107	98	89
Other Surgeonfishes	111	28	68	63
Other Tunas/Mackerels	98	48	122	98
Other Wrasses	25	6	29	23
Other fishes	1,988	1,122	1,116	1,395
Total [2]	13,579	12,813	12,869	14,104

- Represents zero.   [1] Data do not include recreational harvest in Hawaii or Alaska.   Pacific estimates do not include salmon data collected by state recreational surveys.   [2] Totals may not add exactly due to rounding.   Note: "Harvested" includes dead discards and fish used for bait but does not include fish released alive.
U.S. Department of Commerce, NOAA, NMFS, Fisheries Statistics Division, (301) 427–8103.

Table 15-24.—Fish harvested: Estimated number of fish harvested by marine recreational anglers, by area of fishing and year, Atlantic and Gulf and Pacific Coast, 2010–2013

Area	2010	2011	2012	2013
	Thousands	Thousands	Thousands	Thousands
Atlantic and Gulf: [1]				
Inland	87,947	85,798	84,359	95,723
State Territorial Sea [2]	30,015	31,917	32,318	46,208
Federal Exclusive Ecomomic Zone [3]	9,648	9,898	11,084	15,626
Total	127,610	127,613	127,761	157,557

Area	2010	2011	2012	2013
	Thousands	Thousands	Thousands	Thousands
Pacific: [4]				
Inland	1,983	756	1,135	1,065
State Territorial Sea [2]	8,539	9,167	8,500	9,460
Federal Exclusive Ecomomic Zone [3]	1,742	1,576	2,031	2,007
Total	12,264	11,499	11,666	12,532

[1] Data does not include trips from headboats (party boats) in the South Atlantic or the Gulf of Mexico.   [2] Open Ocean extending 0 to 3 miles from shore, except West Florida (10 miles).   [3] Open ocean extending to 200 miles offshore from the outer edge of the State Territorial Seas.   [4] Data does not include recreational catch from Alaska. Pacific estimates do not include salmon data collected by recreational surveys. Note: "Harvested" includes dead discards and fish used for bait but does not include fish released alive.
U.S. Department of Commerce, NOAA, NMFS, Fisheries Statistics Division, (301) 427–8103.

Table 15-25.—Catfish production: Water surface acre usage by State and United States, 2014–2015

State	Acres intended for utilization during Jan 1-Jun 30					Acres taken out of production during Jul 1-Dec 31 prev. year
	Foodsize	Fingerlings	Broodfish	Currently under or scheduled for:		
				Renovation	New construction	
	Acres	Acres	Acres	Acres	Acres	Acres
2014						
Alabama	17,700	300	60	390	(D)	165
Arkansas	4,900	1,500	210	210	(D)	1,600
California	950	190	115	110	(D)	(D)
Louisiana [1]	625	-	-	(D)	-	(D)
Mississippi	30,300	7,500	1,300	2,100	(D)	4,200
North Carolina	1,200	200	(D)	(D)	(D)	(D)
Texas	2,200	(D)	(D)	(D)	(D)	250
Other States [2]	1,200	630	280	135	445	310
United States	59,075	10,320	1,965	2,945	445	6,525
2015						
Alabama	14,900	250	85	480	65	240
Arkansas	4,200	1,200	195	95	(D)	(D)
California	1,100	185	100	40	(D)	(D)
Louisiana [1]	(NA)	(NA)	(NA)	(NA)	(NA)	(NA)
Mississippi	28,800	7,000	1,500	3,400	(D)	960
North Carolina	1,200	135	35	70	(D)	(D)
Texas	1,800	100	70	105	30	500
Other States [2]	1,510	550	70	80	85	570
United States	53,510	9,420	2,155	4,270	180	2,270

- Represents zero.   (D) Withheld to avoid disclosing data for individual operations.   (NA) Not available.   [1] Included in Other States for 2015 acres intended for utilization during January 1-June 30 and included in Others States for 2014 acres taken out of production during July 31-December 31.   [2] Other States include State estimates not shown and States supressed due to disclosure.
NASS, Livestock Branch, (202) 720–3570.

Table 15-26.—Catfish: Number of operations and water surface acres used for production, 2014–2015, and total sales, 2013–2014, by State and United States

State	Number of operations on Jan. 1		Water surface acres used for production during Jan 1 - Jun 30		Total sales	
	2013[1]	2014[1]	2014	2015	2013	2014
	Acres	Acres	Acres	Acres	1,000 dol-lars	1,000 dol-lars
Alabama	(NA)	(NA)	18,300	15,300	100,892	104,468
Arkansas	(NA)	(NA)	6,800	5,800	27,236	21,295
California	(NA)	(NA)	1,300	1,400	8,697	8,071
Louisiana[2]	(NA)	(NA)	625	(NA)	1,266	(NA)
Mississippi	(NA)	(NA)	44,700	41,000	186,609	189,540
North Carolina	(NA)	(NA)	1,400	1,500	4,436	3,985
Texas	(NA)	(NA)	2,400	2,000	21,859	16,656
Other States[3]	(NA)	(NA)	2,200	2,910	5,739	7,888
United States			77,725	69,910	356,734	351,903

(NA) Not available.   [1] State level number of operations will only be published every five years in conjunction with the Census of Agriculture.   [2] Included in Other States for 2015 water acres and Other States for 2014 total sales.   [3] Other States include State estimates not shown and States supressed due to disclosure.
NASS, Livestock Branch, (202) 720–3570.

Table 15-27.—Catfish: Sales by size category, by State and United States, 2013–2014

Size category and State	Number of fish		Live weight		Sales			
					Total		Average price per pound	
	2013	2014	2013	2014	2013	2014	2013	2014
	1,000	1,000	1,000 pounds	1,000 pounds	1,000 dollars	1,000 dollars	Dollars	Dollars
Foodsize:								
Alabama	62,400	63,400	109,300	105,300	100,556	104,247	0.92	0.99
Arkansas	15,500	9,980	25,300	17,200	23,529	18,232	0.93	1.06
California	1,510	1,340	2,800	2,550	8,624	7,982	3.08	3.13
Louisiana[1]	1,050	(NA)	1,130	(NA)	1,266	(NA)	1.12	(NA)
Mississippi	106,000	97,900	175,300	161,500	171,794	176,035	0.98	1.09
North Carolina	2,750	1,990	4,000	3,400	4,400	3,978	1.10	1.17
Texas	10,200	7,050	15,800	14,300	21,804	16,445	1.38	1.15
Other States[2]	2,400	2,940	3,500	3,248	4,515	5,463	1.29	1.68
United States	201,810	184,600	337,130	307,498	336,488	332,382	1.00	1.08
Broodfish:								
Alabama	(D)	(D)	(D)	(D)	(D)	(D)	(D)	(D)
Arkansas	-	(D)	-	(D)	-	(D)	-	(D)
California	(D)	(D)	(D)	(D)	(D)	(D)	(D)	(D)
Louisiana[1]	-	(NA)	-	(NA)	-	(NA)	-	(NA)
Mississippi	(D)	(D)	(D)	(D)	(D)	(D)	(D)	(D)
North Carolina	-	-	-	-	-	-	-	-
Texas	-	-	-	-	-	-	-	-
Other States[2]	40	46	212	268	184	324	0.87	1.21
United States	40	46	212	268	184	324	0.87	1.21
Stockers:								
Alabama	(D)	(D)	(D)	(D)	(D)	(D)	(D)	(D)
Arkansas	(D)	(D)	(D)	(D)	(D)	(D)	(D)	(D)
California	(D)	-	(D)	-	(D)	-	(D)	-
Louisiana[1]	-	(NA)	-	(NA)	-	(NA)	-	(NA)
Mississippi	55,400	47,300	6,900	4,800	6,831	5,808	0.99	1.21
North Carolina	(D)	(D)	(D)	(D)	(D)	(D)	(D)	(D)
Texas	(D)	(D)	(D)	(D)	(D)	(D)	(D)	(D)
Other States[2]	18,490	23,380	2,533	2,354	3,207	3,114	1.27	1.32
United States	73,890	70,680	9,433	7,154	10,038	8,922	1.06	1.25
Fingerlings and fry:								
Alabama	530	2,450	17	41	89	221	5.25	5.40
Arkansas	13,400	8,100	481	278	1,227	798	2.55	2.87
California	350	860	11	10	55	76	5.00	7.60
Louisiana[1]	-	(NA)	-	(NA)	-	(NA)	-	(NA)
Mississippi	132,000	141,000	3,800	4,800	7,828	7,440	2.06	1.55
North Carolina	(D)	(D)	(D)	(D)	(D)	(D)	(D)	(D)
Texas	(D)	(D)	(D)	(D)	(D)	(D)	(D)	(D)
Other States[2]	9,325	22,620	230	677	825	1,740	3.59	2.57
United States	155,605	175,030	4,539	5,806	10,024	10,275	2.21	1.77

- Represents zero.   (D) Withheld to avoid disclosing data for individual operations.   [1] Included in Other States for 2014.   [2] Other States include State estimates not shown and States suppressed due to disclosure.
NASS, Livestock Branch, (202) 720–0585.

Table 15-28.—Trout: Value of fish sold and distributed, by State (excluding eggs), and United States (including and excluding eggs), 2013–2014

State	Total value of fish sold		Total value of distributed fish	
	2013	2014	2013	2014
	1,000 dollars	*1,000 dollars*	*1,000 dollars*	*1,000 dollars*
Arkansas	-	-	3,438	3,122
California	5,214	4,990	11,199	12,794
Colorado	2,018	1,532	7,946	7,618
Georgia	607	455	1,152	1,259
Idaho	44,573	53,118	6,935	8,972
Michigan	783	619	925	966
Missouri	2,062	2,250	2,669	2,365
New York	557	631	2,688	3,149
North Carolina	6,821	7,888	(D)	(D)
Oregon	(D)	(D)	5,064	5,336
Pennsylvania	5,141	5,571	11,864	6,124
Utah	617	604	5,628	7,550
Virginia	1,357	1,481	1,782	2,087
Washington	(D)	(D)	15,129	20,735
West Virginia	1,255	1,233	(D)	(D)
Wisconsin	1,679	1,537	2,512	2,007
Other States [1]	24,730	20,575	31,144	26,765
United States				
Value excluding eggs	97,414	102,484	110,075	110,849
Value including eggs	106,053	111,258	(NA)	(NA)

- Represents zero. (D) Withheld to avoid disclosing data for individual operations. (NA) Not available. [1] Other States include State estimates not listed and States supressed due to disclosure.
NASS, Livestock Branch, (202) 720–3570.

Table 15-29.—Trout: Egg Sales, United States, 2012–2014

Year	Number of Eggs	Average Price per 1,000 Eggs	Total Sales [1]
	1,000	*Dollars*	*1,000 dollars*
2012	434,090	19.50	8,469
2013	445,805	19.40	8,639
2014	427,125	20.50	8,774

[1] Total sales may not add due to rounding.
NASS, Livestock Branch, (202) 720-3570.

MISCELLANEOUS AGRICULTURAL STATISTICS

Table 15-30.—Trout: Sales by size category, by State and United States, 2013–2014

Size category and State	Number of fish		Live weight		Sales			
	2013	2014	Total [1]		Total [2]		Average price per pound	
			2013	2014	2013	2014	2013	2014
	1,000	1,000	1,000 pounds	1,000 pounds	1,000 dollars	1,000 dollars	Dollars	Dollars
12 inch or longer:								
Arkansas	-	-	-	-	-	-	-	-
California	(D)	1,310	(D)	1,550	(D)	4,697	(D)	3.03
Colorado	250	210	441	404	1,654	1,361	3.75	3.37
Georgia	145	(D)	163	(D)	574	(D)	3.52	(D)
Idaho	30,100	36,100	35,700	42,200	44,268	52,750	1.24	1.25
Michigan	145	105	167	119	618	458	3.70	3.85
Missouri	520	780	620	688	1,538	1,686	2.48	2.45
New York	(D)	(D)	(D)	(D)	(D)	(D)	(D)	(D)
North Carolina	3,310	3,310	3,700	4,050	6,179	6,885	1.67	1.70
Oregon	(D)	(D)	(D)	(D)	(D)	(D)	(D)	(D)
Pennsylvania	870	880	1,050	1,030	4,232	4,408	4.03	4.28
Utah	100	130	151	161	556	531	3.68	3.30
Virginia	430	480	498	489	1,205	1,213	2.42	2.48
Washington	(D)	(D)	(D)	(D)	(D)	(D)	(D)	(D)
West Virginia	440	420	551	518	1,196	1,166	2.17	2.25
Wisconsin	480	410	447	403	1,466	1,394	3.28	3.46
Other States [3]	4,380	4,050	13,178	9,021	27,688	18,530	2.10	2.05
United States	41,170	48,185	56,666	60,633	91,174	95,079	1.61	1.57
6 inch-12 inch:								
Arkansas	-	-	-	-	-	-	-	-
California	(D)	(D)	(D)	(D)	(D)	(D)	(D)	(D)
Colorado	190	(D)	92	(D)	339	(D)	3.69	(D)
Georgia	(D)	(D)	(D)	(D)	(D)	(D)	(D)	(D)
Idaho	(D)	(D)	(D)	(D)	(D)	(D)	(D)	(D)
Michigan	(D)	(D)	(D)	(D)	(D)	(D)	(D)	(D)
Missouri	500	460	179	177	440	460	2.46	2.60
New York	85	80	30	37	179	170	5.95	4.60
North Carolina	(D)	(D)	(D)	(D)	(D)	(D)	(D)	(D)
Oregon	(D)	(D)	(D)	(D)	(D)	(D)	(D)	(D)
Pennsylvania	440	510	180	190	853	1,045	4.74	5.50
Utah	(D)	(D)	(D)	(D)	(D)	(D)	(D)	(D)
Virginia	(D)	(D)	(D)	(D)	(D)	(D)	(D)	(D)
Washington	850	1,890	221	470	749	1,208	3.39	2.57
West Virginia	(D)	(D)	(D)	(D)	(D)	(D)	(D)	(D)
Wisconsin	130	70	48	36	209	138	4.35	3.84
Other States [3]	1,560	2,135	625	862	2,444	2,767	3.91	3.21
United States	3,755	5,145	1,375	1,772	5,213	5,788	3.79	3.27

Size category and State	Number of fish		Live weight		Sales			
	2013	2014	Total [1]		Total [2]		Average price per 1,000 fish	
			2013	2014	2013	2014	2013	2014
	1,000	1,000	1,000 pounds	1,000 pounds	1,000 dollars	1,000 dollars	Dollars	Dollars
1 inch-6 inch:								
Arkansas	-	-	-	-	-	-	-	-
California	(D)	(D)	(D)	(D)	(D)	(D)	(D)	(D)
Colorado	55	(D)	2	(D)	25	(D)	451	(D)
Georgia	(D)	(D)	(D)	(D)	(D)	(D)	(D)	(D)
Idaho	(D)	(D)	(D)	(D)	(D)	(D)	(D)	(D)
Michigan	(D)	(D)	(D)	(D)	(D)	(D)	(D)	(D)
Missouri	220	260	12	16	84	104	380	400
New York	(D)	(D)	(D)	(D)	(D)	(D)	(D)	(D)
North Carolina	(D)	40	(D)	2	(D)	17	(D)	421
Oregon	(D)	(D)	(D)	(D)	(D)	(D)	(D)	(D)
Pennsylvania	160	350	5	9	56	118	348	336
Utah	(D)	(D)	(D)	(D)	(D)	(D)	(D)	(D)
Virginia	(D)	(D)	(D)	(D)	(D)	(D)	(D)	(D)
Washington	(D)	(D)	(D)	(D)	(D)	(D)	(D)	(D)
West Virginia	(D)	(D)	(D)	(D)	(D)	(D)	(D)	(D)
Wisconsin	50	45	1	1	4	5	86	110
Other States [3]	6,005	7,655	151	178	858	1,373	143	179
United States	6,490	8,350	171	206	1,027	1,617	158	194

- Represents zero. (D) Withheld to avoid disclosing data for individual operations. [1] Due to rounding, total number of fish multiplied by the average pounds per unit may not exactly equal total live weight. [2] Due to rounding, total number or live weight multiplied by average value per unit may not exactly equal total sales. [3] Other States include State estimates not listed and States supressed due to disclosure.
NASS, Livestock Branch, (202) 720-3570.

Table 15-31.—Refrigerated warehouses: Gross refrigerated space by type of warehouse, United States, biennially, October 1993–2011 [1][2]

Type	1995	1997	1999	2001	2003
	1,000 Cubic Feet				
General:					
Public	1,741,585	2,043,908	2,146,643	2,251,943	2,357,080
Private and Semiprivate	674,649	683,372	756,505	788,853	802,454
Total	2,416,234	2,727,280	2,903,152	3,040,796	3,159,535
Apple:					
Public	23,419	23,907	21,690	14,183	12,517
Private and Semiprivate	647,993	675,838	680,736	712,412	723,499
Total	671,412	699,745	702,426	726,595	736,016
Total, all	3,087,646	3,427,025	3,605,578	3,767,394	3,895,551

Type	2005	2007	2009	2011 [3]	2013
	1,000 Cubic Feet				
General:					
Public	2,435,773	2,498,198	2,900,511	3,028,243	3,076,959
Private and Semiprivate	771,725	821,998	894,463	931,117	978,426
Total	3,207,497	3,320,194	3,794,974	3,959,354	4,055,385
Apple:					
Public	9,270	8,170	23,474	....	....
Private and Semiprivate	711,951	683,798	613,118	....	....
Total	721,221	691,968	636,593	....	....
Total, all	3,928,718	4,012,162	4,431,567	....	....

[1] Warehouse space is defined as all space artificially cooled to temperatures of 50 degrees F. or less, in which food commodities are normally held for 30 days or longer.   [2] Totals may not add due to rounding.   [3] Apple discontinued in 2011.
NASS, Livestock Branch, (202) 720–8784.

Table 15-32.—General storages: Gross and usable cooler and freezer space, by State and United States, October 1, 2013[1]

State	Cooler		Freezer		Total	
	Gross	Usable	Gross	Usable	Gross	Usable
			1,000 Cubic Feet			
Alabama	2,574	2,294	34,152	28,805	36,727	31,100
Alaska	(D)	(D)	(D)	(D)	2,590	2,127
Arizona	4,488	3,422	14,034	11,706	18,522	15,128
Arkansas	(D)	(D)	(D)	(D)	95,508	81,894
California	217,084	173,659	339,687	282,109	556,771	455,768
Colorado	2,260	1,828	21,471	17,615	23,732	19,443
Connecticut	(D)	(D)	(D)	(D)	6,018	5,099
Delaware	(D)	(D)	(D)	(D)	30,752	23,873
Florida	99,091	74,381	178,318	150,258	277,409	224,638
Georgia	60,442	48,146	182,851	150,222	243,293	198,368
Hawaii	(D)	(D)	(D)	(D)	(D)	(D)
Idaho	(D)	(D)	(D)	(D)	60,948	51,507
Illinois	29,650	25,524	177,456	141,592	207,107	167,116
Indiana	(D)	(D)	(D)	(D)	105,223	89,051
Iowa	18,617	13,230	72,098	59,991	90,716	73,222
Kansas	7,588	4,913	39,972	29,451	47,560	34,364
Kentucky	(D)	(D)	(D)	(D)	23,165	19,683
Louisiana	943	812	11,186	9,600	12,129	10,412
Maine	(D)	(D)	(D)	(D)	12,420	9,363
Maryland	4,637	3,908	34,689	29,284	39,326	33,192
Massachusetts	12,855	10,513	81,357	68,916	94,212	79,429
Michigan	11,924	9,657	85,414	69,966	97,338	79,623
Minnesota	25,355	17,405	75,049	60,508	100,403	77,913
Mississippi	(D)	2,024	(D)	17,189	23,406	19,214
Missouri	23,091	19,445	84,009	70,236	107,100	89,681
Montana	507	408	724	578	1,231	986
Nebraska	6,080	3,208	48,876	38,322	54,956	41,530
Nevada	(D)	(D)	(D)	(D)	(D)	(D)
New Hampshire	(D)	(D)	(D)	(D)	8,352	6,672
New Jersey	53,089	48,279	108,823	86,916	161,912	135,195
New Mexico	(D)	(D)	(D)	(D)	4,967	3,592
New York	34,892	28,369	69,897	58,293	104,788	86,662
North Carolina	(D)	(D)	(D)	(D)	70,887	61,699
North Dakota	(D)	(D)	(D)	(D)	10,325	7,800
Ohio	4,992	3,992	75,735	63,241	80,727	67,233
Oklahoma	836	694	9,333	7,401	10,169	8,095
Oregon	14,024	11,878	112,679	89,696	126,703	101,575
Pennsylvania	42,643	32,557	200,633	176,070	243,293	208,627
Rhode Island	(D)	(D)	(D)	(D)	(D)	(D)
South Carolina	(D)	(D)	(D)	(D)	27,659	21,778
South Dakota	(D)	(D)	(D)	(D)	11,673	7,125
Tennessee	2,991	2,080	53,159	44,809	56,150	46,889
Texas	42,035	32,203	177,118	143,208	219,153	175,411
Utah	10,102	9,094	28,736	23,682	38,838	32,776
Vermont	(D)	(D)	(D)	(D)	(D)	(D)
Virginia	18,150	14,213	51,185	45,171	69,334	59,384
Washington	15,120	10,850	185,698	151,163	200,819	162,012
West Virginia	(D)	(D)	(D)	(D)	(D)	(D)
Wisconsin	90,083	70,255	129,622	109,559	219,705	179,815
Wyoming	-	-	-	-	-	-
Other States	54,756	41,634	460,522	364,873	21,386	15,244
United States	910,899	720,875	3,144,483	2,600,430	4,055,385	3,321,308

- Represents zero.   (D) Withheld to avoid disclosing data for individual operations.   [1] Totals may not add due to rounding.

NASS, Livestock Branch, (202) 720–8784.

Table 15-33.—Alaska crops: Acreage harvested, volume harvested, and value of production, 2005–2014

Year	Oats for grain	Barley for grain	All hay	Potatoes	All vegetables [1]
			Acreage harvested		
	Acres	*Acres*	*Acres*	*Acres*	*Acres*
2005	900	4,300	21,000	780	351
2006	800	4,200	20,000	840	341
2007	1,000	3,900	23,000	870	326
2008	500	3,400	18,000	780	347
2009	900	4,400	20,000	740	336
2010	800	4,200	20,000	750	327
2011	1,000	4,800	19,000	720	(NA)
2012	900	4,300	22,000	650	(NA)
2013	400	3,300	20,000	620	(NA)
2014	1,000	5,100	18,000	620	(NA)
			Volume harvested		
	Bushels	*Bushels*	*Tons*	*Cwt.*	*Cwt.*
2005	58,000	208,000	30,000	166,000	57,833
2006	28,000	157,000	22,000	186,000	55,573
2007	47,000	158,000	31,000	176,000	47,340
2008	13,000	99,000	20,000	135,000	40,197
2009	37,000	183,000	23,000	137,000	43,420
2010	48,000	185,000	24,000	150,000	45,740
2011	80,000	175,000	22,000	134,000	(NA)
2012	59,000	207,000	27,000	140,000	(NA)
2013	15,000	110,000	15,000	130,000	(NA)
2014	57,000	217,000	25,000	155,000	(NA)
			Value of production		
	Dollars	*Dollars*	*Dollars*	*Dollars*	*Dollars*
2005	148,000	759,000	7,200,000	3,403,000	3,507,000
2006	69,000	557,000	5,500,000	3,757,000	3,302,000
2007	132,000	577,000	8,370,000	3,538,000	3,072,000
2008	39,000	446,000	6,300,000	3,348,000	2,954,000
2009	113,000	814,000	7,130,000	3,315,000	3,155,000
2010	161,000	814,000	7,320,000	3,570,000	3,470,000
2011	276,000	788,000	6,600,000	3,176,000	(NA)
2012	212,000	1,107,000	8,505,000	3,864,000	(NA)
2013	56,000	594,000	5,925,000	3,055,000	(NA)
2014	211,000	1,183,000	9,625,000	3,565,000	(NA)

(NA) Not available.   [1] Excludes greenhouse-grown vegetables.
NASS, Crops Branch, (202) 720–2127.

Table 15-34.—Crop ranking: Major field crops, rank by production, major States, 2014

Rank	State	Corn, grain	State	Soybeans	State	All wheat
		1,000 bushels		*1,000 bushels*		*1,000 bushels*
1	IA	2,367,400	IL	547,680	ND	347,068
2	IL	2,350,000	IA	505,730	KS	246,400
3	NE	1,602,050	IN	307,440	MT	209,470
4	MN	1,177,800	MN	305,340	SD	131,260
5	IN	1,084,760	NE	288,900	WA	108,460
6	SD	787,360	MO	260,400	ID	93,717
7	MO	628,680	OH	254,100	CO	89,812
8	OH	610,720	SD	229,950	NE	71,050
9	KS	566,200	ND	202,515	TX	67,500
10	WI	485,160	AR	160,500	MN	66,468
	US	14,215,532	US	3,968,823	US	2,025,651

Rank	State	Winter wheat	State	Durum wheat	State	Other spring wheat
		1,000 bushels		*1,000 bushels*		*1,000 bushels*
1	KS	246,400	ND	28,223	ND	291,650
2	MT	91,840	MT	13,330	MT	104,300
3	CO	89,300	AZ	7,992	SD	71,680
4	WA	85,280	CA	2,625	MN	64,900
5	NE	71,050	ID	737	ID	34,580
6	TX	67,500	SD	180	WA	23,180
7	SD	59,400			OR	3,744
8	ID	58,400			CO	512
9	OK	47,600			UT	432
10	IL	448,900			NV	60
	US	1,377,526	US	53,087	US	595,038

Rank	State	Sorghum, grain	State	Barley	State	Oats
		1,000 bushels		*1,000 bushels*		*1,000 bushels*
1	KS	199,800	ID.	51,700	SD	9,300
2	TX	137,250	MT	44,660	WI	8,680
3	OK	17,360	ND	35,845	MN	7,875
4	AR	16,005	WY	7,276	ND	7,665
5	NE	13,120	CO	6,696	IO	3,520
6	SD	9,450	WA	6,300	PA	3,480
7	LA	8,928	AZ	4,000	MI	2,760
8	CO	8,400	PA	3,550	NY	2,520
9	MS	8,400	MD	3,465	OH	2,457
10	MO	7,373	MN	3,120	ME	2,170
	US	432,575	US	181,542	US	69,684

Rank	State	All cotton	State	Peanuts	State	Rice
		1,000 bales		*1,000 pounds*		*1,000 cwt.*
1	TX	6,013	GA	2,423,100	AR	111,957
2	GA	2,500	FL	668,000	CA	36,993
3	MS	1,035	AL	553,600	LA	32,658
4	NC	1,005	TX	488,950	MO	14,540
5	AR	820	SC	410,400	MS	14,096
6	CA	755	NC	399,900	TX	10,791
7	AL	660	MS	124,000		
8	SC	520	VA	82,650		
9	AZ	492	OK	44,000		
10	TN	492	NM	15,500		
	US	16,084	US	5,210,100	US	221,035

Rank	State	All hay, baled	State	Alfalfa hay, baled	State	Other hay, baled
		1,000 tons		*1,000 tons*		*1,000 tons*
1	TX	11,746	CA	5,693	TX	11,130
2	CA	7,513	SD	4,370	MO	6,400
3	MO	7,100	ID	4,251	OK	5,280
4	SD	6,665	WI	4,125	KY	4,200
5	OK	6,121	MT	3,885	TN	3,850
6	NE	6,028	ND	3,465	KS	2,720
7	ND	5,460	NE	3,403	NE	2,625
8	MT	5,381	MN	3,190	AR	2,440
9	KS	5,000	IA	2,916	VA	2,420
10	ID	4,881	CO	2,516	SD	2,295
	US	139,923	US	61,451	US	78,472

Rank	State	All tobacco	State	Dry edible beans	State	Potatoes
		1,000 pounds		*1,000 cwt.*		*1,000 cwt.*
1	NC	453,860	ND	8,795	ID	130,320
2	KY	214,280	MI	4,375	WA	100,300
3	VA	57,651	NE	3,916	WI	27,500
4	TN	52,155	MN	2,886	ND	27,200
5	GA	34,500	ID	2,229	CO	22,857
6	SC	33,180	WA	1,881	OR	21,784
7	PA	22,250	CA	1,061	MI	17,550
8	OH	4,300	CO	835	MN	16,200
9	CT	(D)	WY	799	ME	16,160
10	MA	(D)	MT	603	CA	13,481
	US	876,415	US	28,910	US	440,498

NASS, Crops Branch, (202) 720–2127.

Table 15-35.—U.S. crop progress: 2014 crop and 5-year average

[In percent]

Week-ending date	Winter wheat							
	Planted		Emerged		Headed		Harvested	
	2014	Avg	2014	Avg	2014	Avg	2014	Avg
2013: [1]								
Sep 8	5	5						
Sep 15	12	12						
Sep 22	23	24						
Sep 29	39	40	12	15				
Oct 20	79	79	53	54				
Oct 27	86	85	65	64				
Nov 3	91	90	78	73				
Nov 10	95	93	84	80				
Nov 17	....	....	89	85				
Nov 24	....	....	93	89				
2014:								
Apr 13	....	....	....	....	5			
Apr 20	....	....	....	....	9	17		
Apr 27	....	....	....	....	18	26		
May 4	....	....	....	....	29	35		
May 11 ...	....	....	....	....	44	46		
May 18 ...	....	....	....	....	57	58		
May 25 ...	....	....	....	....	70	69		
Jun 1	....	....	....	....	79	78		
Jun 8	....	....	....	....	86	85	9	12
Jun 15	....	....	....	....	92	90	16	20
Jun 22	....	....	....	....	96	94	33	31
Jun 29	....	....	....	....	....	....	43	48
Jul 6	....	....	....	....	....	....	57	60
Jul 13	....	....	....	....	....	....	69	68
Jul 20	....	....	....	....	....	....	75	75
Jul 27	....	....	....	....	....	....	83	80
Aug 3	....	....	....	....	....	....	90	85
Aug 10 ...	....	....	....	....	....	....	95	90

Week-ending date	Spring wheat							
	Planted		Emerged		Headed		Harvested	
	2014	Avg	2014	Avg	2014	Avg	2014	Avg
2014:								
Apr 13	6	11						
Apr 20	10	19						
Apr 27	18	30	5	9				
May 4	26	41	7	17				
May 11 ...	34	53	12	27				
May 18 ...	49	68	24	40				
May 25 ...	74	82	43	57				
Jun 1	88	88	67	72				
Jun 8	95	93	80	82				
Jun 15	....	....	91	90				
Jun 22	....	....	98	95	10	16		
Jun 29	....	....	....	....	26	29		
Jul 6	....	....	....	....	47	47		
Jul 13	....	....	....	....	69	68		
Jul 20	....	....	....	....	84	85		
Jul 27	....	....	....	....	93	93		
Aug 3	....	....	....	....	97	97		
Aug 10 ...	....	....	....	....	....	....	6	21
Aug 17 ...	....	....	....	....	....	....	17	33
Aug 24 ...	....	....	....	....	....	....	27	49
Aug 31	....	....	....	....	....	....	38	65
Sep 7	....	....	....	....	....	....	58	78
Sep 14 ...	....	....	....	....	....	....	74	86
Sep 21 ...	....	....	....	....	....	....	86	92
Sep 28 ...	....	....	....	....	....	....	94	96
Oct 5	....	....	....	....	....	....	96	99

See footnote(s) at end of table.

Table 15-35.—U.S. crop progress: 2014 crop and 5-year average—Continued

[In percent]

Week-ending date	Rice							
	Planted		Emerged		Headed		Harvested	
	2014	Avg	2014	Avg	2014	Avg	2014	Avg
2014:								
Apr 6	15	19						
Apr 13	25	31	9	12				
Apr 20	32	44	16	24				
Apr 27	45	56	25	35				
May 4	57	65	39	47				
May 11	75	73	53	58				
May 18	87	82	69	66				
May 25	95	91	80	77				
Jun 1			89	86				
Jun 8			93	92				
Jun 15			99	96				
Jun 22					3	5		
Jun 29					9	9		
Jul 6					17	14		
Jul 13					24	22		
Jul 20					32	33		
Jul 27					42	44		
Aug 3					60	58		
Aug 10					71	70		
Aug 17					88	81	7	11
Aug 24					94	89	11	17
Aug 31					97	94	17	26
Sep 7							26	36
Sep 14							36	45
Sep 21							46	53
Sep 28							59	62
Oct 5							70	71
Oct 12							82	78
Oct 19							91	85
Oct 26							96	91

Week-ending date	Corn													
	Planted		Emerged		Silking		Dough		Dented		Mature		Harvested	
	2014	Avg	2014	Avg	2014	Avg	2014	Avg	2014	Avg	2014	Avg	2014	Avg
2014:														
Apr 13	3	6												
Apr 20	6	14												
Apr 27	19	28	3	6										
May 4	29	42	7	13										
May 11	59	58	18	25										
May 18	73	76	34	42										
May 25	88	88	60	64										
Jun 1	95	94	80	80										
Jun 8			92	90										
Jun 15			97	96										
Jun 22														
Jun 29					5	9								
Jul 6					15	18								
Jul 13					34	33								
Jul 20					56	55								
Jul 27					78	75	17	16						
Aug 3					90	88	36	29						
Aug 10					96	95	54	46	11	16				
Aug 17							70	63	22	27				
Aug 24							83	78	35	43				
Aug 31							90	89	53	59	8	16		
Sep 7							95	94	69	74	15	26		
Sep 14									82	85	27	39	4	9
Sep 21									90	92	42	54	7	15
Sep 28									96	97	60	70	12	23
Oct 5											77	81	17	32
Oct 12											87	89	24	43
Oct 19											93	94	31	53
Oct 26											96	97	46	65
Nov 2													65	73
Nov 9													80	80
Nov 16													89	88
Nov 23													94	92

See footnote(s) at end of table.

Table 15-35.—U.S. crop progress: 2014 crop and 5-year average—Continued

[In percent]

Week-ending date	Sorghum									
	Planted		Headed		Coloring		Mature		Harvested	
	2014	Avg	2014	Avg	2014	Avg	2014	Avg	2014	Avg
2014:										
Apr 6	11	17								
Apr 13	20	21								
Apr 20	23	23								
Apr 27	27	26								
May 4	28	29								
May 11	36	33								
May 18	39	39								
May 25	46	47								
Jun 1	56	57								
Jun 8	67	71								
Jun 15	75	83	17	18						
Jun 22	88	90	19	22						
Jun 29	93	96	21	23						
Jul 6	98	99	23	26	15	20				
Jul 13			30	29	21	22				
Jul 20			42	34	26	25				
Jul 27			47	43	28	28				
Aug 3			55	54	35	30				
Aug 10			65	66	39	33	30	24		
Aug 17			76	76	44	37	31	26		
Aug 24			86	85	52	44	34	27		
Aug 31			92	91	61	54	37	29	25	24
Sep 7			95	95	69	65	40	33	26	25
Sep 14					79	75	45	37	28	27
Sep 21					87	83	51	44	30	29
Sep 28					93	89	59	54	32	33
Oct 5					95	93	67	64	37	38
Oct 12							77	74	41	44
Oct 19							85	83	48	51
Oct 26							91	91	56	60
Nov 2							94	95	65	70
Nov 9							96	97	75	80
Nov 16									83	87
Nov 23									88	91

Week-ending date	Soybeans											
	Planted		Emerged		Blooming		Setting Pods		Dropping Leaves		Harvested	
	2014	Avg	2014	Avg	2014	Avg	2014	Avg	2014	Avg	2014	Avg
2014:												
Apr 27	3	4										
May 4	5	11										
May 11	20	21										
May 18	33	38	9	11								
May 25	59	56	25	27								
Jun 1	78	70	50	45								
Jun 8	87	81	71	62								
Jun 15	92	90	83	77								
Jun 22	95	94	90	87								
Jun 29			94	94	10	10						
Jul 6			98	97	24	21						
Jul 13					41	37						
Jul 20					60	56	19	17				
Jul 27					76	72	38	31				
Aug 3					85	83	57	48				
Aug 10					92	91	72	65				
Aug 17					95	95	83	79				
Aug 24							90	89				
Aug 31							95	95	5	7		
Sep 7									12	17		
Sep 14									24	32		
Sep 21									45	53	3	8
Sep 28									69	71	10	17
Oct 5									83	84	20	35
Oct 12									91	91	40	53
Oct 19									95	97	53	66
Oct 26											70	76
Nov 2											83	83
Nov 9											90	91
Nov 16											94	96
Nov 23											97	98

See footnote(s) at end of table.

Table 15-35.—U.S. crop progress: 2014 crop and 5-year average—Continued

[In percent]

Week-ending date	Cotton, Upland									
	Planted		Squaring		Setting Bolls		Bolls Opening		Harvested	
	2014	Avg	2014	Avg	2014	Avg	2014	Avg	2014	Avg
2014:										
Apr 6	6									
Apr 13	8	9								
Apr 20	9	12								
Apr 27	13	18								
May 4	16	25								
May 11	30	34								
May 18	46	48								
May 25	62	64								
Jun 1	74	81	5	6						
Jun 8	89	91	8	10						
Jun 15	95	96	14	16						
Jun 22			25	27	3	6				
Jun 29			36	42	7	10				
Jul 6			53	60	12	16				
Jul 13			70	74	24	25				
Jul 20			85	82	38	37				
Jul 27			87	89	49	51				
Aug 3			95	95	68	66				
Aug 10					83	80				
Aug 17					88	88	7	9		
Aug 24					90	93	12	12		
Aug 31					96	96	19	18		
Sep 7							31	27		
Sep 14							39	37	6	7
Sep 21							51	49	8	9
Sep 28							58	60	10	13
Oct 5							64	70	15	18
Oct 12							73	79	22	24
Oct 19							77	85	29	31
Oct 26							86	90	42	41
Nov 2							91	95	50	51
Nov 9							95	97	62	64
Nov 16									69	74
Nov 23									77	83

Week-ending date	Barley								Oats							
	Planted		Emerged		Headed		Harvested		Planted		Emerged		Headed		Harvested	
	2014	Avg	2014	Avg	2014	Avg	2014	Avg	2014	Avg	2014	Avg	2014	Avg	2014	Avg
2014:																
Apr 13	16	14							35	47						
Apr 20	25	23							43	55	30	38				
Apr 27	33	33	11	8					53	63	37	45				
May 4	46	44	17	16					57	71	42	53				
May 11	55	56	29	27					69	79	51	62				
May 18	68	69	37	40					78	88	61	73	27	21		
May 25	84	82	57	55					89	94	72	82	30	31		
Jun 1	93	89	76	69					95	97	86	90	32	34		
Jun 8	97	93	86	82							92	94	37	40		
Jun 15			92	91							96	98	45	50		
Jun 22			99	95	17	13							57	61		
Jun 29					31	25							69	73		
Jul 6					61	44							80	83		
Jul 13					83	67							90	92	11	16
Jul 20					92	86							95	97	16	24
Jul 27					96	95									26	35
Aug 3															40	49
Aug 10							17	17							52	64
Aug 17							31	31							66	76
Aug 24							43	50							74	86
Aug 31							58	68							80	93
Sep 7							81	82							86	97
Sep 14							91	90							92	99
Sep 21							95	95							96	100

See footnote(s) at end of table.

Table 15-35.—U.S. crop progress: 2014 crop and 5-year average—Continued

[In percent]

Week-ending date	Sunflower				Sugarbeets			
	Planted		Harvested		Planted		Harvested	
	2014	Avg	2014	Avg	2014	Avg	2014	Avg
2014:								
Apr 13					5	15		
Apr 20					11	29		
Apr 27					16	47		
May 4					23	56		
May 11					31	71		
May 18	1	6			52	84		
May 25	12	18			87	95		
Jun 1	26	33			99	97		
Jun 8	52	51						
Jun 15	71	70						
Jun 22	83	84						
Jun 29	91	93						
Jul 6	98	97						
Sep 21							10	8
Sep 28							13	13
Oct 5			1	9			41	26
Oct 12			5	18			74	45
Oct 19			11	30			79	64
Oct 26			30	43			87	78
Nov 2			50	54			94	89
Nov 9			70	69			98	96
Nov 16			80	81				
Nov 23			86	98				

Week-ending date	Peanuts					
	Planted		Pegging		Harvested	
	2014	Avg	2014	Avg	2014	Avg
2014:						
Apr 27	7	5				
May 4	14	15				
May 11	26	29				
May 18	43	49				
May 25	68	68				
Jun 1	84	82				
Jun 8	93	90				
Jun 15	96	96	9	4		
Jun 22			16	12		
Jun 29			27	24		
Jul 6			44	39		
Jul 13			60	54		
Jul 20			73	67		
Jul 27			83	77		
Aug 3			91	86		
Aug 10			94	92		
Aug 17			98	96		
Sep 14					3	4
Sep 21					7	8
Sep 28					12	15
Oct 5					21	25
Oct 12					33	38
Oct 19					51	52
Oct 26					65	65
Nov 2					79	76
Nov 9					88	86
Nov 16					94	92
Nov 23					97	95

[1] Planted the preceding fall.
NASS, Crops Branch, (202) 720–2127.

Appendix I
Telephone Contact List

Appreciation is expressed to the following agencies for their help in this publication. The information offices are listed to provide help to those users who require additional information about specific tables in this publication.

Agricultural Marketing Service:
USDA/AMS
Room 2619 South Bldg.
Washington, DC 20250
202–720–8998

Agricultural Research Service:
USDA/ARS
5601 Sunnyside Ave
Bldg 1, Rm 2251
Beltsville, MD 20705–5128
301–504–1636

Animal and Plant Health Inspection Service:
USDA/APHIS
4700 River Rd
Riverdale, MD 20737
301–851–4100

Center for Nutrition Policy and Promotion:
USDA/CNPP
3101 Park Center Drive
Alexandria, VA 22302
703–305–7600

Economic Research Service:
USDA/ERS
355 E Street, S.W.
Washington, DC 20024-3221
202–694–5050

Farm Credit Administration:
FCA
1501 Farm Credit Dr.
McLean, VA 22102
703–883–4056

Farm Service Agency:
USDA/FSA
Room 4078 South Bldg.
Washington, DC 20250
202–720–7163

Food and Nutrition Service:
USDA/FNS
3101 Park Center Drive, Room 914
Alexandria, VA 22302
703–305–2062

Foreign Agricultural Service:
USDA/FAS
Room 5076 South Bldg.
Washington, DC 20250
202–720–7115

Forest Service:
USDA/FS
2nd Floor Central Wing, Yates Bldg.
Washington, DC 20250
202–205–8333

National Agricultural Statistics Service:
USDA/NASS
Room 5038 South Bldg.
Washington, DC 20250
202–720–3878

National Marine Fisheries Service:
USDC/NOAA/NMFS
1315 East/West Highway,
SSMC III - Room 12405
Silver Spring, MD 20910–3282
301–427–8103

Natural Resources Conservation Service:
USDA/NRCS
Room 6121 South Bldg.
Washington, DC 20250
202–720–2182

Risk Management Agency:
USDA/RMA
Room 403
Kansas City, MO 64133-4675
816–926–1805

Rural Business-Cooperatives Service:
USDA/RECD/RBS
Room 4801 South Bldg.
Washington, DC 20250
202–720–1019

Rural Utilities Service:
USDA/RD/RUS
Room 5144 South Bldg.
Washington, DC 20250
202–720–1255

INDEX

INDEX

INDEX